# The Lithic Assemblages of Qafzeh Cave

Erella Hovers

OXFORD
UNIVERSITY PRESS
2009

# OXFORD

UNIVERSITY PRESS

Oxford University Press, Inc., publishes works that further
Oxford University's objective of excellence
in research, scholarship, and education.

Oxford   New York
Auckland   Cape Town   Dar es Salaam   Hong Kong   Karachi
Kuala Lumpur   Madrid   Melbourne   Mexico City   Nairobi
New Delhi   Shanghai   Taipei   Toronto

With offices in
Argentina   Austria   Brazil   Chile   Czech Republic   France   Greece
Guatemala   Hungary   Italy   Japan   Poland   Portugal   Singapore
South Korea   Switzerland   Thailand   Turkey   Ukraine   Vietnam

Copyright © 2009 by Oxford University Press, Inc.

Published by Oxford University Press, Inc.
198 Madison Avenue, New York, New York 10016

www.oup.com

Oxford is a registered trademark of Oxford University Press



Library of Congress Cataloging-in-Publication Data

Hovers, Erella.
The lithic assemblages of Qafzeh Cave / Erella Hovers.
p. cm.
Includes bibliographical references and index.
ISBN 978-0-19-532277-4 1. Paleolithic period—Israel—Qafzeh Cave.
2. Tools, Prehistoric—Israel—Qafzeh Cave. 3. Excavations (Archaeology)—Israel—
Qafzeh Cave. 4. Qafzeh Cave (Israel)—Antiquities. I. Title.
GN772.32.I75H68  2009
933—dc22      2008029865

9 8 7 6 5 4 3 2 1
Printed in the United States of America
on acid-free paper

# Preface

Qafzeh Cave has been a focus of research since the first campaign of excavations at the site in 1933–1935, conducted jointly by René Neuville, then the French consul to the British mandate of Palestine, and Moshe Stekelis. As is often the case in our discipline, the skeletal remains found associated with material cultural finds from both Upper and Middle Paleolithic became the main topic of discussion. These remains provided the initiative for the renewal of excavations at the site by Bernard Vandermeersch in 1965–1979 (Ofer Bar-Yosef joined this effort in the years 1977–1979), when additional Mousterian layers, containing artifacts, faunal remains, and human skeletal remains were found on the terrace in front of the cave. The taxonomy, phylogeny, and chronology of the Qafzeh hominins have kept generations of researchers on their academic toes and were at the center of heated debates. The dating of the Qafzeh hominins in fact culminated a long scientific debate about the phylogenetic relationship of anatomically modern humans and the Neanderthals. Regardless of one's position on the question of modern human origins, it has to be acknowledged that the early dates of the hominin-bearing layers of Qafzeh played an important—some would argue, a crucial—role in the scientific revolution that the study of modern human origins has undergone in the last two decades.

Work on the material cultural remains left by the Qafzeh occupants was much more low-keyed. Various researchers (for example, Paul Fish and Arthur Jelinek) have sampled the material from Neuville and Stekelis's excavations inside the cave in order to make a methodological argument or a comparative point. In the 1930s Neuville and Garrod both reconstructed linear developmental trajectories of the Levantine Mousterian, in which observations on the Qafzeh materials were included. Samples from the lithic assemblages recovered during the first excavations at the site were included in somewhat later influential models of cultural changes during the Levantine Middle Paleolithic, for example, those advocated by Copeland (1975) and Jelinek (1982a, 1982b). At the same time, advances in the theory and practice of lithic studies revealed the potential of detailed analyses of lithic remains as a source for understanding technological as well as economic and cognitive aspects of material culture. On a larger scale, the surge of work on modern human origins underlined the unique and intriguing place of the Levant in the bio-geographical trajectories and cultural processes that eventually led to behavioral modernity.

As a consequence of the changes in the scientific worldviews of the paleoanthropological community, the research questions with which I started shifted and changed—mainly, they expanded—in the course of the study. I still regard this work first and foremost as a report on the lithic technological and typological aspects of the assemblages from the terrace of Qafzeh Cave. Yet it seemed to me that the lithics from Qafzeh had to be studied from cultural as well as ecological perspectives. I also thought that they should be placed in the broader context of the trajectories and processes observed during the Middle Paleolithic/Middle Stone Age. The last three chapters of this volume turn to these issues.

I hope that the data and ideas in this volume are useful for students of the Levantine Mousterian and of modern human origins. They were not meant to be, nor can or should they be, finite answers to the big questions. If this volume ends with new questions about the relationship between lithic technology, land use, cultural practices, and the emergence of modernity as we know it, then it has made a contribution.

"No man is an island" when it comes to writing a scientific monograph. The first bunch of thanks goes to Bernard Vandermeersch and Ofer Bar-Yosef, who kindly entrusted me, when I was a Ph.D. candidate, with the lithic assemblages of one of the best known and important sites in the paleoanthropology of modern human origins. Indeed, some of the ideas in this book may be a little more than they bargained for all those years ago....I relied heavily on their good will and bugged them shamelessly for excavation field notes, drawings, and their memories of the excavation, which they shared willingly and generously. I am indebted to both of them for their faith in me and for all the assistance that I received from them, and, not the least, for conducting a field project that after all the years made sense to someone who had not taken part in the excavation.

Very special thanks go to Naama Goren-Inbar, who read every word of the original study and did not let me get away with inconsistencies, unclear sentences, or half-baked ideas. She brought to our discussions the right blend of encouragement, constructive criticism, and friendship that was needed to spur me on. I am very grateful to her for her support over the years. Discussions with Ofer Bar-Yosef usually took place standing up, waiting for the water to boil for the next cup of coffee. There was much flailing of arms and of coffee mugs involved in these conversations, which were always very helpful to me. I am very grateful to Anna Belfer-Cohen, whose views on some of the pertinent issues are diametrically opposite to mine, for letting me bounce ideas off her during many fruitful conversations, and for being my friend. Nigel Goring-Morris provided the perspective on the Middle Paleolithic from the later periods, sharing his uncanny memory of details of the archaeological record. Very warm thanks go to John Speth for his kind words over the years. He always had time to listen, to help think things through, gladly shared his vast knowledge of things lithic and faunal alike, and has been a source of new questions and ideas. I also thank him for his critical reading of the last chapter of this volume.

Many of the students roaming the corridors of the prehistory lab over the years, some of whom became full-fledged colleagues, offered relentless questions and a diversity of perspectives on the Mousterian, Israeli politics, and just about any topic on the face of the earth. Not the least, they provided a reliable supply of coffee. I especially thank Nira Alperson, Hila Ashkenazi, Arik Buller, Ravid Ekshtain, Mae Goder, Leore Grosman, and Gonen Sharon for their curiosity, discussions, and good spirits. There were also long discussions with Liliane Meignen and Steve Kuhn on lithic technology, as well as with Paul Goldberg, Anne-Marie Tillier, and Steve Weiner on other issues related to the Qafzeh project. I thank all of them for sharing with me their thoughts on various aspects of the prehistoric record.

My special thanks go to Yoel Rak for his friendship over the years. He encouraged me to offer this book to OUP, did his best to guide me through the intricacies of anatomical details and evolutionary perspectives on the question of Neanderthals and modern humans, and was a source of advice and encouragement throughout the long process of writing.

The majority of artifact drawings was done by Ofra Lazar. These drawings are used here with the kind permission of Bernard Vandermeersch and Ofer Bar-Yosef. Julia Skidel-Rymer drew plates 17, 20, 23–27, 32, 34, and 38; Leonid Zeiger drew plates 22, 28–29. The base map for the site location map was drafted by Nigel Goring-Morris. The drawings as well as the original rough versions of statistical graphs were expertly digitized and prepared for twenty-first-century publication by Noah Lichtinger. Sue Gorodetzky diligently copy-edited the text. Analysis of the Qafzeh lithics was partially supported by a research grant from the Irene Levi-Sala CARE foundation. Preparation of the volume for print was supported in part by a grant from the Research Committee of the faculty of the Humanities, The Hebrew University of Jerusalem.

Finally, very special thanks are due to my family and friends for their patience throughout the long process of completing this work.

Erella Hovers
Jerusalem, March 2008

# Contents

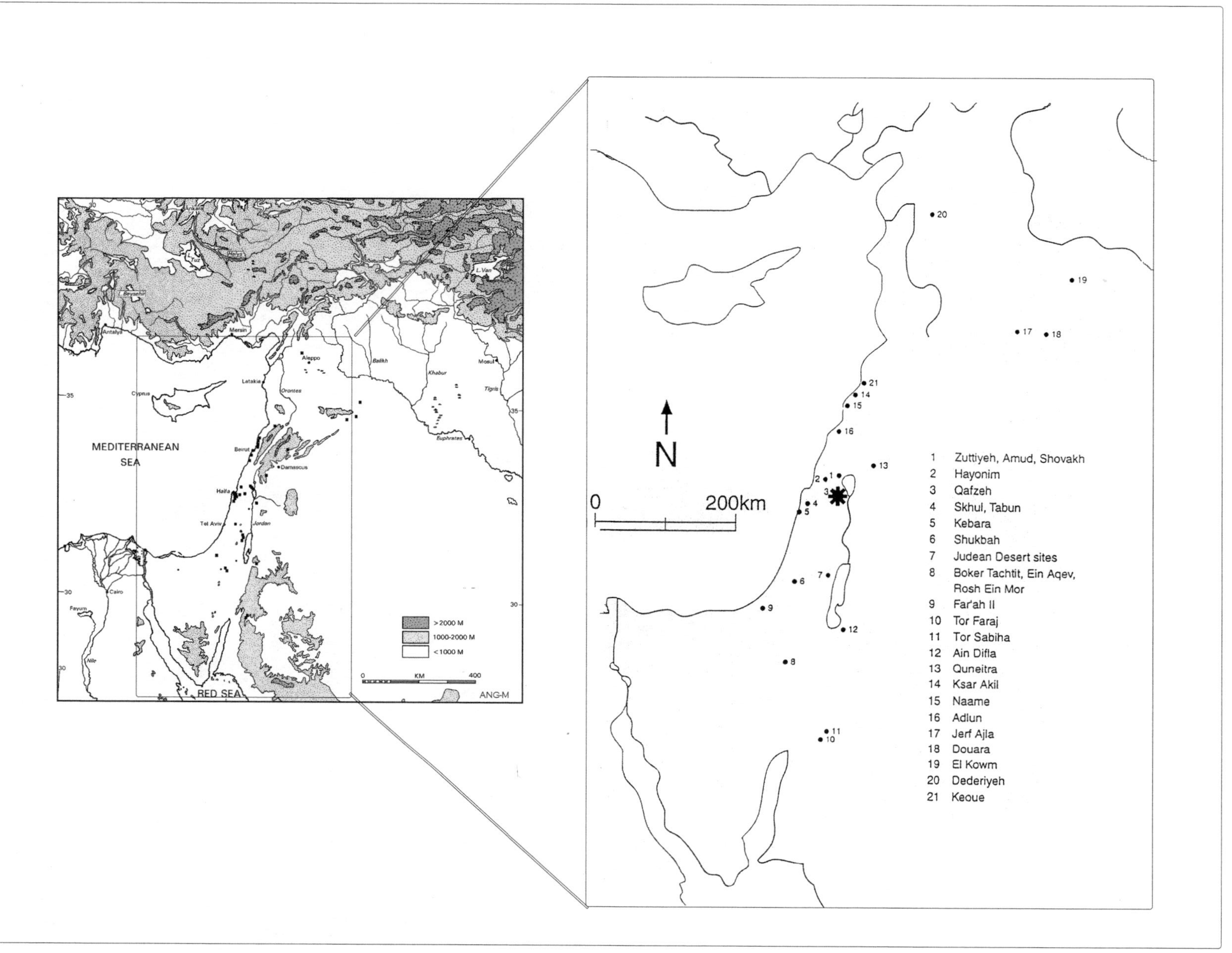



Location map of Qafzeh Cave in the Levant, showing the regional topography and the locations of sites mentioned in the text.

# Foreword

Most Old World prehistorians are aware that Qafzeh cave, located just outside Nazareth, on the eastern slopes of Gebel Qafzeh and overlooking the Jezreel Valley, occupies a special place in the study of human evolution. This is due to early discoveries made by Rene Neuville and Moshe Stekelis during the first series of excavations in the cave in 1932–1935. The first-discovered human fossils were probably a group of intentional burials embedded in deposits that contain stone tool assemblages attributed to the Middle Paleolithic. Surprisingly, the fossils did not resemble the typical Neanderthals known from the Middle Paleolithic contexts of caves and rock shelters in Western Europe. Most striking for contemporary scholars, and during the ensuing years, was the association of human relics, today referred to as Anatomically Modern Humans, with the same tool kits that otherwise in Europe were attributed to Neanderthals. During the 1930s the flint artifacts uncovered in the lower layers at Qafzeh cave were classified as Levalloisian or Levalloisian-Mousterian, a term coined by Dorothy Garrod, a contemporary of R. Neuville and M. Stekelis. The two famous palaeoanthropologists Sir A. Keith and Th. McCown, who were working with D. Garrod in the Mt Carmel caves, suggested that a similar series of fossils be called *Paleoanthropus palestinensis*. By baptizing the fossils with a new name, the researchers wanted to stress that they were different from the European Neanderthals, however, still resembling the earlier fossil classified at the time as Pallaeoanthropines. But while the stone artifacts found in Skhul and Tabun caves in Mt Carmel were published by D. Garrod in her seminal volume (Garrod and Bate 1937), the Middle Paleolithic lithic industry of Qafzeh cave remained unpublished.

Sometimes the fate of a particular aspect of prehistoric research seems to follow the same course over many years. Thus, the collections from the first series of excavations were deposited in two places, the Rockfeller Museum in Jerusalem and the Institute of Archaeology of the Hebrew University, and until 1967 there was no way of studying them according to the original stratigraphic attribution as made by R. Neuville and M. Stekelis. By that time the new series of excavations conducted by one of us (B.V.) had already been underway since 1965. Indeed, again the main target of the excavations in Qafzeh cave was the verification of the stratigraphy, systematically obtaining lithic and faunal remains and in particular uncovering additional human remains. These efforts were successful, new human remains were discovered, and preliminary publications were followed by full reports (Vandermeersch 1981; Tillier 1999).

Less obvious was the issue of the chronological placement of the Qafzeh fossils in the evolutionary sequence. Additional field seasons with the participation of the second author (O.B.Y.) from 1977 through 1979 led us to suggest that instead of dating the fossils to ca. 40,000 to 50,000 years ago, the age estimate given at the time, the deposits in which all fossils were found during the two series of excavations should be dated some 80,000 to 100,000 years ago (Bar-Yosef and Vandermeersch 1981). The confirmation came when the results of dating by a series of TL and ESR readings were published (Valladas et al. 1988; Schwarcz et al. 1988). Soon after that the human internments from Skhul cave were also dated to the same time range, 120,000 to 100,000 years ago (Mercier et al. 1993).

The importance of the Qafzeh and Skhul fossils is underlined by the current paradigm of an African origin of Modern humans, supported by the discovery in Africa of several morphologically similar fossils dated to 200,000 to 150,000 years ago. In this context the Levantine fossils can be seen as marking an important step along the route of dispersal leading African Modern humans into Eurasia. As humans moved bearing their own culture and the learned tradition of making stone tools, the study of the lithic industries is an indispensable component for understanding the demographic process.

We thus were delighted when Erella Hovers took upon herself the tasks of studying several archaeological aspects of Qafzeh cave. First was the enormous task of the lithic assemblages that were collected in the new excavations according to modern standards. Most were located with three coordinates, related to a finer stratigraphy than the original one. Her Ph.D. thesis, extensively revised and updated in this impressive volume, marks a major contribution to the study of Middle Paleolithic industries of the Levant. In addition she published about an incised flake found in the new excavations as well as the ochre remains. All these investigations, carried out with full cooperation and coordination with the excavators, are exemplary joint research that is bringing us closer to a better understanding of the site of Qafzeh cave during the Middle Paleolithic.

None of these studies could have been done without the support that we received during the excavations. We are therefore grateful to the French Ministry of Foreign Affairs, the CNRS, the French Mission in Jerusalem (now know as Centre des Recherches Français de Jérusalem), and in particular to J. Perrot who assisted us in many various ways.

We remember with gratitude the energy of many students and volunteers, digging in the heat of the summer, and working in the evenings. Particularly thanks to A.-M. Tiller and Mario Chech. Many others participated in the study of the Qafzeh cave stratigraphy, lithics, and fauna. For the geological aspects we are grateful to W. Farrand and P. Goldberg, for the dates to H. Vallads and H. P. Schwarcz, for the faunal studies to the late J. Bouchud, G. Haas, E. Tchernov, and recently R. Rabinovich.

Bernard Vandermeersch<br>Ofer Bar-Yosef

## References


Bar-Yosef, O., and Vandermeersch, B. 1981. Notes Concerning the Possible Age of the Mousterian Layers in Qafzeh Cave. In J. Cauvin and P. Sanlaville (eds.), *Préhistoire du Levant,* pp. 281–285. CNRS, Paris.

Garrod, D. A. E., and Bate, D. M. A. 1937. *The Stone Age of Mount Carmel.* Clarendon Press, Oxford.

Mercier, N., Valladas, H., Bar-Yosef, O., Vandermeersch, B., Stringer, C., and Joron, J. L. 1993. Thermoluminescence Date for the Mousterian Burial Site of Es-Skhul Mt. Carmel. *Journal of Archaeological Science* 20: 169–74.

Schwarcz, H. P., Grün, R., Vandermeersch, B., Bar-Yosef, O., Valladas, H., and Tchernov, E., 1988. ESR Dates for the Hominid Burial Site of Qafzeh in Israel. *Journal of Human Evolution* 17: 733–737.

Tillier, A. M. (1999). *Les Enfants moustériens de Qafzeh : Interprétations phylogénétique et paléoauxologique.* CNRS, Paris.

Valladas, H., Reyss, J. L., Joron, J. L., Valladas, G., Bar-Yosef, O., and Vandermeersch, B. 1988. Thermoluminescence Dating of Mousterian "Proto-cro-magnon" Remains from Israel and the Origin of Modern Man. *Nature* 331 : 614–616.

Vandermeersch, B. (1981). *Les Hommes fossiles de Qafzeh (Israël).* CNRS, Paris.

# The Lithic Assemblages of Qafzeh Cave

# 1

## Introduction

Studies of the Middle Paleolithic are closely linked with the question of modern human origins. Historically, the appearance of morphologically modern humans in Europe was conceived as the immediate cause for the emergence of cultural and behavioral modernity. The picture in the Levant has been dramatically different, with Anatomically Modern Humans (referred to throughout the book as "Moderns") appearing on the local scene as early as the Middle Paleolithic. During the Middle Paleolithic in the Levant cultural shifts were not coterminous with biological changes, and behavioral differences between Neanderthals and Moderns are not easily recognized. Consequently, the Levantine Middle Paleolithic record is highly pertinent for understanding the conditions under which behavioral modernity (in itself an elusive term that rests on weak theoretical foundations and is open to many, sometimes contradictory, interpretations) emerged (see Henshilwood and Marean 2003; Kuhn and Hovers 2006).

Recent paleoanthropological research has approached the question of modern human origins with the analytical tools of three scientific disciplines—genetics, human paleontology, and archaeology. Based especially on data from the former two, two main theories of modern human origins have been formulated, with additional "weak" variants of the extreme positions. The "multiregional" or "regional continuity" theory posits that modern humans evolved from regional populations that were initially formed following a dispersal (or dispersals) of *Homo ergaster/erectus* from Africa in the Lower or Middle Pleistocene. Modern humans evolved, according to this model, as a single polytypic species united by extensive gene flow and migrations to the extent that no reproductive barriers were formed (e.g., Clark and Lindly 1989;

Frayer et al. 1993; Wolpoff et al. 1994). This would suggest that European Neanderthals shared their gene pool with contemporaneous African and Levantine populations as well as their successors on the European scene, possibly to this day. Advocates of the "Out-of-Africa" or "replacement" model envision the evolution of a specific human group from an African parent population at some as yet debated time in the late Middle Pleistocene. This group's subsequent dispersal into the rest of the Old World led to replacement of the pre-existing regional populations without genetic admixture (Cann, Stoneking, and Wilson 1987; Caramelli et al. 2003; Noonan et al. 2006; Stoneking 1993; Stringer 1988; Stringer and Andrews 1988). The archaeological record, notably in Europe, has been enlisted to vindicate both theories (e.g., Stringer and Gamble 1993).

Phylogeny, anatomy, and behavior are interconnected, but the pathways of their interactions are largely unknown. In practice, this implies that none of these disciplines can simply borrow or unquestioningly rely on the methods and results obtained by researchers in the other fields. In the 1980s and the early 1990s it seemed that scientists from the three branches of academic inquiry aspired to stand united and form interdisciplinary coalitions in support of one or another theory. Recently, however, paleoanthropology (*sensu lato*) seems to have undergone a process of maturation. Now that the novelty of genetic research on modern human origins is wearing off, reflection on and re-evaluation of a large body of data is paving the way for new insights into the origins of behavioral modernity.

Neither morphological nor genetic data have resolved the phylogeny of Pleistocene *Homo*. This is in large part because the taxonomic significance of morphological and genetic differences between closely related animals is often unclear. Succinctly summarized, such recent studies have demonstrated that the view of cause-and-effect relationships, by which modern anatomy (presumably complete with a modern neurological system) and modern behavior necessarily emerged together, is no longer valid in any geographic region of the Old World. Many independent genetic and anatomical studies are consistent with the notion of Neanderthals as a separate group, possibly reproductively isolated to an extent that justifies their specific designation as *Homo neanderthalensis*. In parallel, although multiple lines of genetic and anatomical data coalesce in Africa as the place of origin of *Homo sapiens*, the mechanisms of its emergence and of its becoming a colonizing species are still being debated. The genetic and fossil data are sometimes interpreted as suggesting the emergence of *Homo sapiens* from a speciation event in Africa, followed by dispersal and subsequent replacement of archaic populations. Such seemingly decisive analyses of modern and fossil human DNA, interpreted as supporting a recent African origin of anatomically modern humans, continue to be challenged on both methodological and interpretive grounds. The data are alternatively viewed as indicating an African origin followed by periods of gene flow. A third view endorses a process of wave diffusion, including hybridization and assimilation at the wave front. Similarly, the chronological framework for such events and processes is as yet unresolved (see Arcadi 2006; Bazin, Glemin, and Galtier 2006; Cann 2001; Caramelli et al. 2003, 2006; Eswaran 2002; Eswaran, Harpending, and Rogers 2005; Harpending et al. 1998; Knight 2003; Krings et al. 1997, 2000; Mellars 2005; Relethford 2001; Templeton 2002; White et al. 2003 for some recent discussions).

Against this background the behavioral and cultural variations that are archaeology's subject matter emerge as being more complex than a straightforward Neanderthal–Modern dichotomy. It is increasingly apparent that biological and cultural changes during the Upper Pleistocene did not necessarily coincide across time and space, nor did they follow a single, repetitive pattern when they occurred (Bar-Yosef and Pilbeam 2000; d'Errico et al. 1998; Hovers 1992; Hovers and Belfer-Cohen 2006; McBrearty and Brooks 2000; Mellars 1989, 1990, 2000; Mellars and Stringer 1989).

It seems, then, that the issue of the origin of modern humans in its broad biological and cultural context can best be studied if approached through multiple independent lines of evidence, rather than by harnessing the different disciplines to serve the dictates of one or another major theory (Hovers 1997, 2006; Kuhn and Hovers 2006). Archaeology cannot be (nor should it be expected to be) a tool for evaluating genetic and physical anthropological models. But it can make its unique contribution by documenting and pondering the variations observed in human behaviors, including mobility, subsistence, social organization, and symbolic systems, and placing them in a long-term, evolutionary context. From this point of view, the Middle Paleolithic presents the researcher with a number of interesting questions.

The conditions, processes, and events that brought on the breakdown (on an evolutionary timescale) of the Middle Paleolithic and enabled the processes of "Upper Paleolithization" are interesting not only because they inform us about our own species. The end of the Middle Paleolithic allows us to ponder, perhaps for the first time in the study of human prehistory against a relatively high-resolution record, how major cultural changes came about and how they were propelled by evolutionary and historical forces. With the Mousterian as its most widespread material cultural manifestation, the Middle Paleolithic presents us, by default of its ca. 200,000-year existence (possibly longer in Africa), with an evolutionary success story. The geographic distribution of the Eurasian Mousterian speaks to its resilience over an array of environments during this long time span, implying that robust mechanisms of adaptation were at work.[1] Regardless of the particular historical scenario that one supports as an explanation for the end of the Mousterian and the onset of the Upper Paleolithic, it is hard to understand this change without elucidating the dynamics of the Mousterian as a system of adaptation. It is unlikely that the Mousterian would have survived the constantly changing world of the late Middle and Upper Pleistocene without a degree of behavioral flexibility and variability, the raw material on which selection acts.

## What Creates Variability?

The specific goal of archaeology is probably best defined as the documentation and explanation of long-term evolutionary changes in human behavior, through its unique access to artifacts as the visible characteristics of these behaviors. Under the basic premise that material culture reflects human behavior, the long-term and widespread phenomenon of the Middle Paleolithic is expected to exhibit variability of material culture that will reflect the variable behaviors of hominins.

Archaeologists have borrowed optimization models from ecological evolution and used them extensively in their attempts to document and explain how the human–environment interface has shaped the behaviors of present and past societies (Foley 1987a; Jochim 1979, 1981; Winterhalder and Smith 1981), relying on a host of simplifying assumptions. Human behavior has been assumed to be omniscient and to have occurred in a homogeneous and unchangeable world. Hence quantifiable flows of energy/matter could be studied in isolation from the social and cultural traits of the system in which they occur (Moore 1983). In assuming an environment that does not change and a cultural matrix that does not influence behavior, formal optimization studies make only a minor contribution to the understanding of long-term cultural evolution (Fitzhugh 2001).

Things are, of course, more complicated in the real world, which is anything but homogeneous in any of its aspects. Out there, the process of adapting to prevailing conditions requires constant evaluation of risks and advantages presented by the environment. Human behaviors in this context are best understood and analyzed as a spectrum of problem-solving strategies that are acted out on the basis of continuous decision making in ever-changing environments. In the case of humans there is an important twist to the conventional wisdom of ecological thought about adaptation: humans have culture.[2] To identify (and hopefully to explain) variability, we need to know something about culture as a source of variation.

One way or another, all decision making and behaviors ensuing from it are the result of the interaction between genetic information stored in the developing organism and the properties of its environments. But organic and cultural evolution are distinct, though interacting, systems of inheritance that are formed and propelled by different mechanisms (Boyd and Richerson 1985; Durham 1991; Ehrlich and Feldman 2003). The transmission of cultural traits, while similar in some important ways to Darwinian inheritance systems (e.g., Durham 1991), differs from them in significant ways (Ehrlich and Feldman 2003). Processes similar to natural selection are important in cultural change, as are copying errors and drift, but processes that have no analogs in genetic evolution also play important roles in cultural evolution (Eerkens and Lipo 2005; Richerson and Boyd 2005:6; papers in Ziman 2000a).

Lamarckian processes of cultural transmission are an obvious example of the difference between genetic and cultural systems of inheritance. Culture is adaptive because the way in which individuals behave is a rich source of information to an observer about which behaviors are adaptive and which are less so. The mechanisms of transmission of information and knowledge are themselves variable. Individuals within a group may learn from one another through cultural transmission by social learning (such as teaching or imitation) or by individual, trial-and-error learning directly from the environment ("acultural" behavior) (Laland 1998; Laland, Odling-Smee, and Feldman 2000; Rogers 1988). Because of its Lamarckian nature, cultural transmission, in most circumstances, allows individuals to adapt more quickly to changing environments than is possible under either a strictly genetic mode of transmission or a system that includes individual learning. Social learning provides individuals with useful information without the inherent risks and costs of trial-and-error learning. It enables access to information about events that these individuals have never experienced personally, about the potential strategies of dealing with such events, and about those strategies that have been tried and are socially acceptable (Alvard 2003; Kameda and Nakanishi 2003). Social learning, however, can get out of hand. If everyone relied fully and solely on imitation, for example, behavior would become decoupled from the environment and the imitated behaviors would no longer be responsive to the conditions of the environment. In other words, the mechanism of information transmission would no longer be adaptive (Richerson and Boyd 2005:12). In sum, mechanisms that govern the acquisition of cultural behaviors are in themselves a form of behavioral plasticity and can be understood in terms of natural selection. Switching between individual and social learning in adjustment to the prevailing conditions increases the mean fitness of populations (Kameda and Nakanishi 2003; Richerson and Boyd 2005:9–10) because it enables emphasis on the quality of information or the rate of transmission according to the tempo of change.

Another major way in which the cultural system of inheritance differs from the genetic one is that culture is not a passive mechanism of adaptation. Genetic inheritance is a dynamic system in that natural selection (combined with mutation and drift) leads to the emergence, and the occasional evolutionary success, of new forms. However, culture does more than this. By amplifying the capacity of humans to shape the sources of natural selection in their environments, culture constructs new ecological niches that they can exploit (Laland, Odling-Smee, and Feldman 2000). This in turn may create a feedback loop that encompasses more potential variation on which selection can operate.[3]

A pertinent point for understanding culture is that as an adaptive system it answers to two masters, interfacing with both the social and the physical environment. Social and cultural infrastructures, created and transmitted through the "second inheritance system" (Whiten 2005b), incorporate different measures of "best fit" and require different modes of achieving them than does the genetic system. The selective pressures of these two systems do not necessarily operate in tandem. Behaviors that may be the preferred solutions for coping with the physical outside world are also subject to internal, cultural and social selective pressures (and vice versa). Decision-making processes, and the actions that emanate from them, obviously need to address the individual's needs for food, heat, and shelter, and the constraints imposed by the environment on obtaining them (e.g., availability and distribution of the desired resources). As archaeologists who deal with physical objects, we are accustomed to infer decision-making processes that respond to this aspect from the material record. But the same behaviors must also satisfy decision criteria anchored in the values and beliefs of the society in which the individual exists. If they fail to respond in any way to both types of selection, behaviors will not survive in the cultural repertoire of a group. At the other extreme, cultural traits can be retained and practiced when they are not "economic" (i.e., do not contribute directly to fitness or to reproductive success) because cultural transmission is strongly structured by conformist biasing. As a result of this duality, problem-solving strategies may be variable even if employed to address similar problems within similar physical environments because they satisfy varying decision criteria, whereas different decision processes may lead to similar acted behaviors (the phenomenon known as equifinality). Despite being an inheritance system that responds to a process similar to natural selection, cultural behavior is context-specific. In order to discuss long-term evolutionary changes, we first have to ask historical questions about how the behaviors reflected in the archaeological record came about (Carrithers 1990; O'Brien and Lyman 2002).

Separating the distinct effects of genes, environment, and culture as determinants of variation of human behavior is a difficult task even in the context of extant societies, not least because the variability of human behavior makes it difficult to discern their respective roles. Even when attempting to explain observed human behavior, the common practice among evolutionary social scientists is to look first to genes and environments as possible causative agents. Culture is proposed as a potential explanation for variation after the other two agents are eliminated. The task of isolating the processes that create variation in the behaviors of humans in the past is obviously more difficult for paleoanthropologists, who cannot observe behavior directly and must work with (what are assumed to be) its material proxies. The practice is nonetheless similar. In a research program that endorses evolutionary processes, and views change as an adaptive response to selective pressures, the challenge of the archaeological record is for us first to identify behavior, and then to decipher why any behavioral strategy may have been advantageous in some circumstances but not in others (see also Kuhn 1995a; Perlès 1992). This is usually done by first addressing behavior as an adaptive response to the environment (see, e.g., Hovers 1997; Schiffer and Miller 1999; and discussion in this volume for a different approach).

Two points require some elaboration before we dive into a discussion of Middle Paleolithic variability. To begin with, is culture a relevant term for discussing the Middle Paleolithic? This is a matter of considerable debate. Many scholars argue that this is at best a moot point in the archaeological record. A more realistic scenario in their view is that culture is a modern phenomenon and was not part of the behavior of earlier hominins (e.g., Binford 1983, 1989; Clark and Riel-Salvatore 2006;

Klein 1995, 2000; Knight, Power, and Watts 1995; Mithen 1996). This notion seems untenable in view of recently accumulated data on cultural transmission and decision making among nonhuman animals, which offer new insights into human prehistory. Arguments for the lack of culture among nonhuman animals are often dependent on semantics: "Define culture one way and it is the exclusive province of human beings; another way, and a multitude of species are deemed worthy of the accolade" (Laland and Hoppitt 2003:150; Whiten 2005a). Characteristics formerly perceived as uniquely human are now known to be shared with other animals, notably primates, and among these primarily chimpanzees. For instance, variability in subsistence behaviors such as nut-cracking or ant-fishing has been shown to be largely unrelated to ecological factors and dictated by the chimpanzees' propensity for cultural (or "cultural," depending on one's take on this issue) behavior stemming from mechanisms of social learning (for discussion of the broader issue, see Byrne 1998; Snowdon 1990; Tomasello and Call 1994; van Schaik and Pradham 2003; Weiskrantz 1988; Whiten et al. 1999).

There are visible differences between human and nonhuman cultures. Human culture is much more likely to be cumulative than animal culture and is characterized by the "ratchet effect," whereby the complexity or efficiency of a behavior increases with time (Hovers and Belfer-Cohen 2006; Tomasello 1994, cited in Laland and Hoppit 2003). While the reasons for these differences are not well established, they cannot be pinned critically or exclusively on mechanisms of transmission (teaching or imitation), language, or perspective-taking (Boesch 2003; Laland and Hoppitt 2003). Possibly, the uniqueness of human culture lies in the fact that it is an emergent property; it takes many willingly interacting participants to form the dynamic processes of social encoding and to transmit by various forms of learning the codes of behavior rather than the behavior itself (Chase 2006). Moreover, the material culture and social behavior of any nonhuman primate are most likely not homologous to those of humans, even if some of the cognitive capacities underlying cultural behaviors occurred before the split between hominins and the great apes (see discussion in Chase 2006:75–82). Some of the cultural behaviors identified today may have formed relatively recently in these animals' evolutionary history.[4] It can, however, be suggested that prehistoric humans were capable of similar types of cultural behavior. Throughout prehistory hominins relied more and more on mechanisms of social learning to facilitate the pooling and sharing of information and to expedite processes of decision making (Dunbar 2003; Humphrey 1976). Against this background, there is no a priori reason to deny the existence of cultural transmission and possibly some form of verbal communication in extinct hominins (e.g., Calvin and Bickerton 2000; Deacon 1997, and references therein).

Moreover, one could argue that it is inconceivable that the variety of reactions to a shifting, unstable natural and social environment were strictly genetically determined in any one complex organism (Ehrlich and Feldman 2003; Pulliam and Dunford 1980). Certainly, this notion is corroborated by an increasing number of studies on intra-site spatial patterning, acquisition and curation of foodstuffs and raw materials, together with symbolic occurrences, in Middle Paleolithic (if not earlier) sites (e.g., Alperson-Afil and Hovers 2005; Chase 1986; d'Errico et al. 2003; Goren-Inbar 1988a; Henry et al. 2004; Henshilwood et al. 2002; Hovers et al. 1995, 2003; Meignen 1994b; Mithen 1990; Roebroeks, Kolen, and Rensink 1988; Speth 2006; Stiner and Kuhn 1992 ).

A second significant point in discussing culture in the context of Middle Paleolithic archaeology is that the craft of manufacturing lithic artifacts, the subject matter of the current analysis, can be transmitted only through social learning, either as active teaching or by imitation. This was probably true of the crudest tools, if chimpanzee studies provide any guidelines, as well as of the more sophisticated morphologies of Acheulean and later stone tools (Ohnuma, Aoki, and Akazawa 1997; Toth et al. 1993). The general trend of increasing complexity and standardization of stone tools during the Lower Paleolithic thus possibly indicates an evolving ability to transmit growing amounts of spatial and mechanical information (see Belfer-Cohen and Goren-Inbar 1994; Robson-Brown 1993).

In sum, the current evidence shows that cognitive and cultural abilities (in addition to physical and environmental forces) that are implicated in the formation of behavioral variability must have been in place during the Middle Paleolithic, and probably earlier. The ability to create and transmit cultural traits is therefore a capacity to reckon with in Middle Paleolithic contexts. This is not to argue that the behaviors of early hominins were necessarily governed by rational or conscious decision-making processes. But then this is not necessarily the characteristic feature of the decision making of extant humans, among whom emotion and decision without due attention have been implicated in economic decision making (Dijksterhuis et al. 2006; Sanfey et al. 2003). (It is for this reason that the term "strategy" is used in the discussion below as an analytical concept rather than as a reference to mental thought processes.) Ecological perspectives likely provide first approximations of this variability, but it is doubtful that they can be the sole (or even the main) explanation of the phenomenon. It is with this caveat in mind that current models attempting to explain Levantine Middle Paleolithic variability should be evaluated.

## The Processes that Formed Mousterian Lithic Assemblages

Broadly speaking, archaeologists have tended to align themselves with one of two approaches in their attempts to pry information from material culture, in general, and stone tools, in particular. One approach relies on patterns of lithic technology to reconstruct population histories, treating stone tools as markers of distinct populations. This point of view encapsulates the assumption that similarity in stone tools stems from their being made by groups belonging to the same culture. Implicit in this view is the assumption that the complexity and sophistication of stone tools reflect the cognitive abilities and the complexity of social organization of the people who made them. The second approach to the study of lithics regards stone tools as adaptive means of tackling environmental demands and constraints, so that changes in lithic assemblages reflect functional responses to environmental shifts. Similarities in the assemblages are analogous to one another, as they arose independently among separate groups responding to similar environmental pressures and challenges. In this case stone tools are not expected to hold much significance as cultural markers and cannot provide clues to the cultural phylogeny of human groups. The "Mousterian debate" of the 1960s is perhaps the best-known clash between these two worldviews, in the wake of which a new approach to variability in prehistoric material culture was constructed.

### The "Mousterian Debate": Culture or Function in Tool Forms?

Archaeological investigations in the first half of the twentieth century were replete with the notion that stone tools reflect the cultural and social groupings of the populations that made them. To archaeologists, who cannot observe the actual process of making things, the ways in which objects had been made and used were a priori evidence of the intent of the implements' makers. This emphasis changed in the second half of the century to the currently common "ecological" approaches to lithics. The debate between François Bordes and Lewis Binford in the late 1960s and the 1970s epitomized this shift in emphasis. An equally important aspect of this debate was that it constituted the first instance in which Middle Paleolithic lithic variability was addressed as such.

Echoing an ongoing "typological debate" in ethnology (Adams and Adams 1991), Bordes and Binford engaged in a debate about the meaning of Mousterian lithics. Both emphasized the intentionality of human actions as the foundation for Mousterian tool morphologies and assemblage compositions, but had very different opinions about the causes for the observed patterns.

As early as 1936, Marcel Mauss had argued that technique, the basic unit of human material culture, is an action that is both effective (i.e., has a role in the social and physical world) and traditional (namely, is learned as part of an inherited cultural package). Very much along the same lines, Bordes considered culture to be the basic unit of reference and viewed collective behavior as an expression of underlying thought patterns and cultural affiliations. He regarded artifact classification as a way to identify the cultural affiliations of the toolmakers. As an archaeologist he had to work with inanimate objects, recovered from archaeological contexts devoid of culturally significant gestures. Therefore his interests focused on variations in the patterning of the material end-products and their cultural meaning.

Bordes devised a system for standardizing the analysis of Middle Paleolithic lithics and of quantifying the observations (e.g., Bordes 1950, 1953c; Bordes and Bourgon 1951) so that assemblages could be compared statistically. The emerging quantified patterns of inter-assemblage typological and technological variation convinced him that several lithic variants could be distinguished from one another. Technological observations were incorporated as quantitative indices into Bordes's criteria for distinguishing the various cultural entities (e.g., Bordes 1950, 1953c; Bordes and Bourgon 1951). Still, it was typological traits (i.e., tool morphologies) that he considered to be the main criteria for identifying these entities. For instance, he combined his originally separate Quina and Ferrassie variants into the "Charentian" group because both were scraper-rich, and despite the notable differences in core-reduction technologies involved in producing each variant (Geneste et al. 1997). The distinction between types relied mainly on the fluctuating frequencies of typological markers (e.g., denticulates, scrapers) and on the occurrence of idiosyncratic tools in some of the variants, e.g., cordiform handaxes and extensively retouched backed knives in the *Mousterién Tradition Acheuléan* (MTA), or limaces in the Charentian Mousterian (see summary in Mellars 1996:320). After rejecting hypotheses of environmental change as the cause of variability, Bordes interpreted changes in type frequencies as stylistic markers of prehistoric cultures (Bordes 1961, 1972, 1973; Bordes and de Sonneville-Bordes 1970). Consequently, he assigned ethnic significance to the typological variability that enabled the recognition of four Mousterian variants (i.e., the MTA, Denticulate, Typical, and Charentian Mousterian).

In contrast to Bordes's "culture history" approach, Binford advocated an "adaptive function" view of the archaeological record, focusing on society rather than culture as the unit of analysis. Binford's attention centered on how people in a society used their technology, how they applied it to the tasks at hand, and what type of artifacts they manufactured and used in the process. To Binford the morphologies of Mousterian lithics and their quantitative patterning spoke of activities with artifacts as a means of adaptation rather than as the outcome of the application of preset, culture-derived mental templates.[5] The initiative for retouching blanks into tools was deemed to be of functional origin, as tool morphologies were shaped in order for the tools to perform particular tasks. Patterns of blank selection were also indications of a functional choice, since "few would disagree that…fabrication plans are guided by some ideas regarding the desired outcomes" (Binford 1978). Thus, the assemblage types identified by Bordes were to Binford material residues reflecting adaptive responses to spatial and temporal changes in the environment. As such, they reflected the nature of activities at the site in which they were found and the nature of the site's occupation (Binford 1973; Binford and Binford 1966). And since the number of solutions to any given problem would be limited by material constraints, these responses were likely to be redundant and to cross temporal and spatial boundaries. Middle Paleolithic lithic variability, therefore, was devoid of ethnic significance (Binford 1972:186–327, 1973:246).

Dibble (1987, 1991a, 1995a) introduced yet another facet to the "Mousterian debate." Looking at the major typological classes recognized by Bordes and accepted by Binford (specifically, the various categories of side-scrapers), he argued that they represented a single continuum of intensifying retouch, the need for which may have risen due to scarcity of suitable raw materials (Braun 2005; Barton 1990; Dibble 1987, 1991a; see the adaptation of this view to other cultural contexts in McPherran 2000; Neeley and Barton 1994). Evaluations of this deterministic hypothesis have been inconclusive (Dibble 1995a; Gordon 1993; Kuhn 1992a). Although this too is a functional/adaptive approach to understanding artifact morphologies, it differs fundamentally from Binford's in that it denies purposeful design of many of the traditional tool types.

## The Concept of "Technological Organization"

There is a broad consensus that technologies are systemic behaviors and that "even the simplest techniques of any primitive society take on the character of a system that can be analyzed, in terms of a more general system" (Levi-Strauss 1976:11). However, there is no unanimous view about the materials and issues that are studied as "technological organization" (see papers in Carr 1994; Torrence 1989b).

The theoretical framework of "technological organization" was constructed (e.g., Binford 1983:87–94, 100, 143) within the general functional/adaptive approach that characterized Binford's earlier attempts at understanding the "Mousterian problem" (Binford 1979, 1980, 1983, 1989;

see also Schiffer 1987). Looking to ethnographic analyses to inform him of the processes leading to the formation of assemblages of material artifacts, Binford emphasized the changing roles of mobility and settlement strategies as behavioral adaptations to varying needs of human groups combined with shifts in resource structure and availability. Such complex interactions seemed to determine the dynamics of technological systems and their signatures (e.g., modes, rates and locations of production, transport, and use and discard of artifacts) in ethnographic situations.

The extensive use of ethnographic observations as analogs for the technological organization of prehistoric peoples is not self-evident and requires justification. To begin with, there are ethical and philosophical questions that are inseparable from the use of ethnographic data in archaeology. Extant hunter-gatherers are not fossilized remains of the Paleolithic, and their behaviors are not residues of the Paleolithic way of life. Furthermore, they cannot be considered a direct analogy for prehistoric behaviors (Gould 1980:29–36; O'Connell 1995; Wylie 1985). The wealth of ethnographic behavioral data is irrecoverable by archaeology. It may (too easily) be projected into the past, but at best such projection would be an unsubstantiated assumption.

This is not an easy problem to tackle, since "no amount of improvement in the knowledge of the present contexts could establish the empirical credibility of the claims an interpretative hypothesis makes about the past" (Binford 1967:10). The variability observed in the behaviors of current hunter-gatherers may have arisen in its present format only with the occurrence of behaviorally modern humans (Kelly 1995:333–338; Klein 1995). The issue bears directly on the question of the variability of material culture in the Middle Paleolithic. Lithic assemblages of this time span are often considered monotonous and relatively homogenous, despite the long duration of the Middle Paleolithic that incorporates many technological shifts (e.g., Kuhn 1995a; Shea 2006a). This is viewed as a significant contrast to the regional variations in the morphologies of similarly used artifacts observed among extant hunter-gatherers who live under variable environmental conditions. It has been suggested that the beginnings of this trend go back to the Upper Paleolithic, when there is little doubt that behaviorally modern humans inhabited most of the Old World (e.g., Klein 1995).

Inferences made from ethnographic observations to the archaeological record are founded on the assumption that past hunter-gatherers were faced with the same types of challenges as are extant ones. Paleolithic groups had to decide and act on access to raw materials, transport of implements, and the optimal ways of orchestrating subsistence-related behaviors, such as procuring food and finding and preparing shelter and fuel under changing conditions. On the assumption that decision-making processes responded to similar types of challenges and survival requirements, the use of economic models within an evolutionary framework provides the tools to overcome the inherently problematic contribution of ethnographic and ethnoarchaeological research to Paleolithic studies. It enables identification of the constraints underlying the observed patterns, so that predictions can be generated and tested to explain the variability in a large number of behaviors, ranging between food-getting technologies, foraging patterns, resource sharing, group composition, territoriality, and the formation of social hierarchies (O'Connell 1995:209–210). The material and behavioral records of modern hunter-gatherer groups have become the frames of reference for model building and for the formulation of hypotheses about the past (Binford 2001 and references; Binford and O'Connell 1984; Galanidou 2000; Kuhn 1995a).

What, then, does the organization of a technological system entail? To answer this question, it is necessary first to define the desired goals and, perhaps more importantly, the constraints of such systems. Technological systems are about problem solving, and the problems that they address involve risk management: how can the risk of failure to obtain resources adequately be minimized? As adequacy is measured in the currencies of time and energy, technological systems are organized so as to minimize expenditure of these currencies compared to the gain in survival potential conferred by the exploited resources (Jochim 1979, 1981, 1983; Torrence 1989a, 1989b). To achieve this goal, prehistoric groups scheduled their movements around the landscape to correspond to the spatio-temporal distribution of their resources, and they used strategies to ensure that the technological aids used to extract resources (i.e., tools designed and made in order to obtain resources from the environment) were available where and when they were needed.

Extractive technologies in the prehistoric past may have used a large number of raw materials. Wood and bone may have been part of human extractive technology from as early as the Lower Pleistocene (e.g., Backwell and d'Errico 2004, 2008; Belitzky, Goren-Inbar, and Werker 1991; d'Errico and Backwell 2003; Goren-Inbar et al. 2000) and certainly since the late Middle Pleistocene, as evidenced by the impressive wooden spears found in several European sites (Oakely et al. 1977; Thieme 1997). For the Mousterian, however, there is little tangible evidence for the use of other raw materials such as bone (see Villa and d'Errico 2001; but also Gaudzinski 1999). The focus of prehistorians on lithics is often blamed on the notoriously incomplete nature of the archaeological record. This is a real enough problem; but lithics were indeed conceived by prehistoric people as functional, technological items characterized by their "for-ness" (Kroes and Meijers 2006).

The archaeological evidence from the Middle Paleolithic onward offers positive evidence of the importance of lithics in extractive technologies, well after other materials had been put to use (e.g., Goring-Morris and Belfer-Cohen 2003; Rots 2002).

With these broadly drawn premises, I now turn to an overview of the Levantine Middle Paleolithic record and the different models aiming to explain its variability.

## The Levantine Middle Paleolithic: An Overview

Different authors have suggested different definitions of the time span of the Levantine Middle Paleolithic and the cultural entities included in it. Some archaeologists consider the group of assemblages known as the Acheulo-Yabrudian as the basal industry of this period (e.g., Jelinek 1982a). Recent studies of both the Acheulo-Yabrudian and the earliest Mousterian, however, suggest that there are significant discontinuities in terms of lithic technology and typology, reflected in the ways of producing flakes and laminar blanks and in the absence of bifaces (e.g., Ashkenazi 2005; Barkai, Gopher, and Shimelmitz 2005; Meignen 2000; Monigal 2002). These justify the view that the beginning of the Middle Paleolithic coincides with the first occurrence of the Mousterian industries (Goren-Inbar 1994).

Now known to have begun some 250,000 years ago, based on thermoluminescence (TL) dates from Tabun and Hayonim Caves (Bar-Yosef 1998a; Mercier and Valladas 2003; Mercier et al. 2007; Valladas and et al. 1998), the Middle Paleolithic period has been studied from the early days of prehistoric research in Israel (appendix 1). The majority of large, stratified cave sites containing remains from this period were first discovered and excavated in the 1920s and 1930s by Garrod (at Tabun, Skhul, Shukba), Neuville (at Qafzeh, the Judean Desert sites), Turville-Petre (in the Amud drainage, Kebara), and Stekelis (Garrod and Bate 1937, 1942; Neuville 1951; Stekelis 1956; Turville-Petre 1932). Some of the major sites were re-excavated and restudied when excavation and retrieval techniques were improved (Bar-Yosef et al. 1992; Copeland 1983a; Jelinek 1977, 1982a; Jelinek et al. 1973; Schick and Stekelis 1977; Vandermeersch 1981). New Mousterian open-air sites were discovered and dug in the Negev, the coastal plain, the Golan Heights, and the Transjordanian plateau, as were caves in Galilee, the Syrian desert, and Lebanon (Akazawa 1979, 1988; Akazawa and Muhesen 2002; Clark et al. 1988; Crew 1976; Gilead 1980, 1988; Gilead and Grigson 1984; Goren-Inbar 1990b; Henry 1995c; Hovers, Rak, and Kimbel 1996; Marks 1976, 1977; Meignen 1998; Munday 1977; Nishiaki 1985; Ronen 1974, 1984; Suzuki and Takai 1970). The renewed and new excavations yielded a wealth of information pertaining to the chronology, human populations, subsistence behavior, site formation processes, and lithic variability, thus establishing the foundation for revised interpretations of human biology and behavior in the Middle Paleolithic Levant.

Findings in the Levant from as early as the 1920s have been pivotal in severing the conceptual Gordian knot between anatomical and cultural modernity (Hovers 1997, 2006). The Eurocentric frame of reference of the 1920s equated Mousterian lithic artifacts with the presence of Neanderthals. Thus, the Zuttiyeh skull, erroneously thought to have been associated with Mousterian lithics, was initially hailed as the first Neanderthal found outside Europe (Turville-Petre 1927), while the discovery of the Tabun C1 Neanderthal skeleton with Mousterian lithics was considered par for the course. Not so with the Skhul human remains, which were found associated with classic Mousterian assemblages, but whose morphological traits were reminiscent of modern *Homo sapiens* (McCown 1934; McCown and Keith 1939). A similar situation was encountered later in Qafzeh Cave (Tillier 1999; Vandermeersch 1981). Subsequent discoveries at the sites of Shanidar, Kebara, Amud, and Dederiyeh did little to resolve the issue.

The human remains found in the Mt. Carmel caves and in Qafzeh Cave raised the question of variation for the first time in the history of paleoanthropology (Wolpoff and Lee 2001). Based on their anatomy the Skhul remains were variably classified, first as belonging to a variant of the Neanderthals ("*Paleoanthropus Palestinensis*," Keith in McCown 1934), and later as intermediate forms between generalized early Neanderthals and modern humans succeeding them ("Proto Cro-Magnon," Howell 1958). Until as late as the 1980s, the Levant was widely regarded as providing the clearest evidence for a transitional phase between Neanderthals and modern humans, with a relatively late date for the transition (Howell 1959; Suzuki and Takai 1970; Wolpoff 1996). The postulated transitional phylogenetic status of the hominins was argued to have been reflected in cultural manifestations as well, specifically in the characteristics of lithic assemblages made by these transitional forms (Jelinek 1982b; Watanabe 1970a).

The notion of transition, congruent with the then-dominant Eurocentric view of human "bio-cultural" evolution, was undermined by anatomical studies (e.g., Rak 1986, 1990; Vandermeersch 1981, 1982; although see Trinkaus et al. 1999), which argued against a view of anagenetic change. A number of physical anthropologists agree that there are two different taxa in the Levantine Middle Paleolithic (e.g., Aiello 1993; Klein 1995; Rak 1993; Vandermeersch 1982). The hominins from Qafzeh and Skhul, and the Tabun C2 mandible (Rak 1998) are identified as anatomically modern humans, while Tabun C1 and the remains from Kebara, Amud, and Dederiyeh Caves are affiliated with the European Neanderthals. According to some researchers (e.g., Rak 1993; Stringer and Gamble 1993), Neanderthals in both regions should be considered members of a distinct species.

An expanding data base of geo-chronological studies now indicates that modern humans antedated or at least were contemporaneous with the Neanderthal-like hominins in the Levant. The age estimates for Skhul and Qafzeh fall 120,000–85,000 years ago, while the Kebara and Amud Neanderthals are dated ca. 70,000–48,000 years ago (Grün et al. 2005; Mercier et al. 1993; Rink et al. 2001; Schwarcz et al. 1988, 1989; Stringer et al. 1989; Valladas et al. 1987, 1988, 1999).

The dating evidence from Tabun is unfortunately contentious because of discrepancies among dating methods (Bar-Yosef 2000; Meignen et al. 2001b). The recently revised TL date of Tabun layer C is 165,000 years ago (Mercier and Valladas 2003). This date would indicate that the Neanderthal C1 pre-dates the known burials of anatomically modern humans found at Qafzeh and Skhul, if the revised Electron Spin Resonance (ESR) age estimates are accepted (Grün and Stringer 2000). However, the Tabun C1 Neanderthal skeleton may be intrusive from layer B into layer C, as hinted by Garrod and Bate (1937) (see discussion in Bar-Yosef and Callander 1999). If so, it could be later than the postulated dates for layer C. Layer B in Tabun is not adequately dated. If the results of recent dating efforts and studies of dental remains are taken at face value (Coppa et al. 2005, 2007), the Neanderthal occupants of Tabun B existed 90,000–80,000 years ago, somewhat earlier than other known Neanderthals in the region. Be that as it may, the anatomically modern mandible C2 was unquestionably found in layer C, stratigraphically somewhat lower than the C1 Neanderthal skeleton (Rak 1998). This situation is minimally congruent with the notion of the two groups' contemporaneity; a more extreme (and realistic, given the resolution of the excavation techniques of the early twentieth century) interpretation of the stratigraphic relationship is that moderns existed in the Levant prior to the Neanderthals, maybe as early as 165,000 years ago.

This TL chronology of Levantine Middle Paleolithic sites, coupled with the anatomical data, is inconsistent with the idea that Neanderthals were the evolutionary forefathers of modern humans, thus refuting the notion of a linear transition between the two taxa. Nonetheless, it has been suggested that all the human remains in the Levant are representatives of a single, highly variable population of modern humans (e.g., Arensburg and Belfer-Cohen 1998; Corruccini 1992; Tillier 2005; Wolpoff and Lee 2001). Such a scenario complies with some variants of the "regional continuity" model (e.g., Clark and Lindly 1989; Frayer et al. 1993; Eswaran 2002; Eswaran et al. 2005; Wolpoff 1989). Alternately, the Qafzeh and

Skhul (and Tabun C2?) hominins could have arrived in the Levant as part of a larger biotic dispersal or diffusion wave (Harpending et al. 1998; Tchernov 1992; Templeton 2002; Walter et al. 2000; White et al. 2003).

Coexistence of Neanderthals and modern humans can no longer be considered a uniquely Levantine trait. Some Neanderthal groups continued to exist in Europe well after the arrival of *Homo sapiens* (Higham et al. 2006; Hublin et al. 1995; Mercier et al. 1991; Schmitz et al. 2002). There are, however, two important differences between the two regions in the patterns of coexistence and overlap during the Middle Paleolithic. First, the time span in which such coexistence occurred in Europe is short compared to the Levant (Conard and Bolus 2003; Mellars 2006). Second, and more pertinent to the business at hand, to date there are no known instances in Europe of modern humans that produced Mousterian lithic assemblages. Moreover, Neanderthal authorship of non–Middle Paleolithic (i.e., Châtelperronian) assemblages has been established in only two cases (at Saint Césaire and Arcy-Sur-Cure; see Bordes 2002; d'Errico et al. 1998; Hublin et al. 1996; Vandermeersch 1984; Zilhão and d'Errico 1999). In contrast, the occurrences of the Mousterian material culture in the Levant cut across taxonomic boundaries. Both populations produced their lithic assemblages by applying Levallois flaking and used a comparable range of typological forms. Additionally, faunal residues found at sites with human skeletal remains show that both groups exploited similar faunal species by hunting (Rabinovich and Hovers 2004; Rabinovich and Tchernov 1995; Speth and Tchernov 1998, 2001; Stiner 2006).

In some respects, the Levantine Middle Paleolithic is not unlike the African Middle Stone Age (MSA), where the use of broadly similar lithic technologies by several non-Neanderthal populations has been recognized over a large geographic scale and a long stretch of time (e.g., Klein 2000; McBrearty and Brooks 2000; Pleurdeau 2003). African hominin fossils that are broadly contemporaneous with the Levantine ones are assigned to several species—*Homo rhodesiensis, Homo helmei,* or *Homo sapiens idaltu* (McBrearty and Brooks 2000; White et al. 2003). These species are thought to have evolved in Africa, although the input of some "backtracking" populations cannot be ruled out (e.g., Dennell and Roebroeks 2005). In contrast, the Levant stands out as a contact area where various Middle Paleolithic human groups that had originated in different continents might have encountered each other. Yet the regional Middle Paleolithic has an "endemic" aspect, with a material culture record that is distinct from those of neighboring regions (e.g., Bar-Yosef 2006: fig. 1). This seeming discrepancy between the postulated evolutionary history of Levantine populations and the trajectories of their material culture bears on the behavioral flexibility of Levantine Middle Paleolithic groups and is informative about processes that enabled the major change that occurred at the end of the period.

## Lithic Variability in the Levantine Middle Paleolithic

To date material expressions of cultural variability in the Levantine Mousterian can be effectively observed mainly in the lithic assemblages, although other behaviors (e.g., burial behavior, hearth construction, hunting strategies, use of space) have recently been studied in this context (Alperson-Afil and Hovers 2005; Henry 2003; Hovers et al. 1995; Meignen et al. 2001a; Rabinovich and Hovers 2004; Speth and Tchernov 2007). The phenomenon has been approached from two distinct worldviews. One was "anagenetic," arguing for a single path of typo-technological change of Mousterian industries throughout the Middle Paleolithic. Neuville's early definitions of Middle Paleolithic lithic assemblages in the Levant conformed with the early European classificatory framework that identified Mousterian and Levallois as two different lithic entities (Neuville 1934: fig. xv).[6] Moreover, only after the publication of the deeply stratified sequences of Tabun and Yabrud was he persuaded that the Mousterian was indeed later than the handaxe industries (Neuville 1951:260–262). Garrod, in turn, emphasized the differences between the Mousterian of the Wadi Mughara caves and the European Mousterian (Garrod 1934:144), recognizing the inadequacy of the Levallois/Mousterian dichotomy in the Levantine context. To indicate the mixture of characteristics in the lithic assemblages of the Levant, she coined the term "Levalloiso-Mousterian" (Garrod and Bate 1937:115).[7] Based on the "key" (Garrod 1934:133) composite sequence of Tabun, Skhul, and el-Wad, Garrod distinguished between Lower and Upper Levalloiso-Mousterian, relying on the "surer test" (compared to lithic typology) of biostratigraphic changes (Garrod and Bate 1937:115).

Both Neuville and Garrod pointed out the differences among the Mount Carmel sites, Judean Desert localities, and Qafzeh. The details of the patterns observed were sometimes contradictory; for example, Garrod noted a decrease over time in the ratio of points to scrapers in Tabun, whereas Neuville observed a reversed pattern at Qafzeh. Still, both researchers described a linear development of industrial phases of the local Mousterian (see also chapter 2).

More recently, Copeland (1975) suggested that variations in the techniques used for Levallois core preparation and frequency shifts of typological classes along the Tabun sequence should be used as a chrono-cultural model for a three-phase sequential change in Mousterian industries of the Levant. Jelinek accepted Tabun as such a model, but recognized only a bipartite division of the sequence (table 1.1; see Jelinek 1982b:74, 1992:256; Ronen 1979). Moreover, he noted that not all the excavated assemblages can be accommodated comfortably into the Tabun model. For example, assemblages from the sites of 'Ain Difla and from the 1960s excavations at Amud Cave showed both Tabun D and B affinities. In the same vein, he viewed the open-air site of Quneitra as an occurrence of a non-Levallois typical Mousterian industry, a variant not known from Tabun. By that time, Garrod had long conceded that "an industry found in isolation cannot be classified as Upper or Lower Levalloiso-Mousterian on the basis of typology alone" (Garrod 1962:234), whereas Copeland herself retracted her linear approach in later publications (e.g., Copeland 1983a). Nonetheless, the model of "Tabun types" is upheld to this day by many archaeologists, albeit with modifications (table 1.1).

Another group of scholars held a radically contrasting, dendritic view of the Levantine Middle Paleolithic. Recognizing five typological variants of the Mousterian, Perrot (1968) adhered to Bordes's ideas about the European Mousterian and identified each such variant as corresponding to a distinct "phylum." He perceived the pattern of variability in the Levantine Mousterian as resulting from a process of branching evolution (*évolution buisonnante*) over time. (Interestingly, Bordes himself did not see this diversity in the Levantine Mousterian.)

Crew (1975) was interested in geographic patterns, specifically interregional comparisons that explored the variation in traits of Levallois products. On this basis, he evaluated the amount and paths of cultural diffusion between the Levantine Mousterian and its Nile Valley and North African counterparts (i.e., the Nubian and Libyan Mousterian). He also looked in some detail at technological differences between coastal and inland sites in the southern Levant (e.g., Kebara, Skhul B, El-Wad G, Tabun D–B, and Shukba versus Erq el-Ahmar E, Abu Sif C–B, Sahba B, Ghar, Rosh Ein Mor, and Nahal Aqev). Although he noted differences on both these geographic scales, he offered no explanations for their occurrences. Skinner (1965), too, saw the variability of the Mousterian as a regional phenomenon. He distinguished between the Zagros Mousterian, typified by high frequencies of retouched tools and low Levallois indices, and the Levantine Mousterian, which he characterized by a moderate to high Levallois component. Skinner identified a higher degree of variability in the Levantine compared to the Zagros Mousterian. Thus, he divided the Levantine Mousterian (his group C) into four industrial types (namely, Abu Sif, Tabun, Yabrud, and Erq el-Ahmar) on typological grounds, including variations in the morphologies of Levallois products. For Skinner these regional differences represented the social and territorial spacing of different Mousterian groups, each of which was associated with its own geographic

**Table 1.1  Division of the Levantine Middle Paleolithic according to the Tabun sequence**

| Author | Phase | Characteristics |
|---|---|---|
| Copeland 1975:329–330 | Phase 1 (Tabun D) | Predominantly single-axis methods of preparation of Levallois cores; laminar, triangular parallel-sided blanks that are struck off along the same axis as the core preparation, evidently by stone hammer; production of heavy flakes and points, some with pronounced bulbs; plain butts common on flakes, blades, and points; relative abundance of retouched Levallois elements. |
| Ronen 1979:302 | Abu Sif facies (Tabun D) | A high proportion of blades and elongated points and a high frequency of Upper Paleolithic elements; relatively few Mousterian tools. |
| Marks 1992b:232 | Early and late early Levantine Mousterian ("Tabun D-type") | Developed unipolar Levallois technology that emphasizes the production of elongated blanks, including many Levallois points; flakes and even shorter points tend to be produced from bipolar Levallois cores; a large range of Levallois techniques, and flakes produced from ovoid centripetally prepared Levallois cores, are not rare; also includes a number of other core reduction techniques, including discoidal through simple single-platform hard-hammer blade production; typologically, only few side-scrapers, moderate frequencies of denticulates, and significant numbers of Upper Paleolithic tools; a temporal trend toward less diverse core reduction strategies and toward blank production from elongated unipolar or bipolar cores; the frequencies of Middle Paleolithic tool types decrease markedly through time to the point of disappearance. |
| Bar-Yosef 1998a:44 | Abu Sifian ("Tabun D-type") | Typical blanks obtained from essentially unipolar convergent cores with evidence for bidirectional flaking; use of both Levallois and non-Levallois methods; minimal preparation of striking platforms; blanks are classified as blades and elongated points. In some cases the appearance of crested blades indicates the use of a prismatic volumetric concept similar to the one that characterizes the Upper Paleolithic blade industries. |
| Copeland 1975:330 | Phase 2 (Tabun C) | Virtual absence (0–2%) of triangular points; the majority of flakes are broad, transverse, oval, or offset types, either centripetally prepared on the dorsal surface or struck off obliquely to the axis of the preparation of the flakes; single-axis cores are virtually absent; very small flakes are abundant; side-scrapers and denticulates are the only common tool types; Upper Paleolithic tools are virtually absent; flakes are used as cores (Nahr Ibrahim pieces are quite common) and cores are reworked into tools; very few retouched Levallois tools. |
| Bar-Yosef 1998a:47 | "Tabun C-type" | Blanks are often oval rectangular, sometimes large flakes, struck from Levallois cores through centripetal and/or bidirectional preparation. Only small numbers of triangular points in definite horizons. |
| Ronen 1979:303 | Tabun C–B facies | Blades are less numerous and the Mousterian components, especially side-scrapers, are more numerous than in the Abu Sif facies. Elongated points are replaced by broad and short points; another group included in this facies is assemblages with a very low number of retouched tools and a dominant Levallois component. |
| Marks 1992b:232 | Late Levantine Mousterian ("Tabun C-type" and "Tabun B-type") | Production of classical ovoid Levallois flakes from centripetally prepared Levallois cores; in addition, some elongated blanks are produced, including some points; on the whole, a wide range of production strategies is used; heavily dominated by side-scrapers and Mousterian points on large and flat flakes; Levallois points and Upper Paleolithic tools are rare; Tabun B type is a combination of D- and C-type; based on Kebara, it has short, wide-based points which become rare in its later phases; Levallois production from unipolar cores with some use of centripetally prepared cores; simple side-scrapers, mostly on thin blanks, are the dominant tool type, with rare Upper Paleolithic tools and denticulates. |
| Copeland 1975:332 | Phase 3 (Tabun B) | Monotonous and standardized production of Levallois points; technological characteristics combine those of phases 1 and 2: the points are struck from either single-axis or centripetally prepared cores; the flakes are light and thin, resembling those of the earlier phase 2, but more laminar and narrow forms prevail. |
| Bar-Yosef 1998a:47 | "Tabun B-type" | Blanks removed mainly from unipolar convergent Levallois cores. Typical products are broad-based Levallois points, commonly with a *chapeau de gendarme* striking platform and a special tilted (*concorde*) profile. Flakes and blades are produced as well. |

region. Perrot, Skinner, and Crew alike inferred some degree of contemporaneity of the Levantine Mousterian variants that each of them defined.

At this point it would be useful to have a somewhat more detailed idea of the assemblages that are the subject matter of such contrasting interpretations (see also table 1.1). One important aspect of the Levantine Mousterian is that it is usually lightly retouched, both quantitatively (the number of retouched pieces) and qualitatively (the intensity of retouch), though some exceptions do occur, notably in the earlier Mousterian (see Hovers 2001; Meignen et al. 2006 and references therein). Among the retouched pieces, the range of tool forms is rather limited. Scrapers dominate the formal tools, and among them simple scrapers (often convex) are the norm (Goren-Inbar and Belfer-Cohen 1998). There have been claims for a chrono-typological change from earlier assemblages with an emphasis on end-scrapers and burins to later ones with an emphasis on Mousterian tools (side-scrapers and retouched points) (Marks 1992a). But despite a degree of variation, typological compositions of the various assemblages place most, if not all, known assemblages within the parameters of Bordes's typical Mousterian (Bordes 1981:83).

This relative typological monotony of Levantine Mousterian assemblages is tied to a theme that commonly emerges in studies of the Middle Paleolithic, despite the typological variations described by Bordes and acknowledged (to various degrees) by more recent researchers (e.g., Delagnes and Meignen 2006 and references therein). Over a long stretch of time Mousterian groups across the Eurasian landscape shared the use of Levallois flaking technologies coupled with a number of redundant tool morphologies. This clearly contrasts with the diverse technological adaptations known among current hunter-gatherer groups in comparably variable environments (Kuhn 1995a), whose tool kits are notably responsive in design and shape to the variations in properties of the targeted prey species (e.g., Lee 1979; Oswalt 1976). Moreover, use-wear analyses have shown the Mousterian tool kit to consist of unspecialized technological aids for general processing and manufacturing purposes (Anderson-Gerfaud 1990; Beyries 1987, 1988; Shea 1989, 1991). Stone tools especially designed as part of an "extractive technology" (in the sense of Binford and Binford 1966), specifically for food acquisition, are scarce. Stone (Levallois) points in Levantine Mousterian assemblages have been claimed to be specialized hafted hunting weapons (Shea 1988, 1991, 1993), but use-wear analyses are inconclusive. Some studies have indicated that even these allegedly specialized artifacts were used in a rather generalized manner (e.g., Plisson and Beyries 1998; Roler and Clark 1997; Shea 1989, 1991, 1993). And yet, the archaeological record demonstrates that Mousterian people in the Levant (as elsewhere) were capable foragers despite their non-specialized tools and their apparent lack of responsiveness to particular environmental conditions. Mousterian groups in Eurasia were successful hunters of medium-sized and large game as well as smaller animals (Bocherens et al. 2005; Chase 1986; Gaudzinski and Roebroeks 2000; Klein 1995, 2000; Marean and Kim 1998; Shea 1997; Speth and Tchernov 1998, 2001; Stiner 2002). They were presumably competent at exploiting other types of resources as well, for which there is rare, if any, archaeological evidence. That these abilities are not reflected immediately and directly in the diversity of stone tools is a puzzling feature of the Mousterian in the Levant and elsewhere.

If not specialized tool kits for specific resources, what were the means that enabled the long-term successful subsistence behavior of Mousterian groups? One solution may have been the adjustment of land-use patterns (i.e., the size of exploited territories and the timing, frequency, and scale of movement) to variations in the availability and abundance of prey species, to enhance capture success. In other words, the cultural means of adaptation to variations in the resource base would have been through shifts and reorganization of a comprehensive system of exploiting lithic resources rather than the production and use of special tools. The latter strategy would have entailed, for instance, variations in lithic raw material procurement patterns, followed by adjustments in raw material economy (i.e., use and discard patterns). Indeed, this type of compensation for the minimal role of design in subsistence-related technology may have been the one favored by at least some Neanderthal populations in Europe (e.g., Kuhn 1995a; Stiner and Kuhn 1992). In the Levant, seasonal differences in resource distributions and availability would not be as dramatic as in more northern latitudes. Secondly, and perhaps more important to the current discussion, the Levant is highly variable in terms of topography and climate, and offers a large number of diverse habitats and ecological niches to be exploited over a relatively small geographic extent. Variations in the availability and abundance of resources in the various ecological niches could be efficiently negotiated by group or individual mobility, which would also have brought people to the proximity of useful raw material and would require less elaborate organizational strategies. An altogether different strategy would involve a broadening of the dietary niche to include resources that could be exploited without specialized procurement technologies, for example, going after sessile faunal species or non-faunal resources (e.g., Lev, Kislev, and Bar-Yosef 2005; Madella et al. 2002; Speth and Tchernov 2003; Stiner and Tchernov 1998). Yet other alternative solutions could have emphasized hunting behaviors that were based on social cooperation rather than on technology-assisted strategies (Shea 1998).

## Why Look at Qafzeh Cave for Clues about Lithic Variability?

Qafzeh Cave is one of the most important locales known today in the Levant, if not globally. The site's initial claim to fame was based on the recovery of, and early age estimates for, the skeletal remains of anatomically modern humans, who nonetheless produced Mousterian industries. Specimens assigned to the same hominin type and associated with similar industries were found at Skhul, at a somewhat earlier date. However, the lithic assemblages from Skhul, excavated in the late 1920s and selectively curated, do not allow the kind of detailed study attempted here. And while it is true that anatomically modern humans from the MSA in South Africa are dated to a slightly earlier date than Qafzeh, human remains in the South African sites of Klasies River Mouth and Border Cave are not as well preserved, and their stratigraphic provenience is sometimes problematic (Grün and Stringer 1991; Grün, Beaumont, and Stringer 1990; Grün, Shackleton, and Deacon 1990; Sillen and Morris 1996).[8] Qafzeh is the only Eurasian site at which the lithic assemblages of Mousterian-making Moderns can be studied stratigraphically and compared to those of Neanderthals. It should be clear from the ongoing discussion that this places the assemblages of Qafzeh in a unique position to act as test cases for many of the hypotheses derived from the explanatory models. The study of the lithic assemblages from the Mousterian layers of the terrace of Qafzeh Cave (hereafter referred to as "Qafzeh Cave") provided an opportunity to address the problem of lithic variability in the Levantine Mousterian by attempting to discern, describe, and explain the effects of ecological and cultural processes on lithic variability within a single site. The insights gained from this case study, as well as available information from a number of other sites, are then used to make inferences about the possible operative mechanisms that created variability in the Levantine Mousterian.

This approach stems from the notion that a complex, multivariate phenomenon may be more easily stripped down to its basic elements if the number of causative agents is reduced. The study of the lithic assemblages of Qafzeh Cave looks at inter-assemblage variability, as the various non-contemporaneous assemblages clearly represent different occupations. But by studying the assemblages from a single geographic locale some factors are eliminated (or at least greatly reduced as influential forces) from the discussion, allowing a clearer view of other sources of variability. Similarly, using the sample from Qafzeh Cave reduces the degree of uncertainty about the biological affiliation of the tool makers. The taxonomic identity of the human populations from Qafzeh (and Skhul) is the least debatable in the period's record, since even those who recognize only a single population in the Levant (e.g., Arensburg and Belfer-Cohen 1998; Corruccini 1992; Wolpoff 1996:604–608) view it as a highly variable population of modern humans rather than Neanderthals.

Of course, it would be naïve to argue that any single set of archaeological finds is fully informative about such complex systems. But the longest journey starts with a single step, and I perceive this work as one step in what I hope is the right direction for understanding Middle Paleolithic lithic variability.

# 2

## Premises and Concepts Underlying
## the Study of the Qafzeh Lithics

### The Sample

The assumption underlying prehistoric research is that all the finds derived from asedimentologically discrete stratigraphic horizon at a given locality have temporal and spatial unity and constitute a discrete assemblage (Clarke 1979). This is clearly a relative, heuristic premise rather than an absolute measure of contemporaneity, as contexts that represent genuine, human life situations are rarely encountered in the prehistoric record (as discussed by Adler, Prindiville, and Conard 2003). A vast literature, drawing on empirical studies from numerous geographic regions and different time periods, has dealt with these questions (e.g., Bordes 1975; Clark and Kleindienst 2001; Leakey 1971; Villa 1983).

The extent to which archaeological data resemble a real-life scenario is largely dependent on site formation processes. Archaeological deposits, more often than not are palimpsests (Binford 1982), documenting the long-term recurrent operation of cultural systems in any single locale. Many complex and diverse natural processes, as well as anthropogenic ones, affect the formation of the archaeological record during and after deposition. Natural processes may include hydraulic action, bioturbation by burrowing and denning animals, trampling, chemical diagenesis that affects both bones and sediments, or paleo-geochemical conditions that differentially affect artifacts across the site's space. Humans, too, contribute to the complexity of formation processes by using the same locale differently during various occupation episodes, carrying out different activities throughout the site's space (and thus leading to seemingly different assemblages in various areas), or digging into archaeological deposits and disturbing them, to name only a few

examples (e.g., Binford 1978, 1979, 1980, 1983; Goldberg and Sherwood 2006; Karkanas et al. 2000; Schiegl et al. 1994, 1996; Schiffer 1987; Weiner, Goldberg, and Bar-Yosef 1993). High-resolution sites that were created and abandoned within an individual life span or during a short, uninterrupted occupation (resulting in considerable success in refitting artifacts) are rarely encountered in the vast Paleolithic time frame. A few examples of such sites are Nahal Nizzana XIII (Davidzon and Goring-Morris 2003), Far'ah II (Gilead 1988), Maastricht (de Loecker 1994), Lokalalei 2C (Delagnes and Roche 2005), Abric Romani (Vaquero and Pasto 2001; Vaquero et al. 2001). In most cases, however, it is assumed that the most narrowly defined stratigraphic horizon forms the minimal indivisible unit of analysis.

This practice was upheld in the current analysis. The lithic artifacts originated from horizons defined by changes in sedimentation processes (Vandermeersch 1981) or by arbitrary divisions (O. Bar-Yosef, pers. comm.) and are considered to be discrete assemblages that represent at least as many occupations as stratigraphic horizons. Twenty-four such horizons were discerned in the Qafzeh terrace (see chapter 3 for details), of which the lower ten had accumulated within the time span of 109.9 ± 9.9 to 82.4 ± 7.7 thousand years ago (Valladas et al. 1988; Schwarcz et al. 1988). An analysis of sedimentation processes by Farrand (1979) suggested that the rate of deposition at Qafzeh was relatively high. If this is correct, the dates bracketing the early part of the sequence may provide an exaggerated maximal extension of the time frame for the duration of its deposition. But even in a scenario of rapid accumulation it is likely that each archaeological assemblage at Qafzeh does not represent a single, nor even necessarily a continuous (again, in the narrowest, "real life" sense) human occupation. Given the complexities of site formation processes, each of the Qafzeh assemblages may have accumulated over a number of years and possibly represent more than a single occupation event, notwithstanding the claim for high rates of deposition at the site. Each assemblage may reflect a mosaic of possibly different behaviors. Therefore, although Qafzeh is a single site in the geographic dimension, its archaeological sequence represents multiple occupations in the temporal dimension. In this sense, the study carried out here deals with inter- rather than intra-assemblage phenomena.

Such caveats determined my approach to the study of the Qafzeh assemblages. Sample sizes often constitute a problem in the analyses of archaeological materials in that they are insufficient for meaningful statistical testing. This is particularly true when the assemblages are broken down into many categories in the course of a detailed analysis. Archaeologists sometimes tend to agglomerate finds from consecutive stratigraphic horizons in order to compensate for this problem. In the case of Qafzeh, too, sample sizes obtained from single assemblages were at times too small for a useful statistical treatment of certain variables. However, agglomeration of data from several discrete assemblages into a single larger sample was deemed archaeologically unwarranted, given the considerations outlined above. Lumping assemblages into a single, larger sample was considered a valid research tactic only when great archaeological similarity among any two stratigraphically successive assemblages suggested strong behavioral similarities. As it turned out, this was never the case throughout the study.

The body of data used in this study derived from the analysis of lithic assemblages excavated from the terrace sequence of Qafzeh Cave in the 1960s and 1970s. The excavation was conducted according to a grid of 1 m² squares and finds larger than 15 mm were registered in three coordinates within their squares. In addition, all the sediments excavated from 5-cm spits were sieved through a 1.5 mm mesh, so that smaller lithics (and bones) were collected with reference to grid squares and elevations. These systematic collection procedures ensured the inclusion in the study of all size fractions.

## Understanding Reduction Processes

The explanation of lithic variability involves ever-expanding tiers of interpretation, starting with the objects themselves and ending with the reconstruction of past social and economic behaviors. In the following (after Isaac [1981] 1996), I approach the interpretation of lithic variability as a stepwise process that attempts to address potential explanatory factors in a hierarchical sequence, in which each analysis is a stepping stone for the next. Residual variance unaccounted for by a given fundamental explanatory factor is carried over to the next step, to attempt its explanation by the next factor.

The fundamental explanatory factor in this analysis is the process of manufacturing artifacts, specifically the mechanical and physical constraints of raw material, and the effects of techniques (e.g., the type[s] of hammerstones used in the process of reduction) and of the actions themselves (e.g., platform shaping, core preparation, and shaping), on the morphological and metrical patterns seen in the assemblage. The insights obtained at this level enable us to formulate questions about the residual variance and move on to address abstract questions about the intentionality of blank and tool designs, and how they operated as part of hominins' overall problem-solving strategies. This basic information requires detailed descriptive and analytical documentation of the assemblages.

Esteem for technical reports is declining in recent scientific practice. Research in prehistoric archaeology has often been oriented toward specific problems, and analysts have focused narrowly on those particular attributes and variables that were deemed informative for those specific goals. "[C]ondescension [was] expressed towards monographs and their authors…The works are dismissed as exercises in 'mere description'…monographs do not emerge as the vanguard of creative novelty" (Gould 1989:97–100). This is an unfortunate attitude, especially in the historical sciences where the detailed description provides the database that transcends into the intangible phenomenon that one aims to explain. The monograph is the foundation for reconstructing a three-dimensional world from fragmented and incomplete evidence (and that, indeed, is the aim of research in archaeology, paleontology, or geology). This is not to say that assemblage description is objective or devoid of theoretical presuppositions. Nevertheless, a detailed, basic description is the closest that historical scientists can come to allowing their colleagues to better evaluate interpretations, to use the data in a critical and informed manner, and to rely on them as a foundation for further research. Where the subject of discussion is behavior, an abstract phenomenon even when observed in real time, presenting as many as possible obtainable archaeological facts is fundamental to any discussion. The first set of analyses in this volume thus focuses on a detailed description of the lithic assemblages from Qafzeh Cave.

The most reliable way to reconstruct lithic reduction strategies is to engage in large-scale refitting studies. This is like hitting the "rewind" button on a VCR: one can observe actions in reverse order, often beginning from the core—the last piece left from a reduction sequence—and working backwards, sometimes to the initial raw material nodule. Sequential steps thus identified can sometimes be traced to individual knappers and differences of their levels of know-how (e.g., Bleed 2002; Davidzon and Goring-Morris 2003; Marder 2002; Pigeot 1990). However, although refitting is probably as close as one can get to observing prehistoric behavior, artifact conjoining is unfortunately not a viable option in most cases. Assemblages from Levantine cave sites usually contain occasional refits, but large-scale conjoining operations are unfeasible and possibly, given the complex formation histories of the sites, not even a plausible research method. Most of the lithic assemblages are found in horizons that do not comply with a "Pompeii premise," representing dynamic anthropogenic processes (e.g., artifact export and import into a site) or being affected by complex post-depositional processes.

In place of refitting, I have relied in this analysis on a combination of conceptual and analytical procedures. This helped to quantify the insights from technological analyses so that they could generate testable hypotheses about the robustness of the observations and their behavioral significance (e.g., Dibble 1995c).

## Attribute Analysis

Acquisition of primary data was conducted through the use of an attribute analysis (e.g., Isaac 1977). This descriptive technique aims to achieve a better understanding of the internal structure and characteristics of the assemblage under study. In practice the same series of characteristics (attributes) is compiled for each artifact. For each attribute there is a list of attribute states that represent the perceived possibilities for describing the characteristic under observation. These attribute states are defined in a way that adequately encompasses the variation of the said property of the artifact. A property of a lithic artifact is then assigned an attribute from the list. Normally, any attribute of a single specimen is assigned a single attribute state. Thus, each artifact can be described by its typological, technological, and stylistic attributes, or by relationship among attributes.

The selection of attributes is based on the accumulated experience of previous researchers, as known from published works (Bar-Yosef and Goring-Inbar 1993:72), as well as on the particular questions posed by the specific characteristics of any studied assemblage. As noted by Bar-Yosef and Goring-Inbar (1993), this is not always a calculated strategy. Personal intuition and familiarity with the material play a role in the researcher's decisions about the attributes to be studied, with the list of both attributes and attribute states being continuously revised and re-evaluated during analysis. A principle of attribute analysis is that each artifact is described independently from others in the assemblage. Moreover, observations on

any given attribute are typically assigned independently of each other. In this manner the attribute analysis helps to document and describe a large number of permutations of attributes that convey the variation within the assemblage. Quantification of the data then leads to the identification of patterns that can be studied and tested statistically for meaningful relationship and correlations. Technological and stylistic variables used in the analysis (appendices 2–4) are similar to those employed by previous researchers of Levantine Paleolithic collections (to name but a few, Bar-Yosef et al. 1992; Crew 1975, 1976; Goren 1981; Goren-Inbar 1985, 1990a; Munday 1977).

The use of an attribute analysis in the study of Mousterian assemblages does not necessarily contrast with the use of Bordes's type-list, perceived primarily as a system of classification (Bar-Yosef 1998b; Hovers 1997). Bordes's method (Bordes 1961; Bordes and Bourgon 1951) for analyzing Eurasian lithic assemblages revolutionized the study of Middle (and Lower) Paleolithic assemblages. By studying the complete assemblage, including unretouched pieces, Bordes expanded considerably the notions of lithic guide fossils that were prevalent in the late nineteenth and early twentieth centuries (Sackett 2000). The application of simply constructed quantification methods enabled a degree of standardization in the treatment, as well as the presentation of the assemblages, facilitating comparisons between sites (see also Bar-Yosef and Goren-Inbar 1993). Relying on both a standardized type-list and standardized quantification of data, *La Méthode Bordes* has become a standard tool for describing Middle Paleolithic lithic assemblages. Recent critiques of the method (e.g., Bisson 2000; Debénath and Dibble 1994; Geneste et al. 1997) take issue with Bordes's interpretations of the analyzed assemblages rather than with the analytical tools themselves. For the sake of comparability with previously studied sites, the typological attributes for the Qafzeh assemblages consist of the classical Bordesian type-list, with only slight modifications (chapter 6). However the various types are treated as just another set of attribute states within a large number of variables examined by the attribute analysis. In this way it is possible to examine relationships and correlations between the "type" attribute and other attributes, and to evaluate the behavioral implications and cognitive validity of types. The treatment of types is, of course, part of the exploration of broader scale, more complex patterns and relationships that convey information about the structure of the assemblages and the decisions involved in forming them.

A final comment on the quantitative treatment of data in this study is required here. The statistical distributions of most variables used in the analyses were not normal. Whenever tests were applied to sets of data, I opted to use nonparametric tests (Siegel 1956; see discussion in Sharon 1990).

## A *Chaîne Opératoire* Approach

As a series of actions that progress through time (Bleed 2001), the manufacture of lithic artifacts is a technological process that is especially conducive to sequence modeling. The physical action of making stone tools forms an irreversible reductive process comprising a series of structured steps.[1] The removal of each flake in the sequence of reduction is singular and cannot be repeated with exactly identical time and space coordinates.

While the *chaîne opératoire* is essentially a sequence model that is used extensively in studies of Eurasian Paleolithic lithics, it is also a conceptual and analytical tool that meshes lithic production with the social and cultural domains of a society of stone tool knappers. It is essentially its claim for this broader worldview that distinguishes it from other sequence models used to grasp how hominins made stone tools (Hovers 2004a; see Shott 2003). The underlying assumption of the *chaîne opératoire* approach is that technology cannot be separated from the overall social and physical well-being of a society (Mauss 1936). Hence, material products derive from, and represent, a cultural pool of templates and knowledge, expressed as technological behaviors that are characteristic of a society. Technological artifacts bear socioeconomic implications and also testify to the cognitive abilities of their makers (Karlin and Joulien 1994; Karlin, Bodu, and Pelegrin 1991; Perlès 1992).

André Leroi-Gourhan expanded on Mauss's work by linking the idea of abstract knowledge with the action that is necessary to make material artifacts (Leroi-Gourhan 1964). The sequence of actions involved in the production of technological artifacts encompasses what might be called strategic planning versus tactical action. The first stage of the process is a purely abstract process of decision making. Selection of the forms, materials, and sequences of action relies on the available, socially obtained, information and preferences (mental templates) relating to these issues (Pelegrin 1990:118). These mental models are the decision criteria against which the manufacturer of a technological object weighs his choice of actions. This is followed by the (still mental) tactical, target-specific planning, structuring, and sequencing of the series of physical actions necessary to materialize the decisions taken in the first stage of the technological process. This is referred to as know-how (*savoir-faire*) (Pelegrin 1990). It is only then that the action itself takes place. Strategic planning and know-how both derive from, and therefore express, the cultural pool of technological knowledge. The artifacts produced at the end of this sequential process are cultural artifacts. They are physical manifestations of a society's cultural pool (Lemonnier 1992). This chain of culturally mediated sequential mental and physical operations that create technological objects is the *chaîne opératoire*, which Leroi-Gourhan introduced as a tool for the study of prehistoric technologies (Audouze 2002). The last stage of the process of making technological items, which results in the physical artifacts, is the step that is observed archaeologically. Any inferences that archaeologists can make about the abstract processes implicated in technological decision making derive from products of this stage.

Because the *chaîne opératoire* approach makes a priori assumptions about societal and cultural infrastructures that underline and shape the technological system, it is in essence an anthropological rather than archaeological concept. The many ethnological case studies describing operational sequences of agricultural practices and the making of pottery or stone tools (e.g., Gosselain 1998; Lemonnier 1993; Roux 2003; Stout 2002) document the diversity and complexity of the interactions between societal infrastructure and technological systems. The use of the *chaîne opératoire* approach in prehistoric studies thus requires some sort of middle ground that can link it to the archaeological objects with which archaeologists deal. If such linking principles are not found, the *chaîne opératoire* can be criticized as a naïve and "unscientific" approach, in that it makes the assumption that Paleolithic societies functioned similarly to social groups of the present and formed societal pools of knowledge in the same manner. On the practical level, since it is evidently a tricky business in dynamic, living societies, one may wonder about the potential of this kind of analysis in static archaeological contexts, if refitting cannot be carried out (Hovers 2004a).

One way out of this conundrum is by recognizing that the *chaîne opératoire* is a dynamic, hierarchical process. Its technological and cultural aspects must not be conflated. While they are two related facets of a complex process, they are not inseparable, so that each facet can be addressed independently by means of the archaeological record (Hovers 2004a). One may be able to reconstruct the technical know-how related to lithic production by identifying the reduction process from patterning of the artifacts' properties. This does not necessitate a priori assumptions about a unifying cultural and societal infrastructure.

Whether this know-how is a reflection of a cultural pool of behaviors, and therefore of a *chaîne opératoire* in the original, anthropological sense of the term, is a separate question that hinges on the existence of purposeful choice. The pool of technological knowledge of a society reflects significant choices that each society has to make, whether they are compatible or not with other choices (Levi-Strauss 1976:1). If, for example, individuals in a group have a number of raw materials and techniques equally available to them and equally efficient for their intended tasks, "identification of the most frequently recurring of these choices enables the archaeologist to characterize the technical traditions of the social group" (Bar-Yosef et al. 1992:511). One cannot make an argument for cultural behavior without first addressing the issue of the technological reduction process, but the reverse is not true.

In Qafzeh Cave, as in many other Levantine Middle Paleolithic sites, refitting was not a feasible research procedure.[2] The heuristic methodology adopted for this study links the quantified information assembled from the attribute analysis with the information provided by the sequential framework of sequence models.[3] In that lithic reduction is a directional and irreversible process, it is possible to make predictions from the relative sizes, shapes, amount of cortical cover, number of dorsal scars and many other characteristics of detached artifacts, as described by the attribute analysis,[4] that are likely affected by the item's place in the reduction sequence. Separate, dissimilar lithic artifacts can be related to one another temporally and causally.

## The Levallois Flaking System

The Levantine Mousterian is rich in Levallois products. The Levallois system is the single most important formal system of prepared core flaking that can be recognized in Levantine assemblages throughout the Middle Paleolithic of the region, with blade-oriented and discoidal systems lagging far behind quantitatively.

The term "Levallois" is one of the most familiar to any student of lithics, as it has had a long history of use. This history is quite checkered. To begin with, the evolutionary origins of the concept of Levallois flaking are not clear. Some archaeologists opt for its emergence in Africa and its global spread as part of world colonization by *Homo helmei* (Foley and Lahr 1997). Others see the worldwide occurrence of Levallois technology as the result of a series of temporally and geographically disparate, discontinuous, and possibly autochthonous processes (as summarized by White and Ashton 2003). It is argued in some cases to have developed technologically out of Late Acheulean bifaces (DeBono and Goren-Inbar 2001; Rolland 1995; Tryon, McBrearty, and Texier 2005), which share with Levallois technology some morphological and technological features. For others, "the development of the full Levallois concept represents…the erosion of boundaries between and the integration of two existing [Acheulean] systems, the practical fusion of *façonnage* [shaping] and *débitage* [flaking] into a new dynamic" (White and Ashton 2003:605).

While the question of Levallois origins is clearly of importance in the evolutionary and historical contexts, it is less crucial when discussing bona fide Middle Paleolithic assemblages. Regardless of its exact evolutionary history, Levallois technology is recognized as a dominant feature of lithic technology throughout the Old World from around 300,000 years ago until the end of the Middle Paleolithic around 30,000 years ago.[5] For the purposes of this study, the important questions are (1) what constitutes the Levallois flaking system, and (2) how can it be clearly recognized in the archaeological record. Chazan (1997) presented an efficient summary of recent discussions of these questions, and the interested reader will find references to most instructive works dealing with such questions. The following paragraphs touch upon those issues that are most pertinent to the current study.

As stated by Van Peer (1992) in his extensive discussion of the "Levallois problem," "Levallois" has meant different things to different people. Copeland (1983b) pinpointed the problem in the shift from a restrictive point of view of the Levallois concept to the more modern, broad view, in which the definitions are general. In her opinion this has led to a wide divergence of views as to what constitutes Levallois. Thus, Commont's definition of Levallois in the early twentieth century already emphasized careful bifacial preparation and the faceting of striking platforms (Commont 1909, cited in Chazan 1997). Bordes adopted the first of these criteria, rejected the second, and added a third criterion, stating that the desired flake's morphology was predetermined by core shaping. The latter, of course, is not an exclusive characteristic of Levallois flaking and therefore is not a good characterization of this particular flaking system. Another serious problem with this criterion is that it assumes the ability of modern analysts to determine the intentions of the prehistoric knapper.

Bordes's definition and its many variants have gained much popularity among scholars of Middle Paleolithic lithics. However, they do not offer technological attributes that are specific enough for a clear definition of Levallois as opposed to other prepared core-flaking technologies. How can an analyst determine the way in which a flake or a blade was meant to be produced by a Middle Paleolithic knapper? Marks and Volkman (1983) have shown through refitting studies that artifact morphology alone is not a solid enough indication of an item's origins in a Levallois reduction sequence. Clearly, Levallois has to be addressed as a dynamic system rather than on the basis of discrete artifacts that represent only a part—and a small one at that—of the reduction process.

Geneste (1985) and Boëda (1990, 1995; Boëda et al. 1990) initiated refitting and replication studies that advanced understanding of Levallois reduction as a process of core modification, exploitation, reorganization, and reuse.[6] In this framework Levallois reduction methods did not produce only Levallois products, but unavoidably led to the production of flakes that may have been predetermined (because they played a specific role in the reduction process) and yet were not the desired end-products of the process. Moreover, Levallois end-products could be obtained through variable flaking methods and modes, differing from one another in the organization of the core's surface in preparation for flaking and in the number of artifacts that could be removed from a single core-flaking surface.

Perhaps the most significant achievement of the attempts to redefine Levallois as a flaking system is the set of criteria that constitutes a "recipe" for preparing a Levallois reduction sequence, based on replications of the sequences. These are phrased in relation to technological characteristics rather than to the analyst's understanding of a knapper's psyche. The specifics of the technological criteria are discussed in some detail in chapter 4, which deals with the study of the cores from Qafzeh. It is important to stress here that these criteria translate into tangible, observable properties of the cores and the detached flakes, which in turn help us to accept or reject them as Levallois products.

While this serves to reduce some of the ambiguities discussed by Van Peer (1992), the premises underlying the formulation of the technological criteria of Levallois flaking also raise new questions about the nature and definition of Levallois. On the practical side and on the lowest theoretical level, the technological criteria for defining Levallois are visible mostly on cores and are far less clear where flakes are concerned (see also Dibble 1995c). Defining flakes as Levallois or non-Levallois remains very much a subjective matter, on which analysts often disagree (e.g., Perpère 1986). Flakes rather than cores, however, form the majority of archaeological lithic finds in most contexts.

On the level of archaeological classification, Boëda's approach to the Levallois system broadens its definition to such a degree that one needs to wonder about the "limits of Levallois." Do all the criteria have to be fulfilled by the knapper, and recognized archaeologically, before a Levallois flaking system is identified? For example, raw material properties may be such that some stages of the technological process are not relevant. Kuhn (1995b) raised this question with regard to the Pontinian assemblages in Italy, in which the shape and size of beach pebbles combined to prohibit elaborate core preparation, while at the same time providing the necessary core geometry for Levallois flaking. The same question can be asked with regard to cores-on-flakes in Middle Paleolithic assemblages, since flakes by definition have the two parallel faces that are one of the Levallois prerequisites (e.g., Delagnes 1995; Hovers 1997, 2007; see chapter 4). The last question, and probably a more crucial point of contention, is that of redundancy in knapping methods. A central tenet of Boëda's approach is that such redundancy

does not occur within an assemblage, and different flaking methods will be used only if different end-products are desired. Moreover, each core is supposedly knapped by the same Levallois method from beginning to end of the reduction sequence. In other words, Boëda argued that the knapper has little mental or dextral flexibility while knapping. While simplifying the job of the analyst (Chazan 1997), adoption of these tenets comes at the expense of a nuanced understanding of the behaviors involved in lithic production and of the agents shaping such behaviors. This approach, in fact, may well promote a tendency to turn the variety of Levallois flaking methods[7] discussed in recent literature into rigid guide fossils that are associated unreservedly with specific periods, geographic regions, or human populations (see also Bar-Yosef 1991).

Similarly, the knapping process (including the particular Levallois knapping process) is often divided into behavioral categories: raw material procurement, the shaping of striking platforms, decortication, initial blank production, core reshaping, late blank production, selection of blanks for tools, tool retouch, tool maintenance (resharpening), and finally discard. These behavioral categories are represented through the variables examined in an attribute analysis and in their quantitative patterning (as described, e.g., by Tostevin 2000, 2003). These commonsensical, intuitive categories are easily discernible during refitting studies or in the lithic material produced in replications. When dealing with archaeological materials, however, they are merely arbitrary analytical units. In order to avoid imposing such preconceived ideas on the studied assemblages, I have refrained from addressing and presenting the quantitative patterns according to such behavioral categories.

Given these problematic aspects of the *chaîne opératoire* approach to Levallois flaking, its premises serve in this study as null hypotheses that should be tested. The technological features are "translated" into specific characteristics that are measured or observed, the distribution and patterning of which are described by quantification of the attributes in the attribute analysis. The seemingly unrelated observations are connected to the various methods and modes of Levallois flaking systems, as elucidated by the studies of refitting and replication of Mousterian core-reduction strategies. This procedure enables the interpretation of statistical data as reflecting the dynamic, variable nature of flaking modes and methods. The three data chapters in this volume reflect the three major observable categories of lithic residues at a site. Chapter 4 describes the cores, whereas chapters 5 and 6 describe the unretouched and retouched artifacts. As a "known variable," the cores are used as a starting point: their characteristics are used to formulate expectations about the reduction sequences that could have resulted in the observed core assemblage. The predictions are then compared against the data from the flaked items. In a similar manner, it is possible to compare the characteristics of retouched and unretouched artifacts in order to identify and understand selection patterns. However, these are not perceived, or treated, as rigid, formal behavioral categories (in the sense of Tostevin 2000, 2003); hence the flexibility and variability of knapping procedures are not masked by preconceptions about the behavioral significance of the technological procedure.

## The Organization of Lithic Production and Use

The use of quantified data on the Qafzeh lithics, interpreted in view of experimental work on lithic fracture mechanics and on the basis of understanding of sequential reduction processes, is likely to reveal the effects of physical and mechanical laws governing the actual process of lithic reduction. These are expected to explain some of the variability seen in the Qafzeh assemblages as the results of the matter–energy interface. In the stepwise approach adopted here, the next question is whether some of the residual variability results from the manner in which the production and use of lithics were incorporated into the organizational strategies of Qafzeh's Middle Paleolithic inhabitants.

The concept of "reverse engineering" (Dawkins 1995:120–122; Dennett 1995) is useful for understanding of the role of lithic artifacts as part of dynamic organizational behaviors. The underlying assumption of this engineering principle is that artifacts are designed intelligently and economically for a defined purpose. An engineer trying to understand the workings of an unfamiliar object takes it apart in order to discover the problem that this implement would be good at solving. The archaeologist, too, assumes for the sake of discussion that the lithics under study were designed intelligently for a purpose and were used economically and intelligently. The next logical step is to identify for which problems these objects were designed, and how the lithics functioned as technological, problem-solving objects (see Bleed 1986).

A technological system encompasses "the selection and integration of strategies for making, using, transporting, and discarding tools and the material needed for their manufacture and maintenance" (Nelson 1991:57). Mobile groups adjust to fluctuations in the distribution of resources by movements organized in response to the seasonal availability and spatial clustering of desired resources, and/or by considered positioning of settlements in relation to the locations of crucial resources (food, water, heat) (e.g., Jochim 1976, 1979, 1981). This in itself requires intimate knowledge of the environment in a

group's territory, which may be achieved through investment in individual and group information-gathering activities culminated by group decision making about the best steps to be taken (Johnson 1978; Moore 1983; Reynolds 1978). A complementary strategy for reducing the risk of failure in resource exploitation is the use of extractive technology. Lithic artifacts clearly fall within this domain of organizational behavior.

The use of extractive technology, however, comes with a price tag (Ugan, Bright, and Rogers 2003) because it complicates the organizational system. In the world of hunter-gatherers, activities are organized primarily around the temporal and spatial distribution of resources. In order to use technological aids, hunter-gatherers have to invest additional time and energy in seeking and procuring appropriate raw materials, storing this information for the future in the societal information pool, and turning the raw material into useful artifacts. Clearly, the production and use of extractive tools are pointless if they are not positioned in the right spatio-temporal relationship with subsistence resources. Thus, technology-getting activities are organized so as to maximize the benefits of subsistence opportunities and are subjugated to them. Hence, the strategies for achieving a viable technological organization through lithics are influenced by three main parameters: the types of activities in which tools are used, the predictability of demand for tools over time and across geographic distance (e.g., Bamforth 1986; Barton 1990; Binford 1977, 1979, 1989; Bleed 1986; Kelly 1988, 1992; Kelly and Todd 1988; Kuhn 1993, 1994; Marks 1988; Shott 1989b), and the spatial distribution of raw materials for manufacturing tools in relation to those of the resources scheduled to be exploited (e.g., Andrefsky 1994; Bamforth 1986). The organization of lithic technology is about the implementation of decision criteria as to the most efficient tactics of manipulating these parameters in the most gainful manner.

The tactical responses of Paleolithic hunter-gatherers to these factors would have depended on the degree of spatial overlap between raw material and subsistence resources. Scarcity of raw material, leading to the risk of failing to supply the technology needed for optimal resource harvesting, is seemingly a function of the distance between the place of raw material procurement and its place of use. Because the distributions of raw material and subsistence resources normally do not overlap, some curation of the former is expected to occur. Bamforth (1986) modeled two curational behaviors—recycling ("remaking of an implement into a different kind of tool"; Odell 1996:59) and maintenance (a behavior designed to extend the use life of an artifact; Shott 1989a). Both these behaviors are conscious choices of hunter-gatherers who give priority to their mobility schedules over constraints of raw material accessibility (Nelson 1991).

An important factor shaping the technological systems of Paleolithic hunter-gatherers would have been the size and structure of the territory in which they moved. Transport distances would have influenced the amount of transported lithic mass, as well as the shape of transported lithic packages. In a highly mobile system over large and partly unknown territories, where access to raw material could not always be anticipated, hunter-gatherers might have opted for curating and transporting relatively small masses of artifacts already prepared for use ("personal gear"; Binford 1979). This would have minimized the risk of failure to exploit unexpectedly encountered resources, as well as the cost of carrying around bulky and heavy lithic packages. If in possession of accurate information about the scheduling of resources and their spatial distribution, the same group could opt to transport large lithic masses to certain localities that were expected to be a focus of lithic production ("provisioning of place"), thus reducing the investment in repeated trips to obtain raw material.

The anticipated exploitation of mobile as opposed to sedentary resources would have determined the ability of an individual or a group to invest in maintenance of their tool kits and keeping them in readiness. The use of sedentary resources obviously incurs more downtime, and a maintainable technological system would have bestowed adaptive advantages. Here investment in the design of specialized, "expensive" tools might have been reduced in favor of versatile tools that could be maintained and recycled if they went out of commission. The exploitation of mobile resources would have required high readiness. Under such conditions hominins would have favored reliable technological systems, investing in advance time and energy in the production of overdesigned artifacts that could be counted on to function when needed. Similarly, the length of the period of resource availability (e.g., year-round as opposed to seasonal) would have influenced patterns of mobility and technological strategies.

In sum, a single group might have shifted its subsistence and therefore its mobility strategies, in response to ecological and/or social circumstances, switching from foraging to collecting and back to foraging within an annual cycle (e.g., Binford 1980; Kelly 1995 with references). This in turn would demand that the organization of technology-assisted subsistence tactics be dynamic in order to maximize resource exploitation.

As a problem-solving behavior, lithic technological organization would have been responsive to environmental dynamics on both "real life" (e.g., seasonal cycles of resource availability and abundance) and evolutionary (e.g., climatic cycles) scales. The decision criteria employed when endorsing particular organizational strategies were shaped by the amount and quality of information about both the physical environment and the presence and behavior of other social groups (e.g., Moore 1983; Perlman 1985; Reynolds 1978; Richter 2000). The knowledge and know-how required for stone tool making are part of the pool of socially transmitted information about culturally acceptable ways of dealing with the challenges of the environment, based on a society's previous experience. But, as we have already seen, socially transmitted information may become decoupled from prevalent environmental conditions. This translates into some interesting expectations with regard to the patterns left in the archaeological record by lithic reduction processes and by the technological organization of lithics. Knowledge about the specific modes and methods of lithic manufacture that is transmitted vertically down the generations may have nothing to do with environmental dictates. Variations in the occurrence of preferred manners of reduction and in the morphologies of individual artifacts (especially if achieved at the time of tool manufacture, as advocated by Bordes) may result from conservative, culturally defined mental templates and not correlate well with long-term trends of environmental variables (Shennan 1991). However, some aspects of the lithic assemblages (e.g., relative frequencies of tool types, the frequencies of cores vs. debitage vs. debris, etc.) manifest the efforts of hunter-gatherers to optimize resource exploitation through the production and transport of lithic technological aids (or the raw material to produce them) across the landscape. These reflect adjustments to perceived or predicted situations and are more responsive to ecological conditions. The characteristics of the lithic assemblages can therefore be used to understand the economic challenges posed by the environments of the group that shaped the lithic assemblages.

We now have in hand the middle range theory that connects lithics with human behavior. Based on the amassed data from ethnography and on ecological and economic theory, it is now possible to formulate a number of hypotheses that explain the archaeological patterns from parsimony and to derive some test implications that can be examined against the specific archaeological record under study.[8] One reasonable way of testing such ideas about technology is to establish associations between archaeological correlates of organizational behavior and the characteristics of subsistence resources in the same archaeological assemblage.

Rational, economic technological behavior cannot explain the entire spectrum of variation seen in Qafzeh Cave. This is not entirely surprising, since parsimony is not "a fact of the way nature works but a reflection of our frequent inability to grasp and deal with the complexities of the real world" (Speth 2004:161). However, this testing of relatively simple cause-and-effect ideas about lithic organization leads to the recognition that the organization of the lithic assemblages of Qafzeh may have been influenced by decision-making processes that do not satisfy rational, economic criteria. As in the previous step of the analysis, unexplained residual variability is moved one step up the scale of explanatory models, to the question of whether cultural behavior may have been responsible for the observed patterns in the Qafzeh record.

Of course, organizational behaviors are cultural practices as well (as discussed above at some length). At this stage I was interested in the notion that some lithic organizational strategies, through the operation of mechanisms of cultural transmission over time, may have become sufficiently insensitive to the selective pressures of the external environment. How much of the organizational decision making of Qafzeh's hominins responded to societal rather than environmental factors, and what might be the processes that led to it?

Finally, the broadest and most speculative tier of inquiry that this study touches upon is the explanation of Levantine Middle Paleolithic lithic variability in view of the results from the study of the Qafzeh assemblages. The wealth of data accumulated from new excavations and newly discovered Middle Paleolithic sites in the Levant (appendix 1) emphasizes the complexity of human interactions in the region during this time. Research programs focusing on understanding the chronology and site formation processes of Levantine Middle Paleolithic sites have demonstrated that the pace of cultural change was slower than previously believed. The newly understood duration of Mousterian times poses new questions about the mode and patterns of culture change within the Middle Paleolithic and across its boundaries with preceding and succeeding periods (e.g., Goren-Inbar and Belfer-Cohen 1998; papers in Hovers and Kuhn 2006). The search for "meaningful, *explained* order has yet to be discovered, if, indeed, it is present" (Munday 1976b:1; original emphasis); this is as valid today (albeit in a different way) as it was thirty years ago, when the search was first started.

Here I address the question of whether the operative mechanisms that are implicated in creating the variability at Qafzeh can parsimoniously explain temporal and geographic lithic variation in the Levant, and how (if at all) they relate to human biological diversity in the region. This is not a trivial question when placed against the "reality" of the Middle Paleolithic Levant. Due to its immense ecological variability over a small geographic space, the Levant is in many ways ideal for examining how Mousterian lithic technology was structured as an ecological behavior that responded to prevailing environmental conditions. And since Levantine Middle Paleolithic populations were probably not taxonomically identical, it is possible to look at variability in lithic technology and how it might have been structured differently between groups simply because people were genetically different.

A number of models have been constructed in the past in attempts to explain the variability of Levantine Middle Paleolithic lithic assemblages. While they have never been explicitly associated with any particular theoretical currents in the archaeological discipline, their intellectual ties are with the adaptive function or culture history approaches discussed above.

## Ecologically Oriented Models

Some of the models examine various ecological aspects as the cause for lithic variability. By default, such models implicitly incorporate optimization approaches to the organization of lithic technologies. Originating from a systemic framework, these models are sometimes interwoven with one another, but are still specific enough to enable the formulation of concrete hypotheses and their test implications.

### Lithic Technological Variability Shaped by Paleoclimatic Shifts

In the greater scheme of things, climatic shifts have caused changes in environmental parameters to which some human behaviors have responded. Hence, climate changes likely played a role in determining some of the patterning of the archaeological lithic manifestations of such behavior. The literature on the European Middle Paleolithic is rich in such scenarios (e.g., Rolland 1981; Rolland and Dibble 1990; van Andel and Davies 2003, and references therein). The paleoclimatic model posits that climatic conditions controlled trends of variability in Levantine Middle Paleolithic assemblages. This model is almost inseparable from climatic determinism. Along these lines Munday (1979) suggested that Mousterian technological changes in the Negev were responsive to shifts in subsistence intensity and regional mobility patterns, which in their turn were propelled by long-term climatic changes. Specifically, Munday argued that more complex traits of lithic artifacts (e.g., highly faceted platforms, convergent scar patterns) would occur in periods of climatic amelioration, when subsistence pressures were alleviated and mobility was reduced, allowing the adoption of a "high preparatory input technology." This resulted in the production of elongate debitage. Less complex, unidirectional flaking, reflecting a shift to "low preparatory input technology," and broad debitage stemming from centripetal flaking were correlated with times of increased mobility due to aridification (Munday 1979:98). Munday further suggested that this was the operative mechanism inducing lithic variability in the whole of the Levant. Significantly, the overall pattern of change is not predicted to be linear, since climate changes occur cyclically. The hypothesis derived from this model predicts that contemporaneous assemblages will demonstrate similar core-reduction methods if they are located in a single climatic regime.

Recent research on eastern Mediterranean paleoclimates (as summarized, e.g., by Almogi-Labin, Bar-Matthews, and Ayalon 2004) has amassed a significant amount of new data that are pertinent to the time span addressed in this work. The details of this research and its contribution to testing models of climate-driven technological variability are discussed in chapters 7 and 8.

*Lithic Technological Variability as Response to Raw Material Constraints*

Behaviors that incorporate the use of lithic technological aids are sensitive to raw material constraints such as availability and quality. The acquisition, transportation, and curation of raw material in its various forms (e.g., natural nodules, cores, tool blanks, or shaped tools) are major components of the lithic technology organizational system, since it is the manipulations of these particular aspects that allow hunter-gatherers to use their tools exactly when and where they are needed, which is in turn dictated by the nature of the subsistence resources. Raw material limitations may affect core-reduction methods as well as assemblage composition (see Andrefsky 1994; Bamforth 1986; Brantingham et al. 2000; Dibble 1991a, 1995b; Rolland and Dibble 1990). Where high-quality lithic resources are abundant and scattered over the landscape, there is less pressure to economize on raw material and to curate the artifacts and use them exhaustively. The opposite is not necessarily true if the available lithic resource is of lesser quality: if a raw material is not usable, groups or individuals may elect to invest time and energy in the search, design, and curation of more appropriate but less accessible materials. High-quality flint is expected to be exploited for artifacts used as part of extractive technology, since these are acutely important for an individual's or a group's livelihood. Such raw materials will be sought, sometimes with great investment, and the tools made from them will be carefully designed, both for the task at hand and with a view to prolonging their use as much as possible. People tend to curate and reuse such artifacts until they are heavily reduced. With increasing distance from raw material sources, the products will be less cortical and smaller, amounts of retouch that express the extent of utilization will increase, and core size will decrease. On the other hand, low-quality flint will be employed for artifacts that are more generalized (e.g., notches). Because there is no special time invested in search for low-quality flint, it is often derived from sources near the site. Generalized tools thus tend to be associated with local, on-site production and are expected to be less curated.

Munday's model attempts to explain lithic variability in the Middle Paleolithic sites of the Negev along similar lines. It proposes that lithic technology was variably organized so as to provide appropriate blanks in task specific and habitation sites distanced from raw material sources, while at the same time attempting to minimize the costs of raw material transport to the consumer localities by designing blanks that were optimal in terms of the ratio between their mass and their desired properties. This variability is expressed in the properties of the resultant debitage (e.g., dimensions, preparatory attributes such as striking platform types, and density of scar patterns; Munday 1976b:128), which tend to vary in a predictable manner with distance from the raw material source.

Two hypotheses are derived from this model. First, it is expected that sites that are closer to raw material sources will have longer and wider debitage than those located away from flint exposures. This will respond to the need to minimize transportation costs. But the further away a consumer site from the source of raw material, the greater the need to curate the nodules or blanks, to compensate for unavailability of raw material and to delay future costly trips to the source. This requires that blanks be larger so that they can be retouched and maintain serviceable dimensions. Thus, the second hypothesis derived from Munday's raw material model predicts that longer blanks will be preferred for retouch, regardless of a site's proximity to raw material sources (Munday 1976b:134–138; Crew 1976; Marks 1988).

*Lithic Technological Variability Shaped by Settlement and Mobility Patterns*

The model explains lithic variability as stemming from the occupation of different types of sites. Assemblages in caves and rock shelters exhibit different compositions and degrees of utilization from those of open-air sites. Caves and rock shelters would have a greater appeal as settlement locales during periods or in seasons of relatively harsh climatic conditions. At such times they would be settled even if distant from lithic raw material sources. In addition, during such times mobility would be reduced so that visits to the raw material sources become fewer. In landscapes that were familiar and exploited regularly, humans would be able to predict such situations, and prehistoric groups would have organized their technological activities to compensate for such difficulties. A step in this direction would have involved curation and transport of raw material in various forms into the cave. Another effect of such situations would be a higher tendency toward conservation and recycling of raw material, entailing more intensive or efficient core-reduction modes and methods as well as more frequent and intensive recycling and resharpening of blanks.

Several hypotheses derive from this model. First, one would expect a correlation between intensity of cave occupation and climatic conditions. Although logically this hypothesis is testable, in practice this may be problematic. Since the history of research in the Levant (and indeed in many other regions) shows that work is too often biased toward cave sites, a reliable comparison of the tendency to occupy cave versus open-air site occupation may not be possible.

Another expectation derived from the model is that assemblages from caves and rock shelters will show higher frequencies of retouched tools than those from open-air sites (Rolland and Dibble 1990). Additionally, if indeed there is a higher tendency toward recycling tools in caves and rock shelter contexts, individual blanks are expected to be heavily retouched. This means that certain tool types (e.g., double, convergent, or Quina scrapers) should occur in caves and rock shelters in higher frequencies than in open-air sites, possibly at the expense of notches, denticulates, or lightly retouched flakes.

Finally, it is expected that the two types of occupation will differ in the relative proportions of high-quality blanks to cores and lesser quality artifacts because of curation and the transport of high-quality blanks into the caves. For instance, the geometry and dimensions of Levallois cores and blanks provide high potential utility relative to their mass, making them cost-effective in contexts of transport (Kuhn 1994). Hence, we may expect to find relatively more Levallois implements in contexts that favor curation and transport.

*Lithic Technological Variability as a Response to Functional Needs*

This model has been expanded and transformed into the conceptual framework of "technological organization" (see above), which in fact integrates and incorporates also the three models discussed thus far. In its original form the functional model, as phrased by Binford and Binford (1966), asserts that typological variability, resulting in the patterned variability of assemblage types observed in the Middle Paleolithic, reflects sets of specific tasks for which particular tool types were used. The nature and frequency of these tasks are in turn dependent on subsistence resource structure in the vicinity of any given site in the season of occupation. The implication of this hypothesis is that particular tool types should bear evidence for a specific manner of use. Assemblages formed in task-specific sites are predicted to be less diverse than those found in base camps or occupation sites. Because resources and their occurrence in space would have changed when the local environments changed, the tendency to produce

particular tool types is predicted to co-vary with paleoenvironmental conditions.

Shea (1998) formulated a spin-off model. Based on the assertion that Levallois points were tools designed for hunting, their use would vary in different ecological zones of the Levant because of the different patterning of faunal resources in each zone. Stone spear points would have been advantageous mainly in intercept hunting, in which technological activities are planned in advance, and disadvantageous in encounter hunting, where there is less planning and anticipation and the investment in technological hunting aids may be too costly. The model suggests that the organization of hunting activities will bear a marked geographic signature. Technology-assisted intercept hunting would have been more frequent in the Irano-Turanian steppe interior of the Levant, where sites are expected to contain more Levallois points (and pointed forms in general). In the Mediterranean woodland ecological zone along the coast and in the northern Levant, advance planning is argued to have been less crucial, and therefore points are predicted to be less frequent. Hunting technology would then be based on a plethora of other technologies that were not related to the use of lithics and are therefore less visible archaeologically.

## Models of Taxonomy-Driven Variability

A worldview that has been referred to in the context of attempting to explain lithic variability in a number of archaeological periods holds that there is a direct and intimate relationship between the taxonomic affiliation of human groups and their cultural behaviors, linking technological variability to biological variation. Stone artifacts are perceived as a "phenotypic" expression of biological taxonomy (e.g., Foley 1987b). For instance, in attempting to provide a comprehensive framework for summarizing variation in the Paleolithic, Clark (1970) suggested that some generalities could be seen across the range of lithic assemblages in the modes in which stone tools were manufactured. He defined five technological modes. Foley and Lahr (2003) argue for a phylogeny of these broad technological systems that echoes that of hominins. Similarly, the uniquely close overlap in temporal span of the Oldowan techno-complex and of *Paranthropus boisei* in the prehistoric record led Wood (1997) to the conclusion that *Paranthropus boisei* was the maker of the Oldowan assemblages in East Africa, even though fossils of other hominin genera are known from segments of this temporal range. Leakey (1971) carefully weighed the possibility that the appearance of the Acheulian in Olduvai Gorge was linked to the occurrence of a new hominin species, *Homo erectus,* in Olduvai, whereas the preceding Oldowan assemblages had been produced by *Homo habilis.* Of course, the best known expression of this way of thinking about the links between biology and technology is the notion of a Middle-to-Upper Paleolithic transition in Europe, long believed to reflect a dramatic cultural revolution due to the evolution (or arrival) of modern humans and the disappearance of the Neanderthals (see above).

In these examples the idea of a close causal relationship between human taxonomy and culture is the basis for explaining changes in lithic technology. Models developed along similar lines for the Middle Paleolithic are relevant only in relation to the Mousterian of the Levant, where they set out to explain variability within a single industrial complex. Each group of Levantine Middle Paleolithic hominins is expected to be associated with specific sets of technological processes or properties, which it would not have shared with the other group. The implication of this hypothesis is that, in addition to skeletal remains, Neanderthals and modern humans can be recognized archaeologically from their material culture remains, specifically lithics; namely, lithic technologies are "species-specific" traits.

Along these lines, Jelinek (1977) emphasized a diachronic trend of reduction of width/thickness ratio of complete flakes along the Tabun sequence, showing that the production of thinner debitage increased with time. He applied the model to other stratified sites with hominin skeletal remains and concluded that the temporal change was related to the replacement of Levantine Neanderthals by modern humans with superior manual dexterity. Supposedly, this latter trait gave modern humans better control over the shape and dimensions of the flakes while preparing their stone tools (Jelinek 1982a, 1982b).

Another variant of the biological model emphasizes behavioral rather than inherent differences between the two populations. Differences in lithic technology are assumed to stem not so much from the inability of a population to produce specific artifacts as from the fact that it adjusted to its environment by a behavior inherently different from that of the other group. This required different equipment and hence different lithic production methods. Neanderthals were argued to have relied on different mobility strategies from those of modern humans and to have emphasized "technology-aided" hunting. Their lithic tool kits and the reduction techniques used to produce it would differ from those of the Moderns in a consistent, identifiable manner (Lieberman and Shea 1994; Shea 1998).

Finally, a recently suggested scenario for the interaction between Moderns and Neanderthals in the Levant argues that there was no real lithic variability in the Levantine Mousterian, which was rather monotonous and lacked technological innovations. Shea (2006a) proposes instead that the lithic technology in the Levant is recursive and consists of a limited number of variations on a restricted number of shapes and forms. The lack of a distinct technological edge on the part of either one of the two populations led by necessity to short periods of coexistence and competition followed by alternate regional population extinctions. Only the introduction of new lithic technologies with the onset of the Upper Paleolithic tilted the balance in favor of Moderns fresh out of Africa with new and more sophisticated tool kits and symbolic behaviors.

Since the testing of biology-driven hypotheses requires that hominin remains be present on site, such hypotheses can be examined in only a limited number of sites.

## Culture History Models

While recognizing the important impact of ecologically driven variability, models that endorse culture history as a plausible approach to explaining patterns in material culture tend to emphasize the significant role of cultural templates and traditions in shaping variability. For many researchers (e.g., Clark and Riel-Salvatore 2006), the enormous time span of the Mousterian precludes the discussion of cultural traditions. Yet the fact remains that culture history models are called upon to explain exactly the same phenomenon, namely conservatism of material culture over long stretches of prehistoric time. With regard to the Levantine Mousterian, Crew (1975:427) noted that lithic production methods were conservative, "at least more so than morphology and the frequency of occurrence of the artifacts created by the methods."

Hypotheses explaining the variability (or lack thereof) in material cultural as the result of cultural traditions typically emerge when alternative explanations are rejected (Bordes's approach to typological variability clearly falls within this worldview). Only more recently have such approaches led to hypotheses that attempted to explain the demographic and social background to the stability or changes in material culture systems.

### A Hypothesis of Cultural Tradition

Meignen and Bar-Yosef (1988, 1992) have argued that the technological variability in the Levantine Mousterian was expressed in the preference of a particular Levallois core-reduction method in any given assemblage. They posited that this resulted from distinct, diehard technological traditions (in the sense of Lemonnier 1986). They further implied that typological variability in Levantine Mousterian assemblages was a reflection of tactical, short-term functional needs, which vary from one place to another, rather than of any stylistic or traditional behavior (Meignen and Bar-Yosef 1992). Archaeologically, one should expect each assemblage (if it is shown or can be assumed to represent an undisturbed archaeological context) to be predominated by a single core-reduction method and mode (though some variety may occur). Additionally, no consistent, redundant co-occurrences of particular typological tool kits with specific reduction practices are predicted. Logically, however, if such patterned co-occurrences do appear, their presence is not sufficient grounds to refute the hypothesis and reject the model.

This model of technological variability being propelled by adherence to technological traditions does not inform us about temporal relationships or, by implication, about distinct cultural groups using the discrete technological repertoires. Different technological traditions can be present at the same time (as argued by Bordes for the European Mousterian on typological grounds) or evolve sequentially from one another, or appear in a region's prehistoric record in distinct temporal frames as a result, for example, of population influx. For the Levantine Mousterian specifically, Meignen and Bar-Yosef (1992) hypothesized that variability would occur along the lines of Copeland's tripartite division of the Levantine Mousterian by "Tabun phases" (table 1.1), the implication being that a single, relatively large, cultural group existed in wide geographic areas of the Levant at any given moment in the Middle Paleolithic. The resultant hypothesis predicts, therefore, that technological traditions were adopted sequentially by a group or groups, and that in any given slice of time a single technological tradition should exist in the Levant (Bar-Yosef 1994:40).

# 3

## Qafzeh Cave: The Region and the Site

**The Region**

The cave of Qafzeh is located on the southwest flank of Gebel Qafzeh (Har Qedumim) in the Central Lower Galilee, 2.5 km south of Nazareth, and some 35 km from the modern Mediterranean shoreline.

### Geology and Geomorphology

The Galilee is a region of complex geological structure, characterized by a high frequency of faulting and numerous other tectonic features that are dated to various periods (Freund 1978). These faulting events shaped many of the geomorphic features of the region, which is divided into two major units: the Lower Galilee (up to 600 m above mean sea level [a.m.s.l.]) and Upper Galilee (1000–1200 m a.m.s.l.); they are separated by the Beit HaKerem Valley (Biq'at Beit HaKerem) (only 150 m a.m.s.l.).

The Lower Galilee is divided into three distinct geological and geomorphologic sub-units.

1. The western Lower Galilee is an area of rounded, low-lying hills, built of Eocene chalks (the Alonim-Shefar'am Hills), at an elevation of 200–250 m a.m.s.l. The impenetrable chalky lithology has led to the development of dispersed and shallow drainage systems, in turn leading to a highly dissected landscape. The slopes are rugged because of the nari crust that has developed on the chalky rocks, and they are devoid of deep soil coverage.
2. The eastern Lower Galilee consists of the Timrat limestone, the eastern facies of the Eocene deposits, in which the dominant rock is a fine-grained, dense, and hard limestone (Greenberg 1963). Exposures of

this unit are found as far west as Nazareth, some 2.5–3 km from the site of Qafzeh. The Timrat limestone underlies Neogene basalts (the Lower and Cover Basalt), exposed only in restricted areas in the southeast Lower Galilee in the form of plateaus and valleys tilting moderately to the southwest. The tilted basalt plateaus terminate abruptly on the east due to faulting associated with the Dead Sea Rift system. More recent Plio-Pleistocene faults can also be seen in this area. Another component of the Neogene is a thin (25 m at most) sedimentary column of detritic limestone and laminar crystalline limestone.

3. The central Lower Galilee is the highest area in the Lower Galilee and has a highly complex geological structure. It is one of only two anticlinal regions in the whole of the Galilee. This anticline, of Turonian-Senonian age, was later intersected by faults, mostly of Neogene age, that are aligned in an east–west direction. As a result, the central Lower Galilee consists of a set of blocks that were tectonically tilted from south to north. This has created a network of ridges and valleys, in which anticlines are abruptly terminated by horsts and grabens.

The Nazareth Hills form the southernmost of the central Lower Galilee ridges and are divided in their turn into four parallel mountain ridges. Gebel Qafzeh is part of the southernmost of these ridges, the Kesulot-Migdal Ha'emek ridge, the southern flanks of which form the boundary between the Galilee Mountains and the Jezreel Valley. The escarpment facing the Jezreel Valley is a combination of echelon faulted blocks rather than a major fault line. Undoubtedly, some of those faults were first active in Turonian times and rejuvenated in

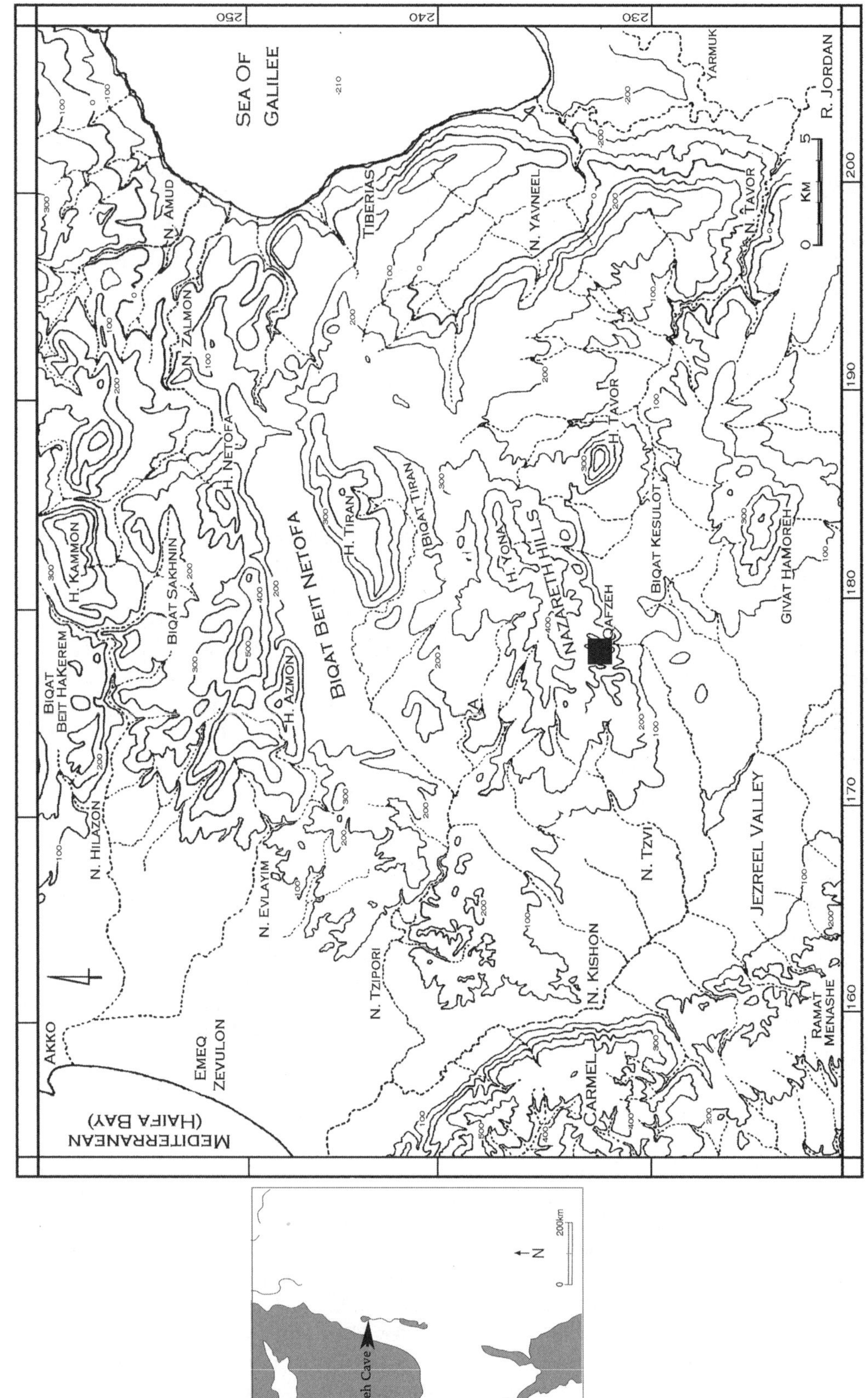


**Figure 3.1** Location and topographic positioning of Qafzeh Cave. The cave's location is marked with a shaded square. (Base topographic map courtesy of A. Nigel Goring-Morris)

later (post-Neogene?) periods of tectonic activity (Weiler 1968:77). Gebel Qafzeh itself is a half-dome created by folding that is probably tephrogenic.

The majority of rocks exposed in the central Lower Galilee are carbonates (e.g., limestone, dolomite, and marls) dating from the Lower Cenomanian to the beginning of the Tertiary (Weiler 1968). The Judea Group (Cenomanian-Turonian) sediments extend over most of the area and mainly include hard dolomites that are responsible for the rugged and sometimes steep terrain of the region. The Sakhnin dolomite (of Upper Cenomanian age) is the main lithological component of the Gebel Qafzeh structure (Weiler 1968: fig. 1). Like other dolomites of the Judea Group, it is very vulnerable to karstic processes, and Qafzeh Cave is carved into this rock formation. Flint bands and nodules form part of the sedimentary sequences of the Eocene deposits (the Ma'lul Formation) to the west and north of Qafzeh Cave (Greenberg 1963). The nari crusts that appear in many places are commonly associated with the chalks and marls of these Eocene sediments.

The eastern part of the central Lower Galilee consists of Senonian to Paleocene sediments of the Mt. Scopus Group, represented by a series of chalks (the Har Zefat and Ein Zeitim Formations), shales, and marls (the Biria Formation).

The valleys within the Nazareth Hills, as well as those separating the ridges of the central Lower Galilee, are filled with alluvial Quaternary deposits and recently developed soils.

## Climate

The Mediterranean climate of the Lower Galilee is characterized by a single rainy season. Amounts of rainfall decline with increasing distance from the Mediterranean Sea and increase with altitude. The eastern part of the region is thus hotter and drier than the western and central parts. As a rule, the amount of rainfall is larger on west-facing slopes than on the slopes facing east. The mean annual rainfall in the Nazareth area is 500–600 mm (Katsenelson 1985), with rains spread over only 40–50 days, from November through March. However, on a multi-annual average, there are 240 nights during the year in which the relative humidity is close to 100%, causing dew and thus contributing to a higher precipitation balance.

The annual mean temperature in the Nazareth Hills is 19°C. January is the coldest month, with a mean monthly temperature of 10°C, and frosts are very rare. On average, temperature exceeds 35°C on only ten days during the year.

The highest relative humidity occurs in the winter (December and January) (Aloni and Orshan 1972: fig. 2).

The mean daily relative humidity is only 55–60% in the hottest month and somewhat higher (60–65%) in the annual mean (Maneh 1985) .

## Soils

The soils of the Lower Galilee develop out of the local rocks, and their characteristics are determined by the rate of erosion of the rock and the rate of leaching. The soils, which belong to the terra rossa, pale rendzina, and brown rendzina association (Dan 1988), require Mediterranean climatic conditions for their pedogenesis (Rabikovitch 1981).

Terra rossa is a fine-grained, reddish-brown, non-calcareous soil that forms on the hard limestone and dolomite typical of the Judea Group lithology. The soil is shallow and many rock exposures appear in its vicinity, as is the case with the immediate area of Qafzeh Cave. However, when the soil fills "pockets" in the rocks it may be quite deep. Pale rendzina soils are loamy, brown to light gray in color, and highly calcareous, and are typical of rocks of the Mount Scopus Group. Brown rendzina is a dark, fine-textured, and non-calcareous soil, rich in organic matter. It develops on nari crusts, hard chalk, and occasionally hard limestone of the Eocene Ma'lul Formation.

Grumosols (reddish-brown, clayey, and dry soils) tend to develop on the Neogene basalt flows in the eastern Lower Galilee.

## Vegetation

Because of the small variation in climate, edaphic factors play a major role in determining the distributions of certain plant communities in the area. However, understanding of the region's vegetation is hampered by the fact that the original Mediterranean vegetation has undergone severe degradation and destruction. As a result of this process, the nature of the climax plant communities and of the succession stages leading to them can at best be speculated on.

Three climax plant associations have been identified in the Lower Galilee. One is the *Quercus ithaburensis–Styrax officinalis* association, which appears as a park forest. It is distinguished by a rich herbaceous layer of both perennial and annual herbs. This plant association grows mainly on the dark brown rendzina soils rich in organic material, and therefore occupies relatively low and dry habitats. Aloni and Orshan (1972) suggested that this plant association dominated the valleys in the past.

The *Quercus calliprinos–Pistacia Palaestin* association is restricted to altitudes above 270 m a.m.s.l. and to terra rossa soils. It appears on all the Central Lower Galilee ridges. This is the typical plant association of the mountainous region of the Nazareth Hills. On the slopes of the mountains the dominant association is that of *Ceratonia siliqua–Pistacia lentiscus,* which appears

**Figure 3.2** View of Qafzeh Cave from the southwest. The arrow points to the cave's opening. (Photograph: Ofer Bar-Yosef ©Qafzeh Excavation archives)

as a three-tiered gallery forest on the southern slopes. The typical variant of this forest also includes *Rhamnus palaestinus* and *Calycotome villosae,* with a large number of grasses (Aloni 1984) . This forest appears at elevations of 0–400 m a.m.s.l., on terra rossa and rendzina soils. On the south facing slopes of the Nazareth Hills, the gallery forest degrades into Mediterranean garigues dominated by *Sarcopoterietum spinosi* and *Calycotome villosae* (Zohary 1980:340–343). Thus, the immediate vicinity of Qafzeh Cave is characterized by widely spaced trees and frequent shrubs and herbaceous plants (figure 3.2).

## The Site

Qafzeh Cave is situated on the left bank of Wadi el-Haj at an elevation of 220 m a.m.s.l. The narrow ephemeral channel develops an increasingly steep slope as it descends into the Jezreel Valley. From the location of the cave, the channel drops some 100 m in elevation over a distance of less than one kilometer, cutting deeply into the bedrock before reaching the valley floor below.

The cave is a remnant of a karstic solution opening. The chimney connecting it with the plateau surface above is presently filled with rubble that has spread as a talus fan inside the cave (Farrand 1979:377; Vandermeersch 1981:22, fig. 4). The inner space consists of a single, large and high-vaulted chamber some 21 by 17 m in maximum dimensions, with its main opening toward the west.

**Figure 3.3** Map of excavated areas in Qafzeh Cave terrace and the entrance to the inner cave area, showing also the lateral distribution of hominid remains (see text for stratigraphic details). Triangles show burials; rectangles, skeletal remains of adults; circles, remains of infants (Hovers et al. 2003).

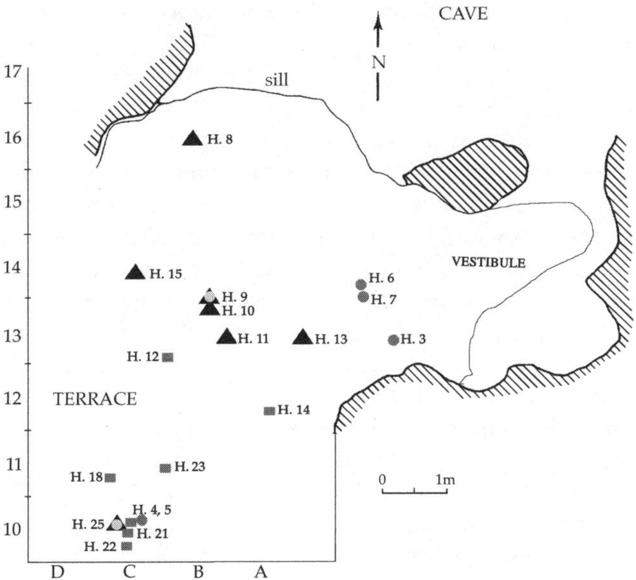


The cave is connected with the open area in front of it (hereafter "the terrace") by a broad vestibule (figure 3.3). This is an area measuring 4 by 5 m just inside the present drip line, which is covered by archaeological sediments. It is blocked to the east by a rocky sill some 2 m higher than the vestibule floor, thus preventing a physical correlation between the cave and the outer part. The only part of the site that lies in the open air is the terrace, a large area covered with sediments, the boundaries of which are not clearly known (it measures at least 12 by 15 m). The sediment cover above the bedrock in this part of the cave consists solely of anthropogenic deposits.

## History of Research

### *Neuville and Stekelis Excavation (1933–1935)*

The site was discovered and brought to the attention of R. Neuville by the geologist Heinz A. Lewonstan in the early 1930s (S. Weiner, pers. comm. 1997).[1] In 1933 Neuville conducted the first sounding at the site with M. Stekelis. Work concentrated on the inner chamber of the cave, but Neuville and Stekelis also excavated half of the surface area of the vestibule. The terrace was only sampled (figures 3.3. and 3.4).

Neuville (1951:179) described a sequence of thirteen layers over a 6.5 m section (published in Vandermeersch 1981 as figs. 4, 5). The two youngest layers (A–B), of historical date, overlie three layers (C–E) dated to the Upper Paleolithic. The latter units consisted of brown silt and contained numerous angular limestone fragments, a phenomenon that was in sharp contrast to the sediments of the lower layers in the sequence (F–L).

On the basis of the lithic assemblages, Neuville defined layers F–L as Middle Paleolithic. With the exception of layer F all these layers contained hearths, and all were rich in phosphates, implying high diagenetic rates and bone destruction. Faunal remains indeed appeared in negligible amounts and were mainly concentrated in a specific area of the vestibule. Layer M (the lowest unit in the excavation) was found only in the terrace test pit and was archaeologically sterile. On the bedrock was a 10 cm thick horizon of phosphate (Neuville 1951:256).

Although he did not describe the assemblages from Qafzeh in detail, Neuville pointed out several major differences between the Middle Paleolithic assemblages of Qafzeh and those retrieved during Garrod's excavations on Mt. Carmel as well as his own work in the Judean Desert (Neuville 1951:183–184). Specifically, Neuville noted that in Qafzeh there were low frequencies of elongated (as opposed to triangular) points. Another characteristic of the assemblages was the proliferation of thin, well-prepared, faceted striking platforms. In contrast, thick and unfaceted platforms were more common in the

**Figure 3.4** Qafzeh Cave at the time of Neuville's excavations. Note the unexcavated terrace in front of the cave, where Vandermeersch's excavations concentrated in the 1960s and 1970s. (Photograph: Moshe Stekelis ©Archives of the Institute of Archaeology, The Hebrew University of Jerusalem)

Mt. Carmel sites. Another difference was the low ratio of side-scrapers to points at Qafzeh as opposed to the various layers in Tabun (Neuville 1951:181–182).

Adhering to the view that development was a gradual, linear process, Neuville (1934: pl. xv) followed Garrod and applied the ratio of points to scrapers within an assemblage as a typological tool for differentiating the Lower from the Upper Levalloiso-Mousterian (Garrod and Bate 1937:115; see chapter 1). He applied this ratio in a somewhat modified form to determine the typological identity of the assemblages of Qafzeh. Not only did Neuville accept the distinction between Levalloisian and Mousterian Middle Paleolithic industries as a real one (see chapter 1), but he also attempted to divide the so-called "Levalloisian" into sub-stages.[2] According to this (now obsolete) division, he considered layers L–J of Qafzeh to be Lower Levalloisian, and layer I was defined as Middle Levalloisian. While he considered layers L and K to be chronologically comparable to Tabun E, Qafzeh layers J and I, as well as layer H (Upper Levalloisian in Neuville's scheme) were believed to be contemporaneous with the Lower Levalloiso-Mousterian of Tabun D. Neuville believed Qafzeh layer G (Upper Levalloisian) to be of Tabun C age, while layer F (Mousterian, in which the ratio of points to scrapers reached almost 4) was perceived as contemporaneous with Tabun B (Neuville 1951:260). This typology-based division was also in accord with a faunal break that had been observed between layers G and F at Qafzeh and layers C and B at Tabun (chapter 1). More recent paleontological and paleoenvironmental analyses (e.g., Garrard 1982:168) verified Bate's observation that *Dicerorhinus mercki*, which Garrod and Bate considered to be a faunal marker of the earlier part of the Middle Paleolithic sequence (Garrod and Bate 1937:115; Neuville 1951:180, 257–261) indeed disappeared between the earlier and later Mousterian at Tabun. However, Garrard did not concur with Bate that a major faunal break occurred between the deposition of layer C and layer B at Tabun.

The remains of five human skeletons were found in layer L (Vandermeersch 1981:23, 30; see below). The hope of augmenting the hominin sample was the main reason for the return to the site in the 1960s.

### Vandermeersch's Excavation (1965–1979)

Work at Qafzeh was resumed in 1965 by a French team, directed by Bernard Vandermeersch, joined by Bar-Yosef in 1977. Efforts focused on both the inner chamber and the terrace. Fifteen layers (13–0) were identified in the cave chamber itself, of which only two (layers 13–12) contained a Middle Paleolithic industry. The terrace in front of the cave, which was sampled systematically for the first time, revealed a sequence of twenty-four sedimentological layers (I–XXIV, top to bottom; see also below), all of which contained Middle Paleolithic lithic assemblages.

*Stratigraphy.* Vandermeersch (1981) described in detail the stratigraphic column that he excavated inside the cave and on the terrace. Neuville had excavated out the part of the sequence that physically connected Middle Paleolithic sediments inside the cave and on the outer side of the drip line, whereas the rocky sill that separates the terrace from the inner chamber made it difficult to establish a stratigraphic correlation between the two areas dug by Vandermeersch himself. Given this history of research and the cave's natural structure, it was necessary to describe the stratigraphic sections separately for each excavated area during the 1960s project. At a relatively late stage a marker horizon was recognized on both sides of the sill, and this served as the basis for correlation between the Middle Paleolithic sequences of the terrace and the inner chamber (table 3.1).

The *cave sequence* consists of fifteen layers, numbered sequentially from top to bottom (0–13) with Arabic numerals (Vandermeersch 1981:27). Layers 13–12 included a rich Mousterian industry, equivalent to Neuville's Upper Levalloisian. These layers were composed of fine-grained, highly weathered sediments. The erosion and redeposition of the sediments of these horizons had caused the dissolution of bones by water leaching and chemical weathering

and the accumulation of secondary phosphates (Farrand 1979:380). A large number of artifacts bore signs of water abrasion, indicating reworking of the Mousterian layers within the cave (Bar-Yosef and Vandermeersch 1981).[3]

A clear unconformity, marked by color and degree of weathering, separates layers 13–12 from the overlying series (Farrand 1979). Layers 11–7 form a single ensemble, characterized by its brown color and fine-grained sediments (Farrand 1979:379). These horizons are of Upper Paleolithic age (Bar-Yosef and Belfer-Cohen 2004; Ronen and Vandermeersch 1972). Layer 6, also of Upper Paleolithic age, resembles the underlying ones in sediment color but is much stonier and appears to be a colluvium deposit issuing from the chimney shaft. A time gap seems to have occurred between the deposition of layer 7 and that of layer 6 (Farrand 1979:379). Layers 4–1 are of possible Neolithic (layer 4) and historical date.

The *terrace sequence* (figure 3.5) encompasses twenty-four layers numbered sequentially (from top to bottom) with Roman numerals. There were no traces of occupations postdating the Middle Paleolithic, and all the lithic assemblages are Mousterian. Table 3.2 presents details of the excavated areas and volumes as estimated from the original field notes and drawings.

The terrace sediments consist almost exclusively of limestone bedrock rubble, rather angular and unaffected by chemical weathering, with only minor amounts of sand-silt-clay matrix (Farrand 1979:377). The upper layers are firmly cemented with secondary calcium carbonate as a result of their exposure to rainfall and weathering. With the exception of a few layers, heavy minerals are rare in the terrace sediments. Where they do appear in significant quantities, these are easy-weathering minerals (Farrand 1979). Their presence is an additional indication of the negligible effect of chemical weathering on the cave's deposits. Deposits of the lower layers are loose, friable, and noticeably mechanically weathered. All in all, the sedimentological evidence suggests a rapid accumulation of sediments (see below).

Bar-Yosef and Vandermeersch (1981) and Vandermeersch (1981) described the terrace sequence as follows:

III.  Brecciated chunks of sediment preserved against the wall.

IV–VIIb.  Recently (mechanically) disturbed Mousterian layers.

VIII.  A hard, gray-green, layer. A clear extension of layer 12 in the cave, this layer was the single key for stratigraphic correlation of the terrace and cave deposits. The only stratigraphic unconformity observed in the terrace sequence is that between this layer and the underlying layer IX. This unconformity appears to be equivalent to that observed

**Table 3.1  The correlation between the Mousterian layers of Qafzeh's terrace and inner chamber**

| Vandermeersch's excavation | | Neuville's excavation | |
|---|---|---|---|
| TERRACE | CAVE | TERRACE | CAVE |
| VIII | 12 | | G, H, I |
| ? | 13 | | J (upper) |
| XVII–XIX | ? | L | |

*Note*: After Vandermeersch 1981.

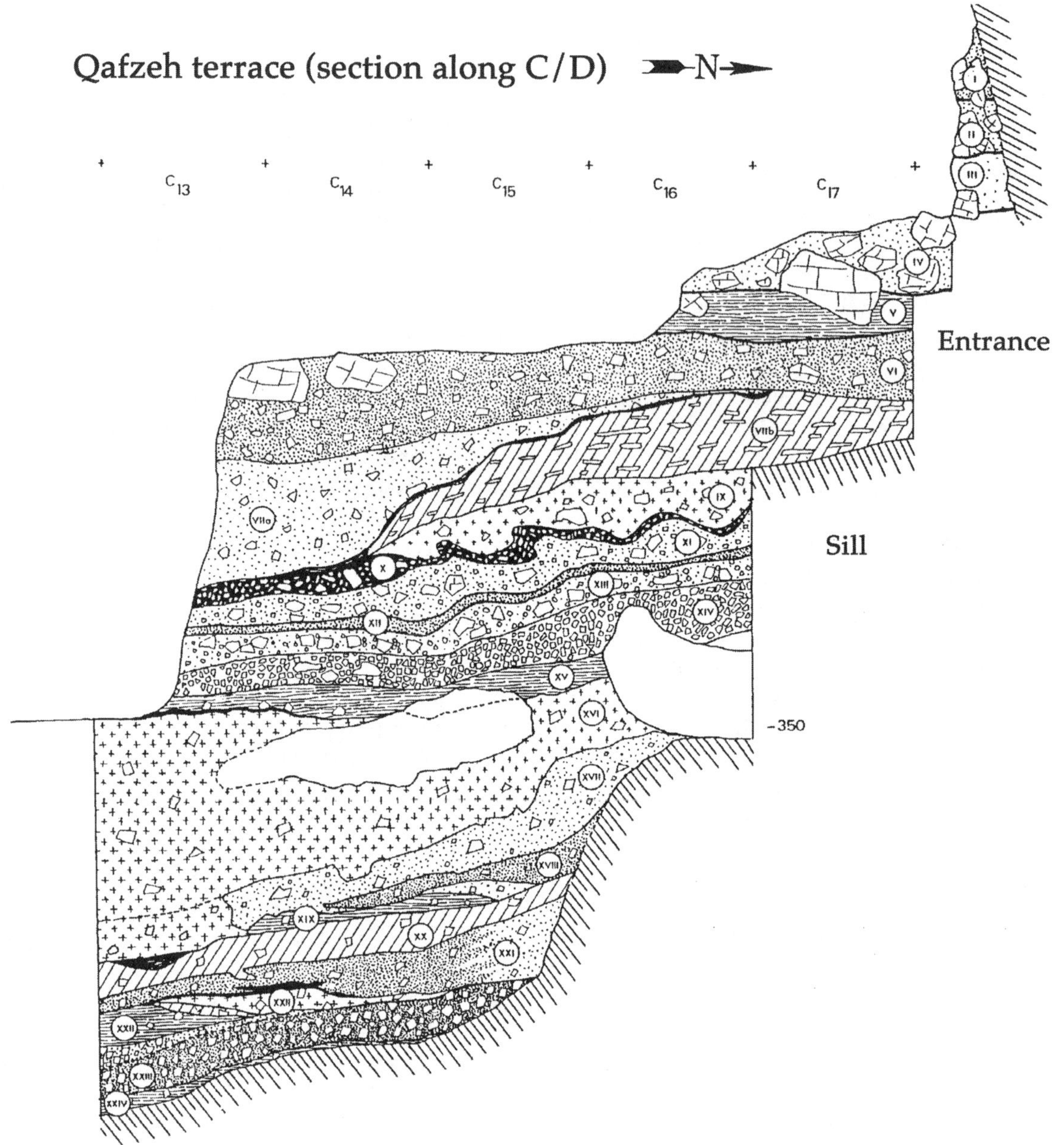


**Figure 3.5**   A generalized stratigraphic section of Qafzeh Cave terrace (after Vandermeersch 1981: fig. 6).

between layers 11 and 12 inside the cave (Farrand 1979:378).

IX.    A hard, gray calcareous breccia, cut by a channel in layer VIIa.

Layers X–XIV were *éboulis* horizons that included a rich lithic industry.

X.    A thin black layer with weathered limestone nodules and traces of many hearths.

XI.    A dense layer of calcareous gravels, some of large dimensions, in a matrix of brown silt.

XII.    A dense layer of calcareous gravels in a matrix of brown silt.

XIII.    As layer XI, but the gravels were larger.

XIV.    A yellow sediment composed of small calcareous gravels and the sand originating from their disintegration.

XV.    Consisted of clayey silt with calcareous gravels. It contained extended patches of white ash, *éboulis*,

**Table 3.2  Area, thickness, and volume of excavated layers on the terrace of Qafzeh Cave**

| Layer | Area | Thickness | Volume | Layer | Area | Thickness | Volume |
|---|---|---|---|---|---|---|---|
| III | 0.40 | 0.35 | 0.14 | XV | 22.00 | 0.25 | 5.50 |
| IV | 1.70 | 0.30 | 0.45 | XVa | | | |
| V | 3.50 | 0.27 | 0.95 | XVb | 5.50 | 0.12 | 1.10 |
| VI | 4.50 | 0.55 | 2.48 | XVf | 7.00 | 0.23 | 1.61 |
| VII | | | | XVII | 16.75 | 0.20 | 3.35 |
| VIIa | 7.50 | 0.40 | 3.00 | XVIIa | 1.10 | 0.05 | 0.056 |
| VIIb | 5.50 | 0.32 | 1.75 | XVIII | 8.75 | 0.09 | 0.80 |
| VIII | | | | XVIIIa | 0.75 | 0.12 | 0.09 |
| IX | 2.50 | 0.30 | 0.75 | XIX | 13.50 | 0.23 | 3.10 |
| X | 6.50 | 0.17 | 1.10 | XX | 8.00 | 0.13 | 1.04 |
| XI | 1.50 | 0.29 | 2.32 | XXI | 7.50 | 0.30 | 2.25 |
| XII | 3.00 | 0.12 | 1.56 | XXII | 9.00 | 0.13 | 1.08 |
| XIII | 19.50 | 0.25 | 4.90 | XXIII | 5.20 | 0.23 | 1.20 |
| XIV | 11.50 | 0.25 | 2.90 | XXIV | 7.50 | 0.09 | 0.67 |

*Note*: Area is in square meters, thickness in meters, and volume in cubic meters.

large quantities of artifacts and a small amount of microfauna. The characteristics of this layer were interpreted by Bar-Yosef and Vandermeersch (1981:281) as indicative of an intensive human occupation. Large mammal bones occur in higher frequencies than in the underlying layers.

XVa. Same as layer XV, but darker in color, with smaller and denser gravels.

XVI. A very hard, black gray brecciated layer, over 1 m thick in places. Water infiltration in the Mousterian layers within the cave resulted in a tunnel that descended from the cave's entrance through layers XV to XX on the terrace and created the brecciated zone of this layer.

Layers XVII–XXIV consist of *éboulis* and sand with remains of hearths, small amount of artifacts, large quantities of microfauna and human burials.

XVII. Calcareous gravels with patches of black silt and traces of hearths.

XVIII. A surface of yellow gravels, almost sterile archaeologically.

XIX. Brown silt with weathered gravels.

XX. Yellow *éboulis*, heavily weathered; this layer was archaeologically almost sterile.

XXI. Small gravels in a brown gray sediment. Traces of many hearths.

XXII. Small weathered gravels in a grayish sediment.

XXIII. Yellow *éboulis*.

XXIV. Gravels in a brownish silt with remains of hearths.

Extensive utilization of the cave entrance is indicated in layers VII–X and XVII–XX by the abundance of microscopic wood fragments (Goldberg 1980:163).

*Previous Lithic Studies*. Samples of both the cave and terrace lithic assemblages were characterized by Boutié (1989) as typical Levantine Mousterian, despite some technological and typological differences between the two samples. Technological Levallois indices (IL) ranged between 12.3 and 24.3 for the terrace assemblages, but were much higher (29.5–35.6) for the cave assemblages. The most common blanks among the Levallois elements were flakes, showing a dominant centripetal preparation (51.2% and 42.7% for the terrace and cave, respectively), with some bipolar (21.9%, 26.8%) and unipolar (15.3%, 18.5%) flaking. High frequencies (between 33.8% and 66.1%) of faceted platforms were recorded in both areas.

The relative frequency of blades and points (combined) is somewhat higher in the cave assemblages than it is in the terrace collections: laminar indices (Ilam) are 24.6–35.4 and 14.6–33.7, respectively. The higher tendency for the production of elongated pieces observed in the cave assemblages is enhanced by the larger number of Levallois points in the cave (Boutié 1989:220), although their frequencies are quite low (15.5% and 13.9%). This latter observation accords with Neuville's description of the cave's Middle Paleolithic industry. However, the high ratio of points to Levallois flakes and scrapers mentioned by Neuville has not been encountered by Boutié in the cave assemblages from the newer excavations. Since Neuville identified, curated, and studied Levallois blanks (Neuville 1951:180–183), this discrepancy between the two records cannot be explained as resulting simply from differential selection on his part.

Given the stratigraphic indications that the Middle Paleolithic sequence within the cave postdates most of the terrace's stratigraphic column, it is necessary to identify which of the differences between the assemblages from the two parts of the cave are due to cultural changes, and which may reflect organizational differences. This task is complicated by the post-depositional processes that affected the cave's deposits. Still, Boutié (1989:221) suggested that the Qafzeh terrace and cave assemblages were homogeneous and did not show any internal diachronic evolution. He placed them with the Tabun B–C industries. Fish (1979) reached similar conclusions based on his study of samples from the Mousterian deposits inside the cave. Other scholars (e.g., Meignen and Bar-Yosef 1992), following Copeland (1975) in favoring a tripartite (as opposed to bipartite) division of the Tabun sequence, regard the Qafzeh assemblages as "Tabun C-type" industries.

*Studies of the Large Fauna.* The first study of the large fauna was conducted by Bouchud (1974) on material from Vandermeersch's excavation in 1965–1969 and some material from the first series of excavations. None of the faunal specimens excavated inside the cave (N = 437) derived from a Mousterian context (Bouchud 1974: tab. III). Of the 506 identified bones from the terrace's Mousterian sequence, the highest overall frequency (32.8%) was of red deer (*Cervus elaphus*). The stratigraphic distribution of those bones, however, was not homogeneous. This species was dominant in the younger layers (XV–XI), where it comprised roughly 40% of all the faunal elements. In contrast, the most common medium-sized to large mammal in the older layers (XXIII–XVI) was the gazelle (*Gazella gazella),* whose bones comprised 22% of the identified elements. Other species represented in the sample were wild cattle (*Bos primigenius* at 20.15%), ibex (*Capra ibex* at 12.84%), fallow deer (*Dama mesopotamica*), wild pig, horse (*Equus mauritanicus*), rhinoceros, hartebeest, and camel (*Camelus dromedarius*). Bouchud (1974:96–97) rejected the identification of the rhinoceros remains at Qafzeh as those of the steppe-dwelling *Dicerorhinus mercki* and assigned these remains to the smaller, woodland species, *D. hemitoechus.* The most common carnivore was the spotted hyena, and there were also remains of panther (*Panthera pardus*).

A recent revision of the faunal sample (Rabinovich and Tchernov 1995) also encompasses bone splinters identifiable only to body size groups, never studied by Bouchud. The species composition derived from this enlarged sample of 1,472 identified bones (all from the terrace layers) differs slightly from that described earlier by Bouchud. According to this new analysis, the dominant species in the Qafzeh sequence are *Cervus elaphus* and *Dama mesopotamica.* Roe deer (*Capreolus capreolus*), previously unrecognized, and gazelle are fairly infrequent. Wild goat (*Capra aegagrus)* actually outnumbers the gazelle, possibly as a result of the rocky nature of the site's vicinity. The new analysis also differs from Bouchud's in the greater diversity of equid species. Interestingly, the most abundant

equid is the North African *E. cf. tabeti* (Eisenmann 1992; Tchernov 1998: tab. 3). Also noteworthy is the relatively high number of ostrich (*Struthio camelus*) eggshells.

## Hominin Remains

Skeletal remains of five Middle Paleolithic hominins were discovered outside the drip line of the cave (figure 3.3) during excavations in September 1934. The individuals Q3, Q6, and Q7 were found close to one another and at the same level. As reconstructed from the field notes and diaries of Neuville and Stekelis, they derived from layer L in Neuville's stratigraphic scheme. Specimens Q4 and Q5 were found in brecciated deposits on the terrace, at a lateral distance of a few meters from the other cluster (Vandermeersch 1981:32). Although these two skeletons also derived from layer L, they occurred in different stratigraphic positions, with Q5 being deposited some 70 cm below Q4. Boule (cited in Vandermeersch 1981:19) recognized in the skeletons a mixture of primitive and evolved anatomical features similar to that found in the Skhul group (McCown and Keith 1939).

The renewed excavations by Vandermeersch yielded additional hominin skeletal remains. Specimens Q9–Q25 (Q16–Q18 and Q23 being isolated teeth) originated from layers XXII–XVII (Vandermeersch 1981:32), while no human skeletal remains were recovered from the upper layers of the terrace sequence (XV–I).[4] Eleven individuals were infants, ranging in ontogenetic age from perinatal to adolescent (Tillier 1999).

Several paleopathologies were observed in the skeletal remains of various individuals from Qafzeh. On the left calcaneum of Qafzeh 8 there is a fracture, typically located in the middle of the bone, accompanied by additional lesions. The injury has been attributed to a penetration wound to the calcaneum. After a period of immobilization, if the injury was not treated medically, permanent hypertension of the foot would set in, and the injured person would be able to move around only with the help of a crutch of some sort. The right foot of Qafzeh 9 was affected by *hallux valgus,* a deformation of the big toe that causes the toe to tilt toward the small toes and a bony lump to appear on the inside of the foot (a "bunion"). This pathology is painful when shoes are worn on the afflicted foot and has in fact been ascribed to this modern practice. The case of Qafzeh 9 (and other Pleistocene instances of this pathology), however, suggest that it may also derive from other reasons (Dastugue 1981).

Two cases of paleopathologies have been observed in children. The child Qafzeh 13 suffered a frontal lesion that was caused either by an intentional blow or by a hard, narrow object, most likely a flint tool. Despite the severity of the injury, the skull displays healing marks, indicating that the child survived the trauma (Dastugue 1981) for a short time (the estimated age of death of this individual is ca. ten months [Tillier 1999:30]). Finally, Tillier et al. (2001) reported that Qafzeh 12, a 3-year-old child (by modern human reference standards) exhibited abnormal pre-death features in the skull (e.g., enlargement of the frontal and parietal regions, abnormal morphology of the temporal bone, pronounced asymmetries of the frontal lobe and of the occipital region that seem to be the result of differential development of the cerebral hemispheres, and peculiarities in the skull vascularization system). Combined with the hypotrophy and shortness of the upper limb bones, these features are consistent with hydrocephaly.

The abundance of skeletal remains at Qafzeh may be explained partly by the fast accumulation of sediments and by brecciation that occurred soon after deposition; these processes may have slowed down the rate of bone diagenesis and dispersion. The highest concentration of skeletons (12 specimens) was in layer XVII (Neuville's layer L). As table 3.2 shows, this is not merely a statistical artifact of the excavated volume. It is mainly due to this concentration that the site earned its name as an early cemetery. At least six cases (= 7 individuals) are identified as intentional burials (Belfer-Cohen and Hovers 1992). These include the only double burial known to date from any Middle Paleolithic site in the world, presumably a mother and a child (Q9 and Q10), buried in an elongated dug out pit; and an internment of a child (Q11) with red deer antlers as a burial gift (Vandermeersch 1970). Interestingly, artifacts that are potentially of symbolic nature were found only in the stratigraphic horizons that yielded the skeletal remains, an association that is interpreted to be of symbolic nature (Bar-Yosef and Vandermeersch 1993; Hovers, Vandermeersch, and Bar-Yosef 1997; Hovers et al. 2003; Taborin 2003; Walter 2003).

Boule's initial analysis placed the first Qafzeh Middle Paleolithic skeletons and the Skhul remains in a problematic taxonomic position, as Neanderthals with some modern features. Their existence was taken to reflect either hybridization between Neanderthal and anatomically modern populations or contemporaneity of two populations (Howell 1958, 1959). With the augmentation of the human skeletal sample in the 1960s, all the adult and immature individuals from Qafzeh were defined as anatomically modern humans (Tillier 1999; Vandermeersch 1981).

Vandermeersch (1982) suggested that these hominins evolved locally from a late *Homo erectus/Homo heidelbergensis*, represented by the Zuttiyeh partial cranium. Stringer and Andrews (1988) proposed a similar hypothesis. Some researchers view the Qafzeh (and Skhul) group as morphologically and phylogenetically distinct from the Neanderthals (Rak 1990, 1993; Rak, Kimbel, and Hovers 1994; Stringer 1988; Stringer and Gamble 1993; Tattersall 1995). Others (e.g., Arensburg and Belfer-Cohen 1998; Wolpoff and Lee 2001) argue for a highly variable

single population of modern humans in the Levant. Klein (1999) summarizes evidence for a mixture of anatomical traits of the Qafzeh (and Skhul) hominins: "As a group, the Qafzeh-Skhul skulls are highly variable in their expression of chins, vertical foreheads, rounded occipitals, parietal bossing, and other modern features, and in some important aspects, such as strongly developed brow ridges, large teeth, and a tendency to pronounced alveolar prognathism, they tend to recall more archaic humans" (Klein 1999:402, and references therein). However, he sees significant differences in the hand morphologies of the Qafzeh hominins compared to Neanderthals (Klein 1999:387 with references; although see Niewoehner et al. 2003; more on this in chapter 9). Overall, Klein designates the Qafzeh-Skhul groups as "nearly modern humans." White et al. (2003) pointed out some morphological resemblance of Qafzeh 6 to the recently discovered late Middle Pleistocene *Homo sapiens idaltu* from the Middle Awash, though they state clearly that the latter is intermediate between the more primitive morphology of the earlier African specimens (such as Bodo and Kabwe) and the more derived morphology of Klasies and Qafzeh, which they seem to consider as modern humans (White et al. 2003:745). This discovery reopens the discussion on the taxonomic affinities of the Qafzeh hominins and about their fate (more on this in chapters 9 and 10).

## Chronology

The modern anatomical affinities of the Qafzeh hominins, the indications of intentional burials, and the Mousterian context in which they were found raised the need for a reliable dating of the Qafzeh Mousterian in order to understand the biological and cultural complexities of the Middle Paleolithic period in the Levant.

In the absence of absolute dates, the chronology of Qafzeh had been based on comparison with the dating of Tabun. Following Garrod and Bate, Neuville (1951:261) dated the Middle Paleolithic sequences at both sites to "Pluvial C" (the Würm glaciation) by typological and faunal comparisons. Jelinek placed all the Qafzeh assemblages at the very end of the Levantine Mousterian sequence on the basis of the alleged trend of reduction in variance of flake thickness through time (Jelinek 1982a:1374). He associated the beginning of deposition of Tabun D (= unit IX) with the beginning of glacial conditions and equated it with Marine Isotope Stage (MIS) 4 (ca. 75,000 years ago). The end of Tabun's Mousterian sequence was assumed to have occurred between 50,000 and 40,000 years ago (Jelinek 1982a:1373, fig. 3). According to this scheme, Jelinek proposed a similar age for Qafzeh, well within the Würm glaciation. Farrand (1979: fig. 6) supported this scheme by proposing that deposition at Qafzeh started ca. 70,000 years ago with the terrace occupation and ended by 55,000 years ago in a hiatus comparable to, but longer than, the Tabun C/D break (Jelinek et al. 1973).

Other lines of evidence, however, pointed to an older age for the Qafzeh Mousterian. The micromammalian community of Qafzeh was thought to display a great similarity to the Acheulian and Acheulo-Yabrudian fauna of Tabun layers F and E (Tchernov 1989). At least two murid genera found at Qafzeh (*Mastomys baeti* and *Arvicanthis ectos*) were African archaic species. Qafzeh is the only Middle Paleolithic site outside Africa in which both were recorded. On the other hand, cricetines, whose arrival in the near East was an important biochronological event (Tchernov 1989) appear in later sites but are completely absent from Qafzeh (Tchernov 1992:162, 175). Based on these data, Tchernov (1989:31–33) antedated layers XXI–XIV to the time span of Tabun D (as it was known at that time) and placed them in MIS 5, ca. 95,000 years ago. A similar age for the Qafzeh Mousterian was suggested by a compilation of stratigraphic and paleoclimatic data (Bar-Yosef and Vandermeersch 1981), with a suggested age of ca. 100,000 years for the occupations of Qafzeh XXIV–XV, Naamé, Tabun D, and Hayonim early E.[5] The erosional phenomena encountered at the top of Tabun D and of Qafzeh IX were associated with the onset of pluvial conditions at the beginning of MIS 4 (80,000–70,000 years ago), which in its turn caused renewed karstic solution in the caves. The archaic microvertebrates found at Qafzeh XXIV–XV were assumed to have disappeared at this time.

The first radiometric dates for Qafzeh, albeit not unanimously accepted, were obtained by amino acid racemization (Bada and Helfman 1976; Masters 1982). They suggested a time range of MIS 4 and 3 for the Mousterian sequence (68,000 years ago for layer XXII; 40,000–39,000 years ago for layer XVII). It was suggested that discrepancies observed between the various dated materials (human versus animal bones) resulted from depositional variables and from limitations of the dating method, neither of which could be fully controlled for (Farrand 1994; Masters 1982).

Finally, two series of Thermoluminescence (TL) and Electron Spin Resonance (ESR) age estimates have placed the lower part of the Qafzeh sequence in the last interglacial (table 3.3), affirming the great antiquity of the site and of modern humans in the Levant (Schwarcz et al. 1988; Valladas et al. 1988).

The first attempts at radiometric dating of Qafzeh understandably focused on the horizons that had contained the hominin remains. Hence layers XV–III remained undated. Given both the hiatus of an unknown duration between layers IX and VIII, and the likelihood that rates of sediment accumulation were not necessarily identical throughout the sequence, it is impossible to date layers XIV–III accurately. If the rate of deposition for the lower layers is assumed to be representative of the whole stratigraphic sequence, it would seem that age estimates obtained by both dating methods imply a high rate of sedimentation, with some 4.5 m of deposits accumulating within 10,000 years. Amino acid racemization attempts on ostrich eggshell indicated a slower rate of accumulation but have not yielded any absolute ages for the Qafzeh sequence (Brooks, Kokis, and Hare 1992). The question of rate of deposition may remain unanswered, since, despite the fact that Vandermeersch identified the remains of hearths in some of the upper layers (e.g., layer X), these deposits did not yield a large number of burned artifacts (Hovers 1997; I will return to this point below, as it is significant in the context of the current discussion). Of these, an even smaller number originated from existing stratigraphic profiles (pers. obs. 1997), a situation that prevents reliable dosimetry. It is therefore doubtful that valid TL dating of layers XV–III will become feasible in the near future.

Both the TL and the ESR age estimates of Qafzeh were criticized by Jelinek (1992) and Farrand (1994), who were concerned with the reliability of these methods, newly introduced at the time. Aitkin and Valladas (1992) responded to these critiques with convincing statistical and analytical arguments for the reliability of TL dating at the site. Another potential source of errors in TL dating was the geochemical history of the sediments. Recent studies have shown that the diagenesis of ashes creates a variety of chemical paleoenvironments, which in turn influence differently the dose rates measured in the sediments. Heterogeneous diagenetic stages may introduce much "noise" and become a major source of errors in TL (and ESR) dating (e.g., Mercier et al. 1995). Recent work at Qafzeh has shown that sediments in the dated lower layers of the terrace have not undergone substantial diagenesis and are chemically relatively homogeneous, thus affecting less crucially the reliability of the dating (S. Weiner, pers. comm. 2004). On the whole, the early age estimates for the hominin-bearing lower layers at Qafzeh are acceptable because they are analytically and methodologically well established and controlled for.

**Table 3.3  Average TL and ESR dates of layers XXIV–XV at Qafzeh**

| TL (average) | ESR EU (average) | ESR LU (average) |
| --- | --- | --- |
| *LAYERS XXIII–XVII* | *LAYERS XXI–XV* | *LAYERS XXI–XV* |
| 92 ± 5 thousand years ago | 96 ± 13 thousand years ago | 115 ± 15 thousand years ago |

## Paleoenvironments and Settlement Patterns

The radiometric age estimates place the early occupations of Qafzeh Cave in the second half of MIS 5, which on current evidence lasted 128,000–74,000 years ago). Recent paleoclimatic studies based on speleothems from several caves in Israel have indicated that the second half of this period was characterized by minimal values of $\delta^{18}O$ and $\delta^{13}C$. Temperature as well as rainfall would have been relatively high compared to the present. Accordingly, the record indicates the presence of C3 vegetation, which does not grow in arid conditions, in the Eastern Mediterranean. Periods of particularly high rainfall have been documented at 124,000–119,000, 108,000, 100,000, 85,000, and 79,000 years ago in the Mediterranean ecological zone (see Bar-Matthews and Ayalon 2001; Bar-Matthews et al. 1999; Bar-Matthews, Ayalon, and Kaufmann 2000; Frumkin, Ford, and Schwarcz 1999).

The composition of the macromammalian community as a whole allows the reconstruction of an ecotone in which parkland and forest species formed the dominant portion of faunal remains at Qafzeh (Haas 1972; Tchernov 1992: fig. 10.4). Gazelles were more common in the lower layers, thus supporting the evidence for an open savanna landscape. The faunal indications of woodland habitats increased over time and were especially clear in the upper layers, in which red deer comprised the most common single species (Bouchud 1974; Rabinovich and Tchernov 1995). As Qafzeh Cave lies in the Mediterranean climatic zone, the change in species composition possibly corresponded to the shifts in quantities and intensity of regional rainfall as documented in cave deposits that reflect this type of climate (Bar-Matthews and Ayalon 2001; Bar-Matthews et al. 1999; Bar-Matthews, Ayalon, and Kaufmann 2000).

Tchernov (1998) characterized the fauna of Qafzeh by the absence of Palearctic elements and the increase in frequencies of Arabian and East African elements in the microvertebrates compared to earlier Middle Paleolithic horizons in the Levant. The vast majority of micromammalian species (up to 95%) consisted of batha and dry savanna elements, which led to the reconstruction of an open, dry landscape near the site at the time of layers XXIV–XV. Some of the large mammalian species (e.g., *Alcelaphus buselaphus*, *Equus tabeti*, *Dicerorhinus hemitoechus*, *Camelus dromedarus*) and the presence of *Struthio camelus* also appear to reflect similar conditions. The composition of the (micro)faunal community at Qafzeh was taken as evidence for a northward expansion of African and Saharo-Arabian biotic zones (Tchernov 1992:175, fig. 10.5; 1998), a somewhat problematic assertion in view of the composition of the large mammal assemblage and the paleoclimatic conditions emerging from the work of Bar-Matthews and colleagues. Tchernov has accepted that micromammalian bones originated from the pellets of birds of prey, mainly the barn owl (*Tito*

*alba*), which refrains from shared habitation with humans. This very territorial bird normally has a hunting area that may range between several hundred meters up to 2–3 km (Andrews 1990:178). If indeed the barn owl was responsible for the deposition of micromammalian bones at Qafzeh, it would be difficult to accept the suggestion (Jelinek 1982b) that these bones represented relict faunal communities that were hunted by owls in the Dead Sea Rift Valley, a distance of ca. 25 km as the crow flies.

## Implications for Settlement and Mobility Patterns

The co-occurrence of hominin remains (some of which are burials) and microvertebrates in the lower layers of Qafzeh (XXIV–XVII) is in striking contrast to their absence from the upper layers (Bar-Yosef and Vandermeersch 1993). The occurrence of microvertebrates intuitively suggests that habitation at the site at the time of their inclusion in the deposits was ephemeral and intermittent. Seasonality studies based on cementum growth in gazelle teeth seem to back up this intuition, yielding patterns that indicate seasonal spring and summer occupation in layers XXIV–XVI (Lieberman and Shea 1994). This was interpreted as reflecting a residential, circulating mobility pattern of the human groups at Qafzeh at the time, so that the locality was used for a short duration before the occupants moved out as a group to another site within their annual home range. In contrast, cementum studies on samples from layers XIV–VII led to the reconstruction of a year-round occupation at the site during that time (Lieberman 1993; Lieberman and Shea 1994), supposedly leading to more extensive periods of occupation. If microvertebrates were indeed introduced to the site by nocturnal birds of prey (see above), the suggested seasonality pattern for these layers may explain the paucity of their remains in the upper layers.

Other correlates of settlement intensity and mobility patterns do not appear to uphold the suggestions raised by the cementum analysis. The high frequencies among the microvertebrates from layers XXIV–XV of *Mastomys baeti*, considered to be a commensal animal that thrives on human refuse (Tchernov 1984), do not accord with the notion of ephemeral occupations in layers XXIV–XVII. Tchernov (1984) in fact suggested a semi-sedentary mode of occupation, based on the occurrence of this rodent species.[6] Another interesting pattern is that carnivore activity in the Middle Paleolithic layers of the terrace is negligible in comparison to that seen within the cave during the Upper Paleolithic (Rabinovich et al. 2004). As carnivores and humans do not co-habit in caves, this may indicate more intensive (and prolonged?) human occupation during the earlier of the two periods.

Bar-Yosef and Vandermeersch (1993) hypothesized that the main settlement at the time of deposition of layers

XXIV–XVII was in a nearby as yet unknown site, whose inhabitants used Qafzeh Cave as their burial ground. The exclusive stratigraphic association of relatively large amounts of ochre with the hominin remains is consistent with the pigment's symbolic use in contexts of burial ritual (Hovers et al. 2003) and congruent with such an interpretation. Finally, the presence of a small number of sea shells in the lower layers of Qafzeh, brought from the Mediterranean coast some 30 km to the west, may hint at the extent of the territory annually exploited by the Qafzeh hominins, at least at the time of the earlier occupations (Bar-Yosef and Vandermeersch 1993).

Use-wear analyses, which encompass variable proportions of the flakes and flake tools in each lithic assemblage (ranging from 38.6% in layer XIX to 74.6% in layer XVII), indicated that lithics were used mainly for light-duty wood-working, butchery, and hide-working (Shea 1991: tabs. 5.24–5.39). Layer XV, which exhibited higher frequencies of Levallois points, was considered an exception to this general rule; the points were interpreted as hafted projectiles used in hunting operations. This phenomenon was claimed to reflect a higher intensity of technology-assisted hunting. If the use-wear observations are accepted and the interpretation of the points as part of complex hunting tools is valid, the occurrence of points in the layer XV assemblage may be indicative of a significant change in the subsistence behavior of hominins at Qafzeh. In fact, this pattern in the lithic assemblages, combined with the results of the cementum studies, was taken to indicate a major change in the identity of the population inhabiting the site, from modern humans to Neanderthals (Lieberman and Shea 1994), despite the lack of any human remains in the upper layers.

Recent work has revealed some fundamental flaws in the methodological and analytical aspects of the cementum analysis (Stutz 2002), thus undermining its conclusions and opening the question of mobility patterns and their shifts throughout the record of Qafzeh.

# 4

# Lithic Production: 1. The Cores

## Beginning at the End: Cores as a Key to Understanding Lithic Variability

Cores in a lithic assemblage bear indications of the manner in which they were last flaked. They are informative about knapping procedures employed during the most recent stage of their usage. Often the reasons for discontinuing their exploitation (among which may be discard due to physical fault in the raw material or core exhaustion) can also be deciphered. Just how much information can be derived from cores about the earlier stages of reduction is more difficult to establish. It is likely that a single *knapping concept* (e.g., Levallois) was used throughout the reduction process of any given core. This does not mean necessarily that the methods and modes of flaking (see below) remained unchanged throughout the whole sequence. When lithic reduction was initiated on small nodules, size restrictions would constrain the number of core reshaping cycles and thus the exploration of any technological repertoire to its fullest extent. In such instances, core reduction would likely be limited to the single set of tactics initially opted for. On the contrary, where raw material was ubiquitous and came in the form of large nodules, flint knappers could often be more flexible and several methods of flaking might have been used along the process of working on a single core, hampering our attempts to reconstruct reduction processes based on core properties. It is here that the use of a combination of attribute analysis and the *chaîne opératoire* concept is most powerful. The deviation between debitage characteristics as anticipated from core characteristics and those seen in the actual debitage in a flake population helps us to evaluate and understand the degree of flexibility and variability of the lithic tactics employed during core reduction, and to understand the possible causes of such variation (e.g., changes in the efficiency of core reduction, changes in shape and size of the desired end-product, etc.).

Viewed from an economic point of view, a dynamic lithic production system may be described as struggling to achieve a balance between two polarities. On the one end, there is the need to extend the utility of the core over time by removing a larger number of smaller flakes. This contrasts with the other end, namely, the attempt to extend the duration of use of the products by detaching fewer and larger flakes, each of which can be undergo cycles of resharpening and reuse before being discarded. Depending on the distances that lithics have to be transported, on the degree of certainty that lithic resources can be found when new tools are needed, and on the nature of subsistence resources (i.e., whether they are sedentary and anticipated or mobile and unpredictable), the knapper decides whether the cores or the detached flakes should become the curated elements of the technological system and uses the appropriate technological system accordingly (Baumler and Speth 1993; Kuhn 1995a; Nelson 1991; see chapter 2). However, these two radically different organizational tactics—or other, intermediate ones—can be achieved through a number of flaking methods within a single flaking concept.

Because the Levantine Mousterian is often rich in Levallois products, it seemed that analysis of assemblage variability should primarily concentrate on the technological and organizational advantages and drawbacks of products of this flaking system in comparison with other knapping systems. Following recent work (e.g., Boëda 1991, 1993, 1995; Geneste 1985; see chapter 2 for discussion), the understanding of Levallois flaking revolves around a number of concrete technological criteria, which define the practical manifestations of the Levallois concept. Given the attention that this issue has received in recent literature (e.g., Boëda 1991, 1993, 1995; Boëda, Geneste, and Meignen 1990; Van Peer 1992), I present below only a brief summary of the pertinent points.

Fundamental to the understanding of the Levallois concept is the perception that the core is organized according to well-defined principles of surface–volume relationships. A Levallois core is shaped into two asymmetrical convex surfaces that intersect at a single plane. Additional operational principles underlie the shaping of the core throughout the reduction sequence. The two surfaces of the core are hierarchical: one is shaped to be the flaking (debitage) surface and the other is an auxiliary (yet obligatory) surface used for preparing removals from the primary surface. The roles of the two surfaces are not interchangeable.

The flaking surface is constructed so that the products knapped off it are predetermined by the core's geometry. This is achieved by shaping the lateral and distal convexities of the core's flaking surface, which in turn dictate the morphology of the flake to be removed. The convexities on the core's surface need to be preserved (or renewed) in order to perpetuate the Levallois process throughout the core's use life. Convexities can be achieved by application of a number of tactics that depend on the specific method and mode of Levallois flaking used by the knapper. This is also the case for the shaping of the core's striking platform. In this latter case, however, it is imperative that the core's flaking surface be modified so as to create a hinge (*charnière*) at the intersection with the preparation surface (Boëda 1995: fig. 4.18). The removal of flakes starts at this hinge, when the flakes are detached at a more-or-less right angle to the hinge. The flake's plane of fracture is parallel or sub-parallel to the intersection plane of the two surfaces (as in fact dictated by the geometry of the core as defined above), which explains the need to reorganize the convexities of the flaking surface as the process of reduction progresses and the original surface is corrupted by use. Finally, at the time of striking the core, a hammerstone impacts the core not directly on the hinge between the two surfaces but slightly below it, on the surface of the core's striking platform (Boëda 1995: fig. 4.19).[1]

Other core properties are not considered defining criteria of the Levallois flaking sequence. Whether the desired products were flakes, blades, or points; how the core's circumference was used to prepare the flaking surface; and whether the flaking surface was prepared for the removal of a single, preferential flake or for the detachment of a number of similarly sized artifacts are characteristics that pertain to the particular technological nuances of the Levallois system.

Two methods of flaking can be applied within the Levallois flaking system. In a *lineal* flaking method, the core is designed for the removal of a preferential, large flake from a Levallois flaking surface. The removal of a lineal flake corrupts the geometry of the flaking surface of a Levallois core, leading to one of three outcomes: (1) the core may be discarded; (2) it may be used further without remanagement of its geometry (in which case it will not be used as a Levallois core); or (3) its striking platforms and the distal and lateral convexities may be reshaped in order to produce another Levallois flake. A core exploited through the *recurrent* method produces several flakes from any given flaking surface. The flakes are somewhat smaller than a preferential flake. More than in the case of preferential flakes, the plane of fracture of recurrent flakes must be parallel to the flaking surface so that its geometry allows further removal of Levallois products without having to rebuild the convexities and striking platform. After the removal of a few flakes the flaking surface must be rearranged. Alternately, core exploitation may continue without applying the flaking principles of Levallois flaking, or the core is discarded (see Boëda 1986; Boëda, Geneste, and Meignen 1990 for a detailed discussion of the notions of lineal and recurrent Levallois methods).

Another aspect of variability within the Levallois system resides in the modes of shaping the core's flaking surface. Shaping of the surface and the controlled removal of the desired flakes can be conducted from the core circumference toward the center of the flaking surface, in which case it constitutes the centripetal Levallois flaking mode. Alternately, only parts of the core's striking platform may be used from either a single direction (the unipolar mode of Levallois flaking) or two opposing parts of the core's striking platform can be exploited (a bipolar mode of Levallois flaking, referred hereafter as "bipolar" flaking).[2]

Theoretically, any detached products can be obtained through any combination of Levallois methods and modes. In reality, Levallois flakes are by far the most "generalized" products and indeed can be obtained through applying any Levallois configuration, whereas an efficient production of blades and points requires more attention to flaking modes. Convergent and unipolar modes may be the least-effort solutions (in terms of core shaping) for the production of points and blades, respectively.

Other formal flaking systems (e.g., laminar production) are characterized by different technological criteria that define the cores and products. Cores and debitage that derive from such systems are not frequent in the Qafzeh assemblages, as the following analysis shows.

## Variation in Core Forms

Among the cores of the Qafzeh assemblages, some closely correspond to the criteria of the Levallois concept and are therefore identified as Levallois cores. All the cores that do not bear evidence for Levallois flaking are loosely grouped under the term "non-Levallois."[3] Whether these two groups indeed reflect two different technological systems, and the role of such putative systems in the organizational scheme of the lithic assemblages, are questions of interest within the framework of this study.

The cores included in each category consist of several variants, and typological variability can be significant. This introduces a methodological problem because sample sizes per layer are often small. The inventory of cores is shown separately for each assemblage (table 4.1). Analyses were first carried out on each assemblage separately, and the technological trends and variation in core types were examined in a stratigraphic context. As typological and technological variations throughout the sequence were found to be minimal, it became archaeologically feasible to agglomerate the samples from the individual layers into a single large sample for the sake of some statistical treatments. In most cases, however, detailed analyses are presented both for the total sample and separately for some of the larger core assemblages.

To facilitate comparison with previously studied assemblages in the Levant, the typological classification used in this analysis follows the system advocated by Bordes (1961, 1980). As discussed in chapter 2, Bordes's definitions were technologically somewhat ambiguous (see also Meignen 1993). This led to the widespread notion that only cores bearing the scar of a single dominant flake, centralized on the core's flaking surface (the classical "horse-shoe" scar pattern), qualified as Levallois cores. Cores exhibiting the scars of several similar-sized predetermined flakes that originated from the core's circumference were termed "discoidal" and presumed to be only weakly related to the Levallois system.[4] Within the new understanding of Levallois, however, such cores are seen as having been obtained by recurrent centripetal Levallois flaking. As currently defined, discoidal cores exhibit a different surface–volume relationship from that of Levallois cores. The use of the two core surfaces is non-hierarchical, which in turn necessitates flake removals at more obtuse flaking angles in relation to the intersecting plane (Boëda 1993: fig. 1; Goren-Inbar 1990a; see, however, papers in Peresani 2003). The distinction between "discoidal" and "recurrent centripetal Levallois" is maintained in the current analysis of the Qafzeh cores.

To maintain comparability with older analyses, I used Bordes's terms for Levallois cores in their literal sense. Cores are classified according to the morphology of

the last Levallois removal observed on the flaking surface. "Levallois core for points" is the term used to describe cores on which points were the last debitage removed. These could have been produced by either a lineal method (in which case the classical point shape and Y-pattern appear on the core), or a recurrent one (by which a series of residual triangular scars, often truncating one another, is preserved on the core surface).

Two types of cores are added to Bordes's list: "core-on-flake" (Goren-Inbar 1988b, 1990a; Hovers 2007; see below) and "fragment." The latter are cores on which no part of any striking platform is preserved.

The frequencies and descriptive statistics of dimensions for each type are shown in tables 4.1 and 4.2.

## Levallois Cores

The core assemblages are dominated by items with the technological characteristics of the Levallois technology. Levallois cores, produced by hard-hammer flaking, outnumber non-Levallois cores at a ratio of 1.45 across assemblages (table 4.1).

The organization of scar patterns on the cores' flaking surfaces serves to identify the methods and modes of reduction just prior to discontinuing the use of the core. A detailed classification of scar patterns (see appendix 2) reveals a high degree of variability. This can, however, be collapsed into five broad categories. All the patterns demonstrating that flakes prior to the last removal had originated from a restricted part of the core's striking platform and were directed in the same orientation (i.e., "unipolar," "opposed") are grouped in the "unipolar" category of scar patterns. In this case, the scars on the flaking surface are parallel to the core's long axis (as defined in appendix 2) and derive from the part of the core's striking platform from which other flakes had been removed. In the second instance, the scars are still parallel to the core's long axis but originate from the opposite edge of the core. A "unipolar convergent" organization of the scars on the core's flaking surface is indicated by only two scar patterns: "convergent" and "convergent and side." The preparation of lateral convexities for a convergent flaking method precludes the use of the lateral sides of the core as part of the striking platform (Boëda, Geneste, and Meignen 1990:67). Indeed, removals that were perpendicular to the convergent scars on the core's surface were always small and seem to have been intended for localized, small-scale maintenance of the lateral convexities rather than for the overall organization of the flaking surface.

A "bipolar" exploitation of the core is implied by "bipolar," "unipolar and opposed," and "convergent and opposed" scar patterns, when two opposing parts of the core's striking platform were used. A "unipolar and

**Table 4.1  Frequencies of core types in the Qafzeh assemblages**

**A. Levallois**

| Layer | Flakes | | Points | | Blades | | Varia | | Amorphous | | Fragments | | Total |
|---|---|---|---|---|---|---|---|---|---|---|---|---|---|
| | N | % | N | % | N | % | N | % | N | % | N | % | N |
| III | 1 | 100.00 | | | | | | | | | | | 1 |
| IV | 2 | 100.00 | | | | | | | | | | | 2 |
| VI | 1 | 100.00 | | | | | | | | | | | 1 |
| V | 5 | 71.43 | 1 | 14.29 | 1 | 14.29 | | | | | | | 7 |
| VII | 5 | 100.00 | | | | | | | | | | | 5 |
| VIIa | 18 | 85.71 | 2 | 9.52 | | | | | | | 1 | 4.76 | 21 |
| VIIb | 5 | 100.00 | | | | | | | | | | | 5 |
| VIII | 1 | 50.00 | 1 | 50.00 | | | | | | | | | 2 |
| IX | 25 | 96.15 | | | 1 | 3.85 | | | | | | | 26 |
| X | 2 | 66.67 | 1 | 33.33 | | | | | | | | | 3 |
| XI | 27 | 96.43 | | | | | | | | | 1 | 3.57 | 28 |
| XII | 26 | 92.86 | | | | | 1 | 3.57 | 1 | 3.57 | | | 28 |
| XIII | 36 | 85.71 | 4 | 9.52 | 1 | 2.38 | | | | | 1 | 2.38 | 42 |
| XIV | 27 | 93.10 | 1 | 3.45 | 1 | 3.45 | | | | | | | 29 |
| XV | 110 | 83.96 | 18 | 13.74 | 1 | 0.76 | | | 1 | 0.76 | 1 | 0.76 | 131 |
| XVa | 18 | 94.74 | 1 | 5.26 | | | | | | | | | 19 |
| XVb | 3 | 100.00 | | | | | | | | | | | 3 |
| XVf | 10 | 100.00 | | | | | | | | | | | 10 |
| XVII | 28 | 93.33 | | | | | 1 | 3.33 | 1 | 3.33 | | | 30 |
| XVIII | 1 | 100.00 | | | | | | | | | | | 1 |
| XIX | 15 | 100.00 | | | | | | | | | | | 15 |
| XXI | 8 | 100.00 | | | | | | | | | | | 8 |
| XXII | 6 | 100.00 | | | | | | | | | | | 6 |
| | 380 | | 29 | | 5 | | 2 | | 3 | | 4 | | 423 |

**B. Non-Levallois**

| Layer | Globular | | Prismatic | | Pyramidal | | Amorphous | | Varia | | Fragments | | Total |
|---|---|---|---|---|---|---|---|---|---|---|---|---|---|
| | N | % | N | % | N | % | N | % | N | % | N | % | N |
| III | | | | | | | | | 2 | 40.00 | 3 | 60.00 | 5 |
| IV | | | | | | | 2 | 50.00 | 2 | 50.00 | | | 4 |
| V | | | | | | | 1 | 14.29 | 4 | 57.14 | 2 | 28.57 | 7 |
| VI | | | | | | | | | | | 2 | 100.00 | 2 |
| VII | | | | | | | | | 2 | 50.00 | 2 | 50.00 | 4 |
| VIIa | 1 | 14.29 | | | | | 1 | 14.29 | 4 | 57.14 | 1 | 14.29 | 7 |
| VIIb | | | | | | | 2 | 22.22 | 4 | 44.44 | 3 | 33.33 | 9 |
| VIII | | | | | | | | | 1 | 50.00 | 1 | 50.00 | 2 |
| IX | | | | | | | 2 | 11.76 | 9 | 52.94 | 6 | 35.29 | 17 |
| X | | | | | | | | | 2 | 100.00 | | | 2 |
| XI | | | | | | | 4 | 25.00 | 11 | 68.75 | 1 | 10.55 | 16 |
| XII | | | | | | | 2 | 22.22 | 6 | 66.67 | 1 | 11.11 | 9 |
| XIII | | | | | | | 5 | 23.80 | 12 | 57.14 | 4 | 19.05 | 21 |
| XIV | | | 1 | 12.50 | 1 | 12.50 | 2 | 25.00 | 4 | 50.00 | | | 8 |
| XV | 5 | 13.51 | | | | | 4 | 10.81 | 25 | 67.58 | 3 | 8.11 | 37 |
| XVa | | | | | | | 2 | 33.33 | 3 | 50.00 | 1 | 16.67 | 6 |
| XVf | | | | | | | | | 2 | 100.00 | | | 2 |
| XVII | | | | | | | 1 | 14.29 | 4 | 57.14 | 2 | 28.57 | 7 |
| XIX | | | | | | | | | 7 | 100.00 | | | 7 |
| XXI | | | | | | | 1 | 33.33 | 1 | 33.33 | 1 | 33.33 | 3 |
| XXII | | | | | | | | | 4 | 100.00 | | | 4 |
| TOTAL | 6 | | 1 | | 1 | | 29 | | 109 | | 33 | | 179 |

(continued)

**Table 4.1    (continued)**

**C. on-flakes**

| Layer | Levallois | | Non-Levallois | | Total | |
|---|---|---|---|---|---|---|
| | N | % | N | % | N | % |
| III | 2 | 100.00 | | | 2 | 100.00 |
| IV | 4 | 66.67 | 2 | 33.33 | 6 | 100.00 |
| V | | | 2 | 100.00 | 2 | 100.00 |
| VI | | | 6 | 100.00 | 6 | 100.00 |
| VII | 1 | 33.33 | 2 | 66.67 | 3 | 100.00 |
| VIIa | 3 | 33.33 | 6 | 66.67 | 9 | 100.00 |
| VIIb | 2 | 25.00 | 6 | 75.00 | 8 | 100.00 |
| VIII | | | 4 | 100.00 | 4 | 100.00 |
| IX | 10 | 45.45 | 12 | 54.55 | 22 | 100.00 |
| X | 2 | 28.57 | 5 | 71.43 | 7 | 100.00 |
| XI | 8 | 32.00 | 17 | 68.00 | 25 | 100.00 |
| XII | 8 | 34.78 | 15 | 65.22 | 23 | 100.00 |
| XIII | 12 | 33.33 | 24 | 66.67 | 36 | 100.00 |
| XIV | 7 | 58.33 | 5 | 41.67 | 12 | 100.00 |
| XV | 52 | 44.08 | 66 | 55.92 | 118 | 100.00 |
| XVa | 5 | 71.43 | 2 | 28.57 | 7 | 100.00 |
| XVf | 2 | 33.33 | 4 | 66.67 | 6 | 100.00 |
| XVII | 3 | 37.50 | 5 | 62.50 | 8 | 100.00 |
| XIX | | | 6 | 100.00 | 6 | 100.00 |
| XXI | 3 | 50.00 | 3 | 50.00 | 6 | 100.00 |
| XXII | 1 | 33.33 | 2 | 66.67 | 3 | 100.00 |
| XXIV | 1 | 100.00 | | | 1 | 100.00 |
| TOTAL | 126 | 39.38 | 194 | 60.62 | 320 | 100.00 |

opposed" pattern suggests that relatively small parts of the opposing flake scars were preserved on the core's surface at the phase of its use just before discard. However, it indicates that in earlier phases a bipolar reduction mode was practiced.

Finally, a number of scar patterns indicate a "centripetal" use of the core-flaking surface. Among these, "unipolar and side," "opposed and side" represent the initial stages of a centripetal flaking, in which parts of the core's circumference had already been used but the continuous use of the platform had not yet been completed. By the same logic, "bipolar and side" reflects a more advanced stage of the same process. The "dominant and centripetal" and "centripetal" dorsal scar patterns indicate a culmination of the process. The last two patterns appear to correspond to the use of the lineal and recurrent Levallois methods, respectively. This dichotomy, however, may not be a real phenomenon in the case of Qafzeh (see below).

Levallois cores of the Qafzeh terrace assemblages are characterized by the dominance of centripetal core reduction modes (figure 4.1a), with a significantly lower representation of bipolar and convergent modes. The use of unipolar recurrent methods is barely discernible on the

cores, with the exception of a few, well-characterized cores for points, exploited by the convergent and recurrent method (see below).

*Levallois Cores for Flakes*

Levallois cores for flakes form ca. 91% of Levallois cores on raw material blocks (this value drops to 70% if cores-on-flakes exploited by Levallois methods are included [table 4.1 and below]). In all the layers, the mean number of scars is high and is similar for the two surfaces in this core type (table 4.3). These high mean values suggest that Levallois cores for flakes were exploited intensively over several cycles of reduction as a tactic of extending the core's utility. However, the strict hierarchical differentiation between the roles of the two core faces is always clear.

Cortical cover is absent from the flaking face in 97% of the cores, while varying amounts of cortex appear on the other face in 71% of the pieces (table 4.3). Combined with the similar mean values of the scar numbers on the two faces, this implies that smaller flakes were removed from the face bearing more cortex. Flakes were removed

**Table 4.2  Descriptive statistics of core measurements**

**A.  All cores by type[a]**

| Core Type | | Length | | | Width | | | Thickness | | | Weight | | | Elongation index[b] | | |
|---|---|---|---|---|---|---|---|---|---|---|---|---|---|---|---|---|
| Type | N | $\bar{X}$ | s.d | s.e. | $\bar{X}$ | s.d. | s.e. | $\bar{X}$ | s.d. | s.e. | $\bar{X}$ | s.d. | s.e. | $\bar{X}$ | s.d. | s.e. |
| Lev. flakes | 304 | 46.78 | 12.87 | 0.74 | 49.43 | 13.83 | 0.79 | 21.91 | 9.01 | 0.52 | 58.37 | 50.26 | 2.89 | 1.08 | 0.22 | 0.10 |
| Lev. points | 25 | 44.04 | 9.86 | 1.97 | 41.16 | 8.44 | 1.69 | 18.12 | 6.42 | 1.28 | 33.40 | 22.30 | 4.46 | 0.96 | 0.22 | 0.04 |
| Lev. blades | 4 | 55.50 | 14.39 | 7.19 | 59.75 | 27.23 | 13.62 | 27.25 | 7.59 | 3.79 | 119.1 | 122.5 | 61.26 | 1.05 | 0.22 | 0.11 |
| Lev. on-flake | 97 | 43.64 | 9.53 | 0.97 | 42.72 | 10.92 | 1.11 | 12.40 | 3.83 | 0.39 | 26.65 | 14.94 | 1.54 | 1.01 | 0.27 | 0.03 |
| Prismatic | 1 | 30.00 | — | — | 24.00 | — | — | 27.00 | — | — | 20.70 | — | — | 0.80 | — | — |
| Pyramidal | 1 | 33.00 | — | — | 28.00 | — | — | 33.00 | — | — | 26.70 | — | — | 0.85 | — | — |
| Globular | 5 | 33.80 | 7.26 | 3.25 | 39.40 | 8.59 | 3.84 | 32.20 | 10.62 | 4.75 | 50.50 | 37.13 | 16.60 | 1.17 | 0.16 | 0.07 |
| Amorphous | 11 | 44.27 | 21.39 | 6.45 | 44.18 | 16.92 | 5.10 | 28.27 | 15.30 | 4.61 | 73.26 | 105.6 | 30.47 | 1.14 | 0.40 | 0.12 |
| Varia | 93 | 41.53 | 13.33 | 1.38 | 44.69 | 13.85 | 1.44 | 22.37 | 9.30 | 0.96 | 47.90 | 57.40 | 5.95 | 1.13 | 0.38 | 0.04 |
| On-flake | 151 | 46.69 | 12.09 | 0.98 | 44.34 | 13.13 | 1.07 | 14.53 | 5.87 | 0.48 | 34.16 | 32.70 | 2.67 | 1.00 | 0.35 | 0.03 |

[a]Measurements are for complete pieces only. Metric measurements in mm, weight in grams.
[b]Computed as WIDTH/LENGTH of the core (see Appendix 2 for methodology of core measurements).

**B.  Levallois cores for flakes (selected layers)[c]**

| Layer | | Length | | | Width | | | Thickness | | | Weight | | | Elongation index[b] | | |
|---|---|---|---|---|---|---|---|---|---|---|---|---|---|---|---|---|
| Layer | N | $\bar{X}$ | s.d | s.e. | $\bar{X}$ | s.d. | s.e. | $\bar{X}$ | s.d. | s.e. | $\bar{X}$ | s.d. | s.e. | $\bar{X}$ | s.d. | s.e. |
| VIIa | 15 | 48.53 | 13.79 | 3.56 | 48.47 | 13.48 | 3.48 | 20.80 | 9.21 | 2.38 | 57.50 | 60.47 | 16.16 | 1.01 | 0.19 | 0.05 |
| IX | 20 | 51.10 | 17.30 | 3.87 | 53.95 | 19.29 | 4.31 | 27.50 | 13.12 | 2.93 | 72.58 | 59.84 | 13.73 | 1.07 | 0.24 | 0.05 |
| XI | 19 | 49.89 | 9.09 | 2.08 | 52.11 | 11.04 | 2.53 | 22.84 | 6.28 | 1.44 | 65.32 | 30.22 | 6.93 | 1.05 | 0.18 | 0.04 |
| XII | 18 | 48.33 | 15.76 | 3.71 | 53.17 | 14.01 | 3.30 | 20.61 | 8.47 | 2.00 | 73.23 | 70.66 | 16.65 | 1.14 | 0.20 | 0.05 |
| XIII | 33 | 43.45 | 10.88 | 1.89 | 48.18 | 12.36 | 2.15 | 20.48 | 6.94 | 1.21 | 50.12 | 42.00 | 7.31 | 1.12 | 0.20 | 0.04 |
| XIV | 24 | 46.92 | 11.44 | 2.33 | 47.96 | 12.62 | 2.58 | 23.38 | 9.66 | 1.97 | 64.06 | 45.14 | 9.21 | 1.04 | 0.22 | 0.05 |
| XV | 95 | 43.32 | 11.34 | 1.16 | 46.54 | 12.84 | 1.32 | 20.36 | 8.01 | 0.82 | 46.08 | 36.97 | 3.79 | 1.10 | 0.25 | 0.03 |
| XVII | 22 | 53.14 | 11.40 | 2.43 | 53.86 | 12.82 | 2.73 | 24.64 | 8.97 | 1.91 | 73.32 | 47.76 | 10.18 | 1.07 | 0.24 | 0.05 |

[c]Layers with more than 15 complete pieces only. Measurements are for complete pieces only. Metric measurements in mm, weight in grams.

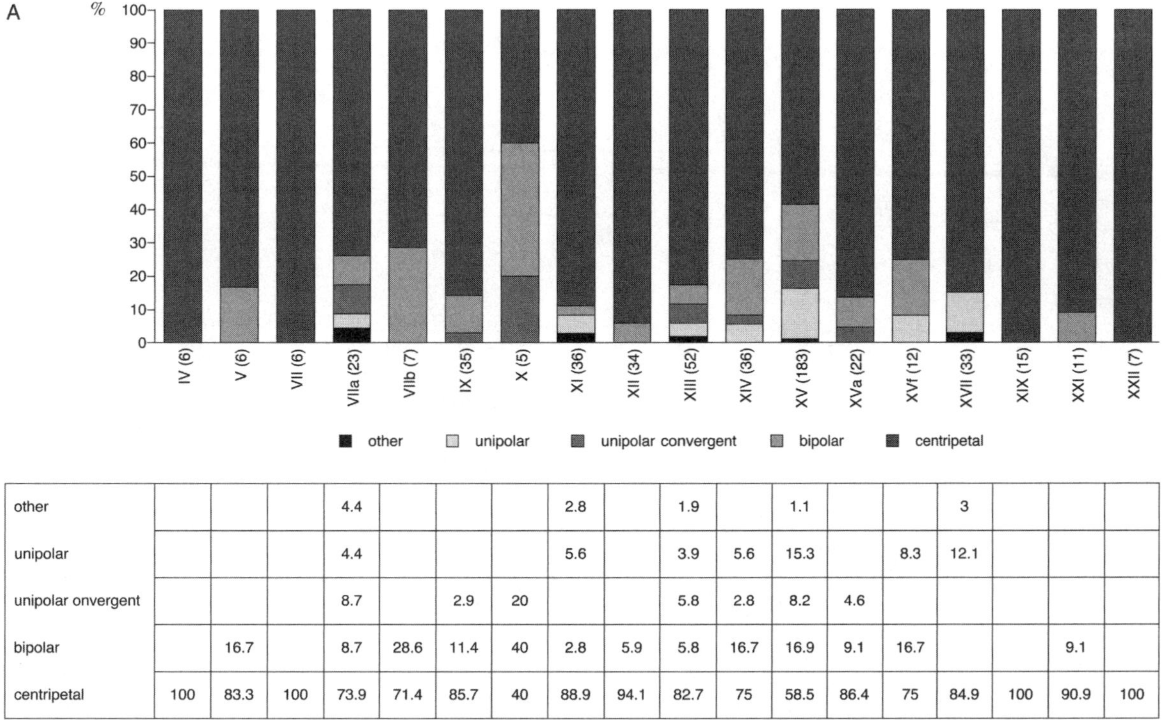



|  | IV (6) | V (6) | VII (6) | VIIa (23) | VIIb (7) | IX (35) | X (5) | XI (36) | XII (34) | XIII (52) | XIV (36) | XV (183) | XVa (22) | XVf (12) | XVII (33) | XIX (15) | XXI (11) | XXII (7) |
|---|---|---|---|---|---|---|---|---|---|---|---|---|---|---|---|---|---|---|
| other |  |  |  | 4.4 |  |  |  | 2.8 |  | 1.9 |  | 1.1 |  |  | 3 |  |  |  |
| unipolar |  |  |  | 4.4 |  |  |  | 5.6 |  | 3.9 | 5.6 | 15.3 |  | 8.3 | 12.1 |  |  |  |
| unipolar onvergent |  |  |  | 8.7 |  | 2.9 | 20 |  |  | 5.8 | 2.8 | 8.2 | 4.6 |  |  |  |  |  |
| bipolar |  | 16.7 |  | 8.7 | 28.6 | 11.4 | 40 | 2.8 | 5.9 | 5.8 | 16.7 | 16.9 | 9.1 | 16.7 |  |  | 9.1 |  |
| centripetal | 100 | 83.3 | 100 | 73.9 | 71.4 | 85.7 | 40 | 88.9 | 94.1 | 82.7 | 75 | 58.5 | 86.4 | 75 | 84.9 | 100 | 90.9 | 100 |

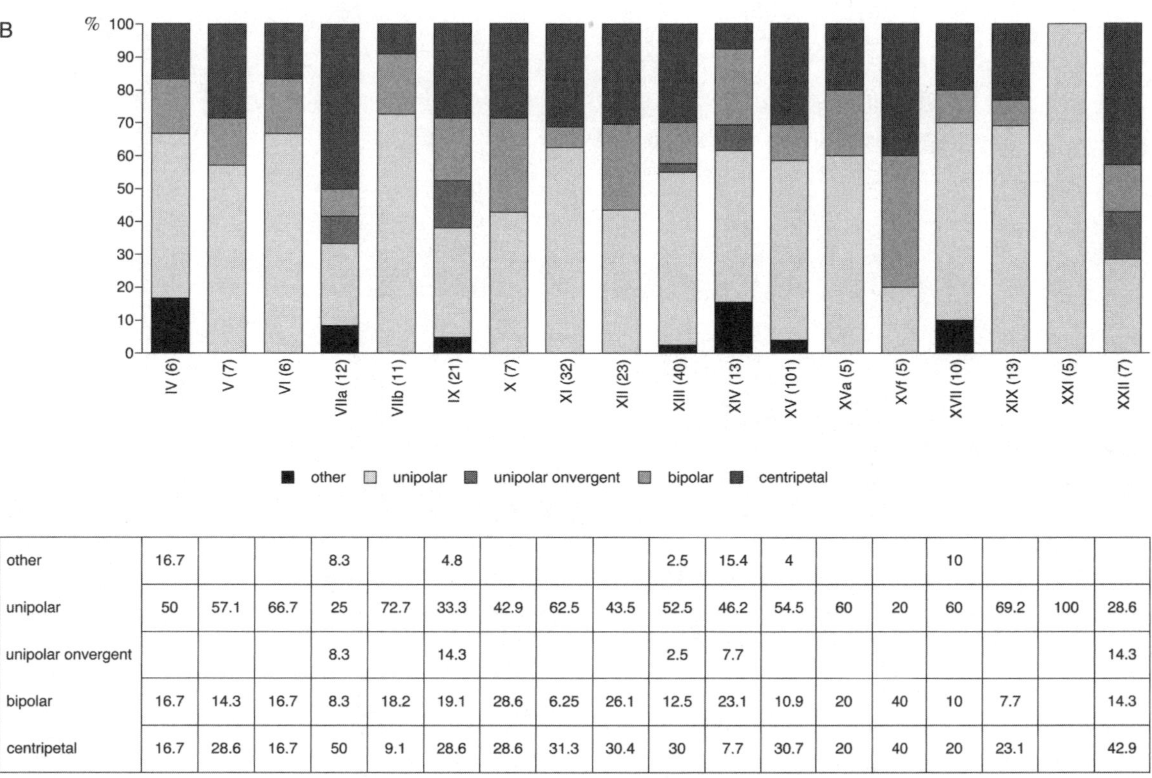



|  | IV (6) | V (7) | VI (6) | VIIa (12) | VIIb (11) | IX (21) | X (7) | XI (32) | XII (23) | XIII (40) | XIV (13) | XV (101) | XVa (5) | XVf (5) | XVII (10) | XIX (13) | XXI (5) | XXII (7) |
|---|---|---|---|---|---|---|---|---|---|---|---|---|---|---|---|---|---|---|
| other | 16.7 |  |  | 8.3 |  | 4.8 |  |  |  | 2.5 | 15.4 | 4 |  |  | 10 |  |  |  |
| unipolar | 50 | 57.1 | 66.7 | 25 | 72.7 | 33.3 | 42.9 | 62.5 | 43.5 | 52.5 | 46.2 | 54.5 | 60 | 20 | 60 | 69.2 | 100 | 28.6 |
| unipolar onvergent |  |  |  | 8.3 |  | 14.3 |  |  |  | 2.5 | 7.7 |  |  |  |  |  |  | 14.3 |
| bipolar | 16.7 | 14.3 | 16.7 | 8.3 | 18.2 | 19.1 | 28.6 | 6.25 | 26.1 | 12.5 | 23.1 | 10.9 | 20 | 40 | 10 | 7.7 |  | 14.3 |
| centripetal | 16.7 | 28.6 | 16.7 | 50 | 9.1 | 28.6 | 28.6 | 31.3 | 30.4 | 30 | 7.7 | 30.7 | 20 | 40 | 20 | 23.1 |  | 42.9 |

**Figure 4.1**  Frequencies of scar patterns on Levallois cores. A: Levallois cores. B: non-Levallois cores. (Layers with N > 5; see text for explanation)

**Table 4.3**  Number of scars and amount of cortical cover on flaking and preparation surfaces of Levallois cores for flakes

| Layer | Number of scars: flaking surface | | | | Number of scars: preparation surface | | | | Amount of cortex: flaking surface | | | | Amount of cortex: preparation surface | | | | | |
|---|---|---|---|---|---|---|---|---|---|---|---|---|---|---|---|---|---|---|
| | N | $\bar{X}$ | s.d. | s.e. | N | $\bar{X}$ | s.d. | s.e. | N | 1 | 2 | 3 | N | 1 | 2 | 3 | 4 | 5 |
| All[a] | 301 | 13.33 | 5.15 | 0.30 | 301 | 14.11 | 5.43 | 0.31 | 304 | 97.37 | 1.97 | 0.66 | 303 | 2871 | 20.79 | 24.75 | 20.79 | 4.95 |
| VIIa | 15 | 13.53 | 5.91 | 1.53 | 15 | 12.60 | 5.53 | 1.43 | 15 | 100.00 | — | — | 15 | 13.33 | 6.67 | 53.33 | 26.27 | — |
| IX | 20 | 15.75 | 5.30 | 1.19 | 20 | 16.05 | 8.48 | 1.90 | 20 | 95.00 | — | 5.00 | 20 | 40.00 | 5.00 | 5.00 | 30.00 | 10.00 |
| XI | 19 | 14.37 | 3.79 | 0.87 | 19 | 17.00 | 5.81 | 1.33 | 19 | 100.00 | — | — | 19 | 26.62 | 20.45 | 26.39 | 19.70 | 4.83 |
| XII | 18 | 13.56 | 4.53 | 1.07 | 18 | 15.06 | 4.94 | 1.16 | 18 | 100.00 | — | — | 18 | 27.28 | 33.33 | 27.78 | 11.11 | — |
| XIII | 33 | 14.24 | 5.08 | 0.88 | 33 | 15.79 | 5.83 | 1.01 | 33 | 93.94 | 3.03 | 3.03 | 33 | 18.18 | 30.30 | 24.24 | 24.24 | 3.03 |
| XIV | 24 | 14.61 | 0.15 | 1.02 | 23 | 12.00 | 5.29 | 1.10 | 23 | 95.83 | 4.17 | — | 24 | 20.83 | 20.83 | 29.17 | 25.00. | 4.17 |
| XV | 95 | 13.83 | 4.61 | 0.47 | 95 | 13.89 | 4.55 | 0.47 | 95 | 98.95 | 1.05 | — | 95 | 38.95 | 18.95 | 22.11 | 14.74 | 5.26 |
| XVa | 12 | 13.83 | 5.94 | 1.71 | 12 | 12.50 | 4.44 | 1.28 | 14 | 92.86 | 7.14 | — | 14 | 7.14 | 35.71 | 35.71 | 21.43 | — |
| XVII | 22 | 14.36 | 5.45 | 1.16 | 22 | 15.23 | 5.74 | 1.22 | 22 | 95.45 | 4.55 | — | 21 | 38.10 | 19.05 | 28.57 | 9.52 | 4.76 |
| XIX | 10 | 11.70 | 9.81 | 3.10 | 10 | 11.90 | 5.57 | 1.76 | 10 | 90.00 | 10.00 | | 10 | 0.00 | 30.00 | 20.00 | 30.00 | 20.00 |

*Note*: Categories for "amount of cortex": 1: no cortex; 2: 1–25% cortex; 3: 26–50% cortex; 4: 51–75% cortex; 5: 76–100% cortex. Frequencies of each group are given as percentages.
[a] All assemblages, complete pieces only.

from the preparation surface in order to obtain appropriate striking angles on the designated flaking surface and were by-products of the desired end-results of the flaking process. Although these flakes may have been used as functional tools (retouched or not), their morphologies and sizes would not have been planned in advance.

As anticipated from the data in figure 4.1 and table 4.1, most of the Levallois flake cores (72.84% of the complete items) bear the patterns of centripetal modes of reduction (table 4.4). Cores exhibit intensive exploitation of the margins, commonly with over 70% of the core circumference used as a striking platform. In only 57 cases (ca. 18%), mainly within the "limited platform" (i.e., non-centripetal) flaking modes, did flake removal occur along a non-continuous platform. Some flake cores may have been cores for points in earlier stages of exploitation. Such cores bear convergent and unipolar scar patterns with remnants of scars of typical points that can still be detected and with typical preparations of point cores (see below). In their last phase of exploitation, however, no attempt was made to readjust their lateral convexities in order to remove successive points, and the last detachments were those of rounded, relatively large flakes, hence their classification as "cores for flakes."

*Lineal and Recurrent Flaking*. Both lineal and recurrent flaking methods were employed in the various assemblages of Qafzeh. The former method was used to produce preferential flakes, which are relatively large (table 4.5, column 12). When combined with centripetal flaking, as was typically the case in Qafzeh, an extensive, continuous striking platform was shaped around the core's circumference before the desired flake was removed. Detachment of preferential flakes left a large remnant scar, usually occupying more than 50% of the core's flaking surface (table 4.5 column 10; plates 1:1–2, 2:1, 3:1, 6:1, 10:20, 35:9–10, 46:9) and necessitating its reshaping before additional flakes could be removed.

In contrast, there were two ways to create the typical striking platform that encompasses most of the core's circumference when applying centripetal recurrent flaking. On some of the cores, the initial flaking was bipolar, and the two striking platforms were connected into a continuous one in the course of continued core use (e.g., plates 1:3, 3:3, 5:2). A second way of exploiting a core through recurrent centripetal flaking was by slightly rotating the core after each flake removal (plates 2:5, 4:4, 7:1, 8:4), a method that also yielded cores with extensive, centripetally prepared platforms. Similarly sized Levallois flakes were removed off the flaking surface, using a progressively increasing portion of the core's circumference as the platform from which flakes were detached (plates 1:3–4, 2:3, 5, 4:4, 5:1–2, 6:2, 4, 7:1, 8:4, 8, 10:9, 11:4, 19:8, 35:9). Given the need to conserve the core's surface convexities and to avoid the formation of large and deep negative scars, the flakes were smaller than those detached by the lineal method (table 4.5 columns 1–8).

Boëda, Geneste, and Meignen (1990:56) have argued that cores exploited by recurrent methods are expected to be more heavily utilized than lineally worked cores. This pattern is not observed in the Qafzeh assemblages, where the sizes of cores exploited by the two methods (as judged from scar patterns) are similar (mean surface area = 2,328.5 and 2,382.9 mm², length = 45.6 and 44.9 mm for complete cores flaked by the lineal and recurrent methods, respectively). Core thickness, which is directly affected by the degree of core exhaustion, is practically identical for cores exploited by the two methods (for the lineal group: 20.75 ± 8.3, N = 143; for the recurrent group: 21.7 ± 9.1, N = 217; Kolmogorov-Smirnov test: 0.5730, $p > .9999$). This suggests

**Table 4.4  Levallois cores for flakes: scar patterns and intensity of use of core striking platform**

| Layer | | Unipolar | | | Convergent | | | Bipolar | | | Centripetal | | | Flaked/core circumference[a] | | |
|---|---|---|---|---|---|---|---|---|---|---|---|---|---|---|---|---|
| 3 | N | 1 | 2 | 3 | 1 | 2 | 3 | 1 | 2 | 3 | 1 | 2 | 3 | 3 | 4 | 5 |
| VIIa | 15 | | | 1 | | | | 1 | | | 1 | 3 | 9 | 0.74 | 0.26 | 0.07 |
| IX | 20 | | 1 | | | 2 | | 1 | 2 | | | 2 | 18 | 0.90 | 0.18 | 0.04 |
| XI | 19 | | | | | | | | | | | 1 | 18 | 0.93 | 0.14 | 0.03 |
| XII | 18 | | | | | | | 1 | | | | 1 | 16 | 0.85 | 0.16 | 0.04 |
| XIII | 33 | | | | | | | | | | | 5 | 26 | 0.86 | 0.22 | 0.04 |
| XIV | 24 | | | | | 1 | 1 | 1 | 2 | | | 7 | 11 | 0.65 | 0.26 | 0.05 |
| XV | 95 | 3 | 2 | 2 | | 1 | | | 6 | 5 | 4 | 18 | 54 | 0.73 | 0.23 | 0.02 |
| XVII | 22 | | | | | | | | | | | 1 | 20 | 0.85 | 0.18 | 0.04 |

*Note*: Only unbroken cores. 1: flakes removed from 1–33% of core's margin; 2: flakes removed from 34–66% of core's margin ; 3: exploitation of 67–100% of core margin. Frequencies are in absolute numbers.
[a] Ratio of the exploited margin of the core to the total core's circumference

that recurrent methods were used more frequently during earlier stages of the reduction sequence, whereas lineal flaking may have been used more frequently during the last stage(s) of the use lives of cores (see also Boëda, Geneste, and Meignen 1990:68). Similar behaviors have been noted in other Levantine Mousterian assemblages such as Keoue Cave in Lebanon (Nishiaki and Copeland 1992). If this reconstruction of lithic reduction practices is valid, it suggests that the bulk of the lithic assemblages of Qafzeh were produced through a remarkably homogeneous technological system, primarily employing recurrent centripetal Levallois flaking.

A valid test of this hypothesis cannot be based solely on patterns observed on the abandoned cores but rather requires refitting of extensive reduction sequences. I noted above that this was not a viable research strategy for the Qafzeh assemblages. However, the hypothesized shifts in flaking methods bear clear implications for the expected relative frequencies of dorsal face scar patterns of the debitage and how they should co-vary with various measures of flake size. The plausibility of the hypothesized technological practices can therefore be evaluated based on the analysis of the debitage (chapter 5).

Some use of recurrent uni/bipolar modes is evident in the existence of flake cores bearing unipolar scars (tables 4.4, 4.6; cf. Boëda, Geneste, and Meignen 1990:61–62), but this appears to have been unsystematic in the last stages of core use.

*Discontinuing Core Use.* Most centripetal cores were abandoned when their length and width reached values between 30–60 mm (79% and 74%, respectively; table 4.5). Yet despite the relatively long use lives implied by the intensive use of the core margins and surfaces, centripetal cores are somewhat larger on average than cores exploited by other modes (the difference is not statistically significant), notwithstanding the large discrepancy in sample sizes (table 4.6; e.g., plates 1:2–3, 7:1).

The frequencies of cores within the size range of 30–60 mm deviate slightly from those expected in a normal distribution, where only 75% and 70% (for length and width, respectively) of the cores are expected to fall in the specified range. The distribution curves of both length and width of unbroken centripetally worked Levallois cores are leptokurtic, indicating that values for both measures are clustered around the central mean, with only a slight tendency toward larger artifacts (median = 46.0, 49.0 mm, kurtosis = 1.47, 1.72, skewness = 0.85, 0.87), respectively for the two measurements). This suggests that the use of centripetal cores may have been discontinued when a broadly-defined size threshold had been reached. Once the critical dimensions had been encountered, cores were considered inadequate for further Levallois production.

However, the discontinuation of the use of Levallois cores in general, and of Levallois cores for flakes in particular, does not reflect a simple, immediate response to absolute size limitations. In some cases flake removal was

**Table 4.5  Mean size and relative surface area of last-removed Levallois flakes**

| Layer | Scar Pattern | | | | | | | | | | | |
| --- | --- | --- | --- | --- | --- | --- | --- | --- | --- | --- | --- | --- |
| | Centripetal – initial | | | | | Centripetal | | | | Centripetal – preferential flake | | |
| | 1 | 2 | 3 | 4 | 5 | 6 | 7 | 8 | 9 | 10 | 11 | 12 |
| | N | % surface[b] | N | $\bar{X}$ length | N | % surface[b] | N | $\bar{X}$ length | N | % surface[b] | N | $\bar{X}$ length |
| VIIa | 2 | 16.59 | 3 | 20.33 | 3 | 13.71 | 4 | 23.50 | 7 | 45.59 | 9 | 32.67 |
| IX | 1 | 14.15 | 2 | 24.00 | 11 | 18.41 | 14 | 20.43 | 6 | 26.93 | 7 | 25.43 |
| XI | 1 | 21.24 | 1 | 39.00 | 10 | 24.53 | 17 | 22.94 | 4 | 55.43 | 5 | 43.20 |
| XII | 2 | 29.65 | 3 | 19.33 | 9 | 12.18 | 14 | 19.50 | 3 | 54.81 | 4 | 32.75 |
| XIII | 3 | 17.18 | 3 | 21.67 | 12 | 19.94 | 15 | 22.53 | 14 | 50.29 | 15 | 30.27 |
| XIV | 2 | 24.59 | 2 | 26.00 | 6 | 15.42 | 7 | 16.43 | 11 | 52.18 | 12 | 32.17 |
| XV | 15 | 26.71 | 15 | 25.54 | 21 | 24.18 | 30 | 20.07 | 27 | 46.51 | 39 | 29.08 |
| XVa | — | — | — | — | 8 | 15.13 | 9 | 20.44 | 3 | 51.05 | 3 | 37.33 |
| XVII | 4 | 25.17 | 4 | 27.50 | 8 | 13.48 | 9 | 15.33 | 10 | 49.55 | 12 | 38.58 |
| XIX | — | — | 1 | 22.00 | 2 | 30.68 | 3 | 29.67 | 3 | 57.66 | 8 | 42.50 |
| TOTAL | 34 | **26.52** | 39 | **25.54** | 104 | **19.49** | 148 | **21.13** | 96 | **48.04** | 124 | **21.19** |

[a]Breakdown of scar patterns included in the CENTRIPETAL mode only, due to the paucity of other flaking modes.
"Initial centripetal" refers to the scar patterns "unipolar and side," "opposed and side," and "bipolar and side," conceived here as possible initial stages for fully centripetal flaking. Note the small sample sizes for the detailed categories in some layers.
[b]% of surface represents the ratio between the surface area of the last scar of Levallois removal (computed as LENGTH x WIDTH of the scar) to the total surface of the core (computed as LENGTH x WIDTH of the core). Only complete cores for which scar sizes and scar pattern were recorded are included.

**Table 4.6  Levallois cores for flakes: Descriptive statistics of measurements, broken down by scar patterns on flaking surface**

| | Unipolar | | | Unipolar convergent | | | Bipolar | | | Centripetal | | |
|---|---|---|---|---|---|---|---|---|---|---|---|---|
| | N | $\bar{X}$ | s.d | N | $\bar{X}$ | s.d. | N | $\bar{X}$ | s.d. | N | $\bar{X}$ | s.d. |
| Length | 9 | 44.11 | 7.90 | 3 | 50.33 | 16.26 | 19 | 43.95 | 12.45 | 270 | 47.19 | 12.94 |
| Width | 9 | 43.78 | 16.00 | 3 | 46.33 | 7.57 | 19 | 45.58 | 16.86 | 269 | 50.14 | 13.47 |
| Thickness | 9 | 17.22 | 5.24 | 3 | 24.33 | 3.79 | 19 | 20.63 | 9.60 | 270 | 22.16 | 9.10 |
| Weight | 9 | 37.00 | 23.80 | 3 | 59.83 | 36.20 | 19 | 55.29 | 68.73 | 268 | 59.72 | 49.66 |

*Note*: Complete cores only. As some scar patterns are represented only by small sample sizes, they are shown here despite the lack of statistical validity.

evidently continued after the critical size had been reached (as discussed below), resulting in very small, exhausted cores. In other cases, however, the cores were abandoned before they were exhausted. The latter claim is supported by the mean values of the angles measured between the two core surfaces in all the layers (ranging between 77° and 79°; layers XII and XVII are exceptions, with respective means of 74.7° and 75°). Whereas core exhaustion results, among other features, in loss of adequate flaking angles, many of the cores in the Qafzeh assemblages still had acute angles between the hierarchical surfaces that allowed further exploitation of the striking platforms.

A critical factor of core discard may have been core geometry, as reflected by the length and width ratios. Values of the cores' elongation index (table 4.2a–b) indicate that Levallois cores for flakes, most of which bear centripetal scar patterns, were discarded when their length and width measurements were more or less similar. It may be that cores were discarded at the stage when any further preparation of flaking surface convexities would have resulted in Levallois flakes that were too small for their anticipated functions. This is supported by data on the sizes of the latest removed Levallois flakes (represented by the negative scars on a core's surface), which suggest that those predetermined, controlled flakes were in fact rather small. The length of 55% of the last-removed Levallois scars falls in the range of 20–39 mm, most of which are within the range 20–29 mm. Another third fall in the range of 10–19 mm (figure 4.2a). Only in four layers are the scars of preplanned flakes smaller (figure 4.2f–h, j), and then in very low frequencies. Taken together with the data on the cores themselves, these frequencies indicate that the knapper operated within a narrow range, most likely close to the lower limit of acceptable sizes for the end-products. The pattern of discard of Levallois flake cores (of all flaking modes) suggests that in the last stage(s) of the reduction process the knapper opted to produce flakes of critical minimum dimensions at the expense of the number of flakes removed off a flaking surface. This preference may explain the shift from recurrent to lineal methods toward the end of the reduction sequence.

Whereas Levallois flaking was likely discontinued when the size and geometric configurations of the cores became unfavorable in terms of controlling flake shape and size, the cores themselves continued to serve as a source of serviceable flakes by removal of small "non-Levallois" (i.e., loosely controlled) flakes, the production of which did not require structured technological steps of core shaping. Negative scars of small flakes, clearly postdating the last-removed Levallois flake, occur on 41.22% of Levallois cores for flakes. These scars tend to be broad and short as a result from the lack of preparation prior to their removal, and their length and width distributions clearly distinguish them from the predetermined Levallois flakes (figure 4.3). The highest frequency of small negative scars appears on cores from which preferential flakes were removed; 47.18% of these cores bear such additional small scars (e.g., plates 2:1, 12:9, 35:10). Comparable scars occur on only 35% of the cores that had been worked by recurrent methods. This preference is not random and may represent an attempt to enhance the use of raw material when relatively large Levallois flakes have been removed in the previous stage of core exploitation.

Given their range of sizes, most of these small flakes were classified formally as "chips" and were not studied in detail. The occurrence of a small number of Levallois flakes and points of similar sizes is noteworthy (plates 20:1–4, 26:1–2, 32:3–4 and chapter 5). In some Levantine Mousterian assemblages the production of small Levallois products is argued to be a systematic *chaîne opératoire* (e.g., at the Mousterian site of Umm el-Tlel in Syria; Bourguinon 1996). It is not clear whether this was the case in the Qafzeh assemblages as well. Cores-on-flakes (discussed below in detail) could have been a possible source of such small items. Alternately, the small artifacts may have been by-products of the manufacture of large Levallois flakes. In this case, their production may not have followed the Levallois technological criteria and their Levallois morphology is incidental.

Finally, Levallois cores for flakes were sometimes discarded because of hinge fractures that occurred during the last attempt to detach a flake (e.g., plate 47:37). In such instances a considerable volume of the remaining core would normally have had to be sacrificed in order to rearrange the core's convexities, considerably reducing the possibility of removing a sizable Levallois flake. These

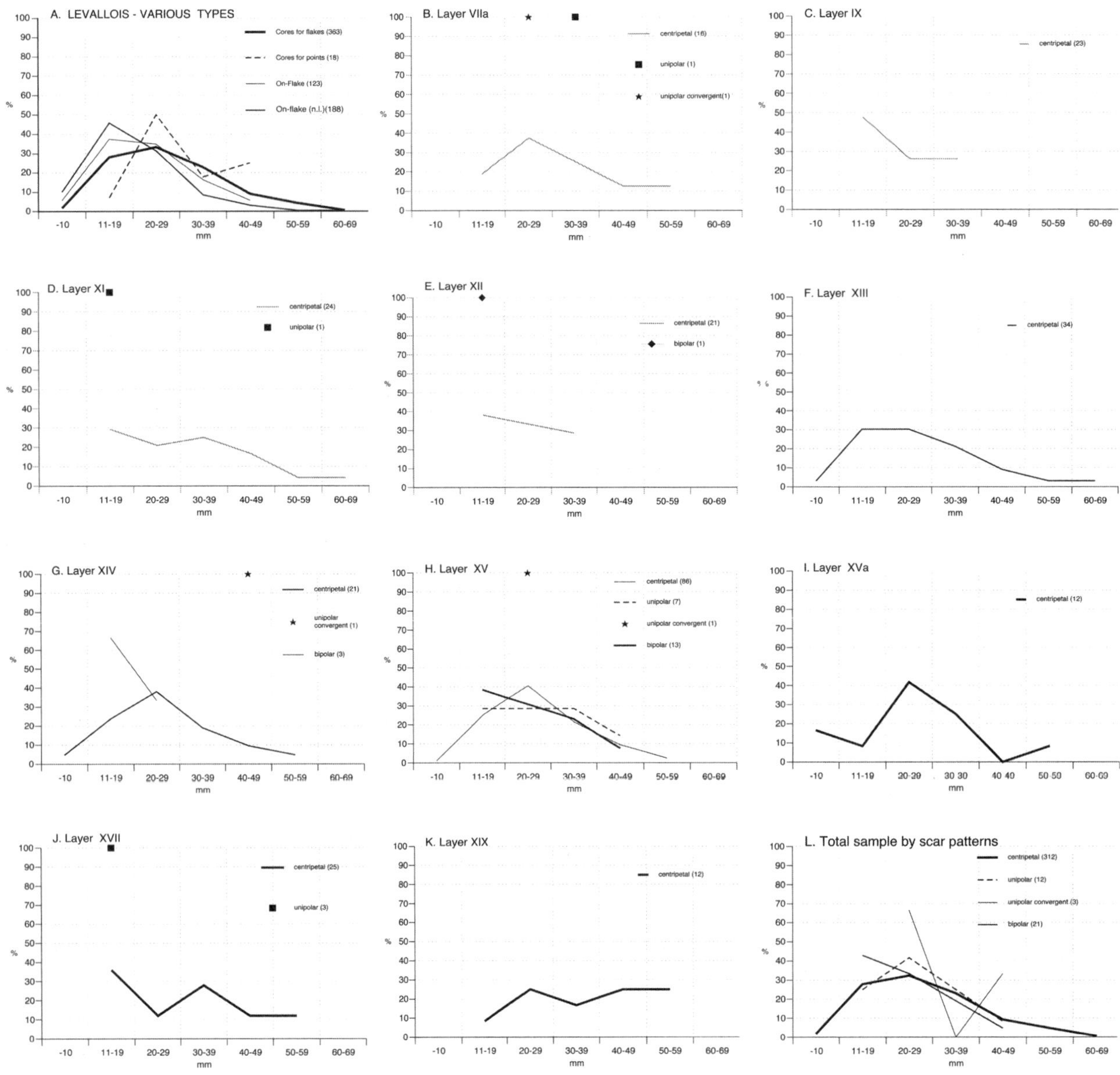

**Figure 4.2** Frequency distributions of length of scars of last-removed Levallois flakes.

knapping accidents are not very common, suggesting that both hammerstone weight and the force of the blow were skillfully judged (Sollberger 1994). On a broader comparative level, it is worth noting that hinge fractures seem to be more common in Levantine Mousterian assemblages dominated by centripetal as opposed to bipolar or unipolar flaking modes (Ekshtain 2006).

*Levallois Cores for Blades*

Levallois cores for blades and points occur in the Qafzeh assemblages in small numbers (table 4.1a), which preclude separate statistical analyses for each type. Only two specimens of the five blade cores encountered in the sample

exhibit the scar patterns expected in the case of preplanned blade production (parallel in layer XIV and bipolar in layer V) (table 4.4). When centripetal scar patterns occur on blade cores, they reflect the application of recurrent centripetal flaking from discontinuous parts of the core's circumference in earlier stages of reduction (i.e., "bipolar and side" and "unipolar and side"; see, e.g., plate 5:3). The number of scars observed on the two faces of each of the blade cores is close to the average of the number of scars on flake cores, and flakes and blades were detached continuously from over 45% of the core circumference rather than from one or two defined regions. These properties are not typical of systematic production of laminar Levallois debitage (e.g., Meignen 1994a), but they may occur infrequently

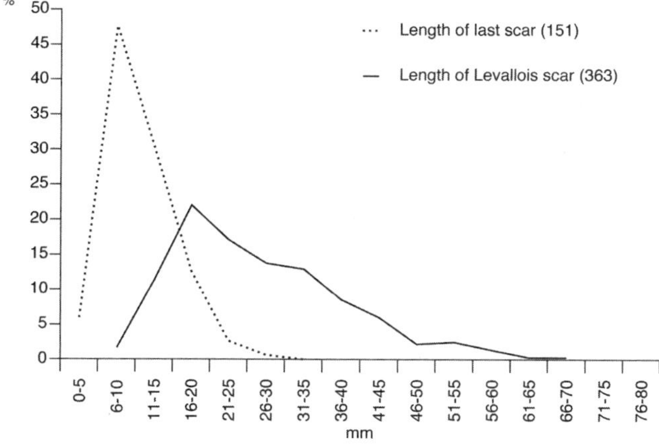



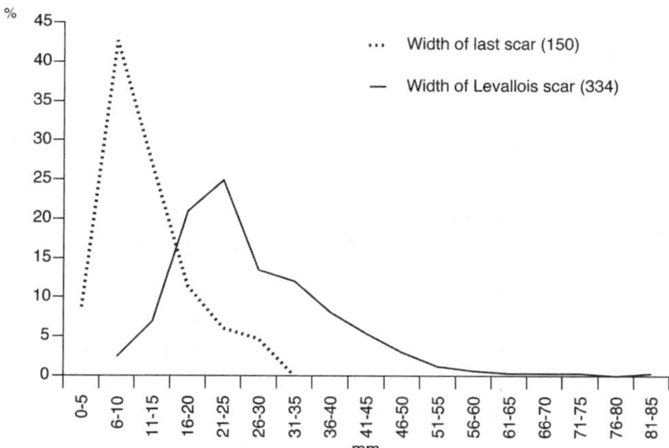



**Figure 4.3** Distribution of length and width of last scars compared to those of last Levallois scars (on Levallois cores for flakes).

during the use life of a centripetally worked core for flakes (Boëda, Geneste, and Meignen 1990:68, figs. 18:2–3, 19:5–7). Indeed, a small number of flake cores in the Qafzeh assemblages bear discernible blade scars from an early phase of core reduction, followed by flake detachments (e.g., plate 4:6). Levallois cores for blades in the Qafzeh assemblage do not represent a *chaîne opératoire* designed specifically for blade production. Flakes and blades seem to have been removed alternately from the same core using a single production mode.

## Levallois Cores for Points

The classical method for flaking Levallois points is the lineal one, with a single point removed from each prepared surface. The preparation of the flaking surface may be initially centripetal or unipolar, followed

by removal of two convergent flakes originating from a limited area of the striking platform. After these are struck from the two lateral parts of the core, the core's striking platform is carefully shaped, sometimes with a protruding region that serves to control the energy of the blow during detachment and to channel it to the triangular area defined on the core's surface by the previous removals. Finally the central flake, its triangular and pointed shape defined by the earlier removals and bearing an inverted Y-shaped dorsal face scar pattern (Tixier, Inizan, and Roche 1980: fig. 8) is detached. This flake often has a protruding striking platform known as *chapeau de gendarme*.[5]

The convergent recurrent method of Levallois flaking is a distinct flaking method (e.g., Boëda, Geneste, and Meignen 1990; Meignen 1995) designed to achieve the removal of several points or triangular flakes off a single surface and from a single, limited striking platform. In this method, core initialization starts with decortication by elongated unidirectional removals, producing some completely cortical large blanks and plunging (*outrepassants*) flakes; later a large striking platform that is often limited to the proximal part of the core is prepared; then lateral and distal convexities are established by the removal of large, slightly twisted and plunging lateral flakes (*éclats débordants*), often with cortical backed edges. A series of several points is then removed successively, moving from one lateral edge of the prepared striking platform to the other and always originating from the same striking platform. The points removed from the lateral edges are slightly asymmetrical in plan and transversal views and are slightly twisted. The process of preparing convexities and removing points is repeated for each successive flaking surface. The abandoned core will bear the remnants of triangular (or sub-triangular) negative scars that often intersect one another. Occasionally, a preferential flake may be removed from the center of the core at the last stage of core exploitation.

The vast majority of Levallois cores for points were recovered from the assemblage of layer XV. Their occurrence in other assemblages is rather sporadic (table 4.1a). Most of the specimens from Qafzeh exhibit unipolar-convergent (hereafter "convergent") and bipolar scar patterns (table 4.4). A few items bear the remains of initial centripetal flaking (e.g., bipolar and side). A mean ratio of 0.46 between used-to-available core circumference is high for the convergent recurrent method, in which usually only up to one-third of the core's circumference, located in its proximal part, is prepared and used for point removal (Meignen 1995: fig. 8). This value reflects the application of additional modes (e.g., bipolar) in point production in some of the Qafzeh assemblages. The mean number of scars (table 4.7) is also relatively high compared to point cores made by the convergent

**Table 4.7  Levallois cores for points: Number of scars and their relative size**

| Number | Number of scars: Flaking surface | | | Number of scars: Preparation surface | | | % surface: Flaking surface | | | Length of dominant scar | | |
|---|---|---|---|---|---|---|---|---|---|---|---|---|
| | $\overline{X}$ | s.d. | s.e. | $\overline{X}$ | s.d. | s.e. | $\overline{X}$ | s.d | s.e. | $\overline{X}$ | s.d. | s.e. |
| 25 | 8.16 | 3.12 | 0.62 | 9.80 | 5.39 | 1.08 | 39.47 | 16.15 | 3.30 | 30.28 | 9.25 | 1.85 |

recurrent method, but it is significantly lower than the average for centripetally prepared Levallois cores (table 4.3; Kolmogorov-Smirnov [K-S] test: 27.33, p < .0001 for flaking surface; K-S 18.08, $p$ = .0002 for the preparation surface).

Most of the point cores in the Qafzeh assemblages (17 out of 29) exhibit on their flaking surface the negative scar of a preferential Levallois point or triangular flake, commonly removed from the center of the flaking surface. In a few instances points may have been detached from the lateral side of the main striking platform. Such scars, however, rarely occupy a large part of the core's surface. The removal of a preferential point at the last stages of core use is not unknown in assemblages in which the convergent recurrent method was employed, although the frequency of this phenomenon at Qafzeh is higher than that reported from other Levantine sites (e.g., Kebara; Meignen 1995).

Yet another technological difference between point cores in Qafzeh and well-executed cores for points in other sites is the relatively small investment in the shaping of the platforms. There are only three instances in all the assemblages where the striking platforms were shaped into protruding morphology (in plan view) that facilitates point removal (plate 9:3).

Point cores have a narrower aspect than flake cores, expressed in the higher values of the elongation index (table 4.2). However, the mean sizes of both core types are similar. Cores in a convergent recurrent system such as that of Kebara Cave are often intensively exploited and reduced to very small sizes (Bar-Yosef et al. 1992; Meignen 1995). At Qafzeh, however, these cores are not totally exhausted. The reason for discarding most of these cores appears to be the flat geometry of the flaking surface achieved at the last stage of removal, which inhibited continued detachment of points. As with flake removals, potential blank size seems to have been an important factor in the decision to abandon point cores at this stage.

Unlike the blade cores discussed above, the characteristics of Levallois cores for points suggest that these cores derive from a *chaîne opératoire* different from that of Levallois cores for flakes. The methods and modes of Levallois flaking differ between the two core groups. At the same time, the point cores have some traits that set them apart from similar items in point-oriented flaking systems.

## Non-Levallois Cores

Very few well-defined types are included in this group (table 4.1b), the majority of artifacts being grouped in the "varia" category.

Prismatic cores, with a single striking platform (and to a lesser degree pyramidal cores as well) are closely associated with systematic blade production in the Upper Paleolithic industries of the Levant. The flaking concepts employed in their production are very different from those of the Levallois system (Boëda 1988; Tixier, Inizan, and Roche 1980). Single-platform cores are relatively numerous in some early Mousterian contexts where laminar production occurs side-by-side with the Levallois system of flaking, and their frequencies in some sites are as high as 20% (e.g., Nahal Aqev; Munday 1976b: tab. 5.11). However, prismatic and pyramidal cores occur sporadically in practically all Mousterian assemblage in the Levant, suggesting that the technical know-how was part of the repertoire of Mousterian knappers (Goren-Inbar and Belfer-Cohen 1998; Marks and Monigal 1995; Meignen 1994a, 1998, 2000). In Qafzeh these cores are rare (table 4.1), which seems to indicate lack of interest (rather than technical inability) in producing systemic laminar blanks. As blade production is said to be more efficient in terms of both the number of blanks removed from a single core and the length of the obtained cutting edge, the disinterest in laminar production (if borne out by debitage assemblages) is potentially significant in terms of technological organization, especially in view of recent studies on this topic (Eren et al. 2008).

Globular cores are spherical in shape, although not necessarily exploited over the whole circumference of their striking platform. The thickness of globular cores in the Qafzeh assemblages is on average higher than that of Levallois cores (table 4.2a) and small amounts of residual cortex appear on half of the cores. Additionally, striking platforms were not completely used. These observations are not consistent with Meignen's (1993:293) suggestion that globular cores may be completely exhausted Levallois cores. Indeed, it is difficult to see how Levallois cores can acquire a globular morphology if the geometric configuration of Levallois flaking is applied throughout the reduction sequence. Globular cores may therefore represent rare instances of opportunistic, expedient flaking (Parry and Kelly 1987).

Most of the cores classified as "amorphous" (18 out of 29) are broken, and none of the pieces can be traced back to a formal system of core modification. The scar patterns on the cores' surfaces could not be identified in many cases. Where discernible, unipolar scar patterns are the most frequent. The cores were exploited over less than 50% of the piece's margin, and the mean number of scars (8.9 over the whole core [N = 26]) is significantly lower than on the Levallois cores for flakes. In this case, too, the cores appear to be the residues of an expedient flake production system.

In contrast, at least some of the cores grouped as "varia" may have been used as Levallois cores at the beginning of their reduction. Somewhere along their use lives, however, the Levallois technological criteria were abandoned, and the cores were then used to produce non-Levallois flakes. On ca. 23% of the items in this category, there are indications for their original use as Levallois cores. Most of these come from assemblages in the upper layers (above layer XV), in which 50% of the "varia" cores could be identified as former Levallois cores. Six other items (5% of the "varia") have retouched edges. In these cases it is not clear whether the pieces were used as tools before or after their exploitation as cores. In most "varia" cores less than 66% of the core's circumference was used as a striking platform. The mean number of scars is relatively low ($\bar{X}$ = 8.61, s.d. = 4.44, N = 93) and most negative scars are small (the mode being 11 mm).

Based on these data, "varia" cores appear to reflect extensive flaking, employed mainly for obtaining quantities of flakes rather than products of predetermined sizes and shapes. That rejected Levallois cores (and, possibly, retouched tools) were occasionally recycled as informal cores may be an expression of stress of some kind in relation to the availability of raw material.

## Cores-on-Flakes

The notion that certain forms of modified flakes were in fact used as cores has been present in Levantine Middle Paleolithic studies since artifacts from Jerf Ajla were described as truncated-faceted flakes (Schroëder 1969:396–403) by the technique later dubbed "Nahr Ibrahim" (Solecki and Solecki 1970). This term describes flakes on which there are clear signs of removal of small flakes on one of the flake's faces, usually the ventral one. This in turn serves as a prepared striking platform for flake removals on the opposite face of the flake. Such removals can appear on limited parts of the flake's circumference as unipolar or bipolar flake detachments (e.g., from one

or both of the flake's tips) (plates 5:1, 9:1–2, 18:12–13, 37:4, 39:5, 40:7, 10) or on the whole circumference of the flake (plates 4:2, 10:10, 33:9, 11, 35:9, 46:10).

Debates as to whether these modified flakes were "specific oriented products" (i.e., tools; Dibble 1984b; Schroëder 1969:398) or cores exploited by a specialized technique focused mainly on the small size of the resultant flakes (Crew 1976:109–111). The problem is twofold. The first issue is whether Middle Paleolithic hominins produced small flakes intentionally. The second, related question is how lithic analysts can distinguish between unintentional small flakes, consensually accepted to be integral to most lithic assemblages, versus intentional small flakes.[6]

Given the latter difficulty, Dibble and McPherron (2006:777–778) recently suggested that intentionality of small flake detachment can be studied from the cores rather than the flake attributes, and especially by comparisons between the products from various core types. Earlier works had not addressed in detail the epistemological issues raised by Dibble and McPherron. Still, various researchers had voiced similar analytical concerns and had taken steps in line with those advocated by them. The analysis of the nodule cores in Qafzeh (above) clearly shows that small flakes were intentional in that cores were knapped with the specific aim of removing small flakes after Levallois production had ceased. Studies of a number of Eurasian assemblages support the interpretation of truncated-faceted pieces as cores-on-flakes, showing that the final size of the last detached flakes could not be differentiated between nodule cores and cores-on-flakes (Goren-Inbar 1988b; Hovers 2007; Munday 1977:44; Nishiaki 1985). The absence of use wear on truncated-faceted pieces sampled from assemblages in Qafzeh, Quneitra, and Kebara is consistent with their understanding as sources of flakes rather than as tools (J. Shea, pers. comm. 1991), in as much as negative evidence can be relied upon.

Several technological phenomena require special attention when identifying intentional removal of small flakes (and, by implication, of cores-on-flakes). Small flakes detached spontaneously during knapping (leaving bulbar scars on the parent flake) may morphologically resemble Kombewa flakes[7] and cause the occurrence of artifacts resembling "Kombewa cores" (e.g., Dibble and McPherron 2006: fig. 1:11). Incidental Kombewa flakes (Dag and Goren-Inbar 2001) similarly lead to inflated numbers of what appear to be intentional small flakes (and Kombewa cores) in an assemblage. For the purpose of this analysis, I included within the category of "cores-on-flakes" only pieces from which three or more flakes had been removed, and only when the removal of a flake off a flake-core relied on the geometry of scars and ridges left by the previous flake removal(s). It should be noted that an elaborate preparatory phase is not part of this definition of cores-on-flakes. When such preparation existed, the cores-on-flakes were identified as Nahr Ibrahim cores.

### Blank Selection

The issue of manufacture and use of cores-on-flakes should be approached from two different perspectives (Hovers 2007). Flakes detached from "regular" nodule cores are perceived as *end-products* of a lithic reduction process; although transforming flakes into retouched tools requires techniques of shaping (*façonnage*), the retouched flake is still perceived as an end-product. On the other hand, when a flake is transformed into a core, it becomes a *source of raw material* for producing additional flakes. The physical properties of the new raw material package require adjustments to the technological practices applied to other raw materials. In this sense, the use of cores-on-flakes entails a separate and discrete *chaîne opératoire* (Goren-Inbar 1990a; Hovers 2007).

A property of cores-on-flakes that distinguishes them from nodule cores is the relatively short use life anticipated for them. In most contexts, the volume of a flake is significantly and very clearly lower than that of nodule cores. Since the volume of flakes usually did not permit many cycles of maintenance and use when exploited as cores, knappers had to balance the need to maximize the number of detached flakes against an anticipated short use life. One way to resolve these seemingly opposing needs was to focus on flakes with characteristics that provided a workable compromise. This suggests that blank selection played a major role in the technological system that relied on cores-on-flakes.

The selection of flakes to be used as cores was not random in the Qafzeh assemblages. Cores-on-flakes often bear a large amount of cortex (table 4.8) when compared to the entire flake population (table 5.2), suggesting a preference of primary flakes as potential core blanks. In some cases, limestone lenses were observed on both faces of the flake. This suggests that the selected flakes had originated from nodules with a thick cortical cover that penetrated into the block itself. The first flakes removed from such blocks tend to be thick and grainy, and likely would have been less effective as extractive tools.

Additionally, 26 retouched tools (8.1% of all cores-on-flakes) and a few core management pieces were recycled into cores-on-flakes. Thirty cores-on-flakes (9.3% of the total number) bear retouch on edges that are not related to their use as cores (e.g., plate 40:7, 10). That artifacts were recycled in 17% of the cases is suggestive of economizing on raw material.

A selection criterion that stands out is that of flake size. Cores-on-flakes are on average larger than whole unretouched flakes (tables 4.9, 5.9a–c). The mean length of all unbroken flakes (N = 10135) is 37.12 mm, while that of all complete cores-on-flake is 45.50 mm (N = 248; s.d. = 11.24, s.e. = 0.71). Cores-on-flakes are also on average wider ($\bar{X}$ = 43.71; N = 248, s.d. = 12.31, s.e. = 0.78) than the rest of the flake population ($\bar{X}$ = 18.67, N = 15,638). Similarly, there appears to be a clear selection of the thickest flakes to be used as cores (tables 4.9, 5.9c). This predilection for large dimensions may also explain the preference for primary flakes, which were often large compared to non-cortical flakes, and for recycling of tools, which were usually made on the largest blanks in the assemblages (as discussed in chapter 6). The preference for larger size suggests that many flakes were selected from the population of Levallois flakes, the mean dimensions of which resemble those of the cores-on-flakes (cf. table 5.3). Observations on the dorsal face characteristics of the cores-on-flakes (discussed below) support this notion.

Additional insights about the selection process are gained from the comparison between nodule cores and cores-on-flakes. Although the limited sample size of both core groups for any individual assemblage hampers a meaningful layer-by-layer comparison, data for individual assemblages (tables 4.2, 4.9) show an overall pattern that is repeated in all the assemblages throughout the

**Table 4.8  Cores-on-flakes: Number of scars and amount of cortical cover on flaking and preparation surfaces**

| Type | Number of scars: Flaking surface | | | | Number of scars: Preparation surface | | | | Amount of cortex: Flaking surface | | | | | Amount of cortex: Preparation surface | | | | | |
|---|---|---|---|---|---|---|---|---|---|---|---|---|---|---|---|---|---|---|---|
| | N | $\bar{X}$ | s.d. | s.e. | N | $\bar{X}$ | s.d. | s.e. | N | 1 | 2 | 3 | 4 | N | 1 | 2 | 3 | 4 | 5 |
| Lev. | 96 | 11.51 | 5.40 | 0.55 | 96 | 9.00 | 4.55 | 0.46 | 86 | 88.66 | 6.19 | 4.12 | — | 74 | 76.29 | 7.22 | 10.31 | 3.09 | 3.00 |
| N.L. | 150 | 7.89 | 4.24 | 0.35 | 149 | 7.95 | 4.40 | 0.36 | 131 | 86.75 | 8.61 | 3.97 | 0.66 | 90 | 59.60 | 14.57 | 13.91 | 8.61 | 3.30 |
| Lev. for flakes | 301 | 13.33 | 5.15 | 0.30 | 301 | 14.11 | 5.43 | 0.31 | 304 | 97.37 | 1.97 | 0.66 | — | 303 | 28.71 | 20.79 | 24.75 | 20.79 | 4.95 |

*Note*: Lev.: Levallois; N.L.: non-Levallois. Complete pieces only. 1: no cortex; 2: 1–25% cortex; 3: 26–50% cortex; 4: 51–75% cortex; 5: 76–100% cortex. Frequencies of each group given as percentages. Levallois/non-Levallois cores-on-flakes: Kolmogorov-Smirnov (K-S) test for number of scars on flaking surface: 22.68 at p < .0001; K-S test for number of scars on preparation surface: 3.56 at p = .3366.

stratigraphic section. There is no statistically significant difference in mean length of nodule cores and cores-on-flakes ($\bar{X} = 46.78$, N = 304; $\bar{X} = 45.50$, N = 248, Levallois cores for flakes and cores-on-flake, respectively; K-S test result: 2.24, $p = .6536$). On the other hand, cores-on-flakes are significantly narrower than are Levallois cores for flakes (mean width: $\bar{X} = 43.71$, N = 248; $\bar{X} = 49.93$, N = 303, respectively; K-S test: 24.97, $p < .0001$). Such comparisons suggest that flake width rather than length may have been a critical constraint on the selection of flakes as core blanks.

Judging from the shapes of the last scars observed on cores-on-flakes, the products detached were primarily flakes. Although the mean size of these scars is smaller than that observed on large cores (table 4.10), the length distributions do not differ significantly between the two groups (figure 4.2a).

There were two broad tactics of exploiting flakes as cores, identifiable as Levallois and non-Levallois approaches. Within each approach, the treatment of the core followed the technological concepts that were applied to the nodule cores.

All flakes exhibit by definition some technological requisites of Levallois flaking, as their ventral and dorsal faces constitute two parallel to sub-parallel surfaces intersecting at a plane. Thus, flakes in general enable the detachment of additional flakes with relatively small investment in the shaping of the core. In addition, the dorsal face is usually a more or less convex surface. The latter property is directly associated with Levallois flakes, the convex dorsal faces of which are formed when the flakes are detached from Levallois nodule cores. When Levallois flakes were used as blanks for cores, the numerous dorsal

face scars on Levallois flakes (tables 4.8, 5.4) a priori provided the guiding ridges that oriented and shaped the morphology of the end-products. The most significant selection criterion favoring Levallois flakes as core blanks may have been their initial large dimensions in comparison to non-Levallois blanks. The geometry of Levallois flakes perpetuated the removal of additional Levallois flakes, as it facilitated their detachment off the flake-turned-core (termed here "Levallois core-on-flake") with relatively little investment in core shaping. Cores-on-flakes exhibiting such Levallois preparation were normally flaked from an extensive length of the flake margins, resulting in high frequencies of centripetal scar patterns (table 4.4).

Non-Levallois cores-on-flakes, on the other hand, bear a small number of scars (table 4.8). Their striking platforms are significantly less utilized and are not worked as extensively as Levallois cores-on-flakes, and platform preparation may not occur at all (the K-S test results [19.48, $p = .000$] reveal significant differences between the two core groups). This may explain their somewhat larger size (tables 4.2, 4.9).

The production of points from cores-on-flakes reflects an interesting deviation from the technological practices used for point removal from nodule cores, being opportunistic without relying on a structured flaking method. In the assemblages of layers XV (seven cores-on-flakes), XIV and XIX (one artifact in each layer), small pointed flakes were obtained when the properties of the core-flakes suited the removal of triangular, relatively elongated products. In some cases, the existing scars on the dorsal face of the flake-core were used to direct the blow and determine the pointed shape, but in other cases, fractures

**Table 4.9  Descriptive statistics of cores-on-flakes: Selected layers**

|  | Layer | | Length | | | Width | | | Thickness | | | Weight | | |
|---|---|---|---|---|---|---|---|---|---|---|---|---|---|---|
|  |  |  | $\bar{X}$ | s.d. | s.e. | $\bar{X}$ | s.d. | s.e. | $\bar{X}$ | s.d. | s.e. | $\bar{X}$ | s.d. | s.e. |
| IX | All | (16) | 48.12 | 9.24 | 2.31 | 45.75 | 14.62 | 3.65 | 12.59 | 4.00 | 1.00 | 32.24 | 29.32 | 7.33 |
|  | L. | (8) | 42.75 | 5.42 | 1.92 | 42.50 | 9.17 | 3.24 | 11.75 | 3.99 | 1.41 | 21.70 | 4.83 | 1.71 |
|  | N.L. | (8) | 53.50 | 9.35 | 3.31 | 49.00 | 18.70 | 6.61 | 13.25 | 4.13 | 1.46 | 42.75 | 35.59 | 14.00 |
| XI | All | (23) | 42.78 | 8.89 | 1.85 | 45.57 | 11.44 | 2.32 | 14.90 | 5.70 | 1.19 | 30.50 | 13.17 | 2.75 |
|  | L. | (7) | 41.57 | 5.13 | 1.94 | 49.57 | 8.02 | 3.03 | 12.29 | 4.86 | 1.84 | 28.53 | 11.61 | 4.39 |
|  | N.L. | (16) | 43.31 | 10.22 | 2.55 | 43.81 | 12.06 | 3.02 | 16.06 | 5.79 | 1.45 | 31.36 | 14.06 | 3.52 |
| XII | All | (19) | 42.84 | 9.04 | 2.08 | 45.79 | 7.08 | 1.63 | 15.42 | 5.27 | 1.21 | 33.81 | 20.18 | 4.63 |
|  | L. | (7) | 38.29 | 7.45 | 2.82 | 44.71 | 6.95 | 2.63 | 14.57 | 3.78 | 1.43 | 28.91 | 14.34 | 5.42 |
|  | N.L. | (12) | 45.50 | 9.09 | 2.62 | 46.42 | 7.39 | 2.13 | 15.92 | 6.08 | 1.76 | 36.66 | 23.02 | 6.64 |
| XIII | All | (19) | 47.00 | 13.62 | 4.67 | 43.68 | 15.19 | 3.49 | 14.63 | 10.30 | 2.34 | 44.72 | 70.18 | 16.10 |
|  | L. | (7) | 39.71 | 12.35 | 4.67 | 35.00 | 8.76 | 3.31 | 12.57 | 4.50 | 1.70 | 22.39 | 18.07 | 6.83 |
|  | N.L. | (12) | 51.25 | 12.92 | 3.73 | 48.75 | 16.12 | 4.65 | 15.83 | 12.58 | 3.63 | 57.75 | 85.90 | 24.80 |
| XV | All | (97) | 44.44 | 10.04 | 2.02 | 41.82 | 11.23 | 1.14 | 12.90 | 4.29 | 0.44 | 26.89 | 15.77 | 1.61 |
|  | L. | (54) | 44.84 | 9.78 | 1.49 | 42.65 | 12.20 | 0.19 | 12.23 | 4.00 | 0.61 | 26.19 | 14.95 | 2.31 |
|  | N.L. | (43) | 44.13 | 10.31 | 1.40 | 41.17 | 10.47 | 1.42 | 13.43 | 4.47 | 0.61 | 27.44 | 16.49 | 2.24 |

*Note*: Unbroken items only; layers selected by sample sizes (cf. table 4.1). L.: Levallois; N.L.: non-Levallois.

**Table 4.10  Descriptive statistics of scars of last-removed flakes**

| Core type | Number | Length | | | Width | | |
|---|---|---|---|---|---|---|---|
| | | $\overline{X}$ | s.d | s.e. | $\overline{X}$ | s.d. | s.e. |
| Cores-on-flakes: Levallois | 123 | 21.49 | 9.10 | 0.82 | 17.91 | 6.79 | 0.64 |
| Cores-on-flakes: Non-Levallois | 188 | 19.09 | 9.43 | 0.69 | 18.01 | 8.60 | 0.66 |
| Levallois cores for flakes | 351 | 25.82 | 11.21 | 0.60 | 25.99 | 11.06 | 0.62 |

Note: K-S test between Levallois and non-Levallois cores-on-flakes: 5.64, p = .1195; K-S test between Levallois cores for flakes and Levallois cores-on-flakes: 12.21, p = .0045; K-S test between Levallois cores for flakes and non-Levallois cores-on-flakes: 33.81, p < .0001

in the flake were exploited for the same purpose. Points were removed off the convex ventral faces of hinged primary flakes or from the lateral part of a large and plain striking platform of the flake-core. The blanks removed from cores-on-flakes would morphologically be Levallois points. Given the size of the scars, they would be smaller than points removed from nodule cores.

The end-products of Levallois and non-Levallois technologies differed in their properties. Given the sizes of negative scars, flakes removed from Levallois cores-on-flakes were on average longer than those extracted from non-Levallois items (table 4.10). Regardless of the flaking technology, the last-removed flakes from cores-on-flakes were similar in size (see K-S results in table 4.10) and somewhat smaller than those detached from the large Levallois cores for flakes (table 4.10).

The *chaîne opératoire* leading to the production and use of cores-on-flakes appears expedient at first glance because it capitalizes on readily available raw material (flakes). It may also seem informal because it reflects minimal investment in core preparation. Some authors emphasize these properties of cores-on-flakes as proxies for reduced settlement mobility in the Levantine Mousterian (e.g., Wallace and Shea 2006). This is not the case in Qafzeh. Within this seemingly expedient organization of the lithic technology, the choice of suitable flake blanks to be used as cores was specific and calculated, enabling reduced investment in core shaping in the later stages of the process. The technological systems responded to the physical characteristics of the pre-selected raw material packages and were applied in a flexible, rather than rigidly predetermined way (Hovers 2007).

## Summary

The analysis of cores leads to the identification of four reduction strategies in the Qafzeh assemblages. The most common is the use of nodule cores and their reduction by either Levallois or non-Levallois flaking systems. In the former case, the recurrent centripetal method was used to produce mainly flakes. A specialized reduction strategy for point production was employed during the time of deposition of layer XV alongside the reduction methods for flake production. Point production may have occurred more sporadically in some of the younger assemblages.

Based on the evidence from the cores, laminar production was very sporadic throughout the sequence of Qafzeh, although it was clearly a known technological concept.

Most large cores that could not be identified as Levallois cores are nevertheless thought to have originated from a Levallois flaking system, based on their technological characteristics. Truly expedient cores are rare among the large cores.

A separate *chaîne opératoire* involved the expedient use (in the sense of Nelson 1991) of flakes as cores for further removal of blanks. The flakes were selected from among the on-site flake populations of the various stratigraphic horizons, and their exploitation was carried out by the reduction methods executed on the large cores.

The strategies of flake production, as reflected in the cores, were designed for maximal exploitation of raw material, but not at all costs. Some of the tactics employed may superficially seem expedient. Thus, while the use of cores-on-flakes underlines a tendency to economize on raw material and to enhance the number of available and usable flakes, it nonetheless conforms with the technological preferences exhibited by the nodule cores, with little compromise on the qualities of the desired products (size, shape, and probably sharpness, although this property is of course not reflected in the cores themselves). In order to achieve the two seemingly opposing goals of maximal raw material exploitation and well-shaped desired products, lithic technological practices had to be flexible. The emphasis on Levallois core technology, as reflected in the ubiquity of Levallois cores, is consistent with the goals of minimizing raw material waste while at the same time maximizing productivity in terms of total numbers of blanks and amount of cutting edge produced (Brantingham and Kuhn 2001).

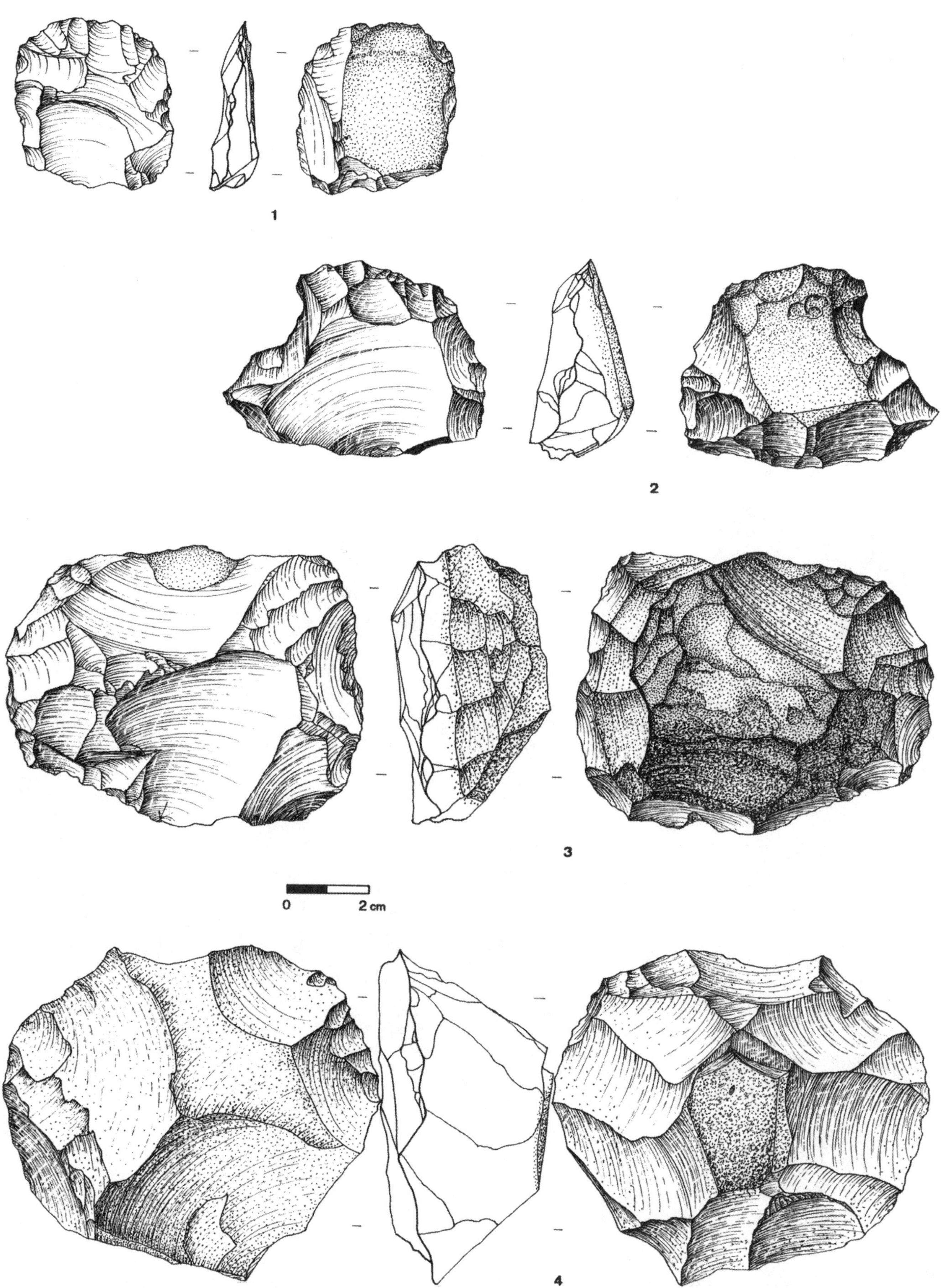

**Plate 1**  Layer XIX: 1–4: Levallois cores for flakes. Item 4 is heavily stained with ochre (Hovers et al. 2003).

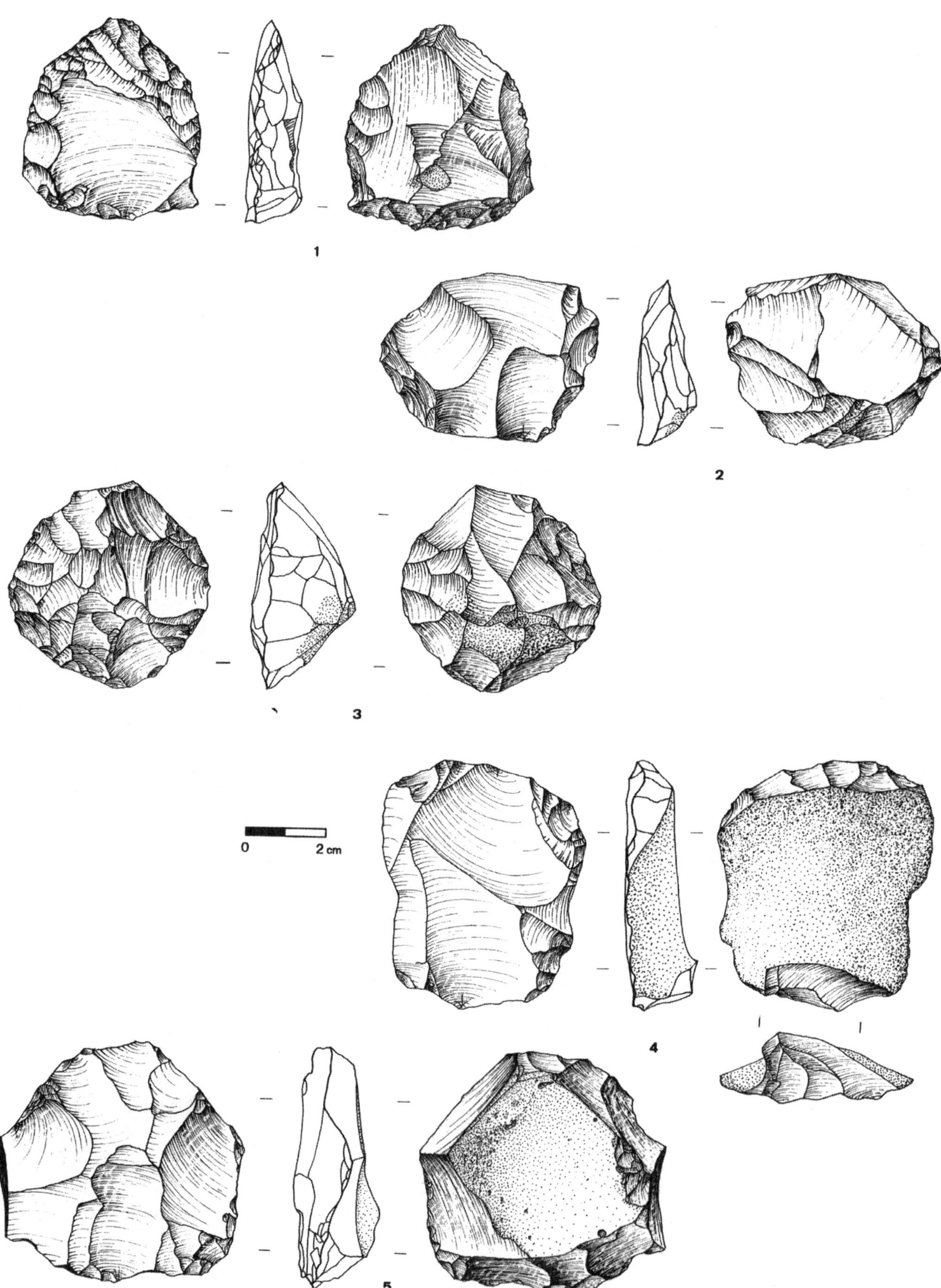

**Plate 2**    Layer XVII: 1, 2–5: Levallois cores for flakes; 2: Levallois core, varia.

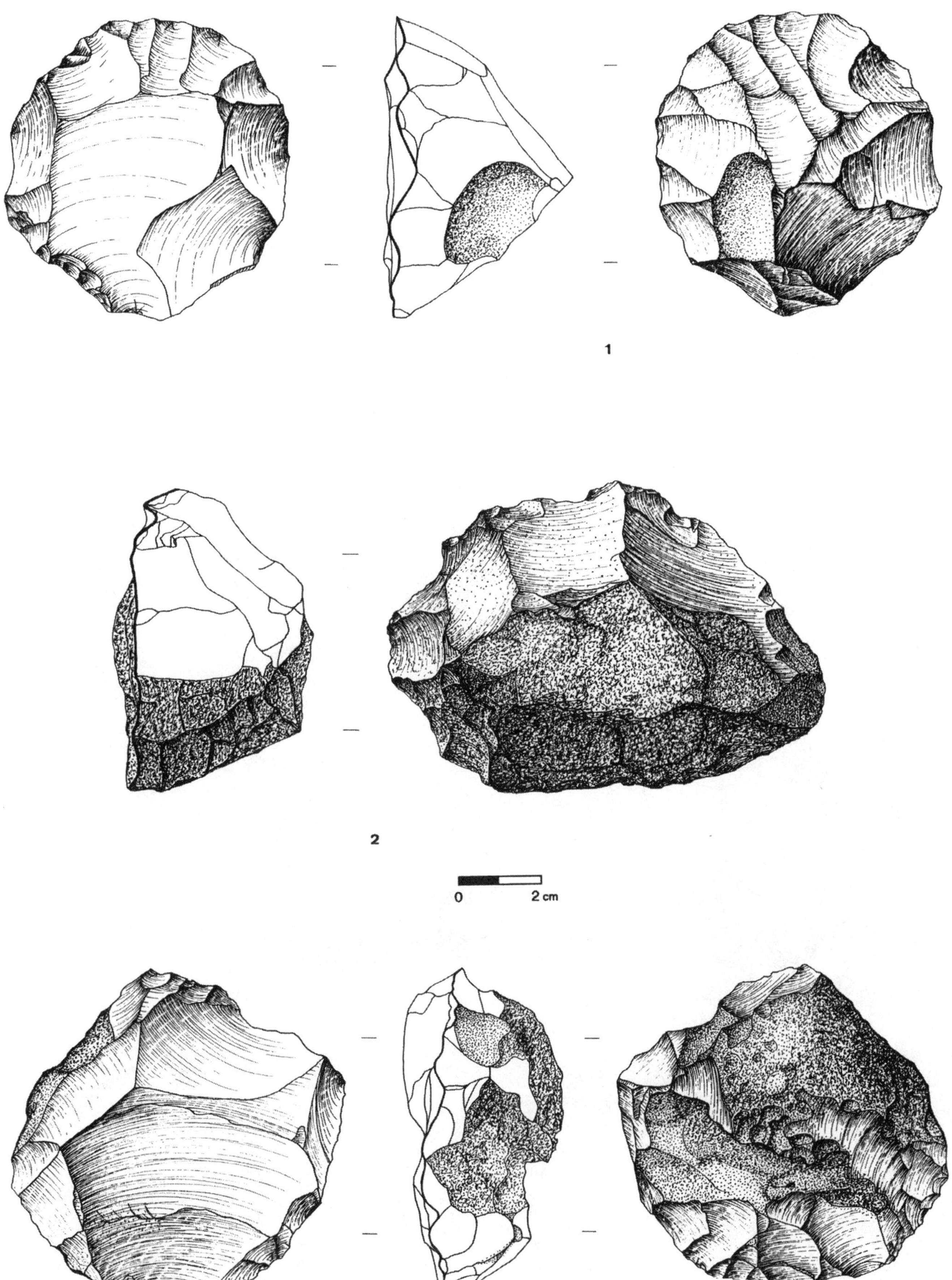

**Plate 3**  Layer XVII: 1–3: Levallois cores for flakes.

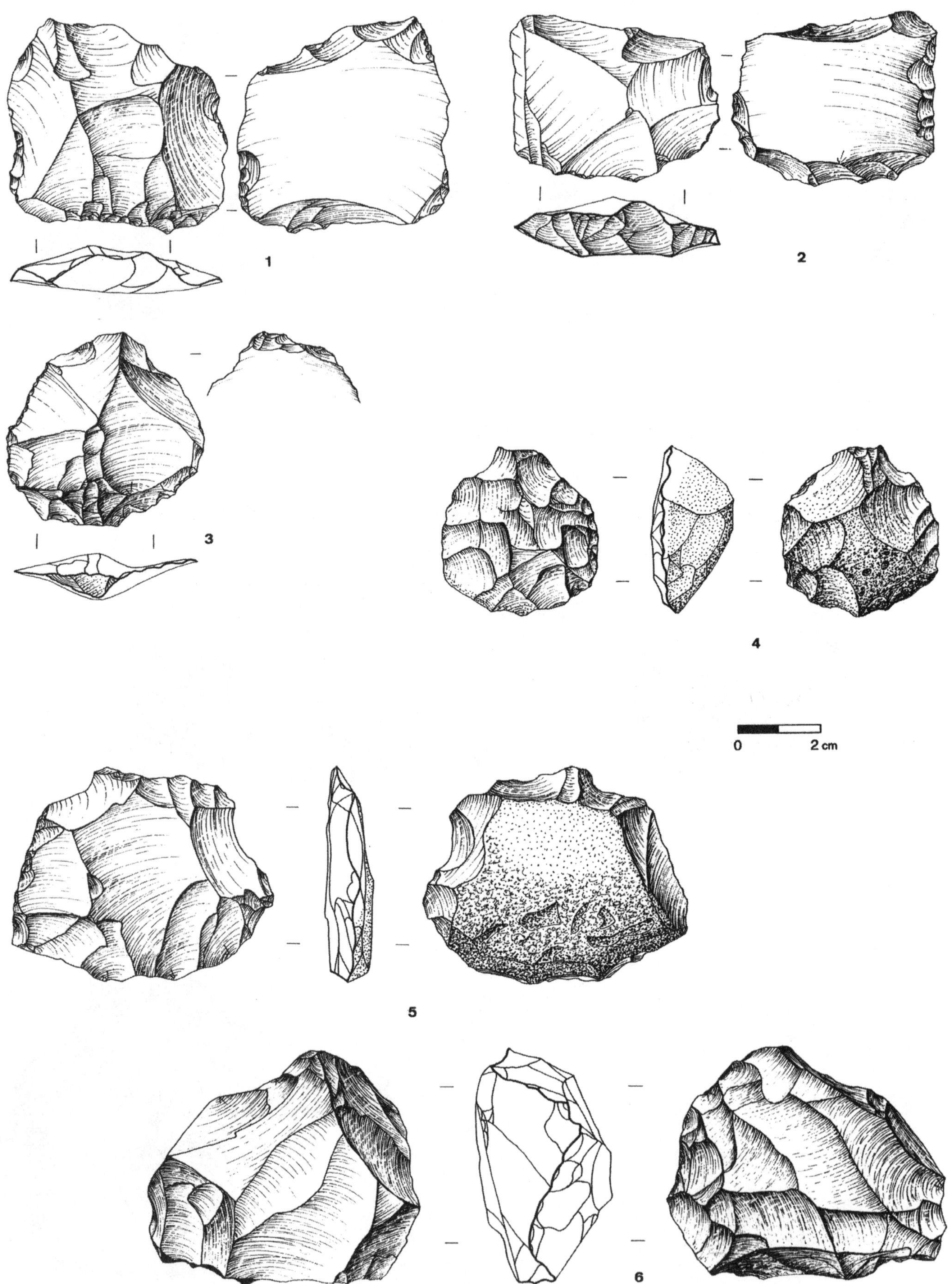

**Plate 4** Layer XIV: 1–2: Cores-on-flakes; 3: Varia (retouched); 4–5: Levallois cores for flakes; 6: Levallois core for blades.

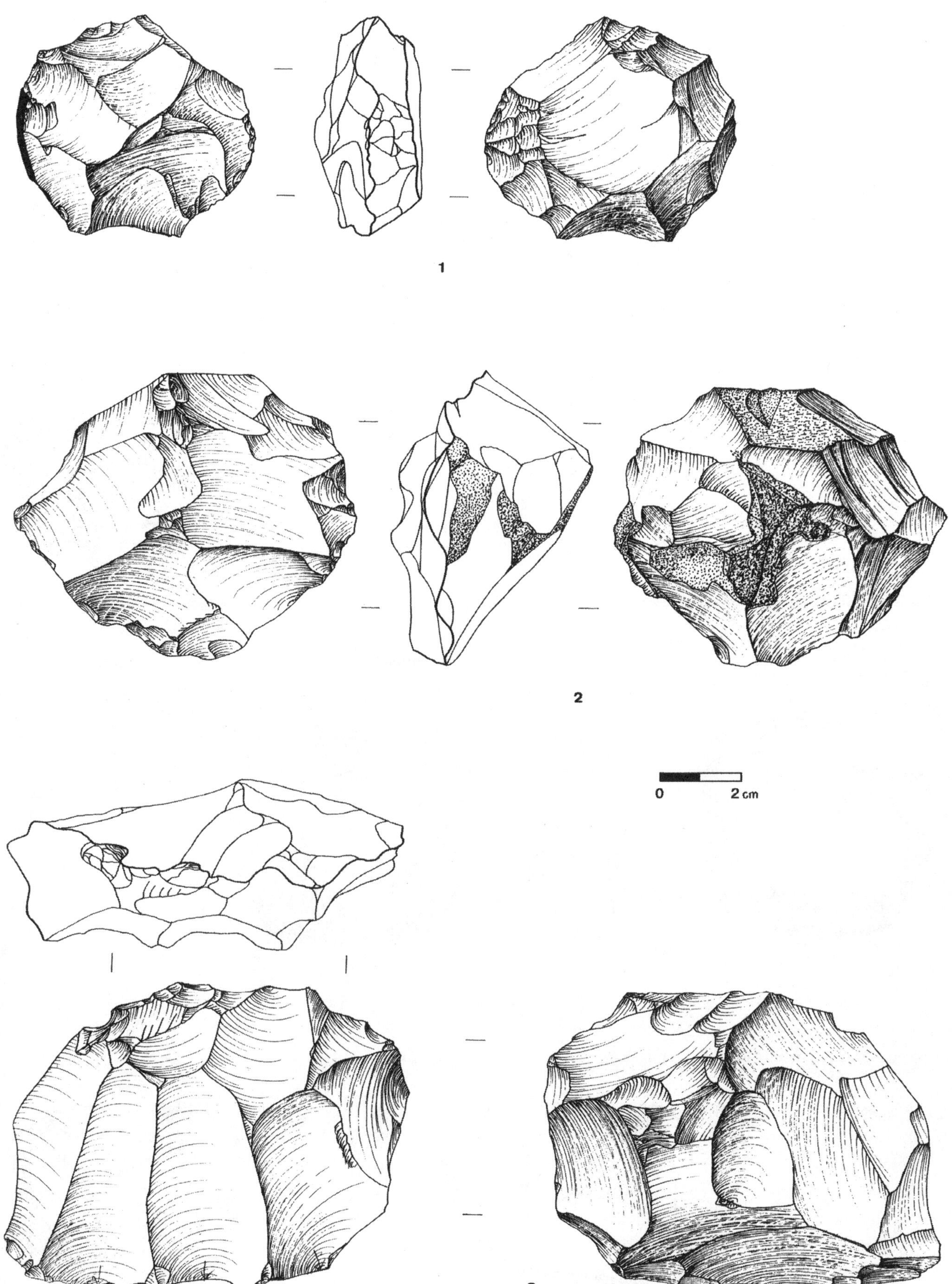

**Plate 5**   Layer XIII: 1–2: Levallois cores for flakes; 3: Levallois core for blades.

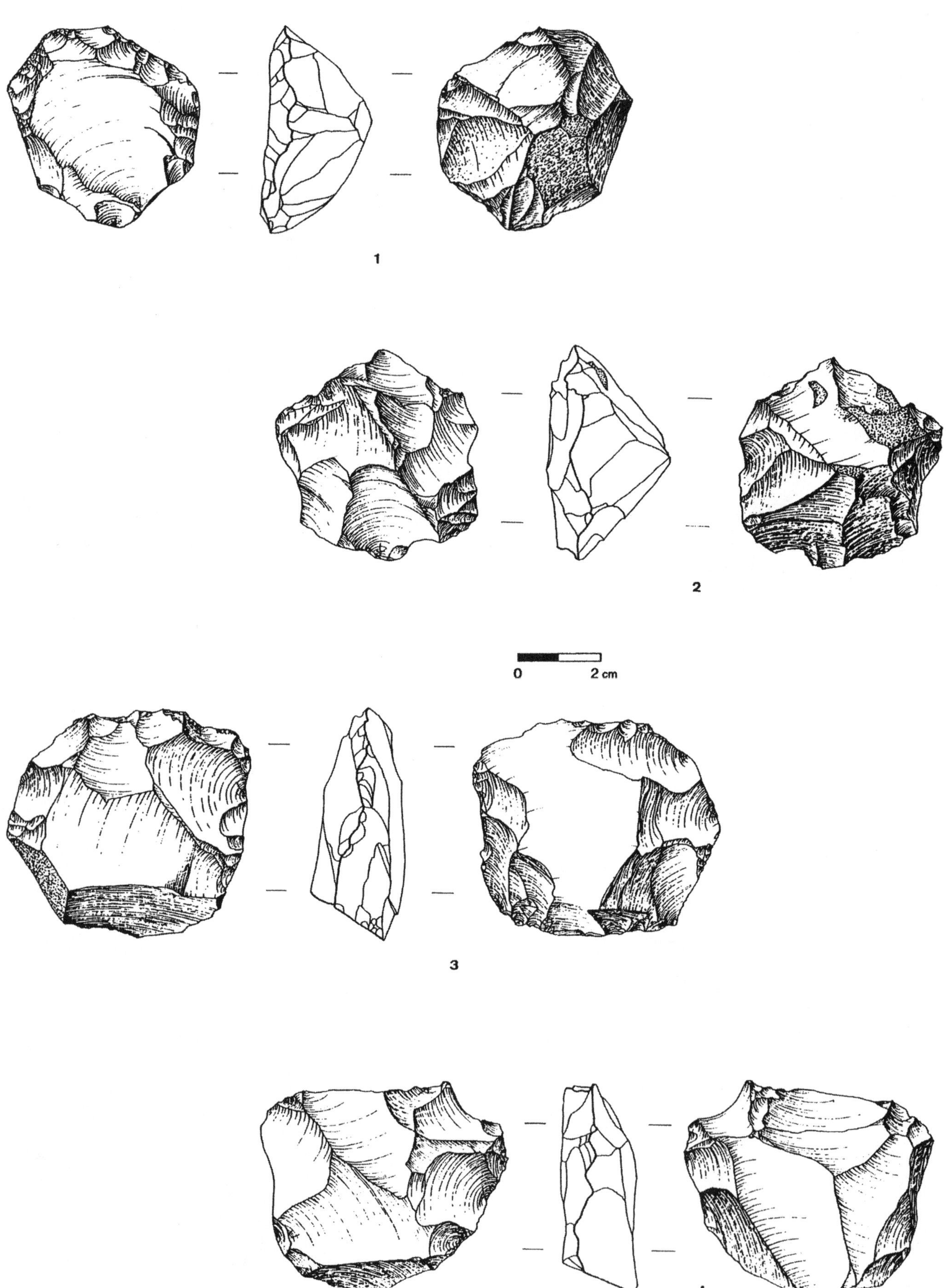

**Plate 6** Layer XI: 1–4: Levallois cores for flakes.

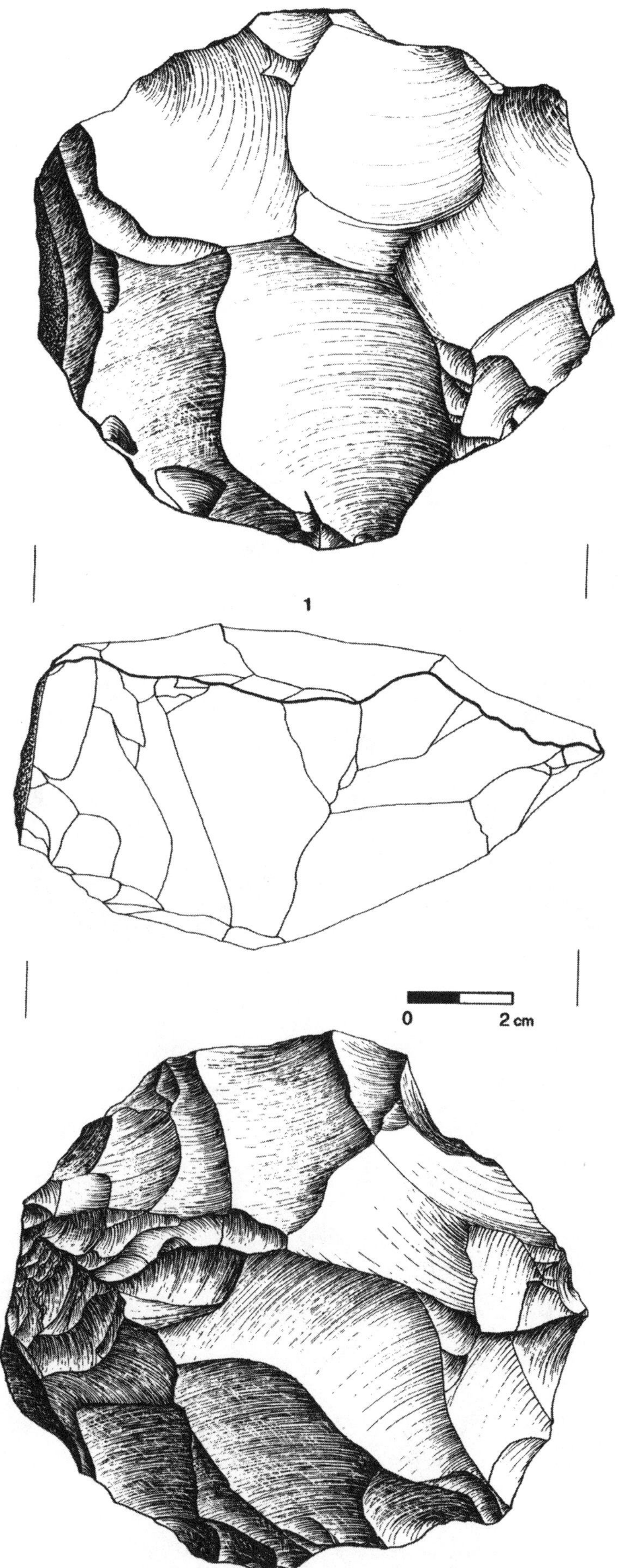

**Plate 7**    Layer XI: 1: Levallois core for flakes.

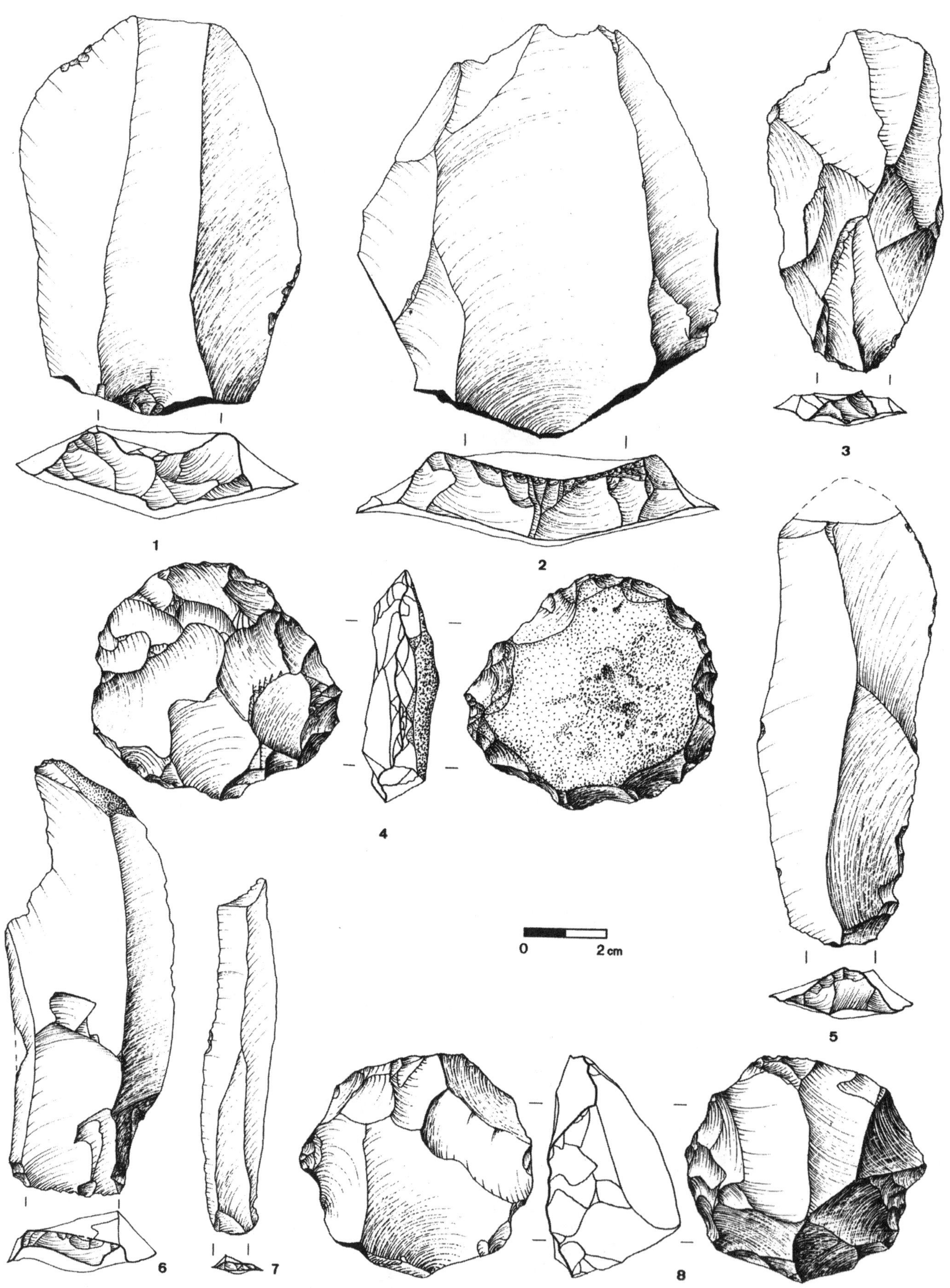

**Plate 8**   Layer IX: 1–3: Levallois flakes; 5–7: Levallois blades; 4, 8: Levallois cores for flakes.

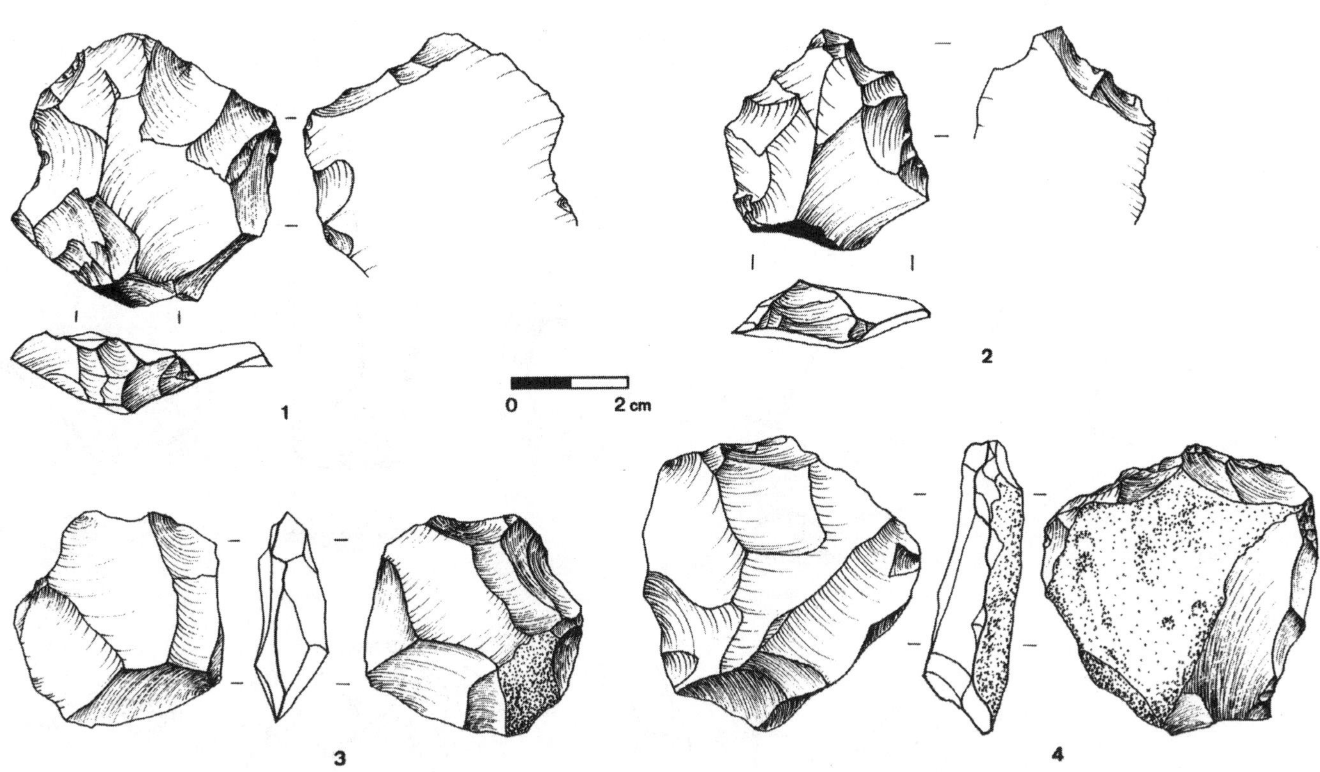

**Plate 9** Layer VIIa: 1: Core-on-flake; 2: Truncated flake; 3–4: Levallois cores for flakes.

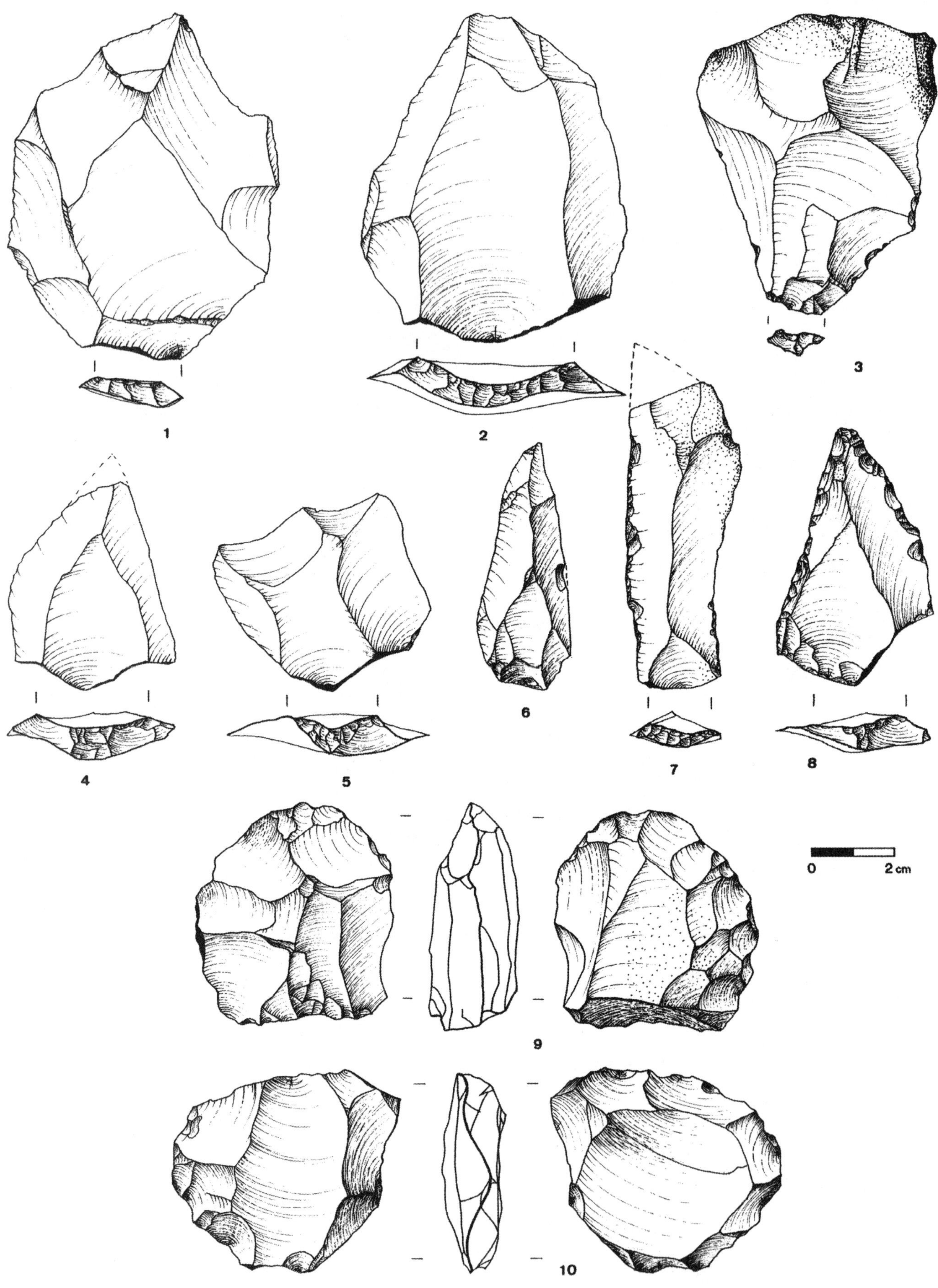

**Plate 10** Layer VII: 1–3, 5: Levallois flakes; 2: Levallois flake (triangular); 4: Levallois point; 6: Levallois blade; 7: Single straight side-scraper; 8: Convergent scraper; 9: Levallois core for flakes; 10: Core-on-flake.

# 5

## Lithic Production: 2. The Debitage

### Blanks as Indicators of Reduction Sequences

Research in empirical disciplines tends to focus on units of analysis that can be defined by particular criteria (Adams and Adams 1991; papers in Ramenofsky and Steffen 1998). In Paleolithic archaeology, that analytical focus was supplied for a long time by retouched artifacts grouped into "types," regardless of the fact that unretouched artifacts constituted the quantitative bulk of most assemblages. Today it is unthinkable that lithic assemblages could be studied without taking into account the component of the unretouched flaked pieces (debitage). This change in the approach to the study of the Middle Paleolithic can be traced back to François Bordes, who introduced the study of complete assemblages through quantitative methods (see chapter 1). White Bordes recognized that unretouched elements embodied information about the technological process that could not be gleaned from the analysis of retouched "types" alone. Bordes's recognition of Mousterian cultural variants was based first and foremost on the relative distributions of retouched artifact groups, considered them in tandem with the patterning of key technological characteristics in both the retouched and unretouched components of any given assemblage.

The adoption by other analysts of a more comprehensive approach to the study of lithics is tied to shifts in research interests. Much of the early research had focused on identification and description of prehistoric cultures through types as cultural markers. Bordes himself, in fact, perceived the properties of unretouched items as reflecting material culture traditions of Middle Paleolithic hominin groups and their regional patterning (see also Fish 1981). Yet when contemporary researchers engage in the lithic analysis of complete assemblages, it is because they are concerned with dynamic processes and with explanations of adaptive processes and how they effected change through time. Evidence from use-wear studies indicates that "waste" (as unretouched artifacts were known for many years) was used by Paleolithic people throughout most prehistoric periods for various tasks, emphasizing the importance of debitage as an element to be reckoned with in lithic analysis. The study of debitage became a foundation for reconstructing and understanding a plethora of prehistoric behaviors, ranging from raw material economics and their role in subsistence patterns, through settlement and mobility behaviors, to cognitive abilities.

The production of lithic artifacts clearly involves intentionality on the part of the tool makers. Still, it would be foolhardy to argue that each and every artifact found in archaeological contexts is pre-planned.[1] Actualistic studies and refitting analyses suggest that production of predetermined artifacts usually involves the detachment of unplanned pieces as well. Unintended pieces may be spontaneously detached (e.g., when the knapper attempts to prepare a striking platform or to retouch) or result from flaking accidents (e.g., Dag and Goren-Inbar 2001; Ekshtain 2006; Geneste 1985; Madsen and Goren-Inbar 2004). Theoretical considerations from the physics of fracture mechanics and neurological principles guiding perceptual-motor coordination (e.g., Cotterell and Kamminga 1987; Pelegrin 2005; Roux and David 2005) are consistent with such observations.

Flake attributes reflect the technological steps employed during the reduction of a core for the purpose of obtaining control over the shape, size, and sharpness of any specific flake. The statistical distributions of morphometric properties of flakes in an assemblage speak volumes about intentionality and the planned, desired shapes and sizes. But those flake properties are also influenced by the specific technologies employed during core reduction. The complexity of dorsal face scar patterns helps us to understand those technologies, in that it is associated with flaking systems, methods and modes of production, and reflects the intensity of core surface exploitation and possibly the core's use life, two properties that can be related to economic factors of lithic exploitation. Striking platform attributes reflect the degree of investment in the preparation carried out to achieve control over the shape and size of the detached items. In reduction strategies that were less formal than the Levallois system and of a more haphazard nature, the amount of preparation would be smaller, and striking platforms and dorsal face patterns are expected to be less effort-intensive. Again, one must remember that in any reduction strategy, flake attributes may change unintentionally because of raw material geometry or as a result of mechanical linkage with intentionally applied flaking methods.

Given the caveats mentioned above with regard to the identification of intentionality, the first task to be tackled in the study of the Qafzeh lithics was to try to understand how the artifacts were manufactured and what factors dictated their properties. Such factors involve, for example, fracture mechanics and the properties of raw material as much as the intention of the knapper. The detailed analysis, which attempts to take on these issues, describes properties of the lithic artifacts and how they change through time.

Did the four reduction sequences recognized through the study of the Qafzeh cores yield flakes with distinct properties that can be identified as the deliberate goals of the separate flaking processes? To answer this question, I begin

from the simplest model of variability in Levallois production (as discussed in chapters 1 and 4). Assuming that in each assemblage only one Levallois reduction method was applied, and that this method did not change through the process of reduction, what would be the expected properties of the resultant, desired flakes? Several predictions are formulated about certain properties of final products of the various reduction sequences, which in turn will help to assign them to the various reduction sequences inferred from the core assemblages. I use this analytical tactic to assess the distance between the model's expectations and the realities reflected in the archaeological samples.

Flake attributes are then described in an attempt to identify their possible interrelationships and to determine which of these affect other characteristics, and in what way. The relationships among traits are examined against expectations from flaking experiments, refitting, and physical models of flint knapping. The comparison makes it possible to assess the degree and causes of intentionality and flexibility in flake production by the Qafzeh hominins. After phenomena associated with the physical production of the artifacts are clarified, we can address questions about why artifacts were made, what were their respective roles in social and economic systems of the Qafzeh hominins, and how these roles may have changed through time (these issues are discussed mostly in chapter 7).

## Expected Flake Characteristics

No systematic attempts at refitting were made, though there is evidence for some conjoining potential in a few assemblages (e.g., plate 34:5). Hence predictions of the

**Table 5.1  Flake attributes predicted by core analyses**

| Reduction strategy/ method and mode | Cortex on dorsal face | Scar pattern | Striking platform | Flake length | Core management |
|---|---|---|---|---|---|
| Levallois centripetal recurrent | < 25% | Centripetal | All types | Relatively long but also some that are < 10 mm[a] | Plunging *éclats débordants*, pseudo-Levallois |
| Levallois convergent recurrent | < 25% | Unipolar-convergent | Faceted, occasional chapeau de gendarme, few cortical or plain | Large | Naturally backed knives, *éclats débordants, outrepassants* |
| Levallois (on-flake) | Mostly < 25%, some with up to 50% | Centripetal, bipolar, seldom unipolar | Faceted | Slightly smaller than "regular" flakes | Not expected |
| Non-Levallois (on-flake) | < 25%, some with up to 50% | Unipolar, centripetal | Plain, occasionally dihedral | Relatively small | Not expected |
| Non-Levallois | < 25%, some with up to 50% | Unipolar | Plain, dihedral | Relatively small | Various informal core trimming elements, including occasional ridge blades from prismatic cores. |

[a] Values derived from length of last-removed Levallois scar and/or of the smaller scars removed after it (cf. figure 4.3).

flake properties that may originate from any flaking strategy have to be founded on the characteristics of the cores and are at best probabilistic. The expected combinations of flake attributes, based on core analyses, are shown in table 5.1.

## Levallois and Non-Levallois Blanks

In this study, flaked artifacts are categorized as being derived from a Levallois, a non-Levallois or an indeterminate technological system. This task is less straightforward than one would hope, especially given the long history of Levallois as a technological concept. I mentioned in previous chapters that specific technological criteria for Levallois exist mainly for the cores. In contrast, formal recognition of Levallois blanks has been a consistent problem in Middle Paleolithic research. Although the notion of predetermination is key in many of the treatments of Levallois blanks, the morphological and technological traits that are deemed essential for recognizing such predetermined artifacts are hardly ever treated specifically and coherently by researchers (Bar-Yosef and Dibble 1995; Van Peer 1992:1–8). Dibble (1989) hypothesizes that predetermination of Levallois blanks should lead to higher standardization of their shape and size traits when compared to non-Levallois blanks. In an assemblage-level study, he compared and tested statistically the differences between predetermined flakes (Levallois flakes and biface trimming flakes) and "regular" flakes for which no production technique could be identified. This analysis did not reveal statistically meaningful differences between the three classes of artifacts, which in Dibble's view cast doubt on predetermination as a diagnostic trait of Levallois products.

As defined by Boëda (1986; 1991:42–50), Levallois flakes can be recognized because they are predetermined products: in a given assemblage they will present well-defined morphometric and technological characteristics that require intentionality and pre-planning. This definition of Levallois flakes is admittedly vague and is reminiscent of earlier ambiguous attempts to define Levallois (as discussed in chapter 1). However, given the clearer criteria that define Levallois cores, it is possible to derive from them some concrete characteristics of the debitage. In the study of the Qafzeh assemblages, predetermination of Levallois flakes is not a starting point of the analysis, but I have rather tried to isolate and identify the technological traits that are expected from the application of the abstract Levallois concept. The "Levallois-ness" of each flake is not assumed but emerges from its specific characteristics.

When worked by a Levallois system, the volume of the core is exploited repeatedly through the use of a surface.[2] Accordingly, resultant flakes are relatively flat and thin. They often have a slightly concave longitudinal ventral profile, the result of their axis of removal being sub-parallel to the slightly convex prepared flaking surface of Levallois cores. On their dorsal face, the flakes bear complex scar patterns that reflect the modification of convexities and represent predetermined flakes, which themselves predetermined the shape of the next flake removed (in many cases both; Boëda 1991:44, 71; 1993). Since the hammer blow that removes Levallois flakes off the core's flaking surface impacts below the striking platforms, Levallois flakes are less likely to have punctiform, thin, or crushed striking platforms and more likely to have discernible, measurable platforms. Whether a platform is faceted, plain, or cortical is a different question that has to do with specific methods and modes of flaking and not with the Levallois flaking concept as such. Similarly, attempts to establish quantitative criteria for the recognition of Levallois products have been only partly successful (Perpère 1989) because the sizes of the pre-planned flakes in an assemblage depend on initial raw material size (e.g., Kuhn 1995b) and on the specific Levallois modes and methods applied to it. Metrics alone cannot constitute a diagnostic criterion of Levallois debitage.

Ambiguities clearly abound. Some artifacts resulting from the use of discoidal flaking methods can be perceived as Levallois debitage, since the clear differences between the two knapping concepts are seen in core rather than flake populations (Boëda 1991, 1993:397–398; Ohnuma 1990; see chapter 4). However, since the core analyses indicate that discoidal flaking was uncommon in the Qafzeh assemblages, this is a negligible problem for the current study.

Recognition of the second, non-Levallois category is based on a negative feature, that is, the lack of Levallois characteristics. Non-Levallois flaking systems may by definition include a number of formal reduction strategies (e.g., blade-oriented technologies). These, however, were rarely observed among artifacts classified in the non-Levallois category. Only one group of products, Kombewa flakes, could be differentiated within the non-Levallois category in the assemblages. Their frequencies range between 0.11% of all debitage (layer XVII) and 3.55% (layer XXI), but are usually less than 1% per assemblage. A similar phenomenon was observed at Quneitra (Goren-Inbar 1990a: fig. 50) and at Kebara Cave (L. Meignen, pers. comm.). These artifacts are considered by-products of the Levallois flaking system (Geneste 1985). Some of them may have resulted from the reduction sequences of cores-on-flakes, as the majority of Kombewa flakes fall in the size range of the scars seen on such cores. Their sporadic occurrence in the Qafzeh assemblages, combined with the fact that very few of them were retouched into tools (e.g., plate 17:6), indicate that their appearance was indeed incidental.

Addressing the issue of recognizing Levallois blanks, Copeland (1983b) suggested that difficulties occurred in the Levant mainly in the context of assemblages with a (relatively) significant laminar component. Rather than enforcing a typological definition on technological items, she proposed the use of a third classificatory category, "indeterminate," to be assigned to technologically ambiguous artifacts. Additional work, however, indicated that such difficulties are eminent also in flake-dominated assemblages (e.g., Goren-Inbar 1990a:83, 114). Similar difficulties rose during the analysis of the Qafzeh assemblages, the rarity of blades notwithstanding (see below). Therefore, an "indeterminate" category was included in the technological classification of debitage. The relative frequencies of this technological category are a minor factor of the technological variation over time (figure 5.1a), hence artifacts of indeterminate technological affinities were grouped with the "non-Levallois" group for the majority of the analyses (unless stated otherwise). The category of Levallois flakes throughout the analysis pertains to blanks that were unambiguously produced by Levallois flaking tactics. The Levallois index (IL) presents the relative frequencies of such artifacts in any given assemblage.

Values of IL in the Qafzeh assemblages are variable and fluctuate among layers. The highest frequencies of Levallois items occur in the older assemblages (XXII–XVII). Slightly lower values are encountered in layers XIV, XII, and X, while the lowest values are observed in the youngest assemblages (but also in layers XVa, XVf; figure 5.1a), showing a diachronic decrease in the use of Levallois flaking. The trend, however, is weak and the decrease is not consistent. Overall, there is a high similarity among the assemblages in terms of the relative frequencies of blanks associated with the three recognized technological groups (figure 5.1b).

## Debitage Characteristics

### Dorsal Face Traits

The characteristics of the dorsal faces of flakes and flake tools are described by three variables. The first quantifies the amount of cortex on the dorsal face and the other two describe the number of scars left by previously removed flakes and their spatial organization. Given the technological variability encompassed in the Levallois flaking system, these observations are important for a more precise identification of the methods and modes of Levallois flaking that had been employed. Observations on dorsal face

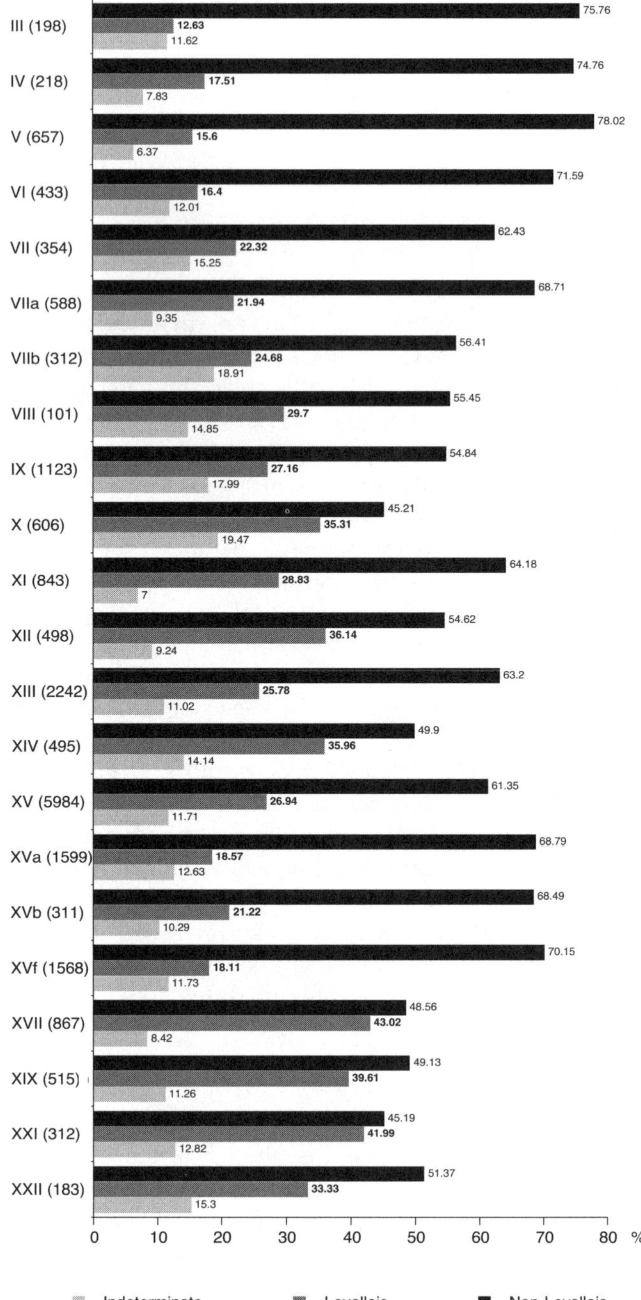


**Figure 5.1a**  Frequencies of blanks according to flaking technologies.

traits help to understand the flexibility of the Levallois flaking throughout the process of flake production (Boëda, Geneste, and Meignen 1990). Finally, when combined with other attributes (such as metrics), dorsal face characteristics are also informative about the intensity of core exploitation at the stage of flake removal off the core.

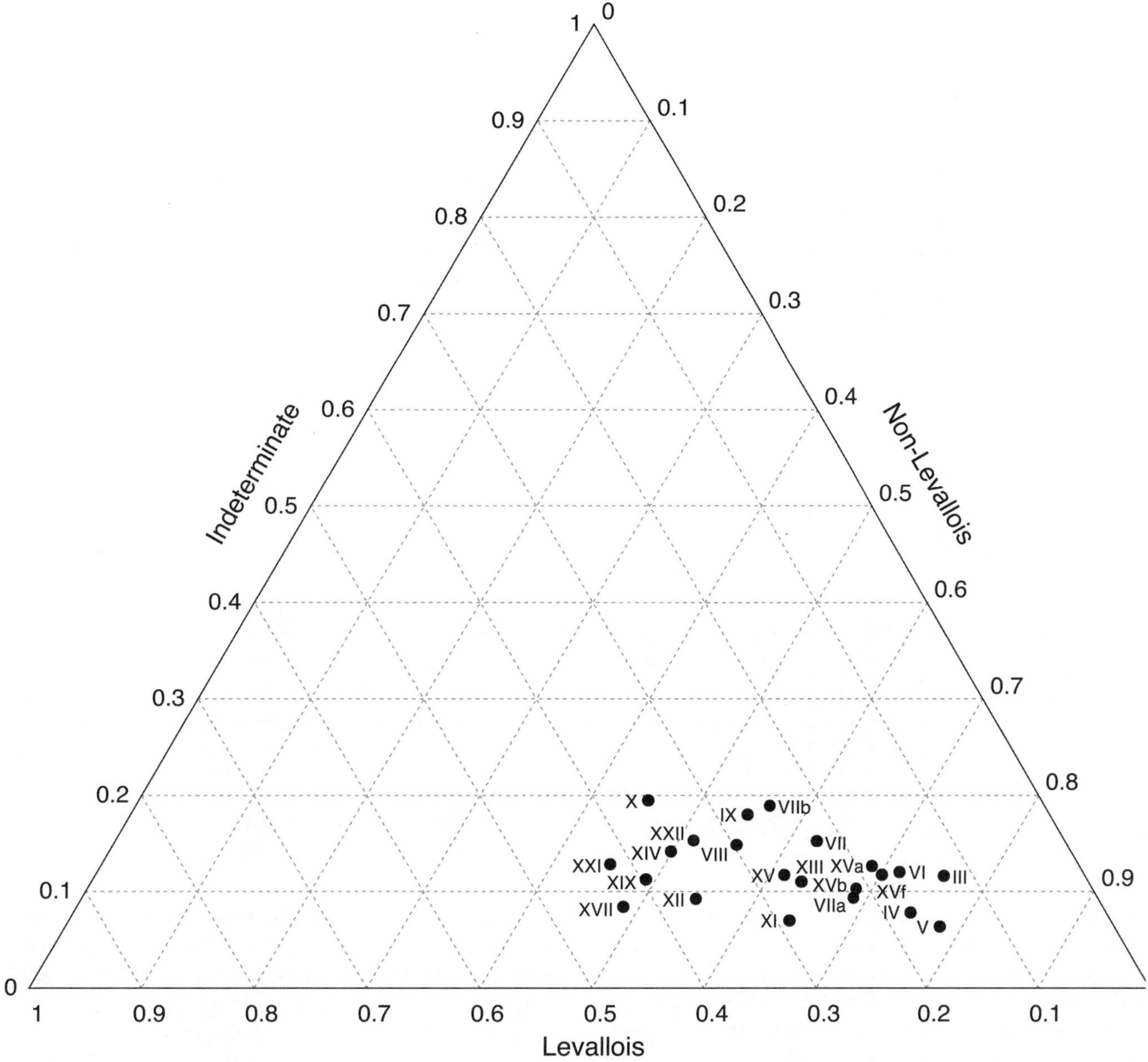

**Figure 5.1b** Clustering of the assemblages according to relative frequencies of flaking technologies. Note the similarity among assemblages, despite the variations shown in figure 5.1a.

*Amount of Cortex*

The majority of flakes and tools in the assemblages bear no cortex. Highly cortical pieces (50–100% cortex) are relatively few (table 5.2, figure 5.2a, b). Pieces with less than 50% of dorsal face cortex account for 25–30% of the flakes, while frequencies of cortex-free flakes are ca. 65%. These patterns are common to all of the layers, although somewhat higher frequencies of cortical flakes are observed in the lower part of the sequence (layers XIV–XXIV, with the exceptions of layers XVb, XVf; table 5.2). Levallois debitage in all layers exhibits higher frequencies of cortex-free pieces than non-Levallois or core management pieces (table 5.2). When cortex exists on the dorsal face of Levallois debitage, it exceeds 50% of surface area in only three assemblages.

Tested or minimally decorticated blocks are very rare in the Qafzeh assemblages. They do not occur at all in layers III, IV, V, VII, VIIb, VIII, XVb, or XXII–XXIV. In layers X and XII they form 1.3% and 1.4%, respectively, of the whole assemblage, and in the rest of the assemblages they

**Table 5.2  Frequencies of cortex on dorsal face: Flake assemblages**

| Layer | Number | Dorsal face cortex | | |
| --- | --- | --- | --- | --- |
| | | NO CORTEX | 1–50% CORTEX | 51–100% CORTEX |
| III | 197 (25) | 66.5 (84.0) | 29.4 (16.0) | 4.1 |
| IV | 215 (38) | 66.5 (89.5) | 31.6 (10.5) | 1.9 |
| V | 654 (98) | 71.3 (88.8) | 24.9 (11.2) | 3.8 |
| VI | 432 (71) | 68.5 (81.7) | 26.3 (18.3) | 5.1 |
| VII | 351 (79) | 67.5 (88.6) | 27.9 (11.4) | 4.6 |
| VIIa | 590 (128) | 58.6 (77.3) | 37.1 (22.7) | 4.2 |
| VIIb | 306 (77) | 67.3 (88.3) | 27.7 (11.7) | 4.9 |
| VIII | 99 (29) | 61.6 (86.2) | 34.6 (13.8) | 4.0 |
| IX | 1,115 (306) | 65.1 (85.3) | 31.0 (14.7) | 3.9 |
| X | 594 (213) | 66.2 (82.6) | 30.1 (17.4) | 3.7 |
| XI | 820 (240) | 67.8 (85.0) | 27.2 (15.0) | 5.0 |
| XII | 483 (178) | 64.6 (81.5) | 31.3 (18.5) | 4.1 |
| XIII | 2,207 (578) | 68.7 (82.0) | 27.8 (18.0) | 3.6 |
| XIV | 494 (178) | 60.3 (83.1) | 32.6 (12.9) | 7.1 |
| XV | 6,023 (1606) | 63.7 (85.7) | 29.7 (14.3) | 6.6 |
| XVa | 1,576 (295) | 65.4 (85.8) | 28.4 (14.2) | 6.3 |
| XVb | 293 (65) | 66.6 (90.8) | 29.3 (9.2) | 4.1 |
| XVf | 1,525 (283) | 68.1 (90.8) | 27.7 (9.2) | 4.1 |
| XVII | 859 (372) | 65.5 (80.7) | 26.8 (18.3) | 7.7 (1.1) |
| XIX | 514 (204) | 67.7 (80.4) | 26.5 (19.6) | 5.9 |
| XXI | 312 (131) | 64.7 (76.3) | 28.5 (22.0) | 6.7 (1.5) |
| XXII | 178 (60) | 64.0 (86.7) | 25.9 (13.3) | 10.1 |
| XXIV | 69 (26) | 73.9 (84.6) | 15.9 (11.5) | 10.2 (3.9) |

*Note*: All debitage and tools. Core management elements (e.g., core trimming elements, *éclats débordants*, etc.) as a rule exhibit cortical cover between 1 and 50%, with rare exceptions, mainly where core trimming elements are concerned. A few pieces with high cortical cover occur in very small numbers (usually one piece) in layers VII, VIIa, X, XI, XII, XIII, XV (13 such elements), XVf, XVII, and XXI. Comparative data for Levallois debitage alone are given in parentheses. Frequencies rounded to first decimal.

occur in frequencies well under 1% of the whole assemblage. In layers XIV and XV a few of the blocks are heavier than 100 grams. These are the only instances in which the shape and size of the original nodules are apparent.

Combined, these data imply that the initial stages of core reduction took place outside the site. Throughout the occupation of Qafzeh, raw material had been brought into the site as partially decorticated blocks (more on this in chapter 7).

*Scar Patterns on Dorsal Face*

A large variety of scar patterns were recognized on the debitage and tools in the various assemblages (appendix 3, table 5.3a–b). The notion that flaking strategies remain constant within any given assemblage is treated in this study as a hypothesis rather than a paradigm. In such an analytical context, detailed observations reveal information about flexibility and the variability of flaking methods and modes that would otherwise be masked under fewer categories of dorsal face scar directions.

Both Levallois and non-Levallois groups exhibit a large diversity of scar patterns, two of which appear mainly in the non-Levallois group. The "indeterminate" pattern occurs in relatively high frequencies (7–17.4%) in the non-Levallois population, as opposed to the Levallois group (0–3.8%). Another scar pattern, observed only in the non-Levallois group, is "cortical," describing flakes with a dorsal face that is completely covered by cortex. By definition, therefore, this pattern cannot be observed on Levallois flakes.

The "dominant and centripetal" pattern is relatively rare in most of the assemblages, in which the vast majority of artifacts exhibiting a "centripetal" dorsal scar pattern originate from a recurrent system. While flakes bearing "centripetal" scar patterns could have originated from the preparatory stages of a lineal flaking method, they would have been accompanied by a larger number of flakes bearing "dominant and centripetal" dorsal scar patterns. Indeed, this is the case for the oldest assemblages. It should be noted that the frequencies of scar patterns observed on the cores (figure 4.1a, b) are not consistent

**Figure 5.2** Frequencies of cortex. A. On the dorsal faces of unretouched artifacts. B: On dorsal faces of retouched tools (assemblage with N ≥ 20 are shown).

**Table 5.3  Frequencies of dorsal face scar patterns: Retouched and unretouched blanks**

**A. Non-Levallois**

| Scar pattern | III | IV | V | VI | VII | VIIa | VIIb | VIII | IX | X | XI | XII | XIII | XIV | XV | XVa | XVb | XVf | XVII | XIX | XXI | XXII |
|---|---|---|---|---|---|---|---|---|---|---|---|---|---|---|---|---|---|---|---|---|---|---|
| Indeterminate | 7.0 | 12.4 | 8.3 | 12.2 | 15.3 | 10.3 | 17.4 | 14.1 | 14.6 | 13.4 | 15.6 | 13.9 | 15.9 | 16.9 | 13.2 | 11.1 | 13.6 | 9.4 | 13.8 | 14.4 | 13.8 | 13.5 |
| Cortical | 0.6 | 1.1 | 1.6 | 2.1 | 2.5 | 2.8 | 1.3 | 2.8 | 1.7 | 1.8 | 3.2 | 0.9 | 1.2 | 1.7 | 2.5 | 2.1 | 1.3 | 1.5 | 1.6 | 3.1 | 2.3 | 4.5 |
| Ridged | — | — | 0.7 | — | 0.4 | 0.4 | 0.4 | 1.4 | 0.7 | 0.5 | 2.2 | 3.8 | 1.3 | 2.9 | 0.5 | 0.4 | 0.4 | 0.7 | — | — | — | — |
| Unipolar | 45.2 | 47.5 | 36.9 | 34.1 | 32.7 | 40.3 | 34.5 | 31.0 | 31.9 | 37.0 | 29.9 | 31.5 | 24.0 | 19.2 | 44.1 | 39.8 | 47.1 | 34.1 | 23.7 | 38.1 | 36.5 | 48.6 |
| Parallel | — | 1.7 | 0.5 | — | 0.7 | 1.3 | — | — | 0.2 | 0.3 | 0.2 | — | — | — | 0.4 | 0.2 | 0.9 | 0.6 | 0.4 | 0.3 | — | 1.8 |
| Opposed | 0.6 | 0.6 | 0.9 | 0.8 | 0.7 | 1.5 | 0.9 | — | 1.6 | 0.5 | 0.7 | 0.9 | 0.6 | 1.3 | 0.8 | 1.4 | 0.9 | 1.0 | 1.4 | 0.9 | 1.1 | 0.9 |
| Side | 2.9 | 2.8 | 3.2 | 3.7 | 2.5 | 3.7 | 4.3 | 2.7 | 3.9 | 2.6 | 4.2 | 3.2 | 4.3 | 5.2 | 2.8 | 4.8 | 5.1 | 2.7 | 8.7 | 6.9 | 8.8 | 7.2 |
| Convergent | 7.6 | 1.1 | 6.7 | 5.0 | 5.8 | 6.3 | 3.8 | 4.2 | 3.8 | 2.6 | 0.7 | 0.6 | 0.8 | 1.3 | 4.7 | 3.6 | 3.4 | 6.1 | 0.6 | — | 0.6 | — |
| Convergent and side | 1.2 | 1.1 | 0.4 | 1.1 | — | 0.7 | — | 2.8 | 0.4 | 0.8 | 0.2 | — | 0.4 | — | 0.6 | 0.5 | 1.3 | 0.6 | 0.6 | — | 0.6 | — |
| Bipolar | 8.7 | 4.0 | 5.6 | 7.7 | 7.6 | 4.8 | 4.7 | 9.9 | 8.7 | 11.4 | 3.1 | 5.4 | 4.6 | 4.2 | 5.3 | 6.0 | 5.1 | 8.7 | 2.6 | 7.8 | 7.7 | 4.5 |
| Unipolar and opposed | 7.6 | 11.9 | 10.1 | 8.7 | 10.2 | 9.6 | 11.9 | 12.8 | 12.7 | 8.8 | 10.7 | 10.4 | 13.0 | 9.4 | 6.6 | 9.2 | 7.2 | 10.6 | 4.9 | — | — | — |
| Convergent and opposed | 0.6 | 0.6 | 1.1 | 1.1 | 1.5 | 0.7 | — | — | 0.3 | 0.5 | — | — | 0.3 | — | 0.1 | 0.3 | — | 1.6 | — | — | — | — |
| Unipolar and side | 16.8 | 12.4 | 14.5 | 14.0 | 16.0 | 15.1 | 17.0 | 15.5 | 15.4 | 16.0 | 23.4 | 23.7 | 28.4 | 29.0 | 15.6 | 16.9 | 16.2 | 13.1 | 33.7 | 24.4 | 20.4 | 15.3 |
| Parallel and side | — | — | — | — | — | — | — | — | — | — | 0.2 | — | — | — | — | 0.1 | — | — | 0.2 | — | — | — |
| Opposed and side | 0.6 | 1.1 | 0.5 | 0.8 | 2.2 | 0.7 | 1.3 | 1.4 | 1.0 | 1.6 | 2.5 | 1.6 | 1.7 | 2.9 | 0.9 | 1.3 | 1.3 | 0.9 | 2.8 | 0.3 | 0.6 | 0.9 |
| Bipolar and side | — | 1.7 | 3.6 | 4.5 | 1.8 | 1.5 | 0.9 | — | 2.7 | 1.6 | 2.5 | 2.2 | 2.4 | 3.3 | 1.5 | 1.7 | 1.3 | 3.1 | 3.9 | 1.6 | 1.7 | 0.9 |
| Centripetal | 0.6 | — | 4.9 | 3.4 | — | — | 0.4 | 1.4 | 0.4 | 0.5 | 0.7 | 0.9 | 0.7 | 1.6 | 0.2 | 0.7 | 0.4 | 4.7 | 0.2 | 1.3 | 5.0 | 0.9 |
| Dominant % centripetal | — | — | 0.7 | 0.3 | — | 0.4 | — | — | — | 0.3 | 0.2 | 0.9 | 0.3 | 0.7 | 0.1 | — | — | 0.5 | 0.9 | 0.9 | 1.1 | 1.8 |
| N | 172 | 177 | 447 | 378 | 275 | 457 | 235 | 71 | 813 | 387 | 589 | 317 | 1,657 | 307 | 4,345 | 1,293 | 235 | 1,547 | 493 | 320 | 181 | 111 |

**B. Levallois[a]**

| Scar pattern | III | IV | V | VI | VII | VIIa | VIIb | VIII | IX | X | XI | XII | XIII | XIV | XV | XVa | XVb | XVf | XVII | XIX | XXI | XXII |
|---|---|---|---|---|---|---|---|---|---|---|---|---|---|---|---|---|---|---|---|---|---|---|
| indeterminate | — | — | — | 2.8 | — | — | — | 1.0 | 0.9 | 0.4 | — | 0.7 | — | 1.2 | 1.2 | 0.3 | 1.5 | 0.4 | 1.1 | 1.5 | 3.8 | — |
| ridged | — | — | — | 1.4 | — | — | — | — | — | — | — | 0.4 | — | 1.0 | 5.6 | — | — | 0.7 | — | — | — | — |
| unipolar | — | — | 2.8 | 2.8 | 1.3 | 3.1 | 2.6 | — | 1.4 | 2.1 | 2.2 | 1.4 | 1.1 | 2.7 | 2.4 | 2.4 | 1.5 | 1.8 | 4.6 | 3.9 | 10.7 | 7.0 |
| parallel | — | — | 1.4 | — | — | — | 1.3 | 0.7 | — | 0.4 | — | — | — | — | — | — | — | — | — | 0.5 | — | — |
| opposed | — | — | — | — | 1.3 | — | — | — | — | — | — | — | — | 0.1 | 0.2 | — | — | — | — | — | — | — |
| side | — | 2.6 | — | — | 1.3 | — | 2.6 | 0.7 | 0.9 | 0.4 | 1.1 | 0.4 | 0.6 | 0.7 | — | 1.0 | — | — | 2.7 | 2.0 | 1.5 | — |
| convergent | 28.0 | 15.8 | 25.4 | 14.1 | 10.1 | 17.1 | 15.6 | 7.9 | 12.2 | 5.8 | 7.8 | 3.3 | 10.2 | 25.6 | 18.7 | 10.8 | 9.1 | 11.6 | 4.3 | 5.4 | 3.1 | 1.8 |

|  |  |  |  |  |  |  |  |  |  |  |  |  |  |  |  |  |  |  |  |  |  |  |
|---|---|---|---|---|---|---|---|---|---|---|---|---|---|---|---|---|---|---|---|---|---|---|
| convergent and side | 4.0 | 7.9 | 1.4 | 2.8 | 11.4 | 5.4 | 6.5 | 1.7 | 2.3 | 0.8 | 0.6 | 1.4 | 5.7 | 4.6 | 3.4 | 4.1 | 7.6 | 2.1 | 2.4 | 0.5 | 1.5 | 3.5 |
| bipolar | 12.9 | 29.0 | 11.3 | 15.5 | 15.2 | 17.1 | 15.6 | 26.4 | 22.4 | 10.3 | 10.0 | 9.9 | 7.9 | 17.0 | 19.5 | 13.2 | 6.1 | 18.7 | 7.6 | 9.4 | 13.0 | 13.3 |
| unipolar and opposed | — | 10.5 | 5.6 | 12.7 | 11.4 | 8.5 | 13.0 | 9.6 | 9.4 | 10.7 | 11.1 | 8.2 | 13.0 | 4.8 | 0.9 | 5.1 | 6.1 | 8.8 | 7.3 | — | — | — |
| convergent and opposed | 40.0 | 5.3 | 7.0 | 5.6 | 11.4 | 8.5 | 6.5 | 6.6 | 4.7 | 2.5 | 1.7 | 2.8 | 2.8 | 7.3 | 6.5 | 4.1 | 3.0 | 5.3 | 1.1 | — | 0.8 | 1.8 |
| unipolar and side | 16.0 | 10.5 | — | 8.5 | 6.3 | 17.8 | 11.7 | 10.9 | 13.6 | 11.6 | 11.1 | 12.3 | 16.4 | 12.2 | 13.8 | 9.8 | 16.7 | 13.0 | 25.1 | 18.7 | 13.0 | 13.3 |
| opposed and side | 8.0 | 2.6 | — | — | 2.5 | — | — | 0.3 | 0.5 | 0.4 | 1.1 | 0.7 | 2.3 | 0.8 | 1.0 | 1.5 | 1.4 | 1.4 | 1.6 | 2.5 | 0.8 | — |
| bipolar and side | 8.0 | 5.3 | 11.3 | 14.1 | 5.1 | 9.3 | 12.3 | 13.5 | 7.9 | 6.2 | 10.0 | 11.6 | 7.9 | 9.8 | 11.4 | 9.8 | 15.2 | 12.0 | 10.2 | 10.8 | 5.3 | 5.3 |
| centripetal | 20.0 | 10.5 | 29.6 | 18.3 | 17.7 | 10.1 | 11.7 | 18.5 | 22.9 | 41.5 | 40.0 | 40.6 | 23.7 | 12.0 | 14.1 | 36.2 | 31.8 | 21.8 | 23.7 | 29.1 | 31.3 | 26.3 |
| dominant and centripetal | — | — | 2.8 | 1.4 | 3.8 | 3.1 | — | 2.3 | 0.9 | 6.6 | 3.3 | 6.4 | 8.5 | 1.1 | 1.3 | 2.4 | — | 2.5 | 8.4 | 15.8 | 15.3 | 29.8 |
| N | 25 | 38 | 71 | 71 | 79 | 129 | 77 | 303 | 214 | 242 | 180 | 576 | 177 | 1,608 | 1,361 | 296 | 66 | 284 | 371 | 203 | 131 | 61 |

*Note:* In order to facilitate reading of this table, numbers are rounded to the closest decimal point.

[a] Including points, retouched tools and core management pieces.

[b] Excluding Levallois points and triangular flakes.

## C. Levallois points[c]

| Scar pattern | III | IV | V | VI | VII | VIIa | IX | X | XI | XII | XIII | XIV | XV | XVa | XVb | XVf | XVII | XIX |
|---|---|---|---|---|---|---|---|---|---|---|---|---|---|---|---|---|---|---|
| indeterminate |  |  |  |  |  |  |  |  |  |  |  |  | 3 (1.8) |  |  |  |  |  |
| unipolar |  |  |  |  |  |  |  |  |  |  |  |  | 3 (1.8) |  |  |  |  | 1 |
| convergent | 2 | 2 | 5 |  |  | 4 | 3 | 4 | 2 | 1 | 4 | 8 | 124 (74.7) | 3 | 1 | 2 | 3 | 1 |
| convergent and side |  |  |  |  |  | 1 |  |  |  |  |  |  | 16 (9.6) | 1 |  | 1 | 1 |  |
| bipolar |  | 1 |  |  |  |  |  |  |  | 1 | 1 |  | 1 (0.6) |  |  |  |  |  |
| convergent and opposed |  |  |  |  |  | 2 |  | 2 |  |  | 1 |  | 16 (9.6) |  |  |  |  |  |
| unipolar and side |  |  |  |  |  | 1 |  |  |  |  |  | 1 | 2 (1.2) |  |  |  | 1 |  |
| bipolar and side |  |  |  |  |  | 1 |  |  |  |  | 1 |  | 1 (0.6) |  |  |  |  |  |
| centripetal |  |  |  |  |  |  |  |  |  |  |  | 1 |  |  |  |  |  |  |
| N | 2 | 3 | 5 |  |  | 9 | 4 | 6 | 2 | 2 | 7 | 10 | 166 | 4 | 1 | 3 | 4 | 2 |

*Note:* In order to facilitate reading of this table, numbers are rounded to the closest decimal point.

[c] Frequencies in absolute numbers; for layer XV, relative frequencies in parentheses.

with the notion of lineal reduction methods as the dominant ones in these older assemblages.

Based on the technological criteria suggested by Boëda (1993:398–399) for the Levallois flaking system, several of the detailed classifications of dorsal face scar patterns were collapsed into fewer, broader categories (as was done for the cores in chapter 4). The recalculated frequencies are shown in figure 5.3a.

Within Levallois debitage, the frequencies of the "other" category (which combines the low frequencies observed for the "indeterminate" and "ridge" patterns within the Levallois pieces) are low throughout the whole sequence, as is the case for the unipolar group. A noticeable change in flaking modes occurs within the sequence. The majority (over 50%) of Levallois products in the older layers (XXII–XVa, XIV–XI) were manufactured through a recurrent centripetal exploitation of the core (see details in table 5.3b). From layer X onward there is a marked increase in the frequencies of bipolar scar patterns and a more moderate increase in frequencies of the convergent patterns. High frequencies of bipolar scar patterns were observed also in layer XVf.

The frequency of the "unipolar convergent" category is low to moderate throughout the sequence, with the exception of layer XV, where it reaches 30.2% and is roughly equal to the frequencies of the centripetal and bipolar patterns (figure 5.3a). This is indeed the only assemblage in which Levallois points and triangular flakes—arguably the desired products of this specific Levallois mode (Bar-Yosef et al. 1992; Boëda, Geneste, and Meignen 1990)—are present in significant numbers, forming 23.4% of the Levallois products.[3] The points of layer XV exhibit mainly (but not exclusively) convergent scar patterns (table 5.3c). When these artifacts are omitted from the sample, the frequency of the convergent patterns decreases (table 5.3b). Significantly, the frequency of convergent scar patterns in the layer XV assemblage does not reach those observed in the point-rich units of Kebara, which range between 43.6% and 67.8% (Meignen and Bar-Yosef 1992: tables 9.2, 9.3), or the Negev sites with a high point index (Munday 1976b: tables 6.18, A1.5).

Among the non-Levallois flakes unipolar patterns are the most common (figure 5.3b), with a few exceptions (layers XIII, XIV, and XVII). "Convergent" scar patterns are very rare for this category in all the assemblages.

*Number of Scars on Dorsal Face*

The mean number of dorsal face scars varies between 3.8 (layer XVb) and 5.6 (layer XVII), the mode being 4.6 (table 5.4). When broken down for Levallois and non-Levallois categories, the mean values for Levallois products (ranging from 5.6 in layer IV to 7.6 in layer XVII) are higher than those for the non-Levallois flakes (3.0–4.3, practically below

the range of Levallois products). The number of scars on the dorsal faces of items classified as "indeterminate" falls closer to those observed on the non-Levallois artifacts.

Layer XV exhibits the lowest mean number of dorsal face scars, a pattern that is consistent with the higher use of the Levallois convergent mode in this layer (tables 5.3a–c, 5.4, figure 5.3a, b). The mean number of dorsal face scars on non-retouched Levallois points in this layer falls within the range of the non-Levallois products (N = 164, $\bar{X}$ = 4.2, s.d. = 1.47); when they are omitted from the Levallois sample the mean for this layer increases (N = 1,430, $\bar{X}$ = 6.0, s.d. = 2.3). Triangular flakes, on the other hand, bear an average number of dorsal scars that is closer to the Levallois range (N = 83, $\bar{X}$ = 5.5, s.d. = 2.2).

## Striking Platforms

The role of striking platform properties in the formation of flakes has been amply studied through replication studies and controlled experiments (Andrefsky 1998:88–89; Cotterell and Kamminga 1987; Davis and Shea 1998; Dibble 1998; Dibble and Pelcin 1995; Dibble and Whittaker 1981; Hayden and Hutchings 1989; Pelcin 1997a, 1997b, 1998; Shott et al. 2000; Speth 1972, 1974, 1975). Variable platform traits have been argued to reflect the type of hammer used in flake production or the stage of core reduction. The controlled experiments have revealed some robust co-variation of platform variables with flake morphometric traits. However, "real-life" archaeological assemblages exhibit a tremendous amount of variability in morphological and metric attributes of flakes that is unexplained by the experimentally observed correlations (Dibble 1998; Hovers 1997). These stem from heuristic considerations such as the specific raw material or the morphology of the core at the minute of flake removal, which determines angles of blow, for example. Variability may also be due to the individual preferences of the knappers and their degree of expertise, or to adherence to the socially induced knapping practices of different human groups. The characteristics of debitage striking platforms in the Qafzeh assemblages are described below, followed later in this chapter by an evaluation of their potential effects on flake production.

Replication studies and controlled experiments are not always in agreement on the effects of hammer types on platform characteristics. Identification of the hammer types used for flake production is far from being a simple matter. Diffused bulbs of percussion and lipping on the flake's striking platform are two morphological traits that are usually attributed to soft-hammer percussion (e.g., Bergman and Ohnuma 1983; Ohnuma and Bergman 1982; Wiseman 1993). The occurrence of crushed platforms is used to distinguish the use of hard-hammer techniques in contexts of blade production (e.g., Wiseman 1993: table 5).

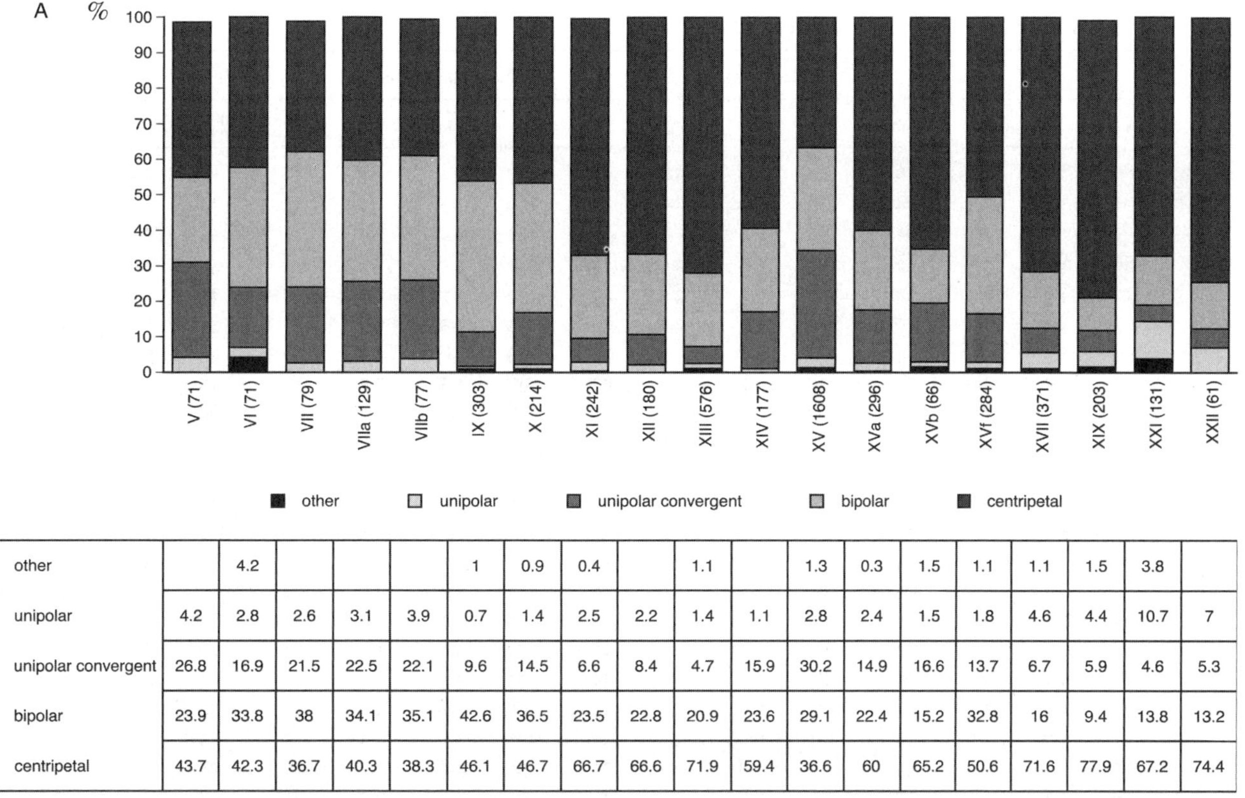

**A**

| | V (71) | VI (71) | VII (79) | VIIa (129) | VIIb (77) | IX (303) | X (214) | XI (242) | XII (180) | XIII (576) | XIV (177) | XV (1608) | XVa (296) | XVb (66) | XVf (284) | XVII (371) | XIX (203) | XXI (131) | XXII (61) |
|---|---|---|---|---|---|---|---|---|---|---|---|---|---|---|---|---|---|---|---|
| other | | 4.2 | | | | 1 | 0.9 | 0.4 | | 1.1 | | 1.3 | 0.3 | 1.5 | 1.1 | 1.1 | 1.5 | 3.8 | |
| unipolar | 4.2 | 2.8 | 2.6 | 3.1 | 3.9 | 0.7 | 1.4 | 2.5 | 2.2 | 1.4 | 1.1 | 2.8 | 2.4 | 1.5 | 1.8 | 4.6 | 4.4 | 10.7 | 7 |
| unipolar convergent | 26.8 | 16.9 | 21.5 | 22.5 | 22.1 | 9.6 | 14.5 | 6.6 | 8.4 | 4.7 | 15.9 | 30.2 | 14.9 | 16.6 | 13.7 | 6.7 | 5.9 | 4.6 | 5.3 |
| bipolar | 23.9 | 33.8 | 38 | 34.1 | 35.1 | 42.6 | 36.5 | 23.5 | 22.8 | 20.9 | 23.6 | 29.1 | 22.4 | 15.2 | 32.8 | 16 | 9.4 | 13.8 | 13.2 |
| centripetal | 43.7 | 42.3 | 36.7 | 40.3 | 38.3 | 46.1 | 46.7 | 66.7 | 66.6 | 71.9 | 59.4 | 36.6 | 60 | 65.2 | 50.6 | 71.6 | 77.9 | 67.2 | 74.4 |

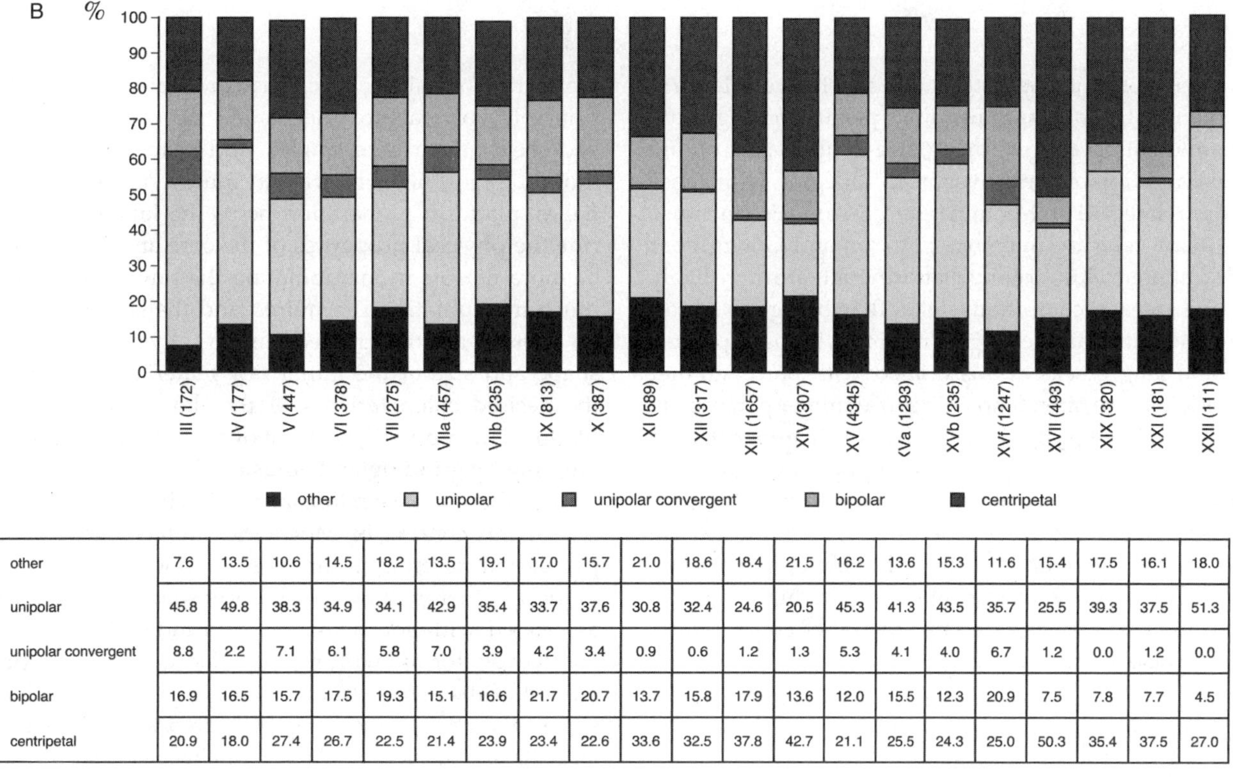

**B**

| | III (172) | IV (177) | V (447) | VI (378) | VII (275) | VIIa (457) | VIIb (235) | IX (813) | X (387) | XI (589) | XII (317) | XIII (1657) | XIV (307) | XV (4345) | XVa (1293) | XVb (235) | XVf (1247) | XVII (493) | XIX (320) | XXI (181) | XXII (111) |
|---|---|---|---|---|---|---|---|---|---|---|---|---|---|---|---|---|---|---|---|---|---|
| other | 7.6 | 13.5 | 10.6 | 14.5 | 18.2 | 13.5 | 19.1 | 17.0 | 15.7 | 21.0 | 18.6 | 18.4 | 21.5 | 16.2 | 13.6 | 15.3 | 11.6 | 15.4 | 17.5 | 16.1 | 18.0 |
| unipolar | 45.8 | 49.8 | 38.3 | 34.9 | 34.1 | 42.9 | 35.4 | 33.7 | 37.6 | 30.8 | 32.4 | 24.6 | 20.5 | 45.3 | 41.3 | 43.5 | 35.7 | 25.5 | 39.3 | 37.5 | 51.3 |
| unipolar convergent | 8.8 | 2.2 | 7.1 | 6.1 | 5.8 | 7.0 | 3.9 | 4.2 | 3.4 | 0.9 | 0.6 | 1.2 | 1.3 | 5.3 | 4.1 | 4.0 | 6.7 | 1.2 | 0.0 | 1.2 | 0.0 |
| bipolar | 16.9 | 16.5 | 15.7 | 17.5 | 19.3 | 15.1 | 16.6 | 21.7 | 20.7 | 13.7 | 15.8 | 17.9 | 13.6 | 12.0 | 15.5 | 12.3 | 20.9 | 7.5 | 7.8 | 7.7 | 4.5 |
| centripetal | 20.9 | 18.0 | 27.4 | 26.7 | 22.5 | 21.4 | 23.9 | 23.4 | 22.6 | 33.6 | 32.5 | 37.8 | 42.7 | 21.1 | 25.5 | 24.3 | 25.0 | 50.3 | 35.4 | 37.5 | 27.0 |

**Figure 5.3** Frequencies of dorsal face scar patterns. A: On Levallois blanks. B: On non-Levallois blanks (see text for details).

**Table 5.4　Mean number of scars on dorsal face of blanks**

| | All | | | | Levallois | | | | Non-Levallois | | | | Indeterminate | | | |
|---|---|---|---|---|---|---|---|---|---|---|---|---|---|---|---|---|
| | N | X̄ | s.d. | s.e. | N | X̄ | s.d. | s.e. | N | X̄ | s.d. | s.e. | N | X̄ | s.d. | s.e. |
| III | 186 | 3.9 | 2.2 | .16 | 25 | 6.4 | 2.4 | .48 | 140 | 3.4 | 1.8 | .16 | 21 | 4.2 | 1.6 | .35 |
| IV | 191 | 3.9 | 1.9 | .14 | 38 | 5.6 | 1.8 | .29 | 140 | 3.3 | 1.5 | .13 | 13 | 5.1 | 1.7 | .47 |
| V | 595 | 4.0 | 2.4 | .84 | 98 | 6.1 | 2.3 | .24 | 453 | 3.4 | 1.6 | .82 | 44 | 4.8 | 1.9 | .28 |
| VI | 386 | 4.2 | 2.3 | .12 | 70 | 6.5 | 2.9 | .34 | 271 | 3.5 | 1.7 | .10 | 45 | 4.6 | 1.8 | .26 |
| VII | 312 | 4.6 | 2.4 | .14 | 79 | 6.7 | 2.3 | .26 | 192 | 3.7 | 1.9 | .14 | 41 | 5.1 | 2.2 | .34 |
| VIIa | 528 | 4.1 | 2.2 | .10 | 129 | 6.2 | 2.1 | .19 | 339 | 3.3 | 1.6 | .09 | 54 | 5.0 | 2.2 | .30 |
| VIIb | 275 | 4.3 | 2.3 | .14 | 76 | 5.7 | 2.1 | .24 | 153 | 3.8 | 2.0 | .16 | 46 | 5.0 | 2.2 | .33 |
| VIII | 99 | 5.2 | 2.9 | .30 | 30 | 6.7 | 3.5 | .63 | 47 | 4.3 | 2.2 | .32 | 15 | 4.8 | 2.1 | .55 |
| IX | 1,004 | 4.4 | 2.3 | .74 | 299 | 6.4 | 2.3 | .13 | 537 | 3.4 | 1.8 | .076 | 168 | 4.5 | 1.8 | .14 |
| X | 545 | 4.6 | 2.5 | .11 | 211 | 6.2 | 2.5 | .17 | 229 | 3.2 | 1.8 | .12 | 105 | 4.3 | 1.7 | .17 |
| XI | 724 | 5.0 | 2.7 | .10 | 229 | 7.1 | 2.6 | .17 | 448 | 4.0 | 2.2 | .10 | 47 | 5.0 | 2.1 | .30 |
| XII | 461 | 5.1 | 3.1 | .14 | 178 | 6.7 | 2.8 | .21 | 246 | 4.2 | 2.9 | .18 | 37 | 3.8 | 2.1 | .34 |
| XIII | 2,095 | 4.9 | 2.7 | .06 | 575 | 7.0 | 2.7 | .11 | 1,304 | 4.1 | 2.2 | .061 | 215 | 4.6 | 2.2 | .15 |
| XIV | 473 | 5.4 | 3.0 | .14 | 177 | 6.5 | 2.5 | .19 | 231 | 4.9 | 3.2 | .21 | 65 | 4.1 | 2.1 | .26 |
| XV | 5,457 | 4.3 | 2.3 | .031 | 1594 | 5.8 | 2.3 | .06 | 3,133 | 3.4 | 2.0 | .04 | 680 | 4.7 | 1.8 | .070 |
| XVa | 1,441 | 4.2 | 2.6 | .07 | 294 | 6.8 | 3.1 | .18 | 968 | 3.3 | 1.8 | .06 | 177 | 4.8 | 1.8 | .14 |
| XVb | 273 | 3.8 | 2.0 | .12 | 65 | 5.8 | 2.1 | .26 | 180 | 3.0 | 1.3 | .10 | 28 | 4.6 | 2.4 | .44 |
| XVf | 1,371 | 4.1 | 2.2 | .06 | 283 | 6.3 | 2.4 | .14 | 922 | 3.4 | 1.7 | .06 | 163 | 4.3 | 1.6 | .12 |
| XVII | 841 | 5.6 | 3.5 | .12 | 373 | 7.6 | 3.7 | .19 | 406 | 4.1 | 2.3 | .12 | 62 | 3.9 | 2.5 | .32 |
| XIX | 481 | 4.6 | 2.6 | .12 | 201 | 6.0 | 2.3 | .16 | 245 | 3.7 | 2.4 | .15 | 35 | 3.1 | 1.8 | .31 |
| XXI | 297 | 4.7 | 2.5 | .15 | 131 | 6.0 | 2.4 | .21 | 138 | 3.8 | 2.1 | .18 | 28 | 2.7 | 1.6 | .30 |
| XXII | 158 | 5.1 | 2.9 | .23 | 56 | 6.8 | 3.3 | .44 | 91 | 4.1 | 2.2 | .23 | 11 | 3.8 | 1.7 | .52 |

*Note*: Only scars ≥ 0.5 cm in maximum dimension were counted.

However, none of the criteria are conclusive. Platform traits caused by hard-hammer direct percussion (e.g., bulb measurements, platform lipping, and the formation of ring cracks) are variable and overlap to a degree with those usually related to soft-hammer percussion (Pelcin 1997a with many relevant references; Sharon and Goren-Inbar 1998). Differences in striking platform traits are more likely probabilistic and continuous rather than being linked categorically with hammer type. Prominent bulbs of percussion and ring cracks are associated with hard-hammer percussion more often than with soft-hammer percussion, and the typical lipping induced by soft-hammer flaking techniques is less common within a population of flakes produced by hard hammers. According to this thinking, most striking platforms in the Qafzeh assemblages are likely associated with direct hard-hammer percussion. They regularly have prominent bulbs, although platform preparation may have weakened the latter effect. Bulbar scars are also a common feature.[4]

*Types of Striking Platform*

How much a platform is modified and prepared prior to flake removal and the specific ways in which it is shaped are technological practices that are not determined by principles of fracture mechanics. On the other hand, because platform size, angles, and shapes influence the morphological and metric attributes of the detached flakes, platform preparation helps the knapper to override the physical properties of the core and flakes and to be more flexible in manipulating the raw material. How much manipulation is required and the specific ways to go about it are determined, among other things, by the shape and size of the initial raw material block and by the desired characteristics of the flakes. Techniques of platform manipulation consist of faceting, polishing, and blunting by grinding and abrasion (Marder 2002 and references therein; Tixier, Inizan, and Roche 1980).

In the context of Mousterian direct hard-hammer percussion, faceting is the most pertinent shaping technique, as other methods of platform shaping are typically associated with soft-hammer, often indirect, percussion. Faceted platforms (with multiple facets caused by preparation of the core's striking platform) thus reflect intensive preparation, which may be geared toward obtaining large flakes (see below). Among the faceted platforms the *chapeau de gendarme* type indicates the most investment, as it involves detailed shaping of the core platform and much attention to preparing the angles and platform dimensions that would determine the morphology of the resultant flake. It has been suggested that, due to the protruding and narrow striking platform, this type of striking platform is associated with unipolar convergent Levallois flaking and with the production of Levallois points (Bar-Yosef et al. 1992:512). Dihedral platforms (with only two facets) suggest a lower investment in platform shaping by detaching fewer, larger, and less accurately placed preparatory flakes; hence, control over the resultant flake morphology is less tight.

The frequencies of prepared platforms (namely, faceted including *chapeau de gendarme* as well as dihedral) are represented by values of the Faceting Index (IF) in table 5.5. The restricted indexc (IFs) shows the frequencies of well prepared platforms, i.e. those defined as faceted and as *chapeau de gendarme.*

Both Levallois and non-Levallois flakes exhibit a diversity of striking platform types (figure 5.4). Patterns within each technological group are broadly repetitive across layers. The only exception is the non-Levallois group in layer VIIa, which exhibits unusual frequencies of striking platform types.

The most frequent category within the non-Levallois group is "missing." Its abundance reflects the high occurrence of proximal breaks in this technological category. Among existing platforms the dominant type is plain, suggesting a simple preparation of the core striking platform. Punctiform platforms are more common in non-Levallois than in Levallois debitage, but their frequencies are always low and cannot be associated with any systematic use of soft hammers or of punch techniques. Faceted platforms, combined with the dihedral and *chapeau de gendarme,* occur in moderate frequencies. The occurrence of *chapeau de gendarme* on non-Levallois pieces is, as expected, sporadic (Tixier, Inizan, and Roche 1980:105).

Cortical platforms are found in higher frequencies within the non-Levallois component of the assemblages (figure 5.4). Such platforms are often taken to represent initial stages of core reduction, when the core still bears large amount of cortex. At Qafzeh, flakes with cortical platforms are not associated exclusively with highly cortical flakes (table 5.6) and do not necessarily occur on artifacts associated with core maintenance (e.g., *éclats débordants* or naturally backed flakes). The occurrence of cortical platforms is consistent with continuous process of cortex removal from cores after the initial testing and decortication stages (which seem to have been carried out off-site; see above). This is corroborated by the presence of many cores that bear cortex residues on at least one face. In the case of Levallois cores, this is usually the preparation face.

Levallois flakes are expected to have a sizable striking platform, which also bears evidence to the intensity of preparation of the core's striking platform. Among the technological criteria defining the Levallois method, Boëda (1993:395–399, fig. 7b) specifies that the point of impact of the hammer on the core should be a few millimeters on the inner side of the *charnière* (i.e., the ridge forming the core's striking platform), with the axis of flaking perpendicular to the core's face. Levallois debitage in all the Qafzeh assemblages is characterized by the high

**Table 5.6  Amount of dorsal face cortex on pieces with cortical platforms**

| Layer | N | 1 | 2 | 3 | 4 | 5 |
|---|---|---|---|---|---|---|
| III | 3 | — | 3 | — | — | — |
| IV | 7 | — | 6 | — | 1 | — |
| V | 6 | — | 5 | 1 | — | — |
| VI | 6 | 1 | 2 | 3 | — | — |
| VII | 11 | 1 | 7 | 1 | 2 | — |
| VIIa | 20 | — | 14 | 3 | 1 | 2 |
| VIIb | 3 | 2 | 1 | — | — | — |
| IX | 21 | 1 | 15 | 4 | — | 1 |
| X | 10 | — | 7 | 2 | 1 | — |
| XI | 15 | — | 13 | 2 | — | — |
| XII | 17 | 2 | 11 | 2 | — | 2 |
| XIII | 47 | 2 | 35 | 9 | — | 1 |
| XIV | 11 | — | 6 | 2 | — | 3 |
| XV | 189 | 8 | 109 | 38 | 18 | 16 |
| XVa | 58 | 3 | 41 | 7 | 5 | 2 |
| XVb | 10 | — | 10 | — | — | — |
| XVf | 23 | — | 14 | 6 | 3 | — |
| XVII | 25 | — | 18 | 6 | 1 | — |
| XIX | 15 | 1 | 10 | 2 | 1 | 1 |
| XXI | 11 | 4 | 4 | — | 2 | 1 |
| XXII | 6 | 2 | 3 | — | 1 | — |

*Note:* Frequencies in absolute numbers: 1: 0%, 2: 1–25%, 3: 26–50%, 4: 51–75%, 5: 76–100% of dorsal face cortical cover.

**Table 5.5  Qafzeh assemblages: IF and IFs (all flakes and tools)**

| Layer | IF | IFs | Layer | IF | IFs |
|---|---|---|---|---|---|
| III | 42.85 | 31.97 | XIII | 49.37 | 39.32 |
| IV | 44.81 | 29.87 | XIV | 56.46 | 47.19 |
| V | 43.50 | 31.34 | XV | 55.78 | 44.24 |
| VI | 43.70 | 32.67 | XVa | 40.57 | 27.36 |
| VII | 49.58 | 41.10 | XVb | 37.28 | 23.24 |
| VIIa | 49.45 | 37.74 | XVf | 36.43 | 24.40 |
| VIIb | 54.59 | 44.90 | XVII | 44.16 | 30.04 |
| VIII | 66.66 | 49.33 | XVIII | 37.14 | 22.86 |
| IX | 57.10 | 45.85 | XIX | 39.07 | 30.59 |
| X | 49.35 | 39.79 | XX | 31.82 | 27.27 |
| XI | 51.41 | 38.30 | XXI | 37.60 | 29.91 |
| XII | 52.40 | 43.05 | XXII | 28.90 | 20.30 |

*Note:* Counts in Appendix 5.

occurrence of faceted platforms (figure 5.4). The occurrence of *chapeau de gendarme* platforms in highest frequencies in layer VIIa is somewhat unexpected, since recurrent convergent flaking is more common in layer XV (figure 5.3, table 5.5).

The few punctiform platforms found on Levallois flakes are likely due to knapping mishaps.

The frequencies of crushed and broken away (nonexistent) platforms are similarly low in both Levallois and non-Levallois debitage. The appearance of crushed platforms in low frequencies in all the assemblages suggests that they mainly result from knapping accidents. Crushing of the striking platform results from hard-hammer percussion at significantly high loads (Speth 1972:38) or from improper placing of the hammerstone on the core (i.e., directly on the *charnière* (Boëda 1993:395), and its occurrence as an intentional technique would be inconsistent with the technological practices involved in Levallois flaking. Accidental crushing of striking platforms may also be the cause of broken platforms, but it is difficult to determine whether these resulted from improper knapping or later use of the flake.

*Angle of Striking Platform*

The properties of the exterior platform angle (EPA), measured at the intersection of the platform surface and the exterior surface of the core (Dibble and Whittaker 1981: fig. 2), are formed before detachment of the flake. All experimental studies of the effects of direct hard-hammer percussion reveal a robust relationship between EPA, on the one hand, and platform thickness and flake length, on the other. EPA in itself (Dibble and Whittaker 1981; Pelcin 1997b) or with other variables (Cochrane 2003) controls the mode of flake termination (i.e., whether it is feathered, hinged, or regular); together with hammer mass and velocity and with angle of blow, it also affects flake length, which increases with increase in EPA values (Dibble and Whittaker 1981; Speth 1975). Yet mechanical requirements of fracture propagation restrict the range of EPA that can be employed for successful flake detachment, so that the relationship between the variables is not linear. When values of EPA increase, variation of flake length increases and the relationship between this variable, platform thickness, and EPA loses its predictive power (Dibble and Whittaker 1981; Speth 1972, 1974). Data on EPA are not dealt with in the current study, as I did not attempt to test further the relationship between EPA and other flake variables.

Several experimental studies have indicated weak negative correlation of variable strength between EPA and interior platform angle (IPA), such that IPA decreases when EPA increases (Cochrane 2003; Dibble and Whittaker 1981). Unlike EPA, the IPA, defined as the angle formed between the platform surface and a line through the point of percussion to the base of the bulb (Dibble and Whittaker 1981: fig. 2), is affected or determined by the detachment of the flake. Most experimental studies identified a direct influence of IPA on the morphometric properties of the flake. On the other hand, IPA is indicative of the fracture initiation type and helps to distinguish between bending and Hertzian flakes (Cotterell and Kamminga 1987:686–691; Pelcin 1997b:1110). It also responds, albeit only partially, to the angle of blow (Dibble and Whittaker 1981). Values of IPA thus provide some insights about the actual process and technique of flaking.

Measurements of IPA (see appendix 3) are often subjective. Regardless of the methods employed, their execution is problematic due to bulb traits (Andrefsky 1998:89–92; Cochrane 2003; Dibble and Whittaker 1981). In this study, angles were measured with a simple goniometer. Each IPA was measured three times, and if the measurements differed by less than five degrees, the results were averaged. Given that a single analyst conducted the research, this low-tech approach should not rule out inter- and intra-assemblage comparisons that are of interpretative value.

The measured angles were grouped into several categories, as shown in figure 5.5. Levallois and non-Levallois blanks show similar distributions with practically identical means and ranges within and among layers. Values of IPA are very rarely lower than 95° and reach as high as 135°. Two frequency peaks (105°–108° and 113°–117°) occur most often within this range, but some variability can be observed. Thus, the curves for layers VIIb, XI–XIII, XVII, and XXI differ from other assemblages in the relatively high frequencies of slightly more obtuse angles, while in layers XIX and XXII there are higher frequencies of relatively acute angles (91°–104°). The apparent stratigraphic clustering of the distributions in assemblages XV, XVa, and XVf may be associated with enhanced production of elongated pieces.[5]

What do such patterns tell us about the flaking techniques? IPA is not a straightforward expression of the complex vectors operating in hard-hammer percussion (Speth 1972, 1975), and it is not a direct result of the angle of blow. IPA values are not a good predictor of the exact angle of blow. Nevertheless, the restricted range of IPA values of the Qafzeh blanks suggests a high degree of control by the knappers over the products, since "with increased control we might also expect increased reproducibility" (Speth 1972:54).

In large part, the range of angle measurements in the analysis overlaps with the range corresponding to experimental angles of blow between 65° and 75° across a range of platform thickness values (Dibble and Whittaker1981: fig. 4, tab. 2; Pelcin 1997b: fig. 3) and to "oblique incidence" in the process of flake removal off a

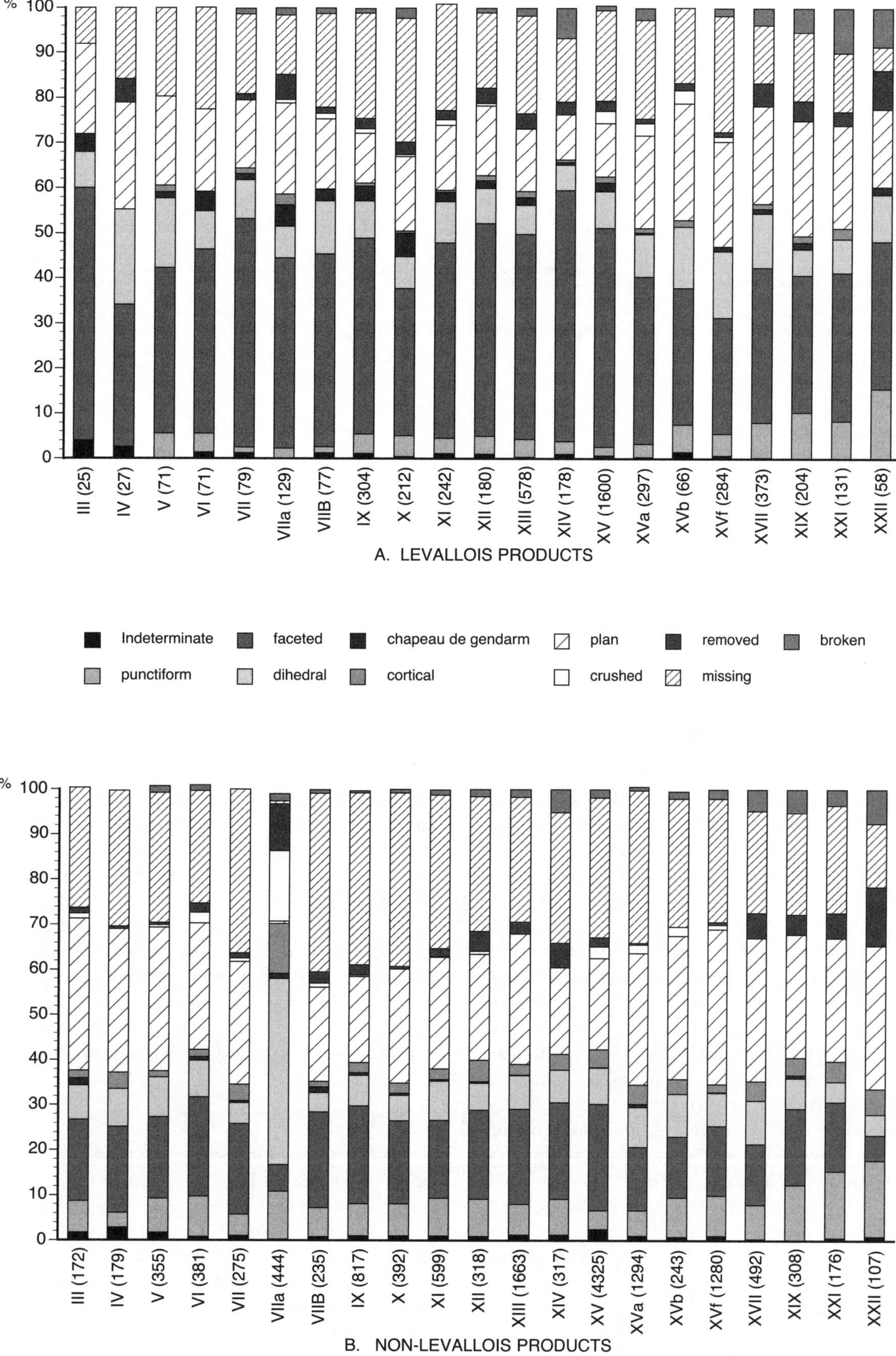

**Figure 5.4** Frequencies of striking platform types of blanks and retouched tools.

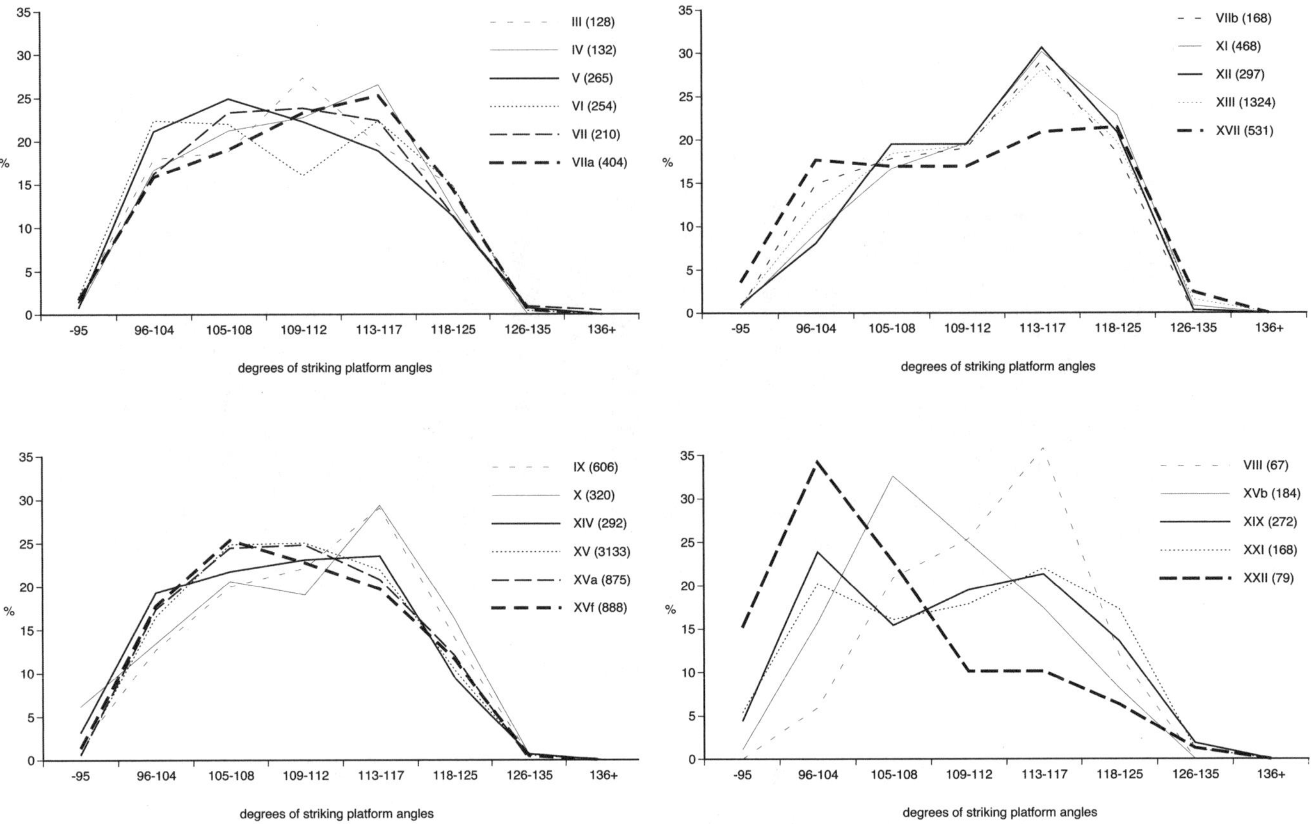

**Figure 5.5** Frequency distributions of interior striking platform angles in the Qafzeh layers.

surface (Speth 1972; see below). Such values of angle of blow would be consistent with the formation of Hertzian flake initiations in general (see above) and with Levallois flaking in particular, as the removal of sub-parallel flakes off a Levallois core involves angles within this restricted range.

Much experimental work carried out on flaking mechanics is concerned with normal incidence of stress waves by vertical percussion. In archaeological contexts, however, spalling off a core involves oblique incidence of the stress wave, in which a flake is detached from the face immediately adjacent to the point of impact that separates the flake from the core surface (Speth 1972:49). The angle of incidence of a stress wave is consciously manipulated by the knapper by varying the angle at which he strikes the platform of the flake and by varying the angle between the platform and the adjacent free face between the processes of core preparation and rejuvenation. IPA is thus influenced by core geometry and by preparation of the core surface and striking platform. Core preparation is expressed by the residue of the core's striking platform on the flake (i.e., the flake's striking platform). This implies that some patterned variation of IPA according to platform types should be expected.

In all the assemblages, the most dramatic difference is between plain, relatively obtuse platforms and faceted ones (table 5.7). Both punctiform and *chapeau de gendarme* platforms show relatively acute means, the latter often exhibiting the most acute angles of all platform types. As discussed above, punctiform platforms are probably accidental in most cases and the extreme angles can be interpreted as resulting from a mistake on the part of the knapper. In contrast, the relatively low angle values of the *chapeau de gendarme* type must be considered to result from the specific preparation of this platform type.

*Platform Size*

Table 5.8 presents the mean dimensions of striking platforms according to platform type (see appendix 3 for measurement system). *Chapeau de gendarme* platforms are in all cases the broadest. Faceted platforms, and sometimes dihedral ones (e.g., layers V, VI, X, XVa, and XXI) are somewhat narrower. Plain platforms are by and large the narrowest type. On the other hand, while in many assemblages *chapeau de gendarme* platforms obtain maximum depth, in other instances (e.g., layers VIIa, X, XI, XV, XVf, XVII, and XXI) faceted, dihedral, and (rarely)

**Table 5.7   Means of angles by striking platform type**

| Layer | 1 | | 2 | | 3 | | 4 | | 5 | | 6 | |
|---|---|---|---|---|---|---|---|---|---|---|---|---|
| | N | $\bar{X}$ | N | $\bar{X}$ | N | $\bar{X}$ | N | $\bar{X}$ | N | $\bar{X}$ | N | $\bar{X}$ |
| III | 11 | 107.09 | 45 | 108.44 | 14 | 109.14 | 3 | 104.33 | 3 | 102.00 | 63 | 110.03 |
| IV | 7 | 111.00 | 43 | 108.30 | 22 | 109.27 | — | — | 6 | 108.67 | 61 | 109.44 |
| V | 32 | 104.84 | 92 | 108.15 | 38 | 108.58 | 1 | 101.00 | 6 | 110.00 | 128 | 108.58 |
| VI | 34 | 104.88 | 98 | 107.30 | 34 | 106.35 | 2 | 107.50 | 6 | 104.83 | 110 | 110.55 |
| VII | 14 | 104.36 | 95 | 107.52 | 19 | 109.26 | 2 | 104.50 | 9 | 107.33 | 85 | 111.14 |
| VIIa | 26 | 112.54 | 166 | 108.60 | 54 | 109.70 | 5 | 108.40 | 18 | 111.94 | 161 | 110.52 |
| VIIb | 16 | 107.44 | 81 | 109.65 | 19 | 109.68 | 5 | 111.00 | 2 | 111.00 | 61 | 111.54 |
| VIII | 2 | 114.00 | 33 | 109.82 | 10 | 110.30 | 4 | 112.50 | 2 | 110.50 | 18 | 111.67 |
| IX | 68 | 107.63 | 304 | 109.27 | 80 | 110.24 | 16 | 107.94 | 21 | 108.90 | 185 | 111.46 |
| X | 32 | 108.31 | 135 | 109.13 | 35 | 111.57 | 13 | 107.38 | 8 | 110.00 | 129 | 111.47 |
| XI | 50 | 108.30 | 203 | 110.70 | 72 | 111.61 | 7 | 108.14 | 14 | 112.07 | 172 | 112.99 |
| XII | 32 | 107.16 | 143 | 110.52 | 33 | 111.30 | 4 | 106.75 | 17 | 110.00 | 100 | 112.35 |
| XIII | 121 | 106.17 | 581 | 110.06 | 150 | 111.56 | 12 | 111.00 | 46 | 109.63 | 535 | 112.20 |
| XIV | 29 | 105.41 | 163 | 107.81 | 33 | 108.76 | 1 | 93.00 | 12 | 107.25 | 76 | 109.51 |
| XV | — | — | 1,569 | 108.20 | 432 | 109.71 | 28 | 108.46 | 146 | 108.79 | 958 | 109.51 |
| XVa | 70 | 107.59 | 276 | 107.59 | 134 | 109.22 | 2 | 104.00 | 50 | 109.24 | 413 | 109.69 |
| XVb | 23 | 105.00 | 52 | 106.71 | 31 | 109.29 | — | — | 10 | 103.80 | 91 | 108.74 |
| XVf | 122 | 106.85 | 252 | 107.52 | 130 | 108.79 | 5 | 105.80 | 20 | 110.85 | 481 | 109.28 |
| XVII | 48 | 100.35 | 186 | 108.64 | 91 | 110.96 | 4 | 108.50 | 25 | 110.72 | 225 | 110.99 |
| XIX | 54 | 98.81 | 104 | 106.09 | 31 | 107.39 | 5 | 109.00 | 13 | 109.54 | 119 | 110.47 |
| XXI | 34 | 104.79 | 67 | 108.73 | 18 | 108.94 | — | — | 10 | 106.30 | 73 | 109.40 |
| XXII | 16 | 96.19 | 25 | 101.00 | 9 | 103.67 | 1 | 92.00 | 5 | 108.20 | 39 | 105.15 |

*Note*: 1: punctiform; 2: faceted; 3: dihedral; 4: *chapeau de gendarme*; 5: cortical; 6: plain.

cortical platforms are deeper. Breadth and depth of striking platforms of Levallois debitage, among which faceted platform are more common (figure 5.4) are significantly larger than those of non-Levallois debitage (Kolmogorov-Smirnov tests show differences at significance levels of $p < .005$ in all assemblages but V and VI). More extensively modified platforms are clearly broader and deeper than untreated ones.

## Morphometrics

Experimental work and replications of Levallois reduction systems have demonstrated that Levallois products tend to be larger than non-Levallois products in the same assemblage. Geneste (1985:262), for example, views this tendency as one of the major reasons for the use of Levallois flaking: "*On cerne ici une des justifications du concept Levallois: la production de supports d'une qualité moyenne supérieure à celle d'un débitage inorganisé où la forme et les dimensions seraiet obtenues 'au hazard.'*" ("One discerns here one of the justifications for the use of a Levallois concept: The production of blanks of better quality compared to the blanks produced through an unorganized production system, in which the shape and size of the products are obtained incidentally.") Differences in size between Levallois and non-Levallois types of debitage are common in many Eurasian assemblages (e.g., Dibble 1995c: tab. 6; Geneste 1985, 1988; Hovers 1998a; Goren-Inbar 1990a; Meignen 1993; Munday 1976b).

Metric measurements of the Qafzeh assemblages are variable. Mean length varies from 27.57 mm (layer V) to 45.44 mm (layer XII), width ranges between 23.06 mm (layer III) and 33.37 mm (layer XXI), and thickness varies from 5.88 mm (layer III) to 8.38 mm (layer XIV) (table 5.9a–c, column 3). Artifact sizes change cyclically throughout the sequence. Larger artifacts occur in the older (XXII–XVII) and mid-sequence (XV–XI, IX) assemblages, in which the artifacts have the largest means for both length and width. Smaller blanks occur in assemblages XVf–XVa and VIIb–III (table 5.9, figure 5.6). Such changes in blank dimensions could result from variation through time in initial size of raw material packages. Alternately, they may stem from differences in flaking methods and modes, which may result in flakes with differing dorsal face scar patterns and of smaller size. This possibility is further explored below.

As both mean length and width of Levallois debitage are higher than those of regular flakes, their mean "flake size" (computed as MAXLEN*MAXWID) is significantly larger than that of regular debitage in all the assemblages

**Table 5.8  Mean breadth and depth of striking platforms types, IF and IFs**

**A.  Platform breadth**

| Layer | Striking platform type | | | | | | | | | | | | | | | | | |
| --- | --- | --- | --- | --- | --- | --- | --- | --- | --- | --- | --- | --- | --- | --- | --- | --- | --- | --- |
| | Faceted | | | Dihedral | | | Chap. de Gend. | | | Cortical | | | Plain | | | K-W test[a] | | IF[b] | IFs |
| | N | X̄ | s.d. | N | X̄ | s.d. | N | X̄ | s.d. | N | X̄ | s.d | N | X̄ | s.d. | H | p | | |
| III | | | | | | | | | | | | | | | | | | 42.85 | 31.97 |
| IV | | | | | | | | | | | | | | | | | | 44.81 | 29.87 |
| V | 132 | 16.66 | 7.68 | 54 | 16.88 | 7.13 | 1 | 35.10 | | 8 | 13.82 | 7.48 | 2.64 | 173 | 12.10 | 42.60 | <.0001 | 43.50 | 31.34 |
| VI | 89 | 18.39 | 10.21 | 33 | 19.95 | 9.35 | 2 | 37.15 | 2.47 | 5 | 11.04 | 5.26 | 104 | 11.69 | 6.22 | 37.05 | <.0001 | 43.70 | 32.67 |
| VII | | | | | | | | | | | | | | | | | | 49.58 | 41.10 |
| VIIa | 160 | 22.97 | 15.16 | 53 | 19.06 | 8.38 | 5 | 37.80 | 17.75 | 10 | 28.23 | 19.73 | 151 | 14.47 | 8.66 | 57.79 | <.0001 | 49.49 | 37.74 |
| VIIb | | | | | | | | | | | | | | | | | | 54.59 | 44.90 |
| VIII | | | | | | | | | | | | | | | | | | 66.66 | 49.33 |
| IX | 277 | 22.18 | 11.06 | 76 | 21.94 | 8.83 | 15 | 30.75 | 9.69 | 18 | 17.01 | 7.68 | 163 | 14.67 | 8.88 | 91.57 | <.0001 | 57.10 | 45.85 |
| X | 134 | 18.76 | 8.48 | 36 | 21.50 | 8.62 | 13 | 35.77 | 9.62 | 7 | 17.56 | 9.62 | 132 | 11.70 | 6.27 | 96.26 | <.0001 | 49.35 | 39.79 |
| XI | 186 | 21.80 | 9.46 | 74 | 19.34 | 8.97 | 7 | 27.41 | 7.82 | 10 | 18.19 | 7.39 | 153 | 12.33 | 7.73 | 105.93 | <.0001 | 51.41 | 38.30 |
| XII | | | | | | | | | | | | | | | | | | 52.40 | 43.05 |
| XIII | 554 | 20.96 | 9.42 | 155 | 19.37 | 9.20 | 12 | 31.82 | 8.21 | 42 | 17.17 | 10.34 | 502 | 11.88 | 7.05 | 304.67 | <.0001 | 49.37 | 39.32 |
| XIV | | | | | | | | | | | | | | | | | | 56.46 | 47.19 |
| XV | 1,739 | 21.92 | 9.54 | 460 | 20.87 | 8.45 | 34 | 35.07 | 9.81 | 160 | 16.97 | 9.72 | 1,012 | 13.76 | 7.49 | 631.57 | <.0001 | 55.78 | 44.24 |
| XVa | 280 | 20.72 | 8.58 | 139 | 21.31 | 9.84 | 2 | 40.95 | 3.32 | 50 | 16.41 | 6.78 | 417 | 12.22 | 6.74 | 228.03 | <.0001 | 40.57 | 27.36 |
| XVb | | | | | | | | | | | | | | | | | | 37.28 | 23.24 |
| XVf | 249 | 19.42 | 9.85 | 134 | 18.91 | 7.65 | 5 | 28.14 | 13.16 | 16 | 16.71 | 6.39 | 482 | 12.36 | 6.67 | 160.65 | <.0001 | 36.43 | 24.40 |
| XVII | 191 | 21.84 | 9.05 | 92 | 19.97 | 8.38 | 4 | 27.65 | 10.34 | 24 | 15.35 | 8.78 | 236 | 13.79 | 7.50 | 109.16 | <.0001 | 44.16 | 30.04 |
| XVIII | | | | | | | | | | | | | | | | | | 37.14 | 22.86 |
| XIX | 109 | 21.50 | 9.74 | 33 | 18.42 | 8.15 | 5 | 42.08 | 19.22 | 14 | 20.51 | 12.95 | 127 | 14.59 | 8.68 | 44.92 | <.0001 | 39.07 | 30.59 |
| XX | | | | | | | | | | | | | | | | | | 31.82 | 27.27 |
| XXI | 69 | 23.55 | 11.45 | 18 | 26.31 | 11.03 | | | | 11 | 18.35 | 14.32 | 73 | 15.45 | 10.31 | 33.20 | <.0001 | 37.60 | 29.91 |
| XXII | | | | | | | | | | | | | | | | | | 28.90 | 20.30 |

[a] Kruskal-Wallis nonparametric one-way analysis of variance. Does not include punctiform, indeterminate, crushed, broken, or missing platforms.
[b] IF calculated from counts in table 5.14.

**B. Platform thickness**

Layer

Striking platform type

| | Faceted | | | Dihedral | | | Chap. de Gend. | | | Cortical | | | Plain | | | K-W test[c] | |
|---|---|---|---|---|---|---|---|---|---|---|---|---|---|---|---|---|---|
| | N | $\bar{X}$ | s.d. | N | $\bar{X}$ | s.d. | N | $\bar{X}$ | s.d. | N | $\bar{X}$ | s.d | N | $\bar{X}$ | s.d. | H | p |
| V | 144 | 4.60 | 2.37 | 55 | 4.03 | 1.68 | 1 | 5.10 | | 8 | 5.18 | 3.57 | 186 | 3.25 | 2.01 | 44.34 | <.0001 |
| VI | 97 | 4.75 | 2.68 | 34 | 4.52 | 2.37 | 2 | 5.30 | 3.54 | 6 | 2.60 | 1.26 | 112 | 3.74 | 2.31 | 16.03 | .0030 |
| VIIa | 164 | 5.08 | 2.47 | 54 | 4.63 | 2.81 | 5 | 4.88 | 2.11 | 11 | 6.37 | 3.44 | 160 | 4.31 | 2.68 | 19.57 | .0006 |
| IX | 305 | 5.33 | 2.40 | 79 | 4.86 | 2.43 | 17 | 5.35 | 1.79 | 19 | 4.77 | 1.80 | 186 | 4.43 | 2.80 | 31.20 | <.0001 |
| X | 141 | 4.55 | 2.05 | 37 | 4.60 | 2.13 | 13 | 5.97 | 1.68 | 8 | 5.95 | 4.78 | 133 | 3.74 | 2.38 | 26.78 | <.0001 |
| XI | 209 | 5.33 | 2.33 | 74 | 4.72 | 2.79 | 7 | 4.30 | 1.61 | 12 | 4.85 | 2.73 | 179 | 3.93 | 2.84 | 52.95 | <.0001 |
| XIII | 612 | 5.47 | 2.39 | 158 | 5.04 | 2.72 | 12 | 6.12 | 1.42 | 44 | 5.50 | 3.12 | 558 | 3.99 | 2.42 | 148.62 | <.0001 |
| XV | 1,782 | 5.38 | 2.28 | 472 | 5.11 | 2.48 | 33 | 5.37 | 1.97 | 165 | 5.27 | 3.18 | 1,057 | 4.27 | 2.43 | 227.46 | <.0001 |
| XVa | 290 | 5.04 | 2.48 | 141 | 4.73 | 2.46 | 2 | 8.20 | 2.55 | 52 | 4.75 | 2.74 | 437 | 3.55 | 2.10 | 96.54 | <.0001 |
| XVf | 266 | 4.81 | 2.16 | 134 | 4.13 | 2.16 | 5 | 4.64 | 1.89 | 17 | 4.61 | 2.00 | 498 | 3.68 | 2.22 | 66.34 | <.0001 |
| XVII | 192 | 5.97 | 2.48 | 93 | 5.60 | 3.14 | 4 | 5.25 | 3.04 | 24 | 4.96 | 2.28 | 237 | 4.52 | 3.02 | 52.30 | <.0001 |
| XIX | 113 | 5.44 | 2.41 | 33 | 5.22 | 3.78 | 5 | 6.86 | 1.70 | 15 | 5.37 | 3.40 | 136 | 4.63 | 3.11 | 18.33 | .0011 |
| XXI | 70 | 6.34 | 2.45 | 18 | 7.41 | 3.62 | | | | 11 | 5.42 | 3.00 | 74 | 5.01 | 3.38 | 19.30 | .0002 |

[c]Kruskal-Wallis nonparametric one-way analysis of variance. Does not include punctiform, indeterminate, crushed, broken, or missing platforms.

(table 5.9, figure 5.6) (Kolmogorov-Smirnov test results are significant at $p < .001$ in all the assemblages). On the whole, length and width are positively but weakly correlated (Spearman's *rho* fluctuates between 0.28 in assemblages III and V and 0.63 and 0.66 in layers XVII and XXI, respectively; analyses carried out on samples of unbroken artifacts, with N > 100; all significant at $p < .05$).

Because length and width do co-vary, I have chosen only one representative dimension (length) for a more detailed analysis. Length distributions for Levallois and non-Levallois debitage form two distinct curves throughout the sequence. The frequency distributions of non-Levallois flakes are typified in most assemblages by a distinct peak of short flakes (< 30 mm) (figure 5.7), forming between 30% and over 50% of this sub-population,

with a few larger flakes occurring in reduced frequencies. The frequency distributions of Levallois flakes exhibit a larger dispersion of length.

Unlike length and width, thickness does not vary considerably between Levallois and non-Levallois debitage (layer VIIb being an exception), and their mean values are close and sometimes overlapping (table 5.9c, figure 5.6). This is somewhat surprising, as the common notion (e.g., Nelson 1991) is that Levallois flakes are thin and provide a sharper working edge compared to non-Levallois blanks. The data presented here suggest that the thinness of Levallois blanks at Qafzeh may be relative to flake size. Levallois blanks were a technological optimization by which two properties were achieved: flakes of large size, combined with a thin and sharp working edge. This assured both long and effective use lives for the flakes (see also chapter 7).

## Core Management Pieces

Under the definition of "core management pieces" are included all the blanks that were removed off the core in order to prepare it for further flake removals. Such elements could then be used (either as blanks or as retouched tools), but the original cause for their detachment was either to maintain the appropriate core geometry during the item's use life (by readjusting it after phases of intensive flake detachment) or to compensate for flaking accidents (see also Ekshtain 2006). In this scenario, the properties of the artifacts do not reflect a desired, preplanned end goal. Rather, the morphometric traits of these items were determined heuristically during reduction, typically influenced by the methods and modes of flaking, and can be associated with various stages of core reduction (Boëda 1986; Boëda, Geneste, and Meignen 1990; Hovers 1998a). In the absence of refitting, the varying frequencies of the specific categories are a most informative source for reconstructing the reduction sequences that were operative on the site.

Table 5.1 presents the expected types of core management pieces. Flakes were selected to be transformed into cores because they either presented a priori the necessary geometric properties (in the case of Levallois cores-on-flakes), or such properties were not deemed important for expedient flaking (in the case of non-Levallois cores-on-flakes). Thus, no core management pieces are expected to originate from this specific *chaîne opératoire*. Any such elements that are found in the assemblages are perceived as resulting from the use of various methods of the recurrent Levallois mode, or from the application of non-Levallois flaking systems, both carried out on large blocks (as opposed to flakes) of raw material.

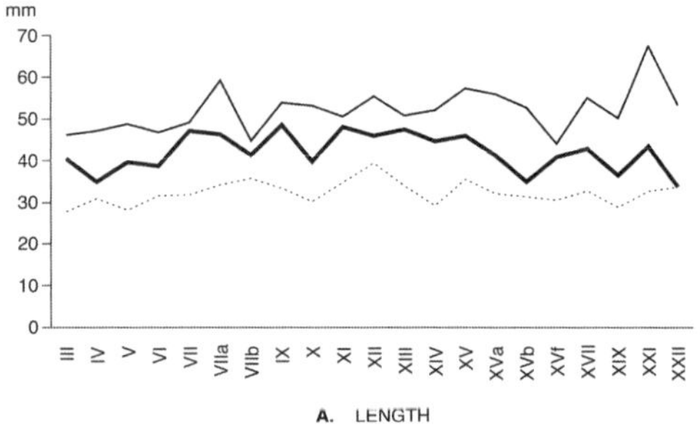



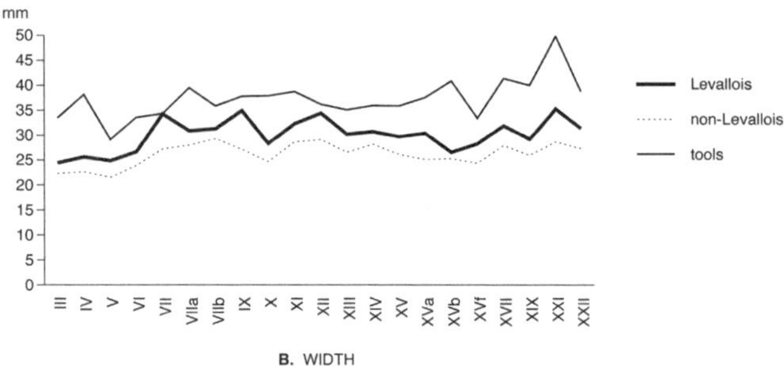



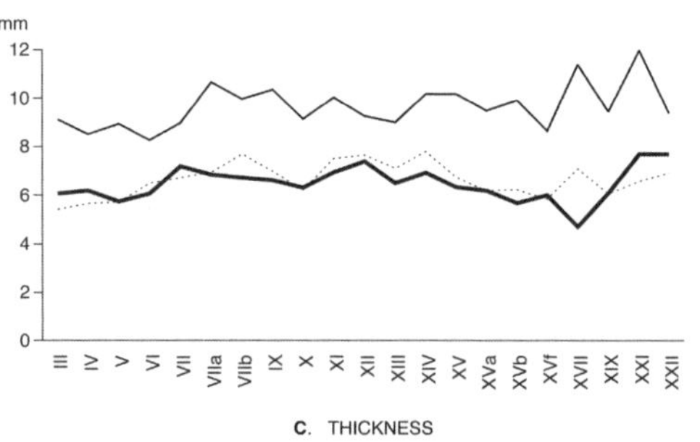



**Figure 5.6** The mean values per assemblage of length (A), width (B), and thickness (C) of retouched tools, Levallois and non-Levallois debitage. Only artifacts unbroken at the measured dimension were included. See table 5.9 for sample sizes and full descriptive statistics.

**Table 5.9  Descriptive statistics of blank dimensions**

**A. Length**

| Layer | All[a] | | | | Tools | | | | Non-Levallois debitage | | | | Levallois debitage | | | |
|---|---|---|---|---|---|---|---|---|---|---|---|---|---|---|---|---|
| | N | $\bar{X}$ | s.d. | s.e. | N | $\bar{X}$ | s.d. | s.e. | N | $\bar{X}$ | s.d. | s.e. | N | $\bar{X}$ | s.d. | s.e. |
| III | 103 | 32.47 | 14.42 | 1.42 | 6 | 46.17 | 18.65 | 7.61 | 67 | 27.79 | 11.90 | 1.45 | 16 | 40.56 | 11.87 | 2.97 |
| IV | 116 | 33.07 | 13.23 | 1.23 | 8 | 47.12 | 8.66 | 3.06 | 82 | 30.89 | 12.31 | 1.36 | 16 | 34.88 | 10.31 | 2.58 |
| V | 309 | 30.83 | 13.41 | 0.76 | 9 | 48.78 | 18.49 | 6.16 | 228 | 28.19 | 11.71 | 0.78 | 51 | 39.67 | 13.81 | 1.89 |
| VI | 242 | 33.98 | 13.22 | 0.85 | 15 | 46.73 | 17.39 | 4.49 | 180 | 31.69 | 11.73 | 0.87 | 34 | 38.68 | 14.78 | 2.53 |
| VII | 160 | 37.58 | 16.10 | 1.27 | 19 | 49.11 | 20.61 | 4.73 | 84 | 31.80 | 11.44 | 1.24 | 37 | 47.08 | 17.78 | 2.92 |
| VIIa | 366 | 39.93 | 17.77 | 0.93 | 26 | 59.23 | 21.23 | 4.16 | 216 | 34.11 | 15.16 | 1.03 | 77 | 46.31 | 15.02 | 1.71 |
| VIIb | 138 | 38.96 | 16.24 | 1.38 | 19 | 44.79 | 13.46 | 3.09 | 73 | 35.73 | 13.72 | 1.61 | 29 | 41.34 | 17.11 | 3.18 |
| IX | 478 | 40.55 | 19.06 | 0.87 | 44 | 53.89 | 22.13 | 3.34 | 245 | 33.39 | 15.60 | 1.00 | 133 | 48.51 | 19.00 | 1.65 |
| X | 290 | 36.61 | 16.29 | 0.96 | 33 | 53.15 | 17.99 | 3.12 | 142 | 30.19 | 13.11 | 1.10 | 82 | 39.77 | 15.37 | 1.70 |
| XI | 380 | 41.81 | 17.35 | 0.89 | 47 | 50.60 | 13.34 | 1.95 | 181 | 34.78 | 14.75 | 1.10 | 101 | 48.06 | 18.17 | 1.81 |
| XII | 245 | 45.44 | 17.67 | 1.13 | 44 | 55.39 | 16.24 | 2.45 | 102 | 39.41 | 15.29 | 1.51 | 69 | 45.99 | 17.61 | 2.12 |
| XIII | 959 | 40.67 | 17.81 | 0.58 | 127 | 50.84 | 16.81 | 1.49 | 483 | 33.94 | 15.53 | 0.71 | 235 | 47.54 | 16.85 | 1.10 |
| XIV | 236 | 44.33 | 16.81 | 1.09 | 44 | 52.14 | 16.91 | 2.55 | 93 | 39.20 | 16.35 | 1.70 | 74 | 44.69 | 15.38 | 1.79 |
| XV | 3,271 | 41.21 | 17.93 | 0.31 | 238 | 57.38 | 16.13 | 1.05 | 1,807 | 35.52 | 16.07 | 0.38 | 925 | 46.00 | 16.78 | 0.55 |
| XVa | 818 | 35.95 | 16.48 | 0.58 | 52 | 55.88 | 18.56 | 2.48 | 561 | 32.10 | 14.49 | 0.61 | 134 | 42.18 | 15.41 | 1.33 |
| XVb | 171 | 33.90 | 14.44 | 1.10 | 4 | 52.75 | 3.76 | 1.89 | 107 | 31.40 | 13.88 | 1.34 | 35 | 34.91 | 11.47 | 1.94 |
| XVf | 805 | 33.40 | 15.04 | 0.53 | 17 | 44.04 | 25.01 | 6.07 | 567 | 30.53 | 12.67 | 0.53 | 137 | 40.83 | 16.69 | 1.43 |
| XVII | 498 | 40.34 | 17.21 | 0.77 | 70 | 55.07 | 18.06 | 2.16 | 207 | 32.74 | 14.01 | 0.97 | 171 | 42.89 | 15.70 | 1.20 |
| XIX | 324 | 34.43 | 15.84 | 0.88 | 24 | 50.21 | 15.58 | 3.18 | 151 | 28.87 | 13.81 | 1.07 | 110 | 36.35 | 14.62 | 1.39 |
| XXI | 200 | 40.72 | 18.89 | 1.34 | 18 | 67.50 | 19.37 | 4.56 | 89 | 32.72 | 14.88 | 1.58 | 69 | 43.46 | 17.33 | 2.09 |
| XXII | 123 | 36.04 | 16.24 | 1.46 | 12 | 53.33 | 22.62 | 6.53 | 64 | 33.69 | 14.27 | 1.78 | 35 | 33.69 | 14.81 | 2.50 |

[a]This category also includes core management pieces, the detailed descriptive statistics of which appear in table 5.11.

**B. Width[a]**

| Layer | All[a] | | | | Tools | | | | Non-Levallois debitage | | | | Levallois debitage | | | |
|---|---|---|---|---|---|---|---|---|---|---|---|---|---|---|---|---|
| | N | $\bar{X}$ | s.d. | s.e. | N | $\bar{X}$ | s.d. | s.e. | N | $\bar{X}$ | s.d. | s.e. | N | $\bar{X}$ | s.d. | s.e. |
| III | 173 | 23.06 | 8.18 | 0.61 | 7 | 33.43 | 14.73 | 5.57 | 133 | 22.28 | 7.36 | 0.64 | 15 | 24.40 | 7.39 | 1.91 |
| IV | 184 | 23.84 | 9.93 | 0.73 | 11 | 38.09 | 11.86 | 3.59 | 139 | 22.62 | 6.90 | 0.76 | 21. | 25.67 | 11.26 | 2.46 |
| V | 556 | 22.21 | 8.31 | 0.35 | 14 | 29.14 | 9.01 | 2.41 | 440 | 21.49 | 28.07 | 0.38 | 73 | 24.84 | 8.83 | 1.03 |
| VI | 361 | 25.16 | 9.50 | 0.50 | 31 | 33.55 | 11.01 | 1.98 | 265 | 23.90 | 8.58 | 0.53 | 50 | 24.64 | 9.54 | 1.35 |
| VII | 273 | 28.98 | 12.38 | 0.75 | 30 | 34.73 | 10.45 | 1.91 | 175 | 27.17 | 11.63 | 0.84 | 45 | 34.24 | 14.64 | 2.18 |
| VIIa | 516 | 29.48 | 12.73 | 0.56 | 46 | 39.48 | 12.25 | 1.81 | 332 | 27.98 | 12.77 | 0.70 | 84 | .30.80 | 10.91 | 1.19 |
| VIIb | 247 | 30.18 | 10.67 | 0.68 | 28 | 35.86 | 10.22 | 1.93 | 150 | 29.33 | 10.64 | 0.87 | 47 | 32.26 | 10.10 | 1.47 |
| IX | 787 | 30.11 | 11.32 | 0.47 | 80 | 37.76 | 12.35 | 1.38 | 450 | 27.13 | 10.06 | 0.47 | 181 | 34.27 | 11.38 | 0.85 |
| X | 418 | 27.53 | 10.61 | 0.52 | 54 | 37.87 | 10.25 | 1.41 | 219 | 24.65 | 9.47 | 0.64 | 103 | 28.29 | 10.29 | 1.01 |
| XI | 584 | 30.85 | 11.78 | 0.49 | 65 | 38.75 | 10.48 | 1.30 | 317 | 28.61 | 11.08 | 0.62 | 143 | 32.24 | 10.54 | 0.88 |
| XII | 364 | 31.57 | 11.82 | 0.62 | 72 | 36.14 | 10.55 | 1.24 | 161 | 29.04 | 12.01 | 0.95 | 89 | 34.38 | 12.14 | 1.29 |
| XIII | 1,577 | 28.39 | 10.44 | 0.26 | 212 | 35.11 | 10.48 | 0.72 | 893 | 26.56 | 9.74 | 0.33 | 303 | 30.18 | 10.82 | 0.62 |
| XIV | 372 | 30.89 | 11.26 | 0.58 | 79 | 35.95 | 12.46 | 1.40 | 154 | 28.17 | 10.39 | 0.84 | 102 | 30.68 | 9.68 | 0.95 |
| XV | 5,157 | 27.72 | 10.31 | 0.14 | 359 | 35.84 | 9.94 | 0.52 | 3,127 | 26.10 | 9.76 | 0.17 | 1,236 | 29.68 | 10.17 | 0.29 |
| XVa | 1,311 | 27.13 | 11.25 | 0.31 | 62 | 37.53 | 12.13 | 1.54 | 955 | 25.64 | 10.34 | 0.33 | 189 | 30.38 | 12.37 | 0.90 |
| XVb | 259 | 26.14 | 10.35 | 0.64 | 6 | 40.83 | 17.72 | 1.75 | 175 | 25.23 | 10.11 | 0.76 | 44 | 26.52 | 8.59 | 1.29 |
| XVf | 1,282 | 25.32 | 10.32 | 0.29 | 28 | 33.39 | 18.46 | 2.92 | 933 | 24.32 | 9.48 | 0.31 | 206 | 28.10 | 11.26 | 0.85 |
| XVII | 667 | 31.40 | 12.96 | 0.50 | 90 | 41.31 | 12.52 | 1.32 | 288 | 27.85 | 11.06 | 0.65 | 232 | 31.89 | 13.12 | 0.86 |
| XIX | 369 | 28.98 | 12.40 | 0.65 | 36 | 40.00 | 15.09 | 2.55 | 168 | 25.92 | 10.97 | 0.85 | 120 | 29.17 | 10.60 | 0.97 |
| XXI | 230 | 33.37 | 15.43 | 1.01 | 25 | 49.80 | 12.82 | 2.56 | 101 | 28.67 | 13.38 | 1.33 | 79 | 35.24 | 15.68 | 1.76 |
| XXII | 137 | 29.98 | 14.68 | 1.25 | 15 | 38.73 | 17.30 | 4.47 | 73 | 27.74 | 14.09 | 1.65 | 38 | 31.32 | 14.86 | 2.41 |

*(continued)*

**Table 5.9   (continued)**

**C.  Thickness**

| Layer | All[a] | | | | Tools | | | | Non-Levallois debitage | | | | Levallois debitage | | | |
|---|---|---|---|---|---|---|---|---|---|---|---|---|---|---|---|---|
| | N | $\bar{X}$ | s.d. | s.e. | N | $\bar{X}$ | s.d. | s.e. | N | $\bar{X}$ | s.d. | s.e. | N | $\bar{X}$ | s.d. | s.e. |
| III | 195 | 5.88 | 2.87 | 0.21 | 9 | 9.11 | 3.44 | 0.15 | 149 | 5.41 | 2.52 | 0.21 | 18 | 6.06 | 2.53 | 0.60 |
| IV | 215 | 5.93 | 3.02 | 0.21 | 14 | 8.50 | 2.90 | 0.78 | 166 | 5.66 | 3.05 | 0.24 | 22 | 6.18 | 2.50 | 0.53 |
| V | 650 | 5.89 | 2.90 | 0.11 | 15 | 8.93 | 3.41 | 0.88 | 528 | 5.71 | 2.78 | 0.12 | 78 | 5.73 | 2.84 | 0.32 |
| VI | 424 | 6.71 | 3.57 | 0.17 | 32 | 8.25 | 3.05 | 0.54 | 322 | 6.49 | 3.54 | 0.20 | 52 | 6.02 | 2.71 | 0.38 |
| VII | 349 | 7.19 | 3.90 | 0.21 | 36 | 8.97 | 3.48 | 0.58 | 235 | 6.71 | 3.96 | 0.26 | 53 | 7.19 | 2.75 | 0.38 |
| VIIa | 581 | 7.49 | 4.23 | 0.18 | 46 | 10.85 | 4.29 | 0.63 | 384 | 6.94 | 4.20 | 0.21 | 94 | 6.84 | 2.61 | 0.27 |
| VIIb | 303 | 7.86 | 3.71 | 0.21 | 38 | 6.97 | 4.20 | 0.66 | 182 | 7.08 | 3.81 | 0.28 | 58 | 6.72 | 2.53 | 0.33 |
| IX | 1,108 | 7.50 | 4.02 | 0.12 | 105 | 10.35 | 4.35 | 0.42 | 684 | 6.98 | 3.81 | 0.20 | 232 | 6.81 | 3.11 | 0.20 |
| X | 598 | 6.73 | 3.19 | 0.13 | 63 | 9.14 | 3.70 | 0.42 | 334 | 6.21 | 3.05 | 0.17 | 152 | 6.31 | 2.74 | 0.22 |
| XI | 833 | 7.90 | 4.11 | 0.14 | 86 | 10.03 | 3.98 | 0.43 | 499 | 7.50 | 4.03 | 0.18 | 178 | 6.94 | 2.96 | 0.22 |
| XII | 495 | 8.14 | 3.94 | 0.18 | 92 | 9.26 | 3.66 | 0.38 | 247 | 7.64 | 3.75 | 0.24 | 111 | 7.79 | 3.37 | 0.32 |
| XIII | 2,213 | 7.78 | 3.80 | 0.08 | 274 | 8.99 | 3.75 | 0.23 | 1,329 | 7.03 | 3.80 | 0.10 | 407 | 6.58 | 2.71 | 0.13 |
| XIV | 495 | 8.38 | 4.05 | 0.18 | 100 | 10.16 | 3.97 | 0.40 | 229 | 7.79 | 3.83 | 0.25 | 122 | 6.91 | 2.85 | 0.26 |
| XV | 6,032 | 7.09 | 3.63 | 0.05 | 393 | 10.17 | 4.18 | 0.21 | 3,739 | 6.74 | 3.49 | 0.06 | 1,361 | 4.91 | 2.50 | 0.07 |
| XVa | 1,585 | 6.54 | 3.59 | 1.09 | 72 | 9.47 | 4.28 | 0.50 | 1,178 | 6.19 | 3.40 | 0.10 | 222 | 6.19 | 2.68 | 0.18 |
| XVb | 308 | 6.46 | 3.53 | 0.20 | 10 | 9.90 | 3.98 | 0.26 | 215 | 6.23 | 3.68 | 0.25 | 48 | 8.67 | 2.35 | 0.34 |
| XVf | 1,534 | 6.15 | 3.41 | 0.09 | 36 | 8.56 | 3.94 | 0.66 | 1,139 | 7.85 | 2.93 | 0.87 | 232 | 6.51 | 3.94 | 0.26 |
| XVII | 861 | 7.83 | 4.72 | 0.16 | 122 | 11.39 | 5.54 | 0.50 | 385 | 7.07 | 4.32 | 0.22 | 285 | 6.71 | 3.32 | 0.10 |
| XIX | 509 | 6.77 | 3.80 | 0.17 | 55 | 8.44 | 4.69 | 0.63 | 246 | 6.07 | 3.51 | 0.23 | 158 | 6.08 | 2.91 | 0.23 |
| XXI | 298 | 8.00 | 4.75 | 0.27 | 38 | 11.97 | 5.84 | 0.95 | 133 | 6.57 | 3.89 | 0.34 | 98 | 7.68 | 3.81 | 0.38 |
| XXII | 167 | 7.56 | 3.97 | 0.31 | 16 | 9.38 | 4.51 | 1.13 | 92 | 6.91 | 3.85 | 0.40 | 47 | 7.68 | 3.83 | 0.56 |

The use of the centripetal recurrent Levallois method results in the occurrence of several types of core management pieces, characteristic of different stages of the reduction sequence (Boëda, Geneste, and Meignen 1990:68; Geneste 1985: tab. 11).

*Naturally backed flakes* (i.e., with lateral or latero-distal cortical cover on the flake's edge) are rare in the preliminary stages of decortication but occur again when the core's lateral convexities are being adjusted further on in the process of removing Levallois debitage. In this latter case, cortex will appear on the lateral rather than the distal end of the blank.

*Éclats débordants* (Beyries and Boëda 1983) are removed from the lateral edge of a Levallois core when the flaking surface is reorganized for continued flaking, and their lateral edges bear residual scars of preparation flakes that had been removed from the preparation face of the core. *Éclats débordants* thus serve a function similar to that of naturally backed flakes. They are expected to occur during relatively advanced stages of Levallois reduction.

*Pseudo-Levallois flakes* (Bordes 1953b), also defined as "*éclats débordants a dos limité*" (Geneste 1985:230; Meignen 1993:280) are additional typical by-products of the more advanced stages of Levallois removals (Boëda, Geneste,

and Meignen 1990:68; Ohnuma 1990). These flakes are designed to correct rather localized irregularities in the geometry of the striking platform of a centripetally worked Levallois core (Boëda 1986). They differ from *éclats débordants* in that their flaking and morphological axes do not overlap.

Occasionally a large flake, designed to remove the whole of the deformed flaking surface, is detached. These *éclats outrepassés* (Tixier, Inizan, and Roche 1980:95) are perceived here as intentional products. These were detached only when intensive use of both the striking platform and the flaking surface of the core had distorted the geometry of the flaking surface. Rejuvenation of the lateral and (mainly) distal convexities required removal of the exploited surface and extensive rearrangement of the flaking surface. Such items are expected to show a large number of dorsal face scars and a complex dorsal face scar pattern. Flakes that are both *débordants* and *outrepassés*, representing a stage of complete rejuvenation of the core's surface, occur very rarely.

All these categories of core management pieces also occur when convergent recurrent Levallois flaking is used, with the exception of the pseudo-Levallois flakes, which tend to be less common (Boëda, Geneste, and Meignen 1990:67). A discernible difference between the

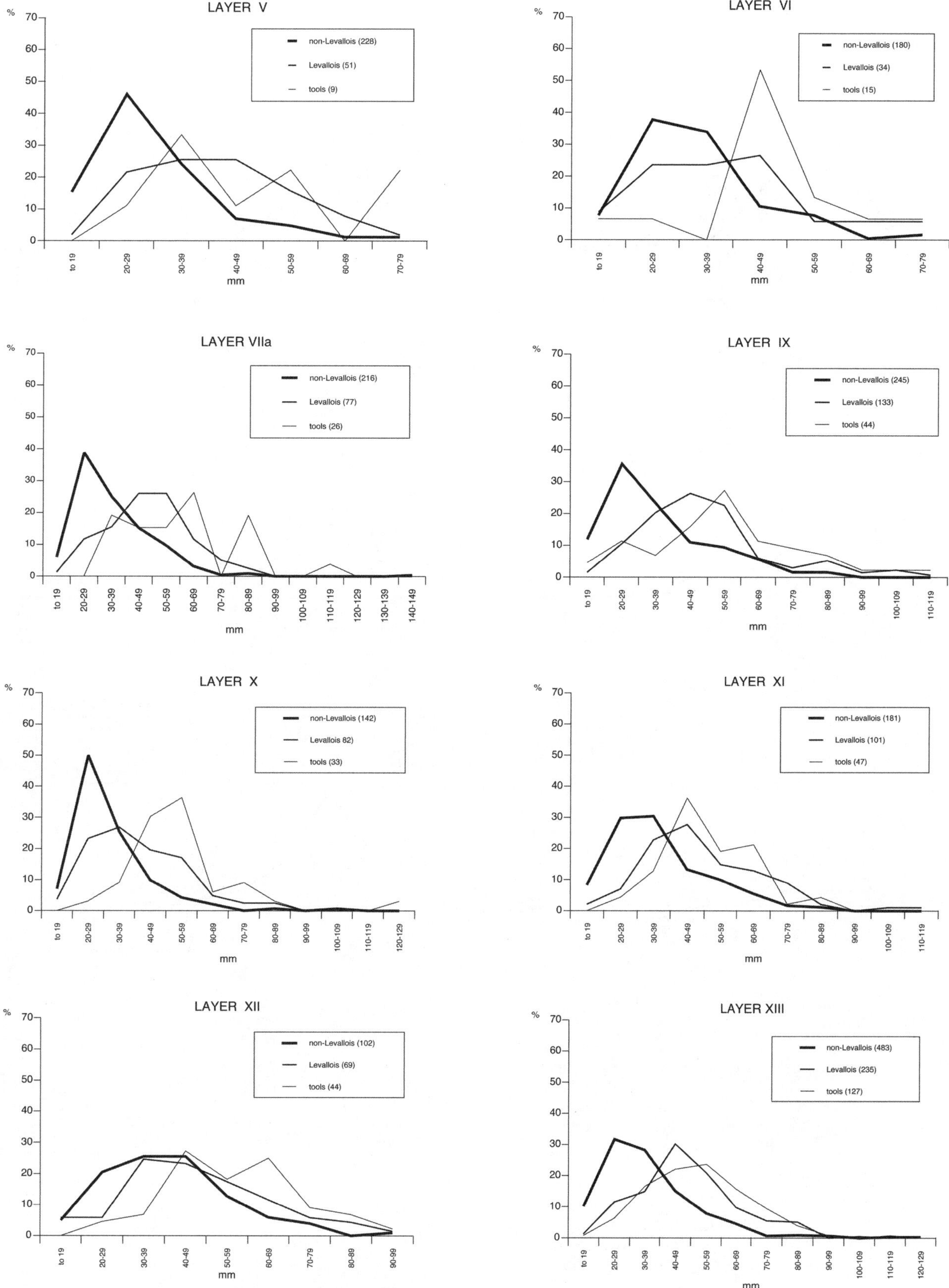

**Figure 5.7** Frequency distributions of the length of tools, Levallois and non-Levallois blanks. Only artifacts unbroken in the length axis are included in the analysis. (*continued*)

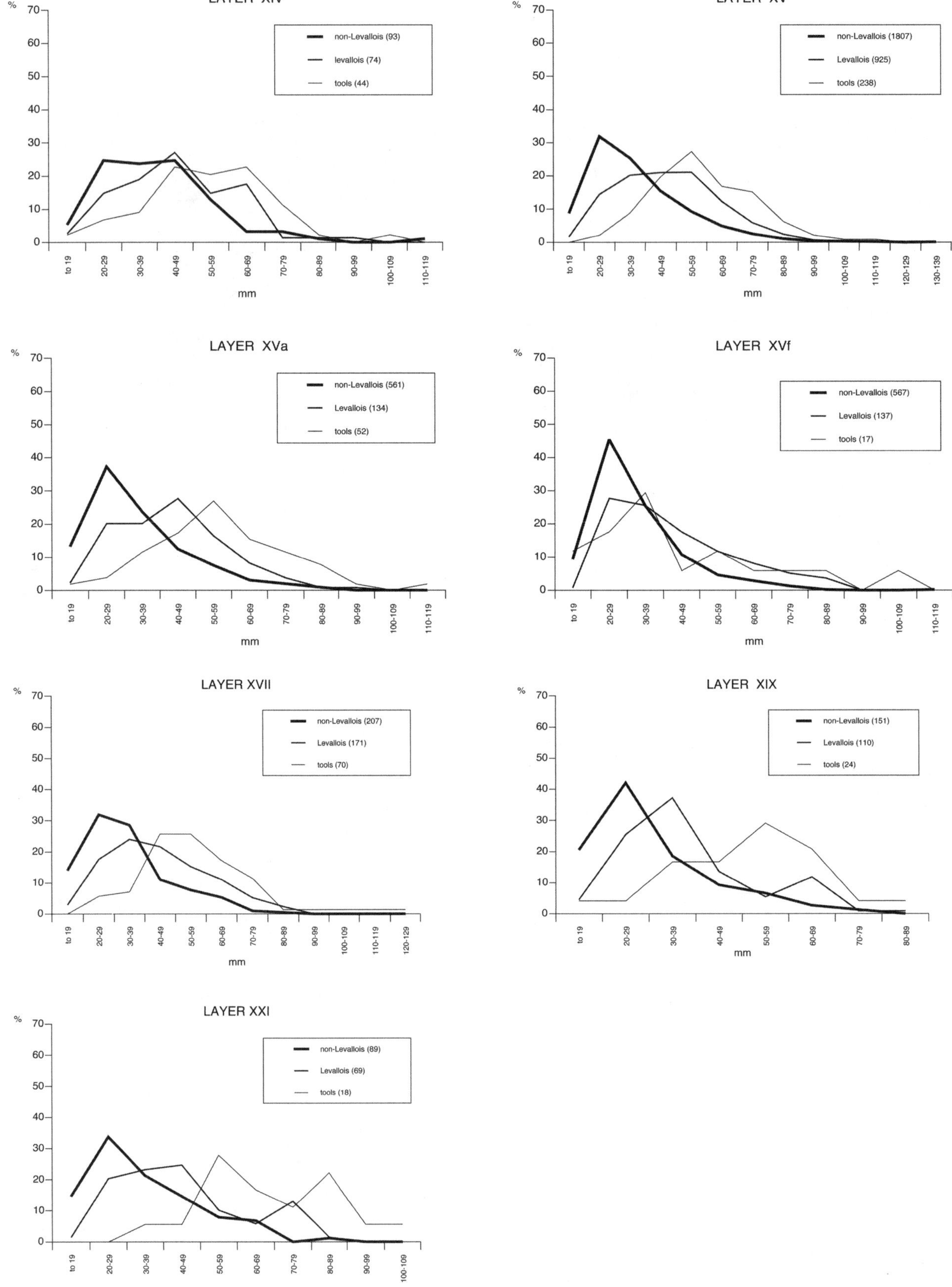


**Figure 5.7** (*continued*)

centripetal and convergent modes of flaking lies in the higher relative frequencies of naturally backed flakes in a unipolar convergent flaking process. In the latter case, the core's striking platform encompasses only a limited part of its circumference, thus leaving large parts of the lateral edges along the preparation surface covered with cortex. Naturally backed flakes and some of the *éclats débordants* may be plunging (*outrepassants*) flakes, perceived as a means to shape the core's distal convexities, especially in unipolar Levallois flaking systems, to facilitate the removal of pointed or triangular elements (Boëda, Geneste, and Meignen 1990).[6] Given the nature of unipolar convergent flaking, the number of scars should be lower than on the homologous pieces removed off centripetally exploited cores, and scar patterns should be less complex.

Other types of Core Trimming Elements (CTE) are associated with non-Levallois flaking systems. Core tablets and ridge blades are used for rejuvenation of prismatic and pyramidal cores and are considered to be characteristic of blade technologies (Tixier, Inizan, and Roche 1980:82, fig. 26). Given that such cores occur only in the layer XIV assemblage (table 4.1b), the compatible core management pieces are expected to occur, if at all, only there. Other non-diagnostic flakes bearing segments of the core's striking platform as part of their dorsal face scars tend to appear mainly where non-Levallois flaking systems were applied. However, some such pieces could be recognized as Levallois flakes (table 5.10), suggesting that they could have been removed during use of this more formal flaking system as well. In the same vein, some of the more typical core management pieces of Levallois flaking do not bear the characteristics of Levallois flakes. This is true mainly of naturally backed flakes (table 5.10).

The magnitude of use of technological modes from which core management pieces are derived is best gauged by their relative frequencies among other types of core management flakes (table 5.10), rather than within the total assemblage (appendix 5). The low frequencies of *éclats outrepassés* (plates 20:8, 34:7) among core management flakes reflect the high degree of technological skills. Despite the intensive exploitation of cores through the use of the recurrent centripetal method, only seldom did the need arise for extensive rejuvenation of core surfaces, rarely involving the combination of *éclats débordants* and *outrepassés* (plates 32:1, 36:3). Moreover, in only one case (the assemblage from layer XV) did this stage occur when cores were still relatively large (60–90 mm long; figure 5.8).

**Table 5.10  Absolute and (relative frequencies) of types of core management pieces**

| Layer | N | 1 | 2 | 3 | 4 | 5 | 6 | 7 |
|---|---|---|---|---|---|---|---|---|
| III | 19 | 2 (10.53) (2) | 13 (68.42) (0) | 3 (15.79) (2) | | | 1(5.26) (0) | 3.2 |
| IV | 13 | 1 (7.69) (1) | 6 (46.15) (1) | 2 (15.38) (2) | 2 (15.38) (1) | 1 (7.69) (1) | 1(5.69) (0) | 2.2 |
| V | 29 | 1 (3.45) (1) | 10 (34.48) (0) | 9 (31.03) (8) | | 1 (3.45) (1) | 8 (27.59) (0) | 3.6 |
| VI | 18 | | 7 (38.89) (0) | 3 (16.67) (2) | | | 8 (44.44) (3) | 2.0 |
| VII | 25 | | 7 (28.00) (0) | 12 (48.00) (6) | | | 6 (24.00) (1) | 1.3 |
| VIIa | 58 | 4 (6.90) (4) | 30 (51.72) (2) | 11 (18.97) (5) | | | 13 (22.41) (1) | 2.1 |
| VIIb | 25 | 1 (4.00) (1) | 6 (24.00) (0) | 10 (40.00) (6) | | | 8 (32.00) (2) | 1.8 |
| IX | 87 | 2 (2.30) (2) | 25 (28.74) (0) | 26 (29.89) (24) | 4 (4.60) (4) | | 30 (34.48) (7) | 2.0 |
| X | 49 | 1 (2.04) (1) | 10 (20.41) (1) | 20 (40.82) (16) | | | 18 (936.73) (5) | 9.8 |
| XI | 71 | | 26 (36.62) (2) | 34 (47.89) (15) | | | 11 (15.49) (0) | 1.6 |
| XII | 46 | | 9 (19.57) (3) | 18 (39.13) (7) | | | 19 (41.30) (9) | 1.2 |
| XIII | 201 | | 56 (27.86) (3) | 105 (52.24) (30) | 2 (1.00) (2) | 6 (2.99) (1) | 31 (15.42) (3) | 3.2 |
| XIV | 44 | 1 (2.27) (1) | 7 (15.91) (1) | 16 (36.36) (7) | | | 20 (45.45) (3) | 1.2 |
| XV | 422 | 10 (2.37) (10) | 228 (54.03) (21) | 105 (24.88) (59) | 10 (2.37) (8) | 2 (0.47) (2) | 67 (15.88) (9) | 2.5 |
| XVa | 110 | 3 (2.73) (3) | 43 (39.09) (6) | 38 (34.55) (23) | 5 (4.55) (3) | 3 (3.73) (2) | 18 (16.36) (1) | 4.4 |
| XVb | 35 | | 16 (45.71) (1) | 14 (40.00) (12) | 1 (2.86) (1) | | 4 (11.43) (1) | 11.7 |
| XVf | 124 | 6 (4.84) (6) | 50 (40.32) (1) | 26 (20.97) (18) | 10 (8.06) (7) | 3 (2.42) (2) | 29 (23.39) (6) | 10.3 |
| XVII | 69 | 5 (2.90) (2) | 11 (15.94) (3) | 12 (17.39) (8) | | | 44 (63.77) (13) | 1.9 |
| XIX | 50 | 1 (2.00) (1) | 5 (10.00) (0) | 11 (22.00) (2) | | | 33 (66.00) (13) | 2.3 |
| XXI | 29 | | 4 (13.79) (0) | 4 (13.79) (1) | 2 (6.90) (1) | | 19 (65.52) (5) | 2.6 |
| XXII | 12 | | 3 (25.00) (1) | 2 (16.67) (1) | | | 7 (58.33) (1) | 1.2 |

*Note*: The number of Levallois artifacts in each category is shown italicized in parentheses. 1: pseudo-Levallois flakes; 2: naturally backed flakes; 3: *éclats débordants*; 4: *éclats outrepassés*; 5: combination of 3 and 4; 6: CTEs; 7: Index of mean intensity of core management, computed as N of core management pieces/N of cores. Only cores on blocks and nodules were counted. For Ns see table 4.1.

Naturally backed flakes and *éclats débordants* are the most common types of core management pieces, while pseudo-Levallois flakes are few (table 5.10). Naturally backed flakes are on average the largest among the core management pieces (table 5.11, figure 5.8), mainly due to the occurrence of a few exceptionally long pieces, but on the whole the curves are continuous and sometimes bimodal (figure 5.9). This suggests that removal of naturally backed flakes occurred throughout the process of core reduction, and not at any specific phase of the process.

In contrast, the small mean sizes of pseudo-Levallois flakes (plate 20:5–7) do indeed reflect the limited length range of these pieces (distributions not shown); they never exceed 50 mm in any of the assemblages and are often not larger than 30 mm. Combined with the paucity of these elements (table 5.10), this suggests that their removal may have taken place during advanced stages of core reduction. The detachment of a blank in which the flaking and symmetry axes do not overlap provided an economic way to modify the core's platforms when it became too small for use of any of the other methods of rejuvenation. In

**Table 5.11**   **Mean length of various categories of core management pieces**

| Layer | Pseudo-Levallois | | | Naturally backed flakes | | | *Éclats débordants* | | | *Éclats outrepassés* | | | combination | | | core trimming elements | | |
|---|---|---|---|---|---|---|---|---|---|---|---|---|---|---|---|---|---|---|
| | N | $\bar{X}$ | s.d. | N | $\bar{X}$ | s.d. | N | $\bar{X}$ | s.d. | N | $\bar{X}$ | s.d. | N | $\bar{X}$ | s.d. | N | $\bar{X}$ | s.d. |
| VIIa | 4 | 42.25 | 7.89 | 23 | 52.61 | 22.14 | 9 | 32.56 | 8.73 | | | | | | | 11 | 40.00 | 13.32 |
| IX | 2 | 31.00 | 0.00 | 12 | 49.67 | 16.62 | 20 | 36.75 | 11.38 | 3 | 42.67 | 11.57 | | | | 19 | 45.11 | 21.41 |
| XI | | | | 19 | 53.16 | 16.15 | 25 | 40.08 | 15.36 | | | | | | | 7 | 49.71 | 25.55 |
| XIII | | | | 33 | 54.61 | 18.14 | 59 | 38.86 | 16.90 | 1 | 32.00 | 0.00 | 4 | 31.50 | 12.12 | 16 | 43.75 | 18.16 |
| XV | 10 | 26.60 | 9.83 | 145 | 55.69 | 17.53 | 78 | 38.77 | 15.59 | 6 | 64.17 | 15.66 | 1 | 50.00 | 0.00 | 49 | 44.73 | 18.71 |
| XVa | 3 | 25.67 | 12.42 | 25 | 49.76 | 17.50 | 29 | 33.97 | 13.77 | 2 | 50.00 | 22.63 | 2 | 29.50 | 0.71 | 10 | 37.60 | 13.64 |
| XVf | 6 | 22.50 | 7.23 | 27 | 43.85 | 16.08 | 18 | 33.06 | 14.74 | 10 | 41.60 | 23.28 | 2 | 57.20 | 16.26 | 20 | 38.80 | 18.85 |
| XVII | 2 | 24.50 | 12.02 | 6 | 50.67 | 15.90 | 8 | 39.12 | 4.92 | | | | | | | 34 | 42.82 | 17.38 |
| XIX | 1 | 27.00 | 0.00 | 5 | 62.00 | 34.45 | 10 | 43.70 | 9.64 | | | | | | | 23 | 35.52 | 14.61 |

*Note*: Only layers in which N of all categories is ≥ 40.

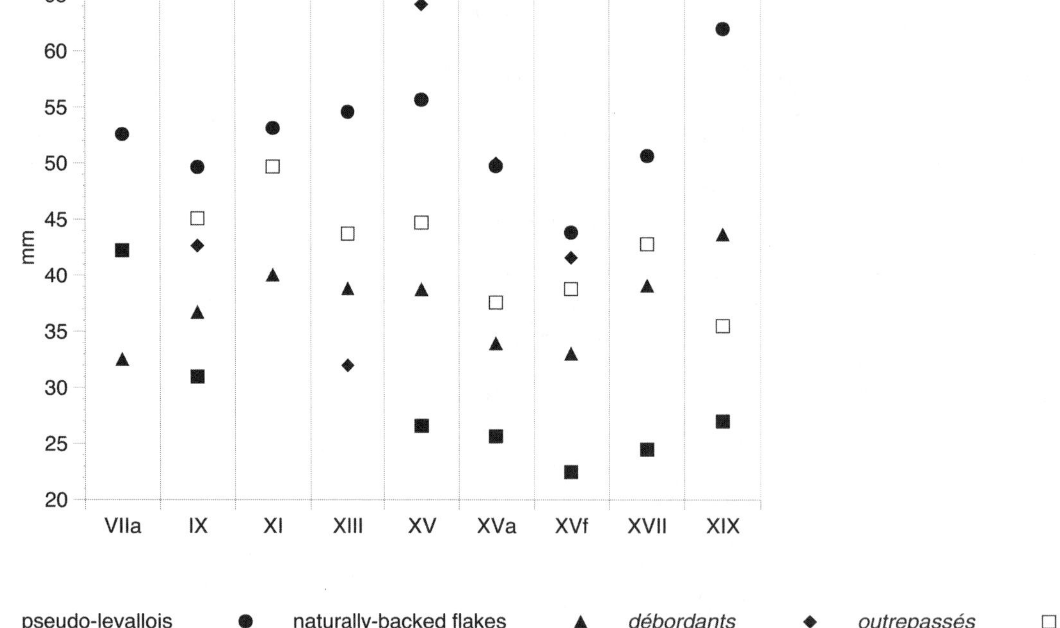


**Figure 5.8**   Mean length of the various categories of core management pieces by layer. Only layers where N of all the categories > 40 are shown.

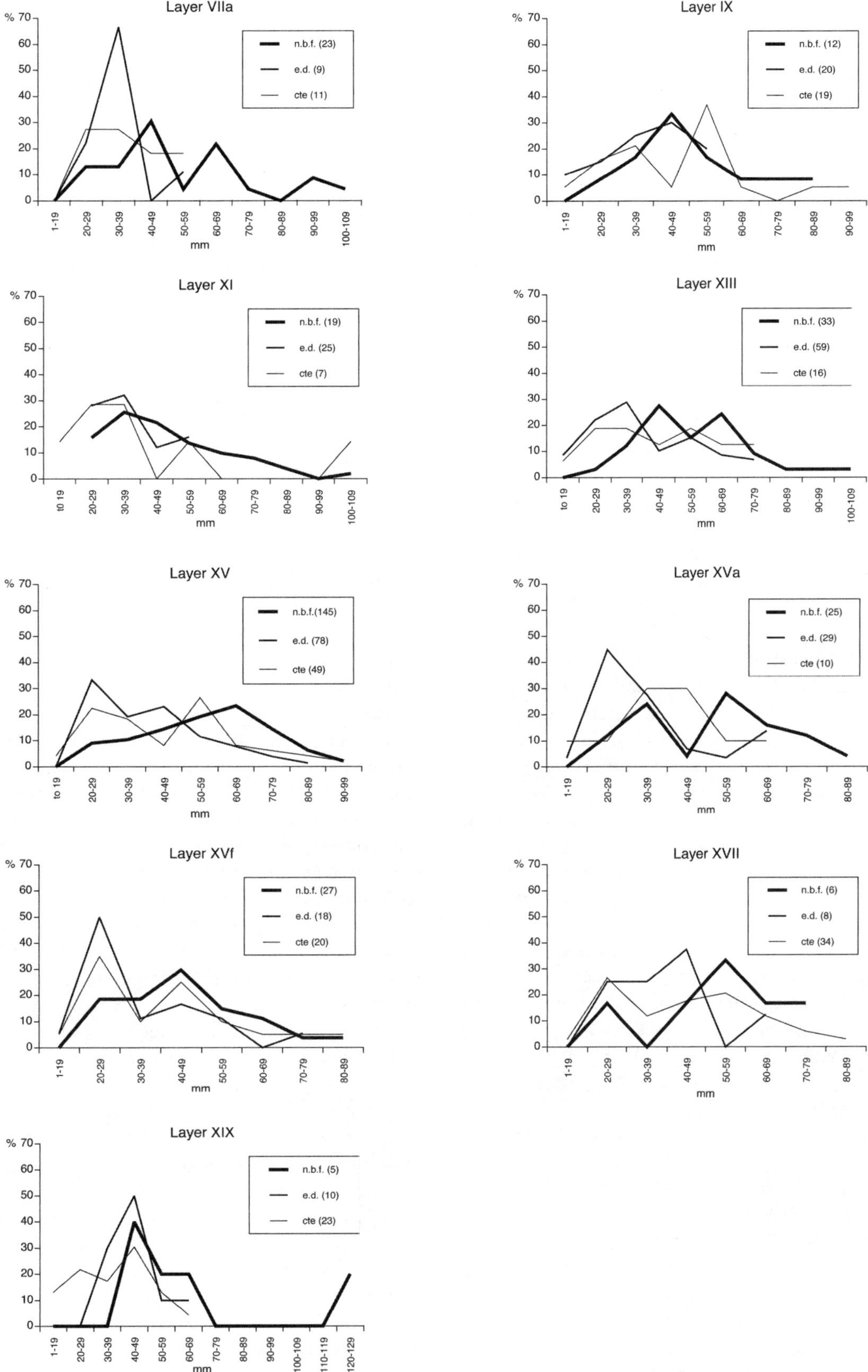

**Figure 5.9** Length distributions of various categories of core management pieces. Only layers where N of all the categories > 40 are shown. n.b.f. = naturally backed flakes; e.d. = *éclats débordants;* cte = core trimming elements.

some of the assemblages that contain pseudo-Levallois flakes, cores are indeed relatively small (table 4.2b). The common dorsal face scar patterns on pseudo-Levallois flakes are centripetal or convergent.

*Éclats débordants* (plates 30:7, 32:1, 36:3), while common in all the assemblages, have a more limited size range than that of naturally backed pieces. Except in layers IX, XVII, and XIX, their length distributions peak in the range of 20–30 mm (figure 5.9). Removal of these elements seems to have been considered effective throughout the reduction process but mostly in its later stages for most core types. Since their technological role overlaps to some degree with that of pseudo-Levallois flakes, the ubiquitous occurrence of *éclats débordants* among core management pieces may explain why pseudo-Levallois flakes do not occur in all the assemblages, despite the similarity in the sizes of Levallois cores for flakes when their use was discontinued (tables 4.1, 4.2a–b). Most *éclats débordants* in each assemblage (32% in layer IX to 100% in layer VIIa, commonly varying around 70%) bear centripetal scar patterns, the mean number of dorsal face scars is commonly six, and they are most likely *éclats débordants primaires,* preceding the removal of a large, preferential Levallois flake (Geneste 1985:232–3). *Éclats débordants secondaires,* bearing the remnant scar of a preferential previously removed flake, are rare in the Qafzeh assemblages. These patterns are in agreement with the flaking methods reflected by core characteristics and support the hypothesis that preferential flakes occurred most often in the last stages of core reduction, rarely followed by additional core rejuvenation.

In the assemblage of layer XV, the high frequency of naturally backed flakes (table 5.10) accords with the relative abundance of cores for points in this assemblage (table 4.1). Their proportion is even higher when retouched pieces are taken into consideration (e.g., plates 16:8, 22:4, 23:3, 4, 35:8, 36:2). Of the complete naturally backed flakes of this assemblage, 61% are of laminar proportions (mean length/width ratio of 2.25). Over 50% (N = 226) bear relatively simple (e.g., unipolar) scar patterns, with a low mean number of scars (3.25 ± 1.96, N = 223), while another 4% bear convergent scar patterns. Additionally, the average length of naturally backed pieces bearing centripetal scar patterns (ca. 17% of all such pieces, N = 27) is very similar in the layer XV assemblage to the mean length of those with other scar patterns (ca. 56 mm), and the mean number of scars on their dorsal faces is only slightly higher (4.23) than that of the other naturally backed elements. Many of the artifacts exhibit the distal and latero-distal cortex, as well as twisted profiles, that are characteristic of the stage of partial decortication in a reduction sequence by the recurrent convergent Levallois method (Boëda, Geneste, and Meignen 1990:67; Meignen 1995). The blanks tend to curve longitudinally but are

rarely plunging (*outrepassants*) (e.g., plates 23:3–4, 25:3–4), suggesting that preparation of the core's distal convexities was less thorough in this assemblage than at other assemblages in which the recurrent convergent method was used (e.g., Kebara IX–X). This is compatible with the shapes of Levallois points in this assemblage, where the "concord" profile, typical of those at Kebara Cave (Bar-Yosef et al. 1992; Meignen 1995), is rare.

Naturally backed flakes in other assemblages are expected to be relatively short. This is typical of core management pieces of this type when they occur in a recurrent centripetal method, since then they mostly occur in the advanced phases of the reduction process (Boëda, Geneste, and Meignen 1990:68). Means and distributions of length confirm this expectation (table 5.11, figures 5.8, 5.9). Although elongated naturally backed flakes appear sporadically in all layers (plates 20:10, 21:12, 30:11–12, 33:8, 34:6, 39:8), most tend to be of non-laminar proportions, with a low mean length/width ratio. Exceptions are the assemblages from layers III, IV, XII, and XIII. In several layers (VI, VII, VIIa) the frequency of centripetal scar patterns is similar to that observed in layer XV, while in another (XVa) it is lower. In the other assemblages, frequencies of centripetal scar patterns are much higher, in some cases more than expected when compared to the whole flake population (figure 5.3), although the mean number of scars on dorsal faces is low (3–4) in all assemblages. Plunging flakes are very few in these assemblages (e.g., plate 20:10), and the occurrence of cortex is most often limited to the lateral edge of the blank. These are typical characteristics of the stage of establishing the core's striking platform for a new cycle of flaking by the recurrent centripetal method.

The technological role of naturally backed pieces and of *éclats débordants* is identical, and both may occur when convergent and centripetal methods of Levallois flaking are applied. The size differences between these two classes in the various assemblages of Qafzeh reflect either differences in core sizes or (more likely) their removal at different stages of the reduction process, and thus they may represent a continuum of flaking. In some assemblages, however, two different reduction strategies seem to occur. This is most clear in the assemblage of layer XV through both the size and characters of naturally backed blanks, as well as the cores and debitage properties. In the same vein, it is possible that the appearance of naturally backed flakes of laminar proportions, combined with the occurrence of a few cores for points in layer XIII, reflects some practice of the convergent mode, although Levallois points are rare (tables 4.1, 5.3; appendix 5). The relative paucity of centripetal scar patterns on naturally backed pieces in layer VIIa may also reflect a similar situation, given that some cores for points and several points do occur in this assemblage (tables 4.1, 5.3).

## Diversity and Flexibility in Lithic Production

The technological characteristics of the flake assemblages vary over time. A general model of this variability, describing the expected combinations of technological attributes, has been proposed (table 5.1) and will now be tested by examining the role of each variable. The treatment of discrete variables may well be too simplistic a means by which to identify and categorize the complex relationships that may occur among the various traits of a flake. Indeed, a number of studies have shown that more complex models, such as multi-step regressions, have considerable predictive powers, for instance, about flake size in relation to flaking order or to initial core size (e.g., Bradbury and Carr 1999; Braun et al. 2005; Carr and Bradbury 2001; Ferraro, Braun, and Tactikos 2006; Shott 1994), thus forming useful analytical tools that provide reflections of complex realities. However, to maintain clarity and to address the effect of each variable, I preferred to examine pairs of variables rather than to use multivariate analyses. Results of the statistical tests are shown only for selected layers, chosen on the basis of their sample size to represent the whole sequence.

Several variables discussed above (e.g., types of striking platforms, scar patterns, or amount of cortex) are best considered as reflecting technological means to achieve a goal, rather than being the goal itself. Other properties, such as size and sharpness, are more likely the desired properties of a detached flake. Analyses of relationships among variables of the first group mainly aim to identify the modes of core reduction employed in each assemblage. In these analyses I also attempt to discern the degree to which the pertinent variables co-vary as an inevitable, deterministic outcome of the particular reduction strategies. At a later stage, I try to estimate the influence that such variables may have on preplanned, desired flake attributes.

### Scar Patterns and Amount of Cortex

Chi-square tests of these two variables were conducted only on debitage, since the retouch on tools might alter the amount of cortex on the dorsal face. For the assemblages of all the layers, with the exception of layer XV, chi-square test values proved invalid due to the high incidence of low expected values. Examination of the standardized residuals, however, confirms the occurrence of the trend predicted in table 5.1.

As a rule, dorsal surfaces with no cortex are over-represented among flakes with centripetal scar patterns. When cortex does occur on flakes with centripetal scar patterns, it often appears as an isolated patch (1–25% of dorsal surface cover) on the distal end or the center of the flake, leaving the flake with a cortex-free, sharp edge.

The relatively common occurrence of centripetal scar patterns on Levallois debitage (table 5.3, figure 5.3) should result in a lower occurrence of cortex on these artifacts (as indeed is the case; table 5.2). Although deviations from this pattern do occur in the Levallois debitage in some assemblages (layers VIIb, IX, XIV, and XV), these are not statistically significant. Examination of the standardized residuals indicated that the occurrence of cortical cover, especially when it covers more than 50% of the surface area, is associated with unipolar scar patterns. Such pieces may be connected mainly with non-Levallois flaking methods (table 5.1) but also with the initial phases of Levallois core reduction.

This model, however, is over-simplistic when recurrent Levallois methods are employed, since flakes bearing "limited platform" scar patterns (i.e., scars that originate from limited, discrete regions on the core) can occur in advanced stages of core reduction. In such a case the incidence of cortical surface cover tends to be under-represented. This can be tested in layer XV, which was the only assemblage to yield valid chi-square test results. In this assemblage debitage pieces with bipolar and convergent dorsal face scar patterns exhibit lower than expected frequencies of high amount of cortical cover (table 5.12a). When the relationship was tested only within Levallois debitage, no particular pairing of variable groups turned out to be significant (table 5.12b). Similar patterns occur in the assemblages of layers VIIa, VIIb, and XIII–XVf, in which either bipolar or convergent scar patterns (or both) are significantly paired with total lack of cortex. However, core variables (chapter 4) and debitage scar pattern frequencies (earlier in this chapter) predicted the use of recurrent unipolar convergent flaking in only a few of these assemblages (e.g., VIIa, XIII, XV). The occurrence of such relationships in other assemblages is thus associated with the use of recurrent centripetal flaking methods.

The pattern suggests that the relationship of amount of cortex and scar patterns within the terrace assemblages is not a deterministic outcome of the use of specific flaking modes. While this may be the case for small cores (Kuhn 1995b), the larger size of cores in the Qafzeh assemblages enabled manipulation of raw material by intentional ordering of removals throughout the reduction sequence. If indeed an attempt was made to avoid the occurrence of cortex on flakes, this goal could be achieved by several tactics within any one flaking strategy.

### Striking Platforms and Scar Patterns

The relationship between striking platform characteristics and dorsal face scar patterns was tested in order to examine a null hypothesis that specific reduction modes are associated with particular types of striking platforms. As scar patterns and striking platform traits are not likely

**Table 5.12  Relationship between the amount of dorsal face cortex and scar patterns in layer XV**

**A.  All debitage[a]**

| % of cortex | Scar pattern | | | | | | | | | | |
|---|---|---|---|---|---|---|---|---|---|---|---|
| | Unipolar | | Convergent | | Bipolar | | Centripetal | | Other | | Totals |
| 0 | 1,006 | −14.9 | 556 | **10.5** | 677 | **7.5** | 798 | 1.9 | 338 | −0.8 | 3375 |
| 1–25% | 433 | **5.3** | 83 | −4.9 | 142 | −2.7 | 233 | 0.5 | 100 | −0.2 | 991 |
| 26–50% | 210 | **8.9** | 12 | −5.7 | 29 | −4.8 | 72 | −1.4 | 38 | 0.2 | 361 |
| 51–75% | 112 | **7.5** | 1 | −5.0 | 10 | −4.2 | 31 | −1.8 | 24 | 1.4 | 178 |
| 76–100% | 55 | **6.9** | 0 | −3.3 | 2 | −3.3 | 5 | −3.3 | 13 | 1.4 | 73 |
| TOTALS | 1,816 | | 652 | | 860 | | 1,139 | | 511 | | 4,978 |

[a] Absolute frequencies and *standardized residuals* of all debitage and retouched pieces. Total sample $\chi$ = 415.47 at $p$ < .0001. Values of the residuals that are significant at p ≤ .05 are bold.

**B.  Levallois debitage only[b]**

| % of cortex | Scar pattern | | | | | | | | | | |
|---|---|---|---|---|---|---|---|---|---|---|---|
| | Unipolar | | Convergent | | Bipolar | | Centripetal | | Other | | Totals |
| 0 | 39 | 0.2 | 388 | 1.6 | 355 | 0.4 | 400 | −1.8 | 14 | −0.6 | 1,196 |
| 1–25% | 5 | −.04 | 42 | −1.5 | 46 | −0.1 | 62 | 1.4 | 3 | −0.8 | 158 |
| 26–50% | 0 | −0.6 | 3 | −0.5 | 2 | −1.0 | 7 | 1.8 | 0 | −0.5 | 12 |
| TOTALS | 44 | | 433 | | 403 | | 469 | | 17 | | 1,366 |

[b] Frequencies and *standardized residuals* of all debitage and retouched pieces. $\chi$ = 6.91 at $p$ > 0.5.

to change in the process of retouch, the relationships between the two attributes were tested for both debitage (excluding core management pieces) and retouched pieces. Results of a chi-square test are invalidated by the frequent occurrence of cells with low expected values (except in layer XV). Within many of the layers the standardized residuals are statistically significant and indicate that patterned relationships between frequencies of scar patterns and of striking platform types are repeated in many of the assemblages.

Centripetal Levallois modes of reduction have been claimed to yield mostly (but not exclusively) flakes with well-prepared (i.e., faceted) platforms. Indeed, it has been suggested that prepared striking platforms are a necessary attribute of Levallois cores and thus of Levallois debitage (Van Peer 1992:56). The alternative hypothesis states that varying striking platforms may occur with varieties of scar patterns. This is based on technological characteristics of recurrent Levallois flaking: the shape of the core's (and thus of the flake's) striking platforms varies along the course of reduction as an outcome of increasing preparation. Moreover, the same types of platforms can result from varying strategies of flaking, in turn resulting in differing scar patterns (e.g., Boëda, Geneste, and Meignen 1990; Geneste 1985; see table 5.1).

Flakes with unipolar scar patterns are associated with plain striking platforms in the assemblages of layers VII, XII–XVa, XVII, and XIX, and with cortical platforms in layers XV, XVII, and XXII. In these assemblages faceted platforms hardly ever occur on flakes with unipolar scar patterns. This supports the notion that the occurrence of these pieces may be attributed either to non-Levallois strategies of flaking (table 5.1) or to initial stages of Levallois production.

Flakes with convergent scar patterns consistently tend to be associated with faceted (significant in layers III, VIIa, XI, and XIII–XVa) and *chapeau de gendarme* (significant in layers V–VI, X, XII, and XV–XVII) platforms. This pattern was not expected on the basis of core characteristics, since cores with convergent scar pattern quite often exhibited platforms that were not carefully prepared, while *chapeau de gendarme* platforms were rarely present.

The specific type of *chapeau de gendarme* has often been associated in Levantine assemblages with the use of the convergent recurrent Levallois method in general, and with the production of Levallois points in particular (Bar-Yosef et al. 1992:512).[7] A chi-square test for Levallois debitage reveals the expected pattern only for the assemblage of layer XV. This supports the hypothesis that recurrent convergent Levallois flaking was used in this assemblage. However, in many other cases *chapeau de gendarme* platforms occur independently of the use of convergent Levallois flaking. Moreover, expectations based on core and scar pattern analyses (table 5.1, figure 5.3) are not borne out by this analysis for layer VIIa (where the *chapeau de gendarme* type is under-represented) and for layer XVII (where it is over-represented). The absence of the expected relationship indicates that the use of *chapeau de gendarme* platforms was not exclusively or even closely associated with the production of Levallois points and convergent scar patterns. Rather, it was used for shaping Levallois flakes as well, likely during the employment of a recurrent centripetal method.

Significant relationships occur between flakes with bipolar scar patterns and faceted (layers VI, XII–XV, and XVf) or dihedral platforms (layers VIIb, XI) in the complete debitage populations. When Levallois debitage was examined as a discrete sub-sample, no significant distributions were detected. This suggests that bipolar flaking was performed from core platforms prepared in any of several manners, and that no single type of core can be considered as their source, contrary to the initial model (table 5.1).

When the whole Qafzeh sample is examined, the combination of centripetal scar patterns and faceted platforms is significantly over-represented only in layers XI, XVa, XVII, XIX, and XXI. In other assemblages there is no significant relationship between any pairing of the two variables. Within the Levallois sub-sample, the distributions of the variables are practically independent, as was expected (table 5.1). In these latter samples there is often a tendency (never statistically significant) for faceted platforms to be slightly over-represented, while cortical, plain, and punctiform ones are somewhat under-represented. An inverse, statistically significant pattern appears in layer XV, in which cortical and plain platforms occur in higher than expected frequencies with flakes bearing centripetal scar patterns. The same holds true of dihedral platforms in layer VIIa.

Flakes with "other" scar patterns are most often associated with punctiform, cortical, and plain platforms. The analysis thus supports the notion that they were derived from the very beginning of a Levallois core reduction, or from cores that were less thoroughly prepared and thus more prone to knapping accidents.

The null hypothesis that there is a clear-cut and rigid association between specific reduction modes and particular types of striking platform is not supported by these data. On the whole, relationship between scar patterns and striking platform types are less than reliable indicators of specific modes of core reduction. The varied patterns observed through the terrace sequence indicate that the relationship is flexible and is not determined by the constraints of any specific reduction mode.

## Striking Platforms and Flake Dimensions

The relationship between flake size and two platform variables, size and type, were examined.

### The Ratio of Flake Surface Area to Platform Area

Speth (1975) demonstrated that when flakes are removed by either vertical or oblique impact, flake length (a variable in computing flake surface area) tends to increase with increased platform thickness up to a point where flaking is no longer possible. After that, if platform thickness increases, flake length plunges very rapidly back toward zero, i.e., flake removal becomes impossible. Dibble and Whittaker (1981:295), too, noted that the "relationship between platform thickness and flake length…begins to break down" under specific conditions.[8] Because platform properties help to control the size of detached blanks (at least up to a certain size limit, as discussed above), the ratio between flake surface area and platform area is perceived to be an important variable in assessing the degree of blank reduction during the process of retouch. Indeed, platform area arguably shows a significant relationship to the original flake surface area (Dibble 1995a:327).

The mean values of platform areas and of flake surface areas of unretouched pieces are highly dispersed in all the Qafzeh assemblages (table 5.13). With low and intermediate values of Spearman's *r*, these correlations indicate that, although positive, the relationship between the two variables is not a linear one. Similar results were reported by Dibble (1995a:326, tab. II) for a large number of Middle Paleolithic assemblages from Eurasia, for which values of *r* range between 0.16 and 0.76 (the mode being around 0.5). Logarithmic transformations of the variables (not shown here) similarly indicated that the predictive power of platform properties is low with regards to both flake length and width, and the relationship between the two variables is not linear.

Superficially, the lack of higher correlations between the two variables seems surprising, in view of experimental work in flaking mechanics. One would expect flakes in archaeological assemblages to exhibit the range of co-varying platform and flake size values. However, the optimal experimental conditions, in which impact height and velocity, impact angle, hammer shape and size, as well as raw material are held constant, are hardly likely to have occurred in the case of an actual assemblage. The relationship between flake area and platform area, as measured in archaeological samples, reflects more than a simple linear relationship and does not appear to be an ideal predictor for the original flake area in the case of reduction by retouch (chapter 6).

### Platform Type and Flake Length

During flaking with a hard hammer, platform faceting is used to increase the friction between the hammerstone and the core surface. This results in less salient bulbs of

**Table 5.13    Means, dispersion measures and correlations of flake surface area and platform area**

| Layer | Flake surface area[a] | | | | Platform area[b] | | | | Correlation | |
|---|---|---|---|---|---|---|---|---|---|---|
| | N | $\bar{X}$ | s.e. | CV | N | $\bar{X}$ | s.e. | CV | $r$[c] | N |
| III | 89 | 751.4 | 50.47 | 0.63 | 72 | 60.5 | 6.34 | 0.89 | 0.48 | 72 |
| IV | 95 | 824.5 | 62.77 | 0.74 | 84 | 64.9 | 7.14 | 1.01 | 0.47 | 84 |
| V | 180 | 736.0 | 40.51 | 0.74 | 140 | 72.3 | 5.82 | 0.95 | 0.52 | 140 |
| VI | 208 | 924.9 | 47.84 | 0.75 | 160 | 78.2 | 5.90 | 0.95 | 0.50 | 160 |
| VII | 123 | 1,292.6 | 103.96 | 0.89 | 110 | 124.8 | 13.73 | 1.15 | 0.51 | 110 |
| VIIa | 314 | 1,248.9 | 59.83 | 0.85 | 257 | 104.7 | 7.76 | 1.19 | 0.57 | 257 |
| VIIb | 102 | 1,211.6 | 83.19 | 0.69 | 87 | 113.4 | 10.17 | 0.84 | 0.52 | 87 |
| IX | 368 | 1,394.1 | 63.99 | 0.88 | 297 | 109.5 | 7.10 | 1.12 | 0.54 | 297 |
| X | 221 | 1,061.1 | 58.22 | 0.82 | 189 | 77.0 | 5.71 | 1.02 | 0.50 | 189 |
| XI | 283 | 1,455.3 | 63.16 | 0.73 | 231 | 98.6 | 6.60 | 1.02 | 0.53 | 231 |
| XII | 164 | 1,576.3 | 80.84 | 0.65 | 127 | 103.0 | 9.24 | 1.01 | 0.45 | 127 |
| XIII | 633 | 1,252.4 | 39.09 | 0.79 | 526 | 95.2 | 4.85 | 1.17 | 0.50 | 526 |
| XIV | 154 | 1,402.7 | 72.11 | 0.64 | 126 | 107.0 | 8.35 | 0.88 | 0.47 | 126 |
| XV | 2,803 | 1,248.6 | 16.85 | 0.71 | 2,346 | 103.1 | 1.87 | 0.88 | 0.56 | 2,346 |
| XVa | 705 | 1,161.1 | 34.50 | 0.79 | 581 | 86.7 | 4.01 | 1.12 | 0.52 | 581 |
| XVb | 157 | 1,022.3 | 67.43 | 0.83 | 133 | 65.8 | 6.38 | 1.12 | 0.48 | 133 |
| XVf | 711 | 991.8 | 31.24 | 0.84 | 562 | 78.0 | 3.41 | 1.04 | 0.47 | 562 |
| XVII | 350 | 1,321.2 | 54.21 | 0.77 | 295 | 96.2 | 6.70 | 1.20 | 0.54 | 295 |
| XIX | 252 | 1,046.2 | 51.66 | 0.78 | 192 | 103.0 | 9.36 | 0.60 | 0.34 | 192 |
| XXI | 160 | 1,424.6 | 90.47 | 0.80 | 115 | 125.5 | 12.33 | 1.05 | 0.56 | 115 |
| XXII | 99 | 1,269.9 | 145.18 | 1.14 | 60 | 103.1 | 14.19 | 1.07 | 0.46 | 60 |

*Note*: Computed on unretouched flakes only.

[a]MAXLEN x MAXWID.

[b]PLATFORM DEPTH x PLATFORM WIDTH.

[c]Spearman's rank order correlation; all values are significant at $p < .000$.

percussion (Speth 1972). Reduction of bulb dimensions in turn increases the amount of material that can be distributed and is conducive to large flakes (Pelcin 1997c:755). It is therefore expected that the higher the investment in platform preparation by faceting, the larger the flakes. I have not used a measure of the degree of platform preparation in this study, but the various platform types are proxies for this trait.

The relationships between platform types and flake length were studied only for debitage (excluding core management pieces), since the process of retouch may affect the length of the original blanks (e.g., truncations, end-scrapers and, in some cases, side-scrapers, as discussed by Dibble 1995a). Crushed and broken platforms, which are most likely unintentional results of hard-hammer percussion (see above), were not included in the following analyses.

A large part of the variance of flake length within each assemblage can be explained by the effects of types of striking platforms, except in layers X, XVII, and XIX (table 5.14). The means of length per type of platform show that debitage pieces with well-prepared platforms tend to be longer than artifacts with other types of platforms. Since the former are often associated with Levallois products

(see figure 5.4 and discussion above), this is consistent with the predicted pattern (table 5.1). Artifacts with *chapeau de gendarme* platforms are on average the longest pieces in any assemblage (with the exception of layer XI).

Faceting plays an important role in reducing the load that is necessary in order to initiate spall fractures with a hard hammer (Speth 1972), but it is not clear how it contributes to the ability to remove longer artifacts. One possibility is that there is a complex, as yet unclear, relationship between the changes in angles of the striking platform, caused partly by faceting, and the length of the detached flakes (Dibble and Whittaker 1981; Speth 1972, 1974, 1975). Possibly, faceting enables better aim of the blow at a small part of the core's striking platform, with the facet ridges monitoring the lateral spread of shear waves and directing the blow to a plane that is closer to being parallel to the core's surface. This is the role employed by the punch in the classical punch technique. The punch technique may not have been efficiently applied to Levallois core types, given the need to use oblique blows in Levallois flaking.

Trends within the Levallois sub-population echo those in the whole population. Levallois artifacts with faceted and *chapeau de gendarme* platforms are longest.

**Table 5.14  Length by type of striking platform**

| Layer | Striking platform type | | | | | | | | | | | | | | | | | | | | |
|---|---|---|---|---|---|---|---|---|---|---|---|---|---|---|---|---|---|---|---|---|---|
| | Punctiform | | | Faceted | | | Dihedral | | | Chap. de Gend. | | | Cortical | | | Plain | | | K-W test[a] | |
| | N | $\bar{X}$ | s.d. | N | $\bar{X}$ | s.d. | N | $\bar{X}$ | s.d. | N | $\bar{X}$ | s.d. | N | $\bar{X}$ | s.d | N | $\bar{X}$ | s.d. | H | $p$ |
| V | 33 | 27.52 | 7.24 | 79 | 36.47 | 13.56 | 30 | 27.40 | 12.59 | | | | 4 | 29.00 | 13.56 | 123 | 28.01 | 12.71 | 26.58 | <.0001 |
| VI | 31 | 31.65 | 11.44 | 69 | 38.78 | 13.37 | 26 | 36.88 | 17.68 | 2 | 56.00 | 19.80 | 6 | 40.17 | 19.15 | 81 | 29.21 | 10.02 | 23.77 | .0002 |
| VIIa | 16 | 31.69 | 13.45 | 95 | 42.37 | 18.90 | 39 | 34.28 | 13.55 | 3 | 43.67 | 18.72 | 14 | 40.46 | 14.81 | 106 | 35.01 | 14.19 | 16.09 | 0066 |
| IX | 35 | 36.37 | 15.19 | 137 | 45.48 | 19.60 | 53 | 32.49 | 16.91 | 8 | 49.38 | 16.42 | 15 | 36.73 | 18.78 | 100 | 34.24 | 16.54 | 38.34 | <.0001 |
| X | 26 | 30.62 | 10.56 | 72 | 36.06 | 15.64 | 19 | 31.95 | 11.56 | 8 | 44.75 | 18.89 | 7 | 31.43 | 18.23 | 83 | 31.42 | 14.06 | 9.49 | .0910 |
| XI | 26 | 35.46 | 13.56 | 89 | 47.19 | 19.55 | 44 | 36.98 | 13.29 | 2 | 44.50 | 3.54 | 9 | 33.67 | 13.38 | 97 | 36.72 | 16.40 | 19.92 | .0013 |
| XIII | 66 | 37.08 | 19.90 | 249 | 44.97 | 17.49 | 79 | 32.33 | 13.61 | 6 | 54.83 | 31.99 | 20 | 37.85 | 15.51 | 254 | 33.75 | 14.29 | 72.56 | <.0001 |
| XV | 147 | 32.46 | 13.04 | 1,072 | 44.42 | 18.01 | 338 | 35.04 | 15.56 | 28 | 50.32 | 10.58 | 127 | 40.54 | 18.96 | 730 | 34.96 | 14.63 | 211.50 | <.0001 |
| XVa | 59 | 32.31 | 15.61 | 164 | 40.10 | 17.18 | 90 | 31.81 | 13.80 | 2 | 43.50 | 19.09 | 43 | 32.40 | 13.81 | 290 | 32.32 | 14.14 | 30.28 | <.0001 |
| XVf | 87 | 31.49 | 12.73 | 158 | 36.37 | 17.47 | 94 | 30.06 | 13.34 | 2 | 41.00 | 25.46 | 17 | 27.06 | 8.61 | 299 | 31.58 | 12.53 | 13.19 | .0217 |
| XVII | 46 | 35.54 | 14.74 | 97 | 42.41 | 18.56 | 55 | 37.15 | 16.61 | 2 | 41.50 | 16.56 | 11 | 33.82 | 12.63 | 139 | 34.84 | 13.54 | 10.12 | .0718 |
| XIX | 37 | 27.70 | 11.04 | 61 | 37.20 | 15.19 | 26 | 27.69 | 10.85 | 1 | 81.00 | | 8 | 34.00 | 20.26 | 99 | 29.74 | 13.30 | 18.43 | .0025 |

*Note*: Unbroken (length) debitage only. Pieces with crushed, broken, indeterminate, or missing striking platforms and core management pieces were excluded from this analysis.
[a]Kruskal-Wallis nonparametric analysis of variance.

Regressions of flake length against platform type were carried out separately for Levallois and non-Levallois sub-populations in each assemblage (details not shown here). These analyses reflect variable effects of platform type on length. In the older assemblages (XVII and XIX), there was a significant effect of striking platform type on the length of the Levallois flakes. This may be related to a somewhat more intentional process of faceting as a prerequisite for detaching long artifacts. Non-Levallois debitage did not reflect this tendency. In other assemblages (e.g., V–VIIa, XI, and XVf), the effect of striking platform type was not significant for the any of the technological categories. In large assemblages (layers IX, XIII, XV, and XVa), the effects are statistically significant for both Levallois and non-Levallois debitage.

Although the variability seen among assemblages is partly influenced by sample sizes, there is a robust, repetitive co-variation between well-prepared platforms and greater flake length. This is in general agreement with the notion that faceting indeed had an effect on the length of the artifacts (see Baumler and Speth 1993:13) and suggests that it may have been conducted with the intention of increasing the length of pre-determined artifacts (i.e., Levallois products).

## Scar Patterns and Flake Morphometrics

### Flake Length/Size

The links between scar patterns and artifact dimensions in Levallois flaking systems have been discussed by a number of workers. Observed relationships were related to mobility patterns. Munday (1979) suggested that longer artifacts required more core preparation and would therefore be more prominent when groups were less mobile and could afford to invest more time in technological investment. Munday's work has shown that more elongated artifacts in the Negev open-air sites were often associated with unipolar and bipolar scar patterns, which in turn suggests that there is a positive relationship between such patterns and artifact sizes. However, he has not tested this relationship formally. Similarly, Kuhn (1995a) and Stiner (1994) have suggested that two basic reduction techniques addressed different economic goals of the flaking process. "Platform core" reduction, in which flakes are removed parallel to the long axis of a core from a limited area on the core's perimeter, tends to maximize the number of flakes removed from a core. On the other hand, centripetal flaking technique puts a premium on the size of the detached blanks. In the Pontinian assemblages of west-central Italy, flakes originating from centripetal reduction strategies (i.e., with centripetal scar patterns) tended to be larger (by as much as 25% in this

specific sample) than those derived from so-called "platform cores," which bear uni- or bipolar scar patterns (Stiner 1994:358). These differences were attributed to different mobility and subsistence behaviors of the artifact makers and users. Other scholars noted similar relationship in other assemblages (e.g., Richter 2000). However, the Qafzeh data are not fully consistent with these observations (the behavioral interpretations of the Qafzeh data are discussed in chapter 7).

Technologically, ridges formed on a core's flaking surface monitor the direction and force of the blow, serving as *nervures guides*. In unipolar (broadly speaking) flaking systems these ridges tend to be relatively elongated, and flakes bearing unipolar scar patterns tend to be longer than flakes detached by centripetal flaking, in which ridges tend to be shorter. That artifacts with convergent scar patterns are in many instances the longest in their respective assemblages (table 5.15, figure 5.10) is expected when unipolar convergent reduction modes are used (Munday 1979). However, flakes with simple unipolar scar patterns are the shortest in each of the Qafzeh assemblages. By the same token, the dorsal scars on flakes with bipolar scar patterns originated from opposing platforms of the core and commonly cut into one another, forming jagged rather than linear guiding ridges, which are therefore relatively short. One might expect flakes with such scar patterns to be short relative to the unipolar ones. And yet flakes with bipolar scar patterns are on average the longest in many of the Qafzeh assemblages (table 5.15, figure 5.10). This in turn suggests that they were often removed in earlier stages of the reduction sequence, before the flaking surface of a core was reduced in size, and less frequently in later stages. Finally, flakes with centripetal dorsal face scar patterns rarely exhibit the highest means of flake length (except for layers XVa and XVII). This can be reconciled with observations on cores, indicating that some of the flakes with centripetal scar patterns were the last to be removed from cores before their use was discontinued. Some flakes with centripetal scar patterns were therefore expected to be relatively short. Moreover, some such flakes were detached from cores-on-flakes, which might have caused the final products to be shorter (figure 4.2a), thus reducing the average length of this sub-population of flakes.

To sum up, although the relationship of dorsal face scar patterns on flake length is statistically significant at $p < .05$ for most of the assemblages (exceptions being layers VI and X), the differences between the categories of dorsal scar patterns are small. The mean length of flakes with different dorsal scar patterns cannot be isolated within one standard deviation in any single assemblage (table 5.15, figure 5.10).

For comparative purposes, scar patterns were also grouped into only two broad categories of "centripetal"

**Table 5.15  Length by dorsal scar patterns**

| Layer | Scar pattern | | | | | | | | | | | | | | | | | | K-W test[a] | |
|---|---|---|---|---|---|---|---|---|---|---|---|---|---|---|---|---|---|---|---|---|
| | Unipolar | | | Unipolar convergent | | | Bipolar | | | Centripetal | | | Other | | | | |
| | N | $\bar{X}$ | s.d. | N | $\bar{X}$ | s.d. | N | $\bar{X}$ | s.d. | N | $\bar{X}$ | s.d. | N | $\bar{X}$ | s.d | H | $p$ |
| V | 105 | 28.28 | 12.58 | 20 | 37.00 | 12.58 | 60 | 31.72 | 11.91 | 73 | 30.16 | 13.85 | 14 | 28.21 | 7.90 | 12.24 | .0156 |
| VI | 80 | 31.08 | 12.38 | 17 | 38.82 | 16.88 | 42 | 35.40 | 10.12 | 56 | 32.30 | 12.74 | 16 | 30.06 | 10.38 | 9.17 | .0569 |
| VIIa | 109 | 33.21 | 13.40 | 36 | 39.14 | 13.15 | 57 | 42.54 | 14.88 | 69 | 39.12 | 19.99 | 16 | 36.19 | 16.40 | 18.66 | .0009 |
| IX | 108 | 41.38 | 17.86 | 21 | 43.76 | 15.00 | 19 | 39.42 | 17.21 | 207 | 37.52 | 19.00 | 20 | 32.60 | 17.08 | 11.72 | .0192 |
| X | 62 | 31.32 | 13.87 | 28 | 35.21 | 18.51 | 64 | 35.75 | 15.59 | 59 | 33.78 | 12.77 | 92 | 9.78 | 12.66 | 3.67 | .4518 |
| XI | 74 | 33.39 | 16.60 | 10 | 47.60 | 15.62 | 59 | 43.54 | 14.25 | 118 | 41.15 | 18.74 | 18 | 37.17 | 14.37 | 23.16 | .0001 |
| XIII | 128 | 32.51 | 15.78 | 20 | 36.70 | 10.30 | 153 | 40.89 | 17.18 | 408 | 39.50 | 17.59 | — | | | 24.22 | <.0001 |
| XV | 916 | 34.75 | 16.21 | 403 | 45.39 | 16.51 | 530 | 45.57 | 16.81 | 685 | 37.86 | 16.75 | 143 | 31.17 | 13.20 | 261.57 | <.0001 |
| XVa | 279 | 32.85 | 14.79 | 50 | 34.48 | 12.74 | 118 | 35.75 | 16.10 | 205 | 35.38 | 15.79 | 28 | 28.71 | 14.62 | 9.92 | .0418 |
| XVf | 277 | 29.88 | 12.44 | 54 | 31.91 | 15.37 | 169 | 36.70 | 15.05 | 145 | 34.35 | 14.47 | 45 | 27.76 | 11.94 | 34.03 | <.0001 |
| XVII | 88 | 34.53 | 14.83 | 17 | 41.41 | 12.50 | 48 | 41.98 | 17.51 | 210 | 37.59 | 15.54 | 13 | 31.08 | 15.11 | 10.13 | .0383 |
| XIX | 86 | 28.12 | 13.29 | 7 | 28.00 | 8.64 | 21 | 30.19 | 14.40 | 138 | 35.17 | 14.62 | 8 | 29.88 | 11.53 | 20.07 | .0005 |

*Note*: Complete (length) debitage only. For details see text. Core management pieces were excluded.

[a] Kruskal-Wallis nonparametric analysis of variance.

and "limited platform" (unipolar, unipolar convergent, and bipolar) flaking methods, and the relationship with flake size (as defined above) explored (figure 5.11). The results are slightly more in line with expectations on the basis of the economic model. Reversals of the expected pattern occur in the assemblages of layers V, IX, XIV, XV, and XVb (figure 5.11). However, the differences in mean flake size between the two groups are very small in most of the assemblages and are practically non-existent within one standard deviation. Moreover, Kruskal-Wallis tests (results not presented here) indicated that the observed variation in "flake size" is not satisfactorily explained as a function of varying scar patterns ($p > .05$ for all but layers XI, XIII, XV, XVII, and XIX). This is true for Levallois debitage as a separate sub-sample as well.

Table 5.16 presents the means of flake size of Levallois and non-Levallois flakes according to the scar patterns on their dorsal faces, while figure 5.12 is a box plot illustrating the spread of flake size values in several assemblages (selected on the basis of large sample sizes). The variation of flake size is quite large in both technological groups, with outliers skewed toward the higher values. The medians for Levallois and non-Levallois samples are statistically different in all cases (the "notches" that correspond to the 95% confidence intervals around the median do not overlap between the populations), as expected from the raw data presented for flake dimensions (see figure 5.6). Yet within each technological group there is an overlap of median values of flake sizes regardless of the modes

of production. In the younger assemblages (V–VIIb), as well as assemblages XI, XIV, XV, and XXI, flakes detached from "limited platform" cores are on average larger than those with centripetal scar patterns (table 5.16). Figure 5.3 shows these to be the assemblages in which unipolar and bipolar scar patterns are relatively frequent (except for XI and XIV). In the older assemblages, in which centripetally flaked Levallois artifacts abound, they are the larger flakes in each assemblage (and, indeed, the largest of the whole sequence).

When combined together, the evidence from the whole sequence suggests that while the use of the Levallois method was designed for obtaining larger flakes, the choice of a specific flaking mode within each assemblage may not have been crucial in respect to size. A similar pattern emerges in the populations of non-Levallois flakes, as could be predicted from the weak but clear co-variation of frequencies of scar patterns in the two technological groups (figure 5.3a–b).

*Blades*

Blades occupy a special place in discussions of the evolution of lithic technologies. In the traditional Eurocentric view of prehistory, the production of laminar blanks has been considered a hallmark of modern behavior. Initially, this traditional view had little to do with any merits of blade production or use per se and relied mostly on the temporal association seen in the European prehistoric record between Upper Paleolithic blade-dominated

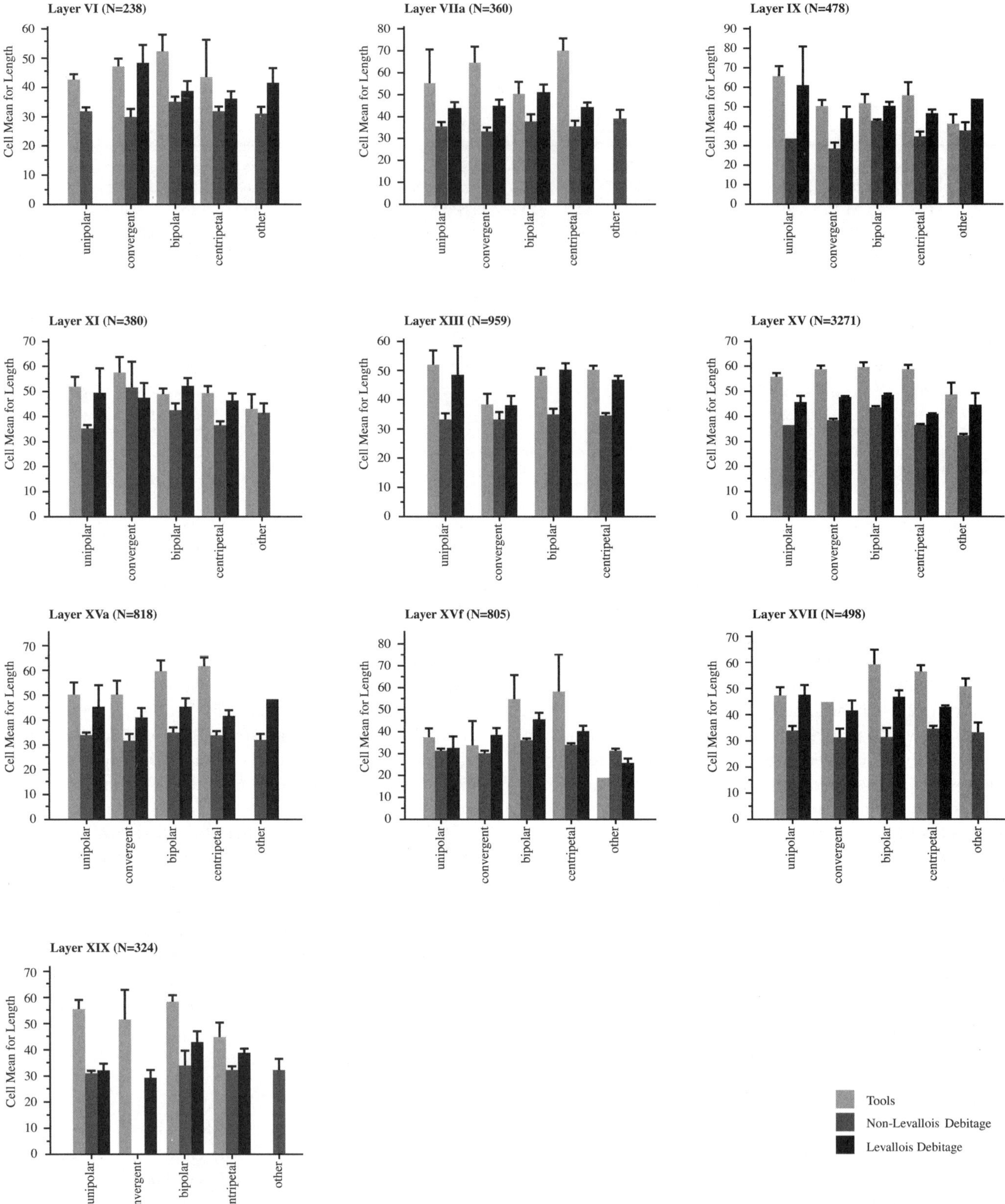

**Figure 5.10**  Mean length of tools and various debitage categories in selected assemblages, broken down by scar patterns. Only artifacts complete in the length dimension were included in this analysis. Error bars: ± 1 standard error.

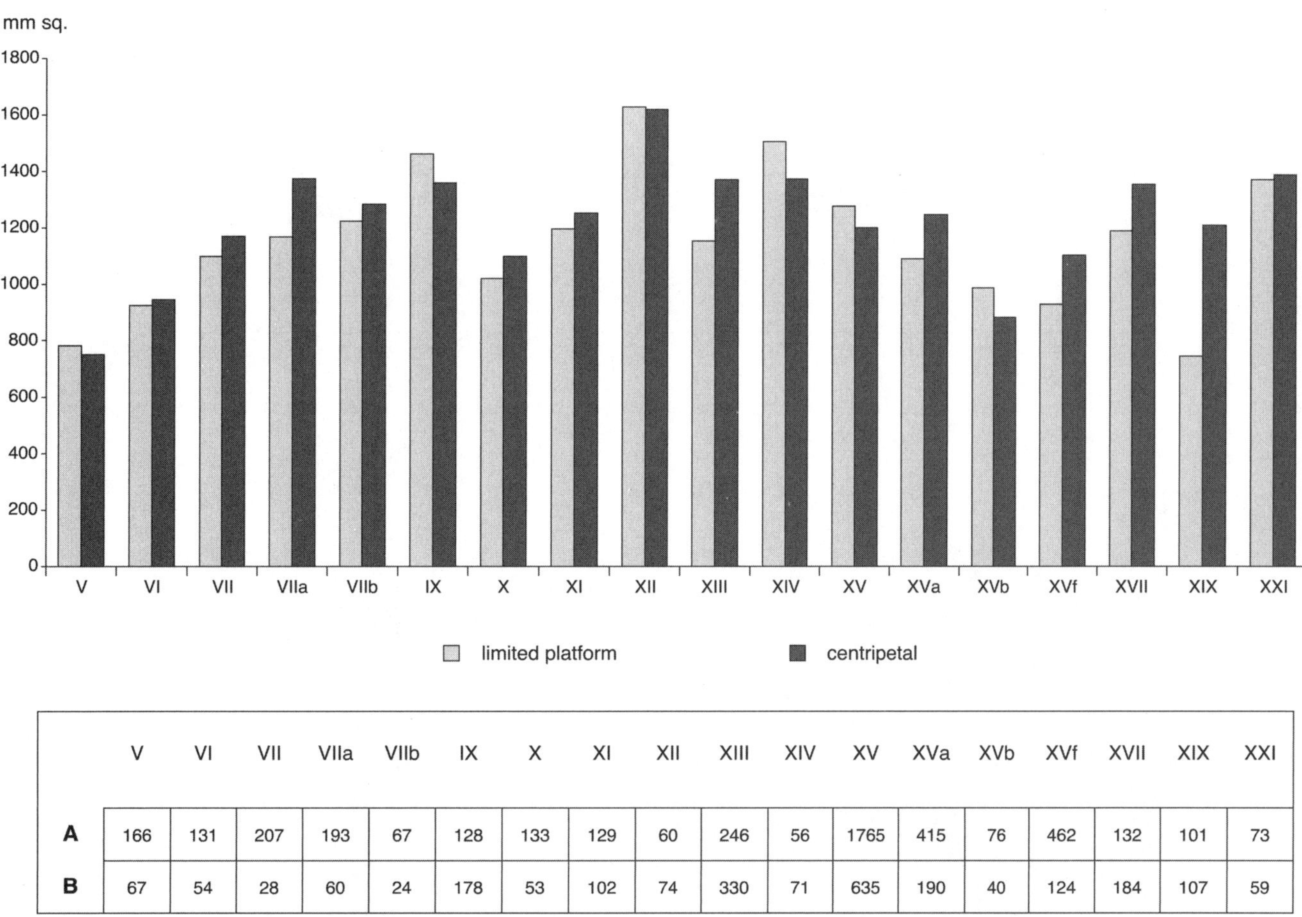

| | V | VI | VII | VIIa | VIIb | IX | X | XI | XII | XIII | XIV | XV | XVa | XVb | XVf | XVII | XIX | XXI |
|---|---|---|---|---|---|---|---|---|---|---|---|---|---|---|---|---|---|---|
| **A** | 166 | 131 | 207 | 193 | 67 | 128 | 133 | 129 | 60 | 246 | 56 | 1765 | 415 | 76 | 462 | 132 | 101 | 73 |
| **B** | 67 | 54 | 28 | 60 | 24 | 178 | 53 | 102 | 74 | 330 | 71 | 635 | 190 | 40 | 124 | 184 | 107 | 59 |

**Figure 5.11**   Mean flake size broken down by schematized dorsal flake scar patterns (see text for explanations of way of schematizing scar patterns and of calculating flake size). Only complete debitage pieces are included. Tools and core management pieces are excluded from this analysis. Absolute frequencies of "limited platform" (A) and "centripetal" (B) scar patterns are shown in the table.

industries and skeletal remains of *Homo sapiens.* This association lent blade production the aura of involving more complicated mental processes and of requiring more demanding skills than the production of Levallois blanks in the preceding Middle Paleolithic. However, neither of these assertions may in fact be valid (Bar-Yosef and Kuhn 1999; Eren et al. 2008). Ongoing research has blurred the clear-cut boundaries between flake- and blade-dominated industries across the Middle-to-Upper Paleolithic transition, pushing back the origins of blade production to earlier than 300,000 years ago. This development casts doubts on the putative modern abilities needed for using  blade-oriented technological systems (Bar-Yosef and Kuhn 1999; Meignen 2000). However, some authorities (e.g., McBrearty and Brooks 2000; McBrearty and Tryon 2006) still associate this technological phenomenon with the origins of biological as well as behavioral modernity.

It is useful in this context to make the distinction between morphological blades (flakes whose length is at least twice their width[9]) and technological blades (which in addition should have parallel or slightly converging lateral edges). While the former may include fortuitous blades, created unintentionally during reduction sequences aiming for other products, production of the latter ("true" blades in the sense of Jelinek 1975) requires special laminar technologies. Upper Paleolithic prismatic blade technology is the best known of a large array of such technologies, but it is not the only one. Other variants of blade production systems exist (e.g., the Amudian or the Hummalian in Levantine contexts; Barkai, Gopher, and Shimelmitz 2005; Meignen 2000; Ronen 1992), and Levallois flaking, too, can be used to produce preplanned blades (Boëda 1990).

Suggestions that blade production possessed inherent advantages suited for advanced, complex, or overwhelmingly efficient technological adaptations came

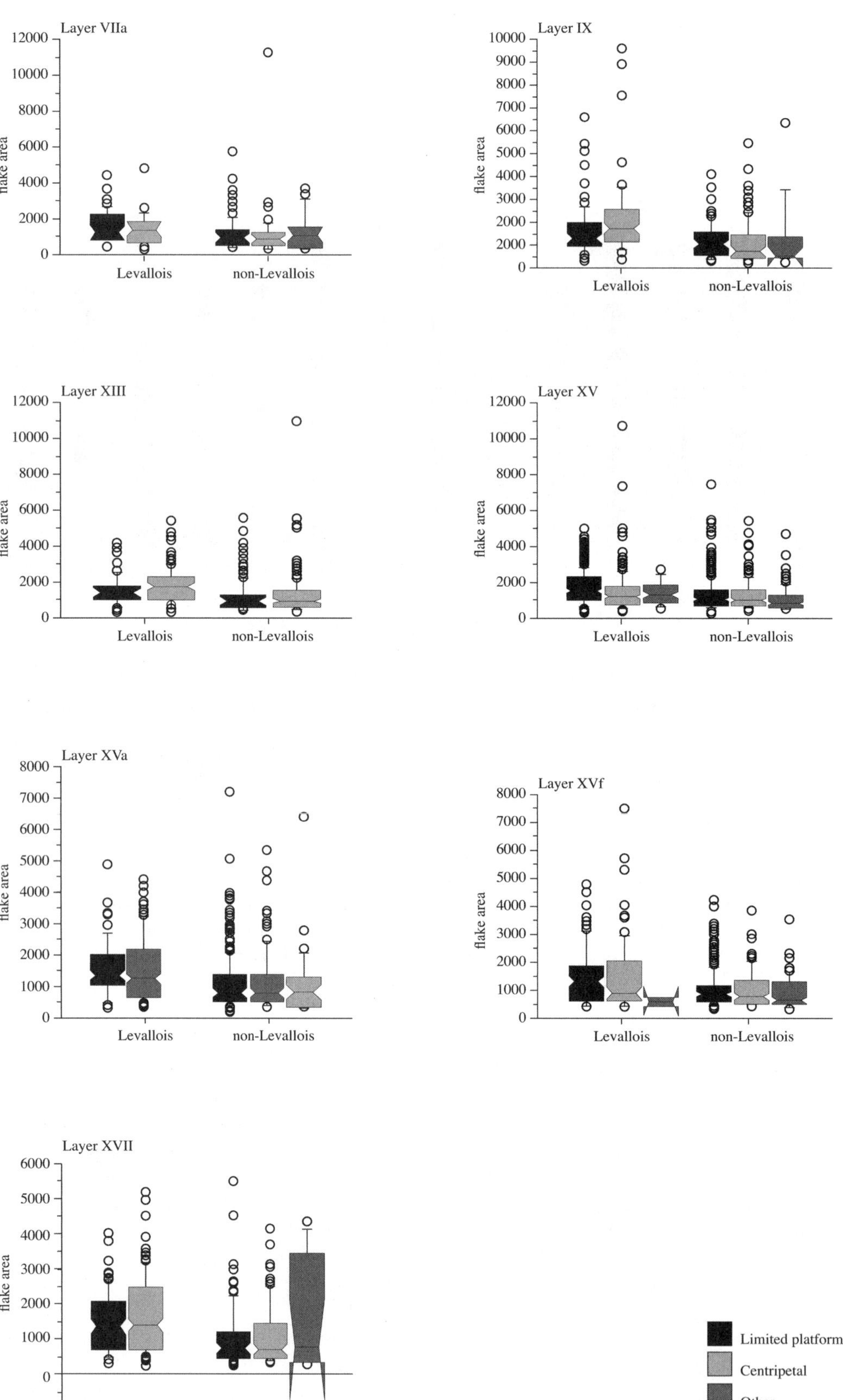

**Figure 5.12** Box plots illustrating the spread of flake size (maximum length x maximum width) values of Levallois and non-Levallois artifacts, broken down by schematized dorsal face scar patterns. See text for detailed explanations. The horizontal lines of each box represent the 10, 25, 50 (median), 75 and 90 percentiles, with a "notch" defining the 95% confidence intervals at the median (McGill, Tukey, and Larson 1978). The open circles show individual cases that form outliers.

**Table 5.16  Flake size of unretouched blanks**

| Layer | Levallois | | | Non-Levallois | | |
|---|---|---|---|---|---|---|
| | Limited platform | Centripetal | Other | Limited platform | Centripetal | Other |
| IV | 1,030 (12) | 1,248 (3) | — | 692 (56) | 839 (8) | 1,474 (5) |
| V | **1,264 (31)** | 875 (19) | — | 673 (135) | 703 (48) | 698 (10) |
| VI | **1,313 (16)** | 1,253 (16) | 1,000 (1) | 871 (115) | 818 (38) | 878 (13) |
| VII | **1,901 (48)** | 1,590 (25) | — | 857 (159) | 971 (53) | 623 (26) |
| VIIa | **1,667 (49)** | 1,487 (21) | — | 997 (144) | 1,314 (39) | 1,189 (15) |
| VIIb | **1,452 (15)** | 1,415 (11) | — | 1,158 (52) | 1,172 (782) | — |
| IX | 1,772 (65) | 2,268 (51) | — | 114 (63) | 995 (127) | 1,315 (13) |
| X | 1,249 (49) | 1,414 (25) | — | 889 (84) | 819 (28) | 798 (6) |
| XI | **1,838 (37)** | 1,763 (56) | — | 1,196 (92) | 1,251 (46) | 1,489 (20) |
| XII | 1,867 (21) | 1,843 (41) | — | 149 (39) | 1,338 (33) | 799 (8) |
| XIII | 1,508 (56) | 1,741 (141) | — | 104 (190) | 1,095 (189) | — |
| XIV | **1,557 (29)** | 1,451 (36) | — | 14 (27) | 1291 (35) | 1,131 (9) |
| XV | **1,649 (593)** | 1,322 (277) | 1,306 (7) | 1,085 (1172) | 1,104 (358) | 887 (112) |
| XVa | 1,539 (49) | 1,523 (70) | 1,274 (1) | 1,046 (366) | 1,085 (120) | 1,111 (22) |
| XVb | 929 (11) | 1,071 (23) | — | 998 (65) | 626 (17) | 963 (8) |
| XVf | 1,360 (73) | 1,446 (56) | — | 849 (389) | 819 (68) | 807 (38) |
| XVII | 1,442 (53) | 1,623 (96) | — | 1,017 (79) | 1,060 (88) | 1,380 (8) |
| XIX | 824 (18) | 1,284 (26) | — | 728 (83) | 1,068 (184) | 1,074 (7) |
| XXI | **1,878 (24)** | 1,635 (36) | — | 1,121 (49) | 1,003 (23) | 1,678 (6) |
| XXII | 1,020 (7) | 1,892 (21) | — | 1,158 (41) | 794 (12) | 1,733 (5) |

*Note*: Means per layer, in mm$^2$; measurements of complete blanks only, excluding core management pieces, rounded to the closest whole number. Absolute frequencies shown in parentheses.

later, when research traditions turned from cultural-historical frameworks to ecologically oriented explanatory models. Attempts were then made to identify the technological adaptations that contributed to the evolutionary success of *Homo sapiens*. The advantages of blades are argued to be most apparent where raw material economy is at a premium. Prismatic (Upper Paleolithic) blade production arguably enables removal of blanks from the whole volume of the core, yielding more laminar blanks and thus presumably more cutting edge length per lithic raw material package than does Levallois blade removal, which concentrates on the exploitation of a single surface of flake detachment, gradually diminishing the core and the size of the products as reduction proceeds. An additional advantage of prismatic blades is the standardization of blank size as a result of the close control it allows during flaking. Such uniformity of products is highly advantageous when preparing the replaceable parts of composite tools (e.g., Bleed 1986; Nelson 1991).

Blades and elongated points (pointed blades) are a significant component of some early Levantine Mousterian ("Tabun D-type") assemblages, such as Tabun IX (Jelinek 1982a, 1982b); Hayonim E (Meignen 1994a, 1998), Abu Sif, Rosh Ein Mor (Bar-Yosef 1998a; Crew 1976), Ain Difla (Lindly and Clark 1987), Douara IV (Nishiaki 1989), Misliya (Weinstein-Evron et al. 2003).

These laminar components derive from a number of flaking systems and concepts (the Levallois as well as an Upper Paleolithic-like laminar system, as well as the contemporaneous Hummalian of El-Kowm [Boëda and Muhesen 1994]). Despite the rather systematic manner of blade production in these assemblages, they are not significantly more standardized in their dimensions than in later Mousterian assemblages, in which blades are clearly by-products of Levallois point and flake manufacture (Ashkenazi 2005), suggesting that they were not replaceable components of composite tools. It has been claimed that blade technologies are more productive in terms of the number of blanks per unit of stone; this claim has been evaluated empirically with regards obsidian pressure flaking (Sheets and Muto 1972) but was recently rejected on the basis of experimental hard hammer percussion of flint (Eren et al. 2008). It is thus difficult to evaluate the possibility that blade production in the earlier Levantine Mousterian was associated with higher mobility of human groups over their territories, which would have favored flaking technologies that boosted blank output per unit of stone mass.

The Qafzeh assemblages are clearly not oriented toward blade production. True blades are practically non-existent in the terrace assemblages, as seen from the paucity of parallel dorsal face scar patterns (table 5.3). Still artifacts with laminar proportions do exist in each of

**Table 5.17**  Frequencies of blades in the terrace assemblages

| Layer | N[a] | N of blades[b] | N of blades[c] | Ilam[d] |
|---|---|---|---|---|
| III | 198 | 45 (22.72) | 39 | 19.70 |
| IV | 218 | 46 (21.10) | 42 | 19.27 |
| V | 657 | 153 (23.28) | 145 | 22.07 |
| VI | 433 | 82 (18.94) | 80 | 18.48 |
| VII | 354 | 44 (12.43) | 37 | 10.45 |
| VIIa | 599 | 105 (17.53) | 89 | 14.85 |
| VIIb | 313 | 26 (8.31) | 26 | 8.31 |
| IX | 1,123 | 121 (10.77) | 103 | 9.17 |
| X | 606 | 75 (12.38) | 64 | 10.56 |
| XI | 846 | 84 (9.93) | 70 | 8.27 |
| XII | 498 | 81 (16.27) | 67 | 13.45 |
| XIII | 2,243 | 285 (12.76) | 236 | 10.52 |
| XIV | 495 | 76 (15.35) | 62 | 12.53 |
| XV | 6,111 | 1,249 (20.44) | 1,063 | 17.39 |
| XVa | 1,602 | 259 (16.17) | 230 | 14.36 |
| XVb | 311 | 44 (14.14) | 38 | 11.22 |
| XVf | 1,572 | 252 (16.03) | 227 | 14.44 |
| XVII | 867 | 104 (12.00) | 97 | 11.19 |
| XIX | 515 | 50 (9.71) | 42 | 8.16 |
| XXI | 312 | 27 (8.65) | 24 | 7.70 |
| XXII | 183 | 23 (12.17) | 20 | 10.58 |

[a] Total number of debitage and tools.

[b] Blade counts and relative frequencies including core management pieces (% out of N in column 2).

[c] Blade counts excluding core management pieces.

[d] % based on Ns in previous column (calculated out of N in column 2).

the Qafzeh assemblages (table 5.17). The number of such pieces used in calculating the "laminar index" (Ilam, table 5.17 column 4) and assessing the "laminar tendency" of each assemblage (Jelinek 1975:304) does not include either blade-proportioned Levallois points or any of the core management pieces (e.g., naturally backed knives), the laminar proportions of which are a by-product of the process of core modification rather than an intended goal.

Unipolar and/or centripetal scar patterns dominate the blade component of all the assemblages (figure 5.13a), bipolar scar patterns being secondary in their frequencies. When compared to the scar patterns observed in the respective total assemblages, values of Ilam do not seem to be related directly to frequencies of uni- and bipolar scar patterns in the assemblages (figure 5.14). Blade-proportioned artifacts are relatively rare in some of the layers in which higher frequencies would be expected on the basis of scar patterns (e.g., layers V, VII, VIIb–X), while surprisingly high values are encountered in assemblages in which centripetal scar patterns are dominant (e.g., layers XII, XIV, and XVII). The high Ilam recorded in assemblages XV–XVa and XVf is consistent with the scar patterns observed in these layers (figures 5.3, 5.14).

Similarly, one might expect that frequencies of Levallois blades within the blade component of each assemblage would rise with the increased occurrence of uni- and bipolar scar patterns (and to a lesser extent, also the convergent; plates 8:5, 7, 17:5, 18:4–8, 21:3–6, 43:5, 46:3, 47:3). Despite this, the highest frequencies of Levallois blades are encountered in the older or mid-sequence assemblages (figure 5.15; plates 14:1, 16:10, 30:8–10), which are dominated by a centripetal flaking mode. Within the Levallois blades, it is not necessarily the uni/bipolar mode that was used for their production (figure 5.13b). However, caution is warranted because of the insufficient sample sizes involved.

The evidence suggests that the shift to increased use of the Levallois bipolar flaking mode in the younger assemblages was not geared toward a more efficient production of laminar elements. Elongated elements in the Qafzeh assemblages are not true technological laminar products, as indicated by the paucity of blade cores and of typical core waste (e.g., ridge blades). The lack of co-variation between scar patterns and the laminar index in the respective assemblages supports this notion. Overall, it seems that blade-proportioned artifacts at Qafzeh were incidental rather than desired products. Given the date of at least some of the Qafzeh assemblages, this is an additional indication that the augmentation of blade production was not a directional long-term shift from the Middle to the Upper Paleolithic, in the Levant or elsewhere in the Old World (Bar-Yosef and Kuhn 1999; Goren-Inbar and Belfer-Cohen 1998; Hovers 1998a; Soriano, Villa, and Wadley 2007).

## Scar Patterns and Relative Thickness

Relative thickness was calculated as "flake size" divided by flake thickness, so that higher ratios indicate thinner flakes and sharper edges. The Levallois and non-Levallois groups are distinct from one another (table 5.18) but overlap within one standard deviation. In assemblages V–VI, VIIa–VIIb, X–XI, and XIV–XVa "limited platform" Levallois flakes are thinner than "centripetal" flakes (mean values for these assemblages are emphasized in the table). When compared with mean flake size (table 5.16), it seems that these relatively thinner flakes do not always occur where "limited platform" flakes are larger than "centripetal" flakes. Thus, in seven instances the observation can be explained by the smaller mean flake size of centripetal flakes in the assemblage, but this is not the case for layers X and XVf, in which centripetally prepared flakes are larger. In the same vein, there are a few instances of larger "limited platform" flakes but thinner centripetal flakes. This suggests that, as in the case of flake size, relatively thin and sharp blanks were prepared using any one of several technological options

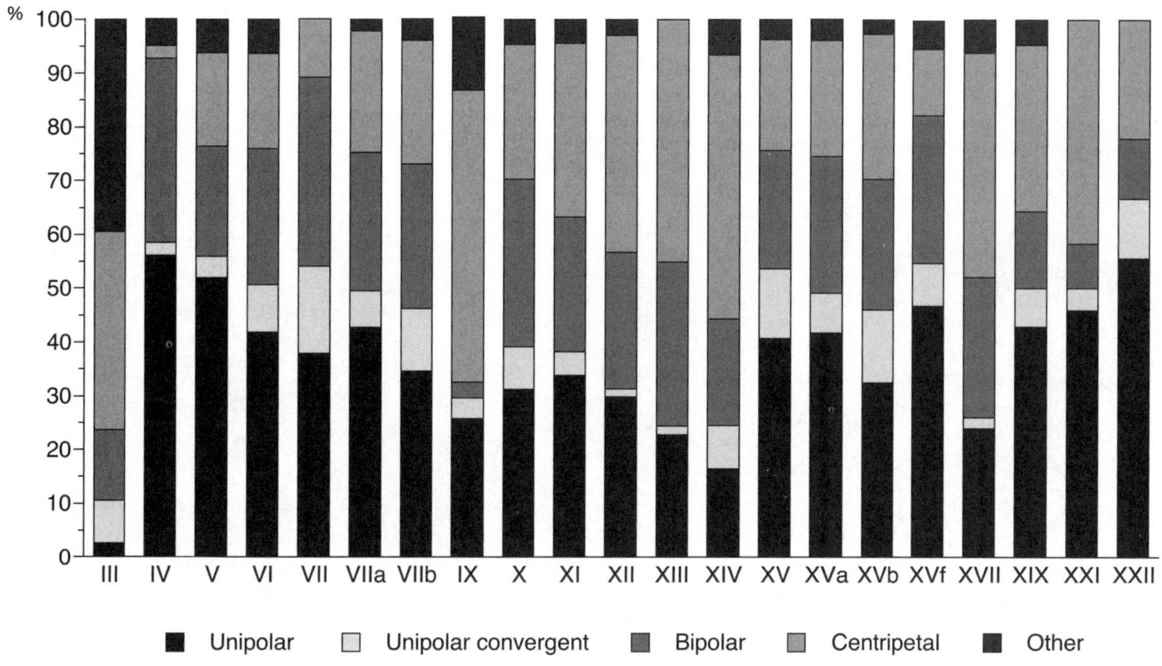


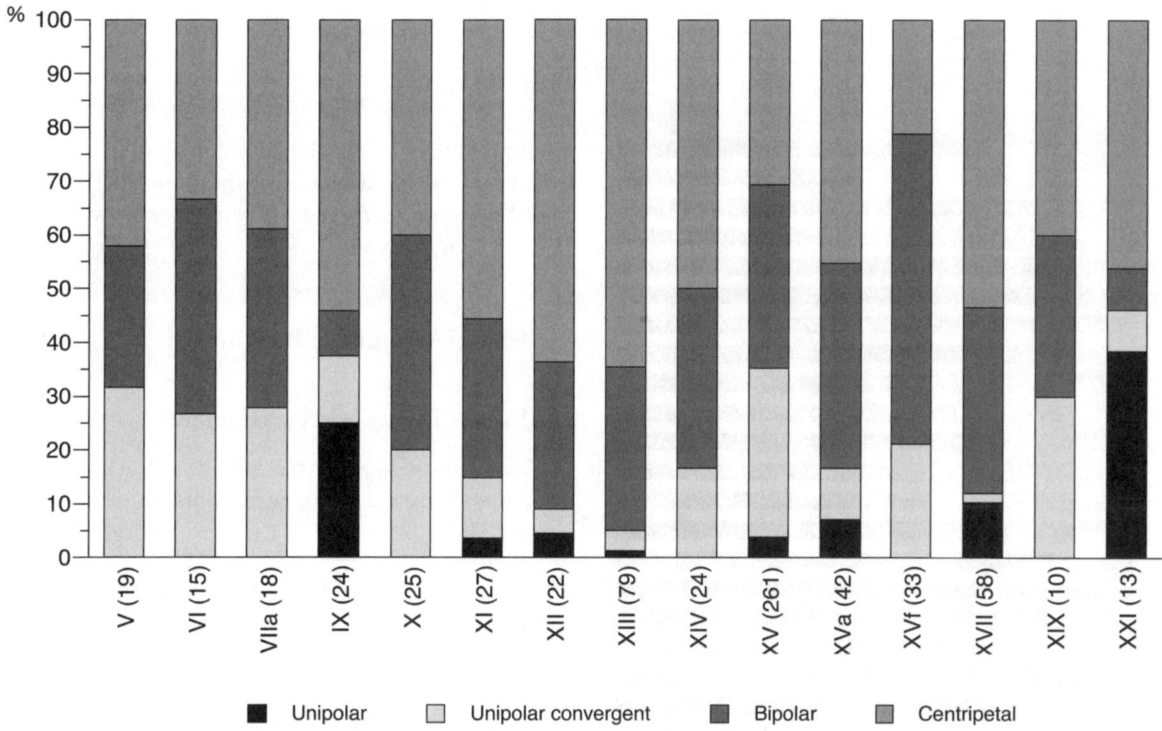


**Figure 5.13**  Frequencies of scar patterns on blades in the Qafzeh assemblages. A: All blades (Ns appear in column 4 of table 5.17). B: Only Levallois blades.

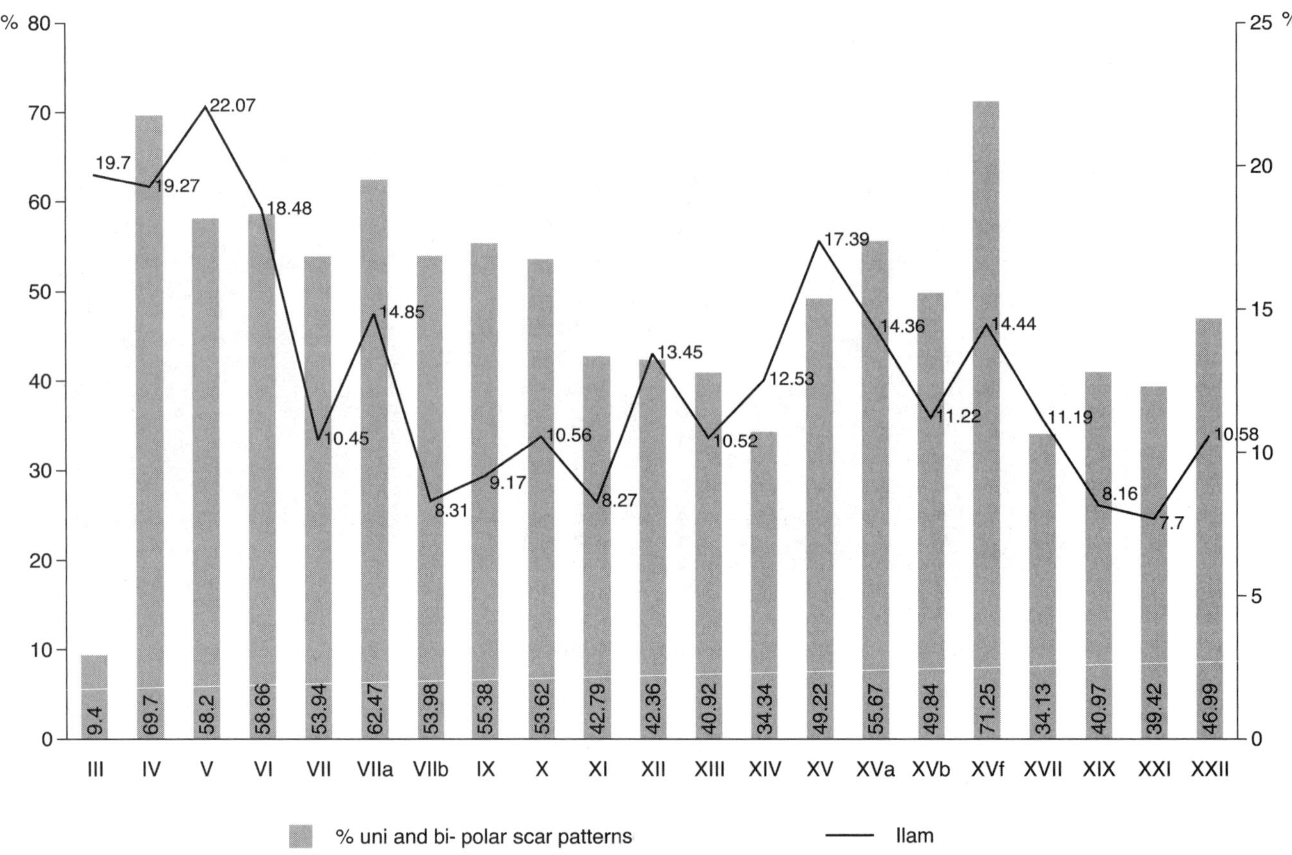



**Figure 5.14** Frequencies of uni- and bipolar scar patterns on debitage (left axis) compared to values of the laminar index (right axis).

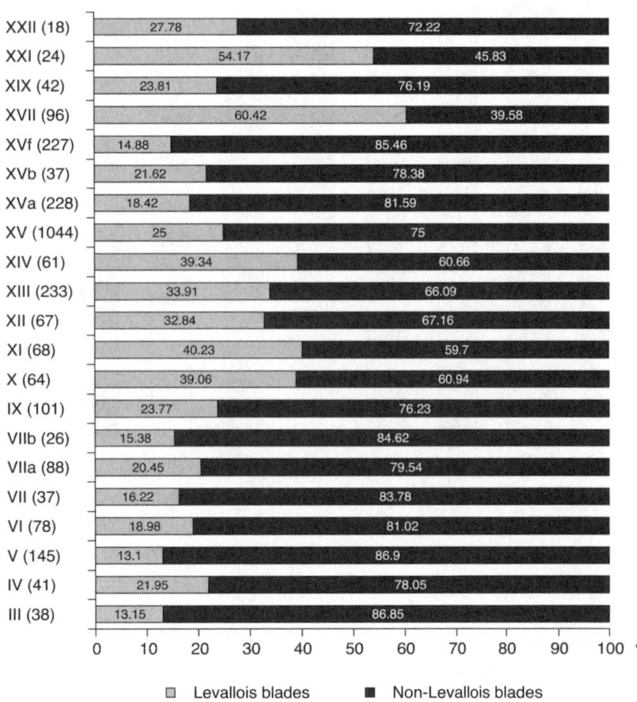



**Figure 5.15** Frequencies of Levallois and non-Levallois blades in the Qafzeh assemblages (calculated from the total number of blades in each assemblage).

encountered within the Levallois system. Obtaining such flakes (presumably the desired products of reduction) did not entail adherence to any specific method or mode of lithic reduction.

## Strategies of Lithic Production

### Modes of Levallois Production

The technological characteristics of flakes and flake tools of the Qafzeh assemblages conform, to a large degree, with those observed in the core assemblages. The flake populations in the lower and mid-sequence assemblages (e.g., layers XI–XIII, XVb, XVII–XXII) exhibit the expected properties of recurrent centripetal Levallois reduction, expressed in the preponderance of centripetal dorsal face scar patterns, well-prepared striking platforms, and large Levallois products, as well as typical core management pieces. In other assemblages of the Qafzeh sequence, there are predictions from the core assemblages that are not borne out, and discrepancies are observed between the flake and core assemblages. In the younger assemblages (X–III, but also XIV–XVa, XVf), Levallois cores for flakes, with characteristic properties

**Table 5.18  Relative thickness of unretouched blanks**

| Layer | Levallois | | | Non-Levallois | | |
|---|---|---|---|---|---|---|
| | Limited platform | Centripetal | Other | Limited platform | Centripetal | Other |
| IV | 149 (12) | 157 (3) | — | 122 (55) | 166 (8) | 100 (4) |
| V | **205 (31)** | **156 (19)** | — | 119 (134) | 111 (48) | 110 (10) |
| VI | **192 (16)** | **183 (16)** | 143 (1) | 136 (115) | 116 (38) | 103 (13) |
| VII | 226 (46) | 203 (25) | — | 135 (158) | 125 (53) | 85 (25) |
| VIIa | **219 (48)** | **203 (21)** | — | 145 (143) | 160 (39) | 133 (12) |
| VIIb | **234 (15)** | **178 (11)** | — | 141 (49) | 140 (13) | — |
| IX | 246 (65) | 285 (51) | — | 141 (62) | 148 (124) | 136 (12) |
| X | **199 (49)** | **198 (25)** | — | 137 (79) | 119 (27) | 107 (5) |
| XI | **243 (37)** | **231 (55)** | — | 134 (89) | 149 (46) | 128 (14) |
| XII | 212 (21) | 251 (41) | — | 184 (39) | 139 (33) | 86 ( 7) |
| XIII | 221 (56) | 248 (139) | — | 150 (187) | 139 (185) | — |
| XIV | **227 (29)** | **213 (36)** | — | 164 (27) | 152 (35) | 102 (9) |
| XV | **245 (587)** | **204 (275)** | 194 (7) | 157 (1160) | 153 (355) | 111 (107) |
| XVa | 229 (48) | 236 (69) | 127 (1) | 154 (364) | 156 (118) | 123 (21) |
| XVb | 190 (11) | 193 (23) | — | 150 (65) | 114 (17) | 92 (6) |
| XVf | **219 (71)** | **212 (55)** | — | 144 (378) | 138 (64) | 111 (37) |
| XVII | 217 (55) | 225 (107) | — | 145 (81) | 136 (98) | 98 (10) |
| XIX | 175 (17) | 209 (69) | — | 122 (83) | 137 (37) | 158 (6) |
| XXI | 199 (24) | 227 (35) | | 146 (48) | 147 (23) | 199 (6) |

*Note*: Means per layer; measurements of complete blanks only, rounded to the closest whole number. Absolute frequencies shown in parentheses. Core management pieces are excluded.

of recurrent centripetal flaking, are the most frequent. "Centripetal" is indeed the single most frequent category of scar patterns in these assemblages, but flakes bearing bipolar scars are also abundant (figure 5.3). Given that in any of the terrace assemblages only a few Levallois cores for flakes exhibit bipolar scar patterns on their flaking surfaces (table 4.4), two possible explanations can be proposed. One posits that bipolar flaking was employed in the earlier phases of the reduction sequence, switching to centripetal recurrent reduction when the cores were reduced to a relatively small size. A second explanation is that the abundance of Levallois flakes with bipolar scar patterns reflects the middle stages of core reduction by Levallois recurrent centripetal methods. The latter possibility is supported by the types and frequencies of core management pieces in the pertinent assemblages (with the possible exception of layer VIIa; see below). It seems that in these assemblages Levallois cores were exploited from limited striking platforms before the preparation of the core's striking platform reached its fullest extent, terminating in a core with centripetal scar patterns on its flaking surface.

The core evidence suggested that in the layer XV assemblage (as well as VIIa, and potentially those of layers XIII–XIV) recurrent unipolar convergent flaking was applied as an additional flaking method. These predictions are clearly borne out in the case of layer XV by the high frequency (12.4%) of Levallois points, the vast majority of which were produced by the convergent method,

among the unretouched Levallois products. Overall, frequencies of convergent scar patterns are far higher in this assemblage than in any other assemblage of the Qafzeh sequence, and naturally backed flakes are the commonest among the core management elements. These lines of evidence combine to suggest that two distinct Levallois methods are reflected in the assemblage of layer XV: one designed for the production of points (and, to a lesser degree, triangular flakes), the other for "regular" Levallois flakes of the Qafzeh sequence. The data for layer VIIa point in the same direction though not as clearly.

## How Valid is the Levallois/non-Levallois Dichotomy in the Qafzeh Assemblages?

Observations on cores and blanks observations tell very different stories about the quantitative importance of Levallois flaking strategies in all the Qafzeh assemblages. Core frequencies indicate that Levallois reduction was the most common way of obtaining detached pieces (primarily flakes) in these assemblages. However, the majority of flakes could not be assigned to Levallois methods, as indicated by the moderate values of IL (figure 5.1a). This discrepancy is not a unique feature of the Qafzeh assemblages among Levantine Mousterian assemblages.

One possible explanation of the discrepancy is that it reflects differential transport of debitage and cores across the landscape. Levallois cores offer an advantageous compromise between mass that needs to be carried and potential removal of flakes with long cutting edges that could well become a mobile component of a Mousterian toolkit (Kuhn 1994), augmenting their numbers in any given assemblage. If that were the case, however, we would expect to see elevated frequencies of Levallois products in these assemblages, especially if (as the data suggest) many of the Levallois cores had long life histories, i.e., had undergone long reduction sequences. In fact, the opposite is true of these assemblages.

Conversely, the redundant patterning of the ratios of Levallois debitage to cores in the assemblages may reflect export of Levallois blanks away from the site, inflating the relative importance of non-Levallois pieces. As we will see in chapter 7, this may have been the case in some cases, for specific Levallois products that were not necessarily the most abundant in these assemblages. Overall, however, the Qafzeh assemblages seem to represent on-site lithic reduction.

Several lines of evidence suggest that the discrepancy is more apparent than real.

1. The major trends of shifts in frequencies of scar patterns observed in the Levallois sub-samples in the various assemblages can also be seen in the non-Levallois flake populations (figure 5.3). The overall higher frequencies of centripetal scar patterns on Levallois debitage in the older assemblages are echoed in the non-Levallois component. By the same token, the highest frequencies of bipolar scar patterns among non-Levallois pieces occur in the assemblages in which this scar pattern is highest in the Levallois component as well. This suggests that at least some of the non-Levallois flakes were removed from the same cores as Levallois flakes, although less attention had been paid to their preparation. The non-Levallois flakes resulted from preparatory and intermediary stages in the process of reduction and rearrangement of the Levallois core.

2. A similar pattern is observed with regard to IPA. The Levallois and non-Levallois groups of debitage show distinct and different distributions of types of striking platforms, with the faceted platforms clearly being more abundant in the former and plain platforms in the latter. IPA indeed seem to differ according to the platform type. Statistically, however, the frequencies and distribution patterns of the means of IPA on flakes associated with the two technological groupings cannot be differentiated. The only exception to this is the assemblage of layer XV. This suggests that the differences are rather small and are statistically valid only in extremely large samples. It is thus unlikely that they reflect conscious differentiation by the knapper between many of the flakes

that are assigned (analytically) to the non-Levallois group and the Levallois debitage.

Comparison of IPA of flakes analytically attributed to Levallois as opposed to non-Levallois strategies shows a clear trend. There is always a higher degree of similarity of the mean values for the two technologies within any specific assemblage than there is within each technological grouping across layers. This implies that both Levallois and non-Levallois flakes could have been removed consecutively from a single core, during alternating phases of removals of predetermined (Levallois) flakes and preparation of the core for a next stage of such removals (non-Levallois flakes). Only minute hand movements would be necessary to adjust the striking angles for each of these purposes, resulting in the observed tendency toward intra-assemblage similarity in striking angles, with a somewhat higher inter-assemblage range.

As flake thickness has been experimentally shown to be highly correlated with impact angles (Dibble and Whittaker 1981; Speth 1972, 1975), the similarity in the means of thickness of Levallois and non-Levallois debitage in each assemblage (figure 5.6c) and in their ranges indirectly supports the argument for an overwhelmingly Levallois reduction process, in the course of which some of the non-Levallois debitage was produced.

3. Length distributions of both Levallois and non-Levallois debitage cover almost identical ranges (figure 5.7). If we accept that blank transport was minimal (see above and chapter 7), the similarity in the shapes of distributions suggests that the two technological groupings were not produced from different-sized nodules of raw materials. The shapes of the two distributions fit the expectations of the nature of the centripetal recurrent Levallois method. Larger flakes were produced (in smaller numbers) at the beginning of the flaking process (Geneste's [1985:250] "phase 2"), as indicated by the tail of lower frequencies of large Levallois flakes. Then a series of several Levallois flakes, similar in size, were removed from each flaking surface of the centripetally prepared core (Boëda 1993; Boëda, Geneste, and Meignen 1990:68). Thus, any single length category of the distribution may include a few similar-sized Levallois flakes. Because the core underwent several cycles of rearrangement and flake removals, and flakes were somewhat reduced in size after each stage of core management, groups of flakes resulting from these consecutive cycles of Levallois production should occur in similar frequencies along a continuous range of the distribution. The highly skewed distributions of non-Levallois elements imply that

many of these may have been removed mainly as auxiliaries, in the process of core reorganization.

Had a lineal mode been used, the presence of larger (but fewer) preferential flakes would be reflected by "troughs" in the higher size range of the distribution. This is in fact the pattern seen in the assemblages of layers XIV, XIX, and XXI, in which the frequencies of the "dominant and centripetal" scar pattern are relatively high (table 5.3). This scar pattern is also significantly represented in cores of layers XIV and XIX. In these assemblages, "troughs" occur at the 50–59 and 60–69 mm length categories (figure 5.7), with a few larger flakes that belong to the initial stages of the core exploitation. These ranges fit the data on the size of last-removed Levallois blanks (table 4.5). Based on the shape of the curves of these assemblages, it is possible that a lineal method had indeed been practiced, alongside a recurrent one.

In sum, the discrepancies between the quantitative importance of Levallois cores among the cores in an assemblage, compared to that of Levallois debitage in an assemblage, is explained partly by the technological practices of the Qafzeh inhabitants when making their stone tools. Specifically, it can be attributed to the extensive use of recurrent centripetal reduction strategy. This flaking strategy is relatively flexible and allows for the exploitation of a whole range of flaking tactics. The resultant flakes vary significantly in any (or all) of their attributes from one stage of the use of a single core to the next. Given the evidence for a long use life of the cores exploited by recurrent centripetal Levallois methods (expressed at Qafzeh by the shapes of length distributions and frequencies of "core management" pieces), the full array of tactics could have been put to use. The implementation of this flaking method would involve the detachment of non-Levallois flakes in phases of core preparation and remanagement (see also Geneste 1985). Although many of these "non-Levallois" flakes are perceived as by-products of a main goal, use-wear analysis suggests that they were used for variable tasks (Shea 1991).

The notion that some of the non-Levallois debitage was produced in the course of Levallois reduction fits the overall evidence that the flaking process was carried out on site most of the time. This, of course, does not rule out the exploitation of exclusively non-Levallois strategies of core reduction. Some core types indicate the use of such strategies in almost every assemblage. Besides, it would be difficult logically to assign all the non-Levallois products to preparatory phases of Levallois flaking strategies. Yet it is difficult to distinguish the intended products of non-Levallois strategies (with the obvious exception of formal laminar systems) from similar ones removed in order to prepare the core during the process of Levallois production. This kind of accurate individual distinction can probably only be obtained by refitting studies.

Most researchers accept that Levallois flaking methods were the favored strategies of Levantine Mousterian hominins for obtaining desired blanks, even if they do not quantitatively dominate the assemblages. The Qafzeh data suggest that in all likelihood Levallois flaking is also quantitatively more widespread than meets the eye. What the current analysis indicates clearly is that the dichotomy of Levallois/non-Levallois in the Qafzeh assemblage (and most probably in other Levantine Mousterian assemblages) is not as clear-cut or dramatic as it sometimes appears.

## Summary

The core and blank populations of the Qafzeh assemblages derive from almost complete on-site reduction sequences. One major method of Levallois flaking—the recurrent centripetal method—was used to produce Levallois debitage, possibly combined with some use of the lineal method in the older assemblages. In each assemblage the specific properties of Levallois flakes, toward the production of which these variations were geared, were obtainable by any of several modes of production. The most critical single variable that affected such flake characteristics was the degree of preparation of the core's striking platform. Technological changes observed throughout the sequence do not involve a major change in reduction strategies. Rather, they exhibit a high degree of technological flexibility within the parameters of one reduction strategy (recurrent Levallois reduction) and, in some cases (layers XV, XIII, and VIIa), the use of several reduction strategies in parallel.

The relationships between parameters such as flake size and form, striking platform angles and shapes, and the complexity of scar patterns, suggest that, within the constraints of the physical processes involved in flint fracture mechanics, the shapes and sizes of the final products were determined by the intent and will of the knappers, who appear to have been able to achieve their morphometric goals by a variety of flaking procedures. As such, the Qafzeh assemblages are an example of the phenomenon of "equifinality."

Another implication of the data concerns the perception of knapping sequences as either continuous or stage-related processes (Tostevin 2006). The data in this chapter suggest that, on different levels, both views are valid. When core convexities were re-created so that Levallois flake production could continue, knappers worked in stages. They diverted from practices and techniques used for flake removal to other techniques used for core management. The switches between flake removal and core maintenance procedures throughout the process of core reduction would have constituted conceptual stages. Other data, such as the relationship between cortical platforms and cortical flakes, suggest that core reduction was perceived as a single continuous process, during which appropriate technical steps were taken to address immediate problems.

The technological indices presented here agree in general with previous ones reported by Boutié (1989), although concrete values may differ to some degree. His work also suggests that technological patterns seen in the terrace assemblages are echoed in the cave assemblages (not analyzed here). However, since the stratigraphic relationships between the majority of the terrace layers and those in the cave suggest different deposition times (chapter 3), it is impractical to hypothesize about the temporal (*sensu stricto*) and occupational relationships between them.

# 6

# Lithic Production: 3. The Retouched Artifacts

## What Mean These Stones—And How Can We Find Out?

The only unambiguous statement about retouched tools that you will hear from prehistorians is that they reflect investment beyond the stage of blank production. Few would doubt that retouch on a lithic blank originated from conscious decisions by prehistoric people, followed by intentional action in order to shape blanks into specific forms; but this is where consensus ends. Once considered cultural and chronological markers of prehistoric people and periods respectively, and hence the backbone of prehistoric analysis, retouched artifacts and their role(s) in the life of Paleolithic groups are now understood in varied (and sometimes conflicting) ways. Tools recovered from archaeological contexts reflect processes of production, possibly transport, probably use, maintenance, and potential reuse, and clearly discard (in the sense of Schiffer 1987:47) or accidental abandonment. But the links between tool manufacture and subsequent use patterns are complex and by no means rigid or constant. There are no compelling a priori reasons to believe that the uses to which tools were put were always the ones that had motivated the knappers to engage in their production in the first place.[1]

Discussion of tool morphologies and their meaning within the context of Middle Paleolithic research requires that Bordes's work be at least considered, if not relied upon, as a methodological venue for studying the relevant assemblages. Bordes created a common set of definitions for Middle Paleolithic artifact types and advocated the use of quantitative comparisons based on relative frequencies of all tool types in an assemblage. Bordes's typology achieved standardization, and thus replicability,

through defined combinations of retouch attributes and flake landmarks. His method of quantitative comparisons of tool type frequencies was intuitively satisfying because it revealed patterning without relying on the traditional, paleontology-derived concept of *fossiles directeur.* Yet Bordes retained the concepts of discrete, unchanging lithic types (Bisson 2000 and references therein).

The basic question about lithic types is whether their morphologies were dictated by the constraints of raw material properties, transport costs, and the practical tasks at hand, so that tool morphologies emerged from continuous processes of modification and shaping as practical needs occurred (i.e., end-goal-directed intentional behavior). An opposing understanding of retouch-imposed morphometrics suggests that tool properties stemmed from rule-governed behaviors, planned and set before retouch began. In this view, retouch was a way to impose intrinsic, culture-imbued properties on lithic blanks (i.e., invest in their "style"). This in turn implies that tools created cultural distinctions meaningful to members of past societies, and therefore can serve as markers of prehistoric social groupings. Finally, there is the question whether economic and "stylistic" aspects of tool manufacture and use were mutually exclusive. Binford (1979) observed ethnographically that tools functioned in three different realms of human life: the practical, the social, and the ideological. But whether this was the case in prehistory, and if so how to pry apart the various meanings of tools, are questions in the focus of ongoing paleoanthropological debates.

Clearly, approaching such questions inevitably requires that "style" in lithic artifacts be understood and defined. While style is not by definition inherent or self-evident in retouched artifacts, they offer archaeologists a good starting point to tackle the issue because they bear clear evidence of some intentional imposition of form. Style is recognized archaeologically by repeated patterning of artifact properties in confined boundaries of time and space. For this reason it is "overdetermination of form" (Byres 1994), or the arbitrary imposition of shape and standardization, that is likely to cause recognizable redundancy in material culture and thus form part of archaeologically visible style (Chase 1991).[2] The key factor in the recognition of style is intentionality. Byres distinguishes between Style 1 (end-goal-directed "material behavior"), which is said to exist when the forms of artifacts are dictated solely by their function, and Style 2 (end-product-directed "material actions"), which is governed by social rules. Regardless of whether retouched tools are formed to conform with one or the other functional templates, artifact forms do not vary as freely as function, raw material, and technology allow because they are culturally overdetermined (Byres 1994:378–379).

Style is active when there is purposeful investment in features that are beyond the demands of physical function and technology, with the intention of conveying and transferring information (Sackett's [1982, 1986] "adjunct style"; Wiessner 1983, 1985; Wobst 1977). Style is perceived as passive when produced without intent to convey information about group identity, age structure, social hierarchy, and other cultural distinctions. In the latter case, stylistic variation may also be isochrestic, in the sense that it consists of an arbitrary choice of one out of a number of equally effective ways of making things (Sackett 1982, 1983, 1986). By definition, isochrestic style is embedded in the process of manufacture itself; later additions or other components of the tool (e.g., the shape or decoration of a haft) must be considered active, adjunct style. Isochrestic style is expressed in attributes of the morphology that are not constrained by raw material properties, the practical function of the tool, or the technology by which it was made.

A central premise of François Bordes's seminal work was that culturally connoted "style" was part and parcel of Middle (and Lower) Paleolithic lithic assemblages. Bordes recognized that form was imposed differentially on various parts of the tools according to their function and clearly acknowledged that rule-governed deliberate retouch was carried out in order to create a utilitarian object (e.g., active cutting or scraping edge, prehension parts; Bordes 1969 cited by Bisson 2000). Still, he repeatedly emphasized that his typological list of sixty-three types was based exclusively on morphology, as he perceived retouched artifacts as "tools," implements whose complete morphology was deliberately devised and then manufactured (i.e., end-product-governed behavior guided by social rules). Bordes carried the notion of "types" as discrete, intentionally produced morphological

units from the level of the artifact to that of the assemblage. He interpreted redundant typological assemblage compositions as the material products of groups with different cultural choices and preferences for style of tool manufacture (Bordes 1961), and adhered to the view that Mousterian inter-assemblage variability reflected ethnic groups, each with different cultural choices. This interpretation of Mousterian lithic assemblages appears simplistic from the perspective of more recent research. Even if we accept that retouched artifacts in later prehistory may carry some form of culture-imbued style, we cannot assume that Lower and Middle Paleolithic behavioral adaptations were similar to those of modern humans (Chase 1991, 2006:136–144).

Bordes's view was challenged by the "functional hypothesis," arguing that Mousterian artifacts were primarily utilitarian and their forms linked to the demands of tasks to be carried out, as dictated by the physical environment (Binford 1973; see chapter 1 for a more detailed discussion). This hypothesis still predicts a measure of correlation between the imposed shape of the artifact and its practical uses, but such predictions were not borne out when tested with use-wear, polish, and edge-damage studies (see summary in Bisson 2000; an exhaustive critique and references in Mellars 1996). On the other hand, the "continuous reduction" model, applied to several tools types (Barton 1990; Dibble 1987; see also below), goes further in that it rejects any notion of rule-governed artifact morphologies, arguing instead for a continuous process dictated by raw material economy and immediate functional needs, specifically length of cutting edges and appropriate edge angles.

Still others are concerned with the variables that Bordes regarded as diagnostic of particular types, arguing that they are inappropriate for understanding the form–function relationship in Mousterian "tools" (mainly sidescrapers). For example, the identification of many scraper types is dependent on the position of the axis of flaking and on edge shape. The former has no direct bearing on function (though it is indicative of patterns related to raw material economy), and the latter has limited functional significance in proportion to the number of combinations of edge shape recognized by Bordes. On the other hand, edge angle, which ethnographic observations point to as a functionally significant variable, is not an explicit diagnostic characteristic of the majority of Bordes's types (backed knives being a possible exception).[3] Thus, a number of archaeologists have chosen to use their own typologies, based on parameters of retouched tools that are different from the ones used by Bordes, e.g., combinations of amounts of cortical cover, types of striking patterns, and dorsal face scar patterns instead of the number, shape, and orientation of retouched edges (Debénath and Dibble 1994; Kuhn 1990a).

Regardless of the particular objections to Bordes's typology, these cycles of critiques and methodological innovations culminate in types. This is not surprising. "Types" are by definition sorting categories, theoretical slots into which entities can be placed in order to differentiate them in some meaningful way from other entities that qualify as members of other types. The starting point for identifying types is their distinctiveness, often recognized intuitively on the basis of morphological variation (Adams and Adams 1991:42–43, 54). Typology is therefore a particular case of classification with inherent subjectivity, its purpose being the sorting of entities for the goal of group comparisons or statistical manipulations (Adams and Adams 1991). Bordes's typology of the Middle Paleolithic (Bordes 1950, 1953a, 1953b, 1954, [1961] 1988; Bordes and Bourgon 1951) fulfills this definition, in that its major types are intuitively recognized "natural entities." Of the number of typological lists currently available to students of Middle Paleolithic lithic variability, it is the longest-lived and most widely used, lending it an advantage in comparative contexts. Given these considerations, the heuristic approach adopted here is that Bordes's typology be conceived as an etic classification, i.e., as a cluster of types designated purely for the convenience of the typologist (Adams and Adams 1991:282). 'La méthode Bordes' ([1961] 1988) is used first and foremost as an analytical research device, aiming to classify a large number of observations and to outline patterns of attribute associations. These serve in turn as the basis for queries into the possible existence of economic and stylistic behaviors that underlie these patterns (Hovers 1997; see also Bisson 2000).

## The Typological Composition of the Assemblages

Slight modifications have been incorporated into Bordes's type-list in order to render it compatible with the Qafzeh assemblages. These changes affected mostly the non-retouched components in this list, i.e., the Levallois blanks, which Bordes included as "types" due to their relative standardized characteristics. Levallois CTE, as well as *éclats débordants, éclats outrepassés,* and their various combinations, to which Bordes did not relate specifically, are included in type 2 (atypical Levallois flake), although their significance is mainly technological (see chapter 5). Levallois blades are grouped with Levallois flakes in type 1.

The broad typological characteristics of the Qafzeh assemblages are presented in figures 6.1–6.4 and in tables 6.1–6.3 (detailed counts for complete assemblages are given in appendix 5).

While sample sizes are commonly small and vary considerably among layers, hampering inter-assemblage comparisons to some degree, the heterogeneity of the internal composition of the retouched tool kits (table 6.3) does not stem solely from differences in sample sizes. Typological differences among the layers are statistically significant (tables 6.1, 6.3).

Despite this variation, there are characteristics that appear to be shared by all the assemblages. A dominant feature is the predominance of unretouched Levallois products (table 6.2a, figure 6.1, real counts). Values of ILty range between 53.88 (layer XIV) and 77.69 (layer V) (sample sizes > 100). (See appendix 4 for the methods of calculating ILty and other typological indices mentioned in this chapter.) Naturally backed knives, yet another unretouched artifact type of technological significance (chapter 5) that Bordes included in the type-list, occur in all the assemblages. They often form a significant component of the restricted tool counts, their frequencies ranging between 7.69 (layer XIV) and 58.82 (layer XVf) (table 6.1, figure 6.1). (The frequencies of these artifacts among all sixty-three types, the "real" count, range between 2.15 [layer XIX] and 15.00 [layer VIIa].)

Frequencies of retouched tools are generally low, ranging in most assemblages between 3% and 9% of the total assemblage (table 6.1 column 4, figure 6.3; see also table 7.1). Retouched tools form up to 17% of the total flake population in rare cases (layers XII and XIV), but usually amount to 8–9% (table 6.3 column 3, figure 6.3). Several types (e.g., Mousterian points, backed knives) are conspicuously rare (or even absent) from all the assemblages.

The Mousterian (II) and Upper Paleolithic (III) groups are each represented in higher frequencies than the Denticulate group (IV). However, when notches (types 42 and 54) are added to form group IVelargi, the frequencies of the less formal tools are similar to those of the more intensively worked artifacts (tables 6.2, 6.3). The frequencies of "miscellaneous" artifacts (type 62) often exceed those of any other single tool type (table 6.1).

The frequencies of the Middle Paleolithic (Mousterian) and Upper Paleolithic groups fluctuate through time, with shifts in the frequencies of the "miscellaneous" group following the trajectory of the Upper Paleolithic (UP) group (figure 6.4b). Thus, three distinct assemblage patterns occur along the sequence (figures 6.2, 6.4a). One is characterized by high relative frequencies of group II, contrasted by the low frequencies of group III and medium to high frequencies of group IV. This type of assemblages is represented by layers VI, IX, X, XI, and XIII. In the second group of assemblages (layers VII, VIIa, and XII), all four typological groups occur in more or less even frequencies. The third pattern characteristically exhibits low frequencies of the Mousterian group, somewhat higher occurrence of the Upper Paleolithic group (often similar to those of the "others" category), and high frequencies of the enlarged group IV (layers XIV–XV and XVf–XXI). This

**Table 6.1   Complete and restricted counts (all layers with N > 50 for complete count)**

| | Type | Layer V | | | | Layer VI | | | | Layer VII | | | | Layer VIIa | | | |
|---|---|---|---|---|---|---|---|---|---|---|---|---|---|---|---|---|---|
| | | N | % real | % rest. | % redc. | N | % real | % rest. | % redc. | N | % real | % rest. | % redc. | N | % real | % rest. | % redc. |
| 1 | Levallois flake | 48 | 42.86 | — | — | 28 | 28.89 | — | — | 43 | 41.74 | — | — | 55 | 27.64 | — | — |
| | Levallois blade | 16 | 14.29 | — | — | 12 | 12.37 | — | — | 4 | 3.88 | — | — | 17 | 8.54 | — | — |
| 2 | Atypical Levallois flake | 7 | 6.25 | — | — | 10 | 10.31 | — | — | 3 | 2.91 | — | — | 15 | 7.54 | — | — |
| | CTE | | 0.00 | — | — | 3 | 3.09 | — | — | 1 | 0.97 | — | — | 15 | 7.54 | — | — |
| | *Éclat débordant* | 8 | 7.14 | — | — | 2 | 2.06 | — | — | 6 | 5.83 | — | — | 3 | 3.30 | — | — |
| | *Éclat outrepassé* | | 0.00 | — | — | | 0.00 | — | — | 1 | 0.97 | — | — | | 0.00 | — | — |
| | Combination | 1 | 0.90 | — | — | | 0.00 | — | — | | 0.00 | — | — | | 0.00 | — | — |
| | *Éclat rebroussé* | 1 | 0.90 | — | — | | 0.00 | — | — | | 0.00 | — | — | | 0.00 | — | — |
| | Combination of *débordant* and *rebroussé* | | 0.00 | — | — | | 0.00 | — | — | 1 | 0.97 | — | — | | 0.00 | — | — |
| 3 | Levallois point | 5 | 4.46 | — | — | | 0.00 | — | — | 1 | 0.97 | — | — | 9 | 4.52 | — | — |
| 4 | Retouched Levallois point | 1 | 0.90 | 4.17 | 7.69 | | 0.00 | 0.00 | 0.00 | | 0.00 | 0.00 | 0.00 | 1 | 0.50 | 1.25 | 2.17 |
| 5 | Pseudo-Levallois flake | 1 | 0.90 | 4.17 | — | | 0.00 | 0.00 | — | | 0.00 | 0.00 | — | 4 | 2.01 | 5.00 | — |
| 6 | Mousterian point | | 0.00 | 0.00 | 0.00 | | 0.00 | 0.00 | 0.00 | | 0.00 | 0.00 | 0.00 | | 0.00 | 0.00 | 0.00 |
| 7 | Elongated Mousterian point | | 0.00 | 0.00 | 0.00 | | 0.00 | 0.00 | 0.00 | | 0.00 | 0.00 | 0.00 | | 0.00 | 0.00 | 0.00 |
| 8 | *Limace* | | 0.00 | 0.00 | 0.00 | | 0.00 | 0.00 | 0.00 | | 0.00 | 0.00 | 0.00 | | 0.00 | 0.00 | 0.00 |
| 9 | Single straight side-scraper | 1 | 0.90 | 4.17 | 7.69 | 2 | 2.06 | 5.40 | 6.67 | 1 | 0.97 | 2.70 | 3.33 | 2 | 1.00 | 2.50 | 4.34 |
| 10 | Single convex side-scraper | | 0.00 | 0.00 | 0.00 | 4 | 4.12 | 10.81 | 13.33 | 3 | 2.91 | 8.11 | 10.00 | 5 | 2.51 | 6.25 | 10.87 |
| 11 | Single concave side-scraper | | 0.00 | 0.00 | 0.00 | 1 | 1.03 | 2.70 | 3.33 | | 0.00 | 0.00 | 0.00 | 2 | 1.00 | 2.50 | 4.34 |
| 12 | Double straight side-scraper | | 0.00 | 0.00 | 0.00 | | 0.00 | 0.00 | 0.00 | | 0.00 | 0.00 | 0.00 | | 0.00 | 0.00 | 0.00 |
| 13 | Double straight-convex side-scraper | | 0.00 | 0.00 | 0.00 | 1 | 1.03 | 2.70 | 3.33 | | 0.00 | 0.00 | 0.00 | 1 | 0.50 | 1.25 | 2.17 |
| 14 | Double straight-concave side-scraper | | 0.00 | 0.00 | 0.00 | | 0.00 | 0.00 | 0.00 | | 0.00 | 0.00 | 0.00 | | 0.00 | 0.00 | 0.00 |
| 15 | Double convex side-scraper | | 0.00 | 0.00 | 0.00 | | 0.00 | 0.00 | 0.00 | | 0.00 | 0.00 | 0.00 | | 0.00 | 0.00 | 0.00 |
| 16 | Double concave side-scraper | | 0.00 | 0.00 | 0.00 | | 0.00 | 0.00 | 0.00 | | 0.00 | 0.00 | 0.00 | | 0.00 | 0.00 | 0.00 |
| 17 | Double concave-convex side-scraper | | 0.00 | 0.00 | 0.00 | 1 | 1.03 | 2.70 | 3.33 | | 0.00 | 0.00 | 0.00 | | 0.00 | 0.00 | 0.00 |
| 18 | Convergent straight scraper | 1 | 0.90 | 4.17 | 7.69 | | 0.00 | 0.00 | 0.00 | | 0.00 | 0.00 | 0.00 | | 0.00 | 0.00 | 0.00 |
| 19 | Convergent convex scraper | | 0.00 | 0.00 | 0.00 | | 0.00 | 0.00 | 0.00 | 1 | 0.97 | 2.70 | 3.33 | | 0.00 | 0.00 | 0.00 |
| 20 | Convergent concave | | 0.00 | 0.00 | 0.00 | | 0.00 | 0.00 | 0.00 | | 0.00 | 0.00 | 0.00 | | 0.00 | 0.00 | 0.00 |
| 21 | *Déjeté* (offset) scraper | | 0.00 | 0.00 | 0.00 | | 0.00 | 0.00 | 0.00 | | 0.00 | 0.00 | 0.00 | | 0.00 | 0.00 | 0.00 |
| 22 | Straight transverse scraper | | 0.00 | 0.00 | 0.00 | | 0.00 | 0.00 | 0.00 | | 0.00 | 0.00 | 0.00 | 1 | 0.50 | 1.25 | 2.17 |
| 23 | Convex transverse scraper | 1 | 0.90 | 4.17 | 7.69 | | 0.00 | 0.00 | 0.00 | | 0.00 | 0.00 | 0.00 | | 0.00 | 0.00 | 0.00 |
| 24 | Concave transverse scraper | | 0.00 | 0.00 | 0.00 | | 0.00 | 0.00 | 0.00 | 1 | 0.97 | 2.70 | 3.33 | | 0.00 | 0.00 | 0.00 |
| 25 | Side-scraper on ventral face | | 0.00 | 0.00 | 0.00 | 4 | 4.12 | 10.81 | 13.33 | | 0.00 | 0.00 | 0.00 | | 0.00 | 0.00 | 0.00 |
| 26 | Abruptly retouched side-scraper | | 0.00 | 0.00 | 0.00 | | 0.00 | 0.00 | 0.00 | | 0.00 | 0.00 | 0.00 | | 0.00 | 0.00 | 0.00 |
| 27 | Side-scraper with thinned back | | 0.00 | 0.00 | 0.00 | | 0.00 | 0.00 | 0.00 | | 0.00 | 0.00 | 0.00 | | 0.00 | 0.00 | 0.00 |
| 28 | Side-scraper with bifacial retouch | | 0.00 | 0.00 | 0.00 | | 0.00 | 0.00 | 0.00 | | 0.00 | 0.00 | 0.00 | | 0.00 | 0.00 | 0.00 |
| 29 | Alternately retouched side-scraper | | 0.00 | 0.00 | 0.00 | | 0.00 | 0.00 | 0.00 | | 0.00 | 0.00 | 0.00 | | 0.00 | 0.00 | 0.00 |
| 30 | Typical end-scraper | | 0.00 | 0.00 | 0.00 | | 0.00 | 0.00 | 0.00 | | 0.00 | 0.00 | 0.00 | | 0.00 | 0.00 | 0.00 |
| 31 | Atypical end-scraper | 2 | 1.79 | 8.33 | 15.38 | | 0.00 | 0.00 | 0.00 | 1 | 0.97 | 2.70 | 3.33 | 2 | 1.00 | 2.50 | 4.34 |
| 32 | Typical burin | | 0.00 | 0.00 | 0.00 | 1 | 1.03 | 2.70 | 3.33 | 1 | 0.97 | 2.70 | 3.33 | 2 | 1.00 | 2.50 | 4.34 |
| 33 | Atypical burin | 2 | 1.79 | 8.33 | 15.38 | 1 | 1.03 | 2.70 | 3.33 | 1 | 0.97 | 2.70 | 3.33 | 1 | 0.50 | 1.25 | 2.17 |
| 34 | Typical borers | | 0.00 | 0.00 | 0.00 | 1 | 1.03 | 2.70 | 3.33 | | 0.00 | 0.00 | 0.00 | 3 | 15.08 | 3.75 | 6.52 |

| # | Type | Layer VIIb | | | | Layer IX | | | | Layer X | | | | Layer XI | | | |
|---|---|---|---|---|---|---|---|---|---|---|---|---|---|---|---|---|---|
| | | N | % real | % rest | % redc. | N | % real | % rest | % redc. | N | % real | % rest | % redc. | N | % real | % rest | % redc. |
| 35 | Atypical borers | | 0.00 | 0.00 | 0.00 | 1 | 1.03 | 2.70 | 3.33 | 1 | 0.97 | 2.70 | 3.33 | | 0.00 | 0.00 | 0.00 |
| 36 | Typical backed knife | | 0.00 | 0.00 | 0.00 | | 0.00 | 0.00 | 0.00 | | 0.00 | 0.00 | 0.00 | | 0.00 | 0.00 | 0.00 |
| 37 | Atypical backed knife | | 0.00 | 0.00 | 0.00 | | 0.00 | 0.00 | 0.00 | | 0.00 | 0.00 | 0.00 | | 0.00 | 0.00 | 0.00 |
| 38 | Naturally backed knife | 10 | 8.93 | 41.66 | — | 7 | 7.22 | 17.95 | — | 7 | 6.80 | 18.94 | — | 30 | 15.08 | 37.03 | — |
| 39 | *Raclette* | | 0.00 | 0.00 | 0.00 | 1 | 1.03 | 2.70 | 3.33 | | 0.00 | 0.00 | 0.00 | 1 | 0.50 | 1.25 | 2.17 |
| 40 | Truncated flake or blade | 1 | 0.90 | 4.17 | 7.69 | | 0.00 | 0.00 | 0.00 | 2 | 1.94 | 5.41 | 6.66 | 5 | 2.51 | 6.25 | 10.87 |
| 41 | Mousterian *tranchet* | | 0.00 | 0.00 | 0.00 | | 0.00 | 0.00 | 0.00 | | 0.00 | 0.00 | 0.00 | | 0.00 | 0.00 | 0.00 |
| 42 | Notch | 2 | 1.79 | 8.33 | 15.38 | 6 | 6.19 | 16.22 | 20.00 | 3 | 2.91 | 8.11 | 10.00 | 3 | 15.08 | 3.75 | 6.52 |
| 43 | Denticulate | 1 | 0.90 | 4.17 | 7.69 | 3 | 3.09 | 8.11 | 10.00 | 5 | 4.85 | 13.51 | 16.66 | 6 | 3.02 | 7.50 | 13.04 |
| 44 | Alternately retouched beaks | | 0.00 | 0.00 | 0.00 | | 0.00 | 0.00 | 0.00 | | 0.00 | 0.00 | 0.00 | | 0.00 | 0.00 | 0.00 |
| 45 | Retouch on ventral face | 1 | 0.90 | — | — | | 0.00 | — | — | 1 | 0.97 | | | 2 | 1.00 | — | — |
| 46–47 | Abrupt and alternate retouch (thick) | | 0.00 | — | — | | 0.00 | — | — | | 0.00 | — | — | | 0.00 | — | — |
| 48–49 | Abrupt and alternate retouch (thin) | | 0.00 | — | — | | 0.00 | — | — | | 0.00 | — | — | | 0.00 | — | — |
| 50 | Bifacial retouch | | 0.00 | — | — | | 0.00 | — | — | | 0.00 | — | — | | 0.00 | — | — |
| 51 | Tayac point | | 0.00 | 0.00 | 0.00 | | 0.00 | 0.00 | 0.00 | | 0.00 | 0.00 | 0.00 | | 0.00 | 0.00 | 0.00 |
| 52 | Notched triangle | | 0.00 | 0.00 | 0.00 | | 0.00 | 0.00 | 0.00 | | 0.00 | 0.00 | 0.00 | | 0.00 | 0.00 | 0.00 |
| 53 | Pseudo-microburin | | 0.00 | 0.00 | 0.00 | | 0.00 | 0.00 | 0.00 | | 0.00 | 0.00 | 0.00 | | 0.00 | 0.00 | 0.00 |
| 54 | End-notched piece | | 0.00 | 0.00 | 0.00 | | 0.00 | 0.00 | 0.00 | | 0.00 | 0.00 | 0.00 | 3 | 15.08 | 3.75 | 6.52 |
| 62 | Miscellaneous | 2 (1) | 1.79 | 8.33 | 15.38 | 8 (5) | 8.25 | 8.11 | 10.00 | 15 (5) | 14.56 | 27.03 | 33.33 | 11 (3) | 5.53 | 10.00 | 17.39 |
| | N | 112 | 24 | 13 | | 97 | 37 | 30 | | 103 | 37 | 30 | | 199 | 80 | 46 | |

| # | Type | Layer VIIb | | | | Layer IX | | | | Layer X | | | | Layer XI | | | |
|---|---|---|---|---|---|---|---|---|---|---|---|---|---|---|---|---|---|
| | | N | % real | % rest | % redc. | N | % real | % rest | % redc. | N | % real | % rest | % redc. | N | % real | % rest | % redc. |
| 1 | Levallois flake | 43 | 37.72 | — | — | 176 | 44.22 | — | — | 106 | 43.44 | — | — | 126 | 41.86 | — | — |
| | Levallois blade | 5 | 4.39 | — | — | 22 | 5.52 | — | — | 21 | 8.61 | — | — | 20 | 6.64 | — | — |
| 2 | Atypical Levallois flake | 8 | 7.02 | — | — | 26 | 6.53 | — | — | 13 | 5.33 | — | — | 25 | 8.31 | — | — |
| | CTE | 8 | 7.02 | — | — | 7 | 1.79 | — | — | 5 | 2.05 | — | — | 6 | 1.99 | — | — |
| | *éclat débordant* | 5 | 4.39 | — | — | 24 | 6.03 | — | — | 15 | 6.15 | — | — | 8 | 2.66 | — | — |
| | *éclat outrepassé* | | 0.00 | — | — | 4 | 1.00 | — | — | 2 | 0.82 | — | — | 1 | 0.33 | — | — |
| | combination | | 0.00 | — | — | | 0.00 | — | — | 1 | 0.41 | — | — | 1 | 0.33 | — | — |
| | *éclat rebroussé* | | 0.00 | — | — | 1 | 0.25 | — | — | 1 | 0.41 | — | — | | 0.00 | — | — |
| | combination of *débordant* and *rebroussé* | | 0.00 | — | — | | 0.00 | — | — | | 0.00 | — | — | | 0.00 | — | — |
| 3 | Levallois point | | 0.00 | — | — | 4 | 1.00 | — | — | 6 | 2.46 | — | — | 2 | 0.66 | — | — |
| 4 | Retouched levallois point | | 0.00 | 0.00 | 0.00 | 1 | 1.00 | 0.85 | 1.10 | | 0.00 | 0.00 | | | 0.00 | 0.00 | |
| 5 | Pseudo-Levallois flake | 1 | 0.89 | 2.43 | — | 2 | 0.50 | 1.69 | — | 1 | 0.41 | 1.44 | — | | 0.00 | 0.00 | — |
| 6 | Mousterian point | | 0.00 | 0.00 | 0.00 | | 0.00 | 0.00 | 0.00 | | 0.00 | 0.00 | 0.00 | | 0.00 | 0.00 | 0.00 |
| 7 | Elongated Mousterian point | | 0.00 | 0.00 | 0.00 | | 0.00 | 0.00 | 0.00 | | 0.00 | 0.00 | 0.00 | | 0.00 | 0.00 | 0.00 |
| 8 | Limace | | 0.00 | 0.00 | 0.00 | | 0.00 | 0.00 | 0.00 | | 0.00 | 0.00 | 0.00 | | 0.00 | 0.00 | 0.00 |
| 9 | Single straight side-scraper | | 0.00 | 0.00 | 0.00 | 3 | 0.78 | 2.54 | 3.30 | 2 | 0.82 | 2.90 | 3.45 | 4 | 1.33 | 4.00 | 5.41 |
| 10 | Single convex side-scraper | 2 | 1.75 | 4.87 | 5.88 | 11 | 2.76 | 9.32 | 12.09 | 9 | 3.69 | 13.04 | 15.51 | 12 | 3.99 | 12.00 | 16.22 |
| 11 | Single concave side-scraper | | 0.00 | 0.00 | 0.00 | 4 | 1.00 | 3.39 | 4.40 | | 0.00 | 0.00 | 0.00 | | 0.00 | 0.00 | 0.00 |
| 12 | Double straight side-scraper | | 0.00 | 0.00 | 0.00 | | 0.00 | 0.00 | 0.00 | | 0.00 | 0.00 | 0.00 | | 0.00 | 0.00 | 0.00 |

(continued)

**Table 6.1**  (continued)

| | Type | Layer VIIb | | | | Layer IX | | | | Layer X | | | | Layer XI | | | |
|---|---|---|---|---|---|---|---|---|---|---|---|---|---|---|---|---|---|
| | | N | % real | % rest. | % redc. | N | % real | % rest. | % redc. | N | % real | % rest. | % redc. | N | % real | % rest. | % redc. |
| 13 | Double straight-convex  side-scraper | 1 | 0.89 | 2.43 | 2.94 | | 0.00 | 0.00 | 0.00 | 2 | 0.82 | 2.90 | 3.45 | | 0.00 | 0.00 | 0.00 |
| 14 | Double straight-concave side-scraper | | 0.00 | 0.00 | 0.00 | | 0.00 | 0.00 | 0.00 | | 0.00 | 0.00 | 0.00 | 1 | 0.33 | 1.00 | 1.35 |
| 15 | Double convex side-scraper | | 0.00 | 0.00 | 0.00 | 1 | 0.25 | 0.85 | 1.10 | | 0.00 | 0.00 | 0.00 | 2 | 0.66 | 1.90 | 2.70 |
| 16 | Double concave side-scraper | | 0.00 | 0.00 | 0.00 | | 0.00 | 0.00 | 0.00 | | 0.00 | 0.00 | 0.00 | | 0.00 | 0.00 | 0.00 |
| 17 | Double concave-convex side-scraper | | 0.00 | 0.00 | 0.00 | 1 | 0.25 | 0.85 | 1.10 | | 0.00 | 0.00 | 0.00 | 1 | 0.33 | 1.00 | 1.35 |
| 18 | Convergent straight scraper | | 0.00 | 0.00 | 0.00 | | 0.00 | 0.00 | 0.00 | | 0.00 | 0.00 | 0.00 | | 0.00 | 0.00 | 0.00 |
| 19 | Convergent convex scraper | | 0.00 | 0.00 | 0.00 | 1 | 0.25 | 0.85 | 1.10 | 2 | 0.82 | 2.90 | 3.45 | | 0.00 | 0.00 | 0.00 |
| 20 | Convergent concave | | 0.00 | 0.00 | 0.00 | | 0.00 | 0.00 | 0.00 | | 0.00 | 0.00 | 0.00 | | 0.00 | 0.00 | 0.00 |
| 21 | Déjeté (offset) scraper | | 0.00 | 0.00 | 0.00 | | 0.00 | 0.00 | 0.00 | 1 | 0.41 | 1.44 | 1.72 | 3 | 1.00 | 3.00 | 4.05 |
| 22 | Straight transverse scraper | | 0.00 | 0.00 | 0.00 | 1 | 0.25 | 0.85 | 1.10 | | 0.00 | 0.00 | 0.00 | | 0.00 | 0.00 | 0.00 |
| 23 | Convex transverse scraper | | 0.00 | 0.00 | 0.00 | | 0.00 | 0.00 | 0.00 | | 0.00 | 0.00 | 0.00 | | 0.00 | 0.00 | 0.00 |
| 24 | Concave transverse scraper | | 0.00 | 0.00 | 0.00 | | 0.00 | 0.00 | 0.00 | | 0.00 | 0.00 | 0.00 | | 0.00 | 0.00 | 0.00 |
| 25 | Side-scraper on ventral face | 1 | 0.89 | 2.43 | 2.94 | 7 | 1.76 | 5.93 | 7.70 | 1 | 0.41 | 1.44 | 1.72 | 4 | 1.33 | 4.00 | 5.41 |
| 26 | Abruptly retouched side-scraper | | 0.00 | 0.00 | 0.00 | | 0.00 | 0.00 | 0.00 | | 0.00 | 0.00 | 0.00 | | 0.00 | 0.00 | 0.00 |
| 27 | Side scraper with thinned back | | 0.00 | 0.00 | 0.00 | | 0.00 | 0.00 | 0.00 | | 0.00 | 0.00 | 0.00 | | 0.00 | 0.00 | 0.00 |
| 28 | Side scraper with bifacial retouch | | 0.00 | 0.00 | 0.00 | | 0.00 | 0.00 | 0.00 | | 0.00 | 0.00 | 0.00 | 1 | 0.33 | 1.00 | 1.35 |
| 29 | Alternately retouched side-scraper | | 0.00 | 0.00 | 0.00 | | 0.00 | 0.00 | 0.00 | | 0.00 | 0.00 | 0.00 | 1 | 0.33 | 1.00 | 1.35 |
| 30 | Typical end-scraper | | 0.00 | 0.00 | 0.00 | 2 | 0.50 | 1.69 | 2.20 | 1 | 0.41 | 1.44 | 1.72 | 2 | 0.66 | 2.00 | 2.70 |
| 31 | Atypicak end-scraper | | 0.00 | 0.00 | 0.00 | 3 | 0.75 | 2.54 | 3.30 | | 0.00 | 0.00 | 0.00 | | 0.00 | 0.00 | 0.00 |
| 32 | Typical burin | 5 | 4.39 | 12.19 | 14.71 | 5 | 1.26 | 4.24 | 5.49 | 2 | 0.82 | 2.90 | 3.45 | 1 | 0.33 | 1.00 | 1.35 |
| 33 | Atypical burin | 1 | 0.89 | 2.43 | 2.94 | 1 | 0.25 | 0.85 | 1.10 | | 0.00 | 0.00 | 0.00 | 3 | 1.00 | 3.00 | 4.05 |
| 34 | Typical borers | | 0.00 | 0.00 | 0.00 | | 0.00 | 0.00 | 0.00 | 1 | 0.41 | 1.44 | 1.72 | | 0.00 | 0.00 | 0.00 |
| 35 | Atypical borers | | 0.00 | 0.00 | 0.00 | 1 | 0.25 | 0.85 | 1.10 | 3 | 1.23 | 4.35 | 5.17 | | 0.00 | 0.00 | 0.00 |
| 36 | Typical backed knife | | 0.00 | 0.00 | 0.00 | | 0.00 | 0.00 | 0.00 | | 0.00 | 0.00 | 0.00 | | 0.00 | 0.00 | 0.00 |
| 37 | Atypical backed knife | 1 | 0.89 | 2.43 | 2.94 | | 0.00 | 0.00 | 0.00 | | 0.00 | 0.00 | 0.00 | | 0.00 | 0.00 | 0.00 |
| 38 | Naturally backed knife | 6 | 5.26 | 14.63 | — | 25 | 6.28 | 21.19 | — | 10 | 4.10 | 14.49 | — | 26 | 8.64 | 26.00 | — |
| 39 | *Raclette* | 1 | 0.89 | 2.43 | 2.94 | 1 | 0.25 | 0.85 | 1.10 | | 0.00 | 0.00 | 0.00 | 2 | 0.66 | 2.00 | 2.70 |
| 40 | Truncated flakes and blades | 5 | 4.39 | 12.19 | 14.71 | 6 | 1.51 | 5.08 | 6.59 | 3 | 1.23 | 4.35 | 5.17 | 7 | 2.33 | 7.00 | 9.46 |
| 41 | Mousterian tranchet | | 0.00 | 0.00 | 0.00 | | 0.00 | 0.00 | 0.00 | | 0.00 | 0.00 | 0.00 | | 0.00 | 0.00 | 0.00 |
| 42 | Notch | 5 | 4.39 | 12.19 | 14.71 | 6 | 1.51 | 5.08 | 6.59 | 8 | 3.28 | 11.59 | 13.79 | 8 | 2.66 | 8.00 | 10.81 |
| 43 | Denticulate | 4 | 3.51 | 9.75 | 11.76 | 12 | 3.02 | 10.17 | 13.19 | 4 | 1.64 | 5.80 | 6.90 | 8 | 2.66 | 8.00 | 10.81 |
| 44 | Alternately retouched beaks | | 0.00 | 0.00 | 0.00 | 1 | 0.25 | 0.85 | 1.10 | | 0.00 | 0.00 | | | 0.00 | 0.00 | 0.00 |
| 45 | Retouch on ventral face | 1 | 0.90 | — | — | 3 | 0.75 | — | — | 2 | 0.82 | — | — | 3 | 1.00 | — | — |
| 46–47 | Abtupt and alternate retouch (thick) | | 0.00 | — | — | | 0.00 | — | — | | 0.00 | — | — | | 0.00 | — | — |
| 48–49 | Abtupt and alternate retouch (thin) | | 0.00 | — | — | | 0.00 | — | — | 1 | 0.41 | — | — | | 0.00 | — | — |
| 50 | Bifacial retouch | | 0.00 | — | — | | 0.00 | — | — | | 0.00 | — | — | | 0.00 | — | — |
| 51 | Tayac points | | 0.00 | 0.00 | 0.00 | | 0.00 | 0.00 | 0.00 | | 0.00 | 0.00 | 0.00 | | 0.00 | 0.00 | 0.00 |
| 52 | Notched triangles | | 0.00 | 0.00 | 0.00 | | 0.00 | 0.00 | 0.00 | | 0.00 | 0.00 | 0.00 | | 0.00 | 0.00 | 0.00 |
| 53 | Pseudo-microburins | | 0.00 | 0.00 | 0.00 | | 0.00 | 0.00 | 0.00 | | 0.00 | 0.00 | 0.00 | | 0.00 | 0.00 | 0.00 |
| 54 | End-notched pieces | | 0.00 | 0.00 | 0.00 | 4 | 1.00 | 3.39 | 4.40 | 2 | 0.82 | 2.90 | 3.45 | 1 | 0.33 | 1.00 | 1.35 |
| 62 | Miscellanious | 11 (3) | 9.65 | 19.51 | 23.53 | 31 (12) | 4.77 | 16.10 | 20.88 | 19 (2) | 7.79 | 24.64 | 29.31 | 22 (9) | 7.31 | 13.00 | 17.57 |
| | N | 114 | | | | 398 | | | | 244 | | | | 301 | | | |
| | | | 41 | 34 | | | 118 | 91 | | | 69 | 58 | | | 100 | 74 | |

| | Type | Layer XII | | | | Layer XIII | | | | Layer XIV | | | | Layer XV | | | |
|---|---|---|---|---|---|---|---|---|---|---|---|---|---|---|---|---|---|
| | | N | % real | % rest. | % redc. | N | % real | % rest. | % redc. | N | % real | % rest. | % redc. | N | % real | % rest. | % redc. |
| 1 | Levallois flake | 67 | 30.04 | — | — | 241 | 32.74 | — | — | 68 | 29.31 | — | — | 727 | 35.27 | — | — |
| | Levallois blade | 13 | 5.83 | — | — | 63 | 8.60 | — | — | 17 | 7.33 | — | — | 223 | 10.82 | — | — |
| 2 | Atypical Levallois flake | 16 | 7.17 | — | — | 57 | 7.74 | — | — | 17 | 7.33 | — | — | 229 | 11.11 | — | — |
| | CTE | 9 | 4.04 | — | — | 10 | 1.36 | — | — | 4 | 1.72 | — | — | 9 | 0.44 | — | — |
| | *éclat débordant* | 7 | 3.14 | — | — | 16 | 2.17 | — | — | 6 | 2.59 | — | — | 59 | 2.86 | — | — |
| | *éclat outrepassé* | 2 | 0.90 | — | — | | 0.00 | — | — | | 0.00 | — | — | 8 | 0.39 | — | — |
| | combination | | 0.00 | — | — | | 0.00 | — | — | | 0.00 | — | — | | 0.00 | — | — |
| | *éclat rebroussé* | 6 | 2.69 | — | — | 6 | 0.82 | — | — | 2 | 0.86 | — | — | 5 | 0.24 | — | — |
| | combination of *débordant* and *rebroussé* | | 0.00 | — | — | | 0.00 | — | — | | 0.00 | — | — | | 0.00 | — | — |
| 3 | Levallois point | 2 | 0.90 | — | — | 7 | 0.95 | — | — | 10 | 4.31 | — | — | 167 | 8.10 | — | — |
| 4 | Retouched levallois point | | 0.00 | 0.00 | 0.00 | 1 | 0.14 | 0.36 | 0.45 | 1 | 0.43 | 1.10 | 1.20 | 4 | 0.19 | 0.71 | 1.24 |
| 5 | Pseudo-Levallois flake | | 0.00 | 0.00 | — | 3 | 0.41 | 1.07 | — | 1 | 0.43 | 1.10 | — | 10 | 0.49 | 1.78 | — |
| 6 | Mousterian point | | 0.00 | 0.00 | 0.00 | | 0.00 | 0.00 | 0.00 | | 0.00 | 0.00 | 0.00 | | 0.00 | 0.00 | 0.00 |
| 7 | Elongated Mousterian point | | 0.00 | 0.00 | 0.00 | | 0.00 | 0.00 | 0.00 | | 0.00 | 0.00 | 0.00 | | 0.00 | 0.00 | 0.00 |
| 8 | Limace | | 0.00 | 0.00 | 0.00 | | 0.00 | 0.00 | 0.00 | | 0.00 | 0.00 | 0.00 | | 0.00 | 0.00 | 0.00 |
| 9 | Single straight side-scraper | 1 | 0.49 | 1.09 | 1.22 | 23 | 3.13 | 8.19 | 10.36 | | 0.00 | 0.00 | 0.00 | 7 | 0.34 | 1.25 | 2.17 |
| 10 | Single convex side-scraper | 13 | 5.83 | 14.29 | 15.85 | 34 | 4.62 | 12.00 | 15.32 | | 0.00 | 0.00 | 0.00 | 18 | 0.87 | 3.20 | 5.57 |
| 11 | Single concave side-scraper | | 0.00 | 0.00 | 0.00 | 8 | 1.09 | 2.83 | 3.60 | | 0.00 | 0.00 | 0.00 | | 0.00 | 0.00 | 0.00 |
| 12 | Double straight side-scraper | | 0.00 | 0.00 | 0.00 | | 0.00 | 0.00 | 0.00 | | 0.00 | 0.00 | 0.00 | | 0.00 | 0.00 | 0.00 |
| 13 | Double straight-convex side-scraper | | 0.00 | 0.00 | 0.00 | 5 | 0.68 | 1.78 | 2.25 | | 0.00 | 0.00 | 0.00 | 1 | 0.05 | 0.18 | 0.31 |
| 14 | Double straight-concave side-scraper | | 0.00 | 0.00 | 0.00 | | 0.00 | 0.00 | 0.00 | | 0.00 | 0.00 | 0.00 | | 0.00 | 0.00 | 0.00 |
| 15 | Double convex side-scraper | | 0.00 | 0.00 | 0.00 | 2 | 0.27 | 0.71 | 0.90 | | 0.00 | 0.00 | 0.00 | 2 | 0.09 | 0.36 | 0.62 |
| 16 | Double concave side-scraper | | 0.00 | 0.00 | 0.00 | | 0.00 | 0.00 | 0.00 | | 0.00 | 0.00 | 0.00 | | 0.00 | 0.00 | 0.00 |
| 17 | Double concave-convex side-scraper | | 0.00 | 0.00 | 0.00 | 1 | 0.14 | 0.36 | 0.45 | | 0.00 | 0.00 | 0.00 | | 0.00 | 0.00 | 0.00 |
| 18 | Convergent straight scraper | | 0.00 | 0.00 | 0.00 | | 0.00 | 0.00 | 0.00 | | 0.00 | 0.00 | 0.00 | | 0.00 | 0.00 | 0.00 |
| 19 | Convergent convex scraper | | 0.00 | 0.00 | 0.00 | 2 | 0.27 | 0.71 | 0.90 | | 0.00 | 0.00 | 0.00 | | 0.00 | 0.00 | 0.00 |
| 20 | Convergent concave | | 0.00 | 0.00 | 0.00 | | 0.00 | 0.00 | 0.00 | | 0.00 | 0.00 | 0.00 | | 0.00 | 0.00 | 0.00 |
| 21 | *Déjeté* (offset) scraper | 2 | 0.90 | 2.20 | 2.44 | 2 | 0.27 | 0.71 | 0.90 | | 0.00 | 0.00 | 0.00 | 1 | 0.05 | 0.18 | 0.31 |
| 22 | Straight transverse scraper | | 0.00 | 0.00 | 0.00 | | 0.00 | 0.00 | 0.00 | | 0.00 | 0.00 | 0.00 | | 0.00 | 0.00 | 0.00 |
| 23 | Convex transverse scraper | | 0.00 | 0.00 | 0.00 | | 0.00 | 0.00 | 0.00 | | 0.00 | 0.00 | 0.00 | | 0.00 | 0.00 | 0.00 |
| 24 | Concave transverse scraper | | 0.00 | 0.00 | 0.00 | | 0.00 | 0.00 | 0.00 | | 0.00 | 0.00 | 0.00 | | 0.00 | 0.00 | 0.00 |
| 25 | Side-scraper on ventral face | 5 | 2.24 | 5.49 | 6.10 | 5 | 0.68 | 1.78 | 2.25 | 1 | 0.43 | 1.10 | 1.20 | 12 | 0.59 | 2.17 | 3.79 |
| 26 | Abruptly retouched side-scraper | | 0.00 | 0.00 | 0.00 | | 0.00 | 0.00 | 0.00 | 1 | 0.43 | 1.10 | 1.20 | 1 | 0.05 | 0.18 | 0.31 |
| 27 | Side-scraper with thinned back | | 0.00 | 0.00 | 0.00 | | 0.00 | 0.00 | 0.00 | | 0.00 | 0.00 | 0.00 | | 0.00 | 0.00 | 0.00 |
| 28 | Side-scraper with bifacial retouch | | 0.00 | 0.00 | 0.00 | | 0.00 | 0.00 | 0.00 | 1 | 0.43 | 1.10 | 1.20 | 1 | 0.05 | 0.18 | 0.31 |
| 29 | Alternately retouched side-scraper | | 0.00 | 0.00 | 0.00 | 3 | 0.41 | 1.07 | 1.35 | | 0.00 | 0.00 | 0.00 | 2 | 0.09 | 0.36 | 0.62 |
| 30 | Typical end-scraper | 3 | 1.35 | 3.30 | 3.66 | 2 | 0.27 | 0.71 | 0.90 | 1 | 0.43 | 1.10 | 1.20 | 2 | 0.09 | 0.36 | 0.62 |
| 31 | Atypicak end-scraper | 2 | 0.90 | 2.20 | 2.44 | 2 | 0.27 | 0.71 | 0.90 | 5 | 2.16 | 5.49 | 6.02 | 11 | 0.53 | 1.96 | 3.40 |
| 32 | Typical burin | 7 | 3.14 | 7.69 | 8.54 | 2 | 0.27 | 0.71 | 0.90 | 6 | 2.59 | 6.59 | 7.23 | 17 | 0.82 | 3.03 | 5.26 |
| 33 | Atypical burin | 1 | 0.49 | 1.10 | 1.22 | 6 | 0.82 | 2.14 | 2.70 | 3 | 1.29 | 3.30 | 3.61 | 16 | 0.78 | 2.85 | 4.95 |
| 34 | Typical borers | 1 | 0.49 | 1.10 | 1.22 | 1 | 0.14 | 0.36 | 0.45 | | 0.00 | 0.00 | 0.00 | 1 | 0.05 | 0.18 | 0.31 |

*(continued)*

**Table 6.1  (continued)**

| | Type | Layer XII | | | | Layer XIII | | | | Layer XIV | | | | Layer XV | | | |
|---|---|---|---|---|---|---|---|---|---|---|---|---|---|---|---|---|---|
| | | N | % real | % rest. | % redc. | N | % real | % rest. | % redc. | N | % real | % rest. | % redc. | N | % real | % rest. | % redc. |
| 35 | Atypical borers | | 0.00 | 0.00 | 0.00 | 2 | 0.27 | 0.71 | 0.90 | | 0.00 | 0.00 | 0.00 | 8 | 0.39 | 1.43 | 2.48 |
| 36 | Typical backed knife | | 0.00 | 0.00 | 0.00 | | 0.00 | 0.00 | 0.00 | | 0.00 | 0.00 | 0.00 | 1 | 0.05 | 0.18 | 0.31 |
| 37 | Atypical backed knife | 1 | 0.49 | 1.10 | 1.22 | | 0.00 | 0.00 | 0.00 | | 0.00 | 0.00 | 0.00 | 3 | 0.15 | 0.53 | 0.93 |
| 38 | Naturally backed knife | 9 | 4.04 | 9.89 | — | 56 | 7.61 | 19.93 | — | 7 | 3.01 | 7.69 | — | 228 | 11.06 | 40.64 | — |
| 39 | *Raclette* | | 0.00 | 0.00 | 0.00 | 7 | 0.95 | 2.49 | 3.15 | 3 | 1.29 | 3.30 | 3.61 | 2 | 0.10 | 0.36 | 0.62 |
| 40 | Truncated flakes and blades | 6 | 2.69 | 6.59 | 7.32 | 8 | 1.08 | 2.85 | 3.60 | 4 | 1.72 | 4.40 | 4.82 | 37 | 1.80 | 6.60 | 11.46 |
| 41 | Mousterian tranchet | | 0.00 | 0.00 | 0.00 | | 0.00 | 0.00 | 0.00 | | 0.00 | 0.00 | 0.00 | | 0.00 | 0.00 | 0.00 |
| 42 | Notch | 4 | 1.79 | 4.40 | 4.89 | 36 | 4.89 | 12.81 | 16.22 | 19 | 8.19 | 20.88 | 22.89 | 47 | 2.28 | 8.38 | 14.55 |
| 43 | Denticulate | 10 | 4.48 | 10.99 | 12.20 | 29 | 3.94 | 10.32 | 13.06 | 15 | 6.47 | 16.48 | 18.07 | 31 | 1.50 | 5.53 | 9.60 |
| 44 | Alternately retouched beaks | | 0.00 | 0.00 | 0.00 | | 0.00 | 0.00 | 0.00 | | 0.00 | 0.00 | 0.00 | 10 | 0.49 | 1.78 | 3.10 |
| 45 | Retouch on ventral face | 4 | 1.79 | — | — | 7 | 0.95 | — | — | 1 | 0.43 | — | — | 19 | 0.92 | — | — |
| 46–47 | Abtupt and alternate retouch (thick) | | 0.00 | — | — | | 0.00 | — | — | | 0.00 | — | — | | 0.00 | — | — |
| 48–49 | Abtupt and alternate retouch (thin) | | 0.00 | — | — | | 0.00 | — | — | | 0.00 | — | — | | 0.00 | — | — |
| 50 | Bifacial retouch | | 0.00 | — | — | 2 | 0.27 | — | — | | 0.00 | — | — | | 0.00 | — | — |
| 51 | Tayac points | | 0.00 | 0.00 | 0.00 | | 0.00 | 0.00 | 0.00 | | 0.00 | 0.00 | 0.00 | | 0.00 | 0.00 | 0.00 |
| 52 | Notched triangles | | 0.00 | 0.00 | 0.00 | | 0.00 | 0.00 | 0.00 | | 0.00 | 0.00 | 0.00 | | 0.00 | 0.00 | 0.00 |
| 53 | Pseudo-microburins | | 0.00 | 0.00 | 0.00 | | 0.00 | 0.00 | 0.00 | | 0.00 | 0.00 | 0.00 | | 0.00 | 0.00 | 0.00 |
| 54 | End-notched pieces | 1 | 0.49 | 1.10 | 1.22 | 4 | 0.54 | 1.42 | 1.79 | 3 | 1.29 | 3.30 | 3.61 | 7 | 0.33 | 1.25 | 1.55 |
| 62 | Miscellanious | 33 (6) | 14.80 | 29.67 | 32.93 | 83 (45) | 13.48 | 13.17 | 16.59 | 36 (16) | 15.52 | 21.98 | 24.10 | 135 (54) | 6.55 | 14.43 | 25.08 |
| | N | | 223 | 91 | 82 | | 735 | 283 | 222 | | 232 | 91 | 83 | | 2061 | 561 | 323 |

| | Type | Layer XVa | | | | Layer XVb | | | | Layer XVf | | | | Layer XVII | | | |
|---|---|---|---|---|---|---|---|---|---|---|---|---|---|---|---|---|---|
| | | N | % real | % rest. | % redc. | N | % real | % rest. | % redc. | N | % real | % rest. | % redc. | N | % real | % rest. | % redc. |
| 1 | Levallois flake | 153 | 40.03 | — | — | 29 | 33.72 | — | — | 170 | 47.22 | — | — | 166 | 39.06 | — | — |
| | Levallois blade | 36 | 9.89 | — | — | 9 | 10.47 | — | — | 31 | 8.61 | — | — | 52 | 12.23 | — | — |
| 2 | Atypical Levallois  flake | 24 | 6.59 | — | — | 8 | 9.30 | — | — | 32 | 8.89 | — | — | 32 | 7.53 | — | — |
| | CTE | 1 | 0.27 | — | — | 1 | 1.16 | — | — | 6 | 1.67 | — | — | 24 | 5.65 | — | — |
| | *éclat débordant* | 23 | 6.32 | — | — | 11 | 12.79 | — | — | 17 | 4.72 | — | — | 3 | 0.71 | — | — |
| | *éclat outrepassé* | 3 | 0.82 | — | — | 1 | 1.16 | — | — | 7 | 1.94 | — | — | 2 | 0.47 | — | — |
| | combination | 1 | 0.27 | — | — | | 0.00 | — | — | 2 | 0.56 | — | — | | 0.00 | — | — |
| | *éclat rebroussé* | 1 | 0.27 | — | — | | 0.00 | — | — | | 0.00 | — | — | 4 | 0.94 | — | — |
| | combination of *débordant* and *rebroussé* | 1 | 0.27 | — | — | | 0.00 | — | — | | 0.00 | — | — | 1 | 0.24 | — | — |
| 3 | Levallois point | 4 | 1.10 | — | — | 1 | 1.16 | — | — | 3 | 0.83 | — | — | 5 | 1.18 | — | — |
| 4 | Retouched levallois point | | 0.00 | 0.00 | 0.00 | | 0.00 | 0.00 | 0.00 | 1 | 0.28 | 1.18 | | | 0.00 | 0.00 | 0.00 |
| 5 | Pseudo-Levallois flake | 3 | 0.84 | 2.70 | — | | 0.00 | 0.00 | — | 6 | 1.69 | 7.06 | — | 2 | 0.47 | 1.65 | — |
| 6 | Mousterian point | | 0.00 | 0.00 | 0.00 | | 0.00 | 0.00 | 0.00 | | 0.00 | 0.00 | 0.00 | | 0.00 | 0.00 | 0.00 |
| 7 | Elongated Mousterian point | | 0.00 | 0.00 | 0.00 | | 0.00 | 0.00 | 0.00 | | 0.00 | 0.00 | 0.00 | | 0.00 | 0.00 | 0.00 |
| 8 | Limace | | 0.00 | 0.00 | 0.00 | | 0.00 | 0.00 | 0.00 | | 0.00 | 0.00 | 0.00 | | 0.00 | 0.00 | 0.00 |
| 9 | Single straight side-scraper | 1 | 0.27 | 0.90 | 1.54 | 1 | 1.16 | 3.85 | 10.00 | | 0.00 | 0.00 | 0.00 | 3 | 0.71 | 2.48 | 2.78 |

| No. | Type | n | % | % | % | n | % | % | % | n | % | % | % | n | % | % | % |
|---|---|---|---|---|---|---|---|---|---|---|---|---|---|---|---|---|---|
| 10 | Single convex side-scraper | 6 | 1.65 | 5.41 | 9.23 | | 0.00 | 0.00 | 0.00 | | 0.00 | 0.00 | 0.00 | 7 | 1.65 | 5.79 | 6.48 |
| 11 | Single concave side-scraper | 1 | 0.27 | 0.90 | 1.54 | | 0.00 | 0.00 | 0.00 | | 0.00 | 0.00 | 0.00 | 2 | 0.47 | 1.65 | 1.85 |
| 12 | Double straight side-scraper | | 0.00 | 0.00 | 0.00 | | 0.00 | 0.00 | 0.00 | | 0.00 | 0.00 | 0.00 | | 0.00 | 0.00 | 0.00 |
| 13 | Double straight-convex  side-scraper | | 0.00 | 0.00 | 0.00 | | 0.00 | 0.00 | 0.00 | | 0.00 | 0.00 | 0.00 | | 0.00 | 0.00 | 0.00 |
| 14 | Double straight-concave side-scraper | | 0.00 | 0.00 | 0.00 | | 0.00 | 0.00 | 0.00 | | 0.00 | 0.00 | 0.00 | | 0.00 | 0.00 | 0.00 |
| 15 | Double convex side-scraper | | 0.00 | 0.00 | 0.00 | | 0.00 | 0.00 | 0.00 | | 0.00 | 0.00 | 0.00 | 1 | 0.24 | 0.83 | 0.93 |
| 16 | Double concave side-scraper | | 0.00 | 0.00 | 0.00 | | 0.00 | 0.00 | 0.00 | | 0.00 | 0.00 | 0.00 | | 0.00 | 0.00 | 0.00 |
| 17 | Double concave-convex side-scraper | | 0.00 | 0.00 | 0.00 | | 0.00 | 0.00 | 0.00 | | 0.00 | 0.00 | 0.00 | | 0.00 | 0.00 | 0.00 |
| 18 | Convergent straight scraper | | 0.00 | 0.00 | 0.00 | | 0.00 | 0.00 | 0.00 | | 0.00 | 0.00 | 0.00 | | 0.00 | 0.00 | 0.00 |
| 19 | Convergent convex scraper | | 0.00 | 0.00 | 0.00 | | 0.00 | 0.00 | 0.00 | | 0.00 | 0.00 | 0.00 | | 0.00 | 0.00 | 0.00 |
| 20 | Convergent concave | | 0.00 | 0.00 | 0.00 | | 0.00 | 0.00 | 0.00 | | 0.00 | 0.00 | 0.00 | | 0.00 | 0.00 | 0.00 |
| 21 | *Déjeté* (offset) scraper | | 0.00 | 0.00 | 0.00 | | 0.00 | 0.00 | 0.00 | | 0.00 | 0.00 | 0.00 | 3 | 0.71 | 2.48 | 2.78 |
| 22 | Straight transverse scraper | | 0.00 | 0.00 | 0.00 | | 0.00 | 0.00 | 0.00 | | 0.00 | 0.00 | 0.00 | | 0.00 | 0.00 | 0.00 |
| 23 | Convex transverse scraper | | 0.00 | 0.00 | 0.00 | | 0.00 | 0.00 | 0.00 | | 0.00 | 0.00 | 0.00 | 1 | 0.24 | 0.83 | 0.93 |
| 24 | Concave transverse scraper | | 0.00 | 0.00 | 0.00 | | 0.00 | 0.00 | 0.00 | | 0.00 | 0.00 | 0.00 | | 0.00 | 0.00 | 0.00 |
| 25 | Side-scraper on ventral face | 2 | 0.55 | 1.80 | 3.08 | | 0.00 | 0.00 | 0.00 | 1 | 0.28 | 1.18 | 3.45 | 2 | 0.47 | 1.65 | 1.85 |
| 26 | Abruptly retouched side-scraper | | 0.00 | 0.00 | 0.00 | | 0.00 | 0.00 | 0.00 | | 0.00 | 0.00 | 0.00 | 1 | 0.24 | 0.83 | 0.93 |
| 27 | Side-scraper with thinned back | | 0.00 | 0.00 | 0.00 | | 0.00 | 0.00 | 0.00 | | 0.00 | 0.00 | 0.00 | | 0.00 | 0.00 | 0.00 |
| 28 | Side-scraper with bifacial retouch | 2 | 0.55 | 1.80 | 3.08 | | 0.00 | 0.00 | 0.00 | | 0.00 | 0.00 | 0.00 | | 0.00 | 0.00 | 0.00 |
| 29 | Alternately retouched side-scraper | | 0.00 | 0.00 | 0.00 | | 0.00 | 0.00 | 0.00 | 1 | 0.28 | 1.18 | 3.45 | | 0.00 | 0.00 | 0.00 |
| 30 | Typical end-scraper | 2 | 0.55 | 1.80 | 3.08 | | 0.00 | 0.00 | 0.00 | | 0.00 | 0.00 | 0.00 | 10 | 2.35 | 8.26 | 9.26 |
| 31 | Atypicak end-scraper | 2 | 0.55 | 1.80 | 3.08 | | 0.00 | 0.00 | 0.00 | 2 | 0.56 | 2.35 | 6.90 | 3 | 0.71 | 2.48 | 2.78 |
| 32 | Typical burin | 3 | 0.82 | 2.70 | 4.61 | 1 | 1.16 | 3.85 | 10.00 | 2 | 0.56 | 2.35 | 6.90 | 1 | 0.24 | 0.83 | 0.93 |
| 33 | Atypical burin | 2 | 0.55 | 1.80 | 3.08 | | 0.00 | 0.00 | 0.00 | 2 | 0.56 | 2.35 | 6.90 | 5 | 1.18 | 4.13 | 4.63 |
| 34 | Typical borers | 2 | 0.55 | 1.80 | 3.08 | | 0.00 | 0.00 | 0.00 | 1 | 0.28 | 1.18 | 3.45 | 3 | 0.71 | 2.48 | 2.86 |
| 35 | Atypical borers | 4 | 1.10 | 3.60 | 6.15 | | 0.00 | 0.00 | 0.00 | | 0.00 | 0.00 | 0.00 | 3 | 0.71 | 2.48 | 2.86 |
| 36 | Typical backed knife | | 0.00 | 0.00 | 0.00 | | 0.00 | 0.00 | 0.00 | | 0.00 | 0.00 | 0.00 | | 0.00 | 0.00 | 0.00 |
| 37 | Atypical backed knife | | 0.00 | 0.00 | 0.00 | | 0.00 | 0.00 | 0.00 | | 0.00 | 0.00 | 0.00 | | 0.00 | 0.00 | 0.00 |
| 38 | Naturally backed knife | 43 | 11.81 | 38.74 | — | 16 | 18.60 | 61.54 | — | 50 | 13.89 | 58.82 | — | 11 | 2.59 | 9.09 | — |
| 39 | *Raclette* | 1 | 0.27 | 0.90 | 1.54 | | 0.00 | 0.00 | 0.00 | | 0.00 | 0.00 | 0.00 | 2 | 0.47 | 1.65 | 1.85 |
| 40 | Truncated flakes and blades | 7 | 1.92 | 6.31 | 10.77 | | 0.00 | 0.00 | 0.00 | 2 | 0.56 | 2.35 | 6.90 | 2 | 0.47 | 1.65 | 1.85 |
| 41 | Mousterian tranchet | | 0.00 | 0.00 | 0.00 | | 0.00 | 0.00 | 0.00 | | 0.00 | 0.00 | 0.00 | | 0.00 | 0.00 | 0.00 |
| 42 | Notch | 11 | 3.02 | 9.91 | 16.92 | 1 | 1.16 | 3.85 | 10.00 | 8 | 2.22 | 9.41 | 27.57 | 19 | 4.47 | 15.70 | 17.59 |
| 43 | Denticulate | 6 | 1.65 | 5.41 | 9.23 | 2 | 2.33 | 7.69 | 20.00 | 1 | 0.28 | 1.18 | 3.45 | 19 | 4.47 | 15.70 | 17.59 |
| 44 | Alternately retouched beaks | | 0.00 | 0.00 | 0.00 | | 0.00 | 0.00 | 0.00 | | 0.00 | 0.00 | 0.00 | | 0.00 | 0.00 | |
| 45 | Retouch on ventral face | 1 | 0.27 | — | — | | 0.00 | — | — | 2 | 0.56 | — | — | 1 | 0.24 | — | — |
| 46–47 | Abtupt and alternate retouch (thick) | | 0.00 | — | — | | | — | — | | 0.00 | — | — | | 0.00 | — | — |
| 48–49 | Abtupt and alternate retouch (thin) | | 0.00 | — | — | | | — | — | | 0.00 | — | — | | 0.00 | — | — |
| 50 | Bifacial retouch | | 0.00 | — | — | | | — | — | | 0.00 | — | — | | 0.00 | — | — |
| 51 | Tayac points | | 0.00 | 0.00 | 0.00 | | 0.00 | 0.00 | 0.00 | | 0.00 | 0.00 | 0.00 | | 0.00 | 0.00 | 0.00 |
| 52 | Notched triangles | | 0.00 | 0.00 | 0.00 | | 0.00 | 0.00 | 0.00 | | 0.00 | 0.00 | 0.00 | | 0.00 | 0.00 | 0.00 |
| 53 | Pseudo-microburins | | 0.00 | 0.00 | 0.00 | | 0.00 | 0.00 | 0.00 | | 0.00 | 0.00 | 0.00 | | 0.00 | 0.00 | 0.00 |
| 54 | End-notched pieces | 1 | 0.27 | 0.90 | 1.54 | | 0.00 | 0.00 | 0.00 | | 0.00 | 0.00 | 0.00 | 1 | 0.24 | 0.83 | 0.93 |
| 62 | Miscellanious | 17 (5) | 17.85 | 39.63 | 55.08 | 5 | 5.81 | 19.23 | 50.00 | 13 (5) | 3.61 | 14.44 | 38.23 | 34 (14) | 8.00 | 25.19 | 18.52 |
| | N | | 364 | 111 | 65 | | 86 | 26 | 10 | | 360 | 85 | 29 | | 425 | 121 | 108 |

*(continued)*

**Table 6.1  (continued)**

| | Type | Layer XIX | | | | Layer XXI | | | | Layer XXII | | | |
|---|---|---|---|---|---|---|---|---|---|---|---|---|---|
| | | N | % real | % rest. | % redc. | N | % real | % rest. | % redc. | N | % real | % rest. | % redc. |
| 1 | Levallois flake | 115 | 49.36 | — | — | 77 | 52.38 | — | — | 35 | 47.95 | — | — |
| | Levallois blade | 9 | 3.86 | — | — | 11 | 7.48 | — | — | 6 | 8.22 | — | — |
| 2 | Atypical Levallois  flake | 24 | 10.30 | — | — | 10 | 6.80 | — | — | 5 | 6.85 | — | — |
| | CTE | 18 | 7.73 | — | — | 5 | 3.40 | — | — | 1 | 1.37 | — | — |
| | *éclat débordant* | 1 | 0.43 | — | — | 1 | 0.68 | — | — | 1 | 1.37 | — | — |
| | *éclat outrepassé* | | 0.00 | — | — | 1 | 0.68 | — | — | 1 | 1.37 | — | — |
| | combination | | 0.00 | — | — | | 0.00 | — | — | 1 | 1.37 | — | — |
| | *éclat rebroussé* | 3 | 1.29 | — | — | | 0.00 | — | — | | 0.00 | — | — |
| | combination of *débordant* and *rebroussé* | 1 | 0.43 | — | — | | 0.00 | — | — | | 0.00 | — | — |
| 3 | Levallois point | 1 | 0.43 | — | — | | 0.00 | — | — | | 0.00 | — | — |
| 4 | Retouched Levallois point | | 0.00 | 0.00 | 0.00 | 1 | 0.68 | 2.44 | | | 0.00 | 0.00 | |
| 5 | Pseudo-Levallois flake | 1 | 0.43 | 1.64 | — | | 0.00 | 0.00 | — | | 0.00 | 0.00 | — |
| 6 | Mousterian point | | 0.00 | 0.00 | 0.00 | | 0.00 | 0.00 | 0.00 | | 0.00 | 0.00 | 0.00 |
| 7 | Elongated Mousterian point | | 0.00 | 0.00 | 0.00 | | 0.00 | 0.00 | 0.00 | | 0.00 | 0.00 | 0.00 |
| 8 | Limace | | 0.00 | 0.00 | 0.00 | | 0.00 | 0.00 | 0.00 | | 0.00 | 0.00 | 0.00 |
| 9 | Single straight side-scraper | | 0.00 | 0.00 | 0.00 | 1 | 0.68 | 2.44 | 2.70 | | 0.00 | 0.00 | 0.00 |
| 10 | Single convex side-scraper | 3 | 1.29 | 4.92 | 5.45 | 2 | 1.36 | 4.88 | 5.41 | | 0.00 | 0.00 | 0.00 |
| 11 | Single concave side-scraper | 2 | 0.86 | 3.28 | 3.64 | | 0.00 | 0.00 | 0.00 | 1 | 1.37 | 4.35 | 5.00 |
| 12 | Double straight side-scraper | | 0.00 | 0.00 | 0.00 | | 0.00 | 0.00 | 0.00 | | 0.00 | 0.00 | 0.00 |
| 13 | Double straight-convex  side-scraper | | 0.00 | 0.00 | 0.00 | | 0.00 | 0.00 | 0.00 | | 0.00 | 0.00 | 0.00 |
| 14 | Double straight-concave side-scraper | | 0.00 | 0.00 | 0.00 | | 0.00 | 0.00 | 0.00 | | 0.00 | 0.00 | 0.00 |
| 15 | Double convex side-scraper | | 0.00 | 0.00 | 0.00 | | 0.00 | 0.00 | 0.00 | | 0.00 | 0.00 | 0.00 |
| 16 | Double concave side-scraper | | 0.00 | 0.00 | 0.00 | | 0.00 | 0.00 | 0.00 | | 0.00 | 0.00 | 0.00 |
| 17 | Double concave-convex side-scraper | | 0.00 | 0.00 | 0.00 | | 0.00 | 0.00 | 0.00 | 1 | 1.37 | 4.35 | 5.00 |
| 18 | Convergent straight scraper | | 0.00 | 0.00 | 0.00 | | 0.00 | 0.00 | 0.00 | | 0.00 | 0.00 | 0.00 |
| 19 | Convergent convex scraper | | 0.00 | 0.00 | 0.00 | | 0.00 | 0.00 | 0.00 | | 0.00 | 0.00 | 0.00 |
| 20 | Convergent concave | 1 | 0.43 | 0.00 | 1.82 | | 0.00 | 0.00 | 0.00 | | 0.00 | 0.00 | 0.00 |
| 21 | *Déjeté* (offset) scraper | | 0.00 | 0.00 | 0.00 | | 0.00 | 0.00 | 0.00 | | 0.00 | 0.00 | 0.00 |
| 22 | Straight transverse scraper | | 0.00 | 0.00 | 0.00 | | 0.00 | 0.00 | 0.00 | | 0.00 | 0.00 | 0.00 |
| 23 | Convex transverse scraper | 1 | 0.43 | 1.64 | 1.82 | | 0.00 | 0.00 | 0.00 | | 0.00 | 0.00 | 0.00 |
| 24 | Concave transverse scraper | | 0.00 | 0.00 | 0.00 | | 0.00 | 0.00 | 0.00 | | 0.00 | 0.00 | 0.00 |
| 25 | Side-scraper on ventral face | 2 | 0.86 | 3.28 | 3.64 | | 0.00 | 0.00 | 0.00 | | 0.00 | 0.00 | 0.00 |
| 26 | Abruptly retouched side-scraper | | 0.00 | 0.00 | 0.00 | | 0.00 | 0.00 | 0.00 | | 0.00 | 0.00 | 0.00 |
| 27 | Side-scraper with thinned back | | 0.00 | 0.00 | 0.00 | | 0.00 | 0.00 | 0.00 | | 0.00 | 0.00 | 0.00 |
| 28 | Side-scraper with bifacial retouch | | 0.00 | 0.00 | 0.00 | | 0.00 | 0.00 | 0.00 | | 0.00 | 0.00 | 0.00 |
| 29 | Alternately retouched side-scraper | | 0.00 | 0.00 | 0.00 | | 0.00 | 0.00 | 0.00 | | 0.00 | 0.00 | 0.00 |
| 30 | Typical end-scraper | 2 | 0.86 | 4.92 | 3.64 | 1 | 0.68 | 2.44 | 2.70 | | 0.00 | 0.00 | 0.00 |

| | | | | | | | | | | | | | |
|---|---|---|---|---|---|---|---|---|---|---|---|---|---|
| 31 | Atypical end-scraper | 7 | 3.00 | 11.48 | 12.73 | 3 | 2.04 | 7.32 | 11.11 | | 0.00 | 0.00 | 0.00 |
| 32 | Typical burin | 3 | 1.29 | 4.92 | 5.45 | 1 | 0.68 | 2.44 | 2.70 | 1 | 1.37 | 4.35 | 5.00 |
| 33 | Atypical burin | 3 | 1.29 | 4.92 | 5.45 | | 0.00 | 0.00 | 0.00 | 1 | 1.37 | 4.35 | 5.00 |
| 34 | Typical borers | | 0.00 | 0.00 | 0.00 | | 0.00 | 0.00 | 0.00 | | 0.00 | 0.00 | 0.00 |
| 35 | Atypical borers | 1 | 0.43 | 1.64 | 1.82 | | 0.00 | 0.00 | 0.00 | | 0.00 | 0.00 | 0.00 |
| 36 | Typical backed knife | | 0.00 | 0.00 | 0.00 | | 0.00 | 0.00 | 0.00 | | 0.00 | 0.00 | 0.00 |
| 37 | Atypical backed knife | | 0.00 | 0.00 | 0.00 | 2 | 1.36 | 4.88 | | | 0.00 | 0.00 | 0.00 |
| 38 | Naturally backed knife | 5 | 2.15 | 8.20 | — | 4 | 2.72 | 9.76 | — | 3 | 4.11 | 13.04 | — |
| 39 | *Raclette* | 1 | 0.43 | 1.64 | 1.82 | | 0.00 | 0.00 | 0.00 | 2 | 2.74 | 8.70 | |
| 40 | Truncated flakes and blades | | 0.00 | 0.00 | 0.00 | | 0.00 | 0.00 | 0.00 | | 0.00 | 0.00 | 0.00 |
| 41 | Mousterian tranchet | | 0.00 | 0.00 | 0.00 | | 0.00 | 0.00 | 0.00 | | 0.00 | 0.00 | 0.00 |
| 42 | Notch | 12 | 5.15 | 19.67 | 28.82 | 11 | 7.48 | 26.83 | | 3 | 4.11 | 13.04 | 15.00 |
| 43 | Denticulate | 11 | 4.72 | 18.03 | 2.00 | 7 | 4.76 | 17.07 | 18.92 | 8 | 10.96 | 34.78 | 40.00 |
| 44 | Alternately retouched beaks | | 0.00 | 0.00 | 0.00 | | 0.00 | 0.00 | 0.00 | | 0.00 | 0.00 | 0.00 |
| 45 | Retouch on ventral face | | 0.00 | — | — | | 0.00 | — | — | | 0.00 | — | — |
| 46–47 | Abrupt and alternate retouch (thick) | | 0.00 | — | — | | 0.00 | — | — | | 0.00 | — | — |
| 48–49 | Abrupt and alternate retouch (thin) | | 0.00 | — | — | 1 | 0.68 | — | — | | 0.00 | — | — |
| 50 | Bifacial retouch | | 0.00 | — | — | | 0.00 | — | — | | 0.00 | — | — |
| 51 | Tayac points | | 0.00 | 0.00 | 0.00 | | 0.00 | 0.00 | 0.00 | | 0.00 | 0.00 | 0.00 |
| 52 | Notched triangles | | 0.00 | 0.00 | 0.00 | | 0.00 | 0.00 | 0.00 | | 0.00 | 0.00 | 0.00 |
| 53 | Pseudo-microburins | | 0.00 | 0.00 | 0.00 | | 0.00 | 0.00 | 0.00 | | 0.00 | 0.00 | 0.00 |
| 54 | End-notched pieces | | 0.00 | 0.00 | 0.00 | | 0.00 | 0.00 | 0.00 | | 0.00 | 0.00 | 0.00 |
| 62 | Miscellaneous | 6 | 2.58 | 9.84 | 10.90 | 8 | 5.44 | 19.51 | 26.62 | 3 | 4.11 | 13.04 | 15.00 |
| | N | | 233 | 61 | 55 | | 147 | 41 | 37 | | 73 | 23 | 20 |

Real counts include retouched flakes, pieces with isolated removal (in type 62); restricted and reduced counts do not include pieces with isolated removals (the number of which out of Miscellaneous is shown in parentheses); reduced frequencies calculated after Jelinek( 1975:303–304).

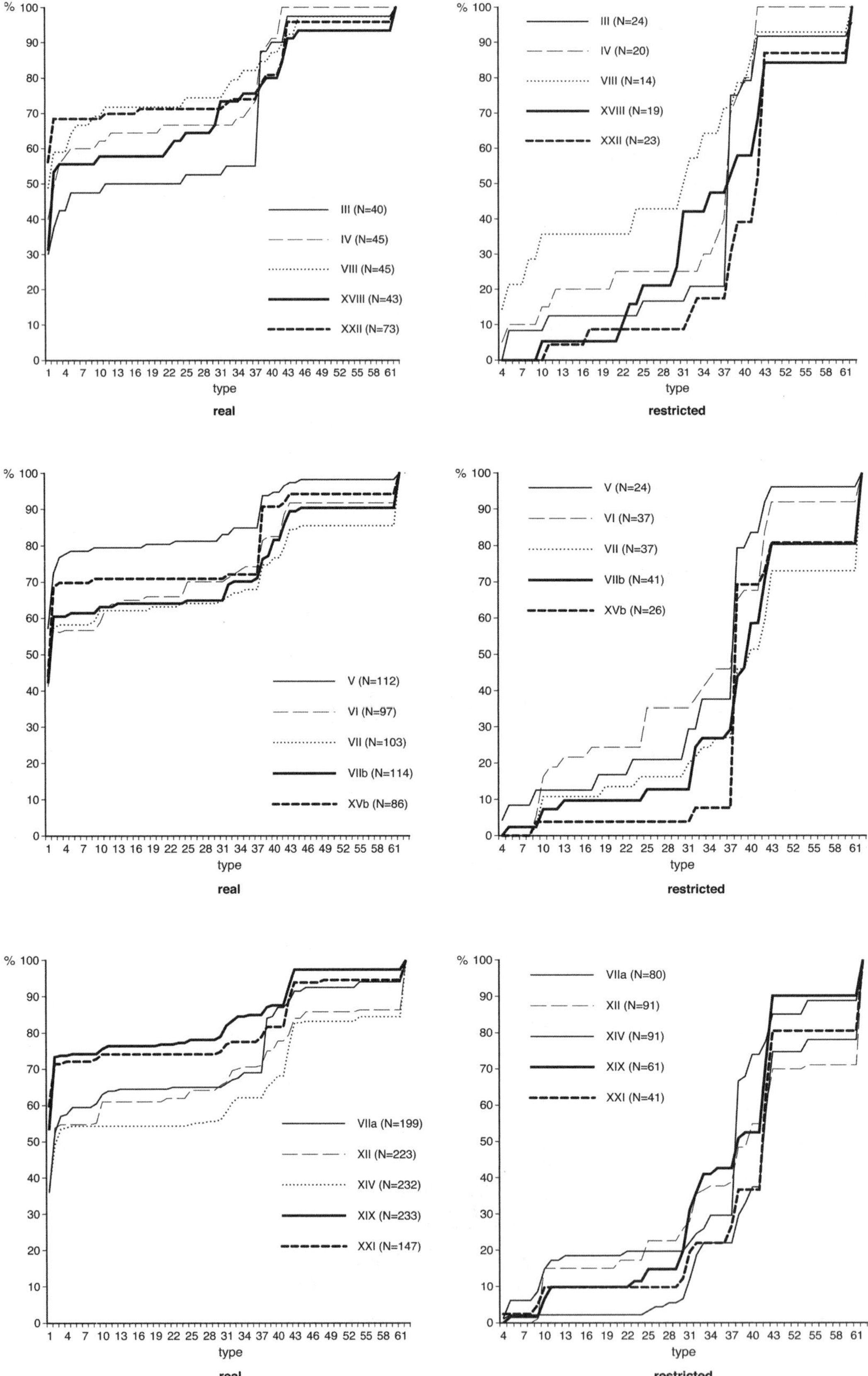

**Figure 6.1** Cumulative graphs showing the real and restricted typological composition of the Qafzeh assemblages. See text for detailed explanations about the calculations involved.

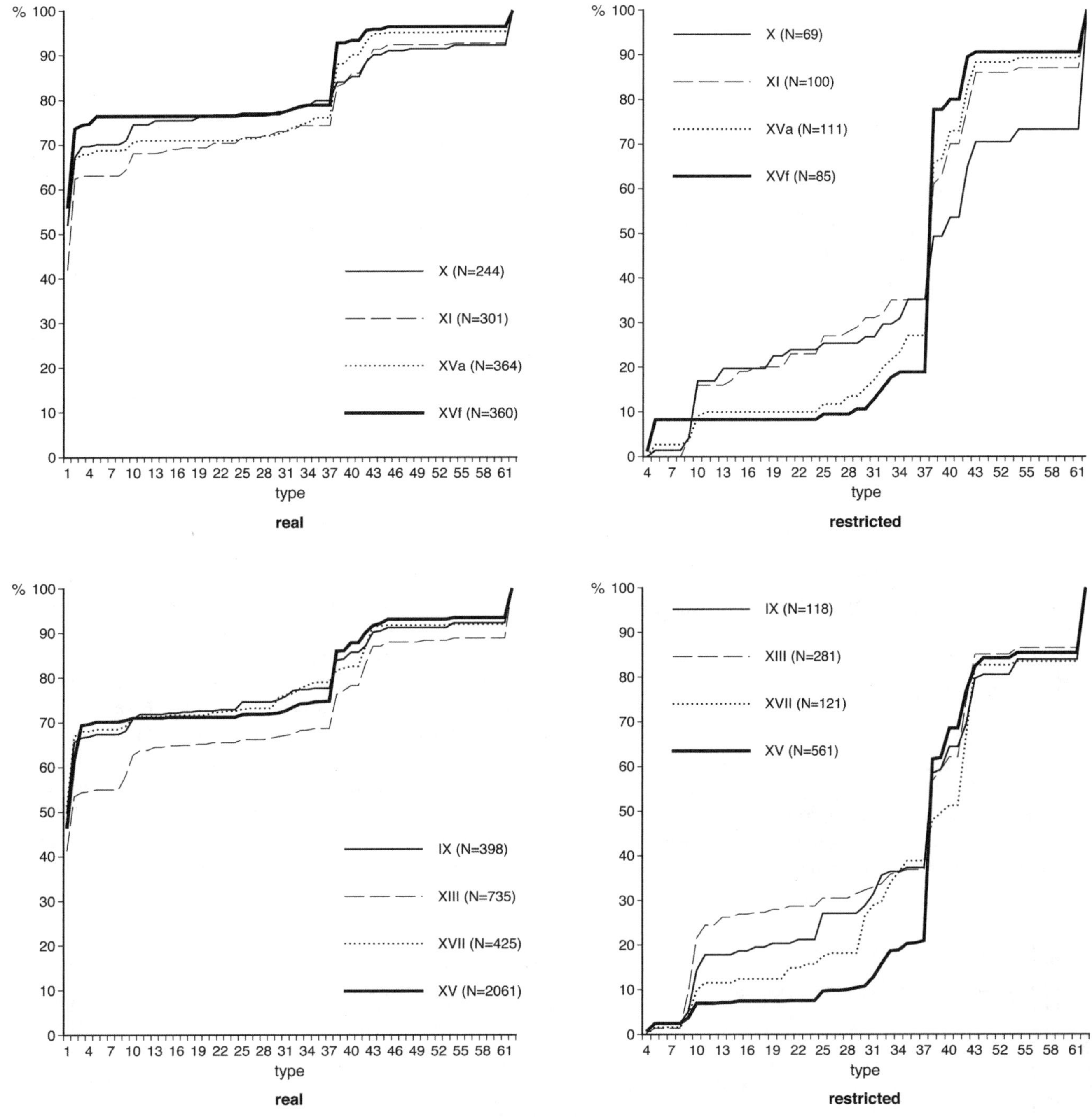

**Figure 6.1**   (continued)

latter pattern characterizes the older assemblages in the Qafzeh sequence (with the addition of layer VIIb).

## Group I

The characteristics of unretouched Levallois flakes and blades were discussed in detail in chapter 5 and need not be reiterated. *Levallois point*s, clearly derived from the use of a Levallois unipolar convergent system of flaking (chapters 4, 5), tend to be relatively long (plates 26:1–5, 8–10, 30:1, 44:1). In layer XV, 19.7% of 122 complete points are of laminar proportions. No other assemblage includes a large enough number of points to enable inter-assemblage comparisons. In both layers VIIa and XIV, the next "point-rich" assemblages (with N = 9, N = 10, respectively), there are no elongated points. Another

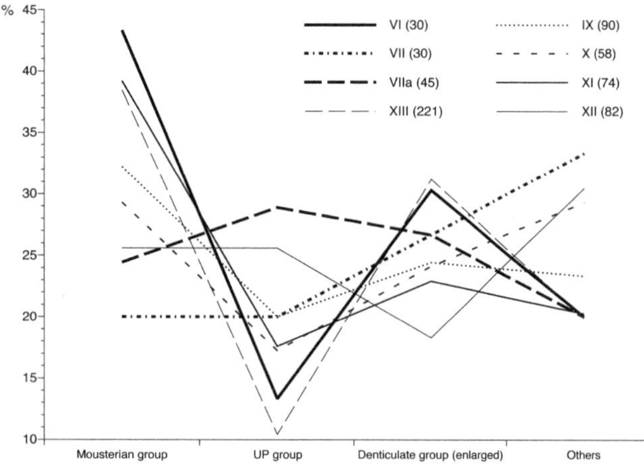

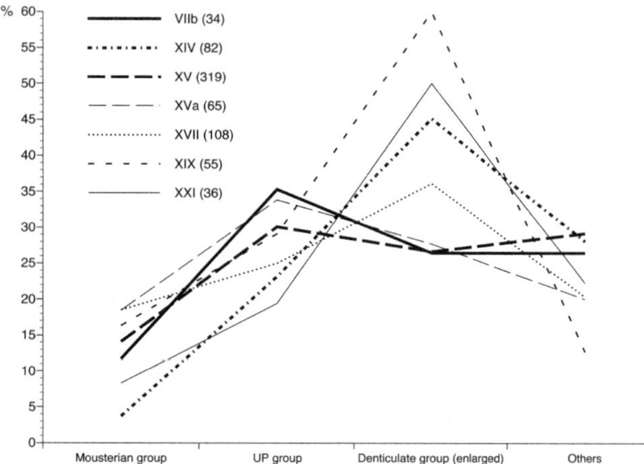

**Figure 6.2** Frequencies of retouched blanks by typological groups. Only assemblages with N ≥ 30 are included in this analysis. See text for details about the compositions of these groups.

characteristic of the points of layer XV is the tendency to remove them off the center of the core's flaking surface.

*Retouched Levallois points* (type 4) hardly occur in any of the assemblages (appendix 5, table 6.1). This characteristic is in line with the overall paucity of Levallois points and triangular flakes in the assemblages (chapter 5). Even in layer XV, retouched Levallois points (N = 4) form only 2.34% of all Levallois elements present in this layer.

## The Mousterian Group (Group II)

This group in the Qafzeh assemblages is composed almost exclusively of *racloirs* (side-scrapers). Hence the value for group II frequencies is often identical to that of IR (index racloirs; see table 6.2b). The lowest value of IR (0.34 in layer XIV) is a rare exception, the common index being ca. 20–30 (for layers with N of tools is > 50).

*Pseudo-Levallois points* (plate 20:5–7) are less with common in the Qafzeh assemblages, despite their alleged abundance in centripetal and discoidal flaking systems (Ohnuma 1990). Morphological regularities of artifacts in this category are a result of their technological role in the flaking process rather than of imposition of form by retouch on lithic blanks. Thus, they have been discussed in more details in chapter 5.

*Mousterian points and limaces* (types 6–8) are virtually absent from any of the assemblages (table 6.1).

*Single convex side-scrapers* (table 6.1; plates 19:1, 24:2, 31:1, 3, 34:2, 37:1, 9–10, 13, 40:9, 46:1, 5, 30:5) are the commonest type of scrapers. Other simple types (plates 10:7, 14:5, 19:6, 9, 23:4, 31:2, 33:5, 12, 41:6, 42:3, 43:6, 8–9) are represented in much lower frequencies. The Qafzeh assemblages share this tendency with most other Levantine

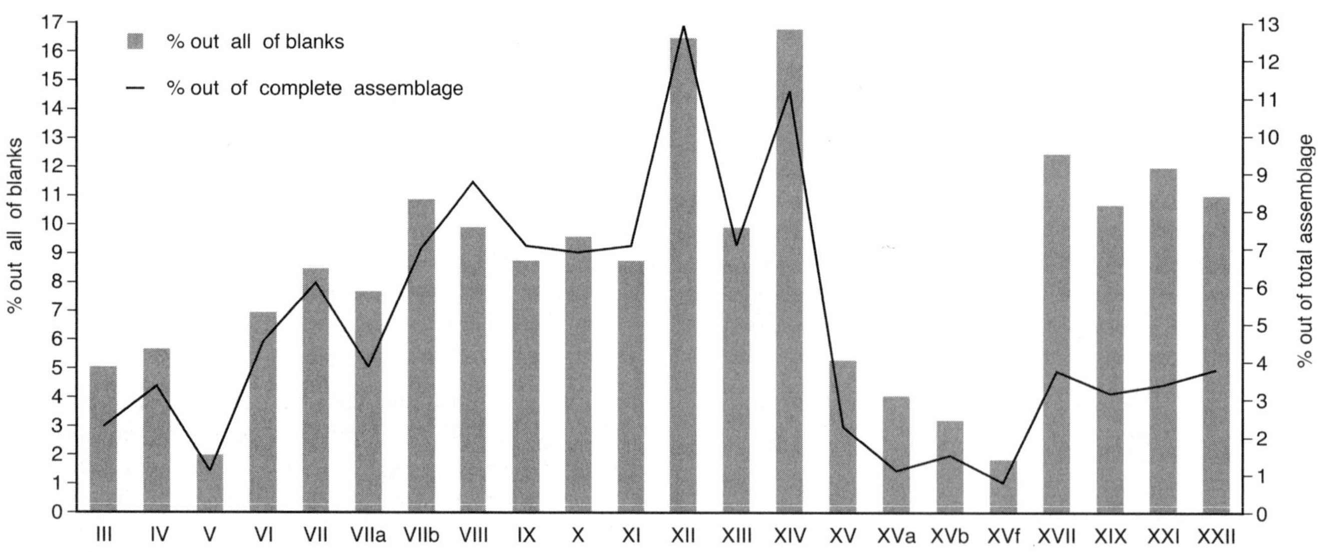

**Figure 6.3** Frequencies of retouched tools out of all flakes and flake tools (left axis); and out of the total number of pieces in an assemblages (including cores and debris) (right axis). See tables 6.2, 6.3, and 7.1 for absolute frequencies.

**Table 6.2a  Typological indices (real)**

| Layer | N | ILty | IR | IRc | IRt | IAu | II | III | IV | IVelargi |
|---|---|---|---|---|---|---|---|---|---|---|
| III | 40 | 50.00 | 5.00 | 0.00 | 0.00 | 0.00 | 10.00 | 5.00 | 7.50 | 7.50 |
| IV | 45 | 60.00 | 6.67 | 2.22 | 0.00 | 4.44 | 8.89 | 8.89 | 0.00 | 8.89 |
| V | 112 | 77.68 | 2.68 | 0.89 | 0.89 | 0.00 | 3.57 | 4.46 | 0.89 | 2.68 |
| VI | 97 | 56.70 | 13.40 | 0.00 | 0.00 | 0.00 | 13.40 | 4.12 | 3.09 | 9.28 |
| VII | 103 | 58.25 | 5.83 | 0.97 | 0.97 | 0.00 | 5.83 | 7.77 | 4.85 | 7.77 |
| VIIa | 199 | 58.37 | 5.53 | 0.00 | 0.50 | 0.00 | 7.54 | 6.53 | 3.02 | 6.03 |
| VIIb | 114 | 60.53 | 3.51 | 0.00 | 0.00 | 0.88 | 4.39 | 9.45 | 3.51 | 7.89 |
| VIII | 39 | 53.85 | 7.69 | 7.69 | 0.00 | 0.00 | 15.38 | 10.26 | 2.56 | 5.13 |
| IX | 398 | 66.58 | 7.29 | 0.25 | 0.25 | 0.00 | 7.79 | 4.52 | 3.02 | 5.53 |
| X | 244 | 69.67 | 6.97 | 1.23 | 0.00 | 0.00 | 7.38 | 4.10 | 1.64 | 5.74 |
| XI | 301 | 62.79 | 9.63 | 1.00 | 0.00 | 0.00 | 9.63 | 4.32 | 2.66 | 5.65 |
| XII | 223 | 54.71 | 9.42 | 0.90 | 0.00 | 0.45 | 9.42 | 8.97 | 4.48 | 6.73 |
| XIII | 735 | 54.55 | 11.16 | 0.54 | 0.00 | 0.00 | 11.97 | 3.13 | 3.95 | 9.39 |
| XIV | 232 | 53.88 | 1.29 | 0.00 | 0.00 | 0.00 | 1.72 | 8.19 | 6.47 | 15.95 |
| XV | 2,061 | 69.43 | 2.18 | 0.05 | 0.00 | 0.19 | 2.67 | 4.61 | 1.50 | 4.12 |
| XVa | 364 | 67.86 | 3.30 | 0.00 | 0.00 | 0.00 | 4.12 | 6.04 | 1.65 | 4.95 |
| XVb | 86 | 69.76 | 1.16 | 0.00 | 0.00 | 0.00 | 1.16 | 1.16 | 2.32 | 3.49 |
| XVf | 360 | 74.72 | 0.28 | 0.00 | 0.00 | 0.00 | 2.22 | 2.50 | 0.28 | 2.50 |
| XVII | 425 | 68.00 | 4.71 | 0.71 | 0.24 | 0.00 | 5.18 | 6.35 | 4.47 | 9.18 |
| XVIIa | 8 | 75.00 | 0.00 | 0.00 | 0.00 | 0.00 | 0.00 | 0.00 | 12.50 | 12.50 |
| XVIII | 17 | 53.33 | 11.11 | 0.00 | 0.00 | 0.00 | 11.11 | 11.11 | 6.67 | 11.11 |
| XIX | 233 | 73.82 | 3.86 | 0.43 | 0.43 | 0.00 | 4.29 | 6.87 | 4.72 | 9.87 |
| XX | 14 | 85.71 | 0.00 | 0.00 | 0.00 | 0.00 | 0.00 | 0.00 | 0.00 | 0.00 |
| XXI | 147 | 72.11 | 2.04 | 0.00 | 0.00 | 1.36 | 2.04 | 4.76 | 4.76 | 12.24 |
| XXII | 73 | 68.50 | 2.74 | 0.00 | 0.00 | 0.00 | 2.74 | 2.74 | 10.96 | 15.07 |
| XXIII | 6 | 62.50 | 0.00 | 0.00 | 0.00 | 0.00 | 0.00 | 0.00 | 0.00 | 12.5 |
| XXIV | 29 | 80.00 | 0.00 | 0.00 | 0.00 | 0.00 | 0.00 | 0.00 | 3.33 | 13.33 |

**Table 6.2b  Typological indices (restricted)**

| Layer | N[a] | IR | IRc | IRt | IAu | I | II | III | IV | IVelargi |
|---|---|---|---|---|---|---|---|---|---|---|
| III | 24 | 8.33 | 0.00 | 0.00 | 0.00 | 0.00 | 16.66 | 8.33 | 12.50 | 12.50 |
| IV | 20 | 15.00 | 5.00 | 0.00 | 10.00 | 5.00 | 20.00 | 20.00 | 0.00 | 0.00 |
| V | 24 | 12.50 | 4.17 | 4.17 | 0.00 | 4.17 | 16.67 | 20.83 | 4.17 | 12.50 |
| VI | 37 | 35.14 | 0.00 | 0.00 | 0.00 | 0.00 | 35.14 | 10.81 | 8.11 | 24.32 |
| VII | 37 | 16.22 | 2.70 | 2.70 | 0.00 | 0.00 | 16.22 | 16.22 | 13.51 | 21.62 |
| VIIa | 80 | 13.75 | 0.00 | 1.25 | 0.00 | 1.25 | 18.75 | 16.25 | 7.50 | 15.00 |
| VIIb | 41 | 9.76 | 0.00 | 0.00 | 2.44 | 0.00 | 12.20 | 29.27 | 9.76 | 21.95 |
| VIII | 14 | 21.43 | 7.14 | 0.00 | 0.00 | 0.00 | 35.71 | 21.43 | 7.14 | 14.29 |
| IX | 118 | 24.58 | 0.85 | 0.85 | 0.00 | 0.85 | 26.27 | 15.25 | 10.17 | 18.64 |
| X | 69 | 24.64 | 4.35 | 0.00 | 0.00 | 0.00 | 26.09 | 14.49 | 5.80 | 20.29 |
| XI | 100 | 29.00 | 3.00 | 0.00 | 0.00 | 0.00 | 29.00 | 13.00 | 8.00 | 17.00 |
| XII | 91 | 23.08 | 2.20 | 0.00 | 1.10 | 0.00 | 23.08 | 22.00 | 10.99 | 16.48 |
| XIII | 281 | 30.14 | 1.42 | 0.00 | 0.00 | 0.35 | 31.21 | 8.16 | 10.28 | 24.47 |
| XIV | 91 | 3.30 | 0.00 | 0.00 | 0.00 | 1.10 | 4.40 | 20.88 | 16.48 | 40.66 |
| XV | 561 | 8.02 | 0.18 | 0.00 | 0.71 | 0.71 | 9.80 | 17.28 | 5.53 | 15.15 |
| XVa | 111 | 10.81 | 0.00 | 0.00 | 0.00 | 0.00 | 13.51 | 19.82 | 5.41 | 16.22 |
| XVb | 26 | 3.85 | 0.00 | 0.00 | 0.00 | 0.00 | 3.85 | 3.85 | 7.69 | 11.54 |
| XVf | 85 | 2.35 | 0.00 | 0.00 | 0.00 | 1.18 | 9.41 | 10.59 | 1.18 | 10.59 |
| XVII | 121 | 16.53 | 2.48 | 0.83 | 0.00 | 0.00 | 18.18 | 22.31 | 15.70 | 32.23 |
| XVIIa | 7 | 0.00 | 0.00 | 0.00 | 0.00 | 0.00 | 0.00 | 0.00 | 14.29 | 14.29 |
| XVIII | 19 | 10.53 | 0.00 | 5.26 | 0.00 | 0.00 | 10.53 | 0.00 | 10.53 | 10.53 |
| XIX | 61 | 14.75 | 1.64 | 1.64 | 0.00 | 0.00 | 16.39 | 26.23 | 18.03 | 37.70 |
| XX | 12 | 0.00 | 0.00 | 0.00 | 0.00 | 0.00 | 0.00 | 0.00 | 0.00 | 0.00 |
| XXI | 41 | 7.32 | 0.00 | 0.00 | 4.88 | 2.44 | 9.76 | 17.07 | 17.07 | 43.90 |
| XXII | 23 | 8.70 | 0.00 | 0.00 | 0.00 | 0.00 | 8.70 | 8.70 | 34.78 | 47.83 |
| XXIII | 3 | 0.00 | 0.00 | 0.00 | 0.00 | 0.00 | 0.00 | 0.00 | 33.33 | 33.33 |
| XXIV | 6 | 0.00 | 0.00 | 0.00 | 0.00 | 0.00 | 0.00 | 0.00 | 16.67 | 66.67 |

[a] Does not include types 1–3, 45–50.

**Table 6.3** Typological groups (retouched pieces only): Absolute, (relative) frequencies, *expected values*, and *standardized residuals*

| Layer | N | a | b | II | | III | | IVelargi | | Others | |
|---|---|---|---|---|---|---|---|---|---|---|---|
| VI | 32 | 6.93 | 4.53 | 13 | (40.63) | 4 | (12.50) | 9 | (28.13) | 6 | (18.75) |
| | | | | *7.22* | **2.48** | *7.38* | **−1.44** | *9.63* | **−0.25** | *7.77* | **−.074** |
| VII | 30 | 8.47 | 6.09 | 6 | (20.00) | 6 | (20.00) | 8 | (26.67) | 10 | (33.33) |
| | | | | *6.77* | **−0.34** | *6.92* | **−0.40** | *9.03* | **−0.41** | *7.29* | **1.17** |
| VIIa | 45 | 7.68 | 3.86 | 11 | (24.44) | 13 | (28.89) | 12 | (26.66) | 9 | (20.00) |
| | [1] | | | *10.15* | **0.31** | *10.38* | **0.94** | *13.54* | **−0.51** | *10.93* | **−0.68** |
| VIIb | 34 | 10.86 | 7.00 | 4 | (11.76) | 12 | (35.29) | 9 | (26.47) | 9 | (26.47) |
| | | | | *7.67* | **−1.52** | *7.84* | **1.72** | *10.23* | **−0.47** | *8.26* | **0.30** |
| IX | 90 | 8.10 | 6.31 | 29 | (32.22) | 18 | (20.00) | 22 | (24.44) | 21 | (23.33) |
| | [1] | | | *20.30* | **2.27** | *20.75* | **−0.71** | *27.08* | **−1.21** | *21.86* | **−0.22** |
| X | 58 | 9.57 | 6.90 | 17 | (29.31) | 10 | (17.24) | 14 | (24.13) | 17 | (29.31) |
| | | | | *13.08* | **1.26** | *13.37* | **−1.08** | *17.45* | **−1.01** | *14.09* | **0.91** |
| XI | 74 | 8.75 | 7.08 | 29 | (39.19) | 13 | (17.57) | 17 | (22.93) | 15 | (20.27) |
| | | | | *16.69* | **3.52** | *17.06* | **−1.15** | *22.27* | **−1.37** | *17.98* | **−.83** |
| XII | 82 | 16.47 | 12.93 | 21 | (25.61) | 21 | (25.61) | 15 | (18.29) | 25 | (30.48) |
| | | | | *18.49* | **0.68** | *18.91* | **0.57** | *24.68* | **−2.40** | *19.92* | **1.35** |
| XIII | 221 | 9.90 | 7.09 | 85 | (38.46) | 23 | (10.41) | 69 | (31.22) | 44 | (19.91) |
| | [1] | | | *49.84* | **6.18** | *51.96* | **−4.87** | *66.51* | **0.40** | *53.69* | **−1.66** |
| XIV | 82 | 16.77 | 11.19 | 3 | (3.69) | 19 | (23.17) | 37 | (45.12) | 23 | (28.05) |
| | [1] | | | *18.49* | **−4.22** | *18.91* | **0.03** | *24.68* | **3.06** | *19.92* | **0.82** |
| XV | 319 | 5.29 | 2.29 | 45 | (14.11) | 96 | (30.09) | 85 | (26.65) | 93 | (29.15) |
| | [4] | | | *71.94* | **−4.18** | *73.56* | **3.40** | *96.00* | **−1.53** | *77.49* | **2.31** |
| XVa | 65 | 4.06 | 1.12 | 12 | (18.46) | 22 | (33.85) | 18 | (27.69) | 13 | (20.00) |
| | | | | *14.66* | **−0.81** | *14.99* | **2.12** | *19.56* | **−0.43** | *15.79* | **−0.83** |
| XVf | 28 | 1.84 | 0.79 | 2 | (7.14) | 9 | (32.14) | 9 | (32.14) | 8 | (28.57) |
| | [1] | | | *6.31* | **−1.97** | *6.46* | **1.15** | *8.43* | **0.24** | *6.80* | **0.53** |
| XVII | 108 | 12.46 | 3.76 | 20 | (18.52) | 27 | (25.00) | 39 | (36.11) | 22 | (20.37) |
| | | | | *24.36* | **−1.05** | *24.91* | **−1.05** | *32.50* | **1.13** | *26.24* | **−0.99** |
| XIX | 55 | 10.68 | 3.16 | 9 | (16.36) | 16 | (29.09) | 23 | (60.00) | 7 | (12.73) |
| | | | | *12.40* | **−1.12** | *12.68* | **1.08** | *16.55* | **1.94** | *13.36* | **−2.04** |
| XXI | 36 | 11.97 | 3.40 | 3 | (8.33) | 7 | (19.44) | 18 | (50.00) | 8 | (22.22) |
| | [1] | | | *8.12* | **−2.07** | *8.30* | **−0.52** | *10.83* | **2.64** | *8.75* | **−0.29** |
| XXII | 20 | 10.99 | 3.80 | 2 | (10.00) | 2 | (10.00) | 11 | (55.00) | 5 | (25.00) |
| | | | | *4.51* | **−1.35** | *4.61* | **−1.40** | *6.02* | **2.45** | *4.86* | **0.07** |

*Notes:* Total chi-square = 156.23; $p < .001$; df – 48.

Layers with N ≥ 20 only. N does not include types 1–3, 5, 38, 45–50 (after Jelinek 1975) and blanks with isolated removals. Frequencies of retouched Levallois points (group I) appear where relevant in square brackets and are added to total counts for calculations of the next two columns. Group I counts were omitted from calculations of relative frequencies and expected values in individual cells, as well as from the total $x^2$ value of the table. Residuals that are statistically significant at $p \le .05$ are in bold face.

a = % from combined numbers of tools and debitage.

b = % from the total presented in the first column of table 7.1.

Middle Paleolithic sites (Goren-Inbar 1990a; Marks 1992a:136). *Double* (plates 15:7, 10, 23:1, 37:11–12, 40:5, 44:3–4), *convergent* (plates 32:6, 40:2), and *offset* (*déjeté*) scrapers (plates 22:3, 33:10, 35:6–7, 37:6–7, 39:7) are few in any single layer (table 6.1, figure 6.5a).

## The Upper Paleolithic Group (Group III)

*End-scrapers* (plates 15:12–13, 16:8, 6, 40:4) are the dominant component of group III, but their frequencies do not drastically exceed those of burins or perforators (plates 19:3, 5, 21:8) (table 6.1, figure 6.5b). *Backed knives* (plates 24:1, 46:4) are absent from practically all the assemblages: IA[u] is nil in most cases. In the few instances in which high values were recorded, this is due mainly to small sample sizes. The paucity of retouched backed knives contrasts the relatively ubiquitous occurrence of naturally backed knives and further emphasizes the different processes of tool production that underlie the appearance of these two types in the assemblages. Atypical forms of *grattoirs*

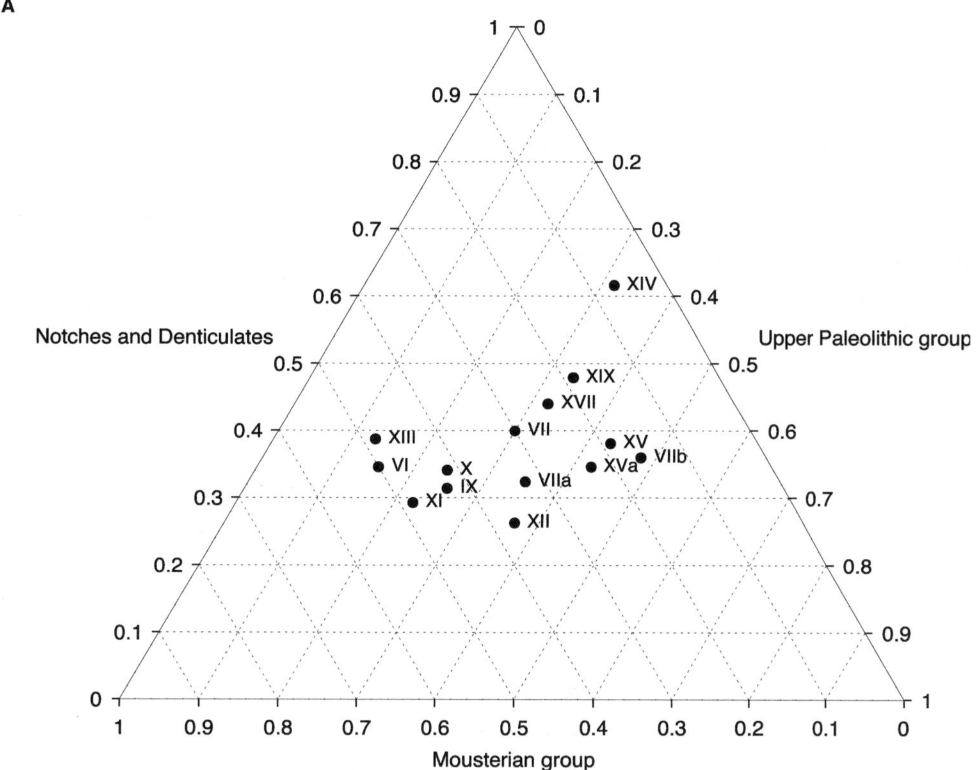


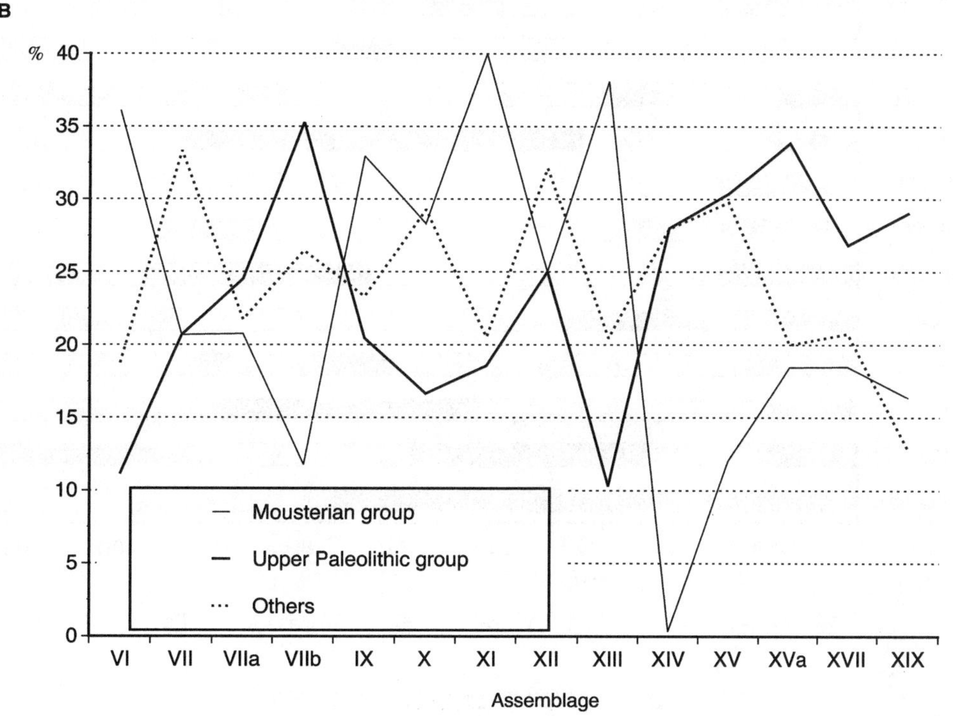


**Figure 6.4** Relationship between typological groups in Qafzeh assemblages. Only assemblages with N ≥ 20 for reduced counts are shown here. A: The clustering of assemblages according to composition of typological groups. B: Co-variation of typological groups in the various assemblages.

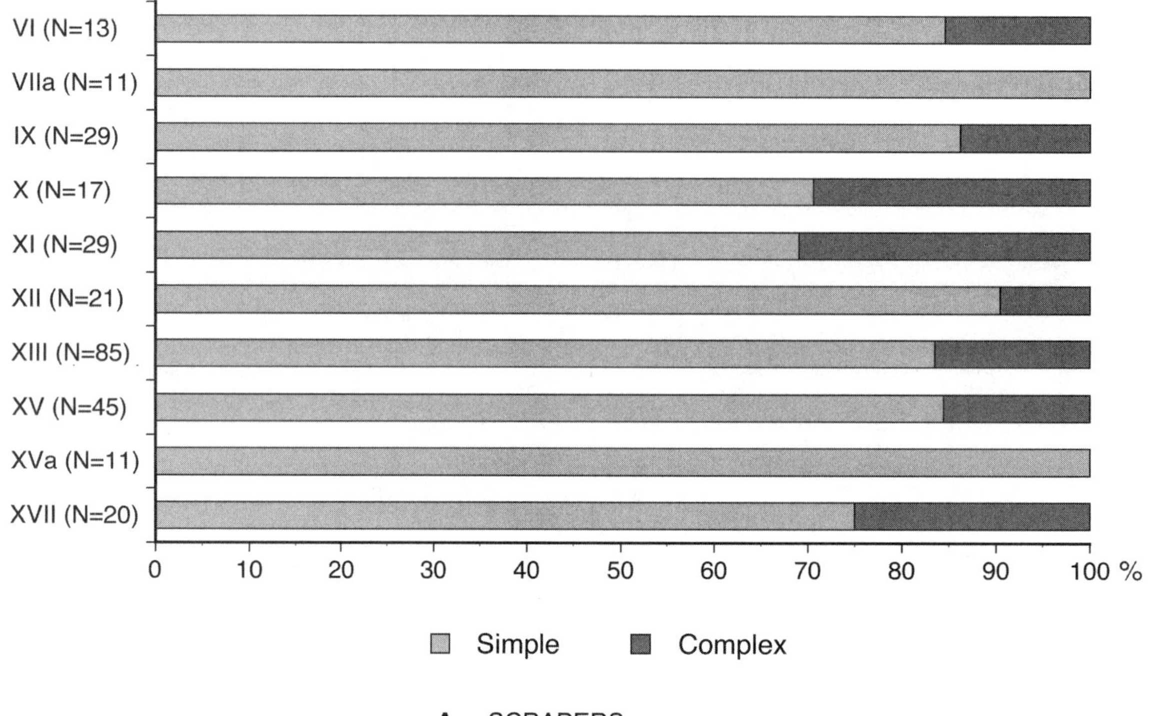

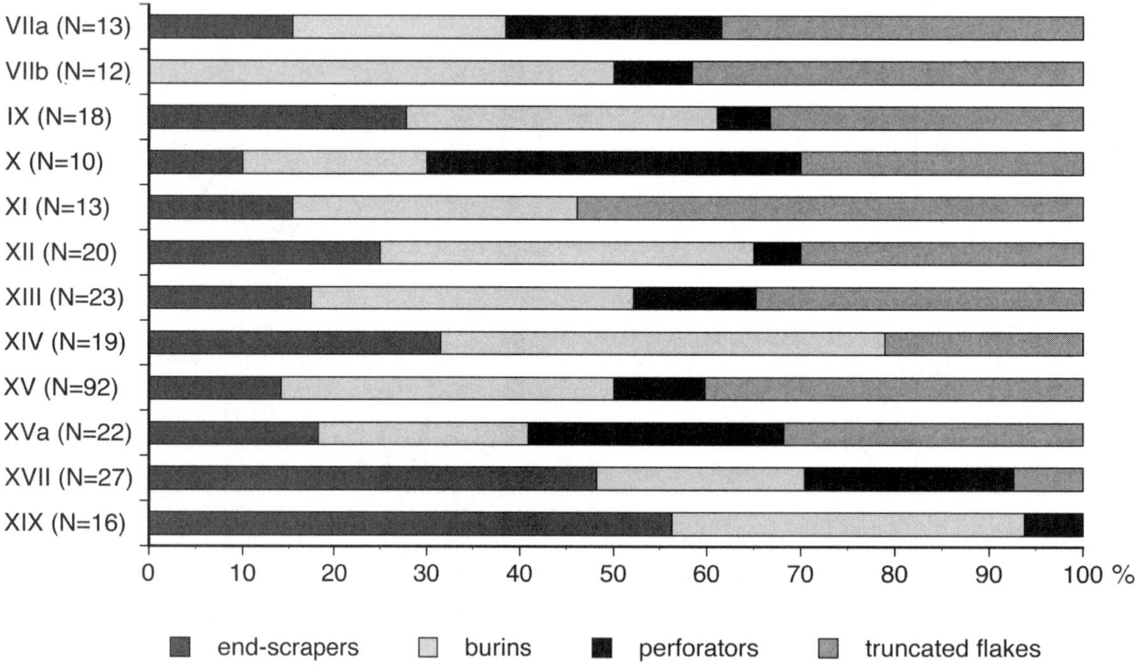


**Figure 6.5** Internal composition of typological groups in selected assemblages. A: Scrapers. "Simple" scrapers include Bordes's types 9–11, 22–28; "Complex" scrapers consist of Bordes's types 12–21, 27, 28.
B: Upper Paleolithic group. Note the small absolute frequencies within group in each assemblage. Only assemblages with N > 10 for the group are included in each analysis.

(end-scrapers) and borers are as frequent as the typical ones (e.g., plates 13:12, 14:2, 6, 15:4, 40:4; table 6.1). A few end-scrapers in layers XIX and XVII, classified here as atypical forms, are reminiscent of Upper Paleolithic carinated scrapers (e.g., plate 13:7–8).

*Burins* are somewhat better executed than the end-scrapers. The vast majority of burins are dihedral or on a natural break (plates 21:7, 22:1–2, 5, 32:2, 35:8, 36:1–2), although burins on truncations do occur (plates 30:14–15, 34:4). Layer XIV is exceptional in that all the burins (N = 9) are on truncations.

*Borers* (plates 15:2, 19:1, 3, 5, 21:8) are well made, with clear tips shaped by retouch on both lateral edges. Several specimens exhibit retouch on only one edge, while the other edge is formed by a break or a single blow on the face opposite the retouch. Such pieces were classified as "alternately retouched beaks" (type 44; plate 22:7). Following the Bordesian convention, such pieces were excluded from group III counts.

*Truncated pieces* (type 40) occur in most of the assemblages (table 6.1, plate 22:4). Many of these were achieved by the use of abrupt or regular retouch. However, some pieces bearing Nahr Ibrahim technique were also considered truncations. When this technique was applied to modify only a small part of the flake's distal/proximal edge so that the two modified faces formed an obtuse angle, and when flake scars indicated that all resultant flakes had been of similar sizes, the artifact was considered a truncated piece (table 6.4; plates 9:2, 23:2, 28:1, 31:4–5, 37:5).

## Notches and Denticulates (Group IVelargi)

*Notches* (plates 15:1, 20:9, 21:1, 12, 30:10, 39:9) are the most frequent tool type in this group, followed by *denticulates* (plates 12:6, 8, 14:3, 15:3, 5, 9, 16:9, 29, 5, 30:13). The relative proportions of frequencies of notches to denticulates vary between 0.5 (layer XII) and 1.74 (layer XV). Specimens of this typological group are normally well executed, with only rare occurrences of Clactonian notches. The frequencies of *end-notched pieces* (type 54; plate 39:4) are low.

## Miscellaneous

A large number of retouched/modified artifacts do not conform with any of Bordes's types. Some of these are classified as *retouched flakes* (type 106; plates 11:2, 12:4–5, 39:12, 41:4, 42:2), since they bear regular and continuous retouch along one or more edges. It should be noted that, while they are recognized as a distinct type, for graphic purposes and Bordesian counts these artifacts were included in Bordes's type 62 (following Goren-Inbar 1990a:63; see appendices 4, 5 for explanation and detailed

counts). Other artifacts classified as *miscellaneous* (Bordes's type 62) exhibit various types of retouch (e.g., flat, abrupt, or mixed retouch) on either edges or tips of flakes. In a few cases *racloir*-like retouch appears on distal ends of flakes.

Two other types of modified flakes were distinguished in the Qafzeh assemblages. These are *flakes with signs of utilization* (type 120; plates 23:2, 29:4, 33:4, 12, 39:10) and *flakes bearing isolated removals* (type 121) on either the dorsal or ventral face. These two non-standardized types occur in almost all assemblages and, although they were omitted from the formal counts (table 6.1), their occurrence enhances the informal character of these assemblages.

### Nahr Ibrahim Technique

Most items included in the *miscellaneous* category were modified by bifacial treatment of the flake. Their process involves the truncation of a flake on one face and then the use of the truncated edge as a striking platform for removals from the other face. First described as "truncated-faceted" or thinned flakes (i.e., conceived as tools; Crew 1976; Schroëder 1969), such artifacts have been viewed as cores by other archaeologists (Goren-Inbar 1988b; Hovers 2007; Munday 1976a; Nishiaki 1985; Solecki and Solecki 1970, who coined the name "Nahr Ibrahim cores").

There has been much debate as to whether this was a technique for removing flakes (*débitage*) off cores-on-flakes or for shaping flakes into tools (*façonnage*). The occurrence of a "truncated-faceted" platform along the whole circumference of the flake, analogous to the preparation of centripetally worked Levallois cores, indeed supports their interpretation as cores. The small size of the flakes compared to cores, as well as that of the resultant secondary flakes, does not rule out the proposition that these were cores (Dibble and McPherron 2006; Goren-Inbar 1988b; Hovers 2007; see plates 20:1–4, 26:1–2, which show intentional Levallois points, albeit miniature in size). Although there is no size difference between flakes selected to be used as cores and those that were modified for other purposes (table 6.4; cf. table 4.9), the distinction between Nahr Ibrahim-associated tools ("miscellaneous" and truncated flakes), on the one hand, and cores-on-flakes, on the other, is based on attributes of the applied retouch and its extent on the core circumference.

In the Qafzeh assemblages, there are several cases in which this technique appears to have been used in order to modify flakes rather than detach new ones (cf. Crew 1976; Dibble 1984b). Such pieces differ from cores in that the scars of the detached flakes cover a relatively small portion of the flake's surface. Several items were defined as *truncated pieces* (type 40; see above). When the surface

**Table 6.4  Frequencies of tools modified by Nahr Ibrahim technique and location of modification**

| Layer | Truncated flake (type 40) | Location of modification[a] | Miscellaneous (type 62) | Location of modification |
|---|---|---|---|---|
| VII | — | | 2 | L |
| VIIa | 2 | D | — | |
| IX | 1 | D | 7 | L (4), D (1), P (1), DP (1) |
| X | 1 | D | 3 | R (1), D (1), P (1) |
| XI | 2 | D | 3 | D (2), P (1) |
| XII | — | | 3 | L |
| XIII | 3 | D (2), P (1) | 7 | L (1), D (4), P (2) |
| XIV | 2 | D | 8 | L (2), P (3), DP (1),  LP (1), PE (1) |
| XV | 12 | D (5), P (3), DP (4) | 43 | L (3), R (1), D (15), P (16), DP (6), RP (1), I (1) |
| XVa | 1 | D | 1 | D |
| XVf | 1 | D | — | |
| XVIII | — | | 2 | R (1), D (1) |
| [b] | $\bar{X}$ length (N = 17) 55.48 | | $\bar{X}$ length (N = 40) 47.96 | |
| [b] | $\bar{X}$ width (N = 22)  39.93 | | $\bar{X}$ width (N = 59) 36.05 | |
| [b] | $\bar{X}$ thick (N = 25)9.27 | | $\bar{X}$ thick (N = 76)  10.54 | |

[a] D: distal, P: proximal, DP: distal and proximal, L: left edge, R: right edge, LP: left and proximal, RP: right and proximal, PE: proximal and two lateral edges, I: indeterminate

[b] Means of  measurements on unbroken artifacts, combined from all assemblages given their high degree of similarity.

area covered by detached flakes was small, and the truncation appeared on a lateral edge, or less than three secondary flakes were removed, the artifacts were classified as *"miscellaneous"* (type 62; plate 28). The two types, while created by the same modification technique, can be distinguished on metrical grounds as well, since there are significant differences in their lengths. However, the small sample size of type 40 precludes a valid formal testing of the hypothesis of different types.

While this modification method is always applied to flakes, slight changes in the angle of intersection between the modified faces of the flake and in the size and spatial organization of the removed flakes can render the object either a core or a tool. Hence, I apply the term "Nahr Ibrahim" in a technological rather than a rigid typological sense, and it does not refer to specific types (e.g., "Nahr Ibrahim cores" or "truncated-faceted pieces"). In this work the term designates a general modification technique employed to modify blanks into tools or, alternately, to exploit them as cores.

## Multiple Tools

The typological list (table 6.1) and commutative graphs (figure 6.1) are presented according to Bordes's method. However, some of the retouched artifacts are multiple tools, i.e., were retouched in a way that enables their classification as several tool types executed on a single blank.

Bordes ([1961] 1988:22) assigned such items to a single type, based on conformity of retouch. By this system, the tool was assigned to one type out of two (or more) on the blank that was more "typically" executed. A second way of assigning types to multiple-type artifacts was based on relative frequencies in the assemblage, so that an artifact was assigned to a type that was less frequent in the studied assemblage. Clearly, such procedures involved loss of information about the frequencies of specific types. Perhaps of more significance, they cause loss of data on potentially favorable combinations of shapes of retouched edges, intensity of retouch, and other variables that are pertinent to understanding the functionality of artifacts and assemblages, raw material economies, and the flexibility of imposition of form. Following Goren-Inbar (1990a), the "second" tools of multiple tools in the Qafzeh assemblages (triple tools were rarely encountered) were also documented. The more typically executed tool of each pair was considered the primary type and included in the traditional typological classifications presented in tables 6.1—6.3. Additional information about these multiple tools is provided below.

Double tools occur in all the assemblages (table 6.5) in relative frequencies that seem independent of the size of the total sample of modified artifacts. Table 6.6 reveals a large variety of type combinations (e.g., plates 12:7, 15:6, 17:1, 19:2, 21:8, 22:6, 23:3, 24:1, 28:1, 30:14, 31:1–4, 37:1, 3, 6, 8, 42:2, 47:6), each occurring in very

**Table 6.5  Frequencies of double tools in the Qafzeh assemblages**

| Layer | 1 | 2 | 3 | 4 |
|---|---|---|---|---|
| III | 6 | 1 | 16.7 | 1 |
| IV | 13 | 2 | 15.4 | — |
| V | 13 | 1 | 7.7 | — |
| VI | 30 | 4 | 13.3 | — |
| VII | 30 | 2 | 6.7 | 1 |
| VIIa | 46 | 6 | 13.0 | 1 |
| VIIb | 34 | 4 | 11.8 | — |
| IX | 91 | 7 | 7.7 | 3 |
| X | 58 | 10 | 17.2 | 3 |
| XI | 74 | 19 | 16.2 | 5 |
| XII | 82 | 13 | 15.9 | 3 |
| XIII | 222 | 37 | 16.7 | 11 |
| XIV | 82 | 10 | 12.2 | — |
| XV | 323 | 23 | 7.1 | 5 |
| XVa | 65 | 6 | 9.2 | 3 |
| XVb | 10 | 2 | 20 | 1 |
| XVf | 29 | 2 | 6.9 | — |
| XVII | 108 | 16 | 14.8 | 5 |
| XIX | 55 | 7 | 12.7 | 2 |
| XXI | 37 | 4 | 10.8 | 2 |
| XXII | 20 | 2 | 10 | — |

*Note*: Retouched pieces only. 1: total number of retouched artifacts (table 6.3); 2: number of double tools out of N in previous column; 3: % of double tools out of N in column 1; 4: number of "simple" scrapers (see figure 6.5) that are paired with other, non-scraper types.

low numbers. (It should be noted that some combinations, represented by a single occurrence each, are not shown in this table.)

There are two trends in this restricted sample. First, retouched flakes tend to co-occur with simple scrapers (types 9, 10, 25; plates 39:12, 41:6). Secondly, notches/denticulates are the most common type occurring in combination with any other tool type (e.g., plates 13:11, 14:4, 15:8, 11, 19:7, 46:6); a similar pattern was noted also in the assemblages from Quneitra (Goren-Inbar 1990a). The most frequent combinations of notches/denticulates are with retouched flakes and with Upper Paleolithic (group III) tools (plates 15:2, 40:4, 43:7). This pattern is inconsistent with suggestions (Gordon 1993:213) that notches should be excluded from the category of functional tools since they were produced for the purpose of hafting elongated and pointed elements (both retouched and unretouched). Possibly their rules were assemblage-specific.

Overall, the combinations of double tools represent the non-formalized aspect that also characterizes the simple tools in the Qafzeh assemblages. Combinations of tool types on the same blank were normally not of the well-executed, more formal types and do not appear to have required higher levels of investment in tool shaping or more rigid imposition of form compared to single tools.

## Blank Selection

The selection of blanks for retouch depends on an array of factors that influence the knapper's decision. One widely discussed factor is the effect of raw material availability and quality (Andrefsky 1994; Bamforth 1991; Baumler and Speth 1993; Bousman 1993; Brantingham et al. 2000; Dibble 1991a, 1991b, 1995b; Jelinek 1991; Kuhn 1995a; Rolland 1981; Rolland and Dibble 1990; a variant of this view [Brantingham 2003] will be discussed in detail in chapter 8).

As discussed in chapters 1 and 2, economic models based on optimization principles are oversimplified depictions of most real situations. Their usefulness in paleoanthropological work in general, and in the context of studying prehistoric technologies in particular, is in the relative ease with which they allow the formulation of testable hypotheses. It is this process that is conducive toward developing more complex models in more advanced stages of research. In this spirit, assuming for the sake of the immediate discussion that tool production is based exclusively on optimization principles (Nelson 1991; Torrence 1983, 1989b), the more abundant and larger the raw material, the less effort will be invested in artifact preparation and in tool maintenance after it has been shaped, all other things being equal (see chapter 7). In such circumstances careful selection for larger or sharper blanks may not occur. In other cases, additional factors may be introduced into the decision-making process. One such factor is the organizational solutions to the problems imposed by limitations on raw material use and by the nature of the intended tasks (Binford 1989), which are ingrained in a group's technological repertoire. In conditions of task-oriented, logistical mobility (Binford 1980; Kelly 1983, 1995), the exclusive and immediate availability of low-quality raw material might cause a dichotomy. Some tool types, arguably those intended for short use, may be executed on inferior-quality but locally available raw materials, while other types, presumably those designed to last longer and to be curated, would be made on better but more exotic stone that was carried (often in the form of ready blanks or partially prepared cores) from greater distances (e.g., Geneste 1985; Meignen 1988; Roebroeks, Kolen, and Rensink 1988). If the latter tools were indeed intended to last longer, it is possible that larger blanks were selected for their manufacture to enable their more exhaustive exploitation. The same tendency of curation may also lead to high retouch intensity (e.g., Hovers 1990b). On the other hand, if a human group was highly mobile and sources of usable

**Table 6.6  Combinations of tool types in multiple tools**

| Types | 9/ | 9/ | 10/ | 10/ | 11/ | 25/ | 30/ | 30/ | 31/ | 31/ | 32/ | 32/ | 34/ | 35/ | 40/ | 40 | 40/ | 42/ | 42/ | 42/ | 43/ | 43/ | 43/ | 45/ | 62/ | 62/ | 62/ | 106/ |
|---|---|---|---|---|---|---|---|---|---|---|---|---|---|---|---|---|---|---|---|---|---|---|---|---|---|---|---|---|
| Layer | 40 | 106 | 42 | 106 | 40 | 106 | 42 | 106 | 42 | 43 | 10 | 43 | 42 | 42 | 10 | /25 | 42 | 42 | 45 | 106 | 40 | 42 | 106 | 106 | 10 | 32 | 43 | 62 |
| III | | | | | | | | | | | | | | | | | | | | | | | | | | | | |
| IV | | | | | | | | | | | | | | | | | | 1 | | | | | | | | | | |
| V | 1 | | | | | | | | | | | | | | | | | | | | | | | | | | | |
| VI | | | | | | | | | | | | | | | | | | 1 | | | | | | | | | | |
| VII | | | | | | | | | | | 1 | | | | | | | | | | | | | | | | | |
| VIIa | 1 | | | | | | | | 1 | | | | | | | | | 1 | | | | | | | | | | |
| VIIb | | | | | | | | | | | | | | | | | | | | | 1 | | | | | | | |
| IX | | | | | | | | | | | | 1 | | | | | | | | | | | | | 2 | | | |
| X | | 1 | | | | | | | | | 1 | | | 1 | 1 | 1 | 1 | | | | | | | | | 1 | | |
| XI | | | | | | | | | | | | | | | 1 | 1 | 1 | | 3 | | | | | | | | | |
| XII | | | 1 | | | 1 | | 1 | | | | 2 | 1 | | | | | | | | | | 1 | | | 1 | | 1 |
| XIII | | 2 | 3 | 5 | | | | | 1 | 1 | | 1 | | | 1 | 1 | | | | 1 | 3 | | 3 | 2 | | | 1 | |
| XIV | | | | | | | | | | | | | | | | | | | 1 | | 1 | 1 | | | | | 1 | |
| XV | | 1 | | 3 | | 1 | | | 1 | 1 | | | | | | | | | | | | | 1 | | | 2 | | 2 |
| XVa | | | | 1 | | | | 1 | | | | | | | | | | | | | | | 1 | | | | | |
| XVb | | | | | | | | | | | 1 | | | | | | | | | | | | | | | | | 1 |
| XVf | | | | | | | | | | | | | | | | | | | | | | | 1 | | | | | |
| XVII | | | | | | | 2 | 1 | | | | | 1 | 1 | | | | | | | 1 | 1 | 1 | | | | | |
| XIX | | | | | 1 | | | | 1 | | | 1 | | | | | | | | | | | 1 | | 1 | | | |
| XXI | | | | | 1 | | | | | | | | | | | | | | | | | | | | 1 | | | |
| XXII | | | | | | | | | | | | | | | | | | | | | | | | 1 | | | | |
| TOTAL | 2 | 4 | 4 | 9 | 2 | 2 | 2 | 3 | 4 | 2 | 3 | 5 | 2 | 2 | 3 | 3 | 2 | 3 | 4 | 10 | 3 | 6 | 5 | 2 | 2 | 2 | 2 | 4 |

*Note*: Type combinations that occur only once were omitted from this table.

128

raw material were expected to be encountered en route, economizing behaviors would be relaxed and the indications of intensive use as described above might not occur. Provisioning-oriented behaviors form the other facet of the same behaviors. From this perspective, the crucial factors informing decisions are whether individuals or sites are to be provisioned, so that there needs to be higher investment of raw material, time, and energy in producing effective tools in advance, with the risk that the products may not be used with maximum efficiency and energy and material resources may be wasted. If more immediate activities are provisioned, the risk of overinvestment in preparing blanks that would not be put to use is reduced.

The mobility and organizational patterns for the various Qafzeh assemblages are discussed more thoroughly in chapter 7. What concerns me in the current context of blank selection is that external limitations on raw material due to changing source locations and shifts in mobility patterns seem to have played only a minor role in any changes in raw material availability through time. Variability in patterns of lithic blank selection in the Qafzeh assemblages (if it occurred at all) is likely to be observed within, rather than among, assemblages.

Below I address the question of whether this variability reflects intentional choices based on the intended functions of the tools or reflects "stylistic" preferences. To assess whether technological aspects played a role in the selection of blanks for retouch, it is necessary not only to describe the patterns among the tools but to show that they diverge from those seen among the unretouched artifacts.[4]

## Selection for Complete Blanks?

As a rule, the lithic artifacts in the various assemblages are well preserved with fresh edges and surfaces (figures 7.4, 7.5). The high frequencies of broken artifacts, occasionally higher than 50% (in layers VIIa, XVb, XIX, XXI, and XXII; figure 6.6), seem to contradict this relatively pristine state of preservation. The vast majority of breaks are "flexion" breaks caused by pressure applied to the item (Bergman and Roberts 1988).[5] Regardless of the type of blank (e.g., blade vs. flake), transversal breaks (i.e., proximal and distal) are the most frequent (figure 6.6). Of these two locations, distal breaks are more common, most likely because the distal part of the blank was usually the thinnest and most vulnerable (see also Goren-Inbar 1990a:78, fig. 55).

Retouched items are relatively more often complete than debitage (table 6.7 columns 1 and 2, figure 6.7). Reversals of this pattern are more frequent in the older assemblages. Moreover, frequencies of complete blanks occur differentially in the various typo-technological groupings. Core management pieces and Levallois debitage in each assemblage seem to have undergone less breakage than have tools and non-Levallois debitage (table 6.7 columns 3–5). The higher frequencies of complete blanks in these two categories are statistically significant. Broken artifacts are associated with the non-Levallois group in most assemblages (table 6.7; standardized residuals not shown).

It is difficult to determine the reasons for the breakage of lithic artifacts in antiquity. The degree of completeness of blanks may reflect taphonomic processes, specific patterns of selection, production, and discard within each assemblage, or a combination of the two. Some of

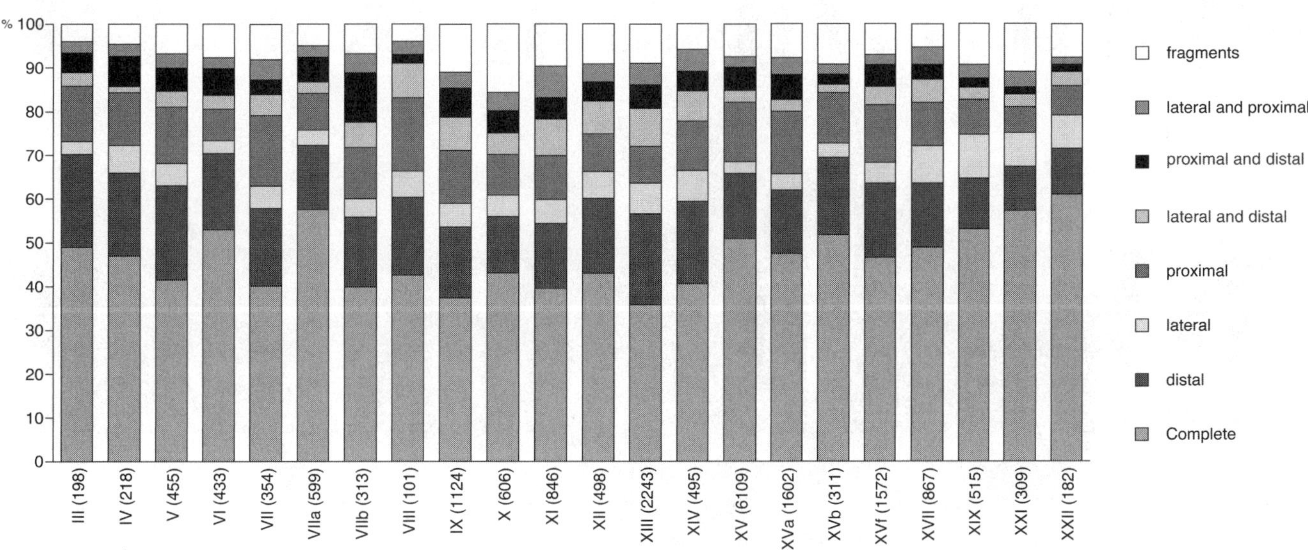



**Figure 6.6** Frequencies of breakage location on debitage and tools.

| Layer | 1[a] | | 2[a] | | 3[a] | | 4[a] | | 5[a] | | $\chi^{2b}$ | $p$ |
|---|---|---|---|---|---|---|---|---|---|---|---|---|
| | N | % | N | % | N | % | N | % | N | % | | |
| III | 189 | 48.2 | 9 | 66.7 | 152 | 41.5 | 18 | 77.8 | 19 | 73.7 | 15.19 | .0017 |
| IV | 203 | 47.3 | 14 | 42.9 | 168 | 42.3 | 22 | 68.2 | 13 | 76.9 | 10.25 | .015 |
| V | 642 | 42.2 | 15 | 60.0 | 535 | 37.4 | 78 | 64.1 | 29 | 72.4 | 33.10 | <.0001 |
| VI | 397 | 53.9 | 35 | 42.9 | 326 | 51.8 | 53 | 62.3 | 18 | 66.7 | 4.80 | **.1873** |
| VII | 318 | 39.0 | 36 | 50.0 | 238 | 30.7 | 55 | 58.2 | 25 | 76.0 | 31.17 | <.0001 |
| VIIa | 548 | 52.9 | 51 | 51.0 | 394 | 51.8 | 96 | 72.9 | 58 | 77.8 | 25.09 | <.0001 |
| VIIb | 274 | 33.2 | 38 | 50.0 | 191 | 34.0 | 58 | 44.8 | 25 | 60.0 | 9.14 | .0275 |
| IX | 1,017 | 31.2 | 106 | 38.7 | 696 | 30.0 | 234 | 49.6 | 87 | 60.9 | 51.64 | <.0001 |
| X | 543 | 42.0 | 63 | 52.4 | 342 | 35.7 | 152 | 48.7 | 49 | 65.3 | 21.70 | <.0001 |
| XI | 758 | 38.7 | 86 | 47.7 | 506 | 30.4 | 181 | 51.9 | 71 | 63.4 | 48.42 | <.0001 |
| XII | 406 | 50.7 | 92 | 45.7 | 249 | 32.5 | 111 | 55.9 | 46 | 63.0 | 26.43 | <.0001 |
| XIII | 1,962 | 35.0 | 278 | 41.0 | 1,351 | 28.6 | 410 | 48.3 | 201 | 51.2 | 82.73 | <.0001 |
| XIV | 395 | 40.8 | 100 | 40.0 | 229 | 31.9 | 122 | 53.3 | 44 | 52.3 | 17.86 | .0005 |
| XV | 5,588 | 51.3 | 396 | 58.0 | 3,790 | 45.0 | 1,376 | 64.0 | 422 | 67.3 | 200.24 | <.0001 |
| XVa | 1,526 | 46.6 | 72 | 66.7 | 1,192 | 43.6 | 224 | 53.6 | 110 | 64.6 | 33.91 | <.0001 |
| XVb | 301 | 53.2 | 10 | 40.0 | 218 | 45.4 | 48 | 70.8 | 35 | 68.6 | 15.03 | .0018 |
| XVf | 1,532 | 47.8 | 36 | 41.7 | 1,171 | 43.5 | 237 | 54.4 | 124 | 63.7 | 25.39 | <.0001 |
| XVII | 744 | 50.2 | 123 | 47.2 | 387 | 45.2 | 288 | 51.7 | 69 | 60.9 | 7.13 | **.0678** |
| XIX | 459 | 55.3 | 55 | 34.6 | 249 | 51.4 | 160 | 55.0 | 50 | 76.0 | 18.65 | .0003 |
| XXI | 274 | 59.1 | 38 | 44.7 | 142 | 56.3 | 103 | 58.3 | 29 | 75.9 | 6.63 | **.0847** |
| XXII | 163 | 61.7 | 20 | 60.7 | 102 | 57.8 | 49 | 59.2 | 12 | 91.7 | 5.22 | **.1563** |

[a] Frequencies of complete blanks in each category. Ns are for total of each category. 1: all debitage; 2: tools (retouched pieces and pieces with isolated removals); 3: non-Levallois debitage; 4: Levallois debitage; 5: all core management pieces.

[b] $\chi^2$ results for complete/broken frequencies in the four categories. df = 3 in all cases. *P*-values indicating that the differences are *not* statistically significant appear in bold face.

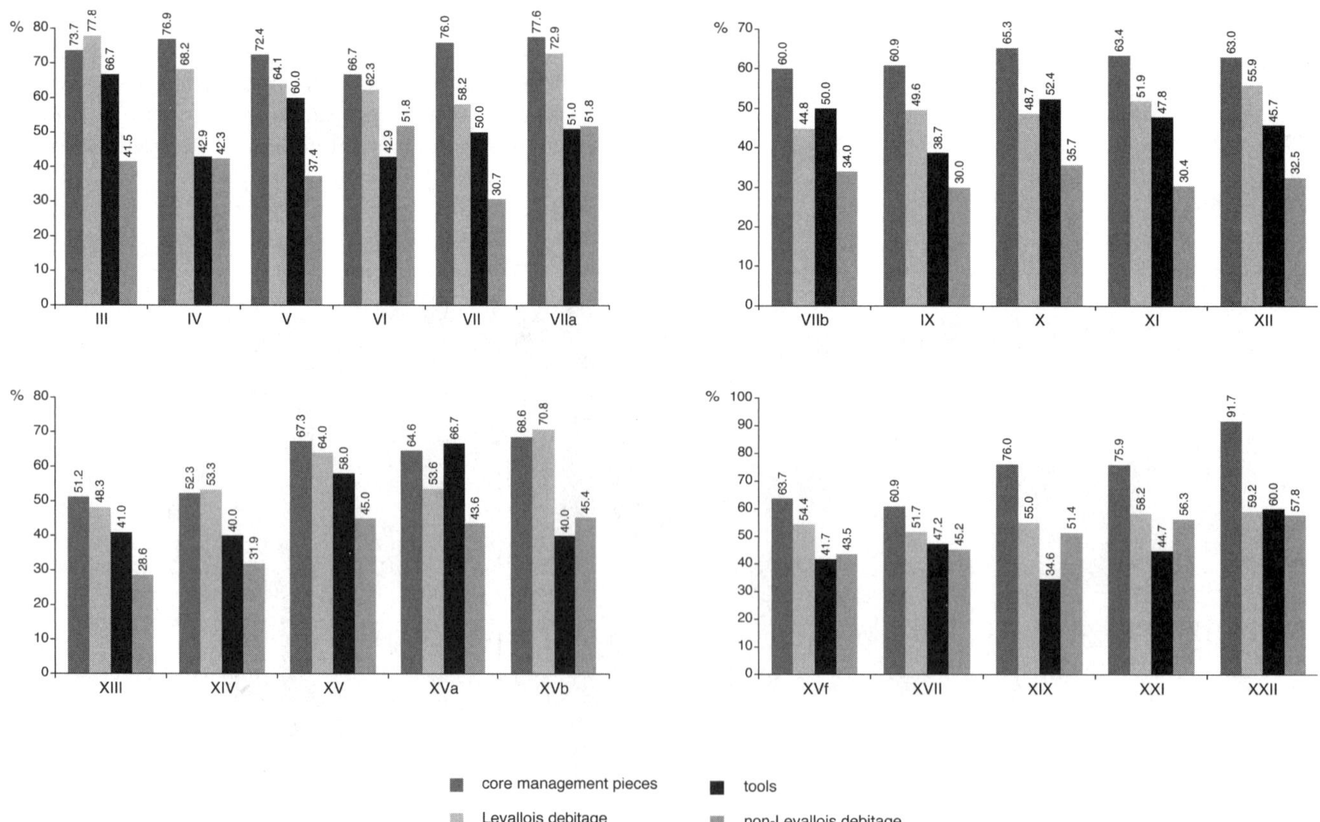



**Figure 6.7**  Frequencies of complete blanks in various categories of the lithic assemblages of Qafzeh.

these processes can be ruled out as the major cause for breakage patterns in the Qafzeh assemblages. Turning to taphonomic processes such as compression of the overlying sediments or trampling as explanatory mechanisms for the breakage patterns (e.g., Bar-Yosef 1993; Gifford-Gonzalez et al. 1985; Hovers 2003; Nielsen 1991) raises more questions than it solves. These processes affect artifacts of different size orders differently (i.e., micro-debitage as opposed to debitage). Yet all the items discussed here fall within the same size order, so size cannot account for the differential breakage pattern among the various typo-technological groups (chapter 5; see also below). A taphonomic explanation to the patterns observed in the Qafzeh assemblages would require that in each assemblage the four classes of artifacts were spatially exclusive, and that breakage occurred as a local, restricted phenomenon. Field observations do not substantiate the first claim, thus refuting also the second.

The breakage patterns observed in the Qafzeh assemblages may reflect a basic pattern of selection of complete blanks to be retouched. The following selection model may explain the differential frequencies of broken flakes and tools:

1. Initial breakage of flakes occurred in varying frequencies during the process of core reduction and flake detachment. Such breakage affected (presumably differentially, because the detachment of desired Levallois blanks was more controlled) both Levallois and non-Levallois pieces. Removals of core management pieces would similarly be highly controlled and thus less prone to accidental breakage during core reduction, simply because the continuation of a core's exploitation depended on their proper removal. Detachment of such pieces, therefore, would have been well calculated.

2. Since the shaping of Levallois blanks occurred during the process of reduction itself, with both dimensions and shape being the goals of the reduction processes, Levallois blanks were often put to use without any further modification/retouch.

3. On the other hand, if non-Levallois blanks were to be used, they would normally require further retouch or modification, since their shapes and dimensions were more random and did not necessarily fit the planned task. Among this group, mostly complete flakes (which tend to be also the largest) were selected for use, and more often than not retouched as well.

4. The selection of complete, relatively large non-Levallois blanks would a priori diminish the frequencies of such pieces within the non-Levallois debitage, resulting in higher frequencies of broken artifacts.

5. Later breakage (mainly of retouched tools and utilized unmodified Levallois blanks) probably

occurred during utilization. Such breaks likely depended on the type of materials to which the artifacts were applied and the motions performed. Breakage of the various typo-technological categories due to the activities in which they were used would be differential only if such activities were radically different. Taphonomic processes, on the other hand, would affect randomly the various categories.

Use-wear studies (Shea 1991) have shown that non-retouched debitage, especially Levallois blanks, had been used as tools in Mousterian sites. Nevertheless, Shea recognized that the highest incidence of use-wear traces occurs among retouched artifacts and Levallois points (Shea 1991:225) in all the sites under study, including Qafzeh. Hence, if breakage were due first and foremost to usage, tools and Levallois blanks would be expected to exhibit higher breakage frequencies than debitage. This prediction is not borne out, suggesting that other processes were in place. The higher ratio of complete to broken blanks among core management pieces may indeed be the result of their not being used as much as "regular" blanks, but could indeed reflect the attention to their shaping during the reduction process.

A model of differential selection that relates to blank completeness appears plausible, as neither taphonomic processes nor use-related breakage are a satisfactory explanation for the breakage patterns seen in the subject assemblages. Indeed, when absolute numbers are examined, the majority of tools are not retouched on Levallois blanks (tables 6.8, 6.10, figure 6.8a). Moreover, in assemblages in which the ratio of complete/broken pieces is higher in the debitage than in the tool sample, this is often concordant with higher frequencies of Levallois blanks among the tools (cf. figure 6.8a, table 6.7). These patterns are consistent with the proposed selection model.

## Selection by Amount of Cortex

The presence of cortex and its amount and position on a blank's dorsal face may have been neutral in the process of tool modification, i.e., various tool types would bear various amounts of cortex so that no clear selection for or against cortical cover can be inferred. Another possible scenario is that some tasks necessitated thinness and sharpness, requiring light weight or homogeneous surfaces (e.g., hunting tools). In such cases cortex would have been perceived as a hindrance and might have been removed either as part of preconceived blank preparation for anticipated tasks (e.g., during Levallois flaking) or by specific selection against cortex-covered blanks for modification as tools. Yet a third scenario posits that the presence of cortex could have been advantageous for some tool types, so that it might have been left purposely on

Table 6.8   Absolute frequencies of Levallois blanks in tool groups

| Layer | Simple scrapers | | Double scrapers | | Convergent scrapers | | Transversal scrapers | | Other scrapers | | End- scrapers | | Burins | | Notches and denticulates | | Other types | |
|---|---|---|---|---|---|---|---|---|---|---|---|---|---|---|---|---|---|---|
| | N | Lev.[a] | N | Lev.[a] | N | Lev.[a] | N | Lev.[a] | N | Lev.[a] | N | Lev.[a] | N | Lev.[a] | N | Lev.[a] | N | Lev.[a] |
| VI | 7 | 2 | 2 | **2** | | | | | 4 | 1 | | | 2 | — | 8 | 4 | 10 | 4 |
| VII | 4 | 2 | | | | | 1 | — | | | | | 1 | — | 3 | 1 | 8 | 3 | 19 | 9 |
| VIIa | 9 | 6 | 1 | 1 | 1 | — | | | | | | | 1 | — | 3 | 1 | 9 | 4 | 25 | 11 |
| VIIb | 2 | 1 | 1 | — | | | | | 1 | 1 | | | | | 6 | 1 | 9 | 1 | 19 | 6 |
| IX | 18 | 10 | 1 | 1 | 2 | 1 | | | 7 | 2 | 5 | 1 | 6 | — | 16 | 6 | 46 | 15 |
| X | 11 | 8 | 2 | 2 | 3 | 3 | | | 1 | — | 1 | — | 2 | 2 | 12 | 3 | 31 | 20 |
| XI | 16 | 11 | 4 | 3 | 3 | 3 | | | 6 | 1 | 2 | 1 | 4 | 2 | 15 | 7 | 34 | 17 |
| XII | 14 | 10 | | | 2 | 2 | | | 5 | 2 | 5 | 2 | 8 | 3 | 14 | 7 | 44 | 24 |
| XIII | 64 | 43 | 7 | 6 | 4 | 2 | | | 8 | 5 | 4 | — | 8 | 1 | 64 | 28 | 114 | 41 |
| XIV | 2 | 2 | | | | | | | | | 6 | 3 | 8 | 3 | 34 | 18 | 48 | 17 |
| XV | 25 | 9 | 3 | 3 | 1 | — | | | 14 | 7 | 13 | 2 | 31 | 5 | 76 | 29 | 220 | 74 |
| XVa | 7 | 7 | | | | | | | 4 | 2 | 3 | 2 | 5 | 1 | 17 | 7 | 34 | 16 |
| XVf | | | | | | | | | 2 | — | 2 | | 4 | 1 | 7 | 4 | 19 | 3 |
| XVII | 11 | 6 | 1 | 1 | 3 | 2 | 1 | 1 | 3 | 2 | 13 | 6 | 5 | 1 | 40 | 18 | 46 | 22 |
| XIX | 5 | 3 | | | 1 | 1 | 1 | — | 2 | — | 9 | 5 | 6 | 2 | 23 | 10 | 8 | 5 |
| XXI | 3 | 2 | | | | | | | | | 4 | 2 | 1 | — | 18 | 10 | 12 | 7 |
| TOTAL | **198** | 122 | **22** | 19 | **20** | 14 | **3** | 1 | **57** | 23 | **69** | 24 | **102** | 24 | **370** | 159 | **729** | 291 |
| [b] | | 86.01 | | 9.56 | | 8.69 | | 1.30 | | 24.76 | | 29.97 | | 44.31 | | 160.73 | | 316.67 |
| [c] | | **4.20** | | **4.09** | | **2.41** | | −0.35 | | −2.62 | | −0.24 | | −4.20 | | −0.21 | | −2.62 |
| % Levallois | | 61.62 | | 86.36 | | 70.00 | | 33.33 | | 40.35 | | 34.78 | | 23.53 | | 42.97 | | 39.92 |

Note: The $\chi^2$ statistic is 64.44 at p ≤ .0001, for a Non-Levallois (N in header)/Levallois comparison for the total raw number per tool group across all the layers.
[a] Number of Levallois blanks out of the total shown in previous column.
[b] Expected values for Levallois blanks in each tool group.
[c] Standardized residuals of Levallois blanks in each tool group. Significant values are shown in bold.

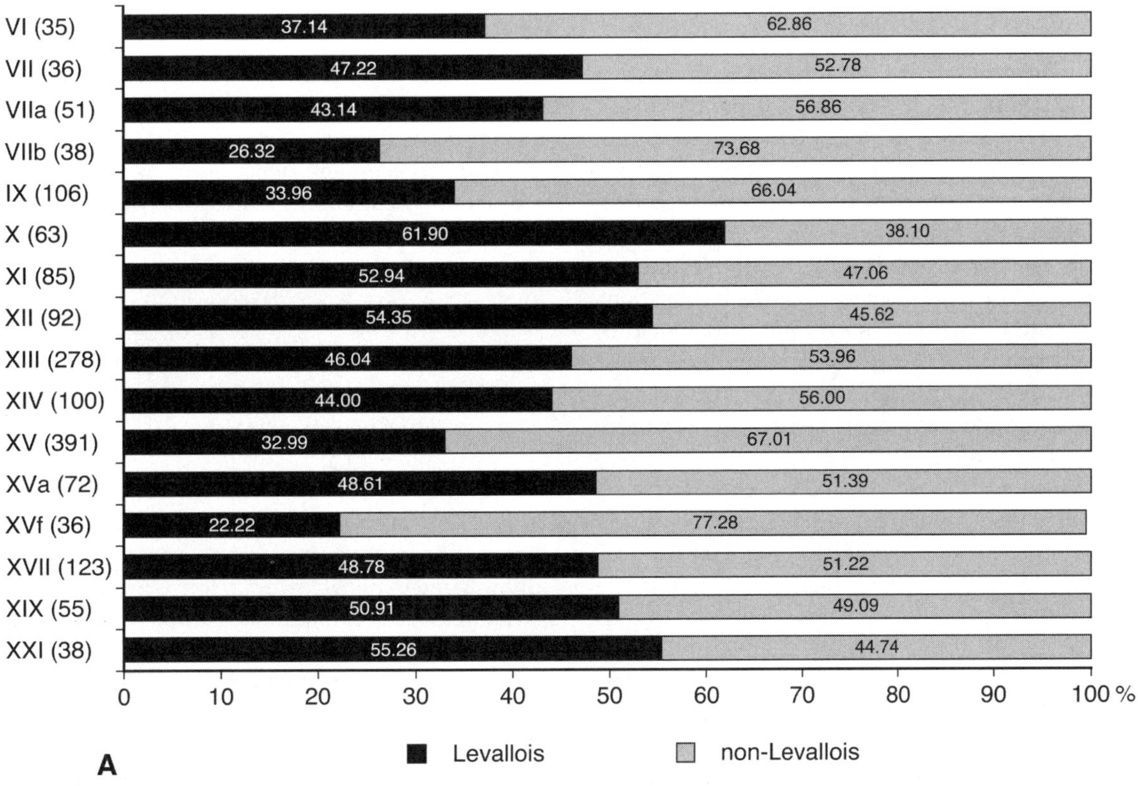


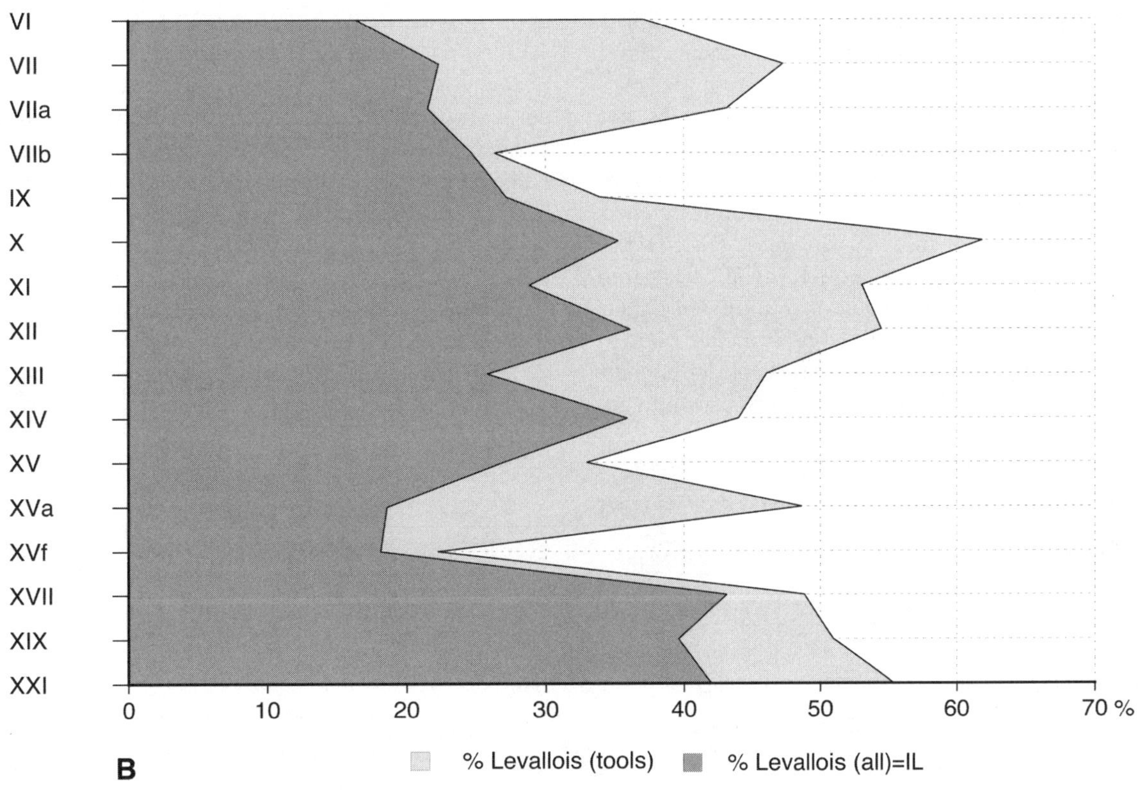


**Figure 6.8** Frequencies of Levallois blanks. A: Among retouched artifacts (including Bordes's types 45 and 121). Only assemblages with N of tools ≥ 30 are shown. B: Among retouched tools, compared to frequencies in the total assemblage (IL).

some predesignated blank types or selected against when available blanks were singled out for further modification. Finally, given that cortical blanks that are removed in the earlier stages of reduction tend to be large compared to other debitage, what appears as a selection for cortical blanks may reflect the tendency to use larger blanks for retouch. While the end-products may be similar in terms of the presence of cortex on tool blanks, the implications of the various paths of action differ significantly. One process invokes preplanning of tool blanks from the earliest stages of the reduction process, rather in line with the Bordesian notion of tools as emic types that require more advance planning and also confer higher risks of overinvestment. The selection (for or against cortical cover) from an existing population of available blanks implies more flexible strategies of blanks shaping and reduces the risk of overinvestment in artifacts that may not, in the end, be used.

To enable statistical treatment of the data, modified and retouched pieces were collapsed into nine categories: all the single scrapers (types 9–11) were grouped as *simple scrapers*, types 12–17 were agglomerated as *double scrapers*, types 18–21 were grouped as *convergent scrapers*, while types 22–24 were designated *transversal scrapers*. All other types of scrapers were included in *other scrapers*. End-scrapers (types 30–31) and burins (types 32–33), *notches and denticulates* (types 42–43) and *other types* (retouched artifacts, including types 45 and 121 that are not encountered in the previous groups) form the remaining tool groups.

The presence of cortical cover on blanks does not appear to have prevented their retouch. The frequencies of retouched artifacts that bear cortex are often only slightly lower than those observed among non-retouched blanks (figure 5.2a-b). In most assemblages (e.g., layers VI–VIIa, IX, and XIII–XXI), the frequencies of cortex-free artifacts are in fact somewhat lower among retouched and modified artifacts than among non-retouched blanks. While the over-representation of cortex on retouched blanks is not statistically significant in any assemblage,

it demonstrates that the presence of cortical cover and its amount did not play a major role in blank selection for further modification.

Cortical elements were used as blanks for all tool types: they occur as single scrapers (plates 24:2, 33:5, 35:5, 40:9, 47:4), burins and end-scrapers (plates 13:8, 15:4, 16:8, 22:1, 5, 30:15, 32:2, 35:8, 36:2), notches and denticulates (plates 11:9, 15:3, 5, 21:12), and double tools (plates 13:11, 15:2, 6, 8, 19:2, 7, 23:3, 33:6, 47:6), as well as other, less common types, e.g., double (plates 15:7, 37:12), convergent (plate 32:6) and offset *(déjeté)* scrapers (plate 22:3), scrapers retouched on the ventral face (plate 19:6, 41:6) and awls (plate 19:3).

Because the distribution of cortex among various retouched pieces appears to be very similar across assemblages, and since sample sizes per assemblage did not allow a meaningful comparison even among the more generalized tool groups, tool samples from all the assemblages were agglomerated in order to examine the use of cortical blanks for production of specific tool classes (table 6.9). This analysis shows some interesting type-related patterns. Non-cortical blanks occur more often among simple scrapes. Less than 10% of these tools exhibit a naturally backed edge opposite the retouched edge (e.g., plates 23:3–4, 40:9), the others bearing cortex on the lateral and central parts of the dorsal face. Burins occur frequently with up to 50% of their dorsal surface covered with cortex, and the "other" category has up to 25% cortical cover. End-scrapers, too, tend to occur more often on cortex-bearing blanks. The observation that notches and denticulates tend to bear less cortex than some Upper Paleolithic types is somewhat surprising, given that the former are usually taken to have been made in a more haphazard and less planned manner than were most other formal tool types (e.g., Geneste 1985; Rolland 1981).

Some of the relationships between tool types and cortical cover are not unique to the Qafzeh assemblages. A tendency to modify Upper Paleolithic tools on cortical blanks has been observed, for example, in the

**Table 6.9   Distribution of cortex cover by generalized tool groups**

| % Cortex/Tool group | N | No cortex | 1–25% cover | 26–50% cover | 51–75% cover | 76–100% cover |
|---|---|---|---|---|---|---|
| Simple scrapers | 201 | 148 (73.63) | 32 (15.92) | 11 (5.47) | 7 (3.48) | 2 (1.49) |
| Double scrapers | 26 | 19 (73.07) | 3 (11.53) | 1 (3.84) | 1 (3.84) | 2 (7.69) |
| Convergent scrapers | 22 | 18 (81.82) | 2 (9.09) | 2 (9.09) | — | — |
| Transversal scrapers | 5 | 4 (80.00) | 1 (20.00) | — | — | — |
| Other scrapers | 64 | 43 (67.18) | 12 (18.75) | 5 (7.81) | 1 (1.56) | 3 (4.69) |
| End-scrapers | 72 | 37 (51.39) | 15 (20.83) | 12 (16.67) | 5 (6.94) | 3 (4.17) |
| Burins | 105 | 40 (38.10) | 36 (34.29) | 19 (18.09) | 4 (3.81) | 6 (5.71) |
| Notches and denticulates | 400 | 243 (60.75) | 75 (18.75) | 47 (11.75) | 18 (4.50) | 17 (4.25) |
| Other tools | 647 | 355 (57.87) | 181 (27.95) | 77 (11.90) | 21 (3.25) | 13 (2.01) |

*Note*: Total $\chi^2$ is not valid due to high number of cells with low expected values.

assemblage of Quneitra (Goren-Inbar 1990a:141–142, fig. 54). Interestingly, in this assemblage, too, denticulates (but not notches) were made on less cortical blanks. Similarly, while the grouping of types in the analysis of the Biache Saint-Vaast assemblage differs from the one employed here, side-scrapers tend to be made on non-cortical elements (Dibble 1995c).

## Size and Shape as Selection Criteria

The mean dimensions of retouched blanks are the largest among flakes in all the assemblages (figure 5.7; table 5.9). Although the mean values of length and width cover practically the same size ranges as do other artifact classes (e.g., Levallois and non-Levallois debitage), there is a clear tendency toward selecting larger artifacts for retouch (the mode being 50–59 mm of length in most assemblages).

These distributions suggest that Levallois elements were preferred for retouch, given their large size compared to non-Levallois blanks. Indeed, the frequencies of Levallois blanks among tools are high. This prediction appears to be borne out by the fact that values of IL in any given assemblage, i.e., the relative frequencies of Levallois blanks in the total assemblage, are lower than their frequencies among tools in that same assemblage (figure 6.8b). Still, Levallois blanks by no means constitute the dominant blank type among the tools (with the exception of layers XI, XII, and XXI; figure 6.8a).

Detailed analysis of the data on Levallois blank frequencies indicates that the higher frequencies of this type of debitage among the tools do not result from an overall, unselective preference of these blanks for the manufacture of all tool types (tables 6.8, 6.10). There is an obvious selection of Levallois pieces to be retouched into side-scrapers, particularly into simple scrapers (61.6% of these tools were made on Levallois blanks).[6] For other tool types, either there was no particular selection or there was

a preference of non-Levallois blanks (see below). The relative high frequencies of Levallois blanks among tools, as opposed to the total assemblage, thus represent stringent criteria for the execution of particular tool types, rather than a generalized need to retouch Levallois pieces due to inadequate morphological or functional properties. Such demanding yet narrowly applied selection criteria may explain the apparent contrast between the "breakage model" presented above, according to which Levallois blanks were retouched less often than non-Levallois blanks, and the relatively high frequencies of retouched Levallois blanks actually observed.

As in the case of cortical cover, the selection pattern seen in the Qafzeh assemblages resembles that identified in other Mousterian assemblages (e.g., Dibble 1995a, 1995c; Goren-Inbar 1988a, 1990a:142; Munday 1976b).

The combination of blank traits of Upper Paleolithic tools suggests a specific selection out of the non-Levallois flakes in any assemblage. This is especially true for burins, only 23.5% of which are made on Levallois pieces. This particular selection is also evident in the fact that burins and (to a lesser extent) end-scrapers were made on cortical pieces, which are relatively rare among Levallois elements (table 6.9; and see table 5.2). In the same vein, blanks with unipolar scar patterns (both Levallois and non-Levallois) are clearly associated with burin production across assemblages (tables 6.8, 6.10, figure 6.9), even though they are under-represented among other tools in the various assemblages (with the exception of layers XIV, XV, and XVa; figure 6.10a). As unipolar scar patterns are rare among Levallois blanks (figures 5.3a, 6.11a), this pattern is again related to reliance on non-Levallois blanks for burin production.

The data shown in figure 6.12b indicate that burins were made on relatively short blanks. The small sample size per assemblage precludes a rigorous statistical testing of these data and allows only identification of general trends, which nonetheless appear robust. Average length of this tool type is restricted to the range of 30–50 mm. Given that the majority of burins were flaked off natural or breakage planes, rather than truncations that would have caused shortening of the blank, the small size of the blanks cannot be attributed to the process of tool shaping. Instead, it appears to represent a true preference of the knappers when selecting blanks for this tool type. A similar tendency was observed at Quneitra (Goren-Inbar 1990a) and at Rosh Ein Mor (Crew 1976).

Notches and denticulates display a larger spread of mean length, associated with a range of mean width that is similar to that of burins (figure 6.12c). This may imply that the overall shape of the flakes played a lesser role (if any) in the process of selecting blanks for such tools. Denticulates tend to be narrower on average than notches, but large standard deviations per sample render

**Table 6.10  Relationship between tool groups and blank technology (expected values and *standardized residuals*)**

| Tool group | Levallois | | Non-Levallois | |
|---|---|---|---|---|
| Simple side-scrapers | 86.01 | **4.20** | 111.99 | **−4.20** |
| Double side-scrapers | 9.56 | **4.09** | 12.44 | **−4.09** |
| Convergent side-scrapers | 8.69 | **2.41** | 11.31 | **−2.41** |
| Transversal side-scrapers | 1.30 | −0.35 | 1.70 | 0.35 |
| Other side-scrapers | 24.76 | **−2.62** | 32.24 | **2.62** |
| End-scrapers | 29.97 | −0.24 | 39.03 | 0.24 |
| Burins | 44.31 | **−4.20** | 57.69 | **4.20** |
| Notches and denticulates | 160.73 | −0.21 | 209.27 | −0.21 |
| Other types | 316.67 | **−2.62** | 412.33 | **2.62** |

*Note*: Total sample $\chi^2 - 69.44$ at $p \leq .0001$. Standardized residuals that are significant at $p \leq 0.5$ are shown in bold.

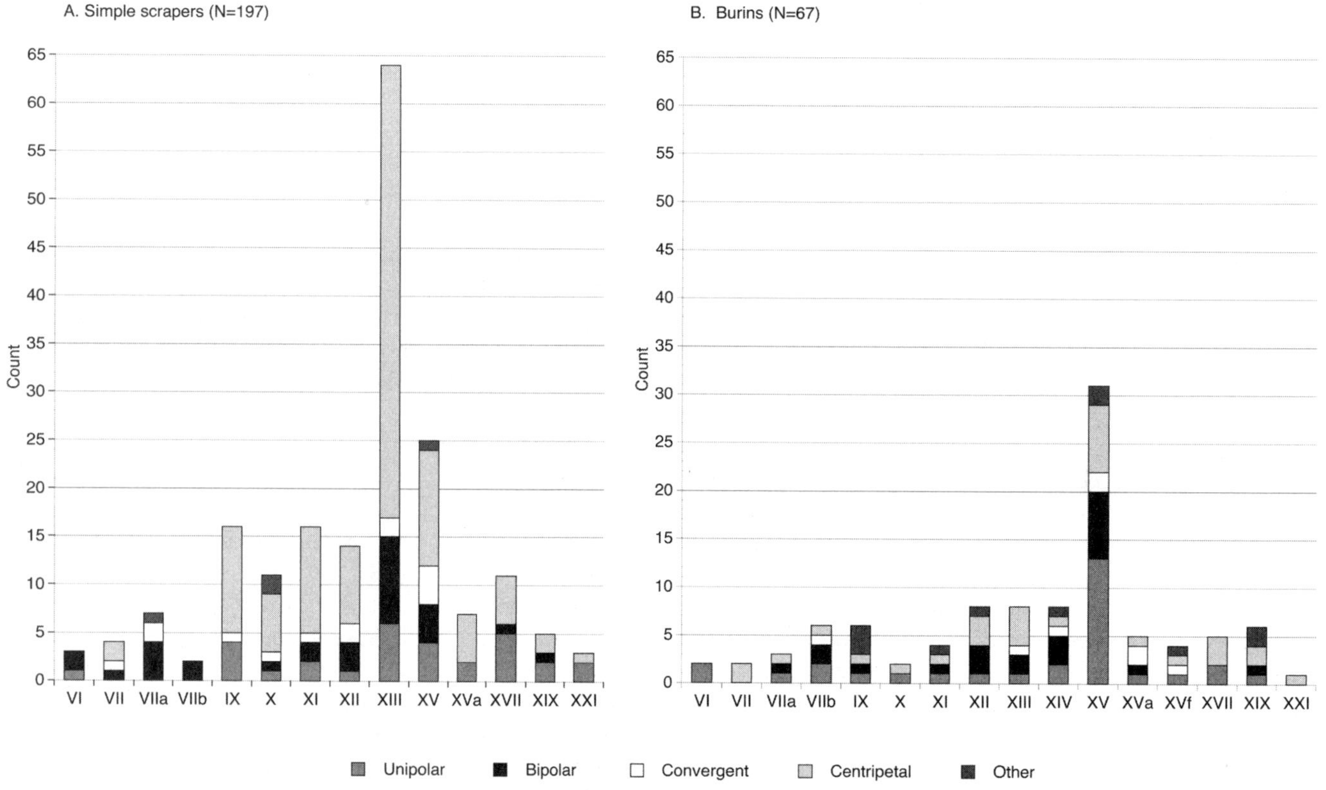

**Figure 6.9**  Frequencies (raw counts) of scar patterns among simple side-scrapers and burins. See text for definition of typological categories.

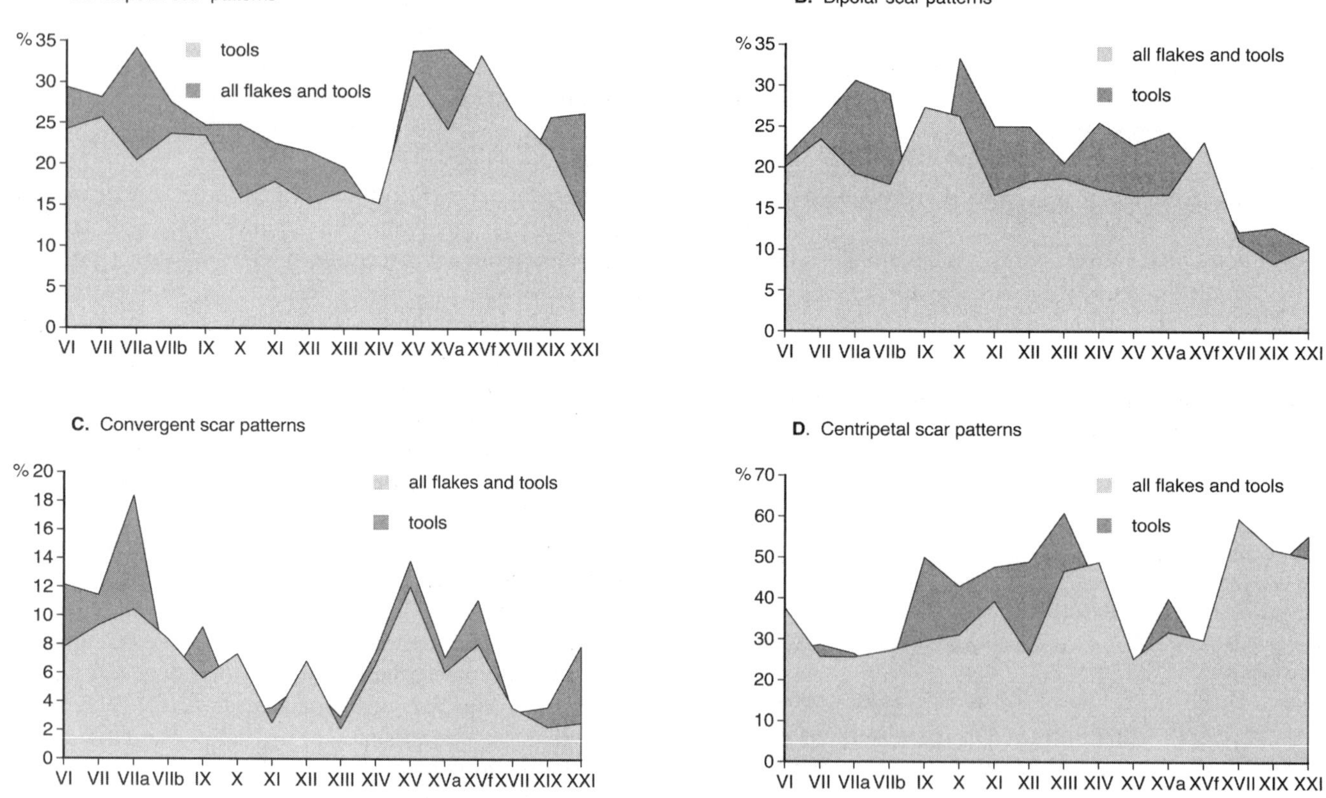

**Figure 6.10**  Comparison of frequencies of scar patterns on debitage and tools in the various Qafzeh assemblages.

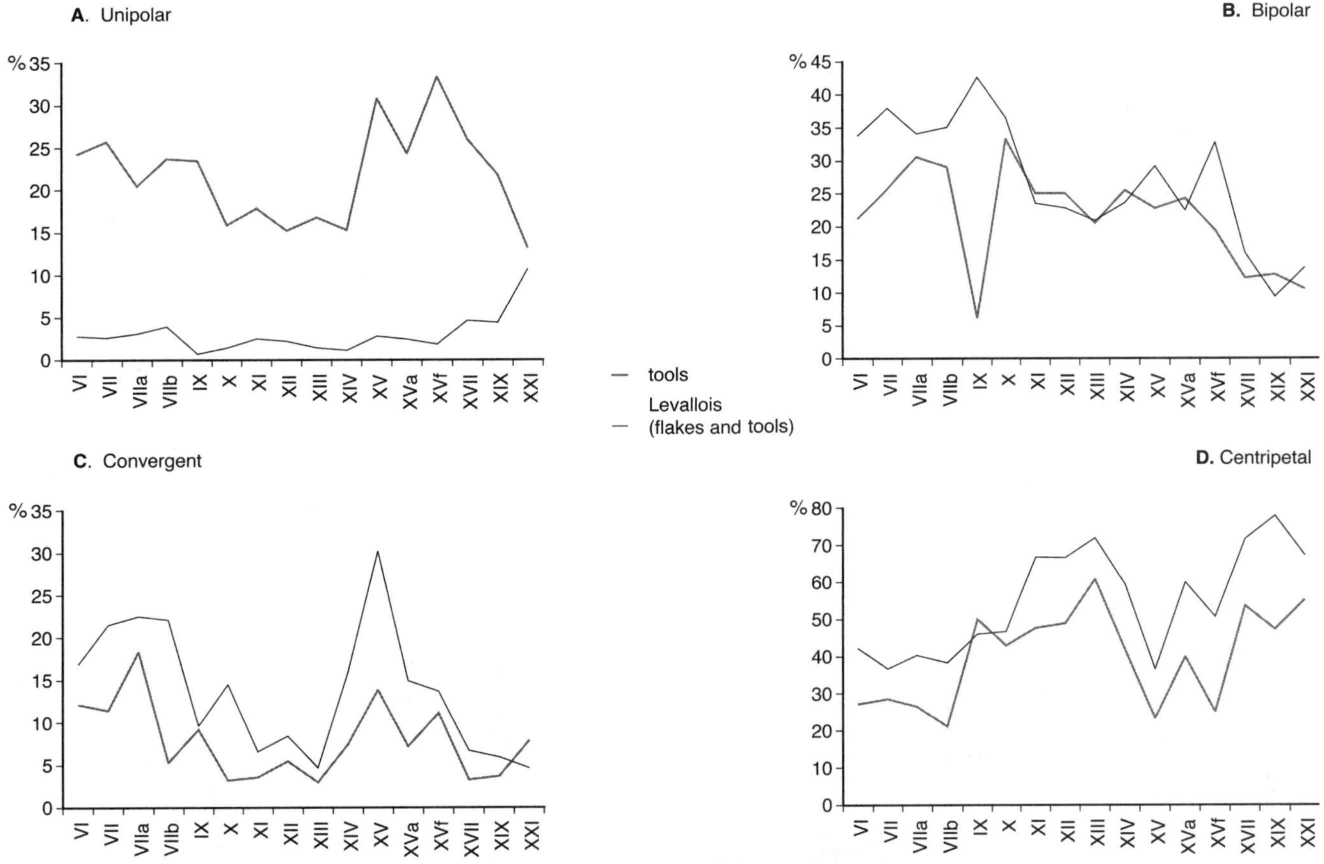

**Figure 6.11** Comparison of frequencies of scar patterns of tools and total Levallois debitage in the various assemblages.

this difference insignificant both statistically and practically. Nor was the choice of blanks oriented toward products of specific flaking systems. Non-Levallois blanks are more frequent than Levallois pieces among notches and denticulates throughout the sequence, echoing the situation in the total flake assemblage. The same is true for scar patterns (Table 6.11). Blanks appear to have been selected at random from whatever artifacts were available, without special regard to their size. This situation is similar to that described for the collection from Ghar, where notched pieces were found to be made on blanks with scar patterns resembling those of the unretouched blanks sample (Gordon 1993). In the latter case, however, Gordon suggested several competing hypotheses to explain this pattern, of which some related to functionality and hafting procedures and one assumed that the observed similarity of scar patterns reflected non-demanding selection criteria. In the case of Qafzeh, relaxed selection criteria with regard to this tool type appear to be the parsimonious explanation of the observed pattern.

"Centripetal" is the largest single category of dorsal face scar patterns in the tool assemblage as a whole, as well as in each of the generalized tool groups (with the exception of burins). However, the association between simple scrapers and blanks with centripetal scar patterns that was observed in the total tool assemblage (table 6.11) does not always hold up when the association of particular scar patterns with specific tool types is broken down by assemblage. In the younger assemblages, in which frequencies of Levallois blanks bearing centripetal scar patterns are relatively lower than those of blanks with bipolar and convergent scar patterns (figure 5.3), simple scrapers are made on a variety of blanks, among which those with centripetal scar patterns are not necessarily dominant (figure 6.9a). On the other hand, there is a strong emphasis on blanks with centripetal scar patterns in the mid-sequence assemblages, where this is the dominant scar pattern mainly within the Levallois component. Combined with the significant tendency toward using Levallois blanks for the production of simple scrapers (table 6.10), the observed pattern indicates that special care was invested in choosing blanks for simple scrapers out of the population of Levallois blanks, but that the particular mode of flaking did not figure prominently in this selection process. This is evident when scar patterns

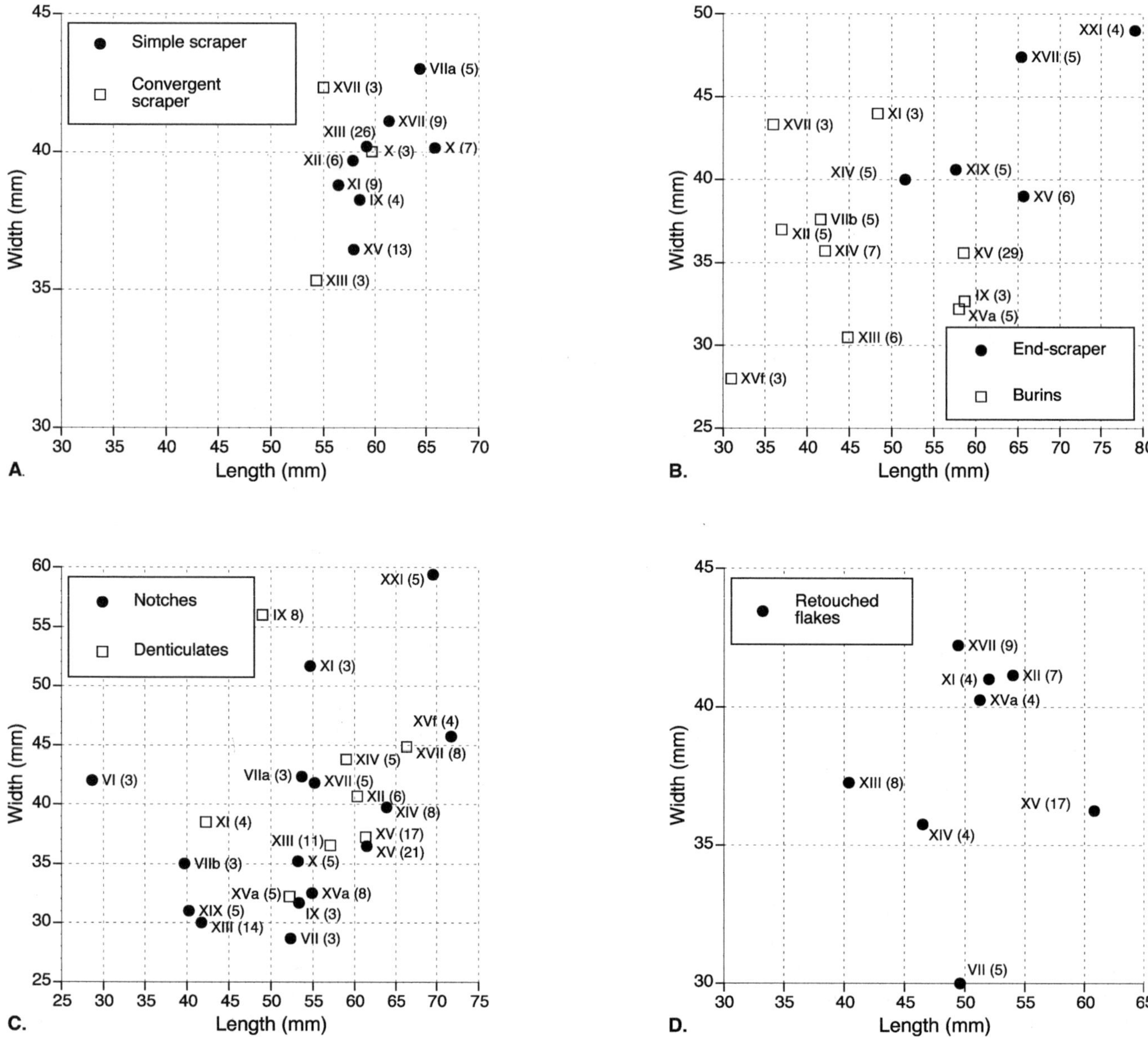

**Figure 6.12** Scatterplot of the mean width and length of various tools groups. Raw counts per typological group per assemblages are very low and prevent rigorous statistical treatment of the data. Only assemblages with N ≥ 3 per tool group are shown here.

of convergent scrapers are compared to other assemblages (e.g., Ghar; Gordon 1993). Indeed, the fluctuations over time of frequencies of blanks with centripetal patterns among tools resemble changes in the total Levallois sample (Figure 6.11d). Similarly, when viewed as a single group, pieces with bipolar and convergent scar patterns often occur in higher frequencies among tools than in the total assemblage (figure 6.10b–c). However, the shape of the curve describing the fluctuations of convergent scar patterns in tools throughout the sequence closely follows the curve for the total Levallois sample (figure 6.11c). Again,

this resemblance suggests that the choice of blanks was made out of the available Levallois population with no special regard to specific production methods.

"Other types" are significantly associated with non-Levallois blanks and with bipolar scar patterns (tables 6.10, 6.11). As in the case of simple scrapers, artifacts in this category appear to have been executed on all types of blanks when broken down by assemblage. Within each assemblage, scar patterns in this tool group are distributed similarly to the distributions of scar patterns within the total assemblage. For this tool group, then, selection

**Table 6.11**  Absolute, (relative) frequencies, expected values and *standardized cell residuals* of scar patterns on blanks of generalized tool groups

| Scar pattern/Type | Unipolar | | Bipolar | | Convergent | | Centripetal | | Other | | Total |
|---|---|---|---|---|---|---|---|---|---|---|---|
| Simple scrapers | 29 | (14.72) | 34 | (17.26) | 15 | (7.61) | 111 | (56.37) | 8 | (4.06) | 197 |
| | 45.72 | −3.02 | 41.72 | −1.44 | 15.86 | −0.24 | 79.20 | 4.94 | 14.49 | −1.89 | |
| Double scrapers | 2 | (9.09) | 5 | (22.72) | 2 | (9.09) | 11 | (50.00) | 2 | (9.09) | 22 |
| | 5.11 | −1.58 | 4.66 | 0.18 | 1.77 | 0.18 | 8.84 | 0.94 | 1.62 | 0.31 | |
| Convergent scrapers | 2 | (8.70) | 4 | (17.39) | 1 | (4.35) | 14 | (60.87) | 2 | (8.70) | 23 |
| | 5.34 | −1.66 | 4.87 | −0.45 | 1.85 | −0.66 | 9.25 | 2.04 | 1.69 | 0.25 | |
| Transversal scrapers | 3 | (50.00) | — | | — | | 3 | (50.00) | — | | 6 |
| | 1.39 | 1.56 | 1.27 | −1.27 | 0.48 | −0.73 | 2.41 | 0.49 | 0.44 | −0.69 | |
| Other scrapers | 15 | (25.42) | 9 | (19.40) | 6 | (5.97) | 23 | (38.98) | 6 | (10.17) | 59 |
| | 13.69 | 0.41 | 14.19 | −1.14 | 5.40 | 0.61 | 23.72 | −0.19 | 4.34 | 0.84 | |
| End-scrapers | 19 | (28.36) | 13 | (19.40) | 4 | (5.97) | 25 | (37.31) | 6 | (8.69) | 67 |
| | 15.55 | 1.02 | 14.19 | −0.36 | 5.40 | −0.64 | 26.94 | −0.49 | 4.93 | 0.51 | |
| Burins | 33 | (32.25) | 23 | (22.55) | 8 | (7.84) | 29 | (28.43) | 9 | (8.82) | 102 |
| | 23.67 | 2.26 | 21.60 | 0.35 | 8.21 | −0.08 | 41.01 | −2.51 | 7.50 | 0.59 | |
| Notches and denticulates | 88 | (22.62) | 77 | (19.79) | 30 | (7.71) | 168 | (43.19) | 26 | (6.68) | 389 |
| | 90.28 | −0.32 | 82.39 | −0.77 | 31.33 | −0.28 | 156.39 | 1.38 | 28.61 | −0.58 | |
| Othertypes | 175 | (24.58) | 169 | (23.74) | 61 | (8.57) | 250 | (35.11) | 57 | (8.01) | 712 |
| | 165.25 | 1.17 | 150.80 | 2.25 | 57.34 | 0.68 | 286.24 | −3.74 | 52.37 | 0.90 | |
| TOTAL | 366 | (23.61) | 334 | (21.18) | 127 | (8.05) | 634 | (40.20) | 116 | (7.36) | 1577 |

*Note*: Total $\chi^2$ is not valid due to a large number of cells with low expected values.

criteria seem to be more relaxed than for the other types. This is not surprising given the eclectic nature of the artifacts included in the groups.

The vast majority of tools (especially the burins; see above) are made on flake-proportioned blanks (table 6.12). This is consistent with the flake-oriented nature of the assemblages (chapter 5; see figure 6.13). The large standard deviations, as well as the large ranges of the length/width ratio, indicate that selection of blanks for retouch did not involve special emphasis on blank laminarity. This may explain why only a few core management pieces, the most laminar elements in most assemblages (table 6.12b), were selected for retouch (1.6–7.5%, with layers XI, XII, XIV, and XVII showing somewhat higher frequencies: 10.1%, 14.8%, 12.0%, and 10.4%, respectively). Where burins exhibit mean measurements of laminar proportions, this is the result of the narrowness of blanks rather than their excessive length (figure 6.12).

The lack of preference for blanks made by any particular reduction mode and method emphasizes the focus on flake size over other selection criteria. The lack of morphological selection criteria among retouched pieces is to be expected. The size of unretouched flakes was found to be independent of the specific methods of core reduction. Large flakes could be obtained by any flaking method preferred by the hominins (tables 5.15–5.18, and accompanying analyses; figures 5.10, 6.13). Given these characteristics of the assemblages, the lack of morphological selection criteria for retouched pieces emphasizes the

focus on flake size over other considerations when blanks were selected for further modification.

A number of ethnographic studies (e.g., Hiscock 2004) describe episodes of tool production in which the process is purposeful in the functional sense (i.e., the knapper intends to extend a tool's use life) but does not embody preplanning of intended morphological forms. The tendencies identified in the Qafzeh assemblages are at odds with such ethnographic studies. On the contrary, they are consistent with prolonged and multi-step procedures of decision making, by which products of certain reduction systems are associated with specific tool types, rather than result from an automated procedure. The reasons for this selection may have been linked with the desire to extend the use lives of these particular tool types, i.e., related to the anticipated functions of the tools and the need (or desire) to curate and move around large blanks that could be maintained and reused over time.

The decision to retouch the larger flakes within a population of pieces of debitage is a pattern that the Qafzeh assemblages share with a large number of both Levantine and European sites (e.g., Zobiste, Fonseigner, Biache Saint-Vasst, Vaufrey, Quneitra, Les Canalettes, the Negev Mousterian sites, among others; Baumler 1988; Dibble 1995c; Geneste 1985, 1988; Goren-Inbar 1988a, 1990a; Meignen 1993; Munday 1976b). The tendency to produce side-scrapers particularly on Levallois blanks is similar to the pattern observed in many French Middle Paleolithic sites (Geneste 1985, 1988; Meignen 1988), as well as in Keoue Cave in Lebanon

**Table 6.12  Length/width ratio of selected tool groups (A) compared to debitage and to Core Management Pieces (B)**

**A.**

| Layer | Simple scrapers | | | | Burins | | | | Notches | | | | Denticulates | | | |
|---|---|---|---|---|---|---|---|---|---|---|---|---|---|---|---|---|
| | N | $\bar{X}$ | s.d | range | N | $\bar{X}$ | s.d | range | N | $\bar{X}$ | s.d | range | N | $\bar{X}$ | s.d | range |
| VI | 2 | 2.11 | 0.07 | 2.06–2.16 | 1 | 1.41 | | | 1 | 2.22 | | | 3 | 0.68 | 0.40 | 0.44–1.14 |
| VII | | | | | 2 | 1.15 | 0.65 | 0.69–1.61 | 3 | 1.74 | 0.32 | 1.50–2.10 | | | | |
| VIIa | 5 | 1.53 | 0.23 | 1.30–1.82 | 2 | 2.09 | 0.55 | 1.71–2.48 | | | | | 3 | 1.30 | 0.53 | 0.77–1.83 |
| VIIb | 1 | 1.13 | | | 5 | 1.12 | 0.30 | 0.82–1.47 | 2 | 1.60 | 0.37 | 1.33–1.86 | 1 | 0.62 | | |
| IX | 4 | 1.60 | 0.38 | 1.13–2.04 | 3 | 2.38 | 1.59 | 1.24–4.20 | 3 | 1.73 | 0.31 | 1.53–2.09 | 6 | 1.06 | 0.48 | 0.52–1.79 |
| X | 7 | 1.67 | 0.50 | 1.07–2.05 | 1 | 1.54 | | | 4 | 1.58 | 0.62 | 1.15–2.48 | 1 | 1.63 | | |
| XI | 9 | 1.50 | 0.38 | 1.11–2.29 | 3 | 1.16 | 0.57 | 0.66–1.78 | 3 | 1.10 | 0.24 | 0.89–1.37 | 4 | 1.15 | 0.49 | 0.64–1.83 |
| XII | 6 | 1.47 | 0.28 | 1.11–1.92 | 5 | 1.42 | 0.76 | 0.52–2.16 | 2 | 1.20 | 0.17 | 1.08–1.32 | 6 | 1.76 | 0.81 | 0.74–2.61 |
| XIII | 26 | 1.51 | 0.32 | 1.05–2.19 | 6 | 1.57 | 0.64 | 0.64–2.17 | 14 | 1.47 | 0.46 | 0.73–2.12 | 11 | 1.61 | 0.46 | 1.13–2.58 |
| XIV | | | | | 7 | 1.26 | 0.51 | 0.43–1.88 | 8 | 1.77 | 0.89 | 0.75–3.75 | 5 | 1.48 | 0.46 | 0.72–1.97 |
| XV | 13 | 1.64 | 0.36 | 1.26–2.42 | 29 | 1.74 | 0.57 | 0.95–3.31 | 21 | 1.75 | 0.56 | 1.14–2.28 | 17 | 1.76 | 0.58 | 0.84–3.16 |
| XVa | 1 | 1.35 | | | 5 | 1.85 | 0.57 | 1.03–2.48 | 8 | 1.82 | 0.67 | 1.15–3.33 | 5 | 1.79 | 0.75 | 0.89–2.69 |
| XVf | | | | | 3 | 1.41 | 1.24 | 0.47–2.81 | 4 | 1.62 | 0.49 | 1.06–2.11 | 1 | 0.88 | | |
| XVII | 9 | 1.53 | 0.40 | 0.92–2.34 | 3 | 0.90 | 0.32 | 0.54–1.12 | 5 | 1.37 | 0.32 | 0.98–1.81 | 8 | 1.51 | 0.55 | 0.96–2.47 |
| XIX | 1 | 0.98 | | | 2 | 1.41 | 0.45 | 1.09–1.73 | 5 | 1.57 | 1.09 | 0.85–3.47 | 2 | 1.55 | 0.04 | 1.50–1.60 |
| XXI | 1 | 1.65 | | | | | | | 1 | 2.22 | | | 3 | 0.68 | 0.40 | 0.44–1.14 |

**B.**

| Layer | Levallois debitage | | | | Non-Levallois debitage | | | | Core management pieces | | | |
|---|---|---|---|---|---|---|---|---|---|---|---|---|
| | N | $\bar{X}$ | s.d | range | N | $\bar{X}$ | s.d | range | N | $\bar{X}$ | s.d | range |
| VI | 33 | 1.54 | 0.63 | 0.57–3.82 | 169 | 1.44 | 0.62 | 0.39–3.89 | 12 | 1.70 | 0.82 | 0.69–3.50 |
| VII | 32 | 1.44 | 0.44 | 0.55–2.54 | 73 | 1.21 | 0.58 | 0.31–3.22 | 19 | 1.42 | 0.61 | 0.52–2.50 |
| VIIa | 70 | 1.59 | 0.55 | 0.64–3.33 | 204 | 1.36 | 0.61 | 0.38–4.00 | 45 | 1.72 | 0.63 | 0.89–3.06 |
| VIIb | 26 | 1.41 | 0.55 | 0.41–2.83 | 65 | 1.38 | 0.72 | 0.50–4.89 | 15 | 1.31 | 0.73 | 0.50–3.08 |
| IX | 40 | 1.47 | 0.54 | 0.66–4.78 | 208 | 1.31 | 0.60 | 0.27–4.00 | 53 | 1.47 | 0.61 | 0.45–3.26 |
| X | 74 | 1.43 | 0.44 | 0.59–2.73 | 122 | 1.33 | 0.50 | 0.50–3.22 | 32 | 1.51 | 0.59 | 0.68–2.88 |
| XI | 94 | 1.48 | 0.60 | 0.61–5.32 | 154 | 1.32 | 0.54 | 0.40–2.85 | 45 | 1.62 | 0.63 | 0.40–3.54 |
| XII | 62 | 1.39 | 0.46 | 0.39–2.56 | 81 | 1.44 | −0.64 | 0.33–3.45 | 29 | 1.83 | 0.79 | 0.67–3.80 |
| XIII | 198 | 1.60 | 0.58 | 0.48–3.93 | 386 | 1.32 | 0.58 | 0.25–3.83 | 103 | 1.71 | 0.76 | 0.40–4.29 |
| XIV | 65 | 1.55 | 0.52 | 0.45–3.21 | 73 | 1.46 | 0.63 | 0.39–3.05 | 23 | 1.83 | 0.72 | 0.64–3.90 |
| XV | 881 | 1.60 | 0.52 | 0.49–4.11 | 1,703 | 1.47 | 0.69 | 0.26–5.27 | 283 | 1.90 | 0.76 | 0.47–4.42 |
| XVa | 120 | 1.46 | 0.49 | 0.67–3.07 | 520 | 1.33 | 0.61 | 0.30–4.10 | 71 | 1.45 | 0.57 | 0.55–2.64 |
| XVf | 129 | 1.51 | 0.58 | 0.60–3.53 | 509 | 1.34 | 0.61 | 0.33–3.89 | 79 | 1.57 | 0.70 | 0.67–4.80 |
| XVII | 149 | 1.48 | 9.57 | 0.45–3.00 | 175 | 1.26 | 0.57 | 0.36–4.06 | 42 | 1.35 | 0.43 | 0.46–2.62 |
| XIX | 88 | 1.33 | 0.49 | 0.35–2.86 | 128 | 1.26 | 0.94 | 0.45–8.50 | 38 | 1.51 | 0.75 | 0.38–3.94 |
| XXI | 60 | 1.33 | 0.47 | 0.64–2.73 | 78 | 1.27 | 0.63 | 0.31–3.86 | 22 | 1.40 | 0.72 | 0.39–3.44 |

*Note*: Mann-Whitney's U is always insignificant for comparisons between tools and Levallois debitage . Mann-Whitney's U is insignificant for comparisons between tools and non–Levallois debitage in layers VI, VIIa–XII, XIV, XVf. In other assemblages it is significant at $0.5 > p \geq .0001$.

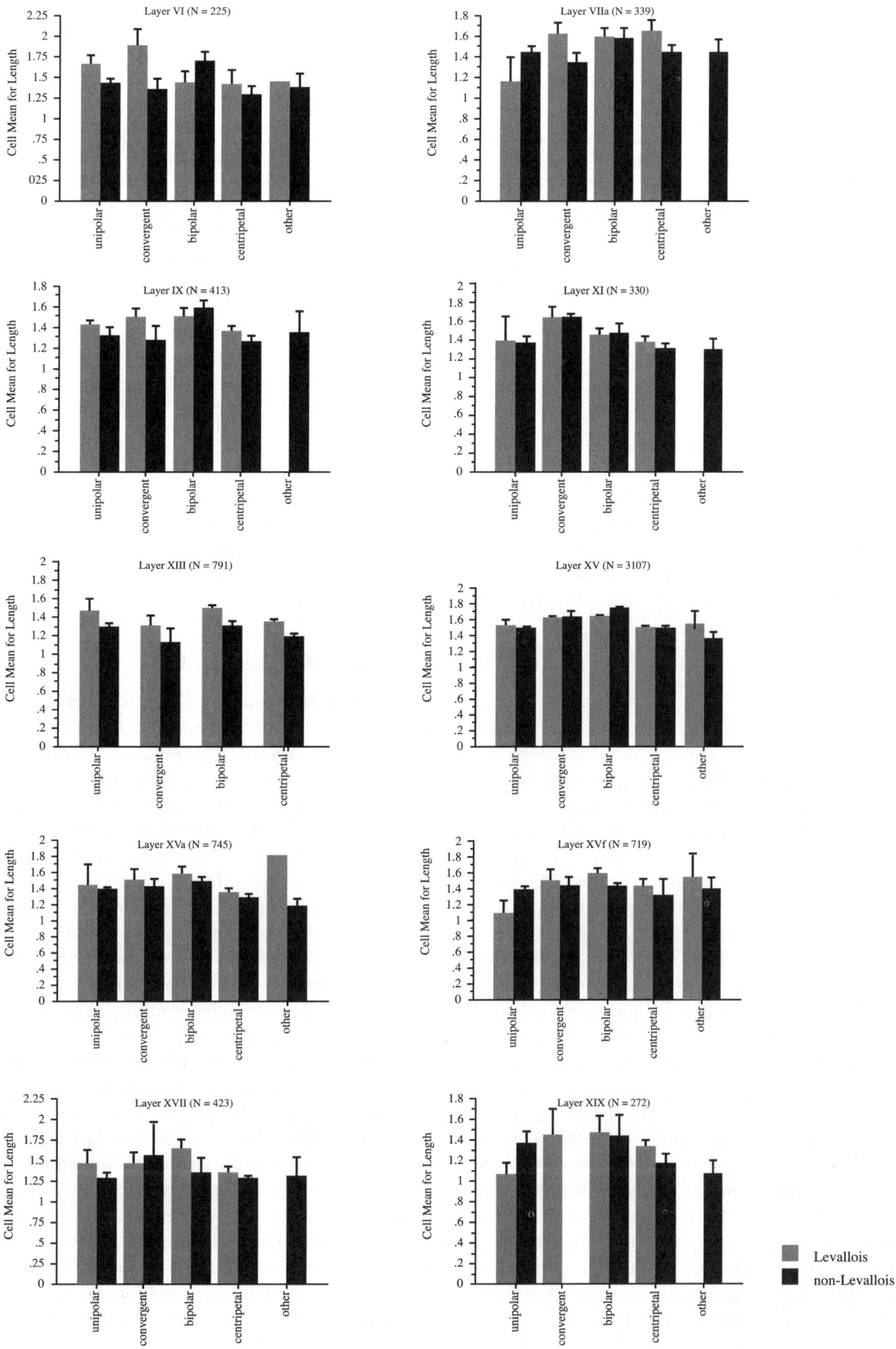

**Figure 6.13**  Laminarity (length/width ratio) of blanks, broken down by flaking systems. Only complete blanks are included.

(Nishiaki and Copeland 1992). However, some aspects of this selection behavior at Qafzeh distinguish it from other Levantine sites. The specific selection of Levallois blanks for simple scrapers is different from that observed at Ghar, where the core reduction strategies (e.g., Levallois vs. non-Levallois) employed to produce the blanks are of secondary importance to dorsal face scar pattern (Gordon 1993:212). At Quneitra, simple scrapers occur mostly on non-Levallois blanks (Goren-Inbar 1990a: fig. 60; Hovers 1990b:163), likely due to the low values of IL; still, the occurrence of Levallois blanks in this group of tools is more pronounced than for other tool types in the assemblage.

## Retouch Characteristics

The analysis of retouch characteristics relates to the retouch of single tools. In the case of multiple tools, the retouch description relates only to the "first" tool. While this results in some loss of information, it was felt that the frequencies of such tools were not high enough to warrant separate treatment. It should be noted that the breakdown of tool groups is somewhat different from that used in analyses of tool morphometrics.

### Edge Angle

Ethnoarchaeological studies (e.g., Hayden 1979b; White, Modjeska, and Hipuya 1977) have reported the existence of preferences for particular ranges of edge angles for particular tasks. As a rule, steeper retouch angles are associated with scraping actions and with the processing of resistant material. More acute angles are used for working with softer materials, mainly in cutting actions. The same studies have shown a considerable degree of overlap in the ranges of angles preferred for different tasks.

Edge angle, or the angle of retouch (i.e., the angle between the ventral face and an imaginary plane running from the tool margin to the termination of the retouch scars), was measured on all tools, including pieces with signs of utilization. Within each separate assemblage the dispersion of values is quite large, with outliers of relatively high values (figure 6.14), but a large degree of homogeneity is encountered among layers. There are no significant differences among the various tool groups. Differences among the means for various tool groups are in the range of 5–10° and are negligible given both the small sample sizes per tool group and the inherent errors in angle measurements. The lack of distinction between tool types is striking against the background of the ethnographic studies mentioned above. It may suggest that tool functions overlapped considerably, a hypothesis that is consistent with the results of low-magnification use-wear studies conducted by Shea (1991) on these assemblages.

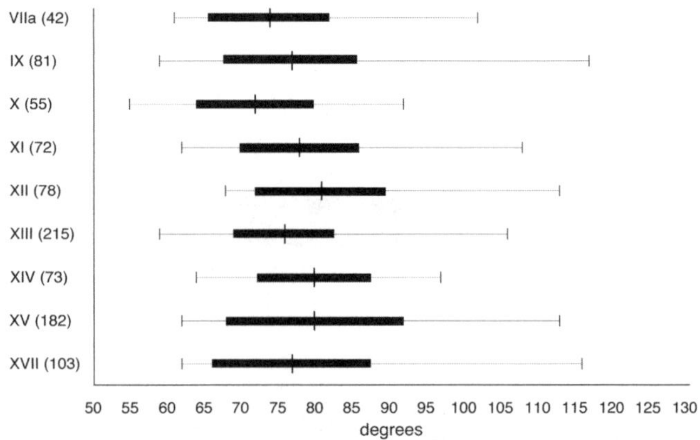



**Figure 6.14** Dispersion of the values of edge angles on retouched tools. Distinction between tool groups within assemblages was statistically insignificant and is therefore not shown here (see text for discussion).

Edge angles also figure prominently in attempts to quantify blank reduction by retouch (e.g., Hiscock and Clarkson 2005; Kuhn 1990). This issue is discussed in more detail below.

### Location of Retouched Edge

The location of retouched edges is described relative to the proximal end of the flake in dorsal view. The sixteen attribute states describing this variable (appendix 3) were collapsed into ten, more generalized categories. More specifically, the detailed categories of "distal and left/right edge" and "distal and both edges" were grouped into "distal and edges," and any combination of retouch on proximal end and edge(s) was included in "proximal and edges." These new attribute states were then broken down by generalized tool groups. Frequencies are shown for selected assemblages (with N > 50) in table 6.13.

A repetitive pattern is seen in the various assemblages. "Simple" retouch locations, in which retouch is confined to one edge/end (i.e., distal, proximal, left or right edge) are the rule in all the assemblages, accounting for 85–90% of retouched edges. Among these, proximal locations are less frequent. The most common combination of complex retouch location is "distal and edges." Some of the associations seen in the assemblages between retouch location and typological groups are the default of the ascribed typology (e.g., a single retouched edge occurs by definition with simple scrapers, distal retouch with end-scrapers, and two edges with double scrapers). In contrast to this trivial correlation, the high association of "simple" retouch locations in other tool types (e.g., retouched flakes, flakes with signs of utilization) is not tautological, and rather underlines the paucity of complex retouch locations in the more formal tools. Indeed, cells in

**Table 6.13  Breakdown of location of retouch by tool type**

**Layer VIIa**

| Type[a] | Distal | Proximal | Left edge | Right edge | Both edges | Convergent | Distal and edges | Proximal and edges | Proximal and distal | Perim. | Total |
|---|---|---|---|---|---|---|---|---|---|---|---|
| Simple scrapers | | | 4 (7.5) | 5 (9.4) | | | | | | | 9 (17.0) |
| Double scrapers | | | | | 1 (1.9) | | | | | | 1 (1.9) |
| End-scrapers | 2 (3.8) | | | | | | | | | | 2 (3.8) |
| Burins | 1 (1.9) | 1 (1.9) | | | | | | 1 (1.9) | | | 3 (5.7) |
| Awls | 3 (5.7) | | | | | | | | | | 3 (5.7) |
| Notches | 1 (1.9) | | 2 (3.8) | 1 (1.9) | | | | | | | 4 (7.5) |
| Denticulates | | 1 (1.9) | 5 (9.4) | | | | | | | | 6 (11.3) |
| Retouched flakes | 1 (1.9) | | 1 (1.9) | 2 (3.8) | 3 (5.7) | | 1 (1.9) | | | | 8 (15.1) |
| Miscellaneous | | | | | | | | | | | |
| Utilization signs | 2 (3.8) | | | | | | | | | | 2 (3.8) |
| Other types | 7 (13.2) | | 3 (5.7) | 1 (1.9) | | | | | | | 11 (20.8) |
| Isolated removal | 3 (5.7) | | | 1 (1.9) | | | | | | | 4 (7.5) |
| TOTAL | 20 (37.7) | 2 (3.8) | 15 (28.3) | 10 (18.9) | 4 (7.5) | | 1 (1.9) | 1 (1.9) | | | 53 (100.1) |

**Layer IX**

| Type[a] | Distal | Proximal | Left edge | Right edge | Both edges | Convergent | Distal and edges | Proximal and edges | Proximal and distal | Perim. | Total |
|---|---|---|---|---|---|---|---|---|---|---|---|
| Simple scrapers | | | 12 (9.9) | 13 (10.7) | | | | | | | 25 (20.7) |
| Double scrapers | | | | | 2 (1.7) | | | | | | 2 (1.7) |
| End-scrapers | 5 (4.1) | | | | | | | | | | 5 (4.1) |
| Burins | 2 (1.7) | 3 (2.5) | | | | | | | | | 5 (4.1) |
| Awls | | 1 (0.8) | | | | | | | | | 1 (0.8) |
| Notches | 3 (2.5) | | 5 (4.1) | 1 (0.8) | | | | | | | 9 (7.4) |
| Denticulates | 2 (1.7) | | 6 (5.0) | 2 (1.7) | | | 1 (0.8) | | | | 11 (9.1) |
| Retouched flakes | 2 (1.7) | 1 (0.8) | 4 (3.3) | 5 (4.1) | | | | | | | 12 (9.9) |
| Miscellaneous | 1 (0.8) | 1 (0.8) | 4 (3.3) | | | | 1 (0.8) | | | | 7 (5.8) |
| Utilization signs | 4 (3.3) | | 5 (4.1) | 8 (6.6) | 1 (0.8) | | | 1 (0.8) | | | 19 (15.7) |
| Other types | 5 (4.1) | 2 (1.7) | | 3 (2.5) | 2 (1.7) | 1 (0.8) | | | | | 13 (10.7) |
| Isolated removal | 3 (2.5) | 8 (6.6) | | | | | 1 (0.8) | | | | 12 (9.9) |
| TOTAL | 27 (22.3) | 16 (13.2) | 36 (29.8) | 32 (26.4) | 5 (4.1) | 1 (0.8) | 3 (2.5) | 1 (0.8) | | | 121 (100.0) |

(*continued*)

**Table 6.13**   (continued)

**Layer X**

| Type[a] | Distal | Proximal | Left edge | Right edge | Both edges | Convergent | Distal and edges | Proximal and edges | Proximal and distal | Perim. | Total |
|---|---|---|---|---|---|---|---|---|---|---|---|
| Simple scrapers | | | 4 (6.0) | 7 (10.4) | | | | | | | 11 (16.4) |
| Double scrapers | | | | | 2 (3.0) | | | | | | 2 (3.0) |
| End scrapers | 1 (1.5) | | | | | | | | | | 1 (1.5) |
| Burins | 2 (3.0) | | | | | | | | | | 2 (3.0) |
| Awls | 3 (4.5) | | | 1 (1.5) | | | | | | | 4 (6.0) |
| Notches | 3 (4.5) | | 6 (9.0) | 1 (1.5) | | | | | | | 11 (16.4) |
| Denticulates | 1 (1.5) | | 2 (3.0) | 1 (1.5) | | | | | | | 4 (6.0) |
| Retouched flakes | 3 (4.5) | | 5 (7.5) | 3 (4.5) | | | 1 (1.5) | | | | 12 (17.9) |
| Miscellaneous | 2 (3.0) | 1 (1.5) | | 1 (1.5) | | | | | | | 4 (6.0) |
| Utilization signs | | | 3 (4.5) | 2 (3.0) | 1 (1.5) | | 1 (1.5) | | | | 7 (10.4) |
| Other types | 2 (3.0) | | 1 (1.5) | 1 (1.5) | | 3 (4.5) | | | | | 7 (10.4) |
| Isolated removal | 1 (1.5) | | | 1 (1.5) | | | | | | | 2 (3.0) |
| TOTAL | 19 (28.4) | 1 (1.5) | 21 (31.3) | 18 (26.9) | 3 (4.5) | 3 (4.5) | 2 (3.0) | | | | 67 (100.0) |

**Layer XI**

| Type[a] | Distal | Proximal | Left edge | Right edge | Both edges | Convergent | Distal and edges | Proximal and edges | Proximal and distal | Perim. | Total |
|---|---|---|---|---|---|---|---|---|---|---|---|
| Simple scrapers | | | 14 (14.4) | 7 (7.2) | | | | | | | 21 (21.6) |
| Double scrapers | | | | | 4 (4.1) | | | | | | 4 (4.1) |
| End scrapers | 2 (2.1) | | | | | | | | | | 2 (2.1) |
| Burins | 1 (1.0) | | | 1 (1.0) | | | 2 (2.1) | | | | 4 (4.1) |
| Awls | | | | | | | | | | | |
| Notches | | | 3 (3.1) | 4 (4.1) | | | | | | | 7 (7.2) |
| Denticulates | | | 4 (4.1) | 2 (2.1) | | | 2 (2.1) | | | | 8 (8.2) |
| Retouched flakes | 1 (1.0) | | 4 (4.1) | 2 (2.1) | | | 1 (1.0) | | | | 8 (8.2) |
| Miscellaneous | 3 (3.1) | 1 (1.0) | | | | | | | | | 4 (4.1) |
| Utilization signs | 1 (1.0) | 3 (3.1) | 7 (7.2) | 6 (6.2) | | | | | | | 17 (17.5) |
| Other types | 6 (6.2) | 1 (1.0) | | 5 (5.2) | | | 4 (4.1) | | | | 16 (16.5) |
| Isolated removal | 1 (1.0) | 2 (2.1) | 1 (1.0) | | | | 1 (1.0) | 1 (1.0) | | | 6 (6.2) |
| TOTAL | 15 (15.5) | 7 (7.2) | 33 (34.0) | 27 (27.8) | 4 (4.1) | | 10 (10.3) | 1 (1.0) | | | 97 (99.8) |

**Layer XII**

| Type[a] | Distal | Proximal | Left edge | Right edge | Both edges | Convergent | Distal and edges | Proximal and edges | Proximal and distal | Perim. | Total |
|---|---|---|---|---|---|---|---|---|---|---|---|
| Simple scrapers | | | 13 (12.0) | 6 (5.6) | | | | | | | 19 (17.9) |
| Double scrapers | | | | | | | | | | | |
| End scrapers | 5 (4.6) | | | | | | | | | | 5 (4.6) |
| Burins | 4 (3.7) | 3 (2.8) | | 1 (0.9) | | | | | | | 8 (7.4) |
| Awls | | | | | | 1 (0.9) | | | | | 1 (0.9) |
| Notches | 1 (0.9) | | 2 (1.9) | 2 (1.9) | | | | | | | 5 (4.6) |
| Denticulates | 2 (1.9) | | 5 (4.6) | 2 (1.9) | | | | | | | 9 (8.3) |
| Retouched flakes | 6 (5.6) | | 8 (7.4) | 6 (5.6) | 1 (0.9) | | | | | | 21 (19.4) |
| Miscellaneous | | | 3 (2.8) | | | | | | | | 3 (2.8) |
| Utilization signs | | 2 (1.9) | 5 (4.6) | 6 (5.6) | 3 (2.8) | | | | | | 16 (14.8) |
| Other types | 4 (3.7) | 3 (2.8) | 3 (2.8) | 1 (0.9) | | 2 (1.9) | | | 2 (1.9) | | 15 (13.9) |
| Isolated removal | 3 (2.8) | 2 (1.9) | 1 (0.9) | | | | | | | | 6 (5.6) |
| TOTAL | 25 (23.2) | 10 (9.3) | 40 (37.0) | 24 (22.2) | 4 (3.7) | 3 (2.8) | | | 2 (1.9) | | 108 (100.2) |

**Layer XIII**

| Type[a] | Distal | Proximal | Left edge | Right edge | Both edges | Convergent | Distal and edges | Proximal and edges | Proximal and distal | Perim. | Total |
|---|---|---|---|---|---|---|---|---|---|---|---|
| Simple scrapers | | | 29 (7.5) | 37 (9.5) | | | | | | | 66 (17.0) |
| Double scrapers | | | 1 (0.3) | | 7 (1.8) | | | | | | 8 (2.1) |
| End scrapers | 4 (1.0) | | | | | | | | | | 4 (1.0) |
| Burins | 4 (1.0) | 2 (0.5) | 2 (0.5) | | | | | | | | 8 (2.1) |
| Awls | | | | | | | 3 (0.8) | | | | 3 (0.8) |
| Notches | 7 (1.8) | | 19 (4.9) | 13 (3.4) | | | | | | | 39 (10.1) |
| Denticulates | 3 (0.8) | 1 (0.3) | 8 (2.1) | 17 (4.4) | | | | | | | 29 (7.5) |
| Retouched flakes | 2 (0.5) | | 9 (2.3) | 13 (3.4) | | | 1 (0.3) | | | | 25 (6.4) |
| Miscellaneous | 6 (1.5) | 2 (0.5) | 4 (1.0) | | | | | | | | 12 (3.0) |
| Utilization signs | 10 (2.6) | 1 (0.3) | 51 (13.1) | 37 (9.5) | 20 (5.2) | | 10 (2.6) | 1 (0.3) | | | 130 (33.5) |
| Other types | 7 (1.8) | | 7 (1.8) | 4 (1.0) | 6 (1.5) | | 2 (0.5) | | | | 26 (6.7) |
| Isolated removal | 6 (1.5) | 8 (2.10 | 8 (2.1) | 12 (3.1) | 2 (0.5) | | 1 (0.3) | 1 (0.3) | | | 38 (9.8) |
| TOTAL | 49 (12.6) | 14 (3.6) | 138 (35.6) | 133 (34.3) | 35 (9.0) | | 17 (4.4) | 2 (0.5) | | | 388 (100.0) |

*(continued)*

**Table 6.13** (continued)

**Layer XIV**

| Type[a] | Distal | Proximal | Left edge | Right edge | Both edges | Convergent | Distal and edges | Proximal and edges | Proximal and distal | Perim. | Total |
|---|---|---|---|---|---|---|---|---|---|---|---|
| Simple scrapers | | 1 (0.9) | | | 2 (1.8) | | | | | | 3 (2.7) |
| Double scrapers | | | | | | | | | | | |
| End scrapers | 6 (5.4) | 1 (0.9) | | | | | | | | | 7 (6.3) |
| Burins | 5 (4.5) | 1 (0.9) | 1 (0.9) | | | | | | | | 7 (6.3) |
| Awls | | | | | | | | | | | |
| Notches | 4 (3.6) | 1 (0.9) | 9 (8.0) | 8 (7.1) | | | | | | | 22 (19.6) |
| Denticulates | 2 (1.8) | | 6 (5.4) | 4 (3.6) | 1 (0.9) | | | 1 (0.9) | | 1 (0.9) | 15 (13.4) |
| Retouched flakes | 1 (0.9) | | 4 (3.6) | 2 (1.8) | | | 2 (1.8) | 1 (0.9) | | | 10 (8.9) |
| Miscellaneous | 1 (0.9) | 3 (2.7) | 2 (1.8) | | | | | | 1 (0.9) | | 7 (6.3) |
| Utilization signs | 3 (2.7) | | 7 (6.3) | 7 (6.3) | 2 (1.8) | | | 2 (1.8) | | | 21 (18.8) |
| Other types | 5 (4.5) | | 1 (0.9) | 1 (0.9) | | | | | | | 7 (6.3) |
| Isolated removal | 4 (3.6) | 2 (1.8) | 1 (0.9) | 4 (3.6) | 1 (0.9) | | 1 (0.9) | | | | 13 (11.6) |
| TOTAL | 31 (27.7) | 9 (8.0) | 31 (27.7) | 26 (23.2) | 6 (5.4) | | 3 (2.7) | 4 (3.6) | 1 (0.9) | 1 (0.9) | 112 (100.2) |

**Layer XV**

| Type[a] | Distal | Proximal | Left edge | Right edge | Both edges | Convergent | Distal and edges | Proximal and edges | Proximal and distal | Perim. | Total |
|---|---|---|---|---|---|---|---|---|---|---|---|
| Simple scrapers | | 1 (0.2) | 17 (3.9) | 21 (4.8) | | | | | | | 39 (8.9) |
| Double scrapers | | | | | 3 (0.7) | | | | | | 3 (0.7) |
| End scrapers | 11 (2.5) | 2 (0.5) | | | | | | | | | 13 (3.0) |
| Burins | 13 (3.0) | 11 (2.5) | 2 (0.5) | 5 (1.1) | | | 1 (0.2) | 1 (0.2) | | | 33 (7.6) |
| Awls | 2 (0.5) | | 1 (0.2) | 1 (0.2) | 1 (0.2) | | 3 (0.7) | | | | 8 (1.8) |
| Notches | 11 (2.5) | 1 (0.2) | 25 (5.7) | 17 (3.9) | | | | | | | 54 (12.4) |
| Denticulates | 2 (0.5) | 2 (0.5) | 14 (3.2) | 12 (2.7) | | | | | | | 30 (6.9) |
| Retouched flakes | 5 (1.1) | | 14 (3.2) | 10 (2.3) | 1 (0.2) | | | | | | 30 (6.9) |
| Miscellaneous | 18 (4.1) | 17 (3.9) | 3 (0.7) | 2 (0.5) | | | | 1 (0.2) | | 6 (1.4) | 47 (10.8) |
| Utilization signs | 6 (1.4) | 2 (0.5) | 30 (96.9) | 21 (4.8) | 5 (1.1) | | 2 (0.5) | 1 (0.2) | | | 67 (15.3) |
| Other types | 28 (6.4) | 9 (2.1) | 17 (3.9) | 6 (1.4) | | | 1 (0.2) | | | 5 (1.1) | 66 (15.1) |
| Isolated removal | 10 (2.3) | 11 (2.5) | 16 (3.7) | 8 (1.8) | | | 2 (0.5) | | | | 47 (10.8) |
| TOTAL | 106 (24.3) | 56 (12.8) | 139 (31.8) | 103 (23.6) | 10 (2.3) | | 9 (2.1) | 3 (0.7) | | 11 (2.5) | 437 (100.2) |

**Layer XVa**

| Type[a] | Distal | Proximal | Left edge | Right edge | Both edges | Convergent | Distal and edges | Proximal and edges | Proximal and distal | Perim. | Total |
|---|---|---|---|---|---|---|---|---|---|---|---|
| Simple scrapers | | 1 (1.3) | 7 (8.8) | 4 (5.0) | | | | | | | 12 (15.0) |
| Double scrapers | | | | | | | | | | | |
| End scrapers | 3 (3.8) | | | | | | 1 (1.3) | | | | 4 (5.0) |
| Burins | 1 (1.3) | 1 (1.3) | 1 (1.3) | 1 (1.3) | | | | 1 (1.3) | | | 5 (6.3) |
| Awls | 4 (5.0) | | | | | | 1 (1.3) | | | | 5 (6.3) |
| Notches | | | 6 (7.5) | 5 (6.3) | | | | | | | 11 (13.8) |
| Denticulates | | | 2 (2.5) | 2 (2.5) | | | 1 (1.3) | | | | 5 (6.3) |
| Retouched flakes | 1 (1.3) | | 4 (5.0) | 3 (3.8) | | | | | | | 8 (10.0) |
| Miscellaneous | 1 (1.3) | 1 (1.3) | 1 (1.3) | | | | | | | | 3 (3.8) |
| Utilization signs | | | 7 (8.8) | 8 (10.0) | | | | | | | 15 (18.8) |
| Other types | 3 (3.8) | 3 (3.8) | 2 (2.5) | | | | | | | | 8 (10.0) |
| Isolated removal | 1 (1.3) | | 2 (2.5) | 1 (1.3) | | | | | | | 4 (5.0) |
| TOTAL | 14 (17.5) | 6 (7.5) | 32 (40.0) | 24 (30.0) | | | 3 (3.8) | 1 (1.3) | | | 80 (100.3) |

**Layer VIIa**

| Type[a] | Distal | Proximal | Left edge | Right edge | Both edges | Convergent | Distal and edges | Proximal and edges | Proximal and distal | Perim. | Total |
|---|---|---|---|---|---|---|---|---|---|---|---|
| Simple scrapers | 2 (1.3) | | 6 (4.0) | 5 (3.3) | 1 (0.7) | | | | | | 14 (9.3) |
| Double scrapers | | | | | 1 (0.7) | | | | | | 1 (0.7) |
| End scrapers | 13 (8.6) | | | | | | | | | | 13 (8.6) |
| Burins | 1 (0.7) | 2 (1.3) | 2 (1.3) | 1 (0.7) | | | | | | | 6 (4.0) |
| Awls | 6 (4.0) | | | | | | | | | | 6 (4.0) |
| Notches | 6 (4.0) | | 2 (1.3) | 11 (7.3) | | | | | | | 17 (11.3) |
| Denticulates | | | 5 (3.3) | 9 (6.0) | 1 (0.7) | | 4 (2.6) | | | | 19 (12.6) |
| Retouched flakes | 2 (1.3) | | 5 (3.3) | 4 (2.6) | 3 (2.0) | | 1 (0.7) | 1 (0.7) | | | 16 (10.6) |
| Miscellaneous | 2 (1.3) | | | 1 (0.7) | | | | | | | 3 (2.0) |
| Utilization signs | 5 (3.3) | | 12 (7.9) | 11 (7.3) | 5 (3.3) | | 2 (1.3) | | | | 35 (23.2) |
| Other types | 1 (0.7) | | 2 (1.3) | 2 (1.3) | 3 (2.0) | | | | | | 8 (5.3) |
| Isolated removal | 4 (2.6) | 1 (0.7) | 2 (1.3) | 2 (1.3) | | | 1 (0.7) | 1 (0.7) | | | 11 (7.3) |
| TOTAL | 42 (27.8) | 3 (2.0) | 36 (23.8) | 46 (30.5) | 14 (9.3) | | 8 (5.3) | 2 (1.3) | | | 151 (100.2) |

*Note*: Absolute frequencies and total percentages.

[a] Simple scrapers in this analysis include Bordes's types 9–11, 25–26, 28–29. Convergent and transversal scrapers are counted with "other types" due to their low frequencies; end-notches (type 54) are counted with notches.

table 6.13 that describe a large number of possible complex combinations of retouch locations are either thinly populated or empty. Combined, these data indicate that the location of the retouched edge is not random.

Retouch on the left edge is more common than on the right edge in all the assemblages (except layer XVII), although the differences are small in most instances. This overall pattern stems from the distribution of these two attribute states among tools other than scrapers, while within the scraper samples the frequencies are somewhat more even.

Burins were mostly executed on distal parts of the blanks, with only rare exploitation of the proximal end for burin spall detachment. In some instances burin blows originated from a lateral edge. Retouch on notches and denticulates is not limited to the lateral edges and occurs on the distal/proximal ends of the blank as well. End-scrapers and awls, on the other hand, are modified strictly on the distal end of blanks (with a single exception for each type in layers XIV and IX, respectively).

Thus, throughout the sequence a high degree of regularity is observed in the location of retouch. For some tool types, particular locations were selected in a consistent manner. The latter pattern deviates from that reported from Lower Paleolithic assemblages (e.g., 'Ubeidiya; Bar-Yosef and Goren-Inbar 1993: tables. 39a–g). However, we should not attribute this difference to a long-term trend toward higher tool standardization in Upper and Epi-Paleolithic assemblages. A common hypothesis (e.g., Mellars 1989, 1996) postulates that modern humans in the Upper Paleolithic had a clearer mental template of flaked stone tools that was manifested in greater tool standardization. Two issues restrict our understanding of this aspect of lithics in the Levantine Mousterian. The first of these is analytical. The published data on Levantine Mousterian assemblages lend the impression that the Qafzeh pattern is by no means unique, but more rigorous comparisons between Middle Paleolithic sites, and between those and Upper Paleolithic sites in the region, are hampered by the lack of quantified data.

Assuming for the moment that tool types in both the Middle and the Upper Paleolithic reflect imposed form, there arise unrelated but fundamental questions as to the higher level of standardization of Upper Paleolithic tool types, and the evolutionary significance of tool standardization in general. Chazan (1995:756) noted that the impression of more standardization in Upper Paleolithic tools may in fact be due to the concentration of retouch on the distal tips of most Upper Paleolithic types. Because the tips are shorter than the lateral edges, this leads to the impression that retouch is more standardized, but he found this standardization to be unrelated to markedly modern traits such as language use. Marks, Hietala, and Williams (2001) tested the hypothesis that

Upper Paleolithic modern humans had a "clearer mental template" of flaked stone tools, manifested in greater tool standardization, by looking at Middle and Upper Paleolithic burins from the Levant and Europe. Their analysis revealed that tools were equally standardized for both metric and non-metric traits. Similarly, Monnier (2006:70–74) found no empirical evidence to support the notion of a gradual increase of standardization in the location of retouch on side-scrapers, notches, and denticulates in various French Mousterian sites.

In the case of the Qafzeh assemblages, the relatively standardized locations of retouch are associated with rather specific selection criteria of blank size. While this may not denote standardization of form, there does appear to be some standardization of process.

## Retouched Face

Retouch was described as occurring either on the dorsal or ventral face, or on both faces. A fourth attribute state, "on edge," relates to instances in which the retouch truncates the edge of the tool, as may be the case with burin blows or steep retouch. The frequencies of various retouched faces are presented in table 6.14. Retouch on the dorsal face is the most common in all the assemblages. This may be a biased pattern, as the distribution of retouched faces in the larger sample of layer XV suggests that the heavily uneven distributions in the other assemblages may be affected by small sample sizes.

Despite this potential distortion, some consistent patterns occur. Various types of side-scrapers are modified as a rule on the dorsal faces of blanks. However, as in the case of "retouch location," some of the most compelling correlations between face of retouch and tool groups stem from the typological definitions themselves. Thus, where ventral face retouch is recorded among side-scrapers, it denotes the occurrence of scrapers on the ventral face, and retouch on both faces correlates with alternately retouched scrapers. Similarly, the association of "miscellaneous" with retouch on the ventral face or on both faces reflects the inclusion in this type of pieces modified by the Nahr Ibrahim technique (see table 6.4). Contrary to these cases, in which an a priori link exists between the retouched face and typological definition, awls exhibit more diversified locations of the retouched face.

Comparison of the data in tables 6.13 and 6.14 shows that dorsal face retouch is more often than not associated with a relatively rigid placement of retouch as defined in planform, while a greater variety of "retouch location" is commonly linked with a larger variation in dorsal/ventral face modification. Blanks with "isolated removals" are exceptional in that they exhibit a striking dominance of modification on the ventral face.

**Table 6.14  Breakdown of location of retouched face by tool group**

**Layer VIIa**

| Type[a] | Dorsal | Ventral | Both | On edge | Total |
|---|---|---|---|---|---|
| Simple scrapers | 9 (18.0) | | | | 9 (18.0) |
| Double scrapers | 1 (2.0) | | | | 1 (2.0) |
| End-scrapers | 1 (2.0) | | | 1 (2.0) | 2 (4.0) |
| Burins | | 1 (2.0) | | 2 (4.0) | 3 (6.0) |
| Awls | 3 (6.0) | | | | 3 (6.0) |
| Notches | 5 (10.0) | 1 (2.0) | | | 6 (12.0) |
| Denticulates | 4 (8.0) | 2 (4.0) | | | 6 (12.0) |
| Retouched flakes | 5 (10.0) | | 3 (6.0) | | 8 (16.0) |
| Miscellaneous | | | | | |
| Other types | 3 (6.0) | 5 (10.0) | 2 (4.0) | | 10 (20.0) |
| Isolated removal | | 2 (4.0) | | | 2 (4.0) |
| TOTAL | 31 (62.0) | 11 (22.0) | 5 (10.0) | 3 (6.0) | 50 (100.0) |

**Layer IX**

| Type[a] | Dorsal | Ventral | Both | On edge | Total |
|---|---|---|---|---|---|
| Simple scrapers | 17 (17.7) | 7 (7.3) | | | 24 (25.0) |
| Double scrapers | 2 (2.1) | | | | 2 (2.1) |
| End-scrapers | 5 (5.2) | | | | 5 (5.2) |
| Burins | | | 3 (3.1) | 3 (3.1) | 6 (6.3) |
| Awls | | | 1 (1.0) | | 1 (1.0) |
| Notches | 6 (6.3) | 4 (4.2) | | | 10 (10.4) |
| Denticulates | 8 (8.3) | 2 (2.1) | 1 (1.0) | | 11 (11.5) |
| Retouched flakes | 8 (8.3) | 4 (4.2) | | | 12 (12.5) |
| Miscellaneous | | | 7 (7.3) | | 7 (7.3) |
| Other types | 3 (3.1) | 2 (2.1) | 1 (1.0) | | 6 (6.3) |
| Isolated removal | | 12 (12.5) | | | 12 (12.5) |
| TOTAL | 49 (51.0) | 31 (32.3) | 13 (13.5) | 3 (3.1) | 96 (100.1) |

**Layer X**

| Type[a] | Dorsal | Ventral | Both | On edge | Total |
|---|---|---|---|---|---|
| Simple scrapers | 10 (17.9) | 1 (1.8) | | | 11 (19.6) |
| Double scrapers | 1 (1.8) | | | | 1 (1.8) |
| End-scrapers | 1 (1.8) | | | | 1 (1.8) |
| Burins | | 2 (3.6) | | | 2 (3.6) |
| Awls | 1 (1.8) | | 3 (5.4) | | 4 (7.1) |
| Notches | 8 (14.3) | 2 (3.6) | | | 10 (17.9) |
| Denticulates | 4 (4.2) | | | | 4 (7.1) |
| Retouched flakes | 11 (19.6) | 1 (1.8) | | | 12 (21.4) |
| Miscellaneous | 1 (1.8) | 1 (1.8) | 2 (3.6) | | 4 (7.1) |
| Other types | 3 (5.4) | 2 (3.6) | | | 5 (8.9) |
| Isolated removal | | 2 (3.6) | | | 2 (3.6) |
| TOTAL | 40 (41.7) | 11 (11.5) | 5 (8.9) | | 56 (99.9) |

**Layer XI**

| Type[a] | Dorsal | Ventral | Both | On edge | Total |
|---|---|---|---|---|---|
| Simple scrapers | 18 (22.5) | 4 (5.0) | | | 22 (27.5) |
| Double scrapers | 4 (5.0) | | | | 4 (5.0) |
| End-scrapers | 2 (2.5) | | | | 2 (2.5) |
| Burins | | 1 (1.3) | 2 (2.5) | 1 (1.3) | 4 (5.0) |
| Awls | | | | | |
| Notches | 5 (6.3) | 3 (3.8) | | | 8 (10.0) |

*(continued)*

**Table 6.14   (continued)**

**Layer XI**

| Type[a] | Dorsal | Ventral | Both | On edge | Total |
|---|---|---|---|---|---|
| Denticulates | 5 (6.3) | 2 (2.5) | 1 (1.3) | | 8 (10.0) |
| Retouched flakes | 6 (7.5) | 2 (2.5) | 1 (1.3) | | 9 (11.3) |
| Miscellaneous | | 1 (1.3) | 3 (3.8) | | 4 (5.0) |
| Other types | 4 (5.0) | 4 (5.0) | 2 (2.5) | 3 (3.8) | 13 (16.3) |
| Isolated removal | | 4 (5.0) | 2 (2.5) | | 6 (7.5) |
| TOTAL | 44 (55.0) | 21 (26.3) | 11 | 4 (5.1) | 80 (100.1) |

**Layer XII**

| Type[a] | Dorsal | Ventral | Both | On edge | Total |
|---|---|---|---|---|---|
| Simple scrapers | 14 (15.1) | 4 (4.3) | 1 (1.1) | | 19 (20.4) |
| Double scrapers | | | | | |
| End-scrapers | 5 (5.4) | | | | 5 (5.4) |
| Burins | 1 (1.1) | 4 (4.3) | | 4 (4.3) | 9 (9.7) |
| Awls | | 1 (1.1) | | | 1 (1.1) |
| Notches | 4 (4.3) | 1 (1.1) | | | 5 (5.4) |
| Denticulates | 4 (4.3) | 4 (4.3) | 1 (1.1) | | 9 (9.6) |
| Retouched flakes | 18 (19.4) | 4 (4.3) | | | 22 (23.6) |
| Miscellaneous | | | 3 (3.2) | | 3 (3.2) |
| Other types | 5 (5.4) | 4 (4.3) | | 5 (5.4) | 14 (15.1) |
| Isolated removal | 1 (1.1) | 5 (5.4) | | | 6 (6.5) |
| TOTAL | 52 (55.9) | 27 (29.0) | 5 (5.4) | 9 (9.7) | 93 (100.0) |

**Layer XIII**

| Type[a] | Dorsal | Ventral | Both | On edge | Total |
|---|---|---|---|---|---|
| Simple scrapers | 64 (24.0) | 5 (1.9) | 3 (1.1) | | 72 (27.0) |
| Double scrapers | 8 (3.0) | | | | 8 (3.0) |
| End-scrapers | 4 (1.5) | | | | 4 (1.5) |
| Burins | 1 (0.4) | 4 (1.5) | | 3 (1.1) | 8 (3.0) |
| Awls | 3 (1.1) | | | | 3 (1.1) |
| Notches | 24 (9.0) | 16 (6.0) | | | 40 (15.0) |
| Denticulates | 19 (7.1) | 6 (2.2) | 4 (1.5) | | 29 (10.9) |
| Retouched flakes | 21 (7.9) | 2 (0.7) | 2 (0.7) | | 25 (9.4) |
| Miscellaneous | 4 (1.5) | 1 (0.4) | 7 | | 12 (4.5) |
| Other types | 11 (4.1) | 12 (4.5) | 3 (1.1) | | 26 (9.7) |
| Isolated removal | 1 (0.4) | 38 (14.2) | 1 (0.4) | | 40 (15.0) |
| TOTAL | 160 (59.9) | 84 (31.5) | 20 (7.5) | 3 (1.1) | 267 (100.1) |

**Layer XIV**

| Type[a] | Dorsal | Ventral | Both | On edge | Total |
|---|---|---|---|---|---|
| Simple scrapers | 1 (1.2) | 2 (2.3) | 1 (1.2) | | 4 (4.7) |
| Double scrapers | | | | | |
| End-scrapers | 6 (7.0) | | | | 6 (7.0) |
| Burins | 1 (1.2) | 3 (3.5) | | 1 (1.2) | 5 (5.8) |
| Awls | | | | | |
| Notches | 15 (17.4) | 4 (4.7) | 2 (2.3) | 1 (1.2) | 22 (25.6) |
| Denticulates | 4 (4.7) | 2 (2.3) | 8 | | 14 (16.3) |
| Retouched flakes | 4 (4.7) | 2 (2.3) | 3 (3.5) | | 9 (10.5) |
| Miscellaneous | 1 (1.2) | 1 (1.2) | 7 (8.1) | | 9 (10.5) |
| Other types | 3 (3.5) | 1 (1.2) | | | 4 (4.7) |
| Isolated removal | | 13 (15.1) | | | 13 (15.1) |
| TOTAL | 35 (40.7) | 28 (32.6) | 21 (24.2) | 2 (2.3) | 86 (100.2) |

(continued)

**Table 6.14   (continued)**

**Layer XV**

| Type[a] | Dorsal | Ventral | Both | On edge | Total |
|---|---|---|---|---|---|
| Simple scrapers | 23 (6.1) | 13 (3.4) | 3 (0.8) | | 39 (10.3) |
| Double scrapers | 1 (0.3) | | | | 1 (0.3) |
| End-scrapers | 10 (2.6) | 13 (3.4) | | 1 (0.3) | 13 (3.4) |
| Burins | 2 (0.5) | 24 (6.3) | 2 (0.5) | 3 (0.8) | 31 (8.2) |
| Awls | 8 (2.1) | 1 (0.3) | | | 9 (2.4) |
| Notches | 43 (11.3) | 11 (2.9) | | | 54 (14.2) |
| Denticulates | 19 (5.0) | 8 (2.1) | 1 (0.3) | 2 (0.5) | 30 (7.9) |
| Retouched flakes | 18 (4.7) | 9 (2.4) | 2 (0.5) | 1 (0.3) | 30 (7.9) |
| Miscellaneous | 7 (1.8) | 3 (0.8) | 41 (10.8) | | 51 (13.5) |
| Other types | 7 (1.8) | 24 (6.3) | 24 (6.3) | 17 (4.5) | 72 (19.0) |
| Isolated removal | 7 (1.8) | 37 (9.8) | 2 (0.5) | 3 (0.8) | 49 (12.9) |
| TOTAL | 145 (38.3) | 132 (34.8) | 75 (19.8) | 27 (7.1) | 379 (100.0) |

**Layer XVa**

| Type[a] | Dorsal | Ventral | Both | On edge | Total |
|---|---|---|---|---|---|
| Simple scrapers | 10 (15.9) | 2 (3.2) | | | 12 (19.0) |
| Double scrapers | | | | | |
| End-scrapers | 3 (4.8) | | 1 (1.6) | | 4 (6.3) |
| Burins | | 3 (4.8) | | 1 (1.6) | 4 (6.3) |
| Awls | 6 (9.5) | | | | 6 (9.5) |
| Notches | 7 (11.1) | 4 (6.3) | | | 11 (17.5) |
| Denticulates | 4 (6.3) | 1 (1.6) | | | 5 (7.9) |
| Retouched flakes | 6 (9.5) | | 1 (1.6) | | 7 (11.1) |
| Miscellaneous | | 1 (1.6) | 2 (3.2) | | 3 (4.8) |
| Other types | 4 (6.3) | 3 (4.8) | | | 7 (11.1) |
| Isolated removal | | 4 (6.3) | | | 4 (6.3) |
| TOTAL | 40 (6.3) | 18 (28.6) | 4 (6.3) | 1 (1.6) | 63 (99.8) |

**Layer XVII**

| Type[a] | Dorsal | Ventral | Both | On edge | Total |
|---|---|---|---|---|---|
| Simple scrapers | 12 (10.4) | 1 (0.9) | 1 (0.9) | | 14 (12.2) |
| Double scrapers | 1 (0.9) | | | | 1 (0.9) |
| End-scrapers | 12 (10.4) | | | | 12 (10.4) |
| Burins | 1 (0.9) | 1 (0.9) | | 3 (2.6) | 5 (4.3) |
| Awls | 3 (2.6) | 2 (1.7) | 1 (0.9) | | 6 (5.2) |
| Notches | 16 (13.9) | 3 (2.6) | | | 19 (16.5) |
| Denticulates | 16 (13.9) | 2 (1.7) | 1 (0.9) | | 19 (16.5) |
| Retouched flakes | 12 (10.4) | 3 (2.6) | 1 (0.9) | | 16 (13.9) |
| Miscellaneous | | 2 (1.7) | 1 (0.9) | | 3 (2.6) |
| Other types | 7 (6.1) | 2 (1.7) | | | 9 (7.8) |
| Isolated removal | 10 (8.7) | | 1 (0.9) | | 11 (9.6) |
| TOTAL | 90 (78.3) | 16 (13.9) | 6 (5.2) | 3 (2.6) | 115 (99.9) |

*Note:* Absolute frequencies and total percentages.

[a] Simple scrapers in this analysis include Bordes's types 9–11, 25–26, 28–29. Convergent and transversal scrapers are counted with "other types" due to their low frequencies; end-notches (type 54) are counted with notches.

## Reduction or Imposed Form
## in the Side-Scrapers of Qafzeh?

The "resharpening model," presented in a series of articles (Dibble 1995a, and references therein; Dibble and Rolland 1992; Rolland and Dibble 1990), is more extreme than other functional or ecological models in that it not only questions Bordes's interpretation of typological variability but undermines its inherent notion of preconceived, emic tool types. Since Mousterian side-scrapers figure prominently in Bordes's type-list and often dominate the assemblages of retouched tools, it is this tool category that is at the focus of discussion (although an attempt was made to apply the reduction model to notches and denticulates as well; see Dibble 1988; Dibble and Rolland 1992).

The model proposes that the various types of side-scrapers are not intentionally created, discrete forms. Rather, these tools are conceived as reflecting various stages in the blank reduction continuum, an idea first voiced with regard to North American lithic assemblages (the "Frison effect"; Jelinek 1976). In this view, scraper retouch is a means to extend a tool's use life by resharpening. The continuous process as originally modeled by Dibble (1987) aims to compensate for the loss of working edge length by using two different resharpening paths. The first postulated path involves addition of working edges, first moving from a single side-scraper to a double side-scraper, then extending cutting edge length through changing the angles of the working edges by resharpening them into convergent forms (convergent scrapers and Mousterian points). The second path of reduction moves through the continuous resharpening of a single edge, gradually shifting by changing the direction of the retouched edge from a single side-scraper to a transversal side-scraper. In essence, all side-scraper morphologies can be accommodated between these two variants of the model. The model relates the length of the continuous reduction process (i.e., the deviation from simple to increasingly exploited blanks, each of which is dubbed a discrete type) to variation in raw material availability and size coupled with group mobility (Rolland 1988; Rolland and Dibble 1990).

More recently, Dibble (1995a) reviewed the reduction model, outlining a series of modified hypotheses and their test implications in response to various critiques voiced since the model's first publication. Assuming that the emphasis in scraper use and maintenance is on the optimal exploitation of a single edge, he posited that scraper morphology could be demonstrated to be responsive to blank form, and thus to core reduction strategies. Comparisons among assemblages are thus irrelevant to a large degree. It is within the assemblage, when scraper forms are evaluated against their (presumably) original technological system, that the validity of the reduction model can be tested. An analytical caveat is that only highly utilized assemblages are appropriate for testing the model's hypotheses because large sample sizes of each scraper class are required (Dibble 1995a:345).

In assemblages in which core reduction strategies resulted in longer blanks, the path leading to elongated pointed forms would be operative. Core reduction strategies that produced short, wide blanks would lead to emphasis on the shift to transversal forms (see also Kuhn 1992a). Offset (*déjeté*) scrapers could originate from either one of the two sequences (Dibble 1988, 1991b). Regardless of the specific path of reduction, the amount of reduction that a particular blank can undergo is a function of its original size. Larger blanks can be used for a longer time, and therefore be subject to more resharpening before the minimum size is reached. Hence, simple scrapers should not be expected to be longer than convergent or transversal ones, even though they have been less heavily reduced. On the contrary, they would be of the same or even smaller dimensions. Were they large enough in the first place, they would be more heavily reduced (Dibble 1995a:330). This statement puts much of the weight of testing the model on reconstructions of the original size of the flake and the degree to which it has been reduced from its original size.

Concurrent with the notion that scraper morphology is responsive to blank form, retouch intensity gains importance in the context of model testing. If blank shape was the main factor in the modification of scraper form, there should be a correlation between the position of the retouched edge(s) and the shape of the original flake. Moreover, one would not expect heavy retouch that created the tool's shape. If, on the other hand, the reduction model is valid, all the scraper classes that are considered late in the reduction continuum should show higher average values of retouch intensity than the less reduced types (Dibble 1995a:328–329).

Assemblages in which only a small portion of blanks was modified into retouched tools will show high proportions of available unmodified blanks, reducing the need to exploit the maximum potential of each retouched blank. The relatively few tools in such assemblages will tend to be only lightly retouched, although a few more heavily reduced blanks may occur. In such circumstances the more reduced forms will not necessarily be shorter than double and single scrapers. Still, all scrapers should, on average, be wider than the unretouched pieces, because blanks that are smaller than the cutoff point of width suitable for scraper retouch will not be selected for modification into scrapers in the first place (Dibble 1995a:325).

Given such restrictions, the lightly utilized Qafzeh assemblages cannot serve to test the model. Regardless, some patterns in the Qafzeh assemblages are of interest in the context of the resharpening model.

## Blank Form and Intensity of Retouch

According to the revised model, scraper form is responsive to the original flake morphology and therefore intensity of retouch should not be correlated with scraper class. The same model also argues that scraper forms believed to be more reduced should be more heavily retouched than the less reduced ones. Both expectations are borne out by the archaeological record of the Levantine Mousterian. Gordon (1993) showed that, contrary to Dibble's argument, Mousterian points in the Ghar collection were not a heavily reduced version of convergent scrapers, but had been created through an independent retouch sequence, applied specifically to pointed and elongated blanks in the assemblage. On the other hand, simple scrapers at Qafzeh were produced on varied blank forms (tables 6.11, 6.12, figure 6.9), although a preference for Levallois blanks could be recognized. (Admittedly, intra-assemblage comparisons are impossible at Qafzeh due to sample size limitations.)

A number of methods were devised for evaluating retouch intensity, relying either on visual assessment and ranking of retouch or on more elaborate quantitative methods, some of which have been tested experimentally (Barton 1990; Baumler and Speth 1993; Dibble 1984b; Gordon 1993; Eren et al. 2005; Hiscock and Clarkson 2005; Jelinek 1988; Kuhn 1990). Ambiguities, however, are inherent in most of those methods (Dibble 1995a:330). For this reason I did not apply any of these methods to the overall lightly reduced Qafzeh samples. On the basis of observation, however, it is clear that some of the simple scrapers have undergone relatively intense retouch (e.g., plates 37:9, 39:8), while some of the forms expected to exhibit high retouch intensity actually present only light retouch (e.g., plates 15:10, 32:1, 40:2; see also Close 1991) comparable to Jelinek's (1988) and Dibble's (1984a) categories 1 (shallow and sometimes discontinuous retouch) and 2 (continuous and moderately invasive retouch) out of four categories of retouch intensity. These instances do not form a concrete argument as regards the resharpening model, but their existence is in obvious contrast to the logic of the model.

## Scraper Morphometrics

Scrapers are the only tool group at Qafzeh in which metric attributes reflect a high degree of standardization. The means of both length and width of scrapers occur in a limited range of values (figure 6.12). A comparison with the mean dimensions of unretouched artifacts (figure 5.6) demonstrates that simple and convergent scrapers are indeed modified on blanks that are on average longer and wider than non-retouched blanks. This is true of double scrapers as well (values not presented in figure 6.12).

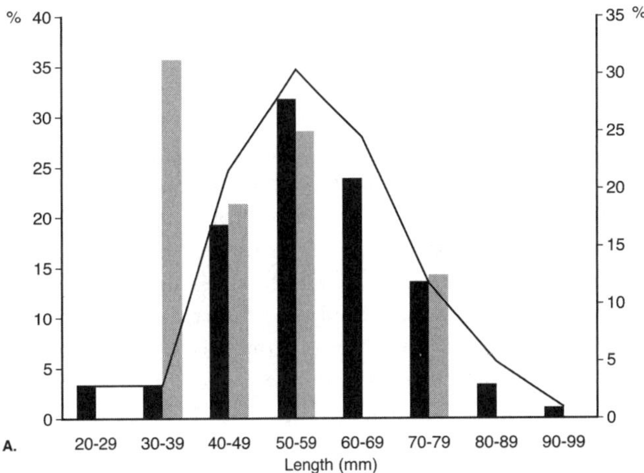



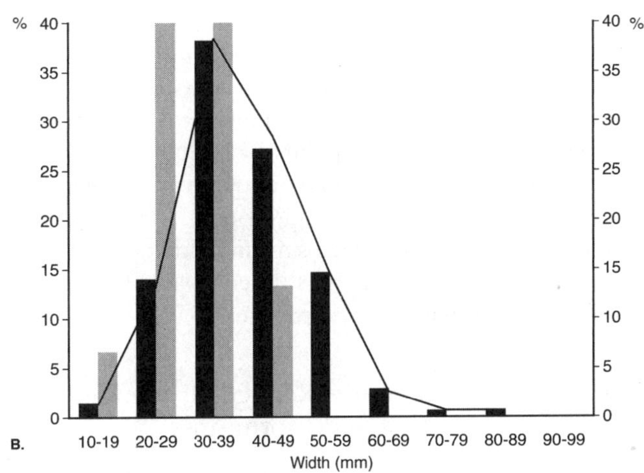



**Figure 6.15** Frequency distribution of length (A) and width (B) of simple and convergent side-scrapers (left axis) and the combined sample (right axis) in the Qafzeh assemblages. Artifacts included in this analysis were not broken at the measured dimension. Artifact frequencies combined from the whole sequence.

The distributions of both length and width of scrapers are unimodal and values tend to concentrate around the mean (less obviously so in the width distribution; figure 6.15). The distributions for convergent scrapers are far from normal, undoubtedly due to the small sample size, and are confined within more limited values than are simple scrapers. The distribution of the combined sample is unimodal and close to normal for both attributes, with no traces of bimodalities that might indicate the existence of two populations.

Such results accord with Dibble's (1984a, 1987, 1995a) resharpening model when applied to a lightly utilized sample. Certainly, the suggestion that scrapers were discarded when their width reached a particular cutoff point cannot be ruled out on the basis of the data presented here. However, observations on metric attributes of scrapers in a complete, non-selected collection from Kunji Cave in the Zagros, dominated by heavily retouched tools (Baumler and Speth 1993:16), and in Grotta di Santa d'Augustino (Kuhn 1992a:124–5) cast doubts on the relevance of metric attributes of single and double scrapers for describing the early stages of a resharpening sequence leading to convergent scrapers. Such is also the case at Quneitra, where the mean width of convergent scrapers is practically identical to that of single scrapers (Goren-Inbar 1990a: table 18, fig. 53).

The mean values of scraper width in the various assemblages at Qafzeh (figure 6.12) are larger than those observed in the Zagros assemblages or Ghar while closer to those of other Levantine, European, and North African assemblages (Baumler and Speth 1993; Close 1991; Dibble 1984b, 1995a; Dibble and Holdaway 1990; Gordon 1993; Goren-Inbar 1990a). Such observations are consistent with the notion that the cutoff points of scraper dimensions, beyond which reduction could not go further, depend on the size and shape of the original unretouched blanks, namely they are assemblage-specific and related to the technological systems of the studied assemblage. Inter-assemblage comparisons are irrelevant.

## Estimating the Amount of Reduction: The Ratio of Flake Surface Area to Platform Area

The realization that the final dimensions of scrapers cannot provide evidence for their reduction history gives much significance to reconstructions of original flake size. What is required is a measure of the amount of reduction that a scraper underwent during the time between the blank's removal from a core and the termination of its use life, due to either discard or accidental loss.

Striking platform width and depth have been suggested to determine overall flake size. Much experimental work (Dibble and Whittaker 1981; Speth 1972, 1974, 1975, 1981) indicates that flake mass derives from four factors: platform depth, EPA, the angle of incidence, and hammer velocity at impact. Since only the former two are measurable to any degree on archaeological materials, the reconstruction of original flake mass is highly problematic (Davis and Shea 1998). Still, if flake size (surface area) is taken as a proxy of flake mass, there should be a predictable ratio between platform size and flake size. Arguing that platform characteristics are not affected by the process of retouch, Dibble (1987) suggested that the ratio between a scraper's platform area and its surface area after retouch

corresponds to the degree of reduction from the original flake: ("[b]ecause of its ability to help control for original blank size, the ratio of surface area to platform area is an important variable in demonstrating scraper reduction"; Dibble 1995a:327–328, tab. II), when compared to the ratios measured on non-retouched flakes.

Recent studies have shown that the relationship of interest is much more complex than was originally understood. Even in controlled experimental conditions, the relationships between the variables that define the flake and platform size are far from linear (Pelcin 1998). Similarly, raw material has a significant effect on the measured ratio. It is possibly this complexity that underlies the long-known fact that reconstructions of original flake sizes and estimates of scraper reduction in archaeological material produced in uncontrolled conditions are at least problematic. For the Qafzeh assemblages, the correlation between flake size (= flake surface area) and platform area of complete, unretouched flakes has been shown to be non-linear (table 5.13 and accompanying discussion). One cannot rely on platform area of scrapers as an indication of the original blank size and, consequently, of the amount and degree of blank reduction associated with particular scraper types. The appeal of the reduction model as an explanation of scraper forms and types is thus reduced.

In view of these data, the claim that the reduction model alone can account for "many, if not most, aspects of assemblage composition variability seen in the Middle Paleolithic of western Eurasia" (Rolland and Dibble 1990:490) is unfounded (cf. Mellars 1996:332–341). It is intuitively clear that retouch intensity reflects to a large degree the attempts made to maximize the use lives of artifacts, but the exact relationship that had been predicted between that variable, the location and shape of retouched edges, and their relationship to reduction strategies is not clear-cut. Scraper morphologies and sizes in the final stages of the tool's life history may reflect continuous reduction; but this in itself does not preclude a long history of intentional selection and preparation of blanks based on criteria of raw material size and availability (Rolland 1981; Rolland and Dibble 1990) as well as functional and stylistic considerations. Indeed, the reduction model as newly phrased (Dibble 1995a) aims to explain more realistic, complex situations than the original, rigid model; it is this simulation of real life that finally renders the derived hypotheses irrefutable.

## Summary

The Qafzeh assemblages commonly demonstrate high values of ILty, relatively low frequencies of retouched tools, and rarity of intensively retouched artifacts. In contrast to these lines of similarity among the assemblages, the typological composition shows variation in tool groups and tool type frequencies throughout the sequence. Still, all the Qafzeh assemblages can be placed within the parameters of Bordes's typical Mousterian (Bordes 1984).

The blanks for retouched pieces were selected from the flake populations available at the time of each assemblage with an emphasis on a relatively large size, a trait that is common to a large number of sites in and out of the Levant. Of all the tool types, only burins and side-scrapers occur on carefully selected blanks with particular properties. The pattern is recurrent in all the assemblages regardless of the frequencies of typological groups. Scrapers especially exhibit well-defined size ranges and tend to be the largest tools. Other tools, such as truncated pieces and pieces with isolated removals, although not as formalized as scrapers, tend to exhibit stability across layers in some stylistic attributes.

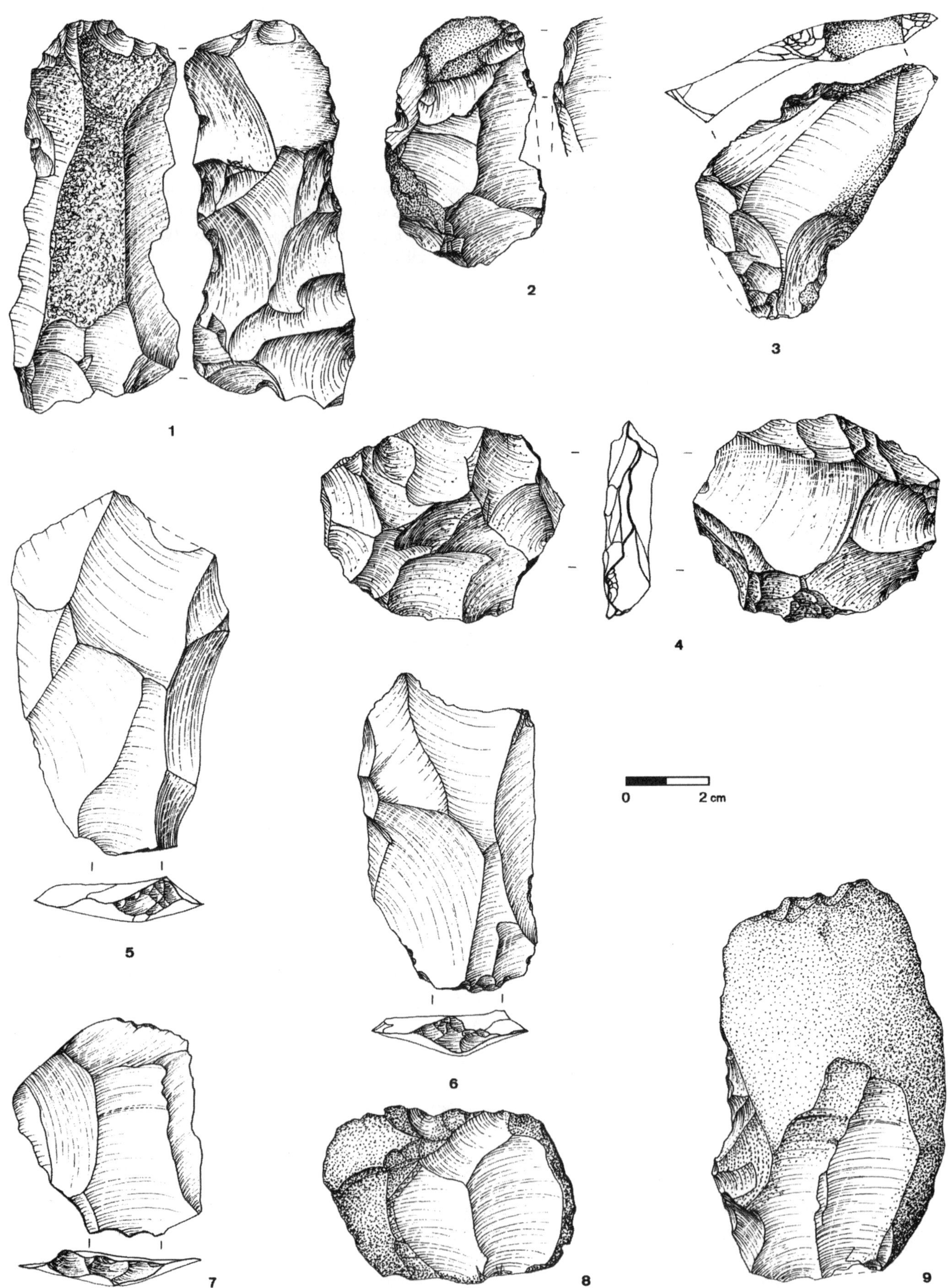

**Plate 11** Layers XXIV–XXII: 1: Core-on-flake; 2: Retouched flake; 3, 9: Denticulate; 4: Levallois core for flakes; 5–6: Levallois flakes; 7: Notch (on Levallois flake); 8: Atypical Levallois flake.

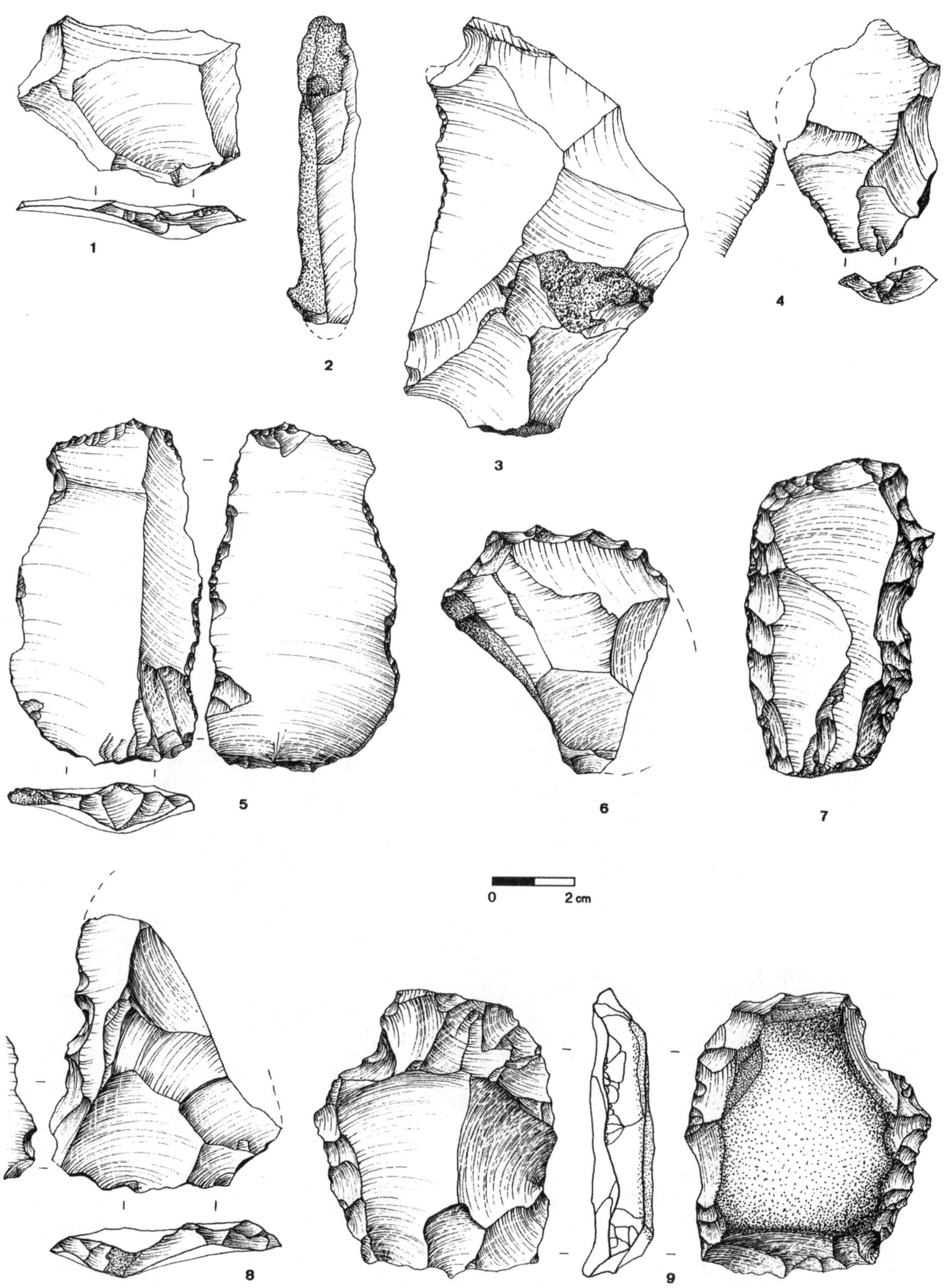

**Plate 12**  Layer XXI: 1: Levallois flake; 2: Blade; 3: Notch (on Levallois flake); 4–5: Retouched flakes;
6, 8: Denticulates; 7: Double convex-concave side-scraper and typical borer; 9: Levallois core for flakes.

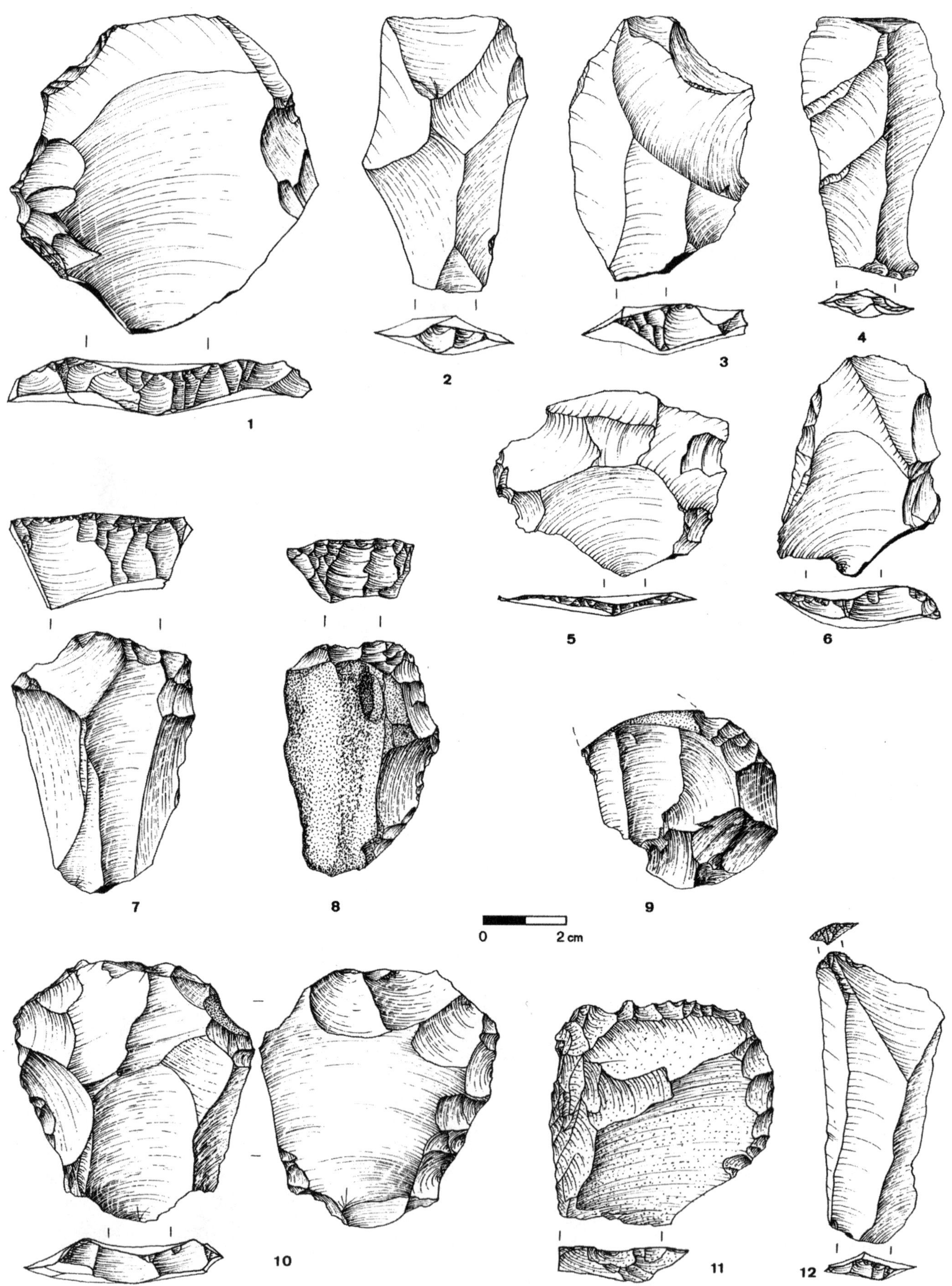

**Plate 13** Layer XIX: 1–6: Levallois flakes; 7–8: Typical end-scrapers; 9: Transversal convex scraper (atypical);
10: Core-on-flake on a side-scraper on the ventral face; 11: Single convex side-scraper and denticulate;
12: Atypical end-scraper.

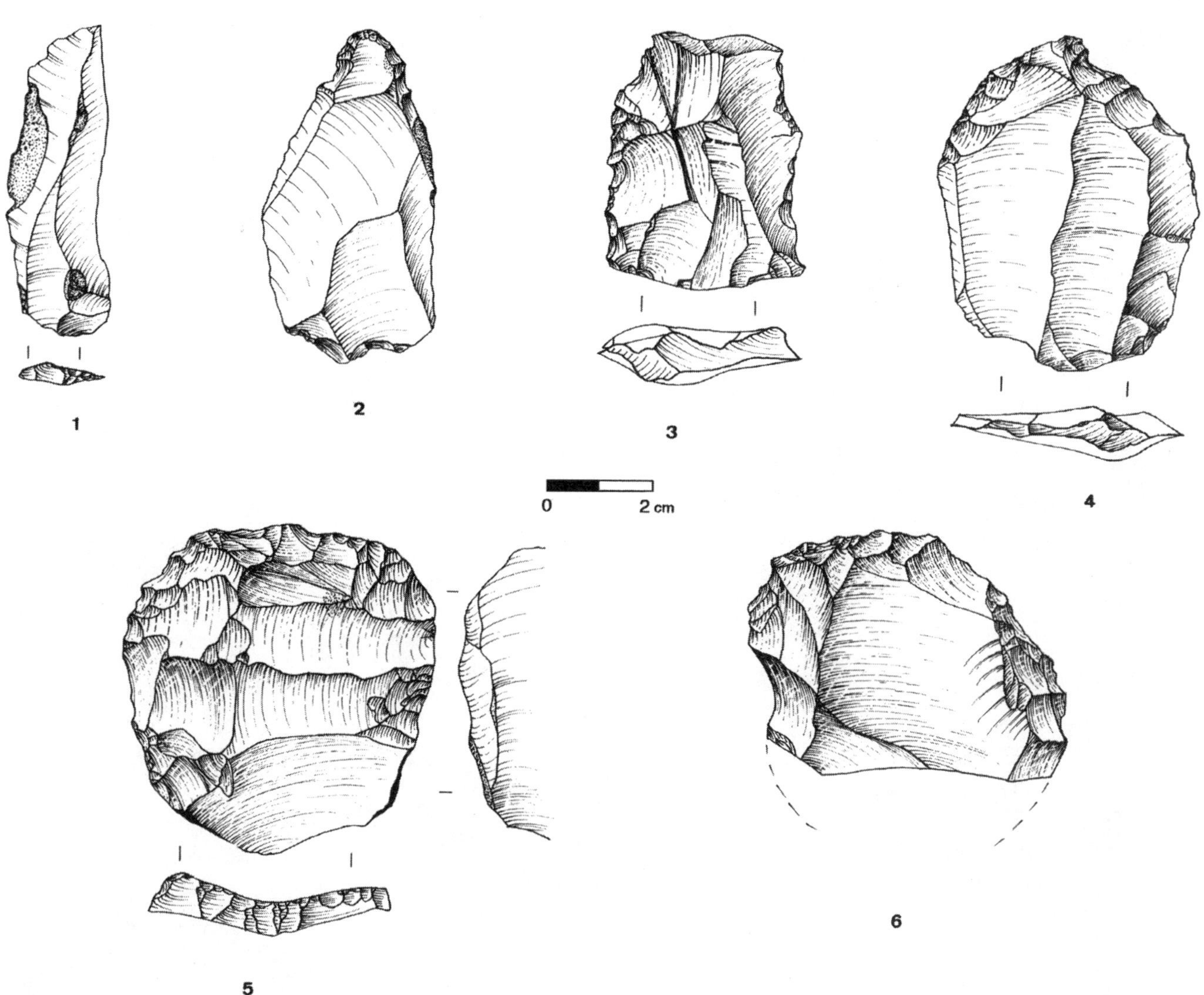

**Plate 14**  Layer XVIIa: 1: Levallois blade; 2, 6: Atypical end-scraper; 3: Denticulate; 4: Single convex side-scraper and a notch; 5: Straight transversal scraper (on bipolar core waste).

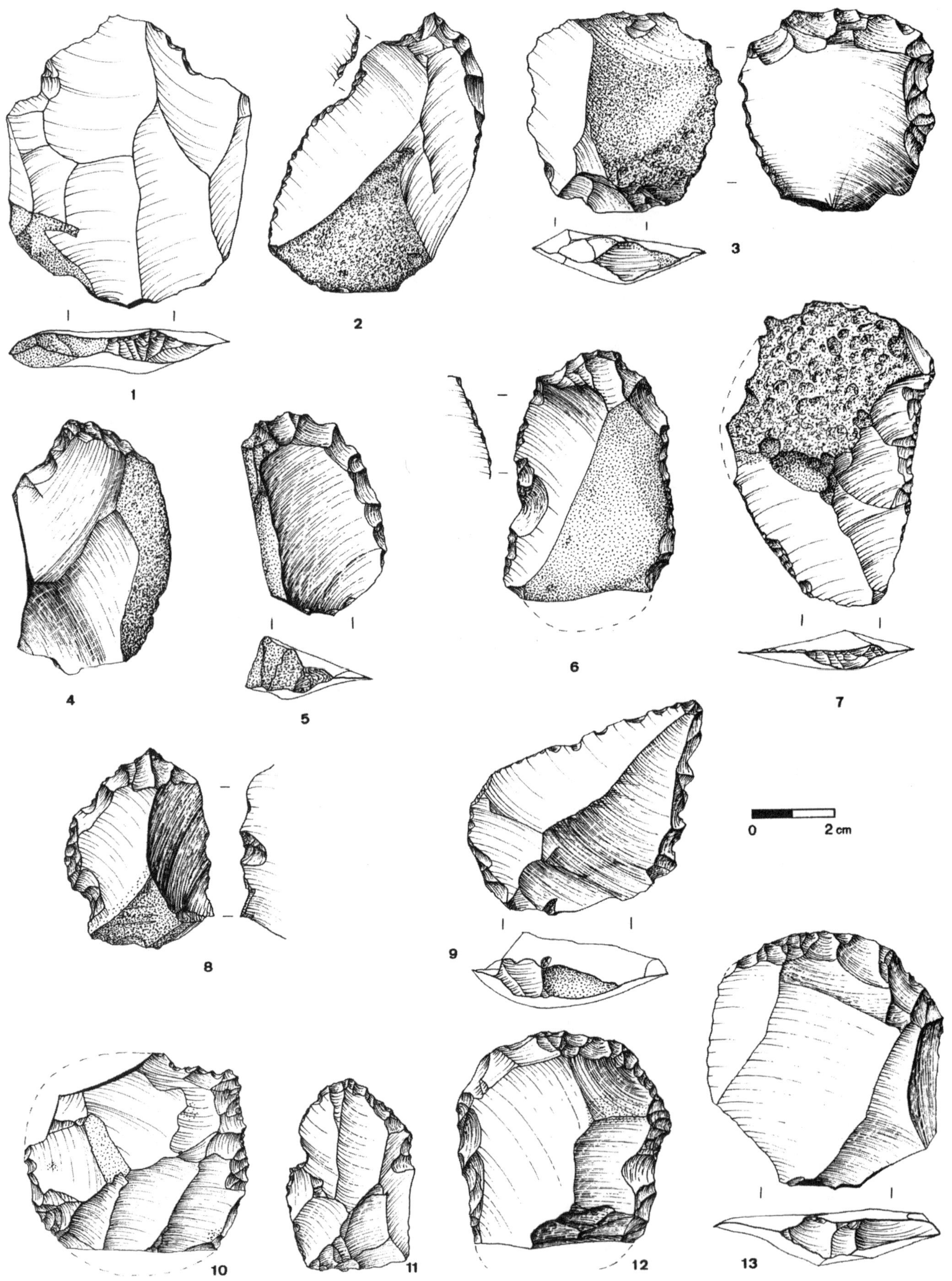

**Plate 15**  Layer XVII: 1, 3, 5, 9: Denticulates (#3 on ventral face); 2: Typical borer and retouched flake; 4: Atypical end-scraper; 6: End-scraper and single straight side-scraper; 7: Double straight-convex side-scraper; 8: Denticulate and a notch on the ventral face; 10: Double convex side-scraper; 11: Offset scraper and a notch; 12–13: Typical end-scrapers.

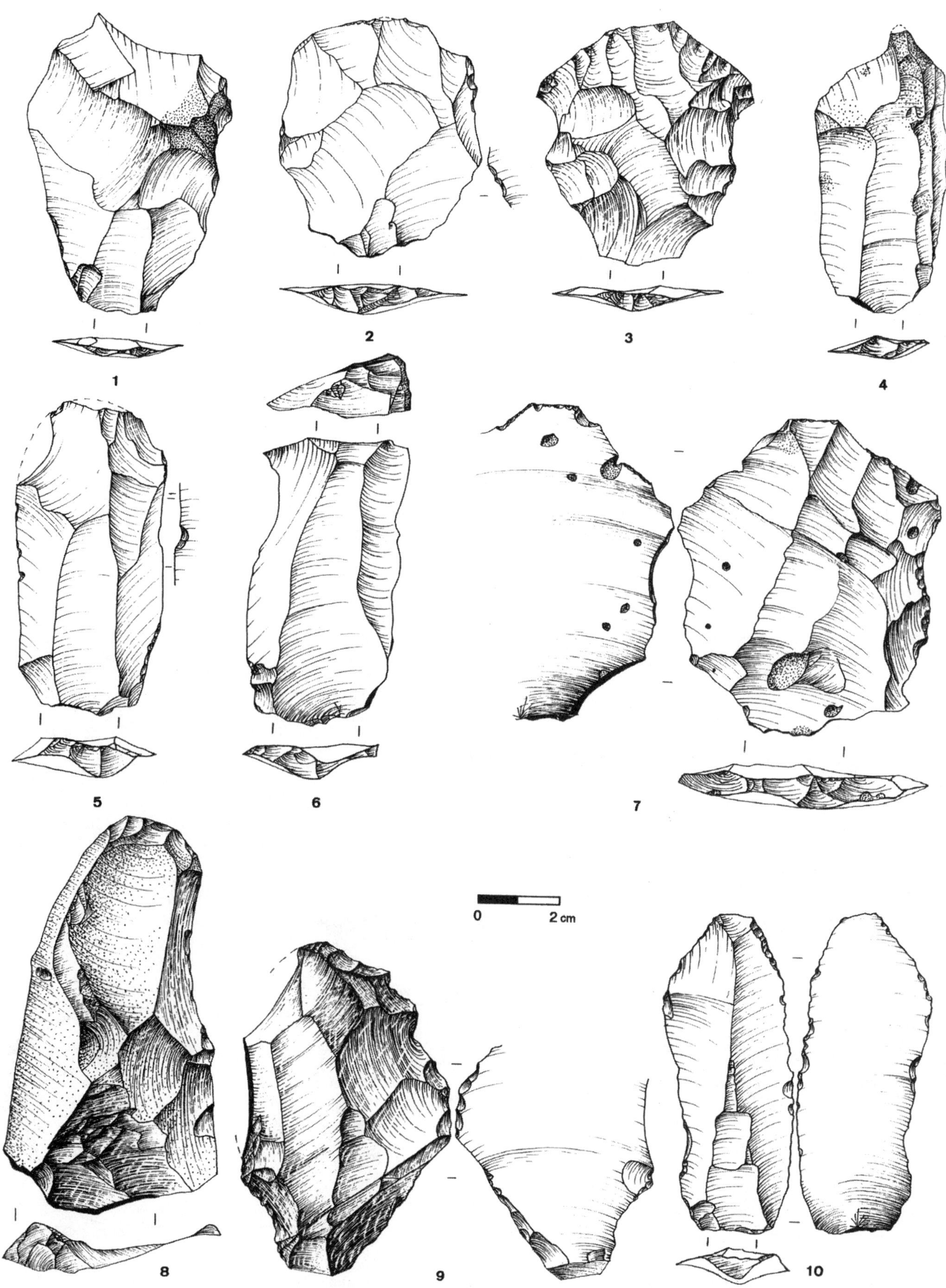

**Plate 16** Layer XVII: 1, 7: Retouched Levallois flakes; 2: Raclette; 3, 6: *éclats outrepassés*; 4: Levallois blade; 5: Levallois flake; 8: Typical end-scraper; 9: Denticulate (massive, with ochre); 10: Retouched blade.

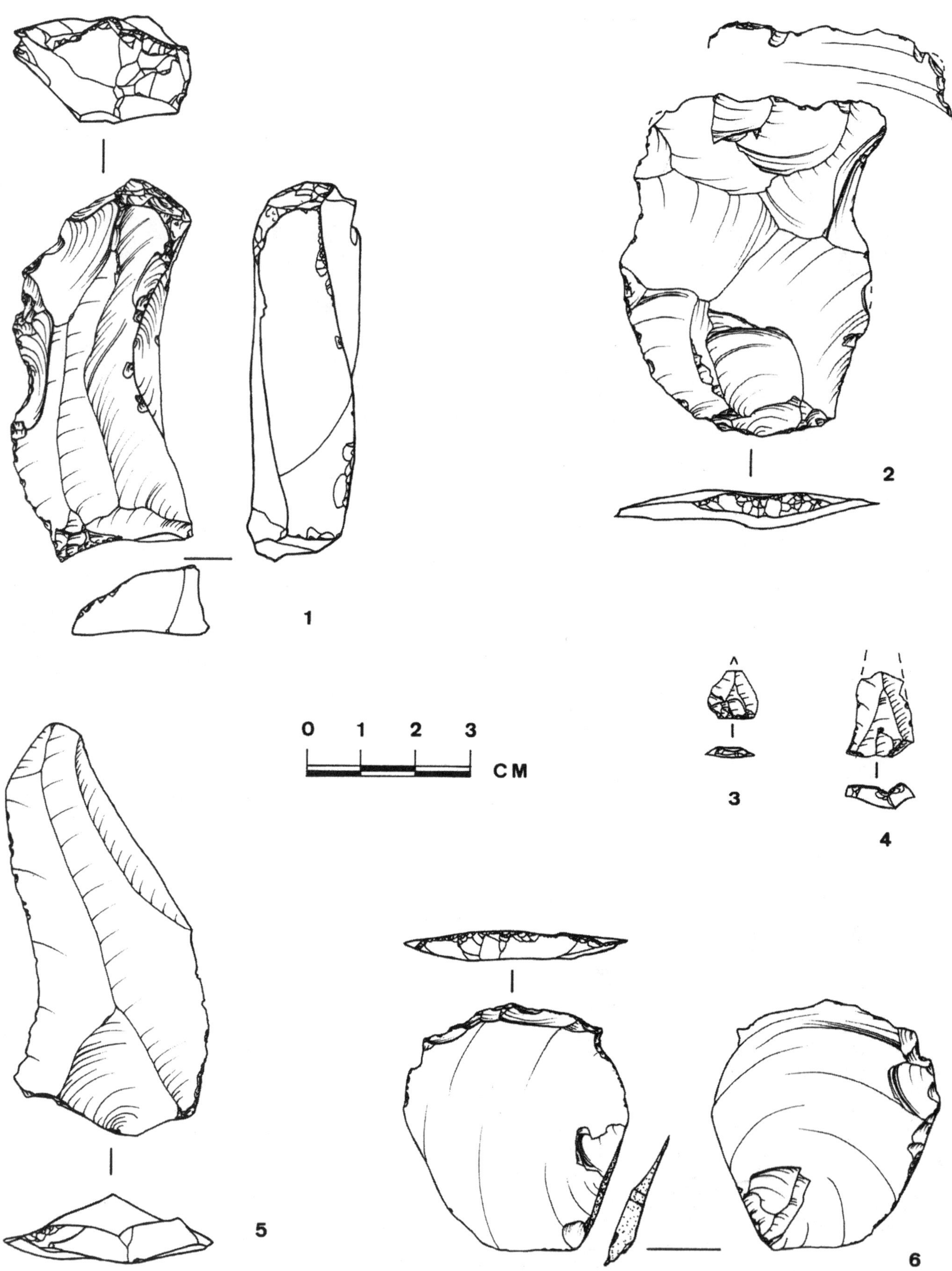

**Plate 17** Layer XVa: 1: Typical end-scraper on retouched flake; 2: Levallois flake; 3–4: Small Levallois points; 5: Levallois blade; 6: Typical end-scraper and an isolated removal on a Kombewa flake.

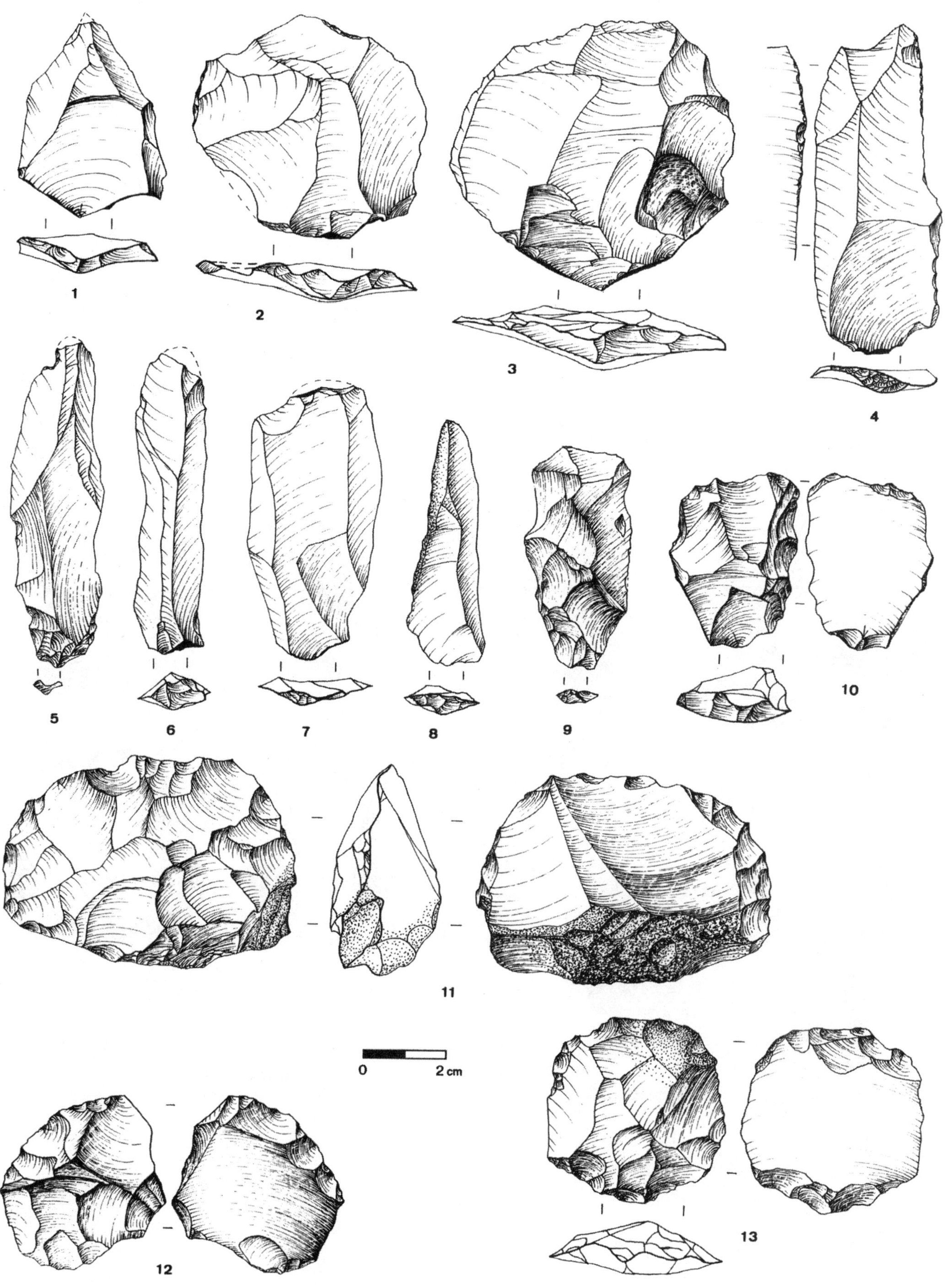

**Plate 18**   Layer XVa: 1: Levallois point; 2–3, 9: Levallois flakes; 4: Retouched Levallois blade; 5: Notch on a Levallois blade; 6–8: Levallois blades; 10, 12–14: Cores-on-flakes.

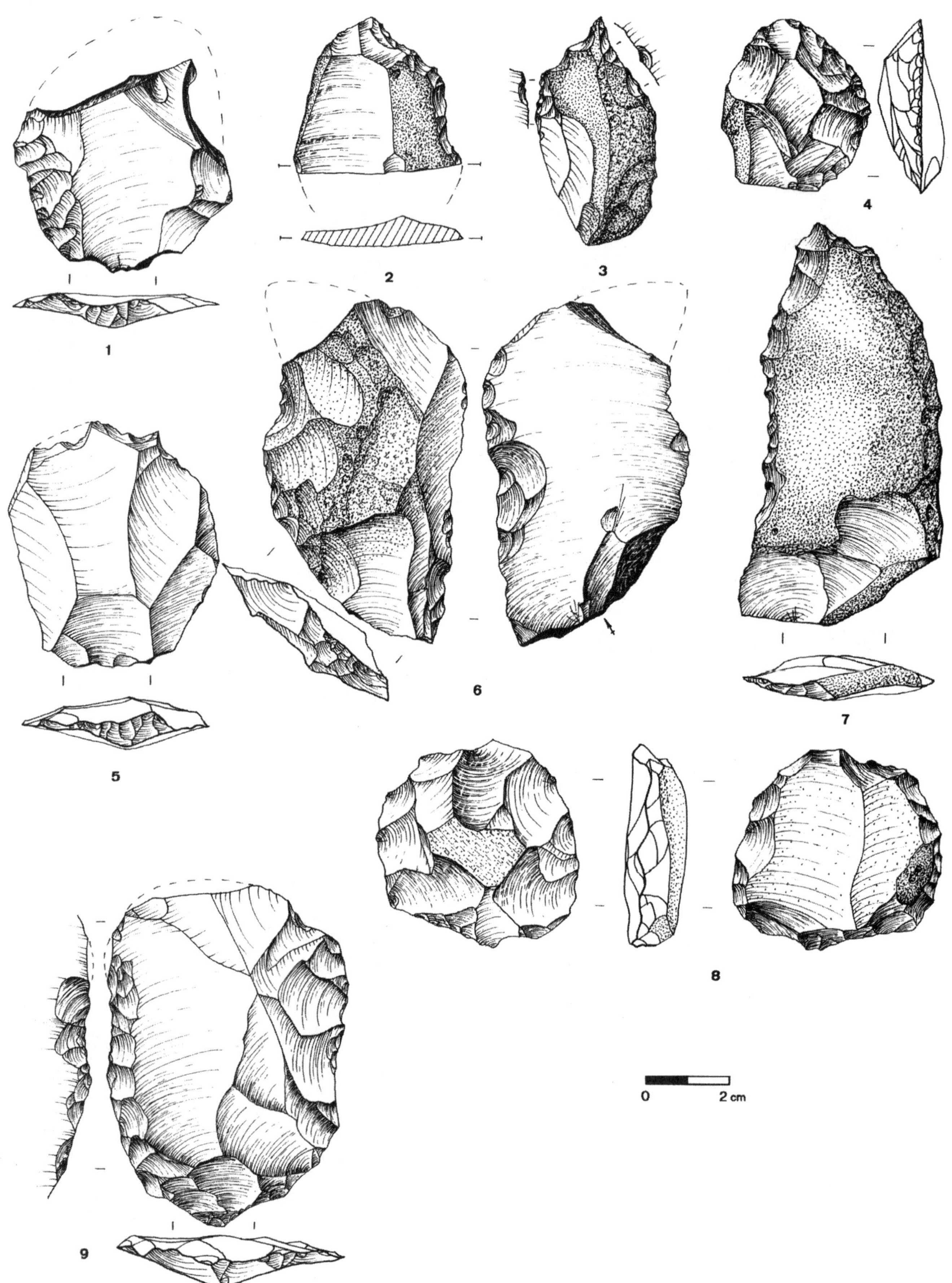

**Plate 19** Layer XVa: 1: Single convex side-scraper; 2: Single convex side-scraper and truncated flake; 3, 5: Typical borers; 4: Typical end-scraper; 6: Side-scraper on the ventral face of a flake; 7: Single convex side-scraper and denticulate; 8: Levallois core for flakes; 9: Side-scraper with bifacial retouch.

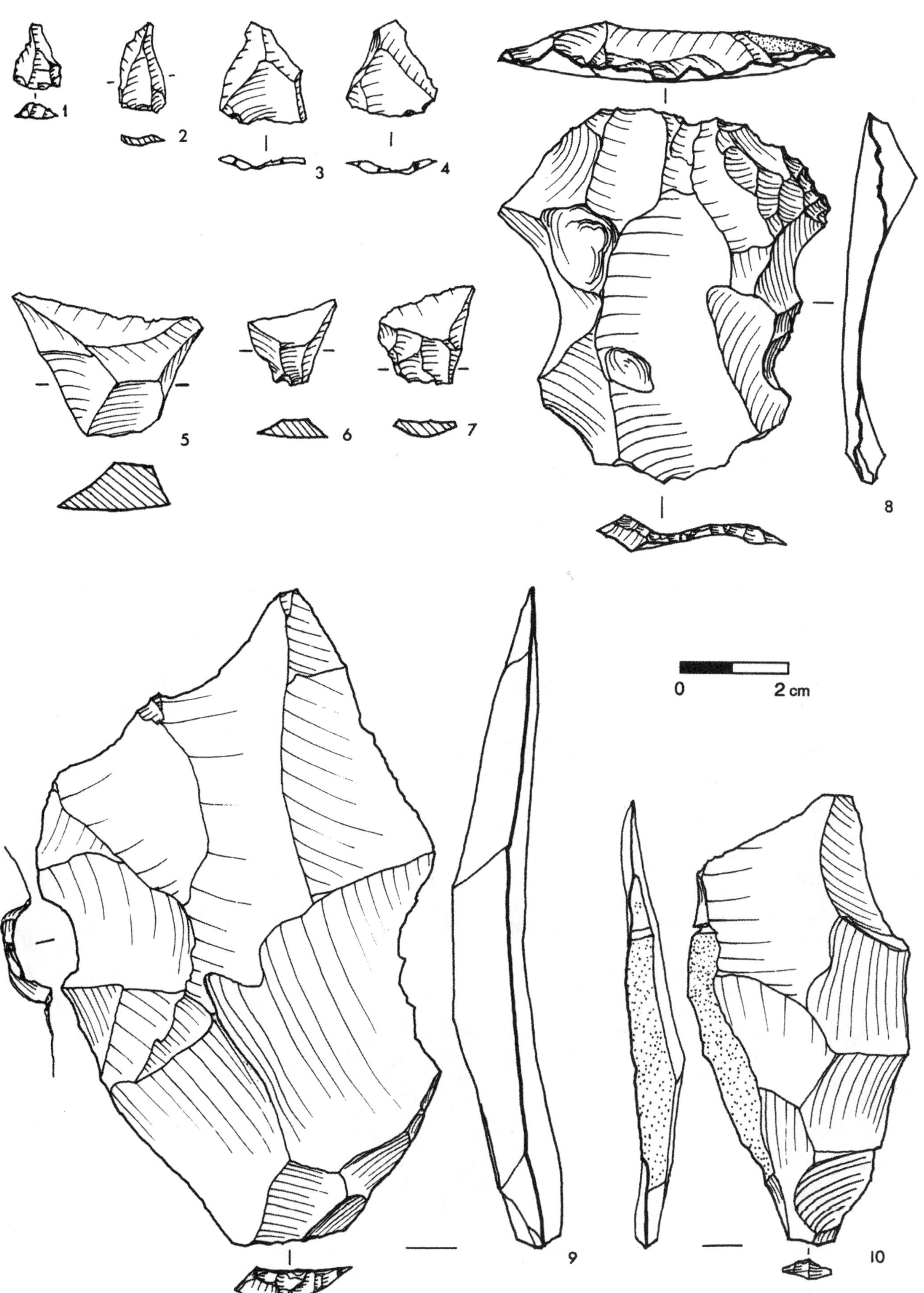

**Plate 20**  Layer XVf: 1–4: Levallois points; 5–7: Pseudo-Levallois points; 8: *Éclat outrepassé;* 9: Notch (on Levallois flake); 10: Naturally backed knife (on a Levallois flake).

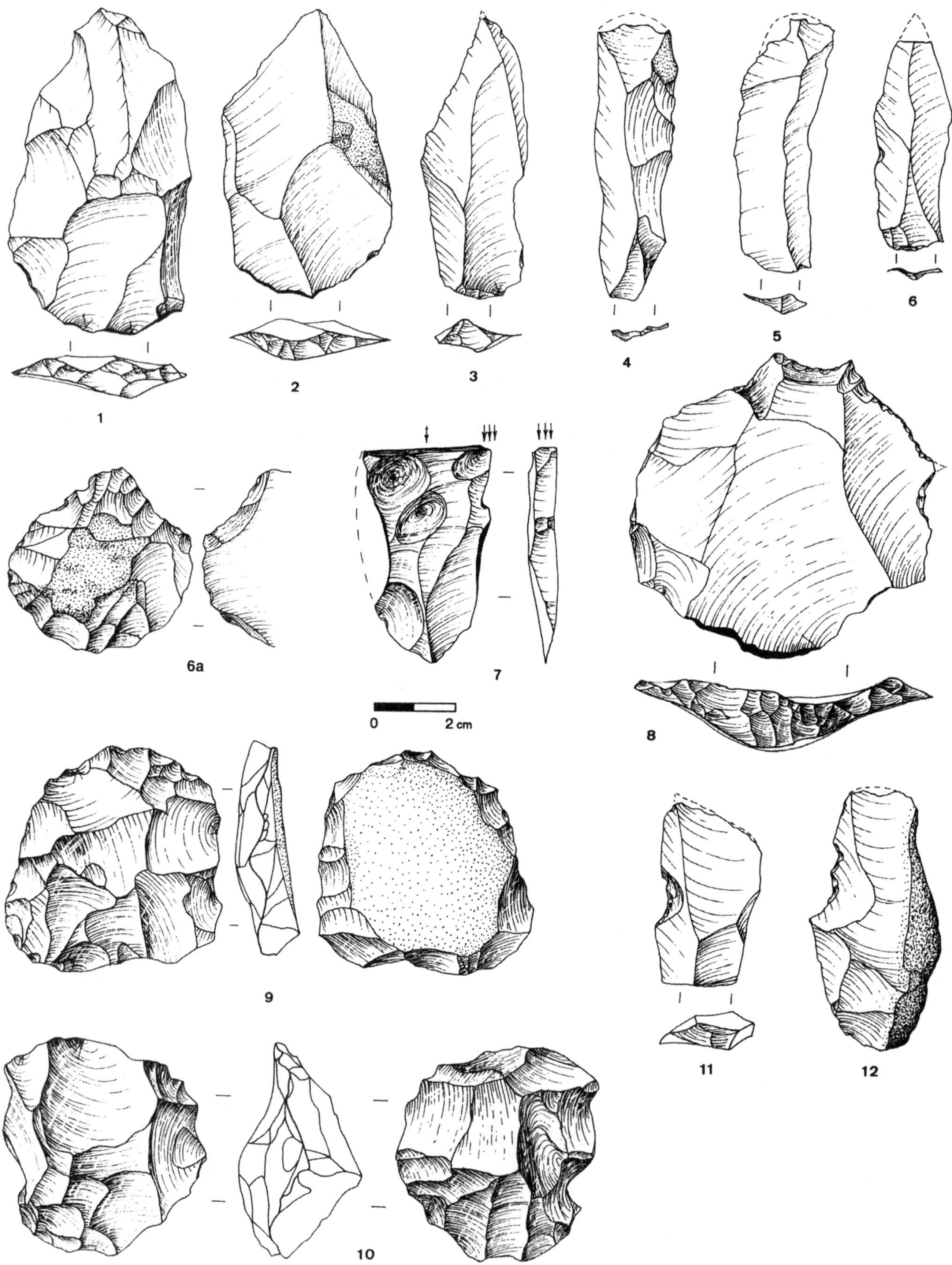

**Plate 21**  Layer XVf: 1–2: Levallois flakes; 3–6: Levallois blades; 6a: Core-on-flake; 7: Typical burin; 8: Two typical borers on Levallois flake; 9: Levallois core for flakes; 10: Discoidal core; 11: Notch; 12: Notch on a naturally backed knife.

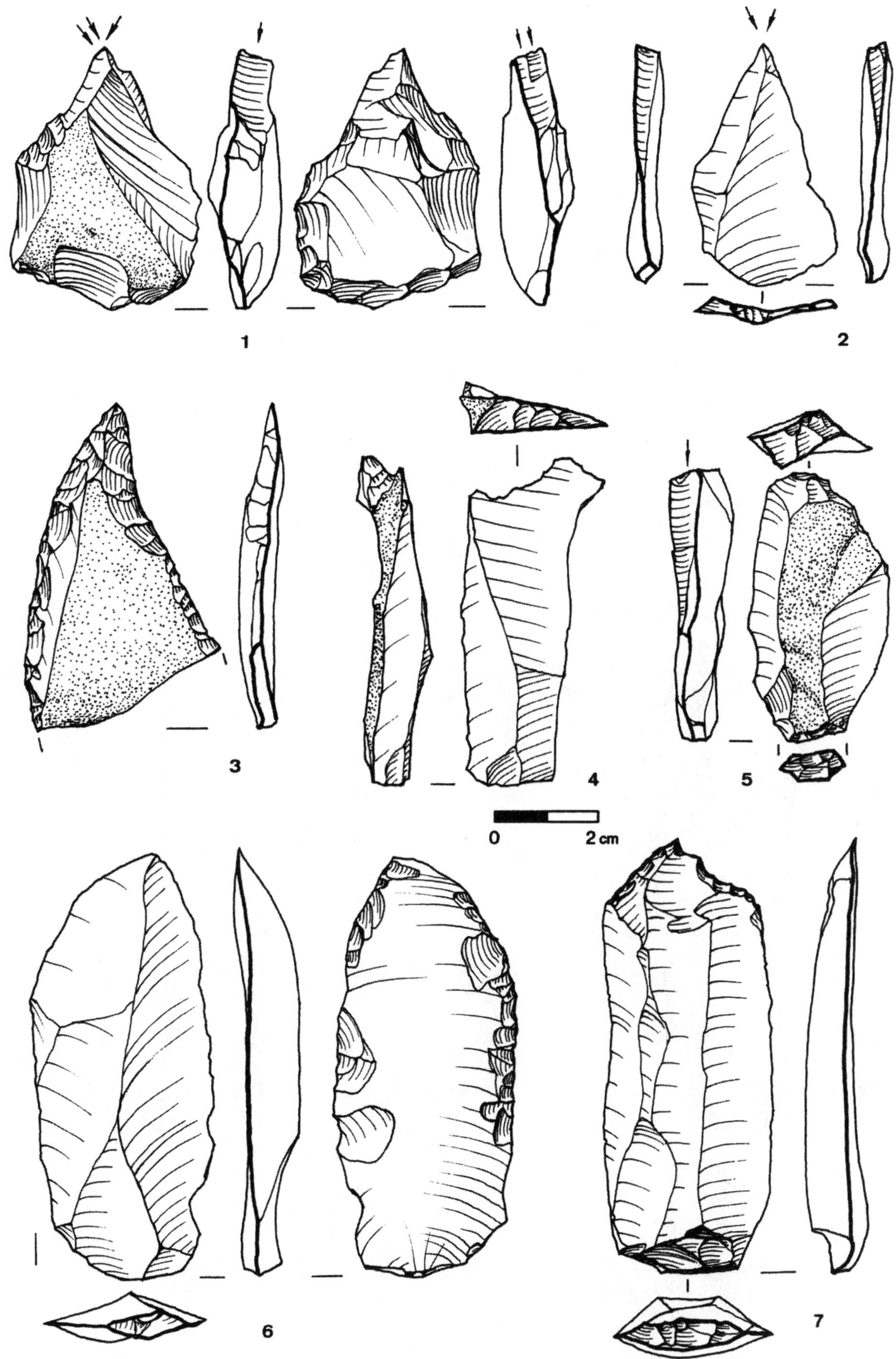

**Plate 22** Layer XV: 1–2, 5: Typical burins (#1 on a broken Levallois cores, #5 on truncation); 3: Offset scraper; 4: Naturally backed knife and truncation; 6: Side-scrapers on ventral face (double tool); 7: Alternately retouched beak.

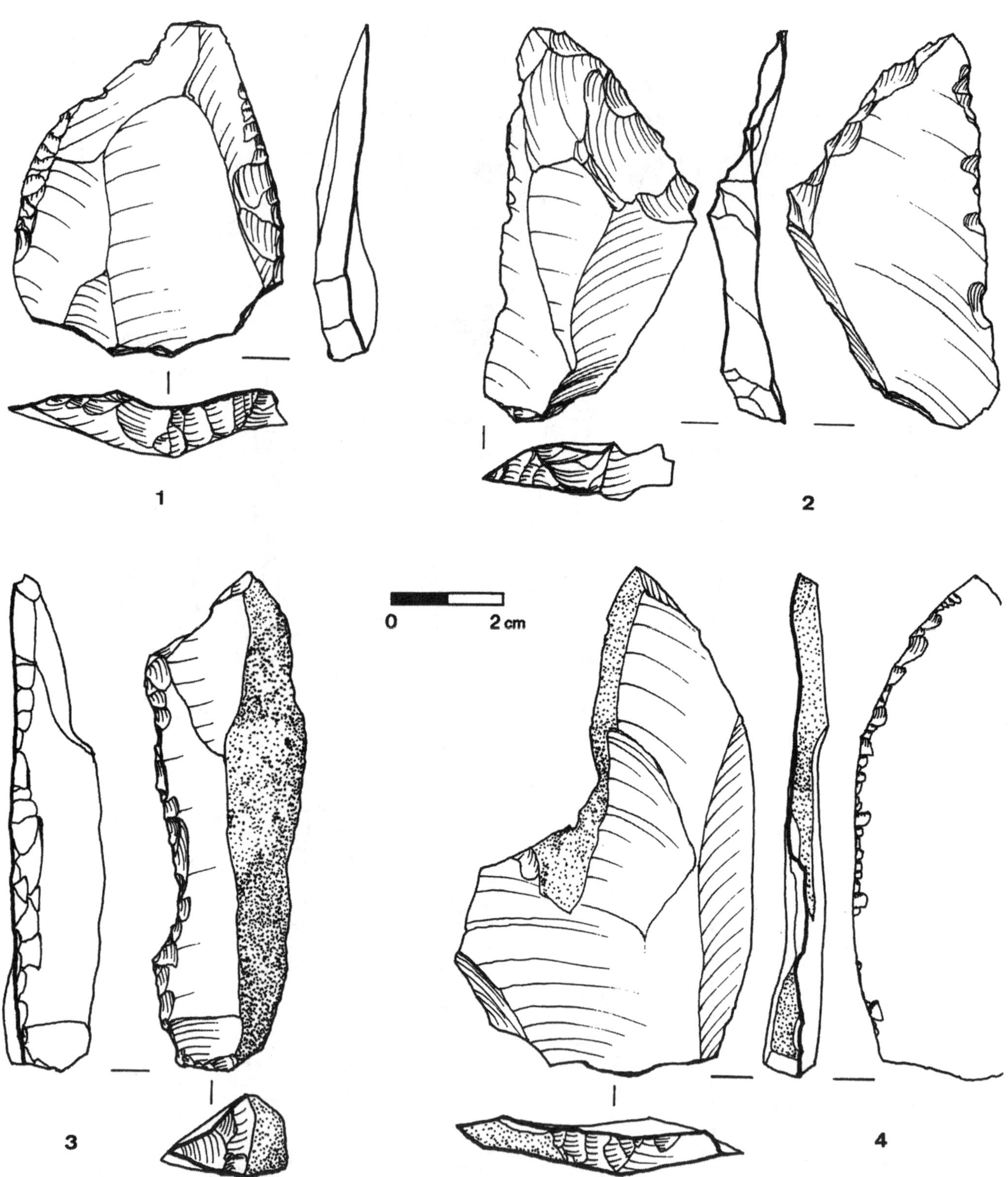

**Plate 23** Layer XV: 1: Convex double side-scraper; 2: Truncated flake (by Nahr Ibrahim technique) and signs of use; 3: Single concave side-scraper and a naturally backed knife; 4: Side-scraper on ventral face.

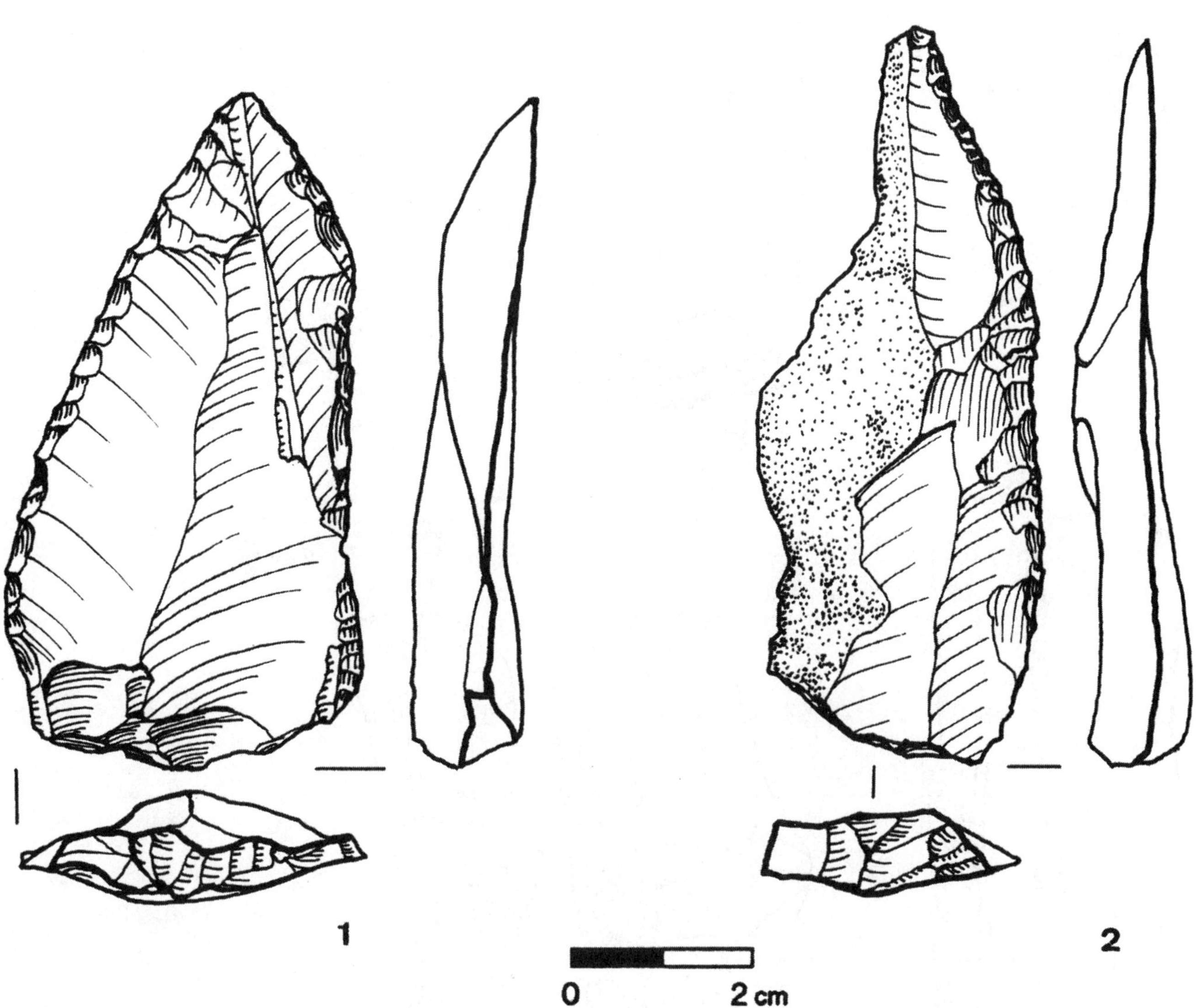

**Plate 24**  Layer XV: 1: Single concave side-scraper and backed knife; 2: single convex side-scraper.

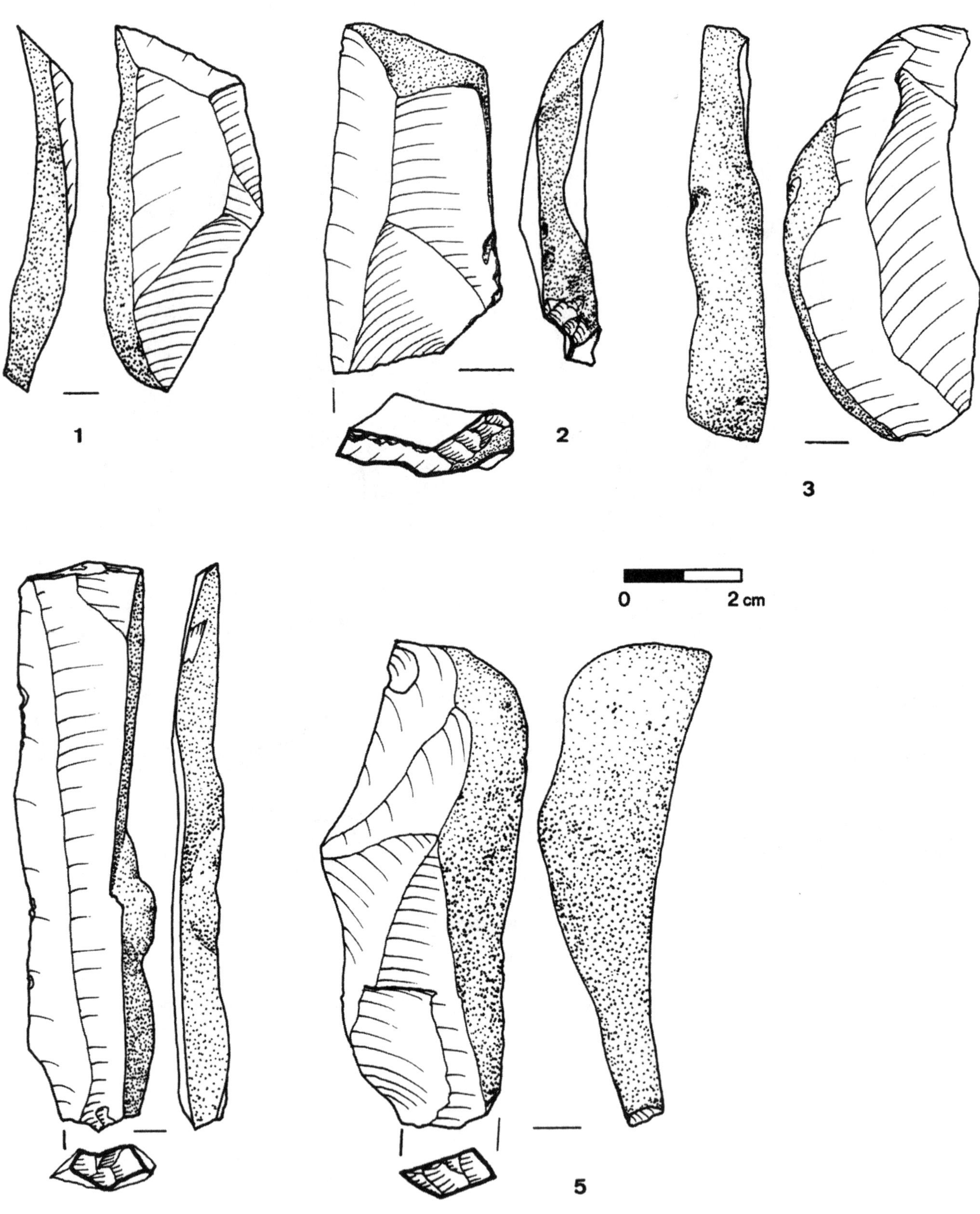

**Plate 25** Layer XV: 1–5: Naturally backed knives.

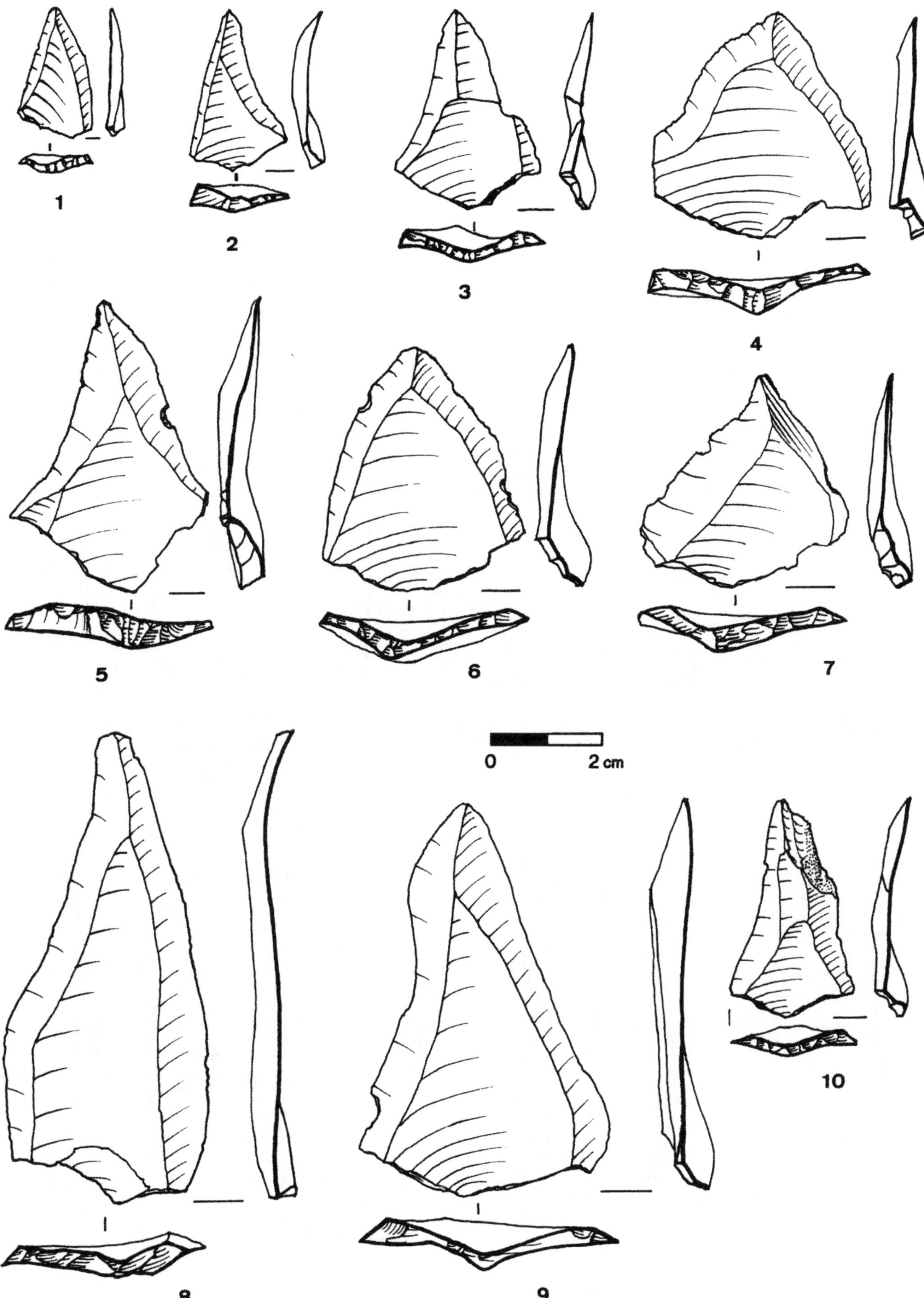

**Plate 26**    Layer XV: 1–10: Levallois points.

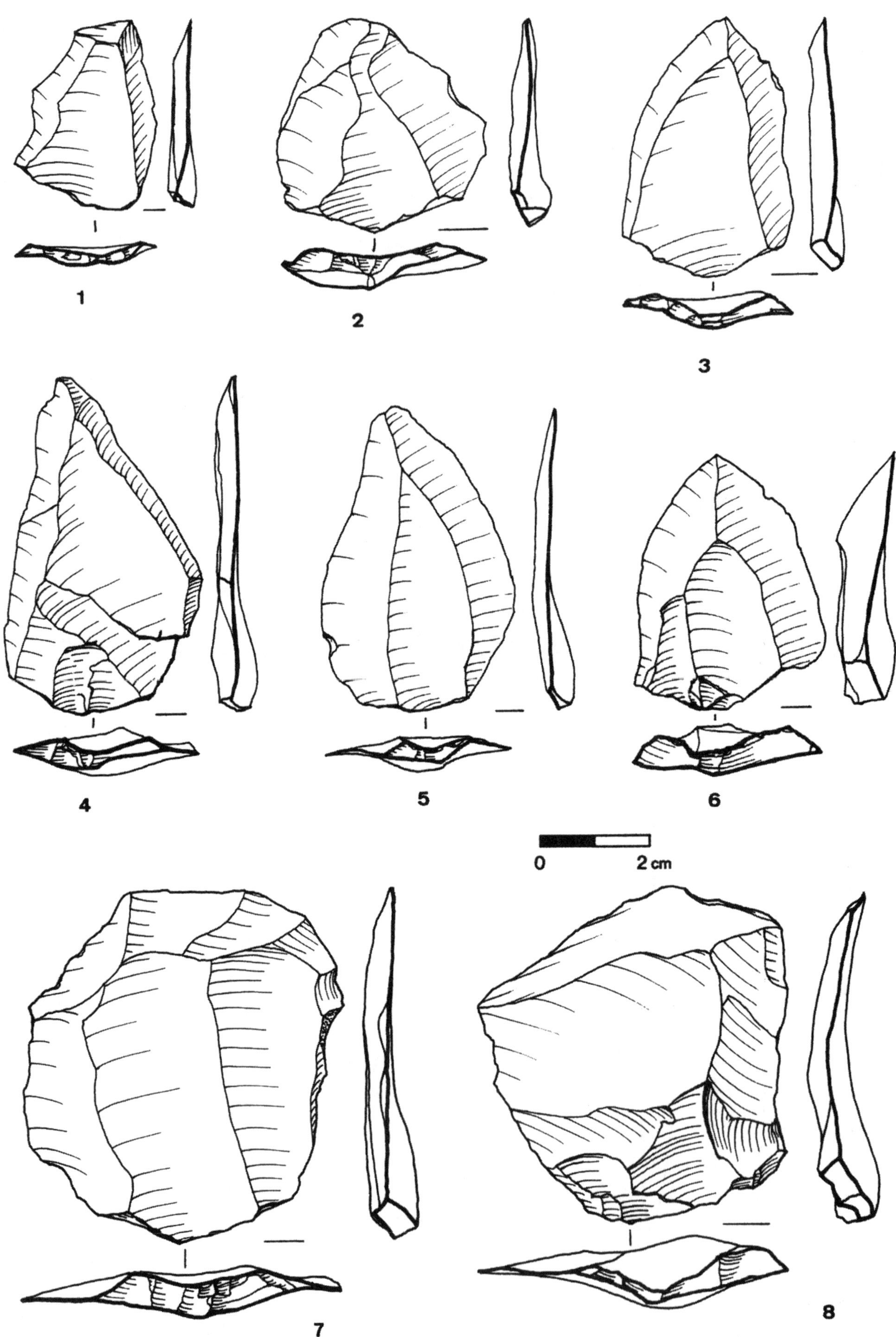

**Plate 27** Layer XV: 1–6: Levallois flakes (triangular); 7: Levallois flake (triangular) with signs of use; 8: Levallois flake.

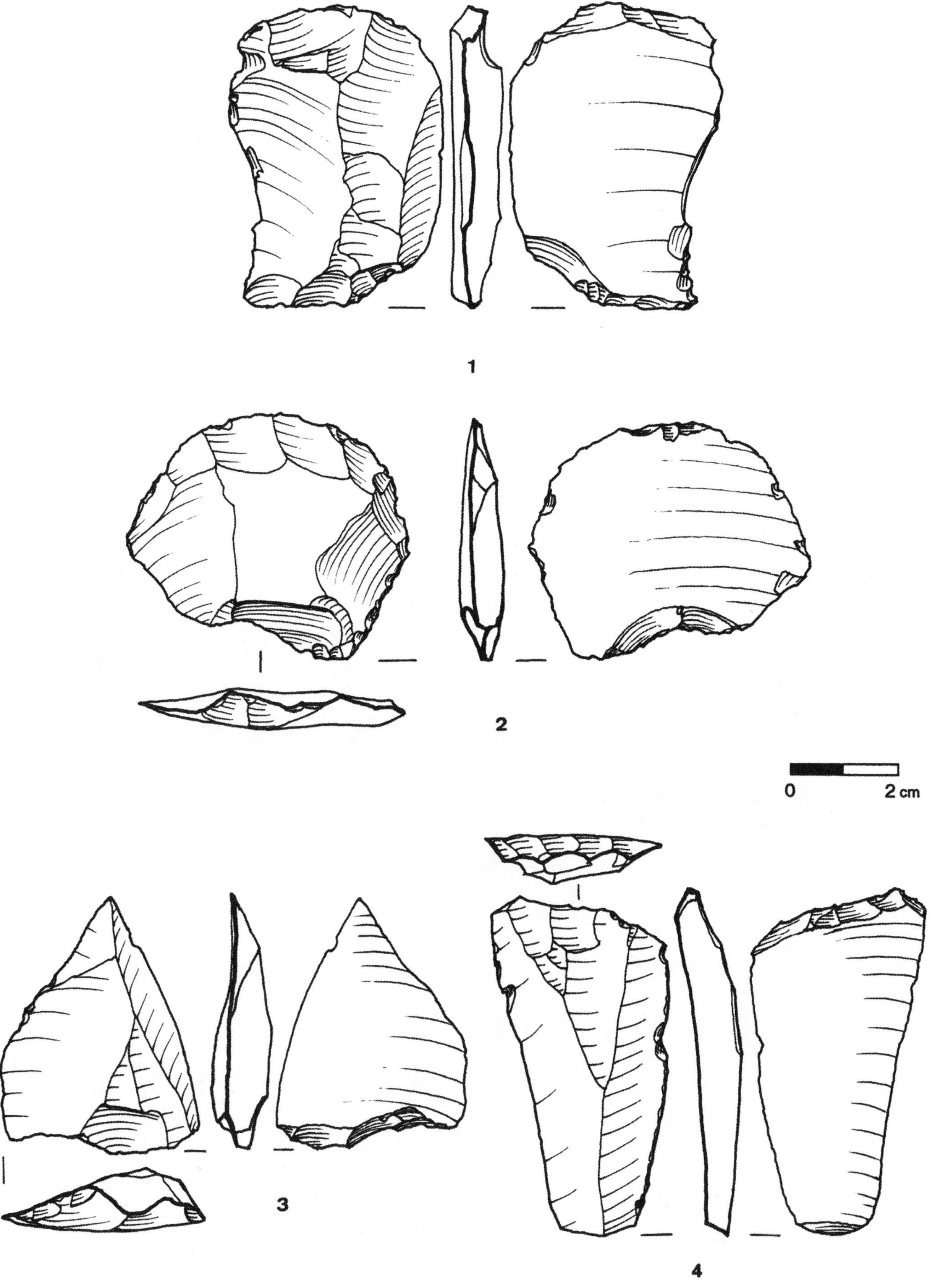

**Plate 28** Layer XV: 1: Double-truncated flake (by Nahr Ibrahim technique); 2, 4: Miscellaneous (modification by Nahr Ibrahim technique); 3: Miscellaneous (modification by Nahr Ibrahim technique) on Levallois point.

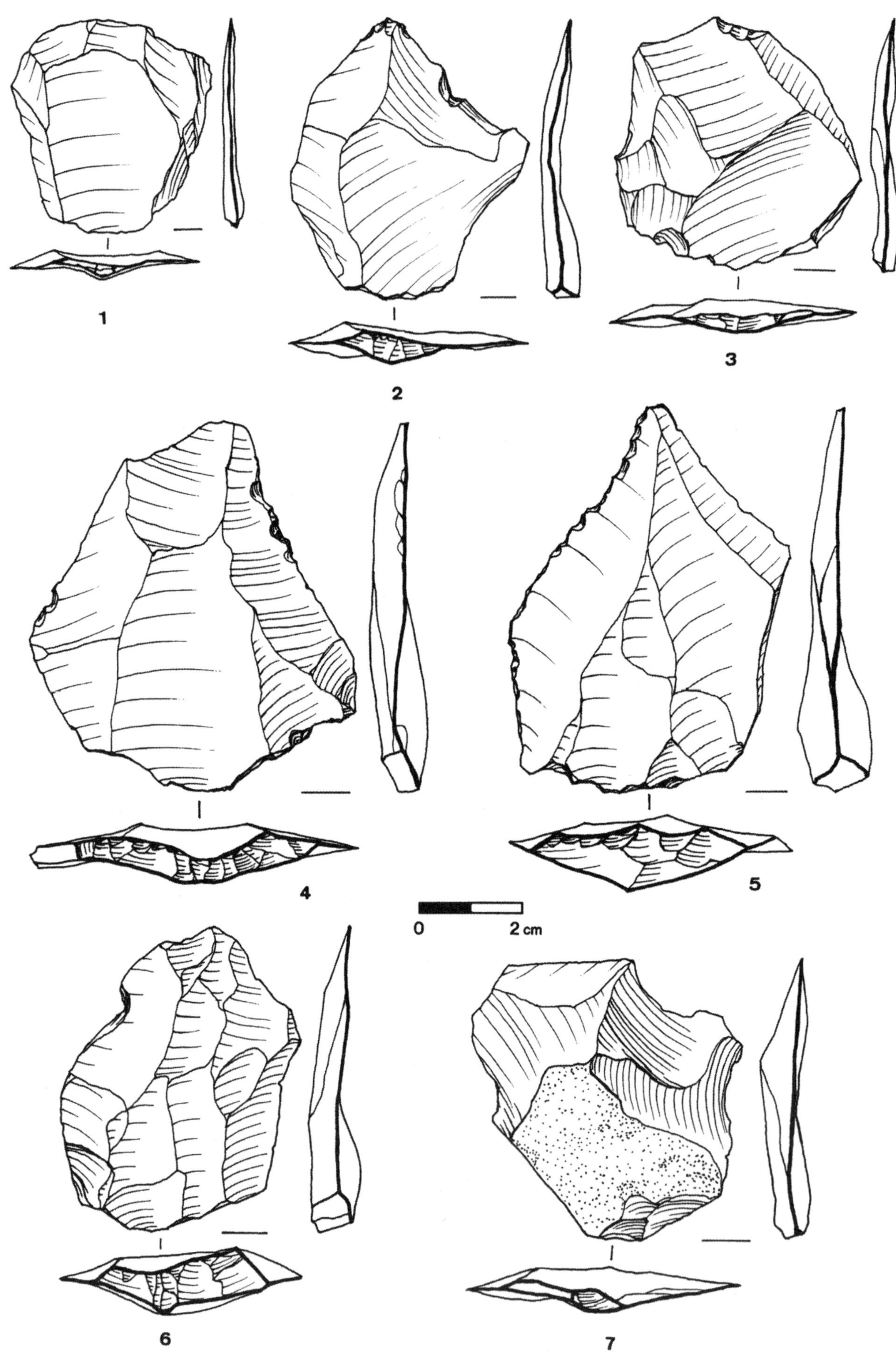

**Plate 29**  Layer XV: 1–4: Levallois flakes; 5: Denticulate (fine retouch) on Levallois flake; 7: Atypical Levallois flake.

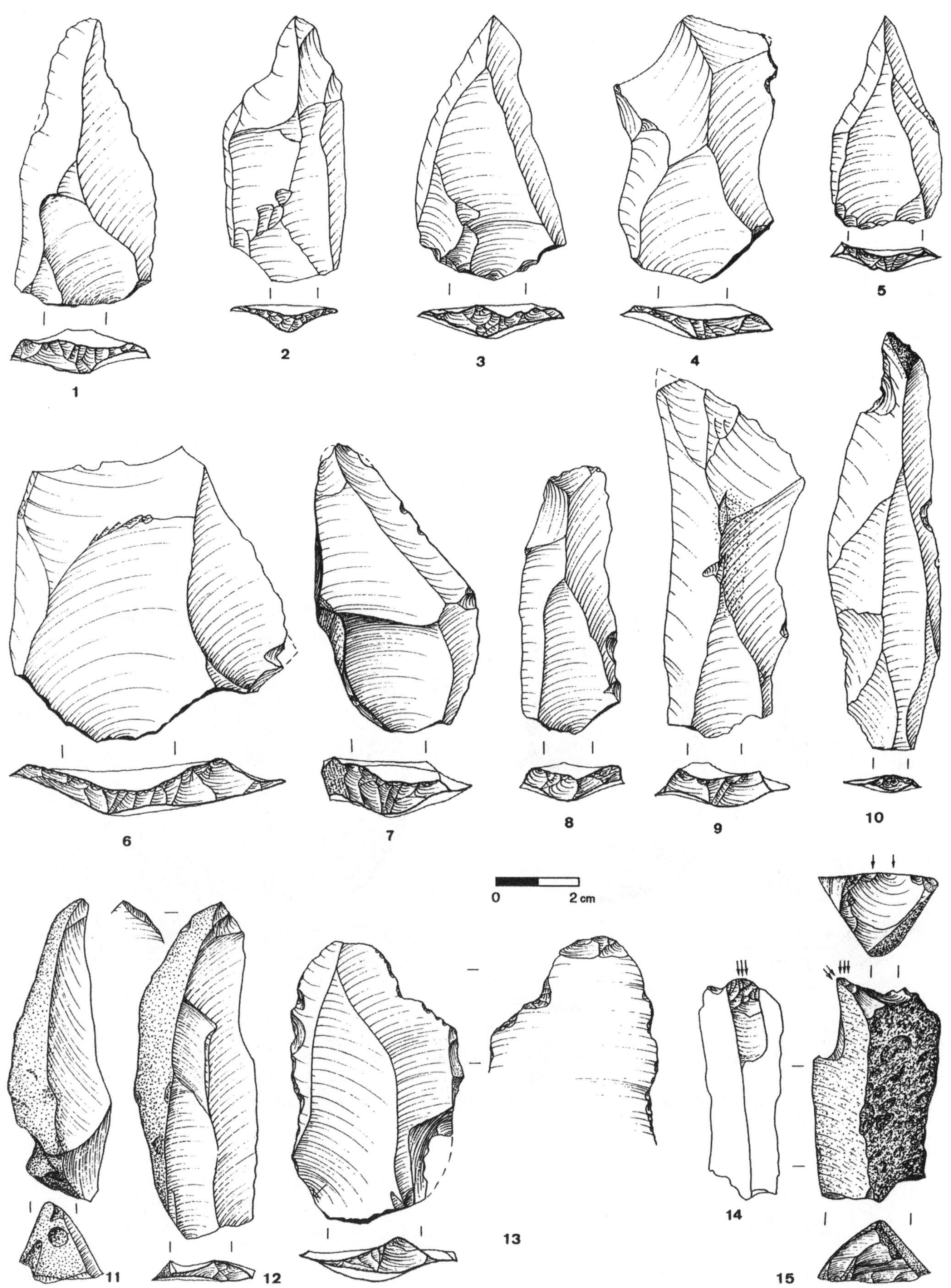

**Plate 30**   Layer XIV: 1, 3, 5: Levallois points; 2, 4, 6: Levallois flakes; 7: *éclat débordant*; 8–9: Levallois blade; 10: Notch on Levallois blade; 11: Naturally backed knife; 12: Burin on truncation and a naturally backed knife; 13: Denticulate and ventral thinning; 14: Typical burin and atypical end-scraper; 15: Typical burin on truncation.

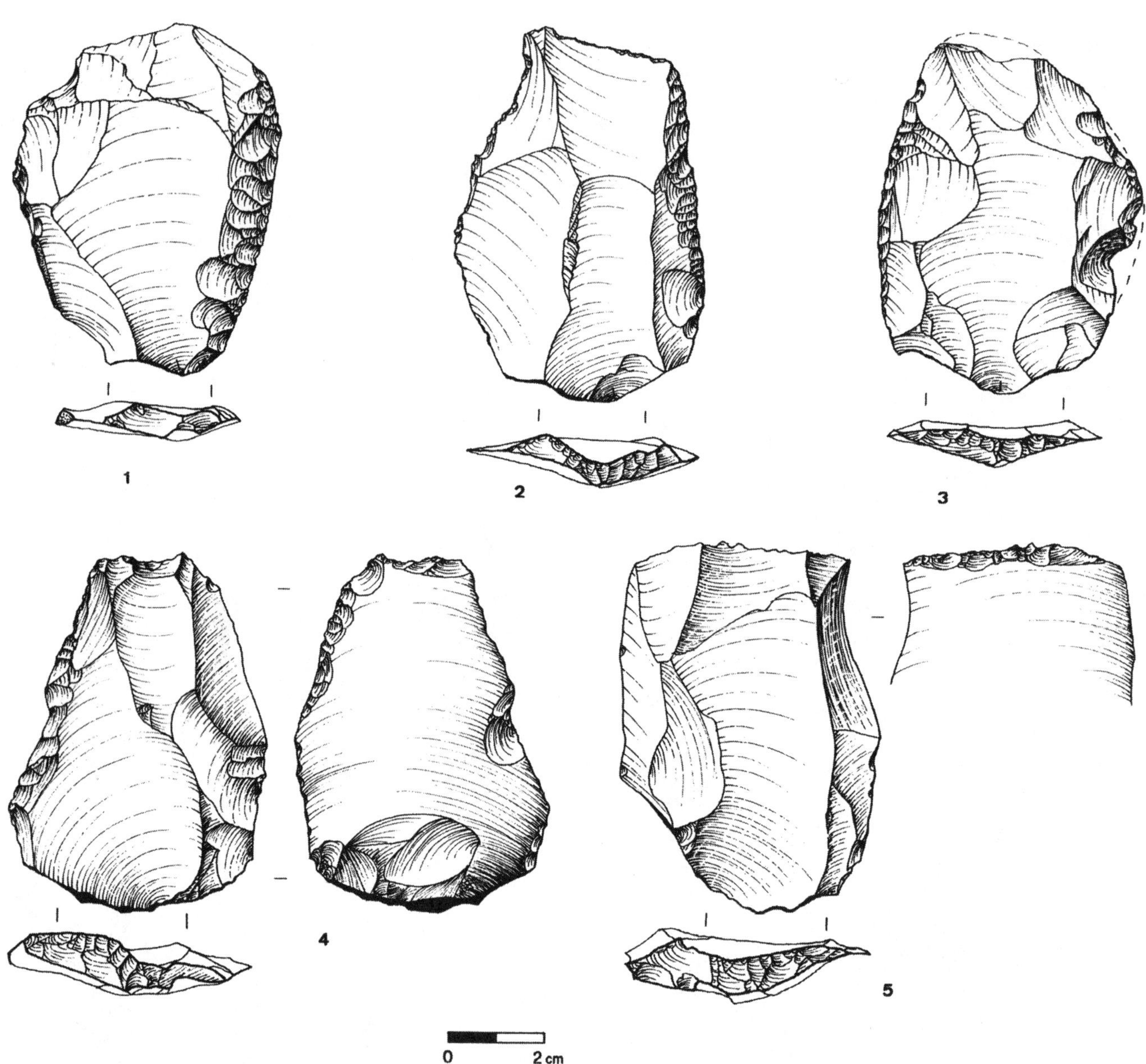



**Plate 31**  Layer XIII: 1, 3: Single convex side-scrapers and retouched flakes; 2: Single straight side-scraper and a denticulate; 4: Single concave side-scraper and a truncated flake (by Nahr Ibrahim technique) and a side-scraper on ventral face; 5: Truncated flake (by Nahr Ibrahim technique).

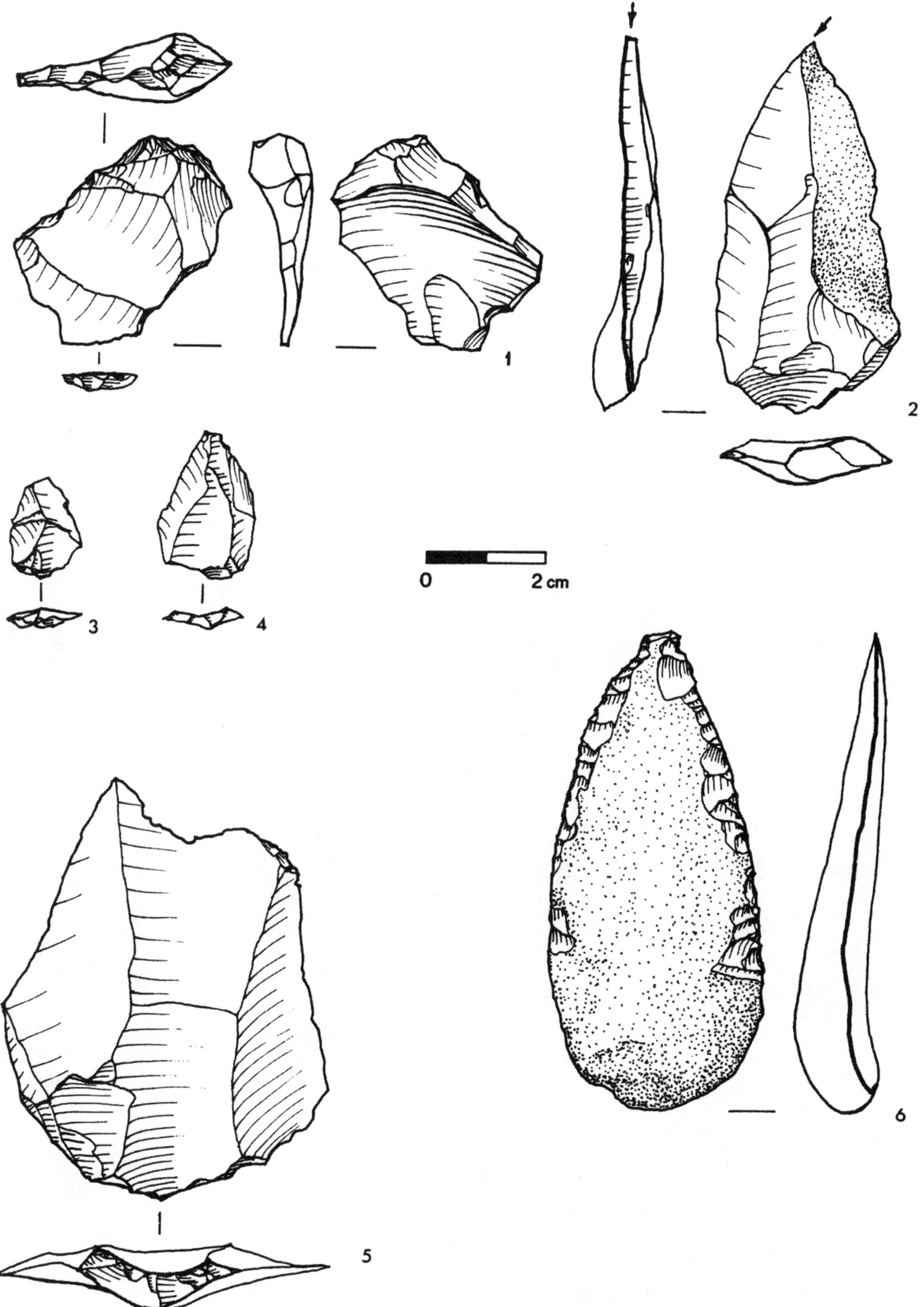

**Plate 32** Layer XIII: 1: *éclat débordant* and *outrepassé*; 2: Typical burin; 3, 5: Levallois flakes; 4: Levallois point; 6: Convergent side-scraper.

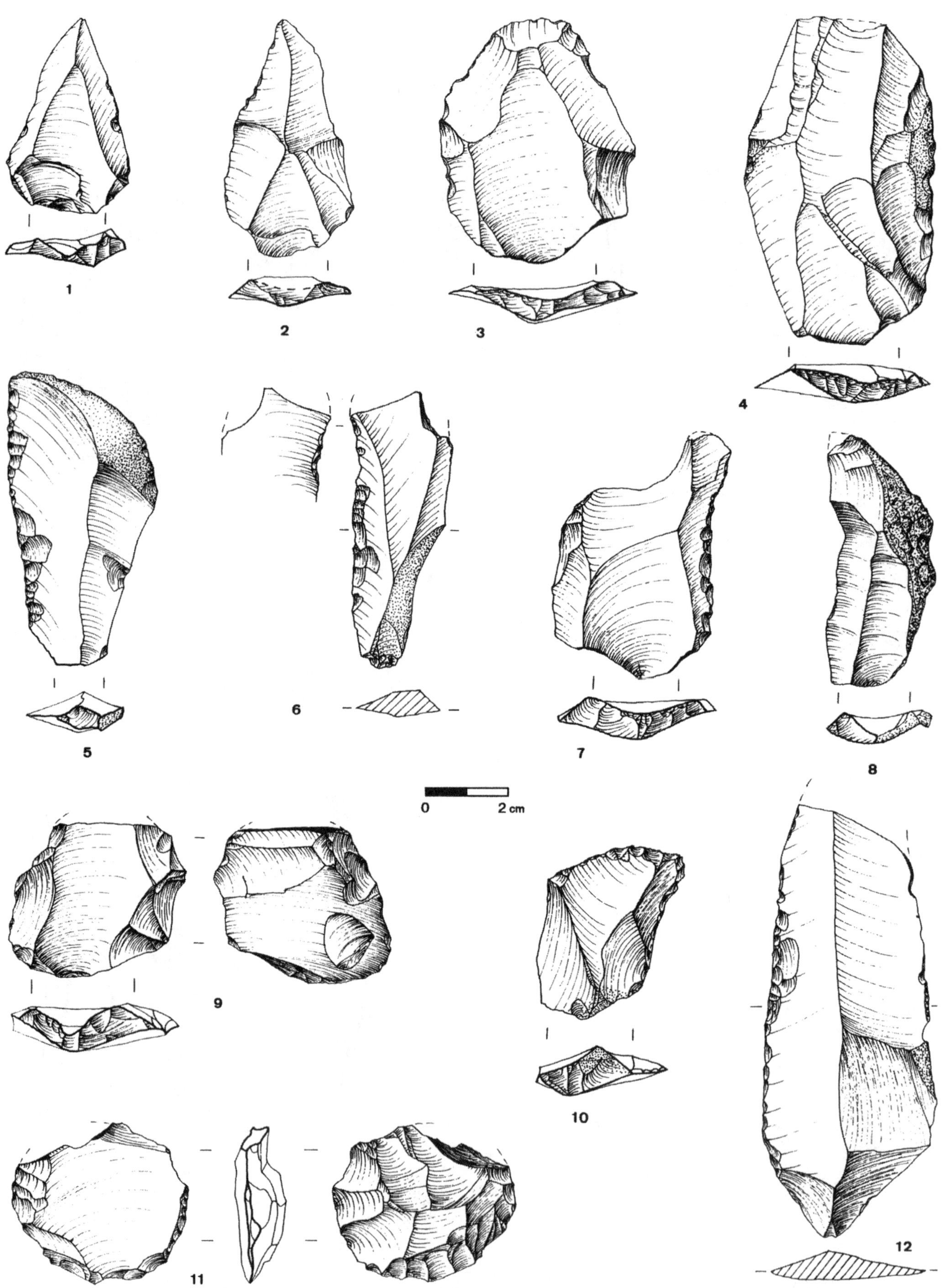

**Plate 33**   Layer XIII: 1: Levallois point; 2–3: Levallois flake (# 2 is a triangular flake); 4: Atypical Levallois flake with signs of use; Single straight side-scraper; 6: Single straight side-scraper and notch on the ventral face; 7: Denticulate; 8: Naturally backed knife on Levallois flake; 99, 11: Cores-on-flakes; 10: Offset scraper; single concave side-scraper with signs of use.

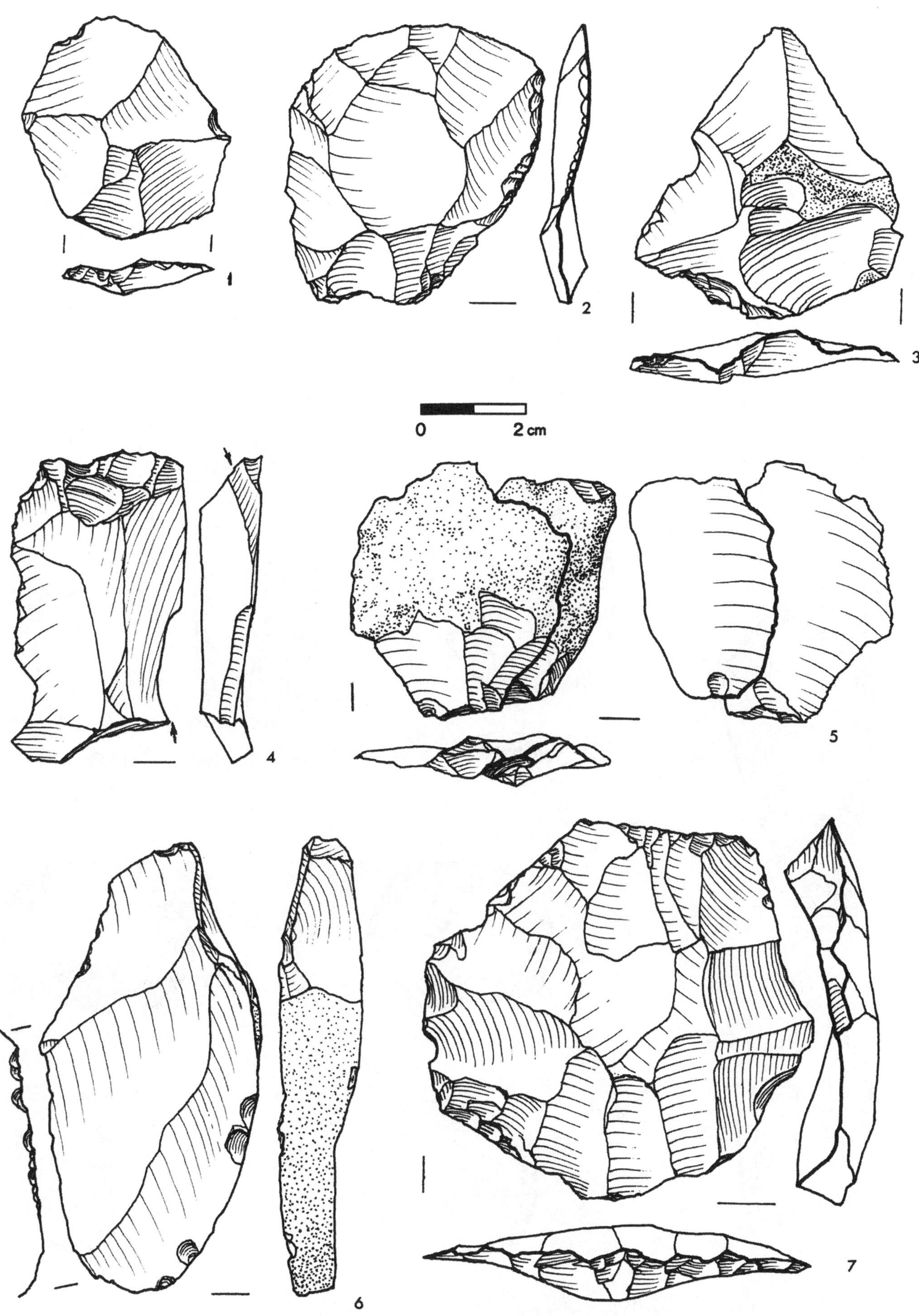

**Plate 34** Layer XII: 1: Levallois flake; 2: Single concave side-scraper; 3: Levallois point; 4: Double burin (both typical); 5: Conjoining (non-Levallois) flakes; 6: Naturally backed knife; 7: *éclat outrepassé*.

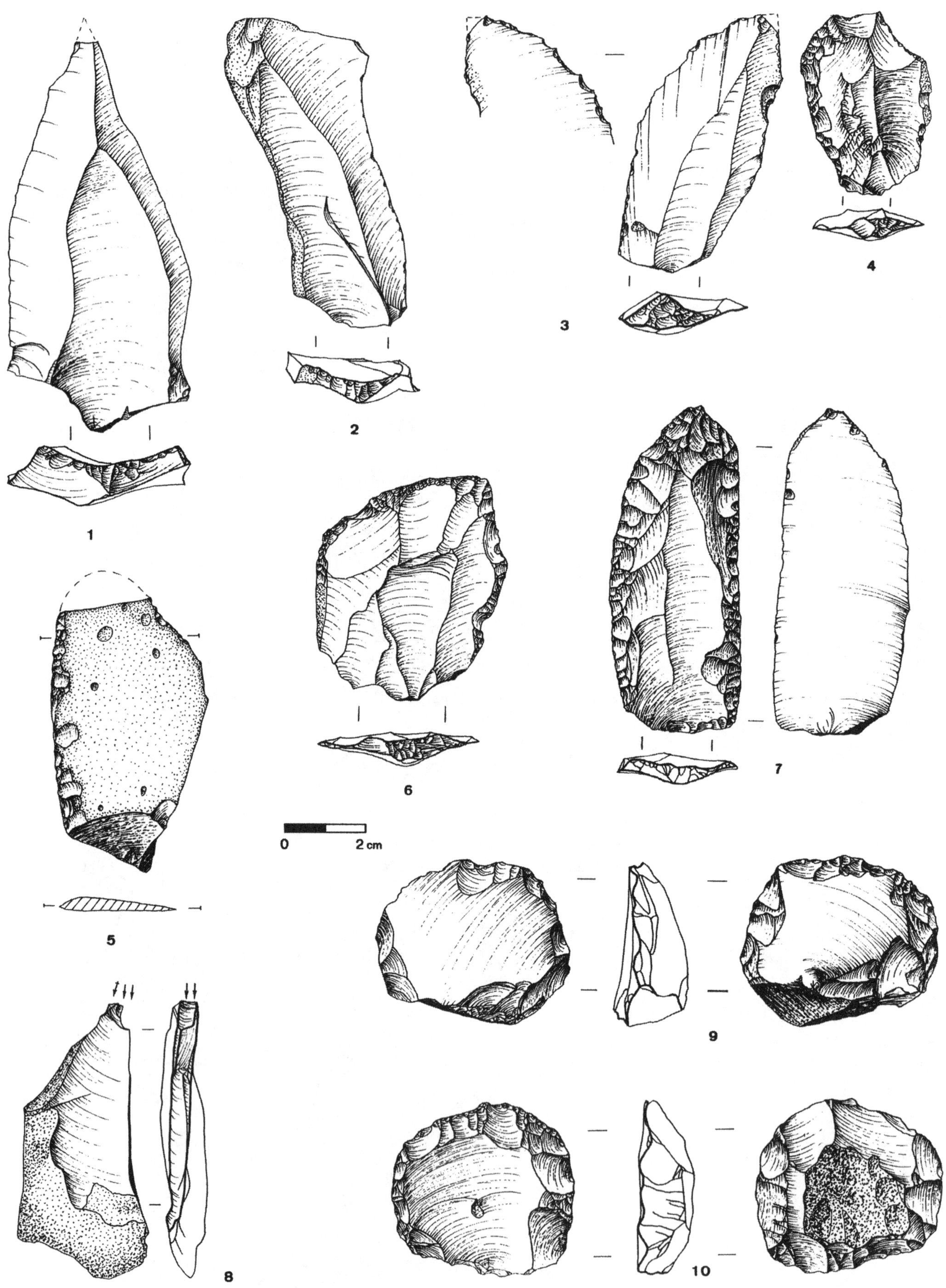

**Plate 35** Layer XII: 1: Levallois point; 2: Naturally backed knife; 3: Notch; 4–5: Single convex side-scraper; 6: Offset side-scraper; 7: Convergent side-scraper; 8: Typical burin; 9–10: Levallois cores for flakes.

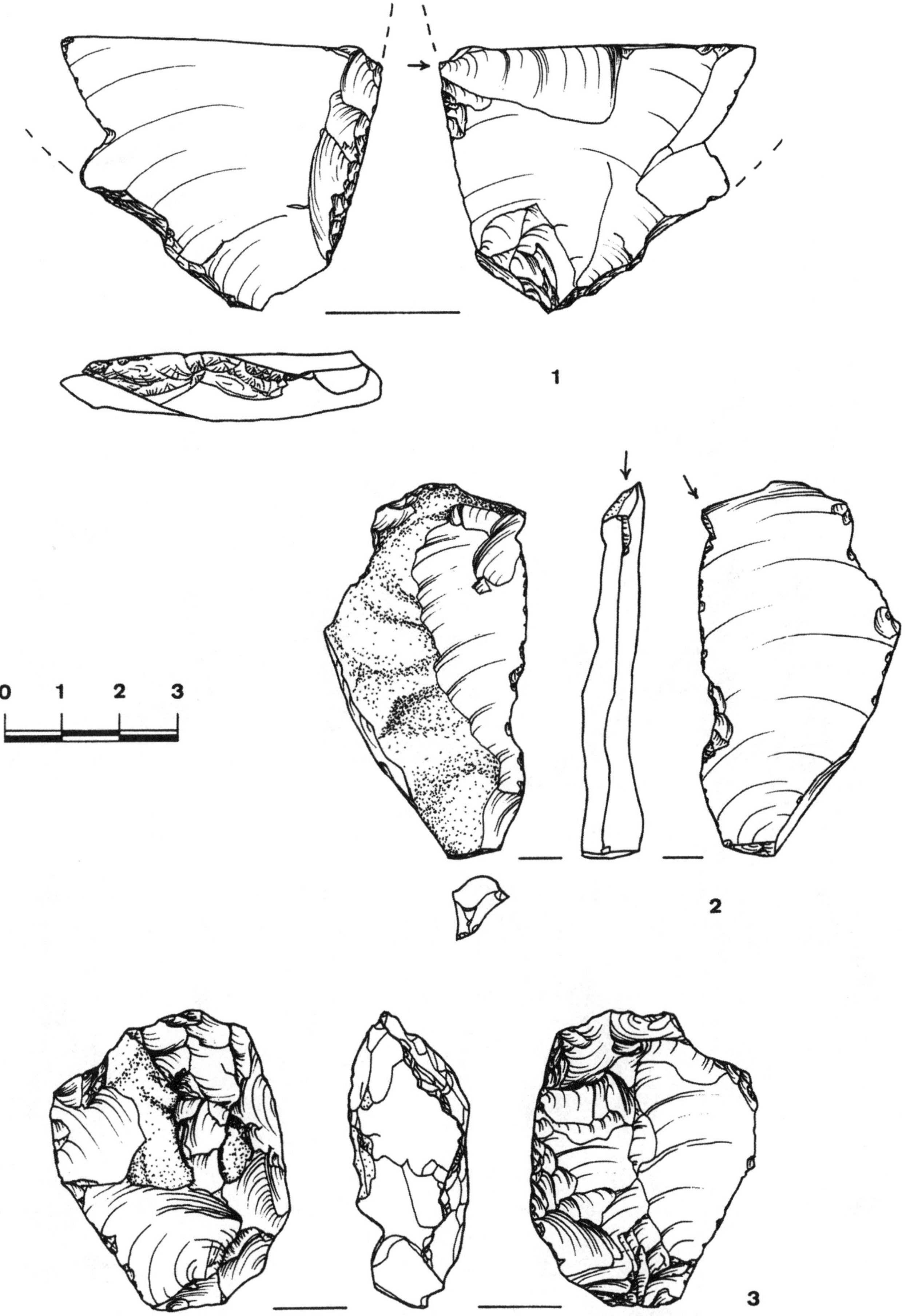

**Plate 36** Layer XI: 1–2: Typical burins (#1 is a ventral burin made on a previous side-scraper); 3: *éclat débordant* and *outrepassé*.

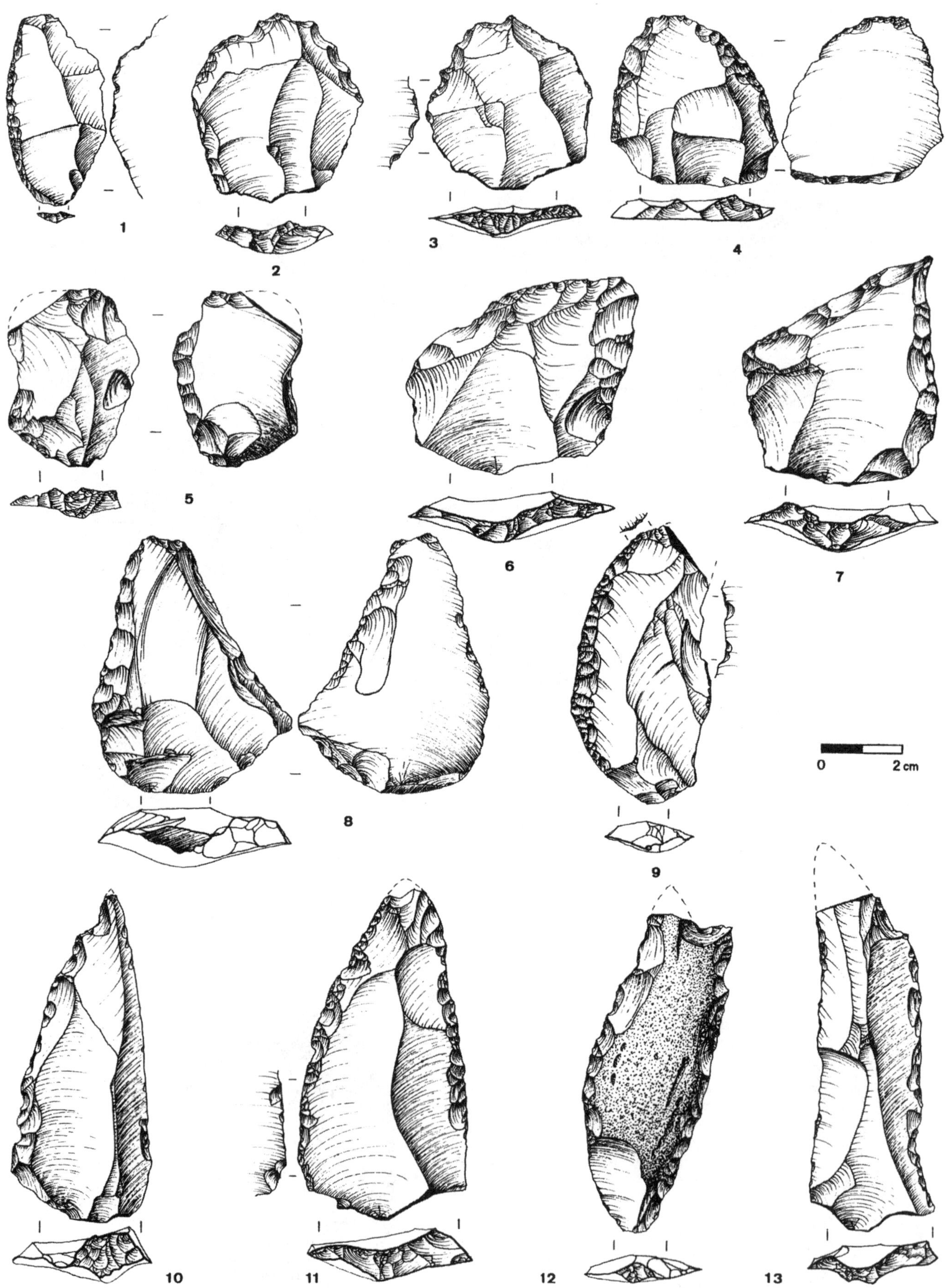

**Plate 37** Layer XI: 1, 9–10, 13: Single convex side-scrapers (# 10 is denticulated); 2–3: Denticulates; 4: Double convex side-scraper and truncated flake (by Nahr Ibrahim technique); 5: Side-scraper on the ventral face and truncated flake (by Nahr Ibrahim technique); 6–7: Offset scrapers; 8: Core-on-flake made on a previous double alternately retouched side-scraper); 11–12: Double convex-concave side-scraper.

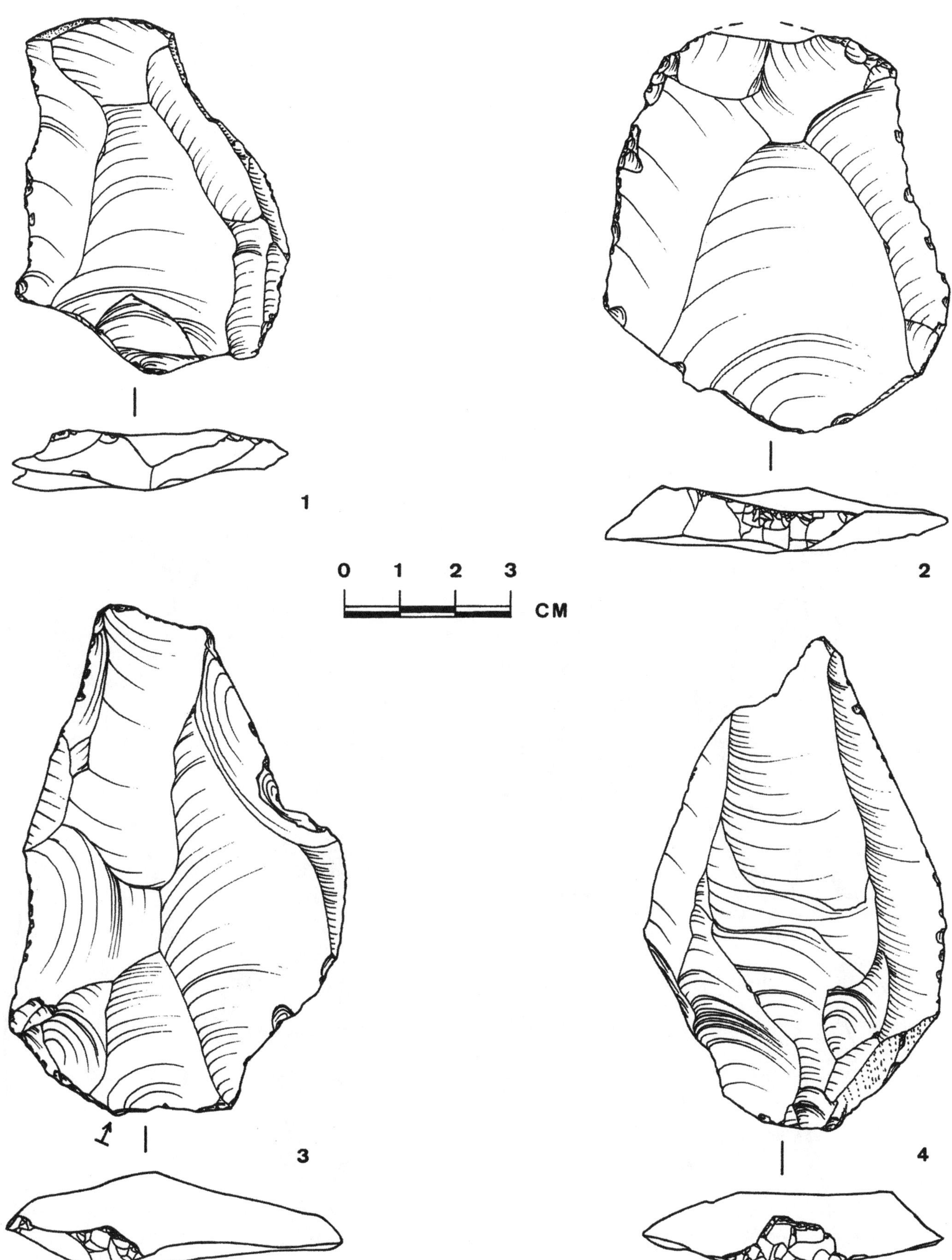

**Plate 38**  Layer XI: 1–4: Levallois flakes.

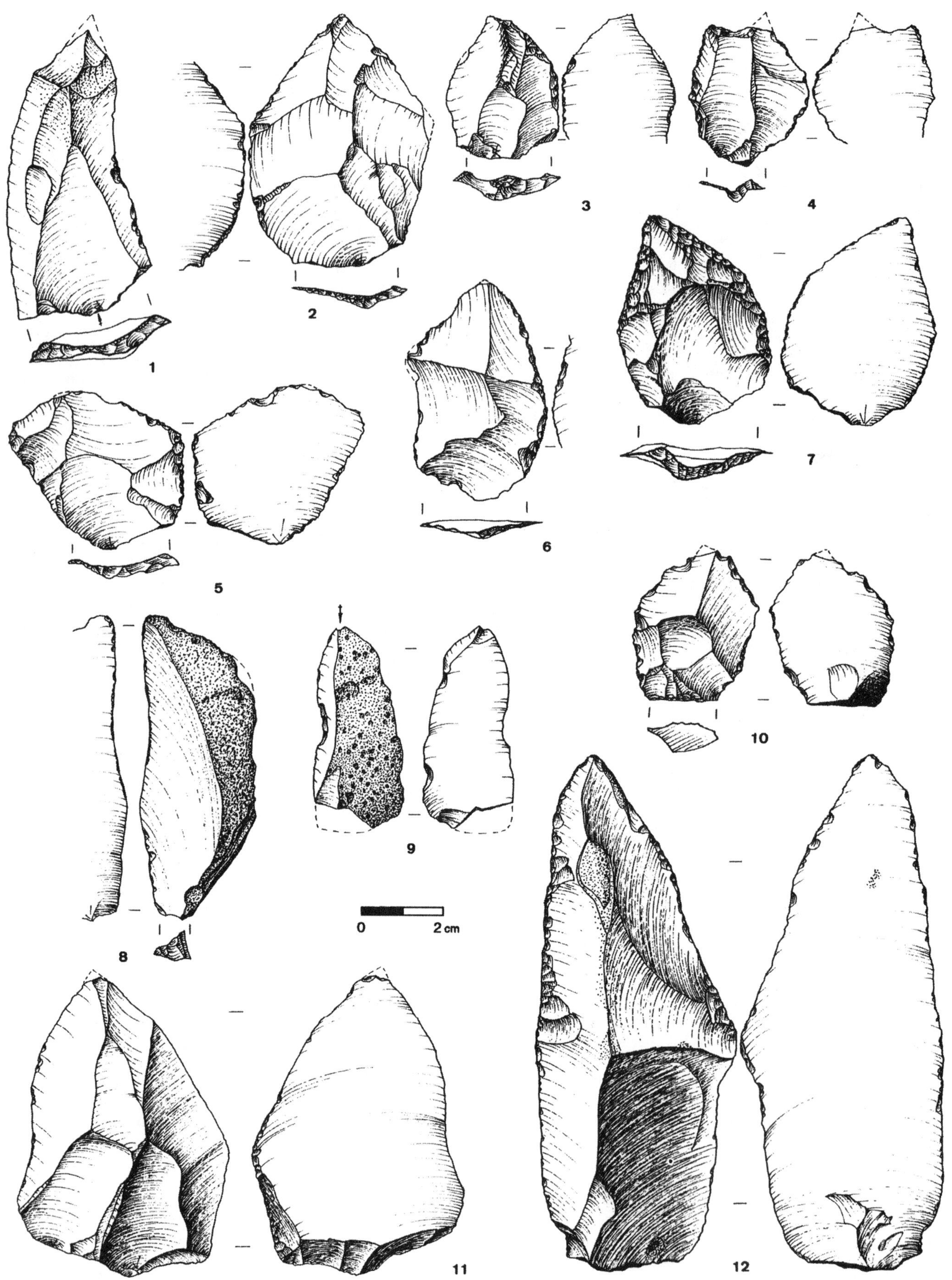

**Plate 39**  Layer X: 1: Levallois point; 2–3, 5: Levallois flakes; 6: Retouched Levallois flake; 7: Offset scraper; 8: Naturally backed knife; 9: Notch; 10: Flake with signs of use; 11: Core-on-flake; 12: Single straight scraper on a retouched flake.

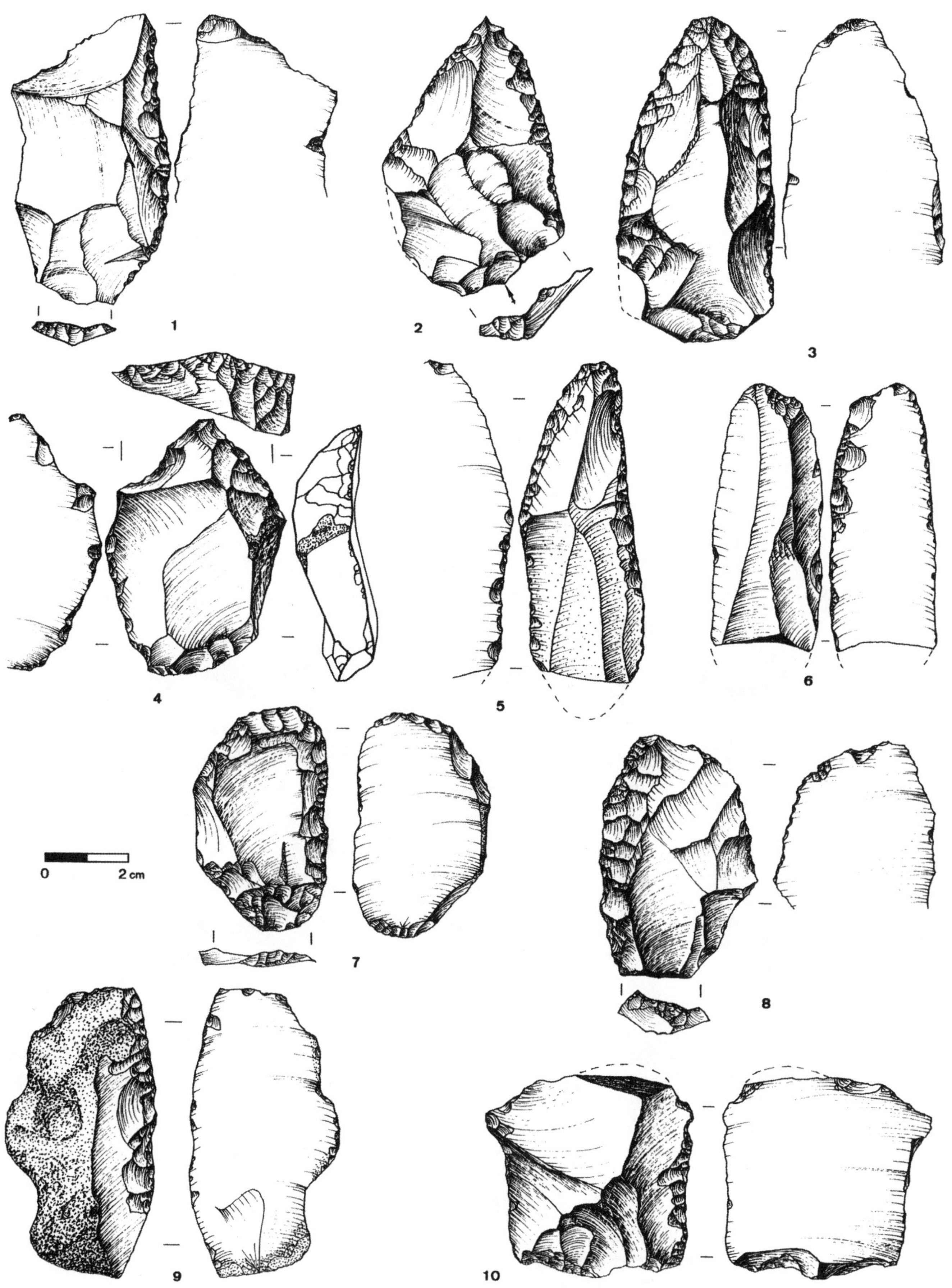

**Plate 40**  Layer X: 1: Burin and single convex side-scraper; 2: Convergent scraper; 3: Convergent scraper and truncation on the ventral face; 4: Typical end-scraper and a notch; 5: Double straight-convex side-scraper; 6: Side-scraper on ventral face and truncation; 7, 10: Cores-on-flakes and single straight side-scrapers; 8: Single convex side-scraper and retouch on ventral face; 9: Single convex side-scraper.

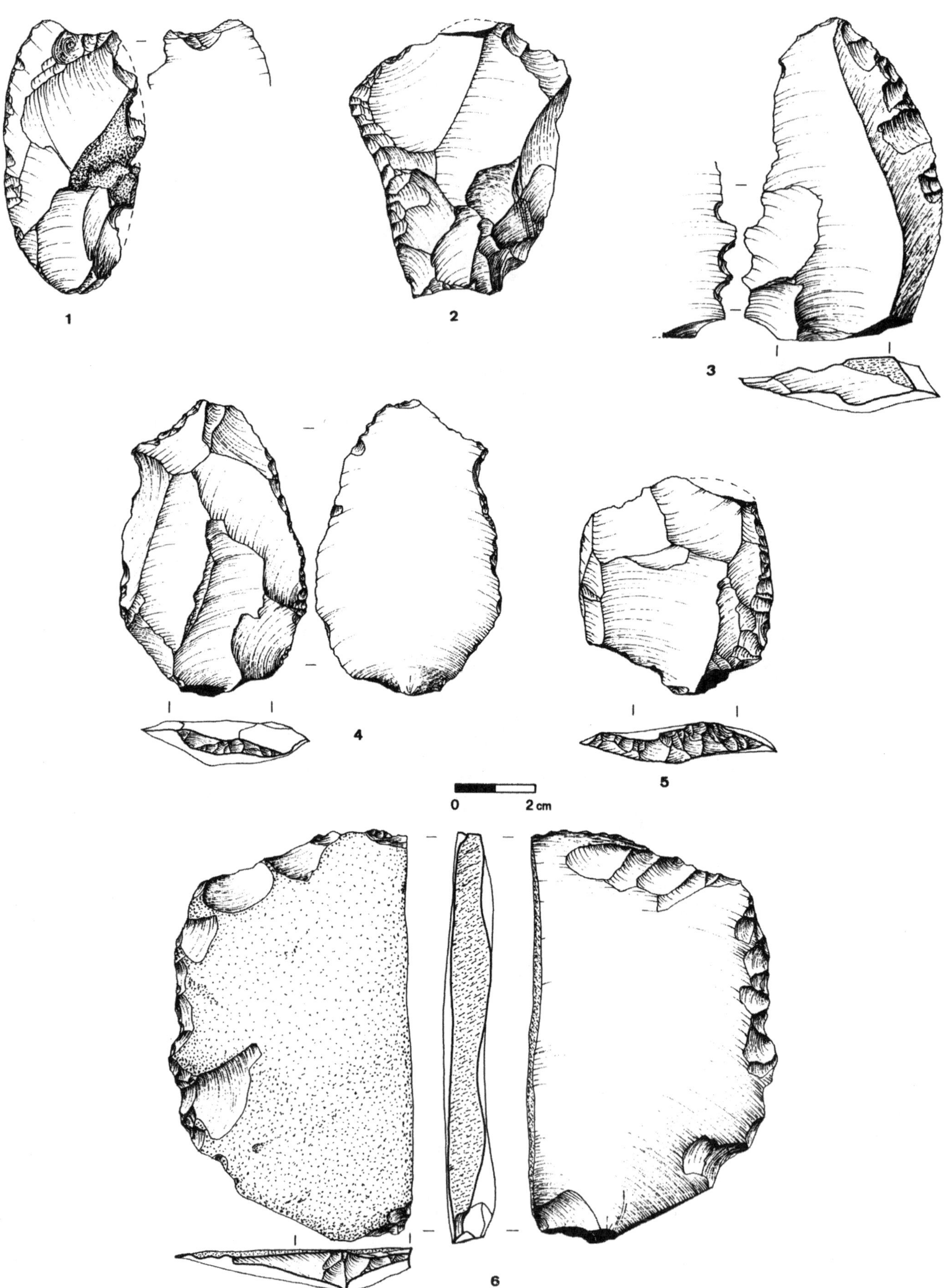

**Plate 41**  Layer IX: 1, 5: Single convex side-scraper; 2: Single concave side-scraper; 3: Single convex side-scraper and a denticulate on ventral face; 4: Retouched flake; 6: Side-scraper on ventral face.

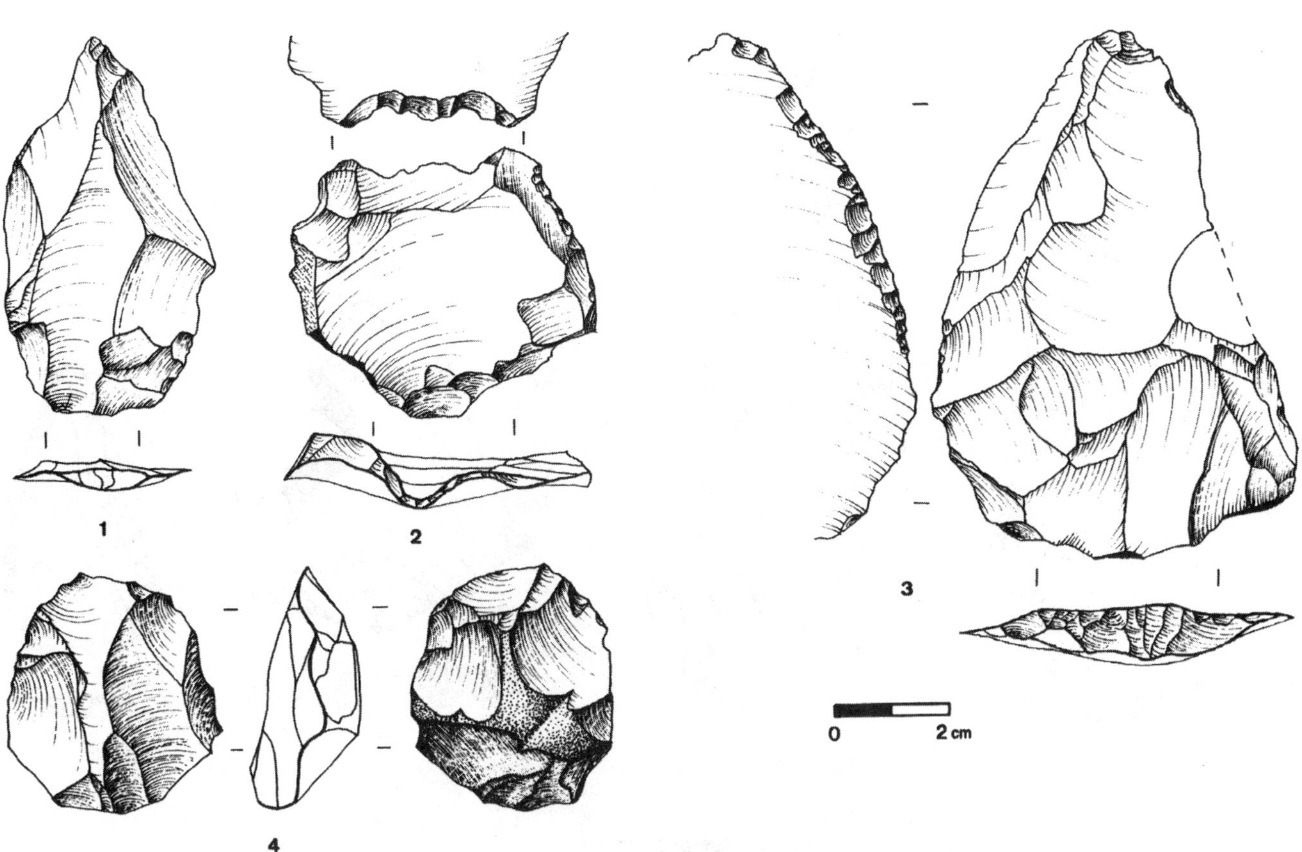

**Plate 42** Layer VII: 1: Levallois flake; 2: Truncated retouched flake; 3: Side-scraper on ventral face; 4: Levallois core for flakes.

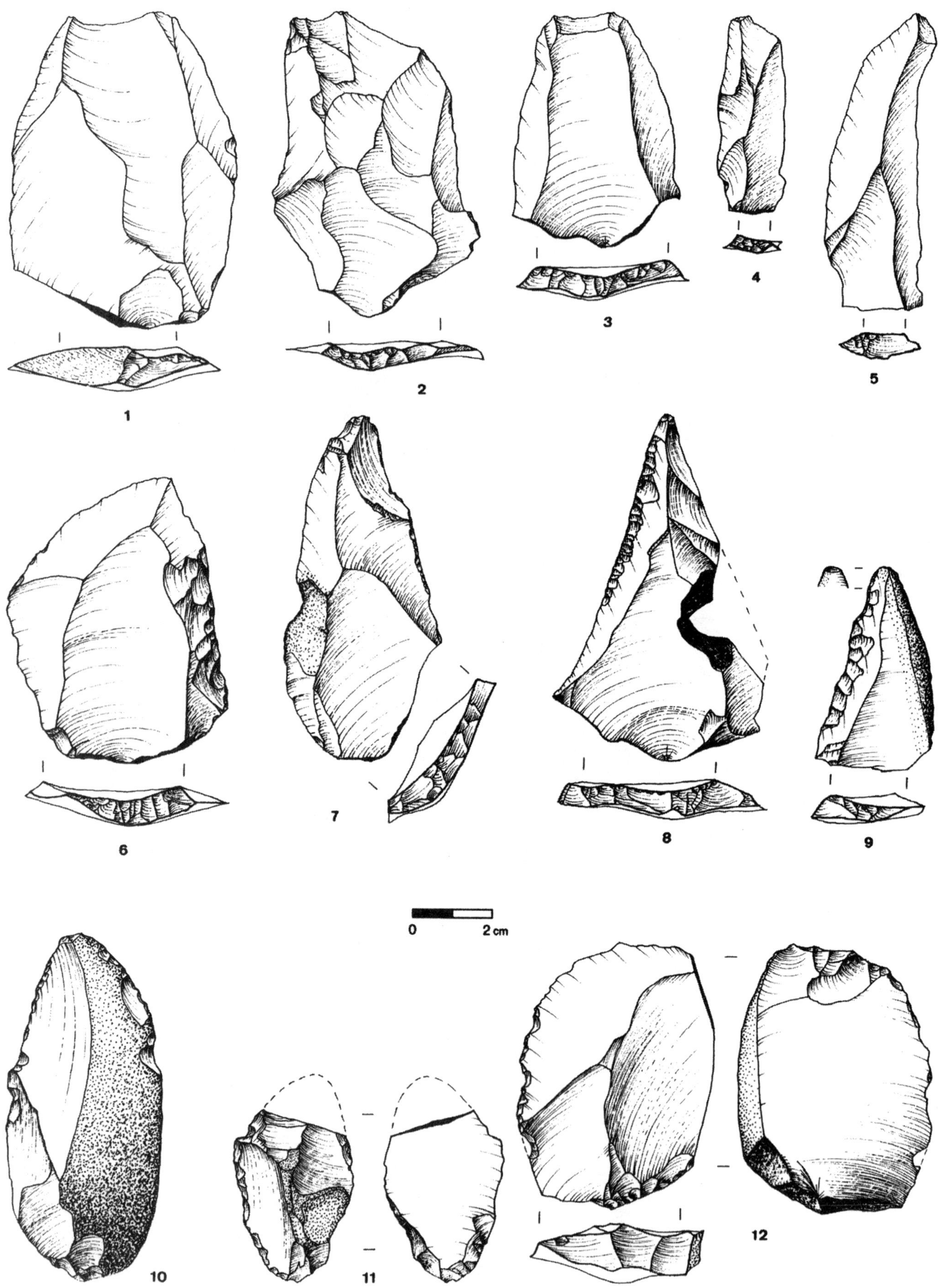

**Plate 43**   Layer VIIa: 1–3: Levallois flakes; 4–5: Levallois blades; 6: Single convex side-scraper; 7: End-notch on a retouched Levallois flake; 8–9: Single concave side-scrapers; 10: Retouched flake; 11: Denticulate on a basally thinned flake; 12: Levallois flake with isolated removals on the ventral face. (#2 and 5 are from Layer VIIb)

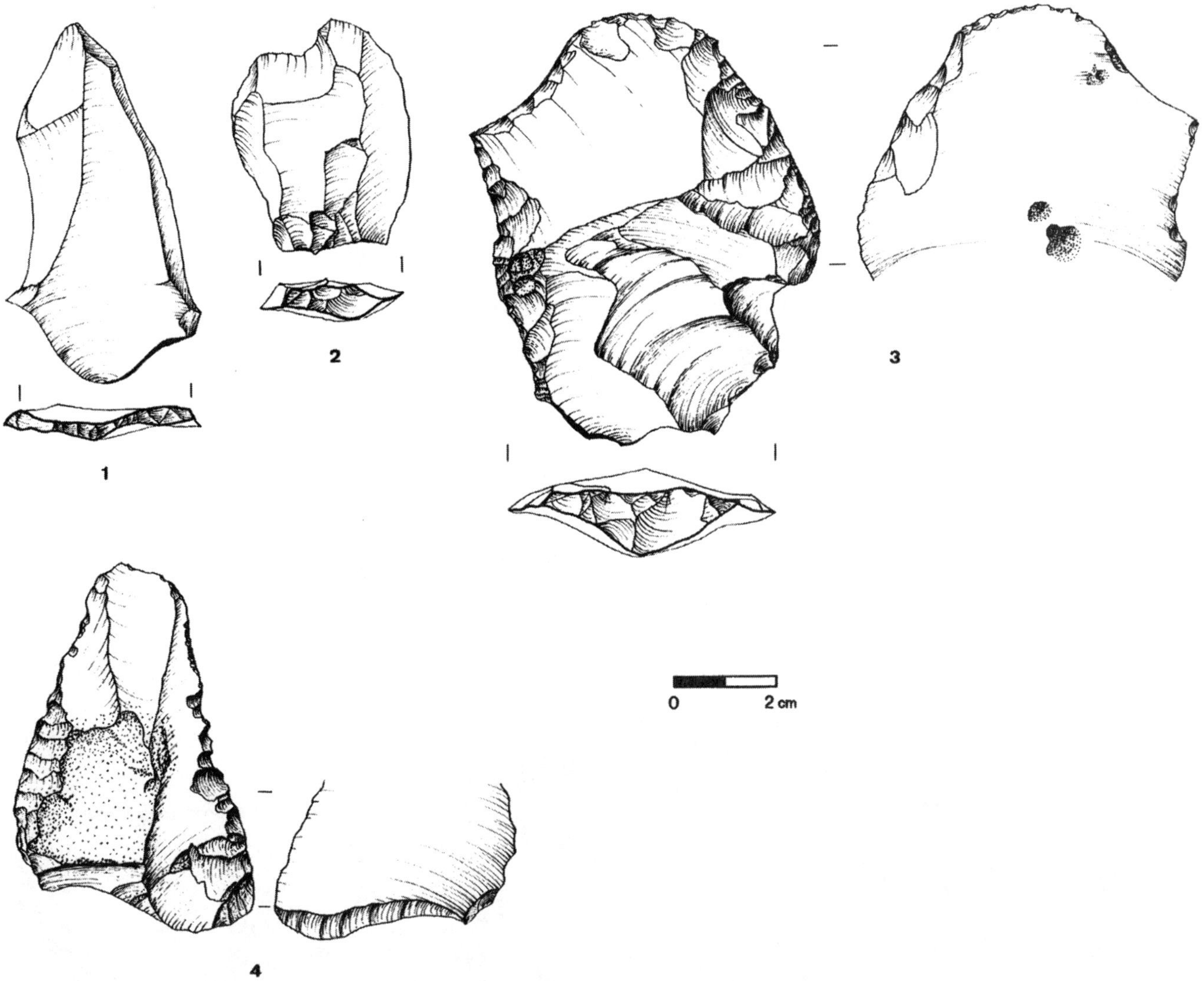

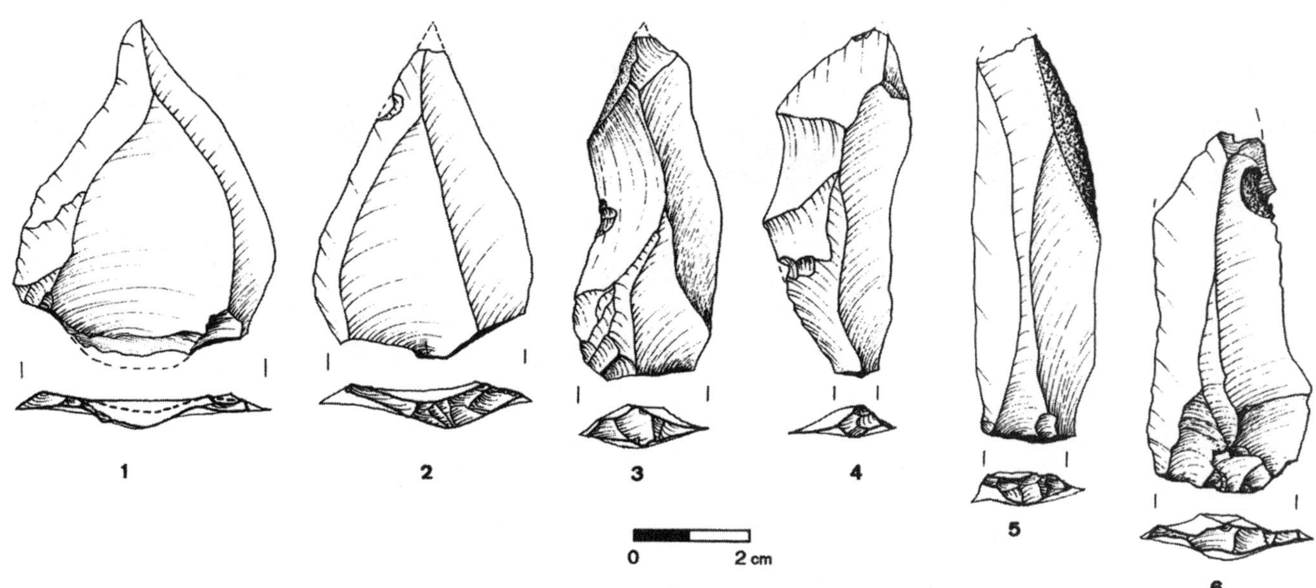

**Plate 44**  Layer VI: 1: Levallois point; 2: Levallois flake; 3: Double straight-convex side-scrapers; 4: Double convex-concave side-scraper.

**Plate 45**  Layer V: 1–2: Levallois points; 2–6: Levallois blades.

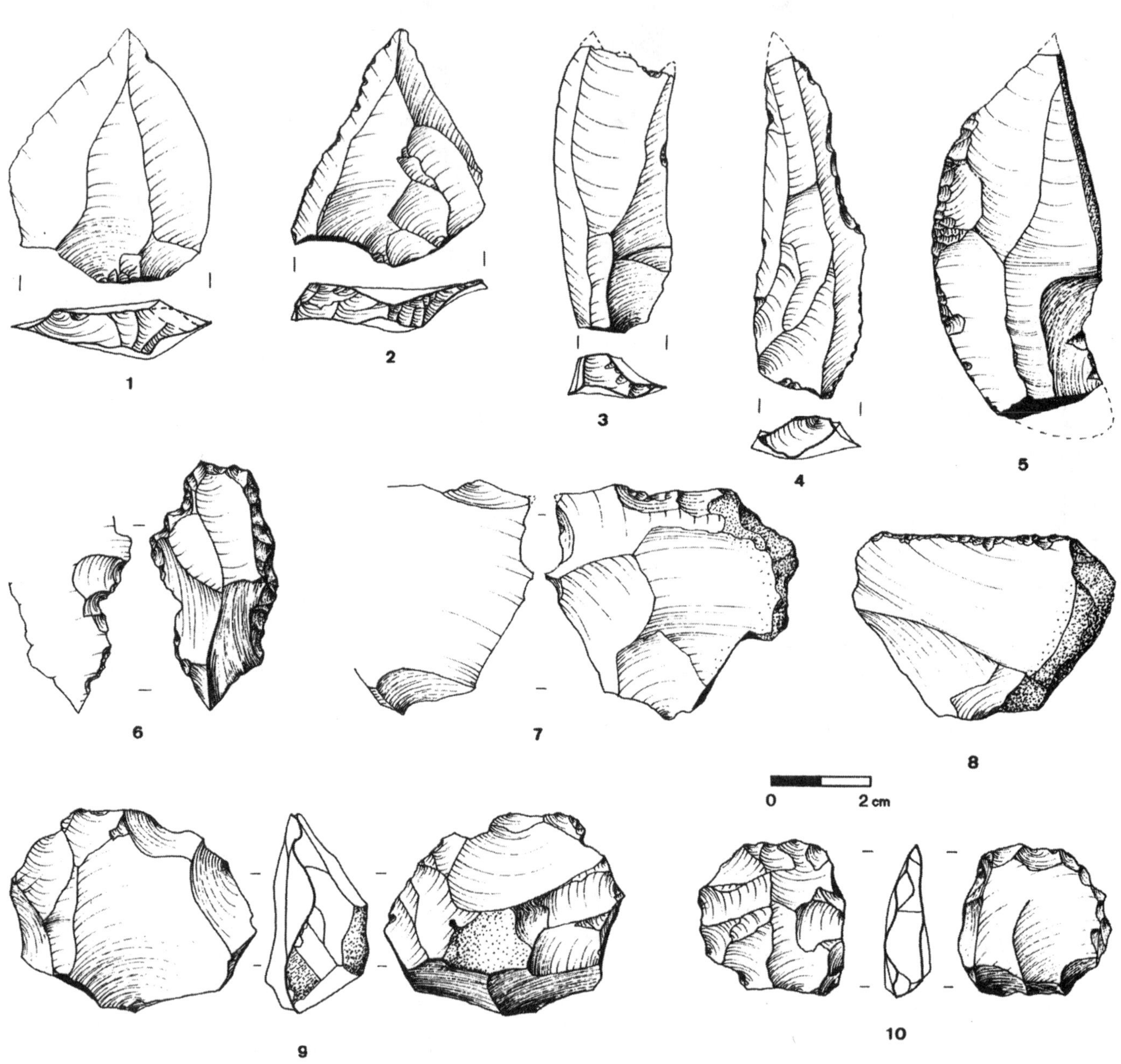

**Plate 46**    Layer IV: 1: Levallois flake; 2: Retouched Levallois point; 3: Levallois blade; 4: Atypical backed knife; 5: Single convex side-scraper; 6: Denticulate on a backed knife; 7: Double notched piece; 8: *Raclette*; 9: Levallois core for flakes; 10: Core-on-flake.

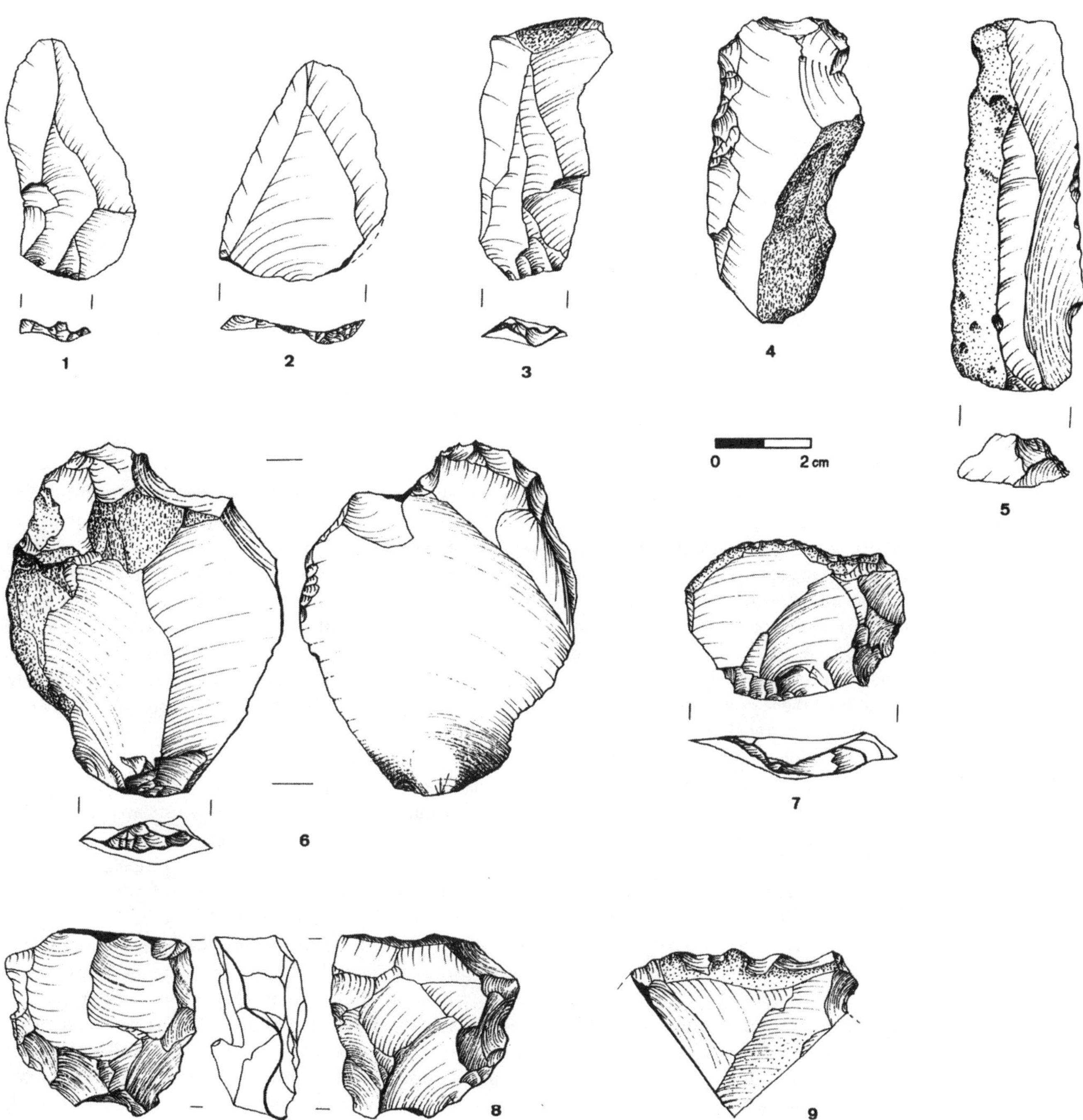

**Plate 47**  Layer III: 1, 3: Levallois blades; 2: Levallois point; 4: Single concave side-scraper; 5: Naturally backed knife; 6: Typical burin (on the ventral face) and end-notch; 7, 9: Denticulates; 8: Discoidal core.

# 7

## The Organization of Lithic Technology at Qafzeh

The analyses of the lithic assemblages of Qafzeh followed the logic of "reverse engineering" (see chapter 2; discussed specifically in relation to lithics and Levallois flaking by Hovers 1997; Sandgathe 2005, among others). The sets of analyses presented in the previous chapters attempted to accomplish the first of two stages involved in thinking about the meaning of ancient artifacts. By looking at the interrelationship of the various properties of the artifacts, I attempted to understand how artifacts were made and how material constraints and production processes affected the respective characteristics of these groups of artifacts. In this chapter I engage in the second question involved in the research strategy of reverse engineering: what could these artifacts do? The strategy of "reverse engineering" was first defined and described within evolutionary studies, where it clearly does not assume "intelligent design" but does ask what ecological survival functions could be answered by the structure of evolutionary designs. In our case, it is the technological designs that we wonder about. Reverse engineering is easiest if artifact structure includes some sort of signature pointing to the function (e.g., through differential use-wear signatures on various artifact types). However, in many cases recognizing the signature of prehistoric artifacts involves some a priori premises and assumptions about their potential functions.

It is not surprising that many paleoanthropologists focus on lithics in their attempts to understand the functioning of prehistoric organizational systems, or that they often consider the exploitation of faunal resources to be the goal served by lithic organizational strategies. Lithics and, to a lesser degree, animal bones are the "hand of cards" dealt to archaeologists (Hovers 1998b). They are the most abundant, the only redundant, and (too often) simply the only type of finds in prehistoric contexts from which inferences can be made. A common premise among paleoanthropologists is that lithics and bones are causally linked in a hierarchical, unequal way, by which the organization of lithic technology is responsive to the spatio-temporal distribution of resources in a group's exploited territory. Models of technological organization emphasize the close connections between subsistence, settlement and mobility patterns, risk management and social factors, and lithic technology (Binford 1977, 1978, 1979; Bousman 1993; Fitzhugh 2001; Geneste 1985; Kelly 1988, 1992; Kelly and Todd 1988; Nelson 1991; Torrence 1989a, 1994).

As discussed in chapters 1 and 2, such models allow the formulation of testable hypotheses about some aspects of hunter-gatherer behaviors. Here I use this conceptual framework to interpret the findings discussed in the previous chapters in the context of the relationship between the organization of lithic technology and other organizational aspects of the behavior of the Qafzeh inhabitants. The aim here is to identify inter-assemblage organizational differences and to discern and explain multi-causal phenomena. In the case of Qafzeh, several non-lithic data sets suggest that the nature of occupations changed throughout the sequence. The retrieval of human skeletal remains from the lower layers, from which microvertebrates (including commensal species) were also recovered, is in striking contrast to the absence of these two classes of finds from the upper layers (Bar-Yosef 1989:171; Bar-Yosef and Vandermeersch 1981). Subsequent research argued that the same dichotomy could be discerned in aspects of paleontology, seasonality, and use-wear traces as well (chapter 3). These findings were interpreted as indications of a major shift in settlement patterns between deposition of the lower (XXVI–XVa) and the upper (XV–VI) layers

(Bar-Yosef and Vandermeersch 1993; Lieberman 1993) and even in the identity of the site's occupants (Lieberman and Shea 1994). It was claimed that the older occupations of Qafzeh (layers XXIV–XVa) were seasonal and ephemeral, involving circulating mobility patterns. In contrast, the settlements of layers XV–VI were deemed permanent, multi-seasonal, and linked with radiating mobility strategies.[1]

Under the premise that lithic technology is intimately linked with settlement and mobility patterns, the organization of lithic technology at Qafzeh can be addressed in light of two general expectations. First, we would expect trends of technological organization to be patterned according to the postulated clear-cut behavioral dichotomy (as opposed to variability) observed along the Qafzeh sequence of occupations on the basis of non-lithic data. Second, we should be able to examine whether specific patterns of lithic organization are compatible with predictions about mobility and subsistence. This chapter examines these issues, first outlining some general premises with regard to lithics in the context of organizational theory and then elucidating some archaeological implications of these premises. This is followed by an interpretation of the findings from Qafzeh against the backdrop of the model's implications. These interpretations capitalize on the detailed analyses is presented in the previous chapters. These allow distinctions between assemblage characteristics that are responsive to the requirements of the mechanical demands of production systems and those that are selected for and obtained to accommodate organizational needs.

## Foraging Behaviors, Form of Mobility, and Lithic Organization

Many of the basic assumptions of technological organization studies are derived from ethnographic research. The application of ethnography-derived models to prehistoric research is a legitimate procedure for creating frames of reference, if several constraints are borne in mind (Binford 2001; see discussion in chapter 1). Ethnographic records and ethnoarchaeological studies from practically all over the globe illuminate the relationship between lithic production and mobility, settlement and economic behaviors, as well as gender, political organization, and the establishment of social order (e.g., Binford 1978, 1986; Binford and O'Connell 1984; Hayden 1979a, 1979b; Hiscock 2004; O'Connell, Hawkes, and Blurton-Jones 1992; Petrequin and Petrequin 2000; Stout 2002; Tindale 1965; Weedman 2002, 2006, to name only a few examples). Limiting the discussion for the moment to the ecological (as opposed to the social and symbolic) perspective of lithic production and use, the point of departure is that subsistence

takes precedence over other activities. Thus, there are predictable links among types of activities and the strategies of providing their technological aids, i.e., raw material economy and mobility (Nelson 1991; papers in Torrence 1983, 1989b).

The organization of lithic technology (as well as other technologies observed in the ethnographic record and assumed for prehistoric contexts) is designed to "make ends meet"; the technological aids necessary for exploiting resources (extractive technologies) must be available at the right time in the right places, i.e., where the resources are located. The use of maintenance technologies (e.g., resharpening, de- or re-hafting) is less constrained by the distribution of subsistence resources and need not overlap spatially and temporally with extractive tasks.

## Raw Material Availability, Mobility Patterns, and the Organization of Lithic Technology

Modeling the effects of lithic raw material organization on behavior is not straightforward, mainly because, in contrast to edible resources, there is no currency with which to measure the fitness-enhancing characteristics of the various raw materials. Despite this, availability (i.e., distance and abundance) and quality of raw material are clearly factors that influence behaviors related to raw material economy (Andrefsky 1994; Dibble 1991a; Munday 1976a, 1976b). Fresh, sharp implements would be preferred for use over extensively consumed artifacts. Such a preference is shared by most extant hunter-gatherers who, when unlimited supplies of raw material are available, tend to manufacture new tools as the need arises rather than modifying dulled or damaged existing ones. Raw material availability is thus defined as the ease of replacing exploited artifacts with fresh ones.

However, availability of lithic raw material is not an absolute or static given of a group's environment or territory because it is defined and then manipulated behaviorally, i.e., it is socially mediated (Hovers 1997; also Ambrose 2006; Minicillo 2006, who engaged in formal modeling of this problem). Availability of lithic raw material is dependent on how knappers perceive their needs in terms of stone quality. If high-quality raw material is desired for the execution of well-shaped tools with standardized morphologies (of either utilitarian or symbolic value to their users), the proximity or abundance of other, low-quality raw materials will not factor into assessments of availability. Group members may still choose to invest time and energy in searching for and/or importing high-quality lithic resources. Low-quality raw material in close proximity may then be exploited to produce less standardized tools, including, for example, unretouched flakes (Andrefsky 1994). On the other hand, when high-quality raw material is found in great abundance and in close vicinity to a given locality, there is little to be gained by making some artifacts on lower-quality raw material or by making and maintaining artifacts in advance of their scheduled use in order to transport them across the landscape (Bamforth 1986; Kuhn 1992a; Marks 1988). Ethnographic and archaeological literature is replete with case studies documenting such behaviors. In the Middle Paleolithic of Europe, Geneste (1985) and Rolland and Dibble (1990) noted the asymmetrical use of high-quality exotic raw materials for scrapers and retouched points as opposed to notches, denticulates, and unretouched flakes made on lower-quality local raw materials. Similar patterns are seen in other archaeological periods. During the Pre-Pottery Neolithic B in the Levant, for example, long, thin and standardized blades that were modified into sickle blades and arrowheads were produced on exotic raw materials from a relatively small number (on each site) of bipolar and naviform cores. In contrast, waste pits at the same sites sometimes contain tens of thousands of pieces of flaking debris and less formalized tools made on the local flint (Goring-Morris 1994; Goring-Morris and Belfer-Cohen 2001).[2]

Availability is also determined by the acceptable costs of having certain raw materials in specific geographic locations at designated times, i.e., adopting acceptable transport tactics from an array of possible such behaviors. As the ongoing discussion makes clear, "acceptable costs" of raw material transport differ according to quality and the need for particular materials for various utilitarian or social uses. One tactic emphasizes the investment of time and energy in transporting raw materials across the landscape from places of abundance to those of shortage, or to localities where there is uncertainty about raw material distribution. Another tactic puts a premium on investment of time and effort in intensive use and reduction (curation) of already available raw material to extend the use lives of artifacts. The choice of one tactic over the other, or the degree to which they are combined, depends to a large degree on the distribution of vis-à-vis subsistence resources (Rolland and Dibble 1990). It is the latter that determine the frequencies and modes of group mobility because it is more difficult for hunter-gatherers to manipulate the scheduling and geographic presence of subsistence resources. Indeed, many researchers have suggested that during Middle Paleolithic times raw material procurement was completely subjected to subsistence activities ("embedded procurement"; Binford 1979; Binford and Stone 1985), and that raw material was brought into sites incidentally to foraging trips (Rolland 1991:188).

The strategies of group mobility determine the types of sites occupied by human groups and consequently influence procedures of lithic manufacture and maintenance as well. When a group practices logistical mobility its main residential sites, i.e. base camps (as defined by Binford 1980), are situated at locations of compromise between the attractions of several dispersed concentrations of resources (Harpending and Davis 1977; Hovers 1988; Jochim 1976, 1979; Wilmsen 1973). Frequency of residential moves decreases while duration of occupations and the predictability of their timing and locations increase. Such conditions alleviate the time stress created by the need to move the group from one resource patch to the next. Hence, maintenance and manufacture tasks are more likely to be associated with base camps where generalized activities and preparation for extractive tasks take place. The stable residential location may be supplied with raw material in bulk to accommodate the lithic technological needs of the group. The base camp thus becomes a predictable "source" of raw material, where need and availability can be easily and safely synchronized. The effort invested in devising technological tactics for obtaining lithic material can be minimized (Nelson 1991:79), and raw material exploitation tends to become more casual, with little evidence for tool renewal or recycling (Parry and Kelly 1987).

The range of raw material transport varies predictably with mobility strategies. Decreased frequency of residential moves results in increased resource depletion in the immediate environment, consequently causing an increase in the range of logistical forays (e.g., Henry 1983; Hovers 1988; Odell 1994; Speth and Scott 1989). If they are indeed tethered strongly to resource acquisition, distances of lithic raw material transport for provisioning the habitation site will be correlated positively with occupation duration.

Transport distances tend to increase with the size of the exploited territory too. Raw material sources may lie well beyond the boundaries of the site exploitation territory used by a band for daily procurement activities (Bailey and Davidson 1983; Hovers 1989). In such circumstances it will be more likely that the subsistence forays and trips for acquisition of lithic raw materials are separated, at least occasionally. Rather than relying on embedded procurement of raw material, trips might be specially designated for obtaining raw materials. Certainly this is a plausible behavior in regions in which suitable lithic sources are uncommon and widely spaced (e.g., Hovers 1990b:164).

Among highly mobile groups practicing residential mobility, lithic manufacture and maintenance tend to be associated with residential camps of short duration rather than with task-specific locations. Tool manufacture on site is more likely to take place when a site is occupied during a season of decreased productivity, when extractive activities are at a low point. Proximity to a source of suitable raw material similarly enhances activities related to tool production. At task-specific locations, on the other hand, time tends to be a precious commodity. In hunting stations, timing is especially crucial for the success of the task and is used first and foremost for obtaining food from the faunal resources. It is less likely that technological activities associated with gear maintenance, such as retooling or recycling, will be carried out in such locations (Nelson 1991:79). Similarly, at faunal procurement sites, the threat of competitors may be too great to allow the investment of time in maintaining lithic gear that requires re-tooling or resharpening. Still, processing activities (i.e., butchery) may occur, possibly with the aim of reducing the cost of transporting the yield back to the habitation site (Metcalfe and Barlow 1992). The preparation of tools to be used on task-specific sites, particularly those involving the procurement of meat by hunting, entails a high investment in the design of reliable tools as a fail-safe mechanism (Bleed 1986; Nelson 1991; Torrence 1983, 1989a; see also below).[3] Reliable tools may be carried around the landscape individually at all times to meet conceivable necessities, and since they entail high investment their users attempt to maximize the duration of their utilization (Binford 1979; Kuhn 1994; Nelson 1991; Shott 1986, 1989a). For instance, curated bifaces were used by residentially mobile groups of North American paleo-Indians both as a source of blanks for future expedient flaking (i.e., cores) and as long-lived tools when raw material was not available near task locations (Kelly 1988; Kelly and Todd 1988). Extractive tasks in the context of high residential mobility thus tend to involve provisioning of individuals (e.g., Binford 1977, 1978) regardless of the mobility strategies employed by the group as a whole. The transport of artifacts carried around by individuals as personal gear is minimally affected by the size of the exploited territory (Kuhn 1995a:29).

Task-specific locations will present signatures similar to those of residential sites when particular activities recur periodically at the same locality (e.g., hunts of seasonally migratory herds). In such instances there may be some caching of raw material for future use, but presumably this will happen on a lesser scale than provisioning behavior in habitation sites.

### Moving Raw Material around the Landscape

Clearly, the organization of lithic technology is a dynamic process with numerous possibilities for behavioral mediation of the limitations and opportunities offered by the natural and social environments. These variations on a theme can be viewed within a framework of three major strategies of technological organization: curation, expediency, and opportunistic behavior.

*Curation,* formally defined as "a continuous property of tools that measures the relationship between maximum [potential] and realized utility" (Shott 1996:268),

characterizes organizational strategies that emphasize the preparation of tools or the hoarding of raw materials in anticipation of shortage. Examples of conditions that are conductive for curation are lack of raw materials/facilities or time stress at the anticipated location of tool use (Torrence 1983). Curation is thus associated either with longer periods of site occupation or with regular moves within a familiar territory, when the scheduling of resources (and therefore of tool use) and their location can be anticipated on the basis of past experience. Curation may be relaxed by provisioning of places, i.e., caching of raw materials of tools to ensure that technological needs are met at the required place and time (Binford 1979; Kuhn 1992b).

Where conditions are unpredictable and there is no a priori knowledge of the structure of raw material or subsistence resources, curation entails provisioning of individuals with tools that are moved around the landscape over greater distances (Binford 1977, 1979). Anticipating circumstances that will not allow tool preparation will lead to the same behavior. This tactic might be employed during the initial exploration of a new territory, within which the resource structure is still unfamiliar (Kelly and Todd 1988). It could also be advantageous where territorial boundaries are not clear, and caches cannot safely be left on site between periods of occupation. Finally, curation through provisioning of individuals is associated with a high degree of residential mobility, in which people are forced to rely on an assembly of tools carried around a landscape with infrequent raw material sources. The assembly of curated tool kits should be responsive to the costs of continuous transport (Nelson 1991), partially alleviated by maximal realization of the potential utility of the artifacts.

*Expediency* is a strategy used where schedules and locations of tool use are predictable. Expediency would be practiced in the anticipation that both sufficient materials and time to conduct tool production and maintenance would to be available at the location of tool use. If raw material was present as part of the geological substrate of a region, significant storing of raw material or caching of prepared tools would not constitute an efficient adaptive strategy, and investment in pre-planned lithic technological activities could be reduced (Nelson 1991:64). For the same reasons, provisioning of individuals is not likely to occur. However, provisioning of a site by creating secondary sources of raw material at the site itself may lead to expedient lithic organization even where raw material is not naturally available.

*Opportunistic* behavior, the third type of organizational strategy, is characterized by responsiveness to immediate conditions and needs without advance planning. Opportunistic behavior depends on the overall distribution of lithic raw material and its geographic overlap with the location of resource use. Mobile gear brought into the location of use may be subjected to unanticipated uses, resulting in modification of tools and cores in a variety of ways not consistent with their original design (Nelson 1991).

The particular organizational strategy adopted by any given group of hunter-gatherers as the optimal means to avoid the risk of technological failure will shift over various temporal scales (annually or seasonally, for example). Also, it will conform to the location of the group within its territorial range.

## Archaeological Implications

The relationships between mobility, resource distribution, settlement patterns, and technological organization have archaeological correlates in terms of tool design and assemblage composition, as well as overall site structure (Nelson 1991:78–87; table 7.1).

Long-duration or frequently occupied residential locations become "artificial" sources of raw material, supplied with raw material in bulk (possibly as cores), which relaxes time constraints on tool preparation. Raw material could be exploited expediently, using core-reduction sequences (or a single sequence producing a variety of flake shapes and sizes) that are not concerned with conservation and transportation costs (Parry and Kelly 1987). With the possible exception of the initial decortication of cores, all the stages of lithic production should occur in these sites. Moreover, cores tend not to be part of a transportable tool kit, due to an inefficient ratio of utility per unit mass (Kuhn 1994), and would remain at the residential site as part of the archaeologically visible assemblage. Since the extent of blank utilization often depends on the task at hand rather than planned maintenance, there should be little evidence for tool renewal or recycling at such sites. On the other hand, retooling of hafted artifacts (if such artifacts were part of the technological gear) presumably took place in habitation sites, resulting in high frequencies of proximal parts of rejected lithic components (Keeley 1982), both retouched and unretouched (e.g., Boëda et al. 1996; Boëda, Connan, and Muhesen 1998b; Friedman et al.1994–5). However, some of the breakage will be associated with manufacture rather than maintenance activities.

If personal gear and curated artifacts were utilized in task-specific sites, they should be characterized archaeologically by the occurrence of later-stage reduction debris and low proportions of waste flakes. Used flakes and small resharpening flakes should occur in high proportions, but tools may be absent, as they would have been removed by users from the sites to other locales (Binford 1979). If the site was the last locale at which tools were used, small, exhausted, and heavily retouched implements are expected. Distal segments of broken artifacts, not salvaged after being broken during use, will be left on site.

Since the organization of technological systems varies across space and time, within and among groups, different modes of settlement or mobility can be represented in a single locale. The principles of logistical and residential organization are thus applied in an attempt to understand the distribution of material remains rather than find perfect archaeological analogies to the sites described in ethnographic literature. This approach disregards taphonomic processes, which certainly affected at least some of the artifact classes discussed above.

## Looking at Inter-Assemblage Variability

The analyses presented in chapters 4–6 dealt with the lithic artifacts in the context of their production processes. The artifacts were categorized as separate and independent classes and were associated probabilistically with particular segments of the reduction sequences. In the absence of large-scale and technologically informative refits, such divisions were deemed necessary to enable some insight into the effects of the actual production processes on artifact characteristics. For the purpose of understanding lithic organization and its changes over time, however, the basic unit of analysis and comparison is the assemblage, in which relationships seen among artifacts can be observed.

As described in chapter 3 (and briefly at the beginning of this chapter), clear differences, supposedly related to mobility, settlement, and subsistence changes, are reflected in the non-lithic finds of the lower layers (XXIV–XV) as opposed to upper layers (XIV–III) of the Qafzeh sequence. Theory-driven relationships between lithic assemblages and those behaviors were discussed above. This middle range theory, and the hypotheses derived from it, informs expectations of the assemblages and the ways in which they change through time.

Comparison of assemblage compositions of the various layers shows a clear temporal segregation of assemblage types. In the older layers (XXII–XV), debris composed mostly of flakes smaller than 20 mm constitutes over 50% of the lithic finds, and tools are 1–4.6% of the total assemblages. Cores and waste are relatively few (table 7.2, figure 7.1). As a group, layers XIV–III contrast with this pattern, although they can be divided into two assemblage "subtypes." In the mid-section assemblages (layers XIV–IX), debris is less than 30% and retouched tools are 7.5–14.5% of the assemblage, while cores and manufacture waste (e.g., cortical elements and core management pieces) are represented in greater frequencies than in both older and younger layers. In the younger assemblages (VIIb–III), the frequencies of tools and frequencies of debris rise again, but not to the same levels as in the older assemblages. Frequencies of debitage are high and are similar to those of the mid-section group of

**Table 7.1**   Archaeologically observed variables of lithic assemblages and their postulated organizational implications

| Variable | Behavioral correlates and predicted relationships in archaeological assemblages | Source |
|---|---|---|
| **Typological variables** | | |
| Frequencies of tool types: simple versus double, convergent, offset and transverse scrapers; notches versus denticulates | Short as opposed to extensive sequences of resharpening as responses to higher/lower degrees of raw material availability. | Dibble 1987; Holdaway McPherron and Roth 1996; Rolland 1996; Rolland and Dibble 1990; Shott 1996. |
| Frequencies of typological groups (for Qafzeh: Upper Paleolithic tools, notches and denticulates, Levallois points); assemblage richness and evenness | Task-specific/logistical sites in circulating/radiating mobility systems. Even as opposed to skewed distribution of tool morphologies as responses to more or less balanced spectrum of activities on site. | Shott 1986. |
| **Assemblage composition** | | |
| Frequencies of modified blanks (retouched tools) in an assemblage | Degree of curation of lithic raw material by use of personal gear (provisioning of individuals in response to changing levels of raw material availability resulting from spatial and/or temporal distribution of human activities in relation to lithic sources). High tool frequencies are postulated to have occurred when raw material sources in exploited territory are known to be unsuitable/scarce, or when there was lesser ability to anticipate timing and location of subsistence activities or availability of raw material sources in exploited territory (e.g., when colonizing new territories, in contexts of high group mobility). | Andrefsky 1994; Bamforth 1986; Binford 1979, 1980; Kuhn 1995; Marks 1988; Nelson 1991. |
| Core frequencies; ratios of tools/cores; *débitage*/cores; frequencies of cortical pieces | Type of settlement and its intensity/degree of mobility/degree of advance technological planning. Technological diversity may be inversely correlated with residential mobility or with degree of risk involved in prey capture. The interplay among these ratios reflects the nature of the site, e.g., as a quarry site (if cores and cortical elements are numerous while retouched tools and non-cortical debitage are few), habitation site (if all the technological categories are present), and/or degree of transport and import of special artifact groups. | Binford 1979, 1980; Kuhn 1995; Nelson 1991 and references therein; Shott 1986. |
| **Technological variables** | | |
| Frequency of Levallois products | Levallois cores are relatively efficient at minimizing raw material waste while at the same time maximizing productivity in terms of total numbers of tool blanks and amount of cutting edge produced. Levallois production is an attempt to increase efficiency of exploitation of high-quality raw material in contexts of high mobility or group movement over relatively long distances. Levallois products were more prone to be moved between sites due to their favorable morphometric properties (ratio of mass to size), either as unretouched blanks or as already retouched blanks (see above, frequencies of retouched tools). Non-Levallois products were the less mobile segment of the technological system, since their production was arguably less constrained by size and shape concerns and they could be made on raw materials of lesser quality. | Andrefsky 1994; Brantingham and Kuhn 2001; Geneste 1985; Kuhn 1994; Shea 1991. |

(continued)

**Table 7.1**  (continued)

| Variable | Behavioral correlates and predicted relationships in archaeological assemblages | Source |
| --- | --- | --- |
| Scar patterns | Responsive to modes and degrees of mobility, often related to subsistence activities. Generally, the tendency toward bipolar flaking is interpreted as responding to more sedentary systems. Correlations between the occurrence of scavenged faunas and dominance of centripetal flaking in some archaeological case studies are interpreted as indications of highly mobile groups with less advance planning, whereas hunting is associated with bipolar flaking and higher degree of planning. Scar patterns are also seen as responsive to specific subsistence activities (e.g., the use of convergent flaking for Levallois point production, which in turn reflects greater emphasis on hunting). | Bar-Yosef et al. 1992; Parry and Kelly 1987; Kuhn 1995; Munday 1979; Shea 1991, 1998; Stiner and Kuhn 1992. |
| Frequencies of blades and points | Emphasis on maintainable versus reliable artifacts in response to anticipated time stress while executing subsistence activities, mainly hunting. Tools designed for use when such time stress is expected to occur should be replaced quickly if necessary, and would be standardized to fit into hafts, etc. Tools designed for longer use tend to "store" potential cutting edges that can be shaped and used as necessary (emphasis is expected to be on size rather than standardized morphology in initial stages of use). | Bar-Yosef and Kuhn 1999; Bleed 1986; Bousman 1993; Nelson 1991 and references therein. |
| Flake size | Degree of mobility. Flake sizes are argued to be related to flaking modes, and since those vary with varying mobility patterns, flake sizes should co-vary with frequencies of the different scar patterns. | Kuhn 1995:111, fig. 4.17. |

*Note*: Modified after Hovers and Raveh 2000.

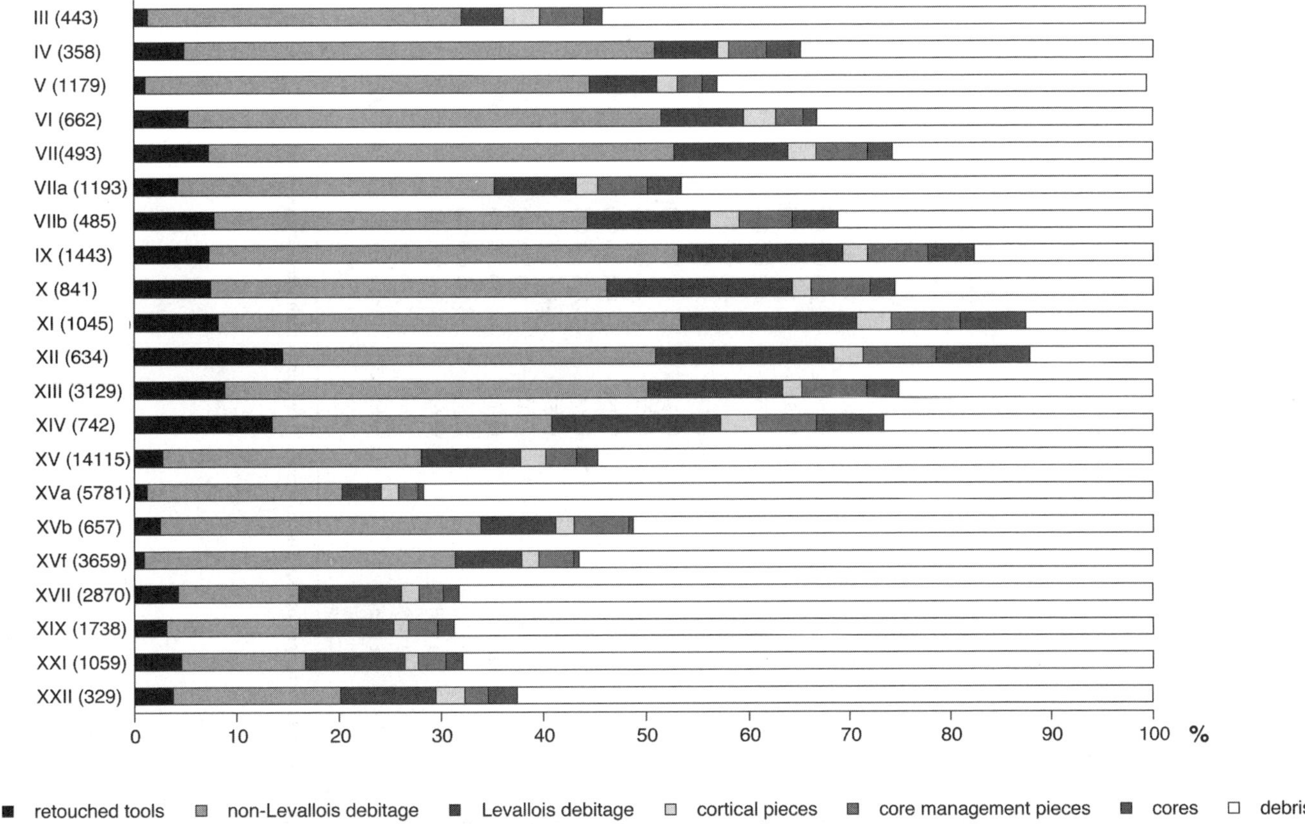



**Figure 7.1**   Composition of the lithic assemblages by layers (See table 7.2 for data)

assemblages. Another difference between the two parts of the section lies in the frequencies of burnt artifacts (figure 7.2a), which are significantly higher in the lower layers ($\chi^2 = 192.58$, $p < .0001$, df = 1), especially in layers XV, XVf, and XVII.

This division in itself displays several patterned co-variations of assemblage traits. When the characteristics of lithic reduction are taken into account, it becomes obvious that the initial bipartite division of the Qafzeh sequence represents only part of the range of diversity and complexity in patterns of both lithic production and technological organization. And yet, for Qafzeh as for many (if not most) Mousterian lithic assemblages, there is an analytical and methodological challenge in pinpointing the variables that make assemblages very similar or highly dissimilar to one another.

The problem is twofold. Bordes's quantitative method (or any similar method, for that matter) indeed provides standardized data that describe single variables, but it does little to help in understanding the complex relationship among variables. Even for single variables, the process of comparison becomes progressively less efficient as the number of assemblages across which this variable is compared grows. It is difficult to judge from such comparative formats where the significant differences lie. Nor does this or similar methods help in assessing the

degree of similarity between any number of assemblages as a "sum" of the behaviors presumably expressed by the quantitative data.

Multivariate approaches (e.g., principal component analysis or cluster analysis) are needed to address this question. Indeed, such methods have occasionally been used in the study of Mousterian assemblage variability (e.g., Binford and Binford 1966; Callow and Webb 1981; Munday 1976b; Würz et al. 2003). The usual procedure of such methods is to analyze either variables or observations, and the results summarize the effects of a number of abstract factors, in themselves a composite of several basic studied variables. In this study, I opted instead to use the multivariate display technique of COPLOT. Within the family of "distance analyses," this variant enables comparison of assemblages on the basis of several types of data derived from any quantifiable aspect of lithic assemblages.[4] After transformation from a multidimensional space to the bi-dimensional graphic space, and after establishing that this transformation does not detract from the quality of the data, variables and observations are used simultaneously to place assemblages at their relative distances from one another. A virtual point at the center of the graph space (the centroid) represents a hypothetical average assemblage, derived from all the variables and observations used in the analysis. The procedure maps observations, such that

**Table 7.2.    Assemblage compositions by general technological categories**

| Layer | Retouched tools | Non-Levallois debitage | Levallois debitage | Cortical pieces[a] | Core management pieces | Cores | Debris | Density[b] |
|---|---|---|---|---|---|---|---|---|
| III (443) | 9 (1.35) | 136 (30.69) | 18 (4.06) | 16 (3.61) | 19 (4.28) | 8 (1.80) | 237 (53.49) | 1,471 |
| IV (358) | 14 (4.90) | 165 (46.00) | 22 (6.14) | 4 (1.11) | 13 (3.63) | 12 (3.35) | 128 (35.75) | 511 |
| V (1179) | 13 (1.10) | 512 (43.42) | 76 (6.61) | 23 (1.95) | 29 (2.45) | 17 (1.44) | 505 (42.83) | 710 |
| VI (662) | 35 (5.29) | 306 (46.22) | 53 (8.00) | 21 (3.17) | 18 (2.71) | 9 (1.36) | 220 (33.23) | 178 |
| VII (493) | 36 (7.30) | 224 (45.43) | 55 (11.15) | 14 (2.83) | 25 (5.07) | 12 (2.43) | 127 (25.76) | |
| VIIa (1193) | 51 (4.27) | 369 (30.93) | 96 (8.04) | 25 (2.09) | 58 (4.86) | 39 (3.26) | 555 (46.53) | 213 |
| VIIb (485) | 38 (7.83) | 177 (36.49) | 58 (11.95) | 14 (2.88) | 25 (5.15) | 22 (4.53) | 151 (31.13) | 191 |
| IX (1443) | 106 (7.34) | 661 (45.80) | 234 (16.21) | 35 (2.42) | 87 (6.02) | 65 (4.50) | 255 (18.67) | 487 |
| X (841) | 63 (7.49) | 326 (38.76) | 152 (18.07) | 16 (1.90) | 49 (5.82) | 12 (2.42) | 223 (26.51) | 646 |
| XI (1045) | 86 (8.22) | 472 (45.16) | 181 (17.32) | 36 (3.44) | 71 (6.79) | 69 (6.60) | 130 (12.44) | 394 |
| XII (634) | 92 (14.51) | 231 (36.43) | 111 (17.50) | 18 (2.89) | 46 (7.25) | 59 (9.31) | 77 (12.15) | 357 |
| XIII (3129) | 278 (8.88) | 1,293 (41.32) | 410 (13.10) | 61 (1.94) | 201 (6.42) | 100 (3.20) | 786 (25.12) | 478 |
| XIV (742) | 100 (13.48) | 203 (27.35) | 122 (16.44) | 26 (3.50) | 44 (5.93) | 49 (6.60) | 198 (26.68) | 188 |
| XV (14115) | 396 (2.80) | 3,562 (25.23) | 1,376 (9.74) | 349 (2.47) | 422 (2.99) | 291 (2.06) | 7,715 (54.66) | 1,117 |
| XVa (5781) | 72 (1.24) | 1100 (19.02) | 224 (3.87) | 96 (1.66) | 110 (1.90) | 32 (0.55) | 4,147 (71.73) | |
| XVb (657) | 10 (2.52) | 206 (31.35) | 48 (7.30) | 12 (1.82) | 35 (5.32) | 3 (0.46) | 343 (52.21) | 286 |
| XVf (3659) | 36 (0.98) | 1,113 (30.41) | 237 (6.47) | 62 (1.69) | 124 (3.38) | 18 (0.49) | 2,069 (56.55) | 988 |
| XVII (2870) | 123 (4.28) | 338 (11.77) | 288 (10.03) | 49 (1.70) | 69 (2.40) | 45 (1.57) | 1,958 (68.22) | 272 |
| XIX (1738) | 55 (3.16) | 225 (12.95) | 160 (9.20) | 25 (1.44) | 50 (2.87) | 28 (1.61) | 1,195 (68.76) | 175 |
| XXI (1059) | 38 (4.59) | 128 (12.08) | 103 (9.73) | 14 (1.32) | 29 (2.74) | 17 (1.61) | 730 (68.93) | 146 |
| XXII (616) | 20 (3.80) | 86 (16.34) | 49 (9.31) | 15 (2.85) | 12 (2.28) | 15 (2.85) | 329 (62.55) | 265 |

$\chi^2 = 6505.72$ at $p < .0001$, df = 120

*Note*: Ns are given for assemblages used in subsequent analyses. "Tools" in these counts do not include types 5 and 38, or artifacts with signs of use. The counts include blanks with retouch on ventral face (Bordes's type 45) and blanks with isolated removals.

[a] Pieces with over 50% of surface covered by cortex (frequencies not included in other counts).

[b] Density per m$^3$ of artifacts larger than 20 mm. Debris not included.

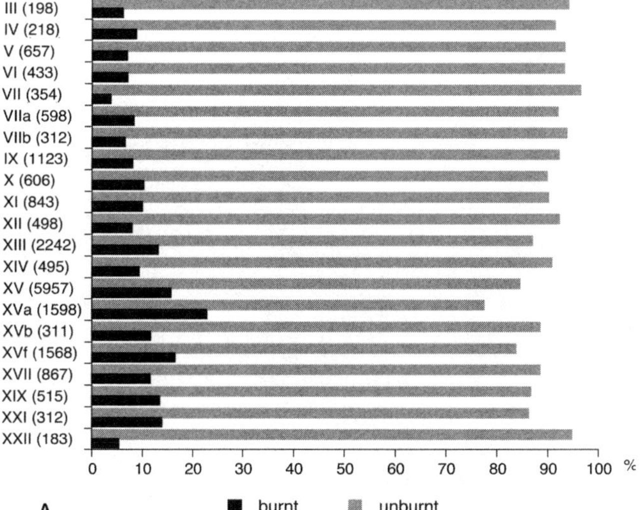



**A.**

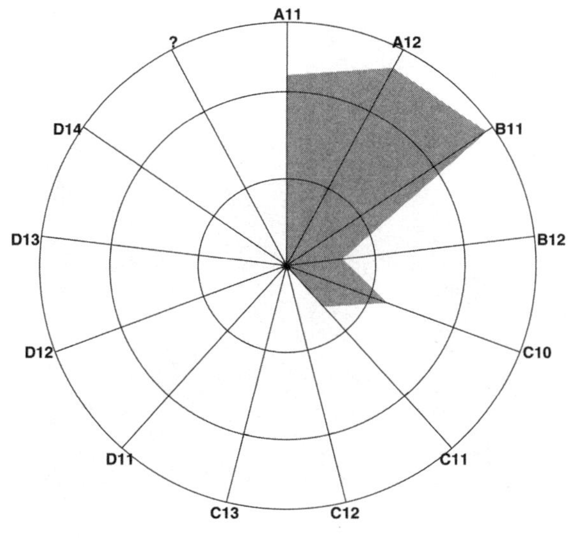



**B.**

**Figure 7.2** Frequencies of burned artifacts. A: Among flakes and retouched tools. B: Frequencies of thermal debris (N = 4,356) in grid squares in layer XV (each concentric circle represents 10%).

the more similar the assemblages (represented as points that are the "sum" of the observations per assemblage), the closer they are to one another on the graph space. The closer an assemblage is to any given arrow (each arrow representing a variable), the higher is the effect of the variable on the location of the assemblage in relation to others. In this manner, the display shows that assemblages clustered in the same group behave similarly with regard to the selected variables. Additionally, the program signifies which of the variables are less or more closely correlated with any other. The angles between arrows signify the degree of correlation between variables such that arrows

depicting highly correlated variables point in roughly the same direction and vice versa. (More details on this technique are available in Hovers and Raveh 2000; Raveh 1992.).

Twenty-one of the Qafzeh assemblages[5] were analyzed in this manner (figure 7.3). Assemblages are dispersed all over the graph space, and none resembles the "average" assemblage (the centroid). This suggests a high degree of inter-assemblage variability. Since assemblages with small samples were winnowed out from this analysis, differences in sample size are not a likely explanation for the high degree of variability, even if this explanation cannot be ruled out completely. The display also shows that variability is not determined by any single variable, nor is it set by a constant set of interrelated variables. The influential attributes that affect the placing of assemblages at varying distances from the hypothetical "average" assemblage differ from one case to the other, indicating that inter-assemblage variability is multicausal.

Two main, readily identified sources of variability are (1) variation in the production process and (2) differences in the ways in which artifacts are used and moved around the landscape. Interpretations of lithic assemblages as reflecting particular types of behavior (table 7.1 and accompanying discussion) often hinge on the interplay among different variables of an assemblage, rather than on comparison of concrete values obtained for any single variable. The graphic display exhibits this interplay clearly and enables immediate appreciation of the facets of variability that require further study.

For some variables, the relationships shown on the graph space are consistent with expectations derived from the technological modeling of Levallois flaking (as discussed at length in chapters 4–6). The negative correlation between IL and the frequencies of unipolar scar patterns on Levallois products is a case in point. However, figure 7.3 also presents other, less predictable relationships among variables. Thus, the display suggests that frequencies of laminar blanks (Ilam), frequencies of Levallois points, and frequencies of bipolar and of convergent scar patterns are closely intercorrelated. These correlations accord with expectations for assemblages in which point production and artifact elongation are emphasized. However, the assemblages at Qafzeh with the highest values of any of these variables are not necessarily closest on the graph space, i.e., they are not necessarily similar to one another. Moreover, there are clear exceptions to the rule, for example, layers VI, XVa, and XVf, in which Ilam is linked with unipolar, rather than convergent or bipolar, scar patterns. These patterns suggest that distances among assemblages were not determined solely, and possibly not even mainly, by straightforward relationships among these technological factors.

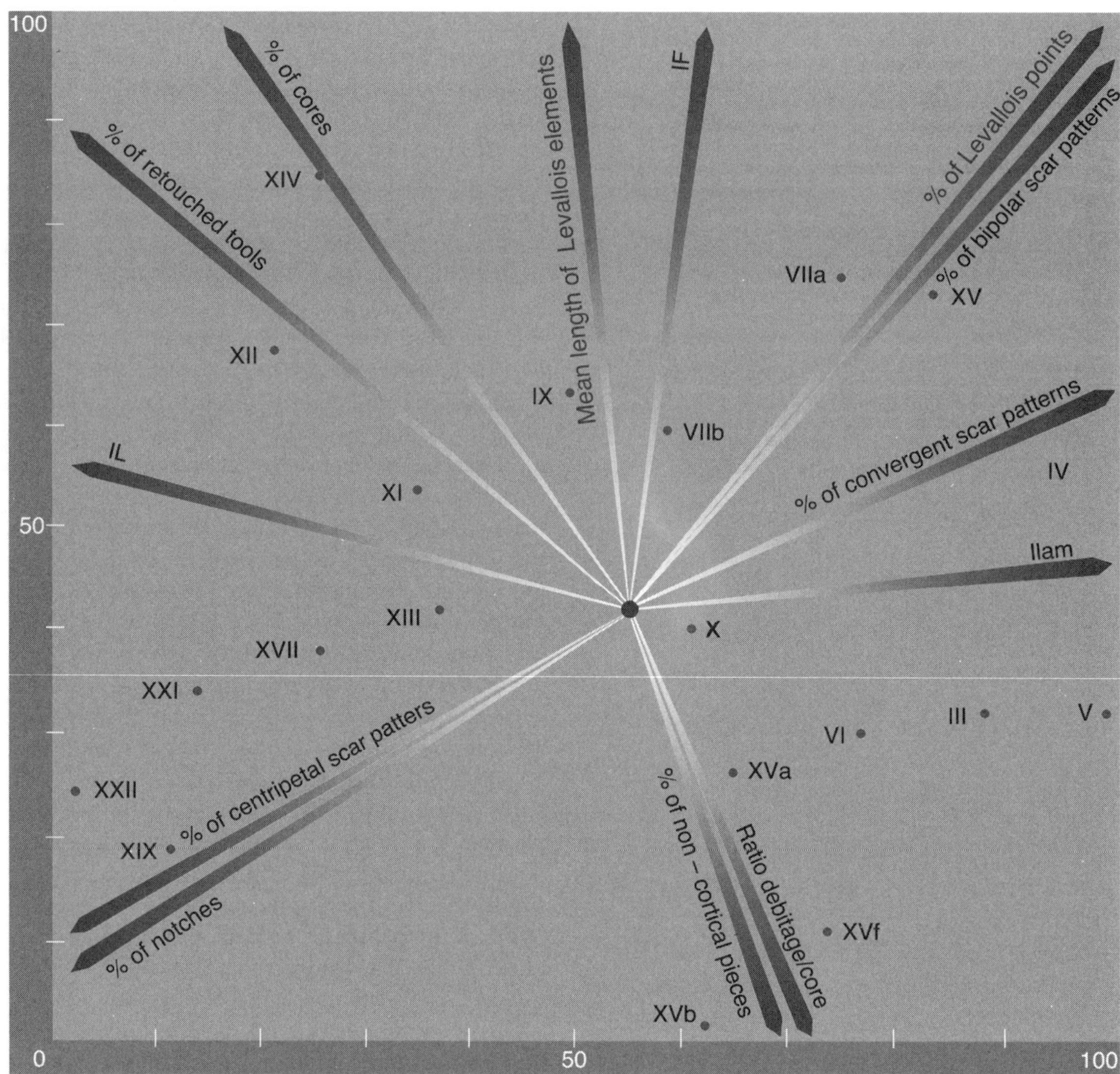


**Figure 7.3**  A COPLOT graphic display of 21 Qafzeh assemblages. Thirteen variables are included in this analysis. The overall goodness-of-fit is very good (coefficient of alienation $[\theta] = 0.11$), indicating that information loss in the transformation from multidimensional to two-dimensional graphic space is acceptable. The set up is schematic and does not depict actual measurements or distances. See text for more details.

The graphic display also shows that the mean length of Levallois products does not correlate directly with any particular mode of flaking (scar pattern variables/arrows). On the other hand, a high correlation is observed between IF and the mean length of Levallois products. While this latter pattern is consistent with predictions from flaking mechanics models, which emphasize the crucial role of striking platform properties in determining blank dimensions (Speth, 1972, 1974; see also Pelcin 1997c), it also implies that the sizes of Levallois artifacts in the assemblages are not a deterministic outcome of specific flaking modes. Similarly, the absence of a strong

correlation between IL and IF suggests that platform faceting was not a prerequisite of Levallois flaking in any of the Qafzeh assemblages. Faceting may have played a significant technological role in achieving specific properties of Levallois flakes during reduction, but it was not an obligatory component of a technical "blueprint." Indeed, variations in the values of IF and mean length of Levallois products are not significant in determining assemblage dissimilarity. On the contrary, frequencies of IL and frequencies of centripetal flaking separate the older from the younger assemblages (layers XXIV–XVII versus XV–III).

Production technology thus appears to explain only part of the variability of the Qafzeh sequence. At least some of that variability should be attributed to factors responsive to the second source of variation considered here, namely differences in lithic organization in response to varying mobility and subsistence behaviors. The analysis highlights the possibility that some of the dissimilarities among assemblages stem from the absence of particular classes rather than the over-representation of others. For example, the negative correlations between core frequencies and debitage/core ratio suggest that the extreme positions on the graph of layers XVb–XVf are the result not of high production rates, but of a paucity of cores.

Rates of tool use, drop, and discard (i.e., use lives) play a major role in the "making" of an assemblage (Ammerman and Feldman 1974; Schiffer 1987; Shott 1989a) and are intimately linked to the overall organization of mobility and subsistence. Assemblage-level analysis of the relationship of such use-life characteristics with the variables that express production practices is needed to understand the organization of lithic technology in the assemblage along the Qafzeh sequence.

## The Organizational Context of Lithic Production and Use in Qafzeh

### Raw Material and Its Sources

In assessing diachronic patterns of lithic raw material selection and use along the sequence of a single site, one must take into account the influence of passing time. Geomorphic processes and/or paleoclimatic events may have changed the visibility of raw material sources or their level of accessibility (Dibble 1991a; Kuhn 1995a). Obviously, such changes can cause discrepancies between what the modern-day observer sees on the landscape and what prehistoric people related to. But time depth may have caused differential availability of raw material also throughout the time of site occupation, leading to changes in strategies of raw material exploitation. In the case of Qafzeh, accumulation of sediments since the Upper Pleistocene, particularly at the margins of the Jezreel Valley, which acts as a regional erosion base, may have masked the existence of raw material sources that were available to the Qafzeh hominins at the time of occupation. Alternately, variations in the frequencies of specific raw materials along a single occupation sequence could result from over-exploitation of a given source due to the intensity of occupation, and the need to shift to another as yet unexhausted raw material exposure (Dibble 1985, 1991a). Assemblages in stratified sites may show diachronic variability that would be comparable to that seen among a series of contemporaneous sites situated differentially in relation to raw material sources.

As it turns out, raw material economies in Qafzeh do not in fact reflect changes in raw material selection patterns throughout the sequence. Flint is practically the only raw material at Qafzeh. Of the 931 cores studied, 920 are made on visibly homogenous flint, the others being made on flint with many limestone inclusions. The latter occur as single items in layers V, IX, XII, XIV, XVII, and XXII, while in layer XV there are five such specimens. Frequencies of flint among the debitage and tools in all layers are over 91% (by number of artifacts), the mode being ca. 97%. Small amounts (1.44–7.07%) of flint with limestone inclusions are present in all layers. Artifacts made on limestone appear in frequencies lower than 1% in twelve of the twenty-six stratigraphic units under study. In only three layers were there artifacts the raw material of which could not be identified, commonly as a result of excessive heating or calcification that greatly altered the items' surfaces.

The assemblages show a high degree of similarity among layers in terms of physical characteristics (figures 7.4, 7.5). This is partly the result of the similar lithologies of the layers, all of which consist of variable proportions of calcareous gravels (Farrand 1979; Vandermeersch 1981). A clear dichotomy is observed between the preservation and patination of cores and those of flakes and retouched flakes; cores always tend to be somewhat more abraded and patinated. The higher degree of abrasion of cores may possibly be explained by the fact that their voluminous, more spherical shapes made them overly prone to small-scale rolling, whereas the flatter and thinner flakes were not susceptible to this type of taphonomic damage. On the other hand, most flakes in all the assemblages are in pristine condition, frequencies of double-patinated and heavily abraded pieces never exceeding 10% in any layer for either variable. Since patina on flint artifacts is caused, among other factors, by micro-organisms that need light for their metabolism (Friedman et al. 1994–5), it is possible that assemblages formed in caves are only marginally affected by patination processes. In addition, severe chemical weathering of heavy minerals in the terrace layers (Farrand 1979) may have destroyed the patina that had accumulated on the artifacts. However, the differences in the degree of patination between cores and flakes are difficult to explain.

The common flint at Qafzeh is tan-brown in color and of high quality, almost devoid of impurities. It is visually homogeneous within and among assemblages, and may well be derived from a limited number of sources (despite the high inter-nodule variability observed in flint; Hovers 1990b). Although no systematic sourcing of raw material has as yet been attempted, this type of flint appears to originate from the flint-bearing beds of the Eocene Ma'lul Formation, currently exposed near Shefar'am, some

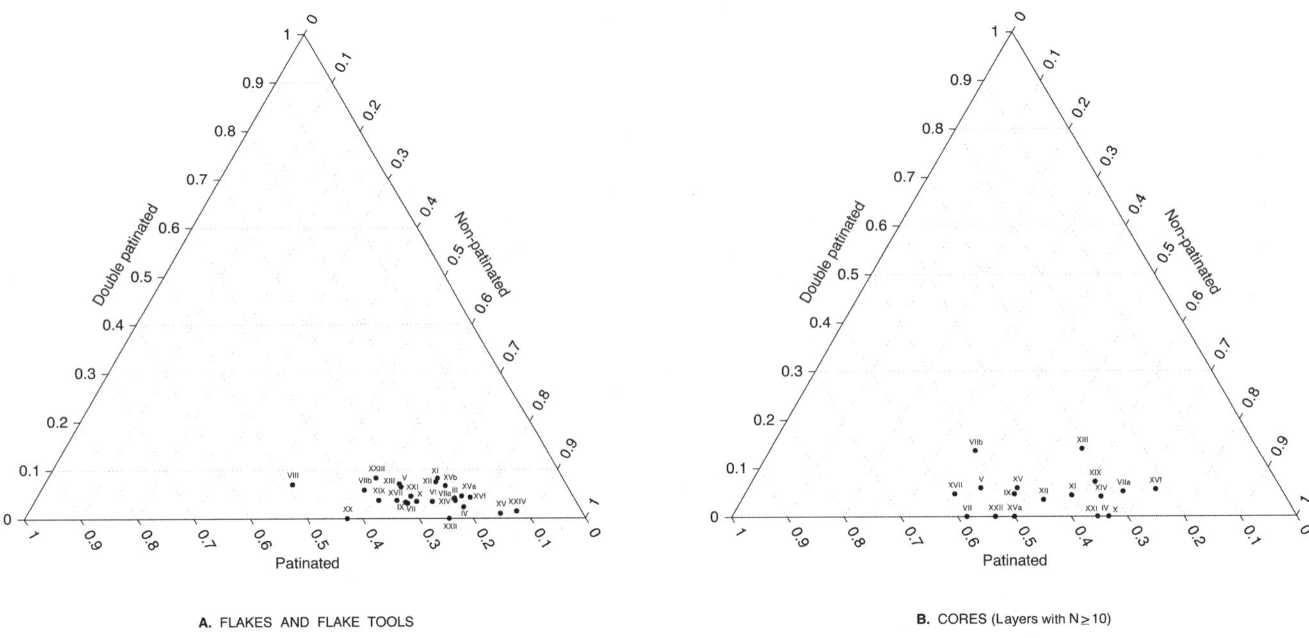

**Figure 7.4**   Triangular scatterplot of frequencies of states of patination.

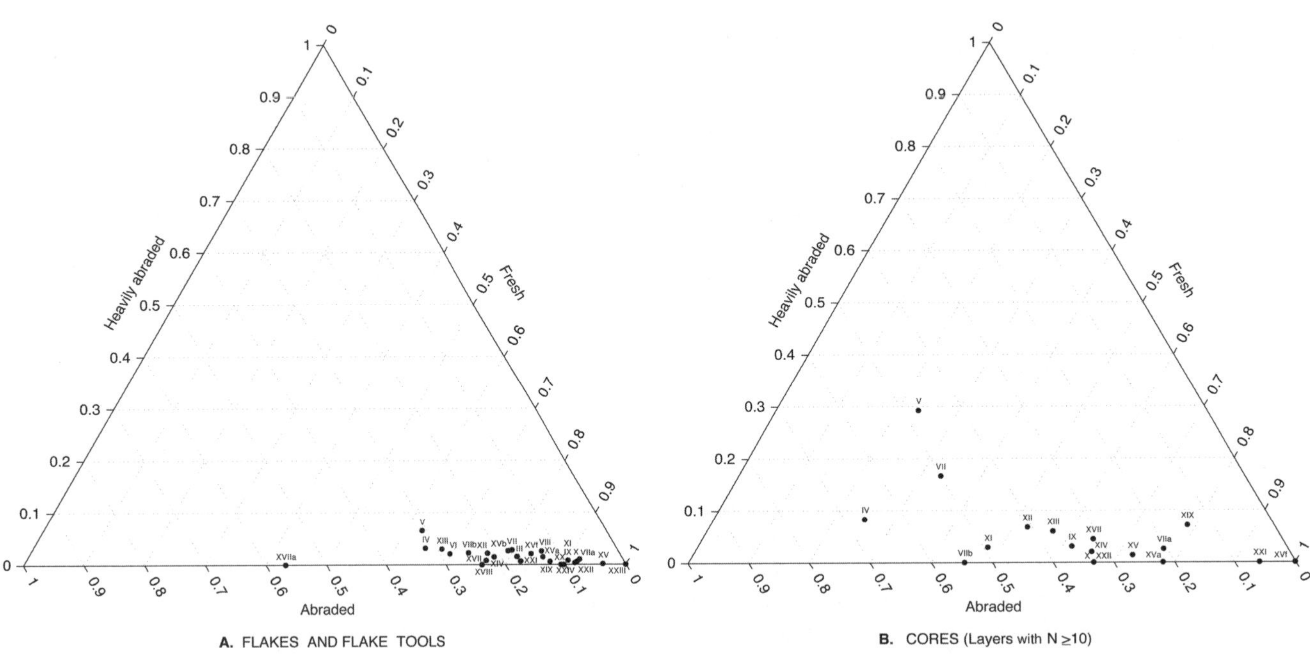

**Figure 7.5**   Triangular scatterplot of frequencies of states of preservation.

12–20 km northwest of the site (Greenberg 1963). Shea (1991:131–132) reports the existence of partially exposed Cenomanian flint nodules at several points along Wadi el-Haj, some within 100 m from the cave. These, however, are of a semi-translucent purple color with waxy texture, and flawed (J. Shea, pers. comm. 1996; pers. obs.), and occur in the cave assemblages only in trace amounts. Brown, good-

quality flint also occurs close to the site, but its appearance in thin bands in the limestone rocks potentially prevented its use for Levallois products (pers. obs.). These data imply selectivity on the part of the Qafzeh hominins with regard to the quality of their raw material.

There is no reliable way of ascertaining the accessibility of flint sources under differing climatic conditions in the past. Still, given Qafzeh's geographic location in the Levant, it can plausibly be argued that sources of raw material known today in the hilly area have never been masked by climate-driven phenomenon (e.g., extensive ice sheets). Nor is there indications of tectonic or volcanic events in the central Lower Galilee region during the late Middle to early Upper Pleistocene, which might have terminated the availability of specific outcrops during the time of occupation.[6] On the whole, the regional geological record is consistent with the picture that emerges from the archaeological data and does not support a model of shifting raw material availability due to paleoenvironmental factors throughout the time of deposition of the Qafzeh sequence. This in turn suggests that observed variations in raw material economies at Qafzeh over time is not biased by geomorphic effects, and should be attributed to social, economic, and technological decisions based on other factors.

## Raw Material Transport

The selectivity observed with regard to raw material quality suggests that raw material acquisition by the Qafzeh hominins was part of an organized technological system. Transport behavior inferred from the lithic finds forms another axis around which arguments for the presence or absence of planned behavior relating to raw material exploitation revolve. The sporadic incidence of small artifacts made on exotic raw material in the assemblages of sites located in areas rich in raw material may cautiously be attributed to accidental loss of personal gear (Binford 1989; Hovers 2001; Kuhn 1992b); for example, the occurrence of isolated flakes of chert in 2.6-million-year-old sites in Gona, Ethiopia, at a relatively large distance from their sources (Semaw et al. 2003), should be interpreted along these lines. On the other hand, the occurrence of bulky stones (e.g., large cores, blocks of raw material) or of lightly utilized pieces made of non-local stones, or the occurrence of imported artifacts in regions containing only raw material of inferior quality, support the inference of planned transport and provisioning of place. The range of such transport is defined through the identification of raw material sources by geological survey and their matching with archaeological artifacts and site distributions (e.g., Féblot-Augustins 1993, 1997; Geneste 1985; Hovers 1990b; Roebroeks, Kolen, and Rensink 1988).

In the case of Qafzeh, the information on raw material sources suggests raw transport of material into the site over a distance exceeding 10 km.[7] This distance is beyond the daily foraging range of most extant hunter-gatherers (Hayden 1981:382, tab. 10; Vita-Finzi and Higgs 1970). In some studies of the European Middle Paleolithic that elucidate the relationship between raw material transport distances and the technological make-up of assemblages, transport distances within the range of 5–20 km

are considered "intermediate" (Féblot-Augustins 1993; Geneste 1985). These studies concluded that only 5–20% of the pieces in an assemblage are likely to have been imported over such distances. When that was the case, they were introduced into the sites in the form of prepared blanks. On the other hand, local flint, transported over distances up to 5 km, occurred abundantly (60–95% of the lithic artifacts), with all or most stages of the reduction sequence being present on site. Finally, tools and blanks brought from distant procurement zones, situated over 20 km away from the site, amount to 5% of the number of artifacts, in the form of preformed cores and finished tools.

Transport behavior at Qafzeh deviates from these expected patterns. Despite the relatively long transport distance, debitage and debris associated with the sequential stages of core reduction (e.g., core management pieces, cortical flakes) occur in each layer (table 7.1, figure 7.1). All or most of the core-reduction process apparently took place on site at all times during the Qafzeh sequence, albeit on notably different scales. Based on experimental work, Geneste (1985:250, 259, tab. 11 and fig. 74) suggested that, when decortication (his "phases 0,1" of six observable reduction phases; Geneste 1985:194–195, fig. 44) occurred on site, the frequencies of highly cortical flakes (i.e., with 50–100% of dorsal face cortical cover) would be ca. 13% in a reduction sequence designed toward the production of Levallois flakes. However, at Qafzeh, frequencies of cortical elements in the terrace layers are substantially lower (table 5.2, figure 5.2). Additionally, these frequencies also encompass cortical core management pieces, which Geneste did not count as cortical elements. The frequencies of cortical pieces at Qafzeh would have been even lower had they been computed with cores being included in the total for each assemblage, as done by Geneste (1985:258, fig. 74). Finally, the frequencies of pieces that are 100% cortical are very low (see table 5.3, the "cortical" category). Such data strongly suggest that the first stages of core reduction (selection of nodules and their preliminary preparation) occurred outside the cave, and that cores were brought into the cave when partially decorticated.

A note of caution, however, is required here. The areas of excavation were limited. If activities were spatially segregated, as seen in other Middle Paleolithic sites (such as Amud, Kebara, Far'ah II, and Tor Faraj; Alperson-Afil and Hovers 2005; Bar-Yosef et al. 1992; Gilead 1988; Henry 2003), products of block decortication on site may not have been sampled by the excavation. However, given the spatial co-occurrence of cores with the various types of debitage, current data are consistent with the null hypothesis that the excavated material is an adequate sample of the total lithic assemblage. This question can only be resolved if and when excavation areas are extended in the future.

That nearly complete reduction sequences occurred on site renders any determination of the amount of blanks and tools transported into the site, that is, of individual provisioning, probabilistic at best. The two archaeological proxies of flake transport to be considered are artifact size, namely identifying artifacts whose size lies outside the normal size range, and distortion of the expected frequencies of various sequential stages of core reduction.

*Blank Size and Transport Behavior*

Where the initial size of raw material packages is both well-defined and small (as in the case of sorted, size-constrained conglomerates or beach pebbles; Baumler and Speth 1993; Kuhn 1995a, respectively), lithic items of exceptionally large size provide a plausible indication of transport from off-site sources. This, however, is not the case for the assemblages of Qafzeh. Here cores were fashioned from nodular flint of variable (boulder-sized) dimensions, so that initial sizes are unknown. The partial decortication of cores before they were brought into the site does imply attempts at a compromise between the desire to acquire large raw material mass and move it to the site for future use and the need to reduce mass when moving raw material over relatively large distances. Together with the paucity of fully cortical pieces, this suggests that

partly decorticated cores were brought to Qafzeh after they had been tested at the raw material source and likely also reduced to a convenient size for carrying.

Cortical pieces are immobile technological elements, left at the sites where they were detached (Geneste 1985). Their presence in the Qafzeh assemblage reflects the process of decortication and shaping of the core as it continued on site. The maximum length of cortical pieces (bearing cortex on 50% or more of their dorsal faces) ranges between 100–120 mm in all the assemblages. Combined with their paucity, this suggests that at all times cores were of a more or less similar (and restricted) size range when first introduced into the site. Based on the few decortication blocks recovered at the site (chapter 5) and on the size of the fully or almost fully cortical pieces, the initial size of such cores may be conservatively estimated as ca. 11–12 cm. Thus, the sizes of flakes detached on site will vary within a range constrained by this value. Flakes larger than this expected size are found in many of the Qafzeh assemblages (table 5.9, figures 5.7–5.9). However, size-based distinction between large flakes produced on site and those that may have been imported into the cave is made difficult by the large variations of flake length and width measurements (see the large standard deviations in table 5.9). To circumvent this

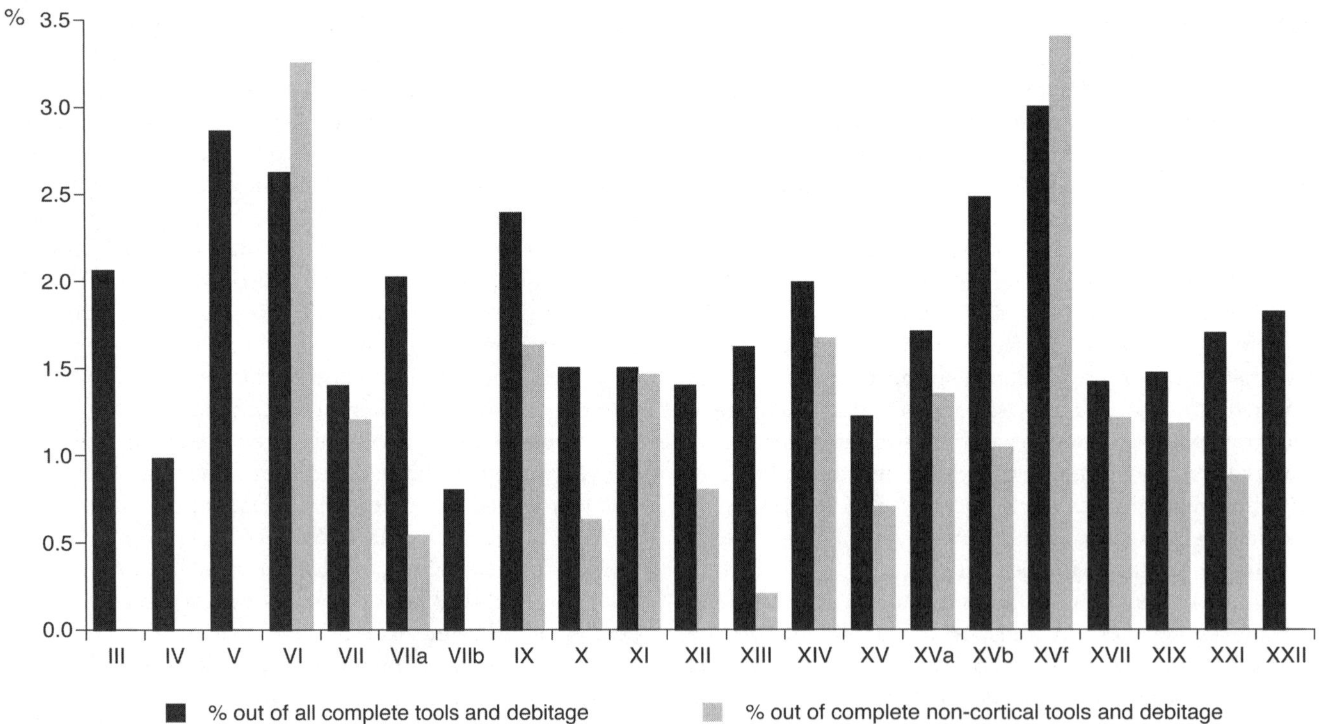



**Figure 7.6**  Percentages of "larger than expected" flakes in the various assemblages. Flakes that fall within this category are those whose length ≥ the mean length + 3 standard deviations in the particular assemblage (see text for further discussion of the statistical procedure and implications).

difficulty, the mean size of unbroken blanks was used as a standard against which flakes of exceptional dimensions were identified. As a precaution due to the large variance, only flakes whose size exceeded the mean length or width of complete flakes by three standard deviations were considered "larger than expected" for the purpose of this analysis.[8] The proportions of exceptionally large flakes in the samples of unbroken flakes and tools from each layer vary from 0.8 to 3.0% (figure 7.6).[9]

Since cortical elements are the less mobile components of lithic reduction products, a fine-tuned measure of blank transport into the site is based on the proportions of "larger than expected" artifacts among non-cortical as compared to cortical elements. Cortex-free flakes tend to be produced in later stages of the reduction sequence and are therefore expected to be smaller on average than cortical pieces. Although cortex-free Levallois flakes are on average larger than other products, this expectation is corroborated at Qafzeh when "flake size" (as defined in chapter 5) of cortical flakes is compared to that of non-cortical pieces (figure 7.7). "Larger than expected" flakes should thus occur less frequently among non-cortical flakes if only minimal transport of blanks into the site took place.

In some assemblages (e.g., layers III–V, VIIb, XXII), there are no excessively large flakes among unbroken, non-cortical elements (usually Levallois flakes, as demonstrated from comparison of data in table 7.3 with figure 5.7). In other instances, such flakes appear in lower percentages than within the assemblage of unbroken pieces, the only exceptions being layers VI and XVf (figure 7.6). These data imply that transport of large flakes or tools as "personal gear," thus curating potentially available working edges in anticipation of future needs, rarely occurred. This pattern is known from other Middle Paleolithic sites, for example, open-air localities in the Nile Valley, where production or import of relatively small Levallois flakes appears to be the normative choice irrespective of distance from raw material sources (Van Peer 1991:139).

*Transport Behavior and Reduction Sequences*

As discussed in chapter 2, experimental and theoretical work on Levallois flaking systems has led to recognition of some inherent properties of reduction sequences carried out by this technology. The properties recognized by such studies enabled the formulation of expectations

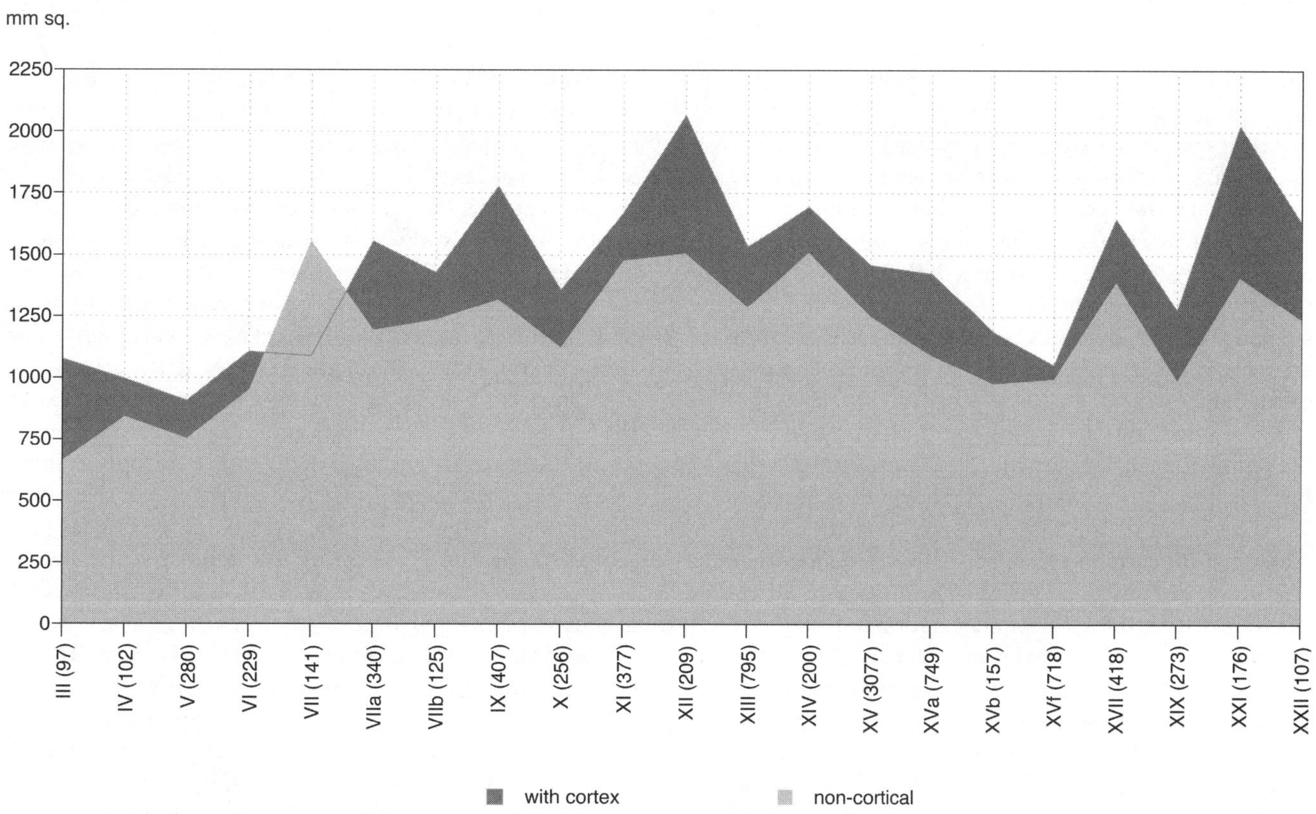


**Figure 7.7** Comparison of mean flake size (see definition of this variable in chapter 5) of cortical vs. non-cortical blanks and tools (only complete pieces included in the analysis).

**Table 7.3   Means, standard deviations, and threshold size for large flakes**

| Layer | Length | | | Width | | |
|---|---|---|---|---|---|---|
| | Mean | s.d. | Mean + 3s.d. | Mean | s.d. | Mean + 3s.d. |
| III | 31.99 | 13.66 | 73.00 | 23.78 | 8.78 | 50.12 |
| IV | 33.51 | 13.76 | 74.79 | 24.40 | 10.89 | 57.07 |
| V | 31.23 | 13.66 | 72.21 | 23.55 | 8.71 | 49.68 |
| VI | 34.39 | 13.34 | 74.41 | 25.91 | 10.04 | 56.03 |
| VII | 37.54 | 16.39 | 86.71 | 31.42 | 14.45 | 74.77 |
| VIIa | 40.00 | 18.00 | 94.00 | 29.80 | 13.07 | 42.87 |
| VIIb | 38.62 | 15.83 | 86.11 | 30.49 | 10.66 | 62.29 |
| IX | 41.26 | 19.66 | 100.24 | 31.19 | 11.95 | 67.04 |
| X | 37.29 | 16.59 | 87.06 | 17.79 | 10.22 | 58.45 |
| XI | 42.73 | 17.11 | 94.06 | 32.53 | 12.05 | 68.68 |
| XII | 46.64 | 17.96 | 100.52 | 33.49 | 12.06 | 69.67 |
| XIII | 41.22 | 17.72 | 94.36 | 29.72 | 10.67 | 61.73 |
| XIV | 45.43 | 17.11 | 96.76 | 32.28 | 11.38 | 66.42 |
| XV | 41.50 | 18.10 | 95.80 | 28.44 | 10.60 | 60.24 |
| XVa | 36.32 | 16.56 | 86.00 | 28.37 | 11.61 | 63.20 |
| XVb | 33.91 | 14.78 | 78.25 | 26.36 | 10.71 | 58.49 |
| XVf | 33.36 | 15.25 | 79.11 | 26.02 | 10.85 | 36.91 |
| XVII | 40.53 | 17.41 | 92.76 | 31.83 | 13.17 | 71.34 |
| XIX | 33.86 | 15.62 | 80.72 | 28.40 | 11.92 | 64.16 |
| XXI | 41.13 | 19.30 | 99.03 | 33.42 | 15.19 | 48.60 |
| XXII | 35.80 | 16.23 | 84.49 | 30.60 | 15.73 | 77.79 |

*Note*: Complete artifacts only.

about the properties of the lithic assemblages and, in turn, allowed the identification of deviations and peculiarities. The discrepancies between the expected and the observed in the Qafzeh assemblages are also helpful in understanding whether transport behavior biased the structure of any of the assemblages. Either the absence of artifacts associated with certain segments of the *chaîne opératoire* or their over-representation in relation to other stages of the sequence allows identification of export and/or import of artifacts in an assemblage. We have seen that some such discrepancies (e.g., the occurrence of bipolar Levallois flakes without bipolar cores) could be explained within the parameters of the reduction sequence itself (chapter 5), but this type of explanation is not always applicable.

The value of the ratio of flakes and tool blanks to cores in each assemblage is heuristically defined here as an "index of flaking intensity." The values of this index fluctuate throughout the sequence. Moderate values were encountered in some of the younger assemblages (layers III, V, and VII) and lower ones were registered in the older assemblages (XXII–XVII) (figure 7.8a). In layers VI, X, and XVa, the index of flaking intensity is high, attaining extreme values in layers XVb and XVf. Returning to the technological discussion in the previous chapters and to figure 7.3, it becomes clear that these fluctuations do not necessarily stem from a single behavior.

Some discrepancies may be related more to production practices than to organizational tactics. For instance, it has been argued (Stiner and Kuhn 1992) that unipolar or bidirectional flaking, expressed by elevated frequencies of unipolar and bipolar scar patterns, enhances the efficiency of flake production, resulting in higher numbers of flakes per core. Based on this suggestion, the values of the index of flaking intensity are expected to co-vary with unipolar or bipolar scar patterns. This co-variation is not clear-cut in Qafzeh. Some assemblages with a relatively high proportion of flakes with bipolar scar patterns do not show the expected high index value (e.g., assemblages IX, X). At the same time, values of the index are high in some assemblages with a relatively low proportion of these scar patterns (e.g., layer XVb). The technological analysis presented in chapter 5, indicating that bipolar scar patterns were in many instances related to centripetal reduction modes, explains this discrepancy in part.

Levallois artifacts require a relatively high investment of time in their production (Shott 1989a), whereas their relative thinness (as defined in chapter 5) enhances their utility per unit mass (Kuhn 1994). As a result, Levallois flakes tend to be the curated, more mobile components within the lithic technological system (Geneste 1985:526). The paucity of Levallois relative to non-Levallois flakes in the Qafzeh assemblages may

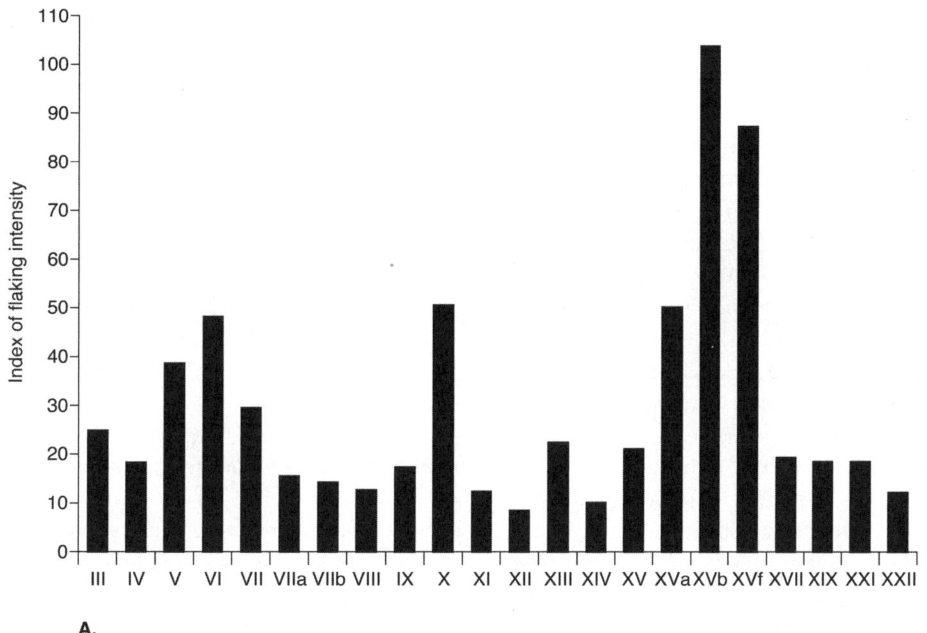



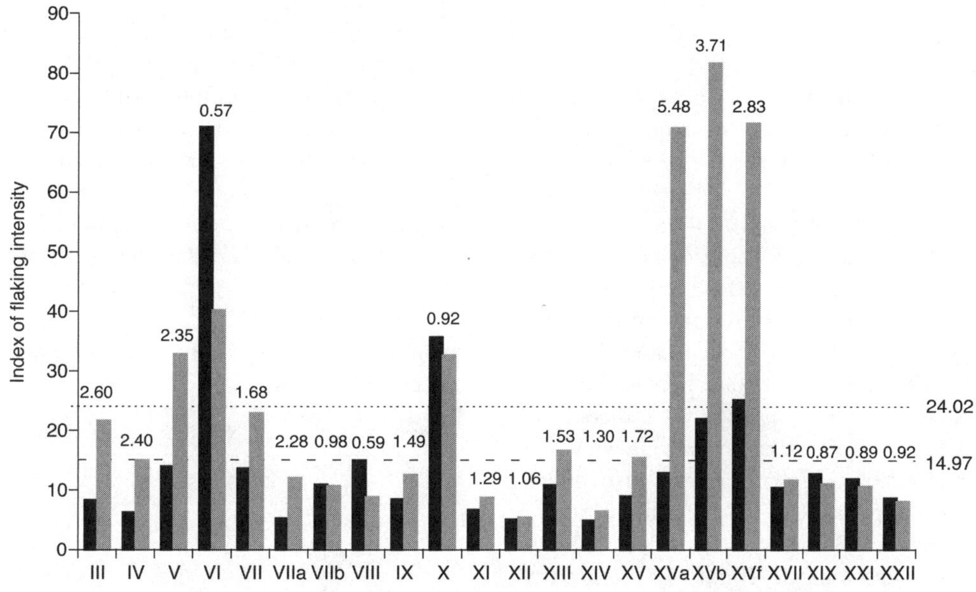



**Figure 7.8** Variations in flaking intensity across assemblages. A: Variation of total numbers of flakes to total number of cores. B: Variation in flaking intensity of Levallois and non-Levallois products in relation to Levallois and non-Levallois cores, respectively. The horizontal lines represent the inter-assemblage mean for each technological group. The ratio between the index value of non-Levallois to Levallois debitage in each assemblage is given at the top of each pair of histograms (see text for more details).

be partly the outcome of the technological steps taken to produce the flakes, where flakes deriving from the Levallois flaking system cannot be recognized as such (discussed in detail in chapter 5). But this could also reflect some export from the production site at Qafzeh to other locales in the exploited territory. Artifact movement in the opposite direction (i.e., into the cave) should also be considered. If the inflated values of the index of flaking intensity in some assemblages stem from import of artifacts, we would expect Levallois artifacts to be the majority of imported elements (cf. Jelinek 1982b:80). In such cases the number of Levallois blanks per core would be expected to be high relative to the number of non-Levallois blanks per core.

Because a substantial number of non-Levallois flakes could have originated from Levallois reduction sequences, an index of flaking intensity for non-Levallois debitage was computed using the total number of cores. The index for Levallois debitage was calculated strictly per Levallois core. Figure 7.8b presents the breakdown of flaking intensity of each category. The horizontal lines indicate across-assemblage means (Levallois: 14.97 ± 14.46; non-Levallois: 24.02 ± 22.58). The ratio of non-Levallois to Levallois debitage in each assemblage is given at the top of each pair of histograms.

The index of flaking intensity of Levallois reduction is higher than that of non-Levallois reduction in layers VI, VIIb, VIII, X, and XIX–XXII. The relatively high value in layer VI appears to reflect a real abundance of Levallois debitage per core (figure 7.8b), rather than a paucity of cores (figure 7.1). The pattern is in agreement with the high proportion of "larger than expected" non-cortical flakes in this layer (figure 7.6), with both trends implying that at the time of this particular occupation Levallois debitage was imported into the site on a perceptible scale. In other assemblages[10] the low values of the indices of the two flaking systems are not as distinct as in layer VI, nor are they corroborated by a high frequency of oversized pieces. In the case of layers XVa–XVf, the high index of flaking intensity (figure 7.8a) very likely reflects the paucity of cores in these assemblages (figure 7.1) rather than over-representation of Levallois products (figure 7.8b). Core management pieces and cortical elements, two types of debitage that are not expected to have been selectively transferred into the site (Geneste 1985), occur in these assemblages. The combination of these two assemblage characteristics implies that core reduction took place on site. Still, some of the cores could have been removed later, possibly to provision other locations exploited by the occupying group or more likely as personal gear. This is consistent with Kuhn's (1994) formal model and cited ethnographic observations, both of which suggest that cores were included in mobile tool kits. This may be related to their functional properties (e.g., as multifaceted

tools in addition to raw material stock), which override their inferior ratio of utility per unit mass.

In the case of Qafzeh it is Levallois points that constitute more reliable clues for recognizing transport into and out of the site than other blank classes, since their manufacture entails particular, visible technological characteristics that are not swamped by the presence of other Levallois products. Cores for points are rare (table 4.1). Additionally, Levallois points are few in relation to other Levallois products (table 7.4) and to the total assemblage of each layer. Point manufacture appears to have occurred mostly outside the site in the majority of cases.[11]

There are a few exceptions, such as layers XV and VIIa. Cores for points form 13.74% (more if cores-on-flakes with point scars are counted) and 9.52% of all Levallois cores in these assemblages, respectively (table 4.1a), whereas the frequencies of points among all the unretouched Levallois products are 12.41% and 9.68%, respectively. While point manufacture was not the main goal of Levallois production in these assemblages, the characteristics of core management pieces (chapter 5) are compatible with on-site flaking of points.

A different situation is observed in layer XIII. Here, too, cores for points form 9.52% of the Levallois cores, but Levallois points account for only 1.90% of all unretouched Levallois products. The occurrence of laminar naturally backed flakes in this assemblage, similar to those of layer XV, suggests on-site point production by convergent Levallois methods (table 5.3, appendix 5). In this case, it seems that Levallois points were removed from the site.

**Table 7.4  Frequencies and indices of flaking intensity of Levallois points**

| Layer | N[a] | N Points | % Points[b] | Points/core |
|---|---|---|---|---|
| V | 76 | 5 | 6.57 | 5.0 |
| VI | 50 | — | — | — |
| VIIa | 94 | 9 | 9.68 | 4.5 |
| VIIb | 56 | — | — | — |
| IX | 228 | 4 | 1.75 | — |
| X | 146 | 6 | 4.11 | 6.0 |
| XI | 173 | 2 | 1.16 | — |
| XII | 98 | 2 | 2.04 | — |
| XIII | 368 | 7 | 1.90 | 1.8 |
| XIV | 112 | 10 | 8.92 | 10.0 |
| XV | 1,346 | 167 | 12.41 | 6.7 |
| XVa | 217 | 4 | 1.84 | 4.0 |
| XVf | 236 | 3 | 1.27 | — |
| XVII | 225 | 5 | 2.22 | — |
| XIX | 149 | 1 | 0.67 | — |
| XXI | 98 | — | — | — |

[a]Unretouched Levallois products.
[b]Percentage from number in column 1.

Levallois points as the hafted parts of thrusting spears (Shea 1989, 1991) would have been personal gear at hunting stations, where discard would have taken place away from the habitation and production site. Points could also have been transported during group movement to other residential sites.

This, in fact, is another case of equifinality, but this time it is observed within the organizational rather than the technological realm of behavior. The outcomes of the two scenarios are the same in terms of archaeological visibility: points are under-represented in the assemblage. However, two very different behaviors might have led to this single outcome. In the first scenario, points would be missing from layer XIII because of the logistical organization of activities or personal curation. In the second scenario, the absence of points would be the outcome of residential mobility strategies.

In layers V, X, and XIV, there are a few cores for points, indicating that point production may have taken place on site (table 7.4). In a recurrent flaking system, it is feasible that the few points retrieved were indeed removed from the single core found in each of these assemblages. The special core management pieces associated with the process do not attest to point production, possibly because their number was too low to be acknowledges as a separate technological phenomenon at the time of analysis.

## Raw Material Consumption

Raw material is primarily consumed during two phases in the use lives of artifacts. The heaviest consumption takes place when the core is reduced into blanks. Further raw material reduction occurs, albeit on a smaller scale, when the products are used as blanks of retouched tools and, finally, if dulled and broken artifacts are remodified or recycled (i.e., used in contexts different from the originally intended use; Shott 1989a:18) as a means of extending their use lives. A knapper can respond to such considerations already at the stage of core reduction by carefully selecting the modes and methods of core reduction. How this control over raw material consumption is exerted depends on the factors deemed crucial by the knapper. The selected reduction sequences may be wasteful in terms of immediate raw material economy, but more efficient in the overall scheme of the anticipated activities and moves of the group. Artifact properties form the basis for inferences about a group's technological behavior.

Depending on the availability of raw material, potential lack of time for artifact knapping, or dearth of information about the nature of future activities (e.g., when moving into new, unknown territories), artifacts may be designed during their removal from the cores to be durable and maintainable, in anticipation of their use for "generalized undertakings that have continuous needs but unpredictable schedules and generally low failure costs" (Bleed 1986:741). Such artifacts are designed to serve as a long-lasting potential stock of cutting edges. This necessitates specific core-reduction modes.

The ability to lengthen an artifact's use life (i.e., artifact maintainability) can be achieved through two different design tactics: versatility and flexibility. Versatile artifact designs can meet a variety of needs without formal change to the artifact (Shott 1986) and are thus expected to exhibit generalized edge forms (e.g., rounded or oval flakes rather than pointed or elongated forms). Use-wear traces tend to be variable because of the variety of tasks performed by these artifacts. Flexible artifacts are those originally produced in generalized form with the notion of later adjustment to a range of uses through changes in their form, that is, retouch. Such changes may be carried out serially, by a sequential reduction/retouch process according to an anticipated order of activities. In this case larger, non-cortical blanks should be selected for use, since they could still be useful after several phases of modification.

Another form of modification is through modular changes, when the order of activities is unanticipated and changes in tool form occur in no particular order. Circumstances of raw material shortage favor versatile designs, which are more economical than flexible designs. Still, in both versatile and flexible designs the emphasis would be on generalized shapes because conversion of specialized forms is expensive (Gould 1983:23) in the currencies of energy, time, and raw material.

### Artifact Design

How lithics (especially pointed specimens) were used by Middle Paleolithic hominins has been extensively debated in the literature (Anderson-Gerfaud 1990; Beyries 1986, 1987; Churchill 1993; Holdaway 1989, 1990; Plisson and Beyries 1998; Shea 1988; Solecki 1992). This debate seems now to be more focused due to analytical advances enabling identification of residues and offering better identification of polishes as well as mechanical damage. A growing body of evidence now suggests that Middle Paleolithic and MSA hominins in various sites applied different hafting materials and techniques to a variety of lithic types, including pointed items, but also retouched and unretouched flakes of various morphologies (Beyries 1988; Boëda, Connan, and Muhesen 1998b; Friedman et al. 1994–5; Lombard 2005; Rots 2002; Rots and van Peer 2006; Shea 1991). Among the influential lithic factors would be tool reliability and its costs in relation to expected returns, the variable brittleness of various lithic raw materials and hence their reliability as hunting weapons. We may assume that tool design in the Middle Paleolithic took into consideration lithic as well as non-lithic components of the tools that likely influenced tool performance, which are usually not preserved archaeologically (e.g., ethnographic examples in Ellis 1997). At Qafzeh it is nonetheless possible to draw some inferences about the design properties embedded in artifacts at the time of their manufacture.

Artifact designs in all the Qafzeh assemblages are consistent with emphasis on maintainability. The shapes of the common core forms, namely centripetal Levallois cores, may not conform to a particular task in the mechanically most efficient way. However, since blank shapes vary with changes in core form throughout the reduction sequence (as discussed in chapter 5), both core and artifacts can be maintained and used for a wide variety of activities (Kelly 1988; Parry and Kelly 1987) in diversified contexts. The occurrence of well-executed but sporadic points in each assemblage indicates that the generalized shapes of artifacts at Qafzeh were intentionally designed in favor of flexibility and/or versatility of tools, most likely in response to the nature of anticipated activities at the site and around it, at the expense of reliable designs for task-specific tools. As discussed above, in a few assemblages there are indications for such tools (i.e., Levallois point production), but these appear to have been exported from the site in most such instances.

The very same properties also satisfy the requirements for easy transport. Transportable tool kits are needed when tools are carried to, rather than made at, the task location (Bamforth 1986; Parry and Kelly 1987; Shott 1986). Such tool kits should be light and small, meaning that they constitute few items (Lee 1979:179 provides an ethnographic example). The constraint on weight dictates the inclusion of versatile or flexible items that can be used to address the variable contingencies of moving over the landscape (Kelly 1988; Kelly and Todd 1988). Levallois cores may form an important component in a mobile tool kit, as they provide flakes that are both thin and have extensive usable edge length relative to unit of mass (chapters 4 and 5). If their use in future extractive tasks away from the site is anticipated, specialized artifacts will be added to the versatile tool kit transported from the habitation and production site to the task locality. The assemblage of layer XIII at Qafzeh, showing indications that Levallois points were carried out of the site, is an example of this approach to raw material consumption.

Design reliability of lithic artifacts is essential in situations in which tool use must be accurately and critically timed, for example, during hunts. Reliable tools tend to be sturdy and bulky (Henry 1995a, b; Nelson 1991), with careful fitting of the tool parts (e.g., the stone tip and the haft). The lithic components are more prone than the non-lithic parts to damage and breakage in the circumstances

in which tools are used.[12] When breakage occurs during use, it will be the damaged stone artifact(s) rather than the whole composite tool that is replaced by a new one because the preparation of the haft is normally the most time-consuming step in this technological process (Keeley 1982). Reliable tool designs emphasize simplicity and standardization at the stage of tool manufacture in order to facilitate emergency replacement procedures (Bleed 1986).

As was shown in chapters 4 and 5, there is a tendency in all the Qafzeh assemblages to adhere to narrow ranges of critical size thresholds and to more or less similar shapes in the process of Levallois flaking. However, the low mean thickness of Levallois products relative to their overall surface area, a repetitive pattern in all the assemblages, renders such blanks more susceptible to breakage during use, and thus less sturdy. This in turn suggests that at all times reliability of design was of less concern during the process of Levallois blank production at Qafzeh.

The paucity of blades in the assemblages supports this inference. Blade production, which arguably allows for a highly efficient ratio of cutting edge length to artifact mass (Sheets and Muto 1972) and for artifact standardization, is one way of obtaining reliable tools. In Qafzeh, not only are blades rare in any given assemblage, but their production has been shown to be a technological side-effect, never a major concern, of the lithic flaking systems of the various assemblages (table 5.17; figures 5.13, 5.15). The highly dispersed values of the metric attributes complement the lack of morphological standardization in these groups of artifacts.

*Artifact Use Lives*

The duration of an artifact's use life depends on the physical properties of a given raw material (i.e., its resistance to various forces of loading and shearing applied during both knapping and use; Braun et al. 2006; Noll 2000) but also on the intensity of its use. Archaeological research has come a long way from the days when only retouched artifacts were considered as artifacts meant for use. Still, because the active parts of lithic artifacts are the edges, retouch remains an important means of evaluating the intensity of the items' use lives. It is taken to reflect purposeful attempts to shape the edge of a blank into a preplanned form or the need to sharpen or strengthen it as use continues.

Retouch demonstrates that the preferred way to obtain usable cutting edges of particular morphology was through resharpening of an existing artifact, rather than by producing a new item. This, too, is the rationalization for the continued use of an already intensively exploited core, despite the small size of the resultant flakes removed in the last stages. The magnitude of retouch would be influenced by the initial suitability of the blank form to the tasks planned for it (i.e., the degree of flexibility assigned to a blank when flaked off a core; see Bamforth 1986) and by overall or immediate scarcity of raw material (Andrefsky 1994).

Raw material consumption can be estimated by sets of data derived from two distinct phases of the flaking sequence. During core reduction itself, raw material consumption can be gauged by the frequency of unexploited cores relative to more thoroughly used ones, as well as the degree of core exhaustion. Consumption of tool blanks in the later stages of the production sequence is apparent in the relative frequency of retouched blanks within the total blank population and by the amount of retouch on those blanks.

One measure of the amount of core reduction is the ratio of "tested" cores (i.e., blocks of raw material that were flaked once or twice to assess the quality of flint) to formal, more completely exploited cores (Geneste 1985; Kuhn 1995a). The former are expected to occur more frequently if raw material was not a critical resource at the time of core reduction. At Qafzeh the ratio is negligible,

choppers and tested cores being practically nonexistent in any of the assemblages (table 4.1). However, this may be related to the fact that raw material was imported into the site after it had been tested at the quarry site. More informative in this context is the fact that globular cores, which appear to have been somewhat more expediently reduced, are extremely few.

It has been argued (Wallace and Shea 2006) that the use of cores-on-flakes tends to be more intensive in assemblages in which raw material is more heavily consumed due to lesser mobility. This is probably an oversimplification with regard to Qafzeh, as well as most other Levantine Mousterian assemblages (Hovers 2007). In the Qafzeh assemblages cores-on-flakes tend to be thicker on average than debitage pieces (compare tables 4.9 and 5.9), attesting to selection for very large flakes (including some primary cortical elements) that had already been present in the assemblage as blanks of such cores. The transformation of flakes into cores thus reflects an improvisation designed to cope with a momentary necessity in a reduced-cost, non-formalized tactic (Binford 1979, 1989).

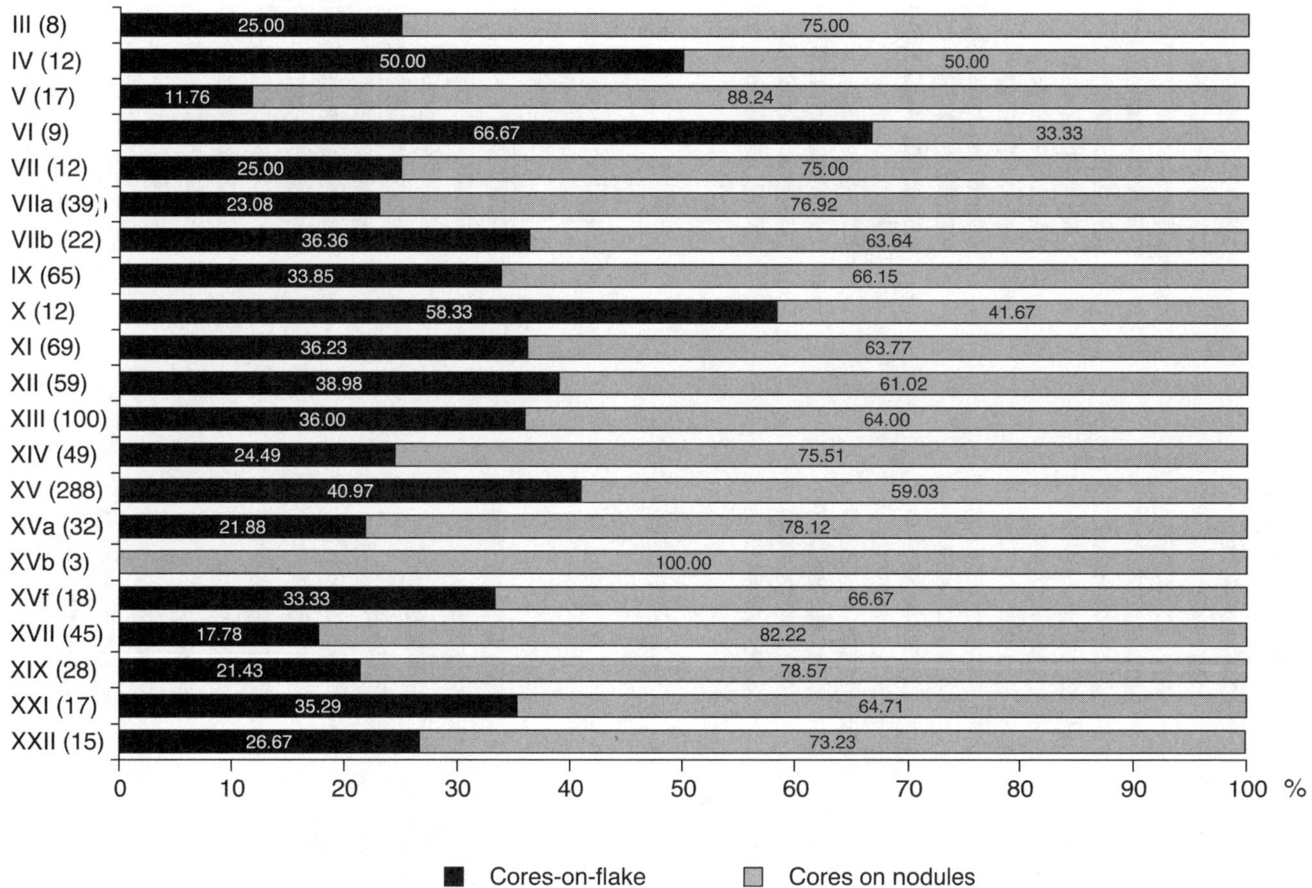



**Figure 7.9** Frequencies of cores on nodules and of cores-on-flakes in the various Qafzeh assemblages (for raw data see chapter 4).

The selection of blanks to be used as cores is non-random and is based on clearly defined selection criteria (chapter 4). The presence of this tactic of blank production is compatible with the lack of expedient core types whose use has incurred more wasteful use of raw material. While the use of cores-on-flakes reflects some level of economizing on raw material, it does not reflect raw material stress.

By the same token, the relative frequencies of cores-on-flakes vary throughout the sequence (notwithstanding the differences in sample sizes), implying that raw material paucity was somewhat more severe at the time of some of the younger occupations (figure 7.9). Given the differences between the two "types" of assemblage compositions, it was expected that the ratio of cores-on-flakes to block cores would differ significantly between the lower (XXII–XV) and the upper (XIV–III) stratigraphic complex. However, the differences in presence of cores-on-flakes from one unit to the other are statistically insignificant ($\chi^2 = 0.19$, $p > .05$, df = 1). Therefore, the limited degree

to which cores-on-flakes are responsive to raw material pressure, their occurrence does not appear to be correlated with the stratigraphic disjunction of assemblage types.

Another set of variables that is prone to changes in the intensity of raw material reduction consists of core dimensions, which are expected to diminish with increasing exploitation. Given the similarity among assemblages in terms of raw material sources and initial transport to the site, a decrease in core dimensions may stand as a proxy for higher exploitation of the cores during the phase of blank production.[13] It is interesting to examine whether changes in core dimensions, if present at all, show positive co-variation with the fluctuations in the ratio of cores-on-flakes to nodule cores, together reflecting heavier demands on raw material.

Levallois cores are longer on average than the total population of nodule/block cores in any given assemblage (figure 7.10a, b), allegedly indicating their more relaxed exploitation (but see below). For each technological class

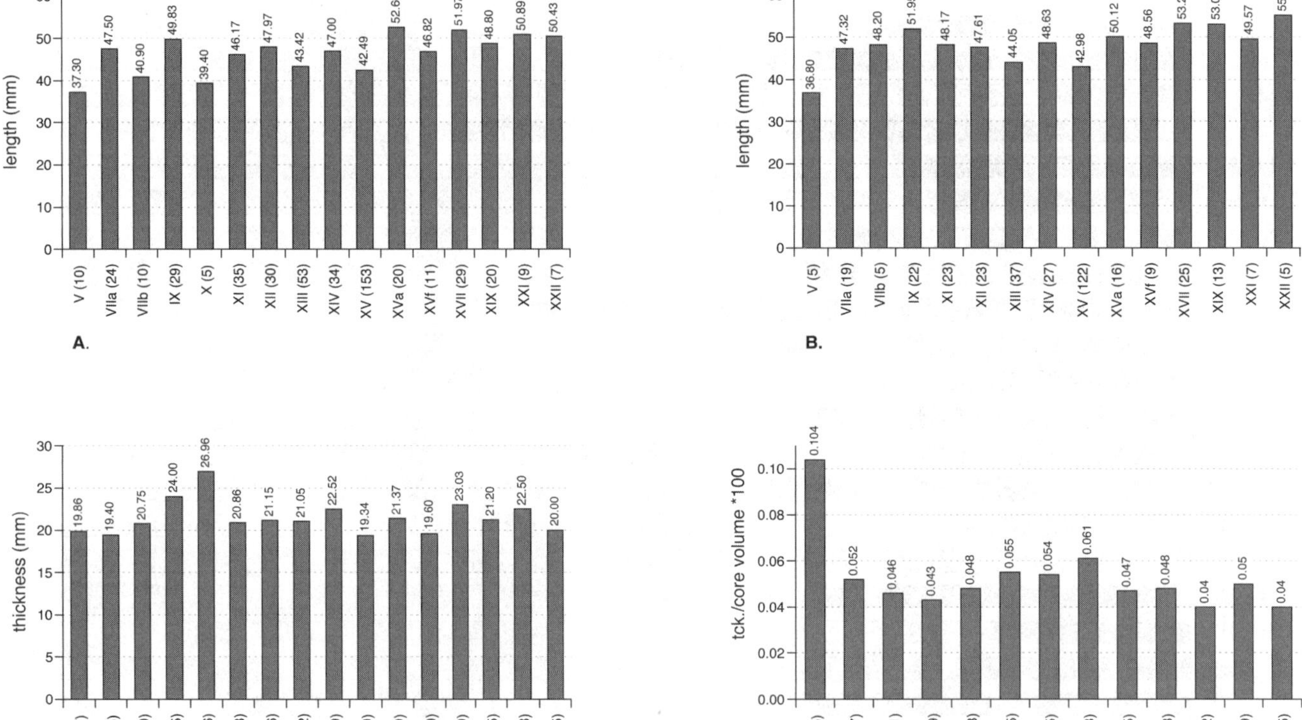

**Figure 7.10** Comparison of mean metric attributes of cores in the various Qafzeh assemblages. A: Mean length of all cores on blocks. B: Mean length of Levallois cores. C: Mean thickness of Levallois cores. D: Mean core exhaustion index of Levallois cores. For analyses A, B, and D only specimens with complete length were included. Only assemblages with N ≥ 5 in the relevant category were included in all the analyses.

there are statistically significant differences among assemblages in the length of cores, although no clear-cut temporal trend is apparent (Kruskal-Wallis H = 51.48, $p < .001$, df = 22; H = 40.88, $p < .01$, df = 21, respectively; but note the small sample sizes available for the younger assemblages). However, Levallois cores are mostly affected by phases of reshaping of the flaking surface. With their bifacially exploited flaking and preparation surfaces, thickness is the most informative dimension as regards intensity of exploitation and exhaustion of Levallois cores. This is especially true when recurrent methods (of any specific mode) are practiced, as the core's thickness decreases directly with each removal.

The relationships between the length and thickness of unbroken Levallois cores are not linear (figure 7.10b, c). The values of mean core thickness are similar in all the assemblages (the mode being ca. 21 mm) regardless of mean core length, or indeed of surface area, and inter-assemblage differences are not statistically significant (H = 22.08, $p > .05$, df = 22). The homogeneity of the core exhaustion index (computed as core thickness divided by core volume; figure 7.10d) throughout the sequence (H = 30.88, $p > .05$, df = 21) indicates that proportionately to their size, cores were reduced very much to the same degree at all times. The high index value for layer V most probably has to do with the small sample size; whereas in layers XIII and XV, it is due to shorter cores rather than to thicker, less utilized ones. These results are in agreement with the suggestion that in all the assemblages Levallois cores were discarded when an average threshold of thickness was reached (chapter 4). Beyond this threshold, removal of appropriate flakes of desired size or shape, while not impossible, was apparently deemed unfeasible. This evidence suggests a technological behavior concerned with raw material deficiency, but not to the extent that threshold criteria were ignored.

The frequency of retouched pieces relative to that of all the unretouched debitage (table 7.5) informs us as to the degree of raw material reduction. This measure is a reflection of the degree of reworking of available blanks and serves as a more reliable indicator of the propensity toward retouch than the frequencies of retouched blanks within the total lithic assemblage. The frequency of retouched elements, or the number of retouched edges, reflect the extent of artifact curation and transport around the landscape in anticipation of future tasks.

Various lines of technological evidence indicate that blanks at Qafzeh were produced on site (chapter 5). We have also seen earlier in this chapter that blank transport into the site was rather limited. The ratio of retouched elements to debitage should therefore be high if concern for

**Table 7.5**  Absolute, (relative) frequencies, and *standardized cell residuals* of retouched and unretouched blanks in the Qafzeh assemblages

| Layer | Retouched | Unretouched | Layer | Retouched | Unretouched |
|---|---|---|---|---|---|
| III | 9 ( 4.55) | 189 (95.45) | XII | 92 (18.47) | 406 (81.53) |
|  | −1.94 | 1.94 |  | **8.29** | **−8.29** |
| IV | 14 ( 6.42) | 204 (93.58) | XIII | 278 (12.39) | 1965 (87.61) |
|  | −1.03 | 1.03 |  | **7.38** | **−7.38** |
| V | 13 ( 1.99) | 640 (98.01) | XIV | 100 (20.20) | 395 (79.80) |
|  | −5.96 | **5.96** |  | **9.67** | **−9.67** |
| VI | 35 ( 8.08) | 398 (91.92) | XV | 396 ( 6.49) | 5709 (93.51) |
|  | −0.19 | 0.19 |  | −6.27 | **6.27** |
| VII | 36 (10.17) | 318 (89.83) | XVa | 72 ( 4.49) | 1530 (95.51) |
|  | 1.26 | 1.26 |  | −5.80 | **5.80** |
| VIIa | 51 ( 8.51) | 548 (91.49) | XVb | 10 ( 3.22) | 301 (96.78) |
|  | 0.16 | −0.16 |  | −3.29 | **3.29** |
| VIIb | 38 (12.18) | 274 (87.82) | XVf | 36 ( 2.29) | 1536 (97.71) |
|  | **2.47** | −2.47 |  | −5.93 | **5.93** |
| IX | 106 ( 9.44) | 1017 (90.56) | XVII | 123 (14.19) | 744 (85.81) |
|  | 1.38 | −1.38 |  | **6.37** | **−6.37** |
| X | 63 (10.40) | 543 (89.60) | XIX | 55 (10.68) | 460 (89.32) |
|  | 1.86 | −1.86 |  | 1.95 | −1.95 |
| XI | 86 (10.17) | 760 (89.93) | XXI | 38 (12.18) | 274 (87.82) |
|  | **1.97** | −1.97 |  | **2.47** | −2.47 |
|  |  |  | XXII | 20 (10.99) | 162 (89.01) |
|  |  |  |  | 1.30 | −1.30 |

*Note*: Total $\chi^2$ = 456.59 at p < .0001, df = 20. Standardized cell residuals that are significant at p < .05 are in bold face.

raw material conservation during core reduction on site was tackled through the use of flexible designs, as argued above. The intensity of retouch of available blanks varies significantly among assemblages. In layers VIIb, XI–XIV, XVII, and XIX, retouched elements are significantly over-represented. In layers V and XVf–XV, the opposite pattern is apparent (table 7.5). Table 6.3 suggests that this is reflected mainly in the tendency to transform generalized blanks into scrapers, emphasized in layers VI, IX, XI, and XIII, leading to statistically significant intra-sequence variation.

Another measure of raw material consumption is the frequency among the tools of artifacts retouched on more than one edge. Composite tools other than complex scrapers do not exhibit any systematically repetitive combinations of "types" or of retouch types (chapter 6) that could suggest intentional, premeditated composite tool forms. There are also no significant size differences between multiple-edged and single-edged tools. As the retouch on the majority of the multi-edged tools is light, the absence of size differences should not be attributed to their reduced dimensions due to extensive use and resharpening. The occurrence of composite tools therefore reflects attempts to utilize the existing cutting edge of a single blank in a more efficient manner and is to some degree an opportunistic behavior of raw material exploitation.

The frequencies of double tools (including double-edged scrapers) are far from being negligible in any layer. They are over-represented in a statistically significant manner, however, in only three assemblages (layers X, XI, and XIII), in all of which, variants of double-edged side-scrapers form a high percentage of the side-scraper group (33.3%, 26.9%, and 24.5%, respectively).

## Inter-Assemblage Variability and Site Function

Within the framework of technological organization studies, lithic assemblage compositions separate occupations on the basis of inferred organizational behaviors (table 7.1). These qualitative typologies serve as baselines for examining archaeological cases, but fail to depict the large amplitude of variation in the lithic assemblages that fall under each category of occupation types. The compositions of the terrace assemblages indeed allow their agglomeration into two distinct groups (layers XXIV–XV and XIV–III) that broadly exhibit different organizational strategies. This has been the basis for many discussions about mobility and settlement patterns along the Qafzeh sequence, coupled at times with inferences about the type of hominins responsible for the different assemblage types (e.g., Lieberman and Shea 1994). Yet the detailed analyses of lithic remains revealed highly variable and complex patterns of technological organization. On the one hand, there is homogeneity that crosses the stratigraphic boundary

between the two groups, while, on the other hand, there is much variation within each assemblage group.

The treatment and use of cores is homogeneous throughout the whole sequence. If, as current data suggest, raw material had to be obtained from a relatively large distance, several possible procurement strategies were open to the cave's inhabitants. Frequent trips could be made to raw material sources in order to obtain flint, ensuring a steady supply by "embedded procurement" whereby flint procurement was incidental to subsistence activities or carried out through task-specific forays within a logistical system of resource acquisition. The evidence in this and previous chapters shows that Qafzeh's occupants opted at all times for a tactical solution of provisioning the site by importing decorticated cores and stockpiling raw material. This enabled the hominins to schedule raw material procurement trips of any type at longer temporal intervals, but is probably also alleviated some of the pressure to economize on raw material.

The lithic assemblages of Qafzeh show a carefully structured combination of conservation strategies during core reduction. Opportunistically flaked cores are extremely rare in these assemblages. On the other hand, core exhaustion due to attempts to maximize blank production is also rare and knapping accidents are a secondary cause for core discard (as discussed in chapter 4), while blanks were purposefully designed to ensure that material for executing predicted tasks would be sufficient. Thus, core abandonment is related primarily to knappers' decisions based on threshold criteria for serviceable, desired blanks. Centripetal flaking modes (in general suitable for raw material conservation; Nelson 1991:76) dominate the core-reduction sequences. When other flaking modes were used, as in layers VIIa, XIII, and XV, they were subsidiary to the main "production line" and applied to specific products, rather than being adopted as the main manufacturing modes of the assemblage. The organization of lithic production at Qafzeh is anything but "expedient manufacture, use and abandonment of instrumental items in the immediate context of use" (Binford 1977:34). Combined, these lithic-related behaviors may indicate that procurement of raw material was a specific task-related activity rather than "embedded" in the acquisition of daily subsistence resources. If the latter was the case, raw material would be collected more frequently and allow for less stringent raw material consumption.

A close look reveals few changes throughout the sequence. IL shows a weak and non-linear, but overall time-trajectoried, decrease in the use of the Levallois technology, concomitant with a lesser emphasis on centripetal flaking. This trend (which is not statistically significant; Fisher's r to z transformation: $r = 0.26$, $p > .05$) does co-occur with a decreasing average length of Levallois flakes (chapter 5), but neither of these changes coincides with the change in assemblage compositions. These patterns imply either reduced emphasis on maintainability as a form of responding to anticipated needs or the use of smaller nodules.

Raw material conservation at the stage of blank use and recycling is far less homogeneous among the various assemblages. Typological characteristics vary considerably along the sequence. The stratigraphic positions of the three classes of assemblages (as defined by typological compositions; figure 6.2) do not co-vary with those of assemblage types based on compositions. Assemblage richness (the number of typological classes represented; Shott 1989b) is fairly similar across assemblages, so that the same typological classes are encountered. Assemblage evenness (the similarity in the frequency distributions of the typological classes within a given assemblage) is low for each assemblage: a single typological class often quantitatively dominates the retouched tools. These variations of assemblage evenness stem from fluctuations in the frequencies of the Mousterian and Upper Paleolithic groups (figure 6.4b).

In the past, attempts have been made to link typological variations along similar lines with intensity of occupation (Rolland 1981; see also Dibble and Rolland 1992; Rolland and Dibble 1990). These authors argued that different retouch angles of side-scrapers affected the attrition rates of two tool classes differentially. In this model side-scrapers, with their lower edge angles, tend to dull more quickly than notches and denticulates, and resharpening of existing side-scrapers or production of new ones is more often required. If activities were carried out with both tool classes for the same length of time, an assemblage would contain more side-scrapers. By this logic, *racloir*-dominated assemblages do not denote proportionately higher amounts of time spent on activities involving those particular tools. Differences in the ratio of side-scrapers to notches (see below) among assemblages represent the intensity of occupation (Rolland and Dibble 1990:487).

Edge angles are similar among the tools at Qafzeh, and since none of the assemblages is dominated by side-scrapers (chapter 6), this model cannot explain the variation at the site. Although this question could have been more closely examined by use-wear studies, such analyses of the Qafzeh lithics (Shea 1991) unfortunately do not touch on the question of functional differences between retouched tool types. Since this is the single available

**Table 7.6  Raw material transport and consumption in the Qafzeh assemblages**

| Layer | Raw material transport | | | | Raw material consumption | | | |
| | EXPORT | | IMPORT | | HIGH | | LOW | |
| | Cores | *Débitage* | Cores[a] | *Débitage* | Cores | *Débitage* | Cores | *Débitage* |
|---|---|---|---|---|---|---|---|---|
| III | | | + | | | | | |
| IV | | | + | | | | | |
| V | | | + | | | | | + |
| VI | | | + | +++ | | + | | |
| VII | | | + | | | | | |
| VIIa | | | + | | | | | |
| VIIb | | | + | + | | ++ | | |
| IX | | | + | | | + | | |
| X | | | + | ++ | | + | | |
| XI | | | + | | + | +++ | | |
| XII | | | + | | + | + | | |
| XIII | | + | + | | + | ++++ | | |
| XIV | | | + | + | | + | | |
| XV | | | + | | + | | | + |
| XVa | + | | + | | | | + | + |
| XVb | + | | + | | | | | + |
| XVf | + | | + | + | | | | + |
| XVII | | | + | | | + | + | |
| XIX | | | + | + | | + | + | |
| XXI | | | + | + | | | | |
| XXII | | | + | + | | | | |

*Note*: "+" represents a statistical test with statistically significant results, or a line of inference that strongly implies a particular conclusion (as detailed in the analysis). The strength of the inference is indicated by the number of "+" signs.
[a] The term "cores" in the context of this column refers to partially decorticated blocks rather than to cores in more advanced stages of reduction.

use-wear study of the Qafzeh materials, it is impossible to address the problem of the varying functions of particular tool types from this perspective. Presumably, the different kinetic properties of tool edges (e.g., of side-scrapers as opposed to denticulates) indicate their use through different motions, and hence for different tasks. In this case, typological differences among the Qafzeh assemblages would reflect changing emphases on various activities rather than being a reliable indication of occupation intensity. The significant differences (table 6.3) within the narrow range of typological variability in the Qafzeh assemblages are caused by variations in assemblage evenness, indicating a degree of "tactical exploitation of the environment in terms of planned strategies" (contrary to Binford 1989:34).

Table 7.6 summarizes the results of the ongoing discussion as a "presence/absence" dichotomy. The "+" symbols in the various columns of the table indicate instances in which either contextual evidence (e.g., cores in all the assemblages; Levallois points in layer XIII) or statistical tests (for instance, the over-representation of retouched artifacts among the flaked blanks in an assemblage) imply a particular behavior with relation to raw material consumption and transport as analyzed in the previous sections. From this summary table it emerges that several organizational strategies played a role in the formation of the Qafzeh assemblages.

Clearly, inferences about technological organization are probabilistic and the identification of any single assemblage as demonstrating specific transport or blank consumption behavior is tentative. I emphasize here that such inferences are relative, in that they are made against the baseline of all the Qafzeh assemblages. The question as to how they are relevant to other assemblages is not discussed at this point.

*Technological Tactics Throughout the Qafzeh Sequence: An Ever-Changing Story*

The overall theme of organization of lithic production at Qafzeh is maintainability of blanks. The manner in which cores were used balances both immediate needs (the need to economize for the duration of site occupation because of distance from raw material sources) against anticipated requirements (the emphasis on size and form of Levallois flakes as "stock" for future modification).

The tactics of achieving blank maintainability in Qafzeh are diversified. Layers XXII–XVII form a cluster in themselves. Centripetal core-reduction modes and flake sizes were accentuated to the extent that in some assemblages lineal rather than recurrent flaking modes were preferred (chapter 5). The small-scale import of Levallois debitage into layers XXII–XIX (figure 7.8) is complementary to the significantly high tendency (layers XIX–XVII)

to retouch tools, mainly into notches and denticulates on non-Levallois blanks (figure 6.2). A similar tactic of raw material parsimony is observed in layer VI, where the transport of Levallois debitage appears to have occurred on a larger scale. In that case blanks were retouched into scrapers, presumably in anticipation of a different set of tasks than was the case for the lower layers. Similarly, in layer VIIb, Levallois debitage appears to have been brought into the site as personal gear. This is coupled with a (statistically) significant preference for retouch of locally produced flakes. The significant occurrence of retouch on Levallois debitage is not random, given that the value of IL in this assemblage is not exceptionally high.

Assemblages XIII–X all exhibit indications of relatively high levels of raw material stress. In layer X, Levallois artifacts were brought into the site, and attempts to extend the use lives of tools are expressed by a higher tendency to produce double-edged tools and apply retouch to large Levallois blanks. Another tactic for maximizing the exploitation of raw material is reflected in the higher than expected frequencies of cores-on-flakes, combined with significantly high frequencies of retouched artifacts in the total flake populations and with double-edged retouch (layers XIII–XI). In layer XIII, this latter tendency is concomitant with intensive retouch of Levallois artifacts, similar to layer X.

The complexity of the interplay between the distribution of activities and the scheduling of raw material acquisition from its sources is illustrated by the fact that in layer XIII, concurrent with the tendency to maximize raw material exploitation on site, there was preparation and export of Levallois points. Given their potential role as hunting weapons, a likely scenario is that these items were transferred to task-specific locations outside the cave and apparently not returned. Superficially contradictory, these two attitudes toward the use of lithic resources in fact complement one another. These characteristics clearly illustrate that processes of lithic production were not solely dictated by the paucity of a single resource but also provide an opportunity to more fully understand the location of Qafzeh Cave within a complex settlement network.

A different tactical approach to economizing on raw material occurs in layers XVf–XV. Retouched blanks are significantly under-represented in these assemblages, perhaps suggesting a more liberal use of raw material. Alternatively, this could reflect a different emphasis on tool design, for example, on versatile, as opposed to flexible, design, as a means to enhance blank maintainability. The patterns observed in the assemblage probably reflect both tactics, as indicated by the reduced values of IL (particularly in layers XVf–XVa) and the rare occurrence of opportunistic cores-on-flakes (layer XVa). Notwithstanding the clear evidence for on-site knapping, the paucity of cores in these assemblages may indicate export of partly reduced cores as a mobile source of serviceable blanks (see Kuhn 1994), that is, provisioning of other locations.

Whereas the focus throughout the occupation at Qafzeh was on activities requiring generalized blank forms, additional tasks were incorporated into the technological repertoire of the layer XV occupation. Although Levallois points were produced on site, their breakage pattern (73.05% of the points are not broken) suggests that they were not used there. The relatively few broken points are possibly those returned for retooling from task-specific locations (proximal parts form 13.77% of the point sample; see Holdaway 1989; Keeley 1982). A plausible interpretation is that points were made on site and stocked there before use at task locations.

The pattern seen in layer XV is discernible, on a smaller scale, in layer VIIa, indicating yet another instance of technological behavior that is associated with hunted meat resources.

*Fauna and Lithics*

So far in this chapter, the variability of lithic assemblages in Qafzeh has been examined in terms of tactics of raw material exploitation. The observed variability (illustrated in figure 7.3) can be linked to tactics of raw material procurement, transport, and consumption and clearly has implications for understanding transport behavior and site function within a larger settlement system. Interestingly, chronological ordering has been shown to be a poor predictor of organizational patterns along this sequence. What might have triggered these changes in organizational behavior? In chapter 2 the hierarchical structure of technological organization was discussed. Strategies of obtaining extractive technologies, as well as tactics of using them, are subservient to the desirability and spatio-temporal availability of subsistence resources within a given physical and social environment (e.g., Kelly 1992; Nelson 1991; Torrence 1989a). It will be useful at this stage to look at ties between lithic organization and the exploited resource structure.

These do not occur as physical facts of the archaeological record and must be inferred. One can at best hope to achieve robust statistical associations, but these do not automatically imply causation. If such associations can be determined, their archaeological explanations will stem from the implications of possible links between behaviors such as foraging techniques and mobility patterns. For instance, the magnitude of group mobility is determined to a large extent by the resource structure. This in turn determines the degree to which people have to rely on portable tool kits and influences the trade-off between transport costs and artifact size, or amount of

reduction and artifact design. This is a complex relationship within a multivariate behavioral system, even before "non-functional" social and cultural variables enter the equation. Hence, the lack of robust associations between resource exploitation and lithic organization may actually lead to new hypotheses regarding the relationship between these two aspects of human behavior than would an association.

In prehistoric research, there has been much theoretical emphasis on the role of faunal resources in subsistence behavior and on their impact on human societies. Meat acquisition (by either hunting or scavenging) has been perceived as a prime mover of technological organization and social behaviors (e.g., Aiello and Wheeler 1995; Ambrose 2001; de Heinzlein et al. 1999; Kuhn 1995a; Kuhn and Stiner 2006; Plummer 2004; Rose and Marshall 1996; Shea 1998; Stanford 1999; Stiner 1994, 2002; Stiner and Kuhn 1992; to name but a few examples). It has been suggested on both theoretical and empirical grounds that variation in technological organization or typological composition is intimately linked with exploitation of faunal resources (Chase 1986; Dibble and Rolland 1992; Kuhn 1995a; Rolland 1981; Stiner 1994). But it is important to recognize that the attention paid to faunal resources is a matter of default as much (if not more) as it is a theoretical attitude (Hovers 1998b), as it stems in part from the simple fact that faunal remains are most often the only subsistence resource archaeologically visible, in the form of bone assemblages.[14]

This is indeed the case at Qafzeh, where fauna is the only known indication of subsistence resources used by the occupants. It was argued that animal bones are distributed differentially in the two parts of the stratigraphic section. Notably the number of macromammal bones is low throughout the section. In the lower part (layers XXIV–XVI), there are few bones of large mammals (NISP = 408), while micromammals abound. The pattern is reversed in the younger layers (XV–III), where large mammals are relatively abundant (NISP = 878), while micromammal bones are practically absent (Rabinovich and Tchernov 1995). Because of extreme differences in sample size per layer, these frequencies need to be standardized by some correlate of occupation magnitude in order to be meaningful. Here the excavated volume (table 3.2) serves as the standardizing factor (see Bar-Yosef 1983; Rafferty 1985 on density and settlement magnitude). Admittedly, this is not a perfect measure, given the possible effects of taphonomic agents on bones (e.g., Rabinovich 1990; Rabinovich and Horwitz 1994; Stiner et al. 2001b; Weiner and Bar-Yosef 1990; Weiner, Goldberg, and Bar-Yosef 1993) and sediment thickness and compactness (Schiegl et al. 1996).

Figure 7.11 shows the densities of lithic items (cores and debris included) and bone remains (NISP; after Rabinovich and Tchernov 1995). The patterns are not compatible with expectations derived from the overall bipartite division of the sequence and the trends for the two find classes are not always synchronized. Lithic and bone densities are positively but not strongly correlated (Spearman's r is 0.59, $p$ < .01; figure 7.11). Layers XXII and XIX–XVII are clustered as relatively "low lithic–high faunal density" assemblages; they share this pattern with layers XII–X in the higher part of the section (figure 7.11). The oldest layers (XXIV and XXIII) form a cluster of overall low-density assemblages, sharing this property with the younger assemblages of layers VI, VIIa, and VIIb. Other assemblages show intermediate values, with higher bone densities but without significant changes or variation in lithic densities. Layers IX, XVf, and XV are exceptions with markedly higher lithic densities compared to other assemblages.

Sample sizes per assemblage are small and do not allow a rigorous examination of the associations between faunal assemblages and lithic technology. Some patterning was detected among assemblages XXII–IX and VIIa–V (layers IV–III, VIIb, and XXIV–XXIII were omitted from the analysis due to sample size limitations). Still, Rabinovich and Tchernov (1995:21) have shown that the number of species in each assemblage was not biased by the small sample size available per assemblage. Wild cattle, red deer or fallow deer are the most abundant species in any assemblage throughout the sequence.

The archaeofaunas of Qafzeh resulted from hunting rather than scavenging (see Rabinovich and Hovers 2004; Speth in Bar-Yosef et al. 1992; Speth and Clark 2006; Speth and Tchernov 1998, 2001; Stiner 2005). The absence of carnivore damage to the bones (less than 1%), the occurrence of cut marks, and the representation of a variety of anatomical elements (though their breakdown by stratigraphic unit is statistically meaningless; Rabinovich and Tchernov 1995: fig. 6), all attest to this effect. Rabinovich and Tchernov (1995:21–23) also note a conspicuous

occurrence of young animals, especially of the smaller species, in the older assemblages (XXII, XXI, and XVII), although they have not tested this statistically. The overall majority of bones are, however, from adult animals. Although age profiles could not be reconstructed, this pattern is reminiscent of prime-dominated death assemblages left by ambush predators, particularly by modern hunter-gatherers (Klein 1982; Stiner 1990:317). The distribution of large animals (Group Sizes A + B) vs. that of smaller animals (Group size C + D)[15] along the bipartite division of the site's stratigraphic column differs significantly ($\chi^2$ = 117.81, $p$ < .0001, df = 16), but there is no detailed stratigraphic patterning of body size preference. Large and medium-sized mammals (aurochs, rhinoceros, equids, red and fallow deer, wild boar, hartebeest; Rabinovich and Tchernov 1995:14) are over-represented in layers XIV and XII–X, while smaller species (wild goat, gazelle, and roe deer) are significantly represented in layers XXI, XIX, XVa, and VI–V (no statistically significant patterns were detected within other assemblages).

Earlier works were able to show clear-cut co-variations between characteristics of lithics and of faunal assemblages and to explain them as resulting from mobility patterns of Middle Paleolithic groups (e.g., Stiner and Kuhn 1992). This is not the case for Qafzeh. Variations in the lithic assemblages are rather extensive and clearly do not respond to the single mode of faunal procurement strategies. No significant co-variation or correlation was found between frequencies of prey size and lithic assemblage characteristics that are responsive to mobility and transport patterns such as oversized blanks, frequencies of retouched pieces or core-reduction methods.

None of the analyses shows clear links between patterns of lithic technological organization and modes of exploitation of faunal resources. Use-wear studies of samples of the lithic assemblages from Qafzeh (chapter 3) support the notion of hunting only for assemblages XV and XVII (12.8% and 3.3% of the total Employed Units [EUs],[16] respectively, with inferred projectile impact); butchery is indicated in all the samples from layers XXIV–XV. As has already been mentioned, no lithic use-wear studies on the younger assemblages are available (Shea 1991: tabs. 5.24–5.39). Levallois points, arguably the extractive tools used to obtain meat (Shea 1988, 1991), were produced only sporadically at Qafzeh, and in one case (layer XIII) appear to have been manufactured for use elsewhere. They also do not appear to have been heavily used, broken, and discarded on site. Additionally, bone densities do not vary strongly with lithic density. The strong statistical associations between specific reduction sequences and patterns of artifact transport over the landscape and strategies of meat procurement that have been reported from the Pontinian of Italy (Stiner 1994) are conspicuously absent from the Qafzeh sample. Also absent are ties between

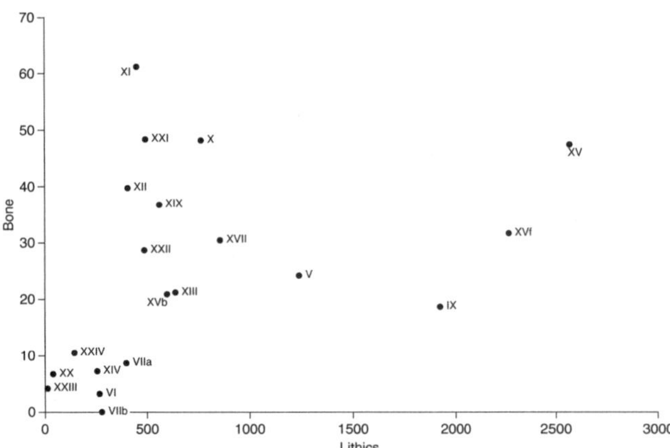



**Figure 7.11** Scatterplot of lithic and bone densities in the Qafzeh assemblages. Axes values are numbers per m³.

specific prey animals and types of tools, like those seen in the Mousterian of Combe-Grenal (Chase 1986).

### Spatial Features

The (admittedly) meager evidence for fire seems at first glance to be the opposite of that expected from the twofold division based on debris and tool frequencies. Inasmuch as the intensity of hearths can be gauged by the frequencies of burnt flint, it is the lower, debris-rich and presumably more ephemeral assemblages (based on lithic densities and on the characteristics of the assemblages as discussed above) that attest to a more extensive use of fire. Although poorly preserved and not recognized macroscopically as a sedimentological component of the stratigraphy (layer XVf being a notable exception; Vandermeersch 1981:27), hearths occurred in the cave. This conclusion is based both on the occurrence of burnt artifacts in all the assemblages and on visual observations at the time of excavation, recognized in hindsight as hearths in various diagenetic stages (O. Bar-Yosef, pers. comm.; S. Weiner pers. comm. 1997; cf. Schiegl et al. 1996).[17]

In layer XV, the distribution of thermal debris (i.e., debris created due to excessive heating of the flint surface) appears to reflect a single hearth location, as ca. 75% of the thermal debris in this layer is concentrated in an area of 3 m² (figure 7.2b). This indirectly hints at the possibility of a hearth (hearths?) with defined spatial boundaries, or that fireplaces may have been built repeatedly over some time in one area of the occupation. Unfortunately, the hypothesis could not be tested in other assemblages, for which provenience data of such debris are unavailable.

Inasmuch as fire intensity and lithic densities are of relevance to the question of settlement duration (e.g., Bar-Yosef et al. 1992; Henry 1995a, 1995c), the indirect lines of evidence for hearths appear to suggest that settlement intensity may have been higher in assemblages XV, XVf, and XIII, possibly because of occupations of longer duration. This is supported by the higher densities of lithics (layers XV and XVf, where the frequencies of burnt artifacts are also highest). The diverse lithic assemblage of layer XV, and the complex processes of artifact transport suggested for layer XIII, support in both cases an interpretation of relatively long-duration occupations, although activities may not have been the same in the two occupations.

## Reconstructing the Broad Patterns: Mobility and Subsistence Systems

The available dates for the lower terrace sequence indicate a time span of around 10,000 years for layers XXIV–XV

(Schwarcz et al. 1988; Valladas et al. 1988), but no dates are available for layers XIV–III. Although the time range of this series of occupations may be relatively short, based on the fast rate of accumulation suggested by Farrand (1979), it probably represents several thousand years. The locale of Qafzeh seems to have had a long-lasting appeal, and thus geologically defined horizons likely constitute palimpsests of many occupations that blended into one another in the course of time. In the specific case of Qafzeh, this process does not seem to have caused a dramatic bias in patterns of technological variation. If the lithic remains of several occupations were technologically and typologically distinct from one another, the observable archaeological assemblage that would result from their mixture would reflect more distinct patterns of intra-assemblage variation than are actually seen (layers XV and XIII are a possible exception, given their more complex technological make-up as discussed above). Hence, while each assemblage in all probability represents more than one occupation, it seems legitimate to treat it as depicting broadly consistent behaviors.

### Why Did Hominins Come to Qafzeh?

The overall evidence of the lithic assemblages suggests that occupation was not intensive during the time of deposition of most layers at Qafzeh, especially when compared to some other (later) sites.[18] Moreover, the lithic (and faunal) evidence suggests that there were variations in occupation intensity and in site function throughout time. Clearly, it was not the existence of shelter per se that dictated occupation intensity, nor did it determine the changing site functions at this locale (or others, for that matter). This raises questions about possible reasons for the repeated occupation of the site of Qafzeh.

Several hypotheses can be formulated to answer this question. Some of these concentrate on the characteristics and accessibility of the exploited resources. Raw material accessibility as a major attraction must be rejected immediately, given the flawed local flint. Indeed, this raw material is hardly used in the assemblages. The previous analyses have shown that Qafzeh was settled despite its distance from adequate raw material exposures. Other resources must therefore have created the major attraction of the site.

Only some of the observed changes in lithic production strategies, artifact transport and intensity of raw material exploitation exhibit temporal trends that conform to the bipartite division of the stratigraphic sequence, in itself based on non-lithic data (i.e., the presence or absence of burials, hearths, ochre, and microvertebrates). Assemblages from layers XXIV–XVII share a number of technological and organizational traits, and may indeed be taken to represent one type of behavior. In these assemblages (as well as in layer XV) the relative frequencies of debris and debitage tend to be higher relative to other lithic categories. These frequencies decline in the younger assemblages, and the same holds for burnt artifacts.

The variability observed among all the other assemblages is far too large, however, to be accommodated within a framework of two contrasting behaviors. Rather, the later assemblages reflect a variety of tactical solutions employed throughout the series of settlements. When they occur in the ethnographic record of hunting and gathering societies, these types of changes are related to attempts on the individual or societal scale to cope with the varying likelihoods of economic risk and uncertainties induced by fluctuations in the natural and societal environment (Bousman 1993; Cashdan 1985; Torrence 1989b; Wiessner 1982).

None of the Qafzeh assemblages furnishes evidence for its being a major hunting or butchery locality. In failing to show clear links between patterns of lithic technological organization and modes of exploitation of faunal resources, the various analyses of the lithic assemblages imply that the organization of technology at Qafzeh did not revolve around the acquisition of faunal food. This is hardly surprising in a Levantine Middle Paleolithic habitation site; in fact, it is the predicted pattern in sites that are not task-specific in a region located in the low-medium latitudes. In terms of both bulk and nutritional value, the emphasis would be on vegetal rather than faunal resources (Bar-Yosef and Meadow 1995:50; Cordain et al. 2000; Hayden 1981; Hovers 1988; Kelly 1983).[19] It is therefore unfeasible to invoke strategies of faunal exploitation as the major cause of technological variability in Qafzeh. While this is not to say that animal resources were not exploited on site (as indicated by both the bones of hunted animals on site and the evidence for butchery), it does imply that they were not the principal motive for the first settlement or later returns.

A possible attraction for hominins might have been specific plant resources. Although the hypothesis that exploitation and processing of plant remains were the main tasks influencing the varying tactics of lithic organization cannot be tested with the available data from Qafzeh,[20] it is sustained by the lithic finds. Use-wear analyses support the notion that activities at Qafzeh (in the older assemblages) focused on procurement and processing of plant remains (Shea 1991), together with butchery of what appears to be sporadic kills. The dominance of this type of use wear is in agreement with the tendency to produce large, generalized flakes that can be used for a variety of tasks. On the other hand, triangular flakes and Levallois points, which arguably exhibit microscopic evidence for both hafting and hunting (Shea 1991; though see Plisson and Beyries 1998), are indeed absent from most assemblages.

Additional lines of inference may be used to investigate the exploited resources at Qafzeh. The immediate vicinity of the cave is presently characterized by widely spaced trees and by the frequent occurrence of shrubs and herbaceous plants (chapter 3), each with edible parts that are available in different seasons. Species composition near Qafzeh at the time of the wet and warm MIS 5 (chapter 3) may be reconstructed as being similar to that of the present. Vegetation clusters at some distance from the cave may have been denser: in the valleys there may have been higher frequencies of herbs and trees belonging to the *Quercus ithaburensis–Styrax officinalis* association (the issue of paleoenvironmental reconstruction is discussed in greater detail in chapter 8). This spatio-temporal variability is consistent with a scenario in which the scheduling of occupational episodes was influenced, and possibly even dictated, by varying plant availability.

Moving away from the cave's immediate vicinity, parts of the site catchment area of Qafzeh can be reconstructed, at least for the time of the older occupations. The catchment area, or the tract of the landscape that was exploited by groups occupying the site in the course of their annual moves (Bailey and Davidson 1983), extended as far as the Mediterranean coast, some 40 km to the west. This is inferred from the presence of marine shells recovered from layer XXIV (a single specimen), XXII (two specimens), and XXI (two specimens) (Bar-Yosef and Vandermeersch 1993; Taborin 2003). All are Mediterranean *Glycymeris* valves that could have been collected from thanatocoenoses along the littoral without special extractive techniques. Along this confirmed east–west transect, several seasonally alternating ecological niches could have been exploited within the group's territory in different seasons. The cave's immediate vicinity would have been but one such location. Recognizing other boundaries of Qafzeh's catchment area, however, is more difficult in the absence of clearly "exotic" materials in the assemblages. Since the terrain toward the north and east was harder to traverse, one may assume that residential moves in these two directions were more limited in frequency and distance (see Bailey and Davidson 1983; Hovers 1988, 1989; Kelly 1995:132–138). Hovers et al. (2003) presented evidence for the procurement of ochre some 6–8 km east of Qafzeh Cave, in the area of Mt. Tabor, whereas the source(s) of flint may be some 12–15 km northeast of the site (see above). Whatever evidence is available, then, points to rather small exploitation territories.

*Occupation and Subsistence Patterns*

Given the numerous variations observed in technological organization of hunter-gatherers, evidence of seasonality cannot in itself be used to make inferences about the modes of mobility of a site's inhabitants. Rather, it should be linked with data on resource structure, lithic technology, and settlement intensity. The ethnographic record suggests that plant-relying groups move in smaller annual territories than groups whose diets are based on game (Kelly 1995:131). The spatio-temporal distribution of vegetal resources in the Levant would have required constant monitoring of resource patches within a group's territory, which in turn factored heavily into the cost of resource exploitation. In the absence of storage techniques, these territories would be exploited thoroughly by frequent residential moves, moving consumers to the resource patch.

Hence, short-distance residential moves over a territory of restricted size are expected to have been the norm for the occupants of Qafzeh (and in general, across the whole of the Middle Paleolithic Levant; chapter 8). The duration of residential camps would have been determined by the degree of spatio-temporal overlap of resources, which could change from one year to another. The behavior of neighboring human groups would also factor into decisions about occupation location and its duration (Kelly 1995; Moore 1983; see Hovers 1988). Shifting to a logistical mode of mobility would have occurred when the spatial overlap among simultaneously required critical resources was not tight (e.g., Tor Faraj, Quneitra; Henry 1995a; Hovers 1990b) or when the geographic location of a site enabled extended occupation, relying on exploitation of different-season resources from one locale within a daily walking distance (e.g., in the Jordan Valley; Hovers 1989).

Lieberman and Shea (1994) suggested that the modes of subsistence and mobility seen in layers XV–III of Qafzeh are strikingly different from those seen in layers XXIV–XVII. A re-evaluation of the interpretation of seasonality data is needed as a first step in attempting to explain this discrepancy. The seasonality data underlying a large part of the argument derive from analyses of cementum increment in gazelle teeth. In a nutshell, this analysis looks at seasonal patterns in the structures of the microscopically distinct incremental layers of cementum, deposited in separate teeth of individual animals (Stutz 2002:1327 and references therein). As cementum deposition stops when the animal is dead, in the case of hunted fauna the latest layer represents the season when the animal was taken.

So what does it really mean when teeth from an assemblage indicate single-season occupation, and how reliable are results showing multiple-season occupation? A re-revaluation of the seasonality data must take into consideration the nature of the archaeological record. It must be borne in mind that the studied teeth constitute small samples derived from sediments that possibly accumulated in the course of several occupations over an unknown stretch of time. When the data suggest a single-season death pattern, the argument for a single-season occupation is credible enough. Even if derived from a post-depositionally mixed sample representing several occupations, these data reflect a real pattern that has not been obscured by taphonomic processes. If the cementum analysis were methodologically and analytically well founded, the older settlements in the Qafzeh sequence would indeed represent single season (spring/summer; Lieberman 1993) occupations.[21] However, if a multiple-season pattern emerges it is very difficult to ascertain that it is a valid pattern rather than the result of admixture from occupations during various seasons. In addition, the seasonality determinations obtained by Lieberman (1993) are accurate only to the nearest three months. This degree of methodological resolution renders it difficult to distinguish long-term multi-seasonal occupations from shorter bi-seasonal ones (Hovers 1997). Hence, the interpretation of the gazelle teeth cementum analysis as reflecting multi-seasonal settlements in layers XV–III is less credible than the patterns inferred from the homogeneous data clusters from layers XXIX–XVII. For all we know, the pattern in the younger layers may reflect a series of occupations that occurred in different seasons.

In addition to the archaeologically problematic nature of such cementum increment studies, recent concerns with their methodological and analytical principles undermine their validity as an archaeological tool (Stutz 2002). The reconstruction of Qafzeh as one of several seasonally-alternating occupations, located along the east–west transect from the cave to the littoral, agrees well with the suggestion of single-season settlements during the time of the older occupations (Lieberman 1993). Indeed, such a pattern would be less understandable if the attraction of the site was due to the presence of faunal resource that had a less distinct seasonal patterning. But given the archaeological and methodological caveats, this agreement between the two types of inferences may not be as robust as it seems at first glance.

Indeed, the lithic evidence is not in complete accord with seasonality studies. The single-season pattern of gazelle deaths in layers XXIV–XVII has been associated with a residential node in a system of circulating mobility (Lieberman 1993; Lieberman and Shea 1994). However, this is not supported by the composition of the lithic assemblages, the typological homogeneity and the low lithic densities. Marks and Freidel (1977) identified the higher residential mobility of the Upper Paleolithic of the Negev (compared to the allegedly more sedentary Middle Paleolithic occurrences) by their typological richness, combined with the presence of products from various stages of core-reduction sequences in the frequencies anticipated by these researchers. In the same vein, Middle

Paleolithic sites in Transjordan (e.g., Tor Sabiha; Henry 1995a, 1995c) or Epi-Paleolithic occurrences in the Negev (Goring-Morris 1987; Marder 2002) were understood as task-specific sites based on their low assemblage diversity. The technological, and especially the typological, homogeneity of the lithic assemblages of layers XXIV–XVII thus contrast with patterns expected in a residential site (e.g., Binford and Binford 1966 on the typological richness of Levantine Middle Paleolithic sites).

The occurrence of microvertebrates (chapter 3) demonstrates that a given locale was occupied by humans only intermittently. However, the substantial occurrence of commensal species such as *Mus spretoides* and *Mastomys baeti* (Tchernov 1984, 1991) does not conform to the pattern of very short ephemeral occupations. In layers XXII–XV such commensals show the highest frequencies among studied Mousterian sites in the Levant (Tchernov 1992).[22] Bar-Yosef and Vandermeersch (1993) suggested that the commensals were brought by birds from a nearby site, located within the flying distance of birds of prey, where the longer-duration occupations would have been located. Most likely the cave of Qafzeh itself did not serve as such a site, because Middle Paleolithic occupation there post-dates the period of accumulation of the bulk of the terrace deposits (table 3.1).

Bar-Yosef and Vandermeersch (1993) also hypothesized that the terrace was used only as a burial ground, that is, a task-specific ("logistical") site. This interpretation accords with the limited range of typological diversity in the lower terrace assemblages, with the fact that faunal density in some of these layers is relatively high, despite of the lack of technological evidence for the production or retooling of reliable extractive tools, and with the presence of ochre and ochre-stained shells (Hovers et al. 2003; Taborin 2003; Walter 2003). It is less successful in explaining the provisioning of the site with raw material in the form of partially decorticated blocks from a relatively long distance. It is possible that the partly exploited cores were left on site between predictably repetitive short-term occupations connected with mortuary behavior. If that were the case, the implication would be that the cave was used only by one group (i.e., territoriality). Another possible explanation is that activities linked with burials were combined with other, more mundane economic behaviors. In this case, site provisioning would have been a viable strategy of raw material exploitation, enabling more economically-oriented occupations of longe-deviation. This is in agreement with the mixed characteristics of the lithic assemblages, which contain elements associated with both logistical and residential sites. The relatively high intensity of burning also accords with this suggestion.

Settlement patterns inferred for the lower layers, rather than pointing to short-duration residential settlements, can be interpreted as associated with logistical task-specific occupations in which a constrained range of activities took place. The settlement of the terrace at these times was, at least in part, the result of social considerations revolving around the existence of burials (more on this in chapter 8).

By the same token, the interpretation of multi-seasonality as a proxy of radiating mobility for the younger occupations is too broad a generalization. Leaving aside the thorny issue of the authenticity of the seasonal pattern itself, the apparent changes between the two stratigraphic blocks are not unambiguous in pointing to extended periods of site occupation. The techno-typological characteristics of the younger assemblages, while different from those of the older assemblages (figures 6.2, 7.1, 7.3), do not demonstrate higher diversity or significant increase in overall occupation intensity in all cases (layers XIII and XV being exceptions). This, however, would have been expected if occupation modes changed toward long-duration occupations. Side-scrapers, while over-represented in some of the younger assemblages, are never the dominant tool class (figure 6.2). In addition, a comparison of the data in figures 6.2 and 7.11 shows that assemblages rich in side-scrapers are not, in most cases, those with high densities of lithic artifacts. Hence, the occurrence of side-scrapers in the various assemblages cannot be considered an indication of more intense occupations along the lines suggested by Rolland and Dibble (1990; Dibble and Rolland 1992).

In all the assemblages of Qafzeh, production is geared toward large, maintainable artifacts, but lithics were not "depleted" (Schiffer 1987; Shott 1989a) and retouch is always light. Shott (1996:272) distinguished between the potential utility of an artifact, the result of its manufacture for a long use life (resharpening and recycling), and its "realized utility," the degree to which the potential was actually exploited. At Qafzeh tools are characterized by light retouch and a low degree of realized utility, suggesting that in none of the assemblages was tool use very extensive. In that Qafzeh was the locale where lithics were manufactured in the first place (notwithstanding cases of import into the site as discussed earlier in this chapter), the minimal exploitation of the potential of the resultant large blanks is suggestive of caching in anticipation of undefined future needs (Binford 1979).

This is illustrated by the combination of well-defined selection criteria and the light retouch on side-scrapers. More than any other tool class, these tools appear to have been designed with a premeditated intention to extend their use lives by using flexible blanks designed to be portable (Kuhn 1994) in anticipation of future activities at the site or away from it. But the lightly retouched scrapers were neither exhausted nor removed for future use off site, and thus do not constitute de facto refuse (Schiffer

1987:89). This implies a short period of occupation, especially if the rate of attrition of scrapers is indeed much higher than that of other tools (Rolland 1981; Rolland and Dibble 1990). These conclusions regarding the duration of occupation are pertinent to the younger assemblages, which contain somewhat higher frequencies of side-scrapers, and support the notion that those were not multiple-season and long-duration occupations.

An alternative explanation of the light retouch is that artifacts were abandoned on the basis of probable failure. This may have occurred when tool users estimated a high likelihood of artifacts being over-used and failing during resource extraction, without opportunity to replace them. This type of tactical decision-making is common in contexts of logistical mobility (Kuhn 1989; see also Binford 1977; Bleed 1986; Kelly and Todd 1988; Torrence 1983). But from this perspective too, the slightly higher retouch frequencies in the younger assemblages compared to the older ones could imply a somewhat higher degree of logistical mobility during the older occupations of the site. This would be consistent with the mobility strategies inferred from the task-specific nature of these earlier occupations. On the other hand, this scenario implies that in the younger occupation, residential rather than logistical mobility tactics were somewhat emphasized. As was the case for the lower assemblages, the lithic characteristics do not correspond neatly with the expected patterns of either a logistical or a residential mobility system.

In the absence of use-wear analyses on artifacts from layers XIV–III (Lieberman and Shea 1994; Shea 1991) indications for a diachronic trend toward technology-assisted hunting from the time of layer XV onward are nonexistent. We have seen that the presence of points in the younger assemblages is suggestive of their import as individual gear rather than systematic reduction sequences aiming to produce hunting weapons. Layers XIII and VIIa may be exceptions to this rule but clearly do not constitute a systematic behavior that characterizes all the assemblages postdating layer X. Moreover, the often-postulated direct relationship between the occurrence of points and hunting does not hold here (table 7.3 and figure 7.11). With the exception of layer XV, which does indeed appear to represent a residential locale, assemblages in which there are indications for point production are associated with only low or medium densities of faunal remains.

The literature on Levantine adaptations contains several models emphasizing seasonal transhumance from higher to lower areas and vice versa (see Henry 1995b; Lieberman and Shea 1994). When combined, the lithic, faunal, and spatial patterns from the upper part of the Qafzeh sequence are suggestive of short-term occupations in different seasons of the year. These indications are informative about mobility within the larger settlement system. That a locale was occupied during various seasons, and not only in the two specific ones expected when seasonal movement over a vertical topographic gradient takes place, weakens the notion of seasonal transhumance as the major mobility strategy of Levantine hominins. It is immaterial in this respect whether archaeologically recognized signatures of multiple-season occupations indeed correspond to seasonality of occupation or result from post-depositional sediment mixture.

## Underlying Factors of Lithic Production and Use: Functional Efficacy or Cultural Tradition?

The ecological emphasis underlying the reverse engineering frame of thought as regards lithics clearly places much emphasis on tool design and technological strategies as tools of adaptation to ecological constraints. When assemblages do not meet expectations of the original scenarios of rational adaptations and ecological reasoning, this is usually explained by alternative organizational, economy-oriented practices. In the case of Qafzeh, rationally planned, patterned co-variations of tool types and flaking procedures point to diverse and fluctuating technological strategies along the sequence of assemblages. Raw material economy is expressed in a number of variations of design features during both flaking and shaping steps of the operational sequence, which sometimes do not seem to work together.

Several possible explanations can be invoked to address the seemingly unrelated variations of flaking (reduction strategies) and shaping (blank modification) tendencies. These may be two behaviors that complement one another, combining to create a single, efficient adaptive behavior. In this case one would still expect some patterned association(s) between the two sets of data. The other possibility is that, while operative within the same technological system, these two facets of lithic technological organization were responsive to different forces, with different (possibly even contradictory) demands on the organization of lithic production and use. In such cases consistent relationships between the behaviors of lithic flaking and shaping may not occur across the stratigraphic sequence. To evaluate the two possibilities, it is necessary first to establish that the patterns are not biased by research methods.

One hypothesis, given the small excavated areas per stratigraphic layer (table 3.2), would be that variations in the evenness of tool types among assemblages resulted from differential use of space, so that different activity areas (and hence different lithic assemblages) were sampled by the excavations. Of course, the best test for this hypothesis would be to enlarge excavated areas in the future. Notwithstanding this caveat, the fact that lithic elements representing all core-reduction steps were recovered from all the assemblages undermines this hypothesis.[23] In sites where lithics reflect spatially segregated activities, elements associated with various steps of the operational sequence are differentially distributed across the excavated space, regardless of the size of the excavated area (e.g., Alperson-Afil and Hovers 2005; see Stapert 1990 for distances and distributions of various-sized artifacts from a real or hypothetical center).[24] Moreover, as typological variation in the Qafzeh assemblages stems mainly from fluctuations in only two tool groups out of the four recognized in each assemblage (the Mousterian vs. Upper Paleolithic groups; chapter 6), it is likely that the variability is a real rather than a statistical artifact. Finally, although sample size affects the richness and evenness that constitute "assemblage diversity" (Shott 1989b), the consistency of stylistic attributes through time appears to be independent of sample size variation and is not linked with quantitative fluctuations in typological compositions.

If biased recovery is ruled out as a causative agent of the technological and typological variations observed in the assemblages along the Qafzeh sequence, then the various types of association seen among tool types, technological practices, and operational chains should be informative about other behavioral forces that affected the technological system. Functional reactions to subsistence requirements do not seem to fully explain the diverse co-variations of flaking and shaping strategies and the variable interpretations of technological organization ensuing from these patterns. The reconstructions suggested earlier in this chapter envision changes through time of settlement patterns, by which different goals of lithic organization were emphasized at different times, necessitating readjustment of economic and technological strategies. Against this variable background, it is significant that at no time did such readjustments involve a major change in the basic strategies of lithic production. A major organizational strategy in the assemblages of Qafzeh is that of blank maintainability, toward which the consistent trends of core-reduction technologies appear to be directed. It is mainly in the varying typological compositions of tool kits that the organizational aspects of the assemblages are reflected.

This statement is not merely a repetition of Binford and Binford's (1966) functional hypothesis. These authors applied their argument for a functional rather than historical-cultural source of variation to a much larger range of typological variability. At Qafzeh this range is restricted to what Bordes called "typical Mousterian" (chapter 6), which in Binford and Binford's explanatory framework would suggest similarity of activities. Indeed, it is a truism of prehistoric research that retouch results from a functional need to shape a blank into a serviceable artifact for future tasks; yet the shapes of individual retouched types do not seem to be conditioned by these tasks, as shown time and again by use-wear studies (Beyries 1988; Shea 1991:230). Another truism, however, is that even if used on the same materials, each "type group" (i.e., burins as opposed to end-scrapers, side-scrapers, notches, or denticulates) would have been used in a different manner (e.g., Binford 1973; Bordes and de Sonneville-Bordes 1970), given the kinetic properties of the shapes and proportions of the used edge (Rolland 1981; Rolland and Dibble 1990). The distinct criteria of blank selection that were applied throughout the Qafzeh sequence to some of these tool groups reflect functional distinctions made on this more general level by the hominins at the site. By the same token, variation among assemblages is also significant on the level of typological groups rather than particular tool types.

Another trait of the Qafzeh assemblages is that tool-kit composition is not influenced directly by raw material stress. Specific typological groups may be overrepresented in some assemblages (table 6.3), but this is not associated with exceptionally high or low frequencies of retouched artifacts in the assemblage (table 7.5). Variations in tool-kit composition appear to be short-term responses to small-scale changes in environmental conditions or functional demands. Given the evidence for the negligible role of faunal food extraction in the Qafzeh assemblages, these conditions may have been those influencing vegetal resources. Admittedly, it is impossible at this stage to formulate specific models that would predict the links between tool groups and such specific conditions.

A markedly different behavior is seen in the Qafzeh hominins' approach to the process of lithic production. Clearly, some blank properties were coveted and obtained with much attention because of their functional advantages in the organizational context of bridging between resource distributions, mobility behavior, and requirements for lithic artifacts. Flake dimensions and the resultant favorable ratio of mass to size were one such characteristic. But the data from Qafzeh do not conform to the view that this property is linked with a particular method of Levallois production (i.e., centripetal flaking), and hence with the particular set of mobility and extractive patterns with which it is assumed to be associated.

Why then did the Qafzeh hominins favor one set of Levallois reduction over others? When searching for explanation of the limited range of lithic production systems, one turns either to the knapper's level of dexterity and skill, or to conscious choices (decision-making) made during blank production and the selection criteria to which such choices respond. In other words, it is time to return again to the approach of *chaîne opératoire*. What interests us here is not the broader social and cultural connotations of the concept as originally devised, but rather *chaîne opératoire* as a process of technological decision making (chapter 2). Unavoidably, this facet of *chaîne opératoire* touches upon questions of cognition, which are not dealt with here.

The execution of complex technological tasks involves the operation of two neuropsychological processes, which are expressed in two fundamental elements (Pelegrin 1990:118). One is "know-how" (*savoir-faire*), which encompasses the intuitive operations that respond to the adequacy of material, geometry, shape, and form. These are assessed unconsciously but constantly during the knapping process through tactile and visual cues, and gestures and energy invested in the technological process are adjusted accordingly. The ongoing analyses of lithic production enable reconstruction of the *chaînes opératoires* prevalent in the Qafzeh assemblages on this level of know-how. The programming and execution of the gestures, which are the part of the operational chain observed directly on archaeological material, can be demonstrated, together with the processes of evaluation, reflection, and decisions involved in lithic production that underlie these final gestures (Karlin, Bodu, and Pelegrin 1991; Pelegrin 1990). This level of technical skill is demonstrated in the accomplished manner in which Levallois flaking was applied.

Shaping the morphologies of core platforms and their angles is a technological practice that reflects "motor know-how" (Lemonnier 1992:6), in which the "mass and quality of the striking tool, as well as the mass and morphological characteristics of the object to be knapped, are appreciated through vision and tactile sensibility. Following that, the orientation and handling of the object by the non-dominant hand, and the strength and trajectory of the gesture carried out by the dominant hand, are 'calculated'" (Pelegrin 1990:118; Pelegrin 2005). "Ideational know-how" provides the mental repertoire of physical objects and the spatial and sequential transformations that can be applied to them, and enables a moment-to-moment evaluation of the outcome of actions in the real world as the basis for additional technical decisions. It is from this repertoire that the knapper makes his decision, that is, chooses his next action and acts overtly upon this choice.[25]

Interestingly, and somewhat counter-expectations, the modes of flaking (i.e., centripetal as opposed to "limited platform") do not appear to have affected the desirable properties of blanks produced at Qafzeh (chapter 5). Instead, control over artifact properties was obtained through emphasis on a few prime factors. The appropriate preparation of the core's striking platform, the application of percussion at well-calculated angles and adjustment of the blow's energy were shown to have affected the dimensional properties of the flakes, likely responding to functional demands imposed by

the way mobility and resource acquisition were organized (i.e., large Levallois flakes were needed as part of the maintainable tool kit). The reliance on platform preparation characteristics as the major dictates of flake size and (to a lesser degree) shape also implies a high degree of "ideational know-how," by which the knapper was able to consider for action a number of spatial and sequential transformations that would ensure satisfactory results. The links between the "knowledge" (i.e., the memorized mental representations of forms and materials) and the "know-how" (the heuristic evaluation of the knapped object) appear to have been flexible and fast, and it was not necessary for the knappers to adhere to a predetermined flaking mode, or to employ specific flaking modes where particular blank characteristics were desired.[26]

Thus, the control and accuracy seen in the technical aspects of core reduction suggest that both facets of *savoir-faire* were operative during the technological processes of core reduction. The operational sequences described in chapters 4–6 are flexible enough to rule out the notion of restricted *savoir-faire* as the reason for the homogeneity seen in the lithic assemblages. The use of similar (if not identical) core-reduction sequences, as seen in the Qafzeh assemblages, cannot be attributed to deficient motor know-how that somehow prevented the knappers from implementing diverse solutions in the course of core reduction. Similarly, one may argue, on the basis of the lithic analyses that the Qafzeh hominins possessed a comprehensive mental "catalogue" of materials and gestures necessary to carry out varied lithic reduction processes. That several Levallois flaking methods can be observed in each assemblage rules out unfamiliarity with alternative courses of action on the level of mental technological repertoires (ideational know-how).

In sum, tool-kit compositions responded to immediate tasks with which the Qafzeh occupants were concerned; the fluctuations in type group frequencies likely followed small-scale changes in extractive resources of interest. Functionally desired characteristics were bestowed on the blanks during flake production through controlled action upon matter. Clearly, in the case of Qafzeh, knapping skills were sufficient to override limitations of raw material or technology and to achieve the desired products. Thus, whatever variation is detected in the assemblages is independent of changes in motor know-how or technological repertoire.

As was shown in chapters 5–6, the various Levallois flaking modes and methods did not seem to have mode-specific favorable influences on functional blank properties. In such circumstances, one might expect a higher degree of evenness in the occurrence of the various Levallois flaking modes and methods within and among assemblages, without preference of any particular single mode. And yet one combination (recurrent centripetal flaking) always dominates the assemblages, despite the obvious familiarity of the knappers with a larger variety of flaking modes and methods.

Against the backdrop of their equal outcome in terms of artifact maintainability, the fact that technological practices at Qafzeh did not occur randomly or evenly suggests that similarity of flaking modes and methods across time reflects some sort of a cultural selective pressure that affected the technological decisions of hominins at the site. What we see in Qafzeh is isochrestic style as defined by Sackett (1982, 1983, 1986; see also Close 1989; Lemonnier 1992): a group's style that is a latent quality, potentially residing in all formal variation in material culture, including variation that is regarded as purely functional in the utilitarian sense. Thus, isochrestic style "may be found in the choice of raw materials, knapping techniques for reducing cores and producing tool blanks, alternative types of marginal retouch and burin spalling" (Sackett 1982:105). In fact, what Sackett described as a general rule and in broad terms, and what emerges from the study of the Qafzeh sequence, is lithic tradition—a set of technological behaviors that are functionally equivalent to others but are chosen by a certain group of people (see Leroi-Gourhan 1945:344–345; Levi-Strauss 1976; see Meignen and Bar-Yosef 1988, 1992; and below). We will return to the questions of whether and how that choice was unconscious, as this may be a point where the formal definition of isochrestism does not apply to the processes envisioned as influential in forming the lithic record of Qafzeh.

It is possible that some characteristics seen among retouched tools reflect a similar trend. Intensity of retouch is a case in point. The selection of larger blanks to be retouched is a characteristic of many, if not all, Middle Paleolithic sites in Eurasia (Dibble 1995b; Goren-Inbar and Belfer-Cohen 1998). Furthermore, in most Levantine Mousterian sites, these large blanks were hardly ever extensively or intensively retouched. In the case of Qafzeh, these two characteristics are more significant with regard to the side-scrapers but also occur with other tool types. Whereas these properties of Levantine Mousterian assemblages have been explained by many archaeologists as a result of the ubiquity of raw material suitable for retouch, this is not the case for Qafzeh, to which raw material was transported from a distance bordering the daily exploitation territory from the site. It could thus also reflect a behavior that is arbitrary with respect to functional tasks or optimization behavior. Similarly, some minor patterns of variation or homogeneity among the retouched tools cannot readily be explained as strictly functional. In particular, the location and faces of retouch of some of the tool types (e.g., isolated removals) may represent arbitrary choices. Comparable suggestions have been made

concerning the occurrence of inverse retouch in the sites of Tor Faraj and Tor Sabiha (Henry 1995b, 1995c), the geometry of Abu Sif points in various early Levantine Mousterian assemblages (Ashkenazi 2005), and retouch attributes on microliths in later prehistoric periods (e.g., Goring-Morris et al. 1996).

The view that lithic assemblages represent cultural traditions has been rejected by some paleoanthropologists as an antiquated and naïve cultural-historical worldview that contradicts evolutionary thought and is therefore unacceptable (e.g., Bisson 2000; Clark and Riel-Salvatore 2006). True, many discussions of these issues employ postmodern, post-processual stances when referring to technological traditions embedded in social systems and perpetuated by social agencies (e.g., Dobres and Hoffman 1994; Pfaffenberger 1992). In parallel, however, a growing body of theoretical work has focused on the emergence of culture as an evolutionary process. Technological practices figure prominently in such discussions as group-level adaptations, adaptive behaviors selected for by the conditions of both physical ("ecological") and social environments.[27]

Technological evolution is only partly analogous to biological evolution. Clearly, it is dependent on "inheritance" of knowledge through time, which is conducive to the well-being and fitness of individuals in all realms of their lives. Importantly, there are "disanalogies" between the biological and technological realms (Ziman 2000b:5; see also Eerkens and Lipo 2005; Jablonka and Lamb 2005; Richerson and Boyd 2005:6). The most obvious difference is that novel forms of artifacts are almost always the products of conscious design aimed for specific goals, at least in their final form. This contrasts with the selection mechanisms that govern biological evolution, which are blind to the ultimate fates of organisms. Technological knowledge and design are transmitted both vertically (to offspring and novices) and horizontally (to siblings and peers) by processes of social and individual learning (Carrithers 1990; Laland 1998; Rogers 1988). Transmission of technological knowledge or of design blueprints and mental templates is deliberate. It is a mechanism of Lamarckian heritability (Jablonka 2000), the plasticity of which in itself confers adaptive advantages (Kameda and Nakanishi 2003; Richerson and Boyd 2005:9–10; see also chapter 1).

Hence, the evolution of technological traits is driven by variation and selection upon it, but these are not blind or natural (Ziman 2000b:6). These biases often stem from the realm of social conventions. While dealing with the question of demographic constraints on the spread of knowledge (inclusive of technological knowledge), Hovers and Belfer-Cohen (2006) emphasize that both modern and traditional societies invest much societal effort in propagation of knowledge that is considered important for social and physical survival. The success of the transmission of practical and abstract knowledge ("motor know-how" and "ideational know-how" of design and process, in the parlance of *chaîne opératoire* research) is dependent on the way they mesh with existing social norms in other realms of life (Richerson and Boyd 2005:29–30). These norms become an important component of the selective pressures that drive cultural evolution and change or enforce technological stability.

This worldview helps explain the observations made throughout this study on the lithic technology of Qafzeh and the way in which its characteristics are patterned over time. It is feasible that the initial emphasis on the use of any core-reduction system, as for technologies, was as an innovation[28] perceived to be an appropriate—perhaps the most appropriate—functional response to the requirement of an organizational system (e.g., Boyd and Richerson 1985, 1992; Durham 1991; Schiffer and Skibo 1987), which in itself mitigated the constraints of the physical environments. As such, it was accepted into the general pool of technological knowledge. The plasticity of cultural transmission would have allowed hominins to change their technological practices and elect to use different flaking methods that would have been more effective when goals of the organizational systems changed with the change in environmental conditions.

The fact that some organizational tactics changed (changing emphases on tool types reflecting differences in tasks and changing emphasis on raw material transport patterns reflecting changes in organization of mobility and settlement patterns) but the technology of lithic production remained constant is suggestive of one of two processes of cultural evolution:

1. Lithic production technology did not change because it was neutral. Retaining the production modes and methods initially used, while not necessarily more effective than others in newly formed environmental circumstances, would not necessarily have been at odds with them. The original technological variant continued to be used side by side with other solutions. Then a process of "drift," which had destroyed the accumulated variation (Neiman 1995) and reached fixation on a single variant, would have led to observed frequency dominance of a given variant. If a variant was not neutral, that is, its use was not adaptive and caused loss of fitness, a second variant would be added as a functional solution and may have replaced it over time. While this scenario is evolutionary in spirit, it is not a cultural evolutionary scenario, because it does not account for the directional, biased selection of technological variants.

2. On the other hand, the persistence of a particular Levallois flaking system in the Qafzeh assemblages would have resulted from repeated choices of individuals[29] to adopt the main theme of social and technological matrices (Dobres and Hoffman 1994). While other manners of flaking were transmitted culturally and were known to the occupants, there would have been a social premium on conforming to the mainstream. Because at Qafzeh artifacts made by the various flaking systems have similar characteristics, the risk in deviation from the norm may have been social rather than functional. To some degree this trend could develop regardless of the ecologically adaptive advantages associated with one system or another, or even despite "non-fatal" maladaptive ecological traits of the socially accepted technology (Dobres and Hoffman 1994; Pfaffenberger 1992; Richerson and Boyd 2005). The overall effect of this process is one of slow change or even stability of technological preferences over time, as changes were socially rejected by directional, biased selection. In this scenario, the expression in the archaeological assemblages of Levallois and non-Levallois flaking systems other than the recurrent centripetal one may correspond to individual practices that did not culminate in innovation and cultural change.

Other variants may be added as functional solutions if the normative technology is unable to fulfill a task, but those would be unlikely to replace the socio-technological normative form of doing things. This explains the pattern seen in layer XV (as well as XIII and VIIa) of Qafzeh, where some of the functional requirements were not met by the prevailing (recurrent centripetal Levallois) technological practice. The "main" lithic production technology was not replaced in total; instead, a second technological system of convergent flaking for point production was put to use contemporaneously with the dominant one.

Both scenarios lead to similar archaeological manifestations. However, it is only the second one that encompasses human decision making, in this case according to criteria of social advantages, and explains how a technological behavior survived as a time-honored tradition, its early functional roots becoming irrelevant to its existence during the later occupations. It is in this context that "isochrestic style" comes to mind. The process of individual choice modeled here to explain the persistence of the technological system at Qafzeh assumes individual choice, but the reason for that choice was unconscious on the part of the decision maker.[30]

Support for the scenario of lithic technological traditions comes from some of the non-lithic finds at

Qafzeh. If indeed the emphasis on a single lithic production mode represents a technological tradition, it would also imply continued occupation by successive groups sharing the same "social representations" (Lemonnier 1986, 1992:79–94). The burials at Qafzeh (Belfer-Cohen and Hovers 1992; Chase and Dibble 1987; Tillier 1990; Vandermeersch 1970), being spatially localized despite the time intervals that must have occurred between individual interments, attest to a tradition of mortuary behavior associated with the specific location (Bar-Yosef 1992; Hovers et al. 1995) and complement the technological pattern.

It may be hypothesized that the initial attraction to the site was probably for reasons of creature comfort such as shelter and specific resources, especially given the cave's topographic location in cliffs overlooking the Jezreel Valley. The steep topography enabled exploitation of several habitats dispersed over a small distance (e.g., the cliffs, the open plain of the valley, and the Lower Galilee hills). In such a location some variation in resource structure would be expected at any time of the year (cf. Hovers 1988, 1989). (Possibly, the cave's continued use through time was associated with specific advantages conferred by this particular resource structure.) The spatio-temporal predictability of resources would have enhanced the benefits associated with territorial defense (Dyson-Hudson and Smith 1978:24–26), in either a direct or a social manner (Cashdan 1983; Endicott and Endicott 1986; Peterson 1975). While territoriality is all in all a social phenomenon, there is ethnographic evidence that rights to a certain territory are often expressed through material symbols. It is noteworthy that a territory is defined by the San as "a sacred place where our fathers and mothers and their fathers and mothers are buried" (Hitchcock and Bartram 1998:31). Thus, the practice of repeated burials may have been related to the need for some expression of group–land association and territorial claim (e.g., Gilead 1989:137), especially when the site was initially occupied by a group in order to access resources during a specific time of the year. The same occupation horizons bear other non-lithic and apparently non-utilitarian finds such as ochre (Hovers et al. 2003; Vandermeersch 1966),[31] shells that may have served as beads (Taborin 2003), and an engraved lithic artifact (Hovers et al. 1997). Each of these items likely attests to the existence of emergent, socially constructed coding, that is, uniquely human cultural systems (as defined by Chase 2006). The fact that all types of finds are clustered in at least some of the earliest horizons at the site supports such assertions (Hovers, Vandermeersch, and Bar-Yosef 1997; Hovers et al. 2003) and is consistent with the establishment of other cultural codes, that is, lithic technological traditions.

The model of traditions appears to run into difficulties with the later occupations at the site, in which there are no burials, ochre, or shells. Instead, function-sensitive properties of the lithic assemblages in these horizons imply varying mobility and settlement modes, possibly in response to different resources to be exploited during various seasons of the year, whereas production systems remained essentially the same as those used in the earlier horizons.[32] This discrepancy suggests that production systems did not respond to physical ecological changes but rather reflect the continued use of traditional technologies. Consequently, assuming that the site was occupied by a new group of hominins, or even by hominins of a different taxon (as argued by Lieberman and Shea 1994), is not a parsimonious explanation of the observed patterns. Instead, it may be speculated in the spirit of the cultural evolution model that the group's claim over the territory of the site had already been established and did not need to be reiterated through physical symbols. The occupation of the particular site became a traditional behavior, in which "the past to which [it] infers imposes fixed...practices, such as repetition" (Hobsbawm 1983:2), embedded in the overall behavioral texture of the larger social unit (see Carrithers 1990:201).

## Summary

The attempt to reconstruct the organization of lithic technology in Qafzeh has employed the concept of reverse engineering, making the working assumption that artifacts were designed and manufactured for some concrete purpose. Through the analyses of artifact properties I have attempted to determine which problems such designs were meant to solve. Organizational changes throughout the sequence are attributed to controlled behavior dependent on arrays of economic decisions unrelated to raw material accessibility, and possibly to social constraints. In lithic production, the emphasis was on maintainability of artifacts, mainly through the use of versatile designs. Aspects of basic design through blank production remained relatively constant. On the other hand, technological tactics of problem solving are not the same throughout the sequence, and there is considerable variability among assemblages.

The strong associations between aspects of lithic technology and faunal exploitation reported elsewhere are not seen in the Qafzeh samples. In this case, it is impossible to invoke patterns of faunal exploitation as the causes for mobility and for adopting particular technological patterns. It is suggested that throughout the sequence the main emphasis of resource exploitation was on vegetal resources, and that the nature of these resources and their modes of exploitation shifted through time. Unfortunately, the resolution of the available paleoenvironmental data is not high enough to enable the formulation of explanations of the specific changes in mobility and settlement patterns.

The reduction sequences and blank modification strategies are suggested to represent two facets of a single technological system, the former being dictated by tradition and style, and the latter by both traditional and functional considerations. Parallels are drawn between lithic tradition and the occurrence of symbolized mortuary tradition, related to group territoriality. The links between these two types of behavior reflect the role of social factors in creating the variability seen in the Qafzeh sequence.

8

# Qafzeh Cave in a Broader Perspective

## Subsistence and Mobility Patterns in the Middle Paleolithic of the Levant

The previous chapters have described how Middle Paleolithic hominins who occupied Qafzeh Cave produced and modified stone tools. The fluctuations in tactics of technological organization were then examined against the distribution of various resources that the occupants seem to have used. This set of analyses revealed variability within what at first glance appeared to be quite uniform technological behaviors. The diversity discerned among the Qafzeh assemblages does not stem from shifts in the application of particular *chaînes opératoires* (although there are some specific examples of this type of variability). Rather, it is expressed mainly in organizational tactics that occasionally shifted against the background of a stable lithic reduction strategy. The complexity of observed behaviors was explained as depicting the dominant role of technological tradition in shaping the lithic assemblages. It was further asserted that the lithic tradition might have emerged initially as a functional response to specific needs, complementing particular mobility and seasonality patterns, but then evolved into a traditional behavior that survived through time without necessarily being dependent on the conditions that enhanced its initial occurrence. Finally, it was argued that independent lines of evidence are consistent with the development of other technological and social traditions, and thus support the suggested interpretation of the lithic finds.

The assemblages of Qafzeh are the residues left by a group or groups of hominins that operated under specific environmental and social constraints. In this chapter, I address the question whether the cultural processes that shaped the Qafzeh assemblages are unique in their period, because the authors of these assemblages were modern humans, or whether cultural norms shaped to a considerable degree the technological behaviors of other groups, as observed in Levantine Middle Paleolithic sites and assemblages. The alternative scenario is that such groups responded to ecological challenges mostly, if not exclusively, by functional cost-effective strategies.

An intuitive answer to the first question would have to be in the negative. This is because tradition as well as territoriality have by default a classificatory aspect, differentiating that which is "ours" from that which is "not ours" (Jochim 1983; Johnson 1982; Sack 1986). These behaviors represent responses to surrounding social entities whose behaviors are sufficiently similar to necessitate socially-based means of mutual separation. If we accept that the Qafzeh assemblages bear signatures of cultural tradition and territorial behavior, as argued in the previous chapter, we have to assume that at least some other contemporaneous groups in the same region had comparable traditions.

This is a stance that requires evaluation through empirical data. As was done with respect to the lithic assemblages of Qafzeh in the previous chapter, the existence of traditions in the Levantine Middle Paleolithic is approached here by attempting to determine to what degree ecological factors explain the observed patterns of variability (reviewed in chapter 1). In chapter 7, the links between patterning of natural resources and the organization of technological behavior were discussed at some length. If formal models, emphasizing environmental factors as the driving force of technological variability, are to be evaluated, it is necessary to understand the physical conditions in which Middle Paleolithic sites existed.

As emphasized in the first chapter of this study, the organizational strategies of human groups respond to environmental, social, and cultural infrastructures, all of which constitute what is referred to here as "human ecology."

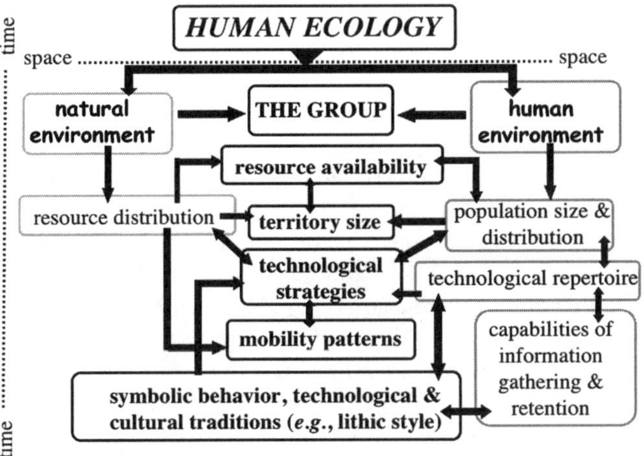


**Figure 8.1** Schematic representation of natural and cultural parameters that interact to form the "human ecology" of hunter-gatherer groups. Time and space variations figure prominently in shaping this variability for extant hunter-gatheres groups. For prehistoric groups, these two dimension change on larger scales due to changes through time in temperature and precipitation and in land configurations following climate fluctuations.

The complex interactions between the two major realms that shape hunter-gatherers' behaviors are shown schematically in figure 8.1. In this much simplified depiction of Hutchinson's (1965) "hyperspace," the natural environment corresponds roughly to the habitat, the variables of which can be measured independently of the species that exploits the specific habitat. The chart flow in this figure is a rough equivalent of the niche—a systemically conditioned, complex, and multidimensional state of a species or a population (Whittaker, Levin, and Root 1973, 1975; and see Binford 2001:32–33). The ecological conditions to which hunter-gatherers respond change temporally and spatially according to the seasonal patterns of resource distributions in the group's area of residence. Both these scales broaden considerably when geological time enters the equation, given that climatic conditions and topographic structure are reconfigured through time.

Given the above, the first step is to outline the environmental background(s) to human adaptations and decision making in the Middle Paleolithic Levant. The role of environment-related economic strategies as well as that of social and cognitive agents in shaping Mousterian variability can then evaluated be against this background.

## The Environmental Context of the Levantine Middle Paleolithic

To understand the environmental context in which Levantine Middle Paleolithic groups operated over 250,000 years, we need to reconstruct the Levantine resource base and how it changed through this time span. The point of departure for such a discussion is the current conditions in the Levant (with an emphasis on the southern part of the region). Once the current framework of mosaic environments in the region is identified and understood, we can use empirical paleoenvironmental and archaeological data to evaluate the roles of dynamic climatic and geomorphologic systems in creating the Middle Paleolithic world.

## The Present-Day Levant

The most distinctive feature of the Levant is its ecological diversity: it is home to a mosaic of ecological niches created by varied topography and climate. This small region (ca. 1,000 km North–South by up to 400 km East–West) is bounded by the Taurus–Zagros mountains to the north, the Mediterranean to the west, the Sinai peninsula to the south, and the Syro-Arabian desert to the east. A longitudinal (i.e., North–South) series of five parallel elevated and low regions occurs across a West–East transect: these are the coastal plain and western piedmont, the mountain range reaching up to 1,000 m above sea level (a.s.l.), the Dead Sea Rift lying below sea level, and the Transjordanian plateau (in the central-south Levant), which rises steeply to elevations between 800 and 2,000 m a.s.l., followed by a gradual eastward descent into Saudi Arabia. Today there are relatively few perennial streams in the region, the most notable being the Tigris, Euphrates, Orontes, and Jordan; springs are common in the Mediterranean zone but widely dispersed in the more arid areas.

Both absolute elevations and topographic steepness affect the pattern and amount of rainfall. However, the major determinant of the seasonal climatic pattern (cold, short, and relatively rainy winters and dry, hot, and long summers) is global atmospheric conditions. The Levantine climate is influenced by two major climatic systems: the Atlantic system, originating to the west of the Levant, and the southeastern African/Western Asian monsoonal system (Almogi-Labin, Bar-Matthews, and Ayalon 2004; Wigley and Farmer 1982). Seasonal (winter) barometric highs, leading to cold and dry spells during the winters, reach the area from the northeast. These varied systems dictate the amount and distribution of precipitation, and hence the occurrence and timing of various food resources across the region. The amount of precipitation and its geographic distribution are directly impacted by orographic effects. Relatively smooth North–South and East–West gradients of rainfall are coupled with a rain shadow effect in the Rift Valley to the east of the mountain range. The outcome of this interplay between climate and topography is a distinct phytogeographic zonation and a mosaic pattern of numerous interfacing ecological niches over relatively small distances.

Resource distributions are dichotomized between the coastal plain and piedmont in the west, where resources can be exploited on a year-round basis, and the inland areas in the east, where the availability of resources depends to a large degree on the existence of springs or lakes. A second vectored change in resource availability occurs as one moves from the wetter north to the drier south, where the 300-mm isohyet annually shifts its position in the northern Negev. South of that line, the decline in mean annual precipitation is sharp.

Although the region's characteristics prescribe varied mosaic environments, this property is not reflected in the variables that characterize environment on a global scale. Effective Temperature (ET), a variable introduced to the anthropological literature by Binford (1980), is derived from the mean temperature (in °C) of the warmest (W) and coldest (C) months in a given region.[1] This variable provides a measure of the intensity of solar radiation as well as its annual distribution, such that low ET values are associated with cold and seasonal environments with short growing seasons and high values are associated with non-seasonal (in terms of temperature), tropical environments with long growing seasons. In the Levant, this proximate measure of productivity reaches a value of about 15 (see Kelly 1995:66–69 for summary and references for this parameter). This value is intermediate between equatorial conditions (where ET is as high as 26) and temperate or Arctic climates (where ET is as low as 8). Of course, this is a rough measure that is insensitive to variations on small geographic scales, and thus is less meaningful on a regional than a global scale. But it makes the point that the effects of seasonality are less pronounced in the Levant than in higher geographic latitudes, a point to which we will return later in the discussion.

The Mediterranean region is a patchwork of habitats (Blondel and Aronson 1999). The characteristics and extent of Mediterranean vegetation are determined by the bimodal seasonal climate regime as well as the soils, which are usually poor in nitrogen and phosphorus (Groves 1991; Rabikovitch 1981). As a rule, habitats and communities in the Mediterranean Basin can be viewed as well-defined "life zones," which in the Levant (as elsewhere in the Mediterranean Basin) correspond to elevational/latitudinal belts due to the numerous mountain ranges (Blondel and Aronson 1999:90). The Near East as a whole is part of the "thermo-Mediterranean life zone," characterized by dense coastal woodlands of wild olive tree (*Olea europaea* subsp. *oleaster*) and carob (*Ceratonia siliqua*). Other frequent components of this vegetation zone are the lentisk (*Pistachia lentiscus*) and laurel (*Laurus nobilis*). Some plants that occur in the western part of the Mediterranean basin within this life zone are not encountered in the Levant (e.g., the cork oak, *Quercus suber*). The northern parts of the Levant are associated with two

other "life zones," the meso- and supra-Mediterranean. The former is characterized by one or two species of evergreen trees (in the eastern Mediterranean these are the oak *Quercus calliprinos* and the pine *Pinus brutia*) dominating a wide variety of woodlands and shrublands. The second "life zone" is typified by a community dominated by deciduous oak forests combined with other deciduous and evergreen trees, some that are cold-sensitive, at elevations between 500 and 1,000 m a.s.l. The variety of Mediterranean vegetation types also includes grasses and steppes, fresh and salt water adaptations that are determined by particular locations in proximity to water bodies and the nature of such water reservoirs, and semi-arid plant communities in the south, on the margins of the desert belt and, due to extreme continental conditions, in the east. In addition to all these variations, there are numerous ecotones between habitats that add to the biodiversity (Blondel and Aronson 1999:133). In the eastern Mediterranean, in particular, annuals play a major role in the diversity of the Mediterranean vegetation, often constituting half of the dominant vegetation present compared to merely 10% in other biomes (Blondel and Aronson 1999:176).

The diversity of Mediterranean forests enhances the food supplies available to generalist foragers (e.g., bears, pigs, and humans). It also provides broad feeding opportunities to browsers (aurochs, deer) and comprises a feeding alternative for adaptable grazers, who may switch to browsing depending on seasonal grass availability. As many as 40 species of trees, many of them nut- or fruit-bearing, can be found in many parts of the Mediterranean Basin (Blondel and Aronson 1999:113). Forests are often interspersed with matorrals, which consist of dense evergreen vegetation reaching up to 4–6 m in height, often characterized by dominance of evergreen shrubs with broad, thick, and stiff leaves, and sometimes with an overstorey of small trees (Blondel and Aronson 1999:118–119; Zohary 1962). This type of plant structure is attractive to animals because it includes a fine-grained mosaic of almost all forms of plant growth and a large number of species. Mattorals regenerate relatively fast if disturbed by agents such as droughts and fires.

Primary productivity (PP) is an additional measure to ET that is used for understanding the ecological context of hunter-gatherers. It refers to the annual above-ground plant production, and as such is clearly a more direct measure of food availability to herbivores (or omnivores, for that matter) than ET. In the Levant, this applies mainly to the woody areas in the northern coastal plain and the western slopes of the central mountain range. However, the PP of pristine Levantine landscapes is not easily estimated on the basis of the present-day Levant because the natural habitat has been constantly and extensively disturbed and manipulated since the onset of agriculture. Mattoral vegetation has replaced forests because of human land-use habits (cultivation, overgrazing, commercial use) and has in turn been disturbed by more recent human activities. In fact, some biogeographers have argued that vegetation formations recognized in the Mediterranean zone (*garrigue, maquis*) may represent progressive stages of forest deterioration rather than original plant formations. It is therefore difficult to assess the original structure of vegetation communities and of faunal resources in the variable physiographic zones of the region.

At present the Mediterranean region hosts some 200 species of mammals, with the highest diversity being recorded in the eastern part of the basin (117 species). Additionally, some 500 species of birds are found in the Levant as either migratory or resident species (Simmons 2004 and references therein). The major faunal groups of the Mediterranean Basin bear a distinct Holarctic signature, with a few elements of Afro-tropical origin (North African mammals being an exception; Blondel and Aronson 1999:31).[2] The great biodiversity of the Mediterranean region as a whole reflects the large number of endemic species (ca. 25% of the species). By definition of endemism, these occur in spatially constrained areas and are not distributed homogeneously over large land tracts within the Mediterranean Basin. Thus, species richness appears low if evaluated on a small spatial scale but is much higher if ecotones between larger (or numerous) subregions or "life zones" are considered (Blondel and Aronson 1999:107–111).

Most Levantine animal species are territorial, or exploit small annual home ranges (Baharav 1974; Nowak and Paradiso 1983), hence they do not shift their territories in accordance with resource distributions. Some species adapt to seasonal resource stress by exploiting diverse habitats, within each of which they have a large range of behavioral adjustments (e.g., the gazelles shift from grazing to browsing according to availability of resources; Baharav 1974, 1981).

As is the case with vegetation, Levantine faunas are greatly disturbed. For example, while browsing animals should be well represented in the Mediterranean forest (e.g., deer), those are not seen in the current faunal communities. Travelers' descriptions throughout the second millennium (as summarized by Bodenheimer 1956; see also, e.g., Tristram 1865) enable a glimpse of some of the recent faunas in the regions. Such descriptions clearly do not provide a full or balanced picture because the travelers were often biased toward hunting grounds, holy places, and other destinations, their descriptions are never quantitative and their taxonomies are sometimes confusing. Still, it is clear that as late as the nineteenth century the visible animals on the landscape included deer (mainly fallow deer), gazelle, wild pigs, wild goats, hares, and a multitude of carnivores (bears, leopards, lions (?), foxes,

wolves, jackals, and hyenas), as well as numerous birds. Today gazelles and wild pigs are still part of the faunal community in only some parts of the Southern Levant, as well as the various canids. Leopards can be observed in very small numbers in the Judean and Negev deserts, where ibex are also found.

## Middle Paleolithic Environments

The topographic and climatic configuration of the Levant as known today was already in place when the first hominins reached the region during the Lower Pleistocene. These settings were further modified during the Pleistocene by a series of tectonics, volcanic eruptions, and combinations of fluvial, limnic, and aeolian processes, as well as attendant deposition and erosion, that further modified local landscapes. Although the details of the physical landscape approached the conditions visible today only in the later Upper Paleolithic, most of the earlier Pleistocene topographic changes were of a localized nature (e.g., the down-cutting of drainages; Goldberg 1976, 1986).

Two major recurrent agents of landscape changes are known from the span of 1.5 million years of human occupation in the Levant. One is the formation and disappearance of a series of lakes within the Rift Valley and on the eastern margins of the Transjordanian/Syrian plateau. Of these, the phase of lake formation that is pertinent to the Middle Paleolithic is the occurrence of Lake Lisan in the central and southern part of the Dead Sea Rift and a smaller lake immediately to the north of it (Bartov et al. 2002; Begin, Ehrlich, and Nathan 1974, 1980; Begin et al. 1985; Druckman, Magaritz, and Sneh 1987; Hazan et al. 2005; Neev and Emery 1967). Lake Lisan first appeared around 70,000 years ago, at the onset of MIS 4, and corresponds in time to the late Middle Paleolithic. Unfortunately, stratigraphic and dating uncertainties do not allow reconstruction of the amplitude and timing of water-level fluctuations during this earlier time of the lake (Bartov et al. 2002, 2003). From 60,000 years ago until the lake's desiccation ca. 16,000 years ago, the "normal" water level was around 265 m below sea level (b.s.l.), but it fluctuated sharply over short, millennial-scale intervals. The water level dropped to about 325 and 320 m b.s.l. at ca. 46,000–45,000 and 38,000 years ago (i.e., the time of the Upper Paleolithic Early Ahmarian industries), respectively, and to 220 m b.s.l. around 30,000 years ago. It reached its all-time high level of approximately 160 m b.s.l. at 26,000 years ago, followed from ca. 25,000 years ago by a gradual decrease in lake level to around 400 m b.s.l. for most of the Holocene. High water levels of Lake Lisan coincide with periods of speleothem formation in the northern Negev desert of Israel, suggesting the southward shift of Mediterranean climatic systems. Indeed, during the wetter periods, inland lakes and springs would provide large amounts of fresh or brackish water. Under glacial conditions, rains would have been restricted to the western part of the Levant, while the inner lakes might have stayed at their interglacial high stand because of lower levels of evaporation (Street and Grove 1979; Vaks et al. 2006; see below).

The two water bodies in the Dead Sea Rift and associated, more localized water bodies on the Rift margins (e.g., Schuldenrein and Clark 2001) would be landscape features with which late Middle Paleolithic hominins had to contend with, in terms of the extent of areas available for exploitation in the Dead Sea Rift, as well as the hindrance of passage along and across the valley. At the same time, lakeshore environments offer diverse ecological niches and habitats that could be exploited (Feibel 2001, 2004).

The other recurring landscape change derives from the cyclic pattern of regressions and transgressions of the sea (Gvirztman et al. 1985; Horowitz 1979; Sanlaville 1981), resulting in expansions of the coastal plain during cold, dry climatic stages. Within the time span of the Middle Paleolithic, the latter are equivalent to MIS 6 (186,000–128,000 years ago) and MIS 4 to mid-3 (74,000–45,000 years ago). Previous estimates of sea level drops to 150 or 125 m b.s.l. may have been exaggerated.[3] The additional terrestrial area exposed when the sea regressed is not easily estimated on the basis of reconstructed sea levels alone, due to local subsidence and tectonics (Flemming and Webb 1986; Rabineau et al. 2006). Moreover, there are now indications that the formation of aeolianites (kurkar) ridges and of paleosols (hamra) co-occurred along the littoral at least from MIS 6 onwards. This undermines traditional scenarios that the two types of deposit represent high and low sea levels, respectively (Frechen et al. 2004 and references therein; Sivan and Porat 2004, and references therein), and consequently hampers accurate reconstructions of the paleogeography of the coastal plain.

The fragmentary paleoclimatic record of the southern Levant as derived from deep sea cores and from pollen studies has been augmented during the last decade by detailed studies of speleothems. Originating from caves in various topographic settings, such research permits high-resolution chronology and sequential records of stable isotope changes as proxies of paleoclimatic conditions (Ayalon, Bar-Matthews, and Kaufman 2002; Bar-Matthews and Ayalon 2001; Bar-Matthews, Ayalon, and Kaufman 1997; Bar-Matthews et al., 2003; Frumkin and Stein 2004; Frumkin, Ford, and Schwarcz 1999; McGarry et al. 2004; Vaks et al. 2003, 2006).

Climatic fluctuations portrayed in both terrestrial and marine records indicate that over the last 400,000 years climate change was regulated by orbital-driven maximum summer insolation cyclicity (Almogi-Labin, Bar-Matthews, and Ayalon 2004 and references therein). During this time span (MIS 11–1), Levantine climatic patterns mainly track those of the Atlantic system, as is the case today, and a high correlation has been established between global climatic events and Levantine conditions. The entire region was subjected to humid and rainy climate during warm interglacial periods, when the Atlantic and monsoonal systems nearly overlapped. During glacial times, the whole region became cool and dry as synoptic configurations shifted. Milder conditions occurred over shorter intervals between these two extremes, contributing to a highly variable climate (Almogi-Labin, Bar-Matthews, and Ayalon 2004). Isotopic records from regions as different as the western flanks of the Judean Mountains, the rain shadow zone on the eastern flanks of the Samaria Hills, high elevations on Mt. Hermon and as far south as the northern Negev desert document the major impact of the Atlantic systems, with differences in isotopic compositions reflecting the specific topographic and geographic locations of individual sequences.

The summer monsoon system penetrated and marginally influenced the southern parts of the Levant mainly during interglacial times, but the major source of rain reaching the northern Negev desert was of eastern Mediterranean origin. There is no synchroneity in monsoonal activity and humidity in the region (Prell and van Campo 1986; Vaks et al. 2006). Humid periods, in which precipitation was sufficient for speleothem formation, are documented mainly during glacial times (MIS 6, MIS 4, MIS 3, and MIS 2) due to the southward shift of the Mediterranean climate systems. Whereas at least 300–350 mm annual rainfall are required for speleothem formation under present-day conditions, lower amounts may have been necessary during glacial times because of lower temperatures and, therefore, evaporation rates. Short intervals of speleothem deposition occurred during interglacial periods. Such humid periods were documented at 200,000–190,000 (MIS 7.1[7a]), 137,000–123,000 and 118,000 (the transitions from MIS 6 to MIS 5 and MIS 5.5 [5e], respectively), and 96,000 and 84,000–77,000 years ago (MIS 5.2, 5.1 [5b–5a], respectively) (Vaks et al. 2006). These periods of deposition, associated with times of sapropel formation in the Mediterranean, represent twice as much rainfall as the present day in the Negev, and higher than any seen in the area during the Holocene. Carbon isotope studies indicate that Mediterranean $C_3$ vegetation penetrated the northern Negev during humid intervals and was mixed with the more arid Irano-Turanian $C_4$ vegetation.

On the other hand, periods of aridity, when no speleothem deposition occurred, were documented in the northern Negev during interglacial and glacial intervals. During Middle Paleolithic times, such arid intervals were registered in the northern Negev during the intervals

150,000–144,000, 141,000–140,000, 117,000–96,000, 92,000–85,000 years ago. These were due both to higher temperature and elevated rates of evaporation and to lower amounts of annual precipitation (Vaks et al. 2006).

The effect of climatic fluctuations in the Mediterranean zone may have been less dramatic. Temperatures during glacial and interglacial periods varied within the range of 2–3°C and were similar to those of the present. Thus, for a single site, Soreq Cave in the Judean mountains, a temperature range of 17°–19°C was calculated for MIS 5c (105,000 years ago), compared to a range of 16°–18°C during MIS 4 (73,000 years ago) and 18°C at present (Bar-Matthews and Ayalon 2001: fig. 8). At this locality, as well as in the Upper Galilee (Peqi'in Cave), periods of high rainfall, causing accumulations of layers rich in organic material in the eastern Mediterranean (figure 8.2), occurred at the same time as observed in the Negev. Extraordinarily high precipitation was inferred for the transition from MIS 6 to MIS 5 (124,000–119,000 years ago), possibly reflecting deluge conditions. Other intervals of pluvial conditions were documented at 108,000 and 100,000, and at 85,000 and 79,000 years ago. Around 54,000 years ago, conditions were again very humid though not as wet as during the MIS 6–5 transition.

Translating the isotopic data into climatic parameters of rainfall and temperatures is a complex procedure with considerable margins of error. Bar-Matthews and Ayalon (2004) have calculated paleo-rainfall amounts for the last 7,000 years, during which variation ranged from 600 mm (about 20% more rainfall than the 500 mm measured today in the western part of the Judean mountains) to 300 mm over a short period during the early Holocene. Importantly, these estimates are based on underlying assumptions about the relationship between isotopic compositions of rainwater in comparison to cave water and about the stability of sea and land surface temperatures. For the Holocene, such assumptions can be checked against other, semi-independent databases (e.g., lake levels, sapropel characteristics) (Bar-Matthews and Ayalon 2004 and references therein; Emies et al. 2000). The conditions during the Pleistocene–Holocene transition (a dramatic rise in temperature and decrease in rainfall values; e.g., Bar-Matthews and Ayalon 2001; CLIMAP 1976; Dayan et al. 1991; Gates 1976) and the extreme aridity and cooling (~6–8° lower than present-day temperatures) of the Last Glacial Maximum (Almogi-Labin, Bar-Matthews, and Ayalon 2004) set the extremes of the amplitude of climatic fluctuations throughout the Pleistocene. However, the paucity of similar corroborative data or their ambiguity for the earlier periods that interest us here prohibit direct projection of calculated Holocene values onto periods of greater antiquity.

The climatic oscillations of the Pleistocene caused alternating advances of forests and open vegetation zones in Europe and the Mediterranean region, whereas in northwestern Africa there were shifts in the locations of Mediterranean forests and semi-deserts (van Andel and Tzedakis 1996). Pollen records in Europe indicate that Mediterranean-type vegetation persisted in southern Europe even during the cooler periods (Urban 2004; van Andel and Tzedakis 1996), effectively creating a mosaic of vegetal landscapes similar to the Mediterranean today (Blondel and Aronson 1999; Finlayson 2004:140–144). These studies indicate that the variability and severity of climatic conditions in the Mediterranean Basin were less drastic than in more northern parts of Europe. While climatic conditions in the Levant were mostly transferred from the mid-high latitudes of the northeast Atlantic and the Siberian high-pressure systems, the amplitude of climate change was certainly lower than in more northern regions. The major drops in Lake Lisan levels seem to correspond to the Heinrich 1–5 cold events (Bartov et al. 2003); some of the events are not recorded in the speleothem records that track the Atlantic rain regime (e.g., the Heinrich 3 and 4 events), while other documented ones are milder than seen in the more northern regions (e.g., the short-term Heinrich 6 event; the Younger Dryas at the close of the Pleistocene; Almogi-Labin, Bar-Matthews, and Ayalon 2004; Bar-Matthews and Ayalon 2004; Bartov et al. 2003. It is important to bear in mind these differences in the magnitude of climatic changes between the Levant and Europe when discussing the possible scenarios of population adaptations and their movements into and out of the Levant at various times during the Middle Paleolithic (see chapter 9).

Importantly, both the global and regional Levantine climatic records show that the orbital-driven cyclic pattern is punctuated by non-cyclic fluctuations on shorter and variable (annual, decadal, centennial, and millennial) scales. It is ironic that the paleoanthropological record, concerned as it is with human activities, lacks the resolution necessary to tie it securely into the high-resolution geological record that depicts such short-term changes, which in turn probably directly influenced the life of hominin groups in the region and their decision-making processes (figure 8.2).

## Resource Structure

Students of the Paleolithic have tended to view faunal food resources as the main influence on the subsistence and mobility patterns of Paleolithic hunters and gatherers. The first and more general reason for this tendency has nothing to do with human behavior and everything to do with the nature of the archaeological record. Bones tend to survive better than other organic remains, so that direct evidence for the use of vegetal resources is limited to a small number of sites with unusual preservation

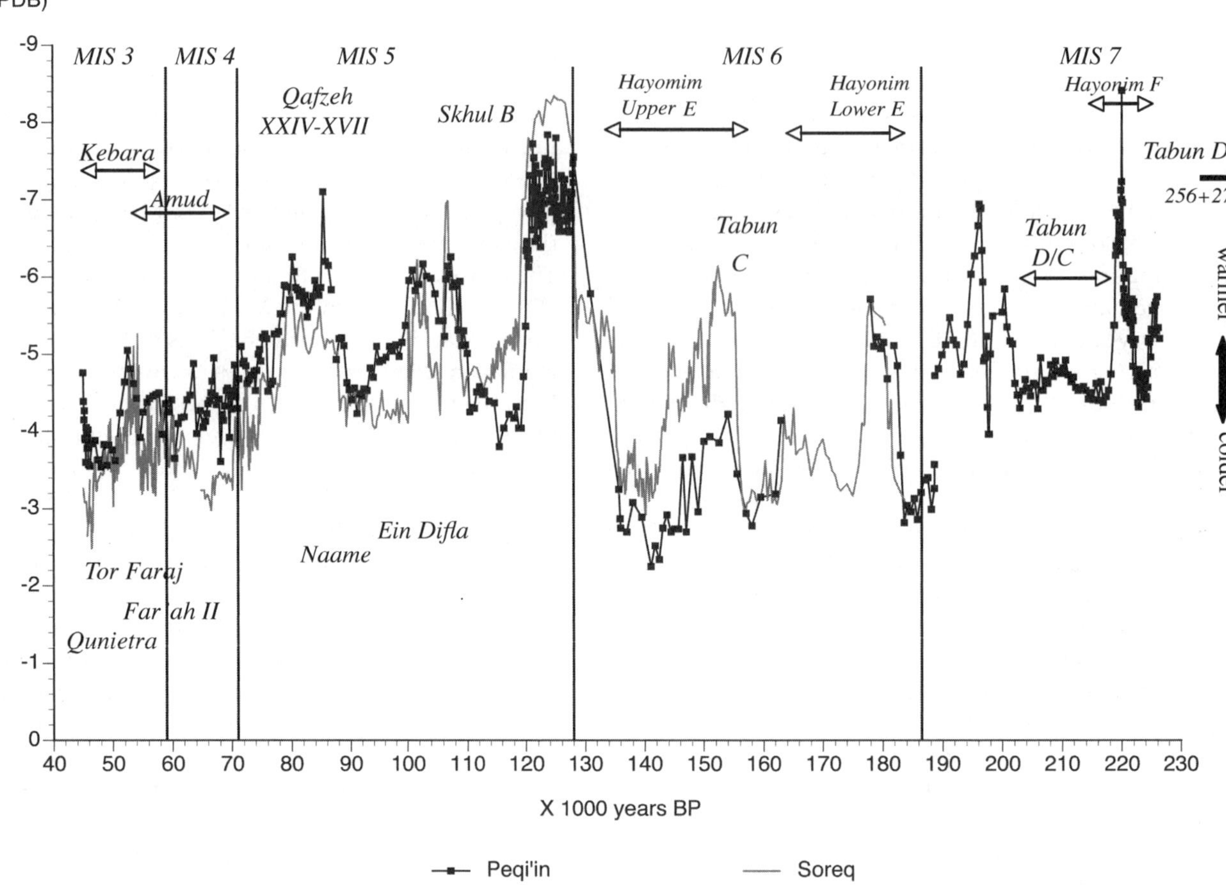


**Figure 8.2** Climatic variation shown against site chronologies. The δ$^{18}$O records from Peqi'in and Soreq caves serve as the proxy for the range and magnitude of climatic changes throughout the Middle Paleolithic period between 230,000 and 40,000 years ago. As discussed in the text, both these records indicate that the eastern Mediterranean climate system was the major climatic influence during the late Middle and early Upper Pleistocene. Dated Middle Paleolithic sites shown here are placed within their chronological ranges (and paleoclimatic contexts) as inferred by various dating methods. Where stratigraphic sequences are dated the arrows show the chronological intervals involved. For the sites of Amud, Kebara, Tabun, Hayonim, Ein Difla, only the TL chronology is shown. Note the millennial scale variations clearly observed in the paleoclimatic record. Paleoclimatic data from Bar-Matthews et al. 2003; site chronologies from Bar-Yosef 1992; Clark et al. 1997; Henry 1995c; Mercier and Valladas 2003; Mercier et al. 2007; Valladas et al. 1986, 1987, 1999; Ziaei et al. 1990).

conditions. Since paleoanthropologists cannot rely on negative evidence, they focus by default on faunal remains and make those the center of their discussion (Hovers 1998b; Madella et al. 2002). More specifically for the Middle Paleolithic, the Eurocentric research tradition has, by definition, linked Middle Paleolithic archaeological entities with Neanderthals. It has been argued that these hominins subsisted within a restricted dietary niche focused on big-game hunting (e.g., Kuhn and Stiner 2006; Stiner 1994, 2002 and references therein).[4] Thus, in most analyses and reconstructions of Middle Paleolithic subsistence and mobility, patterns of game procurement are implicated, whether explicitly or implicitly, in the timing and spatial occurrence of various technological behaviors. This has been the case in both Europe and the Levant (e.g., Chase 1986; Kuhn 1995a; Lieberman and Shea 1994; Speth 2004; Speth and Clark 2006; Stiner and Kuhn 1992; Stiner and Tchernov 1998).

However, the analysis of the lithic technology of the Qafzeh assemblages did not point to such links as important factors in shaping technological behaviors (chapter 7). Instead, it was suggested that variations in raw material economy, settlement patterns, and strategies of resource procurement were responsive to the timing and location of vegetal rather than faunal resources. This deviation from the consensual explanations of technological organization raises the question of whether Qafzeh is exceptional among the Middle Paleolithic contexts in the Levant, or whether (as would be expected from the Levant's geographic location) this pattern was shared by groups occupying other sites. If the latter, we would also want to know how similar or different were the behaviors, and what promoted variability in these behaviors.

As a first step toward clarifying this issue, the overall characteristics of the Levantine Middle Paleolithic resource structure must be determined. It is clear from the previous section that during the Middle Paleolithic there was much variation in climate parameters in the Levant. How did the shifts in rainfall amounts and temperatures across the varied Levantine topography influence the distribution of various resources in space and over time?

The bimodal Mediterranean climate as we know it today began to appear during the late Pliocene (3.2 million years ago) as part of a global cooling trend and became firmly established around 2.8 million years ago. The contrast between the cold-wet and hot-dry seasons has steadily intensified since then (Blondel and Aronson 1999:21). Data from the marine and terrestrial climatic records are consistent with this broad statement. The negligible effect of monsoonal systems precludes the existence of summer rains, and while temperatures and rainfall amounts have changed, the amplitude of seasonal differences may not have been drastically different from that observed today. This implies that ET fluctuated in the range of the present values, influencing the seasonal patterns of resource availability in a similar fashion to present-day conditions. The southward shift of biomes during glacial maxima (possibly as much as 20° in latitude; Blondel and Aronson 1999) meant that Mediterranean vegetation in Europe often survived only as refugia in the south of the continent. This is borne out by circum-Mediterranean palynological evidence that depicts such refugia in various locations such as mountain slopes, large peninsulas, and large river valleys (Blondel and Aronson 1999:27–28; see, e.g., the review of marine pollen cores off the Iberian coast by d'Errico and Sánchez Goñi 2004). During glacial maxima, the geographic extent of Mediterranean vegetation would have been larger and its biodiversity higher because of the land exposed by sea-level drops and claimed by Mediterranean plant communities. The same is true for faunas, in which there was no clear differentiation between Mediterranean and non-Mediterranean communities as far north as the south of France (Blondel and Aronson 1999:27–28). Although vegetation formations in the Levant may have changed through time, plant communities and faunal resources would have remained Mediterranean and offered much of the biodiversity of this phytogeographic world.

These reconstructions, drawn from large-scale databases, are supported by direct finds in the Levant. The first appearance of Mediterranean vegetation communities in the region probably goes back to the early Pleistocene (Blondel and Aronson 1999). Evidence from the rich assemblages of plant remains at the early Middle Pleistocene site of Gesher Benot Ya'aqov, as well as ecological reconstructions (Goren-Inbar et al. 2000, 2004; Goren-Inbar, Werker, and Feibel 2002), directly document the presence of Mediterranean conditions during that time span. The rare macrobotanical remains from Middle Paleolithic sites in the Levant indicate that vegetation assemblages in the north and central Levant during Mousterian times were essentially the same as today's, with gradients in the distributions of vegetation associations being similar (Madella et al. 2002). Paleobotanical finds from Kebara Cave in the Mt. Carmel region (Baruch, Werker, and Bar-Yosef 1992; Lev 1993; Lev, Kislev, and Bar-Yosef 2005) indicate the presence of meso-Mediterranean oak forests in the immediate vicinity of the site, broadly similar to what would have been the natural plant associations in the region today were it not for disturbance by human activities. Phytolith remains from Amud, Kebara, Hayonim, and Tabun Caves are essentially congruent with this scenario (Albert et al. 1999, 2000, 2003; Madella et al. 2002). This reconstruction suggests that some areas of the Mediterranean region may have had rather high primary production.

The vegetal biomass of the Mediterranean coastal plain has been estimated as 160 kg per 1,000 m$^2$ in areas where the typical maquis community of closed Mediterranean forest prevails, through 325 kg per 1,000 m$^2$ in the gallery forest of *Pistacia* and accompanying plants, and up to 770 kg per 1,000 m$^2$ in the open batha and garrigue areas that bear mostly annuals (e.g., grasses, legumes) (Anonymous 1981). Clearly, the amount of plant biomass that is present in a region in an average year is not identical to the amount of plant foods that humans can actually access and exploit in a particular habitat at a given time of the year, given that humans usually concentrate on specific parts of the plants (such as seeds, nuts, or leaves). There are a number of techniques for estimating the potential food available in a habitat (Binford 2001:175–176) but applying them to the meager data currently available would be misleading. The numbers cited here do serve, however, as a rough baseline for the primary production of the various habitats within the Mediterranean region, the degree to which they differed from one another, and which of them may have provided the most diverse and seasonally reliable plant foods.

As with the fauna, the differences between present-day vegetation and that of the Upper Pleistocene are viewed as having been of degree more than of kind. This is especially true for the core Mediterranean zones, though arid and semi-arid parts of the Levant may have shifted more radically between glacial and interglacial primary biomass and faunal distributions, and reconstructions of their environments are more tenuous.[5]

The most frequent finds from archaeological sites that are relevant to issues of environmental reconstructions are, of course, the faunal assemblages. The major faunal groups that are encountered today (or would have been if the fauna had remained pristine and intact) are found in the various archaeozoological assemblages (e.g., Gilead and Grigson 1984; Griggo 1998, 2002; Rabinovich and Hovers 2004; Rabinovich and Tchernov 1995; Speth and Tchernov 1998, 2001; Stiner and Tchernov 1998), although frequencies may shift temporally because of climate fluctuations. As discussed above, incursions of African tropical fauna are relatively rare throughout the Pleistocene in general. The occurrence of the cape hunting dog in the early Mousterian assemblages of Hayonim (Stiner et al. 2001) and the one detected in the Qafzeh assemblages (chapter 3) are among the most notable examples.

Some authors have emphasized the shifts in the quantitative representations of species due to climatic shifts or to behavioral changes (Bate 1937; Davis, Rabinovich, and Goren-Inbar 1988; Speth 2004; Speth and Clark 2006), but these did not significantly change our understanding of the overall patterns of game seasonality and territoriality. As in the present, the flexible adaptations of game animals made them predictable, stable resources, at least in terms of the time and place of their availability, whereas the quality of game would have depended on local conditions on a seasonal as well as annual basis.

In essence, then, both the large-scale models and the direct evidence from sites show that the environmental backdrop to human Middle Paleolithic activity encompassed three life zones of the Mediterranean region: thermo-Mediterranean along the coast and in the south, and meso- and supra-Mediterranean conditions in the north. During wet interglacial times, the southern parts may (where soils were appropriate) have supported vegetation species and diversity that were more similar to the meso-Mediterranean communities. The model of human ecology in the Levant depicts an essentially Mediterranean environment not unlike that of the present that interacted with the social and technological capacities of hominins, determining the constraints and possibilities encountered by these groups.

As is the case in the present day, resources were highly seasonal and spatially clumped. Like today, there was a North–South (and to a lesser degree, a West–East) gradient in rainfall and temperature over small distances, which effectively prolonged the seasonal availability and accessibility of short-time resources. To exploit plant resources fully, human groups in the Levant would have had to move across the landscape in synchroneity with the plants' ripening seasons. These, in turn, would have had rather short periods of spatio-temporal overlap between sub-regions of the Levant, due to the gradients of rainfall and temperatures in the region. On the other hand, game species would have been relatively stationary throughout the year. One should expect some differences between the northern and southern/eastern Levant, since in the latter parts aridity, poor water retention in soils, and accentuated seasonality of plants would have caused higher reliance on animal resources. In the southern and eastern regions, resource availability depended to a large degree on the existence of inland fresh water bodies such as springs or lakes, which could be exploited on a year-round basis under most circumstances. Some gregarious, migratory species (e.g., onagers) are known from the Middle Paleolithic record of the southern Levant; these would have formed large seasonal herds in the vicinity of water sources in drier periods of the year (Gilead and Grigson 1984). Gazelles in arid zones of the Levant tend to cluster (particularly in the summer) in preferred habitats (e.g., in acacia groves; Baharav 1982). At such times, they constitute an abundant and stable food supply, whereas many of the plant foods in the vicinity of gazelle-herding grounds are inedible for humans. To some degree such fauna were a predictable resource, in that the approximate timing of large migrations would have been known to hominins. All of this would have resulted in a higher dependency on faunal resources and scheduling of group moves in accordance with densities of gazelle and/or onagers (less often than gazelle, if the archaeological record is any indication) during the summer.

In the low-medium latitudes of the Levant, the location and availability of plant resources would have been more significant than those of animal resources in determining the timing and extent of group movements (Hayden 1981; Hovers 1988; Kelly 1983; Lieberman 1993) during the Middle Paleolithic. One would thus expect that the organization of subsistence behavior of hominin groups all over the Levant was structured according to plant seasonality, regional differences notwithstanding. Varied responses to environmental challenges lend themselves to interpretation as different tactical decisions rather than fundamental strategic differences among groups.

## Dimensions and Timing of Mobility

The paleoenvironmental patterns reconstructed above influenced two scales of group mobility in the Levant. The first, larger scale is the regional one. It has already been noted that the Levant was probably less accessible from the south during glacial times, when the dry environments of the North African desert would have made human presence or even passage difficult. On the other hand, the Caucasus may have been a formidable obstacle that prevented human occupation during cold periods (e.g., Adler and Tushabramishvili 2004), and thus prohibited passage from Europe to the Levant.

Within the Levant itself, the coastal plain would have enabled a larger number of hominin groups to live off the land. This would have led to long-distance movement across the region, as groups from the arid southern and the eastern parts of the Levant, where conditions were harsh particularly during the dry glacial periods, were attracted to the more lush environment (Bar-Yosef 1992). The expansion of the coastal plain during glacial times would potentially reduce the risk of competing against other migrant or resident groups for territories. Another potential route that may have facilitated population movement on a North–South axis was through the Dead Sea Rift. This route was effectively blocked during the very late Middle Paleolithic, ca. 70,000 years ago, when Lake Lisan filled the major part of the rift (see above), also hampering East–West connections in the process.

The second scale of mobility concerns movement within group territories. The important role of vegetal resources as determinants of group movement begs the question of seasonal moves within a group's home range when adjusting its location in relation to resources. Reconstructing this type of mobility is dependent upon understanding the relationships between trophic levels, body size of organisms, and the size of the effective subsistence range. In the case of humans, the effect of extractive technologies on habitat food characteristics should also be considered (figure 8.1). As a rule, the less abundant the habitat or the higher the trophic level of an organism, the larger the range that the organism must exploit in order to obtain its food. At the same time, it is also apparent that plant species richness, which is tracked to a degree (through a rather complicated relationship) by faunal richness, is strongly conditioned by the global patterning of solar energy distribution, namely, climatic conditions and geographic regimes (e.g., Binford 2001:366–367 and references therein). Although the effects of geographic location are mitigated by cultural factors in the case of humans, such generalizations are still applicable to our genus.

The high investment of meat-dependent groups in hunting of faunal resources—tracking game over long distances away from camp, chasing it down, and transporting the meat back to the camp—is nutritionally and economically justified by the high rates of return involved in animal exploitation. In contrast, foragers who rely primarily on plant gathering cannot afford to invest effort and energy in long-distance procurement. Especially in patchy environments, where resources are spatially clustered and not homogeneously distributed over the landscape, plant resource harvesting must be timed accurately in order to reduce the risk of mistiming extractive activities. This in turn requires continuous monitoring of the group's territory, which can be achieved by exploiting thoroughly small territories through short-distance residential moves (Kelly 1995).

Another factor that gatherers must take into account is the availability and quality of storage capabilities. Plant stands sometime offer bounties that are available during relatively short periods. Investing energy and time in long-distance transport can be economically justified if there are available technologies to extend the resource's shelf-life by storage. Ethnographic hunter-gatherers without storage facilities respond to this organizational challenge by moving consumers to the resource patch (O'Shea 1981), i.e., residential mobility as a form of indirect storage.[6] In this manner they reduce the costs of transport to the consumption site and also ensure that the resource patch can be monitored and guarded against competitors.

Finally, the fact that plants constitute relatively low-return resources often renders their transport to a base camp an inefficient strategy (Kelly 1995; Metcalfe and Barlow 1992). Again, gathering peoples tend to choose more frequent residential moves over short distances in order to reduce transport costs.

Thus, ecological theory predicts, and ethnographic observations confirm, that the sizes of effective subsistence areas and annual home ranges of gathering groups are small. The spatio-temporal availability and predictability of resources also influence the way in which hunter-gatherers structure and organize their socio-economic units. Additional predictions from the relationships between trophic level and size of effective subsistence area pertain to the positioning of hunter-gatherers in relation to their resources. Wilmsen (1973) modeled group social organization, settlement locations, and mobility patterns in relation to the nature of resources. He suggested that when resources are predictable and dense, the optimal "packaging" of human groups will be in the form of intermediately sized groups with low mobility dispersed at equal distances from resource stands. A "central place" for such a group in this type of resource structure will be only suboptimal because territorial defense may become too costly. At the other extreme, where resources are both unpredictable and scarce, the optimal organization of human activities will be in the form of small, highly mobile groups that move around the landscape tapping into resources as they are encountered. In such circumstances, a centrally located, sedentary or semi-sedentary location will not be optimal, since it will be difficult to obtain all the necessary information about the environment, and territorial defense is too expensive. A predictable but scarce resource base is best exploited by small groups that monitor the spatial availability of resources through moderate to high mobility rates. Conversely, unpredictable but dense resources can support large groups for a short time, but temporal availability must be monitored through frequent moves; this type of resource structure thus justifies large, centrally located but highly mobile groups (Dyson-Hudson and Smith 1978; Wilmsen 1973).

The pertinent question in the context of this discussion is whether such general rules can be used to understand the archaeological record of Levantine Middle Paleolithic groups. The focus of the foregoing discussion has been on the most straightforward, simplistic scenarios of the influence of habitat on group decision making, as characterized by optimization analysis (Kelly 1995 and references therein; Smith and Wintherhalder 1992). If one can make the case that the Levantine habitats of the present, characterized as they are by seasonally patchy resource distributions, reflect those of the Middle Paleolithic, this insight may offer the key to understanding important aspects of the organizational behaviors of Levantine Middle Paleolithic groups. This does indeed seem to be the case.

The geographic pattern of increasing reliance on faunal foods as one moves toward the north (see discussion in chapter 7) is a characteristic of the habitat irrespective of the period discussed. In addition, Middle Paleolithic hominins in the Levant appear to have existed in a Mediterranean biome similar to that of the present. This, in turn, implies that these groups probably relied on plants for their staple food supply, and optimization analysis would suggest that their organizational behaviors were structured accordingly. That legume seeds were collected by the inhabitants of Kebara when still green and were inadequately stored (Lev 1993:77)[7] implies that storage was not part of the Middle Paleolithic technological package. Therefore, we may assume that Levantine groups as a rule were not subject to conditions that required deviation from the usual residential mobility strategies of hunter-gatherers.[8]

Group territories in Middle Paleolithic Levantine conditions would have been small and exploited by much the same strategies that modern hunter-gatherers adopt in comparable contexts, that is, by frequent group movements between resource patches. How small were such territories can be determined only by educated guesswork, in the absence of factual evidence. Assessment of territory size requires knowledge of both the size of the population and the carrying capacity of the habitat on which it subsisted. Clearly, the former is an unknown for the Middle Paleolithic, and the latter can be only roughly approximated on the basis of environmental data and estimates of the efficiency of extractive technologies. Based on ethnographic case studies in regions with ETs similar to those of the Levant (14–18), Shea (2004: tab. VI) calculated that an area of 80,000 km$^2$ (the present distribution of Mediterranean woodlands) could support between 5,760 to 9,995 people (based on a median value of seven individuals per 100 km$^2$ or a mean value of twelve

individuals per 100 km$^2$, respectively). If we consider an area of 120,000 km$^2$ (roughly the size of the area in which Middle Paleolithic sites are known), the range is between 8,640 to 14,992 people (according to the same parameters). Although these numbers can be considered only minimum estimates,[9] as such they enable some rough estimates of territory sizes. From these data, it can be speculated that a twenty-five-person band (Wobst 1974:170–173 and references therein) of hunter-gatherers in the Levant could occupy an annual territory as small as 350–400 km$^2$, while a viable population of 500 individuals could exploit a territory of 800–1,000 km$^2$.

In the northern and central Levant, carrying capacity and resource reliability were higher and seasonality more relaxed. Mobility and settlement patterns in such areas probably differed from those in the south. Although in the Mediterranean core area winter would have been relatively harsh in the absence of seeds and fruits, other edible parts of various plants were available (cf. Lev 1993; Lev, Kislev, and Bar-Yosef 2005), so that the area could support human groups (at varying densities according to season) through most, if not all, the year. In the Mediterranean and Irano-Turanian vegetation belts, humans would have aggregated during the winter near the few patches of available vegetal resources (as described for the Shoshone in the Great Plains by Dyson-Hudson and Smith 1978). During the spring and summer, on the other hand, groups would have dispersed among a greater number of available resource clusters. A similarly distinct aggregation-dispersal pattern of human groups may be postulated for the southern and eastern Levant as well, except that in this case the summers would have been the time of large group aggregations in proximity to perennial water courses or water holes. At such times, exploitation territories would shrink because resources were clustered in very few areas, and resource stress would have been higher. In both northern and south/southeastern parts of the Levant, aggregation and dispersion would have taken place in topographically distinct locations, with winter occupations being located at the lower elevations (Bar-Yosef 1992:191; Henry 1995a, 1995b; see also Goring-Morris 1987). These generalized patterns of aggregations and dispersals can be translated into mobility patterns. Larger hunter-gatherer groups are commonly documented as being less residentially mobile (Perlman 1985), drawing on resources obtained by logistical mobility. Smaller groups tend to exploit their environment through residential moves.

Expectations that Middle Paleolithic sites will fall neatly into the predicted "categories" are clearly unrealistic, in view of the inferred practice of mixed mobility strategies by any single group during its annual cycle (Binford 1980; see chapters 1, 7), let alone taphonomic complexities that are inherent in the archaeological record. Still, the paleogeographic reconstruction, despite its glaring drawbacks, serves us well as a baseline against which to examine some ideas, expectations, and predictions about lithic assemblages. We may expect to recognize over the geographic area of the Levant some organizational links between mobility strategies and specific lithic production sequences and raw material economy (chapter 7). Lithic assemblages of residential sites consist of long, complete, or near-complete core-reduction sequences, diversified tool kits, and on-site manufacture and maintenance of standardized and reliable tools (i.e., blades and points produced by specialized technologies), in addition to more generalized ones. Faunal remains in occupations of longer duration are expected to display biased distributions of anatomical parts, given that carcasses of animals hunted or scavenged at ever-increasing distances from a residential camp were more prone to the "schlepp effect."

Where Middle Paleolithic groups dispersed, recovered assemblages would consist of maintainable and portable artifacts (i.e., large and thin relative to their size), intended for generalized continuous use and thus less standardized. Such dispersed groups might have been small residential units, in which case the locations of the occupation may be predicted (e.g., in the highlands of the Mediterranean zone and in the lowlands of the Negev). Alternatively, the smaller groups might occupy task-specific camps within a larger radiating settlement pattern, in which case their location is less predictable, while the assemblage will constitute of relatively monotonous tool kits, and the products of the later stages of core-reduction sequences, as well as many small resharpening flakes. If tools were left at such sites, they might be exhausted and unusable.

Against this background and these expectations, the lithic assemblages of Qafzeh are conspicuously anomalous: the characteristics of the lithic assemblages (chapters 4–6), seasonality patterns and non-lithic indications of occupation intensity in each layer (chapters 3, 7) cannot easily be reconciled with the settlement patterns expected in this specific setting in the central Levant. In this particular case, the explanation of inter-assemblage variability and its inconsistency with ecological conditions was argued to reside in social factors (chapter 7). To examine whether the causes for technological variability in other instances in the Levant resemble in any way those suggested for Qafzeh, these assemblages should be viewed against the backdrop of ecological conditions as well as the technological behaviors that are expected to have taken place in response to them.

## Explanations of Lithic Variability in the Levantine Middle Paleolithic: Do the Models Work?

Testing ecology-related hypotheses derived from formal models (chapter 1) is not a straightforward procedure because of the limitations of the regional databases.

Ideally, the Middle Paleolithic record of an entire region during a given time segment should be examined to identify patterns that allow one to refute the hypotheses. But this is not an easy endeavor in the Levant (or, for that matter, in other regions). The reasons for this are varied.

A technical but nonetheless formidable obstacle to the recognition and explanation of regional patterns in lithic assemblages stems from the history of research and the differences in analytical procedures along a timeline. In a century of Middle Paleolithic studies in the Near East (chapter 1), methods of dealing with the archaeological record have changed, improved, or became geared toward very different sets of research questions. Many of the major questions asked today have already been discussed ad nauseam by earlier writers, but the middle-range research conducted today is very different from that done in the past. We need only compare the excavation and artifact curation principles and methods applied by Garrod in the 1920s with those of modern excavations to realize that many aspects of the databases from these two periods of research can be only broadly compatible. Additionally, as various researchers have focused on variable research questions, the results are not always pertinent to the questions of others, and the data are not necessarily comparable. The plethora of approaches and research interests has, in fact, rendered impossible the construction from published materials of a Levantine database that is sufficiently homogeneous for the identification of statistically robust patterning.

Chapter 2 presented a number of formal models that attempted to explain Mousterian lithic variability through its relationship to environmental variables. An underlying theme of many if not all these models is that they link lithic variability with shifts in the kind and degree of mobility practiced by Mousterian hominins. Each model implicates different factors as the prime movers of the organizational adaptation. If nothing else, the analysis of the Qafzeh material makes it clear that single-variable explanations barely touch on the complexity of Middle Paleolithic organizational behavior. In the following sections, I will discuss and test formally some of these models, which have not so far been subjected to systematic hypothesis testing. These case studies will illustrate the limitations of a rigidly structured, "environmental" approach to the understanding of lithic assemblages.

## Distance from Raw Material Sources and Lithic Variability

The bedrock substrate in the Levant is composed of limestone, and primary sources of flint were widely available throughout the Pleistocene (with the exceptions of the Eilat/Edom mountains in the south and the Golan/Black Desert in the northern and eastern parts of the region, where igneous and volcanic rocks, respectively, dominate). Changes in sedimentation regime and vegetation cover throughout the later Pleistocene notwithstanding, sources of raw material were rarely located more than a day's walk away from any Middle Paleolithic site.

A distance–decay relationship underlies most models attempting to explain the relationship between raw material availability and lithic variability, incorporating aspects of technological organization with the adaptive significance of transport, curation, and discard (e.g., Bamforth 1991; Brantingham 2003; Kuhn 1995b). Munday (1976a, 1976b) was the first to focus on issues of raw material availability and transport costs and their effect on blank characteristics and assemblage compositions in the Levantine Middle Paleolithic, which later received much attention in other regions of the world (e.g., Ambrose 2006; Ambrose and Lorenz 1990; Féblot-Augustins 1993; Geneste 1985; Hovers 1990b; Minichillo 2006; Richter 2000). While he did not focus on source characterization and matching sources with assemblages, Munday developed a "rationing model" of lithic raw material: "Behavior towards the reduction of raw material will change according to the relationship of site location to resource availability and the *amount of work involved in moving raw material between sites*" (1976a:119; emphasis added).

Middle Paleolithic hominins in the Negev arguably had to maximize the number of pieces of debitage carried to sites that (due to the pull of other critical resources, e.g., water) were located away from raw material sources. At the same time they also had to reduce the mass of transported items. According to the model, this was done by moving lithic raw material that had already been worked at the source or in locations along the route from the source; only advanced stages of core reduction were carried out at the destination site.[10] Munday (1976a: tab. 139; 1976b:128) predicted that the mean size of debitage would be inversely correlated with the distance of raw material sources from the consumption sites.

While the predicted trend exists (figure 8.3), it does not explain satisfactorily the variability of blank sizes in either Levallois or non-Levallois debitage. Some 50–60% of the variation in debitage length is explained directly by site distance from raw material ($r^2 = 0.51$, $y = 62.1 - 1.55x$, N = 37; $r^2 = 0.59$, $y = 52.4 - 1.56x$, N = 34 for Levallois and non-Levallois artifacts, respectively), as was also the case with Munday's (1976a:139) specific Negev analysis. Two somewhat overlapping clusters are apparent. One corresponds to distances smaller than 5 km from the source, where larger artifacts occur. The second cluster corresponds to distances of 5–10 km from the studied sites.

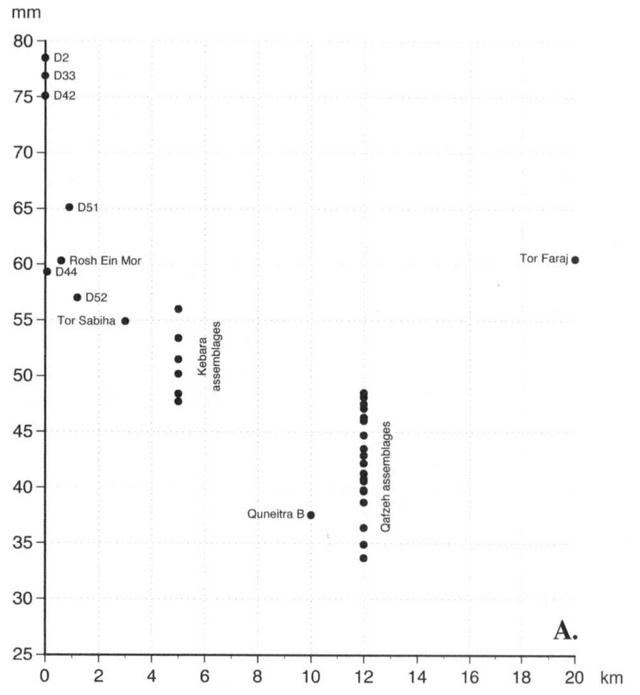


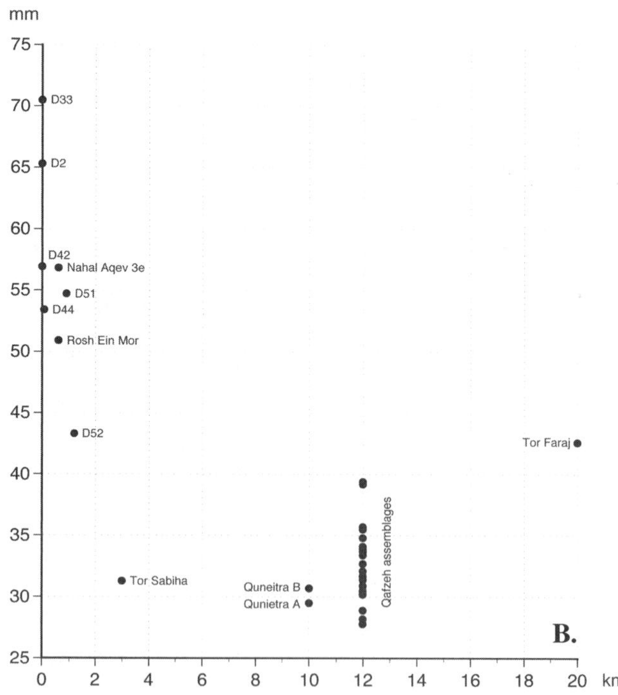


**Figure 8.3** Mean length of Levallois (A) and non-Levallois (B) blanks in Middle Paleolithic assemblages as a function of distance from raw material sources. The identification of raw material sources is based on present-day configurations.

The Qafzeh assemblages serve as an illuminating example. Although raw material was probably procured throughout time from the same source area and transported over the same distance to the site, both Levallois and non-Levallois blanks exhibit a large range of artifact mean length, both smaller and larger than the values predicted by distance from source. Most of the Kebara assemblages, on the other hand, exhibit mean values that are lower than expected. In assemblages that are distant from raw material sources (e.g., Tor Faraj), Levallois and non-Levallois debitage are "over-sized" compared to the model's predicted value,[11] whereas in sites that are close to the source the average artifact length is either relatively large (some of the Negev sites) or small compared to the expected values (Far'ah II).

Similarly, the compositions of Middle Paleolithic assemblages do not seem be strongly correlated with distance from raw material sources. The reduction of cores-on-flakes has been considered a technological strategy for mitigating shortage of raw material due to high mobility that prevented the transport of large cores or required groups to move away from the raw material sources (e.g., Munday 1976a; Wallace and Shea 2006). Munday (1976a:133) saw the relative abundance of cores-on-flakes in an assemblage (specifically those displaying the Nahr Ibrahim technique) as an expression of lithic curation through "remaking of an implement into a different kind of tool" (Odell 1996:59), or in other words, artifact recycling. Accordingly, the production and use of cores-on-flakes in Negev and other Middle Paleolithic assemblages should reflect concerns for raw material conservation correlated with on-site availability of lithic raw material (Bamforth 1986; Binford 1973, 1979). However, frequencies of cores-on-flakes, as well as other assemblage characteristics believed to reflect raw material conservation, do not seem to pattern clearly according to distance from raw material sources (table 8.1; see Hovers 2007 for discussion; and below).[12]

While distance from raw material sources played a role in determining the variability of artifact dimensions, it does not satisfactorily explain the observed variability in this and other aspects of artifact and assemblage compositions. It is possible that other aspects of the natural environment were important in determining the variability, for example, the initial sizes of the raw material packages available for reduction, about which little is known in the absence of sourcing analyses and of large-scale refitting studies. Notwithstanding, disregard of the distance of sites from raw material sources is very likely the prerogative of groups living in an environment rich in lithic sources (a characteristic of the Levantine Middle Paleolithic that differentiates it from the Middle Paleolithic in neighboring regions such as the Zagros). Consequently, distance from raw material sources as such played a relatively minor role in the flexible Levantine Middle Paleolithic decision-making system related to mobility strategies and settlement patterns (e.g., Hovers 2001, 2007; Wallace and Shea 2006).

**Table 8.1  Characteristics of core assemblages in selected Levantine Mousterian sites**

| Site | % of cores[a] (N) | % Cores-on-flakes[b] (N) | Ratio blanks:cores[c] | Distance from raw material sources |
|---|---|---|---|---|
| Amud B1 (1344) | 2.53 (34) | 47.05 (16) | 38.53 | ? |
| Amud B2 (2318)[d] | 1.38 (32) | 53.13 (17) | 71.44 | ? |
| Amud B4 (2084)[d] | 2.06 (43) | 20.93 (9) | 47.47 | ? |
| Quneitra (4587)[e] | 16.24 (745) | 28.72 (214) | 5.16 | 10 km |
| Qafzeh IX (1188)[f] | 5.47 (65) | 33.85 (22) | 17.27 | 10–15 km |
| Qafzeh XIII (2343)[f] | 4.27 (100) | 36.00 (36) | 22.43 | 10–15 km |
| Qafzeh XV (6400)[f] | 4.55 (291) | 40.55 (118) | 20.99 | 10–15 km |
| Qafzeh XVII (912)[f] | 4.93 (45) | 17.78 (8) | 19.27 | 10–15 km |
| Tor Faraj floors I and II (2071)[g] | 5.18 (140) | 57.86 (81) | 18.295 | 20 km |
| Rosh Ein Mor (40875)[h] | 8.77 (3585) | 19.50 (699) | 11.41 | 0.6 km |

[a] Out of raw frequencies of debitage and cores given in column 1 (debris not included).

[b] Out of number of cores.

[c] "Blank" refers here to both debitage and tools on pieces larger than 20 mm in maximal size.

[d] Based on work in progress and likely to change in the future.

[e] Goren-Inbar 1990.

[f] Hovers 1997.

[g] Henry 2003: tab. 4.4.

[h] Crew 1976.

## Does Climate Influence Lithic Variability, and If So, How?

### Climate and Conservation of Raw Material

Some researchers (Dibble 1995a and references therein; Dibble and Rolland 1992; Rolland 1981; Rolland and Dibble 1990) have suggested a model according to which climatic conditions during glacial times created a combination of "local circumstances" (Rolland and Dibble 1990:487) that enhanced the intensity of cave occupations relying on nearby seasonal game aggregations. In turn, the reduced foraging-related mobility led to fewer trips to raw material sources, if raw material acquisition was embedded in subsistence activities. Moreover, under glacial conditions the visibility of raw material sources on the European landscape was reduced by accumulated ice or snow that seasonally (and during glacial times, for prolonged periods) masked the exposures, and accessibility may have been hampered by frozen ground. As a result, assemblages in closed sites are predicted to exhibit high intensity of raw material reduction, with higher frequencies of heavily recycled artifacts and core exhaustion, that is, high frequencies of retouched tools and of heavily reduced blanks.[13]

The model was extended to geographical regions outside Europe, including the Levant (Dibble and Rolland 1992; Rolland and Dibble 1990), where the long sequences of cave sites indicate that human groups repeatedly occupied closed sites over long periods (Copeland 1975; Jelinek 1982a; Mercier et al. 2007). The Levantine Acheulo-Yabrudian assemblages are viewed as the equivalent of the Charentian Mousterian, in terms of both climatic background and the intensity of assemblage reduction (Dibble and Rolland 1992; Rolland and Dibble 1990). However, given current knowledge about Levantine paleoclimatic conditions, the model's initial assumptions are unlikely to be met. Raw material visibility, and hence its accessibility, in all likelihood did not change dramatically either seasonally or within different phases of a glacial cycles. And given the lack of extensive localized seasonal resources such as migrating herds during winter (the harshest season), aggregations of large groups in a few specific locales would not be a viable option for Levantine hominins. Thus, pressure on lithic resources would not be linked to climatic conditions.[14]

Within the Levantine Middle Paleolithic sequence, Tabun IX, Hayonim E, and the sequences from Amud and from Kebara are all dated to glacial periods (MIS 8, MIS 6, and MIS 4–3, respectively). In that frequencies of retouched blanks (relative to the total number of available blanks) reflect the intensity of lithic reduction in an assemblage, the climatic model posits that they should be high in cave sites occupied during cold periods. In the two earlier sequences of Hayonim and Tabun ca. 30% of

the blanks were retouched, inclusive of some intensively retouched Abu Sif points (Jelinek 1982b; Meignen 1998). However, this is not the case in the later assemblages of Kebara XII–X (ca. 3% retouched artifacts; Bar-Yosef et al. 1992) and those of Amud Unit B (between 5–9% in the various sub-units; Hovers 1998). Yet at the late Mousterian open-air site at Quneitra some 26% retouched lithics were observed (Goren-Inbar 1990a). Moreover, with the exception of some Abu Sif points and rare complex scrapers, the Levantine Mousterian technocomplex is characterized by lightly retouched tools,[15] regardless of climatic conditions. The overall pattern is thus inconsistent with the model's expectations (as phrased by Rolland and Dibble 1990:448).

Another hypothesis derived from the climatic model, that raw material consumption will be higher in cave sites than in open-air ones, is similarly not borne out by the Levantine record. There are no discernible preferences for either cave or open-air sites that can be linked with climatic fluctuations throughout the Middle Paleolithic (figure 8.4 and table 8.2).[16] Across assemblages, the frequencies of retouched blanks within the total of available blanks are not associated with the physical type of settlement. While assemblages from Quneitra, Tabun, Hayonim, various layers at Keoue Cave and Ksar Akil exhibit high frequencies of retouch, many other assemblages do not reach 20% of retouched blanks and usually sport much lower values. Mean frequencies of retouched blanks are statistically undifferentiated in cave vs. open-air assemblages, again contrary to the model's expectations (figure 8.4, table 8.2).[17]

By the same token, values of ILty in Levantine Middle Paleolithic assemblages are variable (Goren-Inbar 1990a:139–140) and co-vary inversely to those of IL and the relative frequencies of retouched pieces, both of which tend to increase simultaneously. These quantitative relationships reflect a preference of Levallois blanks for retouch, which was documented for the Qafzeh assemblages in detail (chapter 6; see Dibble 1991a:38). Yet the significantly higher mean value of ILty in cave vs. open-air assemblages (figure 8.4, table 8.2) suggests relatively less modification of Levallois blanks, contrary to the model's expectations. The expected pattern is in fact apparent in only a few assemblages from Ksar Akil in which ILty, but not IL, is extremely low, implying that most Levallois blanks had indeed been retouched or, alternatively, that unretouched Levallois blanks were removed from the site.

The hypothesis that relates raw material consumption to the physical type of sites can be examined by looking at the ratio of the two typological groups (in the Bordesian sense) that represent extreme conditions of blank consumption through retouch. These are group II (the Mousterian group), which in the majority of

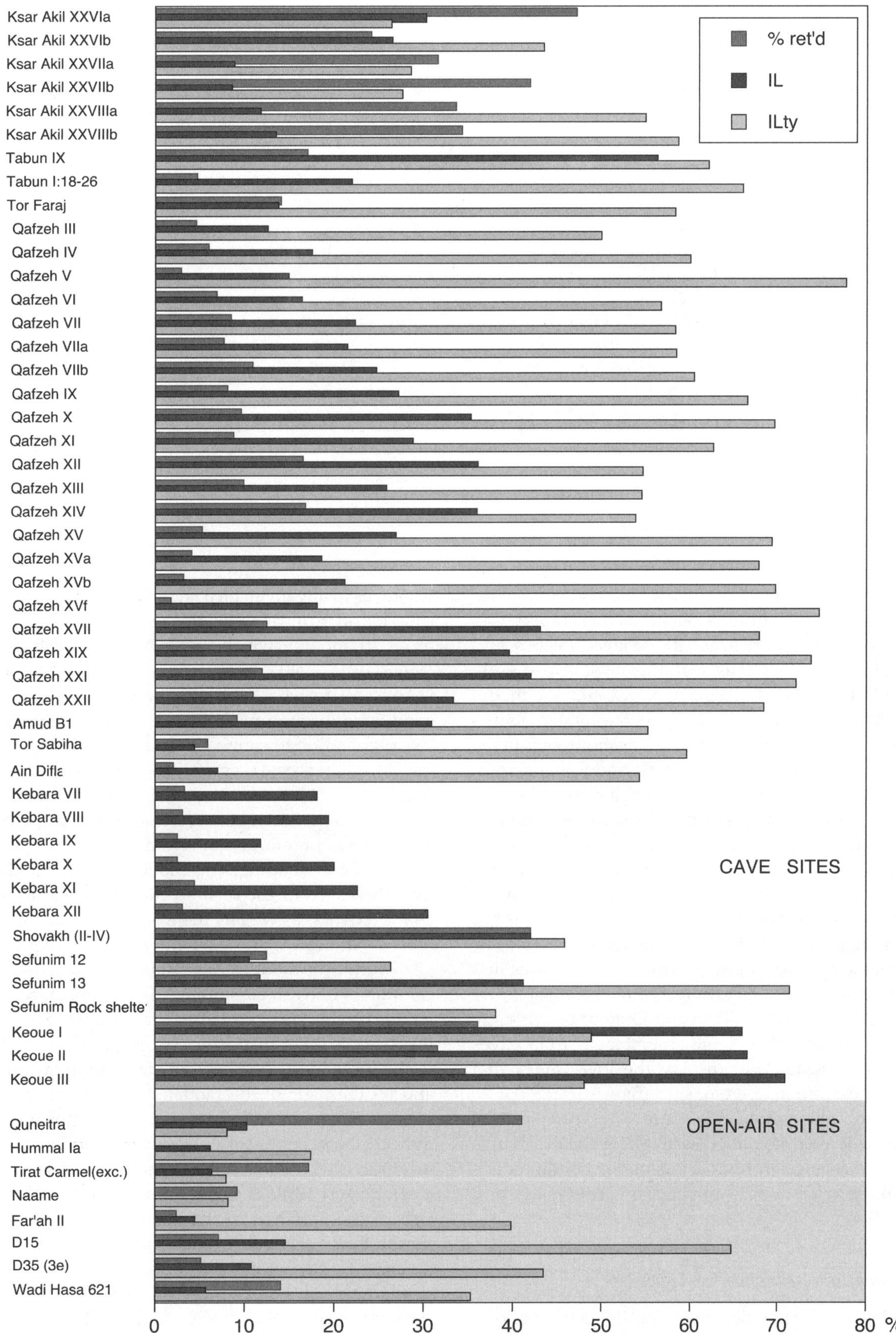


**Figure 8.4**   Values of IL, ILty, and percentages of retouched blanks in various Middle Paleolithic assemblages. See table 8.1 and appendix 1 for data sources.

**Table 8.2  Summary statistics of typological and technological indices of cave and open-air sites**

| | Open-air sites | | | | | Cave sites | | | | |
|---|---|---|---|---|---|---|---|---|---|---|
| | % reto'd | IL | ILty (real) | group IIe | group IVe | % reto'd | IL | ILty (real) | group IIe | group IVe |
| mean | 13.75 | 8.36 | 28.15 | 17.85 | 29.29 | 13.31 | 26.68 | 56.89 | 27.80 | 15.98 |
| s.d. | 13.05 | 3.63 | 21.03 | 10.59 | 9.30 | 11.86 | 15.78 | 13.43 | 20.96 | 11.56 |
| min. | 2.40 | 4.50 | 8.00 | 5.65 | 16.94 | 1.80 | 4.40 | 26.32 | 0.00 | 0.00 |
| max. | 41.00 | 14.60 | 64.90 | 37.47 | 42.11 | 47.20 | 70.90 | 77.70 | 95.00 | 47.83 |
| median | 9.25 | 6.40 | 26.35 | 20.18 | 30.61 | 9.38 | 22.45 | 58.35 | 25.00 | 13.75 |
| N | 7 | 7 | 8 | 7 | 7 | 46 | 46 | 40 | 43 | 42 |

Kolmogorov-Smirnov test for differences of % of retouched tools: 0.47, $p > 0.05$, df = 2

K-S test for differences of IL: 14.07, $0.005 > p > 0.001$, df=2

K-S test for differences of ILty (real): 14.02, $0.005 > p > 0.001$, df = 2

K-S test for differences of Group IIe: 1.79, $p > 0.05$, df = 2

K-S test for differences of Group IVe *elargi*: 9.92, $0.05 > p > 0.001$, df = 2

*Note*: Values for IL, ILty (real), and % of retouched blanks in individual assemblages are shown in figure 8.4. Data used to calculate the descriptive statistics are after Copeland 1985; Gordon 1997; Goren-Inbar 1990a: tabs. 32–34 (omitting the Acheulian sites of Bisitun, Adlun and Kebara [old excavations]); Henry 1995c; Meignen and Bar-Yosef 1991; Nishiaki and Copeland 1992.

Levantine Middle Paleolithic assemblages encompasses mostly simple and lightly retouched side-scrapers (see also Marks 1992a), and group IVe *elargi* (notches and denticulates), which consists of the most expediently retouched blanks in an assemblage. The climatic model predicts that the ratio of side-scrapers (*racloirs*) to denticulates, arguably reflecting the variation among sites in the magnitude of blank reduction (Dibble and Rolland 1992; Jelinek 1988: fig. 11.1; Rolland and Dibble 1990), will be higher in cave assemblages than in open-air assemblages. Indeed, in most cave assemblages group IVe accounts for less than 20% of the retouched artifacts. This is the case in only a third of the open-air assemblages. On the other hand, the values of group II are higher than 20% in 79% of cave assemblages and in 86% of open-air assemblages, with variable and overlapping dispersion measures that cannot be differentiated statistically (table 8.2). Open-air sites like Nahal Aqev (D35) 3e and Quneitra have high, "cave site" ratios, while some assemblages from caves sites (Qafzeh, Ksar Akil) display the low values that would be expected in open-air sites (figure 8.5a).

In sum, the regional database does not support hypotheses derived from models invoking climate change as a major influence on Middle Paleolithic hominin decision making related to raw material conservation and consumption.

## Climate and Core-Reduction Strategies

Munday's (1979) climatic model posits that amelioration of climatic conditions (which in the Levant denotes increased precipitation) led to a decrease in population densities, in turn alleviating the pressure on food resources in any given area and leading to reduced mobility. This in turn allowed the use of "high preparatory input technology which resulted in elongate debitage" (Munday 1979:98).[18] In contrast, broad and short debitage is believed to have been produced during dry climatic conditions through more intensive core exploitation but less preparation, through along-axis and centripetal flaking (Munday 1979:93, fig. 5). The latter method of reduction is associated with higher degrees of mobility over larger areas in search of subsistence resources, which put an excessive premium on investment of time and energy in careful core shaping. This model has generated several hypotheses about the relationships among various lithic characteristics, as well as the effect of climatic factors on these relationships and the nature of mobility patterns.

Munday's model links some particular technological traits within an assemblage. For example, convergent flaking modes are expected to result from the use of well-prepared striking platforms (i.e., high values of IFs) due to the mechanical properties of flint (Munday 1979:3–6), and by the logic of the model should be more frequent in favorable climatic conditions. The regional data sets indicate, however, that this expected relationship is by no means overwhelming in the Levantine Middle Paleolithic assemblages; while it is common and accounts for some 65% of the variation in the available Levantine sample (figure 8.6),[19] exceptions, notably Qafzeh and Quneitra, do exist. By the same token, values of IFs in the various stratigraphic sub-units of Amud cave remain practically constant through time while values of the laminar index (IL) change considerably (Hovers 2004b), whereas blades in Tabun IX (Jelinek 1982b:75) and Hummal Ia (Bergman and Ohnuma 1983:172; see also Meignen 1998: figs. 7, 8)

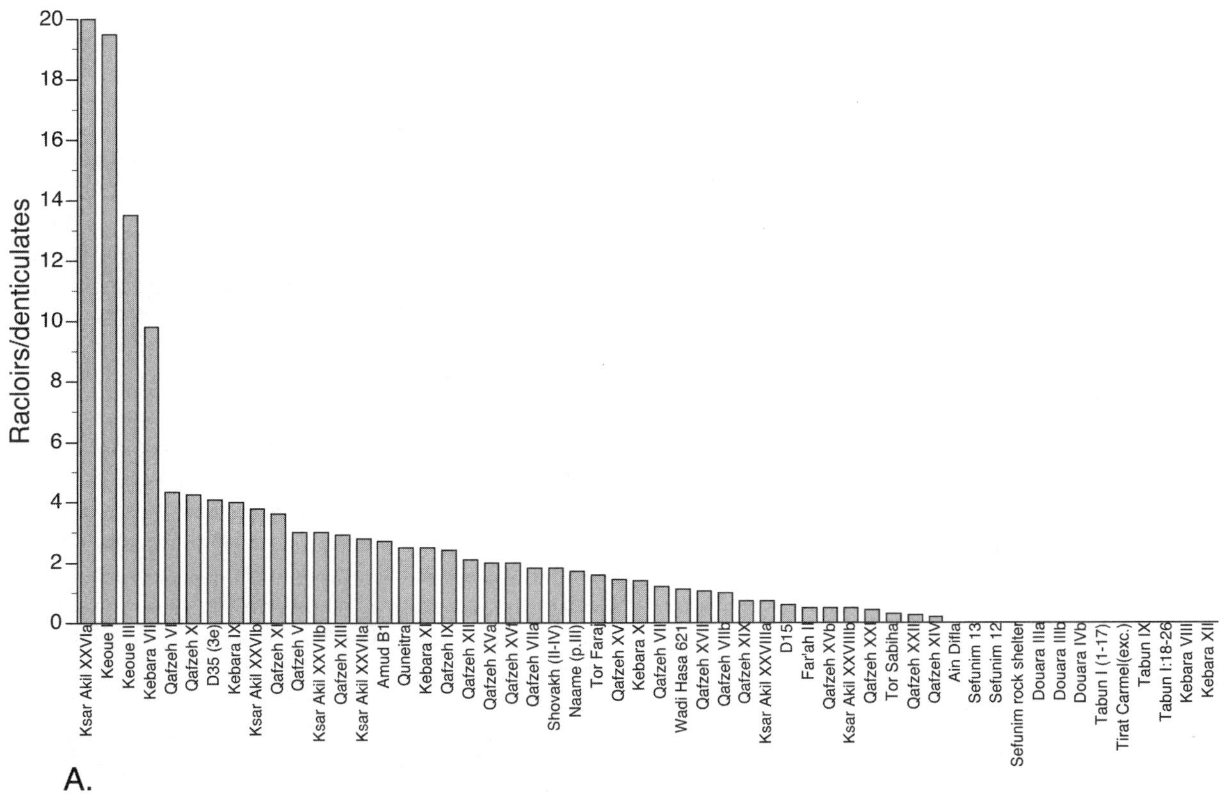


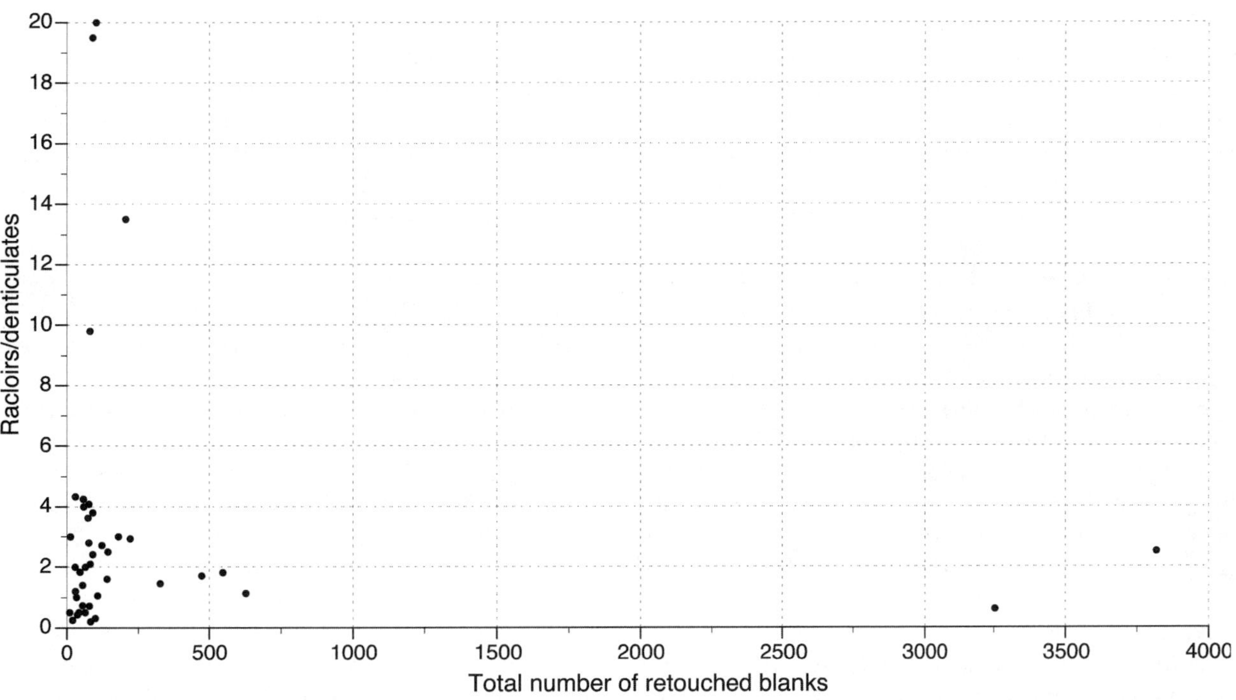


**Figure 8.5** Ratios of denticulates to side-scrapers (A) and the relationship between this ratio and the number of retouched artifacts (B) in various Levantine Middle Paleolithic assemblages.

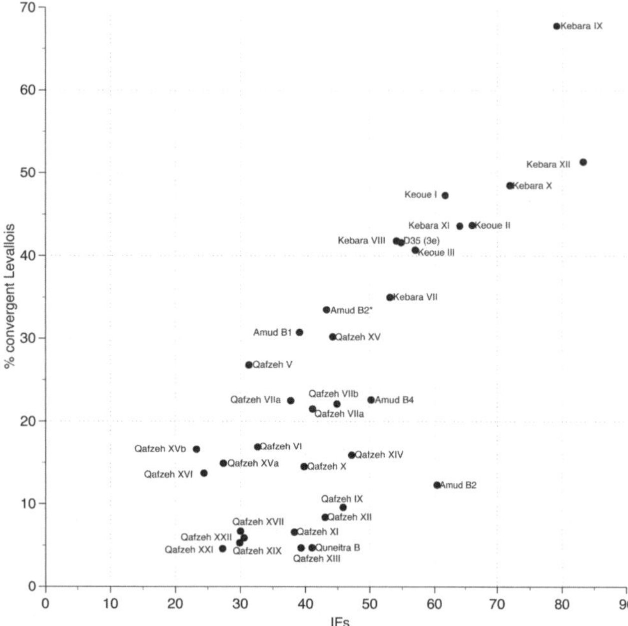


**Figure 8.6** Percent of convergent dorsal face scar patterns on Levallois blanks vs. values of IFs in Levantine Middle Paleolithic assemblages.

exhibit similar or identical frequencies of faceted and plain butts, despite the different modes of preparation.[20]

Since the investment in core platform preparation should lead to larger artifacts when a hard hammer is used (Dibble and Whittaker 1981; Pelcin 1998; Shott et al. 2000; Speth 1972, 1974, 1975), a hypothesis generated from Munday's climatic model is that there should be a positive relationship between flaking mode and length of the end-products. Based on the premise that convergent scar patterns are associated with better prepared artifacts (see above), the test implication of this hypothesis is that blanks with convergent scar patterns should be longer than blanks prepared by other flaking modes, a notion echoed in later research (see Stiner's [1994:358] discussion of the efficiency of "platform reduction techniques" over centripetal ones in producing large flakes). At this time, there are sufficiently specific data to examine this hypothesis from Nahal Aqev (D35) and Qafzeh (table 5.15). While the expected relationship was encountered in both, intra-assemblage differences of the mean length of blanks removed by various flaking modes are small (normally less than 5 mm) for most assemblages involved, with highly overlapping values. Moreover, at Qafzeh the elongation of blanks is related to the degree of platform preparation but not to any specific flaking mode (table 5.14),[21] whereas at Douara IV faceted platforms are associated with a variety of dorsal flake scar patterns, all exploited in the production of elongated pieces (Nishiaki 1989: tabs. 3, 7, 9). Kebara may be another case in which

the pattern does not hold, since in the assemblages from units IX and X artifacts bearing convergent scar patterns combined with extremely well-prepared platforms are the short and broad classical Levallois points (mean L/W in unit X = 1.81; Meignen and Bar-Yosef 1992:141, fig. 9.3; Bar-Yosef et al. 1992: fig. 11).

The regional record thus seems to refute the notion that climatic amelioration and elongated debitage are associated either temporally or causally. High laminar indices occur during both glacial times (MIS 8 or MIS 6; e.g., Tabun IX) and warmer climatic phases (MIS 5c; e.g., 'Ain Difla) (see appendix 6). At times this pattern is combined with elongated points in, of all places, inland localities, such as Hummal Ia in the El-Kowm basin, Douara IV (Nishiaki 1989), and Jerf Ajla F (Schroëder 1969); these were subject to drier and harsher conditions, mainly during glacial phases. In stark contrast to the model's predictions, sites like Quneitra, Qafzeh, and apparently Naamé, all of which enjoyed at all times wetter paleoenvironments than did sites of the arid zone, have well prepared platforms but sparse elongated debitage (Goren-Inbar 1990a:144).

The archaeological data, then, do not support the climatic model as such. Many of the expected relationships either do not occur or are explained by different lithic technological behaviors from the ones enlisted by the model. Lithic variability, insofar as it reflects demographic responses to climatic shifts, must have emerged from flexible reduction processes in which higher investment in platform preparation is linked with a variety of flaking modes through the knappers' choice. The assemblages from Qafzeh, in which this flexibility is more easily observed because of the more detailed analysis employed, do not differ in this respect from other Levantine Mousterian assemblages.

## Lithic Variability and Form–Function Relationship

While it emerged from a powerful statistical analysis of lithic variability in Levantine sites, the functional model (Binford and Binford 1966) was a response to Bordes's explanation of Mousterian variability in southwestern Europe as a cultural phenomenon (Bordes 1972, 1973; Bordes and de Sonneville-Bordes 1970). The model did not question the emic nature of tool types (Binford and Binford 1966; Binford 1978). To the model's devisers, however, these artifacts performed specific functional tasks preassigned by the toolmakers to the tools. The nature and frequency of such tasks were patterned in response to the resource structure in the vicinity of the site at the time of occupation. As tools and blanks were believed to have been manufactured, used, and discarded within a short time span, the repetitive associations of tool types (i.e., assemblage compositions) at any given site were taken to reflect the nature of activities in each locale (Binford 1973:242–253, 1977:266–267, 1989:34–35). If the model's implications with regard to the Levant are stretched *ad absurdum,* the occurrence of a single variant in Levantine sites, the "Typical Mousterian" (chapters 1, 7), suggests that Levantine Middle Paleolithic hominins constantly carried out a limited range of activities when compared to their European counterpart.

The suggested relationship between tool forms and specific functions (e.g., *racloirs* and pointed forms in relation to butchery and processing of animal carcasses; notched and denticulated tools in relation to woodworking) was examined through use-wear analyses. In the Levant, as elsewhere, the expected clear-cut correlations did not appear. Prehistorians had long been qualifying their typological assignations by saying that unretouched artifacts could be used as functional tools, and this was proven by the use-wear studies. In fact, a number of studies indicated that hafting was not exclusive to formal, Levallois points and was associated with a variety of tools and blank forms, including unretouched flakes (Boëda, Connan, and Muhesen 1998; Friedman et al. 1994–5). These findings were not consistent with the model's basic assumption of a rigid, predetermined form–function relationship. Additionally, blanks modified into Bordesian types had been used as multifunctional tools whose roles were also fulfilled by other morphotypes (Anderson-Gerfaud 1990; Beyries 1986, 1988; Shea 1991, 1995). As a rule, these findings put to rest a narrow view of form–function correlations in the Middle Paleolithic.

In the case of Levantine assemblages such correlations revived to some degree when Employed Units (EUs), which are discrete concentrations of use-wear patterns on the blank perimeter, were used as the units of analysis in low magnification analyses rather than the blank itself (Shea 1991). When signs that could refer to light-duty woodworking were thus identified and removed from the sample, form–function correlations improved. This implied that light-duty woodworking was the most generalized activity, for which no special form was required. Other tasks identified by low-magnification use-wear analysis apparently required a more careful selection of artifact forms (Shea 1991:227–231, tab. 6.2).

It is to be expected that a blank's overall shape will determine its kinetic properties and therefore the type of motions through which it can be applied to various materials (Rolland and Dibble 1990; cf. Shea 1991:228 on blades and oval flakes), and that efforts to predetermine blank size will be related to the type of activity envisaged and its predictability. The typological variability along the Qafzeh sequence was interpreted as a reflection of tactical responses to shifts in the nature of tasks performed on site (chapter 7). The emphasis on large Levallois blanks

may have been linked to anticipated tasks that required more careful selection with regard to size and shape. This was most evident in the tendency to select large Levallois blanks for the modification of *racloirs,* but less clear for other tool types (chapter 6). These two patterns are common to most, if not all, of the Levantine Mousterian assemblages, independently of the dominant Levallois flaking modes (e.g., Crew 1976; Fish 1979:141; Gordon 1997; Goren-Inbar 1988a, 1990a; Munday 1976b; Meignen and Bar-Yosef 1992; Nishiaki and Copeland 1992), as well as to a vast number of Mousterian assemblages elsewhere (e.g., Geneste 1985, 1988; Kuhn 1992a; Marks 1968:293; Meignen 1988, 1993). Yet individual morphotypes and their frequencies within assemblages do not appear to bear specific functional significance (Anderson-Gerfaud 1990; Beyries 1987, 1988).

Pointed artifacts of the Levantine Mousterian were argued to be an exception to this rule. In that their shapes are reminiscent of lithic parts of ethnographic weapons, such items drew attention to the possibility that they were part of Paleolithic weaponry. EUs observed during use-wear studies (Shea 1991:141; see also Copeland 1985) include projectile impact fractures and piercing wear on the distal tips that occur exclusively on points, although the same artifacts also bear evidence of maintenance tasks such as cutting and scraping of wood and hides (Plisson and Beyries 1998; Roler and Clark 1997; Shea 1991) and were not used identically in all sites (Lee 1987, cited in Henry 1995c:119–120). These items also bear the highest frequencies of microscopic hafting marks (Shea 1991: tab. 6.2) and thinning retouch on the point's proximal part in some sites (e.g., Henry 1995c:69). The overall combination led to their interpretation as parts of hafted hunting weapons (Shea 1988, 1991, 1993). From a design point of view, spears equipped with stone tips were more advantageous in big-game hunting (Churchill 1993; Shea 1993) than sharpened wooden spears like those known from European late Middle Pleistocene contexts (Movius 1950; Oakely et al. 1977; Thieme 1997). Advocates of points as technological hunting aids emphasize the advantages of triangular blanks, and particularly of broad-based Levallois points, as reliable technological items capable of doing the job for which they were made: cause the death of the prey by lacerations that result in internal hemorrhage. A point embedded between the vertebrae of an equid from the open-air site of Umm el-Tlel in Syria (Boëda et al. 1999) provides unequivocal supporting evidence for the role of points as hunting weapons.[22] Hence, "[t]he percentages of Levallois points [in Levantine Mousterian assemblages]…appear to be relatively accurate predictors of the percentages of EUs referable to extractive activity" (Shea 1991:228, 1993).

The reconstruction suggested above of the structure and distribution of resources implies that points should be more abundant in southern sites, reflecting adaptations to local conditions that favored a high degree of faunal exploitation compared to the Mediterranean zone (see Henry 1995b:129–132; cf. Marks 1989, 1992b). If this is correct, Levantine Mousterian assemblages should exhibit a geographic patterning of point frequencies, with assemblages in the arid and semi-arid zones (in the southern and eastern parts of the Levant) including relatively more hunting-related pointed artifacts than their counterparts in more lush areas. This hypothesis can be examined by looking at the relative frequencies of points within the Levallois component compared to their frequencies within the total assemblage of detached blanks. This will help to clarify whether the points occur in contexts of production, use, or discard (Hovers 1998b).

The relationship between relative frequencies of points within the Levallois component of assemblages and within the total of blanks in each assemblage (table 8.3, figure 8.4) does not merely reflect the swamping of low frequencies of Levallois products by overwhelming numbers of non-Levallois products (which would be represented by low IL values; 'Ain Difla may be an exception to this). The archaeological data only partially bear out the predicted regional differences (table 8.3), as this relationship explains only 27% of the variation in the occurrence of Levallois points in arid zones compared to more northern assemblages ($r^2 = 0.27$, $y = 1.01 + 0.11x$). Many arid zone assemblages do indeed show the expected relatively high frequencies of points among unretouched Levallois products. However, similar frequencies occur in a number of northern assemblages, and the highest frequencies of all occur in Tabun, Keoue, and Ksar Akil,[23] all situated in the Mediterranean core area. The striking difference between sites in the arid zone and those to their north and west lies in the occurrence of some extremely point-poor assemblages in the latter, but never in the south (table 8.3). Moreover, contemporaneous assemblages located in similar environments (e.g., Tor Faraj and Tor Sabiha) sometimes exhibit very different frequencies of the two measures of point abundance, and locations in different paleoenvironmental conditions (e.g., Kebara, Amud, Tor Sabiha) may contain similar values of these indices conditions (table 8.3).

The overall import of these analyses is that geographic location has relatively little to do with the presence of points in assemblages. If, as the ecological reconstructions suggest, hunting of predictable faunal resources was more intensively practiced in the south, these results also undermine the notion that points were geared specifically toward hunting (Hovers 1997; as opposed to, e.g., Shea 1998). Recent experimental work supports this skepticism, showing that short, broad-based points were ideal stone tips of low-speed weaponry (most likely as thrusting weapons; Shea 2006b; but see Ellis 1997 for a cautionary summary of ethnographic uses of stone tips), whereas the morphology of pointed, narrow-based artifacts is functionally disadvantageous for hunting weaponry. Yet it is these narrow, elongated forms that probably served as the multi-purpose tools or knives (Shea, Davis, and Brown 2001) that prevail in the Middle Paleolithic assemblages of the arid zones (Marks 1976, 1977, 1992b; Marks and Monigal 1995). The differences between north and south (as depicted in figure 8.3) become functionally less dramatic. In light of these new insights, claims that have linked the organization of lithic technology to postulated differences in hunting behavior (e.g., Shea 1998) require reconsideration. Variability in the distribution of function-specific lithic hunting aids clearly results from curation and transport across the landscape rather than a simple ratio of production and use within a given locale (Hovers 1998b; Kuhn 1998).[24]

As a rule, single-cause explanations do not deal well with organizational systems in which ecological constraints are negotiated by technological choices rather than by conditioned, rigid human responses.[25] The examples discussed above show clearly that explanations that are closely tethered to optimization models often do not stand scrutiny, since their formulation and subsequent testing necessarily require a high degree of simplification. Thus, they can lead only to crude first approximations when dealing with complex systems that interact with input from numerous and inherently different environments (figure 8.1). It is also true that over a region, variability tends to pattern geographically, so that sequential assemblages derived from a single site tend to resemble one another more closely than any of them resembles an assemblage from another site (Hovers 1997). Each site or assemblage is unique and has its own unique history, and Qafzeh is no exception to that rule.

Having said that, I would still argue that the preceding discussion of explanations of regional lithic variability as being driven by the physical environment has not been an exercise in futility. An important conclusion emerging from the process of formal hypothesis testing is that the elements of lithic organization recognized in a single, relatively short-duration locale (i.e., Qafzeh) are recapitulated on the larger temporal and geographic scale of the regional record. This points to underlying organizational principles in the Levantine Mousterian as a whole, and implies that the principles driving lithic variability in Qafzeh (chapter 7) offer a "window" on Levantine Mousterian lithic variability on a broader scale.

Clearly, it would be naïve to expect that a clear-cut, single organizational Mousterian pattern existed in a region as ecologically diverse and patchy as the Levant, and that lithic assemblages from various localities would be structured in the same manner. Indeed, the pattern that emerges most clearly out of the detailed testing of "ecological" hypotheses is that across-assemblage patterns of lithic organization in Levantine Middle Paleolithic assemblages

**Table 8.3  Proportions of Levallois products in various Levantine Mousterian assemblages**

| Assemblages | Levallois products | | | | % of points[a] |
|---|---|---|---|---|---|
| | N | Flakes | Blades | Unretouched points | |
| **Qafzeh** V | 76 | 72.3 | 21.1 | 6.6 | 0.8 |
| Qafzeh VI | 50 | 76.0 | 24.0 | — | — |
| Qafzeh VIIa | 96 | 72.9 | 17.7 | 9.4 | 1.5 |
| Qafzeh VIIb | 56 | 91.1 | 8.9 | — | — |
| Qafzeh IX | 228 | 88.6 | 9.6 | 1.8 | 0.4 |
| Qafzeh X | 146 | 81.5 | 14.4 | 4.1 | 1.0 |
| Qafzeh XI | 173 | 87.3 | 11.6 | 1.2 | 0.2 |
| Qafzeh XII | 98 | 84.7 | 13.3 | 2.0 | 0.4 |
| Qafzeh XIII | 368 | 81.0 | 17.1 | 1.9 | 0.3 |
| Qafzeh XIV | 112 | 75.9 | 15.2 | 8.9 | 2.0 |
| Qafzeh XV | 1,346 | 70.7 | 16.6 | 12.4 | 2.7 |
| Qafzeh XVa | 217 | 81.6 | 16.6 | 1.8 | 0.3 |
| Qafzeh XVf | 236 | 85.6 | 13.1 | 1.3 | 0.2 |
| Qafzeh XVII | 225 | 88.0 | 23.1 | 2.2 | 0.6 |
| Qafzeh XIX | 149 | 93.3 | 6.0 | 0.7 | 0.2 |
| Qafzeh XXI | 98 | 88.8 | 11.2 | — | — |
| **Kebara** VII[c] | 442 | 73.8 | 19.4 | 6.8 | 1.2 |
| Kebara VIII[c] | 134 | 78.4 | 17.1 | 4.5 | 0.9 |
| Kebara IX[c] | 277 | 63.2 | 22.4 | 14.4 | 1.7 |
| Kebara X[c] | 442 | 63.2 | 22.4 | 14.4 | 2.9 |
| Kebara XI[c] | 740 | 59.3 | 22.6 | 18.1 | 4.1 |
| **Tabun** I (1–17)[d] | 107 | 53.3 | 18.5 | 28.0 | |
| Tabun I (18–26)[d] | 687 | 73.8 | 18.3 | 7.9 | 1.5 |
| Tabun IX[d] | 655 | 23.5 | 42.1 | 34.4 | 14.6 |
| **Amud** B1[e] | 282 | 56.4 | 35.5 | 8.1 | 1.8 |
| **Keoue** I[f] | 93 | 57.0 | 17.2 | 25.8 | 9.5 |
| Keoue II[f] | 32 | 56.3 | 17.2 | 26.5 | 13.2 |
| Keoue III[f] | 199 | 56.2 | 13.5 | 30.3 | 10.8 |
| **Tor Sabiha**[g] | 93 | 52.6 | 11.8 | 36.6 | 1.8 |
| **Tor Faraj** (floors I,II)[h] | 391 | 60.4 | 21.6 | 21.3 | 3.0 |
| **'Ain Difla**[i] | 93 | 39.8 | ?[b] | 60.2 | 2.1 |
| **Ksar Akil** XXVIa[j] | 37 | 100.0 | ? | — | — |
| Ksar Akil XXVIb[j] | 77 | 90.9 | ? | 9.1 | 1.9 |
| Ksar Akil XXVIIa[j] | 38 | 100.0 | ? | — | — |
| Ksar Akil XXVIIb[j] | 77 | 79.2 | ? | 20.8 | 2.5 |
| Ksar Akil XXVIIIa[j] | 105 | 62.9 | ? | 37.1 | 3.9 |
| Ksar Akil XXVIIIb[j] | 114 | 56.1 | ? | 43.9 | 5.6 |
| **Wadi Hasa** 621[i] | 313 | 61.7 | ? | 38.3 | 2.8 |
| **Far'ah II**[k] | 80 | 70.0 | ? | 30.0 | 1.4 |
| **Quneitra** area A[l] | 99 | 75.8 | ? | 23.2 | 1.1 |
| Quneitra area B[l] | 160 | 91.9 | ? | 8.1 | 0.7 |
| **Nahal Aqev** (1)[m] | 133 | 38.5 | 25.4 | 36.1 | 6.1 |
| Nahal Aqev (3d)[m] | 119 | 31.6 | 27.6 | 40.8 | 4.0 |
| Nahal Aqev (3e)[m] | 153 | 22.9 | 39.4 | 37.5 | 4.1 |
| **Rosh Ein Mor**[n] | 5,123 | 43.3 | 24.2 | 32.5 | 3.7 |
| Naamé (p. III)[o] | 375 | 84.3 | 11.5 | 4.3 | 1.3 |

[a] % of unretouched Levallois points out of all flakes and tools.

[b] Blade and flake counts are indistinguishable.

[c] after Meignen and Bar-Yosef 1989; [d] Jelinek 1982b: tab. VI, VIII; [e] Gordon 1997; [f] Nishiaki and Copeland 1992: tab. 8.2; [g] Henry 1995c: tab. 5.3; [h] Henry 2003: tab. 4.4; [i] Clark et al. 1988: tab. 1; [j] Marks and Volkman 1986; [k] Gilead 1980; [l] Goren-Inbar 1990: tab. 17; [m] Munday 1976: tab. 6.18; [n] Crew 1976: tab. 5.1; [o] Fleisch 1970.

underscore the flexibility of their technological organization and show how they manipulated the complex mosaic of regional environmental variables by planning depth and informed decision making (e.g., Goren-Inbar 1988a; Hovers 1997; Kuhn 1992b; Speth 2004).

Having established that the organizational flexibility identified and explained in the case study of Qafzeh can be recognized across the Levantine Middle Paleolithic, the following sections address technological behaviors across the region. The insights from the Qafzeh study serve as guidelines for understanding decision-making processes on a regional scale and their resultant lithic technological organization (cf. Hovers 1998a).

## Reconstructing Land-Use Patterns in the Levantine Middle Paleolithic

The considerations underlying the ecological and economic approaches to lithic organization highlight the subservient role played by lithics in resource acquisition and use. Clearly, we cannot rely on lithics as the only line of evidence for settlement behaviors of Middle Paleolithic hominins, especially given the inherent ambiguities of archaeological evidence with regard to occupation duration and intensity (see below).

Regardless of the particular type of archaeological evidence under discussion, paleoanthropological research, as a historical science that relies heavily on inferences, calls for what in the philosophy of science is known as "consilience of evidence." Consilience is a "jumping together of inductions," when an induction arrived at from one kind of phenomena "coincides with" an induction obtained from a different kind (Snyder 2005). When making inferences from lithics to site occupation, occupation intensity, and technological organization, the principle means that once notions are formulated from the lithic data about land-use patterns from the lithic data, it is paramount that other lines of evidence (sedimentological and faunal data, for example) be examined independently. If hypotheses derived from lithic studies are to be even a modest approximation of the realities of Middle Paleolithic technological organization, they should also "explain…[phenomena] of a kind different from those which were contemplated in the formation of" the hypothesis (Whewell 1858:88, cited in Snyder 2005).[26]

Following the spirit of the principle of "consilience of evidence," land-use patterns hypothesized on the basis of lithic evidence will be reviewed below in light of other data sets.

## Raw Material Provisioning

The economic and ecological premises underlying the study of lithic technological organization are that acquisition of lithic raw material and maintenance of artifacts were manipulated by varying mobility strategies and settlement decisions to accommodate the structure of the resource basis. Thus, decisions about acquisition of raw materials and their distribution through a technological system respond to variable conditions; in turn they set in motion a chain of flexible behaviors (chapters 2, 7).

Recently, Kuhn (1995a) has elegantly rephrased such long-standing premises by characterizing three raw material provisioning categories. Roughly, these correspond to the three modes of technological organization as discussed by Nelson (1991; see discussion in chapter 7).

### Provisioning of Activities

The first strategy caters for "window of opportunity" situations, when unanticipated needs for tools coincide with spatial availability of lithic raw material and with sufficient downtime to engage in stone tool production. In the Levant the ubiquity of flint sources renders this a viable provisioning strategy from the narrow perspective of lithic availability. However, this strategy is too risky in terms of obtaining subsistence resources in an unpredictable environment. It is unlikely that it was used as the sole or main organizational strategy of any group, which may explain why it has been identified only rarely in Levantine Middle Paleolithic assemblages.[27]

Provisioning of activities is opportunistic and reactive, and as such it is less informative about overall organizational principles of Middle Paleolithic groups. The following discussion focuses on the two main provisioning strategies identified in the Levantine Middle Paleolithic, both of which involve active decision making and planning on the part of hominin individuals or groups.

### Provisioning of Individuals

The strategy of provisioning of individuals involves moving blanks or prepared tools around the landscape as part of a personal gear, that is, the curation of specific blanks or cores with specific traits, to be used immediately in unpredictable situations (Binford 1979). Ethnographic evidence and archaeological case studies (see Kuhn 1995a for references) suggest that the more people move their residential locations, the more they have to depend on the provisioning of individuals. This is due to the simple fact that in conditions of high mobility it is harder to predict when or where the needs for tools may arise.

The use lives of mobile tool kits transported by individuals across the landscape are extended through curation, that is, resharpening and recycling (Bamforth 1986; Eren et al. 2005; Geneste 1985, 1988; Kuhn 1992a; Marks

1988; Meignen 1988; Wengler 1991). This requires that tools possess relatively large mass as part of their preconceived design. Thus, the strategy of provisioning individuals with personal gear requires a balance between the cost of transporting large items and the advantages conferred by such artifacts. In the context of Mousterian lithic practices, a favorable utility/mass ratio would be achieved by manufacturing large, thin, and versatile blanks, such as those produced at Qafzeh by centripetal Levallois flaking. Such artifacts are an efficient way to stock raw material for individuals on the move within the context of highly mobile groups that were gearing for contingencies (Kuhn 1994, 1996; Shott 1996).

"Mobile" artifacts can be recognized relatively easily when made of raw materials that are clearly exotic to the assemblage in which the tools are found (e.g., Féblot-Augustins 1993, 1997; Geneste 1985). So far, however, this has not been a very productive research direction in Levantine Middle Paleolithic studies, which have been based mainly on macroscopic observations (see reviews in Delage 2007; Druck 2004; Hovers 1990b). In the absence of appropriate geochemical matching, artifact transport as part of personal gear is usually inferred from the presence of artifacts that do not fit within the metric or technological parameters of their assemblages. For example, curated artifacts were recognized explicitly in some of the Qafzeh assemblages (chapter 7) and at the open-air sites of Rosh Ein Mor (D15) and Nahal Aqev (D35) in the Negev (Crew 1976:86; Marks 1988). When recognized, this provisioning strategy appears to have been linked with the use of points, and hence with hunting-related activities.

The relationship between relatively high frequencies of points within the Levallois component of the lithic technology compared to their frequencies within the assemblage as a whole suggests that these arguably specialized artifacts were moved around as blanks, regardless of size and independently of the reduction methods practiced at the sites to which they were transported (table 8.4). Elongated and pointed Levallois blanks appear to have been imported into Tabun during the time of deposition of unit IX (Ashkenazi 2005; Jelinek 1982b:80), and judging by the paucity of cores suitable for the manufacture of long pointed blades and elongated points, it is likely that laminar blanks were brought into the caves of Abu Sif, Ghar, and Hayonim (lower E) (Gordon 1993: tab. 2; Meignen 1998; Neuville 1951). During the late Mousterian, points were transported, possibly over a considerable distance, to the site of Tor Sabiha (Henry 1995a).

The other facet of this strategy is removal of artifacts from their place of manufacture by individuals anticipating their use in other localities. In some Levantine Middle Paleolithic assemblages, there are indications that tools were indeed manufactured on site and subsequently removed for use. Shea (1991:142) discussed the removal of pointed pieces, allocated to off-site hunting activities, from the assemblages of Qafzeh and of Tabun C.[28] Similar behaviors were recognized at the Negev sites of D44, D45, and D2 (Munday 1976b) and possibly in Kebara VIII (Meignen and Bar-Yosef 1992). In all these cases, point frequencies appear low against technological indications for their on-site production.

### Provisioning of Locations

At the other end of the spectrum of provisioning behaviors is provisioning of places, in which raw materials are brought in bulk to a central place (a cave or an open-air site) to provide the occupants with raw material supply for future use. Systematic lithic manufacture and maintenance activities tend to occur in residential locations rather than in the context of subsistence-extraction activities. Blocks of raw material are transported into such sites, turning them into temporary sources of raw material, which can be exploited for the manufacture of both general and specialized lithic artifacts. The stock of lithic material then acts as a temporary buffer between spatial and temporal discrepancies in the distribution of subsistence resources and raw material sources.[29] As a rule this enables the manufacture of reliable tools, which may require more technological investment, as well as a large spectrum of less specialized artifacts.

This provisioning strategy is advantageous when a land-use system incorporates repeated or extended occupations of specific locations on the landscape. In turn, it forms new sets of decision-making parameters with regard to the acquisition and exploitation of lithic raw material because it alters the spatial relations between subsistence and lithic resources. While foraging trips out of a residential base provide the opportunity to collect and bring back raw materials to the central place (Binford and Stone's [1985] "embedded procurement"), the same provisioning strategy also acts to reduce the linkage between the two activities. The temporary stocks formed at the residential site allow more control through advance planning over raw material availability. This in turn encourages a temporal separation of lithic provisioning trips from subsistence forays, allowing larger amounts of food resources to be moved into residential sites.

Some Levantine Middle Paleolithic lithic assemblages attest to the transport of raw materials as primary blocks, followed by initial exploitation on site. This is indicated by the presence of rejected ("tested") nodules and high frequencies of cortical blanks (Geneste's [1985] "phase 0, 1"). Henry (1995a, 1995c: tab. 5.3) and Bar-Yosef et al. (1992: tab. 1) have reported such finds from Tor Faraj and Kebara, respectively. This, however, is not the most common tactic used within the overall strategy. More

**Table 8.4  Assemblage compositions and distances from raw material sources in some Levantine Mousterian assemblages**

| Assemblage | % Cores[a] | % Tools[a] | Distance from RM sources (km) | Comments |
|---|---|---|---|---|
| Tabun D (IX) | 6.42 | 17.06 | ?[b] | "in unit IX in all beds but one, Levallois elements outnumber other flakes… I would interpret these ratios to mean that most of the flakes in Unit IX were manufactured elsewhere and only a highly selected group of flakes was introduced in the area of the cave that we excavated" (Jelinek 1982b:80) |
| Hayonim lower E | ? | >30[c] | 10, but some artifacts brought from over 30[c] | Each m³ contains ca. 300 lithic pieces and abundant fauna, accumulated over 10/15 thousand TL years (Bar-Yosef 1998a:51) |
| 'Ain Difla | 0.9 | 1.1 | ? | The cores are the kind that would have been carried around and eventually be discarded by mobile forgers. "This in turn implies a degree of uncertainty in the degree to which a forager could predict the location of suitable raw material sources as he…moved about the landscape." Lack of decortication elements would also tend to support the provisioning of highly mobile individuals (Clark et al. 1997:82–83) |
| Tabun I (26–18) | 5.11 | 3.71 | 2.5–6[d] | |
| Qafzeh XXII | 7.61 | 10.99 | 10–15 | |
| Qafzeh XXI | 5.17 | 11.97 | 10–15 | |
| Qafzeh XIX | 5.16 | 10.68 | 10–15 | |
| Qafzeh XVII | 4.93 | 12.46 | 10–15 | |
| Qafzeh XVf | 0.53 | 1.84 | 10–15 | |
| Qafzeh XVb | 0.96 | 3.22 | 10–15 | |
| Qafzeh XVa | 1.96 | 4.06 | 10–15 | |
| Qafzeh XV | 4.55 | 5.29 | 10–15 | |
| Qafzeh XIV | 9.00 | 16.77 | 10–15 | |
| Qafzeh XIII | 4.27 | 9.90 | 10–15 | |
| Qafzeh XII | 10.59 | 16.47 | 10–15 | |
| Qafzeh XI | 7.54 | 8.75 | 10–15 | |
| Qafzeh X | 1.94 | 9.57 | 10–15 | |
| Qafzeh IX | 5.47 | 8.10 | 10–15 | |
| Qafzeh VIIb | 6.58 | 10.86 | 10–15 | |
| Qafzeh VIIa | 6.11 | 7.68 | 10–15 | |
| Qafzeh VII | 3.28 | 8.47 | 10–15 | |
| Qafzeh VI | 2.03 | 6.93 | 10–15 | |
| Qafzeh V | 2.52 | 2.89 | 10–15 | |
| Qafzeh IV | 5.02 | 5.96 | 10–15 | |
| Qafzeh III | 3.88 | 4.55 | 10–15 | |
| Nahal Aqev (D35) 3[e] | 5.19 | 5.18 | ≤1 | |
| Tor Faraj (Floors I and II)[f] | 5.18 | 13.19 | 16–20 | |
| Tor Sabiha[g] | 0.53 | 5.79 | 3 | |
| Kebara XII[h] | 2.30 | 3.13 | ≤5 | |
| Kebara XI[h] | 4.30 | 4.39 | ≤5 | |
| Kebara X[h] | 3.80 | 2.49 | ≤5 | |
| Kebara IX[h] | 4.10 | 2.51 | ≤5 | |
| Kebara VIII[h] | 3.10 | 3.91 | ≤5 | |
| Kebara VII[h] | 1.95 (60.0) | 3.33 | ≤5 | |
| Amud B4[i] | 3.46 | 4.61 | ? | |
| Amud B2[i] | 2.35 | 6.50 | ? | |
| Amud B1[i] | 1.95 | 9.40 | ? | |
| Quneitra A[j] | 18.14 | 40.24 | | |
| Quneitra B[j] | 15.40 | 41.34 | | |
| Rosh Ein Mor[k] | 6.49 | 7.12 | ≤1 | |

*(continued)*

**Table 8.4** (continued)

| Assemblage | % Cores[a] | % Tools[a] | Distance from RM sources (km) | Comments |
|---|---|---|---|---|
| Abu Sif C[l] | | | ? | "Trés peu de nucléus ont été trouvé dans cette couche. Tous sont de type discoidal globuleux....Les éclats de débitage étant également relativement peu abondants" (Neuville 1951:54) |
| Abu Sif B[l] | | | ? | "[nucléus] sont à peine moins rare que dans la couche C" (Neuville 1951:59) |
| Sahba C[l] | | | ? | "Malgré le grand nombre d'éclats de débitage, un seul nucléus a été recueilli" (Neuville 1951:65) |
| Sahba B[l] | | | ? | "Les lames et éclats...Trés abondants...ce niveau n'est pas plus rich en nucléus que le précédent" (Neuville 1951:67) |

[a] "% cores" was calculated without taking the debris (chunks and chips smaller than 20 mm) into the total account. The frequencies of cores-on-flakes out of the total core sample can be found in table 8.1 or are indicated here in parentheses; "% tools" includes only retouched artifacts out of the total of blanks (retouched and unretouched pieces of débitage).
[b] Druck (2004) suggested that lithic raw material found in Tabun D was brought from a distance of some 6 km north of the site. His sample, however, included artifacts from Tabun VI, which is later in time and may represent a fill or an erosive feature of the *in situ* Tabun IX (Mercier et al. 1995: fig. 1). These data, therefore, are not entirely pertinent to the older unit discussed here; [c] Meignen 1998; [d] Druck 2004:52–53; [e] Munday 1976b, 1977; [f] Henry 2003; [g] Henry 1995, 1998; [h] Meignen and Bar-Yosef 1992.; [i] Hovers 1998; [j] Goren-Inbar 1990; [k] Crew 1976; [l] Neuville's drawing show that the excavations of these sites were conducted in the center as well as close to the walls of the caves. The paucity of cores is therefore not a result of differential use of space as seen in Kebara, Amud, and Tor Faraj (Alperson-Afil and Hovers 2005; Bar-Yosef et al. 1992; Henry 2003) in the later part of the Middle Paleolithic.

often, site provisioning took the form of transportation of blocks after their initial decortication, so that few rejected blocks and cortical blanks occur in the assemblage. This is documented both at Qafzeh (see chapters 5, 6) and at other sites, such as 'Ain Difla (Clark et al. 1988:230, tab. 9), Quneitra (Hovers 1990b), D15 and D35 (Crew 1976: tab. 5.1; Munday 1977:45, tab. 2.2).

At the same time, provisioning of locations may lead to changes in manufacturing practices, as people try to maximize the finite stock of raw material while enlarging the intervals between provisioning trips. The exploitation of cores-on-flakes in Levantine Mousterian assemblages is consistent with this scenario (chapters 3, 7; Hovers 2007); as discussed above, the presence of cores-on-flakes is related more to considerations of conservation than to limitations imposed on raw material transport by mass.[30]

As a rule, strategies of lithic raw material provisioning and conservation seem to have been used in tandem and to have balanced one another. Which of the two provisioning strategies was more important in the organizational system of any given group probably depended on the season of occupation and the role of the site in the settlement system, neither of which is readily inferred from the material record in hand.

## Duration of Occupation and Site Functions

Two related but not identical variables, "duration of occupation" and "occupation intensity," figure in discussions of the nature of occupations throughout the Paleolithic. The first term addresses the time elapsed between a group's settling of a site and its subsequent abandonment and pertains to the duration of a single episode of settlement. "Occupation intensity" is a more complex parameter, as it encompasses both "duration of occupation" and the nature of the activities carried out on the site. These in turn may change if and when the role of a given locality in the settlement system of a group changes through time. Yet another variable that factors into "occupation intensity" is the size of the occupying group.

The (usually) limited ability of paleoanthropologists to monitor individual episodes within the depth of archaeological time further confounds matters. An archaeological horizon may represent a single short occupation, whether extensive or intensive (i.e., fewer or more occupants, respectively). But when dealing with palimpsest situations, as is often the case in prehistory, there is blurring of the distinctions between occupations of real or relative short duration, those of longer duration, and very few but intensive occupations through time by large groups (to mention only some of the possible permutations).

Characteristics of lithic assemblages do, however, form the basis for some broad inferences about occupation types and duration. When examining the preplanned components of Levantine Mousterian assemblages (i.e., the Levallois products), the relative frequencies of unretouched "mobile" (points) as opposed to "sedentary" components (flakes and to some degree blades) reflect biases created by various strategies of provisioning. Table 8.3 shows that these frequencies are on the whole similar in a large number of assemblages across the Levant. Flakes normally constitute 50–60%, the rest being divided between varying percentages of points and blades. It thus seems that each such "average" assemblage represents a diverse range of activities (i.e., habitation site), in which hunting or hunting-related tasks (such as retooling) would have been part of the spectrum. Such "mixed" assemblages are the norm in the Levantine Middle Paleolithic. The rather homogeneous assemblages of Qafzeh XXIV–XVII may in fact be relatively rare cases in which a series of task-specific occupations unrelated to hunting can be discerned (in these assemblages the lack of points is not due to transport out of the site; chapter 7).[31]

Low frequencies of points in the assemblages (table 8.3, column 5[32]) and the inferred mixed provisioning behaviors are shared characteristics of most assemblages. These characteristics accord with the ecological settings of the Middle Paleolithic Levant as reconstructed in this work. Since plant resources constituted the main subsistence resource, their distribution would have been monitored constantly in order to make decisions on the timing of relocation of residential camps. On the other hand, Levantine fauna usually occupy relatively stable, rather constant territories and would have been monitored less extensively. Information on faunal resources would have been relatively up-to-date, rendering hunting opportunities relatively more predictable. Provisioning of individuals with mobile, personal gear would be a constant and important feature of Levantine Middle Paleolithic technological organization in most localities, despite the larger size and heavier weight of these artifacts in most instances (see Henry 1995a; Morrow 1996). This is consistent with the faunal evidence, which indicates that hunting rather than scavenging was the main meat procurement strategy of Levantine Middle Paleolithic groups (Boëda et al. 1999; Davis, Rabinovich, and Goren-Inbar 1988; Gilead and Grigson 1984; Griggo 1998, 2002; Rabinovich and Hovers 2004; Rabinovich and Tchernov 1995; Speth and Tchernov 1998; Stiner 2005; Yeshurun, Bar-Oz, and Weinstein-Evron 2007).

The ratio of *racloirs* to denticulates may help to assess the relative differences of duration of occupations in various sites. Side-scrapers and denticulates are consumed during use at different rates. Dibble and Rolland (1992; Rolland and Dibble 1990) argued that scrapers wear out, to the point where a fresh tool is required to carry out a given task, possibly up to four times as fast as denticulates. Where activities requiring both tools were carried out, the ratio of *racloirs* to denticulates is expected to increase as a direct function of the length of occupation. According to this model, the ratio should grow with the number of retouched blanks in an assemblage. This

pattern is documented in a number of European assemblages (Rolland 1981; Dibble and Rolland 1992:12; Jelinek 1988:200), but the Levantine case is evidently different (figure 8.5b). The frequencies of *racloirs* in the assemblages, whether of cave or open-air sites, appear to be unrelated to the number of retouched blanks. The generally higher ratios in cave sites (figure 8.5a) are due to the occurrence of fewer denticulates rather than to significantly higher frequencies of scrapers (as discussed earlier in this chapter), contrary to the model's assertion.

Strategies of core reduction are similarly equivocal. A number of ecological considerations and several case studies (effectively summarized in Kuhn 1995a) often link the strategy of provisioning of places with an emphasis on bipolar or unipolar core-reduction technologies, which are considered typical of relatively long-term occupations. Such expectations are not met in the Levantine Mousterian record. On the contrary, it is the components of the "mobile components" of a lithic assemblage that tend to derive from technological sequences emphasizing unipolar flaking (e.g., Levallois points that are functionally associated with hunting behaviors, as at Qafzeh XIII, Tor Sabiha, D44, D45, D52; pointed and elongated artifacts of standardized designs at Tabun IX, Abu Sif, Hummal, Hayonim E, Douara). Apparently, neither type or duration of occupation, nor provisioning tactics, are linked to specific core-reduction schemes.

Some scenarios (discussed in detail in chapter 7) have outlined specific hypotheses and their clear test implications with regard to core-reduction strategies and the manner of exploitation of faunal resources. In this respect, too, the Qafzeh patterns predict those of the Levantine Mousterian in general. For example, Lieberman and Shea's (1994) model looks at resource depletion due to extended occupations. They suggested that during earlier Middle Paleolithic times sites occupied by hominins (such as Qafzeh) were nodes in circulating mobility systems and were occupied for shorter time spans. The relatively small animals and vegetal foods exploited did not require investment in production of lithic hunting aids. The model goes on to argue that during the late Middle Paleolithic, Levantine caves (specifically, those inhabited by Neanderthals) were the central nodes in a system of radiating mobility and occupied for longer periods. This necessitated the inclusion of large game in the menu, with higher rates of return. The hunting of large game was believed to be the incentive for investment in production of technological hunting aids (stone points).

This model predicts that the faunal compositions of sites occupied for longer duration (i.e., rich in points) will be different, especially in terms of body size groups and of biased distributions of anatomical parts, from those of short-duration sites, in which points are rarer. Such expectations, however, are not borne out by the numerous faunal assemblages now known from the Levantine Middle Paleolithic (Davis, Rabinovich, and Goren-Inbar 1988; Rabinovich 1990; Rabinovich and Hovers 2004; Rabinovich and Tchernov 1995; Speth 2004; Speth and Tchernov 2001; Stiner 2005; Yeshurun, Bar-Oz, and Weinstein-Evron 2007).[33] Far'ah II is again an illuminative case. The recovery of many conjoining pieces from a single "living-floor" is suggestive of a distinct, short-duration occupation. However, the fauna hunted in the very close vicinity of the site (Gilead and Grigson 1984) consists of medium-sized and large animals, while points are rare in the assemblage, possibly because they were transported out of the site. By the same token, Speth and Tchernov (2001) noted that the nature of faunal accumulations in Kebara Cave changed from midden deposits (units XI–IX) to less dense bone accumulations in the later part of the Middle Paleolithic sequence. They interpreted these changes as indicating shifts in intensity or duration of occupation. An increase in frequencies of juvenile gazelle in the later stratigraphic units and a more selective transport of body parts into the cave were attributed to resource depletion in the immediate vicinity of the site. This may have demanded hunting at ever-growing distances from the habitation site to compensate for diminishing returns in closer hunting grounds (Speth 2004; Speth and Clark 2006). Interestingly, the detailed faunal data from Kebara do not point to the seasonality pattern suggested by Lieberman (1993; Lieberman and Shea 1994). Rather than a multi-seasonal signature, there are specific seasonal signatures that change with the change in the function of the site (Speth 2004; Speth and Clark 2006; see below).

In summary, the compositions of Levantine Mousterian assemblages in various geographic locations reflect a "mixed bag" of organizational practices. In practically each case for which some quantitative data are available, different combinations of organizational strategies are inferred. Throughout the temporal and spatial scales of the Levantine Mousterian, the lithic technology demonstrates organizational flexibility, a mixture of structured production and partially expedient use of artifacts, as the optimal technological adaptation to the ecological mosaic of the Levantine environment.

One possible explanation of the divergence of the Levantine record from economic and ecological models is, of course, that the ecological models should be rejected. While this is an easy way out of the conundrum, it may be too extreme a conclusion. It is more likely (leaving aside for the moment the aforementioned oversimplification inherent in models of this type) that the models were designed to explain lithic technological strategies in large regions located in middle latitudes, for example, in North America and (to a lesser degree) Europe. The models' expectations may be less pertinent to the Levant, where

environmental mosaics occur across small distances, seasonality is reduced, and climatic shifts over geological time are less drastic.

## Diachronic Changes of Mobility Patterns: Insights into Territorial Behavior

Throughout the Middle Paleolithic, the lithic aspect of technological organization appears to have consisted of numerous variations on a restricted number of themes. Thus, individual assemblages were shaped by a narrow set of broad organizational strategies, while tactical decisions on the specific manners of manipulating lithic production and use within these broad principles varied in response to specific needs and environmental conditions. Out of this variability, however, a clear trend of temporal changes of land-use patterns emerges.

Although both provisioning of site and provisioning of individuals were used during the 200,000 years of Middle Paleolithic occupation of the Levant, their relative importance seems to have changed through time (Hovers 2001). Because of variations in preservation and research practices, the amount of available information and its quality are not homogeneous for the entire time span involved. The small number of well-studied assemblages from the earlier stages of the Middle Paleolithic may well cause biases in our understanding of the record. Only a handful of sites are securely dated to 200,000 or earlier, whereas MIS 5 is represented by a single well-excavated and meticulously documented site, Qafzeh (table 1.1). Nevertheless, the sites for which multiple data sets are available for analysis show significant similarities in their occupation characteristics.

Assemblages of the Levantine early Middle Paleolithic exhibit high frequencies of pre-planned blanks (e.g., Levallois or laminar products) relative to cores (table 8.4). The few published data suggest that distances to raw material sources were not large, although somewhat longer distances were noted for Hayonim E, where some artifacts derive from sources over 20 km from the site (Druck 2004; Hovers 1990b; Meignen 1998; Shea 1991). At the same time, in most sites frequencies of retouched tools are high and many of the modified blanks show deep, invasive retouch (e.g., Copeland 1985: figs. 3–5; Meignen 1998: figs. 7–8; Neuville 1951: figs. 22–23). These patterns are consistent with transport of blanks into the sites and conservation of raw material through recycling. Given assemblage richness (the number of typological categories) and evenness (the quantitative distribution of the various tool classes), these occupation horizons cannot be characterized as limited-function, task-specific settlements. Instead, the combinations of lithic characteristics suggest relatively ephemeral residential settlements that may have been extensively occupied (either by a small number of people or infrequently over time) by hominins who have moved over relatively large distances between sites.

Densities of lithic and faunal finds, investment in structures and hearths, and spatially patterned distributions of lithic artifacts and bone refuse have long been considered indicators of occupation intensity (e.g., Kelly 1992; Rafferty 1985). However, these data must be evaluated against their depositional contexts and histories, as reflected, among others, by the paleo-geochemical evolution of the sediments. The habitual use of wood fire in Levantine caves, from at least the late Lower Paleolithic onward,[34] has led to complex sets of diagenetic reactions that may have led over time to considerable reduction in the original volume of ashes and to inflated densities of lithic and faunal remains (Albert et al. 1999, 2000, 2003; Bar-Yosef and Vandermeersch 1993; Baruch, Werker, and Bar-Yosef 1992; Karkanas et al. 2007; Meignen et al. 2001a; Shahack-Gross et al. 2008; Schiegl et al. 1996; Weiner, Goldberg, and Bar-Yosef 2002).

Hayonim lower E is possibly the best published example of the settlement characteristics of the Levantine early Middle Paleolithic. In this site, both lithic and faunal remains are thinly distributed throughout the remains of ash deposits, with lithic density in the order of 300 items/ m$^3$ over 10,000–15,000 TL years. Moreover, the advanced diagenetic stage of the ash remains in many parts of the relevant stratigraphic horizons suggest that these low densities may in fact be inflated due to sediment compaction (Schiegl et al. 1996; Weiner, Goldberg, and Bar-Yosef 2002). In parallel, Stiner (2005 and references therein) has argued that the large size of tortoises exploited during the time of Hayonim lower E is an indication of low levels of hominin hunting pressure on these animals. Tortoise populations were not completely eradicated by over-harvesting, thus allowing the population to recover between episodes of human occupation, so that individual tortoises could reach maturity (hence their large sizes). This in turn suggests infrequent occupations of the cave, whereas the low densities of finds imply that the occupations were extensive.

Although few other early Middle Paleolithic sites have been published in similar detail, the available data seem to depict a similarly high degree of residential mobility and extensive occupations. Misliya cave, where the faunal assemblage also reflects stress-free exploitation of large mammals, might be considered a more intensive occupation given the high density of lithics (Yeshurun, Bar-Oz, and Weinstein-Evron 2007). However, diagenetic processes for this site are not yet known and the real significance of its artifact densities remains unclear. Furthermore, as the situation in Hayonim lower E indicates, the presence of a hearth at Misliya (Yeshurun, Bar-Oz, and Weinstein-Evron 2007) does not automatically imply that occupation was long-term or intensive.

The lower part of the Qafzeh sequence, in which assemblage characteristics are indicative of extensive task-specific occupations associated with hearths, is yet another warning against making a straightforward correlation between hearths and occupation intensity.[35]

The record of the late Middle Paleolithic is better documented. As with the early Middle Paleolithic, some patterns are common to all sites, but these patterns differ from those observed in the early sites. As a rule, the strategy of provisioning in practically all the sites seems to have focused on supplying locations rather than individuals. This is expressed in the relatively long and complete reduction sequences in these localities, indicating that nodules were brought in to the localities and processed on site. Where recorded, distances to raw material sources were short (5–10 km from the occupation site, with a bias toward the shorter distances). Thus, in some instances provisioning could have involved "minimum effort" strategies such as "embedded procurement," where raw material had been obtained during subsistence-related forays (Binford and Stone 1985). This is less likely to have been the case where one-way distances to raw material sources exceeded ca. 10 km, typically the distance traversed by modern hunter-gatherers in the course of daily subsistence activities (Hayden 1981: tab. 10). Qafzeh (chapter 7), as well as Quneitra (Hovers 1990b), Tor Faraj (Henry 1995c), and Umm el-Tlel (Boëda, Bourguignon, and Griggo 1998; Boëda, Griggo, and Noël-Soriano 2001), fall within this latter category of sites.

The strategy of provisioning of sites provided hominins with the privilege of flexibility when planning technology-dependent extractive activities. Indeed, lithic assemblages of the late Middle Paleolithic cave sites are usually poor in retouched blanks, although blanks with signs of use are quite common (pers. obs.). Significantly, among the retouched artifacts that do occur, intensively retouched types are rare (Alperson-Afil and Hovers 2005; Hovers 1998a; Meignen and Bar-Yosef 1989). This is also the case in the Negev open-air sites, including Far'ah II. At the same time provisioning of localities necessitated some measure of raw material conservation. One such behavior is the exploitation of flakes, selected from the products available on site, as blanks for cores (Hovers 2007). This behavior, which enabled the sites' occupants to postpone trips to raw material sources (tables 8.1, 8.4), is evident in all sites of the relevant time span.

Provisioning of individuals was probably practiced to some degree and can be recognized when the movement of specific tool types from and to the site can be identified, as was the case in Qafzeh. In other cases, for example in the caves of Amud and Kebara, the amounts of lithics and their densities across the sediment column render it difficult to pry apart the two provisioning strategies, especially given the rarity of formal retouched tools.

Provisioning of individuals is more easily discerned in assemblage compositions of some open-air sites in the Mediterranean zone of the southern Levant. At Quneitra some heavily retouched forms among a relatively large number of retouched items (Goren-Inbar 1990a) may have been carried around the landscape as personal gear and recycled (Hovers 1990b). The open-air (undated) site at Ein Qashish may represent another such instance (Hovers et al. 2008). These instances may be related to the location of sites near water bodies and repetitive activities tied to butchery in an anticipated locale on the landscape. It is important to note, however, that in these sites as well the two provisioning strategies seem to have been in effect (e.g., Hovers 1990b). Personal gear in more arid environments could involve large Levallois points and elongated blanks, albeit not often retouched (e.g., Tor Sabiha, Umm el-Tlel layer VI3b'1; Henry 1995a; Hovers 2001; Meignen et al. 2006 and references therein).

The variability in rates of ash diagenesis in the various sites renders comparisons of lithic and faunal densities at best a crude estimate of the intensity of occupation (Hovers 2001; Meignen et al. 2006). Nevertheless, the shift in the emphasis on provisioning strategies is linked with a significant increase in the densities of lithics in occupation horizons. During MIS 5 densities in the Qafzeh assemblages were around 300 pieces/m$^3$, similar to those observed at Hayonim E, but had been accumulated over only 5,000 TL years. Much higher densities of lithics, over increasingly shorter time spans, were estimated for Kebara during in MIS 4 (1,000–1,200 lithic pieces/m$^3$ over 3,000 TL years was estimated) and Amud (1,000–1,500 pieces/m$^3$ over 1,500 TL during MIS 3). Other contemporaneous sites with relatively diverse lithic assemblages, such as Tor Faraj, contain much lower artifact densities over comparable time spans (Henry 1995c: tab. 7.6), suggesting more ephemeral occupations.[36]

The abundance of micromammalian remains, serving as a rough gauge of occupation intensity (Bar-Yosef 1998a; Hovers 2001), generally decreases from the early to the late Middle Paleolithic, consistent with the notion of increasing occupation intensities.[37] The densities of large mammals, however, co-vary with those of the lithics. Thus, they are relatively low at Hayonim E and Qafzeh (though note again the different time scales of the two sites), and are very high at Kebara and Amud.

A conspicuous difference between early and late Levantine Middle Paleolithic sites is the evidence in the latter for activities that were patterned in space and, furthermore, took place repeatedly in the same locations within the sites. Kebara's "kitchen midden" along the north wall and the consistent occurrence of circular bone concentrations that are tens of centimeters deep point to accumulations over several phases of successive occupations (Bar-Yosef et al. 1992; Schick and Stekelis 1977; Speth

and Tchernov 2001). Hominin remains at Amud were consistently deposited in a particular area of the cave during the accumulation of the two upper stratigraphic sub-units (Hovers et al. 1995).

The intensive and repeated use of hearths is informative. In terms of their small size (25–50 cm in diameter) and combustibles, late Middle Paleolithic hearths are not markedly different from those in early Middle Paleolithic sites (with some larger exceptions, notably at Kebara and Dederiyeh). However, the hearths in late Middle Paleolithic deposits were constructed and used over much shorter time spans than their earlier counterparts. Coupled with the paucity of evidence for special uses of the fires, these variably preserved hearth and hearth features seem to suggest that numerous domestic fires were lit in the sites over time and may have been the focus of various procedures related to intensive use of fauna and a wide range of lithic production activities, some of which were spatially segregated (Alperson-Afil and Hovers 2005; Ekshtain and Hovers 2005; Hovers 2001; Meignen et al. 2001a; Speth 2006; Speth and Tchernov 2003).

Incomplete though it is, the current evidence thus suggests that occupation intensity increased during the Middle Paleolithic, coupled with increasing variability of occupation types, sometimes even within a single locale. Qafzeh represents one instance in which the lithic data point to changes in the role of the locale within a settlement pattern, from task-specific to more generalized occupations. At the much younger locality of Umm el-Tlel, successive occupation horizons indicate shifts from a short-term habitation site with meat processing as the main activity, to a hunting station, to a habitation of a longer duration (Boëda, Griggo, and Noël-Soriano 2001). Similarly, Speth and Tchernov (2001; Speth 2004) noted the fluctuations in the patterns of transport of faunal resources, accumulation intensities and spatial patterning of bone accumulations, as well as seasonality of occupation, between units XI–IX and VIII–VI at Kebara (see above). From these they inferred that the role of Kebara within its settlement system changed over time. Interestingly, the lithics remain relatively unchanged (Meignen et al. 2006; Speth 2004; Speth and Clark 2006; Speth and Tchernov 2001). Comparable patterns, also associated with changes in butchery and transport practices of gazelle and fallow deer, were documented at Amud, albeit on a more moderate scale (Rabinovich and Hovers 2004).

An interesting question is whether shifts in intensity and changes in site roles, over the more than 200 millennia that constitute the Middle Paleolithic and within the late Middle Paleolithic itself, depict a change from residential systems of high mobility to systems of logistical mobility with base camps and "satellite" task-specific localities. This is certainly one way of reading these data. But in considering this question we must also bear in mind the ecological background, which at practically all times favored small groups practicing high residential mobility, and the ambiguities of occupation intensity. These considerations lead to a somewhat different understanding of the data. While occupations of longer duration possibly occurred, complete with accompanying task-specific localities, settlements during the late Middle Paleolithic may not have been fundamentally different from those in the earlier part of the period: namely, short-duration occupations, the palimpsest nature of which results in the impression of increased occupation intensity.[38] High residential mobility and provisioning of place (more commonly associated with logistical mobility and long term occupation) superficially appear to be contradicting organizational strategies, yet this combination of behaviors, as well as various combinations of individual and locale provisioning, is well documented ethnographically (e.g., Gould 1980:71; Kuhn 1995a and references therein).

What appears to have changed drastically during the Middle Paleolithic is the geographic space in which hominin groups moved during the later part of the period. The results of lithic, faunal and "site architecture" analyses, preliminary as they are for many sites, are congruent with the behavior of groups moving regularly over familiar tracts of territories, the size of which allowed, and perhaps necessitated (see below), frequent returns to the same locale (Hovers 2001). The territories traversed, exploited, and occupied by late Middle Paleolithic groups seem to have contracted, which points to higher densities of people on the Levantine landscape.

The notion that demographic shifts were the culprit in the observed change is not seriously contested. Still, there is an ongoing discussion as to whether the postulated increase in population densities represents a real demographic change stemming from significant evolutionary and adaptive changes in technologies or social institutions of late Middle Paleolithic groups. Stiner, Munro, and Surovell (2000) argue on the basis of changes in dietary breadth, predator-prey modeling, and a decline in the body size of Upper Pleistocene tortoises for a pan-Mediterranean increase in the size of human populations toward the end of the Middle Paleolithic.

This proposition runs into difficulties when examined regionally. Changes in the body size of tortoises might be attributed to seasonal, climatic, and taxonomic factors (Speth and Tchernov 2002, 2003). Additionally, reliance on small-bodied animals (including the easy-to-harvest tortoise) as a means of coping with dwindling returns due to over-hunting of large mammals is certainly not reflected in all the faunal assemblages of all late Middle Paleolithic sites (e.g., Amud; Rabinovich and Hovers 2004). The model of population growth is based on evidence of occupation intensity from sites that are

all located in the Mediterranean ecological zone; but sites outside this ecological zone rarely display comparable patterns (even when scaled down against their environmental background). Finally, Upper Paleolithic occupations are in most cases less intense than the large late Middle Paleolithic sites, which probably would not have been the case had a regional trend of population growth occurred. The changes in faunal exploitation at Kebara may suggest intensification, and the consumption of small game, legumes, and grass seeds (Lev, Kislev, and Bar-Yosef 2005; Madella et al. 2002) indeed bring to mind the characteristics of the "broad spectrum revolution" as originally perceived by Flannery (1969). But these data can hardly be construed as evidence of irreversible resource intensification. In fact, the few instances in which relevant data are available may provide glimpses into the staples of Middle Paleolithic existence (and likely in earlier periods as well; e.g., Goren-Inbar et al. 2000) in the Levant and pertain to a "broad spectrum stasis" (Madella et al. 2002; see Flannery 2000).

Given these data, an alternative scenario advocates population pressure mostly or solely in the Mediterranean zone during the late Middle Paleolithic as a temporary and potentially reversible trend triggered by specific historical "episodes" (e.g., influxes of people to the region during this time (Bar-Yosef 2000; Hovers 2001).

When discussing the evidence for hunting pressure and intensification of faunal resources in Kebara, Speth and Clark (2006:31) noted:

> If the over-hunting and intensification we see at Kebara are merely reflections of [a temporary bulge in population numbers], our results, though intriguing, are relevant mostly to issues of local culture history. If, on the other hand, what we see at Kebara is but one localized expression of more fundamental and far more widespread transformations of the economic and social fabric of the late Middle Paleolithic world, then the Kebara evidence becomes at once more interesting and more broadly relevant. We clearly lean toward the latter view, but we have to be honest in admitting that the evidence simply isn't there yet to make our position compelling.

Although the more conservative explanation of Levantine late Middle Paleolithic occupation intensity is not as striking as the "evolutionary" hypothesis, it remains the more acceptable one until additional or better data tip the balance of evidence.

Having said that, even temporary increases in population numbers need to be explained and, as Speth and Clark point out, history rather than evolutionary schemes may have to be invoked. In the case of the Levant, this may have had to do with the relationship between Neanderthal and modern populations in the region (see chapter 9).

Independent of the Neanderthal–Modern question, the discussion of land-use patterns in the Levant points to the dynamics of lithic technological organization throughout the Middle Paleolithic, providing a glimpse into shifts and "transitions" in behavioral patterns.

## The Case for Cultural Traditions

Cultural transmission via social learning is a knowledge-inheritance system that has several advantages over strictly genetic or "acultural" (individual learning) modes of transmission (chapter 1). Participants in a system of cultural transmission have access to information about events that they never experience in the flesh. They can share the knowledge of others about potential strategies to deal with such events and their efficacy after they have been tried and socially accepted (Alvard 2003; Kameda and Nakanishi 2003). In short, individuals that share information transmitted through social learning share sets of mental templates pertaining to their world and potential eventualities in their lives as well as sets of decision criteria that help them assess situations and select their course of action in any given situation.

The decision-making processes and the actions that they set in motion need to address environmentally imposed constraints on satisfying the physical needs of individuals (this is mainly what the previous sections of this chapter have been about). Yet the same behaviors must also satisfy decision criteria that emanate from the values and beliefs of the society in which the individual exists. Behaviors that do not respond to both types of pressure will not survive in the cultural repertoire of a group. Moreover, as cultural transmission is strongly structured by conformist biasing, some cultural traits may be retained and practiced even when they do not contribute directly to fitness or reproductive success. (The theoretical background to cultural inheritance and decision making is reviewed in more detail in chapter 1.)

Socially transmitted information tends to be more effective in slow-changing environments, whereas rapid ecological changes render it much too sluggish to be fully adaptive. This has an immediate bearing on perceiving lithic artifacts (and hence assemblages of lithic artifacts) as products of culturally transmitted technological knowledge. There are no direct links between the physical environment and the morphologies of artifacts at the time of manufacture, which suggests that the process of core reduction and its products (i.e., lithic morphotypes) may bear little relevance to ecological conditions prevailing at the time. On the other hand, the frequencies of lithic types used in particular contexts (including those retouched after being detached) may well be specific responses to predicted or immediately perceived ecological conditions.

We should thus expect links between assemblage compositions and ecological conditions (Shennan 1991).

The ecological hypotheses examined so far have thus focused on assemblage compositions rather than on flaking methods. That these hypotheses are only partially successful in explaining variability strongly implies that factors beyond the physical environment, in addition to affecting reduction sequences, affect compositions of assemblage as well, at least to some degree. This notion is congruent with the duality of problem-solving strategies in a cultural context, where decision criteria accommodate both the physical and the social environments (chapter 1). Problem-solving strategies may be variable even if employed to address similar problems within similar physical environments because they satisfy varying social decision criteria. Conversely, different decision processes may lead to similar behaviors in practice. Despite its being an inheritance system that responds to a natural-selection-like process, cultural behavior is context-specific.

The Qafzeh assemblages once again provide guidelines for prying apart the two types of selective pressures on the decisions underlying lithic production and use. On the one hand, the underlying principles of lithic technological organization and the decision criteria inferred from the study of Qafzeh's lithics are similar to those inferred for other Mousterian assemblages. On the other hand, the case study has demonstrated that technological tradition, embedded in the overall social system (Dobres and Hoffman 1994; Levi-Strauss 1976; Pfaffenberger 1992; Richerson and Boyd 2005), played a major role in forming lithic variability in the Qafzeh assemblages. This combination calls for a closer scrutiny of the role played by technological traditions in forming the Levantine Mousterian beyond Qafzeh.

Relying on distinguishable technological characteristics, Meignen and Bar-Yosef (1992) suggested that Levantine Mousterian lithic assemblages were produced by a number of different *chaînes opératoires*, all of which follow the technological dictates of Levallois flaking. Following Copeland (1975), they noted that in each assemblage one such core-reduction strategy was quantitatively dominant. This is not to say that the prehistoric hominins were unaware of other technological options available to them within the same technological parameters. On the contrary, all the assemblages contain cores and debitage attesting to a number of alternative reduction strategies employed in the production of each single assemblage (Goren-Inbar 1990a; Goren-Inbar and Belfer-Cohen 1998; Hovers 1998a; Meignen and Bar-Yosef 1992). The quantitative dominance in each assemblage of a restricted number of stone knapping technological options cannot be attributed to technological ignorance or to a lack of technological options from which to select. Rather, it suggests that Mousterian hominins made conscious technological choices out of the available options (see Dobres and Hoffman 1994). The fact that core-reduction strategies were occasionally altered during work on the same core (chapter 4; Goren-Inbar and Belfer-Cohen 1998; Marks and Volkman 1986) is indicative of an ability to respond to immediate needs (probably resulting from the constantly changing geometric properties of the core) while still following the prevalent production norms. It is believed that this flexibility of lithic production methods is founded on the generalized, fluid intelligence of Middle Paleolithic hominins (Goren-Inbar and Belfer-Cohen 1998). However, while this cognitive approach explains the mental capacities that enabled the flexible organization of lithic production, it leaves open the question why a narrow range of technological choices was opted for in each assemblage.

Meignen and Bar-Yosef (1992:144) were unable to determine whether particular knapping methods were dictated by external factors (e.g., by functional demands or raw material constraints) or if technological choices were made out of a cultural preference. The case study of Qafzeh provides some insights into this dilemma by demonstrating that several Levallois core-reduction tactics yielded a range of products that were roughly equally efficient in carrying out a range of tasks (chapters 4–6). The use of various reduction strategies did not result in significant differences in blank size or relative thinness, two properties perceived as crucial in the selection of flaking strategies (Kuhn 1994, 1995a; Stiner 1994).[39] Thus, exclusively functional explanations for the use of any particular flaking method should be revoked, enabling the suggestion that the patterned variability of reduction methods stems from cultural rather than purely functional choices. The notion of cultural traditions at work is consistent with the observation that links between reduction sequences and site-use patterns are weak. This is in fact the expected pattern if processes of cultural rather than purely ecological factors shaped the lithic assemblages (Shennan 1991).

As discussed in chapter 7, there is an element of equifinality to the emergence of cultural traditions as observed in the archaeological record. It could stem from "drift," without being guided by cultural preferences. Or it could be the result of repeated, conscious choices by individuals over time and across generations, following mental templates that reflect the norms shared by each individual with his or her social group, even if the reasons for making those choices are unconscious (i.e., isochrestic style). While the specifics differ, variability of lithic reduction strategies in other Mousterian assemblages is patterned much in the same way as at Qafzeh. It is therefore feasible, based on both the case study of Qafzeh and on theoretical considerations (as outlined in chapters 1, 7), that the

variability of reduction sequences in most assemblages reflects adherence to technological traditions, not necessarily constrained by their functional value at the time of manufacture.

A more rigorous test of the traditional hypothesis would require detailed analyses of each assemblage in stratified sites in which several stratigraphic horizons represent a single archaeological period. These serve as appropriate test cases, since the covariance of patterns of technological organization can be followed through time. Examining the available data from such sites (albeit far from sufficient in most cases), several patterns emerge, one of which indicates that the magnitude of variation of core-reduction strategies tends to be more limited across various horizons of any single locale than it is among sites (and see below). Patterns of core reduction that achieve dominance tend to remain quantitatively the most significant throughout the sequence of a single site (e.g., Kebara, Amud, Qafzeh, Rosh Ein Mor, Nahal Aqev[40]; Crew 1976; Hovers 1998, 2004; Meignen and Bar-Yosef 1992; Munday 1977; Ohnuma 1992; Watanabe 1970; chapters 4–6 in this volume), although variations do occur among assemblages.

In evolutionary terms, we are looking at a microevolutionary mechanism that has to do with assimilating innovative behaviors into a social infrastructure and inducing technological change. The pertinent Levantine record may reflect situations in which the frequencies of certain technological operations are inflated through socially biased transmission of some decision criteria at the expense of others (Neiman 1995). Conformity to social norms operates to enhance and preserve the dominance of an adaptively neutral technological variant. Once established, it is likely that these traditional (i.e., stylistic) patterns hold little informational content beyond perpetuating the existing social relationship and norms within a group, given the size and nature of the objects involved (Lemonnier 1992:87; Sackett 1982, 1983, 1986; see, however, Wiessner 1983, 1985; Wobst 1977). Given sufficient time, a different technological variant may be installed as the socially acceptable and hence dominant (but not sole) technological practice. This can happen if the initial technological norm has lost its adaptive neutrality. Culturally induced technological change may also occur when the social "paradigm" was not robust to begin with, exerting weak social pressure for selecting a particular variant. In this case, there will not be sufficient cultural bias to affect individual decision making (Boyd and Richerson 1992:183; Dobres and Hoffman 1994).

Ethnography teaches us that small groups tend to be conservative and resistant to change (e.g., Lepowsky 1991). Moreover, small groups are often unstable and do not accumulate the demographic "critical mass" that would allow the acceptance and stabilization of innovations (Hovers and Belfer-Cohen 2006; Shennan 2002). Given that Middle Paleolithic groups were small, this would suggest that the Middle Paleolithic cultural record was conservative and change across time slow. An archaeological implication of this model is that the stability of technological traditions during the Middle Paleolithic should be inverse to the length of time represented by a stratigraphic sequence: the longer the period of settlement at the site, the higher the probability of change in technological traditions. A review of multi-layer sites demonstrates that this is indeed the case in the Levantine Middle Paleolithic (Hovers et al. 1995). The long Mousterian sequence of Tabun encompasses at least three major technological shifts in core-reduction strategies (the famous "Tabun D-, C-, and B-types").[41] Where the chronological sequences are shorter, the technological behaviors seem to be more homogeneous; the time depth may not have been sufficient for visible accumulations of microevolutionary changes that culminate in cultural (in this case, technological) changes.

In the wake of Garrod's initial thoughts on the Tabun sequence, Copeland (1975) and Bar-Yosef (1998a and references therein), among others, identified the three variants of Tabun as techno-chronological phases concurrent across the whole of the Levant.[42] In other words, over the time span of the Middle Paleolithic, three distinct cultural groups existed successively in the Levant. "Tabun types" could be used as a yardstick for dating Mousterian sites. Very broadly, this approach may be vindicated in the Mediterranean zone of the Levant, as indicated by age estimates and technological analyses of recently excavated and studied sites (appendix 6). The chronological and (many) technological characteristics of Tabun D are replicated in the assemblages of Hayonim lower E (Bar-Yosef 1998a; Meignen 1998) and of Misliya (Weinstein-Evron et al. 2003). The technological characteristics described by Copeland (1975) and Jelinek (1975, 1982b) for Tabun I (26–18) ("Tabun C"), generally match those of Qafzeh, Naamé, and Hayonim upper E. The assemblages of Kebara, Amud, and Tor Faraj are arguably technologically similar to Tabun I (17–1, "Tabun B").

Beyond the boundaries of the Levantine core area, the Tabun model is less effective in predicting typo-technological and chronological associations (Hovers 1997). This is true of Quneitra on the Golan Heights, which displays mainly centripetal, lineal (Goren-Inbar 1990a) reduction and is dated to the time of Amud and Kebara, whereas the "Tabun D-type" assemblage of 'Ain Difla dates to the time of Qafzeh and Tabun C, and the late Mousterian Far'ah II resembles none of the Tabun "types."

Even in the Mediterranean zone of the Levant, variability of core-reduction strategies is not progressive. Some redundancy in the patterning and frequencies of Levallois reduction methods and modes is inevitable, since although Levallois flaking is flexible, the number of technological options of its application is not unlimited. Thus, lithic reduction strategies in any given assemblage are never entirely divorced from those in previous (or contemporaneous) ones. Meignen and Bar-Yosef (1992) discuss at length the difficulties of distinguishing "Tabun D" from "Tabun B" assemblages, given that both exploit unipolar Levallois methods and contain similar products. The Amud assemblages are a typical example, being attributed by Jelinek (1982b) to "Tabun D" on the basis of their significant laminar component, and by Ohnuma (1992) to "Tabun B," due to the occurrence of broad-based points.

And yet a growing number of closely analyzed assemblages has revealed a higher level of diversity in the technological practices within each of the "Tabun-type" technological "phases" (Goren-Inbar and Belfer-Cohen 1998; Hovers 1998). The differences are sometimes subtle. Meignen (1994a, 1998a) describes the particular variations in the application of Levallois and non-Levallois systems designed to produce "Tabun D" industries such as Tabun IX, Hayonim lower E, and Abu Sif (also Ashkenazi 2005; Bar-Yosef 1998a; Copeland 1985). Perhaps the best examples are the assemblages of Kebara and Amud, both of which are identified as "Tabun-B" type assemblages (Meignen 1995; Ohnuma 1992). The difference between the knapping procedures in the two localities are expressed in subtle but consistent differences in the placement of blows on the core's flaking surface in relation to its striking platform (Hovers 1998a; Meignen 1995). It is in such details that the workings of cultural (technological) traditions are visible within the three "cultural phases" defined by the Tabun model, since the end-product would hardly, if at all, differ functionally.

# 9

# Population Dynamics during the Middle Paleolithic Period in the Levant

The issue of Moderns and Neanderthals in the Levant is not the focus of the current work. Yet it is this issue that has long captivated the attention, not to say the imagination, of paleoanthropologists (chapter 1). As the "home" of one of the most important diagnostic groups of skeletal remains, Qafzeh Cave has been at the heart of some of the prolonged and sometimes heated debates on Neanderthal–Modern interactions. It is therefore worthwhile to examine the implications of the lithic assemblages of Qafzeh (chapters 4–7) and their meaning in a broader Levantine context (chapter 8) with regard to the issue of interactions—or lack thereof—between Moderns and Neanderthals in the Levant. In the following discussion, I attempt to re-address, on the basis of current information and recent theoretical advances on the part of both ecologists and archaeologists, some of the premises and assumptions underlying influential models of such relationships.

The discovery of the Skhul skeletal remains together with Mousterian artifacts similar to those associated with the Tabun C1 Neanderthal (and with the European Neanderthals) marked the onset of debates revolving around their taxonomic identity, their relations to Levantine Neanderthals, and the affinities of the latter with the classic European Neanderthals. The discovery in Qafzeh of fossils similar to those of Skhul did little to resolve such disagreements, and debates rage in the literature to this very day. Most if not all researchers in the field accept that the European Neanderthals were different from Upper Paleolithic sapient populations, but not all recognize the Tabun C1, Kebara, Dederiyeh, and Amud skeletal finds as Neanderthal. Arensburg and Belfer-Cohen (1998; Corruccini 1992; Simmons 1994) argue that these remains do not display the distinctive traits that separate Neanderthals from Modern humans. They view the Levantine skeletal remains as belonging to a single population with "a mixed morphology spanning the range between Neandertal (e.g., European) and non-Neandertal (e.g. Asian and African) poles" (Wolpoff 1996:604; Tillier 2005 with regard to Tabun C1). Let others cite similarities of skeletal remains as evidence for admixture (Kramer, Crummett, and Wolpoff 2001; Wolpoff 1996; Wolpoff and Lee 2001). Yet other researchers see in the Levantine Middle Paleolithic two hominin groups, with one taxon sharing a significant number of derived anatomical traits with the European Neanderthals and another (represented by the Skhul-Qafzeh group) that consists of essentially anatomically modern humans, hence the term "proto Cro-Magnon" coined by Howell (1957). References to the Levantine Middle Paleolithic hominins range from attribution to "taxa" with unspecified phylogenetic relationships (e.g., Aiello 1993; Lieberman 1998; Tillier 1992; Trinkaus 1995; Vandermeersch 1992) to the identification of two distinct paleo-species. According to the latter view, the Levantine Neanderthals belong to the Middle Paleolithic population that inhabited Europe (Rak 1993, 1998; Rak, Ginzburg, and Geffen 2002; Rak, Kimbel, and Hovers 1994; Stringer and Andrews 1988) and like their European counterparts would have contributed little to the genetic make-up of extant humans.

Recent paleoanthropological thought has undergone a paradigm shift, not the least because of geochronological evidence of the antiquity of the Skhul-Qafzeh group in the Levant (appendix 6; similar opinions had been voiced on the basis of microfaunal communities, e.g., Tchernov 1992) and in Africa (see Clark et al. 2003; McDougal, Brown, and Fleagle 2005; White et al. 2003). This was combined with an emerging consensus that

Neanderthals and Middle Paleolithic modern humans were the result of allopatric speciation of the genus *Homo* during the late Middle Pleistocene, followed by world colonization of a single population through a series of dispersal events. Molecular data more often than not provide evidence for separate evolutionary histories of Moderns and Neanderthals. While such data are not unequivocal due to the constraints of the fossil and material culture records, there is little indication for admixture of Eurasian archaic hominins such as the Neanderthals with dispersing African populations. (Recent discussions, including some rebuttals of this view from the standpoints of population genetics, paleo-genetics, and dating evidence can be found in Bar-Yosef 1998a, 2000; Cann 2001; Caramelli et al. 2006; Clark et al. 2003; Eswaran 2002; Eswaran, Harpending, and Rogers 2005; Green et al. 2006; Grün and Beaumont 2001; Harpending and Rogers 2000; Harpending et al. 1998; Hublin and Pääbo 2006; Krings et al. 2000; McDougall, Brown, and Fleagle 2005; Noonan et al. 2006; Pearson 2004; Rak 1998; Rak, Ginzburg, and Geffen 2002; Serre et al. 2004; Stringer 2007; White et al. 2003, to mention but a few; see also chapter 1.) Within this emerging view of modern human origins and evolution, the Levant has come to be recognized as a major geographic route of modern human dispersals out of Africa as well as the southern dead-end of Neanderthal geographic expansion (Bar-Yosef 1994:49, 2000; Bar-Yosef et al. 1986; Rak 1993). Additionally, the Levant itself was considered as an alternative origin of anatomically modern humans of the Qafzeh-Skhul group (Stringer 1989:92; Vandermeersch 1982, 1992:37).

The Levantine Middle Paleolithic record is unparalleled in Eurasia in the length of time during which the two populations may have overlapped geographically (Hublin and Pääbo 2006), with Neanderthal and sapient populations producing similar Middle Paleolithic lithic assemblages (as reviewed in some detail in chapter 1). This expands considerably the range of possible models of population dynamics in the region (Hovers 2006), especially since current paleoanthropological thinking accepts for the most part that the two groups were cognitively similar and advanced.[1]

## Linking Anatomy, Lithic Technology, and Mobility Patterns

Against this background, it is not surprising that many researchers implicitly or explicitly dichotomize the Levantine regional material culture record along the Neanderthal–Modern divide, resulting in models of biology-driven variability in behavioral manifestations. In models of this type lithics are perceived as a "phenotypic" expression of taxonomic differences (Foley 1987a, 1987b;

Foley and Lahr 2003; Frayer et al. 1993; Wood 1997; see chapter 2). At the extreme, this is expressed in the inclusion of lithics as a component of taxonomic identification, as first voiced by McCown and Keith (1939) regarding the "Neanderthals" of Skhul. According to this approach "[i] t is difficult to understand how [two populations coexisted], given that they manufactured the same tool industries, utilized the same technology and adapted with the same subsistence patterns unless they became the same people" (Wolpoff 1989:136). This argument is problematic, since it rests on the very same observation that needs to be explained (i.e., similarity of behavior) as the answer to the biological dilemma (Hovers 2006; see discussion of the problems of confounding the biological and cultural domains of enquiry in chapter 1).

As archaeologists, we tend to think from the ground up, and it is probably only natural that explanatory relationships are first sought between the two types of finds that archaeologists unearth: material culture remains and skeletal remains. This raises the practical question of whether technological practices and/or lithic variations can be neatly separated along the biological divide.

This is never an easy task, and certainly not where Levantine Middle Paleolithic hominins are considered. The differences between Neanderthals and AMH occur as a "mosaic" of traits that do not necessarily emerge together. Anatomical complexes changed at different rates: for example, Neanderthals evolved derived facial, dental, and masticatory traits while their pelvic anatomy remained generalized, whereas an opposite pattern was observed among anatomically modern humans (e.g., Bailey and Lynch 2005; Rak 1986, 1990; Rak, Ginzburg, and Geffen 2002; Trinkaus 2006 expresses a variant of this opinion). In this context it is important to bear in mind that the genetically induced differences between Neanderthals and Moderns would have had already been set by the time each population reached the Levant, and therefore reflect their adaptations to their respective environments of origin.[2] These groups most likely underwent some adaptations to the local conditions, but much of their initial (and possibly later) survival in the Levant would have depended on their ability to cope with environmental conditions through behavioral strategies rather than biological adjustments.[3] The similarities in the composition of their lithic assemblages and in their organization of lithic technology are feasibly the outcome of subjecting two groups of large-brained hominins to identical environmental pressures, which in turn led to overlap in their organizational solutions.

As lithic technology is one of the "extrasomatic means of adaptation" of humans, the functionality of technological aids is likely to change so as to complement, enhance, or compensate for anatomical traits. This leaves much room for variability in the structure of the links (if there are any) between technology and anatomy. "Archaeologists cannot regard variation in the archaeological record as a passive measure of physical/ social distance between groups. Nor can they assume that close contact between groups and the incorporation of one group by another will lead to gradual and uniform acculturation" (Jones 1996:71). Although the cultural manifestations of societies of extant humans are highly variable, all these humans undeniably belong to a single biological species. Differences in their behaviors, as well as differential expressions of cognitive characteristics, have to do mostly with cultural norms and particular historical trajectories (Bang, Medin, and Atran 2007; Beller and Bender 2008). Conversely, the existence of cultural similarities does not necessarily imply a close phylogenetic relationship within the *Homo* lineage.

Strict biology-driven models and the hypotheses derived from them have not fared well in the study of Levantine Middle Paleolithic lithic technologies. Jelinek (1977, 1982a) identified in the Tabun sequence a diachronic trend of decreasing variance of flake thickness. This led him to the suggestion that "an orderly and continuous progression of industries...[illustrated by the change from thicker to thinner flakes was] paralleled by a morphological progression from Neanderthal to modern man" (Jelinek 1982a:1374). In this case, the anatomy of hands is implicated as a cause of disparate manual dexterity and hence technological differences between the two hominin types. Yet morphological analyses of the hands of Neanderthals when compared to modern humans did not point to significant differences in precision grip that would have limited their ability to produce thin flakes (Jones, Martin, and Pilbeam 1992; Niewoehner et al. 2003). Ekshtain (2006), who analyzed patterns of flaking accidents and mistakes, did not find compelling indications that Neanderthals in the Levant or in Europe were more prone to such accidents than Middle Paleolithic Moderns. Furthermore, lithic technological studies have indicated that flake thickness in various assemblages did not follow the gross chronological trend (i.e., from Lower to Middle Paleolithic) expected by Jelinek (Gilead 1980; Gilead and Grigson 1984; Goren-Inbar 1985). Finally, the early dates of Qafzeh and Skhul as compared to Kebara and Amud (appendix 6) refute the notion of an "orderly progression" of change, effectively clinching the argument against this model.

A broader understanding of the concept of biology-induced variability has led to a suite of hypotheses, relying on lithics as well as biological phenomena (e.g., cementum analysis in gazelle teeth) as proxies of mobility and settlement characteristics that advocated niche partitioning in accordance with differential specific behaviors of the two hominin groups. In agreement with theoretical expectations (chapter 1), the study of the Qafzeh lithics (chapter 7) suggests that, in that they reflect land-use patterns of

hominin groups, the compositions of lithic assemblages are among the few aspects of lithic organization that are responsive to ecological/environmental conditions. As a rule, this applies to the Levantine Middle Paleolithic as a whole. If, as posited by models of biology-induced lithic variability, such behavioral tactics are causally linked to taxonomic differences, they should pattern according to the taxonomic identity of assemblage-makers.

Studies of Neanderthal functional anatomy suggest that it was designed to absorb high stress levels directly from the environments. Skeletal robusticity and muscular hypertrophy of Neanderthal limbs, it is argued, reflect high levels of stress due to strenuous activity, which may be an outcome of their large range of movement around the landscape (Ruff et al. 1993; Trinkaus 1992, 1995, and references therein). This has often been taken to imply that Middle Paleolithic lithic (and other) technologies played a lesser role in adaptation to environmental stresses, either because Neanderthals were not familiar with them or because they were not able to exploit their advantages fully. (Such notions hark back to deficiencies of Neanderthal compared to Modern human cognition.) Thus, external pressures on Neanderthal biological traits were not alleviated by cultural characteristics, and bone robusticity was maintained despite its high costs (Steegman, Cerny, and Holliday 2002).

Lieberman and Shea (1994) suggested a similar close relationship between the robusticity of Levantine Neanderthal lower limbs (relative to modern humans in Qafzeh and Skhul)[4] and their land-use patterns, which they reconstructed as one of radiating mobility based on gazelle cementum studies. This mobility pattern was viewed by Lieberman and Shea as energetically less efficient than the postulated circular mobility practiced by anatomically modern humans in Qafzeh. This hypothesis did not withstand closer scrutiny. Using cranial vault thickness as a proxy of the levels of physical exercise, Lieberman (1998) found that Neanderthals and AMH experienced roughly equivalent workloads on their lower limbs. This in turn implied that energetic costs associated with movement were roughly equivalent for both populations (see also Trinkaus 1995; Trinkaus and Ruff 1999). These results contradict the premises of the model.

Lieberman and Shea (1994; Shea 1998) also presented an interesting reversal of the thinking about the relationship between bone robusticity and reliance on technology by linking mobility patterns and relatively high bone robusticity with enhanced reliance on extractive lithic technology. Their model posits an association of Neanderthals in the Levant with unipolar convergent Levallois flaking ("Tabun B-type" assemblages), geared toward the production and use of Levallois points. There are now compelling methodological and archaeological reasons for questioning this model (discussed in relation to Qafzeh in particular and the Levantine Middle Paleolithic in general in chapters 7 and 8, respectively; see comments in Shea 1998). Additionally, one may note that the limb anatomy of the European Neanderthals, probably more costly metabolically, did not lead to the archaeological signatures that one observes in the Levant, a fact that argues against deterministic links between Neanderthal anatomy, mobility, and lithics.

None of this is surprising in view of the theoretical and analytical complexities involved in the exercise of explaining the past. If anything, these examples underline the hazards of drawing inferences from an amalgam of disciplines (Hovers 2006; Lieberman and Bar-Yosef 2005). On the other hand, testing hypotheses within the theoretical framework of a discipline, while using its own analytical tools, expands paleoanthropologists' understanding of realms of human existence, even if they are not situated directly within the research questions of that discipline. And so, when dealing with the issue of taxonomy-related differences in mobility patterns, Lieberman (1998) concluded from biological data not linked to material culture finds, that land-use patterns in the Levant were characterized by mobility patterns unrelated to specific anatomies of the hominin taxa involved.

## The Three C's: Coexistence, Competition, Continuity

The conundrum of Modern–Neanderthal relationships in the Levant has also been explored from biogeographic and ecological perspectives. According to the first (Rak 1993), after their allopatric speciation in Europe and Africa, the Levant became the zone of maximum expansion of the home ranges of both Neanderthals and Moderns. Since environmental changes, namely shifts from glacial to interglacial conditions, are thought to be the driving force of expansions and contractions of home ranges, the arrivals of members of the two groups into the Levant would have been asynchronous, and interactions would be minimal. This model attempts to explain a situation, implausible to many, in which two biological groups exploited the same region while preserving their biological distinctiveness. It does not address the issue of similarities or differences in behavioral strategies and their expressions in material culture.

On the other hand, it is this issue of similarities in material culture that drives Shea's (2003) model of competitive exclusion. Ekshtain (2006), Goren-Inbar and Belfer-Cohen (1998), and Hovers (1997, 1998a), among others, have argued that lithic variability in the Levant does not align with the Neanderthal–Modern dichotomy and that, in terms of their technology, these two populations were compatible. This is also evidenced by the faunal remains and analyses of settlement patterns and non-utilitarian behaviors (Hovers 2001 and references therein; Hovers et al. 1995). In this new view of the Levantine Middle Paleolithic record, Neanderthals and Middle Paleolithic Moderns are perceived within the framework of the competitive model as congruent species (although Shea 1991, 1998 presents contrary premises and arguments), assumed to have been unable to co-exist for long periods in a region the size of the Levant. The model further posits alternate dispersal events from Africa or northern Eurasia into the Levant, with short-duration "window of contact," i.e. brief periods of competitive interaction, culminating in the geographic exclusion or physical extinction of one or the other population. After a brief period of competitive coexistence, only a single population remained to inhabit the region until the next influx of competitors occurred.

The biogeographic and competitive models incorporate sets of assumptions and predictions pertaining to the links between anatomy and material culture, the effects of climate and the material culture that would have been left behind according to each scenario (Hovers 2006). For the exploration of such multi-faceted interactions, issues of chronology are key.

## The Relativity of Absolute Chronology

Paleoanthropology faces a perpetual catch. In order to understand long-term evolutionary changes, we first have to ask historical questions about how the behaviors reflected archaeologically came about (Carrithers 1990; O'Brien and Lyman 2002). With very rare exceptions, however, the discipline has not been successful in addressing phenomena on an anthropological, "real time" scale. For deep prehistory, paleoanthropology can establish temporal frames only on a geological and evolutionary timescale (Bordes 1981; Conard and Adler 1997; Hovers 2001; Pettitt 1999; Shea 2003). Yet the questions of interest have a distinct historical flavor to them, relating as they do to "episodes" of interactions and population movements. Hence, when dealing with the possibility of close encounters of human populations, as is the case here, it is best to keep in mind what chronology can and cannot tell us.

Geochronological data for the Levantine Middle Paleolithic derive from a small number of sites, within which only a small fraction of stratigraphic horizons have yielded diagnostic anatomical remains (appendix 6, figure A6.1). The distribution of available age estimates (appendix 6) is spotty, and the statistics associated with each dated sample define broad temporal ranges with many undated intervals. (The analytical and methodological problems of Levantine Middle Paleolithic age estimates and chronologies have been discussed extensively by Bar-Yosef 1998a; Bar-Yosef and Meignen 2001, and references therein.) Comparison of chronological schemes from the late 1980s, 1990s, and the early 2000s shows that as a rule the duration of such undated intervals shortened as new assemblages are dated and new data points fill the gaps. More often than not, the taxonomic affinities of the assemblage makers remain unknown.

A common interpretation of available geochronological data is that they represent a lack of temporal overlap between Neanderthals and AMH. This interpretation of the record is presented as the only way to formulate falsifiable hypotheses (Shea 2003, 2007a). This approach is not without its problems, however, as even "solid data" are sometimes shaky. Take the case of Tabun C, which constitutes ca. 10% of the hominin-yielding stratigraphic horizons. The date of the C1 Neanderthal skeleton and its temporal relationship to other Levantine fossils depends on its stratigraphic assignment and on the date associated with whichever stratigraphic position one accepts. Depending on these two components, Neanderthals can be said to have either slightly predated AMH (based on the TL chronology for Tabun C) or to have been contemporaneous with them (based on the ESR chronology for the same layer). According to both dating methods, the C1 skeleton is earlier than the Amud–Kebara group. If it is assigned a stratigraphic location in Tabun B (Bar-Yosef and Callander 1999), for which no TL age estimates are available, the C1 fossil could be contemporary with the Qafzeh-Skhul group and still older than the late Kebara and Amud Neanderthals. Regardless of any of the above, based on the original excavators' stratigraphic considerations, this fossil postdates the Tabun C2 modern mandible, which is either earlier than the Qafzeh–Skhul group or contemporary with it. Any of these permutations implies, minimally, that Neanderthals existed in the Levant during two separate occupation periods. A more radical reading of the Tabun dates would be that Neanderthals survived in the Levant for a long time.[5] Regardless of the interpretation preferred, the important point here is that the data do not support by default the presence of a single population in the Levant at any given time.

The situation in the Levant differs radically from that in other parts of Eurasia. Where Middle Paleolithic assemblages are attributed to a single hominin taxon, positivist logic is applicable and effective. The hypothesis that Neanderthals were the sole occupants of Europe at any given moment during the Middle Paleolithic has not yet been refuted. Hence, authorship of any cultural remains, even where there are no skeletal remains, is attributed to them. Given the more complex situation in the Levant, one has to accept that when no fossils are associated with lithic assemblages, there is no compelling reason to link the assemblages with one or the other group of hominins. The shortening of temporal gaps between dated sites as new age estimates are obtained underlines the possibility that chronological separation between hominin populations in the Levant may be a matter of interpretation and not a fact of the record.[6] The margins of error in dating are such that even if two fossils belonging to two different species were found in the exact same stratigraphic horizon, the complexity of formation process would prevent us from ascertaining real synchrony. From the point of view of formal science, this means that a hypothesis of discontinuity in the occupation of the Levant by any one group (not to be confused with evolutionary, biological continuity between the two groups) is as falsifiable (or rather, un-falsifiable) as the alternative hypothesis of continuous presence of one or both hominin populations.

The interpretation of geochronological age estimates as solid evidence for vicarism of Moderns and Neanderthals in the Levant has been used as a baseline from which to enlist ecological theories and biogeographic models to construct explanatory scenarios of alternate occupations. If chronological premises are not a given of the Levantine archaeological record, such scenarios can no longer be accepted at face value and their merits as independent lines of reasoning should be re-examined. A consilience of evidence, if achieved, may be used to reconstruct "a modest reality."

## Biogeography of Hominin Dispersals

The biogeographic model of alternate dispersals assumes that different hominins reached the Levant at different times. The effects of climatic shifts are frequently invoked as a mechanism—perhaps, in fact, *the* mechanism—that regulated hominin dispersals to the region over time.

Climate has been stressed as the cause of biogeographic barriers to human movement into the Levant, typically in the context of out-of-Africa dispersals and modern human origins. There has been much emphasis on the role of the Sahara as a biogeographic barrier between Africa and the Levant during dry glacial periods, whereas it is suggested that during humid interglacial periods the desert could sustain humans traversing (and even occupying) it, thus enabling the northward movement of modern humans (Lahr and Foley 1998; Osborne et al. 2008). Supporting paleoclimatic data were provided by Vaks et al. (2007), who show that during the time span 140,000–110,000 years ago the Negev desert in the southern Levant witnessed enhanced amounts of rainfall. Neanderthals, on the other hand, are believed to have been susceptible to arid, cold climatic conditions in their heartland territories during glacial periods, when they expanded their home ranges to more southern territories (as modeled by Rak 1993). Such dispersals would have coincided with periods when the Sahara was presumably impenetrable.

Biogeography seems to offer a regulating mechanism of alternating episodes of population influxes into the Levant from Europe and the African continent, yet climatic conditions may have played a less deterministic role than this model presumes. The Aterian of North Africa attests to human presence in the Sahara in the Upper Pleistocene, a time when no humid intervals could be confirmed for this region (Garcea 2004). Thus, the biogeographic barriers may not have been impenetrable, and some ecological niches in the Sahara could have been exploited over short intervals by traversing hominin groups (Derricourt 2005), enabling movement both into and out of the Levant over extended periods of time.[7] Indeed, evidence from mtDNA studies implies back-migration(s) from the Levant into Africa around 47,000–45,000 years ago (Olivieri et al. 2006), during the dry and cold Heinrich 5 event. This seems to have taken place when Levantine groups were still relying on Middle Paleolithic technologies. The paleoclimatic data from 140,000–110,000 years ago (Osborne et al. 2008; Vaks et al. 2007) have no bearing on the earlier presence of Moderns in the Levant, suggested by any reading of the Tabun sequence. By the same token, it is difficult to explain the southbound movements of Neanderthals as being initiated or regulated by climatic changes as such, given the evidence that at times they successfully occupied rather harsh regions of Eurasia (Hoffecker 1999; Krause et al. 2007).[8]

The biogeographic explanations of alternate occupations are valid if one accepts the "main stream" geochronology of the Levantine Middle Paleolithic. However, when decoupled from these age estimates, the models seem less relevant to the question of Neanderthal–Modern interactions within the Levantine region. Hence, biogeographic considerations do not seem to provide independent evidence to bear on the Neanderthal–Modern question.

## Re-thinking Competition in Levantine Contexts

Competitive scenarios describing the relationship between Levantine Middle Paleolithic hominin populations assume that when a new influx of either hominin group occurred, there was a narrow "window" in time when members of the two populations came into close contact until one outcompeted the other. A second assumption of competitive models for the Levantine Middle Paleolithic is that competition between similar taxa must lead to competitive exclusion (i.e., a biogeographic shift) or extinction of one of the competitors (e.g., Clark et al. 1997[9]), unless competition is alleviated by niche separation through resource partitioning. In the case of hominins, the latter could involve different technologies and/or differential organization of technology. Both of these assumptions merit further scrutiny.

For a competitive relationship to evolve, two (or more) congruent populations must be sympatric and synchronic for some time. The model thus assumes that Moderns and Neanderthals coexisted for at least a brief period when population influxes occurred. Within the

framework of the competitive model, the lack of archaeological evidence for coexistence is explained by suggesting that periods of overlap "were too brief to leave a detectable fossil record" (Shea 2003:177), a statement that obviously is not anchored in the geochronological data as such. The model requires a leap of faith. It argues that population densities were very low (see below) and assumes that the Levantine landscape was inhabited for most of the time by a single population at a time. It also emphasizes the inadequacy of the geochronological evidence to inform us of inter-groups synchrony (Shea 2003, 2006a). Yet the very same model suggests that, within such broad time–space dimensions, there were very concrete, short-duration competitive encounters among populations that were thin over the landscape, ultimately leading to inevitable competitive exclusion or extinction of any of the competitors.

Modern ecological thinking puts into question the inevitability of extinction/geographic dislocation in the Levantine Middle Paleolithic as the result of competition. Such scenarios are possible but not inevitable outcomes of sympatry (Tokeshi 1999:219). Two congruent competitors may stably coexist through their ability to invade one another's habitats and to colonize empty patches (Wang, Zhang, and Liu 2000:632), particularly in heterogeneous, spatially fragmented habitats. The presence of a competing species tends to affect both habitat colonization rates (i.e., it slows down the process) and the perseverance of the competitor. Moreover, the outcomes of inter-species competition depend on its intensity, so that prolonged coexistence is more feasible when competitors are congruent than it is when competition is unbalanced between a strong and a weak competitor (Wang, Zhang, and Liu 2002:498). Another important factor in the emergence of competitive relationship is population densities. If those are kept in check by an extrinsic factor through evolutionary time, competitive tendencies associated with resource scarcities may not evolve (Tokeshi 1999:223).

Competition-regulated, inevitable extinction of hominin lineages in the Levant may have been an appropriate model when Neanderthals were presumed to be weaker challengers to Moderns. As Neanderthals are now accepted to have been congruent competitors on the Middle Paleolithic Levantine stage, this premise can no longer be an axiom from which model building proceeds. Rather, it is a hypothesis that requires independent testing again from consilience of evidence. The relevant topics are levels of competition-generating resource stress and the plausible levels of the inevitable inter-groups friction. These questions can be addressed, albeit indirectly, by looking at the productivity of Levantine environments and their carrying capacity, and how resource structure might influence the territorial packing of hominin groups across the landscape. A distinct but related issue is that of group sizes and population densities.

The diverse, spatially fragmented and productive habitats of the Levant formed conditions that are modeled by ecologists as promoting competitive coexistence. The variable facies of the Mediterranean ecosystem provided large amounts of vegetal biomass that hominins could exploit, whereas other ecosystems, albeit less productive (e.g., in the Negev desert), still produced biomass that could support small, spatially dispersed human groups.[10] In addition, rare botanical remains and more frequent faunal finds suggest that Middle Paleolithic hominins attained a technological level that enabled rudimentary resource intensification through processing to enable safe consumption (e.g., by fire; see chapter 8). The vagaries of seasonality would be mitigated within relatively small territorial ranges by the sharp environmental gradients along both North–South and West–East axes (chapter 8). The spatio-temporal characteristics of habitats would require relatively small annual exploitation territories, which in turn would operate to reduce the levels of inter-group competition.

The most severe resource pressures, and hence highest levels of competition, would have occurred during dry, cold climatic spells in the Mediterranean zone of the Levant. At such times the area along the coastal plain and on the foothills of the mountains would have been more attractive due to the higher stability and durability of its resource structure compared to other ecosystems.[11] Territorial mechanisms and cultural markers may have acted to reduce the levels of friction and competition even during dry periods (Hovers 2001 and references therein). Indications for technological traditions (chapter 8), coupled with the evidence for non-lithic traditions (e.g., purposeful burials, the use of non-utilitarian objects, pigment use), may reflect group cohesion in the context of inter-group dynamics (Hovers 2001, 2006).

In sum, given our current understanding of the environmental and archaeological record of the Levant, conditions in the region could lead to a state of competitive equilibrium, and relatively prolonged coexistence between Moderns and Neanderthals during the Middle Paleolithic would be possible. The fact that dated occupation horizons tend to fill in the chronological gaps between dated hominin-bearing horizons is consistent with this notion. Although competition probably influenced Levantine Middle Paleolithic population dynamics, it may not have played as decisive a role in shaping inter-group relations as the models argue. Moreover, levels of Neanderthal–Modern competition need not have been different from those operating between same-taxon groups, with one probable difference. When separate small groups aggregated, members of the two populations might have competed more actively (see below).

## Continuity and Extinctions

Competitive coexistence of congruent hominin populations in the Middle Paleolithic Levant is a plausible scenario according to both theoretical ecological principles and the archaeological record. Can a case be made, then, for occupational continuity in the region? Clearly, categorical claims favoring this notion should be examined along the same lines of critique as the competitive model. We need to consider the plausibility of such a scenario on the basis of the evidence in hand.

Stochastic extinctions are part of the evolutionary history of small groups due to a variety of changing conditions (e.g., Harpending and Rogers 2000), of which inter-taxa competition is but one. If at any given time during the Middle Paleolithic population size in the Levant stood at extremely low numbers, for example, 1,200 individuals as suggested by Shea (2006a),[12] severe competition among groups is an unlikely scenario. Moreover, if Levantine populations were so small, hominin groups in the Levant hovered on the brink of extinction, perpetually running the risk of not reaching the threshold required for a viable population (see discussion of population sizes in Shennan 2002; Wobst 1974, 1976). This would be especially true if the Levant were a closed region, with population influxes from the south and north restricted if not impossible for very long periods of time. Local extinctions would have occurred independently of the presence of members of a competing hominin taxon.

It is likely that the Levantine Middle Paleolithic has seen its share of local groups going extinct. Rapid demographic crashes would have disrupted continuous social storage of ecological and cultural information (Hovers and Belfer-Cohen 2006; Shennan 2002). The archaeological record of the Levant is suggestive of such instances. Indeed, the record of symbol use at Qafzeh itself is a compelling case of such disruptive episodes (e.g., Hovers et al. 2003). Even if higher population size estimates are used in the model and biogeographic barriers were more permeable (as discussed above) than suggested by Lahr and Foley (1998) and Vaks et al. (2007), small groups would still be likely to experience occasional crashes.[13] In short, the notion that small groups underwent severe demographic crashes is not tethered by default to annihilation of taxonomic lineages.

Arguably, there are some indications for a degree of occupational continuity of the Levant during the Middle Paleolithic. These come from separate disciplines (physical anthropology and archaeology) and are based on a number of lines of inquiry such as anatomical studies, lithic analyses, and study of settlement patterns; thus they provide confirmation of our "modest reality."

Qafzeh Cave figures prominently in the arguments for continuity from the perspective of physical anthropology.

Given the anatomical evidence and ensuing phylogenetic reconstructions, there have been suggestions that the progenitors of the Skhul–Qafzeh "proto Cro-Magnons" should be identified in the population represented by the late Lower Paleolithic Zuttiyeh fossil. This in turn could imply the presence of a locally evolving population throughout the early part of the Middle Paleolithic, at least until the time of Skhul and Qafzeh (Stringer and Andrews 1988; Vandermeersch 1982). Such a model is not informed one way or the other by the geochronological record of the Levantine Middle Paleolithic.

As discussed at length in chapter 8, studies of Middle Paleolithic settlement patterns in the Levant suggest that the number of sites, as well as occupation intensities per site, in general increased through time. Whether this trend is attributed to an evolutionary process of irreversible, gradual pan-Levantine population growth toward the end of the Pleistocene or is perceived as the result of more localized "refugia" conditions, some level of population growth is implied (Hovers 2001; Meignen et al. 2006; Speth and Clark 2006; Stiner 2005; Wallace and Shea 2006). The repeated site occupations, often of high intensity (as detailed in chapter 8), are suggestive of some degree of population stability or slight increase through time, albeit not necessarily as a continuous process throughout the Middle Paleolithic. Thus, the patterns observed in the archaeological record are inconsistent with short-duration peaks in population size due to influx of populations, that were later reduced to the brink of annihilation through strong competition. The difference that may have been made by population influxes to the overall process was one of degree, but not of kind (Hovers 2001).

Perhaps the most ambiguous line of reasoning in favor of some level of occupational continuity derives from general aspects of the Levantine Middle Paleolithic lithic assemblages. As discussed throughout this study with particular reference to Qafzeh, and more generally with regard to the Levantine Middle Paleolithic as a whole, the lithic assemblages reflect what appear to be contrasting trends of conservatism and change. A feature shared by most assemblages is the extensive use of Levallois flaking concepts. Emphases on particular modes of Levallois reduction, however, changed variably through time, such that each "Tabun-type" Mousterian contains more than a one technological variant. Additionally, the Levallois component of the Levantine Mousterian is accompanied by a number of other flaking systems (i.e., the laminar and discoidal systems) used variably throughout the time span of the Middle Paleolithic. Yet the diverse technological make-up of the lithic assemblage is associated with a restricted set of typological forms (Goren-Inbar and Belfer-Cohen 1998; Hovers 1997, 1998; Meignen 2000; Monigal 2002). Although this observation dates back some twenty-five years, it is still largely valid (as discussed in chapter 1).

The Levantine archaeological record exhibits its own trajectories of stability and change, seemingly unaffected by cultural patterns and markers in the regions from whence humans dispersed into the Levant. In and of themselves, the patterns of non-directional change, reduced typological diversity, and paucity of diagnostic types are not exceptional in the context of the Middle Paleolithic, a time span promoted as poor in technological innovations and lithic morphological diversity (e.g., Kuhn and Stiner 1998; Shea 2006a; Stiner 2005). However, when such patterns are viewed against the backdrop of Old World prehistory, from the perspective of a region that had seen population movements from both Europe and Africa they become more intriguing.

Some technological traits, such as Levallois flaking concepts and systems, are shared across vast regions of the Old World, including Africa (e.g., Pleurdeau 2003; Villa, Delagnes, and Wadley 2005), possibly testifying to deep-rooted origins in a technological entity that was ancestral to the Middle Paleolithic/Stone Age. Similarly, systematic production of blades appears at ca. 300,000 years ago or slightly earlier, both in sub-Saharan Africa during the transition from the Early to Middle Stone Age and in the Amudian facies of the Acheulo-Yabrudian in the Levant (Barkai, Gopher, and Shimelmitz 2005 and references therein; McBrearty and Tryon 2006; McBrearty, Bishop, and Kingston 1996; Texier 1996), where it is followed by considerable emphasis on laminar production systems during the early Middle Paleolithic ca. 250,000 years ago (Meignen 1998, 2000), some of which are indeed reminiscent of those seen in Europe.

And yet, technological analyses that go beyond morphology indicate that blade production systems involve an array of regional technological systems that are not shared continuously across vast geographical space. Some techno-morphological concepts, such as the production of elongated pointed blades, were possibly diffused from Africa to the Levant by populations dispersing during the earlier stages of the Levantine Middle Paleolithic before the last interglacial (Brooks et al. 2006; McBrearty, Bishop, and Kingston 1996). Even if that were the case, such elements seem to have undergone their local trajectories of technological change, little influenced or informed by the African subsequent evolution of the same forms (Brooks et al. 2006). Other lithic features remained restricted geographically and temporally. Thus, the typical Nubian Complex is tethered to the lower Nile Valley until the last interglacial, not reaching the Levant during the Middle Paleolithic (Crew 1975; Van Peer 1998). The regionalism of lithic forms, in particular points, has been hailed as a marker of the precocious sub-Saharan African Middle Stone Age record, where points in particular show geographic and temporal diversity of forms and shaping techniques (Clark 1988; McBrearty and Brooks 2000).

These forms are not echoed at all in the Levant. Similarly, multiple regional trajectories of stasis and change become amply evident toward the end of the period in Europe, when Neanderthals in various areas use regional variants of Levallois and other flaking methods as well as relatively local typological forms (e.g., Bar-Yosef and Pilbeam 2000; Delagnes and Meignen 2006; Kuhn 2006; Marks and Chabai 2006). It is difficult to pinpoint any techno-morphological patterns in the lithic assemblages of the Levant that can be linked to specific forms or technologies used by Middle Paleolithic groups north of the region.

In sum, few (if any) of the specific characteristics of neighboring regions occur in the Levant, despite its being the zone into which populations dispersed from both Africa and Europe. On a tentative map marking the territorial boundaries of Middle Paleolithic archaeological cultures, the Levantine Mousterian emerges as a separate phenomenon, readily distinguished from other regional entities (Bar-Yosef 2006:312–315, fig. 1).

This is true of other manifestations of material culture as well. Thus, the choice of raw materials and techniques for the production of shell beads at Skhul is similar to that observed in African Middle Stone Age occurrences and is viewed as part of a pan-African tradition (Vanhaeren et al. 2006). On current evidence, however, Skhul at 120,000 years ago represents the oldest manifestation of a "pan-African" tradition of bead making and use when compared to Blombos (d'Errico et al. 2005) or Taforalt (Bouzouggar et al. 2007). It is therefore not entirely clear where the tradition of shell bead first emerged, especially if one bears in mind the possibility of permeable boundaries (as opposed to biogeographic barriers) discussed above. Similarly, a different tradition, unrelated to the "pan-African" one, is possibly manifested in the layers of Qafzeh dated to 92,000 years ago, possibly as a result of (another?) emerging Levantine tradition. Other non-lithic traits typical of the African record, such as the use of ochre, appear briefly in the Levantine Middle Paleolithic and then disappear (Hovers et al. 2003). This is somewhat reminiscent of the later Upper Paleolithic, when distinct Aurignacian traits indicated dispersal of Aurignacian groups from Europe, followed by short-term persistence of Aurignacian groups in the Levant and culminating in their assimilation into the local Levantine population (Goring-Morris and Belfer-Cohen 2006). Still, the Levantine record differs from the African one in that the sporadic use of ochre in the Levant is clearly conducted in the context of symbolic activities (Hovers et al. 2003), whereas much of the well-documented use of ochre in Africa occurs either in an unclear context (see summary in McBrearty and Brooks 2000) or is primarily utilitarian, with symbolism playing a secondary, implied role (e.g., Lombard 2005, 2007; Wadley 2005a, 2005b).

Undoubtedly, many of the similarities in tool kits of the Levantine Middle Paleolithic derive from their use as technological aid and as adaptive strategies to local conditions (inclusive of a few tactical variants; chapter 8), although it is noteworthy that lithic variability does not appear to be highly responsive to climatic shifts as documented by several lines of evidence. It is also intriguing that point forms that emerged in Africa prior to 100,000 years ago as a means of enhancing hominin adaptive strategies (Brooks et al. 2006) do not seem to have been brought into the Levant by groups of Moderns that (in all the interpretations mentioned in this chapter) dispersed from Africa during the last interglacial, 130,000–90,000 years ago. Two scenarios are possible here. According to the first one, incoming populations never managed to subsist in the Levant long enough to leave their diagnostic marks. Alternatively, the conservatism of lithic morphologies may suggest that incoming groups from either Africa or Europe conformed to local lithic practices and traditions,[14] which in turn would imply some continuity of human occupation in the region despite possible small-scale, local group extinctions. In such a case, the arguable simplicity of the Levantine Middle Paleolithic tool kit (Shea 2006a) has no bearing on the question of identifying dispersing hominin populations. By the same token, the putative differences between the technologies of modern humans and Neanderthals depend on the geochronological scheme that one adopts as a framework for interpretation. If a slightly different chronology is adopted for either one of the two populations, as argued above, this technological dichotomy may equally represent a much broader spectrum of technological variation that may or may not be patterned along the taxonomic dividing line and form chronologically coherent technological clusters. In other words, technological variability does not necessarily stem from recursive population movements and discontinuous occupations.

Interestingly, much of the dynamic of the Middle Paleolithic seems to have continued into the Middle-to-Upper Paleolithic transition and the Upper Paleolithic of the Levant, which is characterized by the relationship between resident populations and those that reached the region around 45,000 years ago. The technological variability of the late Middle Paleolithic likely played a key role in incorporating technological innovations into technological concepts retained from the Middle Paleolithic (Hovers 1998a; Meignen and Bar-Yosef 2002). Early Upper Paleolithic technology should be viewed in terms more of modifications of the underlying Middle Paleolithic concepts than of revolutionary conceptual changes. This is evidenced in the continuation of the Levantine Mousterian notion of a pre-planned, prepared core technology into the Upper Paleolithic, with a shift (rather than the introduction of a brand new concept) from the Middle Paleolithic "surficial" concept of core reduction to a more "volumetric" one observed in the Narrow (N)-fronted cores of the Ahmarian (the first full-fledged Upper Paleolithic entity in the Levant). Production of unretouched Levallois points was replaced by the manufacture of Emireh points with bifacial thinning, in turn rapidly replaced by abrasion of the removal surface of N-fronted cores. The latter enabled more efficient exploitation of the initial volume of the nodule. This low-key innovation was in many ways a conceptual refinement of the Levallois "recurrent" approach. Nonetheless, it led to related improvements (e.g., the production of more functional blanks per unit volume), which are considered the hallmark of Ahmarian technology (Belfer-Cohen and Goring-Morris 2007, in press; Davidzon and Goring-Morris 2003; Goring-Morris and Davidzon 2006). Technologically speaking, the change from Levantine Middle to Upper Paleolithic patterns differs from the preceding Middle Paleolithic record in that some external technological practices were finally absorbed and incorporated into the technological and conceptual infrastructure of local populations, emerging as accepted innovations that became normative (Hovers 1998a). The advantages of some technological innovations, as small as they might have been, could have tipped the balance in the long run and brought about the emergence of Upper Paleolithic technologies.

How these processes are related to the taxonomic identities of the authors of the lithic assemblages (and of other cultural manifestations) remains unclear for both the Middle (in the context of some occupational continuity) and the Upper Paleolithic. As discussed above, neither the region's size nor its resource structure necessitated regular, frequent interactions between competing hominin groups even if a scenario of occupational continuity is adopted. If interactions between Moderns and Neanderthals involved close contacts, they might well have been sporadic enough not to affect the taxonomic distinction of two groups that had gone their distinct evolutionary ways long before they came into contact in the Levant. It is possible that the technological traditions observed archaeologically represent social distinctions (chapter 8) that might have inhibited such contacts on the inter-taxon level. Combined with the alternative interpretations offered here of the other sets of data discussed above, this is a plausible explanation.

It is important to stress here that the above discussion has no bearing on evolutionary continuity of Neanderthals or Moderns, an issue that is better dealt with in the context of anatomical and paleo-genomic studies. In fact, the premise that the two hominin groups moved into the Levant after they had diverged evolutionarily on a significant taxonomic level is at the foundation of this discussion. My intention here was to emphasize that biological distinction should not, and in fact does not, necessarily dictate the type of explanatory models and scenarios for either lithic variability and technological organization in the Levantine Middle Paleolithic, or, on the broader scale, of population dynamics in the Levant.

# Concluding Comments

## Tracing Behavioral Modernity in the Levantine Record

Paleoanthropologists interested in the Middle Paleolithic often emphasize the monotonous nature of the material culture of this period. In the Levant, however, lithic variability is a long-recognized feature of the Middle Paleolithic record. Accordingly, at the core of this study are attempts to identify the unifying rules and processes that led to the diverse facies of a single, clearly defined prehistoric entity, the Levantine Mousterian. The sequence of assemblages from the terrace of Qafzeh Cave has served as the main case study.

The choice of Qafzeh as the focal site for this study responded to several concerns. As a rule, in the majority of Middle Paleolithic sites, detailed analyses of lithic assemblages had served as the main source of information from which models relating to broader issues were constructed. Some aspects of the lithic assemblages in Qafzeh, specifically the predominant reduction sequences, superficially seemed to be unusual compared to many, if not most, Levantine Mousterian sites (particularly cave sites). Additionally, it was the only site in which assemblages authored by Middle Paleolithic anatomically modern humans were excavated systematically (by the standards of modern research) and collected without any selection on the part of the excavators, which in turn enabled a detailed study. Finally, manifestations of behaviors were expressed through several types of non-lithic and non-faunal finds that were almost unknown from other sites of this period. This constellation created an integrated data base that provided independent lines of evidence, which could be used to explore the strengths and weaknesses of inferences as to the causes of lithic variability. Stratigraphic evidence and absolute dating establish the fact that the sequence from Qafzeh terrace does not span the whole duration of the Levantine Mousterian. Nor

does the sequence contain the earliest or latest stages of the Middle Paleolithic period in this region. Still, a review of these assemblages in the broader context of the Levant furnishes some insights into fundamental concerns with regards to the Mousterian phenomenon in the Levant and elsewhere, at the same time leaving open other questions and raising new ones. The patterns and trends of the Levantine record that have been discussed in this study are significant for the understanding of the global Middle Paleolithic record but also in the contexts of conceptual frameworks and epistemological issues pertinent to the archaeological phenomenon.

One immediate implication of the analysis concerns the issue of lithic variability and biological taxonomy. The analysis clearly shows that the range of lithic production technologies seen in the assemblages of Qafzeh falls comfortably within the range of technological repertoires represented by Neanderthal-authored assemblages in Europe (Hovers 1997). The similarity is especially evident where comparable methodologies were used in analysis (e.g., at sites such as Fonseigner, Les Canalettes; see Geneste 1985; Meignen 1993).

The Levant is in some ways an archaeological "controlled-environment laboratory" for the Middle Paleolithic, in which the behaviors of the two populations can be studied against environmental backgrounds that are essentially similar, notwithstanding time-induced changes. In this "laboratory," the premise that biological distinction between the Levantine populations is the source of variability does not pass muster. In fact, lithic production strategies that are heralded as characteristic of many Neanderthal assemblages in the Levant (i.e., the emphasis on convergent flaking and on the production of triangular and pointed pieces) are less comparable to their

Eurasian counterparts than are the Qafzeh assemblages. This mosaic of similarity and differences across geographic distances and different hominin populations speaks volumes about the weakness of notions that link lithic production procedures with biological affinities. Lithic production strategies in the Middle Paleolithic are not taxon-specific and are therefore not diagnostic of a particular biological group. The distinction between Neanderthals and Middle Paleolithic anatomically modern humans as different biological populations or even species, valid as it may be, does not appear to have driven lithic variability. Various levels of variability, which may have enhanced processes of group distinction, are observed between biological taxa but also within assemblages authored by a single hominin taxon (Hovers 1997, 1998a; Goren-Inbar and Belfer-Cohen 1998). This position has recently been endorsed by additional researchers and now serves as the basis for the construction of new hypotheses regarding the nature of the Middle Paleolithic as well as the Middle-to-Upper Paleolithic transition (e.g., Shea 2003; 2006a, 2007b).

From the perspective of the first decade of the twenty-first century, this is not a ground-breaking insight. When discussion is confined to the Middle Paleolithic, the variability seen in Europe during this time, regardless of how it is defined (e.g., Binford 1973; Bordes and de Sonneville-Bordes 1970; Delagnes and Meignen 2006), occurred within a single hominin taxon. From this perspective, the presence of two hominin types in the Levant is anecdotal to the theme of Levantine Middle Paleolithic technological and (as has been argued here) cultural variability. While it would be foolish to argue that these two facets of human evolution are not related, the numerous processes involved are interrelated in ways that are not consistent and not always predictable. Indeed, the difficulty of grasping the fact that material culture and biological evolution and taxonomy have their separate trajectories has led to some of the unsuccessful attempts (discussed in earlier chapters) to reconcile the two records. It is therefore useful to stress that the concept of bio-cultural evolution, implying as it does that the two realms of hominin evolution are driven by the same processes, is conceptually flawed (Hovers 2006).

The analysis of the Qafzeh assemblages suggests that variations in subsistence-related lithic organization were shaped through tactical shifts in mobility and settlement behaviors in response to (primarily) seasonal plant availability. By and large, this result is consistent with predictions from the group of models dubbed "ecological models" throughout this work. The analysis of the production processes of lithic technological aids points to the role of socially driven behaviors that mesh with economic decision making. This suggestion is supported by the "additional" lines of evidence (burials, shell beads, pigment use) provided by the Qafzeh record. Such

technological variations represent processes of cultural selection, likely propelled (and hence biased) by conformism to the technological norms of social groups. Some researchers would not agree that these data provide sufficient evidence for inferring that self-emergent culture (as defined by Chase 2006) had evolved by the Middle Paleolithic. Many archaeologists, however, would accept that lithic variation at this site demonstrates the implementation of transmitted, societal knowledge, indicating that social traditions had emerged and are identifiable in the material record of Qafzeh.

On expanding the scope of the study to encompass the Levantine Middle Paleolithic as a whole, these conclusions were borne out at other sites and for other assemblages. An inference drawn from the Levantine data is that, regardless of temporal range or hominin type, the variability of both lithic production systems and technological organization was governed by two major themes. Responses to the demands of the environment were filtered through the mesh of societal norms. The mechanisms of stabilizing the direction of cultural selections, as discussed in detail with regard to Qafzeh, can be attributed to rigid systems of knowledge transmission that would have reduced significant intra-assemblage technological variation by tagging it as risky and socially costly. This is often the case in small-scale societies (Lepowsky 1991). Thus, much of the patterned variability in the Levantine record may represent, in addition to consideration of functional needs, "adaptation" to social norms and cultural thresholds.

The combined weight of all the types of evidence in Middle Paleolithic sites suggests that the Mousterian record depicts, in addition to successful adjustment to external conditions, the existence of self-defined social units. Such rigid systems of intra-group transmission would have led, over space and time, to the inter-group variation that can be observed in the archaeological record of organizational responses of Middle Paleolithic bands in the Levant. More conspicuous manifestations of group distinction through aspects of the lithic assemblages seem to have occurred within the Mediterranean zone of the central and northern Levant, which at times served as refugia for a number of groups (Hovers 2001). The evidence lends credibility to the suggestion that the same process, although possibly to a lesser degree, occurred in other regions of the Levant, in environmental conditions that dictated lower density, and thus less intensive contacts among groups. Although lithic variability in the Levantine Mousterian as a whole is partly the outcome of organizational responses to the constraints of the physical environment, its impetus derives also from the delineation of social units across time and space.

Here a word of clarification is warranted. The signature of lithic tradition is obviously seen in the variability of production methods adopted and adhered to by specific groups. It is expressed not so much in innovative use of previously unknown technologies but in the consistent use by a group of a few specific variations from the finite number of options encountered within the Levallois flaking system. It is this which lends the record an appearance of monotony and has given rise to suggestions that the lithic record in the Levant reflects "convergence of technological evolution" due to the simplicity of the lithic repertoire (e.g., Shea 2006a). Close analysis has often revealed the nuances that reflect the non-functional ("isochrestic") decisions made during knapping. In fact, a methodological realization stemming from this research is that there is little leeway for shortcuts in the study of Levantine Mousterian lithic variability. Strategic, deductive research is an adequate starting point for dealing with Middle Paleolithic lithic variability. However, the generalities encompassed in the premises of "ecological models" cannot in and by themselves explain the sources of this variability.

In the past, several researchers have pointed out a seeming paradox of the Middle Paleolithic. Its long period of evolutionary success appears inconsistent with the monotony of Middle Paleolithic technology and lithic assemblages, which in turn suggests that Middle Paleolithic technologies "were somewhat less…thoroughly articulated with other domains of life than is the case with the technologies of modern humans" (Kuhn 1995a:174).[1] Middle Paleolithic hominins were not up to the task of integrating various domains of their lives, an ability believed to have been achieved exclusively by modern humans (according to some, it is this ability that defines truly modern humans). The various types of data used in this study, however, do not support the notion that Middle Paleolithic technological behavior was divorced from other aspects of hominin existence. The weight of the Levantine evidence stresses the integrated nature of the technology, social structure, and environmental intelligence of Levantine Moderns and Neanderthals alike (Hovers 1997). Thus, the results of this study of the Levantine Middle Paleolithic are in accord with the conclusions of more recent research on the Middle Paleolithic in general, which has gone a long way toward abolishing notions of Mousterian toolmakers as incomplete prototypes of modern humans (Kuhn and Hovers 2006:8). Thus, perceptions of Middle Paleolithic lithic monotony and variability bear directly on the way in which researchers have looked at the Middle Paleolithic record, what constitutes modern behavior and how "modernity" was "achieved."

There is no comprehensive theory that unifies the approaches of the numerous disciplines concerned with the question of human modernity (Chase 2006; Henshilwood and Marean 2003; Wadley 2001). The yardstick for defining this property of humanity shifts across disciplines and varies among scholars within any single discipline. Since paleoanthropology is no exception to this rule, the definition of "modern humans" and "behavioral modernity" remains one of its most challenging tasks. Researchers rely on an implicit understanding of what is alluded to by using the term "modern" in relation to the archaeological record (Belfer-Cohen and Hovers, n.d.). The infamous "grocery list" approach to the issue (i.e., the recognition of modernity by a list of traits, such as pigment and shell use, symbolic burials, or composite tools made of stone and organic components, among other things) is flawed because it is driven by the empirical record rather than by overarching theory (Henshilwood and Marean 2003). Still, the items on this list keep popping up as important building blocks of other, more sophisticated models.

In the wake of the Eurocentric paradigm, some efforts focus on linking behavioral with anatomical modernity. Klein (1995, 2000) tackled this issue by suggesting that fully modern cognition (and the behaviors that it enabled) emerged when unknown changes in the wiring of the human brain, caused by unspecified genetic mutation(s), rendered it fully modern (see also Noble and Davidson 1993). One can perceive this hypothetical event as compatible with suggested scenarios of cognitive change, such as the relatively sudden, "catastrophic" appearance of language (Bickerton 1990; Chomsky 1986; Klein 1990), the emergence of "enhanced working memory" (Coolidge and Wynn 2005; Wynn and Coolidge 2006, 2007), or the full integration of cognitive processes in the modular brain (Fodor 1985; Mithen 1996). According to Klein's suggestion, the postulated gene-driven change occurred at the end of the MSA among sub-Saharan African populations of *Homo sapiens*. The cognitive change provided these already anatomically modern humans with the evolutionary edge that made them successful colonizers of Eurasia. Bar-Yosef (2002) hypothesized a technological revolution, moving rapidly from a single point of origin to neighboring areas. While the timeline of this model is similar to that proposed by Klein's, the emphasis is on technological innovations rather than on anatomical or neurological ones. A third model (McBrearty and Brooks 2000) posits that African populations of *Homo sapiens* became gradually more and more behaviorally modern during the Middle through Upper Pleistocene. This process is reflected archaeologically in types of finds that are viewed as indications of behavioral modernity, the number of which increases gradually from the later part of the Middle through the Upper Pleistocene.[2] Modern behavior then reached other parts of the Old World 50,000–40,000 years ago, when hominins equipped with fully-modern technologies dispersed out of Africa (see also Shea 2003, 2006a).[3] Finally, some scholars hypothesize that sets of technological innovations were brought about or in fact could not have occurred in the first place without innovations in the social structures of MSA hunter-gatherer groups. For example, Kuhn and Stiner (2006, with comments) suggested that a shift to gendered division of labor, as we know it today, is such a key social change. Gamble views the ability of humans to form social networks on a large geographical scale, a "release from proximity," as a hallmark of modern behavior and a social innovation that enabled the global colonization by humans during the Upper Paleolithic (Gamble 2007:38,, 211–214).

Models of revolutionary change do not fare well against the archaeological record of the Middle, Upper, and Middle-to-Upper Paleolithic in the Levant (Hovers 1997; Belfer-Cohen and Hovers, n.d.). Based on the evidence of lithics, pigment use, burials, or beads and ornaments, all of which figure prominently in defining behavioral modernity, the distinction between the two sides of the transition is fuzzy in many of these aspects.

Systematic blade production does not intrinsically imply a higher degree of planning, dexterity, or capacity for technological complexity, and is no longer perceived as a hallmark of cognitive, behavioral, or anatomical modernity (Bar-Yosef and Kuhn; Boëda 1990; Krin et al. 2008; Hayden 1993). As a rule, blade production technologies of the early Middle Paleolithic (summarized briefly in chapter 9) do not pattern temporally in a way that suggests a preordained evolutionary progression "toward" an Upper Paleolithic technology. Frequencies of blades in the late Levantine Middle Paleolithic decline compared to its earlier counterpart, and the trajectories of frequency shifts through the sequences of various sites are variable (Ashkenazi 2005; Hovers 1998a; Meignen 2000; Monigal 2002).

Still, the overall high level of technological variability in the Levant during the late Middle Paleolithic may have been conducive to (or even a sign of) higher levels of social acceptance of technological innovations (Hovers 1998a; Goren-Inbar and Belfer-Cohen 1998). Irrespective of whether one associates the occurrence of such innovations with autochthonous emergence or with exotic origins (through either demic migration or diffusion of concepts), such innovations did not replace existing Middle Paleolithic Levallois flaking concepts, but rather accrued as a series of small but significant shifts, culminating eventually in full-fledged Upper Paleolithic technology (Belfer-Cohen and Goring-Morris 2007). The recurrent occurrences of lithic practices during the Middle Paleolithic, coupled with the retention of technological traditions during the Initial Upper Paleolithic (IUP) make it difficult to trace diffusion routes or "phylogenetic" relationships between either MSA or Middle Paleolithic lithic industries and those of the Levantine Upper Paleolithic.

Another issue that figures prominently in discussions of the nature and origins of changes at the Middle-to-Upper Paleolithic transition is that of material manifestations related to symbol use. Irrespective of theoretical creeds, most paleoanthropologists accept these as a reliable mark of behavioral and cognitive modernity (Barham 2007). If shown to be non-utilitarian, burials, pigment use, and the use of beads, notwithstanding critiques of their value in assessing hypotheses about cognitive modernity (Wynn and Coolidge 2007), depict complex behaviors that required mental capacities for abstract thinking, synthesizing discrete phenomena into generalizations, and mental plasticity.

The Upper Paleolithic lithic industries of the Levant are seldom accompanied by the manifestations of material culture that are commonly cited as the markings of the modern mind. There is no evidence for mass production of mobile or parietal art. The contexts and frequencies of material manifestations of symbolic behavior in the Levantine Pleistocene record are almost reverse of expectations within a paradigm of a revolutionary transition to "modern behavior." Some of these manifestations are, in fact, archaeologically more visible in the Middle Paleolithic than on the IUP side of "the transition."

Eurasian Middle Paleolithic Neanderthals as well as *Homo sapiens* buried their dead intentionally, sometimes associated with grave goods (Bar-Yosef et al. 1992; Belfer-Cohen and Hovers 1992; Defleur 1993; Hovers et al. 1995; Hovers, Kimbel, and Rak 2000; Tillier 1990); such burials hence have a symbolic aspect. Relying on the criteria that are used for recognizing intentional burials in the Eurasian record (Belfer-Cohen and Hovers 1992), one would have to conclude that burials were not part of the MSA archaeological record. This confounds the question of the origins of this particular practice and the timing of its appearance. (The cut marks on the Herto skulls [Clark et al. 2003] may represent a different tradition of mortuary practices.) And yet, in the Levant burials are almost unknown in the earliest Upper Paleolithic contexts. The first known Upper Paleolithic (and indeed modern humans) burials from the Ahmarian level XII of Ksar Akil date from roughly 40,000–35,000 years ago (Bergman and Stringer 1989; Mellars and Tixier 1989), and are followed by the much younger specimens from the Upper Paleolithic (late Ahmarian) levels at Qafzeh (dated 31,000–27,000 years ago (Bar-Yosef and Belfer-Cohen 2004). From this time burials are unknown till the end of the Upper Paleolithic period at ca. 23,000 years cal BP (Nadel 2002).[4]

Based on ethnographic, experimental, and empirical evidence, ochre in the African MSA has been associated with hafting (Lombard 2007; Wadley 2005b, and references therein). Despite robust evidence for hafting techniques and materials in the Levantine Middle Paleolithic (Boëda, Connan, and Muhesen 1998b; Friedman et al. 1994–5), ochre in the Levant has not been implicated in such contexts. On the contrary, its sporadic occurrence in Qafzeh and its exclusive association with burials and hearths bears a strong symbolic signature. Conversely, elevated quantities of ochre in Upper Paleolithic sites in the Levant are found mainly in mundane contexts and are accompanied by a relative abundance of lithics smeared with ochre, presumably due to use in daily activities (Hovers et al. 2003 and references therein).

Shell beads are one facet of symbolic behavior the manifestations of which in the Levantine Upper Paleolithic are more robust and convincing than those seen in the Middle Paleolithic. Yet here too the change is of degree rather than kind. In both the Middle Paleolithic of the Levant and the MSA the sporadic shell beads (Bar-Yosef Mayer 2005; Bouzouggar et al. 2007; d'Errico et al. 2005; Taborin 2003; Vanhaeren et al. 2006) "indicate that the choice, transport, coloring, and long-term wearing of these items were part of a deliberate, shared, and transmitted non-utilitarian behavior" (Bouzouggar et al. 2007:9969). Thus, beginning at least 120,000 years ago, beads were used as a means of "information technology" (Kuhn and Stiner 2007 following Wobst 1977) on a Pan-Mediterranean, Pan-African scale.[5] When associated with diagnostic hominin remains, Middle Paleolithic shell beads are found with the remains of anatomically modern humans. Still, their numbers increase only marginally across the transition to the Levantine early Upper Paleolithic. Moreover, the later increase of shell bead numbers in Upper Paleolithic sites is gradual (Bar-Yosef Mayer 2005 and references therein) and does not bear the signature of a revolutionary change in the ways of information transmission.

Behaviors that are closely linked with the concept of modern cognitive abilities—a high degree of innovativeness, artistic expressions—occur in a piecemeal fashion in the Levant during and after the Upper Paleolithic as well. Lithic forms, mainly those of microliths, change through time from the early Epi-Paleolithic onward, presumably as adjustments to technological innovations associated with hafting procedures and as expressions of group-specific styles mediating the territorial packing of human groups (Goring-Morris and Belfer-Cohen 1997, 2003). On the other hand, the occurrence of art en masse is of a truly revolutionary nature in the Levantine record. Significantly, it occurs only at the beginning of the Natufian (at about 15, 000 years cal BP), in association with major changes in settlement patterns and subsistence strategies (specifically, the change from mobile hunter-gatherers to mainly sedentary cultivators).

The patterns on both sides of the Levantine Middle-Upper Paleolithic "divide" have some far-reaching implications. To begin with, the Middle Paleolithic record depicts sporadic, erratic occurrences of some modern behaviors that were not incremental "toward" an Upper Paleolithic way of life (Hovers 1997). Various facets of behavioral modernity seem to have been shared by

Neanderthals and Moderns in the Levant, while some were confined to only one of the two populations.

This in turn suggests that the cognitive mechanisms for information storage and processing that enabled modern behavior, e.g., "enhanced working memory" (Coolidge and Wynn 2005), likely emerged within populations that were ancestral to both Neanderthals and Moderns (Belfer-Cohen and Goren-Inbar 1994; Foley and Lahr 1997; Hayden 1993; Hovers 1997; Hovers et al. 1995).[6] Independently, it has been argued that the neural and cognitive faculties (namely, the capacity for information storage or for innovations) that were expressed in archaeologically visible behaviors may have been in place within the hominin line well before they appeared as a normative, standard behavior of human social entities (see Deacon 1989, 1997).[7]

The visibility of material manifestations of modern behaviors in the archaeological record is in itself an indication that those behaviors were assimilated into societal pools of information, where they were transformed into viable innovations that persisted long enough to become a component of the record (Hovers and Belfer-Cohen 2006). Thus, the visibility and frequencies of the so-called "modern" features in the archaeological record are not just a reflection of internal mental capacities, as those seem to have been part of the hominin cognitive make-up before the Middle Paleolithic. The crucial triggers of realizing latent societal capacities and knowledge involved particular external circumstances in each specific instance. The erratic "waning and waxing" of manifestations of behavioral modernity (symbol use, occasional technological innovations) in the Levantine Middle Paleolithic thus demand explanation of the mechanisms that "activated" latent abilities and retained the ensuing behaviors long enough to leave an archaeologically visible mark. A related question would be why these processes did not lead to persistence of the behaviors and their stabilization as a fixed feature of human societies.

In essence, these questions pertain to the stability of societal "proclivity to experiment with new ideas , techniques, devices, and strategies to make inventions into innovations" (Sundbo 1998:20) and systems of information storage and transmission. Once innovative behaviors emerge, their retention and transmission are dependent on cultural mechanisms of transmission (rites, myths, and symbols of social cohesion), the survival of which is related to both social and external conditions (Hovers and Belfer-Cohen 2006). The continuous transmission of knowledge requires a critical demographic threshold to be met and held (Shennan 2001). Indeed, in modern ethnographic contexts, there are intricate correlations between specific ecological constraints, demographic circumstances, and the complexity and diversity of symbolic systems that serve as information storage and transmission mechanisms

(Barham 2007:172). Ecological and social circumstances regulating population densities (e.g., in refugia areas or where large-scale aggregations were not a subsistence necessity, or in large-scale sedentary societies) appear to have had similar correlations with symbolic behaviors in antiquity at different times and in different regions (e.g., Belfer-Cohen 1988; Grosman 2004; Hovers 1990a; Jochim 1983; Keeley 1995). Long-term, continuous low population densities in a given region would have disrupted the networks of exchange and transmission (Barham 2007:172), leading to the disappearance from the archaeological record of evidence for the cultural mechanisms that "stored" innovations and regulated them, even if the occupation of the region was not physically discontinued.

Instability of demographic systems of small-scale groups in the Middle Paleolithic (chapter 9) and the Upper Paleolithic may explain the "non-modern" trajectories of much of the archaeological record of both periods in the Levant. Some of the archaeological expressions of modern behavior occur in the Middle Paleolithic and are discontinued in the Upper Paleolithic, while others occur for the first time only in the later Upper Paleolithic or even the late Epi-Paleolithic; some accepted manifestations of modernity, moreover, are never encountered in the Paleolithic regional record.

By and large, similar patterns can be observed in the regions of the Old World that are considered the powerhouse that generated "modernity," as well as in those deemed the recipients of the behavioral and social changes entailed by the concept. Fluctuations in the stability of demographic systems affected the ability of Middle (and in some places, Upper) Paleolithic human groups to store information over time. This scenario provides a parsimonious explanation for the diverse trajectories of emergence and disappearance of archaeological manifestations of modern behaviors in various regions of the Old World (James and Petraglia 2005; McBrearty and Brooks 2000). The take-home message from the Levantine Upper Pleistocene record is that, despite the continuous attempts of paleoanthropologists to define a single comprehensive package of sweeping traits that mark the emergence of behavioral modernity, it may not have existed as such. We may have been circling around a moving mark.

The Levantine Middle Paleolithic was a period of stasis, i.e., non-directional change. This is not to be confused with lack of dynamism. As a matter of fact, any of the models that one chooses to adopt as a framework for explaining the Levantine Middle Paleolithic presume dynamic changes and active adjustments to ecological and social constraints. Middle Paleolithic hominins in general were successful in surviving in taxing environments and persisted over a long period. In the Levant their challenges may have lain more in the realm of inter-population encounters than of environmental challenges. Either way,

the persistent existence of the Middle Paleolithic entity could not have taken place without the behavioral flexibility and dynamic responses of hominins to the particular challenges of their surroundings. These dynamics, too, often go unrecognized because they were not progressive in nature and did not necessarily evolve toward what eventually became the Upper Paleolithic (Hovers 1997, 2006; Hovers and Belfer-Cohen 2006).

Evolutionary thought provides a theoretical construct of fitness landscapes that may help us understand the combination of non-directional change and dynamic shifts. A "rugged fitness landscape" construct (Palmer 1991) recognizes the existence of variable peaks of sub-optimal fitness values, separated by troughs of low-fitness adaptive states. Populations are driven to fitness peaks that are higher relative to their peak of origin. The landscape can thus host several populations in sub-optimal conditions. Once they reach the closest peak, populations will not move easily, even if a new peak provides greater maximum fitness, because shifting between peaks necessarily involves a reduction in fitness. Harsh environmental or demographic conditions may disrupt the adaptive state and reduce fitness values, displacing a population from its current fitness peak and providing the opportunity for it to begin to scale a higher one that happens to be accessible. Middle Paleolithic groups, both globally and regionally, can be envisioned as occupying a fitness landscape of numerous, comparable fitness peaks. "If…we imagine a very rugged fitness landscape, with many peaks and troughs, then…Middle Paleolithic populations were in fact evolving behaviorally, their fitness was increasing locally, but they happened to be ascending a peak (or more likely several peaks) different from the one that anatomically modern Upper Paleolithic populations eventually climbed" (Kuhn 2006:118).

This work started out as a rather technical inquiry into the record of a single site, distinguished mainly by the fact that the authors of its lithic assemblages were early anatomically modern humans. However, "[n]o one historical trajectory contains enough information to obtain a very good grasp of the processes that affect its own evolution" (Boyd and Richerson 1992:180). The results of a technical study concerned with typo-technological variability required a wider view of the Middle Paleolithic and its place in Levantine prehistory. Thus, the discussion has moved from the record of a single site to a broader discussion of the relationship between technology and land use, to a series of inferences about the links between these realms of hominin life and social organization.

Science is an enterprise of multiple methodologies and paradigms. Evolutionary theory, which provides a wide umbrella for understanding hominin evolution, also yields some key concepts that emphasize the importance of historical approaches in the study of the past

(Boyd and Richerson 1992; Palmer 1991; Richerson and Boyd 2005). Looking at historical processes is not non-evolutionary or unscientific, and it does not necessarily result in "just-so stories" or irrefutable hypotheses. Ultimately, understanding the record of a region requires that one stoops from the heights of theory to look at the historical details. While this is a daunting task in the vast temporal and spatial dimensions of prehistory, it nonetheless has the advantage of making researchers focus on those aspects of the record that are not explicated by the generalities of overarching theory. As this study shows, there are quite a number of such "discrepancies" in the realm of Levantine Middle Paleolithic research. Such cases are not contrary to notions of fitness, adaptation, or evolutionary success. Rather, they require that we reconsider the meaning of these concepts in the context of studying cultural evolution.

It is entirely possible that the end of the Middle Paleolithic phenomenon was due to a set of technological innovations that emerged in a defined core area (Bar-Yosef 2002) where demographic conditions enabled their transformation from inventions to full-fledged, normative innovations, and from whence they diffused. These would have defined the new peaks of fitness values of modern humans. Yet even so, the processes that stabilized such technologies in the archaeological record are far from being unified or even similar. Between 45,000 to 30,000 years ago the Old World witnessed a myriad of "Upper Paleolithic[s]." Some are completely divorced from the material culture of the preceding Middle Paleolithic and may indeed reflect a revolutionary "overthrow" of Middle Paleolithic lifeways. In other cases, new technological practices incorporated local knowledge of the preceding Middle Paleolithic groups. The Levantine record exemplifies the latter process.

Understanding the Middle Paleolithic record is not simply an inquiry into the abilities of hominins "to ascend" to the Upper Paleolithic. At the end of the day, there was nothing preordained in the Upper Paleolithic. The spread and eventual persistence (i.e., evolutionary success) of modern human behavior was played out as a story of historical contingencies that shaped the many forms of things to come. This requires that we learn how hominins applied their abilities in their many local, particular physical and social environments of the Middle Paleolithic and how these circumstances shaped the trajectories of cultural evolution. Daunting as the task may seem, this historical perspective leads paleoanthropologists toward exciting research into the evolution of behavioral modernity.

# Appendix 1

## The History of Excavations in Middle Paleolithic Sites in the Levant: 1925–1999

| | Pre–World War II | | |
|---|---|---|---|
| Site | Excavators, years | Comments | Sources |
| Zuttiyeh Cave | Turville-Petre, 1925 | The work in the Wadi Amud marks the "official" beginning of systematic prehistoric research in the Levant, as well as onset of work on the Middle Paleolithic, since Turville-Petre identified in the lithic assemblages of Zuttiyeh the telltale signs of a Mousterian industry as he knew it from Europe. | Turville-Petre 1927 |
| Shukbah Cave | Garrod, 1928 | | Garrod and Bate 1942 |
| Abu Sif Cave | Neuville, 1928–1932 | | Neuville 1951 |
| Sahba | Neuville, 1928–1932 | | Neuville 1951 |
| Um-Naqos | Neuville, 1928–1932 | | Neuville 1951 |
| Tabban | Neuville, 1928–1932 | | Neuville 1951 |
| Tabun Cave | Garrod, 1929–1934 | Excavation of several areas in the cave's front chamber. Created a 20 m section by removal of large volume by arbitrary horizontal elevation, in spite of recognition of complex stratigraphic features. Recovery of Neanderthal skeleton from layer C (possibly B). | Garrod and Bate 1937 |
| Skhul Cave | Garrod, 1929–1934; McCown, 1933 | Mousterian industry with the remains of numerous human skeletons of modern humans, designated as "Neanderthal Palestinians." | Garrod and Bate 1937; McCown 1934; McCown and Keith 1939 |
| Kebara Cave | Turville-Petre, 1931 | | Turville-Petre 1932 |
| Qafzeh Cave | Neuville and Stekelis, 1933 | | Neuville 1951 |
| Ksar Akil | Murphy, Ewing | | Ewing 1947 |
| Yabrud | Rust | | Rust 1950 |

| | 1950s–1970s | | |
|---|---|---|---|
| *Cave Sites Revisited* | | | |
| Kebara Cave | Stekelis,1953–1957, 1964–1965; Bar-Yosef and Tchernov, 1968 | First excavation of the Mousterian layers of cave, known but practically untouched by Turville-Petre. Discovery of numerous hearths, rich lithic and faunal assemblages. Recovery of fragment of a baby's skeleton, defined as a Neanderthal. | See Bar-Yosef and Vandermeersch 2007 on history of research; Schick and Stekelis 1977 |

(continued)

**(continued)**

| | 1950s–1970s | | | |
|---|---|---|---|---|
| *Cave Sites Revisited* | | | | |
| Qafzeh Cave | Vandermeersch, 1966–1973 | Excavation in cave terrace and chamber according to stratigraphic inclinations. Total collection of faunal and lithic finds. Discovery of numerous skeletal remains of "proto Cro-Magnons." | | Bar-Yosef and Vandermeersch 1981; Vandermeersch 1981, and references therein; Vandermeersch 1982 |
| Tabun Cave | Jelinek, 1967–1971 | Excavation according to stratigraphic inclination. Total collection of faunal and lithic finds. Refinement of controversial stratigraphy. | | Jelinek 1975, 1982a, 1982b; Jelinek et al. 1973 |
| Zuttiyeh Cave | Gisis and Bar-Yosef, 1973 | Limited excavation in breccia to examine stratigraphic sequence; total collection. Support for Garrod's argument for presence of both (Lower, elongated) Mousterian and Acheulo-Yabrudian industries. Confirming association of "Galilee Man" skull with the latter. | | Gisis and Bar-Yosef 1974 |
| *New Cave Sites* | | | | |
| Jerf Ajla | Coon, 1955; Schroëder, early 1960s | First stratified Middle Paleolithic site excavated in the Syrian Desert. Coon's collection consists of selected pieces; piece plotting and complete collection during Schroëder's excavation. An Acheulo-Yabrudian-Mousterian sequence, with high (exceptional) Levallois indices in the latter assemblages. | | Schroëder 1969; Richter et al. 2001 |
| Bezez Cave (also Ras el-Kalb, Abri Zumoffen) | Garrod and Kirkbride 1958–1964 | Bezez Cave contained a long stratigraphic sequence, broadly similar to that of Tabun, dated by shoreline sequences. | | Copeland, 1983a; Saint-Mathurin, 1983 |
| Geula Cave | Wreschner, intermittently in 1958–1964 | Cave with Mousterian remains in the Mt. Carmel area. Total collection of all finds. Lower intensity of occupation and shorter stratigraphic sequence than previously known. | | Wreschner 1967 |
| Amud Cave | Suzuki, 1961 and 1964 | Known but previously unstudied cave in Nahal Amud. Rich lithic assemblage, argued to belong to a single, transitional MP–UP industry. Neanderthal skeleton and taxonomically unassigned human remains | | Suzuki and Takai 1970 |
| Shovakh Cave | S. Binford, 1962 | Known but previously unstudied cave in Nahal Amud. Total collection of all finds. Lithic assemblages used as a case study in support of the argument for functional patterning of Mousterian assemblages. | | Binford 1966; Binford and Binford 1966 |
| Sefunim Cave | Ronen, 1965–1970 | New cave with Mousterian remains in the Mt. Carmel area; total collection of a finds; lower intensity of occupation and shorter stratigraphic sequence than in previously known caves. | | Ronen 1984 |
| Hayonim Cave | Bar-Yosef and Tchernov, 1966 | Long cultural sequence including Middle Paleolithic deposits. Total collection of all finds. | | Arensburg et al. 1990; Bar-Yosef 1979; Stiner 2005 |
| Nahr Ibrahim | Solecki, 1969 | | | Solecki 1970 |
| Keoue Cave | Watanabe, 1970 | | | Nishiaki and Copeland 1992; Watanabe 1970b |
| Douara Cave | Suzuki, 1970; Hanihara, 1974; Akazawa, 1984 | In the Palmyra basin. A long sequence containing two Mousterian layers, partly replicating the stratigraphic sequence of lithic changes at Tabun. Discovery of large hearths and of some botanical remains. | | Akazawa 1988; Nishiaki 1989 |

(*continued*)

*Open-Air Sites*

| | | | |
|---|---|---|---|
| "Mousterian loam," Tirat Carmel | Ronen, 1965,1970 | Systematic collection, excavation. Establishing the existence and regional stratigraphy of open-air Mousterian sites in the coastal plain. | Ronen, 1974, 1977 |
| Naamé | Fleisch, 1966 | Open-air site on the Lebanese coast, situated between two radiometrically dated ancient beaches, and thus was used to estimate date of other assemblages containing similar industry. Industry of large oval flakes. | Fleisch 1970 |
| Negev regional project (Nahal Aqev, Rosh Ein Mor) | Marks, 1968–1975 | A regional approach, viewing sites as components in larger and more complex settlement systems. Open-air sites as the main focus of work. Survey and excavation of selected sites. Association of technological traits as adaptations to changing environmental conditions. | Crew 1976; Marks, 1976, 1977; Munday 1977 |
| Far'ah II | Gilead, 1976–1977 | Northern Negev. Total collection of all finds. Two "living floors," frequent refitting of lithic artifacts. | Gilead, 1980, 1988; Gilead and Grigson 1984 |
| Hummal I | Hours and Sanlaville, 1980 | El-Kowm, Syria. A test pit in a well. Open-air site in the inland zone of the Levant, revealing a long sequence of Acheulo-Yabrudian and a bladey industry similar to Judean Desert sites. | Copeland 1985; Hours 1982 |

1980s–1990s

| | | | |
|---|---|---|---|
| Tor Faraj | Henry, 1979–1984, 1993 | Rock shelter on Transjordanian Plateau. Excavated according to natural layers. Distinct "living floors" and evidence for spatial patterning. | Henry 1995c, 2003; Henry et al. 1996, 2004 |
| Tor Sabiha | Henry, 1979–1984 | Collapsed cave, Transjordanian Plateau. | Henry 1995c |
| Ain Difla | Clark, 1984, 1986, 1992 | Stratified Mousterian deposits in a rock shelter on the Transjordanian Plateau. | Clark et al. 1997 with references therein |
| Kebara Cave | Bar-Yosef, Vandermeersch et. al., 1982–1990 | Excavation according to natural inclinations of stratigraphic units. Recovery of Neanderthal skeleton featuring first fossil hyoid bone and relatively preserved pelvis. Rich lithic and faunal assemblages with spatially differentiated use of space. | Bar-Yosef and Meignen 2007; Bar-Yosef et al. 1992 |
| Amud Cave | Hovers, Rak and Kimbel, 1991–1994 | Enlarging previous excavation. Excavation according to natural inclinations. Total collection of all find classes. Recovery of burial of Neanderthal infant. | Hovers 2004b; Hovers, Rak, and Kimbel 1991; Rak, Kimbel, and Hovers 1994 |
| Dederiyeh Cave | Akazawa, 1991–present | Cave in northern Syria. Recovery of the first Neanderthal in the Northern Levant. | Akazawa and Muhesen 2002; Akazawa et al. 1993 |
| Quneitra | Goren-Inbar, 1982–1983, 1985 | Open-air site on the Golan Heights. Single-horizon occupation. First studied Middle Paleolithic site in basaltic environment in the Levant. | Goren-Inbar 1990b |
| Um e-Tlel | Boëda, 1990–present | Open-air site in the El-Kowm basin. Many Middle Paleolithic horizons. Exceptional preservation. | Boëda and Muhesen 1994; Boëda, Bourguignon and Griggo 1998; Boëda, Connan, and Muhesen 1998 |

# Appendix 2

## Attributes Used in Core Analysis

**I. Provenience**

  A. ID NUMBER OF ARTEFACT
  B. LAYER
  C. GRID
  D. ELEVATION BELOW DATUM

**II. Physical Characteristics**

  A. RAW MATERIAL: 1. flint 2. chert 3. limestone 4. basalt 5. other
  B. STATE OF PRESERVATION: 1. fresh 2. abraded 3. heavily abraded 4. brecciated
  C. PATINATION: 1. non-patinated 2. patinated 3. double-patinated
  D. COMPLETENESS OF BLANK: 1. complete 2. distally broken 3. laterally broken 4. proximally broken 5. lateral and distal break 6. proximal and distal break 7. fragment (no edge preserved) 8. lateral and proximal break 9. indeterminate (when heavily brecciated)
  E. EVIDENCE FOR FIRE: 1. not burnt 2. burnt

**III. Technological Attributes**

  A. METHOD OF FLAKING: 1. Levallois 2. discoidal 3. non-Levallois 4. indeterminate
  B. AMOUNT OF CORTEX ON FLAKING SURFACE (% of total surface area): 1. 0% 2. 1–25% 3. 26–50% 4. 51–75% 5. 76–100%
  C. AMOUNT OF CORTEX ON PREPARATION SURFACE (% of total surface area): 1. 0% 2. 1–25% 3. 26–50% 4. 51–75% 5. 76–100%
  D. NUMBER OF SCARS ON FLAKING SURFACE (ONLY SCARS THAT ARE 5 MM OR MORE IN ANY DIMENSION)
  E. SCAR PATTERN ON FLAKING SURFACE: 1. centripetal dominant 2. intermediate 3. horse shoe 4. Unipolar 5. parallel 6. convergent 7. opposed 8. centripetal 9. convergent and side 10. bipolar and side 11. unipolar and side 12. bipolar 13. convergent and opposed 14. parallel and side 15. unipolar and opposed
  F. SHAPE OF TRANSVERSAL SECTION: 1. flat 2. conical
  G. NUMBER OF STRIKING PLATFORMS
  H. NUMBER OF WORKED FACES (total of faces worked from all striking platforms)
  I. ANGLE BETWEEN STRIKING PLATFORM AND THE DOMINANT SCAR OF FLAKE REMOVED
  J. USE OF NAHR IBRAHIM TECHNIQUE (NIT) ON CORES-ON-FLAKES: 1. yes 2. no

**IV. Metric Measurements**

  A. LENGTH (in the axis of the dominant scar) in millimeters
  B. WIDTH (perpendicular to length) in millimeters
  C. THICKNESS (measured at the thickest point on core) in millimeters
  D. WEIGHT in grams to the nearest decimal point
  E. CIRCUMFERENCE OF CORE in millimeters
  F. LENGTH OF WORKED STRIKING PLATFORM in millimeters (total of all worked striking platform if more than one exists)
  G. STRIKING PLATFORM ANGLE: measured between flaking and preparation surfaces
  H. CORE CIRCUMFERENCE in millimeters (to one decimal point)

I. LENGTH OF DOMINANT SCAR
J. WIDTH OF DOMINANT SCAR (only complete dimensions of the dominant scar were recorded for these two attributes)
K. LENGTH OF LAST SCAR (if dominant scar is not last)
L. WIDTH OF LAST SCAR (if dominant scar is not last)

## V. Core Typology

64. LEVALLOIS FOR FLAKE
65. LEVALLOIS FOR POINTS
66. LEVALLOIS FOR BLADES
67. DISCOIDAL
68. PRISMATIC
69. PYRAMIDAL
70. GLOBULAR
71. AMORPHOUS
72. VARIA
73. ON-FLAKE

74. BROKEN (without any striking platform)

## VI. Stylistic Attributes

A. SHAPE OF STRIKING PLATFORM EDGE: 1. straight 2. convex 3. concave 4. convergent 5. wavy 6. denticulate 7. one tooth 8. indeterminate 9. convex-concave 10. partly broken (if more than one striking platform exists, only the shape of the one from which the dominant scar had been removed is described)

## VII. Core History

A. DOMINANT SCAR LAST TO BE REMOVED: 1. yes 2. no
B. TOOL EXISTING PRIOR TO CORE
C. TOOL CONTEMPORANEOUS OR ADDITIONAL TO CORE

# Appendix 3

## Attributes Used in the Analysis of Flakes and Flake Tools

### I. Provenience

A. ID NUMBER OF ARTEFACT
B. LAYER
C. GRID
D. ELEVATION BELOW DATUM

### II. Physical Characteristics

A. RAW MATERIAL: 1. flint 2. chert 3. limestone 4. basalt 5. other
B. STATE OF PRESERVATION: 1. fresh 2. abraded 3. heavily abraded
C. PATINATION: 1. non-patinated 2. patinated 3. double-patinated 4. calcified
D. COMPLETENESS OF BLANK: 1. complete 2. distally broken 3. laterally broken 4. proximally broken 5. lateral and distal break 6. proximal and distal break 7. fragment (no edge preserved) 8. lateral and proximal break 9. indeterminate
E. EVIDENCE FOR FIRE: 1. not burnt 2. burnt

### III. Technological Attributes

A. METHOD OF FLAKING: 1. Levallois 2. non-Levallois 3. indeterminate
B. AMOUNT OF CORTEX ON DORSAL FACE (% of total surface area): 1. 0% 2. 1–25% 3. 26–50% 4. 51–75% 5. 76–100%
C. NUMBER OF SCARS (ONLY SCARS THAT ARE 5 MM OR MORE IN ANY DIMENSION) ON DORSAL FACE

E. CURVATURE OF THE VENTRAL FACE: 1. straight 2. convex 3. concave 4. irregular 5. indeterminate
F. TYPE OF STRIKING PLATFORM: 1. indeterminate 2. punctiform 3. faceted 4. dihedral 5. chapeau de gendarme 6. cortical 7. plain 8. removed 9. missing 10. broken 11. crushed

### IV. Measurements

A. LENGTH IN FLAKING AXIS (from the striking platform to the distal end of the artifact) in millimeters
B. MAXIMUM LENGTH (along the longest axis) in millimeters
C. FLAKING WIDTH (perpendicular to flaking length) in millimeters
D. MAXIMUM WIDTH (perpendicular to maximum length) in millimeters (artifacts the maximum width or length of which did not exceed 20 mm were not analyzed)
E. THICKNESS (measured at the thickest point on flake except region of the bulb of percussion) in millimeters
G. STRIKING PLATFORM ANGLE: the angle formed between the platform surface and a line through the point of percussion to the base of the bulb (Dibble and Whittaker 1981:286, "interior angle"). The exterior angles (not given in this analysis) show better correlation with artifact's dimensions under experimental conditions, but the interior angle approximates the geometry of the removed flaked in relation to the core's surface.

H. STRIKING PLATFORM DEPTH in millimeters (to one decimal point). Maximum distance between ventral and dorsal faces, measured at the bulb of percussion to the ventral face.

I. STRIKING PLATFORM BREADTH in millimeters (to one decimal point). Distance between the two lateral edges measured at the striking platform.

## V. Typology

See Appendix 4

## VI. Stylistic Attributes

A. TYPE OF RETOUCH: 1. regular 2. scraper like 3. racloir like 4. notch and denticulate 5. indeterminate 6. irregular 7. Quina 8. demi-Quina 9. raclette 10. clactonian notch 11. burin blow 12. Nahr Ibrahim 13. abrupt 14. flat 15. mixed (of any variation) 16. signs of use 17. isolated removals

B. LOCATION OF RETOUCH (PLANAR VIEW): 1. distal 2. proximal 3. obliquely truncated 4. left edge 5. right edge 6. both edges 7. converging 8. distal and two edges 9. edge 13. proximal and left edge 14. indeterminate 15. proximal and distal 16. circular

C. RETOUCHED FACE : 1. dorsal 2. ventral 3. both 4. on edge

D. EDGE ANGLE (ANGLE OF RETOUCH)

E. SHAPE OF RETOUCHED EDGE: 1. straight 2. convex 3. concave 4. convergent 5. wavy 6. denticulate 7. one tooth 8. indeterminate 9. convex-concave 10. partly broken 11. straight-convex 12. straight-concave

# Appendix 4

## Notes on the Typological Classification
## of the Qafzeh Assemblages

Classification was carried out after Bordes (1961, 1972). Some modifications were made in order to record and quantify pertinent types not included in Bordes's type-list. Following Goren-Inbar (1990a), retouched flakes (type 106) were included as a separate type when bearing regular and continuous retouch measuring 1 cm or longer. Another category used here (use-signs, type 120) refers to blanks bearing irregular, often discontinuous use scars or retouch. Type 121 records artifacts with isolated removals. Those may appear on the ventral or dorsal face, in the latter case defined as a distinct retouch type only when the removals were clearly later than the flake production. When the number of such removals coming from one edge of the flake was ≥ 3, the item was considered as a core-on-flake. These three types were accorded specific typological status due to their relative abundance in the Qafzeh assemblages, and are presented in the detailed counts (appendix 5). However, when compiling the indices, typological groups and cumulative graphs, type 106 was included in the counts of type 62, while type 120 was not included in any formal analysis of the retouched tools. Type 121 was included in the real counts but not the restricted and reduced ones (table 6.1). This was done in order to comply with Bordes's method of analysis and presentation and to render the subject assemblages compatible with previously studied ones.

A typological code number was assigned also to non-retouched flakes (type 100) and blades (type 101) and to items of special technological interest (types 113–117) so that their frequencies could be documented.

Chips (flakes < 2 cm) and chunks (blocks with no evidence of being cores or of any flake characteristic) were given a typological number (102, 103 respectively), while type 113 relates to chips resulting from fire cracking. No analysis was conducted on pieces belonging to either one of the three latter types, except counting their absolute frequencies according to provenience in the excavation.

### Calculating Typological Indices and Characteristic Groups

The various indices and typological groups were calculated following Bordes's (1984) method.

*ILty (identical to Group I)* consists of the frequency of artifacts in types 1–4 among the total number of artifacts in the 63 types in the list (real counts). For the restricted counts, this index consists of the relative frequency of artifacts in type 4, out of all artifacts in typological categories excluding #1–3 and #45–50.

*IR (index racloirs)* reflects the relative frequencies of side-scrapers, types 9–29, among all the artifacts in the 63 typological categories; in the restricted counts, the frequency is calculated from all types excluding #1–3 and #45–50.

*IA$^u$ (Index of unifacial Acheulean) = Index of backed knives* depicts the relative frequencies of artifacts classified as types 36 and 37 among all the artifacts classified as types 1–63 (real count) or with the exclusion of types #1–3 and #45–50 (restricted count).

*Group II* is the Mousterian group. It is the relative frequency of all the artifacts in types 5–29 out of the total number of artifacts in 63 categories (real count) or out of all types excluding #1–3 and #45–50 (restricted count).

*Group III* is the Upper Paleolithic group. Its value depicts the relative frequency of all the artifacts in types 30–37 and 40 out of the total number of artifacts in 63 categories (real count) or out of all types excluding #1–3 and #45–50 (restricted count).

*Group IV*, the denticulate group, depicts the relative frequency of denticulates, type 43, out of the total number of artifacts in 63 categories (real count) or out of all types excluding #1–3 and #45–50 (restricted count).

*Group IVelargi* (enlarged) gives the relative frequencies of artifacts in types 42–43 and 54 (notches, denticulates, and end-notched pieces) out of all types excluding #1–3 and #45–50 (restricted count).

# Appendix 5

## Detailed Counts of Debitage and Tools

| | Type/layer | III | IV | V | VI | VII | VIIa | VIIb | VIII |
|---|---|---|---|---|---|---|---|---|---|
| **1** | Levallois flake | *10 (5.05)* | *12 (5.50)* | *48 (7.31)* | *28 (6.47)* | *43 (12.15)* | *55 (9.18)* | *43 (13.74)* | *15 (14.85)* |
| | Levallois blade | *5 (2.53)* | *7 (3.21)* | *16 (2.44)* | *12 (2.77)* | *4 (1.13)* | *15 (2.50)* | *4 (1.28)* | *4 (3.96)* |
| | | 15 (7.58) | 19 (8.71) | 64 (9.75) | 40 (9.24) | 47 (13.28) | 70 (11.69) | 47 (15.00) | 19 (18.81) |
| **2** | Atypical Levallois flake | *1 (0.51)* | — | *7 (1.07)* | *10 (2.31)* | *3 (0.85)* | *15 (2.50)* | *8 (2.56)* | *2 (1.98)* |
| 99* | CTE | — | — | — | *3 (0.69)* | *1 (0.28)* | *1 (0.17)* | *2 (0.64)* | — |
| 113* | éclat débordant | *2 (1.01)* | *2 (0.92)* | *7 (1.07)* | *2 (0.46)* | *6 (1.69)* | *5 (0.83)* | *6 (1.92)* | — |
| 114* | éclat outrépassé | — | *1 (0.46)* | — | — | *1 (0.28)* | — | — | — |
| 115* | combination of 113* and 114* | — | *1 (0.46)* | *1 (0.15)* | — | — | — | — | — |
| 116* | hinged flake | — | — | — | — | — | — | — | — |
| 117* | combination of 113* and 116* | — | — | — | — | *1 (0.28)* | — | — | — |
| | | 3 (1.52) | 4 (1.83) | 15 (2.29) | 15 (3.46) | 12 (3.39) | 21 (3.50) | 16 (5.11) | 2 (1.98) |
| **3** | Levallois point | 2 (1.01) | 3 (1.38) | 5 (0.76) | — | 1 (0.28) | 9 (1.50) | — | — |
| **4** | Retouched point | — | 1 (0.46) | 1 (0.15) | — | — | 1 (0.17) | — | — |
| **5** | Pseudo-Levallois flake | 2 (1.01) | 1 (0.46) | 1 (0.15) | — | — | 4 (0.67) | 1 (0.32) | 2 (1.98) |
| **6** | Mousterian point | — | — | — | — | — | — | — | 1 (0.99) |
| **7** | Elongated Mousterian point | — | — | — | — | — | — | — | — |
| **8** | Limace | — | — | — | — | — | — | — | — |
| **9** | Single straight side-scraper | — | — | 1 (0.15) | 2 (0.46) | 1 (.028) | 2 (0.33) | — | 1 (0.99) |
| **10** | Single convex side-scraper | — | 1 (0.46) | — | 4 (0.92) | 3 (0.85) | 5 (0.83) | 2 (0.64) | — |
| **11** | Single concave side-scraper | 1 (0.51) | — | — | 1 (0.23) | — | 2 (0.33) | — | 1 (0.99) |
| **12** | Double straight side-scraper | — | 1 (0.46) | — | — | — | — | — | — |
| **13** | Double straight-convex side-scraper | — | — | — | 1 (0.23) | — | 1 (0.17) | 1 (0.32) | — |

*Note*: Bordes's type numbers are shown in bold. See appendix 5 for explanation about other type numbers. Asterisks indicate categories of core management pieces that are grouped under type number 2. Frequencies shown in italics are for sub-categories grouped under type 1 and type 2, respectively. Totals of these categories are shown in regular font.

(continued)

| | Type/layer | III | IV | V | VI | VII | VIIa | VIIb | VIII |
|---|---|---|---|---|---|---|---|---|---|
| 14 | Double straight-concave side-scraper | — | — | — | — | — | — | — | — |
| 15 | Double convex side-scraper | — | — | — | — | — | — | — | — |
| 16 | Double concave side-scraper | — | — | — | — | — | — | — | — |
| 17 | Double concave-convex side-scraper | — | — | — | 1 (0.23) | — | — | — | — |
| 18 | Convergent straight scraper | — | — | 1 (0.15) | — | — | — | — | — |
| 19 | Convergent convex scraper | — | — | — | — | 1 (0.28) | — | — | — |
| 20 | Convergent concave | — | — | — | — | — | — | — | — |
| 21 | Déjeté (offset) scraper | — | 1 (0.46) | — | — | — | — | — | — |
| 22 | Straight transverse scraper | — | — | — | — | — | 1 (0.17) | — | — |
| 23 | Convex transverse scraper | — | — | 1 (0.15) | — | — | — | — | — |
| 24 | Concave transverse scraper | — | — | — | — | 1 (0.28) | — | — | — |
| 25 | Side scraper on ventral face | 1 (0.51) | — | — | 4 (0.92) | — | — | 1 (0.32) | 1 (0.99) |
| 26 | Abruptly retouched side-scraper | — | — | — | — | — | — | — | — |
| 27 | Side-scraper with thinned back | — | — | — | — | — | — | — | — |
| 28 | Side-scraper with bifacial retouch | — | — | — | — | — | — | — | — |
| 29 | Alternately retouched side-scraper | — | — | — | — | — | — | — | — |
| 30 | Typical end-scraper | — | — | — | — | — | — | — | — |
| 31 | Atypical end-scraper | — | — | 2 (0.30) | — | 1 (0.28) | 2 (0.33) | — | — |
| 32 | Typical burin | 1 (0.51) | — | — | 1 (0.23) | 1 (0.28) | 2 (0.33) | 5 (1.60) | 1 (0.99) |
| 33 | Atypical burin | — | — | 2 (0.30) | 1 (0.23) | 1 (0.28) | 1 (0.17) | 1 (0.32) | 1 (0.99) |
| 34 | Typical borers | — | 1 (0.46) | — | 1 (0.23) | — | 3 (0.50) | — | — |
| 35 | Atypical borers | — | — | — | 1 (0.23) | 1 (0.28) | — | — | 1 (0.99) |
| 36 | Typical backed knife | — | 1 (0.46) | — | — | — | — | — | — |
| 37 | Atypical backed knife | — | 1 (0.46) | — | — | — | — | 1 (0.32) | — |
| 38 | Naturally backed knife | 13 (6.57) | 6 (2.75) | 10 (1.52) | 7 (1.62) | 7 (1.98) | 30 (5.01) | 6 (1.92) | 1 (0.99) |
| 39 | Raclette | — | 1 (0.46) | — | 1 (0.23) | — | 1 (0.17) | 1 (0.32) | — |
| 40 | Truncated flakes and blades | 1 (0.51) | 1 (0.46) | 1 (0.15) | — | 2 (0.56) | 5 (0.83) | 5 (1.60) | 1 (0.99) |
| 41 | Mousterian tranchet | — | — | — | — | — | — | — | — |
| 42 | Notch | — | 4 (1.83) | 2 (0.30) | 6 (1.39) | 3 (0.85) | 3 (0.50) | 5 (1.60) | 1 (0.99) |
| 43 | Denticulate | 3 (1.52) | — | 1 (0.15) | 3 (0.69) | 5 (1.41) | 6 (1.00) | 4 (1.28) | 1 (0.99) |
| 44 | Alternately retouched beaks | — | — | — | — | — | — | — | — |

*(continued)*

**(continued)**

| | Type/layer | III | IV | V | VI | VII | VIIa | VIIb | VIII |
|---|---|---|---|---|---|---|---|---|---|
| 45 | Retouch on ventral face | — | — | 1 (0.45) | — | 1 (0.28) | 2 (0.33) | 1 (0.32) | 2 (1.98) |
| 46–47 | Abrupt and alternate retouch (thick) | — | — | — | — | — | — | — | — |
| 48–49 | Abrupt and alternate retouch (thin) | — | — | — | — | — | — | — | — |
| 50 | Bifacial retouch | — | — | — | — | — | — | — | — |
| 51 | Tayac points | — | — | — | — | — | — | — | — |
| 52 | Notched triangles | — | — | — | — | — | — | — | — |
| 53 | Pseudo-microburins | — | — | — | — | — | — | — | — |
| 54 | End-notched pieces | — | — | — | — | — | 3 (0.50) | — | — |
| 55 | Hachoir | — | — | — | — | — | — | — | — |
| 56 | Rabot | — | — | — | — | — | — | — | — |
| 57 | Tanged points | — | — | — | — | — | — | — | — |
| 58 | Tanged tools | — | — | — | — | — | — | — | — |
| 59 | Choppers | — | — | — | — | — | — | — | — |
| 60 | Inverse choppers | — | — | — | — | — | — | — | — |
| 61 | Chopping tools | — | — | — | — | — | — | — | — |
| 62 | Miscellaneous | 1 (0.51) | — | — | — | 3 (0.85) | 1 (0.17) | — | — |
| 63 | Bifacial leaf-shaped points | — | — | — | — | — | — | — | — |
| 106 | Retouched flake | — | — | 1 (0.15) | 3 (0.69) | 7 (1.98) | 8 (1.34) | 8 (2.56) | — |
| 120 | Flake with use-signs | 2 (1.01) | 1 (0.46) | 7 (1.07) | 11 (2.54) | 3 (0.85) | 2 (0.33) | 5 (1.60) | 3 (2.97) |
| 121 | Flake with isolated removals | 1 (0.51) | 1 (0.46) | 1 (0.15) | 5 (1.15) | 5 (1.41) | 3 (0.50) | 3 (0.96) | 3 (2.97) |
| 99 | Non-Levallois CTE | 1 (0.51) | 1 (0.46) | 8 (1.22) | 5 (1.15) | 5 (1.41) | 12 (2.00) | 6 (1.92) | 3 (2.97) |
| 100 | Non-Levallois flakes | 118 (59.60) | 134 (61.47) | 403 (61.37) | 251 (57.97) | 201 (56.78) | 321 (53.59) | 162 (51.76) | 46 (45.54) |
| 101 | Non-Levallois blades | 29 (14.65) | 31 (14.22) | 116 (17.65) | 54 (12.47) | 25 (9.60) | 63 (10.52) | 21 (6.71) | 7 (6.93) |
| 105 | Kombewa flake | — | — | 3 (0.46) | 1 (0.23) | 5 (1.41) | 8 (1.34) | 5 (1.60) | 2 (1.98) |
| 108 | Burin spall | 1 (0.51) | — | — | 1 (0.23) | — | — | — | — |
| 113 | Non-Levallois éclat débordant | 1 (0.51) | 1 (0.46) | 2 (0.30) | 1 (0.23) | 6 (1.69) | 6 (1.00) | 4 (1.28) | — |
| 114 | Non-Levallois éclat outrépassé | — | 1 (0.46) | — | — | 2 (0.56) | — | — | — |
| 115 | Non-Levallois combination of 113 and 114 | — | — | — | — | — | 1 (0.17) | — | — |
| 116 | Non-Levallois hinged flake | 2 (1.01) | 2 (0.92) | 7 (1.07) | 11 (2.54) | 4 (1.13) | 5 (0.83) | 2 (0.64) | — |
| 117 | Non-Levallois combination of 113 and 116 | — | — | — | — | — | — | — | — |
| 119 | Thinned flake | — | — | — | — | — | — | — | — |
| **Total** | | 198 (100.00) | 218 (100.00) | 657 (100.00) | 433 (100.00) | 354 (100.00) | 599 (100.00) | 313 (100.00) | 101 (100.00) |

| | Type/layer | IX | X | XI | XII | XIII | XIV | XV | XVa |
|---|---|---|---|---|---|---|---|---|---|
| 1 | Levallois flake | 176 (15.67) | 106 (17.49) | 124 (14.65) | 67 (13.45) | 241 (10.74) | 68 (13.93) | 723 (11.83) | 153 (9.55) |
| | Levallois blade | 22 (1.95) | 20 (3.30) | 20 (2.36) | 13 (2.61) | 58 (2.58) | 17 (3.43) | 223 (3.65) | 36 (2.24) |
| | | 198 (17.63) | 126 (20.76) | 144 (17.02) | 80 (16.06) | 299 (13.33) | 85 (17.17) | 950 (15.50) | 189 (11.79) |
| 2 | Atypical Levallois flake | 26 (2.31) | 13 (2.14) | 24 (2.83) | 16 (3.21) | 54 (2.41) | 17 (3.43) | 229 (3.75) | 24 (1.50) |
| 99* | CTE | 7 (0.63) | 5 (0.83) | — | 9 (1.80) | 7 (0.31) | 3 (0.80) | 9 (0.14) | 1 (0.62) |
| 113* | éclat débordant | 24 (2.13) | 16 (2.64) | 15 (1.77) | 7 (1.41) | 30 (1.34) | 7 (1.41) | 59 (0.97) | 23 (1.43) |

(continued)

**(continued)**

| | Type/layer | IX | X | XI | XII | XIII | XIV | XV | XVa |
|---|---|---|---|---|---|---|---|---|---|
| 114* | éclat outrépassé | 4 (0.35) | 2 (0.33) | 3 (0.35) | 2 ((0.40) | — | — | 8 (0.13) | 3 (0.19) |
| 115* | combination of 113* and 114* | — | 1 (0.17) | 1 (0.12) | — | — | — | — | 1 (0.06) |
| 116* | hinged flake | 1 (0.09) | 1 (0.17) | — | 6 (1.20) | 6 (0.27) | 2 (0.40) | 5 (0.81) | 1 (0.06) |
| 117* | combination of 113* and 116* | — | — | — | — | — | — | — | 1 (0.06) |
| | | 62 (5.34) | 38 (6.27) | 43 (5.08 | 40 (8.03) | 97 (4.32) | 29 (5.86) | 310 (5.10) | 54 (0.88) |
| 3 | Levallois point | 4 (0.35) | 6 (0.99) | 2 (0.24) | 2 (0.40) | 7 (0.31) | 10 (2.02) | 167 (2.73) | 4 (0.25) |
| 4 | Retouched point | 1 (0.09) | — | — | — | 1 (0.04) | 1 (0.20) | 4 (0.65) | — |
| 5 | Pseudo-Levallois flake | 2 (0.18) | 1 (0.17) | — | — | 3 ((0.13) | 1 (0.20) | 10 (0.16) | 3 (0.19) |
| 6 | Mousterian point | — | — | — | — | — | — | — | — |
| 7 | Elongated Mousterian point | — | — | — | — | — | — | — | — |
| 8 | Limace | — | — | — | — | — | — | — | — |
| 9 | Single straight side-scraper | 3 (0.26) | 2 (0.33) | 4 (0.47) | 1 (0.20) | 23 (1.03) | — | 7 (0.12) | 1 (0.06) |
| 10 | Single convex side-scraper | 11 (0.97) | 9 (1.49) | 11 (1.30) | 13 (2.61) | 34 (1.51) | — | 18 (0.30) | 6 (0.37) |
| 11 | Single concave side-scraper | 4 (0.35) | — | — | — | 8 (0.36) | — | — | 1 (0.06) |
| 12 | Double straight side-scraper | — | — | — | — | — | — | — | — |
| 13 | Double straight-convex side-scraper | — | 2 (0.33) | — | — | 5 (0.22) | — | 1 (0.02) | — |
| 14 | Double straight-concave side-scraper | — | — | 1 (0.12) | — | — | — | — | — |
| 15 | Double convex side-scraper | 1 (0.09) | — | 2 (0.24) | — | 2 (0.9) | — | 2 (0.03) | — |
| 16 | Double concave side-scraper | — | — | — | — | — | — | — | — |
| 17 | Double concave-convex side-scraper | 1 (0.09) | — | 1 (012) | — | 1 (0.04) | — | — | — |
| 18 | Convergent straight scraper | — | — | — | — | — | — | — | — |
| 19 | Convergent convex scraper | 1 (0.09) | 2 (0.33) | — | — | 2 (0.9) | — | — | — |
| 20 | Convergent concave | — | — | — | — | — | — | — | — |
| 21 | Déjeté (offset) scraper | — | 1 (0.17) | 3 (0.35) | 2 (0.40) | 2 (0.9) | — | 1 (0.02) | — |
| 22 | Straight transverse scraper | 1 (0.09) | — | — | — | — | — | — | — |
| 23 | Convex transverse scraper | — | — | — | — | — | — | — | — |
| 24 | Concave transverse scraper | — | 1 (0.17) | — | — | — | — | — | — |
| 25 | Side-scraper on ventral face | 7 (0.62) | — | 4 (0.47) | 5 (1.00) | 5 (0.22) | 1 (0.20) | 12 (0.12) | 2 (0.12) |
| 26 | Abruptly retouched side-scraper | — | — | — | — | — | 1 (0.20) | 1 (0.02) | — |

(continued)

**(continued)**

| | Type/layer | IX | X | XI | XII | XIII | XIV | XV | XVa |
|---|---|---|---|---|---|---|---|---|---|
| 27 | Side-scraper with thinned back | — | — | — | — | — | — | — | — |
| 28 | Side-scraper with bifacial retouch | — | — | 1 (012) | — | — | 1 (0.20) | 1 (0.02) | 2 (0.12) |
| 29 | Alternately retouched side-scraper | — | — | 1 (0.12) | 0 | 3 (0.13) | — | 2 (0.03) | — |
| 30 | Typical end-scraper | 2 (0.18) | 1 (0.17) | 2 (0.24) | 3 (0.60) | 2 (0.9) | 1 (0.20) | 2 (0.03) | 2 (0.12) |
| 31 | Atypical end-scraper | 3 (0.27) | — | — | 2 (0.40) | 2 (0.9) | 5 (1.01) | 11 (0.18) | 2 (0.12) |
| 32 | Typical burin | 5 (0.44) | 2 (0.33) | 1 (0.12) | 7 (1.40) | 2 (0.9) | 6 (1.21) | 17 (0.28) | 3 (0.19) |
| 33 | Atypical burin | 1 (0.09) | — | 3 (0.35) | 1 (0.20) | 6 (0.27) | 3 (0.60) | 16 (0.26) | 2 (0.12) |
| 34 | Typical borers | — | 1 (0.17) | — | 1 (0.20) | 1 (0.04) | — | 1 (0.02) | 2 (0.12) |
| 35 | Atypical borers | 1 (0.09) | 3 (0.50) | — | — | 2 (0.9) | — | 8( 0.13) | 4 (0.25) |
| 36 | Typical backed knife | — | — | — | — | — | — | 1 (0.02) | — |
| 37 | Atypical backed knife | — | — | — | 1 (0.20) | — | — | 3 (0.50) | — |
| 38 | Naturally backed knife | 25 (2.26) | 10 (1.65) | 26 (3.07) | 9 (1.80) | 56 (2.50) | 7 (1.41) | 228 (3.73) | 43 (2.68) |
| 39 | Raclette | 1 (0.09) | — | 2 (0.24) | — | 7 (0.31) | 3 (0.60) | 2 (0.03) | 1 (0.06) |
| 40 | Truncated flakes and blades | 6 (0.53) | 3 (0.50) | 7 (0.83) | 6 (1.20) | 8 (0.36) | 4 (0.81) | 37 (0.6) | 7 (0.44) |
| 41 | Mousterian tranchet | — | — | — | — | — | — | — | — |
| 42 | Notch | 6 (0.53) | 8 (1.32) | 8 (0.95) | 4 (0.80) | 36 (1.60) | 19 (3.83) | 47 (0.77) | 11 (0.69) |
| 43 | Denticulate | 12 (1.06) | 4 (0.66) | 8 (0.95) | 10 (2.00) | 29 (1.29) | 15 (3.03) | 31 (0.51) | 6 (0.37) |
| 44 | Alternately retouched beaks | 1 (0.09) | — | — | — | — | — | 10 (0.16) | — |
| 45 | Retouch on ventral face | 3 (0.27) | 2 (0.33) | 3 (0.35) | 4 (0.80) | 7 (0.31) | 1 (0.20) | 19 (0.31) | 1 (0.06) |
| 46–47 | Abrupt and alternate retouch (thick) | — | — | — | — | — | — | — | — |
| 48–49 | Abrupt and alternate retouch (thin) | — | 1 (0.17) | — | — | — | — | — | — |
| 50 | Bifacial retouch | — | — | — | — | 2 (0.9) | — | — | — |
| 51 | Tayac point | — | — | — | — | — | — | — | — |
| 52 | Notched triangle | — | — | — | — | — | — | — | — |
| 53 | Pseudo-microburin | — | — | — | — | — | — | — | — |
| 54 | End-notched piece | 4 (0.35) | 2 (0.33) | 1 (0.12) | 1 (.20) | 4 (0.18) | 3 (0.60) | 7 (0.12) | 1 (0.06) |
| 55 | Hachoir | — | — | — | — | — | — | — | — |
| 56 | Rabot | — | — | — | — | — | — | — | — |
| 57 | Tanged points | — | — | — | — | — | — | — | — |
| 58 | Tanged tools | — | — | — | — | — | — | — | — |
| 59 | Choppers | — | — | — | — | — | — | — | — |
| 60 | Inverse choppers | — | — | — | — | — | — | — | — |
| 61 | Chopping tools | — | — | — | — | — | — | — | — |
| 62 | Miscellaneous | 7 (0.62) | 4 (0.66) | 4 (0.47) | 5 (0.60) | 12 (0.53) | 9 (1.82) | 51 (0.84) | 3 (0.19) |
| 63 | Bifacial leaf-shaped points | — | — | — | — | — | — | — | — |
| 106 | Retouched flake | 12 (1.06) | 13 (2.15) | 9 (1.06) | 22 (4.41) | 26 (1.16) | 11 (2.22) | 30 (0.49) | 9 (0.56) |
| 120 | Flake with use-signs | 21 (1.86) | 7 (1.16) | 19 (2.24) | 18 (3.61) | 133 (5.92) | 24 (4.84) | 72 (1.18) | 16 (1.00) |
| 121 | Flake with isolated removals | | 2 (0.33) | 9 (1.06) | 6 (1.20) | 45 (2.00) | 16 (3.23) | 54 (0.88) | 5 (0.31) |
| 99 | Non-Levallois CTE | 23 (2.04) | 13 (2.15) | 11 (1.30) | 11 (2.20) | 30 (1.33) | 18 (3.63) | 62 (91.01) | 18 (1.12) |
| 100 | Non-Levallois flake | 597 (53.16) | 301 (49.67) | 452 (53.42) | 192 (38.55) | 1,083 (48.28) | 165 (33.33) | 3,098 (50.71) | 987 (61.61) |
| 101 | Non-Levallois blade | 67 (5.96) | 29 (4.79) | 32 (3.78) | 39 (7.83) | 118 (5.26) | 31 (6.26) | 684 (911.19) | 175 (10.92) |
| 105 | Kombewa flake | 15 (1.33) | 3 (0.50) | 2 (0.24) | 1 (0.20) | 11 (0.49) | 2 (0.40) | 28 (0.46) | 11 (0.67) |

*(continued)*

**(continued)**

|  | Type/layer | IX | X | XI | XII | XIII | XIV | XV | XVa |
|---|---|---|---|---|---|---|---|---|---|
| 108 | Burin spall | — | — | — | — | — | 1 (0.20) | 7 (0.12) | — |
| 113 | Non-Levallois éclat débordant | 2 (0.18) | 4 (0.66) | 19 (2.24) | 10 (2.00) | 75 (3.34) | 9 (1.82) | 49 (0.80) | 15 (0.94) |
| 114 | Non-Levallois éclat outrépassé | — | — | 2 (0.24 | 1 (0.20) | 1 (0.04) | 3 (0.40) | 2 (0.03) | 2 (0.12) |
| 115 | Non-Levallois combination of 113 and 114 | — | — | — | — | — | 1 (0.60) | 2 (0.03) | — |
| 116 | Non-Levallois hinged flake | 1 (0.09) | 1 (0.17) | 8 (0.95) | 3 (0.60) | 41 (1.82) | 5 (1.01) | 48 (0.79) | 13 (0.81) |
| 117 | Non-Levallois combination of 113 and 116 |  | — | 1 (0.12) | — | 5 (0.22) | 1 (0.20) | — | 1 (0.06) |
| 119 | Thinned flake | — | — | — | — | 9 (0.40) | 3 (0.60) | — | — |
| **Total** |  | 1,123 (100.0) | 606 (100.0) | 846 (100.0) | 498 | 2,243 (100.0) | 495 (100.0) | 6,109 (100.0) | 1,602 (100.0) |

|  | Type/layer | XVb | XVf | XVII | XVIIa | XVIII | XVIIIa | XIX | XX |
|---|---|---|---|---|---|---|---|---|---|
| 1 | Levallois flake | 29 (9.32) | 170 (10.81) | 166 (19.14) | 5 (13.15) | 3 (7.14) | 8 (13.12) | 115 (22.33) | 9 (32.14) |
|  | Levallois blade | 8 (2.57) | 30 (1.91) | 52 (5.98) | — | 2 (4.76) | 1 (1.64) | 9 (1.74) | — |
|  |  | 37 (11.82) | 200 (12,72) | 188 (21.68) | 5 (13.15) | 5 (11.90) | 9 (14.75) | 124 (24.08) | 9 (32.14) |
| 2 | Atypical Levallois flake | 8 (2.57) | 32 (2.04) | 32 (3.69) | — | 3 (7.14) | 4 (6.56) | 24 (4.66) | 3 (10.71) |
| 99* | CTE | 1 (0.32) | 6 (0.38) | 13 (1.50) | 1 (2.83) | 1 (2.38) | 1 (1.64) | 16 (3.11) | — |
| 113* | éclat débordant | 12 (3.83) | 18 (1.15 | 8 (0.0.92) | — | — | — | 2 (0.39) | — |
| 114* | éclat outrépassé | 1 (0.32) | 7 (0.45) | 7 (0.81) | — | — | — | — | — |
| 115* | combination of 113* and 114* | — | 2 (0.13) | 1 (0.11) | — | — | — | 1 (0.19) | — |
| 116* | hinged flake | 0 | — | 4 (0.46) | — | — | — | 3 (0.58) | — |
| 117* | combination of 113* and 116* | — | — | 1 (0.12) | — | — | — | 1 (0.19) | — |
|  |  | 22 (7.02) | 65 (4.13) | 66 (7.61) |  | 4 (9.52) | 5 (8.20) | 47 (9.12) | 3 (10.71) |
| 3 | Levallois point | 1 (0.32) | 3 (0.19) | 5 (0.58) | — | 1 (2.38) | — | 1 (0.19) | — |
| 4 | Retouched point | — | 1 (0.06) | — | — | — | — | — | — |
| 5 | Pseudo-Levallois flake | — | 6 (0.38) | 2 (0.23) | — | — | — | 1 (0.19) | — |
| 6 | Mousterian point | — | — | — | — | — | — | — | — |
| 7 | Elongated Mousterian point | — | — | — | — | — | — | — | — |
| 8 | Limace | — | — | — | — | — | — | — | — |
| 9 | Single straight side-scraper | 1 (0.32) | — | 3 (0.35) | — | — | — | — | — |
| 10 | Single convex side-scraper | — | — | 7 (0.81) | — | — | 1 (1.64) | 3 (0.58) | — |
| 11 | Single concave side-scraper | — | — | 2 (0.23) | — | — | — | 2 (0.39) | — |
| 12 | Double straight side-scraper | — | — | — | — | — | — | — | — |
| 13 | Double straight-convex side-scraper | — | — | — | — | — | — | — | — |
| 14 | Double straight-concave side-scraper | — | — | — | — | — | — | — | — |

(continued)

**(continued)**

| | Type/layer | XVb | XVf | XVII | XVIIa | XVIII | XVIIIa | XIX | XX |
|---|---|---|---|---|---|---|---|---|---|
| 15 | Double convex side-scraper | — | — | 1 (0.12) | — | — | — | — | — |
| 16 | Double concave side-scraper | — | — | — | — | 1 (2.38) | — | — | — |
| 17 | Double concave-convex side-scraper | — | — | — | — | — | — | — | — |
| 18 | Convergent straight scraper | — | — | — | — | — | — | — | — |
| 19 | Convergent convex scraper | — | — | — | — | — | — | — | — |
| 20 | Convergent concave | — | — | — | — | — | — | 1 (0.19) | — |
| 21 | Déjeté (offset) scraper | — | — | 3 (0.35) | — | — | — | — | — |
| 22 | Straight transverse scraper | — | — | — | — | — | 1 (1.64) | — | — |
| 23 | Convex transverse scraper | — | — | 1 (0.12) | — | 1 (2.38) | — | 1 (0.19) | — |
| 24 | Concave transverse scraper | — | — | — | — | — | — | — | — |
| 25 | Side-scraper on ventral face | — | 1 (0.06) | 2 (0.23) | — | — | 1 (1.64) | 2 (0.39) | — |
| 26 | Abruptly retouched side-scraper | — | — | 1 (0.12) | — | — | — | — | — |
| 27 | Side-scraper with thinned back | — | — | — | — | — | — | — | — |
| 28 | Side-scraper with bifacial retouch | — | — | — | — | — | — | — | — |
| 29 | Alternately retouched side-scraper | — | 1 (0.06) | — | — | — | — | — | — |
| 30 | Typical end-scraper | — | — | 10 (1.15) | — | — | 1 (1.64) | 2 (0.39) | — |
| 31 | Atypical end-scraper | — | 2 (0.13) | 3 (0.35) | — | — | 3 (4.92) | 7 (1.36) | — |
| 32 | Typical burin | 1 (0.32) | 2 (0.13) | 1 (0.12) | — | — | — | 3 (0.58) | — |
| 33 | Atypical burin | — | 2 (0.13) | 5 (0.58) | — | — | — | 3 (0.58) | — |
| 34 | Typical borers | — | 1 (0.06) | 3 (0.35) | — | — | — | — | — |
| 35 | Atypical borers | — | — | 3 (0.35) | — | — | 1 (1.64) | 1 (0.19) | — |
| 36 | Typical backed knife | — | — | — | — | — | — | — | — |
| 37 | Atypical backed knife | — | — | — | — | — | — | — | — |
| 38 | Naturally backed knife | 16 (5.14) | 50 (3.18) | 11 (1.27) | 1 (2.83) | 1 (2.38) | — | 5 (0.97) | 1 (3.57) |
| 39 | Raclette | — | — | 2 (0.23) | — | — | 1 (1.64) | 1 (0.19) | — |
| 40 | Truncated flakes and blade | — | 2 (0.13) | 2 (0.23) | — | — | — | — | — |
| 41 | Mousterian tranchet | — | — | — | — | — | — | — | — |
| 42 | Notch | 1 (0.32) | 8 (0.51) | 19 (2.19) | — | — | 2 (3.28) | 12 (2.33) | — |
| 43 | Denticulate | 2 (0.64) | 1 (0.06) | 19 (2.19) | 1 (2.83) | 2 (4.76) | 1 (1.64) | 11 (2.36) | — |
| 44 | Alternately retouched beak | — | — | — | — | — | — | — | — |
| 45 | Retouch on ventral face | — | 2 (0.13) | 1 (0.12) | — | — | 1 (1.64) | — | — |
| 46–47 | Abrupt and alternate retouch (thick) | — | — | — | — | — | — | — | — |

(*continued*)

**(continued)**

| | Type/layer | XVb | XVf | XVII | XVIIa | XVIII | XVIIIa | XIX | XX |
|---|---|---|---|---|---|---|---|---|---|
| 48–49 | Abrupt and alternate retouch (thin) | — | — | — | — | — | — | — | — |
| 50 | Bifacial retouch | — | — | — | — | — | — | — | — |
| 51 | Tayac point | — | — | — | — | — | — | — | — |
| 52 | Notched triangle | — | — | — | — | — | — | — | — |
| 53 | Pseudo-microburin | — | — | — | — | — | — | — | — |
| 54 | End-notched piece | — | — | 1 (0.12) | — | — | — | — | — |
| 55 | Hachoir | — | — | — | — | — | — | — | — |
| 56 | Rabot | — | — | — | — | — | — | — | — |
| 57 | Tanged point | — | — | — | — | — | — | — | — |
| 58 | Tanged tool | — | — | — | — | — | — | — | — |
| 59 | Choppers | | — | — | — | — | — | — | — |
| 60 | Inverse chopper | — | — | — | — | — | — | — | — |
| 61 | Chopping tool | — | — | — | — | — | — | — | — |
| 62 | Miscellaneous | 2 (0.64) | — | 3 (0.35) | — | — | — | — | — |
| 63 | Bifacial leaf-shaped point | — | — | — | — | — | — | — | — |
| 106 | Retouched flake | 3 (0.96) | 8 (0.51) | 17 (1.96) | 1 (2.83) | 2 (4.76) | 1 (1.64) | 6 (1.17) | 1 (3.57) |
| 120 | Flake with use-signs | 3 (0.96) | 9 (0.57) | 35 (4.03) | — | — | — | 1 (0.19) | — |
| 121 | Flake with isolated removals | — | 5 (0.32) | 14 (1.61) | — | — | — | — | — |
| 99 | Non-Levallois CT | 3 (0.96) | 23 (1.46) | 35 (4.03) | 1 (2.83) | 6 (14.29) | 3 (4.92) | 20 (3.88) | 1 (3.57) |
| 100 | Non-Levallois flake | 183 (58.84) | 948 (60.31) | 314 (36.22) | 23 (60.52) | 16 (38.10) | 23 (37.71) | 198 (38.44) | 12 (42.86) |
| 101 | Non-Levallois blade | 28 (8.95) | 188 (11.95) | 33 (3.81) | 3 (7.90) | 2 (4.76) | 4 (6.56) | 30 (582) | — |
| 105 | Kombewa flake | 3 (0.96) | 7 (0.45) | 1 (0.12) | — | — | — | 7 (1.36) | 1 (3.57) |
| 108 | Burin spall | — | 1 (0.06) | — | — | — | 1 (1.64) | 3 (0.58) | — |
| 113 | Non-Levallois éclat débordant | 2 (0.64) | 8 (0.51) | 4 (0.46) | — | — | — | 9 (1.75) | — |
| 114 | Non-Levallois éclat outrépassé | — | 3 (0.19) | 3 (0.35) | — | — | 1 (1.64) | — | — |
| 115 | Non-Levallois combination of 113 and 114 | — | 1 (0.06) | 1 (0.12) | — | — | — | — | — |
| 116 | Non-Levallois hinged flake | 3 | 24 (1.53) | 11 (1.27) | 2 (5.26) | 1 (2.38) | 1 (1.64) | 11 (2.36) | — |
| 117 | Non-Levallois combination of 113 and 116 | — | — | 1 (0.12) | — | — | — | 1 (0.19) | — |
| 119 | Thinned flake | — | — | 5 (0.58) | — | — | — | 2 (0.39) | — |
| **Total** | | 311 (100.0) | 1,572 (100.0) | 867 (100.0) | 38 (100.0) | 42 (100.0) | 61 (100.0) | 515 (100.0) | 28 (100.0) |

| | Type/layer | XXI | XXII | XXIII | XXIV |
|---|---|---|---|---|---|
| 1 | Levallois flake | 77 (24.91) | 35 (19.23) | 3 (25.00) | 21 (30.44) |
| | Levallois blade | 11 (3.56) | 6 (3.30) | — | 2 (2.90) |
| | | 88 (28.47) | 41 (22.52) | 3 (25.00) | 23 (33.33) |
| 2 | Atypical Levallois flake | 10 (3.23) | 5 (2.75) | 2 (16.67) | — |
| 99* | CTE | 5 (1.62) | 1 (0.55) | — | 1 (1.45) |
| 113* | éclat débordant | 1 (0.32) | 1 (0.55) | — | — |
| 114* | éclat outrépassé | 1 (0.32) | 1 (0.55) | — | — |
| 115* | combination of 113* and 114* | — | — | — | — |
| 116* | hinged flake | — | — | — | — |

(continued)

**(continued)**

| | Type/layer | XXI | XXII | XXIII | XXIV |
|---|---|---|---|---|---|
| 117* | combination of 113* and 116* | — | — | | — |
| | | 17 (5.50) | 8 (4.40) | 2 (16.67) | 1 (1.45) |
| 3 | Levallois point | — | — | — | — |
| 4 | Retouched point | 1 (0.32) | — | — | — |
| 5 | Pseudo-Levallois flake | — | — | — | — |
| 6 | Mousterian point | — | — | — | — |
| 7 | Elongated Mousterian point | — | — | — | — |
| 8 | Limace | — | — | — | — |
| 9 | Single straight side-scraper | 1 (0.32) | — | — | — |
| 10 | Single convex side-scraper | 2 (0.65) | — | — | — |
| 11 | Single concave side-scraper | — | 1 (0.55) | — | — |
| 12 | Double straight side-scraper | — | — | — | — |
| 13 | Double straight-convex side-scraper | — | — | — | — |
| 14 | Double straight-concave side-scraper | — | — | — | — |
| 15 | Double convex side-scraper | — | — | — | — |
| 16 | Double concave side-scraper | — | — | — | — |
| 17 | Double concave-convex side-scraper | — | 1 (0.55) | — | — |
| 18 | Convergent straight scraper | — | — | — | — |
| | Convergent convex scraper | — | — | — | — |
| 20 | Convergent concave | — | — | — | — |
| 21 | Déjeté (offset) scraper | — | — | — | — |
| 22 | Straight transverse scraper | — | — | — | — |
| 23 | Convex transverse scraper | — | — | — | — |
| 24 | Concave transverse scraper | — | — | — | — |
| 25 | Side-scraper on ventral face | — | — | — | — |
| 26 | Abruptly retouched side-scraper | — | — | — | — |
| 27 | Side-scraper with thinned back | — | — | — | — |
| 28 | Side-scraper with bifacial retouch | — | — | — | — |
| 29 | Alternately retouched side-scraper | — | — | — | — |

(continued)

**(continued)**

| | Type/layer | XXI | XXII | XXIII | XXIV |
|---|---|---|---|---|---|
| 30 | Typical end-scraper | 1 (0.32) | — | — | — |
| 31 | Atypical end-scraper | 3 (0.97) | — | — | — |
| 32 | Typical burin | 1 (0.32) | 1 (0.55) | — | — |
| 33 | Atypical burin | — | 1 (0.55) | — | — |
| 34 | Typical borers | — | — | — | — |
| 35 | Atypical borers | — | — | — | — |
| 36 | Typical backed knife | — | — | — | — |
| 37 | Atypical backed knife | 2 (0.65) | — | — | — |
| 38 | Naturally backed knife | 4 (1.29) | 3 (1.65) | — | — |
| 39 | Raclette | — | 2 (1.10) | — | — |
| 40 | Truncated flakes and blade | — | — | — | — |
| 41 | Mousterian tranchet | — | — | | — |
| 42 | Notch | 11 (3.56) | 3 (1.65) | 1 (8.33) | 3 (4.35) |
| 43 | Denticulate | 7 (2.27) | 8 (4.40) | — | 1 (1.45) |
| 44 | Alternately retouched beak | — | — | — | — |
| 45 | Retouch on ventral face | — | — | — | — |
| 46–47 | Abrupt and alternate retouch (thick) | — | — | — | — |
| 48–49 | Abrupt and alternate retouch (thin) | 1 (0.32) | — | — | — |
| 50 | Bifacial retouch | — | — | — | — |
| 51 | Tayac point | — | — | — | — |
| 52 | Notched triangle | — | — | — | — |
| 53 | Pseudo-microburin | — | — | — | — |
| 54 | End-notched piece | — | — | — | — |
| 55 | Hachoir | — | — | — | — |
| 56 | Rabot | — | — | — | — |
| 57 | Tanged point | — | — | — | — |
| 58 | Tanged tool | — | — | — | — |
| 59 | Chopper | — | — | — | — |
| 60 | Inverse chopper | — | — | — | — |
| 61 | Chopping tool | — | — | — | — |
| 62 | Miscellaneous | — | 1 (0.55) | — | — |
| 63 | Bifacial leaf-shaped point | — | — | | — |
| 106 | Retouched flake | 8 (2.59) | 3 (1.65) | 2 (16.67) | 2 (2.90) |
| 120 | Flake with use-signs | — | — | — | — |
| 121 | Flake with isolated removals | — | — | — | — |
| 99 | Non-Levallois CTE | 18 (5.82) | 6 (3.30) | — | — |
| 100 | Non-Levallois flake | 121 (39.16) | 83 (45.60) | — | 32 (46.38) |
| 101 | Non-Levallois blade | 11 (3.56) | 13 (7.14) | — | 3 (4.35) |
| 105 | Kombewa flake | 8 (2.59) | 5 (2.75) | 1 (8.33) | 2 (2.90) |
| 108 | Burin spall | — | — | | — |
| 113 | Non-Levallois éclat débordant | 3 (0.97) | 1 (0.55) | 3 (25.00) | 1 (1.45) |
| 114 | Non-Levallois éclat outrépassé | 1 (0.32) | — | — | 1 (1.45) |

(continued)

**(continued)**

|     | Type/layer | XXI | XXII | XXIII | XXIV |
|-----|------------|-----|------|-------|------|
| 115 | Non-Levallois combination of 113 and 114 | — | 1 (0.55) | — | — |
| 116 | Non-Levallois éclat rebroussé | — | — | — | — |
| 117 | Non-Levallois combination of 113 and 116 | — | — | — | — |
| 119 | Thinned flake | — | — | — | — |
| **Total** | | 309 (100.0) | 182 (100.0) | 12 (100.0) | 69 (100.00) |

# Appendix 6

## Radiometric Dates of Levantine Mousterian Sites

| Site*/layer | ESR (EU) | ESR (LU) | TL | U-Series | Coupled [230]Th/ [234]U/ESR | AAR |
|---|---|---|---|---|---|---|
| Qesem Cave[20] (flowstone in Acheulo-Yabrudian deposit) | | | | 299.70 ± 13.58 | | |
| | | | | 207.21 ± 12.02 | | |
| | | | | 253.88 ± 37.07 | | |
| | | | | 218.52 ± 15.11 | | |
| Post Acheulo-Yabrudian | | | | 217.65 ± 16.61 | | |
| | | | | 152.43 ± 3.29 | | |
| Tabun E[1,2,3] | 176 ± 22 (Ea) | 213 ± 32 (Ea) | *Ed, unit XIII* | 159.1 ± 1.3 (Ea) | 208[+102] | |
| | 180 ± 32 (Eb) | 195 ± 37 (Eb) | 280 ± 21 | 168.1 ± 2.6 (Ea) | [−44] (Ea) | |
| | 198 ± 51 (Ec) | 220 ± 63 (Ec) | 282 ± 26 | | | |
| | 149 ± 17 (Ed) | 191 ± 28 (Ed) | 357 ± 33 | | | |
| | | | 290 ± 28 | | | |
| | | | **302 ± 27 (37) (MEAN)** | | | |
| | | | *Eb, unit XII* | | | |
| | | | 361 ± 31 | | | |
| | | | 314 ± 33 | | | |
| | | | 301 ± 30 | | | |
| | | | 319 ± 30 | | | |
| | | | **324 ± 31 (26) (MEAN)** | | | |
| | | | *Ea unit XI* | | | |
| | | | 222 ± 27 | | | |
| | | | 251 ± 27 | | | |
| | | | 191 ± 22 | | | |
| | | | 271 ± 32 | | | |
| | | | 307 ± 32 | | | |
| | | | 351 ± 33 | | | |
| | | | 296 ± 38 | | | |
| | | | 224 ± 20 | | | |
| | | | 244 ± 29 | | | |
| | | | 279 ± 29 | | | |
| | | | **264 ± 28 (47) (MEAN)** | | | |
| | | | *Ea, unit X* | | | |
| | | | 282 ± 23 | | | |
| | | | 251 ± 21 | | | |
| | | | **267 ± 22 (22) (MEAN)** | | | |

(*continued*)

**(continued)**

| Site*/layer | ESR (EU) | ESR (LU) | TL | U-Series | Coupled $^{230}$Th/$^{234}$U/ESR | AAR |
|---|---|---|---|---|---|---|
| Tabun D[1,2,3] | 122 ± 20 | 166 ± 20 | *Unit IX* | 110.7 ± 0.9 | $143^{+41}_{-28}$ | |
| | | | 243 ± 24 | | | |
| | | | 248 ± 27 | | | |
| | | | 276 ± 29 | | | |
| | | | **256 ± 26 (18) (MEAN)** | | | |
| | | | *Unit V* | | | |
| | | | 237 ± 29 | | | |
| | | | 188 ± 22 | | | |
| | | | 266 ± 35 | | | |
| | | | 198 ± 22 | | | |
| | | | **222 ± 27 (36) (MEAN)** | | | |
| | | | *Unit II* | | | |
| | | | 191 ± 23 | | | |
| | | | 215 ± 23 | | | |
| | | | 183 ± 15 | | | |
| | | | **196 ± 21 (17) (MEAN)** | | | |
| Tabun C[1,2,3] | 102 ± 17 | 119 ± 11 | *Unit I* | 105.4 ± 2.6 | $135^{+60}_{-30}$ | |
| | | | 195 ± 18 | 101.7 ± 1.4 | | |
| | | | 139 ± 14 | 97.8 ± 0.4 | | |
| | | | 168 ± 17 | | | |
| | | | 172 ± 17 | | | |
| | | | 175 ± 18 | | | |
| | | | 179 ± 16 | | | |
| | | | 128 ± 14 | | | |
| | | | **165 ± 16 (23) (MEAN)** | | | |
| Tabun B[1,3] | 86 ± 11 | 103 ± 16 | | 50.7 ± 0.2 | $104^{+33}_{-18}$ sdsad | |
| Tabun B[24] | 82 ± 14 | 92 ± 18 | | | $90^{+30}_{-16}$ | |
| Hayonim F[23] | | | deep sounding | | | |
| | | | *F top* | | | |
| | | | 235 ± 26 | | | |
| | | | 204 ± 17 | | | |
| | | | 224 ± 21 | | | |
| | | | **221 ± 21 (16) (MEAN)** | | | |
| | | | *F base* | | | |
| | | | 205 ± 35 | | | |
| | | | 227 ± 24 | | | |
| | | | 225 ± 21 | | | |
| | | | 183 ± 60 | | | |
| | | | 251 ± 20 | | | |
| | | | 187 ± 20 | | | |
| | | | 221 ± 22 | | | |
| | | | 233 ± 20 | | | |
| | | | 189 ± 20 | | | |
| | | | 175 ± 22 | | | |
| | | | **210 ± 28 (25) (MEAN)** | | | |
| Hayonim E/F[22] | 158 ± 20 | 164 ± 221 | | | | |
| Hayonim Lower E[22, 23] | Central Area | Central Area | Central Area (north) | | | |
| | *unit 4* | *unit 4* | *unit 4* | | | |
| | 160 ± 28 | 160 ± 28 | 157 ± 19 | | | |
| | 177 ± 32 | 182 ± 34 | 208 ± 35 | | | |
| | | | 163 ± 23 | | | |
| | | | **176 ± 26 (28)(MEAN)** | | | |
| | | | Central Area (south) | | | |

(*continued*)

**(continued)**

| Site*/layer | ESR (EU) | ESR (LU) | TL | U-Series | Coupled $^{230}$Th/$^{234}$U/ESR | AAR |
|---|---|---|---|---|---|---|
| Hayonim Lower E[22, 23] (continued) | | | *unit 4* | | | |
| | | | 154 ± 17 | | | |
| | | | 140 ± 16 | | | |
| | | | 151 ± 17 | | | |
| | | | 194 ± 28 | | | |
| | | | 200 ± 29 | | | |
| | | | 105 ± 9 | | | |
| | | | **168 ± 21 (MEAN)** | | | |
| | *unit 5* | *unit 5* | *unit 5* | | | |
| | 200 ± 32 | 211 ± 35 | 160 ± 22 | | | |
| | 172 ± 33 | 175 ± 33 | deep sounding | | | |
| | *unit 6* | *unit 6* | *E base* | | | |
| | 142 ± 30 | 143 ± 30 | 197 ± 18 | | | |
| | 150 ± 21 | 164 ± 26 | 159 ± 13 | | | |
| | 136 ± 25 | 136 ± 25 | 202 ± 28 | | | |
| | 158 ± 28 | 159 ± 28 | **186 ± 20 (24)(MEAN)** | | | |
| | 51 ± 9*** | 51 ± 9*** | | | | |
| Hayonim Upper E[22, 23] | Central Area | Central Area | Central Area (north) | | | |
| | *unit 2* | *unit 2* | *unit 2* | | | |
| | 163 ± 26 | 164 ± 26 | 126 ± 12 | | | |
| | 180 ± 27 | 190 ± 30 | 127 ± 14 | | | |
| | 176 ± 30 | 182 ± 32 | 155 ± 19 | | | |
| | | | 119 ± 12 | | | |
| | | | 114 ± 15 | | | |
| | | | 146 ± 13 | | | |
| | | | 124 ± 12 | | | |
| | | | 125 ± 13 | | | |
| | | | 139 ± 13 | | | |
| | | | 129 ± 11 | | | |
| | | | 125 ± 12 | | | |
| | | | 119 ± 10 | | | |
| | | | **129 ± 13 (12) (MEAN)** | | | |
| | *unit 3* | *unit 3* | *unit 3* | | | |
| | 178 ± 21 | 187 ± 23 | 144 ± 16 | | | |
| | 183 ± 28 | 191 ± 31 | 140 ± 11 | | | |
| | | | 148 ± 18 | | | |
| | | | 146 ± 13 | | | |
| | | | 142 ± 13 | | | |
| | | | 143 ± 14 | | | |
| | | | **144 ± 14 (3) (MEAN)** | | | |
| | | | Central Area (south) | | | |
| | | | *unit 2* | | | |
| | | | 149 ± 15 | | | |
| | | | 163 ± 19 | | | |
| | | | **156 ± 17 (10) (MEAN)** | | | |
| | | | *unit 3* | | | |
| | | | 162 ± 22 | | | |
| | | | 155 ± 15 | | | |
| | | | 169 ± 17 | | | |
| | | | 178 ± 29 | | | |
| | | | 128 ± 14 | | | |
| | | | 144 ± 17 | | | |
| | | | **156 ± 19 (18)(MEAN)** | | | |

(continued)

**(continued)**

| Site*/layer | ESR (EU) | ESR (LU) | TL | U-Series | Coupled [230]Th/[234]U/ESR | AAR |
|---|---|---|---|---|---|---|
| Hayonim C/E[22] | 208 ± 29 | 217 ± 31 | | | | |
| | 208 ± 29 | 204 ± 29 | | | | |
| Skhul[4, 5,3] | 81 ± 15 | 101 ± 12 | 119 ± 18 | 80.3 ± 0.6 | | |
| | | | | 40.4 ± 0.2 | | |
| | | | | 41.4 ± 0.4 | | |
| | | | | 43.0 ± 0.5 | | |
| | | | | 43.5 ± 0.1 | | |
| | | | | 45.5 ± 0.7 | | |
| Ain Difla[6] | | | 105 ± 15 | | | |
| Zuttiyeh, pre-Mousterian[7] | | | | 95.0 ± 10.0 | | |
| | | | | 97.0 ± 13.0 | | |
| Qafzeh XXII[8] | | | 91.2 ± 8.0 | | | |
| | | | 86.6 ± 7.4 | | | |
| | | | 85.4 ± 6.9 | | | |
| Qafzeh XXI[8,9] | 95.9 | 118.0 | 109.9 ± 9.9 | | | |
| | 118.0 | 143.0 | 89.2 ± 8.9 | | | |
| | 73.7 | 94.0 | 90.9 ± 8.7 | | | |
| | 74.2 | 89.1 | | | | |
| | 95.3 | 116.0 | | | | |
| Qafzeh XIX[8,9] | 87.7 | 106.0 | 98.8 ± 8.9 | 88.6 ± 3.2 | | |
| | 99.7 | 112.0 | 82.4 ± 7.7 | 106.4 ± 2.4 | | |
| | 102.0 | 117.0 | 84.9 ± 7.3 | | | |
| | 111.0 | 124.0 | 95.9 ± 8.1 | | | |
| | 107.0 | 128.0 | | | | |
| | 119.0 | 145.0 | | | | |
| | 82.0 | 101.0 | | | | |
| Qafzeh XVIII[8] | | | 87.9 ± 7.2 | | | |
| | | | 89.5 ± 7.0 | | | |
| | | | 93.4 ± 8.2 | | | |
| Qafzeh XVII[8,9] | 95.2 | 103.0 | 94.3 ± 8.8 | | | |
| | | | 106.0 ± 9.6 | | | |
| | | | 107.2 ± 8.8 | | | |
| | | | 89.2 ± 8.4 | | | |
| | | | 87.8 ± 7.2 | | | |
| | | | 100.7 ± 8.2 | | | |
| Qafzeh XV[9] | 91.2 | 112.0 | | | | |
| | 94.2 | 114.0 | | | | |
| | 94.7 | 116.0 | | | | |
| QAFZEH MEAN[8,9] | **96 ± 13.0** | **115 ± 15** | **92 ± 5** | | | |
| Naamé (Enfeen II)[10, 11] | | | | 90.0 ± 20.0 | | |
| | | | | 93.0 ± 5.0 | | |
| Naamé (Naamean)[10] | | | | | | |
| Tor Faraj, Tor Sabiha[12,13,21] | | | 43.8 ± 2.0 | | | 69.0 ± 6.0 |
| | | | 47.5 ± 3.0 | | | |
| | | | 53.8 ± 3 | | | |
| Nahal Aqev, pre-Mousterian travertine[11] | | | | | | |
| Kebara XII[14] | | | 59.9 ± 3.5 | | | |
| Kebara XI[14] | | | 60.0 ± 3.5 | | | |
| Kebara X[14,15] | 60.4 ± 5.9 | 64.3 ± 5.9 | 61.6 ± 3.6 | | | |
| Kebara IX[14] | | | 58.4 ± 4.0 | | | |
| Kebara VIII[14] | | | 57.3 ± 4.0 | | | |

(continued)

(continued)

| Site*/layer | ESR (EU) | ESR (LU) | TL | U-Series | Coupled [230]Th/[234]U/ESR | AAR |
|---|---|---|---|---|---|---|
| Kebara VII[14] | | | 51.9 ± 3.5 | | | |
| Kebara VI[14] | | | 48.3 ± 3.5 | | | |
| Amud B4[17,18] | 68 ± 10 | 73 ± 12 | 75.9 ± 5.3 | | 70.0 ± 11.0 | |
| MEAN | 115 ± 18 | 115 ± 19 | 70.8 ± 3.8 | | 113.0 ± 18.0** | |
| | | | 55.6 ± 4.4 | | 113.0 ± 18.0** | |
| | | | 64.7 ± 4.0 | | | |
| | | | 66.9 ± 4.9 | | | |
| | | | **68.5 ± 3.4** | | | |
| Amud B2[17,18] | 51.5 ± 5.0 | 65 ± 8 | 59.5 ± 1.4 | | 53.0 ± 7.0 | |
| | 66 ± 8 | 77 ± 11 | 52.7 ± 5.5 | | 70.0 ± 10.0 | |
| | 54 ± 7 | 63 ± 9 | 55.4 ± 4.0 | | 59.0 ± 8.0 | |
| | | | 45.6 ± 3.0** | | **61.0 ± 9.0** | |
| | | | 52.4 ± 6.8** | | **(MEAN)** | |
| | | | 44.5 ± 3.9** | | | |
| | | | 44.1 ± 3.1** | | | |
| | | | 53.1 ±5.5** | | | |
| | | | **56.5 ± 3.5 (MEAN)** | | | |
| Amud B1[17,18] | 38 ± 5 | 41 ± 6 | 49.0 ± 4.6 | | 53.0 ± 7.0 | |
| | | | 59.4 ± 5.1 | | | |
| | | | 70.6 ± 8.6 | | | |
| | | | 51.6 ± 6.0 | | | |
| | | | 61.3 ± 10.5 | | | |
| | | | 58.1 ± 4.1 | | | |
| | | | **57.6 ± 3.7 (MEAN)** | | | |
| Far'ah II[19] | 45.6 ± 2.7 | 57.1 ± 4.1 | | | | |
| | 46.2 ± 2.7 | 57.1 ± 4.1 | | | | |
| | 54.4 ± 3.2 | 72.0 ± 4.9 | | | | |
| | 50.1 ± 3.1 | 62.7 ± 4.7 | | | | |
| | **49.1 ± 4.1** | **62.2 ± 7.0** | | | | |
| | **(MEAN)** | **(MEAN)** | | | | |
| Quneitra[16] | 39.2 | 53.9 ± 1.7 | | | | |

* [14]C dates obtained from Middle Paleolithic sites are dubious and therefore were not included in this appendix. Such dates indicate in most cases that the dated material is older than 40,000 or 50,000 years, but are not helpful in terms of understanding the internal chronology of the period.

** Age estimates not used in calculating mean ages of stratigraphic units.

*** This sample is possibly intrusive from younger deposits (Schwarcz and Rink 1998:61–62).

[1] Grün and Stringer 2000; [2] Mercier and Vallada 2003; [3] McDermott et al. 1993; [4] Mercier et al. 1993; [5] Stringer et al. 1989; [6] Barton and Clark 1993; [7] Schwarcz, Goldberg, and Blackball 1980; [8] Valladas et al. 1988; [9] Schwarcz et al. 1988; [10] Bar-Yosef 1992: tab. 11.1; [11] Schwarcz et al. 1979; [12] Henry and Miller 1992; [13] Henry 1995b:108; [14] Valladas et al. 1987; [15] Schwarcz et al. 1989; [16] Ziaei et al. 1990; [17] Valladas et al. 1999; [18] Rink et al. 2001; [19] Schwarcz and Rink 1998; [20] Barkai et al 2003; [21] Henry 1998; [22] Rink et al. 2004; [23] Mercier et al. 2007

## The Chronological Framework

Absolute dates were obtained by various dating methods for only few of the sites, most of them summarized and discussed by Bar-Yosef (1992, 1998a). The use of modern dating techniques served to extend the time span assigned to the Middle Paleolithic period in the Levant, resulting in a chronological reassignment of some assemblages to earlier periods than had previously assumed. When this occurred, dates were pushed one or two glacial cycles back, so that environmental reconstructions suggested for the time of occupation remain essentially the same (see below).

Some dates were perceived unacceptable because of analytical difficulties that were not addressed properly (e.g. Millard and Pike 1999; Richter 2007) or on the basis of archaeological reasoning (e.g., Alperson et al. 2000). Such dates were omitted from this appendix (e.g., the dates of Rosh Ein Mor, Rink et al. 2003; non-destructive dating of the Tabun Neanderthal, Schwarcz, Simpson, and Stringer 1998).

Available age estimates for Mousterian assemblages and sites suggest three temporal clusters: one, ca. 250,000–200,000 years ago, includes Tabun D (Jelinek's unit IX–II) and Hayonim lower E and F (Mercier and Valladas 2003;

Mercier et al. 2007; Rink et al. 2004), the dates of which suggest an early date of at least 220,000 years ago (i.e., comparable to Tabun unit V). These sites are thus assigned to the end of MIS 8 and to MIS 7, respectively. Such dates for Hayonim lower E are supported by the occurrence of some typical, old Palearctic faunal taxa (Tchernov 1981), all of which had disappeared by the time of other Middle Paleolithic occupations. The TL dates for Tabun D seem compatible with sedimentological and palynological evidence, suggesting a period of sea regression and cold climate at the time of accumulation of this stratigraphic unit (Bull and Goldberg 1985; Farrand 1979, 1994; Jelinek 1982;

Jelinek et al. 1973). ESR dates based on a Linear Uptake model yielded dates within MIS 6 and are also in agreement with such evidence; however, they suggest a very quick time span for the accumulation of layers E and D. While not impossible, this is less feasible given the thickness of layer E (Garrod and Bate 1937:65). ESR dates based on the Early Uptake model yielded a date within the time span of MIS 5e for Tabun D and are thus less acceptable.

The second dated cluster consists of Tabun C, Hayonim upper E, Qafzeh (layers XXIV–XV), Naamé, Skhul, and Ain Difla, ranging around 120,000–90,000 years ago, namely, MIS 5d–5a. The dating of Naamé is

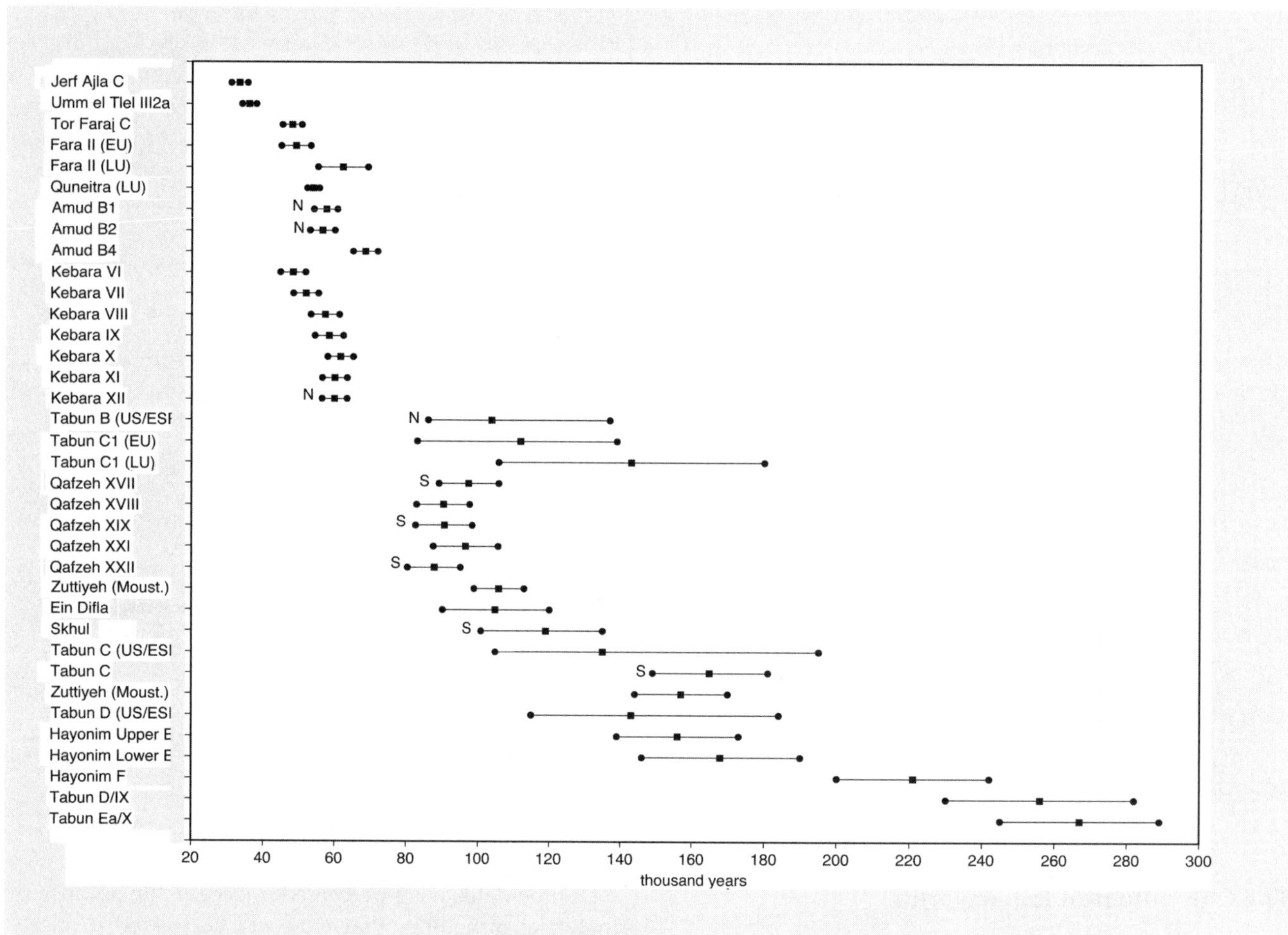



**Figure A6.1**  Age estimates of Levantine Mousterian sites. TL age estimates are shown, unless otherwise specified (for Tabun the results of several dating methods are show due to the large differences between methods). US = Uranium Series. Hominin-bearing horizons are marked by S and N (*H. sapiens* and Neanderthals, respectively). The Tabun C1 specimen is attributed here to Tabun B. See data in the appendix for sources of the values used in the graph.

The Dederiyeh Neanderthal specimens are not shown here because their ages are extrapolated from radiocarbon ages very close to the method's limit (Yoneda et al. 2002). Results of the dating projects in Rosh Ein Mor (Richter 2007; Rink et al. 2003) and from direct dating of the Tabun C1 skeleton (Schwarcz, Simpson, and Stringer 1998) are not included due to methodological and analytical flaws (Alperson et al. 2000; Grün and Stringer 2000; Millard and Pike 1999; Richter 2007).

corroborated by the occurrence in the deposits of the Entean II beach of the west African marine gastropod *Lentigo latus*, formerly named *Strombus bubonius* (Mienis in Galili et al. 2007) that is argued to have arrived to the Mediterranean only during MIS 5e (Gvirztman et al. 1985). At Qafzeh, these dates attain additional reliability due to the composition of the faunal assemblages, characterized by the absence of Palearctic elements and the increase of Arabian and East African elements in the microvertebrate assemblages of layers XXIV–XV. These elements are missing from later assemblages in the Levant (see Tchernov 1992 for the latest written summary; see also chapter 3). Tchernov (1992:164) contended that in spite of the similar dates obtained by various dating techniques for Tabun C and Qafzeh, micromammalian communities in the two sites are fundamentally different and cannot be placed within a single time span. His initial explanation relied on stratigraphic disturbances within the Tabun sequence, which caused confusion in sampling for both faunal and ESR analyses. However, the TL dates for Jelinek's unit I (Garrod's layer C) were obtained from what Tchernov considers to be an undisturbed context, and they range in the same time span suggested by the ESR dates. Since Jelinek did not sample Tabun B (Farrand 1994), ESR dates for this unit, indicating an age similar to those of layer C, cannot be cross-checked against a well-controlled stratigraphic sample. Radiocarbon dates for layer B suggest an age of 39.7 ± 0.8 kyr (Weinstein 1984).

A third cluster of radiometric dates ranges between 70,000 and 50,000 years ago, i.e., MIS 4 (glacial) and MIS 3 (interglacial). Sites dated to this period include Kebara, Quneitra, Tor Faraj, and Tor Sabiha, as well as Amud and Far'ah II. The modern palearctic micromammals found at Kebara and Amud support such age estimates for the two sites.

A number of other sites that as yet have not yielded radiometric dates, or were only dated by radiocarbon dating, were assigned by Bar-Yosef (1992, 1998a) to specific chronological phases based on their typo-technological characteristics. This practice is problematic, given the variability of Levantine Mousterian assemblages (Goren-Inbar and Belfer-Cohen 1998; Hovers 1998a). Notwithstanding this caveat, Jerf Ajla and Douara IV are considered to be equivalent to Tabun D in terms of the lithic industry, hence both are tentatively assigned an MIS 6 date (if the LU model of ESR dating is accepted) or to MIS 8 (based on TL). Similarly, the assignation of Rosh Ein Mor (D15) to MIS 6 rests on its alleged overall lithic resemblance to Tabun D (Marks and Monigal 1995; Munday 1979). Douara III is assigned to the time range of Qafzeh, again on the basis of lithic affinities. Other Negev sites are attributed to MIS 5d–5a, on the basis of geomorphic considerations. The U-series dates for Nahal Aqev (D35), although not obtained directly from the archaeological site, indeed suggest a date within MIS 5a and possibly at the beginning of MIS 4 for Mousterian occupations in the area.

# Notes



1. The concept of adaptation is at the core of processual approaches to the study of culture and cultural change: "as a human being man employs the extrasomatic tradition that we call culture in order to sustain and perpetuate his existence" (White 1959:8). Human behaviors are governed by, and therefore can be explained by, general laws, to which material artifacts can be linked through Middle Range Theory (Binford 1977; Hodder 1986; Patterson 1990; Shennan 1991; Tchauner 1996; Trigger 1989). Thus, prehistoric technologies are an integral part of humans' interface with their environments through cultural behavior, which can be observed archaeologically because the material record is an observable (phenotypic) expression of patterned behaviors of past societies. Kuhn (1995a, following Gould and Lewontin 1979) discusses the differences between "adaptation" (the physiological or behavioral adjustment to prevailing conditions) and "adaptationism" (the tendency to assume that such a process was the source of all variation and change). Archaeologists have been criticized for invariably leaning toward the latter (e.g., Gould 1990). Clearly not all change represents adaptation to identifiable conditions. Yet focusing on adaptive change makes scientific sense because it allows formulation of explanations that can be tested and refuted (see also Hovers 1997, and below).

2. There is a widespread agreement that "culture" (taken as "information capable of affecting individuals' behavior that they acquire from other members of their species through teaching, imitation, and other forms of social transmission"; Richerson and Boyd 2005:5) is important, but it is not at all clearly defined (Richerson and Boyd 2005:249; Whiten 2005a, 2005b). For the immediate discussion, it is the understanding of culture as a system of social transmission that is of importance. This issue is discussed below in more detail.

3. The best example of this process is the intensification of food-getting technologies and the shift to food production (Bar-Yosef and Belfer-Cohen 1992; Belfer-Cohen and Hovers 2005; Madella et al. 2002; Richerson, Boyd, and Bettinger 2001).

4. For instance, Boesch et al. (1994) present compelling evidence for cultural differences in nut-cracking behavior between two populations of chimpanzees, which can be shown to most likely have emerged during the late Pleistocene.

5. In retrospect, Bordes's and Binford's positions heralded the post-processual and processual approaches, respectively.

6. "Mousterian" was characterized by the presence of small or medium flakes removed from small discoidal cores, often retouched into side-scrapers or points, and found exclusively in cave sites. "Levallois" was defined as an industry in which the end-products were detached from large prepared cores, either discoidal or long and rectangular in shape, and were rarely retouched (Breuil and Kozlowski 1931).

7. With the corroboration of Garrod's observations by Bordes's analyses from the 1950s onward, "Mousterian" and "Levallois" came to represent two different, albeit complementary, concepts in Middle Paleolithic lithic studies. "Mousterian" identifies a cultural-historical phenomenon and an analytical unit at the level of a techno-complex. "Levallois" stands for a technological system and is therefore more of a behavioral concept (Bordes 1953c; Bordes and Bourgon 1951). To date, most of the Levantine Middle Paleolithic assemblages are considered to be Mousterian of Levallois facies (though see Jelinek 1992).

8. This situation may have changed with the discovery of *Homo sapiens idaltu* in the Middle Awash, Ethiopia (Clark et al. 2003), but current information on the associated sites and assemblages is preliminary.



## CHAPTER 2

1. It is now clear that the production of the earliest and simplest stone tools, dated to ca. 2.6 million years, already involved planning and structuring of the technical process (e.g., Delagnes and Roche 2005; personal observations).

2. The potential for refitting was recognized for some assemblages, mainly in the lower part of the sequence. The

reconstruction of core-reduction strategies that is presented in the following chapters can possibly be tested in the future by refitting.

3. This is not suggested to be a formal approach, as the methodology is not based on a series of testable hypotheses formulating the relationship between specific variables and their place in the reduction sequence. It is nonetheless useful in the context of work in Levantine Mousterian sites, where refitting is not a viable research option given the immense amounts of lithic artifacts.

4. Bleed (2001:106–107) rightly points out that *chaîne opératoire* models are not set up to deal with natural or taphonomic agents that may influence the way artifacts are found and interpreted by modern researchers. The use of an attribute analysis enables inclusion of variables that reflect such agents (e.g., breakage, patination, abrasion) and allows factoring at least some such agents into the comprehensive analysis.

5. While the first appearance of Levallois dates from at least 300,000 years ago, it did not necessarily occur in every single assemblage from that time onward. In Middle Pleistocene entities, such as the Acheulo-Yabrudian in the Levant, Levallois production does not occur. The same is true of various Middle Paleolithic industries, for example, the Quina Mousterian (e.g., Geneste et al. 1997).

6. Van Peer (1992) also made great analytical and methodological contributions to the understanding of Levallois, which are similar but not identical conceptually to those of Boëda and Geneste.

7. Levallois flaking methods are given special emphasis by their prominent place in the Levantine Mousterian assemblages in general, and in the Qafzeh assemblages in particular.

8. This issue is discussed in detail in chapter 7. Some such archaeological correlates of the variable tactics of lithic organization are summarized in table 7.1).

CHAPTER 3

1. Based on Lewonstan's notes and journals, which came into Weiner's possession after Lewonstan's death.

2. Neuville recognized that the internal division of the so-called Levalloisian was subjective, and that it was not necessarily applicable to all or even most Middle Paleolithic sites (Neuville 1951:183).

3. Lithic artifacts in the Mousterian deposits inside the cave area are found in a context almost devoid of matrix, as if the finer-grained component of the matrix has been removed by water action. This situation makes their densities per volume of sediment seem much higher than they must have been originally.

4. Vandermeersch reports one individual (Q13) from layer XVa. Given its location in the stratigraphic sequence and its depth below datum, this individual probably derives from layer XVII (O. Bar-Yosef, pers. comm. 1997).

5. The latter two sites are now known to be at least one climatic cycle older than Qafzeh (e.g., Mercier and Valladas 2003; Rink et al. 2004).

6. This may be an overestimate, in the absence of studies that attempted to examine the length of human occupation or the amount of anthropogenic refuse needed to draw commensal microvertebrates to a locality and to attach them to it.

CHAPTER 4

1. It has often been maintained that the Levallois flaking surface is based on the exploitation of surface rather than volume. This, of course, is a misunderstanding. It is true, however, that the Levallois flaking concept is based on the exploitation of successive series of flaking surfaces that must be reshaped throughout the process in order to maintain the characteristics of the flakes.

2. This mode of Levallois flaking should not be confused with the bipolar technique, where a single core is placed on a stationary anvil for support and then struck with a large, heavy hammer.

3. Cores of "indeterminate" technology (see appendix 2), usually due to excessive damage to the core surface, were grouped with the latter.

4. Meignen (1995) suggested that within the Levallois system, cores flaked by a lineal flaking method are the classical Levallois cores that Bordes classified as Levallois cores for flakes, points, and so on. She did not suggest any particular typological classification for Levallois cores bearing the signs of a recurrent flaking method, in which several predetermined flakes are removed from a single surface of a Levallois core.

5. The so-called "Nubian" method (Tixier, Inizan, and Roche 1980:50, fig. 9; Van Peer 1992) is a variant of the lineal method that involves an initial centripetal preparation, followed by bipolar removals of *éclats débordants* in order to form the guiding scar ridges. It is commonly associated with a protruding striking platform, and finally the detachment of a point, again from the center of the flaking surface. Nubian cores (and points) are uncommon in the Levantine Mousterian, though they seem to occur in the latest horizons of the Middle-Upper Paleolithic transitional site at Boker Tachtit (Marks and Volkman 1983).

6. Other methodological issues have an impact on these two central questions. The quantitative importance of small flakes in an assemblage is used by Dibble and Mcpherron (2006:778) as a criterion for evaluating the intentionality of small flake production. In turn, the frequency of small flakes in an assemblage depends on the value assigned to the cutoff point that differentiates small from "regular" flakes. Dibble and McPherron define 30 mm as that critical value, whereas in Levantine Middle Paleolithic assemblages thresholds were set at 25 mm (e.g., Crew 1976) and (in more recent analyses, e.g., Gilead 1980; Goren-Inbar 1990a; Hovers 1997, 1998a [and this work]) at 20 mm.

7. Kombewa or Janus flakes have two ventral faces, resulting from their being removed from the ventral face of a flake that serves as a core (Owen 1938; Tixier, Inizan, and Roche 1980).

CHAPTER 5

1. Some of the analytical difficulties involved in identifying intentionality in lithic assemblages have already been touched upon in the previous chapter, in the context of the discussion of cores-on-flakes.

2. Levallois-related literature is replete with references to Levallois flaking as non-volumetric, contrary to laminar systems that are volumetric. Some scholars have gone so far as to define this as the difference between Middle and Upper Paleolithic technologies. This is a misconception. Involving, as it does, the exploitation of a volume of raw material, Levallois is of course a volumetric concept. However, it does differ from other volumetric concepts in that it focuses on a geometric plane, whereas laminar or discoidal flaking concepts involve exploitation of multi-dimensional faces.

3. Points alone are 15% of the Levallois products, identical to the values from Kebara.

4. Hammerstones are rare in the Qafzeh assemblages. Five rounded basalt specimens that could have been used as hard hammers were retrieved from layer XV. Two additional basalt specimens derive from an unknown stratigraphic provenience. Similarly, in most Levantine Mousterian sites hammerstones appear to be very rare. These items are infrequently discussed in published reports on Levantine Middle Paleolithic assemblages (see, however, Goren-Inbar 1990a:134–138). Based on my recent personal observations on the lithic assemblages from Amud Cave, where hammers have yet to be found within samples of tens of thousands of large flakes (> 20 mm), this rarity may reflect a real situation and not simply a research bias.

5. Data are not available from other stratified Levantine Middle Paleolithic sites, although they are available for the single-layer site of Quneitra (Goren-Inbar 1990a: tabs. 18d, 23d). An identical pattern (though not the same specific values) was reported from the Lower Paleolithic site of 'Ubeidiya (Bar-Yosef and Goren-Inbar 1993:170, tab. 34).

6. *Éclats outrepassés*, mentioned earlier in the text, are not identical to *éclats outrepassants*, which are large elongated flakes with a longitudinal convex profile.

7. The proximal end morphology created by *chapeau de gendarme* platforms is often associated with convergent scar patterns on Levallois points. It is perceived as conducive to the hafting of points and their use as the tip of a composite hunting weapon (e.g., Shea 1991). Still, the current work and other studies emphasize the general lack of form and function relationship, whereas Boëda, Connan, and Muhesen (1998b) describe hafting of artifacts with variable proximal morphology (see chapter 8 for further discussion).

8. Note that Speth (1975:204) refers to "platform thickness" as the distance from the edge of the experimental prism (analogous to the core's free face) to the point of impact. This measure is referred to in this study as platform depth and is used in the analysis presented here. Dibble and Whittaker (1981:286) talk about "the thickness of the flake as measured at the point of percussion", as reflected by the distance from the flake's exterior surface (along a line perpendicular to it) to the point of impact. The relationship between platform properties and flake length exhibits similar trends regardless of the differences in definition.

9. A length-width ratio of 2:1 is the most commonly used in the literature (and is the one upheld in this study), although in some cases 2.5:1 or even 4:1 is set as the threshold. The metric distinction between blades and bladelets is also of interest, especially given recent claims for intentional small blank production in the Middle Paleolithic (e.g., Dibble and McPherron 2006), but the paucity of bladelets (with width of unretouched blanks < 12 mm and length < 50 mm) in the Qafzeh assemblages does not justify a detailed discussion of this class of items.

CHAPTER 6

1. Although these questions are obviously pertinent to unretouched artifacts as well, the number of "life-history" phases that a retouched artifact presents is higher.

2. Chase uses the argument to discuss a more general putative relationship between the ability to create the arbitrary (and standardized) forms of retouched artifacts and the cognitive ability to symbolize. This is also the direction discussed by Monnier (2006), who rejects the notion of "mental templates" in retouched tools on empirical and terminological grounds.

3. Bisson (2000) argues that dismissals of the functional hypothesis that concentrate on the inadequacy of the form–function link miss this point and therefore may not be conclusive.

4. This, of course, leaves open the possible selection of unretouched artifacts that had been used. Those need to be identified based on use-wear traces before any questions regarding blank selection can be formed and concrete hypotheses tested.

5. Clear excavation breakage was excluded from the analysis of breakage patterns and their significance. The details of the breakage scar enable reconstruction of the direction of pressure and it is sometimes possible to determine whether the pressure was applied to the ventral or dorsal face of the flake. These details are not quantified or discussed here in detail, but generally it seems that most breaks were caused by pressure on the ventral faces of the artifacts.

6. Although the tendency is stronger for double sidescrapers and for convergent forms, sample sizes are too small to allow clear-cut conclusions in these cases.

CHAPTER 7

1. It was suggested that these postulated differences were correlated with a shift in the taxon of hominins that occupied the site, from Moderns in the older layers to Neanderthals in the upper ones. I will return to this point later. For the time being, it is important to re-emphasize that there are no human skeletal remains in the upper layers.

2. In the PPNB, incipient craft specialization may have played a role in creating the observed patterns. This is clearly not valid for the Middle Paleolithic.

3. Production of the reliable, high-investment artifacts would take place at the habitation sites, as discussed earlier in the text, rather than at the task-specific locations where time is not available for high-investment technological procedures.

4. This procedure deals well with many types of archaeological finds, e.g., quantifiable pottery characteristics or some properties of faunal analyses.

5. Some were omitted due to insufficient sample size.

6. Upper Pleistocene to Holocene alluviation in the valleys may have hidden some flint-bearing horizons closer to the site.

7. Such distances were also documented for other Eurasian and North African Middle Paleolithic sites (Féblot-Augustins

1993, 1997; Geneste 1985; Henry 1995a, 1995b; Roebroeks, Kolen, and Rensink 1988; Wengler 1990).

8. Kuhn (1995a:138), who applied a similar procedure to identify imported blanks in the Italian Pontinian assemblages, used a threshold of twice the mean dimensions. However, as noted above, initial pebble size in this case is easier to identify given the known and limited size range at the raw material source.

9. A comment on this procedure is warranted here. In a large sample normally distributed, 0.14% of the items are larger than "mean plus three standard deviations (s.d.)" (Griffiths 1967:264). In the case of the Qafzeh assemblages, the proportion of flakes larger than the mean plus 3 s.d. is expected to be somewhat higher because the lower tail of the distribution of any measured dimension was set arbitrarily at 20 mm (chapter 5; appendix 2). This procedure, common in lithic analyses of non-microlithic assemblages, distorts the statistical distribution in such a way that it raises the sample mean but lowers the standard deviation.

10. Except in layer VIII, where the small sample size very possibly distorts the pattern.

11. The problem of spatial patterning of activities, discussed earlier in this chapter, is clearly relevant here. As argued above, the joint occurrence of points, cores, and all types of debitage, including cortical elements and core management pieces in the small excavated areas, allows an assumption of unbiased representation of the various categories of lithics in the excavated assemblages.

12. Ellis (1997) emphasized the effects of the varying degrees of brittleness of various lithic raw materials on the degree of their reliability in the context of big game hunting as opposed to hunts of smaller game. Similarly, he addressed the influence of various weapon-assisted hunting techniques (e.g., throwing vs. thrusting) on the choice of materials for producing the points.

13. Cores-on-flakes were omitted from the metric analyses presented below because their dimensions reflect primarily their original size rather than any degree of reduction.

14. Recent nutritional and paleoanthropological studies have undermined the importance of meat acquisition and consumption by indicating that meat may have been a coveted, but in all likelihood not the staple, subsistence resource of human societies (e.g., Cordain et al. 2000; Domínguez-Rodrigo, Egeland, and Barba 2007; Laden and Wrangham 2005; Sponheimer et al. 2006). In the circum-Mediterranean region especially, Middle Paleolithic hominins capitalized on the easy access to and availability of a large spectrum of vegetal resources (Finlayson 2004; Henry et al. 2004; Lev, Kislev, and Bar-Yosef 2005; Madella et al. 2002; Matsutani 1987).

15. Group size categories as designated by Rabinovich and Tchernov (1995).

16. Employed units are the specific areas on the artifact's perimeter on which particular materials and motions have been used (Shea 1991:45–49).

17. Mineralogical and sedimentological work conducted at the site in 1997 confirmed that the lower layers indeed consist of wood ashes typical of Middle Paleolithic fires known from other sites in the Levant (S. Weiner, pers. comm. 2000).

18. Following Bar-Yosef (1998a), lithic density over TL years (taken as calendar years) can be used as a proxy of occupation intensity. The value for Qafzeh is 300/m³ over 5,000 TL years, whereas it is 1,000/m³ over 3,000 TL years and 1,000/m³ over 1,000–1,500 years at the late Middle Paleolithic sites of Kebara and Amud caves, respectively, and 300/m³ over 15,000 TL years at the earlier site of Hayonim Cave (Hovers 2001).

19. This absence of evidence should, of course, be treated cautiously, as such ties may be neither direct nor simple. In the first place, the available data restrict the scope and accuracy of analyses that might otherwise be illuminative on such issues. Another problem, which the Qafzeh archaeological remains clearly share with the majority of prehistoric assemblages, is that of preservation. The recovery of wooden spears in several Late Middle Pleistocene contexts (e.g., Movius 1950; Thieme 1997) obviously raises the possibility that such tools existed in the Levantine Mousterian but have not been preserved archaeologically. If that were the case, associations between hunting weapons and subsistence aspects reflected archaeologically might have taken on a different form and been open to different interpretations than those suggested here. These are, obviously, moot points in the context of the current discussion. Bearing in mind the cautionary notes listed above, the general agreement between the observed patterns and the ones anticipated based on ecological data and models lends credence to the conclusion drawn here.

20. In the absence of macrobotanical remains from the Qafzeh sediments, one avenue for exploring this issue is a study of phytolith remains in the sediments. While taphonomic agents and stratigraphic complexities clearly have to be accounted for, the potential of such studies has been proven in a number of Levantine and other studies (Albert et al. 1999, 2000, 2003; Henry et al. 2004; Madella et al. 2002).

21. This assumes that seasonality patterns observed on the gazelle population reflect those of other species that are represented in the faunal assemblage.

22. The disjunction in the occurrence of microvertebrates in the stratigraphic sequence is also illuminating with respect to settlement patterns and how they changed through time. The absence of microvertebrates from layers XV onward cannot be related to diagenetic or other taphonomic processes, which do not seem to have been differential between layers (P. Goldberg, pers. comm. 1997). Even if differences did occur, scanty remains of the more durable anatomical elements would have been recovered (E. Tchernov, pers. comm. 1997). The absence of micromammalian remains from the upper part of the sequence is most parsimoniously attributed to as yet unclear ecological factors that dictated the behaviors of the predators.

23. The highly uneven tool-kit compositions in the lower layers (figure 7.1) are associated with the largest excavation areas in the sample.

24. Neuville's (1951) initial typo-technological description of the lithic material from the Mousterian layers inside the cave hints at differences between the cave and the terrace assemblages. Since these assemblages are not contemporaneous for the most part, differences between them are not the result of spatial organization of activities between the two parts of the site. Additionally, later work by Boutié (1989) did not support the typological observations (chapter 3), instead identifying similarities between the cave and terrace assemblages.

25. Indeed, the structure of the cognitive processes that constitute the steps of the technological *chaîne opératoire* is

comparable to the architecture of decision-making processes (e.g., Schall 2005).

26. Recent studies have looked at the neurological motor and perceptual mechanisms that are necessary for basic stone tool production (e.g., Stout and Chaminade 2007), at the way in which the human brain evaluates the probability of success of decisions, where success is measured against the subjective desirability of the results (as summarized, e.g., by Glimcher and Rustichini 2004), and at decision making as a process of successive inclusion or exclusion of information (e.g., Levin, Huneke, and Jasper 2000). These studies are clearly pertinent to the processes of flaking as discussed here and are well worth bearing in mind when discussing the notions of "know-how" and "knowledge." They will not be discussed in further detail, since such studies were conducted in relation to simple techniques of making stone tools or to experimental work that is not directly related to lithic studies. In both cases, the implications for the complex flaking procedures involved in Levallois production (i.e., motor skill, perception, evaluation of desirability, and the type and amount of information that is necessary for successful flaking) are at this time conjectural.

27. A long discussion of the theoretical approaches would deviate from the main focus of the current study and will not be attempted here. It should, however, be noted that the social agency and evolutionary approaches to technological behaviors do not contrast as radically as may appear from the pertinent literature. While proponents of social agency models describe how technological behaviors are related to the social background of their practitioners, models of technological evolution attempt to explain the role of such backgrounds in technological stasis and change.

28. The distinction between invention and innovation is of importance here, in that the latter relates to ideas and practices that have been accepted by a group of people and are being used in a normative manner by many members of the community. This in itself may be a process that cannot take place without technological and societal prerequisites. Most importantly, the appearance of an innovation designates by default the existence of a crucial demographic threshold without which an invention cannot become an innovation (Hovers and Belfer-Cohen 2006 and references therein).

29. This does not take into account the possibility that few selected individuals, highly skilled and trained, conducted lithic production on behalf of a group of hominins. For the sake of the current discussion, it is assumed that even in such cases socio-technological parameters would have dictated their choices.

30. It is possible that the long-term pattern at Qafzeh reflects the activities of several groups belonging in the framework of a larger social system. Note that ethnicity cannot be invoked, whereas Sackett's argument is that isochrestic style is linked to ethnic identity. This point must remain moot. It is, in fact, controversial ethnographically as well. For example, stylistic attributes of San artifacts are shared only within large-scale social systems and are not indicative of small-scale socio-political divisions (e.g., Wiessner 1983). Similarly, technical knowledge, and by extension traditions and styles of pottery making among Cameroonian agriculturalists, "appear to circulate mainly in an intra-ethnic manner" (Gosselain 1998:97). On the other hand, in the Mandara Mountains between Cameroon and Nigeria

the irrelevance of ethnic group membership is expressed in the dynamics of artifact production and use, as well as in the archaeologically visible distribution of materials and products (MacEachern 1998:129).

31. The non-utilitarian nature of ochre use is emphasized by the evidence that goethite may have been heated to achieved the typical red color of hematitic ochre (Godfrey-Smith and Ilani 2004).

32. Based on the shared characteristics of the lithic assemblages of the terrace and cave (Boutié 1989), this scenario is applicable to both.



## CHAPTER 8

1. Such that $ET = \dfrac{18W - 10C}{(W - C) + 8}$     (Kelly 1995:66)

2. This is most likely due to the desert barrier present in much of recent geological history and clearly documented for the Pleistocene. The narrow window of opportunity for movements "Out of Africa" has been discussed in relation to both hominin and faunal dispersals (Lahr and Foley 1998; Vaks et al. 2007; see, however, Derricourt 2005 for a less extreme view).

3. Rabineau et al. (2006) argue for sea level drops of 102 ± 6 m on the basis of their work in the Gulf de Lyon, but warn that these estimates are not firmly linked to global fluctuations because they take into account only local subsidence.

4. Isotopic studies underline the role of meat in Neanderthal diets in Europe (e.g., Bocherens et al. 2005; Fizet et al. 1995; Hocket and Haws 2005; Richards and Schmitz 2008; Richards et al. 2000, 2001), but the geographical situation of the Levant makes it more likely that plants were the more common staple foods. As noted by Bar-Yosef and Meadow (1995:50) "Most hunter-gatherer diets in middle latitudes and up to 1,500 m above sea level are based on vegetal resources" (see chapter 7). Even ignoring pertinent critiques and disagreements with the generalization based on isotopic studies (see Hawks 2005; Perez-Perez et al. 2003), it may be hypothesized that Levantine human remains may show different patterns because they responded to different, richer, and less harsh environments. This hypothesis has yet to be tested by isotopic studies of Levantine Middle Paleolithic skeletal remains of both Neanderthals and modern humans.

5. The meager palynological data from the Negev (Horowitz 1976) constitute the only evidence for a significant difference from the present-day pattern, possibly representing a wet interglacial of Middle or Upper Pleistocene age compatible with the patterns reported on by Vaks et al. (2006; see above). The phytolith assemblage from Tor Faraj (Miller-Rosen 2003) may represent the same type of change, whereas the shift from Mediterranean forest in the Middle Paleolithic to dry steppe environments today in the area of Douara Cave (Akazawa 1988) may appear more dramatic than it really was, given the site's location at the ecotone between the mountain ranges (bearing trees until the present) and the open, steppe, basin floor.

6. This point is demonstrated, for example, by Dyson-Hudson and Smith (1978), who discuss how variability in territorial behavior and mobility patterns of Great Plains tribes were directly related to the use of storage technologies. The existence of storage has been perceived by some workers as a diagnostic

of a "second hunter-gatherer economy" characterized by incipient inequality (e.g., Testart 1982). This issue, while important, is not addressed here. The discussion of storage (or rather lack thereof) is restricted here to its role in shaping gatherer-hunter mobility strategies.

7. This conclusion is based on the loss of water content, the reason for the shriveled condition of many of the seeds.

8. Special conditions could have led to other patterns of resource exploitation. For example, a steep elevation gradient over short distances could contribute to easy access to varied resources without the need to move very frequently (see Hovers 1988). Similarly, larger aggregations could lead to increased emphasis on logistical mobility, as happened in the Levant at the close of the Pleistocene, when specific socio-political constraints were formed (Bar-Yosef and Belfer-Cohen 1991).

9. It is not clear from Shea's calculations what proportion of the case studies comes from areas with higher or lower ET compared to the Levant. Additionally, these data derive from groups living in temperate forests and do not habitually use more open areas (Kelly 1995:224–225), which often have higher primary production (Blondel and Aronson 1999). In the Levant, with its densely interwoven mosaic of diverse habitats, carrying capacities may well have been higher. Note also that these values average the size of the Levantine habitable terrain across climatic cycles. During interglacial times, the area available for occupation was reduced due to elevated sea levels.

10. The sites discussed by Munday as respective workshop/quarry sites and "base camp"/habitation sites are situated less than 1 km from one another (table 8.1).

11. The value for Tor Faraj in figure 8.3a is the mean for Levallois points only, other data being unavailable. Still, given the consistent pattern of Levallois flakes being larger than non-Levallois flakes in Levantine assemblages, the inclusion of the latter would not bring the mean length to its predicted value.

12. An inverse relationship apparently exists between frequencies of flaking accidents in some Middle Paleolithic assemblages and distance from raw material sources. It has been hypothesized that this relationship reflects curation of raw material in the context of acquisition of technological skills (Ekshtain 2006). This hypothesis is still untested.

13. The model originally attempted to explain the existence of Mousterian variants described by Bordes (e.g., Rolland 1981; Rolland and Dibble 1990; Dibble and Rolland 1992). The Quina Mousterian, which exhibits an extreme case of blank reduction, is however anomalous in terms of the model, since assemblages are made on local raw material (Bordes [1961] 1988; Turq 1989).

14. Although the Acheulo-Yabrudian is no longer considered part of the Levantine Middle Paleolithic sequence (cf. Goren-Inbar 1994), it is a good test case for the implications of the climatic model with regard to the Levant. Jelinek (1982a) identified facies of the Mugharan/Acheulo-Yabrudian in Tabun with climatic conditions, so that the "Yabrudian" facies, rich in heavily retouched side-scrapers, was associated with stadials within the last interglacial. However, it has recently been argued that Acheulo-Yabrudian stratigraphic sequences encompassing MIS 10–7 may include only a single Acheulo-Yabrudian facies (for example, Qesem Cave; Gopher et al. 2005), apparently independent of climatic fluctuations. Additionally, Acheulo-Yabrudian assemblages are not limited to cave sites (e.g., open-air sites at el-Kowm; Besançon et al. 1982). This contradicts the premises

of the model (Rolland and Dibble 1990:488), which emphasizes caves as the loci of raw material curation through recycling.

15. In only very few assemblages are sample sizes of side-scrapers and the heterogeneity of retouch intensity sufficient to justify calculation of any of the various reduction indices (e.g., Eren et al. 2005; Gordon 1993; Hiscock and Clarkson 2005; Kuhn 1990b).

16. The abandonment and return to cave sites may have been dictated by climatic changes on centennial or decadal-scales. These are not readily observed but may have led to changes in the microenvironments of the caves that could prohibit their occupation (Bar-Yosef and Vandermeersch 1981). However, the isotopic data that reflect these changes suggest that cave occupation may not have been feasible due to excessive water amounts only during the MIS6/5 transition and around 54,000 years ago, at the beginning of MIS 3 (Bar-Matthews et al. 2003).

17. The number of well-studied open-air Mousterian sites is smaller than that of cave assemblages, a situation that reflects research bias rather than a real phenomenon (e.g., Boutié and Rosen 1989; Hovers and Bar-Yosef 1987; Hovers et al. 2008; Ronen 1977). Note that Quneitra is the only open-air assemblage that is highly retouched, so that the high mean of retouched blanks in open-air sites is biased by this assemblage. When it is removed from the total sample of open-air sites, the group mean is reduced to 9.21% of retouched blanks, but the difference between the groups is still statistically insignificant.

18. Interestingly, Marks and Freidel (1977) offered a radically different explanation of incentives for blade production in the Upper Paleolithic of the Negev, whereby it was the higher mobility of groups that put a premium on the use of long debitage.

19. Available data on dorsal face scar patterns are commonly pertinent only to Levallois blanks, which has restricted the inter-assemblage comparisons made here to that fraction of the various assemblages. Note, however, that the data from Quneitra used in this figure (after Goren-Inbar 1990a) are for the whole assemblage.

20. In fact, the laminar products in these two assemblages derive from different flaking concepts (Meignen 2000), which serves only to dissociate the flaking system and methods from the preparatory input toward core modification and from the correlations expected by Munday's ecological model.

21. The size of the initial cores does not appear to have been an influential factor, given that fully cortical elements at both sites are of more or less the same size, indicating similar-sized cores.

22. There is a downside to point production and use, which is the costly maintenance, as these artifacts tend to break easily if they accidentally hit a hard object. An alternative interpretation of use-wear on points is that they had first been designed as multi-purpose tools, and later perhaps recycled into tools (e.g., Anderson-Gerfaud 1990; Holdaway 1990; Plisson and Beyries 1998).

23. The latter assemblage may be biased due to selective retention (Marks and Volkman 1986).

24. That Levallois points may exhibit wear traces nearly five times more often than any other debitage category (Shea 1989) is another indication that they may have been curated objects (cf. Marks and Freidel 1977).

25. Not all the ecological hypotheses attempting to explain inter-assemblage lithic variability could be examined in the context of the study of the Qafzeh lithics, even though it was

perceived and designed as a comparative study (chapter 2). For example, it was impossible to test hypotheses related to the effects of climate change on the properties of the assemblages, given the postulated short time of deposition of this sequence (chapter 3).

26. This principle was employed in the interpretation of the Qafzeh assemblages (chapter 7), and indeed is followed in discussions of behavioral patterns inferred from archaeological finds, albeit implicitly in most cases.

27. Far'ah II may be the only locality where an organizational strategy roughly reminiscent of provisioning of activities can be seen. This is a short-term encampment (hence the high rate of refitting success for this assemblage; see chapter 2) where large ungulates aggregated and were hunted. The availability of raw material and of gregarious equid herds near the water would have been anticipated by Middle Paleolithic groups, so that on-site activities were not fortuitous or incidental. Yet lithic production practices are largely expedient and consistent with provisioning for activities. Lithic raw material sources were located in the immediate vicinity of the site. The aim of lithic production was to obtain cutting edges through on-the-spot reduction of small wadi pebbles (6–10 cm in size based on conjoined cores; Gilead 1988) into a large number of flakes with little regard to shape and size (indicated by low IL values and lack of standardization in manufacture techniques; Gilead 1988; Gilead and Grigson 1984). There are no indications of transport of large or formally shaped artifacts (points or tools) as personal gear in anticipation of the hunt, or of provisioning of the site with large raw material packages from distant sources, to be exploited as the need arose. The use of local limestone nodules also testifies to the expedient nature of the lithic activities. Possibly the paucity of well-planned hunting tools in a kill/butchery site (Gilead 1988, 1995; Gilead and Grigson 1984) suggests that more formal tools used in hunting (e.g., points) might have been removed from the scene as personal gear (Hovers 1997), implying a combination of provisioning strategies by group members.

The assemblage of Quneitra offers a glimpse of a combination of provisioning of places and of activities because of the clear differences in provisioning strategies of local basalts and transported flint (Hovers 1990b) and the different flaking methods applied to each material (Goren-Inbar 1990a; Goren-Inbar and Belfer-Cohen 1998). Cores-on-flakes may reflect the same tactical behavior (Hovers 2007), though the case of Qafzeh may be slightly different (chapters 4, 5). However, even in these cases it might be argued that this is not a completely opportunistic behavior, since the availability of basalt (at Quneitra) or of flakes that could be used as cores (at any site) was anticipated in advance.

28. Given that the functional distinction between "real" points as opposed to pointed forms (Shea, Davis, and Brown 2001) was not made at that time, these assertions should probably be taken with a grain of salt. Still they are partially supported by the current study (e.g., with regard to Qafzeh XIII; see chapter 7).

29. Similar behaviors were arguably identified in some Early Pleistocene sites, interpreted as raw material caches stored for future use (Potts 1988).

30. Cores-on-flakes can also be seen as provisioning of activities, complying with a strategy of making do with whatever

raw material packages are immediately available. The careful consideration given to size and geometry selection of the flakes, however, is not consistent with this scenario (Hovers 2007).

31. In other instances, such as Umm el-Tlel or Kebara, there is evidence that the role of the site in a settlement system changed through time, but when a narrow spectrum of activities is reflected by the assemblages, it is associated with hunting and/or butchering of animal resources (Boëda, Griggo, and Noël-Soriano 2001; Speth 2004).

32. The higher values presented by Lieberman and Shea (1994: table 2) for Kebara and Qafzeh XV include "pointed artifacts" that are not strictly Levallois points and are not included in the current analysis. These differences do not influence the overall pattern.

33. Much of the differences that do exist reflect the powerful signature of taphonomic processes and of hunting choices and availability rather than differences in the modes of acquisition of faunal resources (Rabinovich and Hovers 2004).

34. Controlled use of fire in open-air sites probably goes back to much earlier periods in Africa and the Levant (for a recent review, see Alpreson-Afil and Goren-Inbar 2006).

35. The rich localities of Rosh Ein Mor and Nahal Aqev in the Negev were identified as base camps in settlement systems based on logistical mobility (Marks and Freidel 1977; see discussion in Meignen et al. 2006). Regardless of the nature of the occupation at these sites, their dating (Rink et al. 2003) may be controversial (Hovers 2006; Richter 2007). In any case, the virtual absence of faunal remains precludes a more detailed discussion of the sites and limits the ability to rely on lines of evidence besides lithics.

36. Henry (1998) considered Tor Sabiha, a high-elevation, low-density occupation in Jordan, an ephemeral summer camp. The composition of the site's lithic assemblage may also indicate a task-specific, probably hunting-related, locality (Hovers 1997; Meignen et al. 2006).

37. Because the latter are incorporated in archaeological deposits due to the activity of birds of prey, which are shy of human presence, their frequencies and densities vary conversely to those of anthropogenic remains.

38. That meetings and aggregations took place during the Middle Paleolithic is taken here as granted, despite the absence of archaeological evidence, since biological viability of human groups could not have been ensured otherwise (Wobst 1974, 1976). Such aggregations would have been of short duration. Large social groups are not a natural hominin condition and cause scalar stress that is mediated through complex social mechanisms (e.g., establishment of social and political hierarchies) and/or the creation of cohesive agents (e.g., art; Johnson 1982). Evidence for the former is completely absent from the record of the Levantine Middle Paleolithic, while art occurs very sporadically at best (e.g., Goren-Inbar 1990b:237–238; Hovers, Vandermeersch, and Bar-Yosef 1997; Hovers et al. 2003; Marshack 1996). In the absence of such cohesive agents, aggregations would be rapidly dismantled because of growing social stress and conflicts (cf. Silberbauer 1981:174–180; Tanaka 1980:116–127).

39. Levallois points are admittedly exceptional in this respect. Data from assemblages other than Qafzeh imply that the dimensional and morphological properties of these artifacts were indeed linked to their function. Still, points almost never

constitute the largest component of Levallois products in any given assemblage. This is the case in assemblages where unipolar convergent Levallois production might have been geared toward point production (Meignen and Bar-Yosef 1992), let alone in assemblages where the dominant production methods are not similarly oriented.

40. Munday (1977) suggested that a high degree of technological variability occurred throughout the sequence of Nahal Aqev, but its main component was in assemblage structure rather than radical changes in core-reduction modes. Munday notes correctly that this may have to do with changes in occupation mode.

41. Ksar Akil may be another site where Middle Paleolithic occupation was of considerable length, and it indeed demonstrates a higher degree of core-reduction variation than do other sites (Marks and Volkman 1986; Mellars and Tixier 1989).

42. Garrod (1962) and Copeland (1983a) both qualified in later publications their respective linear approaches to lithic typo-technological variation (see discussion in chapter 1).

CHAPTER 9

1. Suggestions to the contrary were made by Mithen (1994, 1996). Drawing heavily on modular brain and multiple intelligences theories (Fodor 1985; Gardner 1983; Humphrey 1976, 1992), Mithen emphasized that Neanderthal minds were not lacking in the domains of functional or natural history intelligences. The difference from modern brains was, in his view, that they were domain-specific, lacking the fluidity that is the essence of a cognitively modern mind. As a result they would have lacked the ability to anticipate future needs and to engage in planning their activities (Binford 1989; Soffer 1989), or to create arbitrary associations between an object and an idea, i.e., were unable to symbolize (as discussed archaeologically by, e.g., Chase and Dibble 1987). Wynn and Coolidge (2004) take a different tack, arguing for a qualitatively modern cognitive mind in Neanderthals that, like the modern mind, relied on long-term working memory as a centerpiece of problem-solving. They hypothesize that Neanderthal working memory was not as large as that of Moderns (in whom it is enhanced) and could hold in active attention a smaller variety of information. In particular, reduced storage capacity in the phonological loop  would have been a bottleneck in language production. They view this difference in working memory storage size as the reason for the cultural "stasis" throughout the Middle Paleolithic (the issue of "stasis", if at all, and its possible causes is addressed in greater detail in chapter 10). Mithen's view, however, does not withstand the scrutiny of archaeological data (d'Errico 2003; Hayden 1993; Hovers 1997; Marshack 1989; Mellars 1996:357–391; Schepartz 1993). For example, the articulation of technological and symbolic behaviors as seen in Qafzeh (chapter 7) does not greatly differ from what can be seen in Neanderthal sites with regard to burials (Belfer-Cohen and Hovers 1992; Defleur 1993; Garrod and Bate 1937; Rak, Kimbel, and Hovers 1994; Vandermeersch 1970). Wynn and Coolidge's model of Enhanced Working Memory (EWM) in the modern brain has been criticized with regard to the postulated genetic mechanisms underlying it (Martin-Loeches 2006), whereas Beaman (2007) considered their argument to

be "evidentially weak" given observations on neurological patients. Recent suggestions that the FOXP2 gene attained its current, modern structure before Moderns and Neanderthals diverged (Krause et al. 2007) are similarly inconsistent with the view of late emergence of EWM as a specific capacity of *Homo sapiens*.

2. Leaving aside the complexities introduced by exaptations and cooptions, the discussion of which is beyond the scope of this work.

3. For example, the metabolic costs for Neanderthals living in a cold climate would have been immense (Aiello 2003; Churchill 2006; Steegman, Cerny, and Holliday 2002). It is likely that after having moved to the milder climate of the Levant (chapter 8), one of the first adaptations of Neanderthals would have been reduction in the costs of maintaining their (now nonmandatory) robust bodies. The immediate, quicker response would be behavioral, i.e. changes in extractive behavior and associated technological organization. Over time a biological change might have followed. Thus, the lower robusticity of Levantine Neanderthals, cited in support of their being part of a variable gracile sapient population (Arensburg and Belfer-Cohen 1998, with references therein), may be related to such relaxation of environmental pressure.

4. Cortical bone of femoral and tibial diapheses in modern humans of the same period is reported to be significantly thinner (Ben-Itzhak, Smith, and Bloom 1988).

5. The two burials of Neanderthal infants in Dederiyeh Cave were deposited in two distinct stratigraphic layers under different climatic conditions (Akazawa et al. 2004:250). Heeding the caveats of correlating prehistoric time scales and anthropological ones, as discussed in the main text, this evidence is more consistent with scenarios of two Neanderthal occupation phases or of an extended Neanderthal occupation of the Levant than with a scenario of a single, relatively short period in which they existed in the region.

6. This situation is analogous to attempts to identify the biological identity of the makers of late Pliocene Oldowan tools. Because several hominin genera and species are known to have inhabited east Africa at the time, researchers dealing with this period are careful to not assign tool-making ability to one taxon on the basis of chronology alone. That the undated intervals between any two dated points in time are much larger in the Oldowan than is the case in the Middle Paleolithic has no bearing on the principle and interpretation of the respective evidence.

7. One could suggest a scenario by which the deterioration of climatic condition acted as a mechanism that pushed human groups out of the Sahara, to sub-Saharan African and/or north into the Levant, during the shifts from humid interglacial to dry glacial periods. In such a model, dispersal into the Levant may have taken place during transitional periods as well as during full-blown interglacials; climatic conditions would have less of a regulatory role than originally envisioned by biogeographic models.

8. The only archaeologically attested human dispersal from Europe into the Levant, apart from that of Neanderthals, is the much later one of the bearers of the Aurignacian culture (Belfer-Cohen and Bar-Yosef 1999). This may suggest that hominin movements were influenced by a complex plethora of factors in addition to climatic changes.

9. These authors took the argument to the extreme, arguing that the presence of both Neanderthals and Moderns in the Levant testifies to their being a single taxon.

10. Depending on the specific texture and structure of plant communities in the variants of the Mediterranean ecosystem, gross vegetal biomass over 1,000 m² varies from 770 kg, mostly from annuals, in the productive garrigue and batha areas, through 325 kg/1,000 m² in the open gallery forests, to 160 kg/1,000 m² in the closed Mediterranean forest. At an average caloric value of 3.75 Kcal per one kg of vegetal material in the Mediterranean ecosystem, environmental productivity would have set the crucial value of population size across the region closer to the higher end of the range estimated by Shea (Hovers 2006:73 and references therein). Clearly, there would have been some components of the biomass that hominins were unable to use as food; still, the caloric contribution of most habitats would have been adequate to support hominin groups over long parts of the year.

11. It is interesting that during the period of 130,000–80,000 years ago, when a major dispersal from Africa and influx of hominins into the Levant are believed to have taken place (Lahr and Foley 1998; Vaks et al. 2007), humid interglacial conditions would, if anything, have reduced competition for resources.

12. The population densities of 1–38 individuals/100 km² in temperate forests and of 1–19 individuals/100 km² in temperate deserts were used to calculate very low population sizes in the Middle Paleolithic Levant, ranging from 8,400 to 5,700 people, respectively. Shea (2006a) considers even those as overestimates.

13. The sizes postulated on the basis of temperate forests and deserts are likely underestimates because they draw on the ethnographic densities of extant hunter-gatherers in temperate forests or temperate deserts. The analogues are inadequate because these two ecosystems are less productive than the Mediterranean ecosystems of the Levant (Blondel and Aronson 1999).

14. Perlès (2005) discusses the possible reasons for non-transfer of technological and symbolic ideas and objects across the Mediterranean Basin during the Neolithic, implicating local traditions and ideologies that led to local conservatism as the explanation of the phenomenon. While the Mediterranean Neolithic is a far cry from the Levantine Middle Paleolithic, the argument developed in earlier chapters for the existence of technological traditions in the Levantine Middle Paleolithic suggests that some of Perlès's ideas might be pertinent, of course with the proverbial grain of salt, to the current discussion.

CHAPTER 10

1. According to some researchers, however, the technological diversity and innovative streaks seen in European Upper Paleolithic lithic assemblages have been attributed to analytical biases stemming from prejudices (e.g., Reynolds 1990) or from incompatible standards of definition (Chazan 1995).

2. In that the material correlates ascribed to modernity are to be discovered as opposed to being prescribed by theoretical considerations, this scenario is not a formal model (Gamble 2007:38; Henshilwood and Marean 2003; Marean and Assefa 2004).

3. It is in fact doubtful that all aspects of the African MSA clearly depict a gradual broadening of technological innovativeness and proficiency. While the forms of points may have been adjusted through time, in response to changes in hafting technology (Brook et al. 2006; Shea 2006b; Villa and Lenoir 2006), other trends in the realm of lithics are not time-transgressive. The Howeisons Poort (HP) blade-rich assemblages, inclusive of backed-retouched forms, were often promoted as precursors of the "real" Late Stone Age (LSA) in sub-Saharan Africa. Recent research, however, has shown that those assemblages were replaced by flake-dominated MSA III assemblages and only later replaced by the laminar LSA (Soriano, Villa, and Wadley 2007; Villa, Delagnes, and Wadley 2005). In Europe, too, laminar production systems occur as a time-transgressive phenomenon (Delagnes and Meignen 2006; Kuhn 2006).

The use of aquatic resources appears to represent a similar trend. Although reported from the early MSA in South Africa (Marean et al. 2007), it may not have become a stabilized, ongoing innovation in subsistence technology of MSA people as a rule (Klein et al. 2004). Based on isotopic studies, this behavior does not appear to have been a staple of the modern humans who reached Europe in the late Pleistocene. Isotopic signatures suggesting the use of aquatic resources occur in the mid-Upper Paleolithic (Richards et al. 2001).

4. It is implicitly assumed that authors of Levantine IUP and early Upper Paleolithic were modern humans. Strictly speaking, this remains an open question in the absence of IUP and early Upper Paleolithic burials (Gilead 1991).

5. Incised items (Goren-Inbar 1990b; Henshilwood et al. 2002; Hovers, Vandermeersch, and Bar-Yosef 1997; Hovers et al. 2003; Marshack 1996) may also be considered symbolic, i.e., information-encoding devices, though possibly on a smaller spatial scale (see Wobst 1977).

6. Recent findings pertaining to Neanderthal genomics are most parsimoniously interpreted as suggesting that Neanderthals shared with humans the same form of the FOXP2 gene (Krause et al. 2007), a gene that is relevant to the human ability to develop language. This may indicate that language, epitomized as a hallmark of cognitive modernity, may not have been a singular characteristic of "fully-fledged" Moderns. This notion is in agreement with the interpretation of the archaeological data suggested in this study.

7. A major question arising from such models concerns the evolutionary processes that might have selected for such costly yet seemingly unexploited abilities as those that came to be known as "modern cognition." Similar questions were asked in the context of primate studies, when observations on captive chimpanzees indicated that they had cognitive abilities never observed in the wild (Belfer-Cohen and Hovers, n.d.). In response, researchers came up with models that emphasized the role of social factors in exerting selective pressures that favored social ("Machiavellian") intelligence and inventiveness (Dunbar 2003; Humphrey 1976). These are therefore a fundamental part of human cognition. In attempting to explain human cognitive abilities, neurologists, evolutionary psychologists, and cognitive scientists have come up with a myriad of explanations that run the gamut of exaptations, cooptions, and adaptations. A detailed discussion of these is beyond the scope of this work.

# References


Adams, W. Y., and Adams, E. W. 1991. *Archaeological Typology and Practical Reality: A Dialectical Approach to Artifact Classification and Sorting.* Cambridge University Press, Cambridge.

Adler, D. S., and Tushabramishvili, N. 2004. Middle Paleolithic Patterns of Settlement and Subsistence in the Southern Caucasus. In N. Conard (ed.), *Middle Palaeolithic Settlement Dynamics,* pp. 91–132. Kerns Verlag, Tübingen.

Adler, D. S., Prindiville, T. J., and Conard, N. J. 2003. Patterns of Spatial Organization and Land Use during the Eemian Interglacial in the Rhineland: New Data from Wallertheim, Germany. *Eurasian Prehistory* 1: 25–78.

Aiello, L. C. 1993. The Fossil Evidence for Modern Human Origins in Africa: A Revised View. *American Anthropologist* 95: 73–96.

———. 2003. Neanderthal Thermo-Regulation and the Glacial Climate. In T. H. van Andel and W. Davies (eds.), *Neanderthals and Modern Humans in Europe during the Last Glaciation,* pp. 147–156. McDonald Institute for Archaeological Research, Cambridge.

Aiello, L. C., and Wheeler, P. 1995. The Expensive Organ Hypothesis: The Brain and the Digestive System in Human and Primate Evolution. *Current Anthropology* 36: 199–221.

Aitkin, M. J., and Valladas, H. 1992. Luminescence Dating Relevant to Human Origins. *Philosophical Transactions of the Royal Society London B* 337: 139–144.

Akazawa, T. 1979. Middle Paleolithic Assemblages from Douara Cave. In K. Hanihara and T. Akazawa (eds.), *Paleolithic Site of Douara Cave and Paleography of Palmyra Basin in Syria,* pp. 1–30. The University Museum, University of Tokyo, Tokyo.

———. 1988. Ecologie de l'occupation de la grotte de Douara, Syrie, au Paléolithique moyen. *L'Anthropologie* 92: 883–900.

Akazawa, T., and Muhesen, S. 2002. *Neanderthal Burials: Excavations of the Dederiyeh Cave, Efrin, Syria. Studies in Honor of Hisashi Suzuki.* International Research Center for Japanese Studies, Kyoto.

Akazawa, T., Dodo, Y., Muhesen, S., Abdul-Salam, A., Ane, Y., Kondo, O., and Mizoguchi, Y. 1993. The Neanderthal Remains from Dederiyeh Cave, Syria: Interim Report. *Anthropological Science* 101: 361–387.

Akazawa, T., Muhesen, S., Dodo, Y., Kondo, O., Yoneda, M., Griggo, C., and Hakime, I. 2004. Neandertal Burials: Excavations of Dederiyeh Cave, Syria. In O. Aurenche, M. P. Le Mière, and P. Sanlaville (eds.), *From the River to the Sea: The Palaeolithic and the Neolithic on the Euphrates and in the Northern Levant. Studies in Honor of Lorraine Copeland,* pp. 241–270. BAR International Series 1263. Archaeopress, Oxford.

Albert, R. M., Bar-Yosef, O., Meignen, L., and Weiner, S. 2003. Quantitative Phytolith Study of Hearths from the Natufian and Middle Palaeolithic Levels of Hayonim Cave (Galilee, Israel). *Journal of Archaeological Science* 30: 461–480.

Albert, R. M., Weiner, S., Bar-Yosef, O., and Meignen, L. 2000. Phytoliths in the Middle Palaeolithic Deposits of Kebara Cave, Mount Carmel, Israel: Study of the Plant Material Used for Fuel and Other Purposes. *Journal of Archaeological Science* 27: 931–947.

Albert, R. M., Lavi, O., Estroff, L., Weiner, S., Tsatskin, A., Ronen, A., and Lev-Yadun, S. 1999. Mode of Occupation of Tabun Cave, Mt Carmel, Israel during the Mousterian Period: A Study of the Sediments and Phytoliths. *Journal of Archaeological Science* 26: 1249–1260.

Almogi-Labin, A., Bar-Matthews, M., and Ayalon, A. 2004. Climate Variability in the Levant and Northeast Africa during the Late Quaternary Based on Marine and Land Records. In N. Goren-Inbar and J. D. Speth (eds.), *Human Paleoecology in the Levantine Corridor,* pp. 117–134. Oxbow Books, Oxford.

Aloni, R. 1984. The Vegetation of the Lower Galilee. In A. Aloni (ed.), *Vegetation of Israel,* Plants and Animals of the Land of Israel 8, pp. 143–151. Ministry of Defense/The Society for the Protection of Nature, Tel-Aviv (Hebrew).

Aloni, R., and Orshan, G. 1972. A Vegetation Map of the Lower Galilee. *Israel Journal of Botany* 21: 209–227.

Alperson, N., Barzilai, O., Dag, D., Hartman, G., and Matskevich, Z. 2000. The Age and Context of the Tabun I Skeleton: A Reply to Schwarcz et al. *Journal of Human Evolution* 38: 849–853.

Alperson-Afil, N., and Goren-Inbar, N. 2006. Out of Africa and into Eurasia with Controlled Use of Fire: The Evidence from Gesher Benot Ya'aqov, Israel. *Archaeology, Ethnology & Anthropology of Eurasia* 4: 63–78.

Alperson-Afil, N., and Hovers, E. 2005. Differential Use of Space at the Neandertal Site of Amud Cave, Israel. *Eurasian Prehistory* 3: 3–22.

Alvard, M. S. 2003. The Adaptive Nature of Culture. *Evolutionary Anthropology* 12: 136–149.

Ambrose, S. H. 2001. Paleolithic Technology and Human Evolution. *Science* 291: 1748–1753.

———. 2006. Howiesons Poort Lithic Raw Material Procurement Patterns and the Evolution of Modern Human Behavior: A Response to Minichillo. *Journal of Human Evolution* 50: 365–369.

Ambrose, S. H., and Lorenz, K. G. 1990. Social and Ecological Models for the Middle Stone Age in Southern Africa. In P. Mellars and C. Stringer (eds.), *The Emergence of Modern Humans: An Archaeological Perspective,* pp. 3–33. Cornell University Press, Ithaca, N.Y.

Ammerman, A. J., and Feldman, M. W. 1974. On the "Making" of an Assemblage of Stone Tools. *American Antiquity* 39: 610–616.

Anderson-Gerfaud, P. 1990. Aspects of Behavior in the Middle Paleolithic: Functional Analysis of Stone Tools from Southwestern France. In P. Mellars (ed.), *The Emergence of Modern Humans: An Archaeological Perspective,* pp. 389–418. Cornell University Press, Ithaca, N.Y.

Andrefsky, W. 1994. Raw Material Availability and the Organization of Technology. *American Antiquity* 59: 21–34.

———. 1998. *Lithics: Macroscopic Approaches to Analysis.* Cambridge University Press, Cambridge.

Andrews, P. 1990. *Owls, Caves and Fossils: Predation, Preservation and Accumulation of Small Mammal Bones in Caves, with an Analysis of the Pleistocene Cave Faunas from Westbury-Sub-Mendip, Somerset, UK.* University of Chicago Press, Chicago.

Anonymous. 1981. *The Carrying Capacity of the Coastal Plain in Pre-Agricultural Periods.* The Department of Eretz-Israel Studies, University of Haifa, Haifa (in Hebrew).

Arcadi, A. C. 2006. Species Resilience in Pleistocene Hominids that Traveled Far and Ate Widely: An Analogy to the Wolf-like Canids. *Journal of Human Evolution* 51: 383–394.

Arensburg, B., and Belfer-Cohen, A. 1998. Neandertals and Moderns: Re-thinking the Levantine Middle Paleolithic Hominids. In T. Akazawa, K. Aoki, and O. Bar-Yosef (eds.), *Neandertals and Modern Humans in Asia,* pp. 311–322. Plenum Press, New York.

Arensburg, B., Bar-Yosef, O., Belfer-Cohen, A., and Rak, Y. 1990. Mousterian and Aurignacian Human Remains from Hyonim Cave, Israel. *Paléorient* 16: 107–109.

Ashkenazi, H. 2005. Standardization of Blade Production in the Levantine MP. M.A. thesis, The Hebrew University of Jerusalem.

Audouze, F. 2002. Leroi-Gourhan, a Philosopher of Technique and Evolution. *Journal of Archaeological Research* 10: 277–306.

Ayalon, A., Bar-Matthews, M., and Kaufman, A. 2002. Climatic Conditions during Marine Oxygen Isotope Stage 6 in the Eastern Mediterranean Region from the Isotopic Composition of Speleothems of Soreq Cave, Israel. *Geology* 30: 303–306.

Bada, J., and Helfman, P. 1976. Application of Amino-Acid Racemization on Paleoanthropology and Archaeology. Union Internationale des Sciences Préhistoriques at Protohistoriques, IXe Congres, pp. 39–62. Nice.

Baharav, D. 1974. Note on the Population Structure and Biomass of the Mountain Gazelle, *Gazella gazella gazella. Israel Journal of Zoology* 23: 39–44.

———. 1981. Food Habitat of the Mountain Gazelle in Semi-arid Habitats of the Eastern Lower Galilee. *Journal of Arid Environments* 4: 63–69.

———. 1982. Desert Habitat Partitioning by the Dorcas Gazelle. *Journal of Arid Environments* 5: 323–335.

Bailey, G. N., and Davidson, I. 1983. Site Exploitation of Territories and Topography: Two Case Studies from Paleolithic Spain. *Journal of Archaeological Science* 10: 87–116.

Bailey, S. E., and Lynch, J. M. 2005. Diagnostic Differences in Mandibular P4 Shape between Neandertals and Anatomically Modern Humans. *American Journal of Physical Anthropology* 126: 268–277.

Bamforth, D. B. 1986. Technological Efficiency and Tool Curation. *American Antiquity* 51: 38–50.

———. 1991. Technological Organization and Hunter-Gatherer Land Use: A California Example. *American Antiquity* 56: 216–234.

Bang, M., Medin, D. L., and Atran, S. 2007. Cultural Mosaics and Mental Models of Nature. *Proceedings of the National Academy of Science U.S.A.* 104: 13868–13874.

Barham, L. 2007. Modern Is as Modern Does? Technological Trends and Thresholds in the South-Central African Record. In P. Mellars, K. Boyle, O. Bar-Yosef, and C. Stringer (eds.), *Rethinking the Human Revolution,* pp. 165–176. McDonald Institute of Archaeological Research, Cambridge.

Barkai, R., Gopher, A., and Shimelmitz, R. 2005. Middle Pleistocene Blade Production in the Levant: An

Amudian Assemblage from Qesem Cave, Israel. *Eurasian Prehistory* 3: 39–74.

Barkai, R., Gopher, A., Lauritzen, S. E., and Frumkin, A. 2003. Uranium Series Dates from Qesem Cave, Israel, and the End of the Lower Palaeolithic. *Nature* 423: 977–979.

Bar-Matthews, M., and Ayalon, A. 2001. *Eastern Mediterranean Paleoclimate during the Last 250,000 Years as Derived from the Petrography, Mineralogy, Trace Element and Isotopic Composition of Cave Deposits (Speleothems), Israel,* Report GSI/41/2001. Geological Survey of Israel, Jerusalem.

———. 2004. Speleothems as Palaeoclimate Indicators: A Case Study from Soreq Cave, Located in the Eastern Mediterranean Region, Israel. In R. W. Battarbee et al. (eds.), *Past Climate Variability through Europe and Africa,* pp. 363–391. Springer, Dordrecht.

Bar-Matthews, M., Ayalon, A., and Kaufman, A. 1997. Late Quaternary Paleoclimate in the Eastern Mediterranean Region from Stable Isotope Analysis of Speleothems at Soreq Cave, Israel. *Quaternary Research* 47: 155–168.

———. 2000. Timing and Hydrological Conditions of Sapropel Events in the Eastern Mediterranean, as Evident from Speleothems, Soreq Cave, Israel. *Chemical Geology* 169: 145–156.

Bar-Matthews, M., Ayalon A., Kaufman, A., and Wasseburg G. J. 1999. The Eastern Mediterranean Paleoclimate as a Reflection of Regional Events; Soreq Cave, Israel. *Earth and Planetary Science Letters* 166: 85–95.

Bar-Matthews, M., Ayalon, A., Gilmour, M., Matthews, A., and Hawkesworth, C. J. 2003. Sea–Land Oxygen Isotopic Relationships from Planktonic Froaminifera and Speletothems in the Eastern Mediterranean Region and their Implication for Paleorainfall during Interglacial Intervals. *Geochimica et Cosmochimica Acta* 67: 3181–3199.

Barton, C. M. 1990. Beyond Style and Function: A View from the Middle Paleolithic. *American Anthropologist* 92: 57–72.

Barton, C. M., and Clark, G. A. 1993. Cultural and Natural Formation Processes in Late Quaternary Caves and Rock Shelter Sites of Western Europe and the Near East. In P. Goldberg, D. T. Nash, and M. D. Petraglia (eds.), *Formation Processes in Archaeological Sites,* pp. 33–52. Prehistory Press, Madison, Wis.

Bartov, Y., Goldstein, S. L., Stein, M., and Enzel, Y. 2003. Catastrophic Arid Episodes in the Eastern Mediterranean Linked with the North Atlantic Heinrich Events. *Geology* 31: 439–442.

Bartov, Y., Stein, M., Enzel, Y., Agnon, A., and Reches, Z. 2002. Lake Levels and Sequence Stratigraphy of Lake Lisan, the Late Pleistocene Precursor of the Dead Sea. *Quaternary Research* 57: 9–21.

Baruch, U., Werker, E., and Bar-Yosef, O. 1992. Charred Wood Remains from Kebara Cave, Israel: Preliminary Results. *Bulletin de la Société Botanique Française* 139: 531–538.

Bar-Yosef, O. 1979. Excavations in Hayonim Cave (1975–1979). *Mitekufat Haeven* 16: 88–98.

———. 1983. The Natufian in the Southern Levant. In T. C. Young, P. E. L. Smith, and P. Mortensen (eds.), *The Hilly Flanks and Beyond,* pp. 11–42. The Oriental Institute, Chicago.

———. 1989. Upper Pleistocene Cultural Stratigraphy in Southwest Asia. In E. Trinkaus (ed.), *The Emergence of Modern Humans: Biocultural Adaptations in the Later Pleistocene,* pp. 154–180. Cambridge University Press, Cambridge.

———. 1991. The Search for Lithic Variability among Levantine Epi-Palaeolithic Industries. In *25 Ans d'Études Technologiques en Préhistoire,* pp. 319–336. XI Recontres Internationales d'Archéologie et d'Histoire d'antibe. Éditions APDCA, Juan-les-Pins.

———. 1992. Middle Paleolithic Human Adaptations in the Mediterranean Levant. In T. Akazawa, K. Aoki, and T. Kimura (eds.), *The Evolution and Dispersal of Modern Humans in Asia,* pp. 189–215. Hakusen-Sha, Tokyo.

———. 1993. Site Formation Processes from a Levantine Viewpoint. In P. Goldberg, D. T. Nash, and M. D. Petraglia (eds.), *Formation Processes in Archaeological Sites,* pp. 13–32. Prehistory Press, Madison, Wis.

———. 1994. The Contribution of Southwest Asia to the Study of the Origin of Modern Humans. In M. H. Nitecki and D. V. Nitecki (eds.), *Origins of Anatomically Modern Humans,* pp. 23–66. Plenum Press, New York.

———. 1998a. The Chronology of the Middle Paleolithic in the Levant. In T. Akazawa, K. Aoki, and O. Bar-Yosef (eds.), *Neandertals and Modern Humans in Asia,* pp. 39–56. Plenum Press, New York.

———. 1998b. Jordan Prehistory: A View from the West. In D. O. Henry (ed.), *The Prehistoric Archaeology of Jordan,* pp. 162–178. Archaeopress, Oxford.

———. 2000. The Middle and Early Upper Paleolithic in Southwest Asia and Neighboring Regions. In O. Bar-Yosef and D. Pilbeam (eds.), *The Geography of Neandertals and Modern Humans in Europe and the Greater Mediterranean,* pp. 107–156. Peabody Museum of Archaeology and Ethnography, Cambridge, Mass..

———. 2002. The Upper Paleolithic Revolution. *Annual Review of Anthropology* 31: 363–393.

———. 2006. Between Observations and Models: An Eclectic View of Middle Paleolithic Archaeology. In E. Hovers and S. L. Kuhn (eds.), *Transitions before The Transition: Evolution and Stability in the Middle Paleolithic and Middle Stone Age,* pp. 305–325. Springer, New York.

Bar-Yosef, O., and Belfer-Cohen, A. 1991. From Sedentary Hunter-Gatherers to Territorial Farmers in the Levant. In S. A. Gregg (ed.), *Between Bands and States,* pp. 181–202. Center for Archaeological Investigations, Southern Illinois University, Carbondale.

———. 1992. From Foraging to Farming in the Mediterranean Levant. In A. B. Gebauer and T. D. Price (eds.), *Transitions to Agriculture in Prehistory,* pp. 21–48. Monographs in World Archaeology N. 23. Prehistory Press, Madison, Wis.

———— 2004. The Qafzeh Upper Paleolithic Assemblages: 70 Years Later. *Eurasian Prehistory* 2: 145–180.

Bar-Yosef, O., and Callander, J. 1999. The Woman from Tabun: Garrod's Doubts in Historical Perspective. *Journal of Human Evolution* 37: 879–885.

Bar-Yosef, O., and Dibble, H. L. 1995. Preface. In H. L. Dibble and O. Bar-Yosef (eds.), *The Definition and Interpretation of Levallois Technology*, pp. ix–xiii. Prehistory Press, Madison, Wis.

Bar-Yosef, O., and Goren-Inbar, N. 1993. *The Lithic Assemblages of 'Ubeidiya, a Lower Paleolithic Site in the Lower Jordan Valley*, Qedem 34. Institute of Archaeology, Jerusalem.

Bar-Yosef, O., and Kuhn, S. 1999. The Big Deal about Blades: Laminar Technologies and Human Evolution. *American Anthropologist* 101: 322–338.

Bar-Yosef, O., and Meadow, R. H. 1995. The Origins of Agriculture in the Near East. In T. D. Price and A. B. Gebauer (eds.), *Last Hunters—First Farmers*, pp. 39–94. School of American Research, Santa Fe.

Bar-Yosef, O., and Meignen, L. 2001. The Chronology of the Middle Palaeolithic Period in Retrospect. *Bulletin et Mémoires de la Société d'Anthropologie de Paris* 13: 269–289.

————. (eds.) 2007. *Kebara Cave Mt. Carmel, Israel. The Middle and Upper Paleolithic Archaeology. Part I.* American School of Prehistoric Research Bulletin 49. Peabody Museum of Archaeology and Ethnology, Harvard University, Cambridge, Mass.

Bar-Yosef, O., and Pilbeam, D. (eds.) 2000. *The Geography of Neandertals and Modern Humans in Europe and the Greater Mediterranean.* Peabody Museum Bulletin. Peabody Museum of Archaeology and Ethnology, Harvard University, Cambridge, Mass.

Bar-Yosef, O., and Vandermeersch, B. 1981. Notes Concerning the Possible Age of the Mousterian Layers in Qafzeh Cave. In J. Cauvin and P. Sanlaville (eds.), *Préhistoire du Levant*, pp. 281–286. CNRS, Paris.

————. 1993. Modern Humans in the Levant. *Scientific American* 268: 94–99.

————. 2007. The History of Excavations at Kebara Cave. In O. Bar-Yosef and L. Meignen (eds.), *Kebara Cave Mt. Carmel, Israel: The Middle and Upper Paleolithic Archaeology. Part I*, pp. 23–38. American School of Prehistoric Research Bulletin 49. Peabody Museum of Archaeology and Ethnology, Harvard University, Cambridge, Mass.

Bar-Yosef, O., Vandermeersch, B., Arensburg, B., Goldberg, P., Laville, H., Meignen, L., Rak, Y., Tchernov, E., and Tillier, A.-M. 1986. New Data Concerning the Origins of Modern Man in the Levant. *Current Anthropology* 27: 63–64.

Bar-Yosef, O., Vandermeersch, B., Arensburg, B., Belfer-Cohen, A., Goldberg, P., Laville, H., Meignen, L., Rak, Y., Speth, J. D., Tchernov, E., Tillier, A.-M., and Weiner, S. 1992. The Excavations in Kebara Cave, Mt. Carmel. *Current Anthropology* 33: 497–550.

Bar-Yosef Mayer D. E. 2005. The Exploitation of Shells as Beads in the Palaeolithic and Neolithic of the Levant. *Paléorient* 31: 176–185.

Bate, D. M. A. 1937. Palaeontology: The Fossil Fauna of the Wady el-Mughara Caves. In D. E. A. Garrod and D. M. A. Bate (eds.), *The Stone Age of Mount Carmel*, pp. 137–240. Clarendon Press, Oxford.

Baumler, M. E. 1988. Core Reduction, Flake Production and the Middle Paleolithic Industry of Zobiste (Yugoslavia). In H. L. Dibble and A. Montet-White (eds.), *Upper Pleistocene Prehistory of Western Euroasia*, pp. 255–274. University Museum Monographs 54. University of Pennsylvania Press, Philadelphia.

Baumler, M. E., and Speth, J. D. 1993. A Middle Paleolithic Assemblage from Kunji Cave, Iran. In D. I. Olszewski and H. L. Dibble (eds.), *The Paleolithic Prehistory of the Zagros-Taurus Region*, pp. 1–73. University Museum Symposium Series V. The University Museum, University of Pennsylvania Press, Philadelphia.

Bazin, E., Glemin, S., and Galtier, N. 2006. Population Size Does not Influence Mitochondrial Genetic Diversity in Animals. *Science* 312: 570–572.

Beaman, C. P. 2007. Modern Cognition in the Absence of Working Memory: Does the Working Memory Account of Neandertal Cognition Work? *Journal of Human Evolution* 52: 702–706.

Begin, Z. B., Ehrlich, A. and Nathan, Y. 1974. Lake Lisan: The Pleistocene Precursor of the Dead Sea. *Geological Survey of Israel* 63: 1–28.

————. 1980. Stratigraphy and Facies Distribution in the Lisan Formation: New Evidence from the Area South of the Dead Sea, Israel. *Israel Journal of Earth Sciences* 29: 182–189.

Begin, Z. B., Broecker, W., Buchbinder, B., Druckman, Y., Kaufman, A., Magaritz, M., and Neev, D. 1985. Dead Sea and Lake Lisan Levels in the Last 30,000 years: A Preliminary Report. *Israel Geological Survey* GSI/29/85.

Belfer-Cohen, A. 1988. The Appearance of Symbolic Expression in the Upper Pleistocene of the Levant as Compared to Western Europe. In M. Otte (ed.), *L'Homme de Neandertal*, vol. 5: *La Pensée*, pp. 25–29. Universitè de Liège, Liège.

Belfer-Cohen, A., and Bar-Yosef, O. 1999. The Levantine Aurignacian: 60 Years of Research. In W. Davies and R. Charles (eds.), *Dorothy Garrod and the Progress of the Paleolithic: Studies in the Prehistoric Archaeology on the Near East and Europe*, pp. 119–134. Oxbow Books, Oxford.

Belfer-Cohen, A., and Goren-Inbar, N. 1994. Cognition and Communication in the Levantine Lower Palaeolithic. *World Archaeology* 26: 144–157.

Belfer-Cohen, A., and Goring-Morris, A. N. 2007. From the Beginning: Levantine Upper Palaeolithic Cultural Change and Continuity. In P. Mellars, K. Boyle, O. Bar-Yosef, and C. Stringer (eds.), *Rethinking the Human Revolution*, pp. 199–205. McDonald Institute for Archaeological Research, Cambridge.

————. in press. The Shift from the Middle Palaeolithic to the Upper Palaeolithic: Levantine Perspectives. In M. Camps and C. Szmidt (eds.), *The Mediterranean from 50,000 to 25,000 BP: Turning Points and New Directions*, pp. 87–97. Oxbow, Oxford.

Belfer-Cohen, A., and Hovers, E. 1992. In the Eye of the Beholder: Mousterian and Natufian Burials in the Levant. *Current Anthropology* 33: 463–471.

———. 2005. The Ground Stone Assemblages of the Natufian and Neolithic Societies in the Levant: Current Status. *Journal of the Israel Prehistoric Society* 35: 299–308.

———. n.d. 'Modernity,' 'Enhanced Working Memory' and the Middle-to-Upper Paleolithic Transition in the Levant. Paper presented in the Wenner-Gren Symposium on "Enhanced Working Memory," Lisbon, March 2008.

Belitzky, S., Goren-Inbar, N., and Werker, E. 1991. A Middle Pleistocene Wooden Plank with Man-made Polish. *Journal of Human Evolution* 20: 349–353.

Beller, S., and Bender, A. 2008. The Limits of Counting: Numerical Cognition between Evolution and Culture. *Science* 319: 213–215.

Ben-Itzhak, S., Smith, P., and Bloom, R. A. 1988. Radiographic Study of the Humerus in Neandertals and *Homo sapiens sapiens*. *American Journal of Physical Anthropology* 77: 231–242.

Bergman, C. A., and Ohnuma, K. 1983. Technological Notes on Some Blades from Hummal Ia, El-Kowm, Syria. *Quartär* 33/34: 171–180.

Bergman, C. A., and Roberts, M. A. 1988. Flaking Technology at the Acheulian site of Boxgrove, West Sussex, England. *Revue Archéologique de Picardie* 1–2: 105–113.

Bergman, C. A., and Stringer C. B. 1989. Fifty Years After: Egbert, an Early Upper Palaeolithic Juvenile from Ksar Akil, Lebanon. *Paléorient* 15: 99–111.

Besançon, J., Copeland, L., Hours, F., Muhesen, S., and Sanlaville, P. 1982. Prospection géographique et préhistorique dans le bassin d'El Kowm (Syrie). Rapport préliminaire. *Cahiers de l'Euphrate* 3: 9–26.

Beyries, S. 1986. Approche fonctionelle de l'outillage provenant d'un site paléolithic moyen du nord de la france: Corbehem. In A. Tuffreau and J. Somme (eds.), *Chronostratigraphie et faciès culturels du Paléolithique inférieur et moyen dans l'Europe du nord-ouest* pp. 219–224. Supplément 26 au Bulletin d'Association Française pour l'étude du Quaternaire. Société Préhistorique Française, Paris.

———. 1987. *Variabilité de l'industrie lithique au Moustérien: Approche fonctionnelle sur quelques gisements françai*, BAR International Series 328. Oxford.

———. 1988. Functional Variability of Lithic Sets in the Middle Palaeolithic. In H. L. Dibble and A. Montet-White (eds.), *Upper Pleistocene Prehistory of Western Euroasia*, pp. 213–225. University Museum Monograph 54. The University Museum, University of Pennsylvania Press, Philadelphia.

Beyries, S., and Boëda, E.1983. Étude technologique et traces d'utilisation des "éclats débordants" de Corbehem (Pas-de-Calais). *Bulletin de la Société Préhistorique Française* 80: 275–279.

Bickerton, D. 1990. *Language and Species*. Karoma, Ann Arbor.

Binford, L. R. 1967. Smudge Pits and Hide Smoking: The Use of Analogy in Archaeological Reasoning. *American Antiquity* 32: 1–12.

———. 1972. *On Archaeological Perspective*. Seminar Press, New York.

———. 1973. Interassemblage Variability: The Mousterian and the Functional Argument. In C. Renfrew (ed.), *The Explanation of Culture Change*, pp. 227–254. Duckworth, London.

———. 1977. Forty-Seven Trips: A Case Study in the Character of Archaeological Site Formation Processes. In R. V. S. Wright (ed.), *Stone Tools as Cultural Markers*, pp. 24–36. Australian Institute of Aboriginal Studies, Canberra.

———. 1978. *Nunamiut Ethnoarchaeology*. Academic Press, New York.

———. 1979. Organization and Formation Processes: Looking at Curated Technologies. *Journal of Anthropological Research* 35: 255–273.

———. 1980. Willow Smoke and Dogs' Tails: Hunter-Gatherer Settlement Systems and Archaeological Site Formation. *American Antiquity* 45: 4–20.

———. 1982. The Archaeology of Place. *Journal of Anthropological Archaeology* 1: 1–31.

———. 1983. *In Pursuit of the Past: Decoding the Archaeological Record*. Thames and Hudson, London.

———. 1986. An Alyawara Day: Making Men's Knives and Beyond. *Journal of Archaeological Science* 51: 547–562.

———. 1989. Isolating the Transition to Cultural Adaptation: An Organizational Approach. In E. Trinkaus (ed.), *The Emergence of Modern Humans: Biocultural Adaptations in the Later Pleistocene*, pp. 18–41. Cambridge University Press, Cambridge.

———. 2001. *Constructing Frames of Reference: An Analytical Method for Archaeological Theory Building Using Hunter-Gatherer and Environmental Data Sets*. Berkeley: University of California Press.

Binford, L. R., and Binford, S. R. 1966. A Preliminary Analysis of Functional Variability in the Mousterian of Levallois Facies. *American Anthropologist* 68: 238–295.

Binford, L. R., and O'Connell, J. 1984. An Alyawara Day: The Stone Quarry. *Journal of Anthropological Research* 40: 406–432.

Binford, L. R., and Stone, N. 1985. "Righteous Rocks" and Richard Gould: Some Observations on a Misguided "Debate." *American Antiquity* 50: 151–153.

Binford, S. R. 1966. Me'arat Shovakh (Mugharat esh-Shubabiq). *Israel Exploration Journal* 16: 18–32; 96–103.

Bisson, M. 2000. Nineteenth Century Tools for Twentieth-First Century Archaeology? Why the Middle Paleolithic Typology of Francois Bordes must be Replaced. *Journal of Archaeological Method and Theory* 7: 1–48.

Bleed, P. 1986. The Optimal Design of Hunting Weapons: Maintainability or Reliability. *American Antiquity* 51: 737–747.

———. 2001. Trees or Chains, Links or Branches: Conceptual Alternatives for Consideration of Stone Tool Production and Other Sequential Activities. *Journal of Archaeological Method and Theory* 18: 101–127.

Bleed, P. 2002. Obviously Sequential, but Continuous or Staged? Refits and Cognition in Three Late Paleolithic Assemblages from Japan. *Journal of Anthropological Archaeology* 21: 329–343.

Blondel, J., and Aronson, J. 1999. *Biology and Wildlife of the Mediterranean Region.* Oxford University Press, Oxford.

Bocherens, H., Drucker, D. G., Billiou, D., Patou-Mathis, M., and Vandermeersch, B. 2005. Isotopic Evidence for Diet and Subsistence Pattern of the Saint-Césaire I Neanderthal: Review and Use of a Multi-source Mixing Model. *Journal of Human Evolution* 49: 71–87.

Bodenheimer, S. F. 1956. *Animal Life in Biblical Lands: From Stone Age to the End of the Nineteenth Century.* Vol. 2. Jerusalem: Mosad Bialik (in Hebrew).

Boëda, E. 1986. Approche technologique du concept Levallois et évaluation de son champ d'application à travers trois gisements saaliens et weischeliens de la France septentrionale. Ph.D. thesis, Université de Paris X.

———. 1988. Le Concept laminaire: Rupture et filiation avec le concept Levallois. In M. Otte (ed.), *L'Homme de Nèadnertal,* vol. 8, pp. 41–59. ERAUL, Liège.

———. 1990. De la surface au volume: Analyse des conceptions des débitages Levallois et laminaire. In K. Farizy (ed.), *Paléolithique Moyen Récent et Paléolithique Supérieur Ancien en Europe,* pp. 63–68. Mémoires de Musée de Préhistoire d'Ile-de-France 3.

———. 1991. Approche de la variabilité des systèmes de production lithique des industries du Paléolithique inférieur et moyen: Chronique d'une variabilité attendue. *Technique et Culture* 17–18: 37–79.

———. 1993. Le débitage discoïde et le débitage Levallois récurrent centripète. *Bulletin de la Société Préhistorique Française* 90: 392–404.

———. 1995. Levallois: A Volumetric Construction, Methods, a Technique. In H. L. Dibble and O. Bar-Yosef (eds.), *The Definition and Interpretation of Levallois Technology,* pp. 41–68. Monographs in World Archaeology 23. Prehistory Press, Ann Arbor.

Boëda, E., and Muhesen, S. 1993. Umm El Tlel (El Kowm, Syrie): Étude préliminaire des industries lithiques du Paléolithique moyen et supérieur. *Cahiers de l'Euphrate* 7: 47–91.

———. 1994. Umm el Tlel (el-Kowm, Syrie): Etude préliminaire des industries lithiques du paléolithique moyen et supérieur 1991–1992. *Cahiers de l'Euphrate* 7: 47–91.

Boëda, E., Bourguignon, L. and Griggo, C. 1998. Activités de subsistance au Paléolithique moyen: Couche VI3b' du gisement d'Umm el Tlel (Syrie). In J.-P. Brugal, L. Meignen, and M. Patou-Mathis (eds.) *Economie préhistorique: Les Comportements de subsistance au Paléolithique,* pp. 243–258. Recontres Internationales d'Archéologie et d'Historie d'Antibe. Editions CNRS, Sophia Antipolis.

Boëda, E., Connan, J., and Muhesen, S. 1998. Bitumen as Hafting Material on Middle Paleolithic Artifacts from the el-Kowm Basin, Syria. In T. Akazawa T., K. Aoki, and O. Bar-Yosef (eds.), *Neandertals and Modern Humans in Asia,* pp. 181–204. Plenum Press, New York.

Boëda, E., Connan, J., Dessof, D., Muhesen, S., Mercier, N., Valladas, H., and Tisnerat, N. 1996. Bitumen as a Hafting Material on Middle Paleolithic Artefacts. *Nature* 380: 336–338.

Boëda, E., Geneste, J.-M., Griggo, C., Mercier, N., Muhesen, S., Reyss, J.-L., Taha, A., and Valladas, H. 1999. A Levallois Point Embedded in the Vertebra of a Wild Ass (Equus africanus): Hafting, Projectiles and Mousterian Hunting Weapons. *Antiquity* 73: 394–402.

Boëda, E., Geneste, J.-M., and Meignen, L. 1990. Identification de chaînes opératoires lithiques du Paléolithique ancien et moyen. *Paléo* 2: 43–79.

Boëda, E., Griggo, C., and Noël-Soriano, S. 2001. Différents modes d'occupation du site d'Umm el Tlel au cours du paléolithique moyen (El Kowm, Syrie centrale). *Paléorient* 27: 13–28.

Boesch, C. 2003. Is Culture a Golden Barrier between Human and Chimpanzee? *Evolutionary Anthropology* 12: 82–91.

Boesch, C., Marchesi, P., Marchesi, N., Fruth, B., and Joulian, F. 1994. Is Nut Cracking in Wild Chimpanzees a Cultural Behaviour? *Journal of Human Evolution* 26: 325–338.

Bordes, F. 1950. Principes d'une méthode d'étude des techniques de débitage et de la typologie du Paléolithique ancien et moyen. *L'Anthropologie* 54: 19–34.

———. 1953a. Notules de typologie paléolithique: I. outils moustériens à fracture volontaire. *Bulletin de la Société Préhistorique Française* 50: 224–226.

———. 1953b. Notules de typologie paléolithique: II. pointes levalloisiennes et pointes pseudo-levalloisiennes. *Bulletin de la Société Préhistorique Française* 50: 311–313.

———. 1953c. Levalloisien et Moustérien. *Bulletin de la Société Préhistorique Française* 50: 226–235.

———. 1954. Notules de typologie paléolithique: III. pointes moustériennes, racloirs convergents et déjétes, limaces. *Bulletin de la Société Préhistorique Française* 51: 336–339.

———. 1961. Mousterian Cultures in France. *Science* 134: 803–810.

———. [1961] 1988. *Typologie du Paléolithique ancien et moyen.* Presses du CNRS, Paris.

———. 1972. *A Tale of Two Caves.* Harper and Row, New York.

———. 1973. On the Chronology and Contemporaneity of Different Paleolithic Cultures in France. In C. Renfrew (ed.), *The Explanation of Culture Change,* pp. 217–226. Duckworth, London.

———. 1975. Sur la notion de sol d'habitat en préhistoire paléolithique. *Bulletin de la Société Préhistorique Française* 72: 139–144.

———. 1980. Le Débitage Levallois et ses variantes. *Bulletin de la Société Préhistorique Française* 77: 45–49.

———. 1981. Vignt-cinq ans apres: Le Complexe moustérien revisité. *Bulletin de la Société Préhistorique Française* 78: 77–87.

———. 1984. *Leçons Sur le Paléolithique: Le Paléolithique en Europe.* Cahiers du Quaternaire N. 7 II. Editions CNRS, Paris.

Bordes, F., and Bourgon, M. 1951. Le Complexe moustérien: Moustérien, Levalloisien et Tayacien. *L'Anthropologie* 55: 1–23.

Bordes, F., and de Sonneville-Bordes, D. 1970. The Significance of Variability in Palaeolithic Assemblages. *World Archaeology* 2: 61–73.

Bordes, J.-G. 2002. Chatelperronian/Aurignacian Interstratification at Roc de Comb and Le Piage: Lithic Taphonomy and Archaeological Implications. *Journal of Human Evolution* 42: A7–A8.

Bouchud, J. 1974. Étude préliminaire de la faune provenant de la grotte de Djebel Qafzeh près de Nazareth (Israël). *Paléorient* 2: 87–102.

Bourguinon, L. 1996. Un moustérien tardif sur le site d'Umm el-Tlel (bassin d'El Khowm, Syrie): exemples des niveaux IIbase et III2A. In E. Carbonell and M. Vaquero (eds.), *The Last Neandertals, the First Anatomically Modern Humans: A Tale about the Human Diversity*, pp. 317–336.

Bousman, C. B. 1993. Hunter-Gatherer Adaptations, Economic Risk and Tool Design. *Lithic Technology* 18: 59–86.

Boutié, P. 1989. Étude technologique de l'industrie moustérienne de la grotte de Qafzeh (près de Nazareth, Israël). In O. Bar-Yosef and B. Vandermeersch (eds.), *Investigations in South Levantine Prehistory*, pp. 213–230, BAR International Series 497. Oxford.

Boutié, P., and Rosen, S. A. 1989. Des gisements moustériens dans le Neguev central: résultats préliminaires de prospections récentes. In O. Bar-Yosef and B. Vandermeersch (eds.), *Investigations in South Levantine Prehistory*, pp. 147–168, BAR International Series. Oxford.

Bouzouggar, A., Barton, N., Vanhaeren, M., d'Errico, F., Collcutt, S., Higham, T., Hodge, E., Parfitt, S., Rhodes, E., Schwenninger, J.-L., Stringer, C., Turner, E., Ward, S., Moutmir, A., and Stambouli, A. 2007. 82,000-year-old Shell Beads from North Africa and Implications for the Origins of Modern Human Behavior. *Proceedings of the National Academy of Science U.S.A.* 104: 9964–9969.

Boyd, R., and Richerson, P. J. 1985. *Culture and the Evolutionary Process.* University of Chicago Press, Chicago.

———. 1992. How Microevolutionary Processes Give Rise to History. In M. H. Nitecki and D. V. Nitecki (eds.), *History and Evolution*, pp. 179–210. State University of New York Press, Albany.

Bradbury, A. P., and Carr, J. P. 1999. Examining Stage and Continuum Models of Flake Debris Analysis: An Experimental Approach. *Journal of Archaeological Science* 26: 105–116.

Brantingham, P. J. 2003. A Neutral Model of Stone Raw Material Procurement. *American Antiquity* 68: 487–509.

Brantingham, P. J., and Kuhn, S. L. 2001. Constraints on Levallois Core Technology: A Mathematical Model. *Journal of Archaeological Science* 28: 747–761.

Brantingham, P. J., Olsen, J. W., Rech, J. A., and Krivoshapkin, A. I. 2000. Raw Material Quality and Prepared Core Technologies in Northeast Asia. *Journal of Archaeological Science* 27: 255–271.

Braun, D. R. 2005. Examining Flake Production Strategies: Examples from the Middle Paleolithic of Southwest Asia. *Lithic Technology*.

Braun, D. R., Plummer, T., Bishop, L., Ditchfield, P., and Ferraro, J. 2006. Kanjera South: Pliocene Technological Diversity. Paper presented in the Symposium "Interdisciplinary Approaches to the Oldowan," 71st Annual Meeting of the Society of American Archaeology, Puerto Rico, April 2006.

Braun, D. R., Tactikos, J. C., Ferraro, J. V. and Harris, J. W. K. 2005. Flake Recovery Rates and Inferences of Oldowan Hominin Behavior: A Response to Kimura 1999 and Kimura 2002. *Journal of Human Evolution* 48: 525–531.

Breuil, H., and Kozlowski, L. 1931. Études de stratigraphies Paléolithiques dans le nord de la France, la Belgique, et l'Angleterre. *L'Anthropologie* 41: 449–488.

Brooks, A. S., Kokis, J. E., and Hare, P. E. 1992. Dating the Origins of Modern Humans, 1st Paleoanthropology Society Meeting, Pittsburgh.

Brooks, A., Yellen, J. E., Nevell, L., and Hartman, G. 2006. Projectile Technologies of the African MSA: Implications for Modern Humans Origins. In E. Hovers and S. L. Kuhn (eds.), *Transitions before The Transition: Evolution and Stability in the Middle Paleolithic and Middle Stone Age*, pp. 233–255. Springer, New York.

Bull, P. A., and Goldberg, P. 1985. Scanning Electron Microscope Analysis of Sediments from Tabun Cave, Mount Carmel, Israel. *Journal of Archaeological Science* 12: 177–185.

Byres, M. 1994. Symboling and the Middle-Upper Paleolithic Transition: A Theoretical and Methodological Critique. *Current Anthropology* 35: 369–399.

Byrne, R. 1998. The Early Evolution of Creative Thinking: Evidence from Monkeys and Apes. In S. J. Mithen, (ed.), *Creativity in Human Evolution and Prehistory*, pp. 110–124. Rutledge, London and New York.

Callow, P., and Webb, R. E. 1981. The Application of Multivariate Statistical Techniques to Middle Paleolithic Assemblages from Southwestern France. *Revue d'Archéometrie* 5: 129–138.

Calvin, W. H., and Bickerton, D. 2000. *Lingua ex Machine: Reconciling Darwin and Chomsky with the Human Brain.* MIT Press, Cambridge, Mass.

Cann, R. L. 2001. Genetic Clues to Dispersal in Human Populations: Retracing the Past from the Present. *Science* 291: 1742–1748.

Cann, R. L., Stoneking, M., and Wilson, C. A. 1987. Mitochondrial DNA and Human Origins. *Nature* 325: 31–37.

Caramelli, D., Lalueza-Fox, C., Condemi, S., Longo, L., Milani, L., Manfredini, A., de Saint Pierre, M., Adoni, F., Lari, M., and Giunti, P. 2006. A Highly Divergent mtDNA Sequence in a Neandertal Individual from Italy. *Current Biology* 16: R630–R632.

Caramelli, D., Lalueza-Fox, C., Vernesi, C., Lari, M., Casoli, A., Mallegni, F., Chiarelli, B., Dunpanloup, I., Bertranpetit, J., Barbujani, G., and Bertorelle, G. 2003. Evidence for a Genetic Discontinuity between Neandertals and 24,000 year-old Anatomically Modern Europeans. *Proceedings of the National Academy of Science U.S.A.* 100: 6593–6597.

Carr, P. J. (ed.) 1994. *The Organization of North American Prehistoric Chipped Stone Tool Technologies.* Archaeological Series 7. International Monographs in Prehistory, Ann Arbor, Mich.

Carr, P. J., and Bradbury, A. P. 2001. Flake Debris Analysis, Levels of Production, and the Organization of Technology. In W. Andrefsky, Jr. (ed.), *Lithic Debitage: Context, Form, Meaning,* pp. 126–146. University of Utah Press, Salt Lake City.

Carrithers, M. 1990. Why Humans have Cultures. *Man (n.s.)* 25: 189–206.

Cashdan, E. 1983. Territoriality among Human Foragers: Ecological Models and an Application to Four Bushman Groups. *Current Anthropology* 24: 47–66.

———. 1985. Coping with Risk: Reciprocity among the Basarwa of Northern Botswana. *Man* 20: 222–242.

Chase, P. G. 1986. *The Hunters of Combe-Grenal: Approaches to Middle Paleolithic Subsistence in Europe,* BAR International Series 286. Oxford.

———. 1991. Symbols and Paleolithic Artifacts: Style, Standardization, and the Imposition of Arbitrary Form. *Journal of Anthropological Archaeology* 10: 193–214.

———. 2006. *The Emergence of Culture: The Evolution of a Uniquely Human Way of Life.* New York, Springer.

Chase, P. G., and Dibble, H. L. 1987. Middle Paleolithic Symbolism: A Review of Current Evidence and Interpretations. *Journal of Anthropological Archaeology* 6: 263–296.

Chazan, M. 1995. The Language Hypothesis for the Middle-to-Upper Paleolithic Transition. *Current Anthropology* 36: 749–768.

———. 1997. Redefining Levallois. *Journal of Human Evolution* 33:719–735.

Chomsky, N. 1986. *Knowledge of Language: Its Nature, Origin and Use.* Praeger, New York.

Churchill, S. E. 1993. Weapon Technology, Prey Size Selection, and Hunting Methods in Modern Hunter-Gatherers: Implication for Hunting in the Palaeolithic and Mesolithic. In G. L. Peterkin, H. M. Bricker, and P. Mellars (eds.), *Hunting and Animal Exploitation in the Later Palaeolithic and Mesolithic of Eurasia,* pp. 11–24. Archaeological Papers of the American Anthropological Association 4.

———. 2006. Bioenergetic Perspectives on Neanderthal Thermoregulatory and Activity Budgets. In K. Harvati and T. Harrison (eds.), *Neanderthals Revisited: New Approaches and Perspectives,* pp. 113–133. Vertebrate Paleobiology and Paleoanthropology Series. Springer, Dordrecht.

Clark, G., 1970. *Aspects of Prehistory.* University of California Press, Berkeley.

Clark, G. A., and Lindly, J. T. 1989. A Case of Continuity: Observations on the Biocultural Transition in Europe and Western Eurasia. In P. A. Mellars and C. B. Stringer (eds.), *The Human Revolution: Behavioural and Biological Perspectives on the Origins of Modern Humans,* pp. 626–676. Edinburgh University Press, Edinburgh.

Clark, G. A., and Riel-Salvatore, J. 2006. Observations on Systematics in Paleolithic Archaeology. In E. Hovers and S. L. Kuhn (eds.), *Transitions before The Transition: Evolution and Stability in the Middle Paleolithic and the Middle Stone Age,* pp. 29–56. Springer, New York.

Clark, G. A., Schuldenrein, J., Donaldson, M. L., Schwarcz, H. P., Rink, W. J., and Fish, S. K. 1997. Chronostratigraphic Contexts of Middle Paleolithic Horizons at the 'Ain Fifla Rockshelter (WHS 634), West-Central Jordan. In H. G. K. Goebel, Z. Kafaki, and G. O. Rollefson (eds.), *The Prehistory of Jordan, II: Perspectives from 1997,* pp. 77–100. Ex Oriente, Berlin.

Clark, G., Lindly, J., Donaldson, M., Garrard, A., Coinman, N., Schuldenrein, J., Fish, S., and Olszewski, D. 1988. Excavations at Middle, Upper and Epipaleolithic Sites in the Wadi Hasa, West-Central Jordan. In A. N. Garrard and H. G. Gebel (eds.), *The Prehistory of Jordan: The State of Research in 1986,* pp. 209–285, BAR International Serieos 396(i). Oxford.

Clark, J. D. 1988. The Middle Stone Age of East Africa and the Beginnings of Regional Identity. *Journal of World Prehistory* 2: 235–305.

Clark, J. D., and Kleindienst, M. R. 2001. The Stone Age Cultural Sequence: Terminology, Typology and Raw Material. In J. D. Clark (ed.), *Kalambo Falls Prehistoric Site,* vol. 3, pp. 34–65. Cambridge University Press, Cambridge.

Clark, J. D., Beyene, Y., WoldeGabriel, G., Hart, W., Renne, P. R., Gilbert, H., Defleur, A., Suwa, G., Katoh, S., Ludwig, K. R., Boisserie, J.-R., Asfaw, B., and White, T. W. 2003. Stratigraphic, Chronological and Behavioral Contexts of Pleistocene Homo Sapiens from the Middle Awash, Ethiopia. *Nature* 423: 747–752.

Clarke, D. L. 1979. Toward Analytical Archaeology: New Directions in the Interpretive Thinking of British Archaeologists. In Colleagues (ed.), *Analytical Archaeologist,* pp. 145–179. Academic Press, London.

CLIMAP 1976. The Surface of the Ice Age Earth. *Science* 191: 1131–1137.

Close, A. E. 1989. Identifying Style in Stone Artefacts: A Case Study from the Nile Valley. In D. O. Henry and G. H. Odell (eds.), *Alternative Approaches to Lithic Analysis,* pp. 3–26. Archeological Papers of the American Anthropological Association no. 1. American Anthropological Association.

———. 1991. On the Validity of Middle Paleolithic Tool Types: A Test Case from the Eastern Sahara. *Journal of Field Archaeology* 18: 256–269.

Cochrane, G. W. G. 2003. On the Measurement and Analysis of Platform Angles. *Lithic Technology* 28: 13–25.

Conard, N., and Adler, D. S. 1997. Lithic Reduction and Hominid Behavior in the Middle Paleolithic of the

Rhineland. *Journal of Anthropological Research* 53: 148–175.

Conard, N. J., and Bolus, M. 2003. Radiocarbon Dating the Appearance of Modern Humans and Timing of Cultural Innovations in Europe: New Results and New Challenges. *Journal of Human Evolution* 44: 331–371.

Coolidge, F. L., and Wynn, T. 2005. Working Memory, its Executive Functions, and the Emergence of Modern Thinking. *Cambridge Archaeological Journal* 15: 5–26.

Copeland, L. 1975. The Middle and Upper Palaeolithic in Lebanon and Syria in the Light of Recent Research. In F. Wendorf and A. Close (eds.), *Problems in Prehistory: North Africa and the Levant,* pp. 317–350. Southern Methodist University Press, Dallas.

———. 1983a. The Paleolithic Industries at Adlun. Section III: The Levalloiso-Mousterian of Bezez Cave level B. In D. Roe (ed.), *Adlun in the Stone Age: The Excavations of D.A.E. Garrod in the Lebanon, 1958–1963,* pp. 261–366, BAR International Series 159 (ii). Oxford.

———. 1983b. Levallois/Non-Levallois Determinations in the Early Levant Mousterian: Problems and Questions for 1983. *Paléorient* 9: 15–27.

———. 1985. The Pointed Tools of Hummal Ia (El-Kowm, Syria). *Cahiers de l'Euphrate* 4: 177–189.

Coppa, A., Grün, R., Stringer, C., Eggins, S., and Vargiu, R. 2005. Newly Recognized Pleistocene Human Teeth from Tabun Cave, Israel. *Journal of Human Evolution* 49: 301–315.

Coppa, A., Manni, F., Stringer, C., Vargiu, R., and Vecchi, F. 2007. Evidence for New Neanderthal Teeth in Tabun Cave (Israel) by the Application of Self-Organizing Maps (SOMs). *Journal of Human Evolution* 52: 601–613.

Cordain, L., Miller, J. B., Eaton, S. B., Mann, N., Holt, S. H., and Speth, J. D. 2000. Plant–Animal Subsistence Ratios and Macronutrient Energy Estimations in Worldwide Hunter-Gatherer Diets. *American Journal of Clinical Nutrition* 71: 682–692.

Corruccini, R. C. 1992. Metrical Reconsideration of the Skhul IV and IX and Border Cave 1 Crania in the Context of Modern Human Origins. *American Journal of Physical Anthropology* 87: 433–445.

Cotterell, B., and Kamminga, J. 1987. The Formation of Flakes. *American Antiquity* 52: 675–708.

Crew, H. L. 1975. An Evaluation of the Relationship between the Mousterian Complexes of the Eastern Mediterranean: A Technological Perspective. In F. Wendorf and A. E. Marks (eds.), *Problems in Prehistory: North Africa and the Levant,* pp. 427–435. SMU Press, Dallas.

———. 1976. The Mousterian Site of Rosh Ein Mor. In A. E. Marks (ed.), *Prehistory and Palaeoenvironments in the Central Negev, Israel. Vol 1.: The Avdat/Aqev Area, Part 1,* pp. 75–112. SMU Press, Dallas.

Dag, D., and Goren-Inbar, N. 2001. An Actualistic Study of Dorsally Plain Flakes: A Technological Note. *Lithic Technology* 26: 105–117.

Dan, J. 1988. The Soils of the Land of Israel. In Y. Yom-Tov and E. Tchernov (eds.), *The Zoogeography of Israel: The Distribution and Abundance at a Zoogeographic Crossroads,* pp. 95–128. Dr. W. Jung Publisher, Dordrecht.

Dastugue, J. 1981. Pièces pathologiques de la "nécropole" moustériénne de Qafzeh. *Paléorient* 7: 135–140.

Davidzon, A., and Goring-Morris, A. N. 2003. Sealed in Stone: The Upper Paleolithic Early Ahmarian Knapping Method in the Light of Refitting Studies at Nahal Nizzana XIII, Western Negev, Israel. *Journal of the Israel Prehistoric Society* 33: 75–205.

Davis, S. J. M., Rabinovich, R., and Goren-Inbar, N. 1988. Quaternary Extinctions and Population Increase in Western Asia: The Animal Remains from Biq'at Quneitra. *Paléorient* 14: 95–105.

Davis, Z. J., and Shea, J. J. 1998. Quantifying Lithic Curation: An Experimental Test of Dibble and Pelcin's Original Flake-Tool Mass Predictor. *Journal of Archaeological Science* 25: 603–610.

Dawkins, R. 1995. *River Out of Eden: A Darwinian View of Life.* Phoenix, London.

Dayan, T., Simberloff, D., Tchernov, E., and Yom-Tov, Y. 1991. Calibrating the Paleothermometer: Climate, Communities, and the Evolution of Size. *Paleobiology* 17: 189–199.

de Heinzlein, J., Clark, J. D., White, T., Hart, W., Renne, P. R., WoldeGabriel, G., Beyene, Y., and Vrba, E. 1999. Environment and Behavior of 2.5 Million-Year-Old Bouri Hominids. *Science* 284: 625–629.

de Loecker, D. 1994. On the Refitting Analysis of Site K: A Middle Palaeolithic Findspot at Maastricht-Belvedere (the Netherlands). *Ethnographische-Archaeologisch Zeitschrifte* 35: 107–117.

Deacon, T. W. 1989. The Neural Circuity Underlying Primate Calls and Human Language. *Human Evolution* 4: 367–401.

———. 1997. *The Symbolic Species: The Co-Evolution of Language and the Brain.* Norton, New York.

Debénath, A., and Dibble, H. L. 1994. *The Handbook of Paleolithic Typology, Vol. 1: The Lower and Middle Paleolithic in Europe.* University Museum Press, Philadelphia.

DeBono, H., and Goren-Inbar, N. 2001. Note on a Link between Acheulian Handaxes and the Levallois Method. *Journal of the Israel Prehistoric Society* 31:9–23.

Defleur, A. 1993. *Les Sépultures Mousteriénnes.* CNRS éditions, Paris.

Delage, C. 2007. Chert Availability and Prehistoric Exploitation in the Near East: An Introduction. In C. Delage (ed.), *Chert Availability and Prehistoric Exploitation in the Near East,* pp. 1–17, BAR International Series 1615. Archaeopress, Oxford.

Delagnes, A. 1995. Variability within Uniformity: Three Levels of Variability within the Levallois System. In H. L. Dibble and O. Bar-Yosef (eds.), *The Definition and Interpretation of Levallois Technology,* pp. 201–212. Monographs in World Archaeology N. 23. Prehistory Press, Madison, Wis.

Delagnes, A., and Meignen, L. 2006. Diversity of Lithic Productions Systems during the Middle Palaeolithic in France: Are There Any Chronological Trends? In E. Hovers and S. L. Kuhn (eds.), *Transitions before The Transition: Evolution and Stability in the Middle Paleolithic and Middle Stone Age,* pp. 85–107. Springer, New York.

Delagnes, A., and Roche, H. 2005. Late Pliocene Hominid Knapping Skills: The Case of Lokalalei 2C, West Turkana, Kenya. *Journal of Human Evolution* 48: 435–472.

Dennell, R., and Roebroeks, W. 2005. An Asian Perspective on Early Human Dispersal from Africa. *Nature* 438: 1099–1004.

Dennett, D. 1995. *Darwin's Dangerous Idea.* Simon and Schuster, New York.

d'Errico, F. 2003. The Invisible Frontier: A Multiple Species Model for the Origin of Behavioral Modernity. *Evolutionary Anthropology* 12: 188–202.

d'Errico, F., and Backwell, L. R. 2003. Possible Evidence of Bone Tool Shaping by Swartkrans Early Hominids. *Journal of Archaeological Science* 30: 1559–1576.

d'Errico, F., and Sánchez Goñi, M. F. 2004. A Garden of Eden for the Gibraltar Neandertals? A Reply to Finlayson et al. *Quaternary Science Reviews* 23: 1210–1216.

d'Errico, F., Henshilwood, C., Lawson, G., Vanhaeren, M., Tillier, A.-M., Soressi, M., Bresson, F., Maureille, B., Nowell, A., Lakarra, J., Backwell , L., and Julien, M. 2003. Archaeological Evidence for the Emergence of Language, Symbolism, and Music: An Alternative Multidisciplinary Perspective. *Journal of World Prehistory* 17: 1–70.

d'Errico, F., Henshilwood, C., Vanhaeren, M., and van Niekerk, K. 2005. *Nassarius kraussianus* Shell Beads from Blombos Cave: Evidence for Symbolic Behaviour in the Middle Stone Age. *Journal of Human Evolution:* 3–24.

d'Errico, F., Zilhão, J., Julien, M., Baffier, D., and Pelegrin, J. 1998. Neanderthal Acculturation in Western Europe? A Critical Review of the Evidence and its Interpretation. *Current Anthropology* 39 (supplement): S1–S44.

Derricourt, R. 2005. Getting "Out of Africa,": Sea Crossings, Land Crossings and Culture in the Hominin Migrations. *Journal of World Prehistory* 19: 119–132.

Dibble, H. L. 1984a. Interpreting Typological Variation of Middle Paleolithic Scrapers: Function, Style or Sequence of Reduction? *Journal of Field Archaeology* 11: 431–436.

———. 1984b. The Mousterian Industry from Bisitun Cave (Iran). *Paléorient* 10: 23–34.

———. 1985. Raw Material Variation in Levallois Flake Manufacture. *Current Anthropology* 26: 391–393.

———. 1987. The Interpretation of Middle Paleolithic Scraper Morphology. *American Antiquity* 52: 109–117.

———. 1988. Typological Aspects of Reduction and Intensity of Utilization of Lithic Resources in the French Mousterian. In H. L. Dibble and A. Montet-White (eds.), *Upper Pleistocene Prehistory of Western Europe,* pp. 181–197. University Museum Monograph 54. University of Pennsylvania Press, Philadelphia.

———. 1989. The Implication of Stone Tool Types for the Presence of Language during the Lower and Middle Palaeolithic. In P. Mellars and C. Stringer (eds.), *The Human Revolution: Behavioural and Biological Perspectives on the Origins of Modern Humans,* pp. 415–431. Edinburgh University Press, Edinburgh.

———. 1991a. Local Raw Material Exploitation and its Effects on Lower and Middle Paleolithic Assemblage Variability. In A. Montet-White and S. Holen (eds.), *Raw Material Economies among Prehistoric Hunter-Gatherers,* pp. 33–46. University of Kansas Publications in Anthropology. University of Kansas, Lawrence.

———. 1991b. Mousterian Assemblage Variability on an Interregional Scale. *Journal of Anthropological Research* 47: 239–257.

———. 1995a. Middle Paleolithic Scraper Reduction: Background, Clarification, and Review of the Evidence to Date. *Journal of Archaeological Method and Theory* 2: 299–368.

———. 1995b. Raw Material Availability, Intensity of Utilization, and Middle Paleolithic Assemblage Variability. In H. L. Dibble and M. Lenoir (eds.), *The Middle Paleolithic Site of Combe-Capelle Bas (France),* pp. 289–315. The University Museum, University of Pennsylvania, Philadelphia.

———. 1995c. Biache-Saint-Vaast, Level IIa: A Comparison of Approaches. In H. L. Dibble and O. Bar-Yosef (eds.), *The Definition and Interpretation of Levallois Technology,* pp. 93–116. Monographs in World Archaeology N. 23. Prehistory Press, Madison, Wis.

———. 1998. Comment on 'Quantifying Lithic Curation: An Experimental Test of Dibble and Pelcin's Original Flake-Tool Mass Predictor,' by Zachary J. Davis and John J. Shea. *Journal of Archaeological Science* 25: 611–613.

Dibble, H. L., and Holdaway, S. J. 1990. Le Paléolithique moyen de l'abri sous roche de Warwasi et ses relations avec le moustérien du Zagros et du Levant. *L'Anthropologie* 94: 619–642.

Dibble, H. L., and McPherron, S. 2006. The Missing Mousterian. *Current Anthropology* 47: 777–803.

Dibble, H. L., and Pelcin, A. W. 1995. The Effect of Hammer Mass and Velocity on Flake Mass. *Journal of Archaeological Science* 22: 429–439.

Dibble, H. L., and Rolland, N. 1992. On Assemblage Variability in the Middle Paleolithic of Western Europe. In H. L. Dibble and P. Mellars (eds.), *The Middle Paleolithic: Adaptation, Behavior, and Variability,* pp. 1–28. University Museum Monograph 72. The University Museum, University of Pennsylvania, Philadelphia.

Dibble, H. L., and Whittaker, J. C. 1981. New Experimental Evidence on the Relation between Percussion Flaking and Flake Variation. *Journal of Archaeological Science* 8: 283–296.

Dijksterhuis, A., Bos, M. W., Nordgren, L. F., and van Baaren, R. B. 2006. On Making the Right Choice: The Deliberation-Without-Attention Effect. *Science* 311: 1005–1007.

Dobres, A.-M., and Hoffman, C. R. 1994. Social Agency and the Dynamics of Prehistoric Technology. *Journal of Archaeological Method and Theory* 1: 211–258.

Domínguez-Rodrigo, M., Egeland, C. P., and Barba, R. 2007. *Deconstructing Olduvai.* A Taphonomic Study of the Bed I Sites. Springer, Dordrecht.

Druck, D. 2004. The Exploitation of Flint Resources throughout the Sequence of Prehistoric Cultures in Nahal Mea'rot, Mt. Carmel. M.A. thesis, University of Haifa. (Hebrew).

Druckman, Y., Magaritz, M., and Sneh, A. 1987. The Shrinking of Lake Lisan, as Reflected by the Diagenesis of its Marginal Oolite Deposits. *Israel Journal of Earth Sciences* 36: 101–106.

Dunbar, R. I. M. 2003. The Social Brain: Mind, Language, and Society in Evolutionary Perspective. *Annual Review of Anthropology* 32: 163–181.

Durham, W. H. 1991. *Coevolution: Genes, Culture, and Human Diversity.* Stanford University Press, Stanford.

Dyson-Hudson, R., and Smith, E. 1978. Human Territoriality: An Ecological Reassessment. *American Anthropologist* 80: 21–41.

Eerkens, J. W., and Lipo, C. P. 2005. Cultural Transmission, Copying Errors, and the Generation of Variation in Material Culture and the Archaeological Record. *Journal of Anthropological Archaeology* 24: 316–334.

Ehrlich, P., and Feldman, M. W. 2003. Genes and Cultures: What Creates our Behavioral Phenomena? *Current Anthropology* 44: 87–107.

Eisenmann, V. 1992. Systematic and Biostratigraphical Interpretation of the Equids from Qafzeh, Tabun, Skhul, and Kebara (Acheulo-Yabrudian to Upper Paleolithic of Israel). *Archaeozoologia* 5: 43–62.

Ekshtain, R. 2006. A Comparative Study of Knapping Accidents in the Levantine Mousterian. MA thesis. Institute of Archaeology, The Hebrew University of Jerusalem, Jerusalem.

Ekshtain, R., and Hovers, E. 2005. Patterns of Hearth Location in Amud Cave (Israel): Potential and Limits of Various Analytical Tools. Paper presented in the workshop on spatial archaeology, Neuwied, Germany, April 2005.

Ellis, C. J. 1997. Factors Influencing the Use of Stone Projectile Points. In H. Knecht (ed.), *Projectile Technologies,* pp. 37–74. Interdisciplinary Contributions to Archaeology. Plenum Press, New York.

Emies, K.-C.,Struck, U., Schulz, H.-M.,Rosenberg R., Bernasconi, S. Erlenkeuser, H., Sakamoto, T., Maretínez-Ruiz, R. 2000. Temperature and Salinity Variations of Mediterranean Sea Surface Waters over the Last 16,000 Years from Records of Planktonic Stable Oxygen Isotopes and Alkenone Unsaturated Ratios. *Palaeogeography, Palaeoecology, Palaeoclimatology* 158: 259–280.

Endicott, K., and Endicott, K. L. 1986. The Question of Hunter-Gatherer Territoriality: The Case of the Batek of Malaysia. In M. Biesele, R. Gordon, and R. Lee (eds.), *The Past and Future of !Kung Ethnography: Critical Reflections and Symbolic Perspectives. Essays in Honor of Lorna Marshall,* pp. 137–161. Helmut Buske Verlag, Hamburg.

Eren, M. I., Greenspan, A., and Sampson, C. G. 2008. Are Upper Paleolithic Blade Cores More Productive than Middle Paleolithic Discoidal Cores? A Replication Experiment. *Journal of Human Evolution* 55: 952–961.

Eren, M. I., Dominguez-Rodrigo, M., Kuhn, S. L., Adler, D. S., and Bar-Yosef, O. 2005. Defining and Measuring Reduction in Unifacial Stone Tools. *Journal of Archaeological Science* 32: 1190–1201.

Eswaran, V. 2002. A Diffusion Wave out of Africa: The Mechanism of the Modern Human Revolution? *Current Anthropology* 43: 749–774.

Eswaran, V., Harpending, H., and Rogers, A. R. 2005. Genomics Refutes an Exclusively African Origin of Humans. *Journal of Human Evolution* 49: 1–18.

Ewing, J. F. 1947. Preliminary Note on the Excavations at the Palaeolithic Site of Ksar Akil, Republic of Lebanon. *Antiquity* 21: 186–196.

Farrand, W. R. 1979. Chronology and Palaeoenvironment of Levantine Prehistoric Sites as seen from the Sediment Studies. *Journal of Archaeological Science* 6: 369–392.

———. 1994. Confrontation of Geological Stratigraphy and Radiometric Dates from Upper Pleistocene Sites in the Levant. In O. Bar-Yosef and R. Kra (eds.), *Late Quaternary Chronology and Paleoclimates of the Eastern Mediterranean.* Radiocarbon, pp. 33–53.

Féblot-Augustins, J. 1993. Mobility Strategies in the Late Middle Palaeolithic of Central Europe and Western Europe: Elements of Stability and Variability. *Journal of Anthropological Archaeology* 12: 211–265.

———. 1997. *La Circulation des matières premières au Paléolithique.* ERAUL 75. Université de Liège, Liège.

Feibel, C. S. 2001. Archaeological Sediments in Lake Margin Environments. In J. K. Stein and W. R. Farrand (eds.), *Sediments in Archaeological Contexts,* pp. 127–148. University of Utah Press, Salt Lake City.

———. 2004. Quaternary Lake Margins of the Levant Rift Valley. In N. Goren-Inbar and J. D. Speth (eds.), *Human Paleoecology in the Levantine Corridor,* pp. 21–36. Oxbow, Oxford.

Ferraro, J., Braun, D. R., and Tactikos, J. 2006. Contextualizing Oldowan Lithic Strategies: A Biological Perspective. Paper presented in the electronic symposium "Core Reduction, Chaîne Opératoire and Other Methods: the Epistemologies of Different Approaches to Lithic Analysis." San Juan, Puerto Rico.

Finlayson, C. 2004. *Neanderthals and Modern Humans: An Ecological and Evolutionary Perspective.* Cambridge University Press, Cambridge.

Fish, P. R. 1979. *The Interpretive Potential of Mousterian Debitage.* Anthropological Research Papers 16. Arizona State University, Tucson.

———. 1981. Beyond Tools: Middle Paleolithic Debitage Analysis and Cultural Inference. *Journal of Anthropological Research* 37: 374–386.

Fitzhugh, B. 2001. Risk and Invention in Human Technological Evolution. *Journal of Anthropological Archaeology* 20: 125–167.

Fizet, M., Mariotti, A., Bocherens, H., Lange-Badré, B., Vandermeersch, B., Borel, J. P., and Bellons, G.

1995. Effect of Diet, Physiology, and Climate on Carbon and Nitrogen Stable Sitopes of Collagen in a Late Pleistocene Anthropic Paleosystem: Marillac, Charente, France. *Journal of Archaeological Science* 22: 67–79.

Flannery, K. V. 1969. Origins and Ecological Effects of Early Domestication in Iran and the Near East. In P. J. Ucko and G. W. Dimbleby (eds.), *The Domestication and Exploitation of Plants and Animals*, pp. 73–100. Duckworth, London.

Flannery, K. V. 2000. Comment on "The Tortoise and the Hare: Small Game Use, the Broad Spectrum Revolution, and Paleolithic Demography" by M. C. Stiner, N. D. Munro and T. Surovell. *Current Anthropology* 41: 64–65.

Fleisch, S. J. 1970. Les Habitats du paléolithique moyen a Naamé (Liban). *Bulletin du Musée de Beyrouth* 23: 25–93.

Flemming, N. C., and Webb, C. O. 1986. Tectonic and Eustatic Coastal Changes during the Last 10,000 Years Derived from Archaeological Data. *Z. Geomorphology, N. F.* 62 (Supplement): 1–29.

Fodor, J. A. 1985. Précis of *The Modularity of the Mind. The Behavioral and Brain Sciences* 8: 1–42.

Foley, R. 1987a. *Another Unique Species.* Longman Scientific and Technical, New York.

———. 1987b. Hominid Species and Stone-Tool Assemblages: How Are They Related? *Antiquity* 61: 380–392.

Foley, R., and Lahr, M. M. 1997. Mode 3 Technologies and the Evolution of Modern Humans. *Cambridge Archaeological Journal* 7: 3–36.

———. 2003. On Stony Grounds: Lithic Technology, Human Evolution, and the Emergence of Culture. *Evolutionary Anthropology* 12: 109–122.

Frayer, D. W., Wolpoff, M. H., Thorne, A. G., Smith, F. H., and Pope, G. G. 1993. Theories of Modern Human Origins: The Paleontological Test. *American Anthropologist* 95: 14–50.

Frechen, M., Neber, A., Tsatskin, A., Boenigk, W., and Ronen, A. 2004. Chronology of Pleistocene Sedimentary Cycles in the Carmel Coastal Plain of Israel. *Quaternary International* 121: 41–52.

Freund, R. 1978. Geology. In A. Itzhaki (ed.), *The Lower Galilee and the Kinneret Region.* Israel Guide 3, pp. 9–14. Keter/Ministry of Defense, Jerusalem (Hebrew).

Friedman, E., Goren-Inbar, N., Rosenfeld, A., Marder, O., and Burian, F. 1994–5. Hafting during Mousterian Times: Further Evidence. *Journal of the Israel Prehistoric Society* 26: 8–31.

Frumkin, A., and Stein, M. 2004. The Sahara–East Mediterranean Dust and Climate Connection Revealed by Strontium and Uranium Isotopes in a Jerusalem Speleothem. *Earth and Planetary Science Letters* 217: 451–464.

Frumkin, A., Ford, D. C., and Schwarcz, H. P. 1999. Continental Oxygen Isotopic Record of the Last 170,000 Years in Jerusalem. *Quaternary Research* 51: 317–327.

Galanidou, N. 2000. Patterns in Caves: Foragers, Horticulturalists, and the Use of Space. *Journal of Anthropological Archaeology* 19: 243–275.

Galili, E., Zviely, D., Ronen, A., and Mienis, H. K. 2007. Beach Deposits of MIS 5e High Sea Stand as Indicators for Tectonic Stability of the Carmel Coastal Plain, Israel. *Quaternary Science Reviews* 26: 2544–2557.

Gamble, C. 2007. *Origins and Revolutions: Human Identity in Earliest Prehistory.* Cambridge University Press, Cambridge.

Garcea, E. A. A. 2004. Crossing Deserts and Avoiding Seas: Aterian North African–European Relations. *Journal of Anthropological Research* 60: 27–53.

Gardner, H. 1983. *Frames of Mind: The Theory of Multiple Intelligence.* Basic Books, New York.

Garrard, A. N. 1982. The Environmental Implications of a Re-analysis of the Large Mammal Fauna from the Wadi el-Mugharat Caves, Palestine. In J. L. Bintliff and W. van Zeist (eds.), *Palaeoclimates, Palaeoenvironments and Human Communities in the Eastern Mediterranean Region in Late Prehistory*, pp. 165–187. BAR International Series 133. Oxford.

Garrod, D. A. E. 1934. The Stone Age of Palestine. *Antiquity* 8: 133–150.

Garrod, D. A. E. 1962. The Middle Paleolithic of the Near East and the Problem of Mount Carmel Man. *Journal of the Royal Anthropological Institute of Great Britain and Ireland* 92: 232–251.

Garrod, D. A. E., and Bate, D. M. A. (eds.), 1937. *The Stone Age of Mount Carmel* I. Clarendon Press, Oxford.

———. 1942. Excavations at the Cave of Shukbah, Palestine, 1928. *Proceedings of the Prehistoric Society, N.S.* 8: 1–15.

Gates, W. L. 1976. Modeling the Ice-Age Climate. *Science* 191: 1138–1144.

Gaudzinski, S. 1999. Middle Paleolithic Bone Tools from the Open-Air Site Salzgitter-Lebenstedt (Germany). *Journal of Archaeological Science* 26: 125–141.

Gaudzinski, S., and Roebroeks, W. 2000. Adults Only. Reindeer Hunting at the Middle Palaeolithic Site Salzgitter-Lebenstedt, Northern Germany. *Journal of Human Evolution* 38: 497–521.

Geneste, J.-M. 1985. *Analyse lithique d'industries moustéri-ennes du Périgord: Une approche technologique des comportements des groupes humains au Paléolithique moyen.* Thèse doctorat, Université de Bordeaux.

———. 1988. Les Industries de la Grotte Vaufrey: Technologie du débitage, économie et circulation de la matière première lithique. In J.-P. Rigaud (ed.), *La Grotte Vaufrey à Cenac et Saint-Julien (Dordogne): Paléoenvironments, chronologie, et activités humaines*, pp. 441–517. CNRS, Paris.

Geneste, J.-M., Jaubert, J., Lenoir, M., Meignen, L., and Turq, A. 1997. Approche technologique des moustériens charentiens du sud-ouest de la France et du Languedoc oriental. *Paléo* 9: 101–142.

Gifford-Gonzalez, D. P., Damrosch, D. B., Damrosch, D. R., Pryor, J. R. L., and Thunen, R. L. 1985. The

Third Dimension in Site Structure: An Experiment in Trampling and Vertical Displacement. *American Antiquity* 50: 803–818.

Gilead, I. 1980. A Middle Palaeolithic Open-Air Site near Tell Far'ah, Western Negev: Preliminary Report. *Israel Exploration Journal* 30: 52–62.

———. 1988. Le Site moustérien de Fara II (Neguev septentrional, Israël) et le remontage de son industrie. *L'Anthropologie* 92: 797–807.

———. 1989. Review of Les Hommes de Mallaha (Eynan) Israel. Les Sépultures. *Journal of the Israel Prehistoric Society* 22: 132*–138*.

———. 1991. The Upper Paleolithic in the Levant. *Journal of World Prehistory* 5: 105–154.

———. 1995. Problems and Prospects in the Study of Levallois Technology in the Levant: The Case of Fara II, Israel. In H. L. Dibble and O. Bar-Yosef (eds.), *The Definition and Interpretation of Levallois Technology,* pp. 79–92. Monographs in World Archaeology. Prehistory Press, Ann Arbor, Mich.

Gilead, I., and Grigson, C. 1984. Far'ah II: A Middle Palaeolithic Open-Air Site in the Northern Negev, Israel. *Proceedings of the Prehistoric Society* 50: 71–91.

Gisis, I., and Bar-Yosef, O. 1974. New Excavation in Zuttiyeh Cave, Wadi Amud, Israel. *Paléorient* 2: 175–180.

Glimcher, P. W., and Rustichini, A. 2004. Neuroeconomics: The Consilience of Brain and Decision. *Science* 306: 447–452.

Godfrey-Smith, D. I., and Ilani, S. 2004. Past Thermal History of Goethite and Hematite Fragments from Qafzeh Cave Deduced from Thermal Activation Characteristics of the 110 Centigrade TL Peak of Enclosed Quartz Grains. *Revue d'Archéométrie* 28: 185–190.

Goldberg, P. 1976. Upper Pleistocene Geology of the Avdat / Aqev Area. In A. E. Marks (ed.), *Prehistory and Palaeoenvironments in the Central Negev, Israel.* Vol. 1: *The Avdat/Aqev Area, part 1,* pp. 25–55. SMU Press, Dallas.

———. 1980. Micromorphology in Archaeology and Prehistory. *Paléorient* 6: 159–164.

———. 1986. Late Quaternary Environmental History of the Southern Levant. *Geoarchaeology* 1: 225–244.

Goldberg, P., and Sherwood, S. C. 2006. Deciphering Human Prehistory through the Geoarcheological Study of Cave Sediments. *Evolutionary Anthropology:* 15: 20–36.

Gopher, A., Barkai, R., Shimelmitz, R., Khalaily, H., Lemorini, C., Hershkovitz, I., and Stiner, M. C. 2005. Qesem Cave: An Amudian Site in Central Israel. *Journal of the Israel Prehistoric Society* 35: 69–92.

Gordon, D. 1993. Mousterian Tool Selection, Reduction, and Discard at Ghar, Israel. *Journal of Field Archaeology* 20: 205–218.

Gordon, M. 1997. Technological and Typological Aspects of Layer B1 in the Late Mousterian Site of Amud Cave. M.A. thesis, The Hebrew University, Jerusalem (Hebrew).

Goren, N. 1981. The Lithic Assemblages of Ubeidiya, Jordan Valley. Ph.D. thesis, The Hebrew University of Jerusalem.

Goren-Inbar, N. 1985. The Lithic Assemblage of the Berekhat Ram Acheulian Site, Golan Heights. *Paléorient* 11: 7–28.

———. 1988a. Notes on "Decision Making" by Lower and Middle Palaeolithic Hominids. *Paléorient* 14: 99–108.

———. 1988b. Too Small to be True? Reevaluation of Cores on Flakes in Levantine Mousterian Assemblages. *Lithic Technology* 17: 37–44.

———. 1990a. The Lithic Assemblages. In N. Goren-Inbar (ed.), *Quneitra: A Mousterian Site on the Golan Heights,* pp. 61–167, Qedem 31. Institute of Archaeology, Jerusalem.

———. (ed.) 1990b. *Quneitra: A Mousterian Site on the Golan Heights,* Qedem 31. Institute of Archaeology, Jerusalem.

———. 1994. The Lower Palaeolithic of Israel. In T. E. Levy (ed.), *The Archaeology of Society in the Holy Land,* pp. 93–109. Leicester University Press, London.

Goren-Inbar, N., and Belfer-Cohen, A. 1998. The Technological Abilities of the Levantine Mousterians: Cultural and Mental Capacities. In T. Akazawa, K. Aoki, and O. Bar-Yosef (eds.), *Neandertals and Modern Humans in Western Asia,* pp. 205–222. Plenum Press, New York.

Goren-Inbar, N., Alperson, N., Kislev, M. E., Simchoni, O., Melamed, Y., Ben-Nun, A., and Werker, E. 2004. Evidence of Hominin Control of Fire at Gesher Benot Ya'aqov, Israel. *Science* 304: 725–727.

Goren-Inbar, N., Feibel, C. S., Verosub, K. L., Melamed, Y., Kislev, M. E., Tchernov, E., and Saragusti, I. 2000. Pleistocene Milestones on the Out-of-Africa Corridor at Gesher Benot Ya'aqov, Israel. *Science* 289: 944–947.

Goren-Inbar, N., Werker, E., and Feibel, C. S. 2002. *The Acheulian Site of Gesher Benot Ya'aqov, Israel.* Vol 1: *The Wood Assemblages.* Oxford: Oxbow Books.

Goring-Morris, A. N. 1987. *At the Edge: Terminal Pleistocene Hunter-Gatherers in the Negev and Sinai,* BAR International Series 361. Oxford.

———. 1994. Aspects of the PPNB Lithic Industry at Kfar HaHoresh, near Nazareth, Israel. In H. G. K. Gebel and S. K. Kozlowski (eds.), *Neolithic Chipped Stone Industries of the Fertile Crescent,* pp. 427–443. ex Oriente, Berlin.

Goring-Morris, A. N., and Belfer-Cohen, A. 1997. The Articulation of Cultural Processes and Late Quaternary Environmental Changes in Cisjordan. *Paléorient* 23: 71–93.

———. 2001. The Symbolic Realms of Utilitarian Material Culture: The Role of Lithics. In I. Caneva, C. Lemorini, D. Zampetti, and P. Biagi (eds.), *Beyond Tools,* pp. 257–271. SENEPE 9. ex Oriente, Berlin.

———. 2003. Why Microliths? Microlithization in the Levant. In R. G. Elston and S. L. Kuhn (eds.), *Thinking Small: Global Perspectives on Microlithization,* pp. 58–68. American Anthropological Association, Santa Fe.

———. 2006. A Hard Look at the 'Levantine Aurignacian': How Real is the Taxon? In O. Bar-Yosef and J. Zilhão (eds.), *Towards a Definition of the Aurignacian. Proceedings of the Workshop on "The Upper Palaeolithic and the Aurignacian,"* pp. 297–314. ASPR Monograph Series. Brill Academic Publishers, Boston.

Goring-Morris, A. N., and Davidzon, A. 2006. Straight to the Point: Upper Palaeolithic Ahmarian Lithic Technology in the Levant. *Anthropologie* 44: 93–111.

Goring-Morris, A. N., Henry, D. O., Phillips, J. L., Clark, G. A., Barton, C. M., and Neeley, M. P. 1996. Patterns in the Epipalaeolithic of the Levant: Debate after Neeley and Barton. *Antiquity* 70: 130–147.

Gosselain, O. P. 1998. Social and Technical Identity in a Clay Ball. In M. T. Stark (ed.), *The Archaeology of Social Boundaries,* pp. 78–105. Smithsonian Institute Press, Washington.

Gould, R. A. 1980. *Living Archaeology.* Cambridge University Press, Cambridge.

Gould, S. J. 1983. *The Panda's Thumb: More Reflections in Natural History.* Penguin Books.

———. 1989. *Wonderful Life: The Burgess Shale and the Nature of History.* W.W. Norton and Company, New York.

———. 1990. Down on the Farm. *New York Review of Books,* January 18: 26–27.

Gould, S. J., and Lewontin, R. C. 1979. The Spandrels of San Marco and the Panglossian Paradigm: A Critique of the Adaptationist Programme. *Proceedings of the Royal Society of London B* 205: 281–298.

Green, R. E., Krause, J., Ptak, S. E., Briggs, A. W., Ronan, M. T., Simons, J. F., Du, L., Egholm, M., Rothberg, J. M., Paunovic, M., and Pääbo, S. 2006. Analysis of One Million Base Pairs of Neanderthal DNA. *Nature* 444: 330.

Greenberg, Y. 1963. The Eocene of Kefar Hahoresh-Illut Region and its Correlation with the Eocene of Northern Israel. *Israel Journal of Earth Sciences* 12: 147–158.

Griffiths, J. C. 1967. *Scientific Methods in Analysis of Sediments.* McGraw-Hill, New York.

Griggo, C. 1998. La Faune moustérienne du site d'umm el Tlel (Syrie). Étude préliminarie. Fouilles 1991–1993. *Cahiers el l'Euphrates* 8: 11–25.

———. 2002. Faunal Remains from Dederiyeh Cave, 1993 through 1996 Excavations. In T. Akazawa (ed.), *Neanderthal Burials: Excavations of the Dederiyeh Cave, Afrin, Syria,* pp. 63–74. International Research Center for Japanese Studies, Kyoto.

Grosman, L. 2004. Computer Simulations of Variables in Models of the Origins of Agriculture in the Levant. Ph.D. thesis, The Hebrew University of Jerusalem.

Groves, R. H. 1991. The Biogeography of Mediterranean Plant Invasions. In R. H. Groves and F. di Castri (eds.), *Biogeography of Mediterranean Invasions*, pp. 427–438. Cambridge University Press, Cambridge.

Grün, R., and Beaumont, P. B. 2001. Border Cave Revisited: A Revised ESR Chronology. *Journal of Human Evolution* 40: 467–482.

Grün, R., and Stringer, C. B. 1991. Electron Spin Resonance and the Evolution of Modern Humans. *Archaeometry* 33: 153–199.

———. 2000. Tabun Revisited: Revised ESR Chronology and New ESR and U-series Analyses of Dental Material from Tabun C1. *Journal of Human Evolution* 39: 601–612.

Grün, R., Beaumont, P. B., and Stringer, C. B. 1990. ESR Dating Evidence for Early Modern Humans at Border Cave in South Africa. *Nature* 344: 537–539.

Grün, R., Shackleton, N., and Deacon, H. J. 1990. Electron-Spin-Resonance Dating of Tooth Enamel from Klasies River Mouth Cave. *Current Anthropology* 31: 427–432.

Grün, R., Stringer, C., McDermot, F., Nathan, R., Porat, N., Robertson, S., Taylor, L., Mortimer, G., Eggins, S., and McCulloch, M. 2005. U-Series and ESR Analyses of Bones and Teeth Relating to the Human Burials from Skhul. *Journal of Human Evolution* 49: 316–334.

Gvirztman, G., Shachnai, E., Bakler, N., and Ilani, S. 1985. Stratigraphy of the Kurkar Group (Quaternary) of the Coastal Plain of Israel. *Geological Survey of Israel, Current Research* Vol. 1983/84: 70–82.

Haas, G. 1972. The Microfauna of the Djebel Qafze Cave. *Paleovertebrata* 5: 261–270.

Harpending, H., and Davis, H. 1977. Some Implications for Hunter-Gatherer Ecology Derived from the Spatial Structure of Resources. *World Archaeology* 8: 275–286.

Harpending, H., and Rogers, A. R. 2000. Genetic Perspectives on Human Origins and Differentiation. *Annual Review of Genomics and Human Genetics* 1: 361–365.

Harpending, H., Batzer, M. A., Gurven, M. L. B., Rogers, R., and Sherry, S. T. 1998. Genetic Traces of Ancient Demography. *Proceedings of the National Academy of Science U.S.A.* 95: 1961–1967.

Hawks, J. 2005. Neandertals Noshed on Mammoth Meat? http://johnhawks.net/weblog/fossils/neandertal/ neandertal_mammoth_diet_2005.html

Hayden, B. (ed.) 1979a. *Lithic Use-Wear Analysis.* Academic Press, New York.

———. 1979b. *Paleolithic Reflections: Lithic Technology and Ethnographic Excavation among Australian Aborigines.* Australian Institute of Aboriginal Studies, Canberra.

———. 1981. Subsistence and Ecological Adaptations of Modern Hunter-Gatherers. In R. S. O. Harding and G. Teleki (eds.), *Omnivorous Primates: Gathering and Hunting in Human Evolution*, pp. 344–421. Columbia Press, New York.

———. 1993. The Cultural Capacities of Neanderthals: A Review and Re-evaluation. *Journal of Human Evolution* 24: 113–146.

Hayden, B., and Hutchings, W. K. 1989. Whither the Billet Flake? In D. Amick and R. Mauldin (eds.), *Experiments in Lithic Technology*, pp. 235–258, BAR International Series 528. Oxford.

Hazan, N., Stein, M., Agnon, A., Marco, S., Nadel, D., Negendank, J. F. W., Schwab, M. J., and Neev, D. 2005. The Late Quaternary Limnological History of Lake Kinneret (Sea of Galilee), Israel. *Quaternary Research* 63: 60–77.

Henry, D. O. 1983. Adaptive Evolution within the Epi-Paleolithic of the Near East. In F. Wendorf and A. E. Close (eds.), *Advances in World Archaeology* II, pp. 99–160. Academic Press, New York.

———. 1995a. The Influence of Mobility Levels on Levallois Point Production, Late Levantine Mousterian, Southern

Jordan. In H. L. Dibble and O. Bar-Yosef (eds.), *The Definition and Interpretation of Levallois Technology*, pp. 185–200. Monographs in World Archaeology 23. Prehistory Press, Madison, Wis.

———. 1995b. Late Levantine Mousterian Patterns of Adaptation and Cognition. In D. O. Henry (ed.), *Prehistoric Cultural Ecology and Evolution: Insights from Southern Jordan*, pp. 107–132. Plenum Press, New York and London.

———. 1995c. The Middle Paleolithic Sites. In D. O. Henry (ed.), *Prehistoric Cultural Ecology and Evolution Insights from Southern Jordan*, pp. 49–84. Plenum Press, New York and London.

———. 1998. The Middle Paleolithic of Jordan. In D. O. Henry (ed.), *The Prehistoric Archaeology of Jordan*, pp. 23–38, BAR International Series 705. Oxford.

———. (ed.) 2003. *Neanderthals in the Levant: Behavioral Organization and the Beginnings of Human Modernity.* Continuum, London.

Henry, D. O., and Miller, G. H. 1992. The Implications of Amino Acid Racemization Dates of Levantine Mousterian Deposits in the Southern Jordan. *Paléorient* 18: 45–52.

Henry, D. O., Hall, S. A., Hietala, H. J., Demidenko, Y. E., Usik, V. I., Rosen, A. M., and Thomas, P. A. 1996. Middle Paleolithic Behavioral Organization: 1993 Excavations of Tor Faraj, South Jordan. *Journal of Field Archaeology* 23: 31–53.

Henry, D. O., Hietala, H. J., Rosen, A. M., Demidenko, Y. E., Usik, V. I., and Armagan, T. L. 2004. Human Behavioral Organization in the Middle Paleolithic: Were Neanderthals Different? *American Anthropologist* 106: 17–31.

Henshilwood, C. S., and Marean, C. W. 2003. The Origin of Modern Human Behavior: Critiques of the Models and their Test Implications. *Current Anthropology* 44: 627–651.

Henshilwood, C. S., d'Errico, F., Yates, R., Jacobs, Z., Tribolo, C., Duller, G. A. T., Mercier, N., Sealy, J. C., Valladas, H., Watts, I., and Wintle, A. G. 2002. Emergence of Modern Human Behavior: Middle Stone Age Engravings from South Africa. *Science* 295: 1278–1280.

Higham, T., Ramsey, C. B., Karavanic, I., Smith, F. H., and Trinkaus, E. 2006. Revised Direct Radiocarbon Dating of the Vindija G1 Upper Paleolithic Neandertals. *Proceedings of the National Academy of Science U.S.A.* 103: 553–557.

Hiscock, P. 2004. Slippery and Billy: Intention, Selection, and Equifinality in Lithic Artefacts. *Cambridge Archaeological Journal* 14: 71–77.

Hiscock, P., and Clarkson, C. 2005. Experimental Evaluation of Kuhn's Geometric Index of Reduction and the Flat-Flake Problem. *Journal of Archaeological Science* 32: 1015–1022.

Hitchcock, R. K., and Bartram, L. E. J. 1998. Social Boundaries, Technical Systems, and the Use of Space and Technology in the Kalahari. In M. T. Stark (ed.), *The Archaeology of Social Boundaries*, pp. 12–49. Smithsonian Institution Press, Washington.

Hobsbawm, E. 1983. Introduction: Inventing Tradition. In E. Hobsbawm and T. Ranger (eds.), *The Invention of Tradition*, pp. 1–14. Cambridge University Press, Cambridge.

Hockett, B., and Haws, J. A. 2005. Nutritional Ecology and the Human Demography of Neandertal Extinction. *Quaternary International* 137: 21–34.

Hodder, I. 1986. *Reading the Past.* Cambridge University Press, Cambridge.

Hoffecker, J. H. 1999. Neandertals and Modern Humans in Eastern Europe. *Evolutionary Anthropology* 7: 129–141.

Holdaway, S. 1989. Were There Hafted Projectile Points in the Mousterian? *Journal of Field Archaeology* 16: 79–85.

———. 1990. Mousterian Projectile Points: Reply to Shea. *Journal of Field Archaeology* 17: 114–115.

Holdaway, S., McPherron, S., and Roth, B. 1996. Notched Tool Reuse and Raw Material Availability in French Middle Paleolithic Sites. *American Antiquity* 61: 377–387.

Horowitz, A. 1976. Late Quaternary Paleoenvironments of Prehistoric Settlements in the Avdat / Aqev Area. In A. E. Marks (ed.), *Prehistory and Palaeoenvironments in the Central Negev, Israel.* Vol. I: *The Avdat/Aqev Area, part 1*, pp. 57–68. SMU Press, Dallas.

———. 1979. *The Quaternary of Israel.* Academic Press, New York.

Hours, F. 1982. Une nouvelle industrie en Syrie entre l'Acheleén supérieur et le Levalloiso-Moustérien. In *Archéologie au Levant, Recueil a la mémoire de Roger Saidah*, pp. 33–46. Collection de la Maison de l'Orient méditeraneé No. 12, série archéologique. Maison de l'Orient, Lyon.

Hovers, E. 1988. Settlement and Subsistence Patterns in the Lower Jordan Valley from Epi-Palaeolithic to Neolithic Times. M.A. thesis, The Hebrew University, Jerusalem (Hebrew).

———. 1989. Settlement Patterns in the Lower Jordan Valley in the Epi-Palaeolithic and Neolithic Times. In I. Hershkovitz (ed.), *People and Culture in Change: The Second Symposium on Upper Palaeolithic, Mesolithic and Neolithic Populations of Europe and the Mediterranean Basin*, pp. 38–51, BAR International Series 508. Oxford.

———. 1990a. Art in the Levantine Epi-Palaeolithic: An Engraved Pebble from a Kebaran Site in the Lower Jordan Valley. *Current Anthropology* 31: 317–322.

———. 1990b. The Exploitation of Raw Material at the Mousterian Site of Quneitra. In N. Goren-Inbar (ed.), *Quneitra: A Mousterian Site on the Golan Heights*, pp. 150–167, Qedem 31. Institute of Archaeology, Jerusalem.

———. 1992. Review of *The Emergence of Modern Humans: An Archaeological Perspective*, edited by P. Mellars, Cornell University Press, 1990. *Journal of Human Evolution* 22: 155–157.

———. 1997. Variability of Lithic Assemblages and Settlement Patterns in the Levantine Middle Paleolithic: Implications for the Development of Human Behavior. Ph.D. dissertation, The Hebrew University of Jerusalem, Jerusalem.

———. 1998a. The Lithic Assemblages of Amud Cave: Implications for the End of the Mousterian in the

Levant. In T. Akazawa, K. Aoki, and O. Bar-Yosef (eds.), *Neandertals and Modern Humans in Southwest Asia*, pp. 143–163. Plenum Press, New York.

———. 1998b. Comment on "Neandertal and Early Modern Human Behavioral Variability: A Regional-Scale Approach to Lithic Evidence for Hunting in the Levantine Mousterian" by J. J. Shea. *Current Anthropology* 39: S65–S66.

———. 2001. Territorial Behavior in the Middle Paleolithic of the Southern Levant. In N. Conard (ed.), *Settlement Dynamics of the Middle Paleolithic and Middle Stone Age*, pp. 123–152. Tübingen Publications in Prehistory. Kerns Verlag, Tübingen.

Hovers, E. 2003. Treading Carefully: Site Formation Processes and Pliocene Lithic Technology. In J. Martinez, R. Mora, and I. de la Torre (eds.), *Oldowan: Rather More than Smashing Stones: First Hominid Technology Workshop*, pp. 145–164. Treballs d'Arqueologia. Centre d'Estudis del Patrimoni Arqueològic de la Prehistòria. Universitat Autònoma de Barcelona, Barcelona.

———. 2004a. A Needle in a Flake Stack: Reconstructing Lithic Reduction Sequences in Levantine Mousterian Cave Sites. Paper read at Annual Meeting of the Society of American Archaeologists, Montreal, Canada.

———. 2004b. Cultural Ecology at the Neandertal Site of Amud Cave, Israel. In A. P. Derevianko and T. I. Nokhrina (eds.), *Arkheologiya i paleoekologiya Evrasii [Archaeology and Paleoecology of Eurasia]*, pp. 218–231. Institute of Archaeology and Ethnography SB RAS Press, Novosibirsk.

———. 2006. Neandertals and Modern Humans in the Middle Paleolithic of the Levant: What Kind of Interaction? In N. Conard (ed.), *When Neandertals and Moderns Met*, pp. 65–86. Kerns Verlag, Tübingen.

———. 2007. The Many Faces of Cores-on-Flakes: A Perspective from the Levantine Mousterian. In S. P. McPherron (ed.), *Cores or Tools? Alternative Approaches to Stone Tool Analysi*, pp. 42–74. Cambridge Scholars Press, Cambridge.

Hovers, E., and Bar-Yosef, O. 1987. A Prehistoric Survey of Eastern Samaria: A Preliminary Report. *Israel Exploration Journal* 37: 77–87.

Hovers, E., and Belfer-Cohen, A. 2006. "Now You See It, Now You Don't": Modern Human Behavior in the Middle Paleolithic. In E. Hovers and S. L. Kuhn (eds.), *Transitions before The Transition: Evolution and Stability in the Middle Paleolithic and Middle Stone Age*, pp. 295–304. Springer, New York.

Hovers, E., and Kuhn, S. L. (eds.) 2006. *Transitions before The Transition: Evolution and Stability in the Middle Paleolithic and Middle Stone Age*. Springer, New York.

Hovers, E., and Raveh, A. 2000. The Use of a Multivariate Display Technique in the Analysis of Inter-assemblage Lithic Variability: A Case Study from Qafzeh Cave, Israel. *Journal of Archaeological Science* 27: 1023–1038.

Hovers, E., Kimbel, W. H., and Rak, Y. 2000. Amud 7—Still, a Burial: Response to Gargett. *Journal of Human Evolution* 39: 253–260.

Hovers, E., Rak, Y. and Kimbel, W. H. 1991. Amud Cave—the 1991 season. *Journal of the Israel Prehistoric Society* 24: 152–157.

Hovers, E., Rak, Y., and Kimbel, W. H. 1996. Neandertals of the Levant. *Archaeology* January/February: 49–50.

Hovers, E., Vandermeersch, B., and Bar-Yosef, O. 1997. A Middle Palaeolithic Engraved Artefact from Qafzeh Cave, Israel. *Rock Art Research* 14: 79–87.

Hovers, E., Ilani, S., Bar-Yosef, O., and Vandermeersch, B. 2003. An Early Case of Color Symbolism: Ochre Use by Early Modern Humans in Qafzeh Cave. *Current Anthropology* 44: 491–522.

Hovers, E., Malinsky-Buller, A., Ekshtain, R., Oron, M., and Yeshurun, R. 2008. 'Ein Qashish: A New Open-Air Middle Paleolithic Site in Northern Israel. *Journal of the Israel Prehistoric Society* 38: 7–40.

Hovers, E., Rak, Y., Lavi, R., and Kimbel, W. H. 1995. Hominid Remains from Amud Cave in the Context of the Levantine Middle Paleolithic. *Paléorient* 21: 47–61.

Howell, F. C. 1957. The Evolutionary Significance of Variation Varieties of "Neanderthal" Man. *Quarterly Review of Biology* 32: 330–347.

Howell, F. C. 1958. Upper Pleistocene Men of the Southwest Asian Mousterian. In G. H. R. von Koenigswald (ed.), *Hundert jahre Neanderthaler*, pp. 185–198. Kemik en zoom, Utrecht.

———. 1959. Upper Pleistocene Stratigraphy and Early Man in the Levant. *Proceedings of the American Philosophical Society* 193: 1–65.

Hublin, J. J., and Pääbo, S. 2006. Neandertals. *Current Biology* 16: R113–R114.

Hublin, J. J., Ruiz, C. B., Lara, P. M., Fontugne, M., and Reyss, J.-L. 1995. The Mousterian Site of Zafarraya (Andalucia, Spain): Dating and Implications on the Paleolithic Peopling Process of Western Europe. *Comptes Rendus de l'Académie des Sciences, série IIa* 321: 931–937.

Hublin, J. J., Spoor, F., Braun, M., Zonneveld, F., and Condemi, S. 1996. A Late Neanderthal Associated with Upper Palaeolithic Artefacts. *Nature* 381: 224–226.

Humphrey, N. K. 1976. The Social Function of Intellect. In P. P. G. Bateson and R. A. Hinde (eds.), *Growing Points in Ethology*, pp. 303–317. Cambridge University Press, Cambridge.

———. 1992. *A History of the Mind*. Vintage, London.

Hutchinson, G. E. 1965. *The Ecological Theatre and the Evolutionary Play*. Yale University Press, New Haven, Conn.

Isaac, G. L. 1977. *Olorgesailie, Archaeological Studies of a Middle Pleistocene Lake Basin in Kenya*. University of Chicago Press, Chicago.

———. [1981] 1996. Small is Informative: The Application of the Study of Mini-Sites and Least-Effort Criteria in the Interpretation of the Early Pleistocene Archaeological Record of Koobi Fora, Kenya. In B. Isaac (ed.), *The Archaeology of Human Origins. Papers by Glynn Isaac*, pp. 259–268. Cambridge University Press, Cambridge.

Jablonka, E. 2000. Lamarckian Inheritance Systems in Biology: A Source of Metaphors and Models in Technological Evolution. In J. Ziman (ed.), *Technological Innovation as an Evolutionary Process*, pp. 27–40. Cambridge University Press, Cambridge.

Jablonka, E., and Lamb, M. J. 2005. *Evolution in Four Dimensions: Genetic, Epigenetic, Behavioral, and Symbolic Variation in the History of Life*. Life and Mind: Philosophical Issues in Biology and Psychology. MIT Press, Cambridge, Mass.

James, H. V. A., and Petraglia, M. D. 2005. Modern Human Origins and the Evolution of Behavior in the Later Pleistocene Record of South Asia. *Current Anthropology* 46: S3–S27.

Jelinek, A. 1975. A Preliminary Report on Some Lower and Middle Paleolithic Industries from the Tabun Cave, Mount Carmel (Israel). In F. Wendorf and A. E. Marks (eds.), *Problems in Prehistory: North Africa and the Levant*, pp. 279–316. SMU Press, Dallas.

———. 1976. Form, Function and Style in Lithic Analysis. In C. Clealand (ed.), *Culture Change and Continuity: Essays in Honor of James Bennet Griffin*, pp. 19–33. Academic Press, New York.

———. 1977. A Preliminary Study of Flakes from the Tabun Cave, Mt. Carmel. In B. Arensburg and O. Bar-Yosef (eds.), *Eretz-Israel 13*, pp. 87*–96*. Israel Exploration Society, Jerusalem.

———. 1982a. The Tabun Cave and Palaeolithic Man in the Levant. *Science* 216: 1369–1375.

———. 1982b. The Middle Paleolithic in the Southern Levant, with Comments on the Appearance of Modern *Homo sapiens*. In A. Ronen (ed.), *The Transition from Lower to Middle Palaeolithic and the Origin of Modern Man*, pp. 57–104, BAR International Series 151. Oxford.

———. 1988. Technology, Typology and Culture in the Middle Paleolithic. In H. L. Dibble and A. Montet-White (eds.), *Upper Pleistocene Prehistory of Western Euroasia*, pp. 199–212. University Museum Monograph 54. University of Pennsylvania Press, Philadelphia.

———. 1991. Observations on Reduction Patterns and Raw Materials in Some Middle Paleolithic Industries in the Périgord. In A. Montet-White and S. Holen (eds.), *Raw Material Economies among Prehistoric Hunter-Gatherers*, pp. 7–31. University of Kansas Publications in Anthropology 19. University of Kansas, Lawrence.

———. 1992. Problems in the Chronology of the Middle Paleolithic and the First Appearance of Early Modern Homo Sapiens in Southwest Asia. In T. Akazawa, K. Aoki, and T. Kimura (eds.), *The Evolution and Dispersal of Modern Humans in Asia*, pp. 253–275. Hakusen-Sha, Tokyo.

Jelinek, A., Farrand, W. R., Haas, G., Horowitz, A., and Goldberg, P. 1973. New Excavations at the Tabun Cave, Mount Carmel, Israel, 1967–1972: A Preliminary Report. *Paléorient* 1: 151–183.

Jochim, M. B. 1976. *Hunter-Gatherer Subsistence and Settlement: A Predictive Model*. Academic Press, New York.

———. 1979. Breaking Down the System: Recent Ecological Approaches in Archaeology. In M. B. Schiffer (ed.), *Advances in Archaeological Method and Theory 2*, pp. 77–118.

———. 1981. *Strategies for Survival*. Academic Press, New York.

———. 1983. Optimization Models in Context. In J. A. Moore and A. S. Keene (eds.), *Archaeological Hammers and Theories*, pp. 157–172. Academic Press, New York.

Johnson, G. A. 1978. Information Sources and the Development of Decision-Making Organization. In C. L. Redman, M. J. Berman, E. V. Curtin, W. J. Longhorne, Jr, N. M. Versaggi, and C. Wansen (eds.), *Social Archaeology: Beyond Subsistence and Dating*, pp. 87–112. Acedemic Press, New York.

———. 1982. Organizational Structure and Scalar Stress. In C. A. Renfrew, M. J. Rowlands, and B. A. Segraves (eds.), *Theory and Explanation in Archaeology*, pp. 389–421. Academic Press, New York.

Jones, J. S., Martin, R., and Pilbeam, D. (eds.) 1992. *The Cambridge Encyclopedia of Human Evolution*. Cambridge University Press, Cambridge.

Jones, S. 1996. Discourse of Identity in the Interpretation of the Past. In P. Graves-Brown, S. Jones, and C. Gamble (eds.), *Cultural Identity and Archaeology: The Construction of European Communities*, pp. 62–80. Routledge, London.

Kameda, T., and Nakanishi, D. 2003. Does Social/Cultural Learning Increase Human Adaptability? Rogers's Question Revisited. *Evolution and Human Behavior* 24: 242–260.

Karkanas, P., Bar-Yosef, O., Goldberg, P., and Weiner, S. 2000. Diagenesis in Prehistoric Caves: The Use of Minerals that Form *in situ* to Assess the Completeness of the Archaeological Record. *Journal of Archaeological Science* 27: 915–929.

Karkanas, P., Shahack-Gross, R., Ayalon, A., Bar-Matthews, M., Barkai, R., Frumkin, A., Gopher, A., and Stiner, M. C. 2007. Evidence for Habitual Use of Fire at the End of the Lower Paleolithic: Site-Formation Processes at Qesem Cave, Israel. *Journal of Human Evolution* 53: 197–212.

Karlin, C., and Julien, M. 1994. Prehistoric Technology: A Cognitive Science? In C. Renfrew and E. W. Zubrow (eds.), *The Ancient Mind: Elements of Cognitive Archaeology*, pp. 152–164. Cambridge University Press, Cambridge.

Karlin, C., Bodu, P., and Pelegrin, J. 1991. Processus techniques et chaînes opératoires: Comment les préhistoriens s'approprient un concept élaboré par les ethnologues. In H. Balfet (ed.), *Observer L'action technique: Des chaînes opératoires, Pour quoi faire?*, pp. 101–117. CNRS, Paris.

Katsenelson, Y. 1985. *Atlas of Israel*. Survey of Israel , Tel-Aviv, Maps 12–14 (Hebrew).

Keeley, L. H. 1982. Hafting and Retooling: Effects on the Archaeological Record. *American Antiquity* 47: 798–809.

———. 1995. Proto-agricultural Practices among Hunter-Gatherers: A Cross-Cultural Survey. In T. D Price and A. B. Gebauer (eds.), *Last Hunters, First Farmers: New*

*Perspectives on the Prehistoric Transition to Agriculture,* pp. 243–272. School of American Research Press, Santa Fe.

Kelly, R. L. 1983. Hunter-Gatherer Mobility Strategies. *Journal of Anthropological Research* 39: 277–306.

———. 1988. The Three Sides of a Biface. *American Antiquity* 53(4): 717–734.

———. 1992. Mobility/Sedentism: Concepts, Archaeological Measures, and Effects. *Annual Review of Anthropology* 21: 43–66.

———. 1995. *The Foraging Spectrum: Diversity in Hunter-Gatherer Lifeways.* The Smithsonian Institute Press, Washington.

Kelly, R. L., and Todd, L. C. 1988. Coming into the Country: Early Paleoindian Hunting and Mobility. *American Antiquity* 53: 231–244.

Klein, R. G. 1982. Age (Mortality) Profiles as a Means of Distinguishing Hunted Species from Scavenged Ones in Stone Age Archaeological Sites. *Paleobiology* 8: 151–158.

———. 1995. Anatomy, Behavior, and Modern Human Origins. *Journal of World Prehistory* 9: 167–198.

———. 1999. *The Human Career: Human Biological and Cultural Origins.* Chicago University Press, Chicago.

———. 2000. Archeology and the Evolution of Human Behavior. *Evolutionary Anthropology* 9: 17–36.

Klein, R. G., Avery, G., Cruz-Uribe, K., Halkett, D., Parkington, J. E., Steele, T., Volman, T. P., and Yates, R. 2004. The Ysterfontein 1 Middle Stone Age Site, South Africa, and Early Human Exploitation of Coastal Resources. *Proceedings of the National Academy of Science U.S.A.* 101: 5708–5715.

Klein, S. 1990. Human Cognitive Changes at the Middle to Upper Paleolithic Transition: The Evidence of Boker Tachtit. In P. Mellars (ed.), *The Emergence of Modern Humans: An Archaeological Perspective,* pp. 499–516. Cornell University Press, Ithaca, N.Y.

Knight, A. 2003. The Phylogenetic Relationship of Neandertal and Modern Human Mitochondrial DNAs Based on Informative Nucleotide Sites. *Journal of Human Evolution* 44: 627–632.

Knight, C., Power, C., and Watts, I. 1995. The Human Symbolic Revolution: A Darwinian Account. *Cambridge Archaeological Journal* 5: 75–114.

Kramer, A., Crummett, T. L., and Wolpoff, M. H. 2001. Out of Africa and into the Levant: Replacement or Admixture in Western Asia. *Quaternary International* 75: 51–63.

Krause, J., Lalueza-Fox, C., Orland, L., Enard, W., Green, R. E., Burbano, H. A., Hublin, J.-J., Hanni, C., Fortea, J., de la Rasilla, M., Bertranpetit, J., Rosas, A., and Pääbo, S. 2007. The Derived FOXP2 Variant of Modern Humans was Shared with Neandertals. *Current Biology* 17: 1908–1912.

Krings, M., Capelli, C., Tschentscher, F., Geisert, H., Meyer, S., von Haeseler, A., Grossschmidt, K., Possner, G., Paunovic, M., and Pääbo, S. 2000. A View of Neandertal Genetic Diversity. *Nature Genetics* 26: 144–146.

Krings, M., Stone, A., Schmitz, R. W., Kraainitzki, H., Stoneking, M., and Pääbo, S. 1997. Neandertal DNA Sequences and the Origin of Modern Humans. *Cell* 90: 19–30.

Kroes, P., and Meijers, A. 2006. The Dual Nature of Technical Artefacts. *Studies in the History and Philosophy of Science Part A* 37: 1–4.

Kuhn, S. L. 1989. Hunter-Gatherer Foraging Organization and Strategies of Artifact Replacement and Discard. In D. S. Amick and R. P. Mauldin (eds.), *Experiments in Lithic Technology,* pp. 33–45, BAR International Series 528. Oxford.

———. 1990. A Geometric Index of Reduction for Unifacial Stone Tools. *Journal of Archaeological Science* 17: 583–593.

———. 1992a. Blank Form and Reduction as Determinants of Mousterian Scraper Morphology. *American Antiquity* 57: 115–128.

———. 1992b. On Planning and Curated Technologies in the Middle Paleolithic. *Journal of Anthropological Research* 48: 185–214.

———. 1993. Mousterian Technology as Adaptive Response: A Case Study. In G. H. Peterkin, M. Bricker, and P. Mellars (eds.), *Hunting and Animal Exploitation in the Late Palaeolithic and Mesolithic of Europe,* pp. 20–25. Anthropological Papers of the American Anthropological Association 4.

———. 1994. A Formal Approach to the Design and Assembly of Transported Toolkits. *American Antiquity* 59: 426–442.

———. 1995a. *Mousterian Lithic Technology: An Ecological Perspective.* Princeton University Press, Princeton.

———. 1995b. A Perspective on Levallois from a "Non-Levallois" Assemblage: The Mousterian of Grotta di Sant'Agostino (Gaeta, Italy). In H. L. Dibble and O. Bar-Yosef (eds.), *The Definition and Interpretation of Levallois Technology,* pp. 157–170. Monographs in World Archaeology N. 23. Prehistory Press, Madison, Wis.

———. 1996. The Trouble with Ham Steaks: A Reply to Morrow. *American Antiquity* 61: 591–595.

———. 1998. Comment on 'Neandertal and Early Modern Human Behavioral Variability: A Regional-Scale Approach to Lithic Evidence for Hunting in the Levantine Mousterian' by J. J. Shea. *Current Anthropology* 39: S66–S67.

———. 2006. Trajectories of Change in the Middle Paleolithic of Italy. In E. Hovers and S. L. Kuhn (eds.), *Transitions before The Transition: Evolution and Stability in the Middle Paleolithic and Middle Stone Age,* pp. 109–120. Springer, New York.

Kuhn, S. L., and Hovers, E. 2006. General Introduction. In E. Hovers and S. L. Kuhn (eds.), *Transitions before The Transition: Evolution and Stability in the Middle Paleolithic and Middle Stone Age,* pp. 1–11. Springer, New York.

Kuhn, S. L., and Stiner, M. C. 1998. Middle Paleolithic "Creativity": Reflections on an Oxymoron? In Mithen S. (ed.), *Creativity in Human Evolution and Prehistory,* pp. 143–164. Routledge, London and New York.

———. 2006. What's a Mother to Do? The Division of Labor among Neanderthals and Modern Humans in Eurasia. *Current Anthropology* 47: 953–980.

———. 2007. Body Ornamentation as Information Technology: Towards an Understanding of the Significance of Early Beads. In P. Mellars, K. Boyle, O. Bar-Yosef, and C. Stringer (eds.), *Rethinking the Human Revolution*, pp. 45–54. McDonald Institute for Archaeological Research, Cambridge.

Laden, G., and Wrangham, R. 2005. The Rise of the Hominids as an Adaptive Shift in Fallback Foods: Plant Underground Storage Organs (USOs) and Australopith Origins. *Journal of Human Evolution* 49: 482–498.

Lahr, M. M., and Foley, R. 1998. Towards a Theory of Modern Human Origins: Geography, Demography, and Diversity in Recent Human Evolution. *Yearbook of Physical Anthropology* 41: 137–176.

Laland, K. N. 1998. The Evolution of Culture: A Comparative Perspective. In T. Akazawa, K. Aoki, and O. Bar-Yosef (eds.) *Neandertals and Modern Humans in Western Asia*, pp. 427–438. Plenum Press, New York.

Laland, K. N., and Hoppitt, W. 2003. Do Animals Have Culture? *Evolutionary Anthropology* 12: 150–159.

Laland, K. N., Odling-Smee, J., and Feldman, M. W. 2000. Niche Construction, Biological Evolution, and Cultural Change. *Behavioral and Brain Sciences* 23: 131–175.

Leakey, M. D. 1971. *Olduvai Gorge*, vol. 3. Cambridge University Press, Cambridge.

Lee, R. 1979. *The !Kung San: Men, Women, and Work in a Foraging Society*. Cambridge University Press, Cambridge.

Lemonnier, P. 1986. The Study of Material Culture Today: Toward an Anthropology of Technical Systems. *Journal of Anthropological Archaeology* 5: 147–186.

———. 1992. *Elements for an Anthropology of Technology*. Anthropological Papers 88. Museum of Anthropology, University of Michigan, Ann Arbor.

———. (ed.) 1993. *Technological Choices: Transformation in Material Cultures since the Neolithic*. Routledge, London.

Lepowsky, M. 1991. The Way of the Ancestors: Custom, Innovation, and Resistance. *Ethnology* 30: 217–235.

Leroi-Gourhan, A. 1945. *Evolution et techniques. Millieu et techniques (reprinted 1973)*. Albin Michel, Paris.

———. 1964. *Le Geste et la parole* (trans. Anna Bostock Berger, 1993). MIT Press, Cambridge.

Lev, E. 1993. The Vegetal Food of the "Neandertal" Man in Kebara Cave, Mt. Carmel, in the Middle Paleolithic Period. M.A. thesis, Bar-Ilan University, Ramat-Gan (Hebrew).

Lev, E., Kislev, M. E., and Bar-Yosef, O. 2005. Mousterian Vegetal Food in Kebara Cave, Mt. Carmel. *Journal of Archaeological Science* 32: 475–484.

Levin, I. P., Huneke, M. E., and Jasper, J. D. 2000. Information Processing at Successive Stages of Decision Making: Need for Cognitive and Inclusion–Exclusion Effects. *Organizational Behaviour and Human Decision Processes* 82: 171–193.

Levi-Strauss, C. 1976. *Structural Anthropology*, vol. 2. Basic Books, New York.

Lieberman, D. E. 1993. The Rise and Fall of Seasonal Mobility among Hunter-Gatherers: The Case of the Southern Levant. *Current Anthropology* 34: 599–631.

———. 1998. Neandertal and Early Modern Human Mobility Patterns: Comparing Archaeological and Anatomical Evidence. In T. Akazawa, K. Aoki, and O. Bar-Yosef (eds.), *Neandertals and Modern Humans in Western Asia*, pp. 263–275. Plenum Press, New York.

Lieberman, D. E., and Bar-Yosef, O. 2005. Apples and Oranges: Morphological versus Behavioral Transitions in the Pleistocene. In D. E. Lieberman, R. J. Smith, and J. Kelley (eds.), *Interpreting the Past: Essays on Human, Primate, and Mammal Evolution in Honor of David Pilbeam*, pp. 275–296. Bril Academic Publishers, Boston.

Lieberman, D. E., and Shea, J. J. 1994. Behavioral Differences between Archaic and Modern Humans in the Levantine Mousterian. *American Anthropologist* 96: 300–332.

Lindly, J., and Clark, G. 1987. A Preliminary Lithic Analysis of the Mousterian Site of 'Ain Difla (WHS 634) in the Wadi Ali, West-Central Jordan. *Proceedings of the Prehistoric Society* 53: 279–292.

Lombard, M. 2005. Evidence of Hunting and Hafting during the Middle Stone Age at Sibidu Cave, KwaZulu-Natal, South Africa: A Multianalytical Approach. *Journal of Human Evolution* 48: 279–300.

———. 2007. The Gripping Nature of Ochre: The Association of Ochre with Howiesons Poort Adhesives and Later Stone Age Mastics from South Africa. *Journal of Human Evolution* 53: 406–419.

MacEachern, S. 1998. Scale, Style, and Cultural Variation: Technological Traditions in the Northern Mandara Mountains. In M. T. Stark (ed.), *The Archaeology of Social Boundaries*, pp. 107–131. Smithsonian Institution Press, Washington.

Madella, M., Jones, M. K., Goldberg, P., Goren, Y., and Hovers, E. 2002. The Exploitation of Plant Resources by Neanderthals in Amud Cave (Israel): The Evidence from Phytolith Studies. *Journal of Archaeological Science* 29: 703–719.

Madsen, B., and Goren-Inbar, N. 2004. Acheulian Giant Core Technology and Beyond: An Archaeological and Experimental Case Study. *Eurasian Prehistory* 2: 3–52.

Maneh, U. 1985. *Atlas of Israel*. Survey of Israel , Tel-Aviv, Maps 12–14 (Hebrew).

Marder, O. 2002. The Lithic Technology of Epi-Paleolithic Hunter-Gatherers in the Negev: The Implications of Refitting Studies. Ph.D. dissertation, The Hebrew University of Jerusalem, Jerusalem.

Marean, C. W., and Assefa, Z. 2004. The Middle and Upper Pleistocene African Record for the Biological and Behavioral Origins of Modern Humans. In A. Stahl (ed.), *African Archaeology: A Critical Introduction,* pp. 93–129. Blackwell Studies in Global Archaeology. Blackwell, Malden.

Marean, C. W., and Kim, S. Y. 1998. Mousterian Large-Mammal Remains from Kobeh Cave: Behavioral Implications for Neanderthals and Early Modern Humans. *Current Anthropology* 39 (supplement): S79–S113.

Marean, C. W., Bar-Matthews, M., Bernatchez, J., Fisher, E., Goldberg, P., Herries, A. I. R., Jacobs, Z., Jerardino, A., Karkanas, P., Minichillo, T., Nilssen, P. J., Thompson, E., Watts, I., and Williams, H. M. 2007. Early Human Use of Marine Resources and Pigment in South Africa during the Middle Pleistocene. *Nature* 449: 905–908.

Marks, A. E. 1968. The Mousterian Industries of Nubia. In F. Wendorf (ed.), *The Prehistory of Nubia*, pp. 194–314. SMU Press, Dallas.

———. (ed.) 1976. *Prehistory and Palaeoenvironments in the Central Negev, Israel*, vol. 1. SMU Press, Dallas.

———. (ed.) 1977. *Prehistory and Palaeoenvironments in the Central Negev, Israel*, vol. 2. SMU Press, Dallas.

Marks, A. E. 1988. The Curation of Stone Tools during the Upper Pleistocene: A View from the Central Negev, Israel. In H. L. Dibble and A. Montet-White (eds.), *Upper Pleistocene Prehistory of Western Euroasia*, pp. 275–285. University Museum, Philadelphia.

———. 1989. Early Mousterian Settlement Patterns in the Central Negev, Israel: Their Social and Economic Implications. In M. Otte (ed.), *L'Homme de Neandertal*, vol. 6: *La Subsistence*, pp. 115–125. ERAUL. Universitè de Liège, Liège.

———. 1992a. Typological Variability in the Levantine Middle Paleolithic. In H. L. Dibble and P. Mellars (eds.), *The Middle Paleolithic: Adaptation, Behavior, and Variability*, pp. 127–142. University Museum, University of Pennsylvania, Philadelphia.

———. 1992b. Upper Pleistocene Archaeology in the Levant and Adjacent Areas. In T. Akazawa, K. Aoki, and T. Kimura (eds.), *The Evolution and Dispersal of Modern Humans in Asia*, pp. 229–252. Hakusen-Sha, Tokyo.

Marks, A. E., and Chabai, V. P. 2006. Stasis and Change during the Crimean Middle Paleolithic. In E. Hovers and S. L. Kuhn (eds.), *Transitions before The Transition: Evolution and Stability in the Middle Paleolithic and Middle Stone Age*, pp. 121–135. Springer, New York.

Marks, A. E., and Freidel, D. A. 1977. Prehistoric Settlement Patterns in the Avdat/Aqev Area. In A. E. Marks (ed.), *Prehistory and Palaeoenvironments in the Central Negev, Israel*, vol. 2, pp. 131–158. SMU Press, Dallas.

Marks, A. E., and Monigal, K. 1995. Modeling the Production of Elongated Blanks from the Early Levantine Mousterian at Rosh Ein Mor. In H. L. Dibble and O. Bar-Yosef (eds.), *The Definition and Interpretation of Levallois Technology*, pp. 267–278. Monographs in World Archaeology 23. Prehistory Press, Ann Arbor, Mich.

Marks, A. E., and Volkman, P. W. 1983. Changing Core Reduction Strategies: A Technological Shift from Middle to Upper Paleolithic in the Southern Levant. In E. Trinkaus (ed.), *The Mousterian Legacy: Human Biological Change in the Upper Pleistocene*, pp. 13–33, BAR International Series 164. Oxford.

———. 1986. The Mousterian of Ksar Akil: Levels XXIV through XXVIIIb. *Paléorient* 12: 5–20.

Marks, A. E., Hietala, H. J., and Williams, J. K. 2001. Tool Standardization in the Middle and Upper Palaeolithic: A Closer Look. *Cambridge Archaeological Journal* 11: 17–44.

Marshack, A. 1989. Evolution of the Human Capacity: The Symbolic Evidence. *Yearbook of Physical Anthropology* 32: 1–34.

———. 1996. A Middle Paleolithic Symbolic Composition from the Golan Heights: The Earliest Known Depictive Image. *Current Anthropology* 37: 357–365.

Martin-Loeches, M. 2006. On the Uniqueness of Humankind: Is Language Working Memory the Final Piece that Made Us Human? *Journal of Human Evolution* 50: 226–229.

Masters, P. 1982. An Amino Acid Racemization Chronology for Tabun. In A. Ronen (ed.), *The Transition from Lower to Middle Paleolithic and the Origin of Modern Man*, pp. 43–54, BAR International Series 151. Oxford.

Matsutani, A. 1987. Plant Remains from the 1984 Excavations at Douara Cave. In T. Akazawa and Y. Sakaguchi (eds.), *Paleolithic Site of Douara Cave and Paleogeography of Palmyra Basin. Part IV: 1984 Excavations*, pp. 117–122. University of Tokyo Press, Tokyo.

Mauss, M. 1936. Les Techniques du corps. Sociologie et Psychologie, Parts II–VI. In B. Brewster (ed.), *Sociology and Psychology: Essays of Marcel Mauss* (translated 1979). Routledge and Kegan Paul, London.

McBrearty, S., and Brooks, A. S. 2000. The Revolution that Wasn't: A New Interpretation of the Origin of Modern Human Behavior. *Journal of Human Evolution* 39: 453–563.

McBrearty, S., and Tryon, C. A. 2006. From Acheulean to Middle Stone Age in the Kapthurin Formation, Kenya. In E. Hovers and S. L. Kuhn (eds.), *Transitions before The Transition: Evolution and Stability in the Middle Paleolithic and Middle Stone Age*, pp. 257–277. Springer, New York.

McBrearty, S., Bishop, L., and Kingston, J. 1996. Variability in Traces of Middle Pleistocene Hominid Behavior in the Kapthurin Formation, Baringo, Kenya. *Journal of Human Evolution* 30: 363–380.

McCown, T. D. 1934. The Oldest Complete Skeletons of Man. *Bulletin of the American School of Prehistoric Research* 10: 13–18.

McCown, T. D., and Keith, A. 1939. *The Stone Age of Mount Carmel* II. Clarendon Press, Oxford.

McDermott, F., Grün, R., Stringer, C. B., and Hawkesworth, C. J. 1993. Mass-spectrometric U-Series Dates for Israeli Neanderthals/Early Modern Hominid Sites. *Nature* 363: 252–255.

McDougall, I., Brown, F. H., and Fleagle, J. G. 2005. Stratigraphic Placement and Age of Modern Humans from Kibish, Ethiopia. *Nature* 433: 733–736.

McGarry, S., Bar-Matthews, M., Matthews, A., Vaks, A., Schilman, B., and Ayalon, A. 2004. Constraints on Hydrological and Paleotemperature Variations in the Eastern Mediterranean Region in the Last 140 ka Given by the [Delta] D Values of Speleothem Fluid Inclusions. *Quaternary Science Reviews* 23: 919–934.

McGill, R., Tukey, J., and Larson, W. 1978. Variations of Box Plots. *American Statistician* 32: 12–16.

McPherron, S. 2000. Handaxes as a Measure of the Mental Capabilities of Early Hominids. *Journal of Archaeological Science* 27: 655–663.

Meignen, L. 1988. Un exemple de comportement tech-nologique différentiel selon les matières premières: Marillac, couches 9 et 10. In M. Otte (ed.), *L'Homme de Néandertal,* pp. 71–79. Université de Liège, Liège.

———. 1993. Les Industries lithiques de l'abri des Canalettes: Couche 2. In L. Meignen (ed.), *L'Abri des Canalettes: Un habitat moustérien sur les Grands Causses,* pp. 239–328. CNRS, Paris.

———. 1994a. Paléolithique moyen au Proche-Orient: Le Phénomène laminaire, *Les Industries laminaires au Paléolithique moyen,* pp. 125–159. Dossiers de Documentation Archéologique 18. Éditions CNRS, Paris.

———. 1994b. L'Analyse de l'organisation spatiale dans les sites du paléolithique moyen: Structures évi-dentes, structures latentes. *Préhistoire et Anthropologie Mediterranéens* 3: 7–23.

———. 1995. Levallois Lithic Production Systems in the Middle Palaeolithic of the Near East: The Case of the Unidirectional Method. In H. L. Dibble and O. Bar-Yosef (eds.), *The Definition and Interpretation of Levallois Technology,* pp. 361–380. Monographs in World Archaeology 23. Prehistory Press, Madison, Wis.

———. 1998. A Preliminary Report on Hayonim Cave Lithic Assemblages in the Context of the Near Eastern Middle Palaeolithic. In T. Akazawa, K. Aoki, and O. Bar-Yosef (eds.), *Neandertals and Modern Humans in Asia,* pp. 165–180. Plenum Press, New York.

———. 2000. Early Middle Paleolithic Blade Technology in Southwestern Asia. *Acta Anthropologica Sinica* 19: 158–168.

Meignen, L., and Bar-Yosef, O. 1988. Kebara et le Paléolithique moyen du Mont Carmel (Israël). *Paléorient* 14: 123–130.

———. 1989. Nouvelles recherches sur le Paléolithique moyen d'Israël: La Grotte de Kebara, unités VII à XII. In O. Bar-Yosef and B. Vandermeersch (eds.), *Investigations in South Levantine Prehistory,* pp. 169–184. Bar International Series 497, Oxford.

———. 1991. Les Outils lithiques moustériens de Kebara (fouilles 1982–1985). In O. Bar-Yosef and B. Vandermeersch (eds.), *Le Squelette Moustérien de Kebara 2,* pp. 49–85. Cahiers de Paléoanthropologie. CNRS, Paris.

———. 1992. Middle Paleolithic Variability in Kebara Cave, Israel. In T. Akazawa, K. Aoki, and T. Kimura (eds.), *The Evolution and Dispersal of Modern Humans in Asia,* pp. 129–148. Hakusen-Sha, Tokyo.

———. 2002. The Lithic Industries of the Middle and Upper Paleolithic of the Levant: Continuity or Break? *Archaeology, Ethnology & Anthropology of Eurasia* 3: 12–21.

Meignen, L., Bar-Yosef, O., Goldberg, P., and Weiner, S. 2001a. Le Feu au paléolithique moyen: Recherches sur les structures de combustion et le statut des foyers. L'exemple du Proche Orient. *Paléorient* 26: 9–22.

Meignen, L., Bar-Yosef, O., Mercier, N., Valladas, H., Goldberg, P., and Vandermeerch, B. 2001b. Apport des datations au problème de l'origin des hommes mod-ernes au Proche-Orient. In J.-N. Barrandon, P. Guibert, and V. Michel (eds.), *Datation,* pp. 295–313. XXI rencontres internationales d'archéologie et d'histoire d'Antibes. Editions APDCA, Antibes.

Meignen, L., Bar-Yosef, O., Speth, J. D., and Stiner, M. C. 2006. Middle Paleolithic Settlement Patterns in the Levant. In E. Hovers and S. L. Kuhn (eds.), *Transitions before The Transition: Evolution and Stability in the Middle Paleolithic and Middle Stone Age,* pp. 149–169. Springer, New York.

Mellars, P. 1989. Major Issues in the Emergence of Modern Humans. *Current Anthropology* 30: 349–385.

———. 1990. *The Emergence of Modern Humans: An Archaeological Perspective.* Cornell University Press, Ithaca, N.Y.

———. 1996. *The Mousterian Legacy: An Archaeological Perspective from Western Europe.* Princeton University Press, Princeton, N.J.

———. 2000. The Archaeological Records of the Neandertal–Modern Human Transition in France. In O. Bar-Yosef and D. Pilbeam (eds.), *The Geography of Neandertals and Modern Humans in Europe and the Greater Mediterranean,* pp. 35–47. Peabody Museum of Archaeology and Ethnology, Harvard University, Cambridge, Mass.

———. 2005. The Impossible Coincidence. A Single-Species Model for the Origin of Modern Human Behavior in Europe. *Evolutionary Anthropology* 14: 12–17.

———. 2006. A New Radiocarbon Revolution and the Dispersal of Modern Humans in Eurasia. *Nature* 439: 931.

Mellars, P., and Stringer, C. 1989. *Behavioural and Biological Perspectives on the Origins of Modern Humans.* Edinburgh University Press, Edinburgh.

Mellars, P., and Tixier, J. 1989. Radiocarbon-Accelerator Dating of Ksar 'Akil (Lebanon) and the Chronology of the Upper Palaeolithic Sequence in the Middle East. *Antiquity* 63: 761–768.

Mercier, N., and Valladas, H. 2003. Reassessment of TL Age Estimates of Burnt Flints from the Paleolithic Site of Tabun Cave, Israel. *Journal of Human Evolution* 45: 401–409.

Mercier, N., Valladas, H., Bar-Yosef, O., Vandermeersch, B., Stringer, C., and Joron, J.-L. 1993. Thermoluminescence Date for the Mousterian Burial Site of Es-Skhul, Mt. Carmel. *Journal of Archaeological Science* 20: 169–174.

Mercier, N., Valladas, H., Froget, L., Joron, J.-L., Reyss, J.-L., Weiner, S., Goldberg, P., Meignen, L., Bar-Yosef, O., Belfer-Cohen, A., Chech, M., Kuhn, S. L., Stiner, M. C., Tillier, A.-M., Arensburg, B., and Vandermeersch, B. 2007. Hayonim Cave: A TL-Based Chronology for this Levantine Mousterian Sequence. *Journal of Archaeological Science* 34: 1064–1077.

Mercier, N., Valladas, H., Joron, J.-L., Reyss, J.-L., Leveque, F., and Vandermeersch, B. 1991. Thermoluminescence Dating of the Late Neanderthal Remains from Saint-Césaire. *Nature* 351: 737–739.

Mercier, N., Valladas, H., Joron, J.-L., Schiegl, S., Bar-Yosef, O., and Weiner, S. 1995. Thermoluminescence Dating and the Problem of Geochemical Evolution of Sediments—A Case Study: The Mousterian Levels at Hayonim. *Israel Journal of Chemistry* 35: 137–141.

Metcalfe, D., and Barlow, K. R. 1992. A Model for Exploring the Optimal Trade-off between Field Processing and Transport. *American Anthropologist* 94: 340–356.

Millard, A. R., and Pike, A. W. G. 1999. Uranium-Series Dating of the Tabun Neanderthal: A Cautionary Note. *Journal of Human Evolution* 36: 581–585.

Miller-Rosen, A. 2003. Middle Paleolithic Plant Exploitation: The Microbotanical Evidence. In D. O. Henry (ed.), *Neanderthals in the Levant: Behavioral Organization and the Beginnings of Human Modernity*, pp. 156–171. Continuum, London.

Minichillo, T. J. 2006. Raw Material Use and Behavioral Modernity: Howiesons Poort Lithic Foraging Strategies. *Journal of Human Evolution* 50: 359–364.

Mithen, S. 1990. *Thoughtful Foragers: A Study of Prehistoric Decision Making*. New Studies in Archaeology. Cambridge University Press, Cambridge.

———. 1994. From Domain Specific to Generalized Intelligence: A Cognitive Interpretation of the Middle/Upper Paleolithic Transition. In C. Renfrew and E. Zubrow (eds.), *The Ancient Mind: Elements of Cognitive Archaeology*, pp. 29–39. Cambridge University Press, Cambridge.

———. 1996. *The Prehistory of the Mind: A Search for the Origins of Art, Religion and Science*. Thames and Hudson, London.

Monigal, K. 2002. The Levantine Leptolithic: Blade Production from the Lower Paleolithic to the Dawn of the Upper Paleolithic. Ph.D. dissertation, Southern Methodist University.

Monnier, G. F. 2006. Testing Retouched Flake Tool Standardization during the Middle Paleolithic. In E. Hovers and S. L. Kuhn (eds.), *Transitions before The Transition: Evolution and Stability in the Middle Paleolithic and Middle Stone Age*, pp. 57–83. Springer, New York.

Moore, J. A. 1983. The Trouble with Know-it-alls: Information as a Social and Ecological Resource. In J. A. Moore and A. S. Keene (eds.), *Archaeological Hammers and Theories*, pp. 173–191. Academic Press, New York.

Morrow, T. A. 1996. Bigger is Better: Comments on Kuhn's Formal Approach to Mobile Tool Kits. *American Antiquity* 61: 581–590.

Movius, H. L. 1950. A Wooden Spear of Third Interglacial Age from Lower Saxony. *Southwestern Journal of Anthropology* 6: 139–142.

Munday, F. C. 1976a. Intersite Variability in the Mousterian of the Central Negev. In A. E. Marks (ed.), *Prehistory and Palaeoenvironments in the Central Negev, Israel*, Vol. I: *The Avdat/Aqev Area, part 1*, pp. 113–140. SMU Press, Dallas.

———. 1976b. The Mousterian in the Negev: A Description and Explication of Inter-Site Variability. Ph.D. thesis, SMU.

———. 1977. Nahal Aqev (D35): A Stratified, Open-Air Mousterian Occupation in the Avdat/Aqev Area. In A. E. Marks (ed.), *Prehistory and Palaeoenvironments in the Central Negev, Israel*, Vol. II: *The Avdat/Aqev Area, part 2, and the Har Harif*, pp. 35–60. SMU Press, Dallas.

———. 1979. Levantine Mousterian Technological Variability: A Perspective from the Negev. *Paléorient* 5: 87–104.

Nadel, D. (ed.) 2002. *Ohalo II: A 23,000-Year-Old Fisher-Hunter-Gatherers Camp on the Shore of the Sea of Galilee*. Reuben and Edith Hecth Museum, University of Haifa, Haifa.

Neeley, M. P., and Barton, C. M. 1994. A New Approach to Interpreting Late Pleistocene Microlith Industries in Southwest Asia. *Antiquity* 68: 275–288.

Neev, D., and Emery, K. O. 1967. The Dead Sea: Depositional Processes and Environments of Evaporites. *Geological Survey of Israel* 41: 1–147.

Neiman, F. D. 1995. Stylistic Variation in Evolutionary Perspective: Inferences from Decorative Diversity and Interassemblage Distance in Illinois Woodland Ceramic Assemblages. *American Antiquity* 60: 7–36.

Nelson, M. C. 1991. The Study of Technological Organization. In M. B. Schiffer (ed.), *Archaeological Method and Theory 3*, pp. 57–100.

Neuville, R. 1934. Le Préhistoire de Palestine. *Revue Biblique* 43: 237–259.

———. 1951. *Le Paléolithique et le Mesolithique du desert du Judee*. Archives de Musée de Paléontologie Humaine memoire 24. Masson et Cie, Paris.

Nielsen, A. E. 1991. Trampling the Archaeological Record: An Experimental Study. *American Antiquity* 56: 483–503.

Niewoehner, W. A., Bergstrom, A., Eichele, D., Suroff, M., and Clark, J. T. 2003. Manual Dexterity in Neanderthals. *Nature* 422: 369.

Nishiaki, Y. 1985. Truncated-Faceted Flakes from Levantine Mousterian Assemblages. *Bulletin of the Department of Archaeology, the University of Tokyo* 4: 215–226.

———. 1989. Early Blade Industries in the Levant: The Placement of Douara IV Industry in the Context of the Levantine Early Middle Paleolithic. *Paléorient* 15: 215–229.

Nishiaki, Y., and Copeland, L. 1992. Keoue Cave, Northern Lebanon, and its Place in the Context of the Levantine Mousterian. In T. Akazawa, K. Aoki, and T. Kimura (eds.) *The Evolution and Dispersal of Modern Humans in Asia*, pp. 107–127. Hakusen-Sha, Tokyo.

Noble, W., and Davidson, I. 1993. Tracing the Emergence of Modern Human Behavior: Methodological Pitfalls and a Theoretical Path. *Journal of Anthropological Archaeology* 12: 121–149.

Noll, M. P. 2000. Components of Acheulean Lithic Assemblage Variability at Olorgesailie, Kenya. Ph.D. dissertation, University of Illinois.

Noonan, J. P., Coop, G., Kudaravalli, S., Smith, D., Krause, J., Alessi, J., Chen, F., Platt, D., Pääbo, S., Pritchard, J. K., and Rubin, E. M. 2006. Sequencing and Analysis of Neanderthal Genomic DNA. *Science* 314: 1113–1118.

Nowak, R. M., and Paradiso, J. L. 1983. *Walker's Mammals of the World*. 4th edn. Johns Hopkins University Press, Baltimore.

Oakely, K. P., Andrews, P., Keeley, L. H., and Clark, J. D. 1977. A Reappraisal of the Clacton Spear Point. *Proceedings of the Prehistoric Society* 43: 13–30.

O'Brien, M. J., and Lyman, R. L. 2002. Evolutionary Archeology: Current Status and Future Prospects. *Evolutionary Anthropology* 11: 26–36.

O'Connell, J. F. 1995. Ethnoarchaeology Needs a General Theory of Behavior. *Journal of Archaeological Research* 3: 205–251.

O'Connell, J. F., Hawkes, K., and Blurton-Jones, N. G. 1992. Patterns in the Distribution, Site Structure and Assemblage Composition of Hadza Kill-Butchering Sites. *Journal of Archaeological Science* 19: 319–345.

Odell, G. H. 1994. Prehistoric Hafting and Mobility in the North American Midcontinent: Examples from Illinois. *Journal of Anthropological Archaeology* 13: 51–73.

———. 1996. Economizing Behavior and the Concept of "Curation." In G. H. Odell (ed.), *Stone Tools: Theoretical Insights into Human Prehistory*, pp. 51–80. Plenum Press, New York and London.

Ohnuma, K. 1990. An Analysis of the By-Products of Experimental Manufacture of Classical Levallois Flakes. *Al-Rafidian XI*, pp. 113–141. The Institute for Cultural Studies of Ancient Iraq, Kokushikan University, Tokyo.

———. 1992. The Significance of Layer B (square 8–19) of the Amud Cave (Israel) in the Levantine Levalloiso-Mousterian: A Technological Study. In T. Akazawa, K. Aoki, and T. Kimura (eds.), *The Evolution and Dispersal of Modern Humans in Asia*, pp. 83–106. Hakusen-Sha, Tokyo.

Ohnuma, K., and Bergman, C. 1982. Experimental Studies in the Determination of Flaking Mode. *Bulletin of the Institute of Archaeology, London*: 161–170.

Ohnuma, K., Aoki, K., and Akazawa, T. 1997. Transmission of Tool-Making through Verbal and Non-verbal Communication: Preliminary Experiments in Levallois Flake Production. *Anthropological Science* 105: 159–168.

Olivieri, A., Achilli, A., Pala, M., Battaglia, V., Fornarino, S., Al-Zahery, N., Scozzari, R., Cruciani, F., Behar, D. M., Dugoujon, J.-M., Coudray, C., Santachiara-Benerecetti, A. S., Semino, O., Bandelt, H.-J., and Torroni, A. 2006. The mtDNA Legacy of the Levantine Early Upper Palaeolithic in Africa. *Science* 314: 1767–1770.

Osborne, A. H., Vance, D., Rohling, E. J., Barton, N., Rogerson, M., and Fello, N. 2008. A humid corridor across the Sahara for the migration of early modern humans out of Africa 120,000 years ago. *Proceedings of the National Academy of Sciences U.S.A.* 105: 16444–16447.

O'Shea, J. 1981. Coping with Scarcity: Exchange and Social Storage. In A. Sheridan and G. Bailey (eds.), *Economic Archaeology: Towards an Integration of Economic and Social Approaches*, pp. 167–183, BAR International Series 96. Oxford.

Oswalt, W. H. 1976. *An Anthropological Analysis of Food-Getting Technology*. John Wiley & Sons, New York.

Owen, W.E. 1938. The Kombewa Culture, Kenya Colony. *Man* 38: 203–205.

Palmer, R. 1991. Optimization on Rugged Fitness Landscapes. In E. Perelson and S. Kaufman (eds.), *Molecular Evolution in Rugged Fitness Landscapes*, pp. 3–25. Addison, Redwood City.

Parry, W. J., and Kelly, R. L. 1987. Expedient Core Technology and Sedentism. In J. K. Johnson and K. A. Morrow (eds.), *The Organization of Core Technology*, pp. 285–309. Westview Press, Boulder and London.

Patterson, T. C. 1990. Some Theoretical Tensions within and between the Processual and Post-processual Archaeologies. *Journal of Anthropological Research* 9: 189–200.

Pearson, O. M. 2004. Has the Combination of Genetic and Fossil Evidence Solved the Riddle of Modern Human Origins? *Evolutionary Anthropology* 13: 145–159.

Pelcin, A. W. 1997a. The Effect of Indentor Type on Flake Attributes: Evidence from a Controlled Experiment. *Journal of Archaeological Science* 24: 613–621.

———. 1997b. The Formation of Flakes: The Role of Platform Thickness and Exterior Platform Angle in the Production of Flake Initiation and Terminations. *Journal of Archaeological Science* 24: 1107–1113.

———. 1997c. The Effect of Core Surface Morphology on Flake Attributes: Evidence from a Controlled Experiment. *Journal of Archaeological Science* 24: 749–756.

———. 1998. The Threshold Effect of Platform Width: A Reply to Davis and Shea. *Journal of Archaeological Science* 25: 615–620.

Pelegrin, J. 1990. Prehistoric Lithic Technology: Some Aspects of Research. *Archaeological Review from Cambridge* 9: 116–125.

———. 2005. Remarks about Archaeological Techniques and Methods of Knapping: Elements of a Cognitive Approach to Stone Knapping. In V. Roux and B. Bril (eds.), *Stone Knapping: The Necessary Conditions for a Uniquely Hominin Behavior*, pp. 23–33. McDonald Institute for Archaeological Research, Cambridge.

Peresani, M. (ed.) 2003. *Discoid Lithic Technology: Advances and Implications.* Archaeopress, Oxford.

Perez-Perez, A., Espurz, V., Bermudez de Castro, J. M., de Lumley, M.-A., and Turbon, D. 2003. Non-occlusal Dental Microwear Variability in a Sample of Middle and Late Pleistocene Human Populations from Europe and the Near East. *Journal of Human Evolution* 44: 497.

Perlès, C. 1992. In Search of Lithic Strategies: A Cognitive Approach to Prehistoric Chipped Stone Assemblages. In J. C. Gardin and C. S. Peebles (eds.), *Representations in Archaeology,* pp. 223–247. Indiana University Press, Bloomington.

———. 2005. From the Near East to Greece: Let's Reverse the Focus. Cultural Elements that Didn't Transfer. In C. Lichter (ed.), *How Did Farming Reach Europe? Anatolian-European Relations from the Second Half of the 7th through the First Half of the 6th Millennium cal BC.,* pp. 275–290. BYZAS 2, *Veroffentlichung des Deutschen Archaiologischen Instituts Istanbul. Istanbul. Deutsches Archaologisches Institut, Istanbul.*

Perlman, S. M. 1985. Group Size and Mobility Costs. In S. W. Green and S. M. Perlman (eds.), *Archaeology of the Frontier and Boundaries,* pp. 33–50. Academic Press, Orlando.

Perpère, M. 1986. Apport de la typométrie à la définition des éclats Levallois. *Bulletin de la Société Préhistorique Française* 83: 115–118.

———. 1989. Le Frontières du débitage Levallois: Typométrie des éclats. *L'Anthropologie* 95: 837–850.

Perrot, J. 1968. La préhistoire palestinienne. *Supplément au Dictionnarie de la Bible* 8: 186–446. Paris.

Peterson, N. 1975. Hunter-Gatherer Territoriality: The Perspective from Australia. *American Anthropologist* 77: 53–68.

Petrequin, P., and Petrequin, A. M. 2000. *Ecologie d'un outil: La Hache de Pierre en Irian Jaya (Indonesie).* CNRS editions, Paris.

Pettitt, P. B. 1999. Disappearing from the World: An Archaeological Perspective on Neanderthal Extinction. *Oxford Journal of Archaeology* 18: 217–240.

Pfaffenberger, B. 1992. Social Anthropology of Technology. *Annual Review of Anthropology* 21: 491–516.

Pigeot, N. 1990. Technical and Social Actors: Flint Knapping Specialist at Magdalenian Etiolles. *Archaeological Review from Cambridge* 9: 126–141.

Pleurdeau, D. 2003. Porc-Epic Cave (Dire Dawa, Ethiopia) Middle Stone Age: Raw Materials Economy and Technical Behaviour. *L'Anthropologie* 107: 15–48.

Plisson, H., and Beyries, S. 1998. Pointes ou outils triangulaires? Donées fonctionnelles dans le Moustérian levantin. *Paléorient* 24: 5–16, 23–24.

Plummer, T. W. 2004. Flaked Stones and Old Bones: Biological and Cultural Evolution at the Dawn of Technology. *Yearbook of Physical Anthropology* 47: 118–164.

Potts, R. 1988. *Early Hominid Activities at Olduvai.* Aldine de Gruyter, New York.

Prell, W. L., and van Campo, E. 1986. Coherent Response of Arabian Sea Upwelling and Pollen Transport to Late Quaternary Monsoonal Winds. *Nature* 323: 526–528.

Pulliam, H. R., and Dunford, C. 1980. *Programmed to Learn: An Essay on the Evolution of Culture.* Columbia University Press, New York.

Rabikovitch, S. 1981. *The Soils of Israel.* Hakibbutz Ha'meukhad, Tel-Aviv (in Hebrew).

Rabineau, M., Berne, S., Olivet, J. L., Aslanian, D., Guillocheau, F., and Joseph, P. 2006. Paleo Sea Levels Reconsidered from Direct Observation of Paleoshoreline Position during Glacial Maxima (for the last 500,000). *Earth and Planetary Science Letters* 252: 119–137.

Rabinovich, R. 1990. Taphonomic Research of the Faunal Assemblages from the Quneitra Site. In N. Goren-Inbar (ed.), *Quneitra: A Mousterian Site on the Golan Heights,* pp. 189–219. Qedem 31. Institute of Archaeology, Jerusalem.

Rabinovich, R., and Horwitz, L. K. 1994. An Experimental Approach to the Study of Porcupine Damage to Bones: A Gnawing Issue. In M. Patou-Matis (ed.), *Outillage peu elaboré en os et en bois de Cervides IV: Taphonomie,* pp. 97–118. Éditions du CEDARC, Treignes, Belgium.

Rabinovich, R., and Hovers, E. 2004. Faunal Assemblages from Amud Cave: Preliminary Results and Interpretations. *International Journal of Osteoarchaeology* 14:287–306.

Rabinovich, R., and Tchernov, E. 1995. Chronological, Paleoecological and Taphonomical Aspects of the Middle Paleolithic Site of Qafzeh, Israel. In H. Buitenhuis and H.-P. Uerpmann (eds.), *Archaeozoology of the Near East: Proceedings of the Second Symposium of the Archaeozoology of Southwestern Asia and Adjacent Areas,* pp. 5–44. Backhuys Publishers, Leiden.

Rabinovich, R., Bar-Yosef, O., Vandermeersch, B., and Horwitz, L. K. 2004. Hominid–Carnivore Interactions in the Paleolithic Site of Qafzeh Cave, Israel. *Revue de Paléobiology (Muséum d'histoire naturelle de Genève)* 23: 627–637.

Rafferty, J. 1985. The Archaeological Record on Sedentariness: Recognition, Development, and Implications. In M. B. Schiffer (ed.), *Advances in Archeological Method and Theory* 8, pp. 113–156. Academic Press, New York.

Rak, Y. 1986. The Neanderthal: A New Look at an Old Face. *Journal of Human Evolution* 15: 151–164.

———. 1990. On the Differences between Two Pelvises of Mousterian Context from Qafzeh and Kebara Caves, Israel. *American Journal of Physical Anthropology* 81: 323–332.

———. 1993. Morphological Variation in Homo Neanderthalensis and Homo Sapiens in the Levant: A Biogeographical Model. In W. H. Kimbel and L .B. Martin (eds.), *Species, Species Concept and Primate Evolution,* pp. 523–536. Plenum Press, New York.

———. 1998. Does Any Mousterian Cave Present Evidence of Two Hominid Species? In T. Akazawa, K. Aoki, and O. Bar-Yosef (eds.), *Neanderthals and Modern Humans in Western Asia,* pp. 353–366. Plenum Press, New York.

Rak, Y., Ginzburg, A., and Geffen, E. 2002. Does *Homo neanderthalensis* Play a Role in Modern Human Ancestry? The Mandibular Evidence. *American Journal of Physical Anthropology* 119: 199–204.

Rak, Y., Kimbel, W. H., and Hovers, E. 1994. A Neandertal Infant from Amud Cave, Israel. *Journal of Human Evolution* 26: 313–324.

Raveh, A. 1992. *COPLOT: A Graphic Display Method for Multivariate Data Analysis. Technical Report #90025*, Statistics Department, Hebrew University, Jerusalem.

Relethford, J. H. 2001. *Genetics and the Search for Modern Human Origins*. Wiley-Liss, New York.

Remenofsy, A. F., and Steffen, A. (eds.) 1998. Unit Issues in Archaeology: Measuring Time, Space and Material. University Press of Utah Press, Salt Lake City.

Reynolds, R. G. 1978. On Modeling the Evolution of Hunter-Gatherer Decision-Making Systems. *Geographical Analysis* 10: 31–46.

Reynolds, T. E. G. 1990. The Middle-Upper Paleolithic Transition in Southwestern France: Interpreting the Lithic Evidence. In P. Mellars (ed.), *The Emergence of Modern Humans: An Archaeological Perspective*, pp. 262–275. Cornell University Press, Ithaca, N.Y.

Richards, M. P., and Shmitz, R. W. 2008. Isotope evidence for the diet of the Neanderthal type specimen. *Antiquity* 82: 553–559.

Richards, M. P., Pettitt, P. B., Stiner, M. C., and Trinkaus, E. 2001. Stable Isotope Evidence for Increasing Dietary Breadth in the European Mid-Upper Paleolithic. *Proceedings of the National Academy of Science U.S.A.* 98: 6528–6532.

Richards, M. P., Pettitt, P. B., Trinkaus, E., Smith, F. H., Paunovic, M., and Karavanic, I. 2000. Neanderthal Diet at Vindija and Neanderthal Predation: The Evidence from Stable Isotopes. *Proceedings of the National Academy of Science U.S.A.* 97: 7663–7666.

Richards, M. P., Pettitt, P. B., Stiner, M. C., and Trinkaus, E. 2001. Stable Isotope Evidence for Increasing Dietary Breadth in the European Mid-Upper Paleolithic. *Proceedings of the National Academy of Science U.S.A.* 98: 6528–6532.

Richerson, P. J., and Boyd, R. 2005. *Not by Genes Alone: How Culture Transformed Human Evolution*. Chicago University Press, Chicago.

Richerson, P. J., Boyd, R., and Bettinger, R. L. 2001. Was Agriculture Impossible during the Pleistocene but Mandatory during the Holocene? A Climate Change Hypothesis. *American Antiquity* 66: 387–411.

Richter, D. 2007. Advantages and Limitation of Thermoluminescence Dating of Heated Flint from Paleolithic Sites. *Geoarchaeology* 22: 671–683.

Richter, D., Schroeder, B. H., Rink, W. J., Julig, P. J., and Schwarcz, H. P. 2001. The Middle to Upper Paleolithic Transition in the Levant and New Thermoluminescence Dates for a Late Mousterian Assemblage from Jerf el-Ajla Cave (Syria). *Paléorient* 27: 29–46.

Richter, J. 2000. Social Memory among Late Neanderthals. In J. Orschiedt (ed.), *Neanderthals and Modern Humans—Discussing the Transition: Central and Eastern Europe*, pp. 123–132. Neanderthal Museum, Mettmann.

Rink, W. J., Richter, D., Schwarcz, H. P., Marks, A. E., Monigal, K., and Kaufman, D. 2003. Age of the Middle Palaeolithic Site of Rosh Ein Mor, Central Negev, Israel: Implications for the Age Range of the Early Levantine Mousterian of the Levantine Corridor. *Journal of Archaeological Science* 30: 195–204.

Rink, W. J., Schwarcz, H. P., Lee, H. K., Rees-Jones, J., Rabinovich, R., and Hovers, E. 2001. Electron Spin Resonance (ESR) and Thermal Ionization Mass Spectrometric (TIMS) 230Th/234U Dating of Teeth in Middle Palaeolithic Layers at Amud Cave, Israel. *Geoarchaeology* 16: 701–717.

Rink, W. J., Schwarcz, H. P., Weiner, S., Goldberg, P., Meignen, L., and Bar-Yosef, O. 2004. Age of the Mousterian Industry at Hayonim Cave, Northern Israel, Using Electron Spin Resonance and 230Th/234U Methods. *Journal of Archaeological Science* 31: 953–964.

Robson-Brown, K. 1993. An Alternative Approach to Cognition in the Lower Palaeolithic: The Modular View. *Cambridge Archaeological Journal* 3: 231–245.

Roebroeks, W., Kolen, J., and Rensink, E. 1988. Planning Depth, Anticipation and the Organization of Middle Paleolithic Technology: The "Archaic Natives" Meet Eve's Descendants. *Hellinium* 28: 17–34.

Rogers, A. R. 1988. Does Biology Constrain Culture? *American Anthropologist* 90: 819–831.

Roler, K. L., and Clark, G. A. 1997. Use-Wear Analysis of Levallois Points from the 'Ain Difla Rockshelter, West-Central Jordan. In H. G. K. Goebel, Z. Kafafi, and G. O. Rollefson (eds.), *The Prehistory of Jordan, II: Perspectives from 1997*, pp. 101–109. Ex Oriente, Berlin.

Rolland, N. 1981. The Interpretation of Middle Palaeolithic Variability. *Man* 16: 15–42.

———. 1988. Variabilité et classification: Nouvelles données sur le "complexe moustérien." In M. Otte (ed.), *L'Homme de Néandertal*, Vol. 4: *La Technique*, pp. 169–183. ERAUL, Liège.

———. 1991. Review of Quneitra: A Mousterian Open-Air Site on the Golan Heights. *Journal of the Israel Prehistoric Society—Mitekufat Ha'even* 24: 180–190.

———. 1995. Levallois Technique Emergence: Single or Multiple? A Review of the Euro-African Record. In H. L. Dibble and O. Bar-Yosef (eds.), *The Definition and Interpretation of Levallois Technology*, pp. 333–359. Monographs in World Archaeology N. 23. Prehistory Press, Madison, Wis.

Rolland, N., and Dibble, H. L. 1990. A New Synthesis of Middle Paleolithic Variability. *American Antiquity* 55: 480–499.

Ronen, A. 1974. *Tirat Carmel: A Mousterian Open-Air Site in Israel*. Institute of Archaeology, Tel-Aviv University, Tel-Aviv.

———. 1977. Mousterian Sites in Red Loan in the Coastal Plain of Mount Carmel. In B. Arensburg and

O. Bar-Yosef (eds.), *Eretz-Israel 13*, pp. 183*–190*. Israel Exploration Society, Jerusalem.

———. 1979. Paleolithic Industries. In A. Horowitz (ed.), *The Quaternary of Israel*, pp. 296–307. Academic Press, New York.

———. 1984. *Sefunim Prehistoric Sites, Mount Carmel, Israel*, BAR International Series 230. Oxford.

———. 1992. The Emergence of Blade Technology: Cultural Affinities. In T. Akazawa, K. Aoki, and T. Kimura (eds.), *The Evolution and Dispersal of Modern Humans in Asia*, pp. 217–228. Hakusen-Sha, Tokyo.

Ronen, A., and Vandermeersch, B. 1972. The Upper Paleolithic Sequence in the Cave of Qafzeh (Israel). *Quaternaria* 16: 189–202.

Rose, L., and Marshall, F. 1996. Meat Eating, Hominid Sociality, and Home Bases Revisited. *Current Anthropology* 37: 307–338.

Rots, V. 2002. Hafting Traces on Flint Tools: Possibilities and Limitations of Macro- and Microscopic Approaches. Ph.D. thesis. Katholieke Universiteit Leuven, Leuven.

Rots, V., and Van Peer, P. 2006. Early Evidence of Complexity in Lithic Economy: Core-Axe Production, Hafting and Use at Late Middle Pleistocene Site 8-B-11, Sai Island (Sudan). *Journal of Archaeological Science* 33: 360–371.

Roux, V. 2003. A Dynamic Systems Framework for Studying Technological Change: Application to the Emergence of the Potter's Wheel in the Southern Levant. *Journal of Archaeological Method and Theory* 10: 1–30.

Roux, V., and David, E. 2005. Planning Abilities as a Dynamic Perceptual-Motor Skill: An Actualistic Study of Different Levels of Expertise Involved in Stone Knapping. In V. Roux and B. Bril (eds.), *Stone Knapping: The Necessary Conditions for a Uniquely Hominin Behavior*, pp. 91–108. McDonald Institute for Archaeological Research, Cambridge.

Ruff, C., Trinkaus, E., Walker, A., and Larsen, C. 1993. Postcranial Robusticity in Homo, I: Temporal Trends and Mechanical Interpretation. *American Journal of Physical Anthropology* 91: 21–53.

Rust, A. 1950. *Die Höhlenfunde von Jabrud (Syrien)*. Neomünster.

Sack, R. D. 1986. *Human Territoriality: Its Theory and History*. Cambridge Studies in Historical Geography, vol. 7. Cambridge University Press, Cambridge.

Sackett, J. R. 1982. Approaches to Style in Lithic Archaeology. *Journal of Anthropological Archaeology* 1: 59–112.

———. 1983. Style and Ethnicity in Archaeology: The Case for Isochrestism. In M. Conkey and C. Hastrof (eds.), *The Uses of Style in Archaeology*, pp. 32–43. Cambridge University Press, Cambridge.

———. 1986. Isochrestism and Style: A Clarification. *Journal of Anthropological Archaeology* 5: 266–277.

———. 2000. Human Antiquity and the Old Stone Age: The Nineteenth Century Background to Paleoanthropology. *Evolutionary Anthropology* 9: 37–49.

Saint-Mathurin, S. 1983. Preface. In D. A. Roe (ed.), *Adlun in the Stone Age: The Excavations of D.A.E. Garrod in the Lebanon, 1958–1963*, pp. xi–xv. Bar International Series, Oxford.

Sandgathe, D. M. 2005. *Examining the Levallois Reduction Strategy from a Design Theory Point of View*, BAR International Series 1417. Archaeopress, Oxford.

Sanfey, A. G., Rilling, J. R., Aronson, J. A., Nystrom, L. E., and Cohen, J. D. 2003. The Neural Basis of Economic Decision-Making in the Ultimatum Game. *Science* 300: 1755–1758.

Sanlaville, P. 1981. Stratigraphie et chronologie du Quaternaire marin du Levant. In J. Cauvin and P. Sanlaville (eds.), *Préhistoire du Levant*, pp. 21–31. CNRS, Paris.

Schall, J. D. 2005. Decision Making. *Current Biology* 15: R9–R11.

Schepartz, L. A. 1993. Language and Modern Human Origins. *Yearbook of Physical Anthropology* 36: 91–124.

Schick, T., and Stekelis, M. 1977. Mousterian Assemblages in Kebara Cave, Mount Carmel. In B. Arensburg and O. Bar-Yosef (eds.), *Eretz-Israel 13*. Israel Exploration Society, Jerusalem, pp. 97–149.

Schiegl, S., Goldberg, P., Bar-Yosef, O., and Weiner, S. 1996. Ash Deposits in Hayonim and Kebara Caves, Israel: Macroscopic, Microscopic, and Mineralogical Observations and their Archaeological Implications. *Journal of Archaeological Science* 23: 763–781.

Schiegl, S., Lev-Yadun, S., Bar-Yosef, O., El Goresy, A., and Weiner, S. 1994. Silliceous Aggregates from Prehistoric Wood Ash: A Major Component of Sediments in Kebara and Hayonim Caves (Israel). *Israel Journal of Earth sciences* 43: 267–278.

Schiffer, M. B. 1987. *Formation Processes of the Archaeological Record*. University of New Mexico Press, Albuquerque.

Schiffer, M. B., and Miller, A. R. 1999. *The Material Life of Human Beings: Artifacts, Behavior, and Communication*. Routledge, London and New York.

Schiffer, M. B., and Skibo, J. M. 1987. Theory and Experiment in the Study of Technological Change. *Current Anthropology* 28: 595–622.

Schmitz, R. W., Serre, D., Bonani, G., Feine, S., Hilligruber, F., Krainitzki, H., Paäbo, S., and Smith, F. H. 2002. The Neandertal Type Site Revisited: Interdisciplinary Investigations of Skeletal Remains from the Neander Valley, Germany. *Proceedings of the National Academy of Science U.S.A.* 99: 13342–13347.

Schroëder, B. 1969. The Lithic Industries from Jerf Ajla and Their Bearing on the Problem of a Middle to Upper Paleolithic Transition. Ph.D. thesis, Columbia University.

Schuldenrein, J., and Clark, G. A. 2001. Prehistoric Landscapes and Settlement Geography along the Wadi Hasa, West-Central Jordan. Part I: Geoarchaeology, Human Palaeoecology and Ethnographic Modeling. *Environmental Archaeology* 6: 23–38.

Schwarcz, H. P., and Rink, W. J. 1998. Progress in ESR and U-series Chronology of the Levantine Paleolithic.

In T. Akazawa, K. Aoki, and O. Bar-Yosef (eds.), *Neandertals and Modern Humans in the Levant*, pp. 57–67. Plenum Press, New York.

Schwarcz, H. P., Goldberg, P., and Blackball, B. 1980. Uranium Series Dating of Archaeological Sites in Israel. *Israel Journal of Earth Sciences* 29: 157–165.

Schwarcz, H. P., Simpson, J., and Stringer, C. B. 1998. Neanderthal Skeleton from Tabun: U-Series Data by Gamma-Ray Spectrometry. *Journal of Human Evolution* 35: 635–645.

Schwarcz, H. P., Blackwell, B., Goldberg, P., and Marks, A. E. 1979. Uranium Series Dating of Travertine from Archaeological Sites. *Nature* 277: 558–560.

Schwarcz, H. P., Buhay, W. M., Grün, R., Valladas, H., Tchernov, E., Bar-Yosef, O., and Vandermeersch, B. 1989. ESR Dates of the Neanderthal Site, Kebara Cave, Israel. *Journal of Archaeological Science* 16: 653–659.

Schwarcz, H. P., Grün, R., Vandermeersch, B., Bar-Yosef, O., Valladas, H., and Tchernov, E. 1988. ESR Dates for the Hominid Burial Site of Qafzeh in Israel. *Journal of Human Evolution* 17: 733–737.

Semaw, S., Rogers, M. J., Quade, J., Renne, P. R., Butler, R. F., Dominguez-Rodrigo, M., Stout, D., Hart, W. S., Pickering, T., and Simpson, S. W. 2003. 2.6-Million-Year-Old Stone Tools and Associated Bones from OGS-6 and OGS-7, Gona, Afar, Ethiopia. *Journal of Human Evolution* 45: 169–177.

Serre, D., Langeney, A., Cheche, M., Teschler-Nicola, M., Paunovicz, M., Mennecier, P., Hofreiter, M., Possnert, G., and Pääbo, S. 2004. No Evidence of Neandertal mtDNA Contribution to Early Modern Humans. *Public Library of Science, Biology* 2: 313–317.

Shahack-Gross, R., Ayalon, A., Goldberg, P., Goren, Y., Ofek, B., Rabinovich, R., and Hovers, E. 2008. Formation Processes of Cemented Features in Karstic Cave Sites Revealed Using Stable Oxygen and Carbon Isotopic Analysis: A Case Study at Middle Paleolithic Amud Cave, Israel. *Geoarchaeology*.

Sharon, G., and Goren-Inbar, N. 1998. Soft Precursor Use at the Gesher Benot Ya'aqov Site? *Journal of the Israel Prehistoric Society* 28: 55–79.

Sharon, I. 1990. A Note on the Tests of Significance of the Differences between the Size Distribution of Basalt and Flint Flakes. *Cahiers du Quaternaire* 17: 585–592.

Shea, J. J. 1988. Spear Points from the Middle Paleolithic of the Levant. *Journal of Field Archaeology* 15: 441–450.

———. 1989. Tool Use in the Levantine Mousterian of Kebara Cave, Mount Carmel. *Mitekufat Ha'even, Journal of the Israel Prehistoric Society* 22: 15–30.

———. 1991. The Behavioral Significance of Levantine Mousterian Variability. Ph.D. thesis, Harvard University.

———. 1993. Lithic Use-Wear Evidence for Hunting by Neanderthals and Early Modern Humans from the Levantine Mousterian. In G. L. Peterkin, H. M. Bricker, and P. Mellars (eds.), *Hunting and Animal Exploitation in the Later Palaeolithic and Mesolithic of Eurasia*, pp. 189–197. Archaeological Papers of the American Anthropological Association 4.

———. 1995. Lithic Microwear Analysis of Tor Faraj Rockshelter. In D. O. Henry (ed.), *Prehistoric Cultural Ecology and Diversity: Insights from Southern Jordan*, pp. 85–105. Plenum Press, New York and London.

———. 1997. Middle Paleolithic Spear Point Technology. In H. Knecht (ed.), *Projectile Technology*, pp. 79–106. Plenum Press, New York.

———. 1998. Neandertal and Early Modern Human Behavioral Variability: A Regional Scale Approach to Lithic Evidence for Hunting in the Levantine Mousterian. *Current Anthropology* 39 (supplement): S45–S78.

———. 2003. Neandertals, Competition, and the Origin of Modern Human Behavior in the Levant. *Evolutionary Anthropology* 12: 173–187.

———. 2004. The Middle Paleolithic of the East Mediterranean Levant. *Journal of World Prehistory* 17: 313–394.

———. 2006a. The Middle Paleolithic of the Levant: Recursion or Convergence? In E. Hovers and S. L. Kuhn (eds.), *Transitions before The Transition: Evolution and Stability in the Middle Paleolithic and Middle Stone Age*, pp. 171–195. Springer, New York.

———. 2006b. The Origins of Lithic Projectile Point Technology: Evidence from Africa, the Levant, and Europe. *Journal of Archaeological Science* 33: 823–846.

———. 2007a. The Boulevard of Broken Dreams: Evolutionary Discontinuity in the Late Pleistocene Levant. In P. Mellars, K. V. Boyle, O. Bar-Yosef, and C. Stringer (eds.), *Re-thinking the Human Revolution*, pp. 219–232. McDonald Institute for Archaeological Research, Cambridge.

———. 2007b. Behavioral Differences between Middle and Upper Paleolithic Homo Sapiens in the East Mediterranean: The Roles of Intraspecific Competition and Dispersal from Africa. *Journal of Anthropological Research* 63: 449–488.

Shea, J. J., Davis, Z., and Brown, K. 2001. Experimental Tests of Middle Palaeolithic Spear Points Using a Calibrated Crossbow. *Journal of Archaeological Science* 28: 807–816.

Sheets, P. D., and Muto, G. R. 1972. Pressure Blades and Total Cutting Edge: An Experiment in Lithic Technology. *Science* 175: 632–635.

Shennan, S. J. 1991. Tradition, Rationality, and Cultural Transmission. In R. W. Preucel (ed.), *Processual and Postprocessual Archaeologies: Multiple Ways of Knowing the Past*, pp. 197–208. Center for Archaeological Investigations, Southern Illinois University at Carbondale, Carbondale.

———. 2002. *Genes, Memes and Human History: Darwinian Archaeology and Cultural Evolution*. Thames & Hudson, London.

Shott, M. J. 1986. Technological Organization and Settlement Mobility: And Ethnographic Examination. *Journal of Anthropological Research* 42: 15–51.

———. 1989a. On Tool-Class Use Lives and the Formation of Archaeological Assemblages. *American Antiquity* 54: 9–30.

———. 1989b. Diversity, Organization, and Behavior in the Material Record. *Current Anthropology* 30: 283–315.

———. 1994. Size and Form in the Analysis of Flake Debris: Review and Recent Approaches. *Journal of Archaeological Method and Theory* 1:69–110.

———. 1996. The Exegesis of the Curation Concept. *Journal of Anthropological Research* 52: 259–280.

———. 2003. *Chaîne Opératoire* and Reduction Sequence. *Lithic Technology* 28: 95–105.

Shott, M. J., Bradbury, A. P., Carr, J. P., and Odell, G. H. 2000. Flake Size from Platform Attributes: Predictive and Empirical Approaches. *Journal of Archaeological Science* 27: 877–894.

Siegel, S. 1956. *Nonparametric Statistics for the Behavioral Sciences.* McGraw-Hill series in psychology. McGraw-Hill Kogakusha, Ltd., Tokyo.

Silberbauer, G. B. 1981. *Hunter-Gatherers of the Central Kalahari Desert.* Cambridge University Press, Cambridge.

Sillen, A., and Morris, A. 1996. Diagenesis of Bone from Border Cave: Implications for the Age of the Border Cave Hominids. *Journal of Human Evolution* 31: 499–406.

Simmons, T. 1994. Archaic and Modern *Homo sapiens* in the Contact Zones: Evolutionary Schematics and Model Predictions. In M. H. Nitecki and D. V. Nitecki (eds.), *The Origins of Anatomically Modern Humans,* pp. 201–225. Plenum Press, New York.

———. 2004. "A feather for each wind that blows": Utilizing Avifauna in Assessing Changing Patterns in Paleoecology and Subsistence at Jordan Valley Archaeological Sites. In N. Goren-Inbar and J. D. Speth (eds.), *Human Paleoecology in the Levantine Corridor,* pp. 191–205. Oxbow Books, Oxbow.

Sivan, D., and Porat, N. 2004. Evidence from Luminescence for Late Pleistocene Formation of Calcareous Aeolianite (Kurkar) and Paleosol (Hamra) in the Carmel Coast, Israel. *Paleogeography, Paleoclimatology, Paleoecology* 211: 95–106.

Skinner, J. 1965. The Flake Industries of Southwest Asia: A Typological Study. Ph.D. thesis, Columbia University.

Smith, E. A., and Winterhalder, B. 1992. *Evolutionary Ecology and Human Behavior.* Aldine de Gruyter, New York.

Snowdon, C. T. 1990. Language Capacities of Nonhuman Animals. *Yearbook of Physical Anthropology* 33: 215–243.

Snyder, L. 2005. Confirmation for a Modest Reality. *Philosophy of Science* 72: 839–849.

Soffer, O. 1989. The Middle to Upper Palaeolithic Transition on the Russian Plain. In P. Mellars and C. Stringer (eds.), *Behavioural and Biological Perspectives on the Origins of Modern Humans,* pp. 714–742. Edinburgh University Press, Edinburgh.

Solecki, R. 1970. Summary Report of the Columbia University Prehistoric Investigations in Lebanon, Season 1969. *Bulletin de Musée de Beyrouth* 23: 95–128.

———. 1992. More on Hafted Projectile Points in the Mousterian. *Journal of Field Archaeology* 19: 207–212.

Solecki, R. L., and Solecki, R. S. 1970. A New Secondary Flaking Technique at the Nahr Ibrahim Cave Site. *Bulletin du Musée de Beyrouth* 23: 137–142.

Sollberger, J. B. 1994. Hinge Fracture Mechanics. *Lithic Technology* 19: 17–20.

Soriano, S., Villa, P., and Wadley, L. 2007. Blade Technology and Tool Forms in the Middle Stone Age of South Africa: The Howiesons Poort and Post-Howiesons Poort at Rose Cottage Cave. *Journal of Archaeological Science* 34: 681–703.

Spencer, C. S. 1997. Evolutionary Approaches in Archaeology. *Journal of Archaeological Research* 5: 209–264.

Speth, J. D. 1972. Mechanical Basis of Percussion Flaking. *American Antiquity* 37: 34–60.

———. 1974. Experimental Investigations of Hard-Hammer Percussion Flaking. *Tebiwa* 17: 7–36.

———. 1975. Miscellaneous Studies in Hard-Hammer Percussion Flaking: The Effects of Oblique Impact. *American Antiquity* 40: 203–207.

———. 2004. Hunting Pressure, Subsistence Intensification, and Demographic Change in the Levantine Late Middle Paleolithic. In N. Goren-Inbar and J. D. Speth (eds.), *Human Paleoecology in the Levantine Corridor,* pp. 149–166. Oxbow Books, Oxford.

———. 2006. Housekeeping, Neanderthal-Style: Hearth Placement and Midden Formation in Kebara Cave (Israel). In E. Hovers and S. L. Kuhn (eds.), *Transitions before The Transition: Evolution and Stability in the Middle Paleolithic and the Middle Stone Age,* pp. 171–188. Springer, New York.

Speth, J. D., and Clark, J. 2006. Hunting and Overhunting in the Levantine Late Middle Palaeolithic. *Before Farming* 2006/3: Article 1.

Speth, J .D., and Scott, S. 1989. Horticulture and Large Mammal Hunting: The Role of Resource Depletion and the Constraints of Time and Labor. In S. Kent (ed.), *Farmers as Hunters: The Implications of Sedentism,* pp. 71–79. Cambridge University Press, Cambridge.

Speth, J. D., and Tchernov, E. 1998. The Role of Hunting and Scavenging in Neanderthal Procurement Strategies: New Evidence from Kebara Cave (Israel). In T. Akazawa, K. Aoki, and B.-Y. O. (eds.), *Neanderthals and Modern Humans in West Asia,* pp. 223–239. Plenum Press, New York.

———. 2001. Neandertal Hunting and Meat Processing in the Near East: Evidence from Kebara Cave (Israel). In C. B. Stanford and H. T. Bunn (eds.), *Meat-Eating and Human Evolution,* pp. 52–72. Oxford University Press, Oxford.

———. 2002. Middle Paleolithic Tortoise Use at Kebara Cave (Israel). *Journal of Archaeological Science* 29: 471–483.

———. 2003. Paleoclimatic and Behavioral Implications of Middle Paleolithic Tortoise Use at Kebara Cave. In M. Patou-Mathis and H. Bocherens (eds.), *Le Rôle de l'environnement dans les comportements des chasseurs-cueileurs préhistoriques,* pp. 9–21. Acts of the XIVth UISPP Congress, Section 3: Paleoecology. Archaeopress, Oxford.

———. 2007.The Middle Paleolithic Occupations at Kebara Cave: A Faunal Perspective. In O. Bar-Yosef and L.Meignen (eds.), *Kebara Cave, Mt. Carmel, Israel. The Middle and Upper Paleolithic Archaeology Part I,* pp.165–260. American School of Prehistoric Research Bulletin 49. Peabody Museum of Archaeology and Ethnology, Harvard University, Cambridge, Mass.

Sponheimer, M., Passey, B. H., de Ruiter, D. J., Guatelli-Steinberg, D., Cerling, T. E., and Lee-Thorp, J. A. 2006. Isotopic Evidence for Dietary Variability in the Early Hominin *Paranthropus robustus. Science* 314: 980–982.

Stanford, C. B. 1999. *The Hunting Apes: Meat Eating and the Origins of Human Behavior.* Princeton University Press, Princeton, N.J.

Stapert, D. 1990. Middle Palaeolithic Dwellings: Fact or Fiction? Some Application of the Ring and Sector Method. *Paleohistoria* 32: 1–19.

Steegmann, A. T., Cerny, F. J., and Holliday, T. W. 2002. Neandertal Cold Adaptation: Physiological and Energetic Factors. *American Journal of Human Biology* 14: 566–583.

Stekelis, M. 1956. Nouvelles fouilles dans la Grotte de Kebara. *Cronica del IV Congres Internacional de Ciencias Prehistoricas y Protohistoricas,* pp. 385–389. Zaragoza, Madrid 1954.

Stiner, M. C. 1990. The Use of Mortality Patterns in Archaeological Studies of Hominid Predatory Adaptation. *Journal of Anthropological Archaeology* 9: 305–351.

———. 1994. *Honor among Thieves: A Zooarchaeological Study of Neanderthal Economy.* Princeton University Press, Princeton, N.J.

———. 2002. Carnivory, Coevolution, and the Geographic Spread of the Genus Homo. *Journal of Archaeological Research* 10: 1–63.

———. 2005. *The Faunas of Hayonim Cave, Israel: A 200,000 Record of Paleolithic Diet, Demography and Society.* American School of Prehistoric Research Bulletin 48. Peabody Museum of Archaeology and Ethnology, Harvard University, Cambridge, Mass.

———. 2006. Middle Paleolithic Subsistence Ecology in the Mediterranean Region. In E. Hovers and S. L. Kuhn (eds.), *Transitions before The Transition: Evolution and Stability in the Middle Paleolithic and Middle Stone Age,* pp. 213–231. Springer, New York.

Stiner, M. C., and Kuhn, S. L. 1992. Subsistence, Technology and Adaptive Variation in Middle Paleolithic Italy. *American Anthropologist* 94: 306–339.

Stiner, M. C., and Tchernov, E. 1998. Pleistocene Species Trends at Hayonim Cave. In T. Akazawa, K. Aoki, and O. Bar-Yosef (eds.), *Neandertals and Modern Humans in Western Asia,* pp. 241–262. Plenum Press, New York.

Stiner, M. C., Munro, N. D., and Surovell, T. A. 2000. The Tortoise and the Hare: Small-Game Use, the Broad-Spectrum Revolution, and Paleolithic Demography. *Current Anthropology* 41: 39–73.

Stiner, M. C., Howell, F. C., Martinez-Navarro, B., Tchernov, E., and Bar-Yosef, O. 2001a. Outside Africa: Middle Pleistocene *Lycaon* from Hayonim Cave, Israel. *Bollettino della Societa Paleontological Italiana* 40: 293–302.

Stiner, M. C., Kuhn, S. L., Surovell, T. A., Goldberg, P., Meignen, L., Weiner, S., and Bar-Yosef, O. 2001b. Bone Preservation in Hayonim Cave (Israel): A Macroscopic and Mineralogical Study. *Journal of Archaeological Science* 28: 643–659.

Stoneking, M. 1993. DNA and Recent Human Evolution. *Evolutionary Anthropology* 2: 60–73.

Stout, D. 2002. Skill and Cognition in Stone Tool Production: An Ethnographic Case Study from Irian Jaya. *Current Anthropology* 43: 693–722.

Stout, D., and Chaminade, T. 2007. The Evolutionary Neuroscience of Tool Making. *Neuropsychologia* 45: 1091–1100.

Stout, D., Quade, J., Semaw, S., Rogers, M. J., and Levin, N. E. 2005. Raw Material Selectivity of the Earliest Stone Toolmakers at Gona, Afar, Ethiopia. *Journal of Human Evolution* 48: 365–380.

Street, F. A., and Grove, A. T. 1979. Global Maps of Lake-Level Fluctuations since 30,000 BP. *Quaternary Research* 12: 83–118.

Stringer, C. B. 1988. Palaeoanthropology: The Dates of Eden. *Nature* 331: 565–566.

———. 1989. Documenting the Origins of Modern Human. In E. Trinkaus (ed.), *The Emergence of Modern Humans: Biocultural Adaptations in the Later Pleistocene,* pp. 67–96. Cambridge University Press, Cambridge.

———. 2007. The Origin and Dispersal of *Homo sapiens:* Our Current State of Knowledge. In P. Mellars, K. V. Boyle, O. Bar-Yosef, and C. Stringer (eds.), *Rethinking the Human Revolution,* pp. 15–20. McDonald Institute for Archaeological Research, Cambridge.

Stringer, C. B., and Andrews, P. 1988. Genetic and Fossil Evidence for the Origins of Modern Humans. *Science* 239: 1263–1268.

Stringer, C. B., and Gamble, C. 1993. *In Search of the Neanderthals: Solving the Puzzle of Human Origins.* Thames and Hudson, New York.

Stringer, C. B., Grün, R., Schwarcz, H. P., and Goldberg, P. 1989. ESR Dates for the Hominid Burial Site of Es Skhul in Israel. *Nature* 338: 756–758.

Stutz, A. J. 2002. Polarizing Microscopy Identification of Chemical Diagenesis in Archaeological Cementum. *Journal of Archaeological Science* 29: 1327–1347.

Sundbo, J. 1998. *The Theory of Innovation: Enterpreneurs, Technology and Strategy.* E. Elgar, Cheltenham, UK.

Suzuki, H., and Takai, F. (eds.) 1970. *The Amud Man and his Cave Site.* University of Tokyo Press, Tokyo.

Taborin, Y. 2003. La Mer et les prémiers hommes modernes. In B. Vandermeersch (ed.), *Échanges et Diffusion dans la préhistoire Méditerranéenne,* pp. 113–122. Éditions du Comité des travaux historiques et scientifiques, Paris.

Tanaka, J. 1980. *The San Hunter-Gatherers of the Kalahari: A Study in Ecological Anthropology.* University of Tokyo Press, Tokyo.

Tattersall, I. 1995. *The Fossil Trail: How We Know What We Think We Know about Human Evolution.* Oxford University Press, New York.

Tchauner, H. 1996. Middle-Range Theory, Behavioral Archaeology, and Postempiricist Philosophy of Science in Archaeology. *Journal of Archaeological Method and Theory* 3: 1–30.

Tchernov, E. 1981. The Biostratigraphy of the Near East. In J. Cauvin and P. Sanlaville (eds.), *Préhistoire du Levant*, pp. 67–97. CNRS, Paris.

———. 1984. Commensal Animals and Human Sedentism in the Near East. In J. Clutton-Brock and C. Grigson (eds.), *Animals and Archaeology: 3. Early Herders and Their Flocks*, pp. 91–115, BAR International Series 202. Oxford.

———. 1989. The Middle Paleolithic Mammalian Sequence and its Bearing on the Origin of *Homo sapiens* in the Southern Levant. In O. Bar-Yosef and B. Vandermeersch (eds.), *Investigations in South Levantine Prehistory*, pp. 25–42, BAR International Series 497. Oxford.

———. 1991. On Mice and Men: Biological Markers for Long-Term Sedentism; A Reply. *Paléorient* 17: 153–160.

———. 1992. Biochronology, Paleoecology, and Dispersal Events of Hominids in the Southern Levant. In T. Akazawa, K. Aoki, and T. Kimura (eds.), *The Evolution and Dispersal of Modern Humans in Asia*, pp. 149–188. Hakusen-Sha, Tokyo.

———. 1998. The Faunal Sequence of the Southwest Asian Middle Paleolithic in Relation to Hominid Dispersion Events. In T. Akazawa, K. Aoki, and O. Bar-Yosef (eds.), *Neandertals and Modern Humans in Western Asia*, pp. 77–94. Pleunum Press, New York.

Templeton, A. R. 2002. Out of Africa Again and Again. *Nature* 416: 45–51.

Testart, A. 1982. The Significance of Storage among Hunter-Gatherers: Residence Patterns, Population Densities and Social Inequalities. *Current Anthropology* 23:523–537.

Texier, J.-P. 1996. Production en série: Le Debitage de lames de Pierre à 250,000 ans. *Pour la science* 223: 22.

Thieme, H. 1997. Lower Palaeolithic Hunting Spears from Germany. *Nature* 385: 807–810.

Tillier, A.-M. 1990. Une controverse dépassée: L'Existence de pratiques funéraires au Paléolithique moyen. *Les Nouvelles de l'Archéologie* 40: 22–24.

———. 1992. The Origins of Modern Humans in Southwest Asia: Ontogenetic Aspects. In T. Akazawa, K. Aoki, and T. Kimura (eds.), *The Evolution and Dispersal of Modern Humans in Asia*, pp. 15–28. Hakusen-Sha, Tokyo.

———. 1999. *Les Enfants moustériens de Qafzeh: Interprétation phylogénétique et paléoauxologique.* Editions CNRS, Paris.

———. 2005. The Tabun C1 Skeleton: A Levantine Neandertal? *Journal of the Israel Prehistoric Society* 35: 439–450.

Tillier, A.-M., Arensburg, B., Duday, H., and Vandermeerche, B. 2001. An Early Case of Hydrochepalus: The Middle Paleolithic Qafzeh 12 Child (Israel). *American Journal of Physical Anthropology* 114: 166–170.

Tindale, N. 1965. Stone Implement Making among the Nakako, Ngadadjara and Pitjandjara of the Great Australian Desert. *Records of the South Australian Museum* 15: 131–164.

Tixier, J., Inizan, M.-L., and Roche, H. 1980. *Préhistoire de la Pierre Taillée. I. Terminologie et Technologie.* C.R.E.P., Antibes.

Tokeshi, M. 1999. *Species Coexistence: Ecological and Evolutionary Perspectives.* Blackwell Science, Oxford.

Tomasello, M. 1994. The Question of Chimpanzee Culture. In R. Wrangham , W. McGrew, F. de Waal and P. Heltne (eds.),. *Chimpanzee Cultures*, pp. 301–317. Harvard University Press, Cambridge.

Tomasello, M., and Call, J. 1994. Social Cognition of Monkeys and Apes. *Yearbook of Physical Anthropology* 37: 273–305.

Torrence, R. 1983. Time Budgeting and Hunter-Gatherer Technology. In G. Bailey (ed.), *Hunter-Gatherer Economy in Prehistory: A European Perspective*, pp. 11–22. Cambridge University Press, Cambridge.

———. 1989a. Retooling: Towards a Behavioral Theory of Stone Tools. In R. Torrence (ed.), *Time, Energy and Stone Tools*, pp. 57–66. New Directions in Archaeology. Cambridge University Press, Cambridge.

———. (ed.) 1989b. *Time, Energy and Stone Tools.* New Directions in Archaeology. Cambridge University Press, Cambridge.

———. 1994. Strategies for Moving on in Lithic Studies. In P. J. Carr (ed.), *The Organization of North American Prehistoric Chipped Stone Tool Technologies*, pp. 123–136. Archaeological Series 7. International Monographs in Prehistory, Ann Arbor, Mich.

Tostevin, G. B. 2000. Behavioral Change and Regional Variation across the Middle to Upper Paleolithic Transition in Central Europe, Eastern Europe, and the Levant. Ph.D. dissertation, Harvard University.

———. 2003. Attribute Analysis of the Lithic Technologies of Stranska Skala IIIc and IIId in Regional and Interregional Context. In J. Svoboda and O. Bar-Yosef (eds.), *Stranska Skala: Origins of the Upper Paleolithic in the Brno Basin, Moravia, Czech Republic*, pp. 77–118. Peabody Museum of Archaeology and Ethnography, Harvard University, Cambridge, Mass.

———. 2006. Levels of Theory and Social Practice in the Reduction Sequence and *Chaîne Opératoire* Methods of Lithic Analysis. Paper presented in the electronic symposium "*Core* Reduction, *Chaîne Opératoire and Other Methods: the Epistemologies of Different Approaches to Lithic Analysis.*" San Juan, Puerto Rico.

Toth, N., Schick, K. D., Savage-Rumbaugh, E. S., Sevick, R. A., and Rumbaugh, D. M. 1993. Pan the Tool-Maker: Investigations into the Stone Tool-Making and Tool-Using Capabilities of a Bonobo (*Pan paniscus*). *Journal of Archaeological Science* 20: 81–91.

Trigger, B. 1989. *A History of Archaeological Thought.* Cambridge University Press, Cambridge.

Trinkaus, E. 1992. Morphological Contrasts between the Near Eastern Qafzeh-Skhul and Late Archaic Human Samples: Grounds for a Behavioral Difference? In T. Akazawa, K. Aoki, and T. Kimura (eds.), *The Evolution and Dispersal of Modern Humans in Asia,* pp. 277–294. Hakusen-sha, Tokyo.

———. 1995. Near Eastern Late Archaic Humans. *Paléorient* 21(2): 9–24.

———. 2006. Modern Human versus Neandertal Evolutionary Distinctiveness. *Current Anthropology* 47: 597–620.

Trinkaus, E., and Ruff, C. B. 1999. Diaphyseal Cross-Sectional Geometry of Near Eastern Middle Paleolithic Humans: The Tibia. *Journal of Archaeological Science* 26: 1289–1300.

Trinkaus, E., Zilhao, J., and Duarte, C. 1999. The Lapedo Child: Lagar Velho 1 and our Perceptions of the Neandertals. Mediterranean Prehistory Online.

Tristram, H. B. 1865. *The Land of Israel: A Journal of Travels in Palestine Undertaken with Special Reference to its Physical Character.* Society for Promoting Christian Knowledge, London.

Tryon, C. A., McBrearty, S., and Texier, J.-P. 2005. Levallois Lithic Technology from the Kapthurin Formation, Kenya: Acheulian Origins and Middle Stone Age Diversity. *African Archaeological Review* 22: 199–229.

Turq, A. 1989. Approche technologique et économique du faciès Moustérien de type Quina: Etude préliminaire. *Bulletin de la Société Préhistorique Française* 86: 244–255.

Turville-Petre, F. 1927. *Researches in Prehistoric Galilee 1925–1926.* British School of Archaeology in Jerusalem, London.

———. 1932. Excavations in the Mugharat el-Kebara. *Journal of the Royal Anthropological Institute* 62: 271–276.

Ugan, A., Bright, J., and Rogers, A. 2003. When is Technology Worth the Trouble? *Journal of Archaeological Science* 30: 1315–1329.

Urban, B. 2004. Vegetation Response to Climatic Variability during MIS 3 in Europe and its Importance for Expansion of Modern Human Populations and Disappearance of the Last Neanderthals. Paper presented in the conference "Neandertals and Modern Humans Meet?" Blaubeuren, Germany, 7–10 July.

Vaks, A., Bar-Matthews, M., Ayalon, A., Matthews, A., Frumkin, A., Dayan, U., Halicz, L., Almogi-Labin, A., and Schilman, B. 2006. Paleoclimate and Location of the Border between Mediterranean Climate Region and the Saharo-Arabian Desert as Revealed by Speleothems from the Northern Negev Desert, Israel. *Earth and Planetary Science Letters* 249: 384–399.

Vaks, A., Bar-Matthews, M., Ayalon, A., Matthews, A., Halicz, L., and Frumkin, A. 2007. Desert Speleothems Reveal Climatic Window for African Exodus of Early Modern Humans. *Geology* 35:831–834.

Vaks, A., Bar-Matthews, M., Ayalon, A., Schilman, B., Gilmour, M., Hawkesworht, C. J., Frumkin, A., Kaufman, A., and Matthews, A. 2003. Paleoclimatic Reconstruction Based on the Timing of Speleothem Growth and Oxygen and Carbon Isotope Composition in a Cave Located in the Rain Shadow in Israel. *Quaternary Research* 59: 182–193.

Valladas, H., Joron, J.-L., Valladas, G., Arensburg, B., Bar-Yosef, O., Belfer-Cohen, A., Goldberg, P., Laville, H., Meignen, L., Rak, Y., Tchernov, E., Tillier, A.-M., and Vandermeersch, B. 1987. Thermoluminescence Dates for the Neanderthal Burial Site at Kebara in Israel. *Nature* 330: 159–160.

Valladas, H., Mercier, N., Hovers, E., Frojet, L., Joron, J.-L., Kimbel, W. H., and Rak, Y. 1999. TL Dates for the Neandertal Site of Amud Cave, Israel. *Journal of Archaeological Science* 26: 259–268.

Valladas, H., Mercier, N., Joron, J.-L., and Reyss, J.-L 1998. GIF Laboratory Dates for Middle Paleolithic Levant. In T. Akazawa, K. Aoki, and O. Bar-Yosef (eds.), *Neandertals and Modern Humans in Western Asia,* pp. 69–76. Plenum Press, New York.

Valladas, H., Reyss, J.-L, Joron, J.-L., Valladas, G., Bar-Yosef, O., and Vandermeersch, B. 1988. Thermoluminescence Dating of Mousterian 'Proto-Cro-Magnon' Remains from Israel and the Origin of Modern Man. *Nature* 331: 614–616.

van Andel, T. H., and Davies, W. (eds.) 2003. *Neanderthals and Modern Humans in the European Landscape during the Last Glaciation.* McDonald Institute Monographs. McDonald Institute for Archaeological Research, Cambridge.

van Andel, T. H., and Tzedakis, P. C. 1996. Palaeolithic Landscapes of Europe and Environs, 150,000–25,000 years ago: An Overview. *Quaternary Science Reviews* 15: 481–500.

Van Peer, P. 1991. Interassemblage Variability and Levallois Styles: The Case of the Northern African Middle Paleolithic. *Journal of Anthropological Archaeology* 10: 107–151.

———. 1992. *The Levallois Reduction Strategy.* Monographs in World Archaeology 13. Prehistory Press, Madison, Wis.

———. 1998. The Nile Corridor and the Out-of-Africa Model: An Examination of the Archaeological Record. *Current Anthropology* 39, supplement: S115–S140.

van Schaik, C. P., and Pradhan, G. R. 2003. A Model for Tool-Use Traditions in Primates: Implications for the Coevolution of Culture and Cognition. *Journal of Human Evolution* 44: 645–664.

Vandermeersch, B. 1966. Nouvelles découvertes de restes humains dans leas couches Levalloiso-Moustériennes du gisement de Qafzeh (Israël). *Comptes rendus de l'Academie des Sciences* 262D: 1434–1436.

———. 1970. Une sépulture moustérienne avec offrandes découverte dans la grotte de Qafzeh. *Compte rendus de l'Académie des Sciences* 268: 298–301.

———. 1981. *Les Hommes Fossiles de Qafzeh (Israël).* Cahiers de Paléontologie. Éditions du CNRS, Paris.

———. 1982. The First *Homo sapiens sapiens* in the Near East. In A. Ronen (ed.), *The Transition from Lower to Middle Paleolithic and the Origin of Modern Man,* pp. 297–299, BAR International Series 151. Oxford.

———. 1984. The Discovery of the Neanderthal Skeleton of Saint-Césaire. *Bulletins et Mémoires de la Societé d'Anthropologie de Paris* 11: 191–196.

———. 1992. The Near Eastern Hominids and the Evolution of Modern Humans in Asia. In T. Akazawa, K. Aoki, and T. Kimura (eds.), *The Evolution and Dispersal of Modern Humans in Asia,* pp. 29–38. Hakusen-Sha, Tokyo.

Vanhaeren, M., d'Errico, F., Stringer, C., James, S. L., Todd, J. A., and Mienis, H. K. 2006. Middle Paleolithic Shell Beads in Israel and Algeria. *Science* 312: 1785–1788.

Vaquero, M., and Pasto, I. 2001. The Definition of Spatial Units in Middle Paleolithic Sites: The Hearth-Related Assemblages. *Journal of Archaeological Science* 28: 1209–1220.

Vaquero, M., Chacón, G., Fernández, C., Martínez, K., and Rando, J. M. 2001. Intrasite Spatial Patterning and Transport in the Abric Romani Middle Paleolithic Site (Capellades, Barcelona, Spain). In N. Conard (ed.), *Settlement Dynamics of the Middle Paleolithic and Middle Stone Age,* pp. 573–595. Kerns Verlag, Tübingen.

Villa, P. 1983. *Terra Amata and the Middle Pleistocene Archaeological Record of Southern France.* University of California Press, Berkeley.

Villa, P., and d'Errico, F. 2001. Bone and Ivory Points in the Lower and Middle Paleolithic of Europe. *Journal of Human Evolution* 41: 69–112.

Villa, P., and Lenoir, M. 2006. Hunting Weapons of the Middle Stone Age and the Middle Palaeolithic: Spear Points from Sibudu, Rose Cottage and Bouheben. *South African Humanities* 18: 89–122.

Villa, P., Delagnes, A., and Wadley, L. 2005. A Late Middle Stone Age Artifact Assemblage from Sibudu (KwaZulu-Natal): Comparisons with the European Middle Paleolithic. *Journal of Archaeological Science* 32: 399–422.

Vita-Finzi, E., and Higgs, E. C. 1970. Prehistoric Economy in the Mount Carmel Area of Palestine: Site Catchment Analysis. *Proceedings of the Prehistoric Society* 37: 1–37.

Volkman, P. 1983. Boker Tachtit: Core Reconstructions. In A. E. Marks (ed.), *Prehistory and Palaeoenvironments in the Central Negev, Israel: The Avdat/Aqev Area, part 3,* pp. 127–190. SMU Press, Dallas.

Wadley, L. 2001. What is Cultural Modernity? A General View and a South African Perspective from Rose Cottage Cave. *Cambridge Archaeological Journal* 11: 201–221.

———. 2005a. Ochre Crayons or Waste Products? Replications Compared with MSA "Crayons" from Sibudu Cave, South Africa. *Before Farming* 2005/3: Article 1.

———. 2005b. Putting Ochre to the Test: Replication Studies of Adhesives that may have been Used for Hafting Tools in the Middle Stone Age. *Journal of Human Evolution* 49: 587–601.

Wallace, I. J., and Shea, J. J. 2006. Mobility Patterns and Core Technologies in the Middle Paleolithic of the Levant. *Journal of Archaeological Science* 33:1293–1309.

Walter, P. 2003. Charactérisation des traces rouges et noires sur les coquillage perforés de Qafzeh. In B. Vandermeersch (ed.), *Échanges et Diffusion dans la préhistoire Méditerranéenne,* p. 122. Paris: Éditions du Comité des travaux historiques et scientifiques.

Walter, R. C., Buffler, R. T., Henriech, J. B., Guillaume, M., Berhe, S. M., Negassi, B., Libsekal, Y., Cheng, H., Edwards, R. L., Von Cosel, R., N´eraudeau, D., and Gagnon, M. 2000. Early Human Occupation of the Red Sea Coast of Eritrea during the Last Interglacial. *Nature* 405: 65—69.

Wang, J.-L., Zhang, J.-Z., and Liu, X.-M. 2000. Competition and Coexistence in Spatially Subdivided Habitats. *Journal of Theoretical Biology* 205: 631–639.

Wang, J.-L., Wang, F.-Z., Chen, S., and Zhu, M. Y. 2002. Competition and Coexistence in Regional Habitats. *American Naturalist* 159: 498–508.

Watanabe, H. 1970a. A Palaeolithic Industry from the Amud Cave. In H. Suzuki and F. Takai (eds.), *The Amud Man and His Cave Site,* pp. 77–114. Tokyo University Press, Tokyo.

———. 1970b. The Excavations at Keoue Cave, Lebanon: Interim Report. *Bulletin de Musée de Beyrouth* 23: 205–214.

Weaver, T. D., and Roseman, C. C. 2005. Ancient DNA, Late Neandertal Survival, and Modern-Human-Neandertal Genetic Admixture. *Current Anthropology* 46: 677–683.

Weedman, K. J. 2002. On the Spur of the Moment: Effects of Age and Experience on Hafted Stone Scraper Morphology. *American Antiquity* 67: 731–744

———. 2006. An Ethnoarchaeological Study of Hafting and Stone Tool Diversity among the Gamo of Ethiopia. *Journal of Archaeological Method and Theory* 13: 189–238.

Weiler, Y. 1968. Geology of Nazareth Hills and Mount Tabor. *Israel Journal of Earth Sciences* 17: 63–82.

Weiner, S., and Bar-Yosef, O. 1990. States of Preservation of Bones from Prehistoric Sites in the Near East: A Summary. *Journal of Archaeological Science* 17: 187–196.

Weiner, S., Goldberg, P., and Bar-Yosef, O. 1993. Bone Preservation in Kebara Cave, Israel Using On-site Fourier Transform Infrared Spectrometry. *Journal of Archaeological Science* 20: 613–627.

———. 2002. Three-Dimensional Distribution of Minerals in the Sediments of Hayonim Cave, Israel: Diagenetic Processes and Archaeological Implications. *Journal of Archaeological Science* 29: 1289–1308.

Weinstein, M. J. 1984. Radiocarbon Dating in the Southern Levant. *Radiocarbon* 26: 297–366.

Weinstein-Evron, M., Bar-Oz, G., Zaidner, Y., Tsatskin, A., Druck, D., Porat, N., and Hershkovitz, I. 2003. Introducing Misliya Cave, Mount Carmel, Israel: A New Continuous Lower/Middle Paleolithic Sequence in the Levant. *Eurasian Prehistory* 1: 31–55.

Weiskrantz, L. 1988. *Thought Without Language.* Oxford Science Publications. Clarendon Press, Oxford.

Wengler, L. 1990. Économie des matières premières et territoire dans le moustérien et l'Atérian maghrébins: Exemples du Maroc oriental. *L'Anthropologie* 94: 335–360.

———. 1991. Choix des matières premières lithiques et comportement des hommes au Paléolithique moyen, *25 Ans d'Études Technologiques en Préhistoire,* pp. 159–168. XI Recontres Internationales d'Archéologie et d'Histoire d'antibe . Éditions APDCA, Juan-les-Pins.

Whewel, W. 1958. *Novum Organon Renovatum.* John W. Parker, London.

White, J., Modjeska, N., and Hipuya, I. 1977. Group Definitions and Mental Templates: An Ethnographic Experiment. In R. Wright (ed.), *Stone Tools as Cultural Markers,* pp. 380–390. Australian Institute of Aboriginal Studies, Canberra.

White, L. A. 1959. *The Evolution of Culture: The Development of Civilization to the Fall of Rome.* McGraw-Hill, New York.

White, M. J., and Ashton, N. M. 2003. Lower Palaeolithic Core Technology and the Origins of the Levallois Method in Northwestern Europe. *Current Anthropology* 44: 598–609.

White, T. D., Asfaw, B., DeGusta, D., Gilbert, H., Richards, G. D., Suwa, G., and Howell, F. C. 2003. Pleistocene *Homo sapiens* from Middle Awash, Ethiopia. *Nature* 423: 742–747.

Whiten, A. 2005a. Animal Culture Is Real but Needs to be Clearly Defined. *Nature* 438: 1078.

———. 2005b. The Second Inheritance System of Chimpanzees and Humans. *Nature* 437: 52–57.

Whiten, A., Goodall, J., McGrew, W. C., Nishida, T., Reynolds, V., Sugiyama, Y., Tutin, C. E. G., Wrangham, R., and Boesch, C. 1999. Cultures in Chimpanzees. *Nature* 399: 682–685.

Whittaker, R. H., Levin, S. A., and Root, R. B. 1973. Reasons for Distinguishing Niche, Habitat and Ecotope. *American Naturalist* 107:321–338.

———. 1975. Niche, Habitat and Ecotope. *American Naturalist* 109:479–482.

Wiessner, P. 1982. Risk, Reciprocity and Social Influences on !Kung San Economies. In E. Leacock and R. B. Lee (eds.), *Politics and History of Band Societies,* pp. 61–84. Cambridge University Press, Cambridge.

———. 1983. Style and Social Information in Kalahari San Projectile Points. *American Antiquity* 48: 253–276.

———. 1985. Style or Isochrestic Variation? A Reply to Sackett. *American Antiquity* 50: 160–166.

Wigley, T. M. L., and Farmer, G. 1982. Climate of the Eastern Mediterranean and Near East. In J. L. Bintliff and W. van Zeist (eds.), *Palaeoclimates, Palaeoenvironments and Human Communities in the Eastern Mediterranean Region in Later Prehistory,* pp. 3–37, BAR International Series 133(i). Oxford.

Wilmsen, E. N. 1973. Interaction, Spacing Behavior and the Organization of Hunting Bands. *Journal of Anthropological Research* 29: 1–31.

Winterhalder, B., and Smith, E. A. (eds.), 1981. *Hunter-gatherer Foraging Strategies.* Prehistoric Archeology and Ecology Series. Chicago University Press, Chicago.

Wiseman, M. 1993. Lithic Blade Elements from the Southern Levant: A Diachronic View of Changing Technology and Design Process. *Journal of the Israel Prehistoric Society—Mitekufat Haeven* 25: 13–102.

Wobst, M. H. 1974. Boundary Conditions for Palaeolithic Social Systems: A Simulation Approach. *American Antiquity* 39: 147–178.

———. 1976. Locational Relationship in Palaeolithic Society. *Journal of Human Evolution* 5: 49–58.

———. 1977. Stylistic Behavior and Information Exchange. In C. Clealand (ed.), *Culture Change and Continuity: For the Director: Essays in Honor of James B. Griffin,* pp. 317–342. Anthropological Papers 61. University of Michigan Museum of Anthropology, Ann Arbor, Mich.

Wolpoff, M. H. 1989. Multiregional Evolution: The Fossil Alternative to Eden. In P. A. Mellars and C. B. Stringer (eds.), *The Human Revolution: Behavioural and Biological Perspectives on the Origins of Modern Humans,* pp. 62–108. Edinburgh University Press, Edinburgh.

———. 1996. *Human Evolution* (1996–1997 edn). College Custom Series. McGraw-Hill, New York.

Wolpoff, M. H., and Lee, S. H. 2001. The Late Pleistocene Human Species of Israel. *Bulletin et Mémoires de la Société d'Anthropologie de Paris* 13: 291–310.

Wolpoff, M. H., Thorne, A. G., Smith, F. H., Frayer, D. W., and Pope, G. G. 1994. Multiregional Evolution: A World-wide Source for Modern Human Populations. In M. Nitecki and D. Nitecki (eds.), *Origins of Anatomically Modern Humans,* pp. 174–199. Plenum Press, New York.

Wood, B. 1997. The Oldest Whodunnit in the World. *Nature* 385: 292–293.

Wreschner, E. 1967. The Geula Cave, Mount Carmel— Excavations, Finds and Summary. *Quaternaria IX:* 69–90.

Würz, S., le Roux, N. J., Gardner, S., and Deacon, H. J. 2003. Discriminating between the End Products of the Earlier Middle Stone Age Sub-stages at Klasies River using Biplot Methodology. *Journal of Archaeological Science* 30: 1107–1126.

Wylie, E. 1985. The Reaction against Analogy. *Advances in Archaeological Method and Theory* 8: 63–111.

Wynn, T., and Coolidge, F. L. 2004. The Expert Neandertal Mind. *Journal of Human Evolution* 46: 467–487.

———. 2006. The Effect of Enhanced Working Memory on Language. *Journal of Human Evolution* 50: 230–231.

———. 2007. Did a Small but Significant Enhancement in Working Memory Capacity Power the Evolution of Modern Thinking? In P. Mellars, K. Boyle, O. Bar-Yosef, and C. Stringer (eds.), *Rethinking the Human Revolution,* pp. 79–90. McDonald Institute for Archaeological Research, Cambridge.

Yeshurun, R., Bar-Oz, G., and Weinstein-Evron, M. 2007. Modern Hunting Behavior in the Early Middle Paleolithic: Faunal Remains From Misliya Cave,

Mount Carmel, Israel. *Journal of Human Evolution* 53: 656–677.

Yoneda, M., Shibata, Y., Morita, M., Hirota, M., Uchida, M., and Akazawa, T. 2002. Radiocarbon Age Determination of the Dederiyeh Cave Site, Syria: Preliminary Results. In H. Ishida, M. Nakatsukasa, and O. Ogiwara (eds.), *Recent Advances in Anthropology and Primatology,* pp. 31–34. Proceedings of the Joint Congress of the 55th Annual Meeting of Anthropological Society of Nippon and the 17th Annual Meeting of Primate Society of Japan. Kinseisha, Tokyo.

Ziaei, M., Schwarcz, H. P., Hall, C. M., and Grün, R. 1990. Radiometric Dating at the Mousterian Site at Quneitra. In N. Goren-Inbar (ed.), *Quneitra: A Mousterian Site on the Golan Heights,* pp. 232–235. Institute of Archaeology, Hebrew University, Jerusalem.

Zilhão, J., and d'Errico, F. 1999. The Chronology and Taphonomy of the Earliest Aurignacian and its Implications for the Understanding of Neandertal Extinction. *Journal of World Prehistory* 13: 1–68.

Ziman, J. (ed.) 2000a. *Technological Innovation as an Evolutionary Process.* Cambridge University Press, Cambridge.

———. 2000b. Evolutionary Models for Technological Change. In J. Ziman (ed.), *Technological Innovation as an Evolutionary Process,* pp. 3–12. Cambridge University Press, Cambridge.

Zohary, M. 1962. *The Plant Life of Palestine.* Ronald Press, New York.

———. 1980. *Vegetal Landscapes of Israel.* Am Oved, Tel-Aviv (Hebrew).

Zubrow, E. 1989. The Demographic Modeling of Neanderthal Extinction. In P. Mellars and C. B. Stringer (eds.), *Behavioural and Biological Perspectives on the Origins of Modern Humans,* pp. 212–231. Edinburgh University Press, Edinburgh.

# Index

Abric Romani, 16
Absolute dating, *see* Radiometric dating
Abu Sif, 12, 13, 99, 219, 221, 222, 229, 247
Abu Sif point, 192, 210
Acheulian, 26, 40, 212
Acheulo-Yabrudian, 10, 40, 210, 237,
    248, 249, 267, 275, 279
Acquisition
    of food resources, 7, 14, 158, 180, 183,
        186, 191, 218, 277, 280
    of cultural behaviors, 5, 279
Adaptation, 4, 5, 8, 14, 189, 207, 223, 231,
    232, 241, 246, 274
Ahmarian, 139, 299, 243
'Ain Difla, 12, 214, 216, 217, 220, 221, 229
Anatomically modern humans (AMH), 4, 10,
    11, 15, 39, 230, 231, 232, 234, 240, 241, 242,
    244, 245
    see also Moderns in the Levant,
        *Homo sapiens*
Amino Acid Racemization, 40
Amud
    age estimates of, 11, 270–273
    cave of, 10, 11, 12, 169, 202, 203, 209, 212,
        216, 220, 221, 224–225, 226, 228, 232, 234,
        248, 249,
    lithic assemblages from, 209- 211, 217,
        220–221, 229,
    skeletal remains from, 11, 230, 234
Amud, wadi, 247, 248, 276, 277
Amudian, 97, 237
Analogy, 9, 160, 192
Analogous processes, 5, 7, 9, 125, 192, 276, 281,
    282
Aquatic resources, 282
Art, 243, 244, 280
    *see also* Engrave piece, beads
*Arvicanthis ectos*, 40
Ash, 36, 224, 225
    *see also* Wood fire

Assimilation, 4, 239
Aterian, 235

Beads, 194, 238, 241, 243, 244
Behavioral modernity, 3, 97, 240, 242, 243, 244,
    245, 246
Biache Saint Vaast, 135, 139
Bifaces, 10, 20, 159
Bifacial flaking/explitation, 20, 63, 125, 179
Bifacial retouch, Plate 19, 110, 111, 112, 239,
    257–269
Bio-cultural evolution, 10, 241
Bitumen
    *see* hafting; Umm el-Tlel
Blade technologies, 13, 20, 37, 44, 46, 48, Plates
    4–5, Plate 8, Plate 10, Plate 12, Plate 14,
    Plates 16–18, Plate 21, 54, 55–56, 63, 70, 85,
    95, 97, 99–102, 109, 110–117, Plate 30, Plate
    43, Plates 45–47, 162, 176, 207, 212, 217, 219,
    237, 243, 249, 251–256, 276, 279, 282
Blank selection
    for cores-on-flake, 58–59, 177
    for tools, 5, 21,22, 127, 129–142, 148, 154, 167,
        188, 190,192, 215, 276, 280
Blombos Cave, 238
Boker Tachtit, 275
Border Cave, 15
Bordes's typological system, 8, 18, 27, 45, 107,
    108–126, 134, 147, 163, 210, 254
*Bos primigenius*, 38
Botanical remains, 203, 236, 248, 277
Bottleneck, 281
Burial gift, 39
Burial ground, 42, 188
Burials, 11, 12, 33, 37, 39, 41, 42, 185, 188, 194,
    236, 241, 243–244, 249, 281, 282
Butchery, 42, 159, 184, 186, 215, 225, 280

C3 vegetation, 41, 200
C4 vegetation, 200

*Camelus dromedarius*, 38, 41
*Capra*
    *aegagus*, 38
    *ibex*, 38, 199
    *see also* Wild goat
*Capreolus capreolus*, 38
Carnivores, 38, 41, 199
Carnivore activity, 41, 184
*Cervus elaphus*, 38
    *see also* Red deer
Chaîne opératoire
    as a methodological approach, 19, 21, 43, 190,
        191, 193, 275, 277
    as a technical process, 19, 53, 55, 56, 58, 60,
        80, 172, 191
Chapeau de gendarme, 13, 55, 62, 72, 73, 76, 77,
    90, 91, 92, 94, 251, 276
Chimpanzees, 6, 7, 274, 282
Coexistence
    ecological theory of, 235
    of Neanderthals and Moderns, 11, 27, 233,
        235, 236, 239
Cognition, 191, 232, 242, 282,
Cognitive abilities, 6, 7, 19, 61, 244, 276, 282
Cognitive mechanisms/processes, 7, 197, 242,
    244, 277
Colonization, 20, 231, 235, 243
Competition, 27, 159, 205, 233, 235–236, 239,
    282
    Competitive exclusion, 233, 235
Composite tools, 99, 176, 180, 242, 276
Cooptions, 281, 282
Core geometry, 21, 53, 76, 80
Cores-on-flakes, 21, 45, 53, 57–60, Plate 4,
    Plates 10–11, Plate 13, Plate 18, Plate 21,
    80, 94, 125, 126, 174, 177, 178, 182, Plate 33,
    Plate 37, Plates 39–40, 209, 221, Plate 45,
    250, 254, 275, 277, 280
Cultural evolution, 5, 95, 192, 193, 194, 237,
    246, 278